# Present Value of $1 Due at the End of *n* Periods (C

$$PVIF_{k,n} = \frac{1}{(1 + k)^n}$$

| 13% | 14% | 15% | 16% | 17% | 18% | 19% | 20% | 25% | 30% | 35% | 40% | 50% |
|---|---|---|---|---|---|---|---|---|---|---|---|---|
| .8850 | .8772 | .8696 | .8621 | .8547 | .8475 | .8403 | .8333 | .8000 | .7692 | .7407 | .7143 | .6667 |
| .7831 | .7695 | .7561 | .7432 | .7305 | .7182 | .7062 | .6944 | .6400 | .5917 | .5487 | .5102 | .4444 |
| .6931 | .6750 | .6575 | .6407 | .6244 | .6086 | .5934 | .5787 | .5120 | .4552 | .4064 | .3644 | .2963 |
| .6133 | .5921 | .5718 | .5523 | .5337 | .5158 | .4987 | .4823 | .4096 | .3501 | .3011 | .2603 | .1975 |
| .5428 | .5194 | .4972 | .4761 | .4561 | .4371 | .4190 | .4019 | .3277 | .2693 | .2230 | .1859 | .1317 |
| .4803 | .4556 | .4323 | .4104 | .3898 | .3704 | .3521 | .3349 | .2621 | .2072 | .1652 | .1328 | .0878 |
| .4251 | .3996 | .3759 | .3538 | .3332 | .3139 | .2959 | .2791 | .2097 | .1594 | .1224 | .0949 | .0585 |
| .3762 | .3506 | .3269 | .3050 | .2848 | .2660 | .2487 | .2326 | .1678 | .1226 | .0906 | .0678 | .0390 |
| .3329 | .3075 | .2843 | .2630 | .2434 | .2255 | .2090 | .1938 | .1342 | .0943 | .0671 | .0484 | .0260 |
| .2946 | .2697 | .2472 | .2267 | .2080 | .1911 | .1756 | .1615 | .1074 | .0725 | .0497 | .0346 | .0173 |
| .2607 | .2366 | .2149 | .1954 | .1778 | .1619 | .1476 | .1346 | .0859 | .0558 | .0368 | .0247 | .0116 |
| .2307 | .2076 | .1869 | .1685 | .1520 | .1372 | .1240 | .1122 | .0687 | .0429 | .0273 | .0176 | .0077 |
| .2042 | .1821 | .1625 | .1452 | .1299 | .1163 | .1042 | .0935 | .0550 | .0330 | .0202 | .0126 | .0051 |
| .1807 | .1597 | .1413 | .1252 | .1110 | .0985 | .0876 | .0779 | .0440 | .0254 | .0150 | .0090 | .0034 |
| .1599 | .1401 | .1229 | .1079 | .0949 | .0835 | .0736 | .0649 | .0352 | .0195 | .0111 | .0064 | .0023 |
| .1415 | .1229 | .1069 | .0930 | .0811 | .0708 | .0618 | .0541 | .0281 | .0150 | .0082 | .0046 | .0015 |
| .1252 | .1078 | .0929 | .0802 | .0693 | .0600 | .0520 | .0451 | .0225 | .0116 | .0061 | .0033 | .0010 |
| .1108 | .0946 | .0808 | .0691 | .0592 | .0508 | .0437 | .0376 | .0180 | .0089 | .0045 | .0023 | .0007 |
| .0981 | .0829 | .0703 | .0596 | .0506 | .0431 | .0367 | .0313 | .0144 | .0068 | .0033 | .0017 | .0005 |
| .0868 | .0728 | .0611 | .0514 | .0443 | .0365 | .0308 | .0261 | .0115 | .0053 | .0025 | .0012 | .0003 |
| .0768 | .0638 | .0531 | .0443 | .0370 | .0309 | .0259 | .0217 | .0092 | .0040 | .0018 | .0009 | .0002 |
| .0680 | .0560 | .0462 | .0382 | .0316 | .0262 | .0218 | .0181 | .0074 | .0031 | .0014 | .0006 | .0001 |
| .0601 | .0491 | .0402 | .0329 | .0270 | .0222 | .0183 | .0151 | .0059 | .0024 | .0010 | .0004 | .0001 |
| .0532 | .0431 | .0349 | .0284 | .0231 | .0188 | .0154 | .0126 | .0047 | .0018 | .0007 | .0003 | .0001 |
| .0471 | .0378 | .0304 | .0245 | .0197 | .0160 | .0129 | .0105 | .0038 | .0014 | .0006 | .0002 | .0000 |
| .0417 | .0331 | .0264 | .0211 | .0169 | .0135 | .0109 | .0087 | .0030 | .0011 | .0004 | .0002 | .0000 |
| .0369 | .0291 | .0230 | .0182 | .0144 | .0115 | .0091 | .0073 | .0024 | .0008 | .0003 | .0001 | .0000 |
| .0326 | .0255 | .0200 | .0157 | .0123 | .0097 | .0077 | .0061 | .0019 | .0006 | .0002 | .0001 | .0000 |
| .0289 | .0224 | .0174 | .0135 | .0105 | .0082 | .0064 | .0051 | .0015 | .0005 | .0002 | .0001 | .0000 |
| .0256 | .0196 | .0151 | .0116 | .0090 | .0070 | .0054 | .0042 | .0012 | .0004 | .0001 | .0000 | .0000 |
| .0139 | .0102 | .0075 | .0055 | .0041 | .0030 | .0023 | .0017 | .0004 | .0001 | .0000 | .0000 | .0000 |
| .0075 | .0053 | .0037 | .0026 | .0019 | .0013 | .0010 | .0007 | .0001 | .0000 | .0000 | .0000 | .0000 |
| .0041 | .0027 | .0019 | .0013 | .0009 | .0006 | .0004 | .0003 | .0000 | .0000 | .0000 | .0000 | .0000 |
| .0022 | .0014 | .0009 | .0006 | .0004 | .0003 | .0002 | .0001 | .0000 | .0000 | .0000 | .0000 | .0000 |

# INTRODUCTION TO FINANCIAL MANAGEMENT

# INTRODUCTION TO FINANCIAL MANAGEMENT

**Jeff Madura**
University of Central Florida

**E. Theodore Veit**
University of Central Florida

**West Publishing Company**
St. Paul     New York     Los Angeles     San Francisco

## Complete Teaching Package to Accompany Introduction to Financial Management

- **Instructor's Manual with Test Bank**

- **Solutions Manual**

- **Menu-Driven Diskette** Used to solve Computer-Assisted Problems at the end of selected chapters. Requires no other software or working knowledge of computer usage. Free to adopters.

- **Template Diskette** For LOTUS 1-2-3 and VP Planner. Sets up the spreadsheet structure allowing students to solve the Computer-Assisted Problems contained in the text. Free to adopters.

- **Study Guide** Written by Jacobus T. Severiens (Kent State University). Provides a comprehensive overview of each chapter. Multiple choice, true-false, fill-in-the-blank questions, along with numerical problems are included in a trial exam for each chapter.

- **Transparencies** A set of acetate transparencies illustrating example problems presented in the text is provided. In addition to these acetate transparencies, transparency masters are also available containing figures and tables, end of chapter solutions and solutions to computer-assisted problems.

- **Computerized Testing**

This text was set in Aster, Avant-Garde, and Helvetica by G & S Typesetters. Maggie Jarpey copyedited the manuscript and prepared the index. Alice B. Thiede, Carto-Graphics, prepared the art.

The cover photograph was supplied by Steve Krongard, The Image Bank. Roslyn M. Stendahl, Dapper Design, Minneapolis, Minnesota, designed the cover.

Copyright © 1988    By WEST PUBLISHING COMPANY
50 W. Kellogg Boulevard
P.O. Box 64526
St. Paul, MN 55164-1003

**Library of Congress Cataloging-in-Publication Data**

Madura, Jeff.
    Introduction to financial management / Jeff Madura, E. Theodore Veit.
        p.    cm.
    Bibliography: p.
    Includes index.
    ISBN 0-314-65664-2
        1. Corporations—Finance.    I. Veit, E. Theodore.    II. Title.
HG4026.M335    1988
658.1'5—dc19                                                    87-29510
                                                                    CIP

To Mary Madura
        and
To Marcia, Shawn, and Erica Veit

# BRIEF CONTENTS

# CONTENTS

## PART 7    WORKING CAPITAL MANAGEMENT    535

# PREFACE

This text has been structured to provide a clear explanation of the theory of financial management and to demonstrate how that theory is applied to real world situations. The goal of the text is to enable students to apply the theory that they learn in managerial situations. This text can be used either in an undergraduate introductory course or at the MBA level. It provides broad coverage of numerous concepts and comprehensive coverage of the most critical topics. Its flexible design enables instructors to focus on the critical concepts that require the most classroom attention without having to spend additional classroom time on material that is adequately covered by the text.

## ORGANIZATION OF THE TEXT

The organization of the text allows concepts to build upon each other. Part 1 identifies the organization and goals of firms and describes the financial environment in which firms must operate. Part 2 describes two important financial tools (time value of money and risk and return). It also describes the valuation process, which is critical to financial management because of its influence on corporate policies. Part 3 focuses on financial analysis and planning, which enable financial managers to evaluate historical performance and forecast future performance. Part 4 describes how capital budgeting (the acquisition of long-term assets) is conducted. Part 5 explains the decisions to finance the acquisition of long-term assets, while Part 6 describes the specific means by which long-term funds can be obtained. Part 7 focuses on the management of short-term assets and liabilities (working capital management). Part 8 covers specialized topics in financial management. Part 9 offers a synthesis of the most critical concepts explained throughout the text.

Because each part of the text is self-contained, it can be restructured to fit various lecture organizations. For example, Part 7 (working capital management) can be moved forward, and Parts 2 (tools and concepts) and 3 (financial analysis) can be postponed until later in the course. Some professors may wish to assign the specialized topics in Part 8 as required reading but not cover them in class. Other chapters may be treated in the same way to allow more in-class time for the most critical concepts.

## KEY FEATURES OF THE TEXT

This text offers several features designed to enhance the learning process. The most important of these features are described below.

### Focus on Maximization of Shareholder Wealth

While most financial management texts explicitly state that the goal of the firm is to maximize shareholder wealth, this text goes beyond that by explaining how the material in each chapter affects shareholder wealth.

### Comparing Theory and Practice

Most chapters provide insight into how financial managers perform their tasks in the real world. Where appropriate, the results of recent surveys are summarized to explain how financial managers handle various policy decisions. This feature allows students to compare the theory and practice of financial management.

### Real World Examples

Examples of actual firms that have implemented the policies under discussion are presented throughout the text to reinforce the application of theory to practice.

### Tax Reform Act of 1986

Chapter 2 covers the important and relevant aspects of the Tax Reform Act of 1986. This chapter has been carefully reviewed for accuracy and clarity by tax experts. The Tax Reform Act of 1986 is also fully integrated throughout the remainder of the text. End-of-chapter problems, as well as numerical examples within each chapter, also reflect the new tax laws.

### Lists of Key Terms

The "key terms" used in each chapter appear in boldface type in the text and are defined at the end of the chapter. These lists reinforce the meaning of each term and provide a convenient reference for the students. A separate Index to Key Terms enables students to find definitions quickly.

### Summaries of Equations

The equations used in each chapter are summarized at the end of the chapter. The variables are identified, and each equation's use is briefly described. These summaries provide students with a convenient reference source for studying the material.

## Questions and Problems

Discussion questions appear at the end of each chapter. These questions are designed to reinforce the concepts presented in the chapter. Many of the questions require students to apply the concepts presented in the chapter to different situations.

Every chapter containing analytical content has a large number of end-of-chapter problems that vary in their degree of difficulty. Problems for which answers have been provided at the end of the book are indicated by color numbers.

## Self-Test Problems

Each chapter containing analytical problems also has a number of self-test problems; step-by-step solutions to these problems appear at the end of the text. These self-test problems prepare students to work additional end-of-chapter problems.

## Computer-Assisted Problems

A number of chapters contain a set of computer-assisted problems, which complement the other end-of-chapter problems because they account for uncertainty. Furthermore, the computer-assisted problems provide students with experience in using sensitivity analysis, probability distributions, and simulation. They also allow students to spend less time on computations and more time on decision making.

## References

A list of references is included at the end of each chapter. These references have been selected because of their contributions to the development of some aspect of financial management. Many of them offer a more comprehensive background on the concepts discussed in the chapter.

# ANCILLARY MATERIALS

The following ancillary materials are available to adopters.

## Instructor's Manual

The instructor's manual contains lecture outlines and a test bank of multiple choice questions created directly from the text. In formulating the questions, the authors of the text have expended considerable effort to avoid ambiguity and to ensure that each question has only one correct answer. These questions can be used for major tests and quizzes.

### Solutions Manual

The solutions manual contains answers to all end-of-chapter questions and solutions to all end-of-chapter problems and computer-assisted problems.

### Study Guide

The study guide, written by Jacobus T. Severiens of Kent State University, provides a comprehensive overview of each chapter. Multiple choice, true-false, and fill-in-the-blank questions, along with numerical problems, are included in the trial exam for each chapter. Students can take the trial exam to determine whether they have a thorough understanding of the material in each chapter. The type and difficulty level of the questions are consistent with the text and the test bank.

### Computerized Test Bank

The test questions in the Instructor's Manual are also available on Wes-Test II magnetic tape for use on mainframe computers. In addition, Micro-Test II diskettes are available to adopters who want to produce tests using Apple, IBM PC, or TRS 80 microcomputers.

### Computer Software

Students may work the computer-assisted problems with a microcomputer using either of the two options available free of charge with this text:

■ Option one is the Menu-Driven Diskette, a self-contained computer package that is entirely menu driven and does not require the use of any other software. Neither advance knowledge of the computer nor the use of any documentation manual is required.
■ Option two is the Template Diskette, containing a set of programs that will run with Lotus 1-2-3, VP Planner, or several other popular spreadsheet packages.

### Transparencies

A set of acetate transparencies illustrating example problems presented in the text is available. Because the acetate transparencies provide a step-by-step procedure, instructors can focus on the conceptual aspects of the problems without being concerned about notation and other specifics that can interrupt a presentation when the procedure is written on a blackboard. In addition to these acetate transparencies, transparency masters containing figures and tables, solutions to end-of-chapter problems, and solutions to computer-assisted problems are also available.

## ACKNOWLEDGMENTS

We have benefited from the helpful comments and suggestions of many people. The Department of Finance faculty at the University of Central Florida helped improve our earlier drafts. Special thanks are extended to

John M. Cheney, Sharon S. Graham, Susan C. LeBlanc, Naval K. Modani, and Wallace W. Reiff. In addition, D. Dale Bandy of the School of Accounting provided valuable comments and suggestions.

We also benefited from the suggestions of professors at other universities who reviewed chapters for us. In alphabetical order, they are

Jack E. Adams, University of Arkansas at Little Rock
Henry C. F. Arnold, Seton Hall University
William L. Ashley, San Jose State University
Robert T. Aubey, University of Wisconsin—Madison
James C. Baker, Kent State University
Gurudutt M. Baliga, University of Delaware
Scott Besley, University of South Florida
Randall S. Billingsley, Virginia Polytechnic Institute and State University
Robert L. Black, University of Texas at Austin
Keith E. Boles, University of Missouri at Columbia
Gerald A. Blum, University of Nevada at Reno
P. R. Chandy, North Texas State University
John T. Emery, California State University, Fullerton
Keith Wm. Fairchild, University of Texas at San Antonio
Indra J. C. Guertler, Babson College
Hal Heaton, Brigham Young University
Steven C. Isberg, Northern Illinois University
R. L. Johnson, New Hampshire College
Ray G. Jones, Jr., Appalachian State University
Peter E. Koveos, Syracuse University
Susan C. LeBlanc, University of Central Florida
James T. Lindley, University of Alabama
Judy Maese, New Mexico State University
David M. Maloney, University of Virginia
Carl B. McGowan, Jr., Bentley College
William J. McGuire, Eastern Kentucky University
Angela M. McLain, University of Mississippi
Z. Lew Melnyk, University of Cincinnati
Ben H. Nunnally, University of North Carolina at Charlotte
Coleen C. Pantalone, Northeastern University
S. Ghon Rhee, University of Rhode Island
Jack H. Rubens, Cleveland State University
Murray Sabrin, Ramapo College
Michael Schellenger, Appalachian State University
Robert L. Schweitzer, University of Delaware
Louis O. Scott, University of Illinois
R. Stephen Sears, University of Illinois
Jacobus T. Severiens, Kent State University
Michael E. Solt, Santa Clara University
Stanley R. Stansell, University of Mississippi
A. Charlene Sullivan, Purdue University
Robert J. Sweeney, Marquette University
Skip Swerdlow, University of Nevada at Las Vegas
Richard J. Teweles, California State University, Long Beach
Pochara Theerathorn, Wichita State University
Jack W. Trifts, University of South Carolina
Alan L. Tucker, University of Tennessee
Joanne Turner, Ohio State University
Douglas Wilson, University of Massachusetts—Boston

We would also like to thank our typists, especially Judy Ryder and Raymonde Toland, who endured countless special requests from us. Support in many ways was also provided by Sherry Spring and Judy Distler.

The people at West Publishing Company also deserve special thanks for their time and effort. In particular, our editor, Dick Fenton, greatly influenced the final product. We sincerely appreciate his knowledge of the market and his insight regarding numerous text features and ancillaries. Esther Craig, our developmental editor, was also extremely helpful in expediting the text review process.

We would also like to thank other individuals who, in various ways, inspired us to write this text or made our task easier: E. Joe Nosari, professor of finance, Florida State University; Mark Thornton, controller, Barnett Bank; Lynn Thornton, independent appraisal analyst; and Don Toland, Westinghouse Corporation.

Finally, our parents, Arthur and Irene Madura and Ed and Sally Veit, provided considerable moral support. Our families, Mary Madura and Marcia, Shawn, and Erica Veit, tolerated us over the entire book-writing process, a feat that may have been even more difficult than writing the book itself.

# PART 1

# INTRODUCTION

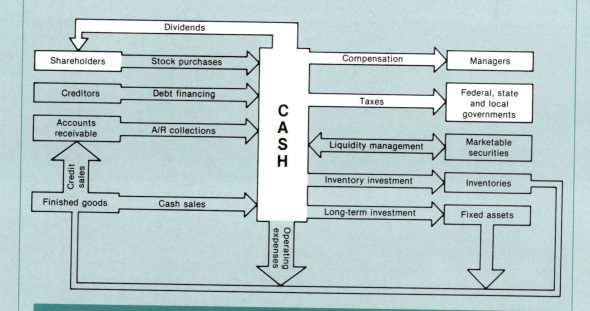

The diagram above illustrates both the major functions of financial management and the main sources and uses of funds for a firm. The diagram will recur throughout the text to identify in schematic form the main topics discussed in each part; the topics receiving attention in each part are represented by the uncolored areas of the diagram.

Part 1 provides a glimpse of the environment in which financial managers must operate. Chapter 1 describes the main functions and goals of a firm. Although most financial managers will have a variety of secondary objectives, their primary goal should be to maximize the wealth of shareholders.

Chapter 2 describes legal forms of businesses and the federal tax laws, both of which are important aspects of the environment in which management must work. Firms must choose the form of business that is most beneficial for them, while taxes affect the cash flows firms receive as well as the cost of raising funds and the cost of acquiring assets.

# CHAPTER 1

# OVERVIEW OF FINANCIAL MANAGEMENT

## FINANCIAL MANAGEMENT GOALS IN PERSPECTIVE

At International Paper Company's annual shareholders' meeting in 1987, a very important investor criticized the firm's management. The investor was a representative of the College Retirement Equities Fund (CREF), which manages a pension portfolio of common stock valued at about $30 billion. This portfolio includes a substantial investment in shares of International Paper Company common stock. The CREF representative specifically criticized International Paper's management for trying to prevent other firms from taking over the company. His concern was that the preventive measures taken by International Paper's management may have been designed more to benefit the managers of the firm than the shareholders.

Similarly, prior to General Motors' 1987 annual shareholders' meeting, GM's chairman, Roger Smith, was criticized by some stockholders for providing executives with large cash bonuses during periods when corporate performance was poor. In an effort to avert further criticism at the meeting, the company implemented several policy changes. One of the most significant changes was to declare that executive bonuses would be made in the form of GM common stock rather than cash. This change was designed to provide managers with an incentive to make decisions that maximize the price of the firm's common stock.

Do the shareholders of International Paper Company, General Motors, and other corporations have a right to criticize the firm's managers? Why are managerial objectives not always similar to shareholders' objectives? What can be done to prevent potential conflicts of interest? This chapter addresses these and other related questions.

*Source:* "The Battle for Corporate Control," *Business Week*, May 18, 1987, pp. 102–9.

Every business is faced with making financial decisions, from corporate giants such as IBM and Exxon to the grocery store around the corner. Although the tools used to make these decisions may be different for firms of different size, the financial principles and concepts are much the same for all firms. This book explains those principles and concepts and shows how they can be applied in analyzing individual situations in order to make rational financial decisions.

This chapter begins with a brief description of the broad area of finance, followed by a discussion of how financial management fits into the organizational structures of firms. The corporate form of business is emphasized throughout most of this text because the vast majority of business revenues are generated by corporations rather than partnerships and proprietorships.[1] After the subject of organizational structure has been addressed, the goals of firms and, finally, the major functions of the financial manager are discussed.

## WIDE WORLD OF FINANCE

Most schools of business offer a wide assortment of courses in finance. Although this text is concerned with financial management (the finance-related aspects of managing businesses), it is only one of several broad areas of finance in which financial experts specialize. Table 1.1 provides a partial listing of these areas.

Financial management, the first area of specialization listed in the table, overlaps with and is related to the other areas. Similarly, all the other areas overlap to a certain extent with the rest. For example, in managing a business, the financial manager must be familiar with how security analysts and individual investors view the firm's stocks and bonds (the investments specialty). In addition, firms generally establish a relationship with a bank or other institution for the purpose of obtaining loans and receiving the benefit of other services offered by those institutions (the

---

TABLE 1.1  **Specialty Areas in Finance**

■ *Financial management:* Managing the financial aspects of a for-profit business (also called business finance).

■ *Investments:* Analyzing alternative securities in which to invest and managing investment portfolios.

■ *Financial institutions:* Background and management of banks, insurance companies, and other institutions that play a major role in the financial markets.

■ *Financial services:* Providing services to individuals to help them improve their financial well-being. These services include personal financial planning, personal income taxes, estates and trusts, investments, real estate, insurance, and so forth.

■ *Public finance:* Managing the financial aspects of government organizations.

---

1.  A description of all three forms of business organization (proprietorships, partnerships, and corporations) is provided in Chapter 2.

financial-institutions specialty). Because of the overlapping of areas, students of financial management are introduced to most of these other specialty areas of finance. Many colleges and universities offer a variety of finance courses in all these areas, permitting students to more closely examine financial services, investments, financial institutions, and so forth. Likewise, while this text focuses on financial management, it also provides some background in the other areas of finance.

## FINANCIAL MANAGEMENT IN THE ORGANIZATIONAL STRUCTURE

Figure 1.1 provides an organizational view of a typical manufacturing corporation. Notice that stockholders are at the top of the chart. As the owners of the firm, they retain ultimate authority and control of the firm's activities. Just under the stockholders is the board of directors, which is elected by the stockholders. The stockholders have the power to replace members of the board whose performance is deemed unsatisfactory. The board of directors appoints the firm's president and other key officers and provides guidelines for managing the firm. If the officers fail to perform adequately, they can be replaced by the board.

As Figure 1.1 indicates, financial management is just one of at least three aspects of a firm's operation. Marketing and production are two others. All must operate effectively if the firm is to operate effectively.

Much interaction is required among the marketing, finance, and production areas. For example, in order to establish the level of production, the production manager must receive input from the marketing division about the expected level of future sales. In order to estimate the level of sales, the marketing manager must work with the financial manager to determine the appropriate credit policies for the firm. Numerous other as-

**FIGURE 1.1**
**Typical Organizational Structure for a Manufacturing Corporation**

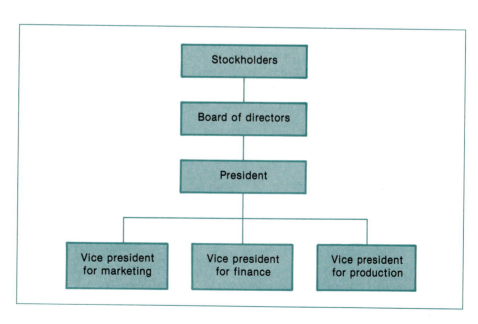

pects of interdepartmental activity require managers in each functional area of the firm to be familiar with the activities of all other functional areas.

## GOALS OF THE FIRM

Before management can make any decisions, it must identify the goals of the firm. Although some firms may have specific goals peculiar to their organizations, the primary goal for most firms is to **maximize shareholder wealth.** Other goals are important, too, but are usually subordinate to this goal.

### Maximizing Shareholder Wealth

As shown in Figure 1.1, the ultimate authority and responsibility for a firm rests with the stockholders. Since most investors purchase common stock primarily as a means of increasing their wealth, and since a firm's management works for the stockholders, the goal of management should be to maximize shareholder wealth. Executives of companies commonly make statements confirming this as the primary goal. For example, the cover of the 1985 BF Goodrich annual report states: "BF Goodrich will have changed more during 1985 and 1986 than it has over the last 50 years combined. The objective of this change is to increase shareholder wealth." Similarly, the 1986 annual reports of firms such as Coca Cola, Pillsbury, Quaker Oats, Avon, and Con Agra specifically state that the firms' objective is to increase shareholder wealth.

The wealth of shareholders is directly affected by both the market price of the common stock they own and the dividends they receive. (As demonstrated in Chapter 4, the market price of common stock reflects, among other things, investors' expectations regarding dividends that will be paid in the future.) Since the price of a firm's common stock reflects both aspects of investor returns, the goal of management is to maximize the value of the firm's common stock.[2] The goal of maximizing shareholder wealth by maximizing the value of the firm's common stock is the central theme in each chapter of this text.

### Firm Profits

Maximizing firm profits is often mistaken as the primary goal of the firm. While increasing firm profits is important to firms, it is not the primary goal, because shareholder wealth can actually decline despite rising profits. The explanation for this centers around the risk-return trade-off that is

---

2. Although the value of a firm's common stock (what it is really worth) and its market price can be different in an imperfect market, management has no control over the difference. Therefore, management can only attempt to maximize the value of the stock and hope that investors price it fairly. In a perfect market, value and market price are identical.

so important in finance. Investors are willing to purchase risky invest-ments only if they expect to be compensated with a higher return. The greater the risk, the higher the return must be.

| | |
|---|---|
| **Example** | Consider a firm that expects to have earnings per share (EPS) next year of $1.00. The firm's management may be able to increase EPS next year to $1.25, but only if it takes some additional risks that could result in losses to the firm and the stock-holders. The stockholders may be unwilling to accept those risks. If most of them sell their common stock as a result, the price of the stock will decline (not only be-cause of the increased sales, but also because fewer potential investors will want to purchase the shares). Therefore, even if the firm does realize the higher EPS, the increased risk incurred by the firm has lowered the wealth of the stockholders as a result of the declining price of the stock. |

Since the price of common stock reflects both the return generated and the risk incurred by firms, maximizing the price of a share of stock is the primary goal. And since this primary goal is determined by the profit-ability generated and the risk assumed by the firm, they (profits and risk) are also important objectives of the firm.

## Social Responsibility

Should the primary goal of the firm be to achieve social goals such as im-proving the well-being of employees, customers, the community, and so-ciety in general? In other words, should **social responsibility** be the primary goal? To address this question, consider a firm that elects to undertake a number of costly social activities. The cost of these activities must be borne by someone. It could be borne by the firm's customers through higher prices charged by the firm for its product. In a competitive environ-ment, firms that raise their prices so that customers bear these costs may experience lower sales and lower employment within the firm, a socially unacceptable consequence, and one that could even result in bankruptcy if sales are severely affected.

As an alternative, the firm could elect to keep its prices unchanged and simply operate with lower profits, in which case the cost of the social pro-grams is borne by the stockholders. However, only investors who are will-ing to receive a lower than competitive return would invest in such a firm. While the public is very generous in its support of charitable organiza-tions, most people seek high returns and low risk for their investments. In-deed, it is the drive for profits that allows our capitalistic economy to func-tion so well.

The previous discussion does not mean that businesses cannot be so-cially responsible and still function. Most businesses demonstrate social responsibility in a number of ways and for several reasons. First, commu-nities, states, and the federal government establish minimum rules of ac-ceptable social behavior. These laws, statutes, and ordinances cover zoning, waste disposal, safety, and many other subjects. They help ensure that all businesses meet certain minimum standards of social responsibility. In 1985 Celanese Corporation spent $12 million on projects designed to help the firm comply with federal, state, and local environmental control regulations.

A second aspect of social responsibility involves the *voluntary* social activities of firms. These activities can take many forms: safety and health programs for employees that go beyond those required by law or union contracts, corporate donations to charitable organizations, corporate sponsorship of local or national nonprofit organizations, and support for the arts.

Firms may have two reasons for making expenditures for these types of activities. One reason, recognized by most, is the need to contribute to the betterment of the community and society in which they operate. A second reason may be to enhance the image of the firm in the eyes of its customers.

The amounts spent on socially desirable activities are substantial. For example, in 1986 Pillsbury Company offered cash contributions of $6.7 million to a variety of programs focused on youth needs and hunger. Rockwell International Corporation contributed $12.3 million in the same year in support of higher education, health, culture, and civic organizations. Also in 1986, Campbell Soup Company contributed $3.4 million to 500 health, educational, and charitable activities, and Du Pont contributed $32.9 million to over 350 colleges and universities and to various health and service groups. Yet these examples are but a few of the many charitable contributions made by firms each year.

Another aspect of social responsibility concerns a firm's normal business activity. Successful firms produce and sell products to satisfy the needs of society. If the product is of poor quality, the price is too high, or the product is not desired by the public, the firm will not survive. In producing products, firms employ people, provide employees with wages and other employee benefits, and in most cases provide a pleasant work environment for employees. Although these contributions to society are frequently overlooked in an environment where infrequent corporate indiscretions and abuses are trumpeted in the headlines of newspapers, they are important and should not be taken for granted by society.

## Maximizing Management Wealth

For small firms, the managers and the owners are frequently the same people. However, for medium and large firms, the managers generally act as *agents* for the owners of the firm (the stockholders). The more widespread the firm's common stock, the less direct contact the owners have with management. The more removed the owners are from management, the greater the potential conflict of interest faced by the firm's managers. This conflict can be described in terms of management making decisions that may benefit themselves at the expense of the stockholders. These decisions may involve managers consuming greater perquisites and/or managers making their own jobs easier. Such decisions may directly conflict with the goal of maximizing shareholder wealth.

Another conflict of interest can arise when management initiates a **leveraged buyout (LBO),** in which the firm's management borrows money to purchase all shares of the firm's common stock, and the managers become the owners of the company. The company is "taken private," meaning the shares no longer trade publicly. The objective of management is to make a profit by purchasing all of the firm's shares near the current market price, taking action to improve the prospects for firm profitability, then reselling the shares to the public at a higher price in order to generate a profit for themselves. Since management intends to make a profit on the difference between the price it pays to purchase the firm's common stock and the price it receives when it sells those shares, there is an incentive for management to purchase the stock at the lowest possible price. As a result, managers may be tempted to take action that reduces the price of the firm's stock prior to initiating the LBO. Unfortunately, such activities do appear to take place.

Stockholders can take several actions in an effort to reduce the **agency problem** (when managers act for themselves rather than the owners). One of the most basic actions is the threat of firing. Although it is difficult for stockholders in firms with wide distribution of their common stock to gather sufficient votes to replace management, such has occurred—and there appears to be an increase in such activity in recent years.

A second possible strategy stockholders can use to motivate managers to maximize shareholder wealth is to tie a substantial proportion of management's total compensation to the performance of the firm. This can be done through the use of **executive stock options,** which grant managers the option to purchase the firm's common stock at a fixed price. Over 90 percent of large U.S. corporations offer stock options to some employees.[3] If the firm performs well, causing the price of the stock to rise above the fixed option price, the managers can purchase the stock at a discount from the current price. As an example of the potential profitability of executive stock options, in 1986 Donald E. Peterson, chairman of Ford Corporation, not only received $2 million in salary and bonuses, but also realized an additional $2.4 million by exercising stock options.

Executive stock options lost much of their appeal during the 1970s as a result of the poor overall stock market performance. When the stock market is performing poorly, even the stocks of firms with strong performance may not rise. As a result, managers may not be adequately compensated for their performance during such periods.

More recently, **performance shares** have increased in popularity as a means of providing management incentives. Under this plan, managers are granted shares of common stock based on firm performance as measured by the growth rate of earnings, return on equity, return on assets, or some other performance measure. Management can benefit from this program in two ways. First, by achieving certain goals, managers receive shares of the firm's stock free of cost. Second, as a result of the firm's strong performance, the price of the firm's stock is likely to rise, increasing the

---

3. See "Firms Trim Annual Pay Increases and Focus on Long Term," *Wall Street Journal,* April 10, 1987, 25.

## FINANCIAL MANAGEMENT IN PRACTICE

### MAXIMIZE SHAREHOLDERS' WEALTH OR MANAGERS' WEALTH?

An article by Benjamin J. Stein in a recent issue of *Barrons* questioned the behavior of managers who participate in leveraged buyouts (LBOs).*

According to Stein, "[I]nvariably, the companies [that are the subject of leveraged buyouts] emerge from the LBO laboratory a few months or years later at values that endow the creators of the LBO, the financers of the deal and the managers involved, with spectacular profits." As evidence of this, Stein identifies several recent LBOs and estimates the returns made by the creators of those LBOs.

| LBO | Estimated Return |
| --- | --- |
| Gibson Greetings and Anchor Hocking | 10,000% |
| Beatrice | $5 billion on an investment "in the millions" |
| Amsted Industries | 5,000% |
| Metromedia | $3 billion on an investment "in the millions" |
| Kaiser Aluminum | 4,000% |
| Malone & Hyde | $400 million on an investment "of a few million" |

\*  Benjamin J. Stein, "Shooting Fish in a Barrel," *Barrons*, January 12, 1987.

Stein suggests the reason why LBOs are so profitable is a combination of (1) the failure of managers to act in the best interests of the stockholders and (2) the inability of securities analysts to determine the value of firms. When analysts undervalue shares of common stock, the stock sells at a price that is lower than it should be. The managers close to the firm's operations may recognize the true value of the firm and decide to take advantage of the situation by purchasing all of the stock from the shareholders. Prior to doing that, moreover, the managers may reduce the firm's earnings by artificial means (accounting manipulations) so that the market price of the stock will decline even more. The managers then borrow large sums of money to purchase all of the shares of the firm's stock, using the firm's assets as collateral for the loan. Once the company is fully owned, they begin to take whatever action is necessary to increase the value of the firm's stock. This action frequently involves the sale of some of the firm's assets. The firm is then "taken public" by selling the shares at a much higher price than was paid for them. Says Stein, "It is a sad commentary on the psyche of the American manager that most frequently he seems to aggressively manage only when the results go straight to him without the intermediation of stockholders."

value of the shares owned by the managers. A disadvantage of this management incentive, however, is that managers may be motivated to take actions that increase firm profitability in the short-run (in order to receive performance shares) at the expense of achieving long-run goals.

A third method of incentive compensation involves the payment of cash bonuses for achieving certain goals. Prior to 1987 Chrysler Corporation paid executives cash bonuses that were tied to various performance measures. However, in 1987 Lee Iacocca announced plans to tie compensation to the value of the firm's common stock, presumably to more closely tie executive compensation to the goal of shareholder wealth maximization. Many firms offer more than one of the incentive programs described here, while other firms develop specialized incentives that meet their own needs.

## FUNCTIONS OF FINANCIAL MANAGEMENT

Figure 1.2 indicates that the office of the vice president for finance generally consists of two components. The controller component is normally responsible for cost accounting, financial accounting, tax accounting, and budgeting. These important functions help provide information to management about the historical activities of the firm and the firm's current situation, and they help to develop plans for future operations. The other finance functions normally come under the treasurer. These functions, the main topics of this text, are working capital management, capital budgeting, and capital structure management. Figure 1.3 shows how they are related to the firm's balance sheet.

**Working capital management** involves managing both the current assets of the firm (cash, marketable securities, accounts receivable and inventories) and the current liabilities (accounts payable, accrued wages and taxes, and notes payable). These are important activities that require a large portion of the financial manager's time. **Capital budgeting** involves the acquisition and disposition of the firm's fixed assets. This activity is extremely important to firms, since fixed assets generally involve large and irrevocable expenditures. **Capital structure management** involves making decisions on the proportion of long-term funds that come from debt sources and equity sources. The proportion of equity funds obtained from preferred stock and common equity is also a capital structure decision. Part of this decision is related to the firm's dividend policy. That is, a decision to retain some or all of the firm's earnings rather than paying it all out as dividends is a decision that effectively results in the acquisition of additional common equity as a source of financing. After these important decisions have been made, a final aspect of capital structure management involves the use of the capital markets to raise the necessary funds.

A fourth function of financial management, not identified in Figure 1.3,

**FIGURE 1.2**
Typical Organization of the Office of the Vice President for Finance in a Firm

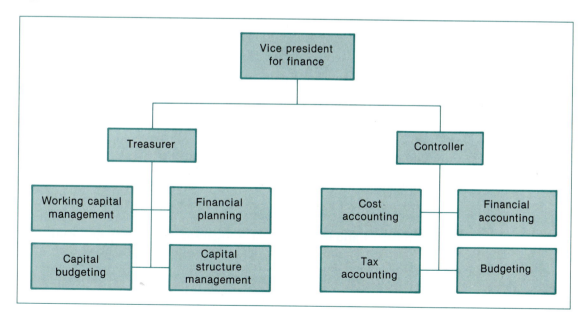

FIGURE 1.3
**Functions of Finan-
cial Management**

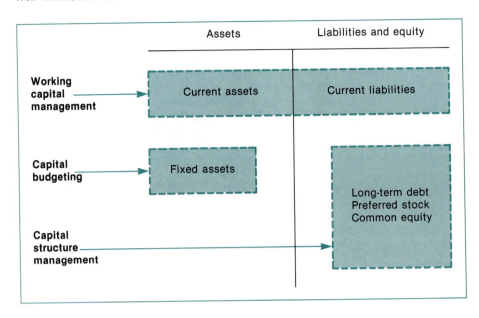

is **financial analysis and planning.** This function involves (1) evaluating the firm's current financial situation, (2) determining what the firm's financial situation should be in the future, and (3) deciding how the firm will achieve the desired financial situation.

Virtually every page in this text addresses one of the four finance functions described here or introduces the student to the tools necessary to perform these functions. Since the goal of the firm is to maximize shareholder wealth by maximizing the value of the firm's common stock, all of the finance functions should be carried out in a manner that is consistent with that goal.

## ORGANIZATION OF THE TEXT

Part I of this text introduces the goals of the firm (Chapter 1) and the financial environment in which financial managers must operate (Chapter 2). The discussion of the financial environment describes the different forms of businesses and introduces the system of federal income taxes.

Part II of this text explains the various tools that can be used to facilitate managerial decision-making: the time value of money (Chapter 3), valuation of financial assets (Chapter 4), and the assessment of risk and return (Chapter 5).

Part III discusses techniques used to evaluate corporate performance and improve managerial decisions. This includes a discussion of how to use ratio analysis and sources and uses of funds statements (Chapter 6), how to construct and interpret cash budgets and pro forma financial statements (Chapter 7), and how to analyze and interpret the breakeven point and degree of operating leverage (Chapter 8).

Part IV describes how the proposed acquisition of fixed assets and other capital investments are evaluated and how the final accept-or-reject decision is made (Chapters 9 through 11). Part V describes how firms finance their assets. This part begins with a discussion of how to determine the cost of financing projects (Chapter 12). Next, the impact of using various financing sources on the firm's risk, return, and value is addressed in Chapter 13. The use of dividend policy as a source of financing is presented in Chapter 14.

Part VI identifies the major sources of financing and describes the characteristics of each. It also discusses how firms enter the capital markets to raise funds. Chapter 15 considers debt sources of financing, while Chapter 16 describes common stock and preferred stock as sources of financing. Chapter 17 explains how the firm enters the financial markets to issue new securities, and Chapter 18 describes leasing as a source of capital. Chapter 19 discusses how the use of warrants, convertibles, and options can affect the cost of long-term funds.

Part VII explains the importance of managing working capital (current assets and current liabilities) and the appropriate techniques to manage it. This part begins with an overview of working capital management (Chapter 20) and is followed by a discussion of how to manage individual current assets and current liabilities: cash and marketable securities (Chapter 21), inventories and accounts receivable (Chapter 22), and major sources of short-term funds (Chapter 23). A comparison of Parts IV through VII reveals that Part IV focuses on long-term assets, Parts V and VI focus on long-term liabilities and equity, and Part VII focuses on current assets and current liabilities.

Part VIII applies the core concepts covered earlier to selected topics. Chapter 24 addresses the special situations faced by small businesses in managing their finances; Chapter 25 presents the major issues surrounding mergers and divestitures; Chapter 26 looks at how the firm is affected by bankruptcy and failure; and Chapter 27 discusses the financial aspects of international business. Throughout the text, the integration of financial management concepts is explained. For further reinforcement, Part IX presents a synthesis of financial management concepts.

## KEY TERMS

**Agency problem** The inability of stockholders to assure that management will act in the best interests of the stockholders and not themselves. Agency costs are incurred to maintain programs that encourage managers to make decisions that satisfy shareholder goals rather than their own goals.

**Capital budgeting** A function of financial management involving the acquisition and disposition of the firm's fixed assets.

**Capital structure management** A function of financial management that involves deciding the proportion of long-term funds that emanate from long-term debt, preferred stock, common equity, and other long-term sources.

**Executive stock options** A means of compensat-

ing firm managers. It involves granting managers the right to purchase shares of the firm's stock at a fixed price. If the firm performs well, so that the stock price rises, the managers can exercise those options and purchase stock at below-market prices.

**Financial analysis and planning** This function of the financial manager involves evaluating the firm's current financial situation, determining the desired financial situation, and deciding how the firm will achieve that desired situation.

**Leveraged buyout (LBO)** The purchase of a firm by an individual or group using mostly borrowed funds. The firm's assets are used as collateral for the loan.

**Maximizing shareholder wealth** This is the primary goal of the firm's management, since the shareholders own the firm and management works for the shareholders.

**Performance shares** A means of compensating firm managers that involves granting them shares of common stock based on the attainment of specified goals.

**Social responsibility** The responsibility of firms to improve the well-being of employees, customers, the community, and society in general.

**Working capital management** A function of financial management requiring decisions about a firm's current assets and current liabilities.

## QUESTIONS

**Q1-1.** Why are most firms socially responsible?

**Q1-2.** Describe leveraged buyouts, and indicate how they can adversely affect shareholder wealth.

**Q1-3.** Describe how executive stock options can reward managers for good performance.

**Q1-4.** What are the common ways in which firms obtain funds for long-term investment?

**Q1-5.** What is the generally accepted primary goal of a firm? Why should this be the primary goal?

**Q1-6.** Why is the goal of maximizing profits not necessarily consistent with the goal of maximizing shareholder wealth?

**Q1-7.** Why is the goal of being socially responsible not necessarily consistent with the goal of maximizing shareholder wealth?

**Q1-8.** What is the agency problem?

**Q1-9.** How do firms encourage managers to maximize shareholder wealth?

**Q1-10.** Describe the major specialty areas of finance, and identify how they overlap with each other.

**Q1-11.** Although the stockholders of a firm have ultimate authority over the firm, they seldom exercise their authority to replace directors and managers. Why is that so?

**Q1-12.** What advantage do performance shares have over executive stock options as a method of compensation?

**Q1-13.** At a recent board meeting for Century Hospital, one of the board members suggested a new strategy: "Century Hospital should accept all patients without insurance under any conditions. This will advertise the hospital's willingness to help society and increase the desire of investors to purchase shares of the hospital's stock." Comment on the board member's suggestion.

**Q1-14.** STAR Corporation has just organized ten-kilometer races in ten different cities in an effort to promote exercise and good health. There is no entrance fee, and there is a $1,000 award to every winner, plus a free pair of STAR running shoes to the top twenty runners of every race. Can STAR Corporation provide such benefits to society and simultaneously maximize shareholder wealth?

**Q1-15.** Assume that you plan to take a job with a small growing corporation upon graduation. Your job is to identify the best location in the United States for a firm branch and then to move to that location in order to manage the branch. Explain why your decision might not be consistent with the goals of the corporation. How can the corporation change the process so that a decision is made that is consistent with the firm's goals?

**Q1-16.** Tom Fitzgerald plans to work for a bank in the corporate loan department one year from now. He has no plans to learn financial management, since he will not be pursuing a job as a financial manager. Comment on his reasoning.

## REFERENCES

Anthony, Robert N. "The Trouble with Profit Maximization." *Harvard Business Review* 38 (November–December 1960): 126–34.

Beranek, William. "Research Directions in Finance." *Quarterly Review of Economics and Business* 21 (Spring 1981): 6–24.

Branch, Ben. "Corporate Objectives and Market Performance." *Financial Management* 2 (Summer 1973): 24–29.

Cooley, Phillip L. "Managerial Pay and Financial Performances of Small Business." *Journal of Business* 52 (September 1979): 267–76.

Davis, Keith. "Social Responsibility Is Inevitable." *California Management Review* 19 (Fall 1976): 14–20.

Donaldson, Gordon. "Financial Goals: Management vs. Stockholders." *Harvard Business Review* 41 (May–June 1963): 116–29.

———. "Financial Goals and Strategic Consequences." *Harvard Business Review* 63 (May–June 1985): 57–66.

Findlay, M. Chapman, III, and G. A. Whitmore. "Beyond Shareholder Wealth Maximization." *Financial Management* 3 (Winter 1974): 25–35.

Findlay, M. Chapman, III, and E. E. Williams. "A Positivist Evaluation of the New Finance." *Financial Management* 9 (Summer 1980): 7–17.

Jensen, Michael C., and William H. Meckling. "Theory of the Firm: Managerial Behavior, Agency Costs and Ownership Structure." *Journal of Financial Economics* 3 (October 1976): 305–60.

Lewellen, Wilbur G. "Management and Ownership in the Large Firm." *Journal of Finance* 24 (May 1969): 299–322.

Meckling, William H., and Michael C. Jensen. "Reflections on the Corporation as a Social Invention." *Midland Corporate Finance Journal* 1 (Fall 1983): 6–15.

Seitz, Neil. "Shareholder Goals, Firm Goals and Firm Financing Decisions." *Financial Management* 11 (Autumn 1982): 20–26.

———. "What Should We Teach in a Course in Business Finance?" *Journal of Finance* 21 (May 1966): 411–15.

Weston, J. Fred. "Developments in Finance Theory." *Financial Management*, 10th anniversary issue (1981): 5–22.

# CHAPTER 2

# BUSINESS ORGANIZATIONS AND TAXES

## BUSINESS TAXES IN PERSPECTIVE

Ninety-five of the 604 profitable major U.S. firms monitored by Tax Analysts (a nonprofit organization) paid no U.S. federal income tax for 1985. Among those firms were Westinghouse Electric Corporation, Mobil Corporation, and Phillips Petroleum Company. The average tax rate of the other firms in the sample varied widely among firms and industries. Certain types of wholesalers and tobacco firms had the highest rates, while oil firms and railroads had the lowest. The average tax rate for all the firms in the study was 18.7 percent in 1985 versus 23.2 percent in 1984, even though the highest marginal tax rate for corporations was 46 percent in both years. Tax-law changes since 1985 have attempted to ensure that all profitable firms pay taxes.

Even with the recent changes, substantial differences remain in the tax rates applied to the income of various firms. Since some firms may pay 44 percent (or more) of their taxable income to federal, state, and local taxing authorities in 1988, management must consider the tax consequences when making decisions. A firm's tax rate can affect decisions about the sources of capital it uses, the investments it makes in financial assets and plant and equipment, the dividends it pays to its stockholders, and many other aspects of its operations.

How are different sources of income taxed? How can the use of different depreciation methods affect which expenses are tax-deductible and which are not? This chapter addresses these and other questions about the tax implications of financial decisions made by management.

Businesses must operate within the legal environment provided by federal, state, and local governments. Two of the most important aspects of the legal environment are (1) the legal forms of business permitted (proprietorships, partnerships, and corporations) and (2) tax rules. To maximize the wealth of its owners (whether shareholders, partners, or proprietors), a business must assume its most advantageous form and focus on maximizing after-tax profits rather than before-tax profits. Focusing on an increase in revenues without considering the tax implications may actually decrease after-tax profits. This can lead to a decrease in the wealth of the owners.

## FORMS OF BUSINESS ORGANIZATION

The three different forms of business organizations—proprietorships, partnerships, and corporations—are listed in Table 2.1 with the number and average size (in revenues) of each in the United States in 1983. Notice that 70 percent of U.S. business firms were proprietorships, while only 10 percent were partnerships and another 20 percent were corporations; yet proprietorships received less than 7 percent of all business revenues. Almost 90 percent of all business revenues were generated by corporations and the remaining 3 percent by partnerships. This illustrates that corporations tend to be larger businesses than proprietorships or partnerships.

There are both advantages and disadvantages to each form of business organization, many of which relate to the size of the firm. For example, small firms frequently benefit from the low organizational costs of being a proprietorship or partnership. If the firm grows, the need for capital can literally force the firm to incorporate. The principal advantages and disadvantages of each form of business are discussed below and summarized in Table 2.2.

### Proprietorships

A **proprietorship** is an unincorporated business owned by one person. In many locations, the only legal requirements for starting a proprietorship are to (1) obtain an occupational license and (2) observe local zoning re-

**TABLE 2.1** Types of Business Organizations in the United States: 1983

| | Number | Percent of Total Firms | Revenues (Billions of $) | Percent of Total Revenue |
|---|---|---|---|---|
| Proprietorships (nonfarm) | 10,703,000 | 70.2% | $ 465 | 6.6% |
| Partnerships | 1,541,000 | 10.1 | 243 | 3.5 |
| Corporations | 2,999,000 | 19.7 | 6,334 | 89.9 |
| Total | 15,243,000 | 100.0% | $7,042 | 100.0% |

*Source:* U.S. Department of the Treasury, Internal Revenue Service, *Statistics of Income, 1985 Business Income Tax Returns,* and *Statistics of Income, 1985 Corporation Income Tax Returns* (Washington, D.C.: U.S. Government Printing Office).

**TABLE 2.2**    **Key Characteristics of Different Forms of Business Organization**

|  | Proprietorship | Partnership | Corporation |
|---|---|---|---|
| *Organizational costs* | Lowest | Intermediate | Highest |
| *Income tax treatment* | Income is taxed as personal income to the proprietor | Income is taxed as personal income to the partners | Income is taxed twice: as corporate income and as dividend income to stockholders when distributed |
| *Privacy of company information* | Records can remain confidential | Records can remain confidential | When the stock is traded publicly, significant amounts of information must also be made public |
| *Liability of owners* | Unlimited | Unlimited for general partners but limited to the initial investment for limited partners | Limited to the initial investment |
| *Ease of raising capital* | Limited to proprietor's resources | Limited to the resources of the partners | Best business form for raising capital |
| *Continuity of the business* | Company dies when the proprietor dies | Special provisions may or may not be made to continue the firm upon the death of a partner | Business continues to exist upon the death of an owner |
| *Transferability of ownership* | May be transferred but is not liquid | May require approval of all partners and has limited liquidity | More easily transferred; good liquidity |

*Note:* Although key characteristics are identified in this table, some more subtle differences are discussed in the body of the text.

strictions. The owner of a proprietorship (the proprietor) *is* the business. That is, all debts of the business are debts of the owner, and any profit or loss to the business is profit or loss to the owner. Indeed, proprietors file *personal income tax* returns with the Internal Revenue Service (IRS), declaring the revenue and expenses of the business as their own. Individual income tax rates are applied to the net income of the proprietorship.

**Advantages of Proprietorships**    The main advantages of proprietorships include the following:

1. Organizational costs are lower for proprietorships than for the other forms of business. As indicated earlier, licensing by the local community may be required. In addition, licensing may be necessary for the sale or production of certain products, and the firm may need to collect state or local sales taxes. There is little additional government regulation of proprietorships.
2. The income of a proprietorship is taxed just once whereas the income of corporations is normally taxed twice.
3. Generally, losses incurred in a proprietorship can be deducted for tax

purposes from income received by the proprietor from other sources. Conversely, owners of corporations generally cannot deduct losses incurred by the corporation from their personal income, although there are exceptions to this rule.

**4.** For most proprietorships, there is no requirement to make public the financial and other records of the firm. This permits the proprietorship to operate in relative privacy.

**Disadvantages of Proprietorships** Along with their advantages, proprietorships have some disadvantages.

**1.** The proprietor is personally responsible for all of the liabilities of the firm. Proprietors are, therefore, said to have unlimited liability.
**2.** It is difficult to raise large amounts of money in a proprietorship. Raising outside *equity* funds means giving up the proprietorship form of organization (there is no longer a single owner). The amount of financing available to a proprietorship is limited to the amount the proprietor invests plus the amount the proprietor can borrow.
**3.** The life of a proprietorship is limited to the life of the proprietor. Since the proprietor and the business are one, when the proprietor dies, the proprietorship legally ceases to exist.

## Partnerships

A **partnership** is very much like a proprietorship except there is more than one owner. While partnerships in the United States have an average of approximately five partners, most partnerships have fewer. At the other extreme, some partnerships have hundreds of partners.

There are two principal types of partnerships, general and limited. Most are **general partnerships,** which are owned and managed by all the partners, each of whom has unlimited liability. Most general partnerships are governed by *articles of partnership*, which are agreements between the partners. Although the agreements can be either oral or written, written agreements are strongly recommended. The articles of partnership should clearly detail all aspects of the partnership including the time and money each partner is to contribute, salary provisions, how to divide profits and losses, how to dissolve the partnership, the disposition of partnership interests when one partner dies, and all other relevant matters.

In a **limited partnership,** one or more general partners have unlimited liability, but other partners, who do not participate in the management of the business, are limited in their liability. The limited partners share in the profits and the losses of the business, but only to the extent of their investment. For tax purposes, losses resulting from limited partnership investments cannot be used to offset income from other sources such as salaries, stocks, and bonds. Losses can only be used to offset income from similar investments. In addition, the liability of limited partners is also limited to their investment. Each limited partnership organization must have at least one general partner who manages the firm. The general partner normally receives a salary, participates in the profits and losses of the firm, and has unlimited liability.

Limited partnerships are very popular forms of organizations, particularly for developing and managing large real estate investments and for oil and gas development and production. They are more expensive to establish than general partnerships due to greater government regulation and control; for example, the sale of limited partnership interests is highly regulated by both federal and state agencies. Nevertheless, limited partnerships usually find it easier to raise large amounts of capital, because limited partners have limited liability, and also because they normally can sell their share of ownership more easily than partners in a typical general partnership. The better marketability of limited partnership shares results from the large number of limited partnership units that are typically issued, the availability of more information about limited partnerships as required by government regulation, and efforts by the creators of limited partnerships to make the units more marketable to help attract investors.

**Advantages of Partnerships**     The principal advantages of partnerships include the following:

1. Organizational costs are generally lower for partnerships than for corporations (although they can be higher than for proprietorships due to the need to draw up articles of partnership). However, this advantage pertains mainly to general partnerships, which typically have no more government regulation than proprietorships, and not to limited partnerships, which typically are subject to considerable government regulation.
2. The income of a partnership is taxed just once, as personal income to the partners (similar to a proprietorship).
3. Since general partnerships are privately owned, information about the firm is private, just as it is for proprietorships.
4. Compared to proprietorships, partnerships have access to more capital. First, more equity can normally be invested since there are two or more owners available to make the investments. Second, more credit may be available to general partnerships since two or more owners are responsible for any debts of the firm. Third, limited partnerships can raise large amounts of capital by selling limited partnership interests of the firm to the public.
5. A partnership may find it easier to retain good employees than a proprietorship because of the opportunities employees have to become full partners. Also, the partnership may offer the promise of unlimited life for the business by providing in the partnership agreement for continued operation and reorganization of the firm upon the death of a partner.

**Disadvantages of Partnerships**     In addition to the advantages, partnerships present certain disadvantages.

1. Like proprietors, each general partner is personally responsible for all the liabilities of the firm. If only one general partner has resources, he or she may be called upon to satisfy all of the liabilities of the partnership, regardless of which partner obligated the firm.
2. Although partnerships can normally raise more capital than proprietorships, they have access to less capital than corporations.

3.  It may be more difficult to transfer a general partner's ownership than the ownership of a proprietorship or a corporation if prior consent of the other partners is required (this requirement can be specifically voided in the partnership agreement).

## Corporations

A **corporation** is a legal entity that is separate and distinct from its owners (the stockholders). As an artificial being, a corporation is treated as a legal person in the eyes of the law. Therefore, it can sue and be sued, it can own property, it can enter into legal contracts, and it can be punished for crimes committed.

The *stockholders* of a corporation own the corporation and retain ultimate responsibility for the company's success or failure. They elect the members of the *board of directors*, who are responsible for establishing the general policies of the firm. One of the directors' responsibilities is to elect the *president* and other key officers, who are then given the responsibility of managing the firm on a day-to-day basis. If the board of directors becomes displeased with the performance of the key officers, the board has the power to replace them. Similarly, if the stockholders become displeased with the performance of members of the board of directors, the stockholders can replace the directors in the next election. In some corporations, one individual or a handful of individuals may serve in all three capacities, as stockholder, member of the board of directors, and key officer of the firm.

In order to incorporate a business, an individual or group must adopt a corporate *charter* and file it with the state government where the corporation is to be chartered. The charter describes important aspects of the corporation, such as the name of the firm, the names and addresses of the members of the board of directors, information about the common stock issued, and a description of the activities of the firm in addition to other information. Also, the organizers of the corporation must establish *bylaws* providing management with general guidelines for managing the company. The bylaws include provisions on a variety of topics, including how members are to be elected to the board of directors, what management committees are to be formed, and how future changes can be made to the bylaws.

**Advantages of Corporations**  Among the major advantages of corporations are the following:

1.  Corporations have unlimited lives. Since corporations themselves are legal entities, the death of an owner of the firm's common stock does not result in the dissolution of the corporation. Instead, the common stock is transferred to another individual or organization who then receives all benefits and responsibilities of ownership.
2.  Owners of corporations normally have limited liability. Therefore, if an investor purchases the common stock of a company, the maximum amount the investor can lose is the value of the investment. The limited liability feature of common stock reduces the risk of purchasing common stock and enhances the value of common stock. This limit on the liability of investors

does not exist for proprietors or general partners, although it does exist for limited partners.

**3.**   In many situations, an investment in common stock can be sold very quickly and easily and for only a small transaction fee. Indeed, investors in large, publicly traded companies can sell their stock in minutes by placing orders with their stockbrokers. For nonpublicly traded firms, the seller of the common stock may have some difficulty finding a buyer. Once a buyer has been found, however, the seller only needs to sign the stock over to the purchaser to complete the transaction. This ease of transfer is perceived by investors as reducing their risk. As a result, the value of common stock is enhanced.

**4.**   When a firm's stock is actively traded, it is very easy to determine the value of the stock for buyout or estate valuation purposes. Determining the value of a proprietorship or partnership, on the other hand, can be a very difficult and expensive undertaking.

**5.**   Corporations have an advantage over the other forms of business in raising capital because of the lower risk to investors resulting from the limited liability feature and the ease of selling one's ownership, and because of the perpetual life of the corporation. And because it is easier for corporations to raise capital, they can support more rapid growth than other forms of business.

**Disadvantages of Corporations**   Despite their advantages, corporations also have certain disadvantages.

**1.**   Corporate income is subject to double taxation. After subtracting all eligible expenses from revenues, the corporation pays taxes on the remaining amount (taxable income). What is left after paying taxes (net income) belongs to the stockholders; and if dividends are paid to stockholders from net income, the amount paid is taxed a second time as personal income to the stockholders.

**2.**   Organizational expense normally is greater for the corporate form of business than the other forms due to the necessity of creating a corporate charter and filing it with the secretary of state. Some expense may also be incurred in establishing bylaws. In many states, however, individuals can incorporate small businesses through an attorney for $600 or less, barring complications.

**3.**   When the stock of a corporation trades publicly, the investing public has the right to inspect the company's books, within certain limits. As a result, firms may be obligated to reveal more about their operations than they would like. This lack of privacy is considered by some people to be a disadvantage.

## CORPORATE INCOME TAXES

Both incorporated and unincorporated businesses are affected directly by federal, state, and local taxes. The major taxes paid by businesses are property taxes, social security taxes, unemployment taxes, and income taxes. The tax that most affects the financial decisions of firms is the fed-

## FINANCIAL MANAGEMENT IN PRACTICE

### COPING WITH CHANGING TAX LAWS

Changing tax laws are a fact of life with which businesses must learn to live. The following commentary addresses the sweeping tax revisions that were passed into law in 1986.* Although written before final passage of the tax law, the opinion expressed is still relevant today.

"Congress is in the process of passing the most significant tax reform measure since the 1954 [Tax] Code was enacted. Taking almost two years to complete, the Tax Reform Act of 1986 (Act) is a bipartisan legislative effort touching every American taxpayer. The changes are so pervasive that the income tax laws will now be referred to as the Internal Revenue Code of 1986.

"The announced goal of reform was in large part to remove tax considerations from economic decision making. And even though generally not effective until January 1, 1987, the new rules are already causing taxpayers and tax practitioners

alike to rethink their long-held assumptions about investments now that many tax subsidies have been removed.

"The linchpin of the new Federal income tax code is its dramatic lowering of rates for individuals and businesses. More than 6 million individuals who will pay 1986 taxes will pay no such taxes in 1988, and more than half of all taxpayers will pay no higher than a 15% rate. Although the remaining individual taxpayers will be paying taxes at a stated 28% rate, surcharges and phase-outs could substantially increase their effective rates over the stated rate.

"The new code is intended to be revenue neutral, i.e., it brings in the same revenue over a six-year period as current law. This means that rate reductions must be financed through base broadening. Although the top corporate rate has been reduced from 46% to 34%, Federal revenue from business taxes will increase by a total of more than $120 billion dollars over a six-year period. The sheer magnitude of the new business tax burdens will inevitably increase tax considerations in economic decision making, contrary to the stated goal of tax reform."

*Reprinted, with permission of the copyright holder, from *Tax Reform—1986: An Analysis of the Internal Revenue Code of 1986*, published by Ernst & Whinney.

eral income tax, since this is normally the largest in size, and also because it can be altered substantially by management decisions.

The legality of an income tax on individuals and businesses was formalized in 1913 by the passage of the Sixteenth Amendment to the U.S. Constitution (temporary taxes had been in effect at various times prior to 1913). Under this amendment, Congress was given the authority to enact tax laws to be interpreted by the U.S. Treasury Department and enforced through the Internal Revenue Service. Congress frequently changes the tax laws. In some years these changes are relatively minor, and in other years they are major. The most recent major revision was the Tax Reform Act of 1986, which was designed to simplify the tax structure by reducing the number of deductions and credits that can be taken by some taxpayers while simultaneously reducing the tax rates.

The tax laws specify several different taxable entities: individuals, corporations, and fiduciaries (estates and trusts). Although proprietorships, partnerships, and some corporations are subject to individual income

**TABLE 2.3**  **Income Statement: Le Blanc Industries, Year-Ended December 31, 1988**

| Line | | | |
|---|---|---:|---:|
| 1. | Sales ........................................................ | | $1,000,000 |
| 2. | Less: Cost of goods sold ................................. | | 680,000 |
| 3. | Gross profit ............................................... | | 320,000 |
| 4. | Less: Operating expenses ................................ | | 120,000 |
| 5. | Operating profit .......................................... | | 200,000 |
| 6. | Other taxable income and expenses | | |
| 7. | Interest income .................... | 20,000 | |
| 8. | Gain on the sale of equipment ....... | 10,000 | |
| 9. | Interest expense ................... | (80,000) ................... | (50,000) |
| 10. | Profit before taxes ....................................... | | 150,000 |
| 11. | Less: Federal income taxes .............................. | | 41,750 |
| 12. | Net income .............................................. | | 108,250 |

taxes, most business earnings are subject to corporate income taxes. For that reason, only corporate income taxes are discussed in this text.

The purpose of this section is not to make the reader an expert in corporate income tax, but rather to introduce some key tax provisions that financial managers must understand in order to enhance the after-tax profits of the firm. This is an important ingredient in maximizing the wealth of the firm's owners.

Businesses are required to pay taxes on their profits only, not on all of their revenue. Therefore, the costs of operating a business are deducted from revenue before the tax liability is calculated. This information can be presented in tabular form as a firm's income statement.[1] Table 2.3 presents a simplified example for Le Blanc Industries. Basically, all business expenses are deducted from the firm's revenues for the year, then other sources of taxable income are added, and other deductible expenses are subtracted. What remains is taxable income. By applying the appropriate income tax rates to that income, the firm determines its tax liability for the year.

## Revenues and Expenses

The following paragraphs provide a brief discussion of each tax-deductible expense item for Le Blanc Industries.

**Sales (or Net Sales)**  Returns and allowances plus discounts granted to customers are deducted from gross sales to determine net sales.

**Cost of Goods Sold**  The cost to a firm of producing or acquiring the product it sells is the firm's cost of goods sold. This amount is a tax-deductible

---

1.  Most firms generate two different income statements. One complies with IRS rules and is designed to take advantage of favorable tax provisions. A second income statement is subjected to different accounting rules and is presented to stockholders and the general public to report the firm's operating performance. This practice of reporting different income statements is legal.

expense and is subtracted from a firm's sales to determine its gross profit. For Le Blanc Industries, cost of goods sold is $680,000.

**Operating Expenses**  All firms have some operating expenses associated with producing and selling their products. These expenses include such things as depreciation, executive and secretarial salaries, sales commissions, office supplies, electricity, and telephone. Subtracting operating expenses from gross profit results in operating profit.

**Other Taxable Income and Expenses**  Some taxable income is realized and some expenses incurred from activities that are not part of the firm's normal operations. Three such items are identified on Lines 7, 8, and 9 of Table 2.3: interest income, a gain from the sale of equipment, and interest expense. Other items might include such things as dividend income from stock owned and losses from the sale of bonds. Adding the net amount of other income to operating profit and subtracting other expenses results in profit before taxes. It is this amount on which the tax liability is based.

## Tax Calculation

The applicable tax rates are applied to the firm's profit before taxes to determine the firm's tax liability. Table 2.4 shows the rates applicable to corporate income in 1988. Notice that higher tax rates are applied to higher levels of income, except for the final category, where the tax rate decreases to a flat rate on all income when taxable income exceeds $335,000. Despite this decrease in the tax rate when income is above $335,000, the average tax rate does not decrease. The reason is that the 34 percent rate indicated in that final category is applied to *all* of the firm's income, not just the amount in excess of $335,000. Conversely, a firm with say, $330,000 of taxable income, has the 39 percent rate applied to only $230,000 of its taxable income. The first $100,000 is taxed at the lower rates shown in Table 2.4. Applying these tax rates to Le Blanc Industries results in a federal income tax liability of $41,750, as indicated in Table 2.5.

To reinforce the calculation of a corporation's tax liability, consider Madison Industries and Nelson, Inc., which generated profit before taxes of $64,000 and $2,530,000, respectively. The tax liabilities for these firms

**TABLE 2.4**  **Tax Rates Applicable to Corporate Income: 1988**

| Taxable Income | Applicable Tax Rate |
|---|---|
| Not more than $50,000 | 15% |
| $50,001 to $75,000 | 25 |
| $75,001 to $100,000 | 34 |
| $100,001 to $335,000 | 39 |
| Firms with income over $335,000 pay a flat tax of 34 percent on all taxable income. | |

*Note:* These rates are also applicable for the second half of 1987.

**TABLE 2.5** **Tax Liability Calculation: Le Blanc Industries**

Given: Taxable income is $150,000.

| | |
|---|---:|
| The first $50,000 is taxed at 15% . . . . . . . . . . . . . . . . . . . . . . . . . . . . . . . . . . . . . . . . . . . | $7,500 |
| The next $25,000 is taxed at 25% . . . . . . . . . . . . . . . . . . . . . . . . . . . . . . . . . . . . | 6,250 |
| The next $25,000 is taxed at 34% . . . . . . . . . . . . . . . . . . . . . . . . . . . . . . . . . . | 8,500 |
| The remaining $50,000 is taxed at 39% . . . . . . . . . . . . . . . . . . . . . . . . . . . . . . | 19,500 |
| Total tax liability . . . . . . . . . . . . . . . . . . . . . . . . . . . . . . . | $41,750 |

**TABLE 2.6** **Tax Liability Calculation: Madison Industries and Nelson, Inc.**

| | |
|---|---:|
| Madison Industries with profit before tax of $64,000 | |
|     The first $50,000 is taxed at 15% | $7,500 |
|     The remaining $14,000 is taxed at 25% | 3,500 |
|         Total tax liability | $11,000 |
| Nelson, Inc., with profit before tax of $2,530,000 | |
|     The entire $2,530,000 is taxed at 34% | $860,200 |

are calculated in Table 2.6 as $11,000 for Madison Industries and $860,200 for Nelson, Inc.

## Average Tax Rate versus Marginal Tax Rate

It is important to understand the difference between a firm's average tax rate and its marginal tax rate. The **average tax rate** is the average rate applied to all of a firm's taxable income. It is determined by dividing the total tax liability by taxable income. For Madison Industries and Nelson, Inc., the average tax rates are

Madison Industries

$$\text{average tax rate} = \frac{\$11,000}{\$64,000} = 17.2\%$$

Nelson, Inc.

$$\text{average tax rate} = \frac{\$860,200}{\$2,530,000} = 34.0\%$$

A firm's **marginal tax rate** is the tax rate applied to the next dollar of taxable income. This rate is important for firms to consider when making financial decisions since the marginal tax rate is applied to any additional income generated by the decision. Consider three firms with taxable income of $60,000, $200,000, and $500,000. If the firm with taxable income of $60,000 makes a decision that increases taxable income, the next dollar of income will be taxed at a 25 percent rate. For the firms with taxable income of $200,000 and $500,000, the next dollar of income will be taxed at 39 percent and 34 percent, respectively. Notice that firms with taxable income exceeding $335,000 have average tax rates equal to their marginal tax rates (34 percent). This is because the 39 percent tax rate that is applied to taxable income between $100,001 and $335,000 gradually increases the firm's average tax rate. When the 335-thousandth dollar has been taxed, the firm's average tax rate has risen to 34 percent. Since any additional taxable income is subjected to a 34 percent marginal tax rate, the average tax rate remains at 34 percent.

It might appear from the preceding discussion that all firms have marginal tax rates of 15 percent, 25 percent, 34 percent, or 39 percent. Such is not the case, however, for two reasons. First, although state income taxes are not discussed here, each state imposes taxes on corporate income. For firms with 34 percent marginal federal tax rates, the combined state and federal marginal tax rate may be 44 percent or higher. Obviously, state taxes cannot be ignored, but since state income tax laws are all different, it is not appropriate to address them here.

A second reason why a firm's marginal tax rate may differ from the rates identified in this chapter is because of the alternative minimum tax, which can markedly increase a firm's tax rate.

**Alternative Minimum Tax**   To ensure that all profitable firms pay a fair share of the nation's tax burden, Congress has imposed an **alternative minimum tax** (AMT). Without this tax, some businesses could use certain tax deductions such as charitable contributions, accelerated depreciation, tax-exempt interest on certain bonds, and other tax-preference items to avoid paying even small amounts of taxes. (*Tax-preference* items are expenses and revenues that are afforded favorable tax treatment). The AMT rules are complex, requiring a set of computations entirely separate from the regular tax liability. For that reason, they are not addressed in this text.

The 1986 tax law altered the existing AMT provisions in a manner that increased the tax substantially for capital-intensive corporations and firms with certain other characteristics. Financial managers should be aware of how the AMT affects their respective firms, since it has the potential of increasing the firm's marginal and average tax rates.

## Important Tax Rules

The key rules as to how specific items of income and expense are taxed are important to numerous financial decisions. Some of these rules existing at the time of this writing are discussed briefly here. However, since tax laws frequently change, it is necessary for financial managers to remain abreast of the current tax laws.

**Depreciation Expense**   Depreciation represents the portion of a firm's fixed asset costs that is allocated to expenses during an accounting period. The Internal Revenue Code specifies how much depreciation expense can be taken each year.

Firms currently have a choice of two different methods of depreciating their assets.[2] The first is called the *modified accelerated cost recovery system*,[3] which we will refer to as the *modified ACRS system*. The alternative

---

2.   The rules presented here apply to property put into use after December 31, 1986.
3.   The accelerated cost recovery system applies to certain assets placed in service prior to January 1, 1987. This system was modified by the Tax Reform Act of 1986.

**TABLE 2.7** Modified Accelerated Cost Recovery System (ACRS): Asset Classes and Depreciation Method

| Asset Class (Recovery Period) | Depreciation Method | Types of Assets |
|---|---|---|
| 3-year | 200% declining-balance | Small tools used in manufacturing |
| 5-year | 200% declining-balance | Autos, light trucks, and computer equipment |
| 7-year | 200% declining-balance | Office furniture, machinery, and equipment |
| 10-year | 200% declining-balance | Special assets (longer-lived equipment) |
| 15-year | 150% declining-balance | Special assets (i.e., telephone distribution plants) |
| 20-year | 150% declining-balance | Special assets (i.e., municipal sewers) |
| 27½-year | Straight-line | Residential rental property |
| 31½-year | Straight-line | Nonresidential real property |

method provides for *straight-line depreciation* over a specified recovery period. In the discussion that follows, a brief presentation of the two methods is made. The reader should be aware that there are numerous exceptions to the material presented here, and some of the rules are simplified here for ease of presentation. It is also important to recognize that assets placed in service prior to 1987 continue to be depreciated under the methods that were in effect at the time they were put into service. Some of the earlier depreciation methods differ substantially from today's methods.

Under the **modified ACRS** system, each depreciable asset falls into one of eight classes, based on its recovery period. Each asset class is required to use either the 200 percent declining-balance method, the 150 percent declining-balance method, or the straight-line method. Table 2.7 provides a description of the eight asset classes and indicates the applicable depreciation methods.

The Internal Revenue Code specifies that all assets in the first six classes are assumed to be placed in service and disposed of in the middle of the year regardless of the *actual* date. Because of this, firms can take only one-half of one year's depreciation in the first year of ownership. An additional one-half of one year's depreciation is then taken in the year following the class life. For example, a portion of the cost of a 3-year asset remains to be depreciated in Year 4, and a portion of the cost of a 5-year asset remains to be depreciated in Year 6.

Although the 200 percent and 150 percent declining-balance methods result in larger depreciation expenses in the earlier years of an asset's life, straight-line depreciation produces greater depreciation in the later years. At the point where the amount of depreciation becomes greater for the straight-line method than for the accelerated method, the firm may cross over to the straight-line method in order to increase its depreciation ex-

**TABLE 2.8**  **Annual Depreciation Percentages Using the Modified Accelerated Cost Recovery System: Up to 20-Year Class**

| Year | 3-Year Class | 5-Year Class | 7-Year Class | 10-Year Class | 15-Year Class | 20-Year Class |
|------|------|------|------|------|------|------|
| 1 | 33.00% | 20.00% | 14.28% | 10.00% | 5.00% | 3.75% |
| 2 | 45.00 | 32.00 | 24.49 | 18.00 | 9.50 | 7.22 |
| 3 | 15.00 | 19.20 | 17.49 | 14.40 | 8.55 | 6.68 |
| 4 | 7.00 | 11.52 | 12.49 | 11.52 | 7.69 | 6.18 |
| 5 | | 11.52 | 8.93 | 9.22 | 6.93 | 5.71 |
| 6 | | 5.76 | 8.93 | 7.37 | 6.23 | 5.28 |
| 7 | | | 8.93 | 6.55 | 5.90 | 4.89 |
| 8 | | | 4.46 | 6.55 | 5.90 | 4.52 |
| 9 | | | | 6.55 | 5.90 | 4.46 |
| 10 | | | | 6.55 | 5.90 | 4.46 |
| 11 | | | | 3.29 | 5.90 | 4.46 |
| 12 | | | | | 5.90 | 4.46 |
| 13 | | | | | 5.90 | 4.46 |
| 14 | | | | | 5.90 | 4.46 |
| 15 | | | | | 5.90 | 4.46 |
| 16 | | | | | 3.00 | 4.46 |
| 17 | | | | | | 4.46 |
| 18 | | | | | | 4.46 |
| 19 | | | | | | 4.46 |
| 20 | | | | | | 4.46 |
| 21 | | | | | | 2.25 |

*Note:* Some percentages have been rounded so that columns total 100%.

pense in the later years. In order to simplify the calculation of annual depreciation, Table 2.8 presents the applicable percentage of an asset's depreciable basis that can be recovered each year. (The *depreciable basis* is the cost of the asset including any transportation and installation costs.) This table reflects the so-called half-year rule and the crossover from accelerated to straight-line depreciation in the appropriate years. Notice that this table applies only to assets in the first six classes.

As an example of how to determine the amount of depreciation taken each year using Table 2.8, consider an asset purchased by Costello Corporation that has a depreciable basis of $100,000 and falls into the 5-year class that appears in Table 2.9. Column 1 indicates each of the six years during which depreciation can be recovered on the asset. Column 2 of Table 2.9 indicates that 20 percent of the asset's depreciable basis can be depreciated in the first year, 32 percent in the second year, and so on. Column 3 indicates the depreciable basis, which remains the same each year, and Column 4 indicates the actual dollar amount of depreciation that can be recovered each year on the depreciable asset. The values in Column 4 are determined by multiplying the percentages in Column 2 by the depreciable basis in Column 3. Notice that depreciation takes place over a six-year period for this asset, even though it is in the 5-year class.

Table 2.8 does not provide depreciation percentages for assets in the two remaining classes: the $27\frac{1}{2}$-year and $31\frac{1}{2}$-year classes. This is because the assumption of midyear purchase does not apply to those asset classes. Instead, depreciation is to be taken based on the actual number of months

**TABLE 2.9**  Annual Depreciation Using the Modified Accelerated Cost Recovery System: Costello Corporation

Given: Asset's depreciable basis: $100,000
        Asset's designated recovery period: five years

| (1) Year | (2) Applicable Depreciation Percentage | (3) Depreciable Basis | (4) (2) × (3) Year's Depreciation |
|---|---|---|---|
| 1 | 20.00% | $100,000 | $20,000 |
| 2 | 32.00 | 100,000 | 32,000 |
| 3 | 19.20 | 100,000 | 19,200 |
| 4 | 11.52 | 100,000 | 11,520 |
| 5 | 11.52 | 100,000 | 11,520 |
| 6 | 5.76 | 100,000 | 5,760 |
| | | | $100,000 |

in which the asset is in service during the year. Appendix A presents a discussion of how assets in the 27½-year and 31½-year classes are depreciated. The remainder of our discussion here is limited to assets with a maximum class life of twenty years.

As an alternative to using the modified ACRS system, firms may elect to use **straight-line depreciation** over the asset's class life. When this method is used, the asset's entire cost is depreciated, including the estimated salvage value. The assumption of placing the asset in service and disposing of it at midyear also applies to this method. As a result, half of one year's depreciation is taken in the initial year of service, and the other half of one year's depreciation is taken in the year following the class life.

Most firms prefer to use the modified ACRS method because of the larger amounts of tax-deductible depreciation it provides in the early years of an asset's life. However, firms expecting to experience low tax rates in the short term but higher tax rates in future years may prefer to incur the less rapid depreciation provided by the straight-line method in the early years. In this way, the tax-reduction benefits provided by high levels of depreciation are reserved for later years when the firm's tax bracket is higher.

**Interest and Dividends**  As indicated earlier, interest paid by a firm is treated as a tax-deductible expense. Since the payment of interest reduces the amount of taxes the firm must pay, it, in effect, reduces the cost of borrowing to the firm.

Conversely, the payment of dividends on both preferred stock and common stock is not considered to be a cost of doing business, but rather a return on the owners' investment in the firm, and is therefore not tax-deductible. The fact that dividends are not tax-deductible contributes to making equity sources of funds more expensive than debt sources (Chapter 12 discusses the cost of all sources of capital to the firm).

When a firm receives interest on loans it has made, that interest is fully taxable. However, when a firm receives dividends on its investments in preferred or common stock of other domestic corporations, the firm is eligible for the *dividends-received deduction*, which exempts 80 percent of all dividends received by corporations from federal income taxes. Thus, if a corporation earns $100,000 of dividends on stocks it owns, only $20,000 of it is taxed as income.

The reason for the dividends-received deduction is to avoid triple taxation. Assume Corporation A owns common stock in Corporation B. Corporation B generates some income on which it pays taxes, then pays a dividend from its net income. If Corporation A is fully taxed on the dividend it receives from Corporation B, taxes would be paid on that same revenue a second time. Then, when Corporation A pays a dividend, it becomes income to Corporation A's stockholders, and they must pay personal income taxes on it. Were it not for the dividends-received deduction, part of Corporation B's income would be fully taxed three times: once as Corporation B's income, again as Corporation A's income, and still again as dividend income to the stockholders of Corporation A.

### Capital Assets

For most firms, stocks, bonds, and real estate are **capital assets** because they are not bought and sold in the normal course of business. When a firm sells capital assets for more than it paid, the *gain* from the sale of those assets is taxed as ordinary income. Prior to 1987, preferential tax treatment was given to gains from the sale of capital assets that were held for longer periods of time. This is no longer the case. The handling of capital losses is subject to special rules that are not presented here.

### Gains and Losses from the Sale of Depreciable Assets

When a firm sells a depreciable asset, the difference between the selling price and the *book value* (cost minus depreciation) of the asset represents a gain or loss to the firm. If the asset has been fully depreciated, book value is zero. If the asset is sold before it is fully depreciated, it is assumed to be sold at midyear, and only half of the year's depreciation can be expensed. When the asset is sold for less than its book value, the loss incurred is deducted from ordinary income. When a depreciable asset is sold for more than its book value, the difference is a gain that is taxed as ordinary income. It does not matter if the selling price is above or below the original purchase price. The entire difference is taxed as ordinary income.

### Operating Losses

When firms incur operating losses (that is, when before-tax profit is negative), those losses can be carried back three years or forward fifteen years to offset taxable income in other years. Thus a loss incurred in the current year can be used to offset an equal amount of taxable income earned in a previous year. The firm must first carry the loss back three years to offset any taxable income in that year. If some losses still remain, the firm can bring them forward a year to offset taxable income two years earlier. If losses still remain, the firm can offset taxable income one year earlier. If losses still remain, the firm can wait until the next year to offset taxable income in that year. The losses can be carried forward a maximum of fifteen years.

This carryback/carryforward provision is designed to reduce the negative impact taxes can have on firms with volatile profits. For example, if a firm has $50,000 of taxable income for three straight years, under the cur-

**TABLE 2.10**  Carryback/Carryforward Provisions Applied to Operating Losses: Abbott, Inc.

| Year | Before Carryback/Carryforward | | After Carryback/Carryforward | |
| :---: | :---: | :---: | :---: | :---: |
| | Taxable Income | Taxes | Taxable Income | Taxes |
| 1984 | $500,000 | $170,000 | 0 | 0 |
| 1985 | 400,000 | 136,000 | 0 | 0 |
| 1986 | 350,000 | 119,000 | 0 | 0 |
| 1987 | (1,900,000) | 0 | 0 | 0 |
| 1988 | 450,000 | 153,000 | 0 | 0 |
| 1989 | 550,000 | 187,000 | 350,000 | 119,000 |
| 1990 | 600,000 | 204,000 | 600,000 | 204,000 |

rent tax structure it must pay a 15 percent tax on that income every year. This would result in total tax payments of $22,500 over the three years. If, however, another firm has $350,000 of taxable income in one year followed by a loss of $100,000 in each of the following two years, the total tax liability would be $119,000 ($350,000 × .34) in the absence of the carryback and carryforward provisions. This larger tax bill is experienced despite the fact that the second firm's average taxable income is the same as that of the first firm, $50,000 per year.

Table 2.10 illustrates the carryback/carryforward provisions. In this example, Abbott, Inc., had taxable income for a number of years before incurring a loss in 1987. The loss incurred in that year is first carried back to offset the taxable income in year 1984, then it is used to offset the taxable income in 1985 and 1986. This means that at the end of 1987, this firm would apply for a refund of the $425,000 it paid in taxes during the years 1984 through 1986. At this point, the firm still has $650,000 of operating losses ($1,900,000 − $500,000 − $400,000 − $350,000) that it can carry forward into future years. In 1988 the firm realizes taxable income of $450,000 before considering the losses being carried forward. Since the losses carried forward exceed the taxable income for 1988, the firm will pay no taxes in that year. This leaves $200,000 of losses that have not yet been used to offset taxable income. The remaining $200,000 can be used in 1989 to offset an equal amount of taxable income. The adjusted taxable income in 1989 is $350,000, and only $119,000 in taxes will be paid that year. Since there are no additional losses to carry forward, the taxable income and level of taxes in 1990 are unaffected.

Because of the carryback/carryforward provisions, an operating loss in the current year normally benefits the firm by an amount equal to the loss times the firm's tax rate (this assumes that the firm either had taxable income in the past or will have taxable income in the future that can be offset). Therefore, for analysis purposes, it is common to recognize this benefit in the form of a negative tax. For example, a firm with a 34 percent tax rate and taxable income of minus $500,000 realizes a tax liability of minus $170,000. This is determined by multiplying 34 percent times the $500,000 loss. As a result, the firm's net profit after tax is negative $330,000 (the numbers in parentheses indicate negative values).

| | |
|---|---|
| Profit before taxes | ($500,000) |
| Less: Federal income taxes (34%) | (170,000) |
| Net profit after taxes | ($330,000) |

**Accumulated Earnings Tax**   Because of the double taxation of corporate income (first as corporate income, then as dividend income to stockholders), it is tempting for small firms to avoid paying dividends, particularly when it is known that the firm's stockholders do not need additional current income. This accumulation of wealth within the firm tends to increase the market value of the firm's common stock and permits profits to be taken and income to be realized (by selling the stock) when desired by the stockholders, perhaps during retirement, when the stockholder's tax bracket is lower. Some small firms may use accumulated earnings to make loans to stockholders or purchase assets that can be used by stockholders. To prevent firms from accumulating earnings to help stockholders avoid paying taxes on dividends, the IRS imposes a special surtax on excessive accumulations of earnings. **Excessive earnings accumulations** are defined only as profits retained by the firm in excess of "reasonable business needs." This rather imprecise definition makes it difficult for the IRS to enforce the surtax.

**S Corporations**   A corporation that elects to be taxed as a partnership is an **S corporation.** Its income is taxed as personal income to the shareholders regardless of whether or not the shareholders actually receive any cash distributions from the firm. The advantage of an S corporation to the stockholders is that the firm can benefit from the corporate form of business organization while avoiding the double taxation that affects the stockholders of regular corporations (called C corporations).

In order to qualify as an S corporation, a firm must possess certain characteristics of a small firm, such as having no more than thirty-five stockholders, and having individual stockholders as opposed to institutional stockholders. One disadvantage of owning an S corporation is the higher tax rate applied to certain levels of income. Owners of small businesses should consider all advantages and disadvantages of S and C corporations before selecting either form.

**Tax Payment Dates**   Corporations that expect to have a tax liability of $40 or more during a given year are required to pay taxes quarterly during the year. Those with fiscal years ending December 31 must estimate the tax liability for the entire year and pay one-fourth of the estimated amount on April 15. The other three installments are due June 15, September 15, and December 15. Since the exact tax liability is not known until after December 31, the firm has until March 15 of the following year to file its tax returns, either applying for a refund if too much has been paid, or paying any additional amount due. Firms substantially underestimating their tax liabilities for the year may be assessed penalties by the IRS.

## Depreciation and Cash Flow

A firm's *cash flow from operations* is defined as the net amount of cash made available to the firm as a result of conducting normal operations. Table 2.11 indicates the income statement for La Rosa Industries in 1988. The purpose of this table is to illustrate the source of cash flow from operations. It is assumed here that all sales are for cash and that all expenses, except for depreciation, are cash expenses paid at the time they are incurred. La Rosa Industries had $2,000,000 of cash flow into the firm from sales during 1988. Cash expenses totaled $1,437,000 during the year. These cash expenses include cost of goods sold, operating expenses, interest, and taxes. They do not include depreciation, since depreciation is a noncash expense.

Subtracting total cash expenses from total revenue results in cash flow from operations. For La Rosa Industries, cash flow from operations was $563,000 ($2,000,000 minus $1,437,000). This same value is determined in Table 2.11 by adding the firm's depreciation to net income. Thus, in general, adding depreciation to net income results in cash flow from operations, although in most firms this is an approximation only, since sales are not normally all cash sales, and all cash expenses are not normally paid when incurred. This example also illustrates why depreciation is considered to be a source of funds.

## The Importance of Taxes in Financial Management

The tax provisions that have been presented have tremendous influence on the decisions made by financial managers, especially in the following three broad areas: acquiring assets, determining capital structure, and paying dividends versus retaining earnings.

**Acquiring the Firm's Assets**  The process of planning for the acquisition of long-term assets is referred to as *capital budgeting*. The tax aspects of capital budgeting are very important since only projects that provide an acceptable level of return on an *after-tax* basis are worth considering. The

**TABLE 2.11  Income Statement: La Rosa Industries, Year-End December 31, 1988**

| | |
|---|---:|
| Sales | $2,000,000 |
| Less: Cost of goods (excluding depreciation) | 1,000,000 |
| Gross profit | 1,000,000 |
| Less: Operating expenses | 200,000 |
| Less: Depreciation | 200,000 |
| Less: Interest | 50,000 |
| Profit before taxes | 550,000 |
| Less: Taxes (34%) | 187,000 |
| Net profit after taxes | 363,000 |
| Plus: Depreciation | 200,000 |
| Cash flow | 563,000 |

after-tax return is affected by such things as the firm's marginal tax rate, the tax savings from depreciation deductions, the impact of taxes on the gains or losses from selling depreciable assets, and the tax-deductible nature of other expenses related to adopting the project (such as training of personnel).

Decisions regarding investment in money market securities, bonds, and common stock are also greatly affected by taxes. For example, the income from some assets is fully taxable, while the income from other assets is only partially taxable (as in the case of dividends), or fully tax-exempt (as in the case of municipal bonds).

**Determining the Firm's Capital Structure**   A firm's capital structure is its mixture of long-term sources of financing. This mixture frequently includes long-term debt, preferred stock, and common equity. In raising long-term funds, the firm must consider the tax-deductible nature of the compensation (interest and dividends) it pays for those funds, as well as other factors. As indicated earlier, the tax-deductible nature of interest can reduce the cost of debt relative to the cost of equity, an important factor to be considered in determining the proportion of total funds to be raised with debt.

**Paying Dividends versus Retaining Earnings**   Since dividends are paid from after-tax profits, the tax liability of the firm is unaffected by the level of dividends paid. However, the firm's stockholders may have a strong preference either for or against the receipt of dividends based on their personal tax situation. If they have high marginal tax rates, they may prefer low dividends in order to postpone taxation until some time in the future. If the stockholders have low current income and low marginal tax rates, they may prefer higher dividends to provide a source of income. Thus, the dividend policy implemented can be influenced by the tax characteristics of investors.

## SUMMARY

Two of the most important aspects of the legal environment in which businesses operate are the legal forms of business permitted and the tax code with which businesses must comply. The three principal forms of business organization—proprietorships, partnerships, and corporations—each have both advantages and disadvantages. Proprietorships are unincorporated businesses that are owned by one individual. That individual *is* the business. The principal advantages of the proprietorship are the ease with which they can be started and the favorable tax treatment of the firm's earnings. The principal disadvantages are the unlimited liability of the owner, and the difficulty raising large amounts of capital.

Partnerships are unincorporated businesses that are owned by more than one person. They have advantages similar to those of proprietorships, including ease in starting the business and favorable tax treatment. The principal disadvantages are the unlimited liability of the partners (although there are exceptions to this), and difficulty in transferring ownership.

Corporations are legal entities that are separate from their owners. As such, they provide the owners with limited liability. A second advantage of the corporate form of business is the ease with which owners can transfer their ownership. The principal disadvantages of the corporate form of business are the cost of incorporation and the double taxation of corporate income.

It is important for business managers to understand how their decisions affect the firm's taxes, since stockholders benefit only from the after-tax profits of the firm. The marginal tax rate of the firm is of particular importance since it indicates the tax rate applicable to additional taxable income generated by the firm.

Depreciation of assets is important to firms in deciding whether or not to purchase depreciable assets. The more rapidly the asset is depreciated, the lower the firm's taxes will be in the early years of ownership.

Both dividend and interest income are taxable to the firm, although dividend income is subject to the dividends-received deduction. Special provisions exist for handling operating losses and accumulated earnings. Although taxes are important in numerous aspects of firm operations, they are particularly important in the acquisition of firm assets, in determining the mixture of long-term sources of financing, and in determining the firm's dividend policy.

## KEY TERMS

**Alternative minimum tax** A special tax paid by firms that would otherwise pay very little tax as a result of receiving large deductions for charitable contributions, accelerated depreciation, tax-exempt interest on certain bonds, and other tax-preference items.

**Average tax rate** The mean tax rate that is applied to the firm's aggregate taxable income. It can be found by dividing the firm's total tax liability by taxable income.

**Capital assets** Stocks, bonds, real estate, and other assets that are not bought and sold by the firm as part of its normal business.

**Corporation** A type of organization that is a legal entity, separate from its owners (stockholders).

**Depreciation** A method of expensing a portion of the cost of fixed assets over time.

**Excessive earnings accumulations** When firm earnings are retained (as opposed to being paid out as dividends) beyond the reasonable business needs of the firm, they may be deemed excessive by the IRS. A surtax is imposed on the excess amount.

**General partnership** An unincorporated business that is owned and managed by all of the partners, each of whom share unlimited liability. This is the most common type of partnership.

**Limited partnership** A special type of partnership wherein one or more partners have limited liability and one or more partners must be a general partner having unlimited liability.

**Marginal tax rate** The tax rate that is applied to the next dollar of taxable income.

**Modified ACRS** An asset-depreciation method specified in the tax code that permits rapid depreciation of an asset's value in the early years. ACRS stands for "accelerated cost recovery system."

**Partnership** An unincorporated business owned by more than one person. There are two types: limited partnerships and general partnerships.

**Proprietorship** An unincorporated business owned by one person.

**S corporation** A small, incorporated business that is permitted to pay taxes as a partnership instead of a corporation, provided the firm meets certain requirements.

**Straight-line depreciation** A method of expensing an *equal* portion of the value of an asset each year over its useful life.

## QUESTIONS

**Q2-1.** Which form of business organization is preferred based on the following characteristics? Why?

**a.** Organizational costs
**b.** Income tax treatment
**c.** Privacy of company information
**d.** Liability of owners
**e.** Ease of raising capital
**f.** Continuity of the business
**g.** Transferability of ownership

**Q2-2.** Why do most large firms adopt the corporate form of business while most small firms are proprietorships and partnerships?

**Q2-3.** From the perspective of the investor, how does ownership of a limited partnership interest differ from owning shares of common stock?

**Q2-4.** Under what circumstances is a firm's marginal tax rate (1) greater than its average tax rate, (2) less than its average tax rate, and (3) equal to its average tax rate?

**Q2-5.** Under what circumstances might a firm want to use straight-line depreciation on an asset that is eligible for depreciation under the modified ACRS system?

**Q2-6.** Describe how the payment and receipt of dividends and interest are handled by corporations for tax purposes.

**Q2-7.** How do corporations handle operating losses and losses from the sale of depreciable assets?

**Q2-8.** What are the two main reasons why firms accumulate earnings instead of paying them out as dividends? What characteristics distinguish those firms most likely to accumulate earnings within the firm?

**Q2-9.** Derive the depreciation percentage for assets in the 3-year class under the modified ACRS method, using the 200 percent declining-balance method and the crossover to straight-line when appropriate.

**Q2-10.** What is the rationale for permitting S corporations to exist?

## SELF-TEST PROBLEMS

Solutions to self-test problems appear on p. S1.

**SP2-1.** What is the tax liability, average tax rate, and marginal tax rate for each of the following firms?

| Firm | Taxable Income |
|------|----------------|
| A | $74,500 |
| B | 350,000 |
| C | 85,000 |
| D | 210,000 |

**SP2-2.** Cheeks, Inc., is about to purchase an asset in the 7-year class with a depreciable basis of $2.5 million.

**a.** Calculate the annual depreciation using the modified ACRS method.
**b.** Calculate the annual depreciation using straight-line depreciation and assuming a 7-year life.

**SP2-3.** In 1988 Sampson, Inc., had sales of $2 million, received interest income of $100,000, and received dividends of $50,000. In addition, it sold a fully depreciated machine for $20,000, paid interest of $150,000, paid dividends of $200,000, incurred operating expenses of $320,000, and cost of goods sold was $1.2 million. What was Sampson's tax liability for the year?

## PROBLEMS

**P2-1.** Irving Industries had taxable income of $300,000 while Dawkins, Inc., had taxable income of $95,000.

**a.** Find each firm's tax liability.
**b.** What is the average tax rate for each firm?
**c.** What is the marginal tax rate for each firm?

**P2-2.** Using the modified ACRS method, find the annual depreciation on the following assets:

**a.** An asset in the 3-year class with a depreciable basis of $250,000.
**b.** An asset in the 7-year class with a depreciable basis of $430,000.

**P2-3.** Find the annual depreciation on an asset with a depreciable basis of $1.5 million. Use straight-line depreciation over a useful life of five years.

**P2-4.** The taxable income for Jordan Industries in recent years is indicated in the following list. These figures do not reflect the effect of carryback or carryforward provisions. Indicate the adjusted taxable income for each year.

| Year | Taxable Income | Adjusted Taxable Income |
|------|------|------|
| 1983 | $500,000 | |
| 1984 | 800,000 | |
| 1985 | 1,400,000 | |
| 1986 | 1,000,000 | |
| 1987 | (2,500,000) | |
| 1988 | 600,000 | |
| 1989 | (300,000) | |
| 1990 | (700,000) | |
| 1991 | 900,000 | |
| 1992 | 1,000,000 | |

**P2-5.** Barkley Enterprises purchased a $3,000,000 machine in the 15-year class. Assuming the firm has a 34 percent marginal tax rate, what will its tax liability be on the asset if it sells the machine for $1.6 million in the eighth year of ownership?

**a.** Assume the use of the modified ACRS method.
**b.** Use straight-line depreciation and a useful life of fifteen years.

**P2-6.** Determine the tax liability and average tax rate for each of these situations:

**a.** Bird Corporation had before-tax profit from operations of $100,000. In addition, it sold depreciable assets with a book value of $200,000 for $150,000, had capital gains of $40,000, paid dividends of $60,000, and received interest payments of $30,000.

**b.** In its first year of operation, McHale Industries had before-tax profit from operations of $150,000. In addition, it paid interest of $120,000, received $300,000 of dividends on its investments, and sold a depreciable asset for $250,000 that had a book value of $330,000.

**P2-7.** Find the book value of an asset at the time of its sale if it were purchased for $5 million and sold during the fifth year of ownership.

**a.** Use the modified ACRS method, and assume the asset is in the 15-year class.
**b.** Use the straight-line method, and assume a 13-year recovery period.

**P2-8.** Ewing, Inc., had taxable income as indicated below. These figures do not reflect the effect of the carryback and carryforward provisions. Assuming a 34 percent average tax rate each year, describe what the firm will do in years 1986 through 1990 as a result of the carryback and carryforward provisions. Discuss each year separately.

| Year | Before-tax Income | Tax |
|------|-------------------|-----|
| 1983 | $5,000,000 | $1,700,000 |
| 1984 | 8,000,000 | 2,720,000 |
| 1985 | 12,000,000 | 4,080,000 |
| 1986 | (10,000,000) | 0 |
| 1987 | 6,000,000 | 2,040,000 |
| 1988 | 9,000,000 | 3,060,000 |
| 1989 | (15,000,000) | 0 |
| 1990 | 7,000,000 | 2,380,000 |

**P2-9** Gilmore Industries received $15,000 in interest and $25,000 in dividends on its investments last year. In addition, it had revenue from product sales of $325,000 and received $32,000 from the sale of a depreciable asset. The depreciable asset had been purchased four years earlier for $130,000, it is in the 5-year class, and the modified ACRS method of depreciation is used. Cost of goods sold for the year was $200,000, and the firm had operating expenses of $35,000. Gilmore paid $10,000 in interest and another $10,000 in dividends. What is Gilmore's tax liability?

**P2-10.** Rambus Recording Company had before-tax income from operations of $5.3 million during a recent year. Additional revenues of $50,000 came from dividends and $15,000 from interest. Rambus sold some common stock it owned for $900,000 and some bonds for $1.2 million. The cost basis on those assets was $700,000 and $1,000,000, respectively. Rambus also sold a depreciable asset during the year (7-year class and modified ACRS). It had been purchased in February three years earlier for $750,000 and was sold for $78,000. Rambus paid $27,000 in interest during the year and $50,000 in dividends. What is Rambus's tax liability?

## REFERENCES

Fama, Eugene F., and Michael C. Jensen. "Organizational Forms and Investment Decisions." *Journal of Financial Economics* (March 1985): 347–50.

———. "Separation of Ownership and Control." *Journal of Law and Economics* 26 (October 1983): 301–25.

———. "The Effects of a Firm's Investment and Financing Decisions on the Welfare of its Security Holders." *American Economic Review* 68 (June 1978): 272–84.

*Federal Tax Course.* Chicago: Commerce Clearing House, Inc., 1987.

*Federal Tax Course.* Updated annually. Englewood Cliffs, NJ: Prentice-Hall, 1987.

*Federal Taxation.* Dane Publications, Inc. Houston, TX, 1986.

Fisher, Bruce D., and Michael J. Phillips. *The Legal Environment of Business.* 2d ed. West Publishing Co. 1986.

Green, Richard C., and Eli Talmor. "The Structure and Incentive Effects of Corporate Tax Liabilities." *The Journal of Finance* 40 (September 1985): 1095–1114.

Haugen, Robert A., and Lemma W. Senbet. "Corporate Finance and Taxes: A Review." *Financial Management* (Autumn 1986): 5–21.

Vandell, Robert F., and Jerry L. Stevens. "Personal Taxes and Equity Security Pricing." *Financial Management* 11 (Spring 1982): 31–40.

## RECOVERY PERCENTAGES FOR ASSETS IN THE 27½-YEAR AND 31½-YEAR CLASSES: MODIFIED ACRS METHOD

The amount of depreciation taken each year on 27½-year and 31½-year assets is dependent on the number of months those assets are in service during the year. Tables 2A.1 and 2A.2 provide the depreciation percentage for each year of an asset's life based on the month of purchase.

**TABLE 2A.1**
Depreciation Percentage for
27½-Year Assets
(Residential Real Estate)

| | Month Placed in Service | | | | | |
|---|---|---|---|---|---|---|
| Year | Jan | Feb | Mar | Apr | May | Jun |
| 1 | 3.48 | 3.18 | 2.88 | 2.58 | 2.27 | 1.97 |
| 2–27 | 3.64 | 3.64 | 3.64 | 3.64 | 3.64 | 3.64 |
| 28 | 1.88 | 2.18 | 2.48 | 2.78 | 3.09 | 3.39 |
| 29 | 0 | 0 | 0 | 0 | 0 | 0 |

| | Month Placed in Service | | | | | |
|---|---|---|---|---|---|---|
| Year | Jul | Aug | Sep | Oct | Nov | Dec |
| 1 | 1.67 | 1.36 | 1.06 | .76 | .45 | .15 |
| 2–27 | 3.64 | 3.64 | 3.64 | 3.64 | 3.64 | 3.64 |
| 28 | 3.64 | 3.64 | 3.64 | 3.64 | 3.64 | 3.64 |
| 29 | .05 | .36 | .66 | .96 | 1.27 | 1.57 |

**TABLE 2A.2**
Depreciation Percentages for
31½-Year Assets
(Nonresidential Rental Property)

*Month Placed in Service*

| Year | Jan | Feb | Mar | Apr | May | Jun |
|------|------|------|------|------|------|------|
| 1 | 3.04 | 2.78 | 2.51 | 2.25 | 1.98 | 1.72 |
| 2–31 | 3.17 | 3.17 | 3.17 | 3.17 | 3.17 | 3.17 |
| 32 | 1.86 | 2.12 | 2.39 | 2.65 | 2.92 | 3.17 |
| 33 | 0 | 0 | 0 | 0 | 0 | .01 |

*Month Placed in Service*

| Year | Jul | Aug | Sep | Oct | Nov | Dec |
|------|------|------|------|------|------|------|
| 1 | 1.46 | 1.19 | .93 | .66 | .40 | .13 |
| 2–31 | 3.17 | 3.17 | 3.17 | 3.17 | 3.17 | 3.17 |
| 32 | 3.17 | 3.17 | 3.17 | 3.17 | 3.17 | 3.17 |
| 33 | .27 | .54 | .80 | 1.07 | 1.33 | 1.60 |

To illustrate the use of Tables 2A.1 and 2A.2, consider a 27½-year asset that is placed in service in October 1987 at a cost of $500,000. The dollar amount of depreciation for each year is indicated in the following table.

| (1) Year | (2) Depreciation Percentage (from Table 2A.1) | (3) Depreciable Basis | (4) (2) × (3) Dollar Amount of Depreciation |
|------|------|------|------|
| 1 | .76 | $500,000 | $3,800 |
| 2–27 | 3.64 | 500,000 | 18,200 |
| 28 | 3.64 | 500,000 | 18,200 |
| 29 | .96 | 500,000 | 4,800 |

## PROBLEMS (Appendix 2A)

**2A-1.** Malone Enterprises recently purchased a building that is in the 31½-year class. If the building has a depreciable basis of $5.2 million, how much depreciation would the firm write off each year under the modified ACRS method? (Assume November 30 was the date of purchase of the building.)

**2A-2.** Maxwell-Cummings Industries purchased a commercial building for $450,000 and began depreciating it as a 27½-year class asset. How much depreciation can be expensed each year under the modified ACRS method if Maxwell-Cummings placed the building in service on February 2?

# PART 2

# VALUATION TOOLS AND CONCEPTS

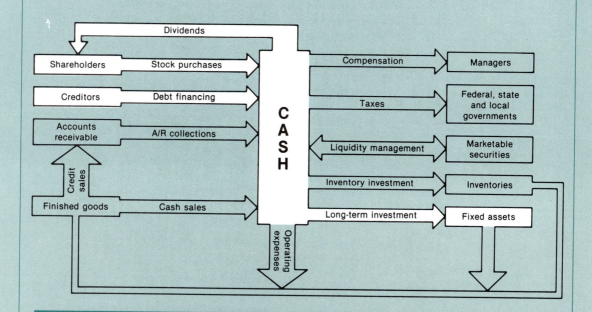

Chapters 3 through 5 focus on the tools that can be applied to a variety of financial management functions. These tools are normally used to assess the value of long-term investments. Chapter 3 describes the time value of money. An understanding of this important concept is necessary for several chapters that follow.

Chapter 4 explains how to value long-term securities such as bonds, preferred stock, and common stock. These securities provide a source of long-term funds for firms. An understanding of how securities are valued by investors is an important prerequisite to making good management decisions. Chapter 5 explains how risk can be incorporated into the valuation process.

# CHAPTER 3

# TIME VALUE OF MONEY

## TIME VALUE IN PERSPECTIVE

Six first round draft picks in the 1987 National Football League draft are listed in the following table along with their contract offers as of June 1987. It is obvious that Vinny Testaverde's contract terms are superior to those of the other players. What is not so obvious, however, is which of the remaining five players has the next best contract. Would you rather have D. J. Dozier's higher signing bonus and lower base salary or Shawn Knight's lower signing bonus and higher base salary? When you fully understand the time value of money, you will be able to make such decisions on a rational basis.

| Player | Team | Signing Bonus | Base Salary | | | |
|--------|------|---------------|-------------|---|---|---|
| | | | Year 1 | Year 2 | Year 3 | Year 4 |
| D. J. Dozier | Minnesota | $ 500,000 | $100,000 | $125,000 | $ 150,000 | $ 200,000 |
| Shane Conlan | Buffalo | 400,000 | 125,000 | 150,000 | 175,000 | 200,000 |
| Tony Woods | Seattle | 400,000 | 120,000 | 150,000 | 180,000 | 230,000 |
| Shawn Knight | New Orleans | 400,000 | 150,000 | 175,000 | 200,000 | 250,000 |
| Vinny Testaverde* | Tampa Bay | 2,000,000 | 600,000 | 800,000 | 1,000,000 | 1,200,000 |
| Roger Vick | New York Jets | 425,000 | 125,000 | 165,000 | 195,000 | 222,000 |

*The signing bonus also includes the reporting bonus. The actual contract offer includes base salaries of $1.2 million and $1.4 million in years 5 and 6, respectively.

Source: USA Today, June 26, 1987, p. 8c.

Most decisions made by financial managers involve the flow of funds into and out of the firm. The timing of these cash flows is important, since dollars received earlier can be reinvested earlier to begin earning an additional return for the firm. Since differences in the value of cash flows can result from timing differences, financial managers must be able to measure these differences in order to make their long-run investment and financing decisions. Determining value differences resulting from timing are also important in making decisions about current assets and current liabilities. Techniques for measuring the *time value of money* are described in this chapter. The application of these techniques to financial decision making is demonstrated in subsequent chapters. This chapter is divided into four major parts, each applicable to a particular set of financial problems:

- Future value of a lump sum
- Present value of a lump sum
- Future value of an annuity
- Present value of an annuity

## FUTURE VALUE OF A LUMP SUM

The **future value of a lump sum** refers to the dollar amount of interest (plus the original principal) that accumulates over time when invested at a specified rate of interest. For example, if you deposit $100 into a savings account at 6 percent annual interest, you will have $106 in your account after one year. Students can solve this problem in their heads by multiplying $100 by 6 percent to determine the amount of interest earned ($6.00). This interest is then added to the original $100, yielding $106. Another way to solve this problem is to recognize that you will have 106 percent of your original deposit after one year, 100 percent representing your deposit and 6 percent representing the interest earned. This method can be displayed algebraically as follows:

$$\text{future value} = \$100(1 + .06)$$
$$= \$100(1.06)$$
$$= \$106$$

What will you have if you leave the $100 in the savings account for two years? After one year you have an amount equal to $100(1 + .06), or $106, in your account. During the second year, you earn 6 percent interest on that entire amount; therefore the amount in the account after the second year is 106 percent of $100(1 + .06), which is written as follows:

$$\text{future value} = \underbrace{\$100(1 + .06)}_{\substack{\text{amount in the} \\ \text{account after} \\ \text{one year}}}\underbrace{(1 + .06)}_{106\%}$$

$$= \$100(1 + .06)^2$$
$$= \$112.36$$

After two years, the amount in the account will be $112.36. This includes the original deposit of $100, plus $12.36 interest. Six dollars of the interest is earned in the first year and $6.36 in interest during the second year. The interest earned in the second year represents 6 percent of the initial deposit (6 percent of $100 equals $6), plus 6 percent of the interest that accumulated during the first year (6 percent of $6 equals $.36). When interest is earned on interest, it is known as **compound interest.**

If you were offered a choice of receiving $100 today or $111 two years from today, which would you prefer, assuming you could earn 6 percent interest on all funds over the next two years. By determining the value of both amounts at the same point in time (two years from today), a decision can be reached. If you receive the $100 today and invest it at 6 percent interest, it will grow to $112.36 in two years. Since this value is higher than the alternative $111 you would receive two years from today, you would prefer to receive the $100 today.

Recall that the future value of $100 deposited for two years at 6 percent interest can be presented as follows:

$$\text{future value} = \$100(1 + .06)(1 + .06)$$

$$= \$100(1 + .06)^2$$

This equation can be generalized and used for all problems where a lump sum is invested for a specified period of time at a stated rate of interest:

$$FV = P(1 + k)^n \qquad \textbf{(3.1)}$$

where $FV$ = future value of a lump sum

$P$ = principal or lump sum

$k$ = annual interest rate

$n$ = the number of years (or periods) the principal is invested

To illustrate the use of Equation 3.1, consider the future value of $500 deposited in a savings account at 10 percent interest for three years. The future value can be found as follows:

$$FV = \$500(1 + .10)^3$$

$$= \$500(1.331)$$

$$= \$665.50$$

There are two principal methods for determining the value of $(1 + k)^n$ used in the previous problem. Hereafter this value is referred to as the *future value interest factor,* or *FVIF.*

The first method requires the use of a calculator with the function $(y^x)$, where the value of $y$ becomes $(1 + k)$ and the value of $x$ becomes $n$. Since in this problem, $k = 10\%$ and $n = 3$, a calculator generates the value 1.3310.

The second method of finding the value of $(1 + k)^n$ is to use Table 3.1. This table is an excerpt from Table A located at the back of the text. It reveals a matrix of values, with the variable $n$ down the left column and the

TABLE 3.1  **Future Value Interest Factors (*FVIF*) for Selected Interest Rates and Periods**

| n | k = 3% | k = 6% | k = 8% | k = 9% | k = 10% | k = 12% | k = 15% |
|---|--------|--------|--------|--------|---------|---------|---------|
| 1 | 1.0300 | 1.0600 | 1.0800 | 1.0900 | 1.1000 | 1.1200 | 1.1500 |
| 2 | 1.0609 | 1.1236 | 1.1664 | 1.1881 | 1.2100 | 1.2544 | 1.3225 |
| 3 | 1.0927 | 1.1910 | 1.2597 | 1.2950 | 1.3310 | 1.4049 | 1.5209 |
| 4 | 1.1255 | 1.2625 | 1.3605 | 1.4116 | 1.4641 | 1.5735 | 1.7490 |
| 5 | 1.1593 | 1.3382 | 1.4693 | 1.5386 | 1.6105 | 1.7623 | 2.0114 |
| 6 | 1.1941 | 1.4185 | 1.5869 | 1.6771 | 1.7716 | 1.9738 | 2.3131 |
| 7 | 1.2299 | 1.5036 | 1.7138 | 1.8280 | 1.9487 | 2.2107 | 2.6600 |
| 8 | 1.2668 | 1.5938 | 1.8509 | 1.9926 | 2.1436 | 2.4760 | 3.0590 |
| 9 | 1.3048 | 1.6895 | 1.9990 | 2.1719 | 2.3579 | 2.7731 | 3.5179 |
| 10 | 1.3439 | 1.7908 | 2.1589 | 2.3674 | 2.5937 | 3.1058 | 4.0456 |

variable $k$ across the top row. To determine the value of $(1 + k)^n$, look down the left-hand column for the appropriate value of $n$. Then read across that row until you reach the column headed by the appropriate value of $k$. The value under the appropriate $k$ column and in the appropriate $n$ row is the *FVIF*. For our problem where $k = 10\%$ and $n = 3$, the value of $(1 + k)^n$ is 1.3310 using Table 3.1. This is the same value determined by using the calculator.

The longer that funds remain in a savings account, the greater the value of the accumulated funds. This can be verified in Table 3.1 by looking down any column. For any given value of $k$, the *FVIF* is higher for higher values of $n$. Similarly, the higher the rates of interest earned on deposits, the higher is the future value of the funds in the account. Therefore, for any row in Table 3.1, the *FVIF*s are greater for higher values of $k$. Figure 3.1 illustrates the effect of $n$ and $k$ on *FVIF*.

As a final example of finding future values, assume that you have received an $8,000 commission for selling some real estate. How much will you have after seven years if you invest this money and earn 12 percent interest annually?

$$FV = P(1 + k)^n$$

$$= \$8,000(1 + .12)^7$$

$$= \$8,000(FVIF)$$

$$= \$8,000(2.2107)$$

$$= \$17,686$$

From the information given, you can determine that you will have $17,686 after seven years.

## Compounding Frequency

Thus far the examples have all assumed that interest is compounded annually; that is, interest is credited to the account one time each year. The procedure just presented can be adjusted to solve problems where interest

**FIGURE 3.1**
Future Value of
$1,000 Based on
Various Rates and
Maturities

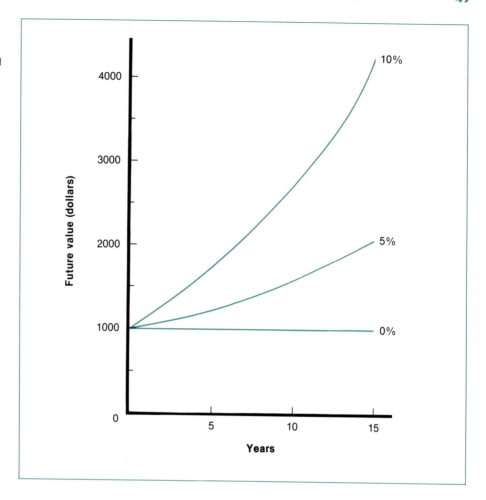

is compounded more frequently. Consider the original example of a $100 deposit for one year at 6 percent interest where interest is compounded annually. Now assume interest is compounded semiannually (twice a year). This means that interest will be credited to the account at midyear, so that during the second half of the year, interest will be earned on both the original principal and on the interest earned during the first half of the year. In this example, the $100 deposited in a savings account will be credited with $3 interest after six months (since the annual interest is 6 percent, only 3 percent interest will be earned for half a year). At the end of the second six-month period, another 3 percent interest will be credited to the account. This time, interest will be earned on the entire $103 that was in the account during that second six-month period. Therefore, the interest earned during the second six-month period will be $3.09 (3% × $103). Total interest earned for the year is $6.09 ($3 + $3.09). After one year, the account balance is $106.09.

In solving this problem, annual interest was divided by 2 (the number of times a year interest is compounded) to determine the interest rate for each subperiod. Additionally, the number of periods was multiplied by 2 to reflect the number of semiannual periods during which interest would be earned on the account. Similar steps are taken when compounding occurs more frequently than twice a year. That is, the interest rate is divided by the number of times a year interest is compounded, and the number of years is multiplied by the number of times each year interest is compounded. Equation 3.2 indicates the adjustments necessary to solve problems where **intrayear compounding** applies:

$$FV = P\left(1 + \frac{k}{m}\right)^{nm} \tag{3.2}$$

where $m$ = number of times each year that interest is compounded.

Equation 3.2 is applied as follows to the example of a $100 deposit at 6 percent interest (compounded semiannually) for one year:

$$FV = P\left(1 + \frac{k}{m}\right)^{nm}$$
$$= \$100\left(1 + \frac{.06}{2}\right)^{1 \cdot 2}$$
$$= \$100(1 + .03)^2$$
$$= \$100(FVIF)$$
$$= \$100(1.0609)$$
$$= \$106.09$$

After the compounding adjustments have been made, Table 3.1 can be used to find that the $FVIF$, reflecting $k = 3\%$ and $n = 2$, is 1.0609.

As a final example of intrayear compounding, consider the case of Nancy Morgan, who invested $5,000 in an investment on which she expects to earn a 24 percent annual return, compounded quarterly. What total value will she accumulate by the end of two years?

$$FV = P\left(1 + \frac{k}{m}\right)^{nm}$$
$$= \$5,000\left(1 + \frac{.24}{4}\right)^{2 \cdot 4}$$
$$= \$5,000(1 + .06)^8$$
$$= \$5,000(1.5938)$$
$$= \$7,969$$

Nancy would have $7,969 after two years if her investment is compounded quarterly; but how much would Nancy have if she could earn 24 percent interest compounded *daily* for two years?

$$FV = \$5,000\left(1 + \frac{.24}{365}\right)^{2 \cdot 365}$$

$$= \$5,000(1.6158)$$

$$= \$8,079$$

Since the value of the *FVIF* in this last example cannot be obtained from Table 3.1, a calculator must be used. Notice that the increased compounding frequency results in more rapid accumulation of interest on the initial investment.

## Solving for the Number of Periods

There are four variables in Equation 3.1. If any three of the variables are known, the fourth can be determined. For example, how long must a $100 deposit remain in an account earning 8 percent annually in order to accumulate $136.05? Plugging the known variables into Equation 3.1 allows the future value interest factor to be isolated on one side of the equation:

$$FV = P(1 + k)^n$$

$$\$136.05 = \$100(1 + .08)^n$$

$$1.3605 = (1 + .08)^n$$

Since the *FVIF* is 1.3605, and the value of $k$ is known, Table 3.1 can be used to determine $n$. Find the column headed "$k = 8\%$," then read down that column until you find the value closest to 1.3605. That exact value can be found in the row where $n = 4$. Therefore, the answer is four years.

## Solving for the Interest Rate

Assume you have $10,000 to deposit in a savings account and you hope to accumulate $30,000 in thirteen years. What annual rate of interest would you need to earn in order to accumulate that amount? By plugging the known variables into Equation 3.1, you can solve for the *FVIF* as follows:

$$FV = P(1 + k)^n$$

$$\$30,000 = \$10,000(1 + k)^{13}$$

$$3.0 = (1 + k)^{13}$$

Since these calculations have set the value of $(1 + k)^{13}$ equal to 3.0, Table 3.1 can be used to determine the value of $k$. Look down the left-hand column for $n = 13$ (the value of $n$ given in the problem). Read across that row (left to right), looking for a *FVIF* of 3.0. In this case, the exact value of 3.0 cannot be found. However, the values 2.7196 and 3.0658, representing 8 percent and 9 percent, respectively, surround the interest factor we are seeking. Depending on the desired degree of accuracy, there are several ways to describe the correct answer. The answer can be described as "close to 9 percent" or "between 8 percent and 9 percent." If greater accuracy is called for, *interpolation*[1] may be used to estimate the interest rate. If a very precise answer is called for, the interest rate can be determined algebraically directly from Equation 3.1:

$$3.0 = (1 + k)^{13}$$

$$1.0882 = (1 + k)$$

$$.0882 = k$$

Therefore, you must earn 8.82 percent interest on your $10,000 of savings to accumulate $30,000 by the end of thirteen years.

## Growth Rates

The future value problems analyzed thus far have all centered around funds on which interest is earned. However, the same framework can be used to calculate growth rates. In finance, it is frequently necessary to determine the *compound annual growth rate* of net income, earnings per share, stock prices, and other series of data. Assume that NCU Corporation paid a dividend of $1.00 per share in 1980 and $2.31 in 1986. It is tempting to take the total growth as a percentage (131 percent) and divide by the number of years of growth (6 years) to get an annual growth rate of 21.8 percent. However, this method ignores compounding (see what the results are if you begin with $1.00 and increase it every year for six years at a rate of 21.8 percent). The compound annual growth rate of the dividend can be determined using Equation 3.1, in which $k$ is now the growth rate instead of a rate of interest, $P$ is the beginning dividend, and $FV$ is the value to which the dividend has grown. We can solve for $k$ as follows:

---

1.  The following equation can be used to estimate the value of either the interest rate $(k)$, or the interest factor $(IF)$ using interpolation:

$$\frac{k - k_L}{k_H - k_L} = \frac{IF - IF_L}{IF_H - IF_L}$$

Here, the symbols $H$ and $L$ stand for the next higher or next lower interest rate or interest factor than the desired value. For example, the previous problem required determining the value of $k$ that is consistent with $n = 13$ and a $FVIF$ of 3.0000. This can be found using Table 3.1 and by solving for $k$ as follows:

$$\frac{k - 8\%}{9\% - 8\%} = \frac{3.0000 - 2.7196}{3.0658 - 2.7196}$$

$$k = 8.81\%$$

This same technique can be used to estimate interest factors. It can also be used to estimate time periods by substituting values of $n$ for $k$ in the equation.

$$FV = P(1 + k)^n$$

$$\$2.31 = \$1.00(1 + k)^6$$

$$2.31 = (1 + k)^6$$

From Table 3.1, the compound annual growth rate is approximately 15 percent.

## PRESENT VALUE OF A LUMP SUM

It was suggested earlier that Equation 3.1 can be used to find the value of *FV*, *k*, and *n*. The fourth variable, *P*, also can be found when the other three variables are known. However, solving for *P* (the *present value* of some future amount, or **present value of a lump sum**) is so important in finance, that instead of using Equation 3.1 to find it, a separate equation is used in which the terms in Equation 3.1 are rearranged to isolate *P* on the left side of the equation:

$$P = FV\left[\frac{1}{(1 + k)^n}\right] \tag{3.3}$$

This equation can be used to find the value today of a lump sum that is expected to exist in the future. For example, assume a firm can purchase an investment that will provide a $25,000 cash receipt three years from today. How much would the firm be willing to pay for the investment if it requires a 12 percent return? Stated differently, what is the present value of the $25,000 future lump sum? By specifying 12 percent as a required rate of return on the investment, it is assumed that any funds committed to the investment could earn 12 percent interest if invested elsewhere. Twelve percent is the value of *k* and is called the **discount rate** since it is used here to discount, or reduce, the value of the future lump sum to its current value. The present value of $25,000 discounted back three years at 12 percent interest can be found as follows:

$$P = FV\left[\frac{1}{(1 + k)^n}\right]$$

$$= \$25,000\left[\frac{1}{(1 + .12)^3}\right]$$

$$= \$25,000(.7118)$$

$$= \$17,795$$

The value in brackets is referred to as the *present value interest factor* (*PVIF*) and can be found using a calculator or by using Table 3.2, which is an excerpt from Table B located in the back of the text. This table is used in a manner very similar to the way Table 3.1 is used. That is, given the values of *n* and *k*, the *PVIF* can be determined from the table. In the problem just described where *n* = 3 and *k* = 12 percent, the *PVIF* can be found

**TABLE 3.2    Present Value Interest Factors (*PVIF*) for Selected Interest Rates and Periods**

| *n* | *k* = 3% | *k* = 6% | *k* = 8% | *k* = 10% | *k* = 12% | *k* = 15% |
|---|---|---|---|---|---|---|
| 1 | .9709 | .9434 | .9259 | .9091 | .8929 | .8696 |
| 2 | .9426 | .8900 | .8573 | .8264 | .7972 | .7561 |
| 3 | .9151 | .8396 | .7938 | .7513 | .7118 | .6575 |
| 4 | .8885 | .7921 | .7350 | .6830 | .6355 | .5718 |
| 5 | .8626 | .7473 | .6806 | .6209 | .5674 | .4972 |
| 6 | .8375 | .7050 | .6302 | .5645 | .5066 | .4323 |
| 7 | .8131 | .6651 | .5835 | .5132 | .4523 | .3759 |
| 8 | .7894 | .6274 | .5403 | .4665 | .4039 | .3269 |
| 9 | .7664 | .5919 | .5002 | .4241 | .3606 | .2843 |
| 10 | .7441 | .5584 | .4632 | .3855 | .3220 | .2472 |

by looking down the left-hand column of Table 3.2 until $n = 3$ is reached. Reading across that row, the value .7118 is found under the column headed by 12 percent.

The value \$17,795 determined in the preceding equation represents the amount the firm will have to pay for the investment in order to realize a 12 percent return. If the firm can pay less than \$17,795 for the investment, the return will exceed the required rate of return, so the firm would be wise to purchase the investment. If the firm must pay more than \$17,795, the return will be less than 12 percent, so the firm should decide not to purchase the investment.

Although different equations have been presented for calculating future value and present value, it should be noted that any problem that can be solved using Equation 3.1 can also be solved using Equation 3.3, and vice versa. This holds true for solving for any of the four variables (*FV*, *P*, *k*, and *n*). For example, the previous problem can be solved using Equation 3.1 as follows:

$$FV = P(1 + k)^n$$

$$\$25,000 = P(1 + .12)^3$$

$$\$25,000 = P(1.4049)$$

$$\$17,795 = P$$

When Equation 3.1 is used to solve a problem, Table 3.1 or Table A at the back of the text must be used. When Equation 3.3 is used, Table 3.2 or Table B must be used. However, the *PVIF* also can be found by dividing 1 by the *FVIF* for the same values of $k$ and $n$. Conversely, the *FVIF* can be found by dividing 1 by the *PVIF*.

It is apparent from Table 3.2 that as the value of $k$ increases, the *PVIF* decreases, resulting in a lower present value of the future amount. This indicates that a higher discount rate results in a lower present value of the future amount. Similarly, as the value of $n$ increases, the *PVIF* decreases, resulting in a lower present value of the future amount. This indicates that when the amount to be received is farther in the future, the present value of that amount is lower. Figure 3.2 illustrates the relationship between the *PVIF* and both $k$ and $n$.

As a final example of how to find the present value of a lump sum, consider the case of Rudecki Corporation, a small real estate developer that is deciding whether to purchase a small lot near downtown Tampa for $20,000. Rudecki expects to be able to resell the lot in two years for $30,000. Ignoring property taxes, transaction costs, and so forth, should Rudecki purchase the lot if it requires a 15 percent return?

One way to solve this problem is to determine the present value of the $30,000 that is expected to be received from the investment in two years and compare this to the purchase price. The required rate of return of 15 percent should be used as the discount rate in this problem.

$$P = FV\left[\frac{1}{(1 + k)^n}\right]$$

$$= \$30,000\left[\frac{1}{(1 + .15)^2}\right]$$

$$= \$30,000(.7561)$$

$$= \$22,683$$

Since the present value of $30,000 discounted back two years at 15 percent is $22,683, Rudecki Corporation would earn a 15 percent return if the lot were purchased for that amount and sold two years later for $30,000. Since the lot can be purchased for less than that amount ($20,000), the return would be higher than 15 percent. Therefore, the firm should purchase the lot.

**FIGURE 3.2**
**Present Value of $1,000 Based on Various Rates and Maturities**

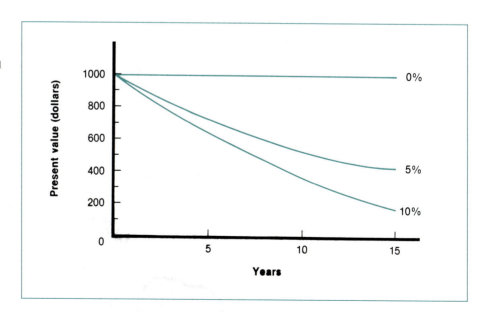

# FUTURE VALUE OF AN ANNUITY

Thus far this chapter has focused on determining the future value and present value of lump sums. In this section, and in the one that follows, the future value and present value of annuities are discussed. An **annuity** is a stream of equal payments at regular intervals. An **ordinary annuity** is one in which the first payment is made at the end of the first period, and the annuity ends at the time the last payment is made.

Since annuities are frequently encountered in finance, it is useful to have a framework for determining their value. As an example, assume that you decide to deposit $100 into a savings account at the end of each of the next three years. You expect to earn 6 percent interest on the account, and you want to determine the total value of the account at the end of the three years. Stated differently, you want to determine the future value of a three-year $100 annuity at 6 percent interest. This situation is illustrated in Figure 3.3. The first $100 deposit is made at the end of the first year and earns interest for only two years, since the annuity ends at the end of the third year. Since the savings account earns 6 percent interest (compounded annually), the first $100 deposit will have grown to $112.36 by the end of the annuity period ($112.36 is the future value of a $100 lump sum earning 6 percent interest for two years). The $100 deposited at the end of the second year earns interest for only one year (from the end of the second year until the end of the third year). During that time, its value will increase to $106.00. The third deposit, made at the end of the third year, earns no interest during the annuity period, since the annuity ends at the time the third deposit is made.

Since the **future value of an annuity** is the value to which the total principal and interest payments have grown during the annuity period, we can sum all of the future value amounts that were previously determined. That is, $112.36 + $106.00 + $100.00 = $318.36. Thus, the future value of a three-year $100 annuity at 6 percent interest is equal to $318.36. Of this amount, $300 is principal, and $18.36 is interest that has been earned on the principal. Instead of finding the future value of each annuity payment separately and summing them, Equation 3.4 can be used to find the future value of an annuity more directly.[2]

---

2. The future value of an annuity can be described algebraically as

$$FVA = A(1 + k)^{n-1} + A(1 + k)^{n-2} + \ldots + A(1 + k)^0$$

where $FVA$ is the future value of an annuity, $A$ is the annuity payment, and $n$ is the number of periods in the annuity. This expression can be reduced to

$$FVA = A[(1 + k)^{n-1} + (1 + k)^{n-2} + \ldots + (1 + k)^0]$$

and

$$= A \sum_{t=1}^{n} (1 + k)^{n-t}$$

(Note continued on next page)

**FIGURE 3.3**

Determining the
Future Value (*FV*)
of a Three-Year
$100 Annuity at
6 Percent Interest

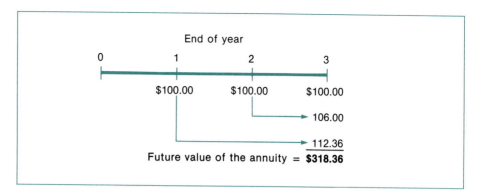

End of year

Future value of the annuity = **$318.36**

$$FVA = A\left[\frac{(1 + k)^n - 1}{k}\right] \qquad\qquad (3.4)$$

where $FVA$ = future value of an annuity

$A$ = annuity payments or receipts

The value enclosed in brackets is called the *future value interest factor of an annuity,* given $k$ and $n$ ($FVIFA_{k,n}$). Its value can be found by using a calculator, by using Table 3.3 in this chapter, or by using Table C at the back of the text.[3]

Equation 3.4 and Table 3.3 can be used to solve the annuity problem described above, which asked for the future value of a three-year $100 annuity at 6 percent interest:

$$FVA = A(FVIFA_{k,n})$$

$$= \$100(FVIFA_{k=6\%,n=3})$$

$$= \$100(3.1836)$$

$$= \$318.36$$

To reinforce the concept of the future value of an annuity, work the following sample problem before looking at the solution. Jim Bradford plans to deposit $2,000 into a savings account at the end of each of the next ten years to accumulate a nest egg for retirement. If he can earn 12 percent

---

It can be shown that

$$\sum_{t=1}^{n} (1 + k)^{n-t}$$

is equivalent to

$$\left[\frac{(1 + k)^{n-1}}{k}\right]$$

3.   This value can also be determined by summing the nonannuity *FVIF*s for $n - 1$ periods and then adding 1.0.

TABLE 3.3   Future Value Interest Factor of an Annuity (*FVIFA*) for Selected Interest Rates and Periods

| n | k = 3% | k = 6% | k = 8% | k = 10% | k = 12% | k = 15% |
|---|--------|--------|--------|---------|---------|---------|
| 1 | 1.0000 | 1.0000 | 1.0000 | 1.0000 | 1.0000 | 1.0000 |
| 2 | 2.0300 | 2.0600 | 2.0800 | 2.1000 | 2.1200 | 2.1500 |
| 3 | 3.0909 | 3.1836 | 3.2464 | 3.3100 | 3.3744 | 3.4725 |
| 4 | 4.1836 | 4.3746 | 4.5061 | 4.6410 | 4.7793 | 4.9934 |
| 5 | 5.3091 | 5.6371 | 5.8666 | 6.1051 | 6.3528 | 6.7424 |
| 6 | 6.4684 | 6.9753 | 7.3359 | 7.7156 | 8.1152 | 8.7537 |
| 7 | 7.6625 | 8.3938 | 8.9228 | 9.4872 | 10.089 | 11.067 |
| 8 | 8.8923 | 9.8975 | 10.637 | 11.436 | 12.300 | 13.727 |
| 9 | 10.159 | 11.491 | 12.488 | 13.579 | 14.776 | 16.786 |
| 10 | 11.464 | 13.181 | 14.487 | 15.937 | 17.549 | 20.304 |

interest on those funds, how much money will be in the account after ten years?

$$FVA = A(FVIFA_{k,n})$$

$$= \$2{,}000(FVIFA_{k=12\%,n=10})$$

$$= \$2{,}000(17.549)$$

$$= \$35{,}098$$

Therefore, Jim would expect to accumulate $35,098 in the account by the end of ten years.

## Solving for the Annuity Amount

Annuity problems involve the interaction of four variables. When given any three of these variables, we can solve for the fourth. For example, suppose Jim Bradford (in the previous example) decides that he needs to accumulate more than $35,098 to supplement his future retirement income. He wants to accumulate at least $50,000 over the next ten years. If he still uses the assumption of a 12 percent return on his savings, how much will he need to deposit in his savings account each year to accumulate the desired amount? Since he needs to end up with $50,000, that amount becomes the future value of an annuity.

$$FVA = A(FVIFA_{k,n})$$

$$\$50{,}000 = A(FVIFA_{k=12\%,n=10})$$

$$\$50{,}000 = A(17.549)$$

$$A = \$2{,}849.17$$

Therefore, Jim will need to deposit $2,849.17 into his savings account at the end of each of the next ten years and earn 12 percent interest on those deposits to accumulate the desired $50,000.

## Solving for the Interest Rate

Assume now that Jim has decided he will be unable to save $2,849.17 each year. Instead, he expects to be able to save and invest a maximum of $2,500 each year. What rate of interest would he neeed to earn in order to accumulate $50,000 after ten years? To answer this question, Equation 3.4 can be used to solve for the value of $k$:

$$FVA = A(FVIFA_{k,n})$$

$$\$50{,}000 = \$2{,}500(FVIFA_{k=?,n=10})$$

$$20.0 = (FVIFA_{k=?,n=10})$$

Since the *FVIFA* and the number of years in the annuity are known, Table 3.3 can be used to find the value of $k$. In the left-hand column for the value $n = 10$, read across that row for a *FVIFA* equal to 20.0. Although there is no *FVIFA* in the table equal to 20.0, the *FVIFA* for 15 percent is very close to it (20.304). This implies that Jim will need to earn almost 15 percent interest on his deposits in order to accumulate $50,000 in ten years.

With annuities it is not possible to solve for the variable $n$ unless $n$ is an integer. When $n$ includes a fraction, it implies that the last payment is for only a fraction of the stated annuity amount. When this is true, an annuity no longer exists. Consequently, such problems are not presented in this text.

# PRESENT VALUE OF AN ANNUITY

The previous section described how to find the future value of an annuity as of the date the annuity ends. Finding the **present value of an annuity** involves determining the value today of all the future annuity payments. As discussed earlier, future dollar amounts are worth less money today. Accordingly, the present value of an annuity should be worth less than the sum of the annuity payments.

For example, if a lump-sum investment today will generate $100 at the end of each of the next three years, how much would you be willing to pay for that investment if you require a 6 percent return? To solve this problem, you must find the value today (present value) of each annuity payment using 6 percent as the discount rate.

One way to solve this problem is to find the present value of each annuity receipt individually and sum the results. This procedure is illustrated in Figure 3.4. Notice that each of the three cash receipts is discounted back to present value. On the time line in Figure 3.4, today is the end of Year 0 or the beginning of Year 1. The first payment must be brought back one year, the second must be brought back two years, and the third must be brought back three years. When added together, the result is the present value of the annuity (in this case, $267.30). This means that if the investment is purchased today for $267.30 and held for three years, the rate of return to the investor, based on the receipt of $100 per year for three years, will be 6 percent. If this investment can be purchased for less than $267.30, the return to the investor will be greater than 6 percent. If the

**FIGURE 3.4**

**Determining the Present Value (PV) of a Three-Year $100 Annuity Using a 6 Percent Discount Rate**

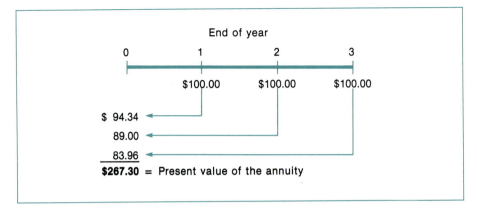

price of the investment exceeds $267.30, the investment will generate less than a 6 percent return.

Equation 3.5 can be used to find the present value of an annuity without the necessity of multiple calculations:[4]

$$PVA = A \left[ \frac{1 - \frac{1}{(1 + k)^n}}{k} \right]$$  (3.5)

where $PVA$ = present value of an annuity.

The value in brackets is called the *present value interest factor of an annuity*, given $k$ and $n$ ($PVIFA_{k,n}$). Its value can be found for selected values of $k$ and $n$ in Table 3.4 and in Table D at the back of the text, or it can be determined with the help of a calculator.[5]

---

4. The present value of an annuity can be described algebraically as

$$PVA = A \left[ \frac{1}{(1 + k)^1} \right] + A \left[ \frac{1}{(1 + k)^2} \right] + \ldots + A \left[ \frac{1}{(1 + k)^n} \right]$$

This expression can be reduced to

$$PVA = A \left[ \frac{1}{(1 + k)^1} + \frac{1}{(1 + k)^2} + \ldots + \frac{1}{(1 + k)^n} \right]$$

$$= A \sum_{t=1}^{n} \left[ \frac{1}{(1 + k)^t} \right]$$

It can be shown that

$$A \sum_{t=1}^{n} \left[ \frac{1}{(1 + k)^t} \right]$$

is equivalent to

$$A \left[ \frac{1 - \frac{1}{(1 + k)^n}}{k} \right].$$

5. This value can also be found by summing the nonannuity *PVIF*s for $n$ periods.

TABLE 3.4 **Present Value Interest Factor of an Annuity (PVIFA) for Selected Interest Rates and Periods**

| n | k = 3% | k = 6% | k = 8% | k = 10% | k = 12% | k = 15% |
|---|---|---|---|---|---|---|
| 1 | .9709 | .9434 | .9259 | .9091 | .8929 | .8696 |
| 2 | 1.9135 | 1.8334 | 1.7833 | 1.7355 | 1.6901 | 1.6257 |
| 3 | 2.8286 | 2.6730 | 2.5771 | 2.4869 | 2.4018 | 2.2832 |
| 4 | 3.7171 | 3.4651 | 3.3121 | 3.1699 | 3.0373 | 2.8550 |
| 5 | 4.5797 | 4.2124 | 3.9927 | 3.7908 | 3.6048 | 3.3522 |
| 6 | 5.4172 | 4.9173 | 4.6229 | 4.3553 | 4.1114 | 3.7845 |
| 7 | 6.2303 | 5.5824 | 5.2064 | 4.8684 | 4.5638 | 4.1604 |
| 8 | 7.0197 | 6.2098 | 5.7466 | 5.3349 | 4.9676 | 4.4873 |
| 9 | 7.7861 | 6.8017 | 6.2469 | 5.7590 | 5.3282 | 4.7716 |
| 10 | 8.5302 | 7.3601 | 6.7101 | 6.1446 | 5.6502 | 5.0188 |

Equation 3.5 and Table 3.4 can be used to find the present value of the annuity described earlier, a three-year $100 annuity at 6 percent:

$$PVA = \$100(PVIFA_{k=6\%,n=3})$$
$$= \$100(2.673)$$
$$= \$267.30$$

This answer is identical to that found when each annuity receipt was discounted back to present value separately.

In order to reinforce these concepts, solve the following problem. Smith Corporation has the opportunity to purchase a security that promises to pay $10,000 at the end of each of the next seven years. What is the maximum dollar amount Smith Corporation can pay for this investment if an 8 percent return is required?

$$PVA = A(PVIFA_{k,n})$$
$$= \$10,000(PVIFA_{k=8\%,n=7})$$
$$= \$10,000(5.2064)$$
$$= \$52,064$$

If Smith Corporation pays $52,064 for the investment, it will earn the required 8 percent return over the seven-year period.

## Solving for the Discount Rate

Once again, there are four variables in Equation 3.5, and given any three, the value of the fourth can be determined (except for n when it includes a fraction of a year). For example, suppose Smith Corporation was able to purchase the investment just described for only $48,680. What rate of return would Smith expect to earn on the investment? (Recall that the investment promises to pay $10,000 at the end of each of the next seven years.)

$$PVA = A(PVIFA_{k,n})$$

$$\$48,680 = \$10,000(PVIFA_{k=?,n=7})$$

$$4.868 = PVIFA_{k=?,n=7}$$

From Table 3.4, $k = 10\%$. Therefore, if Smith Corporation purchases the investment for $48,680, it will earn a 10 percent annual return on its investment over the seven-year period.

## Solving for the Annuity Amount

Equation 3.5 is frequently used to determine the size of loan payments necessary to repay an **amortized loan** where equal payments are made over a specified period. This type of problem requires solving for the value of $A$ in Equation 3.5. Assume that Jones Corporation borrows $20,000 from a bank and promises to repay the loan by making equal annual payments (an annuity) at the end of each of the next four years. These payments are to include both 15 percent interest on the declining loan balance plus increasing principal payments. The size of the loan payments can be determined by solving for the value of $A$:

$$PVA = A(PVIFA_{k,n})$$

$$\$20,000 = A(PVIFA_{k=15\%,n=4})$$

$$\$20,000 = A(2.855)$$

$$A = \$7,005.25$$

If Jones Corporation makes four annual payments of $7,005.25, it will repay the entire $20,000 of loan principal plus 15 percent interest on all outstanding borrowed funds after making the four payments. This is illustrated in Table 3.5. At the end of the first year, a loan payment of $7,005.25 is made (Column 3). Interest on the borrowed amount is paid first ($3,000 in Column 4), and the remaining payment amount is used to reduce the balance of the loan (Column 5). The new loan balance ($15,994.75 in Column 6) is the amount on which interest must be paid during the second

**TABLE 3.5**    **Schedule of Payments for a $20,000 Amortized Loan at 15 Percent Interest for Four Years**

| (1) | (2) | (3) | (4) | (5) | (6) |
|---|---|---|---|---|---|
| Year | Loan Principal | Loan Payment | Interest (15% of Principal) | Principal Reduction | Loan Balance |
| 1 | $20,000.00 | $7,005.25 | $3,000.00 | $4,005.25 | $15,994.75 |
| 2 | 15,994.75 | 7,005.25 | 2,399.21 | 4,606.04 | 11,388.71 |
| 3 | 11,388.71 | 7,005.25 | 1,708.31 | 5,296.94 | 6,091.77 |
| 4 | 6,091.77 | 7,005.25 | 913.77 | 6,091.48 | .29 |

year. A portion of the loan payment made at the end of the second year goes toward paying interest due on the loan ($2,399.21 in Column 4), and the remaining amount ($4,606.04 in Column 5) is applied to the loan principal. Each successive loan payment includes smaller payments of interest and larger principal payments. The last payment (at the end of the fourth year) is designed to cover both interest due for that year and the remaining principal. Due to rounding, a loan balance of 29 cents remains after the final payment. This additional amount is normally added to the final payment made by the borrower.

### Relationship between the Present and Future Values of Annuities

It was indicated earlier that any time-value problem involving lump sums can be solved using either the future value of a lump-sum formula or the present value of a lump-sum formula. *This is not the case when annuities are involved.* The analyst must identify the one correct formula to use in solving the problem. As a practical matter, once you recognize that an annuity is involved, you should ask yourself if you are given, or if you need to determine, the *future value* of an annuity. If neither is the case, ask yourself if you are given, or if you need to determine the *present value* of an annuity. The answer should be yes to one of those questions, and it will indicate the appropriate equation and table to use.

## OTHER TIME-VALUE CONSIDERATIONS

The following time-value problems do not fit into the framework presented thus far.

### Uneven Cash Flow Streams

Consider an investment that is expected to provide cash receipts of $100 in the first year, $200 in the second year, and $300 in the third year. How can you find the present value of that investment if you require a 10 percent return? The annuity formula is not useful here since the cash flows are uneven. Instead, the present value of each lump sum must be computed separately and then summed. This procedure is illustrated in Table 3.6, where the present value of this uneven stream is determined to be $481.58.

TABLE 3.6  **Present Value of an Uneven Cash-Flow Stream**

| Year | Receipts | | PVIF (10%) | | Discounted Cash Flow |
|---|---|---|---|---|---|
| 1 | $100 | × | .9091 | = | $ 90.91 |
| 2 | 200 | × | .8264 | = | 165.28 |
| 3 | 300 | × | .7513 | = | 225.39 |
| | | | PV | = | $481.58 |

## Present Value of a Perpetuity

A **perpetuity** is an annuity that never ends. For example, an investment that is expected to pay $100 every year forever is a perpetuity. To find the present value of all the expected cash receipts is not as difficult as it might seem, since the cash receipts that will be received far in the future have very little value today. In fact, $100 received seventy-five years from today is worth only one-half of 1 cent today using a 14 percent discount rate. In addition, since you would never receive your principal back, you do not need to find its present value. As a result, the present value of a perpetuity can be found using the following equation:[6]

$$PVP = \frac{A}{k} \qquad (3.6)$$

where $PVP$ = present value of the perpetuity

$A$ = the annuity payments or receipts

$k$ = the discount rate

For example, the present value of a $100 perpetuity (received annually) using a 14 percent discount rate can be found as follows:

---

6.  Equation 3.6 can be derived as follows:

$$PVP = \sum_{t=1}^{n} \frac{A}{(1 + k)^t} \qquad (1)$$

where $n$ continues to infinity. This can be rewritten as

$$PVP = A\left[ \frac{1}{(1 + k)^1} + \frac{1}{(1 + k)^2} + \cdots + \frac{1}{(1 + k)^n} \right] \qquad (2)$$

Multiplying both sides of Equation 2 by $(1 + k)$ results in

$$PVP(1 + k) = A\left[ 1 + \frac{1}{(1 + k)^1} + \frac{1}{(1 + k)^2} + \cdots + \frac{1}{(1 + k)^{n-1}} \right] \qquad (3)$$

Subtracting Equation 2 from Equation 3 yields

$$PVP(k) = A\left[ 1 - \frac{1}{(1 + k)^n} \right] \qquad (4)$$

As $n$ approaches infinity, the value of

$$\frac{1}{(1 + k)^n}$$

approaches zero. Therefore, Equation 4 approaches

$$PV(k) = A$$

$$PV = \frac{A}{k}$$

$$PVP = \frac{A}{k}$$

$$= \frac{\$100}{.14}$$

$$= \$714.29$$

### Present Value of a Series of Annuities

Consider an investment that is expected to generate cash inflows of $200 at the end of each of the next three years, and $300 at the end of each of the four years following that. What would be the value of this investment if the firm requires a 10 percent return? This problem involves a series of annuities and cannot be solved as other annuity problems were solved. The answer could be found by discounting each cash flow separately (seven separate present-value-of-a-lump-sum problems) and summing the results. A much quicker solution is to find the value of each annuity today, separately, and then sum the two values. Recognize, however, that the present value of each annuity is the value of that annuity at the time the annuity begins, not necessarily the value today. To illustrate, Figure 3.5 presents a time line identifying these cash flows. The first annuity begins at the end of Year 0, and its present value is $497.38, found as follows:

$$PVA = \$200(PVIFA_{k=10\%,n=3})$$

$$= \$200(2.4869)$$

$$= \$497.38$$

The present value of the second annuity, however, is the value at the time that the annuity begins, which is the end of the third year. The value of this annuity at the end of the third year is $950.97, found as follows:

$$PVA = \$300(PVIFA_{k=10\%,n=4})$$

$$= \$300(3.1699)$$

$$= \$950.97$$

**FIGURE 3.5**
**Determining the Present Value (PV) of a Series of Annuities**

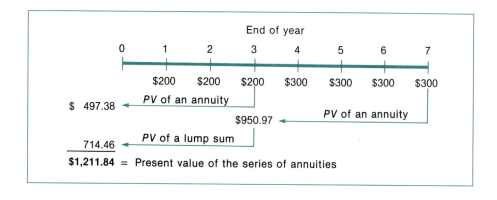

Since this value now represents a lump sum three years in the future, it can be brought back to the present using the present-value-of-a-lump-sum formula:

$$P = FV\left[\frac{1}{(1 + k)^n}\right]$$

$$= \$950.97\left[\frac{1}{(1 + .10)^3}\right]$$

$$= \$950.97(.7513)$$

$$= \$714.46$$

The value of both annuities have now been converted to values in today's dollars.[7] Their sum represents the total value of the investment: $497.38 + $714.46 = $1,211.84.

## The Concept of Annuity Due

An **annuity due** differs from an ordinary annuity only in the timing of the payments or receipts. An annuity due assumes that the payments are made at the beginning of each period instead of at the end, and the annuity ends one year after the last payment has been made. This assumption is appropriate for certain types of finance situations such as lease payments, which are normally made in advance of each lease period.

For a problem involving the future value of annuity due (*FVAD*), one more year of interest will accumulate on each payment. Therefore, the future value interest factor that applies to an annuity due situation will reflect $n + 1$ periods. When that annuity factor has been found, 1.0 should be deducted to remove the principal payment that is not made.[8]

For example, the future value of a three-year $100 annuity due at 6 percent interest is

---

7.  There are a number of other ways to solve this problem, including the following:

a.  Find the present value of a seven-year $300 annuity. Then subtract the present value of a three-year $100 annuity from that.

b.  Add the present value of a three-year $200 annuity to the present value of a four-year $300 annuity found as follows:

$$300(PVIFA_{k=10\%,n=7} \text{ minus } PVIFA_{k=10\%,n=3})$$

c.  Add the present value of a seven-year $200 annuity to the present value of a four-year $100 annuity that has subsequently been brought back three years as a lump sum.

8.  Equation 3.4 would be adjusted to

$$FVAD = A\left[\frac{(1 + k)^{n+1} - 1}{k} - 1\right]$$

where *FVAD* = future value of an annuity due.

$$FVAD = \$100[(FVIFA_{k=6\%, n=3+1}) - 1]$$

$$= \$100[(4.3746) - 1]$$

$$= \$100(3.3746)$$

$$= \$337.46$$

For a problem involving the present value of an annuity due ($PVAD$), each deposit or receipt must be discounted back one less year. As a result, the present value of the annuity will be greater by a factor of $1 + k$. That is, after identifying the $PVIFA$ for an ordinary annuity, multiply $1 + k$ times that amount to determine the $PVIFA$ for an annuity due.[9]

For example, the present value of a three-year $100 annuity due at 6 percent interest is

$$PVAD = \$100(PVIFA_{k=6\%, n=3})(1 + .06)$$

$$= \$100(2.6730)(1.06)$$

$$= \$283.34$$

## SUMMARY

Financial managers must be able to calculate present and future value amounts in order to analyze and solve a variety of problems. Present and future values are influenced by the cash amounts involved, the interest rate (or discount rate), and the number of periods. Table 3.7 summarizes these relationships for each of the four basic types of time-value problems.

Perhaps the most difficult task in solving time-value problems is identifying the appropriate equation to use. The following steps can help in this identification.

**TABLE 3.7**  **Time-Value-of-Money Relationships**

| Increase in | Impact on Present Value of Lump Sum | Impact on Future Value of Lump Sum | Impact on Present Value of Annuity | Impact on Future Value of Annuity |
|---|---|---|---|---|
| Cash amounts | Increase | Increase | Increase | Increase |
| Interest rate ($k$) | Decrease | Increase | Decrease | Increase |
| Number of periods ($n$) | Decrease | Increase | Increase | Increase |

---

9. Equation 3.5 can be adjusted to

$$PVAD = A\left[\frac{1 - \frac{1}{(1 + k)^n}}{k}\right](1 + k)$$

where $PVAD$ = present value of an annuity due.

**TABLE 3.8**

| Task | Equation to Use | Solve for |
|------|-----------------|-----------|
| 1. Find the future value of a lump sum with annual compounding. | $FV = P(1 + k)^n$ | FV |
| 2. Find the future value of a lump sum with compounding more than once a year. | $FV = P\left(1 + \dfrac{k}{m}\right)^{nm}$ | FV |
| 3. Find the interest rate at which a lump sum would accumulate to a specified amount at a future point in time. | $FV = P(1 + k)^n$ | k |
| 4. Find the number of periods it would take to accumulate a specified lump sum at a given interest rate. | $FV = P(1 + k)^n$ | n |
| 5. Find the value today of a future lump sum. | $P = FV\left[\dfrac{1}{(1 + k)^n}\right]$ | P |
| 6. Find the future value of an annuity. | $FVA = A(FVIFA_{k,n})$ | FVA |
| 7. Find the size of annuity payments necessary to achieve a specified lump sum in the future. | $FVA = A(FVIFA_{k,n})$ | A |
| 8. Find the rate of interest necessary to accumulate a specified lump sum over a given time period. | $FVA = A(FVIFA_{k,n})$ | k |
| 9. Find the present value of a series of annuity payments. | $PVA = A(PVIFA_{k,n})$ | PVA |
| 10. Find the rate of return being earned on an annuity-type investment. | $PVA = A(PVIFA_{k,n})$ | k |
| 11. Find the size of the annuity payments necessary to generate a specified rate of return on an investment (i.e., bank loan). | $PVA = A(PVIFA_{k,n})$ | A |
| 12. Find the present value of an uneven stream of cash flows. | $P = FV\left[\dfrac{1}{(1 + k)^n}\right]$ <br> The total cash flow amount for each period is a lump sum. Determine the present value of each lump sum separately and add the results. | P |
| 13. Find the present value of a perpetuity. | $PVP = \dfrac{A}{k}$ | PVP |

*Step 1.* Determine if the problem involves an annuity. If it does not, then it is a lump-sum problem that can be solved using either Equation 3.1 or 3.3. Be certain to use the correct table with the equation selected. If the problem involves an annuity, go to Step 2.

*Step 2.* Determine whether you are given or must solve for the future value of an annuity. If so, use Equation 3.4 to solve the problem. If not, go to Step 3.

*Step 3.* Determine whether you are given or must solve for the present value of an annuity. If so, use Equation 3.5 to find the solution.

Table 3.8 provides a comprehensive list of different types of time-value problems and the method of solving each. Students may wish to refer to it to assure that the correct approach has been selected for a particular problem.

## KEY TERMS

**Amortized loan** A loan that is to be repaid in equal payments at regular intervals. Payments include both interest and principal amounts.

**Annuity** A stream of equal payments made or received at regular intervals.

**Annuity due** A stream of equal payments made at the beginning of each period.

**Compound interest** When interest is earned during a period on interest that had been earned during a previous period.

**Discount rate** The rate at which a lump-sum payment or stream of payments is discounted in order to determine the present value of the payment(s).

**Future value of a lump sum** The value of a lump sum at a specified time in the future. This value includes both principal and accumulated interest.

**Future value of an annuity** The value of a stream of equal payments at regular intervals at a specified time in the future. This value includes both principal and accumulated interest.

**Intrayear compounding** A situation where interest is compounded more than one time each year.

**Ordinary annuity** A stream of equal payments made at the end of each period.

**Perpetuity** A stream of equal payments at regular intervals that continues indefinitely.

**Present value of a lump sum** The value today of a future lump-sum amount.

**Present value of an annuity** The value today of a future stream of equal payments at regular intervals.

## EQUATIONS

**Equation 3.1**     **Future Value of a Lump Sum**

$$FV = P(1 + k)^n$$     **(p. 47)**

where $FV$ = future value of a lump sum
$P$ = principal or lump sum
$k$ = annual interest rate
$n$ = number of periods the principal is invested

This equation can be used to find the future value of a given dollar amount, including both principal and interest earned during the investment period. It can also be used to find interest rates, investment periods, and growth rates.

**Equation 3.2**     **Future Value of a Lump Sum with Compounding More Than Once a Year**

$$FV = P\left(1 + \frac{k}{m}\right)^{nm}$$     **(p. 50)**

where $m$ = the number of times per year that interest is compounded.

This equation is similar to Equation 3.1, except that it adjusts for compounding more than one time each year.

**Equation 3.3**        **Present Value of a Lump Sum**

$$P = FV\left[\frac{1}{(1 + k)^n}\right]$$        **(p. 53)**

This equation can be used to determine the value today of a future lump sum, as-suming a return could be earned on that sum during the intervening period. It can also be used to solve for any of the other three variables that are in the equation.

**Equation 3.4**        **Future Value of an Annuity**

$$FVA = A\left[\frac{(1 + k)^n - 1}{k}\right]$$        **(p. 57)**

where $FVA$ = future value of an annuity
       $A$ = annuity payments or receipts

This equation computes the future value of a stream of equal periodic payments, considering both the principal and interest that accumulate over time. When given some future amount, this equation can be used to find the size of the annuity pay-ments, or the interest rate necessary to accumulate that amount over a given period.

**Equation 3.5**        **Present Value of an Annuity**

$$PVA = \left[\frac{1 - \dfrac{1}{(1 + k)^n}}{k}\right]$$        **(p. 60)**

where $PVA$ = present value of an annuity.

This equation is used to determine the value today of a stream of equal periodic payments expected in the future. Alternatively, it can be used to find the size of loan payments on an amortized loan and the rate of return expected from a given investment.

**Equation 3.6**        **Present Value of a Perpetuity**

$$PVP = \frac{A}{k}$$        **(p. 64)**

where $PVP$ = present value of a perpetuity.

This equation can be used to find the present value of a stream of equal payments at regular intervals that are expected to continue to infinity.

## QUESTIONS

**Q3-1.** Explain the relationship between interest rates and the future value of a lump sum, other things held constant.

**Q3-2.** Explain the relationship between the discount rate and the present value of a lump sum, other things held constant.

**Q3-3.** Explain the relationship between the number of years and the present value of a lump sum, other things held constant.

**Q3-4.** If you wanted to work a present-value-of-a-lump-sum problem using table values, but you only had the future-value-of-a-lump-sum table, how could you derive the *PVIF*?

**Q3-5.** What is the difference between an annuity and a perpetuity?

**Q3-6.** Graph the present value of $500 over a ten-year period at 5 percent and 10 percent. Why do the lines have different slopes?

**Q3-7.** What effect does more frequent compounding have on the present value of a lump sum? Why?

**Q3-8.** Suppose you want to find the value of an investment paying $100 in Year 1, $200 in Year 2, and $300 in Years 3 through 10. What alternative methods are there for finding the value of the investment?

**Q3-9.** If you deposit $50 into a savings account at the *beginning* of each of the next five years at a specified rate of interest, how could you find the future value of the annuity?

**Q3-10.** If you wanted to reduce the present value of an annuity, would you use a larger or a smaller discount rate? Why?

**Q3-11.** Gala Construction Company received two requests for the completion of identical work. Both jobs would take three years to complete. Yet one contract would provide the firm equal payments spread over a ten-year period while the other contract offered equal payments over a three-year period. Describe the method the construction company should use to compare the offers.

**Q3-12.** Spark, Inc., has set a goal of increasing the asset size of its firm from $3 million today to $5 million in four years. It wants to know how much it must grow at a steady quarterly rate in order to achieve its goal. Describe the method this firm should use to determine the appropriate quarterly growth rate.

## SELF-TEST PROBLEMS

Solutions to self-test problems appear on p. S1.

**SP3-1.** Patton Company has invested in a newsletter business that is expected to generate payments as indicated below.

| End of Year | Payment |
|:---:|:---:|
| 1 | $     0 |
| 2 | 0 |
| 3 | 25,000 |
| 4 | 40,000 |
| 5 | 40,000 |
| 6 | 60,000 |
| 7 | 70,000 |

Determine the present value of these payments using a 12 percent discount rate.

**SP3-2.** Janutis, Inc., plans to invest $1,000 at the end of each of the next eight years. It expects to earn a 9 percent return on each investment made. How much will it have accumulated after eight years?

**SP3-3.** Your goal is to accumulate savings of $100,000. Determine the number of years it will take for you to save this amount under the following conditions:

**a.** You deposit $9,000 into a savings account today, and it earns an annual interest rate of 11 percent.
**b.** You deposit $12,000 into a savings account today, and it earns an annual interest rate of 11 percent.
**c.** You deposit $22,000 into a savings account today, and it earns an annual interest rate of 6 percent.

**SP3-4.** Determine the following:

**a.** The future value of a $7,000 deposit today that earns 9 percent annually over the next four years.
**b.** The amount you must deposit today in an account promising 9 percent annual interest over four years in order to accumulate $11,000.
**c.** The annual interest rate necessary so that a $7,000 deposit today would accumulate to $11,000 in four years.

**SP3-5.** You expect to receive $50,000 at the end of each of the next three years from an investment you will make today.

**a.** What is the maximum amount you should pay for this investment if you require a 14 percent return?
**b.** If the investment is priced at $110,000, what would be the annual return on this investment?
**c.** If the investment is priced at $110,000, what amount would you need to receive at the end of each of the next three years in order to give you a 14 percent return?

**SP3-6.** Munster, Inc., expects to receive even cash flows of $8,000 at the end of each of the next seven years from a project it has purchased. This project will also generate cash flows of $12,000 at the end of each of Years 8 through 12. What is the present value of this project based on a required return of 16 percent?

**SP3-7.** As a result of winning the lottery, Sandy Maduski must choose between receiving $8,000 per year for 10 years or receiving a lump-sum payment today. What lump-sum amount would be equally desirable if Sandy could invest that amount at 17 percent?

**SP3-8.** Jayhawk Corporation is considering an investment that would generate $25,000 at the end of Year 1, $40,000 at the end of Year 2, and $55,000 at the end of Year 3. Jayhawk will make the investment only if it can expect to earn an annual return of at least 20 percent. What is the maximum amount Jayhawk should pay for this investment?

## PROBLEMS

**P3-1.** Determine the future value of your $5,000 savings deposit if it earns 12 percent interest annually for six years.

**P3-2.** Determine the future value of your $2,000 savings deposit if it earns 8 percent interest compounded semiannually for three years.

**P3-3.** What annual rate of interest would you need to earn in order for your $4,000 savings account to increase to $6,000 in three years?

**P3-4.** A firm needs to accumulate $500,000 in three years to expand its business. How much should it set aside now if the firm expects to earn 9 percent interest compounded annually?

**P3-5.** A firm needs to accumulate $200,000 in five years to expand its business. How much should it set aside now if it can earn 8 percent interest compounded quarterly?

**P3-6.** A firm plans to purchase an asset that will generate revenues of $50,000 two years from today. How much would the firm be willing to pay for this asset if it requires a 14 percent return?

**P3-7.** An investment company plans to purchase gold, currently priced at $400 per ounce. It expects gold to be worth $750 per ounce in four years. Should the company purchase the gold if it requires an 18 percent compound annual return?

**P3-8.** You deposit $4,000 in a bank at the end of each of five years. How much money will be in the account after the fifth year if it earns 11 percent annual interest?

**P3-9.** How much money must you deposit in a bank account at the end of each of the next twenty years in order to accumulate a total of $200,000 if you earn 10 percent interest on your deposits?

**P3-10.** You deposit $5,000 into a savings account at the end of each of ten years. What interest rate would you need to earn in order to accumulate $80,000?

**P3-11.** Scarlet Corporation has the opportunity to make an investment that would return $15,000 at the end of each of the next ten years. What is the maximum amount Scarlet would be willing to pay for this investment if it requires a 13 percent return?

**P3-12.** If you can purchase an investment for $10,000 that is expected to pay you $2,000 at the end of each of the next nine years, what rate of return would you earn?

**P3-13.** A firm plans to borrow $50,000 from a bank and repay the loan in equal installments at the end of each of the next fifteen years. Each installment includes 8 percent interest on the declining balance, plus principal (an amortized loan). What should the amount of the periodic payments be?

**P3-14.** An investment is expected to provide $2,000 at the end of the first year, $4,000 at the end of the second year, and $9,000 at the end of the third year. How much would you be willing to pay for this investment if you require a 20 percent return?

**P3-15.** An investment will provide $20,000 at the end of each of the next six years and $40,000 at the end of each of the following four years. Determine the value of this investment if you require a 14 percent return.

**P3-16.** Nancy Baker Enterprises has found an investment that will pay $4,000 annually, forever. What is the value of this investment based on a required rate of return of 11 percent?

**P3-17.** How long would it take to double your money at 4 percent interest?

**P3-18.** UVA Corporation plans to invest $20,000 at the end of each year into a special fund that will provide retirement benefits to employees in the future. What will be the value of this fund after eight years if the interest rate earned on it is 14 percent?

**P3-19.** UCONN Corporation plans to invest $300,000 in a project that would generate even cash inflows at the end of each of seven years. What size cash flow would be necessary each year in order for UCONN to earn a 15 percent return?

**P3-20.** USC Corporation plans to deposit $11,915 into a bank account at the end of each of the next nine years. What interest rate must be earned on the funds in order to accumulate $200,000 at the end of the nine years?

**P3-21.** Seminole Corporation plans to borrow funds from a bank at 10 percent. It will have $15,000 available at the *beginning* of each of the next four years to pay interest on the loan balance plus repay principal (an amortized loan). What is the maximum amount Seminole Corporation can borrow if it wants to have fully repaid the loan in four years?

**P3-22.** OSU Corporation plans to purchase a new machine in five years that will cost $90,000. How much cash would it need to deposit in an interest-earning account at the end of each year if it wants to accumulate the full $90,000 by that time (assume an interest rate of 10 percent)?

**P3-23.** Vandy Corporation borrows $150,000 from a bank and will repay the loan in equal annual payments at the end of each of the next six years. These payments will include 12 percent interest on the declining loan balance plus principal payments. What is the size of the annual loan payments?

**P3-24.** IU Corporation is considering making an investment that would generate $10,000 of cash at the end of each of the next ten years. What is the maximum amount the firm can pay for this investment if it requires a 12 percent rate of return?

**P3-25.** Bulldog Corporation plans to make an investment that is expected to generate cash flows of $10,000 at the end of the first year, $20,000 at the end of the second year, and $50,000 at the end of the third year. What is the maximum amount that Bulldog Corporation should pay for this investment if it requires an 8 percent return?

**P3-26.** Hurricane Corporation plans to make an investment that will generate a $3,000 perpetuity. If it requires a 10 percent rate of return, what is the maximum amount it should pay for this investment?

**P3-27.** Cornhusker Corporation plans to make an investment that will generate $8,000 at the end of each of the first six years, and $14,000 at the end of each of the following four years. If it requires a 15 percent rate of return, what is the maximum amount that it should pay for this investment?

**P3-28.** Gopher Corporation has borrowed $100,000 from a bank and promises to repay the loan by making equal annual payments at the end of each of the next five years. These payments are to include both 13 percent interest on the declining loan balance, plus principal payments (an amortized loan). What is the annual loan payment amount?

**P3-29.** War Eagle Corporation plans to borrow $76,000 from a bank, promising to repay the loan by making equal annual payments at the end of each of the next four years. The payments are to include interest on the declining loan balance, plus principal payments. The payment amount required by the bank is $25,000.

**a.** What is the interest rate on this loan?
**b.** Construct an amortization schedule similar to Table 3.5.

**P3-30.** Gator Corporation has made two bank deposits simultaneously. The first was for $100,000 and will earn 11 percent per year. The second was for $70,000 and will earn 12 percent per year. How much will the combined deposits accumulate to in six years?

**P3-31.** UNLV Corporation plans to make an investment of $100,000 that will earn 9 percent per year for three years. It will then use the accumulated amount to invest in a small business. What return on the business must be achieved in order to accumulate $300,000 after nine more years?

**P3-32.** Lynn Thornton hopes to accumulate $1 million over a twenty-year period. She expects to earn 11 percent per year on equal investments of $10,000 made at the end of each of the next twenty years. She is also making a separate lump-sum investment of $200,000. What rate must she earn on this lump-sum investment so that when combined with the annuity, she will accumulate $1 million in twenty years?

**P3-33.** Value Curve Enterprises expects to deposit $10,000 at the end of each of seven years into its pension fund. For the ten years after that, Value Curve expects to increase the deposits to $15,000 per year. Finally, in the thirteen years after that, it expects to deposit $7,000 per year. If Value Curve can earn 9 percent interest on all deposits, how much would be in the pension fund at the end of this thirty-year period?

**P3-34.** Badger Corporation is an investment company that is considering the purchase of a condominium overlooking Waikiki Beach. It expects that it could earn $20,000 per year (after accounting for costs) from renting this condo out. Badger Corporation plans to keep the condo for ten years, at which time it hopes to sell the condo for $400,000. Five years from now the condo will need to be renovated, at a cost of $100,000. The condo is priced at $300,000 today. Badger's required rate of return for this investment is 18 percent. Should Badger Corporation make the investment? Explain.

**P3-35.** Hobbs Company expects to receive payments of $30,000 at the beginning of each of the next seven years. Hobbs believes that it can earn 9 percent on any available funds. What is the present value of the payments to Hobbs Company?

**P3-36.** Morton, Inc., has arranged a contract in which it will receive an "annuity due," representing $85,000 per year for twelve years. Morton, Inc., could earn 8 percent on any available funds. What is the present value of the annuity due?

**P3-37.** Finn Corporation is considering investing $10,000 every year in a money market investment on which it expects to earn 7 percent interest each year. If it makes the first investment today and makes six more at the beginning of each of the next six years, how much will be accumulated after eight years?

**P3-38.** You are planning to retire in thirty-five years. Thus far, you have accumulated $10,000 in a bank account earning 6 percent interest. When you retire, you would like to withdraw $30,000 from the account at the end of each of the following twenty-five years. After the last withdrawal, your bank account balance will be zero. How much must you deposit at the end of each of the next thirty-five years to be able to do this? Assume the bank account will continue to earn 6 percent interest.

# CONTINUOUS COMPOUNDING

If a deposit is compounded continuously, the number of times per year (or period) that interest is compounded approaches infinity. In this case, $(1 + k/m)^{nm}$ approaches $e^{kn}$, where $e$ is defined as

$$e = \lim_{m \to \infty} \left(1 + \frac{1}{m}\right)^m$$

and $\infty$ represents infinity.

The value of $e$ is approximately 2.71828. The future value of a lump sum with continuous compounding can be solved as follows:

$$FV = P\left(1 + \frac{k}{m}\right)^{nm}$$

$$= P\, e^{kn}$$

For example, if a $10,000 deposit was compounded continuously at an annual rate of 11 percent, the future value of this lump sum after five years would be

$$FV = \$10,000(2.71828)^{(.11)(5)}$$

$$= \$17,332.52$$

As a basis of comparison, the future value of the $10,000 deposit is $16,850.58 if it is compounded annually.

# CHAPTER 4

# FINANCIAL ASSET VALUATION

## VALUATION IN PERSPECTIVE

During the week of June 22, 1987, the price of Golden Nugget, Inc. common stock increased $2.50 per share (24.7 percent), while the price of Financial Corporation of America declined $1.75 per share (26.9 percent). During the same week, a bond issued by Kimberly Clark rose in price by $33.75 (3.6 percent), while a bond issued by Ford Credit Corporation declined in price by $23.75 (2.5 percent). Similarly, the price of Bethlehem Steel Corporation preferred stock rose $37\frac{1}{2}$ cents per share (1.9 percent), while the price of a preferred stock issued by Commonwealth Edison declined $1.25 per share (1.5 percent).

In any given day, week, month, or year, some financial assets increase in price while others decline. The changes in securities' prices can be substantial even during short periods of time. Since the goal of management is to maximize shareholder wealth, it is important for management to understand what factors affect the price of the firm's common stock. It is also important for managers to understand the factors that affect the value of the firm's bonds and preferred stock because the higher the value of these securities, the less expensive it is for the firm to raise additional capital.

What factors affect security prices? What, if anything, can management do to influence the price of its firm's securities? This chapter addresses these and other questions concerning the value of financial assets.

Investors must be able to determine the value of financial assets (such as bonds, preferred stock, and common stock) in order to know the maximum price they are willing to pay. After investors decide on the price they are willing to pay for an asset, they can place orders with stockbrokers to purchase or sell that asset; these orders will affect the asset's supply and demand and therefore its market price. That is, if a particular common stock is selling for $10 a share, but investors determine its true value to be $12, they will continue to purchase the stock until the price rises to $12.

Firms would like investors to place a high value on the securities they issue since this will result in higher market prices, which will benefit shareholders and management in two ways. First, securities with a high value allow the firms to raise additional funds in the financial markets at a lower cost, resulting in higher profits. Second, maximizing the value of common stock is consistent with maximizing shareholder wealth, which is the primary goal of management.

As will be shown later, decisions made by management affect the value investors place on the firm's financial assets. Therefore, it is critical for management to understand how investors determine value. The process of determining the value of an asset is called the **valuation** process.

## VALUATION BASICS

There are a number of ways to assess the value of an asset. For example, the **market value** of the asset is the dollar price that can be received from the sale of an asset in the marketplace. This value is determined by the supply of and demand for the asset. For many stocks and bonds, recent market prices are reported in the financial pages of many newspapers.

The **liquidation value** of an asset refers to the dollar amount that would be received from the sale of the asset if it were sold separately as opposed to being sold as part of a going concern. When this term is used to describe the value of common stock, it refers to the dollar amount that would remain if all of a firm's assets were sold separately and all liabilities repaid with the proceeds of the sale. What remains would belong to the stockholders and is generally reported on a per share basis. Since the value of a firm's assets are generally worth more as a going concern than they are separately, the liquidation value of a firm's common stock is normally well below its market value.

The **book value** of an asset refers to its value as it appears on the balance sheet of the firm. Therefore, it is a historical value as opposed to a current value. When the term is used to describe common stock, it refers to the amount of owner's equity in the firm (total assets minus total liabilities) and is generally reported on a per share basis.

The **intrinsic value** of an asset is a measure of its *fair value*. Although the actual intrinsic value may never be known, investors estimate it and compare it to the current market value (price) of the asset. If the estimate of intrinsic value exceeds an asset's market value, investors would consider purchasing the asset. If the market value exceeds the estimated intrinsic value, investors would not consider purchasing the asset.

The preceding discussion of intrinsic value assumes that the financial markets are less than perfectly efficient. If they were perfectly efficient, the market value of all assets would be equal to their respective intrinsic values. This occurs because in a perfectly efficient market, investors would be able to accurately evaluate and act on all new information about individual assets so quickly that the price of the asset would adjust instantly to reflect all new information. Therefore, in a perfectly efficient market, market value and intrinsic value should always be equal.

A controversy surrounding the degree of market efficiency continues, although most experts acknowledge that the financial markets are not perfectly efficient. For our purposes, the degree of efficiency is not as important as an understanding of how financial assets are valued by the investing public. In the remainder of this text, the term *value* refers to the intrinsic value estimated by investors (unless stated otherwise).

The intrinsic value of financial assets (bonds, preferred stock, common stock, and others) can be estimated by calculating the present value of all the cash receipts expected from ownership. The steps necessary to do this are as follows:

*Step 1.* Estimate the future cash receipts expected from ownership of the asset.

*Step 2.* Determine the required rate of return on the asset. This rate reflects several factors, including the riskiness of the asset (the greater the risk of an asset, the higher the return required by investors).

*Step 3.* Determine the present value of the expected future cash receipts using the required rate of return as the discount rate.

It is important to recognize that the results of asset valuation are only as accurate as the estimates of cash flow and the required rate of return. Since both variables are uncertain in most cases, the estimate of value is also uncertain and should be treated accordingly.

## BOND VALUATION

Before discussing the actual valuation of bonds, it is important to gain an understanding of their major characteristics. More detailed information about bonds is provided in Chapter 15.

### Par Value, Coupon Rate, and Maturity

The **par value** (or face value) of a bond is the amount of money the issuing firm must pay to the owner of the bond when the bond matures. It is not necessarily equal to the market value or price of a bond, although when a bond is originally sold by a company, the price is normally very close to par value. For the vast majority of bonds issued by corporations, par value is $1,000. Par value is also useful in determining the dollar amount of interest paid to bondholders as described in the following paragraph.

The **coupon rate** of a bond describes the dollar amount of interest paid to the owner of a bond as a percent of par value. Therefore, multiplying the coupon rate by the bond's par value results in the dollar amount of interest paid to the bondholder each year. This amount is fixed, regardless of the price paid for the bond by the original owner or its subsequent owners. For example, a firm that issues a bond with a par value of $1,000 and an 11 percent coupon rate promises to pay the owner of the bond $110 (11 percent × $1,000) in interest each year until the bond matures.

Interest is normally paid to bondholders semiannually (half the annual interest is paid every six months.) For the bond just described, the semiannual interest is $55. Investors generally prefer to receive half the annual interest after just six months instead of waiting twelve months to receive all of the interest for the year. In this way, the investors can reinvest the earlier payment to earn an additional return during the second six months, resulting in semiannual compounding of interest.

The **maturity date** of a bond is the date the investor is eligible to receive payment of the bond's par value from the issuer. It is also the date on which the bondholder ceases to earn interest on the bond.

## An Example of Bond Valuation

To illustrate bond valuation, consider a bond issued by P. Corum Enterprises having a par value of $1,000, a five-year life, and an 11 percent coupon rate. For simplicity, assume interest is paid annually. The description of this bond reveals that the expected cash payments to the owner of the bond include $110 at the end of each of the next five years, plus an additional $1,000 at the end of the fifth year. The value of this bond to an investor who requires a 10 percent return is determined as follows:

*Step 1. Identify the expected cash receipts of the bondholder.* These expected cash receipts are described with the help of a time line in Figure 4.1.

*Step 2. Determine the required rate of return on the bond.* As indicated earlier, the required rate of return on a financial asset reflects several factors, including the risk of the investment. The required rate of return is discussed in detail later in this chapter and is assumed to be 10 percent in this example.

*Step 3. Find the present value of the expected cash receipts.* At this point we know the expected cash receipts and the required rate of return on the bond issued by P. Corum Enterprises. To find the value of the bond, we need to calculate the present value of the expected cash receipts using the

**FIGURE 4.1**
**Expected Cash Receipts from a $1,000 Par Value Bond Having an 11 Percent Coupon and Five Years until Maturity (Assumes Annual Interest Payments)**

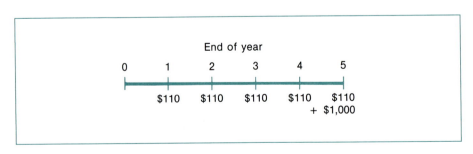

required rate of return as the discount rate. This process can be described algebraically as follows:

$$V_b = \sum_{t=1}^{n} I \left[ \frac{1}{(1 + k_b)^t} \right] + M \left[ \frac{1}{(1 + k_b)^n} \right] \qquad \textbf{(4.1)}$$

where $V_b$ = value of a bond

$\quad\quad I$ = annual dollar amount of interest paid on the bond

$\quad\quad M$ = maturity value (par value) of the bond

$\quad\quad k_b$ = required rate of return on the bond

$\quad\quad n$ = number of years until maturity

$\quad\quad t$ = time period

Equation 4.1 simply tells us to find the present value of the annual interest payments (an annuity) and add them to the present value of the maturity value of the bond (a lump sum). Using the same present value symbols developed in Chapter 3, we can restate Equation 4.1 to read as follows:

$$V_b = I(PVIFA_{k_b,n}) + M(PVIF_{k_b,n}) \qquad \textbf{(4.2)}$$

The value of the bond issued by Corum can now be found using Equation 4.2 to find the present value of the five-year, $110 annuity, plus the present value of the $1,000 lump-sum payment at maturity:

$$V_b = \$110(PVIFA_{k_b=10\%,n=5 \text{ yrs.}}) + \$1,000(PVIF_{k_b=10\%,n=5 \text{ yrs.}})$$

$$= \$110(3.7908) + \$1,000(.6209)$$

$$= \$416.99 + \$620.90$$

$$= \$1,037.89$$

Therefore, the value of this bond is $1,037.89. This represents the maximum amount investors would be willing to pay for the bond. If they pay exactly that amount for the bond, they will earn the required 10 percent return.

## Semiannual Compounding

As indicated earlier, most bonds pay interest semiannually as opposed to just once a year. If the bond issued by P. Corum Enterprises paid interest semiannually, the bond would have greater value to investors since the interest payments received at midyear could be reinvested to earn an additional return. Adjustments can be made in Equation 4.1 to reflect the payment of interest twice a year. The following steps reflect the necessary changes:

1. Divide the annual dollar amount of interest ($I$) by 2 to adjust the annual interest payments down to semiannual payments.
2. Divide $k_b$ by 2 to reflect the rate of return that is required in each semiannual period.
3. Multiply $n$ by 2 to reflect the total number of semiannual payments to be received by the bondholder and the number of semiannual periods over which the maturity value must be discounted.

These changes transform Equations 4.1 and 4.2 into Equations 4.3 and 4.4, respectively:

$$V_b = \sum_{t=1}^{2n} \frac{I}{2}\left[\frac{1}{\left(1 + \frac{k_b}{2}\right)^t}\right] + M\left[\frac{1}{\left(1 + \frac{k_b}{2}\right)^{2n}}\right] \tag{4.3}$$

and

$$V_b = \frac{I}{2}\left(PVIFA_{k_b/2,\ 2n}\right) + M\left(PVIF_{k_b/2,\ 2n}\right) \tag{4.4}$$

Assuming semiannual interest payments, the value of the bond issued by P. Corum Enterprises can be determined as follows (a 10 percent required rate of return is still assumed):

$$V_b = \frac{\$110}{2}\left(PVIFA_{k_b/2=5\%,\ 2n=10\text{ periods}}\right) + \$1{,}000\left(PVIF_{k_b/2=5\%,\ 2n=10\text{ periods}}\right)$$

$$= \$55(7.7217) + \$1{,}000(.6139)$$

$$= \$1{,}038.59$$

Therefore, the value of the bond is $1,038.59 assuming semiannual compounding. This is a slightly higher value than that found using annual compounding. The higher value is due to the benefit investors enjoy from receiving half of each year's interest earlier and thus being able to reinvest it earlier to begin earning an additional return.

Note that the assumption of semiannual compounding is applied to both the interest payments and the maturity value of the bond. Even though the maturity value will not be received in semiannual payments, the idea is to determine what the maturity value of the bond is worth today, assuming that if you had that amount today, it could be invested to earn interest compounded semiannually between now and the maturity date.

To investors, the bond issued by P. Corum Enterprises has a value of $1,038.59 (using semiannual compounding). That is, investors would expect to earn a 10 percent return on their investment if they purchase the bond for $1,038.59. Investors can compare this perceived value of the bond to the market price to determine whether or not to purchase it. If the market price is $1,025, they would buy the bond, since its value exceeds its market price (in other words, the bond is undervalued by the market). If the market price is $1,050, they would not buy the bond, since its value is less than its purchase price.

## Expected Return on a Bond
## (Yield to Maturity)

The previous section showed that investors would receive a 10 percent return on the bond in question if they purchased it for $1,038.59 and held it until maturity. The expected return on a bond that includes both the interest payments and the gain or loss at maturity is called the **yield to maturity (YTM)**.[1] The *YTM* can be calculated by solving for the discount rate that equates the present value of the future cash receipts from a bond to the current price of the bond. *YTM* is normally difficult to compute since it requires solving for the variable $k_b$ in Equation 4.1. Unfortunately, there is no easy way to isolate the variable $k_b$ on one side of the equation. In the absence of a calculator programmed to solve this problem, trial and error may be the only practical way to find the *YTM*.[2] A trial-and-error example follows:

| | |
|---|---|
| **Example** | Find the *YTM* of a bond with an 8 percent coupon, a market price of $911.33, and six years to maturity. Assume semiannual compounding. |

An initial estimate of the *YTM* can be determined from the price of the bond and the coupon rate. If the bond sells at par value, the *YTM* is equal to the coupon rate. If the bond sells at a price below par value, the *YTM* exceeds the coupon rate; and vice versa. The greater the difference is between the price of the bond and par value, the greater the difference between the coupon rate and *YTM*, other things being equal. Similarly, the shorter the time is to maturity, the greater the difference between the coupon rate and *YTM*, other things being equal. (Since these factors are specifically considered in the shortcut method for estimating *YTM* as described in footnote 2, the reader may wish to use that method to establish an initial estimate of the *YTM*.)

Try 12 percent. Since the bond in this example sells at a discount from par value, the *YTM* must exceed the eight percent coupon rate. Try 12 percent first to

---

1. The *YTM* is the rate of return earned by bond investors, assuming the bond is held until it matures, and assuming the investor reinvests all interest payments at the same *YTM*. If interest rates decline after the bond is purchased, the interest payments will be reinvested at lower rates, causing the actual return to the investor to be less than the bond's original *YTM*. Conversely, an investor who reinvests the interest payments at rates exceeding the bond's original *YTM* will realize an actual return that exceeds the *YTM*.

2. The following shortcut method for estimating yield to maturity is less accurate than the regular method, since it does not consider the time value of money.

$$YTM = \frac{I + \dfrac{M - P}{n}}{\dfrac{P + M}{2}}$$

where *YTM* = yield to maturity

    *I* = annual interest in dollars

    *M* = maturity value of the bond

    *P* = market price of the bond

    *n* = number of years until maturity

see if it is the *YTM*. Find the present value of the expected cash receipts using 12 percent as the discount rate.

$$V_b = \frac{\$80}{2}\left(PVIFA_{k_b=6\%,n=12 \text{ periods}}\right) + \$1,000\left(PVIF_{k_b=6\%,n=12 \text{ periods}}\right)$$

$$= \$40(8.3838) + \$1,000(.4970)$$

$$= \$335.35 + \$497$$

$$= \$832.35$$

Since $832.36 is below the market price of the bond, 12 percent is not the *YTM*. To increase the present value of the cash receipts to equal the price of the bond, try a lower discount rate.
   Try 10 percent:

$$V_b = \frac{\$80}{2}\left(PVIFA_{k_b=5\%,n=12 \text{ periods}}\right) + \$1,000\left(PVIF_{k_b=5\%,n=12 \text{ periods}}\right)$$

$$= \$40(8.8633) + \$1,000(.5568)$$

$$= \$354.53 + \$556.80$$

$$= \$911.33$$

Since the present value of the cash receipts is equal to the price of the bond ($911.33) using a 10 percent discount rate, 10 percent is the yield to maturity of the bond.

**Using *YTM* to Make Investment Decisions**   As discussed earlier, investors can make an investment decision by comparing their estimated value of a bond to its market price. A second way to make this decision is to compare the *YTM* on a bond to the investor's required rate of return on the bond. When the *YTM* is greater than or equal to the required rate of return, investors will purchase the bond. When the *YTM* on a bond is lower than the required rate of return, investors should not purchase the bond. The decision made by comparing the required rate of return to the expected rate of return (*YTM*) always agrees with the decision arrived at by comparing the value of the bond to its market price.

## Bond Prices: Discounts and Premiums

When bonds sell at a market price above par value, they are said to sell at a *premium* relative to par value. When they sell below par value, they sell at a *discount* from par value. Recall the valuation problem involving a bond issued by P. Corum Enterprises that has a $1,000 par value, an 11 percent coupon, and five years until maturity. If investors had a required return of 11 percent, the bond would sell for $1,000 (par value). This is true because investors would receive interest payments each year equal to their required rate of return, and they would receive their original investment back at maturity. If investors required a 12 percent return on that same bond, they would have to pay something less than $1,000 for it. For example, if they paid $963.21 for the bond, they would still receive $110 each year on their investment. Their **current yield** (defined as annual interest divided by the initial investment) would be $110/$963.21, or 11.4 percent. In addition, at maturity, the investor would receive $1,000 (par value), which would exceed their purchase price by $36.79. This additional gain, when annualized and adjusted for the time value of money, would bring the total annual return to the investor up to 12 percent. If investors required only a 10 percent return, they would be willing to pay more than par value for the bond described in this example.

## PREFERRED STOCK VALUATION

Preferred stocks are very much like bonds in that they typically pay the owner a fixed amount of compensation each year.[3] One way they differ from bonds, however, is that most do not mature. Preferred stocks and other assets that promise to pay a fixed amount of compensation forever are called **perpetuities.** Recall from Chapter 3 that the value of a perpetuity is the present value of all future cash receipts, where the cash receipts are constant to infinity. Equation 4.5 describes the valuation of preferred stock.

$$V_p = \sum_{t=1}^{\infty} D_p \frac{1}{(1 + k_p)^t} \qquad (4.5)$$

where $V_p$ = value of preferred stock

$D_p$ = annual dividend on preferred stock in dollars

$k_p$ = required rate of return on preferred stock

$t$ = time period

Equation 4.5 can be reduced to the following:[4]

$$V_p = \frac{D_p}{k_p} \qquad (4.6)$$

**Example**

UNF, Inc., has an issue of preferred stock outstanding that pays an annual dividend of $9.75. If an investor requires an 11.5% return on that preferred stock, what is the stock's value?

---

3. Some preferred stocks pay a variable dividend, some are convertible into common stock, and still others have sinking fund provisions. These provisions and others are not typical and are ignored in this chapter. These special provisions are discussed in detail, however, in Chapter 16.

4. Recall that the proof of this equation was presented in Chapter 3 as part of the discussion of perpetuities. The symbols have been changed in this chapter to conform to a specific type of perpetuity, preferred stock.

$$V_p = \frac{D_p}{k_p}$$

$$= \frac{\$9.75}{.115}$$

$$= \$84.78$$

Investors interpret the results of preferred stock valuation in the same manner as they interpret the results of bond valuation. That is, if the value is greater than or equal to the market price, investors would purchase the stock. If the value is below the market price, investors would not purchase the stock, or they would sell it if they owned it.

## Expected Return on Preferred Stock

The expected return on preferred stock is easy to calculate. A rearrangement of terms in Equation 4.6 to isolate $k_p$ results in the following equation:

$$\hat{k}_p = \frac{D_p}{V_p} \tag{4.7}$$

Here, $\hat{k}_p$ (called "$k_p$ hat") is the *expected* return, as opposed to $k_p$ without the hat in Equation 4.6, which represents the *required* rate of return. In Equation 4.7, $V_p$ no longer represents the value of the preferred stock, but rather the market price of the preferred stock.

---

**Example**

Find the expected rate of return on a preferred stock that pays a $4.25 annual dividend and currently sells for $47.22.

$$\hat{k}_p = \frac{D_p}{V_p}$$

$$= \frac{\$4.25}{\$47.22}$$

$$= 9.0\%$$

---

Once investors have determined the expected rate of return, they can compare it to their required rate of return ($\hat{k}_p$ versus $k_p$) to make the investment decision. The stock would be purchased only if the expected return was greater than or equal to their required rate of return. The buy-sell decision using the expected return criterion will always agree with the decision arrived at by comparing the value of the preferred stock to its market price.

## COMMON STOCK VALUATION

The value of common stock, like the value of bonds and preferred stocks, is the present value of all future cash flows. However, two important differences exist. First, the dividend on common stock is not constant, forcing investors to *forecast* future dividends. Second, for most issues of common stock, investors expect to realize a significant proportion of their return from price appreciation in addition to the receipt of dividends (there are some exceptions to this). Several different approaches to common stock valuation are presented here. These approaches generally differ based upon the length of the expected period of investment (*holding period*) and the pattern of expected dividend receipts.

The basic model for common stock valuation is

$$P_0 = \frac{D_1}{(1 + k_s)^1} + \frac{D_2}{(1 + k_s)^2} + \cdots + \frac{D_\infty}{(1 + k_s)^\infty} \qquad (4.8)$$

where $P_0$ = value of common stock

$D_1, D_2, \ldots, D_\infty$ = dividends expected in years 1 through infinity

$k_s$ = required rate of return on common stock

This model suggests that investors must forecast annual dividends to infinity and then discount them back to present value at the required rate of return in order to estimate the value of common stock. For investors who expect to own common stock for a limited period rather than holding it to infinity, the appreciation of the stock's price may be a more important source of return than the receipt of dividends. This situation is specifically recognized in the valuation model that follows.

### Limited-Holding-Period Model

When a stock is to be held for a limited period of time and the future selling price can be forecasted with some degree of accuracy, the value of the stock can be viewed as the present value of the expected dividends during the holding period plus the present value of the expected future selling price of the stock:

$$P_0 = \frac{D_1}{(1 + k_s)^1} + \frac{D_2}{(1 + k_s)^2} + \cdots + \frac{D_n + P_n}{(1 + k_s)^n} \qquad (4.9)$$

where $P_n$ = the price of the stock at the end of the $n$th period.

**Example**

An investor expects QRS Corporation to pay a $1.00 dividend on its common stock next year and $1.10 in the following year. He expects to sell the stock after two years at a price of $27.50 per share. If his required rate of return on the stock is 15 percent, what is the value of the stock today?

$$P_0 = \frac{\$1.00}{(1 + .15)^1} + \frac{\$1.10 + \$27.50}{(1 + .15)^2}$$

$$= \$.87 + \$21.63$$

$$= \$22.50$$

---

Although this appears to deviate from the concept that the value of common stock is the present value of all future dividends, it does not. The future selling price of the stock that must be estimated reflects the present value of all dividends to be paid from the date it will be sold to infinity. Therefore, the concept that the value of common stock today is the present value of all future dividends holds.

## The Constant-Growth Model

In some situations it is reasonable to assume that the dividend paid on a common stock will grow at a fairly constant rate each year. When this is the case, a simplified version of Equation 4.8 can be used for common stock valuation. This constant-growth-rate model (also called the *Gordon model* after Myron Gordon, who developed it) is described in Equation 4.10.[5]

$$P_0 = \frac{D_1}{k_s - g} \tag{4.10}$$

---

5.  Equation 4.10 can be derived algebraically from Equation 4.8 as follows:
    Restate Equation 4.8 to

$$P_0 = \frac{D_0(1 + g)^1}{(1 + k_s)^1} + \frac{D_0(1 + g)^2}{(1 + k_s)^2} + \cdots + \frac{D_0(1 + g)^\infty}{(1 + k_s)^\infty} \tag{1}$$

Multiply both sides of this equation by $(1 + k_s)/(1 + g)$, then subtract Equation 1 from the result:

$$\frac{P_0(1 + k_s)}{1 + g} - P_0 = D_0 - \frac{D_0(1 + g)^\infty}{(1 + k_s)^\infty} \tag{2}$$

When $k_s > g$ (an important assumption of this model), the second term on the right side of the equation approaches zero, leaving

$$P_0 \frac{1 + k_s}{1 + g} - 1 = D_0 \tag{3}$$

Algebraically,

$$P_0 \frac{(1 + k_s) - (1 - g)}{1 + g} = D_0 \tag{4}$$

$$P_0(k_s - g) = D_0(1 + g) \tag{5}$$

$$P_0 = \frac{D_1}{k_s - g} \tag{6}$$

where $g$ = the growth rate of the common stock dividend, assumed to be constant to infinity.

This model can be used only in situations where constant growth of the dividend to infinity is forecasted. Of course, $D_1$ cannot be equal to zero, or the value of the stock would be undefined, and $k_s$ must exceed $g$ (if it does not, a negative or undefined value would result). When one or more of the aforementioned assumptions does not hold true, an alternative valuation model must be used. (One alternative common-stock-valuation model is presented in Appendix A at the end of this chapter.)

Since Equation 4.10 requires the use of some highly restrictive assumptions (such as constant growth), this model only can be used in special situations. However, it does an excellent job of describing the sources of value of common stock: the level of the dividend, the required rate of return, and the dividend growth rate. For this reason, the constant-growth model will be used throughout the text to describe the impact of management decisions on the value of common stock. It should also be noted that regardless of the specific valuation technique employed by an investor, and regardless of the specific source of return to the investor (whether from dividends or from price appreciation), the ultimate source of return to an investor is the firm's dividend (an exception to this would be if the firm is liquidated, in which case the firm's assets are the ultimate source of investor return).

In Equation 4.10, $g$ was defined as the growth rate of the firm's dividend. In order for the dividend to increase at the constant growth rate $g$, the firm's earnings per share (EPS) must also increase by at least that rate, since dividends are paid from earnings. It is assumed in this analysis that EPS grows at the same rate, $g$. Additionally, a constant dividend growth rate will result in a constant growth rate of the price of a share of stock, given certain restrictive conditions. That is, if the denominator of Equation 4.10, consisting of the required rate of return and the growth rate remains constant, while the numerator grows at a constant rate, $g$, the value of $P_0$ would also grow at the constant rate, $g$.

Since $g$ is the growth rate of the dividend, the following relationship holds:

$$D_1 = D_0(1 + g)^1$$

and

$$D_2 = D_0(1 + g)^2$$

and so on.

If last year's dividend $(D_0)$ was $1.00 per share, and the dividend growth rate is 10 percent, the dividends in Year 1 $(D_1)$ and Year 2 $(D_2)$ are expected to be $1.10 and $1.21, respectively:

$$D_1 = \$1(1 + .10)^1$$
$$= \$1.10$$

and

$$D_2 = \$1(1 + .10)^2$$
$$= \$1.21$$

---

**Example**

Godiva Industries paid a dividend last year of $2.23 per share. Assuming a constant dividend growth rate of 8 percent and a required rate of return of 13 percent, what is the value of Godiva Industries' common stock?

$$P_0 = \frac{D_1}{k_s - g}$$

$$= \frac{\$2.23(1 + .08)^1}{.13 - .08}$$

$$= \frac{\$2.41}{.05}$$

$$= \$48.20$$

---

From the perspective of common stock investors, if the value of common stock is greater than or equal to the market price of the stock, its purchase should be considered, since it is undervalued. Conversely, if the value of the stock is lower than the market price, investors should not purchase the stock, and they should sell it if they own it. Some words of caution to prospective investors are necessary here. The results of common stock valuations are estimates and highly subjective. Additionally, the procedure described here has been greatly simplified.

## Expected Return on Common Stock

Owners of common stock generally expect to earn a return from the receipt of cash dividends and from price appreciation. This total return can be described algebraically by solving for $k_s$ in Equation 4.10. This solution is reported here as Equation 4.11.

$$\hat{k}_s = \frac{D_1}{P_0} + g \qquad\qquad (4.11)$$

The variable $\hat{k}_s$ (called "$k_s$ hat") now represents the *expected* return on common stock, instead of the *required* return. The ratio $D_1/P_0$ specifies the expected **dividend yield,** which is the rate of return the investor expects to receive from the cash dividend. The variable $P_0$ in this ratio is the market price of the stock as opposed to the value of the stock as it was defined in Equation 4.10. The variable $g$ is still the growth rate, but in this case it specifically represents the growth rate of the price of the stock, which provides the second component of return to the investor. Although not demonstrated here, it can be shown that the long-run growth rate of the price of the stock is equal to the long-run growth rate of the firm's dividend, given certain assumptions.

To illustrate the use of Equation 4.11, assume that Lewis Industries is expected to pay a $1.37 dividend on its common stock next year. The stock currently sells for $17.25 per share. The dividend has increased at an 8 percent compound annual rate during the past ten years, and this growth is expected to continue in the future. The expected return on Lewis Industries common stock is

$$k_s = \frac{D_1}{P_0} + g$$

$$= \frac{\$1.37}{\$17.25} + 8\%$$

$$= 15.9\%$$

After calculating the expected rate of return, investors can make their investment decisions by comparing this figure to their required rate of return. When the expected return is greater than or equal to the required rate of return, investors should consider purchasing the stock. When the expected return is less than the required rate of return, investors should not purchase the stock, and they should sell it if they own it.

## Alternative Approach to Common Stock Valuation

Most practitioners determine the value of common stock by estimating an appropriate price-earnings (P/E) ratio (also called an *earnings multiple*), which is then multiplied by the firm's earnings per share to arrive at an estimate of the value of the firm's common stock. For example, a stock with EPS of $1.00 and an estimated P/E ratio of 10 has a value of $10. If the price of the stock is currently $9, the stock is considered to be undervalued. The reason why it is undervalued could be described in terms of its current earnings multiple of 9 ($9/$1), which is below what the analyst thinks it should be.

Although this procedure appears to be very different from the common stock valuation procedures described earlier in the chapter, it is not. In order to estimate a firm's P/E ratio, the analyst must first estimate the variables that affect this ratio: the ratio of dividends to earnings, the growth rate of dividends and earnings, and the required rate of return on the stock. Notice that two of these variables are the same as those used earlier to find the value of common stock.

## DETERMINING CASH RECEIPTS AND REQUIRED RATES OF RETURN

In valuing all financial assets, two key variables must be estimated: future cash receipts and required rates of return. A brief discussion of how each is determined follows.

## Forecasting Future Cash Receipts

For bonds and preferred stock, future cash receipts are specified. For common stock, cash receipts are not specified and must be forecasted by investors. A variety of techniques can be used to forecast future dividends. One of the more popular methods involves making a detailed forecast of the economic environment in which a company will operate, followed by an analysis and forecast of how the industry in which the company operates will perform. Finally, an analysis and forecast of the individual company's earnings capability is conducted. To learn more about forecasting dividends, students should consider taking a course in investments.

## Determining Required Rates of Return

In valuing financial assets, the required rate of return is a critical variable. Given the expected cash flows, higher required rates of return (discount rates) result in lower asset values. Earlier in the chapter, the required rate of return was given for various valuation problems. The required rate of return on asset $j$, $(k_j)$, can be described as the risk-free return $(R_f)$, plus a risk premium $(PREM_j)$. The **risk-free rate of return** is the return one can receive on an asset that is void of default risk. Many analysts use the return on U.S. Treasury securities to represent the risk-free rate, since Treasury securities are void of default risk. The **risk premium** is the portion of the required rate of return on an asset that compensates the investor for assuming risk. Owners of different assets incur different levels and types of risk. The greater the riskiness of the asset under consideration, the higher the risk premium and the higher the required rate of return will be. The remainder of this section addresses the specific risks incurred by the owners of different types of financial assets.

**Risk of Investment in Bonds**   Bond investments are subject to default risk and interest rate risk. **Default risk** is the risk to the investor that interest and principal will not be paid when due. This could happen if the firm experiences financial difficulty, and the result could be a large loss for the bondholder. Default risk can be evaluated by the investor through careful financial analysis. However, not only does the investor run the risk of the firm defaulting on its obligations, but a mere change in the market's perception of the firm's default risk can reduce the market value of existing bonds by increasing investor required rates of return (discount rates) on those bonds.

Interest rate risk is the risk that interest rates, including the risk-free return, will rise after a bond has been purchased. This can happen either because of changes in the supply and demand for loanable funds, or because the expected level of inflation changes. When one or both of these components increase, the required rate of return rises, and bond values decline. This is an important source of risk to bond investors.

Interest rate risk affects the market value of some bonds more than others. The values of bonds with low coupon rates and long maturities are more sensitive to market interest rate movements than bonds with high coupons and short maturities. Evidence of the relationship between bond

**TABLE 4.1** Value of Bonds with Different Coupon Rates at Various Required Rates of Return (Par Value Is $1,000 and Maturity Is Ten Years)

| Required Rate of Return | Coupon Rate | | | |
|---|---|---|---|---|
| | 8% | 10% | 12% | 14% |
| 8% | $1,000 | $1,136 | $1,272 | $1,408 |
| 10 | 875 | 1,000 | 1,125 | 1,249 |
| 12 | 771 | 885 | 1,000 | 1,115 |
| 14 | 682 | 788 | 894 | 1,000 |

**TABLE 4.2** Value of Bonds with Different Maturities at Various Required Rates of Return (Par Value Is $1,000 and Coupon Is 10 Percent)

| Required Rate of Return | Maturity | | | |
|---|---|---|---|---|
| | 5-Year | 10-Year | 15-Year | 20-Year |
| 8% | $1,081 | $1,136 | $1,173 | $1,198 |
| 10 | 1,000 | 1,000 | 1,000 | 1,000 |
| 12 | 926 | 885 | 862 | 850 |
| 14 | 859 | 788 | 752 | 733 |

price volatility and both the coupon and maturity of bonds is presented in Tables 4.1 and 4.2. Table 4.1 shows how the values of bonds with different coupon rates change when investors' required rates of return change (presumably due to changing market rates of interest). All of the bonds have an assumed par value of $1,000 and ten-year maturity. For a bond with an 8 percent coupon, the price declines 31.8 percent (from $1,000 to $682) when the required rate of return rises from 8 percent to 14 percent. Given the same change in required rate of return, a bond with a 14 percent coupon declines only 28.9 percent (from $1,408 to $1,000).

Table 4.2 illustrates the effect of changing interest rates on the value of bonds with different maturities. All the bonds displayed in Table 4.2 have a par value of $1,000 and a coupon rate of 10 percent. The price of the bond with a five-year maturity declines 20.5 percent (from $1,081 to $859) as investors' required rates of returns increase from 8 percent to 14 percent. For the bond with a twenty-year maturity, the value declines 38.8 percent (from $1,198 to $733).

Since bonds with lower coupons and longer maturities have more volatile prices, investors desiring low risk should consider purchasing bonds with high coupons and short maturities. Of course, higher potential returns that could result from declining interest rates would be sacrificed. A measure that considers both the maturity and coupon of a bond is known as *duration*. Among other things, duration is a useful indication of the volatility of bond prices. Appendix B to this chapter provides a brief introduction to the concept of duration.

**Risk of Investment in Preferred Stock**    Default risk and interest rate risk are also major sources of risk incurred by owners of preferred stock. However, the level of interest rate risk is not influenced by either the size of the dividend or the time to maturity because most preferred stocks never mature. Consequently, interest rate risk on preferred stock is exclusively dependent on changes in market rates of interest.

Investors in preferred stock also incur the risk that the firm will be unable to pay the stated dividends when they are due. The extent of this default risk can be determined by investors in the same way that they determine the risk of firms being unable to pay interest on debt: through financial analysis. Since interest on debt must be paid before dividends on preferred stock can be paid, investment in preferred stock is generally more risky than an investment in bonds.

**Risk of Investment in Common Stock**    While investors in bonds and preferred stock expect to receive a fixed amount of compensation at regular intervals, investors in common stock normally expect to receive a small regular dividend that increases periodically, plus a capital gain from price appreciation. Although the dividend can be very important to investors (it is the ultimate source of value), price appreciation frequently provides the greatest return. Since dividends are paid on common stock only after all interest has been paid on debt and all required dividends have been paid on preferred stock, common stock is a more risky investment. In addition, there is no legal obligation for firms to pay any dividends on common stock.

The main source of risk to investors in common stock results from

- Decreases in the growth rate ($g$) of firm earnings and dividends, which can reduce the value of common stock.
- Increasing *uncertainty* surrounding a firm's earnings and dividends. This would increase investors' required rates of return on the individual common stock, which can reduce the value of common stock.
- Increases in the required rates of return on common stock in general. This would cause a general decline in stock prices (a *bear market*) that could reduce the value of individual stocks, regardless of the profitability and growth of the individual firms.

In summary, the required rate of return on each asset has two components, the risk-free rate and an additional return to compensate investors for assuming the risk peculiar to the asset in question. Both of these components can be estimated subjectively by the investor after careful financial analysis.

## SUMMARY

It is important for financial managers to understand how financial assets are valued by investors. This helps them understand how the firm's decisions affect the value of the firm's securities. The value of a financial asset is the present value of all the expected cash receipts discounted at the investor's required rate of return. When investors believe the value of an asset is greater than or equal to its market price, they will purchase the asset. When the market price is greater than the asset value, the investors will

## FINANCIAL MANAGEMENT IN PRACTICE

### VALUATION TECHNIQUES USED BY INVESTMENT BANKERS

A study performed by Moses and Cheney provides some insight into how investment bankers determine the value of common stock.* This is an important aspect of investment banking, since the price at which a new public offering is sold depends on the results of the valuation process. The study consisted of collecting and analyzing the responses of investment bankers to a questionnaire. Eighty-six percent of the investment bankers responding to a question about the techniques used to determine stock value indicated that they always use the price-earnings ratio approach. Conversely, only 6 percent of the respondents indicated that they always use the

*Edward Moses and John Cheney, "The Use of Capital Market Theory in Pricing Unseasoned Equity Issues." Presented at the Eastern Finance Association Meeting, April 1980.

present-value-of-cash-flow approach to valuation. When the latter approach is used, very few investment bankers (7 percent) consider an infinite stream of cash flows. Instead, most estimate a finite stream of cash flows and a future selling price two or more years into the future.

A third approach is always used by another 6 percent of the respondents in which they estimate the expected dividend yield and capital gain that would result for three or more years in the future if stock is sold at various possible prices. The total return that would result is then assessed to determine its adequacy.

The study also indicated that the use of systematic risk to determine the appropriate discount rate to use in the valuation process is much less common than using a combination of measures of business and financial risk.

not purchase the asset, or they will sell it if they own it. The same decision will be made if investors compare their expected rate of return to their required rate of return on the asset.

Forecasting future cash receipts and determining required rates of return are critical to the valuation process. Because bonds and preferred stock normally provide stable cash flows at regular intervals, the cash flows resulting from these investments are easy to forecast. For common stock, estimating cash flows is more difficult, since the level of dividends paid is normally related to the level of future earnings, which must be forecasted. The required rate of return on an asset is determined subjectively and is equal to the risk-free return plus an additional amount based on the risk of the specific asset.

## KEY TERMS

**Book value**  The value of a firm according to the firm's balance sheet. It is calculated by subtracting total liabilities from total assets and is based on historical costs.

**Coupon rate**  The annual interest paid on a bond. It is specified as a percentage of the bond's par value.

**Current yield**  The annual interest on a bond as a percentage of the bond's market price.

**Default risk**  The risk to a creditor that the debtor will be unable to pay interest and principal when due.

**Dividend yield**  The annual dividend on a stock described as a percentage of the stock's market price.

**Interest rate risk**  The volatility of investment returns resulting from fluctuating interest rates.

**Intrinsic value**  The true value of an asset. When

estimated by financial analysts and compared to market price, it is the basis for the purchase or sale of financial assets.

**Liquidation value** The value of a firm that would remain for stockholders if the firm's assets were sold separately and all creditors were repaid.

**Market value** The value of an asset as determined by the price at which the asset has been sold or could be sold in the market.

**Maturity date** The date on which a bondholder ceases to earn interest on a bond. The bondholder is also entitled to receive payment of the bond's par value on this date.

**Par value** The stated value of a security as specified by the issuer. For a bond, it is the amount of money a firm must pay to the owner of a bond when it matures.

**Perpetuity** An investment that pays a fixed an-

nual dollar amount to investors, and never matures.

**Risk-free rate of return** The return available on assets that are void of risk. The rate of return on U.S. Treasury bills is generally recognized as a proxy for the risk-free rate of return.

**Risk premium** The return required on an asset, over and above the risk-free rate. The amount of risk premium is based on the riskiness of the asset.

**Valuation** The process of determining the value of assets.

**Yield to maturity (YTM)** The percent return promised to a bondholder if the bond is held to maturity. The YTM considers both the annual interest as a percentage of the bond's price, and any capital gain or loss realized at maturity.

## EQUATIONS

**Equation 4.1**    **Value of a Bond: Annual Interest Payments**

$$V_b = \sum_{t=1}^{n} I \left[ \frac{1}{(1 + k_b)^t} \right] + M \left[ \frac{1}{(1 + k_b)^n} \right] \qquad \textbf{(p. 81)}$$

where $V_b$ = value of a bond

$I$ = annual dollar amount of interest paid on the bond

$M$ = maturity value (par value) of the bond

$k_b$ = required rate of return on the bond

$n$ = number of years until maturity

$t$ = time

This equation can be used to find the value of a bond using the assumption of annual interest payments. It can also be used to find the yield to maturity by solving for the value of $k_b$, where $V_b$ becomes the market price of the bond.

**Equation 4.3**    **Value of a Bond: Semiannual Interest Payments**

$$V_b = \sum_{t=1}^{2n} \frac{I}{2} \left[ \frac{1}{\left(1 + \frac{k_b}{2}\right)^t} \right] + M \left[ \frac{1}{\left(1 + \frac{k_b}{2}\right)^{2n}} \right] \qquad \textbf{(p. 82)}$$

where all variables were defined above.

Using the more realistic assumption of semiannual interest payments on a bond, Equation 4.3 can be used to find the value of a bond ($V_b$) when the required rate of return is given. It can also be used to find the bond's yield to maturity ($k_b$), when the price of the bond is given.

**Equation 4.5**  **Value of Preferred Stock: Basic Equation**

$$V_p = \sum_{t=1}^{\infty} D_p \, \frac{1}{(1 + k_p)^t}$$  **(p. 85)**

where $V_p$ = value of preferred stock

$D_p$ = annual dividend on preferred stock in dollars

$k_p$ = required rate of return on preferred stock

The value of preferred stock is the present value of all future dividends to be received by the investor, discounted at the investor's required rate of return. This relationship is described in Equation 4.5.

**Equation 4.6**  **Value of Preferred Stock: Simplified Equation**

$$V_p = \frac{D_p}{k_p}$$  **(p. 85)**

where all variables were defined above.

The value of preferred stock is the present value of all the preferred stock dividends to infinity. Equation 4.6 determines that value.

**Equation 4.7**  **Expected Return on Preferred Stock**

$$\hat{k}_p = \frac{D_p}{V_p}$$  **(p. 86)**

where $\hat{k}_p$ = expected return on preferred stock
$V_p$ = market price of preferred stock

Equation 4.7 results from the rearrangement of terms in Equation 4.6. Now, however, $k_p$ has a "hat," indicating that it is the expected return as opposed to the required return, and $V_p$ now represents the current market price of the stock rather than the value to the investor.

**Equation 4.8**  **Value of Common Stock: Basic Equation**

$$P_0 = \frac{D_1}{(1 + k_s)^1} + \frac{D_2}{(1 + k_s)^2} + \cdots + \frac{D_\infty}{(1 + k_s)^\infty}$$  **(p. 87)**

where   $P_0$ = value of common stock

$D_1, D_2$, etc. = annual dividend on common stock in periods 1, 2, etc., out to infinity

$k_s$ = required rate of return on common stock

The value of a share of common stock is equal to the present value of all future dividends that will be received from the ownership of that stock. While Equation 4.8 illustrates this important relationship, it has little practical application in its current state (see Equations 4.9 and 4.10).

**Equation 4.9**          **Value of Common Stock: Limited Holding Period**

$$P_0 = \frac{D_1}{(1 + k_s)^1} + \frac{D_2}{(1 + k_s)^2} + \cdots + \frac{D_n + P_n}{(1 + k_s)^n}$$          **(p. 87)**

where $P_n$ = price of common stock at the end of period $n$
$D_n$ = dividend paid in period $n$

When a common stock is to be held for a limited period of time and the future selling price can be forecasted along with the dividends during the holding period, Equation 4.9 can be used to find the value of the stock.

**Equation 4.10**          **Value of Common Stock: Constant Growth**

$$P_0 = \frac{D_1}{k_s - g}$$          **(p. 88)**

where $g$ = growth rate of the dividend, which is assumed to be constant to infinity ($g$ is also the growth rate of earnings per share and the growth rate of the price of the stock)

When the dividend on common stock is assumed to be constant to infinity, Equation 4.8 can be reduced to Equation 4.10. The value of the common stock is still equal to the present value of all future dividends, but the assumption of a constant dividend growth rate simplifies the calculation.

**Equation 4.11**          **Expected Return on Common Stock**

$$\hat{k}_s = \frac{D_1}{P_0} + g$$          **(p. 90)**

where $P_0$ = current market price of a share of common stock (note that in Equation 4.10, $P_0$ was the value of common stock)

When the assumption of a constant dividend growth rate can be made, the expected return to investors in a common stock is the dividend yield ($D_1/P_0$), plus the growth rate of the price of the stock ($g$).

## QUESTIONS

**Q4-1.** Describe the steps required to find the value of a financial asset.

**Q4-2.** Why is bond valuation easier for the analyst than common stock valuation?

**Q4-3.** Describe the procedures one must follow to determine the yield to maturity on a bond.

**Q4-4.** Investors can decide whether or not to purchase a bond by either calculating its value or by calculating its yield to maturity. How is the decision made based on each of those figures?

**Q4-5.** Why is the mathematics of preferred stock valuation so much easier than the mathematics of bond valuation?

**Q4-6.** The variable $g$ can represent several things. What are they? How are they related to each other?

**Q4-7.** What assumptions are necessary in order to use the constant-growth valuation model?

**Q4-8.** Define the following variables and describe their relationship to each other: $D_0$ and $D_1$.

**Q4-9.** Briefly describe the major factors that affect the riskiness of bonds, preferred stock, and common stock.

**Q4-10.** Briefly describe the earnings-multiple approach to common stock valuation. How is it similar to the present-value-of-future-dividends approach?

**Q4-11.** If a firm increases the percent of total earnings it pays out in dividends, how would the following factors most likely be affected: future growth rate of the dividend, future price appreciation, and future dividend yield (the ratio of dividend to price)?

**Q4-12.** How might each of the following affect the variables in the constant growth valuation model (consider each separately): (1) market rates of interest rise; (2) the firm's sales begin to rise at a slower rate; (3) the firm experiences financial difficulty; (4) the firm's expenses rise faster than it can increase its prices?

## SELF-TEST PROBLEMS

Solutions to self-test problems appear on p. S1.

**SP4-1.** Phyllis Lentz Industries recently issued a $1,000 par value bond with a 14.6 percent coupon and twenty years to maturity. Bonds of comparable risk, maturity, and coupon currently sell to yield 14 percent (their yield to maturity).

**a.** Find the value of the bond assuming annual interest payments.
**b.** Find the value of the bond assuming semiannual interest payments.
**c.** Find the yield to maturity on the bond if it currently sells for $917 (assume annual compounding).
**d.** If the price of the bond subsequently increases to $1,195.58, what would be the yield to maturity (assume semiannual compounding)?

**SP4-2.** WCU, Inc., preferred stock pays an annual dividend of $12.35.

**a.** What is the value of this preferred stock if you require a 10.5 percent return?
**b.** If the stock currently sells for $137.50 a share, what is your expected return?

**SP4-3.** The common stock of K. Corum Cosmetics, Inc., currently sells for $8.25 a share. You expect it to pay a $.43 annual dividend next year, which should increase at a constant 9 percent rate in the future.

**a.** If you require a 13 percent return, what is the value of the stock?
**b.** What is the expected return on K. Corum Cosmetics common stock?

**SP4-4.** Tom Callihan is a securities analyst with a major brokerage firm. A stock he is currently analyzing has a history of dividend payments as follows:

| Period | Dividend |
| --- | --- |
| Last year | $2.45 |
| 2 years earlier | 2.29 |
| 3 years earlier | 2.14 |
| 4 years earlier | 2.00 |

Tom expects this same pattern of dividend growth to continue indefinitely.

**a.** If Tom requires a 16 percent return on the stock, what is the stock's value?
**b.** What is Tom's expected return on the stock if it currently sells for $32.75?

## PROBLEMS

**P4-1.** Jim Hughes is considering investing in a bond having a $1,000 par value, a $9\frac{3}{4}$ percent coupon, and fifteen years until maturity. Jim requires a 12 percent return on the bond.

**a.** Find the value of the bond if it pays interest annually.
**b.** Find the value of the bond if it pays interest semiannually.
**c.** Find the yield to maturity on the bond assuming annual interest payments and a current price of $790.05. Should Jim purchase the bond?
**d.** Find the yield to maturity on the bond assuming semiannual interest payments and a current price of $980.43. Should Jim purchase the bond?

**P4-2.** Joyce Cleaver owns the preferred stock of NCS, Inc. The preferred stock pays a $9.35 dividend annually and currently sells for $62.75.

**a.** What is Joyce's expected return on NCS, Inc., preferred stock?
**b.** What is the value of NCS, Inc., preferred stock if Joyce requires a 14 percent return?

**P4-3.** Dorothy Poole recently purchased 100 shares of USF Industries for $25 a share. She expects USF to pay a $1.95 dividend per share next year, and she forecasts continued growth of the earnings, dividends, and the price of the stock at a constant 9 percent rate in the future.

**a.** What is the value of each share of USF Industries common stock if Dorothy requires a 13 percent return?
**b.** What is the expected return on USF Industries common stock?

**P4-4.** Chester Enterprises common stock paid a dividend of $.95 a share last year and $.75 five years earlier. The growth rate of the dividend demonstrated during this period is expected to continue in the future.

**a.** What is the value of Chester Enterprises common stock if you require a 15 percent return?
**b.** What is the expected return on Chester Enterprises if it currently sells for $11 a share?

**P4-5.** Anderson Aviation Corporation issued a twenty-year $1,000 par value bond five years ago. It has an 11.5 percent coupon, pays interest semiannually, and currently sells for $844.92. What is the bond's yield to maturity?

**P4-6.** The preferred stock of Bandy Enterprises currently sells for $87.50 per share. It is a 9 percent preferred stock and has par value of $100. What is the expected return on the stock?

**P4-7.** Kaminsky Corporation paid a $3.25 dividend per share last year. Investors require a 15 percent return on the stock, and the dividend is expected to grow at a constant 12 percent rate in the future. What is the value of the stock?

**P4-8.** Phillips Industries has a $1,000 par value bond outstanding that has a 12.6 percent coupon. It has twelve years remaining until maturity and pays interest semiannually. What is the value of this bond to an investor who requires a 10 percent return?

**P4-9.** What is the value of a preferred stock that pays a $2.30 annual dividend if you require a 12 percent return? The par value of the preferred stock is $25.

**P4-10.** What is the expected return on a common stock that sells for $55 per share and is expected to pay a quarterly dividend of $1.50 next year? The dividend is expected to grow at a constant rate of 7 percent each year.

**P4-11.** A bond issued by Grierson Corporation has a 10.6 percent coupon, pays interest semiannually, and matures in twelve years. If the current yield on the bond is 16.54 percent, what is the expected yield to maturity?

**P4-12.** Kelliher Corporation has 100,000 shares of preferred stock and 1,000,000 shares of common stock outstanding. Net income for Kelliher last year was $2 million, and earnings per share of common stock was $1.50. What is the value of Kelliher Corporation preferred stock if investors require a 9 percent return?

**P4-13.** The history of dividends paid on Salter Enterprises common stock is as follows:

| Year | Dividend |
| --- | --- |
| 1987 | $2.86 |
| 1986 | 2.65 |
| 1985 | 2.45 |
| 1984 | 2.27 |
| 1983 | 2.10 |

After evaluating this common stock, you feel it is appropriate to require a 7 percent risk premium. What is the value of the common stock if the risk-free rate of return is 5 percent? (Assume that the same pattern of dividend payment is expected to continue in the future).

**P4-14.** The preferred stock of Zax Company pays an annual dividend of $4.00 and currently sells for $34.00.

a. What is the expected return to investors on this stock?
b. What is the value of Zax Company preferred stock if investors require a 16 percent return?

**P4-15.** Bill Patton plans to invest in a bond having a $1,000 par value, a 9 percent coupon, and ten years until maturity. Bill requires a 14 percent return on the bond.

a. Find the value of the bond if it pays interest annually.

**b.** Find the value of the bond if it pays interest semiannually.

**c.** Find the yield to maturity on the bond assuming semiannual interest payments and a current price of $790. Should Bill purchase the bond?

**P4-16.** Max, Inc., common stock is expected to pay a dividend of $1.95 per share next year. The growth rate of the firm's earnings, dividends, and the price of the stock is expected to continue at a constant 6 percent rate in the future.

**a.** What is the value of each share of Max, Inc., common stock if investors require a 10 percent return?

**b.** What is the expected return on Max, Inc., common stock if it currently sells for $50 a share?

**P4-17.** What is the expected return on a common stock that sells for $30 per share and is expected to pay a quarterly dividend of $.90 next year? The dividend is expected to grow at a constant rate of 5 percent each year in the future.

**P4-18.** A bond issued by Casey Corporation has an 11.8 percent coupon, pays interest semiannually, and matures in fifteen years. If the current yield on the bond is 13.0 percent, what is the expected yield to maturity?

**P4-19.** Yoder Corporation has 200,000 shares of preferred stock and 3,000,000 shares of common stock outstanding. Net income for Yoder last year was $5 million, and earnings per share of common stock was $1.20. What is the value of Yoder Corporation preferred stock if investors require a 11 percent return?

**P4-20.** The history of dividends paid on Mantle Corporation common stock is as follows:

| Year | Dividend |
| --- | --- |
| 1987 | $2.65 |
| 1986 | 2.50 |
| 1985 | 2.36 |
| 1984 | 2.23 |
| 1983 | 2.10 |

If investment in this common stock requires a 7 percent risk premium, what is the value of the common stock? Assume that the risk-free rate of return is 7 percent and that the same pattern of dividend payments is expected to continue in the future.

## COMPUTER-ASSISTED PROBLEMS

An explanation of the techniques used in the following problems is presented in Chapter 5.

**CP4-1.** Spector Corporation is considering the purchase of some Carmel, Inc., common stock. Spector estimates that (1) Carmel's dividend will grow at a constant rate of 3 percent per year to infinity, and (2) next year's dividend per share will be $2.00. Spector's required rate of return on the stock is 15 percent.

**a. Sensitivity of Stock Values to Growth Rates**   Estimate the value of Carmel's stock. Would you purchase the stock given a market price of $18 per share? Explain.

If the growth rate were 4 percent, how would this affect the estimated stock value? What if the growth rate were 2 percent? Would any of these scenarios lead to the purchase of the stock if its market price were $19 per share? Explain.

**b. Sensitivity of Stock Values to Investor Required Rates of Return**   If the risk of investment in Carmel common stock really warrants a 16 percent required return, how would this affect the price of Carmel's stock? What if the required return were 14 percent? Would either of these scenarios lead to purchase of the stock if its market price is $17 per share? Explain.

**c. Sensitivity of Stock Values to Growth Rates and Required Returns**   Is the estimated value of Carmel stock more sensitive to the possible growth rates or dividends described in Parts a and b? Explain.

**d. Sensitivity of Stock Values to Growth Rates and Required Returns**   What would the value of Carmel stock be under the most optimistic conditions regarding the growth rate and required return? What would the stock value be under the most pessimistic conditions? Would either of these conditions lead to a stock purchase if the market price of the stock is $19 per share? Explain.

**e. Probability Distribution**   Assume the following probability distribution for the growth rate and required return:

| Growth Rate | Probability | Required Return | Probability |
|---|---|---|---|
| 2.0% | 20% | 13.0% | 10% |
| 3.0 | 40 | 14.0 | 20 |
| 4.0 | 30 | 15.0 | 40 |
| 5.0 | 10 | 16.0 | 20 |
| | | 17.0 | 10 |

Given that Carmel's expected dividend next year is $2.00 per share, what is the probability that the true value of the stock is greater than $18 per share?

**f. Simulation**   Assume that the growth rate of Carmel's dividend is estimated to be somewhere between 2 percent and 5 percent, while the required return is estimated to be somewhere between 13 percent and 17 percent. Use simulation to determine whether Spector should purchase the stock if it requires at least a 90 percent chance that the stock value exceeds $17 per share.

## REFERENCES

Barnea, Amir, and Dennis E. Logue. "The Valuation Forecasts of a Security Analyst." *Financial Management* 2 (Summer 1973): 38–45.

Chu, Chen-Chin, and David T. Whitford. "Stock Market Returns and Inflationary Expectations: Additional Evidence for 1975–1979." *Journal of Financial Research* 5 (Fall 1982): 261–73.

Elton, Edwin J., and Martin J. Gruber. "Earnings Estimates and the Accuracy of Expectational Data." *Management Science* 18 (April 1972): 409–24.

———. "Valuation and Asset Selection under Alternative Investment Opportunities." *Journal of Finance* 31 (May 1976): 525–39.

Granger, Clive W. J. "Some Consequences of the Valuation Model When Expectations Are Taken to Be Optimum Forecasts." *Journal of Finance* 30 (March 1975): 135–45.

Keim, Donald B., and Robert F. Stambaugh. "Predicting Returns in the Stock and Bond Markets." *Journal of Financial Economics* 17 (December 1986): 357–390.

Lewellen, Wilbur G., and James S. Ang. "Inflation, Security Values, and Risk Premium." *Journal of Financial Research* 5 (Summer 1982): 105–24.

McEnally, Richard W. "A Note on the Return of High-Risk Common Stocks," *Journal of Finance* 29 (March 1974): 199–202.

Nelson, Charles R. "Inflation and Rates of Return on Common Stocks." *Journal of Finance* 31 (May 1976): 471–83.

Norgaard, Richard L. "An Examination of the Yields of Corporate Bonds and Stocks." *Journal of Finance* 29 (September 1974): 1275–86.

Reilly, Frank K., and Thomas J. Zeller. "An Analysis of Relative Industry Price-Earnings Ratios." *Financial Review* (1974): 17–33.

Ricketts, Donald E., and Michael J. Barret. "Corporate Operating Income Forecasting Ability." *Financial Management* 2 (Summer 1973): 53–62.

Rosenberg, Barr, and James Guy. "Beta and Investment Fundamentals." *Financial Analysts Journal* 32 (May–June 1976): 60–72.

# VALUATION MODEL FOR VARIABLE OR SUPERNORMAL GROWTH RATE

It is not unusual for an investor to forecast an earnings and dividend growth rate that changes in the short term and/or intermediate term. This would be typical of a young company whose earnings and dividends expand rapidly as a result of the firm's entry into new markets or from the exploitation of new technologies. Such supernormal growth is temporary, however, since firms eventually reach the maturity stage of their life cycle. In the maturity stage, the growth rate of earnings and dividends typically declines to a level approximating the growth rate of the economy. Under such conditions, forecasting a long-run constant growth rate may be appropriate. A procedure for finding the value of variable-growth-rate companies follows:

$$P_0 = \frac{D_1}{(1 + k_s)^1} + \frac{D_2}{(1 + k_s)^2} + \cdots + \frac{D_n}{(1 + k_s)^n} + \left( \frac{D_{n+1}}{(k_s - g)} \right) \left( \frac{1}{(1 + k_s)^n} \right)$$

(4A.1)

where $n$ = the last year in which the growth rate of the dividend is variable

$g$ = the constant growth rate of the dividend beginning in year $n$

The first part of this model determines the present value of each expected dividend separately during the period of variable or supernormal growth. Next, the present value of all remaining dividends to infinity is calculated as of the start of the constant-growth period. This is done using a variation of the constant-growth valuation equation (4.9). Since this represents the value of the stock at some future point in time (the point where constant growth begins), it must be brought back to today's value before being added to the amount found in the first step.

| Example | Angel Corporation paid a $2 dividend last year. The dividend is expected to grow 15 percent next year and 20 percent the following year before declining to an 8 |

percent growth rate that should continue to infinity. What is the value of the stock if investors require a 12 percent return?

$$P_0 = \frac{\$2\,(1 + .15)}{(1 + .12)^1} + \frac{\$2(1 + .15)\,(1 + .20)}{(1 + .12)^2}$$

$$+ \left( \frac{\$2(1 + .15)\,(1 + .20)\,(1 + .08)}{(.12 - .08)} \right) \left( \frac{1}{(1 + .12)^2} \right)$$

$$= \$63.66$$

# APPENDIX 4B

# DURATION

Duration is a measure of bond price volatility. (The term *duration* has other definitions and uses in bond portfolio management, but they are not discussed here.) We suggest that interested students read, "The Many Uses of Bond Duration," by Frank K. Reilly and Rupinder Sidhu, *Financial Analysts Journal* (July–August 1980): 58–72, for a discussion of other uses of duration.

The value of a bond's duration is determined by the maturity and coupon rate of the bond as well as the required rate of return on the bond. Bonds with long maturities and low coupons have high durations. A high duration indicates that the value of the bond is very sensitive to changes in the required rate of return. The relationship is such that the percent change in bond value is approximately equal to the change in required rate of return times the bond's duration. For example, assume Bond A has a duration of 5 whereas Bond B has a duration of 3. Given a change in the required rate of return of half a percentage point for each bond, the approximate change in value of Bond A would be $\frac{1}{2}$ percent times 5, or 2.5 percent. For Bond B, the same half a percentage point change in the bond's required rate of return would result in a 1.5 percent change in value. For bond investors, duration is a very important measure of price volatility.

## CALCULATING DURATION

Duration is the market price of a bond divided into the present value of all cash flows that have been weighted by the length of time until receipt. That is,

$$D = \frac{\sum_{t=1}^{n} I(t) \left[ \dfrac{1}{(1 + k_d)^t} \right] + M(t) \left[ \dfrac{1}{(1 + k_d)^n} \right]}{\sum_{t=1}^{n} I \left[ \dfrac{1}{(1 + k_d)^t} \right] + M \left[ \dfrac{1}{(1 + k_d)^n} \right]} \tag{4B.1}$$

where $D$ = duration of the bond

$t$ = year of the cash flow

All other variables were defined earlier

**107**

Notice that the denominator of Equation 4B.1 is the value of the bond. The numerator is identical to the denominator, except each interest payment and the maturity value of the bond is multiplied by $t$ before the present value is calculated.

---

| | |
|---|---|
| Example | What is the duration of the bond on page 80 of Chapter 4? This bond had a $1,000 par value, 11 percent coupon, and five-year maturity. Interest is paid annually, the required rate of return is 10 percent, and the value of the bond is $1,038.01. (The value of the bond is the denominator of the duration formula.) |

The value of the numerator is found as follows (annual compounding is generally assumed when determining duration):

| (1) Year of Receipt(t) | (2) Cash Receipt | (3) Time Weighted Cash Receipt (1) × (2) | (4) PVIF 10% | (5) PV of (3) at 10% |
|---|---|---|---|---|
| 1 | 110 | 110 | .9091 | 100.00 |
| 2 | 110 | 220 | .8264 | 181.81 |
| 3 | 110 | 330 | .7513 | 247.93 |
| 4 | 110 | 440 | .6830 | 330.52 |
| 5 | 110 + 1,000 | 5,550 | .6209 | 3,446.00 |
| | | | | $\Sigma$ = 4,306.26 |

Inserting the two values into the duration equation,

$$D = \frac{4,306.26}{1,038.01} = 4.15 \text{ years}$$

---

# PROBLEMS (Appendixes A and B)

**P4A-1.** Whistle Enterprises common stock paid a $6 dividend last year, but the dividend is expected to grow at a 20 percent rate for the next three years. After three years, the growth rate is expected to decline to 10 percent. What is the value of the stock if investors require a 14 percent return?

**P4A-2.** W & M Enterprises is expected to pay a dividend of $1.30 next year. The dividend is expected to grow at a 25 percent rate for the three years after that before declining to 21 percent for the two years after that. In the next year and in every subsequent year the dividend growth rate is forecasted at 16 percent. What is the value of W & M Enterprises common stock if you require a 20 percent return?

**P4B-1.** Determine the duration of a $1,000 par value bond that has a $13\frac{1}{4}$ percent coupon and that matures in three years. Your required rate of return is 14 percent, and the value of the bond is $982.61. (Assume annual compounding.)

**P4B-2.** Gable Corporation issued a $1,000 par value bond four years ago. It has a twelve percent coupon and matures six years from today (it originally had a ten-year maturity). Based on a 15 percent required rate of return, what is the bond's duration? (Assume annual compounding.)

# CHAPTER 5

# RISK AND RETURN

## RISK AND RETURN IN PERSPECTIVE

In 1987 Alcoa announced plans to diversify away from its aluminum businesses. The company's stated goal was to generate half of its revenues from nonaluminum products by 1995. This will help reduce the firm's dependence on business cycle fluctuations and reduce the variability of the firm's net income.

In 1987 Nippon Steel, a Japanese firm, announced the closing of five major blast furnaces over a four-year period. It also announced plans to diversify into other product areas with a long-term goal of reducing its steel products business to 50 percent of its overall business. Once again, an important objective is to reduce the firm's dependence on business cycle fluctuations and reduce the variability of the firm's net income.

Just as these companies are attempting to reduce the variability of their net income, so too do investors attempt to reduce the variability of the returns they realize in their portfolios because the variability of returns is a measure of risk.

What other risk measures are there? Can risk be reduced without reducing expected return? How can risk reduction through diversification affect the ability of firms to obtain funds and the cost of those funds? This chapter provides a framework that can be used to answer these and other questions about the risk of a firm and the investments it makes.

The previous chapter frequently referred to the use of required rates of return as discount rates to find the value of bonds, preferred stock, and common stock. The higher the required rate of return on an asset is, the lower the value of the asset, other things being equal. As explained in Chapter 4, required rates of return on securities consist of the **risk-free rate** of interest ($R_f$), which is the rate that can be earned without incurring risk, plus a risk premium ($PREM_j$). Now we will investigate how the risk of a security is measured and how the risk premium is determined. This information is important input to investors when making investment decisions that affect the prices of the firm's securities. In attempting to maximize the value of a firm's stock, financial managers should understand how investors view their firm's risk and return. In addition, financial managers must be able to evaluate the risk and return of assets the firm is considering purchasing, including both **financial assets** (claims against individuals or organizations promising future payments) and **real assets** (tangible assets such as buildings and equipment). The same principles of risk and return apply to both types of assets although the emphasis in this chapter is on financial assets. The application of risk and return concepts to the acquisition of real assets is emphasized in Chapter 11.

## MEASURING RISK AND RETURN

Risk is the probability that the results of an event will differ from the expected outcome. When purchasing securities, investors incur the risk of receiving a lower return than they expect. For example, assume that you are considering purchasing common stock issued by Secure Corporation. You expect to earn a 10 percent return on the stock next year, but you recognize the return could be as high as 12 percent or as low as 8 percent. Since the actual return could be lower than the expected return, this investment has risk. Another stock issued by Swinger Industries is also expected to provide investors with a 10 percent return. However, this return could be as high as 30 percent or as low as −10 percent. Since the actual return on the Swinger stock could deviate farther from its expected return than that on the Secure stock, the Swinger stock is more risky. It is well documented that most investors are risk averse, meaning they prefer to avoid risk, other things being equal. Since the expected returns on Secure Corporation and Swinger Industries are identical but the risk of Swinger is greater, most investors would prefer to purchase shares of Secure Corporation. Risk-aversion is assumed throughout this text.

### Probability Distributions

Table 5.1 presents probability distributions of possible states of the economy next year and the related returns on Secure and Swinger common stocks. This information is presumed to be provided to an investor by a securities' analyst. Notice that the returns are identical for both stocks if the economy is normal. However, the return on Swinger stock is expected to be higher in an economic boom and lower in a recession than the return on Secure stock.

TABLE 5.1  **Probability Distribution of Returns for Two Alternative Investments:** Secure and Swinger

| State of Economy | Probability of Occurrence | Return on Secure Stock | Return on Swinger Stock |
|---|---|---|---|
| Boom | 20% | 12% | 30% |
| Normal | 60 | 10 | 10 |
| Recession | 20 | 8 | −10 |

## Measuring Expected Return

In Chapter 4, the expected return on common stock was calculated by adding the expected dividend yield to the expected growth rate (see Equation 4.9). In this chapter, probability distributions are used to describe a number of possible investment returns, and the expected return can be determined directly from these probability distributions. The expected return is the weighted average of all possible outcomes, using the probability of each outcome as weights.

$$\hat{k} = \sum_{i=1}^{n} p_i k_i \tag{5.1}$$

where  $\hat{k}$ = expected return on an asset

$p_i$ = probability of the $i$th outcome occurring

$k_i$ = the $i$th outcome (return)

$n$ = number of possible outcomes

**Example**

Given the information in Table 5.1, the expected return on Secure stock is

$$\hat{k} = (20\%)(12\%) + (60\%)(10\%) + (20\%)(8\%)$$
$$= 10\%$$

The expected return on Swinger stock is

$$\hat{k} = (20\%)(30\%) + (60\%)(10\%) + (20\%)(-10\%)$$
$$= 10\%$$

Thus, the expected returns on the stocks are identical.

Figure 5.1 presents bar graphs of the probability distributions of the returns on the Secure and Swinger common stocks. Here, the height of each bar indicates the probability of each outcome, which is specified on the vertical scale. The more widespread the observations are on the hori-

**FIGURE 5.1**
**Discrete Probability Distributions of Returns: Secure and Swinger Common Stocks**

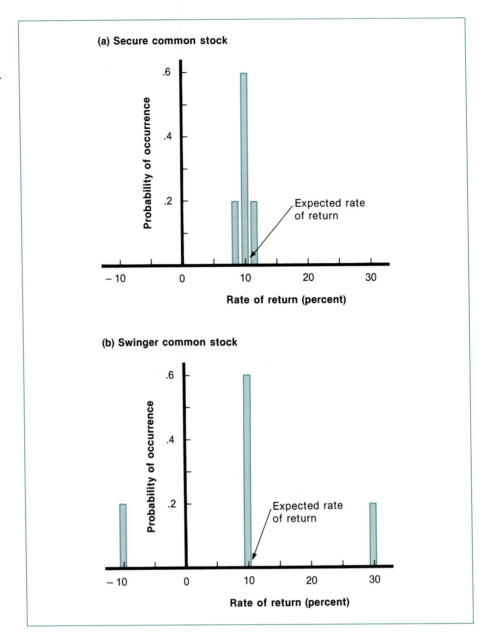

zontal scale, the greater the dispersion of possible returns, and the greater the risk. By observation, it is apparent that the dispersion of returns for Secure stock is less than for Swinger stock.

## Continuous Probability Distributions

The discussion so far has focused on **discrete probability distributions,** where there are a limited number of possible outcomes. In reality, the possible states of the economy are infinite, and, therefore, so are the possible returns on the stocks. If we were to consider all of these possible outcomes

**FIGURE 5.2**
Continuous Probability Distributions of Returns: Secure and Swinger Common Stocks

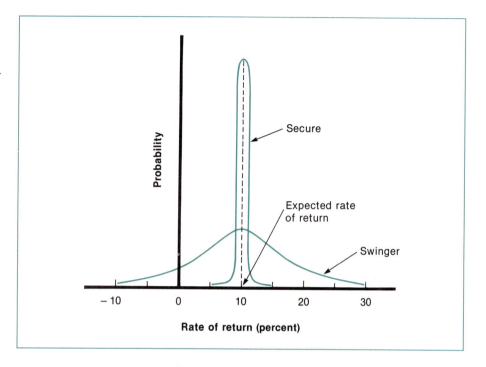

and assign probabilities to each, a greatly expanded probability distribution would result. A **continuous probability distribution** could then be graphed from that information. Continuous probability distributions of returns for Secure and Swinger common stocks are shown in Figure 5.2. The areas under both curves must be equal since they represent 100 percent of all possible outcomes. The tighter (more peaked) a probability distribution is, the lower the dispersion of possible outcomes and the lower the risk. The distributions for Secure and Swinger indicate an expected return of 10 percent on the horizontal scale. However, the tighter distribution of possible returns for Secure stock indicates lower risk. The narrower *range* of possible outcomes for Secure stock (8 percent to 12 percent) also suggests lower risk than for Swinger stock (−10 percent to 30 percent). Given the narrower range of possible outcomes and the higher probabilities assigned to outcomes near the expected outcome (10 percent), the actual return on Secure stock is likely to be closer to its expected outcome than the return on Swinger stock is.

## Measuring Risk

There are many ways for investors to quantify risk, and some of the more popular ones are described here. No single measure is best, since different measures are suited to different situations.

**Variance and Standard Deviation**   As indicated earlier, the risk of an investment can be measured in terms of the dispersion of possible outcomes from the expected outcome. The **variance** of returns ($\sigma^2$) is a measure of dispersion that can be calculated from a probability distribution.

$$\sigma^2 = \sum_{i=1}^{n} (k_i - \hat{k}_i)^2 \, p_i \qquad\qquad (5.2)$$

An alternative measure of risk is the **standard deviation** of returns ($\sigma$), which is the square root of the variance:

$$\sigma = \sqrt{\sigma^2} = \sqrt{\sum_{i=1}^{n} (k_i - \hat{k}_i)^2 \, p_i} \qquad\qquad (5.3)$$

The variance and standard deviation of returns, calculated in Table 5.2, are both less for Secure stock (1.6 and 1.26 percent, respectively) than for Swinger stock (160 and 12.65 percent, respectively). This reinforces the earlier observation that an investment in Secure common stock is less risky than an investment in Swinger.

The symmetrical shape of the probability distributions in Figure 5.2 suggests normal distributions. For this type of distribution, the expected return is in the middle of the range of possible outcomes, where the peak is located. Given a normal distribution, the standard deviation has a very convenient interpretation: 68 percent of all possible outcomes are within one standard deviation of the expected outcome, 95 percent of all outcomes are within two standard deviations of the expected outcome, and 99 percent

**TABLE 5.2  Calculation of Variance and Standard Deviation for Secure and Swinger Common Stocks**

Secure Corporation

| State of Economy | Probability of Occurrence ($p_i$) | Return ($k_i$) | $k_i - \hat{k}$ | $(k_i - \hat{k})^2$ | $(k_i - \hat{k})^2 \, p_i$ |
|---|---|---|---|---|---|
| Boom | 20% | 12% | 2 | 4 | .8 |
| Normal | 60 | 10 | 0 | 0 | .0 |
| Recession | 20 | 8 | −2 | 4 | .8 |
| | | | | $\sigma^2 =$ | 1.6 |
| | | | | $\sigma =$ | $\sqrt{1.6}$ |
| | | | | $\sigma =$ | 1.26% |

Swinger Industries

| State of Economy | Probability of Occurrence ($p_i$) | Return ($k_i$) | $k_i - \hat{k}$ | $(k_i - \hat{k})^2$ | $(k_i - \hat{k})^2 \, p_i$ |
|---|---|---|---|---|---|
| Boom | 20% | 30% | 20 | 400 | 80 |
| Normal | 60 | 10 | 0 | 0 | 0 |
| Recession | 20 | −10 | −20 | 400 | 80 |
| | | | | $\sigma^2 =$ | 160 |
| | | | | $\sigma =$ | $\sqrt{160}$ |
| | | | | $\sigma =$ | 12.65% |

of all outcomes are within three standard deviations. This means that for Secure common stock, there is a 68 percent probability that the actual return will be between 8.74 percent and 11.26 percent (10% ± 1.26%), a 95 percent probability that it will be between 7.48 percent and 12.52 percent (10% ± 2.52%), and a 99 percent probability that it will be between 6.22 percent and 13.78 percent (10% ± 3.78%).

The higher standard deviation of returns for Swinger results in a wider range of possible outcomes for each level of confidence. That is, there is a 68 percent probability of an actual return for Swinger of between −2.65 percent and 22.65 percent, a 95 percent probability of an outcome between −15.30 percent and 35.30 percent, and a 99 percent probability of an outcome between −27.95 percent and 47.95 percent.

Generally, return outcomes are assumed to be normally distributed, or sufficiently close to normally distributed to make the standard deviation and variance useful measures of risk. However, when returns are not normally distributed, other risk measures must be used.

**Coefficient of Variation**    In the previous example, two investments having identical expected returns were compared. When the expected returns on two investments are different, the use of variance and standard deviation to compare the risk of the projects may be inadequate because they fail to consider the amount of risk relative to the expected return. Consider two investments: Investment S is expected to generate a 5 percent return, and Investment T is expected to generate a 20 percent return. Both have standard deviations of 2 percent. Based on standard deviation criteria, the two investments are equally risky. However, one standard deviation from the expected outcome of Investment S represents a 40 percent deviation (2%/5%) from the expected outcome, while one standard deviation from the expected outcome for Investment T represents only a 10 percent deviation (2%/20%) from the expected outcome. Investment T is clearly less risky.

In order to make the risk of the two projects comparable, we can consider the amount of risk per unit of return. A measure of risk called the **coefficient of variation** (*CV*) does just that. It is defined as

$$CV = \frac{\sigma}{\hat{k}} \tag{5.4}$$

**Example**

The coefficients of variation for Secure and Swinger common stock are as follows:

| Stock | $\sigma$ | $\hat{k}$ | $(\sigma/\hat{k}) = CV$ |
|-------|------|------|-----------------|
| Secure | 1.26% | 10% | 1.26%/10% = .126 |
| Swinger | 12.65 | 10 | 12.65%/10% = 1.27 |

As one might expect, Swinger has a higher level of risk than Secure when measured by the coefficient of variation.

## PORTFOLIO RETURN AND RISK

Thus far, the discussion of risk and return has concentrated on individual assets. Since most assets are held in portfolios, however, most investors are concerned with how the addition of assets to a portfolio will affect the portfolio's risk and return.

### Portfolio Return

The return on an investor's portfolio of assets is the weighted average of returns on the individual assets in the portfolio, where the weights are the proportions of the total portfolio invested in each asset. That is, the expected return on a portfolio of assets ($\hat{k}_p$) is

$$\hat{k}_p = \sum_{j=1}^{n} w_j k_j \qquad (5.5)$$

where $w_j$ = the weight or percentage of the total portfolio invested in the $j$th asset

$k_j$ = the expected return on the $j$th asset

$n$ = number of assets in the portfolio

---

**Example**    Assume that a portfolio is composed of two common stocks with weights and expected returns as follows:

| Asset | Weight | Expected Return |
|-------|--------|-----------------|
| Stock C | 20% | 30% |
| Stock D | 80 | 10 |
| | 100% | |

The expected return on the portfolio is

$$\hat{k}_p = (20\%)(30\%) + (80\%)(10\%)$$
$$= 6\% + 8\%$$
$$= 14\%$$

---

### Portfolio Risk

The standard deviation of returns used earlier to measure the risk of individual assets is also applicable to portfolios of assets, since portfolio risk, like the risk of individual assets, can be described as the probability that an outcome will differ from what is expected. The actual return on the portfolio might be lower or higher than the expected return. However, the

TABLE 5.3   **Historical Rates of Return on Stocks M and W and Portfolio MW**

| Year | Returns Stock M | Stock W | Portfolio MW |
|---|---|---|---|
| 1987 | 20% | −5% | 7.5% |
| 1986 | −5 | 20 | 7.5 |
| 1985 | 20 | −5 | 7.5 |
| 1984 | −5 | 20 | 7.5 |
| 1983 | 20 | −5 | 7.5 |
| 1982 | −5 | 20 | 7.5 |
| Mean | 7.5 | 7.5 | 7.5 |
| Standard Deviation | 13.7 | 13.7 | 0.0 |

FIGURE 5.3
Perfect Negative
Correlation and
Portfolio Returns

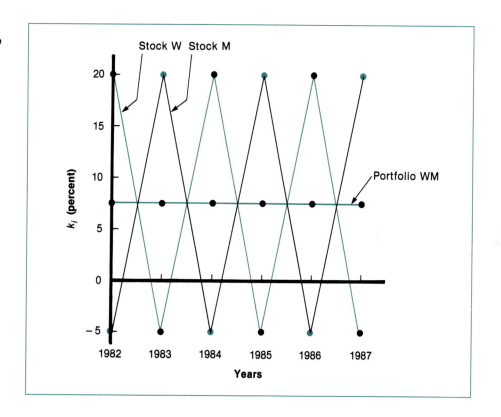

standard deviation of returns on a portfolio is generally less than the average standard deviation of returns on the individual assets in the portfolio. The reason for this lies in the timing of the deviations of the returns on the assets in the portfolio. Table 5.3 presents some historical information about the returns on Stocks M and W and a portfolio consisting of equal investments in both during the previous six years. Notice that both stocks experienced some variability of returns over the six-year period. The mean return is 7.5 percent for both stocks, and the standard deviation of returns is 13.7 percent for both stocks. The returns on Stocks M and W and portfolio MW are presented graphically in Figure 5.3. Notice that the returns on the two stocks move in opposite directions. When one stock's return is below its mean, the other is above its mean. The portfolio return appears as a horizontal line, indicating zero variability of portfolio returns. Clearly, the risk of the portfolio is less than the risk of either asset in the portfolio. This so-called **portfolio effect** is an advantage of diversifying one's portfolio.

The relationship between the variability of returns on two assets over time can be measured using the **correlation coefficient,** a statistical measure that ranges in value from +1.0 in the case of perfect positive correlation (the returns move up and down together) to −1.0 in the case of perfect negative correlation (the returns move in opposite directions). The example of Stocks M and W used earlier illustrated perfect negative correlation. As indicated, perfect negative correlation can eliminate portfolio risk. However, identifying assets with returns that are perfectly negatively correlated and that also provide positive returns may not be possible. Most investors must settle for forming portfolios of assets having returns with low positive correlations. The average correlation of returns between two randomly selected stocks is approximately +.6. Although combining stocks having positively correlated returns will not eliminate risk, it will reduce risk to a level below that of the average standard deviation of the assets in the portfolio.

Unlike the expected return of a portfolio, the expected standard deviation of a portfolio of assets is not the weighted average of the standard deviation of the assets in the portfolio. The standard deviation of portfolio returns is dependent on (1) the weight (proportion) of each asset in the portfolio, (2) the standard deviation of each asset in the portfolio, and (3) the correlation between each pair of assets in the portfolio. As a result, an investor owning more than one asset is more concerned about the risk of the portfolio of assets than the risk of the individual assets in the portfolio—although the risk of the individual assets influences the risk of the portfolio. We can conclude that investors considering the purchase of assets must be concerned about how those assets will interact with the other assets in the portfolio.

The standard deviation of returns on a portfolio ($\sigma_p$) containing two assets can be determined as follows:

$$\sigma_p = \sqrt{w_A^2 \sigma_A^2 + w_B^2 \sigma_B^2 + 2 w_A w_B \sigma_A \sigma_B \rho_{AB}} \qquad (5.6)$$

where   $w_A$ = percentage of the portfolio allocated to Asset A

$w_B$ = percentage of the portfolio allocated to Asset B

$\sigma_A$ = standard deviation of returns for Asset A

$\sigma_B$ = standard deviation of returns for Asset B

$\rho_{AB}$ = correlation coefficient between the returns on Assets A and B

When Equation 5.6 is used to estimate the standard deviation of a portfolio's returns, the historical standard deviations and correlation coefficients of the assets are used to represent the expected standard deviation and correlation coefficients of the assets concerned. However, if either statistic is expected to change in the future, the expected changes should be reflected in the values.

To illustrate the application of Equation 5.6, assume that an investor already owns shares of Chatfield Corporation common stock and is considering the purchase of shares of either Price, Inc., or Samuels Company. The additional asset to be acquired will constitute 50 percent of the portfolio, while Chatfield will make up the other 50 percent. The estimated standard deviation of returns for each of the three assets is .03, while the estimated correlation between Chatfield and Price is .10 and between Chatfield and Samuels is .9. Given this information, the estimated standard deviation of the portfolio consisting of Chatfield and Price common stock is

$$\sigma_p = \sqrt{(.50)^2(.03)^2 + (.50)^2(.03)^2 + 2(.50)(.50)(.03)(.03)(.10)}$$

$$= \sqrt{.000225 + .000225 + .000045}$$

$$= \sqrt{.000495}$$

$$= .0222486$$

In this case, the estimated standard deviation of the portfolio is lower than the estimated standard deviation of either Chatfield or Price common stocks separately. Since the correlation coefficient between the Chatfield and Samuels common stocks is higher (.9), one would expect the standard deviation of the resulting portfolio to be higher. The standard deviation of a portfolio consisting of equal amounts of Chatfield and Samuels common stock is

$$\sigma_p = \sqrt{(.50)^2(.03)^2 + (.05)^2(.03)^2 + 2(.50)(.50)(.03)(.03)(.90)}$$

$$= \sqrt{.000225 + .000225 + .000405}$$

$$= \sqrt{.000855}$$

$$= .02924038$$

As expected, the standard deviation of portfolio returns is greater when the correlation coefficient is larger. If the correlation coefficient were +1.0, then the portfolio's standard deviation would be equal to the weighted average of the standard deviation of the two stocks in the portfolio (.03). If the correlation coefficient were −1.0, then the portfolio would have a standard deviation of zero.

## PORTFOLIO RISK AND THE CAPITAL ASSET PRICING MODEL (CAPM)

It has been demonstrated that, when selecting individual assets, investors must consider not only the expected return and risk of the assets, but also how the assets interact with each other in a portfolio. Although the correlation coefficient defines the interaction of returns between two assets, it is not a very practical measure of each asset's contribution to portfolio risk, because an asset's contribution changes depending upon the other assets in the portfolio.

A generalized framework has been created to help analyze the relationship between risk and return in a portfolio context. This framework, called the **capital asset pricing model** or CAPM, is applicable to both investment analysis and financial analysis.

## Systematic versus Unsystematic Risk

All of the return volatility of an asset (*total risk*) can be classified as being caused by either systematic factors, resulting in *systematic risk,* or by unsystematic factors, resulting in *unsystematic risk.* That is,

$$\text{total return volatility} = \begin{matrix} \text{return volatility} \\ \text{caused by} \\ \text{systematic factors} \end{matrix} + \begin{matrix} \text{return volatility} \\ \text{caused by} \\ \text{unsystematic factors} \end{matrix}$$

or

$$\text{total risk} = \text{systematic risk} + \text{unsystematic risk}$$

**Unsystematic risk** is the return volatility that results from events that affect the returns on one asset or a small group of assets, like an industry. For example, the price of an individual stock (and, therefore, its return) can be affected by labor strikes, the development of new products, cost increases, and numerous other factors. These factors are asset-specific, since they are not expected to simultaneously influence all securities.

The return volatility (risk) of a portfolio resulting from such asset-specific sources can be reduced or eliminated if an investor diversifies his or her portfolio among numerous assets. Although the returns on individual assets in the portfolio will fluctuate as a result of these asset-specific events, just by chance, the unfavorable things happening to some assets in the portfolio are offset by good things happening to other assets in the portfolio. Thus, diversification can reduce or eliminate unsystematic risk.

**Systematic risk** is the return volatility of an asset that results from factors that affect overall stock market movements. If the stock market is rising, most stocks tend to rise along with it, and vice versa. Frequently, the reason why the stock market rises and falls is related to such systematic factors as economic growth, wars, and inflation. In summary, individual stock prices fluctuate based on two influences, factors that are peculiar to the stock, and factors that influence the overall stock market.

In a well-diversified portfolio of common stock, the influence of factors peculiar to individual stocks will not cause fluctuations in portfolio returns. This is because the random nature of events that affect stocks individually cancel each other out. The return volatility that remains in the portfolio is caused by factors that influence the overall market affecting all stocks simultaneously.

How many stocks are necessary to eliminate unsystematic risk? This question is difficult to answer because the number of stocks needed to obtain adequate diversification depends on how the stocks are selected. If they are selected randomly from a large sample, most unsystematic risk is eliminated after selecting just ten stocks. If stocks are selected by some nonrandom means, the portfolio may be biased in favor of assets with similar characteristics and thus lack efficient diversification despite the addition of thirty or more securities.

**FIGURE 5.4**
**Risk Reduction through Diversification**

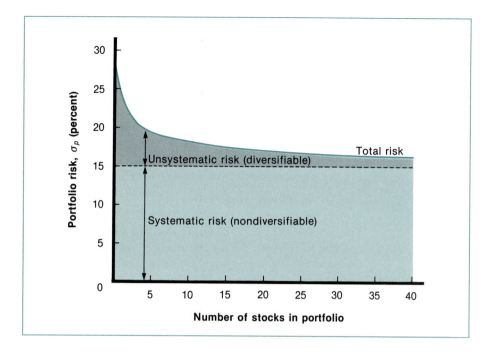

Figure 5.4 presents a graph indicating the reduction in unsystematic risk that results from random selection of stocks. Notice the substantial reduction in unsystematic risk that results as the first few stocks are added. After ten or so stocks have been added, the additional reduction in unsystematic risk is minimal.

## Beta as a Measure of Systematic Risk

When an asset is added to a well-diversified portfolio of assets, only its systematic risk affects portfolio risk. The following discussion explains how the systematic risk of an asset can be measured.

While the returns on most stocks are affected by market fluctuations, the sensitivity of return fluctuations to market fluctuations (level of systematic risk) is different for different stocks. The level of systematic risk of an asset can be measured by analyzing the relationship between the asset's historical returns and the historical returns of a so-called *market portfolio*. Although theoretically the market portfolio consists of all assets (stocks, bonds, real estate, and so on) in proportion to their total value, for purposes of analyzing the systematic risk of a common stock, a stock market index such as the New York Stock Exchange Index or the Standard & Poor's Composite Index of 500 Stocks is generally used as a proxy for the market portfolio.

The sensitivity of the returns on an asset to the returns on the market portfolio is a measure of systematic risk called the **beta coefficient.** For example, if the return on a stock is consistently twice as large as the return on the market, the stock is said to have a high level of systematic risk. This risk can be measured by regressing historical return data of an individual asset (the dependent variable) against historical returns for the market portfolio (the independent variable). The regression equation is specified as

$$k_j = a + b_j k_m + e_j \qquad (5.7)$$

where   $k_j$ = return of the $j$th asset

$a$ = constant

$b_j$ = slope coefficient (beta)

$k_m$ = return of the market index

$e_j$ = error term

The slope coefficient, $b_j$, indicates the sensitivity of the individual asset's returns to the returns on the market. As an example, the returns on Craig Corporation's common stock and the market portfolio for twenty periods are indicated in Figure 5.5. The results of regressing these data reveals a slope coefficient (beta) of 1.56. This roughly implies that a 1 percent return on the market portfolio is expected to be matched by a 1.56 percent return on Craig common stock.

The regression line defining the relationship between the return on the asset and the return on the market portfolio is called the asset's **characteristic line.** For Craig common stock, this line is illustrated in the bottom of Figure 5.5. The slope of the characteristic line is the beta coefficient that defines the linear relationship between the returns on the stock and the returns on the market. Figure 5.6 illustrates the characteristic lines for a high-risk stock (Stock H), a low-risk stock (Stock L), and a stock of average risk (Stock A). The slope of the characteristic line of Stock A is 1.0 indicating that it has risk equal to that of the market. That is, if the market experienced a 1 percent return during a given period, Stock A would be expected to experience a 1 percent return. The slope of Stock H's characteristic line is very steep and the beta coefficient is high (2.0), indicating substantial sensitivity of Stock H's returns to the returns on the market. Stock L's characteristic line is relatively flat, indicating a low beta coefficient (.5) and a low volatility of stock returns relative to the market. Notice that the characteristic lines extend into the third quadrant of the graph, indicating negative returns on both the market and each stock. Since systematic risk is symmetrical, stocks with high beta coefficients experience larger losses than the market and larger losses than low-beta stocks when the market portfolio experiences negative returns.

## Betas of Specific Firms

Table 5.4 lists the betas of eighteen well-known firms. These beta coefficients were reported in *Value Line Investment Survey* in July 1987 on the basis of monthly observations for a five-year period and the use of Standard & Poor's Composite Index of 500 Stocks as a proxy for the market portfolio. Merrill Lynch and other large brokerage firms also publish beta coefficients for use by their customers.

**FIGURE 5.5**

**The Characteristic Line for Craig Corporation**

| Period | Return on Craig Corp Common Stock ($k_j$) | Market Return ($k_m$) | Period | Return on Craig Corp Common Stock | Market Return ($k_m$) |
|---|---|---|---|---|---|
| 1 | 8% | 6% | 11 | 15% | 13% |
| 2 | 11 | 9 | 12 | 10 | 9 |
| 3 | 3 | 5 | 13 | 8 | 7 |
| 4 | −1 | 0 | 14 | 1 | 2 |
| 5 | 0 | 1 | 15 | −3 | −1 |
| 6 | −4 | −3 | 16 | 14 | 12 |
| 7 | 3 | 4 | 17 | 9 | 8 |
| 8 | 5 | 7 | 18 | 12 | 11 |
| 9 | 10 | 10 | 19 | 12 | 10 |
| 10 | 14 | 12 | 20 | 14 | 12 |

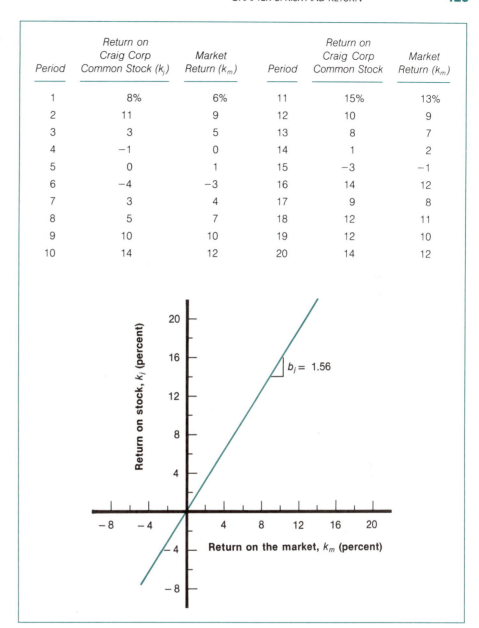

## APPLICATION OF THE CAPM

Rational investors are willing to purchase risky assets only if the expected returns are sufficiently high to compensate for the risk. If investors can eliminate unsystematic risk by diversifying their portfolios, then the only risk requiring compensation is systematic risk. Investors should not expect to receive additional compensation (a risk premium) for the unsystematic risk of an investment. Recognizing this, the CAPM specifies the linear relationship between an asset's risk and its return using beta as a measure of

**FIGURE 5.6**
**Characteristic
Lines Indicating
Stock Betas**

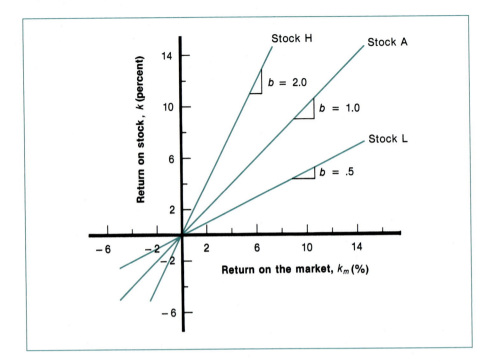

**TABLE 5.4  Beta Coefficients of Eighteen Well-Known Firms**

| Firm | Beta |
|------|------|
| Coca Cola | .90 |
| Dow Chemical | 1.20 |
| Exxon | .80 |
| Family Dollar Stores | 1.10 |
| General Cinema Corporation | 1.15 |
| General Motors | 1.15 |
| Gerber Products | .85 |
| Gerber Scientific | 1.80 |
| Health America Corporation | 1.55 |
| Heinz | .85 |
| Hughes Tool | 1.35 |
| International Business Machines | 1.05 |
| Seagram Company | 1.15 |
| Service Merchandise | 1.40 |
| Tyson Foods, Inc. | .80 |
| United Cable Television Corporation | 1.00 |
| Walgreen Company | 1.10 |
| Xerox Corporation | 1.05 |

*Source: Value Line Investment Survey,* July 4, 1987.

risk. That is, the required return on an asset $(k_j)$ is a function of the prevailing risk-free rate $(R_f)$ and the asset's risk premium $(PREM_j)$:

$$k_j = R_f + PREM_j \qquad (5.8)$$

If an adequate risk premium is not offered on risky assets, investors will purchase risk-free assets instead. The amount of risk premium required depends on the asset's level of systematic risk $(b_j)$. The risk premium can be specified as

$$PREM_j = b_j(k_m - R_f) \qquad (5.9)$$

where $k_m$ = expected return on the market

$b_j$ = beta coefficient of asset $j$

The quantity $(k_m - R_f)$ specifies the *market risk premium*, which is the additional return (above the risk-free rate) that investors expect to receive for investing in a market portfolio. This risk premium can change with time as investor's expectations about the future prospects for returns on a market portfolio change.

---

**Example**

If the expected market return is 12 percent, the risk-free rate is 8 percent, and the asset's beta is 1.00, then the market risk premium is (12% − 8%) or 4 percent, and the risk premium on the asset is also 4 percent:

$$PREM_j = b_j(k_m - R_f)$$
$$= 1(12\% - 8\%)$$
$$= 4\%$$

---

An asset with a beta of 1.00 has a risk level equal to that of the market. Thus, the risk premium for such an asset is the same as the market risk premium. If the beta of an asset is greater than 1, it is riskier than the market portfolio, and investors will require a higher risk premium. For example, the risk premium of an asset with a beta of 1.5, when the risk-free rate is 8 percent and the expected return on the market is 12 percent, is 6 percent:

$$PREM_j = b_j(k_m - R_f)$$
$$= 1.5(12\% - 8\%)$$
$$= 6\%$$

The required rate of return on the asset can be determined by combining the risk-free return and the risk premium of the asset:

$$k_j = R_f + PREM_j$$
$$k_j = R_f + b_j(k_m - R_f) \qquad \text{(5.10)}$$

**Example**

Assume once again that the existing risk-free rate is 8 percent, and the expected return on the market is 12 percent. The required rate of return on an asset with a beta of 1.5 is

$$k_j = R_f + b_j(k_m - R_f)$$
$$= 8\% + 1.5(12\% - 8\%)$$
$$= 14\%$$

This model specifies that the following relationships hold, other things being equal:

**1.** The higher (lower) the risk-free rate, the higher (lower) is the required rate of return on an asset.
**2.** The greater (smaller) the market risk premium, the higher (lower) is the required rate of return on an asset.
**3.** The higher (lower) an asset's level of systematic risk, the higher (lower) is the required rate of return on the asset.

To illustrate how required rates of return on assets vary with their respective levels of systematic risk, Table 5.5 presents the required rates of return for the low-risk, average-risk, and high-risk assets identified in Figure 5.6. All returns presented here are based on a risk-free rate of 8 percent, and an expected return on the market of 12 percent. The risk premium of each asset is also given in the last column. Notice how this premium rises with the asset's beta.

When Equation 5.9 is presented in graphical form, it is called the **security market line (SML)**. Figure 5.7 illustrates the SML using the same risk-free rate and expected return on the market as used in Table 5.5 (8 percent and 12 percent, respectively). Notice that the measure of risk appearing on the horizontal scale is beta, and the required rate of return appears on the vertical scale. The SML begins at the risk-free rate on the vertical scale and

**TABLE 5.5**  **Use of CAPM to Determine the Required Rate of Return on Various Common Stocks** ($R_f$ = 8% and $k_m$ = 12%)

| Stock | Stock Beta | Required Rate of Return | Risk Premium |
|---|---|---|---|
| L | .5 | 8% + .5(12% − 8%) = 10% | 2% |
| A | 1.0 | 8% + 1.0(12% − 8%) = 12% | 4 |
| H | 2.0 | 8% + 2.0(12% − 8%) = 16% | 8 |

**FIGURE 5.7**

Graph of the
Security Market
Line (SML)

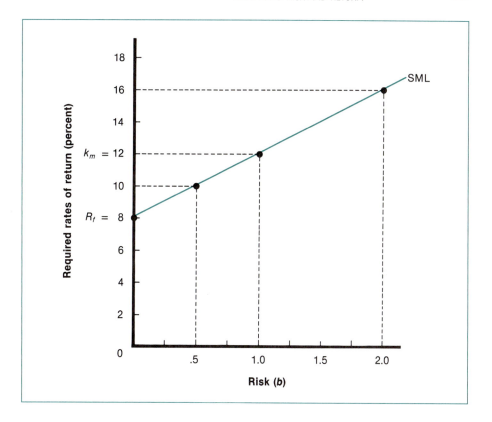

slopes upward to the right. The slope of the SML reflects investors' attitudes towards risk.

The required rates of return on the high-beta, average-beta, and low-beta stocks discussed earlier are identified on the SML in Figure 5.7. The beta coefficient for each stock can be identified on the horizontal scale while the vertical axis indicates the corresponding required rate of return. The required rate of return for each stock is the sum of the risk-free rate (8 percent) plus a risk premium that is different for each value of beta.

The slope of the SML changes over time. For $R_f = 6\%$ and $k_{m1} = 9\%$, if the market risk premium is only 3 percent, the SML is fairly flat, as illustrated by $SML_1$ in Figure 5.8. If the market risk premium is relatively large, say 6 percent (for $R_f = 6\%$ and $k_{m2} = 12\%$) the slope of the SML is greater (as illustrated by the steep-sloped $SML_2$ in Figure 5.8). The steeper slope of the SML results in higher required rates of return at each level of systematic risk. The slope of the SML depends upon a number of factors but basically reflects the attitudes of investors towards risk. If investors become more risk averse (perhaps due to an anticipated recession), the slope of the line will increase, reflecting greater required compensation for each unit of risk assumed.

In addition to changes in the slope of the SML, shifts in the level (y-intercept) of the SML also occur as a result of changes in the risk-free rate of interest. Figure 5.9 illustrates two different security market lines, $SML_1$, which reflects a 6 percent risk-free rate, and $SML_2$, which reflects a $7\frac{1}{2}$ per-

**FIGURE 5.8**
**Changes in the
Slope of the
Security Market
Line (SML)**

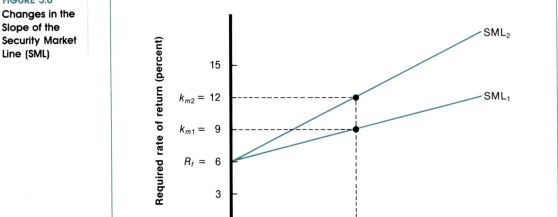

**FIGURE 5.9**
**Changes in the
Level of the
Security Market
Line (SML)**

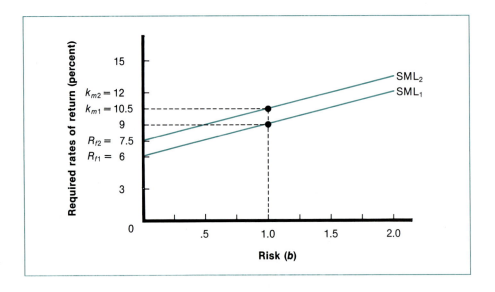

cent risk-free rate. Both SMLs show a 3 percent market risk premium; however, all risky securities require a 1.5 percent higher return, given $SML_2$ as opposed to $SML_1$.

## Limitations of the CAPM

While the CAPM is useful for quantifying the required rate of return on assets, it is not without its limitations. In its purest form, the CAPM is built upon a number of restrictive assumptions: zero brokerage costs, zero taxes, and identical investor expectations about the future. Because these assumptions depart from reality, the CAPM's application to the real world is somewhat questionable. Also, even if the CAPM accurately pinpoints the appropriate required return on an asset, it cannot be applied in its present form (as a single-period model) to the measurement of the risk-return relationship over multiple periods. Furthermore, the CAPM's determination of an asset's required rate of return is highly dependent on estimates of the return on the market ($k_m$) and the beta ($b_j$) of the asset in question. Thus, its results are only as accurate as these estimates.

Despite its limitations, the CAPM serves as a valuable tool for illustrating the relationship between risk and return. In addition, it is widely used by investors to complement other methods for valuing assets. Also, variations of the CAPM have been developed in order to consider additional variables (such as taxes) simultaneously. Much research presently is devoted to developing new models for asset pricing. One such model that has gained considerable attention in recent years, the *arbitrage pricing theory* (*APT*), is briefly discussed in the appendix to this chapter.

## Stock Price Adjustments

Most stock investors attempt to identify and purchase securities having expected returns that exceed their required returns. Such stocks have market prices below their intrinsic values and are described as being *undervalued* by the market. Stock U in Figure 5.10 illustrates the position of an undervalued security within a CAPM framework. This security has a beta coefficient of .5 and a required rate of return of 7.5 percent based on the SML; however, the security is located above the SML, indicating an expected return of 11 percent, which is above the required rate of return. If the stock were located on the SML (making the expected and required returns equal) it would be *in equilibrium*. That is, it would be priced appropriately, and there would be no pressure for price adjustment. Since the asset is above the SML, potential investors will want to purchase the stock and owners of the stock will not want to sell it. The result will be an increase in the price of the stock, which decreases the expected return. The expected return will decrease until it is equal to the required return at point X. For example, assume that Stock U is expected to pay a $1 dividend next year, and the dividend is expected to grow at a constant 5 percent rate in the future. If Stock U's current market price is $16.67, then its expected return based on the constant growth model introduced in Chapter 4 is

$$\hat{k}_s = \frac{D_1}{P_0} + g \qquad (4.11)$$

$$= \frac{\$1.00}{\$16.67} + .05$$

$$= 11\%$$

Market forces will push this stock into equilibrium at point X on the SML through price adjustments. That is, since the demand for Stock U increases

FIGURE 5.10

**Undervalued Securities, Overvalued Securities, and Market Equilibrium**

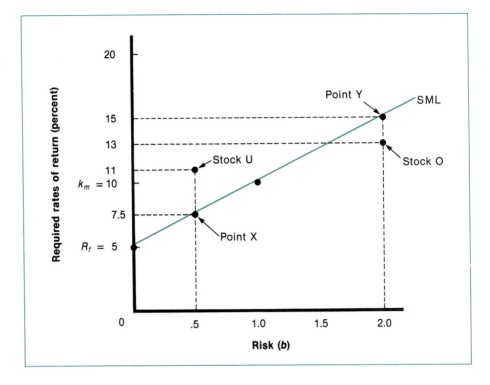

and the supply decreases (investors do not want to sell the stock), the market price will increase until the expected return has reached 7.5 percent. In this case, the expected return reaches 7.5 percent when the price of the stock has risen to $40 per share:

$$\hat{k} = \frac{\$1.00}{\$40.00} + .05$$

$$= 7.5\%$$

The same type of adjustment occurs when a stock is in disequilibrium in the other direction. That is, when the required return exceeds the expected return, the price of the stock declines until the expected return is equal to the required return. At this point, the stock is in equilibrium. This is illustrated in Figure 5.10 with Stock O, which is overvalued. Although it has an expected return of 13 percent, its beta of 2.0 indicates a required rate of return of 15 percent. Investors will sell the stock until its market price decreases sufficiently to increase the expected return to 15 percent at point Y.

## OTHER RISK MEASURES

The risk measures presented thus far are applicable in many areas of finance, not just financial-asset valuation. Additionally, other measures of risk and other techniques for analyzing risk are discussed later in this text.

## FINANCIAL MANAGEMENT IN PRACTICE

### IS THE CAPITAL ASSET PRICING MODEL VALID?

The capital asset pricing model (CAPM) has been a popular model for specifying the relationship between risk and return for years. During this time a substantial amount of research has been directed at testing the validity of the CAPM. One type of test estimates the actual slope of the security market line (SML), based on the average return and the beta of various securities over a historical period. If investors require higher returns on investments exhibiting higher betas, the slope of the SML determined from the application of regression analysis on historical data should be positive and significantly different from zero.

A second type of test attempts to determine whether the risk-return relationship among securities is linear. This test can be conducted by specifying the return on securities as a function of (1) beta and (2) beta squared. Then regression analysis is applied to historical data to determine whether the beta squared term is significant. If so, a nonlinear relationship between risk and return is indicated.

A third test of the CAPM involves the inclusion of factors other than beta as independent variables using returns as the dependent variable. If regression analysis applied to historical data shows that one or more of these other variables are significant, it suggests that beta is not the only determinant of the required rate of return. For example, if unsystematic risk were found to be a significant independent variable, it would suggest that unsystematic risk can also influence the required rate of return on assets.

Results of the tests described above generally support the CAPM. Yet, research conducted by Richard Roll showed reasons why the CAPM cannot be tested.* Although it may be true that the CAPM cannot be validated, financial managers and investment managers frequently use it to determine appropriate required rates of return for corporate projects and investments, suggesting that some financial experts perceive the CAPM to be a useful tool.

*Richard Roll, "A Critique of the Asset Pricing Theory's Tests," *Journal of Financial Economics* 4 (March 1977): 129–176.

---

At this point, it is useful to introduce the techniques of *sensitivity analysis* and *simulation*. Although these techniques may not be as practical for evaluating the risk of financial assets as some other techniques, they can be used in numerous aspects of financial management and thus in various applications throughout this text. For convenience, these techniques are applied here to the evaluation of risk of common stock.

### Sensitivity Analysis

**Sensitivity analysis** can be used to evaluate the uncertainty of returns on an asset by measuring the sensitivity of the asset's return to changes in the factors that influence returns.

Assume the expected return on the common stock of Ricardo Corporation is 15 percent. This estimate is based on the current price of $20 per share, a forecasted dividend next year of $2 per share, and a 5% long-run growth rate. An investor may wish to evaluate the sensitivity of the stock's return to alternative dividends and growth rates. For example, the investor may feel that the dividend next year could be as low as $1.50 per share or as high as $2.50 per share. Additionally, the long-run growth rate could be as low as 1 percent or as high as 9 percent. Given this information, the investor can estimate the expected return under the various possible circumstances. The most likely outcome involves a $2.00 dividend and 5 percent growth rate, resulting in a 15 percent return:

$$\hat{k}_s = \frac{D_1}{P_0} + g$$

$$= \frac{\$2.00}{\$20} + .05$$

$$= 15\%$$

In conducting sensitivity analysis, the investor may want to determine the return that will result if the dividend is $1.50 instead of $2.00 per share. Substituting $1.50 for $2.00 in the preceding equation yields an expected return of 12.5 percent. Similarly, the expected return is 17.5 percent if the dividend is $2.50 per share.

The investor may also want to determine the return if the long-run growth rate is 1 percent or 9 percent. Substituting those values into the expected-return equation (holding $D_1$ constant at $2.00) yields expected returns of 11 percent and 19 percent, respectively. This analysis suggests that the expected return is more sensitive to changes in the growth rate than to changes in the dividend. Consequently, the investor knows to spend more time estimating the growth rate than the dividend. He or she may also wish to monitor growth prospects in the future to identify any changes early.

An additional use of sensitivity analysis involves the estimation of returns for the "best case" and "worst case" scenarios. Using our previous example, the best possible outcome would involve a dividend of $2.50 and a 9 percent growth rate. The worst possible outcome would involve a $1.50 dividend and 1 percent growth rate. These combinations would result in returns to the investor of 21.5 percent and 8.5 percent, respectively. The investor must now determine if he or she is willing to assume the risk implied by these results. Table 5.6 displays a matrix indicating all possible results based on expected future dividends and growth rates.

TABLE 5.6   **Expected Returns on Common Stock under Various Combinations of Dividend and Growth Rates: Ricardo Corporation**

| $D_1$ | Growth Rates | | |
| --- | --- | --- | --- |
| | 1% | 5% | 9% |
| $1.50 | 8.5% | 12.5% | 16.5% |
| 2.00 | 11.0 | 15.0 | 19.0 |
| 2.50 | 13.5 | 17.5 | 21.5 |

FIGURE 5.11
Probability Distributions for Dividends and Growth Rate: Ricardo Corporation

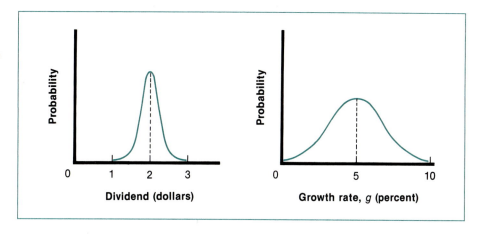

Personal computers make sensitivity analysis easy. The user simply defines the appropriate model to calculate the outcome, then revises the estimates of one or more input variables to determine the resulting outcome.

Sensitivity analysis provides information about risk since assets with returns that are less sensitive to changes in key factors are more likely to provide returns that are closer to the expected outcome. Conversely, assets with returns that are highly sensitive to key factors are more risky.

## Simulation

In some situations, **simulation** can be used in which a distribution of possible outcomes is developed based on possible values of key variables and their probabilities. For example, in the case of Ricardo common stock discussed earlier, the analyst may be able to assign probabilities to the possible future dividend and growth rate such as those displayed in Figure 5.11. Based on the defined probability distributions, the analyst randomly selects a value from each distribution (a value with a 10 percent probability of occurrence would have a 10 percent probability of being randomly selected). The selected values are then used to determine the expected return on the stock. For example, if the dividend value selected is $1.70 and the growth rate selected is 8 percent, the expected return on the stock would be 16.5 percent. After repeating this process numerous times (perhaps 100 or more iterations), the results are used to construct a probability distribution describing the expected return of the stock. The results of simulation conducted on the Ricardo Corporation example are presented in Figure 5.12. In addition to indicating the expected return on the asset, the variance, standard deviation, and coefficient of variation of returns on the project can also be calculated.

Although the application of simulation and sensitivity analysis appears to be quite tedious, computer software packages designed for use on personal computers are available. The computer software accompanying this text includes programs designed to provide experience with simulation and sensitivity analysis.

**FIGURE 5.12**
**Simulation Results:
Ricardo
Corporation**

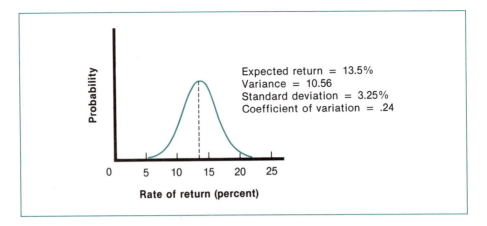

Expected return = 13.5%
Variance = 10.56
Standard deviation = 3.25%
Coefficient of variation = .24

## SUMMARY

Valuation of both real and financial assets is a common task for investors. Because future returns on assets are uncertain, the assessment of an asset's expected return and risk is necessary. However, an asset's risk may be perceived differently when assessed in the context of a portfolio as opposed to when it is assessed individually. If an asset is part of a well-diversified portfolio, only systematic risk is relevant, since proper diversification reduces or eliminates unsystematic risk.

The relationship between the expected return on an asset and its systematic risk can be quantified using the CAPM. The CAPM describes the expected return of an asset as being dependent on the risk-free rate of interest, the expected market return, and the asset's level of systematic risk, beta. The higher these variables are, the higher the risk premium of an asset is, other things equal. Investors in either real or financial assets should purchase only those assets having expected returns that sufficiently compensate for the risk incurred.

## KEY TERMS

**Beta coefficient** A measure of the sensitivity of an asset's returns to changes in market returns.
**Capital asset pricing model** A model used to specify the relationship between risk and return whereby the required return on an asset is equal to the risk-free rate plus a risk premium, and risk is measured by beta.
**Characteristic line** A least-squares regression line indicating the relationship between an asset's returns and the returns on the market. The slope of the line is beta.
**Coefficient of variation** A measure of risk (standard deviation of return per unit of expected return). This measure of risk is especially useful

for comparing assets that have different expected returns.
**Continuous probability distributions** Probability distributions indicating all possible outcomes and their probabilities.
**Correlation coefficient** A statistical measure indicating how two series move in relation to each other. The values range from $+1.0$ to $-1.0$.
**Discrete probability distributions** Probability distributions indicating a limited number of possible outcomes and their probabilities.
**Financial assets** Claims against an individual or organization promising future payments.
**Portfolio effect** The reduction in portfolio risk

resulting from the addition of assets having returns that are not perfectly correlated to those of the other assets in the portfolio.

**Real assets** Tangible assets such as machinery, equipment, and buildings.

**Risk averse** A rational approach to investing in which investors desire to avoid risk or accept risk only when adequately compensated.

**Risk-free rate** The rate of return that can be earned by investors without incurring risk. The prevailing yield on Treasury bills is commonly used as a proxy for the risk-free rate.

**Security market line** A line indicating the relationship between the risk of an asset, as measured by beta, and the required return on the asset.

**Sensitivity analysis** A procedure used to determine how sensitive an outcome is to changes in the values of certain key input variables.

**Simulation** A procedure for developing a distribution of possible outcomes based on probability distributions describing the possible values of certain key input variables.

**Standard deviation** A statistical measure of the variability of a series of data. It is measured as the square root of the variance and used as a measure of risk in finance.

**Systematic risk** The variability of returns on an asset that is caused by factors that tend to affect the returns on the market.

**Unsystematic risk** The variability of returns on an asset that is caused by factors that affect that asset (or a small group of assets) only. This risk is eliminated in well-diversified portfolios.

**Variance** A statistical measure of the degree to which the possible returns deviate from the expected return. It is used as a measure of risk in finance.

## EQUATIONS

**Equation 5.1**    **Expected Return from a Probability Distribution**

$$\hat{k} = \sum_{i=1}^{n} p_i k_i \qquad \textbf{(p. 111)}$$

where  $\hat{k}$ = expected return on an asset
$p_i$ = probability of the $i$th outcome occurring
$k_i$ = return if the $i$th outcome occurs
$n$ = number of possible outcomes

Equation 5.1 is used to determine the expected return on an asset based on a probability distribution. Essentially, Equation 5.1 instructs the analyst to find the weighted average of the possible outcomes using the probabilities of the outcomes as weights.

**Equation 5.2**    **Variance of Returns**

$$\sigma^2 = \sum_{i=1}^{n} (k_i - \hat{k})^2 \, p_i \qquad \textbf{(p. 114)}$$

where $\sigma^2$ = variance of returns
$p_i$, $k$, $k_i$ are defined as in Equation 5.1.

Equation 5.2 is used to find the variance of returns from a probability distribution. The variance is a measure of the dispersion of the possible returns about the expected return.

**Equation 5.3**  **Standard Deviation of Returns**

$$\sigma = \sqrt{\sigma^2} = \sqrt{\sum_{i=1}^{n} (k_i - \hat{k}_i)^2 \, p_i}$$  **(p. 114)**

where $\sigma$ = standard deviation of returns
  $k_i$, $\hat{k}$, $p_i$ are defined as in Equation 5.1.

Equation 5.3 is an alternative measure of risk.

**Equation 5.4**  **Coefficient of Variation**

$$CV = \frac{\sigma}{\hat{k}}$$  **(p. 115)**

where $CV$ = coefficient of variation
  $\sigma$ and $\hat{k}$ are defined as in Equation 5.1.

In Equation 5.4, the coefficient of variation measures the amount of risk (standard deviation) per unit of expected return. This measure is particularly useful when comparing assets having different expected returns.

**Equation 5.5**  **Expected Return on a Portfolio**

$$\hat{k}_p = \sum_{j=1}^{n} w_j k_j$$  **(p. 116)**

where $\hat{k}_p$ = expected return on a portfolio
  $w_j$ = the weight or percentage of the total portfolio allocated to the $j$th asset
  $k_j$ = the expected return of the $j$th asset
  $n$ = number of assets in the portfolio

Equation 5.5 can be used to determine the expected return on a portfolio of assets. It requires multiplying the expected return on each asset in the portfolio by the percentage of each asset in the portfolio and then summing the results.

**Equation 5.6**  **Standard Deviation of Returns on a Two-Asset Portfolio**

$$\sigma_p = \sqrt{w_A^2 \sigma_A^2 + w_B^2 \sigma_B^2 + 2 w_A w_B \sigma_A \sigma_B \rho_{AB}}$$  **(p. 118)**

where  $\sigma_p$ = standard deviation of a two-asset portfolio
  $w_A$ = percentage of total portfolio allocated to Asset A
  $w_B$ = percentage of total portfolio allocated to Asset B
  $\sigma_A$ = standard deviation of returns for Asset A
  $\sigma_B$ = standard deviation of returns for Asset B
  $\rho_{AB}$ = correlation coefficient between the returns of Assets A and B

In Equation 5.6, the standard deviation of portfolio returns reflects the weight and standard deviation of each asset in the portfolio as well as the correlation of returns between each pair of assets in the portfolio. This equation can be used to determine the standard deviation of a portfolio consisting of two assets.

**Equation 5.7**  **Regression Equation to Estimate Beta**

$$k_j = a + b_j k_m + e_j \qquad \text{(p. 122)}$$

where   $k_j$ = return of the $j$th asset
  $a$ = constant
  $b_j$ = slope coefficient (beta)
  $k_m$ = return on a market index
  $e_j$ = error term

Equation 5.7 is the general form of a regression equation. When historical returns on an asset are regressed against market returns, the resulting regression equation is the characteristic line of the asset, and $b_j$ is the asset's beta coefficient.

**Equation 5.8**  **Required Rate of Return on an Asset: General Equation**

$$k_j = R_f + PREM_j \qquad \text{(p. 125)}$$

where   $R_f$ = risk-free rate
  $PREM_j$ = the risk premium of asset $j$

Equation 5.8 defines the required rate of return on an asset as being a function of the risk-free rate of return and the risk premium of the asset.

**Equation 5.9**  **Risk Premium on an Asset**

$$PREM_j = b_j (k_m - R_f) \qquad \text{(p. 125)}$$

where all terms are defined as previously.

Equation 5.9 shows that an asset's risk premium is dependent on the market risk premium $(k_m - R_f)$ and the systematic risk of the asset $(b_j)$.

**Equation 5.10**  **Required Rate of Return on an Asset (CAPM)**

$$k_j = R_f + b_j (k_m - R_f) \qquad \text{(p. 126)}$$

where all terms were defined previously.

Equation 5.10 can be used to estimate the required rate of return on an asset when given the risk-free rate, the market risk premium, and the beta of the asset.

## QUESTIONS

**Q5-1.** Define risk.

**Q5-2.** Explain how a discrete probability distribution differs from a continuous probability distribution.

**Q5-3.** What does the variance indicate about a set of historical returns? Why would an investor be interested in measuring this?

**Q5-4.** If you have ten perfectly positively correlated assets in your portfolio, will they reduce portfolio risk? Explain.

**Q5-5.** Explain how two negatively correlated assets affect portfolio risk.

**Q5-6.** Explain the meaning of unsystematic risk and how diversification affects the level of unsystematic risk in a portfolio.

**Q5-7.** Explain the meaning of systematic risk and how diversification affects the systematic risk in a portfolio.

**Q5-8.** What does a beta of 1.3 suggest?

**Q5-9.** Why does a low beta reflect low risk?

**Q5-10.** Other things equal, how will an increase in the market risk premium affect the required return of assets according to the capital asset pricing model (CAPM)? Why?

**Q5-11.** Other things equal, how will an increase in an asset's beta affect the required return on that asset according to the CAPM?

**Q5-12.** How are the required rates of return on assets affected if the risk-free rate decreases by 3 percent and the differential between the market return and risk-free rate remains constant?

**Q5-13.** Explain why you agree or disagree with this statement: "A risk-averse investor will invest funds only in risk-free ventures."

**Q5-14.** Samito Corporation invested most of its funds in a huge printing machine it uses to provide printing services. It recognizes there is some unsystematic risk associated with this asset but believes that only systematic risk is important, so it has ignored this risk. Explain why you agree or disagree with Samito's perception.

**Q5-15.** Your friend describes perfect negative correlation as follows: "When one asset's returns are negative, the other asset's returns are positive and by the same degree." Explain why this statement is wrong, and clarify the meaning of perfect negative correlation.

**Q5-16.** Describe the steps necessary to use sensitivity analysis in assessing the future return and risk of an asset.

**Q5-17.** Describe the steps necessary to use simulation in assessing the future return and risk of an asset.

## SELF-TEST PROBLEMS

Solutions to self-test problems appear on p. S1.

**SP5-1.** Garret, Inc., plans to invest in Assets Y and Z, which have the following possible returns:

| Economy | Probability | Return on Y | Return on Z |
|---------|-------------|-------------|-------------|
| Boom | 30% | 30% | 16% |
| Stable | 40 | 10 | 9 |
| Recession | 30 | −10 | 1 |

a. Compute the expected return on each asset.
b. Compute the standard deviation of returns for each asset.
c. Compute the coefficient of variation of returns for each asset.
d. If Garret, Inc., uses 60 percent of its funds to purchase Asset Y and 40 percent of its funds to purchase Asset Z, determine the expected return of this portfolio.

**SP5-2.** An investor plans to put 80 percent of his funds in Stock R and the remaining 20 percent in Stock S. Stock R has an expected return of 15 percent and a standard deviation of 3 percent. Stock S has an expected return of 25 percent and a standard deviation of 5 percent. The correlation coefficient between the returns of the two stocks is .9.

a. Determine the expected return of the portfolio.
b. Determine the expected standard deviation of returns on the portfolio.

**SP5-3.** Assume that the risk-free rate of return is 9 percent, the expected market return is 14 percent, the beta of Lancer stock is 1.3, and the beta of Rudi stock is 1.8.

a. Using the capital asset pricing model (CAPM), determine the required return of Lancer stock and Rudi stock.
b. What is the risk premium of Lancer stock and Rudi stock?

## PROBLEMS

**P5-1.** The risk and return of Assets Q and R are described in the form of probability distributions as follows:

| Economy | Probability | Return on Q | Return on R |
|---------|-------------|-------------|-------------|
| Boom | 20% | 19% | 15% |
| Stable | 60 | 13 | 11 |
| Recession | 20 | −4 | 5 |

a. Compute the expected return on each asset.
b. Compute the standard deviation of returns for each asset.
c. Compute the coefficient of variation of returns for each asset.
d. Which asset is riskier? Why? Which asset is preferable? Why?

**P5-2.** Scaler Corporation is considering the purchase of a stock whose return is dependent on the economy as follows:

| Economy | Probability | Return |
|---------|-------------|--------|
| Boom | 30% | 21% |
| Stable | 40 | 16 |
| Recession | 30 | 3 |

a. Determine the expected return of the stock.
b. Determine the standard deviation of returns for the stock.
c. Determine the coefficient of variation of returns for the stock.

**P5-3.** Moose, Inc., is considering an investment whose return distribution is estimated as follows:

| Return | Probability |
|--------|-------------|
| −3% | 15% |
| 0 | 20 |
| 8 | 30 |
| 12 | 20 |
| 15 | 15 |

**a.** What is the expected return of the investment?
**b.** What is the standard deviation of the investment's returns?
**c.** What is the coefficient of variation of the investment's returns?
**d.** If you had the opportunity to make the same investment as Moose, Inc., or the same investment as Scaler Corporation (in the previous question), what would be your choice? Explain.

**P5-4.** The expected return and standard deviation of returns for five investments follow. Based on the coefficient of variation as a measure of risk, which investment is preferred? Explain.

| Project | Expected Return | Standard Deviation of Returns |
|---------|-----------------|-------------------------------|
| 1 | 20% | 4% |
| 2 | 24 | 5 |
| 3 | 30 | 10 |
| 4 | 16 | 2 |
| 5 | 18 | 2 |

**P5-5.** Assume that the probability distribution of returns on Dover stock is normal, with an expected return of 15 percent and a standard deviation of 4 percent. Complete the following statements.

**a.** There is a 68 percent probability that the return will be between _____ percent and _____ percent.
**b.** There is a 95 percent probability that the return will be between _____ percent and _____ percent.
**c.** There is a 99 percent probability that the return will be between _____ percent and _____ percent.

**P5-6.** Assume that the probability distribution of returns on Lima stock is normal, with an expected return of 8 percent and a standard deviation of 4 percent.

**a.** Estimate the probability that the return will be negative. Explain.
**b.** Estimate the probability that the return will exceed 20 percent. Explain.

**P5-7.** An investor plans to allocate 30 percent of her funds to Investment C and the remaining 70 percent to Investment D. The expected returns on C and D are 12 percent and 16 percent, respectively, while the standard deviation of returns are 3 percent and 4 percent, respectively. The correlation coefficient between C and D is estimated to be .4.

**a.** Compute the expected return of the portfolio.
**b.** Compute the standard deviation of portfolio returns.

**P5-8.** Zelter, Inc., uses 60 percent of its funds for its gardening business and 40 percent of its funds to provide landscaping services. The expected return on the gardening business is 20 percent, with a standard deviation of returns of 5 percent.

The expected return of the landscaping services is 16 percent, with a standard deviation of returns of 3 percent. The correlation coefficient between the two businesses' returns is .8.

**a.** Determine the expected return of the combined businesses.
**b.** Determine the standard deviation of returns for the combined businesses.
**c.** Determine the coefficient of variation of returns for the combined businesses.

**P5-9.** Assume that the risk-free rate of return is 7 percent, while the expected market return is 10 percent. The beta of Orbit stock is 2.

**a.** What is the risk premium of Orbit's stock according to the CAPM?
**b.** Using the capital asset pricing model (CAPM), determine the required rate of return on Orbit stock.
**c.** Using the original information, if Orbit's beta decreases to 1.5, how would this affect the risk premium of the stock and the required rate of return?
**d.** Using the original information, if the risk-free rate suddenly increases to 7.5 percent, while the return on the market and Orbit's beta are unaffected, how would this affect the risk premium and the required rate of return?
**e.** Using the original information, if the expectations for the market return change to 12 percent, how would this affect the risk premium and the required rate of return?

**P5-10.** Assume that the risk-free rate of return is 8 percent, the expected market return is 11 percent, and the beta of Morland stock is .9.

**a.** What is the risk premium of Morland stock according to the CAPM?
**b.** Using the capital asset pricing model (CAPM), determine the required rate of return on Morland stock.
**c.** Using the original information, if Morland's beta increases to 1.1, how would this affect the risk premium and the required rate of return of Morland stock?
**d.** Using the original information, if the risk-free rate suddenly decreases to 6 percent, while the return on the market and Morland's beta are unaffected, how would this affect the risk premium and the required rate of return of Morland stock?
**e.** Using the original information, if expectations of market returns decrease to 10 percent, how would this affect the risk premium and the required rate of return of Morland stock?

## COMPUTER-ASSISTED PROBLEMS

**CP5-1.** Chester, Inc., plans to invest in either Asset A or Asset B. The probability distribution of returns for each asset is described as follows:

| Asset A | | Asset B | |
|---|---|---|---|
| *Probability* | *Return* | *Probability* | *Return* |
| 10% | −2% | 5% | −12% |
| 15 | 0 | 15 | −1 |
| 30 | 8 | 40 | 10 |
| 25 | 13 | 25 | 14 |
| 15 | 16 | 15 | 29 |
| 5 | 20 | | |

**a.** Which of the projects would be preferred using the expected return as the sole criterion?

**b.** Which of the projects would be preferred using various measures of risk as the sole criterion?

**c.** Which of the projects would be preferred when return and risk are both considered?

**CP5-2.** Zeero Company has invested in two assets that have the following characteristics:

|  | Asset X | Asset Y |
|---|---|---|
| Expected Return | 12% | 19% |
| Standard Deviation | 3 | 4 |

The correlation coefficient of returns between Assets X and Y is estimated to be .8.

**a. Sensitivity of Portfolio Risk and Return to Asset Composition**   Determine the expected return, standard deviation, and coefficient of variation for a portfolio consisting of 50 percent of each assset.

How would the portfolio return, standard deviation, and coefficient of variation be affected if 20 percent of the funds were allocated to Asset X with the remaining funds allocated to Asset Y? Would you recommend a 50–50 mix or a 20–80 mix? Explain.

**b. Sensitivity of Portfolio Risk to Correlation Estimates**   Using the original information and a 50–50 mix, how would the portfolio return, standard deviation, and coefficient of variation be affected if the correlation coefficient was .6? What if the correlation coefficient was .1? What if it was −.3? Which correlation would be preferable in terms of affecting portfolio performance? Explain.

**CP5-3.** Lefty, Inc., is planning to invest in Asset Z, which is expected to generate a return of 11 percent. Lefty uses the capital asset pricing model to determine the rate of return it should require on such assets. Assume that the risk-free rate is presently 6 percent, the expected market return is 10 percent, and the estimated beta for Asset Z is 1.2.

**a. Sensitivity of Required Return to Beta**   Determine the required rate of return on Asset Z. Should Lefty invest in the asset? Explain.

How would the required rate of return be affected if the asset's beta was estimated to be .9? What if it was 1.3? Would either of these estimates change Lefty's decision? Explain.

**b. Sensitivity of Required Return to Market Return Estimates**   Using the original information, how would the required rate of return on Asset Z with a beta of 1.2 be affected if the expected market return was 9 percent? What if it was 15 percent? Would either of these estimates change Lefty's decision? Explain.

**c. Sensitivity of the Required Rate of Return to Beta and Market Return Estimates**   Is the required rate of return on Asset Z more sensitive to the possible values of beta or the market return? Explain.

**CP5-4. Estimation of Beta**   Assume returns on the market and on Bando Company stock for the last 16 quarters as listed in the table on p. 143. Given this information, determine the beta of Bando stock. Describe the general interpretation of the beta estimated for Bando stock. Is Bando stock more risky or less risky than the market? Why?

| Period | Return on Market | Return on Bando Stock | Period | Return on Market | Return on Bando Stock |
|--------|------------------|-----------------------|--------|------------------|-----------------------|
| 1 | 3.0% | 3.2% | 9 | 2.1 | 2.8 |
| 2 | 1.6 | 1.9 | 10 | 1.4 | 1.5 |
| 3 | −1.4 | −1.8 | 11 | 0.3 | 10.4 |
| 4 | 0.3 | −.5 | 12 | −0.6 | −1.1 |
| 5 | 2.4 | 3.1 | 13 | −2.7 | −3.2 |
| 6 | 3.0 | 3.4 | 14 | 1.3 | 1.5 |
| 7 | 5.2 | 5.7 | 15 | 4.3 | 4.9 |
| 8 | 2.7 | 2.9 | 16 | 2.6 | 2.9 |

**CP5-5. Estimation of Beta**   Use the computer package to determine the beta of a stock assigned by your professor. Use the Standard and Poor's 500 index as a proxy for the market. Returns on the stock and the market can be obtained from a variety of sources in your library.

## REFERENCES

Blume, Marshall, and Irwin Friend. "A New Look at the Capital-Asset Pricing Model." *Journal of Finance* 28 (March 1973): 19–34.

Modigliani, Franco, and Gerald A. Pogue. "An Introduction to Risk and Return: Concepts and Evidence, Part I." *Financial Analysts Journal* 30 (March–April 1974): 68–80.

Mullins, David W., Jr. "Does the Capital Asset Pricing Model Work?" *Harvard Business Review* 60 (January–February 1982): 105–14.

Pettit, R. Richardson, and Randolph Westerfield. "Using the Capital Asset Pricing Model and the Market Model to Predict Security Returns." *Journal of Financial and Quantitative Analysis* 9 (September 1974): 579–605.

Roll, Richard. "A Critique of the Asset Pricing Theory's Tests." *Journal of Financial Economics* (March 1977): 129–76.

Rosenberg, Barr. "The Capital Asset Pricing Model and the Market Model." *Journal of Portfolio Management* 7 (Winter 1981): 5–16.

Rubinstein, Mark E. "A Mean-Variance Synthesis of Corporate Financial Theory." *Journal of Finance* 28 (March 1973): 167–81.

Wagner, W. H., and S. C. Lau. "The Effect of Diversification on Risk." *Financial Analysts Journal* 27 (November–December 1971): 48–53.

Weston, J. Fred. "Investment Decisions Using the Capital Asset Pricing Model." *Financial Management* 2 (Spring 1973): 25–33.

# ARBITRAGE PRICING THEORY

The following discussion is intended to provide the student with an intuitive understanding of the arbitrage pricing theory (APT).[1] Like the capital asset pricing model (CAPM), APT attempts to explain how assets are priced. Both models assume efficient diversification, which eliminates unsystematic risk. The CAPM views risk as the sensitivity of an asset's returns to the returns on a market portfolio. APT identifies several key factors that may affect the level of asset risk. The more sensitive an asset's returns are to the key factors, the higher the risk of the asset and the higher the required return on the asset.

Among the factors identified by researchers as possible sources of risk are (1) unanticipated inflation, (2) unanticipated changes in industrial production, (3) unanticipated changes in risk premiums on assets in general, and (4) unanticipated changes in the shape of the yield curve. Notice that all four factors involve unanticipated events. Under APT, all anticipated events are already reflected in the price and return of the asset. If, however, there is an unexpected change in a key factor, the price of an asset (and hence the return on that asset) will change. Since each asset may have a different sensitivity to the key factors, the change in return will be different for each asset. For example, assume Asset A's return is highly sensitive to unanticipated changes in industrial production, and Asset B's return is not. An unanticipated change in industrial production would substantially change the actual return of Asset A, but it would not affect the actual return of Asset B. This change in return on Asset A represents risk to the investor. Therefore, investors will require a higher return on Asset A than on Asset B (assuming equal sensitivities of both assets to the other factors). Arbitrage conducted by investors results in the pricing of assets such that assets with greater factor sensitivities have higher expected returns, while assets with equal sensitivities have identical returns.

---

1. More rigorous presentations are available in S. Ross, "The Arbitrage Theory of Capital Asset Pricing," *Journal of Economic Theory* 13 (December 1976): 341–60; R. Roll and S. Ross, "An Empirical Investigation of the Arbitrage Pricing Theory," *Journal of Finance* (December 1980): 1073–1103; and W. Sharpe, "Factors Models, CAPMs, and APT," *Journal of Portfolio Management* (Fall 1984): 21–5.

The basic equation describing APT is as follows:

$$R = E + (b1)(f1) + (b2)(f2) + (b3)(f3) + (b4)(f4) + e \qquad \textbf{(5A.1)}$$

where $R$ = actual return on an asset

$E$ = expected return on an asset

$b1, b2$, etc. = sensitivity of an asset's returns to factors 1, 2, etc.

$f1, f2$, etc. = actual values of factors 1, 2, etc.

$e$ = return on unsystematic factors

# PART 3

# FINANCIAL ANALYSIS AND PLANNING

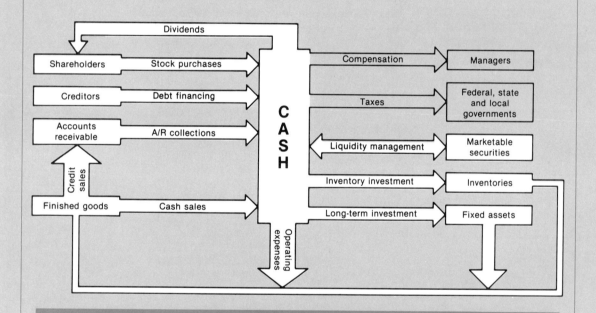

Chapters 6 through 8 focus on the analysis and planning aspects of financial management. Chapter 6 demonstrates how ratio analysis and sources and uses of funds statements can be used to help managers evaluate past performance and forecast future performance. Chapter 7 discusses planning for future financing needs. It explains how the cash budget can be used to anticipate a short-term cash deficiency (or surplus). Chapter 8 explains how the firm is affected by the interaction of fixed costs, variable costs, and revenues. Any policy that affects these variables can affect the firm's risk and profitability.

# CHAPTER 6

# FINANCIAL ANALYSIS

## FINANCIAL ANALYSIS IN PERSPECTIVE

The disappointing performance in 1986 of Allegis Corporation, the parent company of United Airlines, Hertz, and Hilton International, led the firm's management to seek ways to improve profits in 1987 and beyond. Its financial statements suggested that operating expenses were too high relative to revenue and that several areas of the firm's operations were not performing as well as management and stockholders would like.

As a result, Allegis took some cost cutting steps in the first quarter of 1987. This action included laying off more than 1,000 employees and transferring some aircraft and crews to more profitable routes. Those actions (plus some others) are expected to reduce the firm's expenses by $100 million for the year 1987. In July 1987, Allegis an-

nounced sharply improved earnings for the second quarter of 1987 compared to the same quarter a year earlier. Although some of this improvement is attributable to improvement in the airline industry as a whole, much of it resulted from the cost cutting actions taken by Allegis. An analysis of the firm's financial statements also led Allegis to consider selling its nonairline subsidiaries. It was felt that Hertz and Hilton International were not generating sufficient profitability relative to the size of the investment made in those firms.

How firms analyze their financial statements to determine what actions are necessary to improve profitability, reduce risk, and improve the financial soundness of the firm is the subject of this chapter.

An important task of management is to assess its firm's recent performance and evaluate its current and expected future situation. The firm's strengths and weaknesses must be known if management is to exploit the former and minimize the latter in an effort to maximize shareholder wealth. Among the tools managers use to evaluate their firms' performance are ratio analysis, common-size financial statements, and sources and uses of funds statements. By applying these tools to the analysis of the firm's income statement and balance sheet, managements can determine (1) the efficiency with which their firms utilize assets, (2) the ability of their firms to generate profits, and (3) the riskiness of their firms.

This chapter first describes the importance of financial analysis to the firm's managers, creditors, and stockholders. Next, various ratios are presented, discussed, and applied to a hypothetical firm. Sources of information about industry ratios are then identified. Finally, the construction and interpretation of a sources and uses of funds statement are discussed.

## IMPORTANCE OF FINANCIAL ANALYSIS

The purpose of income statements and balance sheets is to inform interested parties about the operations and financial condition of firms. However, these financial statements merely present the facts; an analysis of those facts is necessary in order to arrive at conclusions. **Income statements** indicate the revenues, costs, and profits of firms over a period of time, while **balance sheets** report the book value of assets, liabilities, and owners' equity of firms at a given point in time. It is up to the individual analyst to identify important variables, calculate ratios, evaluate trends, and make comparisons with other firms to accurately assess the firm's financial condition.

It is possible for firms to show high profits on their income statements yet be financially weak according to their balance sheets. It is also possible for firms to show low profits or even losses on their income statements yet be financially strong according to their balance sheets. Because the two statements reveal different financial characteristics, both must be analyzed to afford a complete evaluation of the firm's situation.

Financial analysis is important to everyone involved with the firm, including managers, creditors, and shareholders. The specialized concerns of each group are briefly described in the following sections.

### Managers' Use of Financial Analysis

Managers evaluate their firm's financial statements as a means of monitoring the firm's operations and identifying the firm's strengths and weaknesses. The firm's financial statements can be generated and analyzed as frequently as necessary so that developing problems can be identified and dealt with before they become serious. Managers are also concerned with how the firm's creditors and owners view the firm's financial condition as revealed by the financial statements. Constant monitoring of those statements can suggest actions that will improve their appearance.

### Creditors' Use of Financial Analysis

Creditors conduct financial analysis of firms to determine the probability that the firms will default on loans. Short-term creditors may be most interested in the firm's balance sheet, which indicates the level of liquid assets available to repay loans. Long-term lenders, however, may be just as concerned with the income statement as they are with the balance sheet, since the firm must generate sufficient income in future years to pay interest and repay the loan. Additionally, a firm's balance sheet can deteriorate very quickly if its income statement is not healthy.

### Shareholders' Use of Financial Analysis

Financial analysis is very important to shareholders (and prospective shareholders) who need to know how well their investment (the firm) is performing. Financial analysis may signal to existing shareholders that it is time to replace the board of directors or time to sell their stock in the company. Some shareholders do not take the time to analyze the firms in which they invest. Instead they heed the advice of financial advisors who analyze firms for them.

## INCOME STATEMENTS AND BALANCE SHEETS

Before financial analysis can begin, of course, one must understand the information reported on the income statement and balance sheet. These financial statements are explained briefly here.

### Income Statement

The 19X8 income statement for Zell Corporation, a manufacturing firm, is presented in Table 6.1. *Net sales* is sales adjusted for discounts and returns. *Cost of goods sold* is subtracted from net sales to arrive at gross profit. Then *operating expenses* (composed of selling expense, depreciation expense, and general and administrative expenses) are subtracted from gross profit to arrive at *earnings before interest and taxes* (EBIT). Next, interest expense is subtracted to determine *earnings before taxes*. Finally, taxes are subtracted to determine *net income* (sometimes referred to as *earnings after taxes*). The breakdown of net income into cash dividends paid on common stock and retained earnings is displayed at the bottom of Table 6.1.

### Balance Sheet

The balance sheet for Zell Corporation as of December 31, 19X8, is illustrated in Table 6.2. The assets listed in a balance sheet are separated into *current* and *fixed*. Major current assets include cash, marketable securities, accounts receivable, and inventories. *Cash* primarily represents checking account balances, and *marketable securities* are generally short-term secu-

**TABLE 6.1    Zell Corporation Income Statement, Year Ending December 31, 19X8 (Thousands of Dollars)**

| | | |
|---|---:|---:|
| Net sales | | $8,000 |
| Less: Cost of goods sold | | 3,600 |
| Gross profit | | $4,400 |
| Less: Operating expenses | | |
| Selling expense | $1,600 | |
| Depreciation expense | 300 | |
| General and administrative | 1,800 | |
| Total operating expenses | | $3,700 |
| Earnings before interest and taxes | | $ 700 |
| Less: Interest expense | | 120 |
| Earnings before taxes | | $ 580 |
| Less: Taxes | | 140 |
| Net income | | $ 440 |
| Dividends paid on common stock | | 140 |
| To retained earnings | | $ 300 |

**TABLE 6.2    Zell Corporation Balance Sheet as of December 31, 19X8 (Thousands of Dollars)**

*Assets*

| | |
|---|---:|
| Current assets | |
| Cash | $ 30 |
| Marketable securities | 600 |
| Accounts receivable | 830 |
| Inventory | 400 |
| Total current assets | $1,860 |
| Fixed assets | |
| Plant and equipment | $3,140 |
| Less: Accumulated depreciation | 1,000 |
| Net fixed assets | $2,140 |
| Total assets | $4,000 |

*Liabilities and owners' equity*

| | |
|---|---:|
| Current liabilities | |
| Accounts payable | $ 460 |
| Notes payable | 270 |
| Accrued expenses | 150 |
| Other current liabilities | 200 |
| Total current liabilities | $1,080 |
| Long-term liabilities | |
| Long-term debt | $1,000 |
| Owners' equity | |
| Common stock (100,000 shares at par value of $.80 per share) | $ 80 |
| Additional paid-in capital | 240 |
| Retained earnings | 1,600 |
| Total owners' equity | $1,920 |
| Total liabilities and owners' equity | $4,000 |

rities that can be converted to cash quickly if additional funds are needed. In the interim, those marketable securities will earn interest for the firm. *Accounts receivable* reflect sales that have been made for which payment has not yet been received. As such, accounts receivable are assets, since they represent funds owed to the firm. *Inventories* are composed of raw materials, work-in-progress, and finished goods.

Fixed assets include plant and equipment. Table 6.2 illustrates that *depreciation* is subtracted from plant and equipment to arrive at *net fixed assets.* Depreciation represents the theoretical reduction in the value of assets as a result of their use.

Liabilities and owners' equity are also shown in Table 6.2. Current (short-term) liabilities typically include accounts payable, notes payable, and accrued expenses. *Accounts payable* represent money owed by the firm for the purchase of materials. *Notes payable* represent loans to the firm made by creditors such as banks. *Accrued expenses* reflect amounts owed by firms for labor already used and also taxes owed on past profits. Long-term liabilities are liabilities that will not be repaid within one year. These liabilities commonly include long-term loans from banks and outstanding bond issues.

Owners' equity includes the par value of all common stock issued, additional paid-in capital, and retained earnings. *Additional paid-in capital* represents the dollar amount in excess of par value, received from issuing common stock. *Retained earnings* represents the accumulation of the firm's earnings that are reinvested in assets by the firm rather than being distributed as dividends to shareholders.

Now that the key components of the income statement and balance sheet have been reviewed, the discussion will focus on interpreting these financial statements.

## RATIO ANALYSIS

Analysts can learn much about a firm by merely observing the income statement and balance sheet. The level of net income, total assets, common equity, and so on, all provide useful information. However, by observing certain financial statement items in relation to certain other items, the analyst can learn even more. An analysis that considers the relationships between financial statement variables is called **ratio analysis.**

When conducting ratio analysis, it is important to consider how the ratios have changed over time as well as how a firm's ratios compare to those of other firms in the same industry. Analyzing the ratios over time (*trend analysis*) may indicate an improvement or a deterioration of a given ratio. For example, two firms could have identical ratios in the most recent period, but one firm's ratios might have improved from the prior period while the other firm's ratios might have deteriorated. Analysts would look more favorably on a firm whose ratios had improved.

Comparing a firm's ratios to those of other firms in the same industry, or to an average of the other firms' ratios, can also provide useful information. The analyst can use the industry average as an indication of what the norm is for firms in the industry. Deviations from the norm may be considered either favorable or unfavorable depending upon the size and direction of the deviation.

Financial ratios can be categorized based on the characteristics they measure. This text groups ratios into four such categories:

- Measures of liquidity
- Measures of efficiency
- Measures of financial leverage
- Measures of profitability

A number of ratios can be used to analyze each of these characteristics. In addition to those discussed here, there may be other ratios that provide superior measurements of desired characteristics in given situations. It is also important to recognize that the ratios presented here are particularly useful for analyzing manufacturing firms; an analysis of financial institutions, utilities, transportation firms, and other service industries, however, generally requires the use of some ratios that are substantially different.

### Measures of Liquidity

The **liquidity of a firm** refers to its ability to meet its short-term obligations. Most liquidity measures compare current assets to current liabilities. The greater the level of a firm's current assets relative to current liabilities, the greater the firm's liquidity is. While some interested parties such as short-term creditors may feel the firm can never be too liquid, others, such as stockholders, may not want the firm to have too much liquidity, since current assets typically do not earn high returns for the firm. For this reason, firms attempt to avoid both insufficient and excessive liquidity. Three common liquidity measures are discussed below.

**Net Working Capital**   Net working capital is measured as current assets minus current liabilities. Net working capital for Zell Corporation is as follows:

$$\text{net working capital} = \text{current assets} - \text{current liabilities}$$

$$= \$1,860,000 - \$1,080,000$$

$$= \$780,000$$

It is only natural for larger firms to have higher levels of net working capital. Therefore, this measure has significance only when compared to firms of similar size in the same industry or when used in a trend analysis.

**Current Ratio**   The current ratio uses the same information as net working capital but in a different way. Instead of determining the absolute difference between current assets and current liabilities, the relationship between these two variables is analyzed in true ratio form:

$$\text{current ratio} = \frac{\text{current assets}}{\text{current liabilities}}$$

For Zell Corporation, the current ratio is as follows:

$$\text{current ratio} = \frac{\$1,860,000}{\$1,080,000}$$

$$= 1.7$$

For most firms, current assets exceed current liabilities, resulting in a current ratio greater than 1.0. For Zell Corporation, current assets are about 1.7 times current liabilities. The higher the ratio, the more liquid the firm is. Does a ratio of 1.7 reflect adequate liquidity? That depends on the nature of the firm's operations. An analysis of Zell Corporation's liquidity and other financial ratios is conducted later in this chapter after the individual ratio values have been determined.

**Quick Ratio**   The quick ratio (sometimes referred to as the *acid-test ratio*) requires a slight adjustment in the current ratio. Recall that the current ratio considers *all* current assets to be liquid assets. Yet, inventories are the least liquid of the current assets and may not be easily converted into cash. In order to get a more conservative indication of a firm's liquidity, the quick ratio eliminates inventories from the measure of liquid assets.

$$\text{quick ratio} = \frac{\text{current assets} - \text{inventories}}{\text{current liabilities}}$$

The quick ratio for Zell Corporation is as follows:

$$\text{quick ratio} = \frac{\$1,860,000 - \$400,000}{\$1,080,000}$$

$$= 1.4$$

Because this ratio considers only the more liquid current assets, its value is lower than the current ratio. The greater the value of the quick ratio of a firm, the greater is the firm's liquidity.

## Measures of Efficiency

**Efficiency ratios** (sometimes referred to as *activity ratios*) measure how efficiently a firm manages its assets. Several efficiency ratios are described here.

**Average Collection Period**   When a firm sells its product but does not receive payment immediately, an account receivable is created. Each account receivable represents an expense to the selling firm, since it has invested its money in, but has not received payment for the product. Therefore, a high level of accounts receivable can be costly to the firm. Accounts receivable may become too large if a firm does not collect its receivables in a timely manner. The average collection period is a useful measure of how long it takes the firm to collect payment on its receivables, and it can be determined as follows:

$$\text{average collection period} = \frac{\text{accounts receivable}}{\text{average sales per day}}$$

$$= \frac{\text{accounts receivable}}{\text{annual sales}/360}$$

Notice that *average sales per day* appears in the denominator of this ratio. When available, the denominator should be *average credit sales per day,* since the collection period for cash sales is zero and could bias the ratio. When the level of credit sales is not available to the analyst, the level of total sales may be used.

For Zell Corporation, the average collection period is as follows:

$$\text{average collection period} = \frac{\$830,000}{\$8,000,000/360}$$

$$= 37.4 \text{ days}$$

A high average collection period indicates a firm is receiving payment from its sales too slowly. It is useful to compare the average collection period to the firm's credit terms. If Zell Corporation's credit terms are net 35, an average collection period of 37.4 days would appear to be reasonable. However, if credit terms are net 20, a problem could be indicated.

A shorter collection period is not always better. Zell Corporation could reduce its average collection period if it restricts sales to only those customers that pay on time. However, Zell's sales may decline if some customers are denied trade credit. The optimal credit policy is one that is sufficiently loose to generate a high level of sales, but sufficiently restrictive to avoid extending credit to customers who are likely to cause collection problems. Chapter 22 takes a closer look at credit policy.

**Inventory Turnover**   Generally, firms prefer to support a high level of sales with a low level of inventory. The reason is that the expense of maintaining inventory is directly related to the level of inventory. However, low levels of inventory can be just as expensive as high levels (or more expensive) if they result in shortages or stock-outs that reduce sales. Therefore this ratio can be either too high or too low. To assess the relationship between a firm's inventory position and sales, the inventory turnover ratio can be used:

$$\text{inventory turnover} = \frac{\text{cost of goods sold}}{\text{inventory}}$$

For Zell Corporation, the inventory turnover ratio is as follows:

$$\text{inventory turnover} = \frac{\$3,600,000}{\$400,000}$$

$$= 9.0$$

This ratio suggests that Zell Corporation turned its inventory over nine times during the year. *Cost of goods sold* is used in the numerator instead of *sales* because *cost of goods sold* reflects the value of the inventory sold and does not include the firm's operating expenses and profit, which are included in sales. When cost of goods sold is not available, sales is sometimes used in the numerator as a substitute. *Average inventory* should be used in the denominator when it is available, since inventory can change substantially during the period, and year-end inventory may be abnormally high or low. When average inventory is not available, though, year-end inventory will suffice.

**Total Asset Turnover**   Generally, firms prefer to support a high level of sales with a small amount of assets, which indicates efficient utilization of assets. Firms maintaining excess capacity or excess inventory may be needlessly spending money to maintain those assets. Conversely, an exceptionally high total asset turnover ratio may indicate that the firm is using old, fully depreciated plant and equipment that may be inefficient, or that the plant is operating at full capacity with no ability to increase production (without substantial delay and expense). To measure the efficiency with which firms use their assets, the total asset turnover ratio can be calculated. For Zell Corporation, the total asset turnover ratio is as follows:

$$\text{total asset turnover} = \frac{\text{sales}}{\text{total assets}}$$

$$= \frac{\$8,000,000}{\$4,000,000}$$

$$= 2.0$$

Zell Corporation's sales during the year were twice the level of its total assets. Like all other financial ratios, the total asset turnover should be evaluated over time and in comparison to the industry norm.

## Measures of Financial Leverage

**Financial leverage** refers to the use of borrowed funds to finance a firm's assets. Firms that borrow a large proportion of their funds, as opposed to financing with common equity, have fewer owners of common stock sharing the firm's earnings. However, these same firms incur higher fixed financing costs, which must be paid regardless of the level of firm sales. There are two different types of leverage measures: those that measure the amount of debt used by the firm and those that measure the ability of the firm to service its debt (pay interest and principal when due). The *debt ratio* and the *debt to equity ratio* consider the amount of debt; the *times interest earned ratio* and the *fixed charge coverage ratio* consider the ability of the firm to service its debt.

**Debt Ratio**   The debt ratio indicates the percentage of a firm's total assets that is financed with borrowed funds. For Zell Corporation, the debt ratio is as follows:

$$\text{debt ratio} = \frac{\text{total debt}}{\text{total assets}}$$

$$= \frac{\$2,080,000}{\$4,000,000}$$

$$= 52.0\%$$

Total debt includes both short-term and long-term liabilities. The higher the debt ratio, the greater the proportion of total assets financed with borrowed funds. For Zell Corporation, 52 percent of its total assets are financed with debt sources of funds. If this ratio is too high, it indicates a high level of risk that may be unacceptable to both the owners and creditors of the firm. It may also suggest that the firm will be unable to obtain additional debt financing until this ratio is reduced. In other words, it may restrict the flexibility of the firm in raising funds in the future. To reduce the debt ratio, a firm can issue more shares of common stock, retain more earnings, or sell some assets and use the proceeds to retire some debt. If the debt ratio is very low, it may be viewed negatively by stockholders who want to reap the benefits of higher earnings that financial leverage can produce.

**Debt to Equity Ratio**   To measure the amount of long-term financing provided by debt relative to equity, the debt to equity ratio can be used. For Zell Corporation, the debt to equity ratio is as follows:

$$\text{debt to equity ratio} = \frac{\text{long-term debt}}{\text{owners' equity}}$$

$$= \frac{\$1,000,000}{\$1,920,000}$$

$$= 52.1\%$$

This ratio is similar to the debt ratio in terms of its interpretation except the debt to equity ratio considers only long-term financing. Zell Corporation's long-term debt is 52.1 percent as large as owners' equity (the fact that the debt ratio is very close at 52.0 percent is a coincidence). If this ratio is too high, it suggests there is considerable risk to both creditors and owners of the firm. A high debt to equity ratio may also indicate a lack of future financial flexibility. If the ratio is too low, the stockholders may feel that earnings are suffering from a lack of financial leverage.

**Times Interest Earned**   The financial leverage ratios discussed thus far measure how much debt the firm has. The times interest earned ratio considers the ability of the firm to service its debt. If a firm has a low level of earnings (EBIT) with which to pay interest, a small decrease in EBIT could result in the firm defaulting on its loans, which could lead to bankruptcy. Conversely, a high level of EBIT relative to required interest payments suggests that even if EBIT declines substantially, funds will be available with which to pay interest on the firm's debt. If it is too high, though, stockholders may feel the firm is not taking advantage of the benefits provided by financial leverage. For Zell Corporation, the times interest earned ratio is as follows:

$$\text{times interest earned} = \frac{\text{earnings before interest and taxes}}{\text{annual interest expense}}$$

$$= \frac{\$700,000}{\$120,000}$$

$$= 5.8$$

A times interest earned ratio of 5.8 indicates that the earnings before interest and taxes of Zell Corporation during 19X8 was 5.8 times Zell's interest expense. While this appears to be a comfortable margin, it should be compared to the industry average and the trend analyzed to obtain a better perspective.

**Fixed Charge Coverage**  Like the times interest earned ratio, the fixed charge coverage ratio is a measure of the ability of the firm to pay its fixed financing costs. The only difference is that required lease payments are considered in the same manner as interest payments. The fixed charge coverage ratio is

$$\text{fixed charge coverage} = \frac{\text{EBIT} + \text{lease payments}}{\text{interest} + \text{lease payments}}$$

Since Zell Corporation's financial statements do not indicate the existence of any lease or rental obligations, Zell's fixed charge coverage ratio is identical to its times interest earned ratio.

## Measures of Profitability

Measuring firm profitability is important to the analyst since it provides summary information on the success of the firm's operations during a given period. While the level of net income indicates the dollar amount of profit generated by a firm, the analyst should also know the level of profit relative to (1) the level of sales, (2) the amount of equity invested in the firm, and (3) the level of total assets used to generate those profits. The ratios that measure these relationships follow:

**Gross Profit Margin**  Two of the largest and therefore most important expenses of manufacturing firms are wages and the cost of raw materials. Combined, these expenses constitute *cost of goods sold*. Gross profit margin indicates the percent of each sales dollar remaining after cost of goods sold has been subtracted. Firms would like their gross profit margin to be as high as possible. For Zell Corporation, the gross profit margin is as follows:

$$\text{gross profit margin} = \frac{\text{sales} - \text{cost of goods sold}}{\text{sales}}$$

$$= \frac{\text{gross profit}}{\text{sales}}$$

$$= \frac{\$4,400,000}{\$8,000,000}$$

$$= 55.0\%$$

A gross profit margin of 55 percent for Zell Corporation indicates that 55 percent of each dollar of sales remains after subtracting the cost of producing the product. Gross profit margin should be monitored over time and compared to the industry average to assure that the cost of goods sold does not become excessive.

**Net Profit Margin**   Net profit margin is a measure of the percent of each dollar of sales that flows through to the stockholders as net income. For Zell Corporation, the net profit margin is as follows:

$$\text{net profit margin} = \frac{\text{net income}}{\text{sales}}$$

$$= \frac{\$440,000}{\$8,000,000}$$

$$= 5.5\%$$

Firms having a high volume of sales may find that a low profit margin on sales generates a satisfactory return for the shareholders. Conversely, firms with a low volume of sales may need a higher profit margin to generate a satisfactory return for its shareholders.

**Return on Investment (ROI)**   A firm's return on investment (ROI), also referred to as *return on assets* (ROA), measures the return to the firm as a percentage of the total amount invested in the firm, on a book-value basis. For Zell Corporation, ROI is calculated as follows:

$$\text{return on investment} = \frac{\text{net income}}{\text{total assets}}$$

$$= \frac{\$440,000}{\$4,000,000}$$

$$= 11.0\%$$

ROI provides a broad measure of a firm's performance. Managers generally prefer this ratio to be very high for their firms. However, a high ratio can also mean that the firm is failing to replace worn-out assets. It is possible for firms to generate a high net profit margin but have a low ROI if they have a high level of assets.

**Return on Equity (ROE)**   The return on equity (ROE) measures the return to the common stockholders as a percent of their investment, where the amount of investment is based on book value. For Zell Corporation, ROE is calculated as follows:

$$\text{return on equity} = \frac{\text{net income}}{\text{owners' equity}}$$

$$= \frac{\$440,000}{\$1,920,000}$$

$$= 22.9\%$$

Common stockholders prefer ROE to be very high, since it indicates high returns relative to their investment. However, some policies implemented to increase ROE can also increase risk. For example, using high levels of financial leverage can increase ROE, but high levels of financial leverage also increase the firm's exposure to risk as discussed earlier. Therefore, when ROE is abnormally high, the reasons should be determined.

**Earnings per Share (EPS)**   As the name implies, earnings per share (EPS) indicates the dollar amount of net income earned by the firm for each share of common stock outstanding. For Zell Corporation, EPS is determined as follows:

$$\text{earnings per share} = \frac{\text{net income}}{\text{number of shares of common stock outstanding}}$$

$$= \frac{\$440,000}{100,000 \text{ shares}}$$

$$= \$4.40$$

Unlike most of the other ratios presented here, a comparison of a firm's EPS to that of the industry average is not meaningful. The reason is that discretionary activities of a firm, such as stock splits and the payment of stock dividends (the issuance of additional shares of stock to stockholders at no additional cost), have a direct effect on the EPS reported by the firm, but not on the wealth of shareholders. Comparison of values that can be artificially managed by firms could lead to faulty conclusions, although trend analysis of EPS is useful for analyzing the performance of the firm. Of course, the trend analysis is meaningful only when the firm's EPS figures have been adjusted to reflect the effect of stock splits and stock dividends.

## COMPARISON OF FIRM RATIOS TO AN INDUSTRY AVERAGE

Table 6.3 summarizes how the financial ratios presented here can be interpreted when they are substantially lower or higher than the industry norm. Caution should be exercised when using this table, however, since all possible interpretations are not presented. Also, determining whether the deviation of a firm's ratio from the industry norm is significant must be subjectively determined by the analyst. Some firms feel that if their ratio is in the upper or lower quartile of the ratios of all firms in the industry, there is reason for concern, but such a generalization cannot be applied in all cases.

When analyzing financial ratios, it is important to recognize that there may be a perfectly logical reason why a ratio deviates from the norm. It

**TABLE 6.3   Interpretation of Financial Ratios That Differ from Industry Norms**

| Ratios | Common Interpretation for Low Ratio[a] | Common Interpretation for High Ratio[a] |
|---|---|---|
| *Liquidity ratios* | | |
| Current ratio | Insufficient liquidity | Excessive liquidity |
| Quick ratio | Insufficient liquidity | Excessive liquidity |
| *Efficiency ratios* | | |
| Average collection period | Credit policy is too restrictive | Credit policy is too easy |
| Inventory turnover | Excessive inventory relative to sales | Insufficient inventory relative to sales |
| Total asset turnover | Excessive level of assets relative to sales | Insufficient assets relative to sales |
| *Leverage ratios* | | |
| Debt ratio | Insufficient debt used to finance the firm's assets | Excessive debt used to finance the firm's assets |
| Debt to equity ratio | Insufficient long-term debt relative to equity | Excessive long-term debt relative to equity |
| Times interest earned | Potential cash flow problems, since required interest payments are high relative to the earnings available to pay interest | The firm is able to pay interest on its current debt and may wish to consider assuming additional debt |
| Fixed charge coverage | Potential cash flow problem since required interest and lease payments are high relative to earnings available to pay them | The firm is able to service its debt and lease obligations and may wish to consider assuming additional debt and lease obligations |
| *Profitability ratios* | | |
| Gross profit margin | Cost of goods sold is higher than it should be | The firm has maintained a relatively low cost of goods |
| Net profit margin | Expenses are high relative to the sale price of the product | Expenses are low relative to the selling price of the product |
| Return on investment | Net income is low relative to the amount of assets employed by the firm | Net income is high relative to the amount of assets employed by the firm |
| Return on equity | Net income is low relative to the amount of equity invested in the firm | Net income is high relative to the amount of equity invested in the firm |

[a] As compared to industry norms.

may turn out to be a temporary situation that will reverse itself in the future. For example, a firm may have an abnormally large amount of cash and marketable securities according to both a trend analysis and a comparison to the industry average. Common stockholders may interpret this as evidence of inefficient use of assets, but further investigation may reveal that the firm recently issued new bonds and has not yet used the funds received from that issue for their intended purpose.

Of the two steps in ratio analysis, calculating ratios and interpreting ratios, the second step is clearly more difficult. As indicated earlier, comparing a firm's ratios to the same ratios for other firms in the industry, or to an industry average, can help identify a firm's strengths and weaknesses. Columns 1 and 2 of Table 6.4 identify and define the financial ratios presented in this chapter. Each ratio value for Zell Corporation is shown in Column 3, and the industry averages are provided in Column 4. Based on the information in these two columns, an evaluation of Zell Corporation's ratios relative to the industry average is provided in Column 5. An elaboration of this evaluation follows.

In terms of liquidity, both the current and quick ratios of Zell Corporation are higher than the industry average. This implies that Zell has adequate liquidity. However, the analyst may want to consider whether Zell is maintaining excessive liquidity.

In terms of efficiency, the average collection period for Zell Corporation is more than two weeks longer than the norm for the industry. This could imply that Zell is not managing its accounts receivable efficiently, either because it is (1) providing trade credit to non-creditworthy customers, (2) extending trade credit for longer periods than necessary, or (3) doing a poor job of pursuing overdue accounts. Zell's credit policy needs to be analyzed further to identify the specific source of the problem.[1] The slow collections could account for the higher than normal liquidity, since slow collections would make accounts receivable higher than they should be.

The inventory turnover ratio for Zell Corporation is low relative to the industry. This suggests that Zell uses a relatively large inventory to support its sales. The firm should determine why its inventory level is higher than the norm and consider whether it can reduce it without causing stockouts. Zell's higher than normal inventory level could also help explain the firm's higher than normal liquidity.

The asset turnover ratio for Zell Corporation is slightly below the industry average. It can be improved, however, by reducing inventory and accounts receivable, which appear to be too high.

With regard to financial leverage, the debt ratio is somewhat lower than the industry average. This suggests Zell may be able to raise some additional funds by borrowing if necessary. The debt to equity ratio is substantially lower than that of the industry, implying that the firm obtains a relatively large percentage of its long-term funds from equity compared to other firms in the industry and offering more evidence that Zell Corporation has additional borrowing capacity. The times interest earned ratio is identical to the industry's, however, indicating that an increase in debt

---

1. Information about how to analyze a firm's credit policy is presented in Chapter 22.

TABLE 6.4   **Evaluation of Financial Ratios: Zell Corporation**

| (1) | (2) | (3) | (4) | (5) |
|---|---|---|---|---|
| Ratio | Calculation | Ratio for Zell Corporation | Average for Industry | Evaluation of Zell Corporation Based on Ratio |
| **Liquidity** | | | | |
| Current | $\dfrac{\text{current assets}}{\text{current liabilities}}$ | 1.7 | 1.5 | Good |
| Quick | $\dfrac{\text{current assets} - \text{inventories}}{\text{current liabilities}}$ | 1.4 | 1.0 | Good |
| **Efficiency** | | | | |
| Average collection period | $\dfrac{\text{accounts receivable}}{\text{annual sales}/360}$ | 37 days | 22 days | Bad. Requires further analysis |
| Inventory turnover | $\dfrac{\text{cost of goods sold}}{\text{inventory}}$ | 9.0 | 13.1 | Bad. Requires further analysis |
| Total asset turnover | $\dfrac{\text{sales}}{\text{total assets}}$ | 2.0 | 2.1 | OK |
| **Financial leverage** | | | | |
| Debt ratio | $\dfrac{\text{total debt}}{\text{total assets}}$ | 52% | 55% | Good |
| Debt to equity ratio | $\dfrac{\text{long-term debt}}{\text{owners' equity}}$ | 52% | 67% | OK |
| Times interest earned | $\dfrac{\text{earnings before interest and taxes}}{\text{annual interest expense}}$ | 5.8 | 5.8 | OK |
| Fixed charge coverage | $\dfrac{\text{EBIT} + \text{lease payments}}{\text{interest} + \text{lease payments}}$ | 5.8 | 5.2 | Good |
| **Profitability** | | | | |
| Gross profit margin | $\dfrac{\text{gross profit}}{\text{sales}}$ | 55.0% | 47.0% | Good |
| Net profit margin | $\dfrac{\text{net income}}{\text{sales}}$ | 5.5% | 5.3% | Good |
| Return on investment | $\dfrac{\text{net income}}{\text{total assets}}$ | 11.0% | 11.1% | OK |
| Return on equity | $\dfrac{\text{net income}}{\text{owners' equity}}$ | 22.9% | 25.2% | Bad. Requires further analysis |

would result in a lower times interest earned ratio unless an increase in debt is offset by increasing EBIT.

In terms of profitability, the gross profit margin is substantially higher for Zell Corporation than for the industry average. This suggests that Zell has the ability to keep the cost of goods sold low relative to the price of the product.

The net profit margin and return on investment (ROI) are similar to their respective industry average ratios. Both ratios could be improved, however, by a reduction in inventories and accounts receivable. A reduction in the level of assets would permit Zell to repay some of its debt and reduce its interest expense. The resulting increase in net income and reduction in assets would result in a higher net profit margin and ROI.

Zell's return on common equity (ROE) is lower than the norm. This could result from the use of less leverage than other firms in the industry, which is consistent with the low debt to equity ratio identified earlier.

In summary, it appears that Zell Corporation needs to

- Improve its collection of accounts receivable without reducing sales.
- Reduce its inventory level without causing stockouts.
- Change the sources of long-term financing to include more long-term debt.

Decreasing accounts receivable and inventories will improve Zell's average collection period and inventory turnover. It will also increase net profit margin, ROI, and ROE. Shifting to greater emphasis on long-term debt as a source of financing should also help to increase Zell's ROE.

## Analysis of ROE: The DuPont System

ROE is an important summary measure of a firm's operations since it indicates the return to shareholders as a percent of their total investment in the firm (in book-value terms). In addition, the growth rate of a firm's dividend and stock price is heavily dependent upon the firm's ROE.[2] In order to analyze ROE, analysts frequently compare its components to the same components for the industry average.

ROE can be broken down into two major components, return on investment (ROI) and the equity multiplier (a measure of leverage):

$$\text{ROE} = \text{ROI} \times \text{equity multiplier}$$

$$\frac{\text{net income}}{\text{owners' equity}} = \frac{\text{net income}}{\text{total assets}} \times \frac{\text{total assets}}{\text{owners' equity}}$$

The DuPont System of analysis analyzes ROI by breaking it down into its components, net profit margin and total asset turnover:

---

2. It can be shown that the long-run growth rate of a firm's dividends and stock price is a function of the long-run ROE and the firm's earnings retention rate. Proof of this relationship can be found in most investments texts.

**TABLE 6.5   Components of ROE and ROI: Zell Corporation versus the Industry Average**

|  | ROE | = | ROI | × | equity multiplier |
|---|---|---|---|---|---|
|  | $\dfrac{\text{net income}}{\text{owners' equity}}$ | = | $\dfrac{\text{net income}}{\text{total assets}}$ | × | $\dfrac{\text{total assets}}{\text{owners' equity}}$ |
| Firm | 22.9% | = | 11.0% | × | 2.08 |
| Industry | 25.2% | = | 11.1% | × | 2.27 |

|  | ROI | = | net profit margin | × | asset turnover |
|---|---|---|---|---|---|
|  | $\dfrac{\text{net income}}{\text{total assets}}$ | = | $\dfrac{\text{net income}}{\text{sales}}$ | × | $\dfrac{\text{sales}}{\text{total assets}}$ |
| Firm | 11.0% | = | 5.5% | × | 2.0 |
| Industry | 11.1% | = | 5.3% | × | 2.1 |

$$\text{ROI} = \text{net profit margin} \times \text{total asset turnover}$$

$$\frac{\text{net income}}{\text{total assets}} = \frac{\text{net income}}{\text{sales}} \times \frac{\text{sales}}{\text{total assets}}$$

Since ROI is an important component of ROE, the analyst can first determine if ROI is lower than it should be. If it is too low, the analyst can determine which component of ROI is responsible for the lower value. After identifying the deficient component, it, too, can be subdivided into its components for further analysis.

The top half of Table 6.5 identifies the components of ROE for both Zell Corporation and the industry average. Although Zell's ROI is very close to the industry average, its equity multiplier is substantially lower, suggesting that Zell has less debt than the average firm in the industry. The result is a substantially lower ROE for Zell. To improve its ROE, the firm should consider using more financial leverage.

The lower half of Table 6.5 indicates the components of ROI for both Zell Corporation and the industry average. Although Zell's net profit margin is slightly higher than that of the industry average, its asset turnover is lower. The net result is a slightly lower ROI. To increase ROI, Zell should consider ways to increase its asset turnover. It might explore the disposal of unproductive assets (such as excess inventories and accounts receivable) or methods of increasing sales without increasing its assets.

Figure 6.1 shows ROE and its components and subcomponents. The financial manager can visually identify and calculate how a change in any component affects ROE. This can be useful in determining how a proposed cost-cutting measure, asset acquisition, or other activity will affect the firm's ROE.

## TREND ANALYSIS

As indicated earlier, it is important to analyze firm ratios over time. Each financial ratio for the current year should be compared to the same ratios for one or more earlier years in order to determine if a trend exists, because trend analysis may detect problems that are not revealed by comparing a firm's ratios to the industry average at a single point in time. For example, a firm's most recent profitability ratios may appear to be adequate when compared to the industry. Yet, trend analysis might detect a consistent declining pattern of profits over time. This would call for further examination to determine the reasons for the decline in profit performance, which may lead to solutions for reversing the trend.

An analysis of the trends in a firm's financial ratios may be enhanced if it is compared to the trend for the industry average. As an example, Figure 6.2 shows the return on investment (ROI) for Zell Corporation over the last five years and the industry average ROI over the same period. Notice that Zell's ROI has been declining while the industry average ROI has been rising. This should suggest to Zell Corporation that a problem exists and that if the same trend continues, Zell's ROI will move further below the industry average. This type of trend analysis can be performed on most financial ratios.

**FIGURE 6.1**
**Modified DuPont Analysis Applied to Zell Corporation**

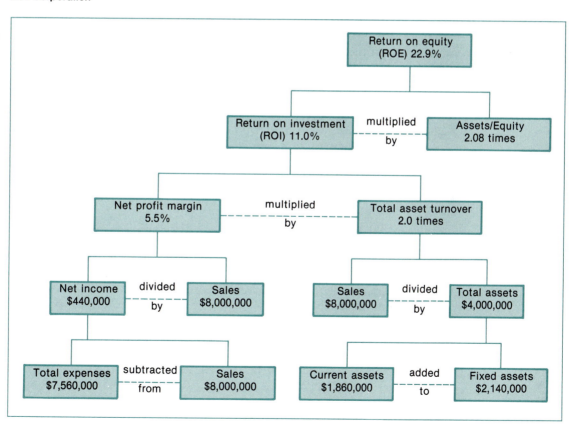

**FIGURE 6.2**
**Trend Analysis of
Return on Invest-
ment and Com-
parison with
Industry Average:
Zell Corporation**

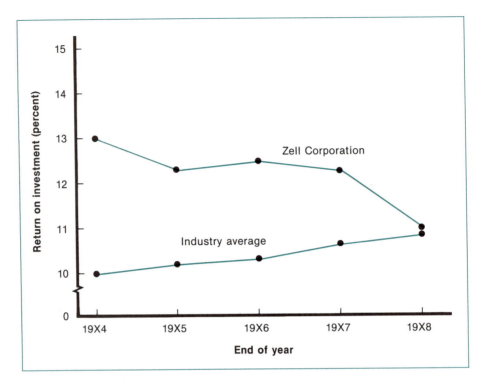

## COMMON-SIZE FINANCIAL STATEMENTS

Analyzing common-size financial statements is a form of ratio analysis that can provide the analyst with additional useful information. **Common-size income statements** measure each item on the income statement as a percentage of sales. When evaluated over time, changes in expense items relative to sales can be detected. Ideally, each expense item will decrease as a percent of sales over time so that net income will rise. However, this is seldom the case. Instead, some expenses rise and some fall from one period to the next. By comparing the common-size income statements for two periods, increases or decreases in each cost category relative to sales can be detected. Analysis of these changes, and investigation into the reasons for each, helps the firm to identify developing problems.

In addition to performing trend analysis, the analyst should compare the firm's common-size income statements against those of the industry average to determine which of the firm's costs are low and which are high relative to sales in comparison to other firms in the industry. This information also helps the firm identify problem areas.

The common-size income statements for Zell Corporation for the years 19X7 and 19X8 are presented in Table 6.6. The industry norm for each income statement item is also provided in this table. Zell's cost of goods sold as a percentage of sales increased from 19X7 to 19X8, which is unfavorable. However, it still remains well below the industry average. Meanwhile, Zell's selling expense has decreased slightly as a percent of sales, and it remains below the industry average. Depreciation expense remains unchanged from the prior year and is close to the industry average. General

**TABLE 6.6**  Common-Size Income Statements: Zell Corporation and Industry Average

| | Zell Corporation, 19X7 | | Zell Corporation, 19X8 | | Industry Average, 19X8: |
|---|---|---|---|---|---|
| | *Actual Figure (Thousands of Dollars)* | *Percent of Sales* | *Actual Figure (Thousands of Dollars)* | *Percent of Sales* | *Percent of Sales* |
| Net sales | $7,500 | 100.0% | $8,000 | 100.0% | 100.0% |
| Less: Cost of goods sold | 3,300 | 44.0 | 3,600 | 45.0 | 53.0 |
| Gross profits | 4,200 | 56.0 | 4,400 | 55.0 | 47.0 |
| Less: Operating expenses | | | | | |
|     Selling expense | 1,553 | 20.7 | 1,600 | 20.0 | 20.3 |
|     Depreciation expense | 285 | 3.8 | 300 | 3.8 | 3.9 |
|     General and administrative | 1,635 | 21.8 | 1,800 | 22.5 | 15.2 |
|     Total operating expenses | 3,473 | 46.3 | 3,700 | 46.3 | 39.4 |
| Earnings before interest and taxes | 727 | 9.7 | 700 | 8.8 | 7.6 |
| Less: Interest expense | 143 | 1.9 | 120 | 1.5 | 1.3 |
| Earnings before taxes | 584 | 7.8 | 580 | 7.3 | 6.3 |
| Less: Taxes | 143 | 1.9 | 140 | 1.8 | 1.0 |
| Net income | 441 | 5.9 | 440 | 5.5 | 5.3 |

and administrative expenses have increased slightly for Zell Corporation and remain well above the industry average. Interest expense declined substantially as a percent of sales; however, it remains above the industry average. Similarly, the tax rate for Zell has declined but remains well above the industry average. Zell's management can utilize this information in an effort to improve its net income in future years by concentrating on controlling the costs that remain above the industry average (particularly general and administrative expenses), and prevent those costs that remain favorable from deteriorating (particularly its cost of goods sold).

Common-size analysis can also be applied to balance sheets, as illustrated for Zell Corporation in Table 6.7. **Common-size balance sheets** show each balance sheet item as a percent of total assets. The common-size balance sheet for Zell Corporation indicates that current assets have increased as a percent of total assets for 19X8. This may indicate an unfavorable situation, since maintaining excess current assets can result in excessive financing costs. The bulk of the increase was from an increase in marketable securities. This has been at least partially offset by a large decrease in accounts receivable. Comparing current assets as a percent of total assets to the industry average reveals that Zell maintains substantially greater current assets than the average firm in the industry. This is true for all individual current assets except cash.

Although net fixed assets have increased in dollar terms, they have declined as a percent of total assets, indicating that Zell's current assets increased more on a percentage basis than its fixed assets. Zell's net fixed assets are low relative to the industry average, which could indicate that Zell is not maintaining its productive facility in good condition or that it has no excess capacity that would permit expanded production if warranted.

On the liabilities and owners' equity side of the balance sheet, current liabilities have increased as a percent of total assets, largely as a result of

TABLE 6.7  **Common-Size Balance Sheets: Zell Corporation and Industry Averages**

|  | Zell Corporation, 19X7 | | Zell Corporation, 19X8 | | Industry Average, 19X8: |
|---|---|---|---|---|---|
|  | Actual Figure (Thousands of Dollars) | Percent of Total Assets | Actual Figure (Thousands of Dollars) | Percent of Total Assets | Percent of Assets |
| *Assets* | | | | | |
| Current assets | | | | | |
| Cash | $    20 | .6% | $    30 | .8% | 2.0% |
| Marketable securities | 300 | 8.6 | 600 | 15.0 | 12.3 |
| Accounts receivable | 820 | 23.4 | 830 | 20.8 | 15.2 |
| Inventory | 360 | 10.3 | 400 | 10.0 | 8.5 |
| Total current assets | $1,500 | 42.9 | $1,860 | 46.5 | 38.0 |
| Fixed assets | | | | | |
| Plant and equipment | $2,700 | 77.1 | $3,140 | 78.5 | 82.0 |
| Less: Accumulated depreciation | 700 | 20.0 | 1,000 | 25.0 | 20.0 |
| Net fixed assets | $2,000 | 57.1 | $2,140 | 53.5 | 62.0 |
| Total assets | $3,500 | 100.0% | $4,000 | 100.0% | 100.0% |
| *Liabilities and owners' equity* | | | | | |
| Current liabilities | | | | | |
| Accounts payable | $  550 | 15.7 | $  460 | 11.5 | 5.5 |
| Notes payable | 190 | 5.4 | 270 | 6.8 | 11.0 |
| Accrued expenses | 10 | .3 | 150 | 3.8 | 3.5 |
| Other current liabilities | 50 | 1.4 | 200 | 5.0 | 5.0 |
| Total current liabilities | $  800 | 22.9 | $1,080 | 27.0 | 25.0 |
| Long-term liabilities | | | | | |
| Long-term debt | $1,080 | 30.9 | $1,000 | 25.0 | 30.0 |
| Owners' equity | | | | | |
| Common stock—par value | $    80 | 2.3 | $    80 | 2.0 | 3.0 |
| Additional paid-in capital | 240 | 6.9 | 240 | 6.0 | 8.0 |
| Retained earnings | 1,300 | 37.1 | 1,600 | 40.0 | 34.0 |
| Total owners' equity | $1,620 | 46.3 | $1,920 | 48.0 | 45.0 |
| Total liabilities and owners' equity | $3,500 | 100.0% | $4,000 | 100.0% | 100.0% |

substantial increases in accrued expenses and other current liabilities. These increases were partially offset by a substantial decrease in accounts payable. The increase in total current liabilities as a percent of total assets was matched by a decrease in long-term debt, common stock, and additional paid-in capital as a percent of total assets. The only long-term source of funds to increase as a percent of total assets was retained earnings.

Zell Corporation also has a slightly higher level of current liabilities as a percent of total assets compared to the industry average. This is accounted for by substantially higher accounts payable, although it is partially offset by substantially lower notes payable. Long-term debt is lower for Zell than the industry average, while common equity is higher. This is consistent with the conclusion arrived at earlier that Zell has low financial leverage.

## LIMITATIONS OF RATIO ANALYSIS

Ratio analysis is very useful for examining a firm's financial situation since it can detect various strengths and weaknesses of the firm. However, some limitations exist that can lead to faulty conclusions:

1. When a firm operates in more than one industry, comparing its ratios to the average for one industry can prove meaningless. Consider a firm that produces sporting goods and tires, operates restaurants, and brews beer. If the firm is compared to the restaurant industry in which the firm has most of its operations, deviations of the firm's ratios from the industry norm may result from the influence of the characteristics of the other industries in which the firm operates.

2. Related to the first item, the industry used as a benchmark for comparison may include firms that are involved in a variety of other businesses. This may distort the average ratios for the industry.

3. Accounting practices vary among firms. Since financial ratios are derived from accounting statements, a firm's financial ratios can deviate from the norm because of differences in accounting methods rather than differences in firm operations. Some corporations have been criticized for using "creative accounting" in order to disguise their true financial situation. Such activities can limit the ability of financial analysts to evaluate the firm. If the analyst is an employee of the corporation being assessed, the problem may be less critical, since additional information can easily be obtained. Analysts outside the firm normally do not have access to such information.

4. While an industry average serves as a convenient benchmark, it lacks relevant information related to the dispersion of financial ratios among all firms within the industry. For this reason, some sources of industry ratios include upper and lower quartiles that the analyst can use as an indication of the range of ratios.

5. Firms whose financial statements vary based on the season of the year may show large deviations from the norm at certain times but not at other times.

6. There can be very sound reasons why a firm's ratios appear to indicate a problem when none exists, and vice versa. Recall the example of a firm that has just sold a new issue of long-term debt. Between the time that the firm receives the proceeds from issuing the bonds and the time that the funds are spent for their intended purpose, the firm may have an exceptionally high current ratio. The analyst observing this could wrongfully conclude that management is doing a poor job of managing the firm's assets.

7. Industry norms are based on past data and are not necessarily indicative of the future. Therefore, management should not feel secure in basing decisions solely on ratio analysis.

8. In some instances, it is important that the industry average ratios be constructed of ratios of firms of comparable size. Indeed, small firms may tend to have substantially different ratios than large firms in the same industry.

## IMPACT OF INFLATION ON FINANCIAL ANALYSIS

High rates of inflation can distort the values contained in financial statements and therefore the results of financial analysis. The primary financial statement distortions are identified below.

1. Under last-in, first-out (LIFO) inventory accounting, a firm's balance sheet reflects the value of old inventory items. This may result in an artificially low value of the firm's inventory on the balance sheet, which can affect the value of the firm's inventory turnover ratio, total asset turnover ratio, and so forth.

Additionally, a firm's net income is distorted when it uses LIFO inventory accounting and it reduces its level of inventory during an accounting period. When this occurs, the cost of goods sold will partially reflect the old low-cost items, causing an understatement of costs and an overstatement of profits. Similarly, switching to first-in, first-out (FIFO) inventory accounting during a given period creates an artificially low cost of goods sold and overstates profits. Although taking these *inventory profits* can increase a firm's reported earnings, it also results in a greater tax liability.

2. High inflation also causes the value of a firm's fixed assets to be understated on the balance sheet, since the value of a firm's plant and equipment is recorded at its purchase price minus depreciation, but inflation tends to increase the value of fixed assets. Since fixed assets may be undervalued, ratios such as return on investment, total asset turnover, and others are distorted.

3. Rising interest rates generally accompany increasing inflation rates. This increase in interest rates tends to reduce the value of bonds. If the value of a firm's debt is reduced below its book value, the debt on the firm's balance sheet and the level of financial leverage will be overstated.

In an effort to help users of financial statements understand the impact inflation has had on specific firms, the Financial Accounting Standards Board (FASB) issued Statement No. 33 calling for large firms to report supplemental unaudited financial statement data reflecting an estimate of the impact of inflation on the firm's financial statements. FASB No. 33 provides specific guidelines for making these estimates.

The controversy continues over the merits of FASB No. 33 and the value of inflation-adjusted data provided by firms. At this writing, the inflation rate is relatively low making such reporting requirements unimportant. However, should the inflation rate rise to double-digit levels once again, the issue of how best to reflect the impact of inflation on financial statements will surely gain more attention.

## SOURCES OF INFORMATION FOR RATIO ANALYSIS

To help perform ratio analysis, industry data can be obtained from a variety of sources. Some of the more common sources follow:

■ *Robert Morris Associates.* A publication entitled *Annual Statement Studies,* published by Robert Morris Associates (RMA), provides financial ratios for many different industries. These ratios are presented for firms of various size so that analysts can compare a firm's ratios to those of firms in the same industry that are of comparable size. The median, upper-quartile, and lower-quartile ratios are given.

Table 6.8 illustrates the type of industry information provided by Robert Morris Associates. A listing of balance sheet items is presented at the top and close to the center column of the page. Income statement items appear below that, and various financial ratios are presented at the bottom of the page. To the left of this column listing are current data, segmented into various columns according to size. The first column represents firms with an asset size of less than $1 million (0–1 MM), the second column represents firms with an asset size between $1 million and $10 million (1–10 MM), and so on. The table shows that a sample of 103 financial statements was used to develop the industry norms for the smallest size group, a sample of 187 statements was used for the second group, and so on.

To the right of the listing of financial statement items and ratios are historical data on the entire sample of firms used to develop industry norms. This information is useful for trend analysis.

■ *Dun & Bradstreet.* Like the *Annual Statement Studies* of Robert Morris Associates, Dun & Bradstreet provides financial ratios for industries and for groups of firms within industries classified by size. However, the industry data of these two services do not match perfectly due to different samples used to represent each industry. In addition, some differences in the types of industries covered also exist.

■ *Prentice-Hall's Almanac of Business and Industrial Financial Ratios.* Although not as thorough as the services mentioned previously, this publication provides useful information on the financial characteristics of many industries.

■ *Quarterly Financial Reports for Manufacturing Companies.* These reports are published by the federal government. They provide financial statement information on a variety of manufacturing firms.

In addition to the preceding sources, some business magazines such as *Business Week, Forbes,* and *Fortune* periodically provide financial information about industries. In many cases, no single source will provide all the information desired, so many analysts use more than one source of industry information as a basis for comparison.

## SOURCES AND USES OF FUNDS STATEMENT

In addition to a firm's financial ratios, its **sources and uses of funds statement** should also be analyzed. This statement indicates how the firm has

**TABLE 6.8**  Example of Industry Ratios

## MANUFACTURERS - GENERAL INDUSTRIAL MACHINERY & EQUIPMENT  SIC# 3561 (64,66,67,69)

### Type of Statement

| Current Data | | | | | Type of Statement | Comparative Historical Data | | | | |
|---|---|---|---|---|---|---|---|---|---|---|
| 7 | 71 | 48 | 12 | 138 | Unqualified | | | | 161 | 138 |
| 5 | 1 | | 1 | 7 | Qualified | | | | 11 | 7 |
| 29 | 56 | 2 | | 87 | Reviewed | DATA NOT AVAILABLE | | | 80 | 87 |
| 44 | 19 | | | 63 | Compiled | | | | 73 | 63 |
| 23 | 36 | 11 | 1 | 71 | Other | | | | 57 | 71 |
| 167(6/30-9/30/85) | | 199(10/1/85-3/31/86) | | | | 6/30/81-3/31/82 | 6/30/82-3/31/83 | 6/30/83-3/31/84 | 6/30/84-3/31/85 | 6/30/85-3/31/86 |

| 0-1MM | 1-10MM | 10-50MM | 50-100MM | ALL | ASSET SIZE | ALL | ALL | ALL | ALL | ALL |
|---|---|---|---|---|---|---|---|---|---|---|
| 103 | 187 | 62 | 14 | 366 | NUMBER OF STATEMENTS | 349 | 411 | 372 | 382 | 366 |
| % | % | % | % | % | **ASSETS** | % | % | % | % | % |
| 9.2 | 6.1 | 6.5 | 6.8 | 7.1 | Cash & Equivalents | 8.1 | 8.8 | 7.9 | 7.7 | 7.1 |
| 32.4 | 29.3 | 23.0 | 24.9 | 28.9 | Trade Receivables - (net) | 28.1 | 25.8 | 27.3 | 29.1 | 28.9 |
| 28.1 | 31.5 | 28.4 | 30.3 | 30.0 | Inventory | 29.1 | 28.0 | 28.7 | 28.5 | 30.0 |
| 1.6 | 2.9 | 3.0 | 1.8 | 2.5 | All Other Current | 2.8 | 3.0 | 2.8 | 2.2 | 2.5 |
| 71.2 | 69.9 | 60.8 | 63.7 | 68.5 | Total Current | 68.2 | 65.6 | 66.7 | 67.6 | 68.5 |
| 22.5 | 22.5 | 31.9 | 24.9 | 24.2 | Fixed Assets (net) | 24.5 | 26.4 | 25.2 | 24.5 | 24.2 |
| .9 | 1.4 | 1.8 | .4 | 1.3 | Intangibles (net) | .7 | 1.0 | 1.0 | .9 | 1.3 |
| 5.4 | 6.3 | 5.6 | 11.0 | 6.1 | All Other Non-Current | 6.7 | 7.1 | 7.1 | 7.0 | 6.1 |
| 100.0 | 100.0 | 100.0 | 100.0 | 100.0 | Total | 100.0 | 100.0 | 100.0 | 100.0 | 100.0 |
| | | | | | **LIABILITIES** | | | | | |
| 8.3 | 13.3 | 8.6 | 4.9 | 10.8 | Notes Payable-Short Term | 8.8 | 8.6 | 9.3 | 10.4 | 10.8 |
| 5.1 | 3.6 | 2.7 | 2.1 | 3.8 | Cur. Mat.-L/T/D | 3.0 | 3.6 | 2.9 | 4.0 | 3.8 |
| 17.9 | 16.3 | 9.8 | 8.2 | 15.4 | Trade Payables | 14.5 | 13.2 | 14.3 | 15.4 | 15.4 |
| 1.2 | 1.5 | .8 | 1.0 | 1.3 | Income Taxes Payable | — | — | — | 1.5 | 1.3 |
| 13.0 | 11.8 | 9.1 | 11.4 | 11.7 | All Other Current | 13.3 | 12.0 | 12.2 | 10.6 | 11.7 |
| 45.5 | 46.5 | 30.9 | 27.7 | 42.9 | Total Current | 39.7 | 37.4 | 38.6 | 41.9 | 42.9 |
| 13.9 | 15.2 | 19.7 | 14.4 | 15.6 | Long Term Debt | 14.6 | 16.1 | 16.3 | 16.1 | 15.6 |
| .9 | .8 | 2.2 | 1.8 | 1.1 | Deferred Taxes | — | — | — | 1.1 | 1.1 |
| 1.6 | 1.8 | 1.8 | 3.2 | 1.8 | All Other Non-Current | 2.3 | 1.9 | 3.0 | 2.2 | 1.8 |
| 38.1 | 35.7 | 45.3 | 52.8 | 38.7 | Net Worth | 43.5 | 44.5 | 42.0 | 38.8 | 38.7 |
| 100.0 | 100.0 | 100.0 | 100.0 | 100.0 | Total Liabilities & Net Worth | 100.0 | 100.0 | 100.0 | 100.0 | 100.0 |
| | | | | | **INCOME DATA** | | | | | |
| 100.0 | 100.0 | 100.0 | 100.0 | 100.0 | Net Sales | 100.0 | 100.0 | 100.0 | 100.0 | 100.0 |
| 35.9 | 31.1 | 31.9 | 28.0 | 32.4 | Gross Profit | 30.4 | 30.8 | 31.1 | 32.3 | 32.4 |
| 30.6 | 26.4 | 26.5 | 22.4 | 27.4 | Operating Expenses | 23.3 | 26.0 | 28.0 | 26.4 | 27.4 |
| 5.2 | 4.7 | 5.4 | 5.5 | 5.0 | Operating Profit | 7.1 | 4.9 | 3.1 | 5.9 | 5.0 |
| 1.6 | 1.2 | 2.0 | 1.2 | 1.5 | All Other Expenses (net) | 1.7 | 1.8 | 1.4 | 1.5 | 1.5 |
| 3.6 | 3.4 | 3.4 | 4.3 | 3.5 | Profit Before Taxes | 5.4 | 3.0 | 1.7 | 4.4 | 3.5 |

### RATIOS

| 0-1MM | 1-10MM | 10-50MM | 50-100MM | ALL | RATIOS | 6/30/81-3/31/82 | 6/30/82-3/31/83 | 6/30/83-3/31/84 | 6/30/84-3/31/85 | 6/30/85-3/31/86 |
|---|---|---|---|---|---|---|---|---|---|---|
| 2.3 / 1.6 / 1.2 | 2.2 / 1.5 / 1.2 | 3.0 / 2.3 / 1.6 | 3.0 / 2.5 / 1.7 | 2.5 / 1.6 / 1.3 | Current | 2.8 / 1.8 / 1.3 | 3.0 / 1.9 / 1.3 | 2.9 / 1.8 / 1.3 | 2.5 / 1.7 / 1.3 | 2.5 / 1.6 / 1.3 |
| 1.3 / .9 / .6 | 1.2 / .8 / .5 | 1.5 / 1.0 / .6 | 1.7 / 1.3 / .8 | 1.3 / .9 / .6 | Quick | 1.4 / 1.0 / .7 | 1.6 / 1.0 / .6 | 1.6 / .9 / .6 | 1.4 / .9 / .6 | 1.3 / .9 / .6 |
| 33 / 11.2, 43 / 8.4, 57 / 6.4 | 41 / 9.0, 54 / 6.8, 65 / 5.6 | 41 / 8.8, 58 / 6.3, 72 / 5.1 | 46 / 7.9, 63 / 5.8, 104 / 3.5 | 39 / 9.3, 51 / 7.1, 65 / 5.6 | Sales/Receivables | 41 / 9.0, 54 / 6.8, 68 / 5.4 | 36 / 10.2, 49 / 7.4, 64 / 5.7 | 43 / 8.4, 57 / 6.4, 72 / 5.1 | 41 / 9.0, 55 / 6.6, 72 / 5.1 | 39 / 9.3, 51 / 7.1, 65 / 5.6 |
| 30 / 12.1, 62 / 5.9, 96 / 3.8 | 53 / 6.9, 87 / 4.2, 135 / 2.7 | 70 / 5.2, 111 / 3.3, 159 / 2.3 | 89 / 4.1, 122 / 3.0, 159 / 2.3 | 48 / 7.6, 83 / 4.4, 130 / 2.8 | Cost of Sales/Inventory | 48 / 7.6, 87 / 4.2, 126 / 2.9 | 45 / 8.1, 83 / 4.4, 130 / 2.8 | 56 / 6.5, 94 / 3.9, 135 / 2.7 | 49 / 7.4, 83 / 4.4, 130 / 2.8 | 48 / 7.6, 83 / 4.4, 130 / 2.8 |
| 19 / 19.5, 31 / 11.6, 54 / 6.7 | 26 / 14.0, 39 / 9.4, 60 / 6.1 | 22 / 16.4, 33 / 10.9, 45 / 8.1 | 20 / 18.3, 30 / 12.1, 34 / 10.7 | 22 / 16.7, 35 / 10.3, 55 / 6.6 | Cost of Sales/Payables | 22 / 16.4, 37 / 10.0, 52 / 7.0 | 17 / 21.3, 29 / 12.5, 49 / 7.4 | 24 / 15.3, 37 / 9.8, 59 / 6.2 | 23 / 15.9, 38 / 9.7, 58 / 6.3 | 22 / 16.7, 35 / 10.3, 55 / 6.6 |
| 6.3 / 11.2 / 23.3 | 4.9 / 8.0 / 16.8 | 2.8 / 4.5 / 8.0 | 2.8 / 3.6 / 4.7 | 4.3 / 7.8 / 16.1 | Sales/Working Capital | 3.8 / 6.4 / 14.1 | 3.7 / 6.4 / 15.9 | 3.4 / 5.8 / 11.6 | 4.3 / 7.2 / 16.6 | 4.3 / 7.8 / 16.1 |
| (88) 6.3 / 3.7 / 1.7 | (167) 6.3 / 2.6 / 1.4 | (57) 6.2 / 3.0 / .9 | (13) 11.3 / 2.7 / 1.6 | (325) 6.4 / 3.0 / 1.4 | EBIT/Interest | (287) 8.6 / 3.2 / 1.5 | (340) 6.0 / 2.2 / 1.0 | (335) 6.0 / 2.5 / .4 | (339) 8.2 / 3.2 / 1.4 | (325) 6.4 / 3.0 / 1.4 |
| (56) 6.1 / 3.2 / .9 | (129) 5.7 / 2.6 / 1.2 | (47) 5.6 / 3.2 / .9 | (11) 7.5 / 4.9 / 1.6 | (243) 6.1 / 3.1 / 1.2 | Net Profit + Depr., Dep., Amort./Cur. Mat. L/T/D | (227) 10.0 / 3.8 / 1.6 | (247) 7.8 / 3.0 / 1.0 | (227) 7.1 / 2.7 / .7 | (244) 6.5 / 2.8 / 1.4 | (243) 6.1 / 3.1 / 1.2 |
| .3 / .5 / 1.2 | .3 / .6 / 1.3 | .5 / .7 / 1.1 | .4 / .4 / .7 | .3 / .6 / 1.2 | Fixed/Worth | .3 / .5 / .9 | .3 / .6 / 1.1 | .3 / .6 / 1.0 | .3 / .6 / 1.1 | .3 / .6 / 1.2 |
| .8 / 1.7 / 4.9 | 1.0 / 2.1 / 4.3 | .6 / 1.2 / 2.2 | .4 / 1.0 / 1.9 | .8 / 1.7 / 4.0 | Debt/Worth | .7 / 1.4 / 2.7 | .6 / 1.3 / 2.6 | .7 / 1.4 / 2.9 | .8 / 1.5 / 3.4 | .8 / 1.7 / 4.0 |
| (96) 44.3 / 24.9 / 7.2 | (176) 44.2 / 17.1 / 4.8 | (61) 29.8 / 15.0 / 1.3 | 21.2 / 16.0 / 7.1 | (347) 41.2 / 17.9 / 5.4 | % Profit Before Taxes/Tangible Net Worth | (343) 34.6 / 22.6 / 8.1 | (402) 29.1 / 13.9 / 1.3 | (356) 27.7 / 11.8 / -3.9 | (360) 39.6 / 20.9 / 8.7 | (347) 41.2 / 17.9 / 5.4 |
| 16.3 / 8.6 / 1.7 | 11.9 / 5.8 / 1.9 | 12.3 / 6.7 / .2 | 11.2 / 7.1 / 3.4 | 13.6 / 6.7 / 1.8 | % Profit Before Taxes/Total Assets | 16.3 / 9.0 / 2.8 | 12.6 / 5.3 / .4 | 10.9 / 5.2 / -3.0 | 14.0 / 8.5 / 2.0 | 13.6 / 6.7 / 1.8 |
| 29.3 / 15.7 / 7.3 | 18.3 / 9.8 / 5.1 | 7.1 / 4.5 / 3.4 | 8.4 / 4.6 / 3.7 | 19.1 / 8.6 / 4.5 | Sales/Net Fixed Assets | 16.9 / 8.0 / 4.5 | 15.1 / 7.4 / 4.1 | 14.7 / 7.5 / 3.9 | 16.4 / 8.3 / 4.4 | 19.1 / 8.6 / 4.5 |
| 3.2 / 2.6 / 1.9 | 2.4 / 1.8 / 1.4 | 1.8 / 1.4 / 1.1 | 1.5 / 1.3 / 1.1 | 2.5 / 1.9 / 1.3 | Sales/Total Assets | 2.3 / 1.8 / 1.4 | 2.3 / 1.8 / 1.3 | 2.2 / 1.6 / 1.2 | 2.5 / 1.8 / 1.3 | 2.5 / 1.9 / 1.3 |
| (92) 1.2 / 1.9 / 3.5 | (164) 1.2 / 2.2 / 4.2 | (57) 2.4 / 3.1 / 4.6 | (12) 1.7 / 2.7 / 4.7 | (325) 1.4 / 2.4 / 4.2 | % Depr., Dep., Amort./Sales | (304) 1.1 / 1.9 / 3.0 | (356) 1.3 / 2.3 / 3.6 | (335) 1.5 / 2.5 / 3.9 | (338) 1.3 / 2.3 / 3.5 | (325) 1.4 / 2.4 / 4.2 |
| (44) 4.8 / 7.4 / 10.7 | (67) 2.5 / 3.8 / 6.2 | | | (113) 2.9 / 4.8 / 8.2 | % Officers' Comp/Sales | (110) 2.1 / 3.8 / 7.3 | (140) 2.7 / 4.6 / 8.4 | (113) 2.9 / 4.3 / 8.6 | (121) 2.6 / 5.4 / 8.6 | (113) 2.9 / 4.8 / 8.2 |
| 128471M | 1135678M | 1891461M | 1372698M | 4528308M | Net Sales ($) | 4939549M | 4809385M | 4277387M | 6237080M | 4528308M |
| 50508M | 629075M | 1341470M | 1020528M | 3041581M | Total Assets ($) | 3217082M | 3365506M | 3197572M | 3608929M | 3041581M |

generated funds (sources) during a given period, and how it has elected to apply those funds (uses). In order to construct such a statement, the analyst must obtain information from both the income statement for the period in question, and the balance sheets at the start and end of the period in question.

The income statement reveals two important sources of funds to the firm and one use. The sources are net income and depreciation (depreciation as a source of funds was discussed in Chapter 2), and the use is the payment of dividends. All other cash inflows reported on the income statement are cancelled out by cash outflows. That is, all cash received as revenue by the firm is paid out as cash expenses except for net income and depreciation, which are said to be funds provided by operations.

Net income belongs to the stockholders and is distributed to them in two ways. One way is through the payment of cash dividends; the other is through the reinvestment of net income back into the firm as an addition to retained earnings. This additional investment in the firm belongs to the stockholders and can be used to purchase additional assets. In summary, the income statement can be used to identify two sources of funds (net income and depreciation), and one use of funds (the payment of dividends). Zell Corporation's income statement (Table 6.1) indicates depreciation of $300,000, net income of $440,000, and dividends paid on common stock of $140,000. This information will be used later as input to the sources and uses of funds statement.

The balance sheet can help identify sources and uses of funds that result from changes in assets, liabilities, and equity accounts. If an asset item on the balance sheet increases during the period in question, it is because the firm has elected to use funds to increase that asset. For example, if a firm's inventories increase by $5,000, the firm has elected to use funds to purchase more inventory. The same logic is used to describe an increase in any asset, fixed or current. An exception to this is cash, which is used as a balancing account in the sources and uses of funds statement presented here. Since the term *funds* is synonymous with *cash* as it is used here, we will observe the net effect of the sources and uses of funds on the cash balance during the period under study.

When a firm's assets decrease during a given period, it represents a source of funds to the firm. For example, if a firm reduces its inventories, it has sold those inventories, and the proceeds from the sale become a source of funds available to the firm for application elsewhere within the firm. In summary, when an asset increases, it is a use of funds; and when it decreases, it is a source of funds.

The reverse is true for liabilities and equity accounts. When a liability or equity account increases, it represents a source of funds to the firm. When they decrease, they are uses of funds. For example, when accounts payable

TABLE 6.9    **Balance Sheet Items as Sources and Uses of Funds**

| Balance Sheet Item | When It Increases | When It Decreases |
|---|---|---|
| Assets | Use | Source |
| Liabilities | Source | Use |
| Equity accounts | Source | Use |

increase, it indicates that the firm has purchased some materials and has not yet paid for them. This "loan" made by the firm's suppliers represents a source of funds. Similarly, when the firm's common stock or long-term debt accounts increase, it implies that the firm has issued some new common stock or bonds, which brings cash (funds) into the firm. When these same accounts decrease, they represent uses of funds to pay accounts payable, repurchase common stock, or to retire some debt. Table 6.9 summarizes when balance sheet items are sources and when they are uses of funds.

Table 6.10 identifies many of the sources and uses of funds for Zell Corporation during a recent period. Each balance sheet item is compared, and the dollar amount of the source or use is recorded in the appropriate column. Notice that total sources from the balance sheet equals total uses. This will always be the case if done correctly. Also notice that some of the items identified as sources and uses here will not appear as such on the actual sources and uses of funds statement (for example, cash and retained earnings).

Now that all sources and uses have been identified from the income statement and balance sheet, everything necessary is available to construct the sources and uses of funds statement for Zell Corporation. Although there is no universally accepted format, this text uses a format that is very popular with financial analysts. The general format is as follows:

> Beginning cash balance
> Plus:    Sources of funds
> Less:    Uses of funds
> Ending cash balance

Before constructing this statement for Zell Corporation, some guidelines are presented.

**1.** Depreciation appears on both the income statement and the balance sheet. If the depreciation for the year suggested by these financial statements differs, the income statement figure should be used since the balance sheet can be affected by the disposal of depreciable assets.

**2.** As indicated earlier, net income is a source of funds to the firm, and it is used to pay dividends and/or to increase retained earnings. Any amount used to increase retained earnings will appear on the comparative balance sheet as a source of funds to the firm. Since this amount is included in net income, which has already been identified as a source of funds, the increase in retained earnings should not be identified again as a separate source. If it is, this same amount will be reported twice. Therefore, when the sources and uses of funds statement is constructed, net income is re-

**TABLE 6.10**  **Determining the Sources and Uses of Funds for the Year Ending December 31, 19X8: Zell Corporation (Thousands of Dollars)**

| Assets | 12/31/X7 | 12/31/X8 | Sources | Uses |
|---|---|---|---|---|
| Current assets | | | | |
| Cash | $ 20 | $ 30 | | $ 10* |
| Marketable securities | 300 | 600 | | 300 |
| Accounts receivable | 820 | 830 | | 10 |
| Inventories | 360 | 400 | | 40 |
| Total current assets | $1,500 | $1,860 | | |
| Fixed assets | | | | |
| Plant and equipment | $2,700 | $3,140 | | 440 |
| Less: Accumulated depreciation | 700 | 1,000 | $300 | |
| Net fixed assets | $2,000 | $2,140 | | |
| Total assets | $3,500 | $4,000 | | |
| | | | | |
| Liabilities and owners' equity | | | | |
| | | | | |
| Current liabilities | | | | |
| Accounts payable | $ 550 | $ 460 | | 90 |
| Notes payable | 190 | 270 | 80 | |
| Accrued expenses | 10 | 150 | 140 | |
| Other current liabilities | 50 | 200 | 150 | |
| Total current liabilities | $ 800 | $1,080 | | |
| Long-term liabilities | | | | |
| Long-term debt | $1,080 | $1,000 | | 80 |
| Owners' equity | | | | |
| Common stock—par value | $ 80 | $ 80 | | |
| Additional paid-in capital | 240 | 240 | | |
| Retained earnings | 1,300 | 1,600 | 300* | |
| Total owners' equity | $1,620 | $1,920 | | |
| Total liabilities and owners' equity | $3,500 | $4,000 | | |
| Total sources and uses of funds | | | $970 | $970 |

*Denotes items not identified as sources or uses on the final statement.

ported as a source of funds, and the increase in retained earnings is not reported as a separate source.

**3.** Normally, the most important sources of funds to firms are net income and depreciation, and the most important uses of funds are the purchase of fixed assets and the payment of dividends. Therefore, these items are normally recorded at the top of their respective groups.

**4.** It is useful to record both the dollar amount of each source and use of funds as well as the percentage of total sources or uses provided by each item.

Table 6.11 presents the sources and uses of funds statement for Zell Corporation for the period ending December 31, 19X8. Beginning cash is taken from Zell's December 31, 19X7 balance sheet. Next, the dollar amount of each source and the percentage of total sources provided by each source are listed. These percentages were determined by dividing the dollar amount of each source by total sources ($1,100,000). All uses of funds are listed next in both dollar amounts and as a percentage of total uses. By adding the total sources of funds to the beginning cash balance and subtracting total uses of funds, the ending cash balance results. The correctness of this figure can be verified by comparing it to the cash balance on the December 31, 19X8 balance sheet.

Interpretation of the sources and uses of funds statement involves evaluating the appropriateness of the sources and uses. For example, a healthy firm should have net income and depreciation as the largest sources of funds, unless the firm has raised substantial amounts of money by issuing new securities. For Zell Corporation, 66.7 percent of total sources of funds come from net income and depreciation. A healthy firm should also be purchasing fixed assets to support future growth and to replace old plant and equipment. For Zell Corporation, the purchase of fixed assets represents the use of 40.0 percent of total sources of funds. This purchase of fixed assets should be financed by a combination of net income, depreciation, and other long-term sources (new long-term debt or equity). Table 6.11 indicates that depreciation will provide sufficient funds to finance most of the new fixed assets, and net income is sufficient to finance the remaining amount after dividends have been paid.

The only remaining items on the sources and uses statement are working capital items. In a healthy firm, current assets generally increase as the firm experiences a need for higher levels of inventories to support sales, higher accounts receivable that result from higher levels of sales, and more cash and marketable securities as the level of transactions increases. In addition, healthy firms experience an increase in the level of current liabilities (other things being equal) as they purchase more materials on trade credit and experience larger wages payable. If an analyst finds that

**TABLE 6.11  Zell Corporation Sources and Uses of Funds Statement for the Year Ending December 31, 19X8 (Thousands of Dollars)**

| | | | |
|---|---|---|---|
| *Beginning cash balance (12/31/X7)* | | $  20 | |
| *Plus: Sources of funds* | | | |
| Funds from operations | | $ 740 | 66.7% |
| Net income | $440 | | 39.6% |
| Depreciation | 300 | | 27.0 |
| Increased notes payable | | 80 | 7.2 |
| Increased accrued expenses | | 140 | 12.6 |
| Increased other current liabilities | | 150 | 13.5 |
| Total sources of funds | | $1,110 | 100.0% |
| | | | |
| *Minus: Uses of funds* | | | |
| Purchase of fixed assets | | $  440 | 40.0% |
| Cash dividends paid | | 140 | 12.7 |
| Increased marketable securities | | 300 | 27.3 |
| Increased accounts receivable | | 10 | .9 |
| Increased inventories | | 40 | 3.6 |
| Reduced accounts payable | | 90 | 8.2 |
| Reduced long-term debt | | 80 | 7.3 |
| Total uses of funds | | $1,100 | 100.0% |
| | | | |
| *Ending cash balance (12/31/X8)* | | $  30 | |

---

### FINANCIAL MANAGEMENT IN PRACTICE

## ANNUAL REPORTS: FACT OR FICTION?

According to an article in *Business Week*, the degree to which a firm's financial condition is emphasized in its annual report depends on the firm's recent performance.* Immediately following a good year, greater emphasis is given to the firm's financial statements, and immediately following a bad year, less attention is drawn to the financial statements. Furthermore, following bad years the firm's financial characteristics are often buried in the annual report by an overload of miscellaneous materials, such as pictures of the corporate headquarters and pictures of numerous managers. Any form of poor performance is often deemphasized. For this reason, both potential and current shareholders might benefit from requesting a copy of the firm's *10-K report* in addition to the firm's annual report. The 10-K report is a factual report publicly traded firms must file with the Securities and Exchange Commission and which they must also make avail-

able to their stockholders. This report normally contains more detailed information about a firm than the annual report, including the following:

**1.** A description of the business or businesses, principal markets served, and importance of patents and licenses.
**2.** The location(s) of principal plants.
**3.** A description of legal proceedings pending against the firm.
**4.** Identification of shareholders that own 10 percent or more of any class of security issued by the firm.
**5.** A description of recent dividend payments and future dividend-payment plans.
**6.** A five-year spreadsheet of historical financial data.
**7.** An analysis of the firm's financial condition.
**8.** A statement of changes in financial position.
**9.** Identification and background of directors and executive officers.

*"Annual Reports, the Good, the Bad, and the Ridiculous," *Business Week*, April 7, 1986, 40.

---

declining current assets are a source of funds or that declining current liabilities are a use of funds, further analysis should be conducted to determine why.

## SUMMARY

A firm's financial condition is of importance to the firm's managers as well as to creditors and stockholders of the firm. Managers evaluate the firm in order to detect weaknesses that can be corrected and strengths that can be exploited. Creditors evaluate the firm with a view toward determining creditworthiness, and stockholders evaluate the firm's performance to determine whether they should buy or sell the firm's common stock.

The key financial statements necessary to perform a thorough evaluation are the income statement, balance sheet, and sources and uses of funds statement. The income statement reports costs, revenues, and earnings over a specified time period. The balance sheet reports the book value of assets, liabilities, and owners' equity at a given point in time. The sources and uses of funds statement helps to identify where the firm has procured funds and how it has elected to use those funds.

Most financial ratios help evaluate one of four characteristics:

- Liquidity
- Efficiency
- Financial leverage
- Profitability

In evaluating a firm's financial ratios, it is useful to compare them to an industry norm and to identify trends over time. This approach can help detect any managerial deficiencies that may require corrective action. Furthermore, it provides useful input for implementing new policies.

## KEY TERMS

**Balance sheet** Financial statement reporting the book value of assets, liabilities, and owners' equity of a firm at a given point in time.

**Common-size balance sheet** Balance sheet reporting each asset, liability, and equity account as a percentage of total assets.

**Common-size income statement** Income statement reporting each expense and revenue item as a percentage of sales.

**Efficiency ratios** Financial ratios that indicate how effectively a firm manages its assets. Also called *activity ratios*.

**Financial leverage** The extent to which a firm uses debt as a source of financing.

**Income statement** Financial statement reporting the revenues, expenses, and income of a firm during a given period.

**Liquidity of a firm** The ability of a firm to meet its short-term obligations.

**Ratio analysis** Analysis of the relationship among various items on a firm's financial statements. It is designed to determine the operating and financial characteristics of the firm over time and in relation to other firms.

**Sources and uses of funds statement** Financial statement indicating how a firm obtained funds and used funds during a given period.

## EQUATIONS

The reader is referred to Tables 6.3 and 6.4 for a summary of the ratios used in this chapter and the interpretation of same.

## QUESTIONS

**Q6-1.** How would creditors' interpretation of a firm's financial ratios differ from the owners' interpretation?

**Q6-2.** How are net income, dividends, and retained earnings related to each other?

**Q6-3.** What is wrong with the statement, "A firm's level of total assets should be equal to its level of total liabilities"?

**Q6-4.** If a firm has the ability to borrow funds from a bank, why should it be concerned with its liquidity ratios?

**Q6-5.** What is the major limitation of using net working capital as a measure of a firm's liquidity?

**Q6-6.** What does a current ratio of 1.2 tell you?

**Q6-7.** Why do analysts evaluate the quick ratio as well as the current ratio?

**Q6-8.** If a firm borrows short-term funds to increase its short-term assets, how does this affect net working capital? How does it affect the current ratio?

**Q6-9.** What does a relatively low inventory turnover ratio suggest about a firm?

**Q6-10.** Why is a high level of financial leverage undesirable?

**Q6-11.** How can a firm have a relatively low debt ratio but a relatively high debt to equity ratio?

**Q6-12.** You and your friend each start your own business, and you both borrow the same amount of money. You run a financial planning business out of a downtown office building, and the product you sell is advice. Your friend purchases imported artwork and sells it on the streets. You and your friend each have the same net sales and net income during the first year, yet some of your expenses on the income statement are much different. How are your income statements likely to differ?

**Q6-13.** Hillcrest Corporation has a quick ratio of 2.4, which is substantially higher than that of other firms in the industry. Can we conclude that Hillcrest is appropriately managing its liquidity? Explain.

**Q6-14.** Warrior Corporation has an average collection period of eight days versus the industry average of twenty-one days. What factors might explain this?

**Q6-15.** Which financial leverage measures would be most appropriate to evaluate a firm's ability to service its debt?

**Q6-16.** Since net income discloses more about a firm's true profitability, why do some measures of profitability use gross profit rather than net income?

**Q6-17.** Indicate whether the income statement, balance sheet, or both, are needed to calculate each of the following financial ratios: (a) times interest earned, (b) inventory turnover, (c) quick ratio, (d) average collection period, (e) return on assets, (f) gross profit margin, (g) debt to equity.

**Q6-18.** The profitability of Lokem Corporation was relatively good when measured by return on investment (ROI), but relatively weak when measured by return on equity (ROE). What might account for this?

## SELF-TEST PROBLEMS

Solutions to self-test problems appear on p. S1.

**SP6-1.** Use the financial statements provided for Kassel Corporation (Tables A and B on p. 182) to determine the following ratios:

**a.** Current ratio
**b.** Quick ratio
**c.** Inventory turnover
**d.** Total asset turnover
**e.** Debt ratio
**f.** Debt to equity

**g.** Times interest earned
**h.** Gross profit margin
**i.** Net profit margin
**j.** Return on investment
**k.** Return on equity

## TABLE A
### KASSEL CORPORATION
### INCOME STATEMENT
### YEAR ENDING DECEMBER 31, 19X9
### (THOUSANDS OF DOLLARS)

| | | |
|---|---:|---:|
| Net sales | | $12,000 |
| Less: Cost of goods sold | | 8,000 |
| Gross profit | | $ 4,000 |
| Less: Operating expenses | | |
|     Selling expense | $1,400 | |
|     Depreciation expense | 600 | |
|     General and administrative | 1,000 | |
|     Total operating expenses | | $ 3,000 |
| Earnings before interest and taxes | | $ 1,000 |
| Less: Interest expense | | 400 |
| Earnings before taxes | | $ 600 |
| Less: Taxes | | 200 |
| Net income | | $ 400 |
| Dividends paid on common stock | | 100 |
| Retained earnings | | $ 300 |

## TABLE B
### KASSEL CORPORATION
### BALANCE SHEET
### AS OF DECEMBER 31, 19X9
### (THOUSANDS OF DOLLARS)

*Assets*

| | | |
|---|---:|---:|
| Current assets | | |
|     Cash | $ 50 | |
|     Marketable securities | 700 | |
|     Accounts receivable | 1,100 | |
|     Inventory | 450 | |
|     Total current assets | | $2,300 |
| Fixed assets | | |
|     Plant and equipment | $5,000 | |
|     Less: Accumulated depreciation | 1,000 | |
|     Net fixed assets | | $4,000 |
| Total assets | | $6,300 |

*Liabilities and owners' equity*

| | | |
|---|---:|---:|
| Current liabilities | | |
|     Accounts payable | $ 700 | |
|     Notes payable | 500 | |
|     Accrued expenses | 100 | |
|     Other current liabilities | 200 | |
|     Total current liabilities | | 1,500 |
| Long-term liabilities | | |
|     Long-term debt | | 1,800 |
| Owners' equity | | |
|     Common stock (100,000 shares | | |
|     at par value of $3 per share) | $ 300 | |
|     Additional paid-in capital | 700 | |
|     Retained earnings | 2,000 | |
|     Total owners' equity | | 3,000 |
| Total liabilities and owners' equity | | $6,300 |

**SP6-2.** Using the following industry norms for the industry in which Kassel Corporation operates, analyze and evaluate Kassel's liquidity, efficiency, financial leverage, and profitability.

INDUSTRY NORMS

| | |
|---|---|
| Current ratio = 1.2 | Times interest earned = 4.0 |
| Quick ratio = .9 | Gross profit margin = 30% |
| Inventory turnover = 15 | Net profit margin = 4% |
| Total asset turnover = 1.7 | Return on investment = 6.8% |
| Debt ratio = .40 | Return on equity = 12.2% |
| Debt to equity ratio = .3 | |

**SP6-3.** Analyze Kassel Corporation's return on equity (ROE) using the DuPont method of analysis. The equity multiplier for the industry is 1.79.

**SP6-4.** Use the income statement and balance sheet provided for Kassel Corporation to construct common-size financial statements.

# PROBLEMS

**P6-1a.** Calculate and analyze the ratios of Barton Corporation (see Tables C and D on p. 184) and provide recommendations for how Barton can improve its performance. Industry norms and historical ratios follow:

INDUSTRY NORMS

| | |
|---|---|
| Current ratio = 2.3 | Debt ratio = .55 |
| Quick ratio = 1.7 | Times interest earned = 4.5 |
| Average collection period = 30 days | Gross profit margin = 30% |
| Inventory turnover = 16.6 | Net profit margin = 3% |
| Total asset turnover = 2.5 | Return on investment = 7.5% |
| Debt to equity ratio = .95 | Return on equity = 16.7% |

HISTORICAL RATIOS: BARTON CORPORATION

| | 19X3 | 19X4 | 19X5 | 19X6 | 19X7 |
|---|---|---|---|---|---|
| Current ratio | 1.1 | 1.5 | 1.7 | 1.8 | 1.9 |
| Quick ratio | .9 | 1.1 | 1.1 | 1.2 | 1.2 |
| Average collection period | 35 days | 34 days | 34 days | 32 days | 31 days |
| Inventory turnover | 15.2 | 14.4 | 13.6 | 13.2 | 12.4 |
| Total asset turnover | 2.5 | 2.3 | 2.3 | 2.1 | 1.9 |
| Debt to equity ratio | .95 | .94 | .93 | .93 | .92 |
| Debt ratio | .5 | .51 | .55 | .62 | .65 |
| Times interest earned | 4.4 | 4.1 | 3.5 | 2.8 | 2.5 |
| Gross profit margin | 29% | 29% | 30% | 28% | 27% |
| Net profit margin | 3.0% | 3.2% | 2.9% | 3.1% | 2.7% |
| Return on investment | 7.5% | 7.36% | 6.67% | 6.51% | 5.13% |
| Return on equity | 15.0% | 14.72% | 14.81% | 17.12% | 14.67% |

**P6-1b.** Analyze Barton's return on equity (ROE) using the DuPont method. (Assume an industry equity multiplier of 2.22.)

**P6-1c.** Create common-size financial statements for Barton Corporation. Offer some recommendations based on comparison to the industry average given in Tables E and F on p. 185.

## TABLE C
### BARTON CORPORATION
### INCOME STATEMENT
### YEAR ENDING DECEMBER 31, 19X8
### (THOUSANDS OF DOLLARS)

| | | |
|---|---:|---:|
| Net sales | | $36,000 |
| Less: Cost of goods sold | | 25,000 |
| Gross profit | | $11,000 |
| Less: Operating expenses | | |
| Selling expense | $5,000 | |
| Depreciation expense | 1,000 | |
| General and administrative | 3,000 | |
| Total operating expenses | | $ 9,000 |
| Earnings before interest and taxes | | 2,000 |
| Less: Interest expense | | 1,000 |
| Earnings before taxes | | $ 1,000 |
| Less: Taxes | | 340 |
| Net income | | $ 660 |
| Dividends paid on common stock | | 200 |
| To retained earnings | | $ 460 |

## TABLE D
### BARTON CORPORATION
### BALANCE SHEET
### AS OF DECEMBER 31, 19X8
### (THOUSANDS OF DOLLARS)

*Assets*

| | | |
|---|---:|---:|
| Current assets | | |
| Cash | $ 1,000 | |
| Marketable securities | 3,000 | |
| Accounts receivable | 3,000 | |
| Inventory | 3,000 | |
| Total current assets | | 10,000 |
| Fixed assets | | |
| Plant and equipment | $12,000 | |
| Less: Accumulated depreciation | 2,000 | |
| Net fixed assets | | 10,000 |
| Total assets | | $20,000 |

*Liabilities and owners' equity*

| | | |
|---|---:|---:|
| Current liabilities | | |
| Accounts payable | $ 2,000 | |
| Notes payable | 2,000 | |
| Accrued expenses | 200 | |
| Other current liabilities | 800 | |
| Total current liabilities | | 5,000 |
| Long-term liabilities | | |
| Long-term debt | | 9,000 |
| Owners' equity | | |
| Common stock (100,000 shares at par value of $10 per share) | $ 1,000 | |
| Additional paid-in capital | 2,000 | |
| Retained earnings | 3,000 | |
| Total owners' equity | | 6,000 |
| Total liabilities and owners' equity | | $20,000 |

## TABLE E
### INDUSTRY AVERAGE
### COMMON-SIZE INCOME STATEMENT
### FOR THE YEAR ENDING DECEMBER 31, 19X8

| | | Industry Average: Percent of Sales |
|---|---|---|
| Net sales | | 100.0% |
| Less: Cost of goods sold | | 70.0 |
| Gross profit | | 30.0 |
| Less: Operating expenses | | |
|     Selling expense | 13.6% | |
|     Depreciation expense | 3.6 | |
|     General and administrative | 7.0 | |
|     Total operating expenses | | 24.2 |
| Earnings before interest and taxes | | 5.8 |
| Less: Interest expense | | 1.3 |
| Earnings before taxes | | 4.5 |
| Less: Taxes | | 1.5 |
| Net income | | 3.0% |

## TABLE F
### INDUSTRY AVERAGE
### COMMON-SIZE BALANCE SHEET
### AS OF DECEMBER 31, 19X8

| Assets | Industry Average: Percent of Total Assets |
|---|---|
| Current assets | |
|   Cash | 3.5% |
|   Marketable securities | 5.2 |
|   Accounts receivable | 20.9 |
|   Inventory | 10.4 |
|     Total current assets | 40.0% |
| Fixed assets | |
|   Plant and equipment | 77.4% |
|   Less: Accumulated depreciation | 17.4 |
|   Net fixed assets | 60.0% |
| Total assets | 100.0% |

| Liabilities and owners' equity | |
|---|---|
| Current liabilities | |
|   Accounts payable | 6.9% |
|   Notes payable | 6.9 |
|   Accrued expenses | 2.7 |
|   Other current liabilities | .9 |
|     Total current liabilities | 17.4% |
| Long-term liabilities | |
|   Long-term debt | 39.4% |
| Owners' equity | |
|   Common stock—par value | 6.9% |
|   Additional paid-in capital | 10.4 |
|   Retained earnings | 25.9 |
|     Total owners' equity | 43.2% |
| Total liabilities and owners' equity | 100.0% |

**P6-1d.** The individual accounts on Barton Corporation's balance sheet as of December 31, 19X7, were identical to those on its 19X8 balance sheet (Table D) except for the following items: accounts receivable and inventory were each $2.5 million; plant and equipment was $10 million; accumulated depreciation was $1 million; accounts payable was $1.5 million; notes payable was $1.96 million; long-term debt was $8 million; and retained earnings was $2.54 million. Construct a sources and uses of funds statement for Barton Corporation for 19X8.

**P6-2a.** Use the financial statements provided for Sunfest Corporation (Tables G and H) to conduct a ratio analysis of that firm. Make recommendations for improving the firm's performance based on your analysis. Industry ratios follow:

### INDUSTRY RATIOS

| | |
|---|---|
| Current ratio = 1.9 | Quick ratio = 1.4 |
| Inventory turnover = 6.1 | Total asset turnover = 3.0 |
| Net profit margin = 2.9% | Times interest earned = 3.2 |
| Return on equity = 17.4% | Return on investment = 8.7% |
| Debt ratio = .50 | |

**P6-2b.** Analyze the components of Sunfest's ROE. Explain why Sunfest's ROE differs from the industry norm. (Assume an industry equity multiplier of 2.0.)

**P6-2c.** The individual accounts on Sunfest's balance sheet as of December 31, 19X8, were identical to those on its 19X9 balance sheet except for the following items: cash was $1.7 million; inventory was $9.2 million; plant and equipment was $7.216 million; accumulated depreciation was $.85 million; accounts payable was $2.95 million; notes payable was $2.5 million; and retained earnings was $5.416 million. Construct Sunfest's sources and uses of funds statement for 19X9.

**P6-3a.** Use the financial statements provided for Fowler Corporation (Tables I and J on p. 188) to conduct a ratio analysis of that firm. Make your recommendations about how the firm's performance can be improved based on your analysis. The industry ratios are indicated in the following table.

### INDUSTRY RATIOS

| | |
|---|---|
| Current ratio = 1.7 | Quick ratio = .8 |
| Inventory turnover = 18.8 | Total asset turnover = 3.5 |
| Return on equity = 13.1% | Times interest earned = 3.4 |
| Net profit margin = 1.5% | Return on investment = 5.25% |
| Debt ratio = .60 | |

**P6-3b.** Analyze the components of Fowler's ROE. Explain why Fowler's ROE differs from the industry norm. (Assume an industry equity multiplier of 2.5.)

**P6-3c.** The balance sheet for Fowler Corporation as of December 31, 19X7, was identical to that for 19X8 (Table J) except for the following items: cash was $.15 million; accounts receivable was $1.1 million; inventory was $1.5 million; plant and equipment was $4.5 million; accumulated depreciation was $.6 million; accounts payable was $.87 million; long-term debt was $2.3 million; common stock was $.9 million; additional paid-in capital was $.5 million; and retained earnings was $.98 million. Construct Fowler's sources and uses of funds statement for 19X8.

## TABLE G
### SUNFEST CORPORATION
### INCOME STATEMENT
### YEAR ENDING DECEMBER 31, 19X9
### (THOUSANDS OF DOLLARS)

| | | |
|---|---|---:|
| Net sales | | $57,800 |
| Less: Cost of goods sold | | 50,980 |
| Gross profit | | $ 6,820 |
| Less: Operating expenses | | |
| Selling expense | $1,700 | |
| Depreciation expense | 500 | |
| General and administrative | 2,000 | |
| Total operating expenses | | $ 4,200 |
| Earnings before interest and taxes | | $ 2,620 |
| Less: Interest expense | | 1,432 |
| Earnings before taxes | | $ 1,188 |
| Less: Taxes | | 404 |
| Net income | | $ 784 |
| Dividends paid on common stock | | 200 |
| To retained earnings | | $ 584 |

## TABLE H
### SUNFEST CORPORATION
### BALANCE SHEET
### AS OF DECEMBER 31, 19X9
### (THOUSANDS OF DOLLARS)

*Assets*

| | | |
|---|---|---:|
| Current assets | | |
| Cash | $ 1,200 | |
| Marketable securities | 3,000 | |
| Accounts receivable | 6,425 | |
| Inventory | 8,700 | |
| Total current assets | | 19,325 |
| Fixed assets | | |
| Plant and equipment | $10,300 | |
| Less: Accumulated depreciation | 1,350 | |
| Net fixed assets | | 8,950 |
| Total assets | | $28,275 |

*Liabilities and owners' equity*

| | | |
|---|---|---:|
| Current liabilities | | |
| Accounts payable | $ 3,450 | |
| Notes payable | 3,000 | |
| Accrued expenses | 3,300 | |
| Other current liabilities | 900 | |
| Total current liabilities | | 10,650 |
| Long-term liabilities | | |
| Long-term debt | | 5,500 |
| Owners' equity | | |
| Common stock (1,000,000 shares | | |
| at par value of $3 per share) | $ 3,000 | |
| Additional paid-in capital | 3,125 | |
| Retained earnings | 6,000 | |
| Total owners' equity | | 12,125 |
| Total liabilities and owners' equity | | $28,275 |

## TABLE I

### FOWLER CORPORATION
### INCOME STATEMENT
### YEAR ENDING DECEMBER 31, 19X8
### (THOUSANDS OF DOLLARS)

| | | |
|---|---:|---:|
| Net sales | | $35,000 |
| Less: Cost of goods sold | | 26,000 |
| Gross profits | | $ 9,000 |
| Less: Operating expenses | | |
|     Selling expense | $2,000 | |
|     Depreciation expense | 400 | |
|     General and administrative | 3,400 | |
|     Total operating expenses | | $ 5,800 |
| Earnings before interest and taxes | | $ 3,200 |
| Less: Interest expense | | 900 |
| Earnings before taxes | | $ 2,300 |
| Less: Taxes | | 780 |
| Net income | | $ 1,520 |
| Dividends paid on common stock | | 400 |
| To retained earnings | | $ 1,120 |

## TABLE J

### FOWLER CORPORATION
### BALANCE SHEET
### AS OF DECEMBER 31, 19X8
### (THOUSANDS OF DOLLARS)

*Assets*

| | | |
|---|---:|---:|
| Current assets | | |
|   Cash | $ 200 | |
|   Marketable securities | 400 | |
|   Accounts receivable | 1,200 | |
|   Inventory | 1,600 | |
|     Total current assets | | 3,400 |
| Fixed assets | | |
|   Plant and equipment | $5,000 | |
|   Less: Accumulated depreciation | 1,000 | |
|     Net fixed assets | | 4,000 |
| Total assets | | $7,400 |

*Liabilities and owners' equity*

| | | |
|---|---:|---:|
| Current liabilities | | |
|   Accounts payable | $ 500 | |
|   Notes payable | 600 | |
|   Accrued expenses | 700 | |
|   Other current liabilities | 200 | |
|     Total current liabilities | | 2,000 |
| Long-term liabilities | | |
|   Long-term debt | | 1,300 |
| Owners' equity | | |
|   Common stock (1,000,000 shares | | |
|     at par value of $3 per share) | $1,000 | |
|   Additional paid-in capital | 1,000 | |
|   Retained earnings | 2,100 | |
|     Total owners' equity | | 4,100 |
| Total liabilities and owners' equity | | $7,400 |

## COMPUTER-ASSISTED PROBLEMS

**CP6-1.** Aztec Corporation expects its net profit margin to be 5 percent, its total asset turnover ratio to be 2.3, and its equity multiplier to be 2.0 next year.

**a. Sensitivity Analysis**   What is Aztec's best estimate of its return on equity (ROE), given the information above? Aztec's management realizes that the firm's net profit margin is uncertain. They feel it could be as low as 4 percent or as high as 6 percent. What would be the firm's ROE for each possible net profit margin?

**b. Sensitivity Analysis**   Aztec's management also recognizes that the firm's total asset turnover ratio is uncertain. Although it is estimated to be 2.3 next year, it could be as low as 2.0 or as high as 2.7. What would Aztec's ROE be for each possible total asset turnover?

**c. Sensitivity Analysis**   Is the estimated ROE more sensitive to the possible values of the net profit margin or the total asset turnover ratio? Explain.

**d. Sensitivity Analysis**   What would the ROE be under the most optimistic conditions regarding the possible values of both the net profit margin and the asset turnover? What would the ROE be under the most pessimistic conditions?

**e. Probability Distribution**   Aztec's management has developed the following probability distributions:

| Total Asset Turnover Ratio | Probability | Net Profit Margin | Probability |
|---|---|---|---|
| 2.0 | 30% | 4% | 20% |
| 2.3 | 40 | 5 | 50 |
| 2.7 | 30 | 6 | 30 |

Aztec is hoping to achieve an ROE of at least 20 percent. Assuming its equity multiplier remains 2.0, would you expect Aztec to achieve its goal? Explain.

**f. Simulation**   Aztec's management just changed its forecasts so that the total asset turnover ratio is expected to be between 1.7 and 2.6, the net profit margin is expected to be between 8 percent and 14 percent, and the equity multiplier is expected to be between 1.8 and 2.3. Do you think that Aztec will achieve its goal of at least a 20 percent ROE? Explain.

**CP6-2.** Use the computer package to calculate the financial ratios and common-size financial statements of Barton Corporation. See Problem 6-1 in the Problems section for that firm's income statement and balance sheet.

**CP6-3.** Obtain financial statements for the last three years (from an annual report or other source) of a company of your choice. Also obtain ratios for the industry in which the company operates. Assess the company's liquidity, efficiency, financial leverage, and profitability using the computer package to expedite the computations. Identify aspects of the firm's operations that need to be improved. Make recommendations about how these improvements can be made.

## REFERENCES

Altman, Edward I. "Financial Ratios, Discriminant Analysis and the Prediction of Corporate Bankruptcy." *Journal of Finance* 23 (September 1968): 598–609.

Altman, Edward I., R. G. Haldeman, and P. Narayanan. "Zeta Analysis and the Prediction of Corporate Bankruptcy." *Journal of Banking and Finance* 1 (June 1977): 29–54.

Baker, Morton, and Martin L. Gosman. "The Use of Financial Ratios in Credit Downgrade Decisions." *Financial Management* 9 (Spring 1980): 53–56.

Beaver, William H. "Financial Ratios as Predictors of Failure." *Empirical Research in Accounting: Selected Studies in Journal of Accounting Research* (1966): 71–111.

Chen, Kung H., and T. A. Shimerda. "An Empirical Analysis of Useful Financial Ratios." *Financial Management* 10 (Spring 1981): 51–60.

Gombola, Michael J., and J. Edward Ketz. "Financial Ratio Patterns in Retail and Manufacturing Organizations." *Financial Management* 12 (Summer 1983): 45–56.

Johnson, W. Bruce. "The Cross Sectional Stability of Financial Ratio Patterns." *Journal of Financial and Quantitative Analysis* 14 (December 1979): 1035–48.

Lewellen, W. G., and R. W. Johnson. "Better Way to Monitor Accounts Receivable." *Harvard Business Review* 50 (May–June 1972): 101–9.

Moore, James S., and Alan K. Reichert. "An Analysis of the Financial Management Techniques Currently Employed by Large U.S. Corporations." *Journal of Business Finance & Accounting* 10 (December 1983): 623–45.

Richards, Verlyn D., and Eugene J. Laughlin. "A Cash Conversion Cycle Approach to Liquidity Analysis." *Financial Management* 9 (Spring 1980): 32–38.

Stone, Bernell K. "The Payments-Pattern Approach to the Forecasting of Accounts Receivable." *Financial Management* 5 (Autumn 1976): 65–82.

# CHAPTER 7

# FINANCIAL PLANNING

## FINANCIAL PLANNING IN PERSPECTIVE

In 1977 Federal Express Corporation had total revenue of $109 million and total assets of $58 million. In the ten years that followed, revenues increased 2,790 percent to more than $2 billion. In order to support this increase in sales, Federal Express experienced a need for rapid growth of its assets. During the same ten-year period, total assets grew 3,700 percent to more than $2 billion. Such rapid growth of assets does not come easily. It requires much planning and analysis to estimate the level of assets required, obtain the financing necessary to acquire those assets, and utilize those assets so that they generate sufficient revenue to compensate the sources of financing.

Some financing needs are temporary and therefore suited to short-term sources such as bank loans. Other needs are permanent and require financing either from internal sources, such as retained earnings, or from external sources, such as the sale of bonds, preferred stock, or additional common stock. Selection of the appropriate source can be as important as identifying the financial need.

This chapter presents methods of planning for both short-term and long-term financing needs. The importance of planning for growth cannot be understated. Many firms with excellent products and growing sales find their growth uncontrolled and their liquidity lacking. Despite their profitability, many such firms enter bankruptcy every year.

The previous chapter illustrated how to determine a firm's financial condition through an analysis and evaluation of its financial statements. This chapter concerns planning for the firm's future financing requirements (both short-term and long-term needs) and forecasting its financial condition. By assessing the potential impact of different sales levels and management policies on the firm's financial statements, managers can identify the financing needs and policies that result in the most desirable financial condition. It is important how a firm's financial statements are viewed by creditors and shareholders. If viewed favorably (in terms of liquidity, efficiency, leverage, and profitability), the firm's stock value may be maximized, and management will have accomplished its primary goal.

The importance of financial planning is often underestimated. Some profitable firms fail to anticipate future temporary cash shortages and default on their obligations as a result. Other firms are unable to adjust to adverse economic conditions quickly enough to avoid large losses because they have not planned for such contingencies. Both can lead to bankruptcy.

Of course, financial planning is not free. Management must be willing to hire qualified people to conduct financial planning, and it must be willing to take whatever action is necessary to improve the firm's situation. For virtually all firms, this cost is an absolute necessity if shareholder wealth is to be maximized.

A primary function of financial planning is to forecast the firm's short-term cash flows and financial statements in order to help answer the following questions:

■ How much cash will the firm need to borrow temporarily during the planning period? What will be the timing of those borrowing needs?

■ What is the expected earnings per share for the firm during the planning period? What factors under the control of management can be altered to improve firm profitability?

■ How much permanent external financing will the firm require over the next one to five years or longer? What sources of financing should be used?

■ How will the firm's creditors and owners view the firm's future financial situation in terms of liquidity, efficiency, leverage, and profitability? What can the firm do now to make the future financial statements more attractive?

This chapter begins with an explanation of how a firm can forecast cash inflows and outflows in the short run and how it can use those forecasts to plan for short-term financing needs. Then it explains how **pro forma financial statements** (or forecasted statements) can be developed and used to help in the long-term planning and decision-making process.

Both aspects of financial planning use forecasted sales as a key input variable. While a number of quantitative techniques can be used to arrive at a sales forecast, the final forecast generally involves subjective judgment. Normally, the sales forecast is constructed using input from the marketing department, production department, and from economic forecasts. Since this chapter focuses on *how to use* the sales forecast for financial planning, rather than on how to develop a sales forecast, we will assume the sales forecast is given.

## CASH BUDGETING

A **cash budget** is constructed from forecasted cash receipts and cash disbursements at regular intervals over some future planning period. A typical planning period is one year, although longer or shorter periods are sometimes used. The cash receipts and disbursements are normally forecasted for each month during the planning period, although weekly or daily subperiods may be used. By comparing expected cash receipts to expected cash disbursements, the firm can determine if and when it will have a cash deficiency. It can also estimate the size of the cash deficiency and how long the deficiency will exist. This information can help the firm arrange for necessary financing in advance by demonstrating to its bank or other lender when and why it expects to need funds, and for how long it expects that need to continue. A well-constructed cash budget shows the bank that the firm has given careful thought to the important task of managing its cash position. Such planning is viewed favorably by lending institutions. The cash budget also indicates when the firm expects to have excess cash, how much excess cash will be available, and for how long, which helps management plan for using these excess funds.

Constructing the cash budget involves the following steps:

*Step 1.* Estimate the cash receipts (inflows) for each subperiod.
*Step 2.* Estimate the cash disbursements (outflows) for each subperiod.
*Step 3.* Find the net cash gain (inflow) or loss (outflow) for each subperiod.
*Step 4.* Add the net gain to (or subtract the net cash loss from) the cash at the start of the subperiod, and subtract interest to be paid on short-term debt. The result is the ending cash balance for the subperiod.
*Step 5.* Compare the expected cash balance for each subperiod to the amount of cash the firm wishes to hold. This latter figure is normally predetermined by the firm. The difference represents either a cash surplus that can be invested, or a cash deficit that the firm must plan to borrow.

### Estimating Cash Receipts

Construction of a cash budget is best illustrated by an example. Neal Corporation has developed a sales forecast for the months of January through July of 19X9 as follows (actual sales for December 19X8 are also indicated).

| Month | Sales (Thousands of Dollars) |
| --- | --- |
| December 19X8 | $ 7,000 |
| January 19X9 | 8,000 |
| February | 10,000 |
| March | 12,000 |
| April | 14,000 |
| May | 16,000 |
| June | 17,000 |
| July | 16,000 |

Assume it is now December 31, 19X8, and the firm would like to develop a cash budget for the next six months. From the historical records

**TABLE 7.1    Schedule of Anticipated Cash Receipts: Neal Corporation (Thousands of Dollars)**

| | Dec 19X8 | Jan 19X9 | Feb 19X9 | Mar 19X9 | Apr 19X9 | May 19X9 | Jun 19X9 | Jul 19X9 |
|---|---|---|---|---|---|---|---|---|
| *Line* | | | | | | | | |
| 1. Total forecasted sales | 7,000 | 8,000 | 10,000 | 12,000 | 14,000 | 16,000 | 17,000 | 16,000 |
| *Cash receipts* | | | | | | | | |
| 2. Cash sales (30% of total) | | 2,400 | 3,000 | 3,600 | 4,200 | 4,800 | 5,100 | |
| 3. Credit sales (70% of total; one-month lag) | | 4,900 | 5,600 | 7,000 | 8,400 | 9,800 | 11,200 | |
| 4. Total cash receipts | | 7,300 | 8,600 | 10,600 | 12,600 | 14,600 | 16,300 | |

maintained by Neal Corporation's credit department, the firm has found that every month about 30 percent of sales are for cash and 70 percent are credit sales. All credit sales have historically been paid for during the month following the sale. The firm expects this same pattern of collections to continue in the future.

Table 7.1 illustrates how Neal Corporation can estimate its cash receipts for January through June. Forecasted sales for each month (and actual sales for December) appear in Line 1 of Table 7.1. The actual sales figure for December is needed to estimate cash receipts for January. During January Neal Corporation expects to receive $2,400,000 from January's cash sales (30% × $8,000,000), as shown in Line 2. In addition, it expects to receive $4,900,000 from December's credit sales (70% × $7,000,000), as shown in Line 3. Cash receipts for January are therefore expected to total $7,300,000, as indicated in Line 4. February's cash receipts are expected to include $3,000,000 from February's cash sales (30% × $10,000,000), and $5,600,000 from January's credit sales (70% × $8,000,000). Cash receipts for March through June are calculated the same way. July's cash receipts are not estimated here since the cash budget being constructed is only for January through June.

Cash can flow into the firm from sources other than sales, such as interest earned on marketable securities, tax refunds from the federal government, and proceeds from issuing securities. Such sources should be considered when forecasting the total cash receipts for the applicable period. Neal Corporation does not expect to receive any such cash flows during this period.

## Estimating Cash Disbursements

Cash disbursements (payments) can occur for a variety of reasons, but the more common cash disbursements are for materials, wages, operating expenses (such as rent and sales commissions), interest and principal payments on long-term debt, taxes, cash dividends, and capital expenditures.

The level of sales can affect the size of these disbursements. Higher sales are normally accompanied by the purchase of more raw materials and the payment of more wages, taxes, and dividends. Higher sales could also require greater capital expenditures to expand capacity and higher interest payments on the funds used to finance the expansion. To illustrate the estimation of total cash disbursements, the following information is provided for Neal Corporation for January through June.

- Each month Neal Corporation purchases materials equal to 40 percent of sales forecasted for the following month. Forty percent of all purchases are on a cash basis, and 60 percent are paid the following month.
- Wages paid each month are estimated to be 20 percent of the subsequent month's sales.
- Fixed operating expenses are expected to be $1 million each month. Other expenses are estimated as follows: January, $.5 million; February, $1 million; March, $1.5 million; April, $2 million; May, $2.5 million; June, $2.5 million.
- Interest payments of $1 million are expected to be paid in February and August each year on the firm's $15 million of long-term debt.
- Capital expenditures of $.5 million in March and $1 million in both April and June are planned.
- Tax payments of $980,000 are anticipated on March 15 and June 15.
- Quarterly dividends of $1,320,000 will be paid in February and May.

Given the above information, a schedule of cash disbursements for January through June has been developed and is presented in Table 7.2. Line 1 indicates the level of sales (given in the problem), and Line 2 indicates the purchase of materials. In December the firm purchased materials equal to 40 percent of forecasted January sales. Of those $3.2 million of purchases, the firm would pay cash for 40 percent of them (40% × $3,200,000 = $1,280,000) in December (Line 3). The remaining $1.92 million of December's purchases (60 percent) would be paid for in January (Line 4). Forty percent of January's purchases of $4 million are to be paid for during January ($1.6 million), while the remaining 60 percent of January's purchases are paid in February ($2.4 million). This same pattern continues through June. Disbursements for wages in January (Line 5) are expected to be 20 percent of February's sales, or $2 million; for February they are 20 percent of March's sales, or $2.4 million, and so on. Placing the remaining disbursements on the schedule of cash disbursements is straightforward and has been done in Table 7.2. The last row in Table 7.2 indicates the total cash disbursements for Neal Corporation for January through June. This information will be used, along with the cash receipts information generated in Table 7.1, to complete the cash budget. Some firms prefer a more detailed breakdown of receipts and disbursements than the one provided in Table 7.2, in order to identify the cash receipts and disbursements for each subperiod as precisely as possible.

## Combining Cash Receipts and Disbursements

To complete the cash budget for Neal Corporation, the following additional information is provided:

**TABLE 7.2  Schedule of Anticipated Cash Disbursements: Neal Corporation (Thousands of Dollars)**

| Line | December 19X8 | January 19X9 | February 19X9 | March 19X9 | April 19X9 | May 19X9 | June 19X9 | July 19X9 |
|---|---|---|---|---|---|---|---|---|
| 1. Forecasted sales | 7,000 | 8,000 | 10,000 | 12,000 | 14,000 | 16,000 | 17,000 | 16,000 |
| 2. Materials purchased (40% of next month's sales) | 3,200 | 4,000 | 4,800 | 5,600 | 6,400 | 6,800 | 6,400 | |
| *Cash disbursements* | | | | | | | | |
| 3. Cash purchases (40% of material purchases) | 1,280 | 1,600 | 1,920 | 2,240 | 2,560 | 2,720 | 2,560 | |
| 4. Credit purchases (60% paid in the month after purchase) | | 1,920 | 2,400 | 2,880 | 3,360 | 3,840 | 4,080 | |
| 5. Wages (20% of next month's sales) | 1,600 | 2,000 | 2,400 | 2,800 | 3,200 | 3,400 | 3,200 | |
| 6. Fixed operating expenses | | 1,000 | 1,000 | 1,000 | 1,000 | 1,000 | 1,000 | |
| 7. Other expenses | | 500 | 1,000 | 1,500 | 2,000 | 2,500 | 2,500 | |
| 8. Interest payments on long-term debt | | | 1,000 | | 1,000 | | 1,000 | |
| 9. Capital expenditures | | | | 500 | | | | |
| 10. Taxes | | | | 980 | | | 980 | |
| 11. Cash dividends | | | 1,320 | | | 1,320 | | |
| 12. Total cash disbursements | | 7,020 | 11,040 | 11,900 | 13,120 | 14,780 | 15,320 | |

TABLE 7.3   **Cash Budget, January 19X9–June 19X9: Neal Corporation (Thousands of Dollars)**

|  | Jan 19X9 | Feb 19X9 | Mar 19X9 | Apr 19X9 | May 19X9 | Jun 19X9 |
|---|---|---|---|---|---|---|
| *Line* |  |  |  |  |  |  |
| 1. Net cash gain (loss) for the month | 280 | (2,440) | (1,300) | (520) | (180) | 980 |
| 2. Minus: Interest on prior month's short-term debt[a] | 0 | 0 | 22 | 35 | 40 | 43 |
| 3. Plus: Beginning cash (before short-term borrowing) | 1,000 | 1,280 | (1,160) | (2,482) | (3,037) | (3,257) |
| 4. Ending cash (before short-term borrowing) | 1,280 | (1,160) | (2,482) | (3,037) | (3,257) | (2,320) |
| 5. Minus: Desired level of cash | 1,000 | 1,000 | 1,000 | 1,000 | 1,000 | 1,000 |
| 6. Cumulative short-term financing |  | 2,160 | 3,482 | 4,037 | 4,257 | 3,320 |
| 7. Excess cash | 280 |  |  |  |  |  |

[a]This value is rounded to the nearest thousand and represents the monthly interest (1 percent per month) on the short-term debt outstanding the prior month (Line 6).

■ At the start of January, Neal Corporation's cash balance is $1 million.
■ Neal Corporation must pay interest each month on any short-term loans that were outstanding in the prior month. A 12 percent annual interest rate applies (1 percent per month). There is no short-term debt outstanding during December 19X8.
■ Neal Corporation wishes to maintain a minimum level of cash of $1 million every month.

The estimated cash disbursements derived in Table 7.1 can now be subtracted from the estimated cash receipts derived in Table 7.2 for each subperiod in order to determine the estimated net cash gain (or loss). This difference appears in Line 1 of Table 7.3, which is the actual cash budget. Henceforth, each month must be evaluated separately before going on to the next month.

The interest paid on short-term debt (Line 2) is calculated based on the outstanding short-term debt the prior month. This amount is subtracted from the net cash gain (or loss) for the month. The cash balance at the beginning of the month (Line 3) also is added. For January there was a net cash gain of $.28 million, and since Neal Corporation had no short-term debt outstanding during December, there is no interest to deduct. The firm started the month with $1 million in cash, so this amount is added to the net cash gain, resulting in ending cash of $1.28 million (Line 4).

The desired level of cash (Line 5) is now subtracted from ending cash to determine if a cash deficiency exists (a deficiency would appear on Line 6). Any excess cash is recorded on Line 7. An entry will be made on only one of these lines for each month. For the month of January, Neal Corporation expects to have excess cash of $.28 million.[1]

For the month of February, the analysis is conducted in the same man-

---

1.   In the event that a corporation plans to invest the excess cash, the interest to be earned on the cash would need to be projected. In our example, any excess cash is maintained as cash.

ner. In February there is an expected net cash loss of $2.44 million. There was no short-term debt in January, so the interest on the prior month's short-term debt is zero. Next, the beginning balance of $1.28 million for February must be added. Notice that the beginning cash balance for February is equal to the ending cash balance for January. The beginning cash balance for any month is always equal to the ending cash balance from the previous month. After the beginning cash balance is added to the net cash loss for February, the ending cash balance for February is negative $1.16 million. Since the company wants to maintain a minimum of $1 million in cash, it will need to borrow $2.16 million in February (Line 6) to bring cash back up to the desired level. Notice that the excess cash that exists in January is used in February, and the firm still needs to borrow money.

Neal Corporation expects to experience another net cash loss in March ($1.3 million). In addition, management expects to pay $22,000 (Line 2) in interest (rounded to the nearest thousand) on the new short-term debt it incurred in February (Line 6). Adding these two outflows to the beginning cash for March (negative $1.16 million) results in an ending negative cash balance for March of $2.482 million. In order to maintain the desired level of cash, Neal Corporation will need to have total short-term financing in March of $3.482 million.

The cash budget for the remaining months is constructed in the same manner. Although we have provided information that will permit construction of the cash budget for only six months, Table 7.4 displays the last two lines of the cash budget for Neal Corporation for those six months *plus* the remaining months of 19X9. Table 7.4 indicates that Neal Corporation expects to be free of short-term debt in January but must begin borrowing in February. The level of short-term debt increases gradually to a high of $4.257 million in May. When analyzing the cash budget, remember that the short-term borrowing figures are cumulative. That is, since $2.16 million is to be borrowed in February, the *additional amount borrowed in March* is only $1.322 million. In April an additional $.555 million will be borrowed ($4.037 million minus $3.482 million). Therefore, the maximum amount of short-term debt outstanding at any time during the year is expected to be $4.257 million in May.

Neal Corporation can expect to begin reducing its short-term debt in June and continue reducing it through October. By November the firm expects to be free of short-term debt and have excess cash of $36,000.

TABLE 7.4 **Selected Cash Budget Information: Neal Corporation, 19X9 (Thousands of Dollars)**

|  | Jan | Feb | Mar | Apr | May | Jun |
|---|---|---|---|---|---|---|
| Cumulative short-term financing |  | 2,160 | 3,482 | 4,037 | 4,257 | 3,320 |
| Excess cash | 280 |  |  |  |  |  |

|  | Jul | Aug | Sep | Oct | Nov | Dec |
|---|---|---|---|---|---|---|
| Cumulative short-term financing | 2,990 | 2,156 | 1,821 | 44 |  |  |
| Excess cash |  |  |  |  | 36 | 170 |

This pattern of increasing short-term debt followed by debt reduction is typical of firms experiencing sales fluctuations resulting from seasonal sales or some other reason. During the period of inventory buildup the need for financing increases. Once cash flows are generated by the sale of the inventory, the short-term loans can be repaid. This type of lending is very common. In fact, the majority of bank loans to businesses are used to finance temporary increases in current assets.

Neal Corporation must convince its bank that it has a legitimate need to borrow up to $4.257 million during 19X9 to support a temporary increase in assets. The firm should also demonstrate to the bank that it expects to be free of short-term debt by the end of the year. If the bank is convinced that these estimates are reasonably accurate, Neal's loan request will likely be approved. Normally, a firm in this situation establishes a *line of credit* with its bank, meaning the bank approves a maximum loan amount for the firm for a specified period of time (in this case, perhaps a maximum loan of $4.257 million for one year). Neal Corporation can then borrow any amount (up to the maximum) at any time during the year. Borrowers can repay any amount they wish during the loan period, and they frequently renew such loan agreements annually. However, it is common for banks to require this type of loan to be reduced to zero for at least one month during the year (this is to ensure that the loan is truly being used for short-term financing purposes).

In summary, the cash budget is a valuable short-term planning tool that can reveal cash deficiencies requiring short-term financing. It can also reveal that a firm will have difficulty repaying its short-term debt within a year and will thus need long-term financing. The cash budget forces the firm to plan its production schedule, purchasing requirements, and other operational requirements. In addition, it permits the firm to anticipate and arrange for its financing needs well in advance.

## ACCOUNTING FOR UNCERTAINTY IN THE CASH BUDGET

Since cash budgeting is based on *estimates* of future cash flows, the results are subject to forecasting error. Recall that many cash flow estimates are based on forecasts of monthly sales. If these forecasts prove to be inaccurate, the estimated ending cash balance for each month will also be inaccurate. Two common methods of accounting for the uncertainty in cash budgeting are *sensitivity analysis* and *simulation*.

### Sensitivity Analysis

Since it is impossible to forecast sales with perfection, it is wise for a firm to estimate a variety of possible sales levels and assess the implications of each possible level on the cash budget. This can be done by constructing a different cash budget for each level of sales. The different cash budgets reveal the sensitivity of the firm's borrowing needs to alternative sales levels—information that is useful in planning for future short-term financing needs.

As an example, management could develop an optimistic, pessimistic, and most likely sales forecast for each month. The cash receipts, disbursements, and ending cash balance could be estimated based on each sales forecast. This cash budgeting process would differ from the earlier example in that three separate cash budget schedules would be developed, indicating the sensitivity of the future ending cash balances to the different possible sales projections. A pessimistic sales forecast might generate a cash budget that shows no need for additional future short-term financing. Conversely, an optimistic sales forecast might generate a cash budget indicating that substantial short-term financing is needed (to support the increased inventories and accounts receivable). The firm should not react to this information by immediately borrowing a large amount of money. However, it may wish to establish contingency plans in case additional funds are needed.

Sensitivity analysis can also be used to develop cash-budget projections based on alternative relationships between variables. That is, the firm can incorporate various "what if" questions into alternative cash budgets. For example:

- What if cash sales are 25 percent of total sales?
- What if fixed operating expenses are 10 percent greater than initially forecasted?
- What if the cost of raw materials is actually 45 percent of next month's sales instead of 40 percent?
- What if wages are actually 25 percent of next month's sales instead of 20 percent?

By using a computer to construct cash budgets, "what if" questions are very easy to address. For example, the original cash budget can be constructed by defining the relationships between all cash-budget variables (for example, cash sales equal 30 percent of total sales, labor costs equal 20 percent of next month's sales, net cash gain or loss equals cash receipts minus cash disbursements, and so on). If the estimate of sales is changed, the entire cash budget can be changed automatically based on the defined relationships.

Similarly, if any of the relationships are redefined (for example, cash sales might be changed to 25 percent of total sales), the computer program will automatically change all necessary cash budget items. Given this flexibility to evaluate alternative possible outcomes, the firm can consider the impact of many possible situations on the cash budget and potential need for short-term financing.

## Simulation

Simulation is an alternative tool for considering the uncertainty of a cash budget that is normally conducted with the help of a computer. Simulation requires the user to define values of the input variables in the form of probability distributions. For example, the sales forecast for January could be input as a probability distribution with a range of $7.6 million to $8.4 million rather than using the point estimate of $8 million. Wage expense could be estimated using a probability distribution with a range between 18 percent and 22 percent of forecasted sales, rather than using a point estimate of 20 percent of sales. For all variables that are uncertain, a probability distribution can serve as the estimate. The more uncertain the financial manager is about the variable's future value, the wider will be the range of the probability distribution.

Once a probability distribution has been established for each relevant input variable, the simulation program is ready to generate alternative cash budgets. Each cash budget is generated in the following manner. The simulation program randomly picks a single value for each variable that has been specified in terms of a probability distribution. Using the defined relationship between all cash budgeting variables, the computer program then calculates a cash budget and provides the "cumulative financing" or "excess cash" as output. The entire process is repeated with the computer again performing its random selection of variables, construction of the cash budget, and output of "cumulative financing" or "excess cash." This process is replicated perhaps 100 times so that 100 possible outcomes are generated. From the various outcomes that result, a probability distribution of possible cumulative financing or excess cash can be derived for each month. These probability distributions can be used by the firm to determine the probability that it may need to obtain short-term financing at the end of any particular month in order to maintain the desired level of cash. The computations involved in generating 100 or more cash budgets, which could take weeks without the assistance of a computer, takes only seconds with a computer.

## PRO FORMA FINANCIAL STATEMENTS

A *pro forma income statement* is a projected income statement for a future period (such as the following year). It can provide management with projections of all income and expense items as well as summary figures such as net income and earnings per share. By analyzing pro forma income statements, financial managers can prepare for future conditions that may arise and, if necessary, take corrective action to improve profitability prior to beginning the period under analysis. The pro forma income statement also provides a benchmark against which actual performance can be measured. If various operating expenses are higher than those forecasted by the pro forma income statement, management can investigate the cause of the deviation and attempt to prevent similar deviations from occurring in the future.

A *pro forma balance sheet* is a projected balance sheet for a specific date in the future (such as one year ahead). It can be used to forecast future liquidity and activity ratios, and some leverage ratios. When used in combination with the pro forma income statement, it can help management forecast efficiency and profitability ratios. An analysis of these ratios may reveal potential problems that, if corrected early, might improve the future balance sheet.

A second function of the pro forma balance sheet is to help management plan for future financing needs. This is a particularly useful function when the planning period extends beyond the period of the cash budget. That is, the pro forma balance sheet may be more useful than the cash budget for projecting long-term financing needs in some cases.

# FORECASTING FINANCIAL STATEMENTS USING THE PERCENT-OF-SALES METHOD

The cash budget can be used to develop pro forma financial statements when the cash budget extends to the end of the period for which the pro forma statements are being constructed. This technique is demonstrated in the appendix to this chapter. When the pro forma period extends beyond the cash-budget period, however, it is necessary to use some other method, such as the **percent-of-sales method.** This method assumes that many of the firm's expenses and balance sheet accounts will remain a constant percent of sales in the future, regardless of the level of sales. For example, if cost of goods sold in the prior period was 75 percent of sales, cost of goods sold in the forecasted period is assumed to be 75 percent times the forecasted sales—provided there is no evidence suggesting this percentage will change in the future.

Application of the percent-of-sales method is limited in two ways, however. First, it makes the implicit assumption that a linear relationship exists between sales and the forecasted variables. Although this may be a reasonable assumption for some variables in the short-run, it is not reasonable for all variables, particularly when long-run forecasts are being made. Generally, the farther into the future the forecast is, the less reliable percent-of-sales forecasts are. A second limitation is that, used in its purest form, the percent-of-sales method does not allow for the application of additional information that may be available to the analyst. For this reason, a practicing analyst must constantly ask the question "how can percent-of-sales forecasts be adjusted to reflect additional known information?" This approach is reflected in the examples and end-of-chapter problems presented in this text. For consistency, unless stated otherwise, the following variables are assumed to remain a constant percent of sales: cost of goods sold, depreciation expense, variable operating expenses, interest expense, cash, accounts receivable, inventories, and accounts payable.

## Constructing a Pro Forma Income Statement

An example of the use of the percent-of-sales method for constructing a pro forma income statement is presented in Table 7.5. The first column of numbers indicates the actual income statement for Neal Corporation in 19X8. The second column of numbers indicates the forecasted income statement. In this instance, an expected increase in sales to $154 million is given. It is assumed that cost of goods sold (excluding depreciation) will change directly with sales. In 19X8, cost of goods sold was 60 percent of sales. If this same relationship is expected to continue during 19X9, cost of goods sold would be 60 percent of $154 million, or $92.4 million.

Two precautionary comments are necessary. First, in this example, the

**TABLE 7.5** Constructing Pro Forma Income Statement Using Percent-of-Sales Method, Ending December 31, 19X9: Neal Corporation (Thousands of Dollars)

|  | | 19X8 Actual | | 19X9 Estimated | Source of the Estimate |
|---|---|---|---|---|---|
| Sales | | $140,000 | | $154,000 | The 19X9 estimate was given. |
| Less: Cost of goods sold (excluding depreciation) | | 84,000 | | 92,400 | 60% of sales in 19X8 |
| Less: Depreciation | | 10,000 | | 10,934 | 7.1% of sales in 19X8 |
| Gross profit | | 46,000 | | 50,666 | |
| Less: Operating expenses | | | | | |
| Fixed | 12,000 | | 12,000 | | Fixed component is unchanged. |
| Variable | 16,000 | | 17,556 | | Variable component was 11.4% |
| Total | | 28,000 | | 29,556 | of sales in 19X8. |
| Earnings before interest and taxes | | 18,000 | | 21,110 | |
| Less: Interest expense | | 2,200 | | 2,464 | 1.6% of sales in 19X8 |
| Earnings before taxes | | 15,800 | | 18,646 | |
| Less: Taxes | | 5,372 | | 6,340 | 34% average tax rate in 19X8 |
| Net income | | 10,428 | | 12,306 | |
| Cash dividend | | 4,400 | | 4,400 | Given: no change |
| To retained earnings | | $ 6,028 | | $ 7,906 | |

relationship established between the variables being forecasted and sales is based entirely on the relationship that existed during the prior year. While the experience of the year just ended may be the most relevant, some firms may want to use the average percent of sales for the preceding two, three, five, or even more years. This will help to minimize the impact of any abnormal relationships that may have existed during one specific year. Conversely, data used two or more years in the past may be less representative of the current situation, in which case the analyst may prefer to rely exclusively on the relationship that existed in the most recent year.

A second precautionary comment is necessary to assure that the reader recognizes the necessity of adjusting the historical percentages. In the current example, cost of goods sold was 60 percent of sales in the prior year. While this may be a good starting point for forecasting cost of goods sold next year, this percentage may be adjusted higher or lower based on information available to the analyst about changes in the sale price of the firm's product or changes in the cost of raw materials or labor. Although the use of more than one year of historical data and the application of additional information is not used in this example, students should be mindful of their use in real-world applications.

Next, the firm must estimate depreciation. This can be done by analyzing the firm's depreciation schedules and forecasting the acquisition of additional fixed assets on which depreciation will be taken in the future. Alternatively, the assumption can be made that depreciation will remain the same percent of sales in the future that it was in the past, an assumption implying that increased sales must be supported by increased capital expenditures. In this example, it is assumed that depreciation remains the same percent of sales in 19X9 as it was in 19X8 (7.1 percent). This results in forecasted depreciation of $10,934,000. Subtracting the estimated cost of goods sold and depreciation from forecasted sales results in forecasted gross profit of $50,666,000.

Some operating expenses are relatively fixed, while others tend to vary with the level of sales. In Table 7.5, the fixed and variable components have been separated. It is assumed in this example that the fixed component remains unchanged, while the variable component remains a constant percent of sales (11.4 percent). This results in forecasted fixed operating expenses of $12,000,000, variable operating expenses of $17,556,000, and total operating expenses of $29,556,000. Earnings before interest and taxes of $21,110,000 results from subtracting total operating expenses from gross profit. Interest expense was 1.6 percent of sales in the previous year. Assuming that interest expense remains the same percent of sales in the forecasted year, interest expense would be $2,464,000. Taxes on earnings can be determined using a 19X9 tax schedule or by estimating the firm's average tax rate during the forecasted period. It is assumed here that the average tax rate will be the same in 19X9 as it was in 19X8. The average tax rate in 19X8 was 34 percent and is determined by dividing 19X8 taxes by 19X8 earnings before taxes ($5,372,000/$15,800,000). Taxes in 19X9 are forecasted to be $6,340,000 based on this 34 percent rate. Forecasted net income can now be determined by subtracting taxes from earnings before taxes ($18,646,000 − $6,340,000 = $12,306,000).

The cash dividend to be paid must be determined by the firm's board of directors. Management can estimate the dividend based on the firm's capital needs and the level of net income. In this example, the dividend is assumed to remain unchanged from the previous year at $4,400,000. The difference between net income and the cash dividend paid ($7,906,000) will be added to retained earnings on the pro forma balance sheet.

The accuracy of the percent-of-sales method depends upon the consistency of the relationship between each expense item and the level of sales. If there is reason to believe these relationships will change in the future, the percentages used should be adjusted to reflect the expected changes.

## Constructing a Pro Forma Balance Sheet

The pro forma balance sheet can also be derived using the percent-of-sales method. First, each balance sheet item must be assessed to determine whether it changes directly with the level of sales. For example, if sales are expected to increase, so will the need for cash, raw materials, accounts receivable, and inventories. Projecting the required increase in those assets is an important part of financial planning. Gross fixed assets may remain unchanged, provided sufficient capacity is available to support forecasted sales. If, however, additional fixed assets are needed to support future sales, the firm will need to acquire the additional assets. Accumulated depreciation will increase by the amount indicated on the pro forma income statement. Next, the firm must forecast all future liability and equity accounts. Some liabilities such as accounts payable and taxes payable increase automatically with sales and are referred to as **spontaneous liabilities.** As sales increase, the firm must purchase more raw materials, increasing its accounts payable. Also, as sales increase, the firm incurs

**TABLE 7.6** **Constructing Pro Forma Balance Sheet as of December 31, 19X9 Using Percent-of-Sales Method: Neal Corporation (Thousands of Dollars)**

|  | Actual Figures 12/31/X8 | Pro Forma Balance Sheet 12/31/X9 | Source of the Estimate |
|---|---|---|---|
| **Assets** | | | |
| Current Assets | | | |
| Cash | $ 1,000 | $ 1,078 | .7% of sales in 19X8. |
| Marketable securities | 500 | 500 | Given: unchanged. |
| Accounts receivable | 4,900 | 5,390 | 3.5% of sales in 19X8. |
| Inventories | 12,000 | 13,244 | 8.6% of sales in 19X8. |
| Total current assets | 18,400 | 20,212 | |
| Fixed assets | | | |
| Gross fixed assets | 63,000 | 83,000 | Given: $20,000 increase. |
| Less: Accumulated depreciation | 30,000 | 40,934 | Based on pro forma income statement. |
| Net fixed assets | 33,000 | 42,066 | |
| Total assets | $51,400 | $62,278 | |
| **Liabilities and owners' equity** | | | |
| Current liabilities | | | |
| Accounts payable | $ 1,920 | $ 2,156 | 1.4% of sales in 19X8. |
| Notes payable | 0 | 0 | Given: No change. |
| Taxes payable | 1,185 | 1,585 | 25% of 19X9 taxes. |
| Other current liabilities | 4,980 | 4,980 | Given: No change. |
| Total current liabilities | 8,085 | 8,721 | |
| Long-term debt (13.33%) | 15,000 | 15,000 | Given: No change. |
| Owners' equity | | | |
| Common stock—par value | 2,000 | 2,000 | Given: No change. |
| Additional paid-in capital | 8,000 | 8,000 | Given: No change. |
| Retained earnings | 18,315 | 26,221 | Increase of $7,906 from pro forma income statement. |
| Total owners' equity | 28,315 | 36,221 | |
| Total liabilities and owners' equity | $51,400 | $59,942 | |

higher profits, a greater tax liability, and therefore a higher amount of taxes payable.

Other liabilities such as bank loans and long-term debt remain unchanged or decrease over time (they may decrease due to the firm making required principal payments). These accounts will increase only if management takes specific action to increase them. Equity accounts are normally expected to remain unchanged, unless management takes specific action to increase them. An exception is retained earnings, which should increase as profits are reinvested in the firm.

Table 7.6 illustrates the construction of a pro forma balance sheet for Neal Corporation using the percent-of-sales method. Much of this analysis is based on the 19X8 relationships between specific balance sheet items and the level of sales. These relationships were used to forecast cash, accounts receivable, inventories, and accounts payable. These balance sheet items are assumed to increase spontaneously with sales. Therefore, Table 7.6 reflects the increases based on the assumption that each item remains the same percentage of sales in 19X9 that it was in 19X8.

Other items, such as marketable securities on the asset side, and notes payable, other current liabilities, long-term debt, common stock, and additional paid-in capital on the liability and equity side, do not change unless the firm specifically takes action to change them. Such decisions would normally be known in advance by the analyst so that the changes could be accounted for on the pro forma balance sheet. For Neal Corporation these items are expected to remain unchanged in 19X9 (as reflected in Table 7.6). The remaining items must be estimated separately.

As indicated earlier, fixed assets may increase if higher sales are forecasted (or if some fixed assets need replacing). In this case, it is assumed that Neal Corporation plans to invest $20 million in additional gross fixed assets. Depreciation for the year can be taken from the pro forma income statement ($10,934,000, as shown in Table 7.5). Since gross fixed assets are expected to increase by $20 million, and accumulated depreciation is expected to increase by $10,934,000, net fixed assets should increase by $9,066,000. Therefore, projected total assets for 19X9 total $62,278,000.

On the liabilities and owners' equity side, only taxes payable and retained earnings remain to be forecasted. Referring to the pro forma income statement (Table 7.5), the total tax liability for 19X9 is estimated to be $6,340,000. Since firms pay taxes quarterly, they normally owe 25 percent of their total tax bill at the end of their fiscal year. That would make taxes payable equal to $1,585,000 (25 percent of $6,340,000). The pro forma income statement also reveals that Neal Corporation expects to add $7,906,000 to its retained earnings. This would increase retained earnings on the pro forma balance sheet to $26,221,000. Liabilities and owners' equity are therefore projected to be $59,942,000.

After forecasts of all assets, liabilities, and equity accounts have been made, it would be a rare coincidence if the balance sheet balanced. Normally, a growing firm will find that the forecasted need for assets to support its rising sales exceeds the firm's internally generated funds. The amount by which the projected value of total assets exceeds the liability and owner's equity value represents the additional outside financing that will be required to support higher levels of sales.

Once the firm has determined from the pro forma balance sheet how much additional financing is necessary, it will consider a variety of financing alternatives, such as obtaining loans, issuing bonds or stock, or reducing its dividends. The firm can consider how each of these sources will affect its financial ratios and select the source that it feels will help maximize shareholder wealth. (Later chapters address the question of which sources are most suitable to the firm under various conditions.) The point here is that the pro forma balance sheet can indicate future financing needs well in advance so the firm has time to plan for additional sources of financing. If the firm feels that the needed funds cannot or should not be raised, it may elect to postpone the acquisition of certain additional assets.

In those cases where the value of liabilities plus owners' equity exceeds the asset value on the pro forma balance sheet, the firm should plan in advance how those excess funds are to be used. Common alternatives are to increase dividends, repay outstanding debt, or repurchase stock.

We can conclude that Neal Corporation expects to need more assets ($2,336,000 worth) to support its 19X9 sales than will be provided by internally generated funds. Therefore, the firm should consider how it will obtain those additional funds. Its major alternatives are to postpone the acquisition of some of the fixed assets it expects to acquire, pay a smaller dividend, borrow the needed money, or issue new preferred or common stock.

## PRO FORMA SOURCES AND USES OF FUNDS STATEMENT

Along with a pro forma income statement and balance sheet, the firm may wish to create a pro forma sources and uses of funds statement. This statement indicates the sources from which the firm expects to acquire funds and how it expects to use those funds. A review of the pro forma sources and uses of funds statement may also reveal potential inefficient uses of funds. Since the information contained in pro forma statements relates to the future, there may be time to correct any inefficiencies that are detected.

As demonstrated in Chapter 6, the sources and uses of funds statement can be developed using the differences in balance sheet items at two different points in time, plus some selected income statement data. Thus, a pro forma sources and uses of funds statement can be developed by comparing the most recent balance sheet to a pro forma balance sheet, and by using the pro forma income statement, in the manner described in the previous chapter.

## ACCOUNTING FOR UNCERTAINTY IN PRO FORMA FINANCIAL STATEMENTS

As with cash budgeting, pro forma financial statements are subject to considerable uncertainty. Because decision-making is sometimes dependent on the assessment of pro forma financial statements, bad decisions could result from inaccurate pro forma statements. While it is virtually impossible to create perfect forecasts, the firm can evaluate and deal with the uncertainty associated with such forecasts. Sensitivity analysis and simulation can be applied to pro forma income statements and pro forma balance sheets in the same manner as they were applied to cash budgets. Using sensitivity analysis, different financial statements can be constructed under various possible assumptions about the level of sales and alternative relationships between sales and various income statement and balance sheet items. The analyst can assess the sensitivity of future income statements and balance sheets to these possible scenarios.

Simulation can allow for the use of probability distributions (rather than point estimates) for the level of sales and the relationships between sales and financial statement items. A simulation program can generate a distribution of possible future values for selected pro forma balance sheet and income statement items, such as net income, total assets, and so forth. Each distribution can then be evaluated to determine the probability of that variable's value being outside some acceptable range.

# FORECASTING TECHNIQUES USED IN FINANCIAL PLANNING

The construction of cash budgets and pro forma financial statements frequently requires analysis of the relationships between individual variables (such as between sales and the level of inventories). Numerous techniques are available to help determine the relationship between any two variables, some of which require only common sense, while others require the application of statistical techniques. Analysts often combine subjective evaluation and statistical analysis to develop forecasts of variables instead of relying exclusively on one technique. Forecasting techniques useful for constructing pro forma financial statements are discussed in the next section.

## Time Series Forecasting

Time series forecasting uses historical values of a variable to forecast the variable's future value. For example, if the level of long-term debt of a firm has been $1 million in each of the last five years, one might expect it to be $1 million next year unless there is some reason to believe there will be a change. In this case, the historical trend shows no change.

Of course, not all variables remain unchanged over time. For those variables that show a somewhat consistent level of growth, it may be reasonable to apply the historical growth rate to the current level in order to forecast the future level. Consider the level of accounts receivable for Harmon Enterprises at the end of each of the past six years:

| Observation Number | End of Year | Accounts Receivable |
| --- | --- | --- |
| 1 | 19X3 | $152,625 |
| 2 | 19X4 | 157,730 |
| 3 | 19X5 | 165,079 |
| 4 | 19X6 | 170,682 |
| 5 | 19X7 | 178,950 |
| 6 | 19X8 | 185,692 |

In this example, the growth rate has been fairly consistent, between 3.3 percent and 4.7 percent every year, with a compound annual growth rate of 4 percent. If the firm forecasts the growth rate next year (19X9) based on this information, it might want to assume a 4 percent growth rate. This would result in an estimate of accounts receivable of 104 percent of the 19X8 level ($185,692), or $193,120.

A similar forecast could have been derived by statistically or graphically defining the implied trend line. For example, Figure 7.1 displays the scatter diagram for the accounts receivable of Harmon Enterprises, and a line of best fit has been constructed on the scatter diagram. By identifying the year 19X9 on the horizontal scale, the analyst can draw a vertical line up to the best-fit line, then a horizontal line to the vertical axis. The point of intersection on the vertical axis, at approximately $193,000, becomes the forecasted level of accounts receivable.

**FIGURE 7.1**
Scatter Diagram
Used to Define the
Trend in Accounts
Receivable: Har-
mon Enterprises

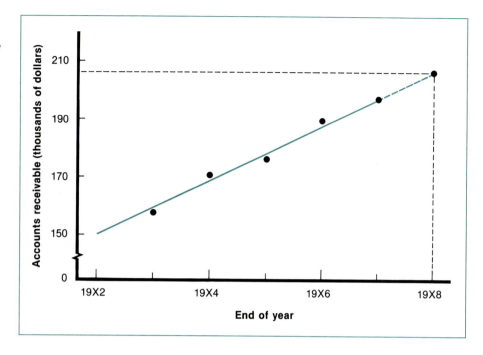

Similarly, time series analysis applied to the accounts receivable data presented previously results in the following regression equation:

$$Y = \$145{,}000 + \$6{,}702.8(X)$$

where $Y$ = dependent variable (accounts receivable)

$X$ = independent variable (observation number)

This regression equation yields an accounts receivable forecast $(Y)$ of $191,920 for 19X9 (Observation 7):

$$\begin{aligned} Y &= \$145{,}000 + \$6{,}702.8(7) \\ &= \$145{,}000 + \$46{,}920 \\ &= \$191{,}920 \end{aligned}$$

## Historical Relationships

Individual variables can be forecasted based on their historical relationships to other variables. For example, as a firm's sales increase, one would expect accounts receivable to increase simultaneously. If the relationship between accounts receivable and sales can be established, the future level of accounts receivable can be estimated based on forecasted sales.

**Ratio Forecasts**  Table 7.7 indicates the levels of accounts receivable and sales for Harmon Enterprises over the past six years (see Columns 2 and 3). Column 4 indicates that accounts receivable represented between 9.9 percent and 10.1 percent of sales in each of the past six years, with a mean of

TABLE 7.7   **Accounts Receivable and Sales (19X2–19X9): Harmon Enterprises**

| (1) | (2) | (3) | (4) = (2)/(3) |
|---|---|---|---|
| Year | Accounts Receivable (AR) | Sales | AR as a Percent of Sales |
| 19X3 | $152,625 | $1,526,250 | 10.0% |
| 19X4 | 157,730 | 1,561,683 | 10.1 |
| 19X5 | 165,079 | 1,667,465 | 9.9 |
| 19X6 | 170,682 | 1,689,921 | 10.1 |
| 19X7 | 178,950 | 1,807,576 | 9.9 |
| 19X8 | 185,692 | 1,856,920 | 10.0 |

10 percent. The stability of this ratio suggests that Harmon Enterprises may wish to forecast accounts receivable for 19X9 based on this relationship. If sales for 19X9 are forecasted to be $1,930,000, then accounts receivable would be forecasted to be 10 percent of $1,930,000, or $193,000. This is similar to the percent-of-sales method used earlier, except that it uses more than one year of historical information to determine the relationship.

**Graphical and Statistical Forecasts**   The same historical sales and accounts receivable information that was presented in Table 7.7 can be used to take a graphical or statistical approach to forecasting accounts receivable. Figure 7.2 presents a scatter diagram of the relationship between sales and accounts receivable for Harmon Enterprises. A line of best fit has also been drawn based on the scatter points. The analyst can now identify the level of forecasted sales on the horizontal scale, draw a vertical line to

**FIGURE 7.2**
**Scatter Diagram Used to Define the Relationship between Sales and Accounts Receivable: Harmon Enterprises**

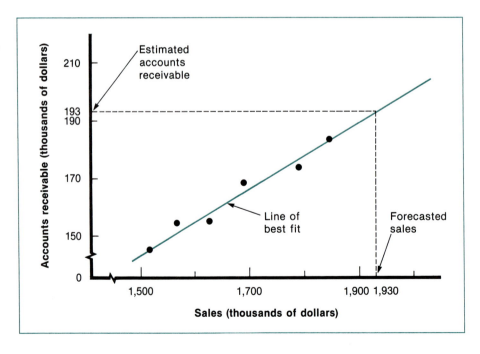

the line of best fit, then draw a horizontal line to the vertical axis. The forecast of accounts receivable can then be read from the vertical scale (approximately $193,000).

Alternatively, the characteristics of the best-fit line can be determined statistically with the help of *regression analysis* similar to the time series regression analysis presented earlier except the independent variable is sales (in this case) instead of time. Using the data presented in Table 7.7, the following regression equation results:

$$Y = \$7,400 + .0956X$$

where $Y$ = dependent variable (accounts receivable)

$X$ = independent variable (sales)

Based on this relationship, if sales are forecasted to be $1,930,000 during the forecasted period, then accounts receivable would be forecasted as follows:

$$
\begin{aligned}
Y &= \$7,400 + .0956X \\
&= \$7,400 + .0956(\$1,930,000) \\
&= \$191,908
\end{aligned}
$$

For greater accuracy, the use of other statistical techniques may be necessary. For example, if the relationship between accounts receivable and sales is not linear, a curvilinear relationship may be defined statistically (see Figure 7.3). Or if accounts receivable are found to be related to more than just one variable (perhaps they are related to both sales *and* the mar-

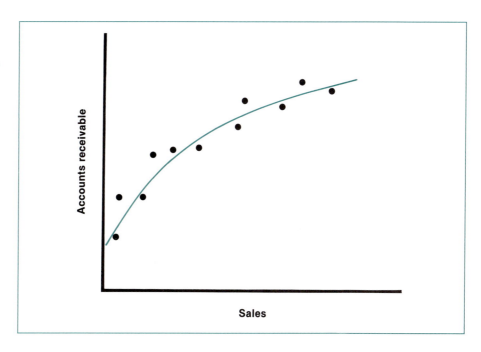

**FIGURE 7.3**
Scatter Diagram Illustrating a Nonlinear Relationship between Accounts Receivable and Sales

---

## FINANCIAL MANAGEMENT IN PRACTICE

### IS FINANCIAL PLANNING REALLY IMPORTANT?

Smaller firms frequently lack the expertise necessary to carry out formal financial planning. Indeed, they may not realize the value of cash budgets and pro forma statements for analyzing potential decisions and controlling operations. Instead, managers of small firms may choose to address problems as they arise.

Larger firms find the financial planning activity to be extremely important. A recent study by Gitman and Maxwell revealed just how important financial planning and budgeting is to a sample of the 1,000 largest U.S. firms.* In that study, financial managers indicated that financial

\* Lawrence J. Gitman and Charles E. Maxwell, "Financial Activities of Major U.S. Firms: Survey and Analysis of Fortune's 1000," *Financial Management* 14 (Winter 1985): 57–65.

planning and budgeting is the most important financial activity in terms of percent of time spent on various activities. Financial planning was considered to be even more important than managing working capital, managing capital expenditures, and raising long-term funds. In terms of the skill levels required for various financial activities, financial planning and budgeting was judged to require more skill than any of the seven other functions listed in the survey (other high-skill-level activities included cash management and long-term financing activities). A final important finding of the study is that the growth prospects for job opportunities for people skilled in financial planning and budgeting are better than for any of the other financial activities listed.

---

ket rate of interest), multiple regression techniques can be used to define the relationship. The multiple regression equation could then be used to forecast accounts receivable. Although forecasting accounts receivable is used as an example here, regression techniques can be used to forecast other variables.

### Subjective Analysis

While the quantitative forecasting techniques described here are valuable tools, each must be used along with subjective judgment. An analyst electing to rely heavily on time series forecasting must consider whether there is any reason to expect that the future trend will differ from the past trend. Similarly, an analyst using historical relationships to make forecasts must consider if there is any reason to believe these relationships are likely to change in the future. For example, an analyst forecasting cost of goods sold may be tempted to rely on its historical relationship with sales. While this relationship may be a good starting point, the analyst must consider any expected changes that may occur in the price of the firm's product, the price of raw materials, or the cost of labor. If a significant change in any of these factors is expected, the historical relationship may need to be adjusted to reflect the expected change.

## SUMMARY

The cash budget is a valuable planning tool that helps a firm estimate its temporary financing needs. By estimating these needs, the firm can make advance arrangements to secure short-term financing. Additionally, the cash budget provides potential lenders with information about the purpose of requested loans as well as the source of revenue that will be used to repay the loans. Because lenders view this type of information favorably, firms providing cash budgets to lenders may increase the probability of their obtaining financing.

The emphasis in Chapter 6 was on analyzing recent income statements and balance sheets. Such analysis can help reveal problems that exist or are beginning to develop. The current chapter discusses how to construct pro forma financial statements, which can be analyzed to identify potential problems before they actually arise. If potential problems can be identified, corrective action can be applied before the problems develop.

All of the financial statements discussed in this chapter can be useful for evaluating the future financial condition of a firm. Various techniques exist for dealing with the uncertainty that is inevitable with financial forecasts.

## KEY TERMS

**Cash budget** A schedule of forecasted cash receipts and cash disbursements used to identify the timing and amount of any excess cash or cash deficiency.

**Percent-of-sales method** A technique for forecasting the value of income statement and balance sheet items. It assumes many items will remain the same percentage of sales in the future as they were in the past.

**Pro forma financial statements** Forecasted financial statements.

**Spontaneous liabilities** Liabilities (such as accounts payable and taxes payable) that increase automatically as sales increase.

**Time series forecasting** Forecasting a variable based on its historical trend.

## QUESTIONS

**Q7-1.** What might cause the actual ending cash balance for a period to be much different from the amount forecasted in a firm's cash budget?

**Q7-2.** What is the purpose of a cash budget?

**Q7-3.** Why might sensitivity analysis be used in cash budgeting?

**Q7-4.** What is the advantage of using simulation in cash budgeting over generating a cash budget from a single point estimate of each input item?

**Q7-5.** How do firms use pro forma income statements?

**Q7-6.** Describe in general terms two techniques for constructing pro forma income statements.

**Q7-7.** How do firms use pro forma balance sheets?

**Q7-8.** If a company's pro forma balance sheet indicates that its total assets exceed its total liabilities next year, what options does the firm have available to it?

**Q7-9.** If a company's pro forma balance sheet indicates less total assets than liabilities next year, what options does the firm have available to it?

**Q7-10.** What information would a pro forma sources and uses of funds statement provide an analyst?

**Q7-11.** How would a policy of lengthening the credit period for a firm's customers affect the firm's cash budget?

**Q7-12.** Should pro forma financial statements be used to make policy decisions, or should policy decisions dictate the numbers in pro forma statements? Explain.

**Q7-13.** Flake, Inc., barely survived a recent recession but since then has increased sales by 30 percent each year. Its controller has created a cash budget covering the next three years, based on the assumption of a 30 percent increase in sales every year. She admits that future sales growth is uncertain but believes this estimate is as good as any, in view of the recent past. Comment on the potential adverse consequences of this assumption.

## SELF-TEST PROBLEMS

Solutions to self-test problems appear on p. S1.

**SP7-1.** Gable Company has developed the following sales projections for the months of January through July 19X9, along with actual sales for December 19X8.

| Month | Sales (Thousands of Dollars) |
| --- | --- |
| December 19X8 | $10,000 |
| January 19X9 | 12,000 |
| February | 10,000 |
| March | 14,000 |
| April | 16,000 |
| May | 16,000 |
| June | 14,000 |
| July | 12,000 |

**a.** Normally, 40 percent of Gable's sales are for cash, while the remaining 60 percent of sales are on credit, payable within one month. Estimate the cash receipts from sales for each of the next six months.

**b.** Use the sales projections provided above along with the following information to estimate Gable's cash disbursements for each of the next six months:

▪ Each month Gable Company purchases materials equal to 50 percent of sales forecasted for the following month. Sixty percent of all purchases are on a cash basis, and 40 percent are paid the following month.

▪ Wages paid each month are estimated to be 10 percent of the subsequent month's sales.

▪ Cash outlays for fixed operating expenses and other expenses are expected to be $1 million per month.
▪ A $4 million capital expenditure is planned for January, and $3 million for February.
▪ Tax payments of $600,000 are anticipated for March and June.

**c.** Use the information you developed in Parts a and b to construct a cash budget for Gable Company. Assume that the firm plans to hold a minimum cash balance of $1 million and that it must pay an annual financing charge of 12 percent (1 percent per month) on any funds borrowed. As of January 1, 19X9, Gable has $1 million in cash and no debt. Interest is paid in the month after the expense is incurred.

**SP7-2.** Given the 19X8 income statement and balance sheet for Mulford Company (Tables A and B on p. 216), use the percent-of-sales method along with the following additional information to develop pro forma financial statements for 19X9:

▪ Sales are forecasted to be $220 million.
▪ Cash dividends are expected to remain unchanged in 19X9.
▪ Gross fixed assets will increase by $33 million in 19X9.
▪ The items marketable securities, notes payable, and other current liabilities will remain unchanged.

**SP7-3.** Based on the pro forma balance sheet developed in SP7-2, determine whether Mulford Company will need additional funds or have excess funds to invest.

## PROBLEMS

**P7-1.** Jordon Company has developed the following sales projections for the months of January through July 19X9 (November's and December's sales are actual):

| Month | Sales (Thousands of Dollars) |
|---|---|
| November 19X8 | $18,000 |
| December 19X8 | 20,000 |
| January 19X9 | 24,000 |
| February | 21,000 |
| March | 18,000 |
| April | 16,000 |
| May | 22,000 |
| June | 24,000 |
| July | 26,000 |

**a.** Jordon has determined that, historically, 30 percent of each month's sales are for cash, 40 percent are paid for in the month following the sale, and 30 percent are paid for in the second month after the sale. Estimate the cash receipts for January through June 19X9.
**b.** Use the sales projections along with the following information to estimate Jordon's cash disbursements for each of the next six months:

▪ Each month Jordon Company purchases materials equal to 40 percent of fore-casted sales for the following month. Fifty percent of all purchases are on a cash basis, and 50 percent are paid the following month.

## TABLE A
### MULFORD COMPANY
### INCOME STATEMENT
### YEAR ENDING DECEMBER 31, 19X8
### (THOUSANDS OF DOLLARS)

| | | |
|---|---:|---:|
| Sales | | $200,000 |
| Less: Cost of goods sold | | 100,000 |
| Less: Depreciation | | 18,000 |
| Gross profit | | 82,000 |
| Less: Operating expenses | | |
| Fixed | 28,000 | |
| Variable | 20,000 | |
| Total | | 48,000 |
| Earnings before interest and taxes | | 34,000 |
| Less: Interest expense | | 4,000 |
| Earnings before taxes | | 30,000 |
| Less: Taxes | | 10,200 |
| Net income | | 19,800 |
| Cash dividend | | 7,000 |
| To retained earnings | | $ 12,800 |

## TABLE B
### MULFORD COMPANY
### BALANCE SHEET
### AS OF DECEMBER 31, 19X8
### (THOUSANDS OF DOLLARS)

*Assets*

| | | |
|---|---:|---:|
| Current assets | | |
| Cash | $ 2,000 | |
| Marketable securities | 1,000 | |
| Accounts receivable | 7,000 | |
| Inventories | 20,000 | |
| Total current assets | | 30,000 |
| Fixed assets | | |
| Gross fixed assets | $150,000 | |
| Less: Accumulated depreciation | 90,000 | |
| Net fixed assets | | 60,000 |
| Total assets | | $90,000 |

*Liabilities and owners' equity*

| | | |
|---|---:|---:|
| Current liabilities | | |
| Accounts payable | $ 3,000 | |
| Notes payable | 1,450 | |
| Taxes payable | 2,550 | |
| Other current liabilities | 8,000 | |
| Total current liabilities | | 15,000 |
| Long-term debt (13.33%) | | 25,000 |
| Owners' equity | | |
| Common stock—par value | $ 4,000 | |
| Additional paid-in capital | 14,000 | |
| Retained earnings | 32,000 | |
| Total owners' equity | | 50,000 |
| Total liabilities and owners' equity | | $90,000 |

- Wages paid each month are estimated to be 15 percent of the subsequent month's sales.
- Cash outlays for fixed operating expenses are expected to be $5 million per month.
- Capital outlays of $3 million are planned for January and March.
- Tax payments of $1 million are anticipated for January and April.
- Quarterly dividends of $2 million will be paid in February and May.

c. Using the information from Parts a and b, develop a cash budget for Jordon Company. Assume that the firm desires to maintain a minimum cash balance of $1.5 million (its current cash balance) and that it incurs an annual financing charge of 12 percent (1 percent per month) on any short-term funds borrowed. Interest is paid in the month after the expense is incurred. Interpret the cash budget.

**P7-2.** Given the 19X8 financial statements for Howard Company (Tables C and D on p. 218) use the percent-of-sales method along with the following information to develop pro forma financial statements for 19X9:

- Sales are forecasted to be $1.6 billion.
- Dividends are expected to increase by 50 percent.
- The average tax rate is 34 percent.
- Gross fixed assets will increase by $100 million in 19X9.
- Marketable securities, notes payable, and the balance sheet item "other current liabilities" will remain unchanged.

What does the pro forma balance sheet suggest to the firm?

**P7-3.** The forecasted sales for January through July 19X9 and actual sales for December 19X8 for Load, Inc., are as follows:

|              Month              |             Sales             |
| ------------------------------- | ----------------------------- |
| December 19X8                   | $200,000                      |
| January 19X9                    | 500,000                       |
| February                        | 400,000                       |
| March                           | 500,000                       |
| April                           | 550,000                       |
| May                             | 600,000                       |
| June                            | 650,000                       |
| July                            | 700,000                       |

Load expects 70 percent of sales to be on a cash basis, while 30 percent are expected to be on a credit basis, payable within one month. It expects its material expenses each month to be 60 percent of the following month's sales. Eighty percent of its purchases are paid in cash, while 20 percent are made on credit, payable in one month. Wages are estimated to be 30 percent of the following month's sales. The following cash outlays are also anticipated:

- Capital expenditures of $100,000 in May.
- Dividend payments of $20,000 in February and May.
- Tax payment of $40,000 in April.

Assume that Load, Inc., currently has $50,000 in cash (its desired level of cash) and no short-term debt. Monthly interest rate on borrowed funds is 1 percent and is paid in the month after the expense has been incurred. Develop a cash budget for Load, Inc. What is the maximum line of credit Load expects to need for 19X9?

## TABLE C
### HOWARD COMPANY
### INCOME STATEMENT
### YEAR ENDING DECEMBER 31, 19X8
### (MILLIONS OF DOLLARS)

| | | |
|---|---:|---:|
| Sales | | $1,500 |
| Less: Cost of goods sold | | 600 |
| Less: Depreciation | | 100 |
| Gross profit | | 800 |
| Less: Operating expenses | | |
|   Fixed | 300 | |
|   Variable | 300 | |
|     Total | | 600 |
| Earnings before interest and taxes | | 200 |
| Less: Interest expense | | 50 |
| Earnings before taxes | | 150 |
| Less: Taxes | | 51 |
| Net income | | 99 |
| Cash dividends | | 30 |
| To retained earnings | | $   69 |

## TABLE D
### HOWARD COMPANY
### BALANCE SHEET
### AS OF DECEMBER 31, 19X8
### (MILLIONS OF DOLLARS)

*Assets*

| | | |
|---|---:|---:|
| Current assets | | |
|   Cash | $  100 | |
|   Marketable securities | 100 | |
|   Accounts receivable | 400 | |
|   Inventories | 400 | |
|     Total current assets | | 1,000 |
| Fixed assets | | |
|   Gross fixed assets | $1,000 | |
|   Less: Accumulated depreciation | 600 | |
|     Net fixed assets | | 400 |
| Total assets | | $1,400 |

*Liabilities and owners' equity*

| | | |
|---|---:|---:|
| Current liabilities | | |
|   Accounts payable | $  200 | |
|   Notes payable | 200 | |
|   Taxes payable | 13 | |
|   Other current liabilities | 87 | |
|     Total current liabilities | | 500 |
| Long-term debt | | 100 |
| Owners' equity | | |
|   Common stock—par value | $  40 | |
|   Additional paid-in capital | 120 | |
|   Retained earnings | 640 | |
|     Total owners' equity | | 800 |
| Total liabilities and owners' equity | | $1,400 |

**P7-4.** The accounts receivable balances for Noonan Company in recent years are indicated in the following table:

| End of Year | Accounts Receivable | Sales |
|---|---|---|
| 19X1 | $ 98,000 | $1,000,000 |
| 19X2 | 104,000 | 1,060,000 |
| 19X3 | 111,000 | 1,110,000 |
| 19X4 | 115,500 | 1,117,000 |
| 19X5 | 132,000 | 1,350,000 |
| 19X6 | 127,900 | 1,280,000 |
| 19X7 | 121,330 | 1,200,000 |

**a.** Analyze the historical growth rates of accounts receivable, and use this to forecast accounts receivable for 19X8.
**b.** Assume that the sales forecast for 19X8 is $1.4 million and for 19X9 is $1.5 million. Use the average percentage of accounts receivable relative to sales to forecast accounts receivable in 19X8 and 19X9.

**P7-5.** The 19X8 financial statements for Atkins Enterprises are indicated in Tables E and F on p. 220. Use the percent-of-sales method to develop a 19X9 pro forma income statement and balance sheet for Atkins, assuming forecasted sales are $30 million. Also assume operating expenses increase directly with sales, dividends increase 8 percent, and marketable securities remains unchanged. Depreciation expense, interest expense, gross fixed assets, and other current liabilities change directly with sales.

**P7-6.** The levels of sales and inventories for Priest Brothers, Inc., for the period 19X2 through 19X8 are indicated in the following table.

| Year-End | Sales | Inventories |
|---|---|---|
| 19X2 | $75,000,000 | $ 9,000,000 |
| 19X3 | 82,500,000 | 9,075,000 |
| 19X4 | 78,375,000 | 10,189,000 |
| 19X5 | 84,645,000 | 10,157,000 |
| 19X6 | 82,106,000 | 9,032,000 |
| 19X7 | 90,316,000 | 11,741,000 |
| 19X8 | 85,800,000 | 10,296,000 |

**a.** Analyze the growth rate of inventories, and use this to forecast the level of inventories for 19X9.
**b.** Graph the relationship between sales and inventories for Priest Brothers. Use this graph to estimate the level of inventories based on forecasted sales of $100 million.
**c.** Assume the following time series regression parameters are determined where inventories are the dependent variable, and time, the independent variable, is measured in terms of observation numbers (19X2 is Observation 1, 19X3 is Observation 2, and so on, where $a = 8,775,286$ and $b = 287,964$). Forecast the level of inventories for 19X9.
**d.** Assume the results of regressing inventories (the dependent variable) against sales (the independent variable) are $a = -2,279,215$ and $b = .1476$. Forecast the level of inventories if sales are $95 million.

**TABLE E**
ATKINS ENTERPRISES
INCOME STATEMENT
YEAR ENDING DECEMBER 31, 19X8
(THOUSANDS OF DOLLARS)

| | |
|---|---:|
| Net sales | $27,500 |
| Less: Cost of goods sold | 20,000 |
| Less: Depreciation | 2,750 |
| Gross profit | 4,750 |
| Less: Operating expenses | 1,650 |
| Earnings before interest and taxes | 3,100 |
| Less: Interest expense | 400 |
| Earnings before taxes | 2,700 |
| Less: Taxes | 918 |
| Net income | 1,782 |
| Dividends paid on common stock | 740 |
| To retained earnings | $ 1,042 |

**TABLE F**
ATKINS ENTERPRISES
BALANCE SHEET
AS OF DECEMBER 31, 19X8
(THOUSANDS OF DOLLARS)

*Assets*

| | | |
|---|---:|---:|
| Current assets | | |
| Cash | $ 500 | |
| Marketable securities | 750 | |
| Accounts receivable | 900 | |
| Inventory | 3,100 | |
| Total current assets | | 5,250 |
| Fixed assets | | |
| Gross fixed assets | $20,000 | |
| Less: Accumulated depreciation | 5,000 | |
| Net fixed assets | | 15,000 |
| Total assets | | $20,250 |

*Liabilities and owners' equity*

| | | |
|---|---:|---:|
| Current liabilities | | |
| Accounts payable | $ 800 | |
| Notes payable | 220 | |
| Taxes payable | 230 | |
| Other current liabilities | 250 | |
| Total current liabilities | | 1,500 |
| Long-term debt | | 2,750 |
| Owners' equity | | |
| Common stock—par value | $ 5,000 | |
| Additional paid-in capital | 5,000 | |
| Retained earnings | 6,000 | |
| Total owners' equity | | 16,000 |
| Total liabilities and owners' equity | | $20,250 |

## COMPUTER-ASSISTED PROBLEMS

**CP7-1.** **Sensitivity of Cash Receipts Schedule to Percent of Cash Sales**  Calculate the expected cash receipts for Problem 7-1 of the Problems section, using the computer package. Next, determine the cash receipts of Jordon Company if Jordon's cash receipts pattern changes so that 60 percent of its sales are for cash, with the balance received in the following month. What if 80 percent of its sales are for cash? Explain how the cash receipts schedule is affected by the adjustment in the percent of cash sales.

**CP7-2.** **Sensitivity of Cash Disbursements Schedule to Percent of Cash Purchases**  Calculate the expected cash disbursements in Problem 7-1 of the Problems section. If the disbursement pattern changes so that 70 percent of these purchases are made with cash, how would the cash disbursements schedule be affected? What if cash purchases were 85 percent of total purchases?

**CP7-3.** **Sensitivity of Net Cash Gain to Percent of Cash Sales and Purchases**  Assume that Jordon Company prefers to generate cash receipts as quickly as possible and prefers to slow disbursements as much as possible. Using the possible scenarios in the two previous problems, determine the net cash gain (or loss) per month under the most optimistic scenario. Also determine the net cash gain (or loss) per month under the most pessimistic scenario. Is there much of a difference under these two extreme scenarios? Explain how the firm can use this information.

**CP7-4.** **Sensitivity of Cash Needs to Percent of Cash Sales and Purchases**  Assume that Jordon Company plans to establish a line of credit that is adequate to cover any necessary financing over the next six months. Develop a cash budget for the optimistic scenario and for the pessimistic scenario as described in the previous problem. From the cash budgets, determine the appropriate line of credit for each scenario.

**CP7-5.** **Sensitivity of Pro Forma Statements to Sales Estimates**

**a.** Construct the pro forma financial statements as required in Problem 7-2 of the Problems section using the computer package. Howard Company realizes there is a possibility that sales could be as high as $1,700,000 or as low as $1,500,000 next year. Create new pro forma income statements and balance sheets if these forecasts are realized. Explain the differences in the amount of additional financing needed for these two scenarios.

**b.** Using the original estimate for sales, explain how earnings after taxes would be affected under each of the following conditions:

**1.** Cost of goods sold is 50 percent of sales
**2.** Fixed operating expenses are $375,000
**3.** The combination of the two conditions described in 1 and 2

**CP7-6.** **Forecasting Accounts Receivable**  Use time series regression analysis to identify the relationship between accounts receivable and the observation number of the data in Problem 7-4 of the Problems section. Based on the relationship identified, develop a forecast of accounts receivable in 19X8 and 19X9.

**CP7-7.** **Forecasting Accounts Receivable**  Use regression analysis to identify the relationship between accounts receivable and sales in Problem 7-6 of the Problems section. Assume that sales are projected to be $1.4 million in 19X8 and $1.5 million in 19X9. Based on your analysis, develop a forecast of accounts receivable in 19X8 and 19X9. Do you think these forecasts will be more accurate than the forecasts developed in the previous problem? Why?

## REFERENCES

Campbell, David R., James M. Johnson, and Leonard M. Savoie. "Cash Flow, Liquidity & Financial Flexibility." *Financial Executive* 52 (August 1984): 14–17.

Chambers, John C., Satinder K. Mullick, and Donald D. Smith. "How to Choose the Right Forecasting Technique." *Harvard Business Review* 49 (July–August 1971): 45–74.

Francis, Jack Clark, and Dexter R. Rowell. "A Simultaneous Equation Model of the Firm for Financial Analysis and Planning." *Financial Management* 7 (Spring 1978): 29–44.

Gentry, James A., and Stephen A. Pyhrr. "Simulating an EPS Growth Model." *Financial Management* 2 (Summer 1973): 63–75.

Hunt, Pearson. "Funds Position: Keystone in Financial Planning." *Harvard Business Review* 53 (May–June 1975): 106–15.

Maier, Steven F., and James H. Vander Weide. "A Practical Approach to Short-Run Financial Planning." *Financial Management* 7 (Winter 1978): 10–16.

Weston, J. Fred. "Forecasting Financial Requirements." *Accounting Review* 33 (July 1958): 427–40.

# CONSTRUCTING PRO FORMA FINANCIAL STATEMENTS FROM CASH BUDGETS

The percent of sales method is useful for constructing pro forma financial statements when the future relationships between sales and certain key financial variables are expected to reflect past relationships. A more complex method of constructing pro forma statements involves using the cash flows identified by the cash budget to forecast key financial variables. This method tends to provide more finely tuned estimates of financial variables at the expense of simplicity. An important prerequisite for using this method is the construction of a cash budget covering the entire period of concern.

## PRO FORMA INCOME STATEMENT

Constructing a pro forma income statement requires a forecast of each income statement item for the desired planning period. Much of this information can come directly from the cash budget, but some cannot. To illustrate, the information used to develop the cash budget for Neal Corporation for the period January through June 19X9 as shown in Tables 7.1 and 7.2, is used here to develop a pro forma income statement covering that same six-month period (see Table 7A.1). Recall that Table 7.1 provides a monthly sales forecast for the period January through June 19X9. The sales forecast for the six-month period is $77 million, the sum of the monthly sales during that period. This becomes the sales figure on the pro forma income statement (Table 7A.1).

The forecasted cost of goods sold would include materials and labor used in the production process. Recall that materials expense is forecasted to be 40 percent of the following month's sales, so that materials purchased in December are part of the cost of goods sold in January. Therefore, total materials cost for the six-month period would be the sum of the materials purchased in December 19X8 through May 19X9 ($30.8 million). The cost of goods sold would also include labor costs associated with production, which amounts to $15.4 million over the six-month period (December through May). The cost of goods sold therefore totals $46.2 million ($30.8 million + $15.4 million). Since depreciation is not included in the

**TABLE 7A.1   Neal Corporation Pro Forma Income Statement Six Months Ending June 30, 1979 (Thousands of Dollars)**

|  | Estimate | Source of the Estimates |
|---|---|---|
| Sales | $77,000 | Cash budget (Table 7.1) |
| Less: Cost of goods sold (excluding depreciation) | 46,200 | Cash budget (includes material purchases from line 2 and wages from line 5 for December 19X8–May 19X9) |
| Less: Depreciation | 5,000 | Given |
| Gross profit | 25,800 | |
| Less: Operating expense | 16,000 | Cash budget (Table 7.2) |
| Earnings before interest and taxes | 9,800 | |
| Less: Interest expense | 1,173 | Cash budget (includes interest on both long-term and short-term debt, including interest on June's short-term debt although it would not be paid until July)[a] |
| Earnings before taxes | 8,627 | |
| Less: Taxes (34%) | 2,933 | Tax rate is given here |
| Net income | 5,694 | |
| Cash dividend | 2,640 | Cash budget (Table 7.2) |
| To retained earnings | $3,054 | |

[a] Interest on long-term debt from Table 7.2 ($1,000,000) plus interest on short-term debt from Table 7.3 ($22,000 + $35,000 + $40,000 + $43,000 + $33,000).

cash budget, the firm must estimate depreciation over the six-month period using (1) depreciation schedules on existing fixed assets and (2) expected depreciation on assets to be acquired in the coming months. For our purposes here, this figure is given as $5 million. Subtracting the cost of goods sold from sales results in gross profit of $25.8 million.

Fixed operating expenses and other expenses can be summed from the cash budget ($16 million). When these total operating expenses are subtracted from gross profits, the result is estimated earnings before interest and taxes of $9.8 million. Over the period of concern, interest on short-term debt is about $.173 million which includes interest on June's short-term debt although it would not be paid until July. Recall from Table 7.2 that interest on long-term debt is $1 million. Total interest expense is therefore $1.173 million. When total interest expense is subtracted from earnings before interest and taxes, the result is earnings before taxes of $8.627 million. The dollar amount of tax on the pro forma income statement cannot be derived from the cash budget. Recall that the cash budget reflects cash flows while the income statement reflects revenues and expenses on an accrual basis. Therefore, the tax *payment* made in March would reflect the firm's tax liability for October through December of 19X8 while the income statement should reflect taxes due on firm profits earned during the period January through June. Based on a 34 percent average tax rate, Neal Corporation would expect to owe $2.933 million in taxes for the January-through-June period, so that net income is estimated to be $5.694 million. The dividend paid by the firm must be decided by the board of directors. In this example, the cash budget reflects the expected dividend payment for the January-through-June period ($2.64 million). The estimated contribution to retained earnings over the six-month period is therefore $3.054 million.

## PRO FORMA BALANCE SHEET

The pro forma balance sheet can also be constructed with the help of the firm's cash budget. This has been done for Neal Corporation using its cash budget (including Tables 7.2 and 7.3) and the balance sheet for the earlier period; Neal's pro forma balance sheet appears as the second column of numbers in Table 7A.2 (the first column of numbers is the actual balance sheet for December 31, 19X8).

Beginning with current assets, cash as of June 30, 19X9, can be taken from the cash budget in Table 7.3. Line 5 of the cash budget indicates that the firm wants to hold a minimum of $1 million in cash. The cash budget also indicates that in June, the firm has no excess cash. Therefore, Neal Corporation would expect to have $1 million in cash as of June 30, 19X9. The value of marketable securities would change from the earlier period if the firm sold securities to obtain needed cash rather than borrowing the funds. It is assumed here that the firm borrows all needed funds and holds its marketable securities for an emergency situation. Therefore the value of marketable securities is expected to remain at $500,000 as of June 30, 19X9.

Recall that 70 percent of each month's sales are credit sales with cash to be received in the following month. Given forecasted sales of $17 million in June, the accounts receivable outstanding at the end of June would be $11.9 million (70% × $17 million). Inventory at the end of the period can be forecasted based on the following relationship: Inventory at the start of the period ($I_s$) plus materials purchased ($m$) plus wages paid ($w$) minus cost of goods sold during the period ($CGS$) results in the ending inventory ($I_e$). For Neal Corporation,

$$
\begin{aligned}
I_e &= I_s + m + w - CGS \\
&= \$12{,}000{,}000 + \$34{,}000{,}000 + \$17{,}000{,}000 - \$46{,}200{,}000 \\
&= \$16{,}800{,}000
\end{aligned}
$$

Summing the value of all the current assets results in $30.2 million.

With regard to long-term assets, the forecast of gross fixed assets is based on the corporate plans for expansion or replacement of existing plant and equipment. This information can also be taken from the cash budget. According to the schedule of anticipated cash disbursements (in Table 7.2), capital expenditures of $2.5 million are planned during the period. Therefore, gross fixed assets will increase to $65.5 million by June 19X9 from 19X8's level of $63 million. The level of depreciation during the period was earlier assumed to be $5 million, resulting in accumulated depreciation in 19X9 of $35 million. Given the projections of gross fixed assets and depreciation, net fixed assets are forecasted to be $30.5 million. Total assets for Neal Corporation at year end 19X9 are forecasted to be $60.7 million.

Current liabilities can also be derived from the cash budget as follows.

**TABLE 7A.2   Neal Corporation Pro Forma Balance Sheet as of June 30, 19X9 (Thousands of Dollars)**

| | Actual Figures 12/31/X8 | Pro Forma Balance Sheet 12/31/X9 | Source of the Estimate |
|---|---|---|---|
| **Assets** | | | |
| Current assets | | | |
| Cash | $ 1,000 | $ 1,000 | Cash budget: Minimum level of cash |
| Marketable securities | 500 | 500 | Given: No change |
| Accounts receivable | 4,900 | 11,900 | Cash budget: 70% of June sales |
| Inventories | 12,000 | 16,800 | Cash budget: $I_s + m + w - CGS$ |
| Total current assets | 18,400 | 30,200 | |
| Fixed assets | | | |
| Gross fixed assets | 63,000 | 65,500 | Cash budget: $2,500 of capital expenditures |
| Less: Accumulated depreciation | 30,000 | 35,000 | Given: $5,000 depreciation during the period |
| Net fixed assets | 33,000 | 30,500 | |
| Total assets | $51,400 | $60,700 | |
| **Liabilities and owners' equity** | | | |
| Current liabilities | | | |
| Accounts payable | $ 1,920 | $ 3,840 | Cash budget: 60% of June purchases |
| Notes payable | 0 | 3,320 | Cash budget: Short-term financing in June |
| Interest payable | 833 | 866 | Accrued interest on June's short-term debt ($33) and long-term debt ($833) |
| Taxes payable | 1,185 | 2,158 | Taxes payable as of December 31, plus taxes from the pro forma income statement, minus taxes paid from the cash budget |
| Other current liabilities | 4,147 | 4,147 | Given: No change |
| Total current liabilities | 8,085 | 14,331 | |
| Long-term debt (13.33%) | 15,000 | 15,000 | Cash budget: No change |
| Owners' equity | | | |
| Common stock—par value | 2,000 | 2,000 | Cash budget: No change |
| Additional paid-in capital | 8,000 | 8,000 | Cash budget: No change |
| Retained earnings | 18,315 | 21,369 | Expected additions to retained earnings from the pro forma income statement are added to retained earnings at the end of the previous period |
| Total owners' equity | 28,315 | 31,369 | |
| Total liabilities and owners' equity | $51,400 | $60,700 | |

Recall that Neal Corporation pays cash for 40 percent of its purchases but delays paying for the remaining 60 percent until the following month. Since material purchases are forecasted to be $6.4 million in June, the accounts payable balance as of June 30 is estimated to be $3.84 million (60% × $6.4 million).

Notes payable on the balance sheet indicate the level of bank loans while the cash budget indicates the level of short-term borrowing necessary for any given month. Therefore, the $3.32 million of short-term financing necessary at the end of June (indicated on the cash budget) can be recorded as notes payable on the pro forma balance sheet. Interest payable includes accrued interest on both short-term and long-term debt. Recall that interest is paid on long-term debt as of February 1 and August 1. As of June 30, Neal Corporation will owe accrued interest on long-term debt for five months (February 1 through June 30). At 13.33 percent (the interest rate on the long-term debt), this amounts to accrued interest of $833,125 (13.33 percent interest for five months on $15 million). In addition, Neal Corporation will owe interest on the $3.32 million of short-term debt outstanding as of June according to the cash budget. When the interest on this amount ($33,200) is added to the interest on long-term debt, the total interest payable is $866,325.

Taxes payable can be calculated using information presented on the cash budget, pro forma income statement, and the balance sheet from the prior period. The balance sheet as of December 31, 19X8, indicates that taxes payable totaled $1,185,000. Adding the expected tax liability for the forecasted period from the pro forma income statement ($2,933,000) brings total taxes payable up to $4,118,000. However, that amount is reduced by the $1.96 million of taxes paid during March and June (see Table 7.2). As a result, taxes payable total $2,158,000 as of the end of June 30, 19X9.

Since there is no indication that other current liabilities will change, these liability balances are assumed to remain unchanged from the end of December 19X8. This results in total current liabilities of $14,331,000.

There was also no indication from the cash budget that long-term debt, common stock, or paid in capital will change during the six-month period of concern. Therefore, these items will remain unchanged on the pro forma balance sheet. Additions to retained earnings can be taken from the pro forma income statement for the period ending June 30, 19X9. The addition to retained earnings is estimated to be $3,054,000, which, when added to the current level of $18,315,000, provides forecasted retained earnings of $21,369,000.

Owners' equity now totals $31,369,000, and total liabilities and owners' equity equal $60,700,000, the same as total assets. Constructing a pro forma balance sheet using the cash budget and the pro forma income statement results in a balance sheet that balances. Using the completed pro forma balance sheet in Table 7A.2 and the pro forma income statement constructed earlier (Table 7A.1), the management of Neal Corporation can now analyze the expected financial condition of the firm and determine if any changes in operations or financing are necessary.

# CHAPTER 8

# BREAKEVEN ANALYSIS AND OPERATING LEVERAGE

## BREAKEVEN ANALYSIS IN PERSPECTIVE

In 1985 when Eric Kobren quit his $70,000 per year job as a marketing director for Fidelity Investments (a mutual fund group), he began his own small business with an investment of $12,000. His product is a monthly investment newsletter that advises mutual fund investors which of Fidelity's many mutual funds to purchase. Is it possible to start a profitable business with an investment of only $12,000? Mr. Kobren thought so because the fixed costs of publishing a newsletter can be kept very low by paying an outside organization to typeset each issue and a printer to produce the final product (the latter expense is partially variable in that it is more expensive to print more copies). The first ad he placed at a cost of $950 brought in sufficient revenue to pay for the ad and for much of the fixed costs necessary to produce and distribute the newsletter.

By keeping fixed costs very low, the breakeven point for the newsletter was very low. That is, relatively few subscribers (at $95 per year) were necessary before all fixed costs were covered and the variable costs for such things as advertising and distribution were also covered. By mid 1987, the newsletter (called *Insight*) had 20,000 subscribers and annual revenues of $1.9 million dollars. Although his fixed costs have since increased as a result of the acquisition of computers and the necessary software to edit and simulate the typesetting process, total production costs remain low at $200,000 per year. Mr. Kobren forecasts 1987 profits for his firm at $500,000.

How can an entrepreneur estimate the level of sales necessary to cover both the fixed and variable costs of a new business? How can the concept of breakeven analysis be applied in large corporations? What factors need to be considered when deciding on the acquisition of assets that will increase fixed costs? These and other questions are addressed in this chapter.

*Source: Wall Street Journal, August 20, 1987.*

The two main topics of this chapter, breakeven analysis and operating leverage, are closely related to each other. Breakeven analysis is a tool of financial analysis and planning in that the **breakeven point** indicates the level of sales necessary for the firm to cover its operating expenses. Firms use this information to plan future operations, and investors use it to help evaluate firm risk.

**Operating leverage** is the extent to which a firm uses fixed operating costs (as opposed to variable operating costs) in its operations. A change in operating leverage can affect the firm's breakeven point as well as other aspects of both risk and return; and, as shown in Chapter 4, the risk-return trade-off influences the value of the firm's common stock and therefore shareholder wealth.

## BREAKEVEN ANALYSIS

The top portion of an income statement indicates the revenues realized and expenses incurred during a given period. Generally, the expense items include the cost of goods sold (raw materials and labor), depreciation, sales expense, and administrative expense. What remains after subtracting these expenses from revenue is **operating profit,** or *earnings before interest and taxes (EBIT)*. Table 8.1 illustrates the top portion of a *pro forma income statement* for a sample firm, Cleaver Industries. This represents the income statement that is expected to result from the sale of a proposed new product.

To facilitate our discussion of breakeven analysis and operating leverage, it is useful to reclassify all expenses into groups based on whether the costs are fixed or variable. **Fixed operating costs** are those that do not change with fluctuations in the level of production and sales. Instead, they are a function of time. For example, rent and depreciation are expenses that firms incur regardless of the number of units sold. Of course, these fixed costs must rise in the long run to support a growing level of sales (the firm will eventually need to acquire more plant and equipment to support increased production). For simplification, the assumption is made here that current capacity is adequate for all levels of sales under consideration. Therefore, fixed operating costs do not change.

Unlike fixed costs, **total variable operating costs** increase directly with sales and are unrelated to the passage of time. For example, raw materials and labor are variable costs because firms will incur those costs directly

TABLE 8.1   **Top Portion of Income Statement: Cleaver Industries**

| | |
|---|---:|
| Sales (110,000 units at $4 per unit) | $440,000 |
| Less: Cost of goods sold | 330,000 |
| Gross profit | 110,000 |
| Less: Depreciation | 20,000 |
| Less: Sales expense | 10,000 |
| Less: Administrative expense | 10,000 |
| Earnings before interest and taxes | $ 70,000 |

**TABLE 8.2  Top Portion of Income Statement Showing Fixed and Variable Costs: Cleaver Industries**

| | |
|---|---:|
| Sales (110,000 units at $4 per unit) | $440,000 |
| Less: Fixed operating costs | 40,000 |
| Less: Variable operating costs | 330,000 |
| Earnings before interest and taxes | $ 70,000 |

for each unit produced and sold. Total variable costs for a firm can be found by multiplying the number of units produced and sold times variable cost per unit.

In practice, some costs are difficult to classify as either fixed or variable since they have some characteristics of each. These costs are called *semi-variable*. For example, some firms pay their salespeople a fixed salary plus bonuses for reaching certain sales goals. The salary portion represents a fixed cost, but the bonuses represent variable costs. For simplification, semi-variable costs are ignored in the remainder of this discussion.

Table 8.2 illustrates the top portion of the income statement for Cleaver Industries after all operating costs have been reclassified as either fixed or variable (sales expense is assumed to be a fixed cost in this example). For a firm with one product, the sales figure that appears in both Tables 8.1 and 8.2 can be found by multiplying the price per unit sold times the number of units sold. Theoretically, the firm can establish any price for its product that it wishes. However, competitive forces make price per unit difficult for management to control. For now, assume the price per unit is constant and dictated by competitive forces. Throughout most of this chapter, the simplifying assumption is made that firms sell one product. This assumption is dropped later.

## Determining the Breakeven Point

Cleaver Industries is considering the production and sale of a new product that it says will reduce gas consumption in automobiles. The firm estimates the following costs and revenue associated with producing the product.[1]

$$\text{price per unit } (p) = \$4.00$$
$$\text{variable cost per unit } (v) = \$3.00$$
$$\text{fixed costs } (F) = \$40,000$$

Every unit that is sold for $4.00 brings in enough revenue to cover the cost of producing that unit ($3.00) and provides an additional $1.00 to help offset fixed costs. This difference between the price per unit and variable cost per unit is called the **contribution margin.** It derives its name from the

---

1. Although variable cost per unit is given here, it can also be calculated from Table 8.1 by dividing total variable costs by the number of units sold.

fact that this is the amount of money from the sale of each unit that will contribute toward covering the firm's fixed operating costs. After all fixed costs have been covered, the contribution margin contributes to EBIT. Since the contribution margin is $1.00 for Cleaver Industries, the firm must sell 40,000 units in order to cover all fixed costs in addition to all variable costs. The breakeven quantity of sales ($Q_b$) is therefore 40,000 units. That is, after subtracting the cost of producing each unit from the price of each unit ($p - v$), the difference is divided into fixed costs ($F$) to see how many units must be sold to cover fixed costs. This can be translated into the general formula:

$$Q_b = \frac{F}{p - v} \qquad \text{(8.1)}$$

This same equation could have been derived algebraically by solving for the quantity of units that equates total revenue and total costs such that EBIT equals zero.

$$\text{total revenue} = \text{total costs}$$
$$pQ = F + vQ$$

solving for $Q$

$$pQ - vQ = F$$
$$Q(p - v) = F$$
$$Q_b = \frac{F}{p - v}$$

Using Equation 8.1 to determine the breakeven point for Cleaver Industries results in

$$Q_b = \frac{\$40,000}{\$4 - \$3}$$
$$Q_b = 40,000 \text{ units}$$

The previous example is analyzed graphically in Figure 8.1. The revenue line starts at the origin of the graph, indicating that revenue is zero when sales are zero. This line slopes upward to the right indicating total revenue ($pQ$) on the vertical scale at each possible level of production and sales on the horizontal scale. For example, at 20,000 units of sales, total revenue is $80,000 (20,000 units × $4.00/unit). Fixed costs are displayed graphically as a horizontal line, indicating that these costs remain constant at $40,000 regardless of the level of sales. The total-variable-cost line indicates the amount of total variable costs ($vQ$) at each possible level of production and sales. For example, at 40,000 units of production and sales, total variable costs are $120,000. The total-cost line indicates fixed costs plus total variable costs for each level of production and sales. At zero units of production and sales, total variable costs are zero, fixed costs are

FIGURE 8.1

**Breakeven Graph:
Cleaver Industries**

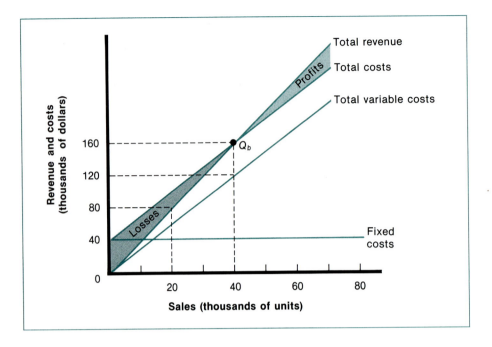

$40,000, and total costs are $40,000. At 40,000 units, total variable costs are $120,000, and fixed costs are $40,000, for total costs of $160,000. The point of intersection of the total-cost line with the revenue line at point $Q_b$ indicates the only point where total costs and total revenue are equal. The point on the horizontal scale directly below this breakeven point indicates the number of units the firm must sell in order to have zero EBIT. At 40,000 units of sales, total costs and total revenues are both equal to $160,000. There is no operating profit or loss, then, at 40,000 units, the breakeven point.

As indicated earlier, profit and loss in the context of breakeven analysis refers to operating profits and losses, or earnings before interest and taxes (EBIT). To calculate EBIT at any level of sales, the estimated total costs ($F$ plus $vQ$) should be subtracted from estimated total revenue ($pQ$). Table 8.3 illustrates the calculation of EBIT for Cleaver Industries at sales of 20,000 units, 40,000 units, and 60,000 units.

While Figure 8.1 graphically illustrates production and sales at 40,000 units (the breakeven point) for Cleaver Industries, Figure 8.2 illustrates the

**TABLE 8.3   Determination of EBIT at Various Levels of Sales: Cleaver Industries**

|  | Level of Sales | | |
|---|---|---|---|
|  | **20,000 Units** | **40,000 Units** | **60,000 Units** |
| Sales revenue ($pQ$) | $80,000 | $160,000 | $240,000 |
| Less: Fixed costs ($F$) | 40,000 | 40,000 | 40,000 |
| Less: Variable costs ($vQ$) | 60,000 | 120,000 | 180,000 |
| EBIT | ($20,000) | 0 | $ 20,000 |

FIGURE 8.2
Breakeven Graph:
Cleaver Industries

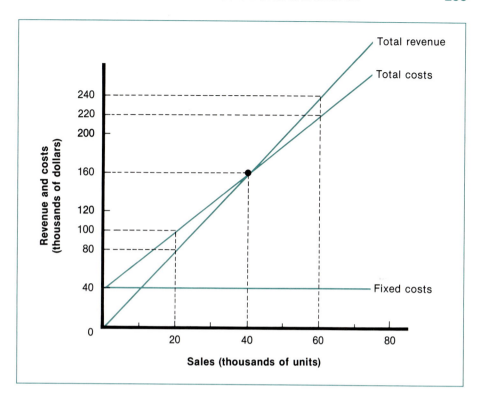

other two levels of sales for which **EBIT** was calculated in Table 8.3 (20,000 and 60,000 units). A vertical line drawn at 20,000 units of sales intersects the revenue line at $80,000 and the total-cost line at $100,000. The result is a $20,000 loss. Conversely, a vertical line drawn at 60,000 units of sales intersects the revenue line at $240,000 and the total-cost line at $220,000, resulting in operating profit of $20,000.

## How the Breakeven Point Is Used

There are a number of uses of breakeven analysis. First, for firms that are planning the production and sale of a new product, the breakeven point will help estimate how much of the product must be sold in order to avoid incurring operating losses on the new product. When combined with a sales forecast, knowledge of this breakeven point can help firms decide whether or not to initiate production of the product. For example, if the management of Cleaver Industries forecasts sales of at least 60,000 units every year in the future, it is worthwhile to continue planning for the production and sale of the new product, since EBIT would be $20,000 at sales of 60,000 units. Indeed, long-term production and sales anywhere to the right of the breakeven point (40,000 units in Figure 8.2) may suggest further consideration of the project is warranted. If, however, the forecast of long-term production and sales is anywhere to the left of the breakeven point, then perhaps the firm should abandon the idea of producing the new product.

Generally, we would expect a firm that is undertaking the production and sale of a new product to experience relatively low sales in the early years (to the left of the breakeven point), with sales rising in later years (to the right of the breakeven point). Losses in early years may be acceptable if the promise of high future profits exists.

Two related uses of breakeven analysis involve (1) planning a new business and (2) assessing the risk of a firm by potential creditors and equity investors. Comparing the breakeven point to forecasted sales provides useful information both to the entrepreneur who is deciding whether to start a new business and to the potential creditors or equity investors who need to evaluate the risk of investment in the firm.

Another use of breakeven analysis is to assess the effect on the firm of altering fixed costs or variable costs. A change in either can alter the firm's breakeven point, so the firm should determine what that breakeven point is prior to making a decision that would alter either or both variables.

### The Cash Breakeven Point (Planning for Losses)

As indicated earlier, firms initiating the production and sale of a new product may not be deterred by the prospect of operating to the left of the profit breakeven point temporarily. This is particularly true if the firm is able to generate sufficient cash from sales to cover its required cash expenditures. That is, even if the firm is operating to the left of the profit breakeven point, there may still be enough cash flowing into the firm from sales to pay the firm's bills. The reason is that depreciation (and perhaps other noncash expenses) is part of total costs but does not involve the outflow of funds from the firm. Therefore, the firm may be able to generate enough cash revenue to pay its expenses even if its EBIT is negative. However, if sales are too far to the left of the profit breakeven point, required cash expenditures will exceed cash receipts.

The minimum level of sales necessary to generate sufficient cash revenue for the firm to pay its required expenses is known as the **cash breakeven point.** In order to find the cash breakeven point ($CQ_b$), one can subtract the firm's noncash expenses ($NE$), from fixed costs (this is where most noncash expenses appear) before dividing by the difference between price and variable cost per unit. Adjusting Equation 8.1 to reflect this results in

$$CQ_b = \frac{F - NE}{p - v} \qquad \text{(8.2)}$$

Applying Equation 8.2 to Cleaver Industries, which had $20,000 worth of depreciation (see Table 8.1), the cash breakeven point becomes

$$CQ_b = \frac{\$40,000 - \$20,000}{\$4 - \$3}$$

$$= 20,000 \text{ units}$$

The cash breakeven point is illustrated graphically in Figure 8.3. The decrease in fixed costs that results from the removal of noncash expen-

**FIGURE 8.3**
**Cash Breakeven Analysis: Cleaver Industries**

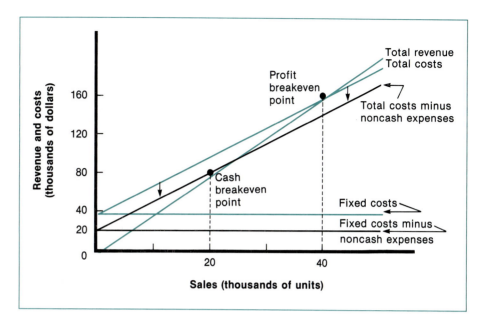

ditures shifts the total-cost line downward to a lower point of intersection with the vertical axis. The intersection of the total-cost line and revenue line is now lower and farther to the left of its original position. The result is a cash breakeven point to the left of the profit breakeven point.

What does a cash breakeven point of 20,000 units and a profit breakeven point of 40,000 units tell us? Between zero units and 20,000 units of sales, the firm expects to not only realize an operating loss but also have insufficient revenue to pay all required cash expenses. If sales are expected to be in this range temporarily, the firm must plan for funding the cash deficiency. If sales are expected to be in this range in the long run, the firm should decide against producing the product.

Between 20,000 units and 40,000 units of sales, the firm would receive enough cash from producing and selling the product to cover required cash expenditures, but it would incur operating losses. The firm can operate within this range of sales at least temporarily without an additional source of cash. However, the revenue within this range is inadequate to cover the depreciation of fixed assets. Therefore, although the firm has sufficient cash to pay its bills if it operates within this range, eventually it must move to the right of the profit breakeven point or it may be unable to replace its plant and equipment when it has been used up.

## Complicating Factors about Breakeven Analysis

**Semi-variable Costs**  As indicated earlier, some costs incurred by the firms are not totally fixed, nor are they totally variable. Such costs can be very difficult to incorporate into breakeven analysis. Although methods of dealing with semi-variable costs in breakeven analysis exist, they are beyond the scope of this text.

**Expense Items with Long-Term Benefits**    Some costs, like those for advertising and research and development, are expensed in the year incurred but may benefit the firm over a number of years. If these items are included in a breakeven analysis that covers only a one-year period, the breakeven point will be higher than it should be. The financial analyst must be aware of this and either adjust the cost figures or evaluate the firm's breakeven point over multiple periods.

**Multiproduct Applications**    Frequently, a firm wishes to determine its breakeven point when a number of different products are produced and fixed costs are shared. When this is the case, it may be difficult or even impossible to allocate the fixed costs between the different products. The greater the number of different products sharing the same costs, the more difficult the problem is.

One simple solution to the multiproduct problem is to group all the products together and find the firm's breakeven point in terms of the dollar volume of sales. Essentially this approach establishes the percent of each sales dollar that remains after variable costs have been covered. This value is the contribution margin on a percentage basis, and it is divided into total fixed costs to find the dollar breakeven point ($D$). The dollar breakeven point ($D$) can now be defined as

$$D = \frac{F}{1 - \dfrac{TV}{S}} \tag{8.3}$$

where   $S$ = total sales in dollars
       $TV$ = total variable operating costs needed to support sales level $S$

The ratio of $TV$ to $S$ represents variable costs as a percent of total sales revenue. Subtracting this percentage (in decimal form) from 1 results in the percent of each sales dollar that is available to pay fixed costs, after variable costs have been covered. Dividing this amount into fixed costs results in the dollar level of sales required for the firm to cover all of its operating costs.

Consider the example of Cleaver Industries once again. Suppose the firm produces and sells twenty different items. Using the information that appears in Table 8.2, the firm's dollar breakeven point can be determined as follows:

$$D = \frac{\$40,000}{1 - \dfrac{\$330,000}{\$440,000}}$$

$$= \$160,000$$

This indicates that Cleaver Industries must generate $160,000 of sales in order to avoid operating losses. Since Cleaver Industries expects sales of $440,000, it should operate well above the breakeven point.

Several additional observations about dollar breakeven analysis are appropriate here. First, this analysis can be particularly useful when his-

**FIGURE 8.4**
**Fixed Cost Line
over a Wide Range
of Output**

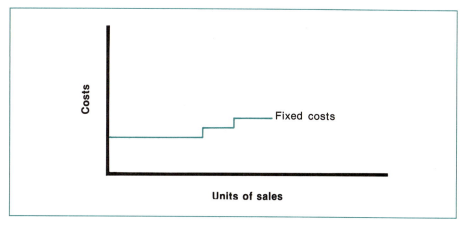

torical information is available. That is, a firm that has incurred operating losses can identify the level of sales, fixed costs, and total variable costs on its income statement, and it can use this information to estimate the level of sales necessary in order to break even. Second, dollar breakeven analysis assumes that as total sales rise, the percentage increase in the sales of all of the firm's products is identical (or they all have identical variable costs per unit). Third, while Equation 8.3 is presented here as a tool for use by multi-product firms, it will work equally well in single-product applications.

**Nonlinear Cost and Revenue Functions**    When fixed costs, variable cost per unit, and sales price per unit remain unchanged over all levels of production and sales, they are represented graphically by straight lines. This was true in the Cleaver Industries example, as indicated in Figure 8.1. While the assumption of linear cost and revenue functions may be valid over a narrow range of alternative levels of sales, they may not be linear over a wide range of sales. Normally this situation would be of concern when firms are conducting long-range planning, since sales can vary greatly over long periods of time.

Firms wishing to increase the number of units they produce must eventually acquire additional plant and equipment, which increases fixed costs. Figure 8.4 shows what the fixed-cost line might look like for a firm considering a wide range of possible sales levels. Notice the fixed-cost line moves up in steps as new plant and equipment are acquired. Due to the severe complications these increases can have on breakeven analysis, they will not be given further consideration in this discussion.

The variable-cost line may be curved over a broad range of possible sales levels, particularly when fixed costs are held constant. For example, Cleaver Industries may expect variable cost per unit to change when there are significant changes in the level of production. An example of this type of relationship is presented in Table 8.4. This information, when plotted on a graph and smoothed, appears as the curved variable-cost line in Figure 8.5. Notice that the line slopes upward but at a decreasing rate as moderate levels of sales are attained. This indicates a decrease in variable cost per unit as economies of scale are achieved. However, as production continues to increase, the total-variable-cost line increases at an increasing

**TABLE 8.4**  **Variable Cost per Unit over a Wide Range of Sales: Cleaver Industries**

| Sales (Thousands of Units) | Variable Cost per Unit | Sales (Thousands of Units) | Variable Cost per Unit |
|---|---|---|---|
| 0–75 | $3.30 | 450–525 | $3.30 |
| 75–150 | 3.20 | 525–600 | 3.40 |
| 150–225 | 3.10 | 600–675 | 3.50 |
| 300–375 | 3.10 | 675–750 | 3.60 |
| 375–450 | 3.20 | 750–825 | 3.70 |
| | | 825–900 | 3.80 |

rate (that is, variable cost per unit increases). This increase occurs because, as the firm approaches full capacity, labor efficiency decreases. Labor inefficiency can result from the payment of overtime wages to production employees, or from having too many workers for the amount of plant and equipment available. The total-cost line reflects the slope and shape of the variable-cost line, and it intersects the vertical axis at the level of fixed costs. In this example, the level of fixed costs is assumed to be constant over the entire range of sales.

The revenue line may also be curved, indicating that as the number of units sold increases, total revenues increase at a decreasing rate. The reason for this is that firms generally must reduce the price per unit of their product to significantly increase the number of units they sell. This nonlinear revenue line is also illustrated in Figure 8.5.

**FIGURE 8.5**
**Nonlinear Operating Breakeven Analysis**

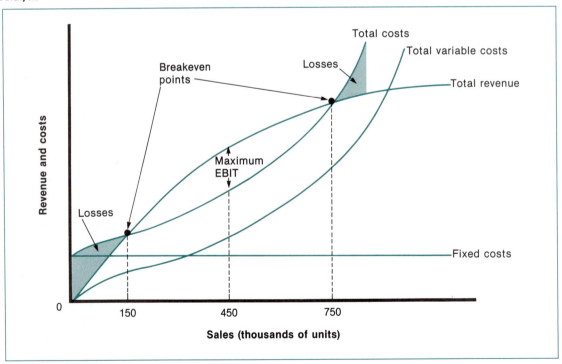

As a result of the nonlinear revenue and total-cost functions, Cleaver Industries now has two operating breakeven points (that is, two points where the total cost line and revenue line intersect). The firm should attempt to produce and sell to the right of the first breakeven point at 150,000 units and to the left of the second breakeven point at 750,000 units. (This can be determined from Figure 8.5, but it cannot be determined algebraically here because insufficient data have been provided.) The optimal level of production and sales is at approximately 450,000 units. This is where the vertical distance between the total-cost line and revenue line is the greatest, resulting in the greatest profit level. Although not demonstrated here, there are methods available to determine the optimal level of production and sales when nonlinear revenue and cost functions are used.

## OPERATING LEVERAGE

Thus far, the measurement and interpretation of the operating breakeven point have been considered. Now we will consider ways of changing the position of the breakeven point (either for the firm or for some new product) by changing the variables that determine it. Although management would normally prefer to decrease the firm's breakeven point, it may consider increasing it instead because of the increased profit potential that would result. More specifically, firms frequently purchase fixed assets that increase the firm's fixed costs in order to reduce variable costs. This trade-off of increased fixed costs for decreased variable costs results in operating leverage. Before analyzing the impact of operating leverage on the firm, let us consider some additional background on the variables that affect the breakeven point and operating leverage.

### Changes in Input Variables

As discussed earlier, the variables that determine the breakeven point are price per unit ($p$), variable cost per unit ($v$) and total fixed costs ($F$). A change in any one of these variables can affect the breakeven point.

**Changes in Price per Unit**   If the firm could increase its selling price per unit without affecting its level of sales, the operating breakeven point would decline. Recall that for Cleaver Industries, $F = \$40,000$, $p = \$4.00$, $v = \$3.00$, and the operating breakeven point is 40,000 units. If the price per unit were increased to $4.60, the breakeven point would decrease to 25,000 units:

$$Q_b = \frac{F}{p - v}$$

$$= \frac{\$40,000}{\$4.60 - \$3.00}$$

$$= 25,000 \text{ units}$$

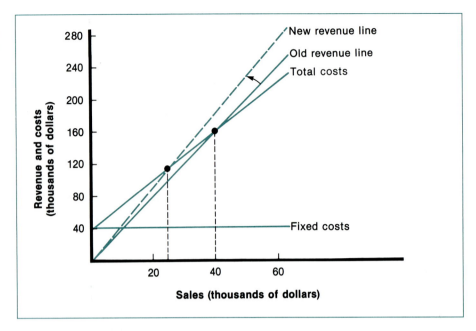

This is also illustrated in Figure 8.6. Notice that the increase in price per unit from $4.00 to $4.60 results in an increase in the slope of the revenue line. The new revenue line (the dashed line), now intersects the total-cost line farther to the left of the original point of intersection.

The situation described here would be desirable for any firm. Not only would it reduce the operating breakeven point, but it would also increase EBIT (or decrease the loss) at each level of sales. Unfortunately, most firms operate in a competitive environment, making it difficult to raise prices without adversely affecting sales.

**Changes in Fixed Costs**   Management frequently makes decisions that affect the amount of fixed costs. Sometimes a manufacturing firm will purchase replacement equipment. For example, a shoe manufacturer may need to replace a worn-out machine with a new machine of the same type. This new equipment represents an additional investment in fixed assets that increases the firm's depreciation (a fixed cost).

Referring again to Cleaver Industries ($F = \$40{,}000$, $p = \$4.00$, and $v = \$3.00$), consider the impact on the firm's operating breakeven point if fixed costs increase from $40,000 to $100,000. This increase in fixed costs increases the breakeven point from 40,000 units to 100,000 units. The new breakeven point is determined as follows:

$$Q_b = \frac{\$100{,}000}{\$4.00 - \$3.00}$$

$$= 100{,}000 \text{ units}$$

This is portrayed graphically in Figure 8.7a by an upward shift in the fixed-cost line and a corresponding shift upward in the total-cost line. The point

**FIGURE 8.7**
Changes in
Operating Break-
even Point Result-
ing from Changes
in Fixed and Vari-
able Costs

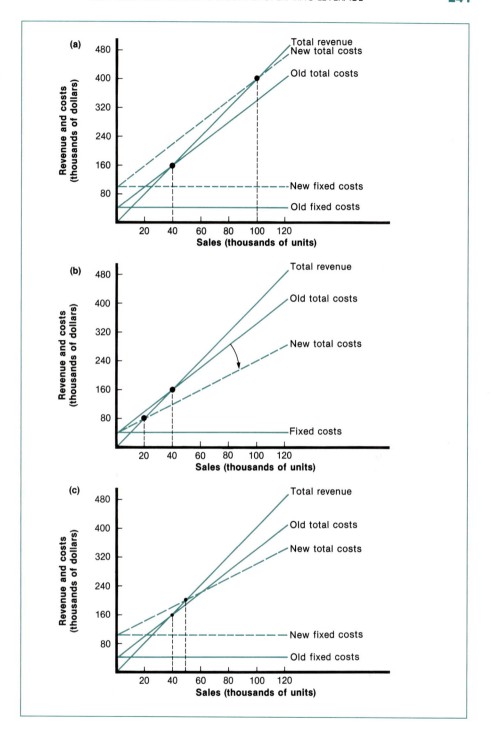

of intersection of the revenue line and total-cost line is now to the right of the previous point of intersection (the breakeven point is higher).

**Changes in Variable Cost per Unit**    Sometimes management is able to reduce variable cost per unit by finding a cheaper supply of raw materials, by reducing labor costs, or by some other means. Decreases in variable cost per unit decrease the firm's breakeven point (other things being equal). Assume Cleaver Industries is able to decrease variable cost per unit from $3.00 to $2.00 while everything else remains unchanged. In this case, the breakeven point would decrease from 40,000 units to 20,000 units:

$$Q_b = \frac{\$40,000}{\$4.00 - \$2.00}$$

$$= 20,000 \text{ units}$$

This change is portrayed graphically in Figure 8.7b as a change in the slope of the total-cost line. Since variable cost per unit has decreased, total variable costs, and therefore total costs, are lower at each level of production and sales. The revenue and total-cost lines now intersect at a point to the left of the previous point of intersection (the breakeven point is lower).

**Simultaneous Changes in Fixed and Variable Costs**    Firms frequently purchase fixed assets that simultaneously increase fixed costs and reduce variable costs. For example, some equipment permits individuals to produce more units of the firm's product than they could without the equipment. This reduces the firm's wage expense (a variable cost). When fixed costs increase while variable cost per unit decreases, the forces that affect the breakeven point tend to work against each other.

Assume that Cleaver Industries has purchased new fixed assets that increase fixed costs from $40,000 to $100,000 but reduce variable cost per unit from $3.00 to $2.00 per unit. As a result, the breakeven point would increase from 40,000 units to 50,000 units as indicated below and in Figure 8.7c:

$$Q_b = \frac{\$100,000}{\$4.00 - \$2.00}$$

$$= 50,000 \text{ units}$$

Management might be willing to accept this increase in the breakeven point in order to increase potential returns. Although fixed costs are higher, once they have been covered by unit sales, additional sales contribute more to profits than previously since the contribution margin (the difference between price and variable cost per unit) is greater. This relationship represents increased *operating leverage* and is illustrated in Figure 8.8. (This figure is similar to Figure 8.7c except that several additional lines have been added.)

Point A on Figure 8.8 represents the operating breakeven point for

**FIGURE 8.8**
**An Illustration of Operating Leverage**

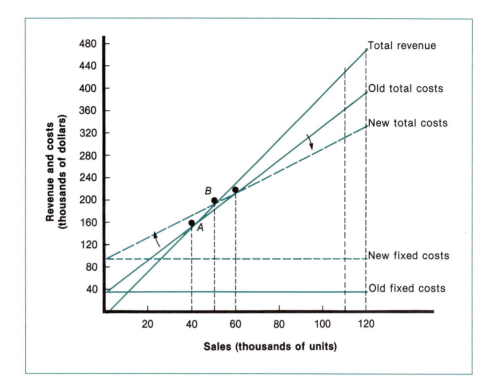

Cleaver Industries before additional operating leverage is added. The additional operating leverage is evidenced by a shift upward in the fixed-cost line, a lower slope on the total-cost line, and a higher vertical intercept for the total-cost line. Point B represents the breakeven point after the addition of more operating leverage. Notice that the new breakeven point is to the right of the old one. Several observations can now be made regarding the level of EBIT (operating profit) given different amounts of operating leverage.

1. At sales of 40,000 units on Figure 8.8, EBIT is zero when the lower operating leverage is used. Given the higher amount of operating leverage, however, the firm would incur losses (the vertical distance between the revenue line and the new total-cost line) at 40,000 units of sales.

2. At sales of 50,000 units, and assuming the smaller amount of operating leverage is used, the firm has a small amount of EBIT (the vertical distance between the revenue line and the old total-cost line). If the greater amount of operating leverage is used, the firm just breaks even.

3. At all levels of sales to the left of 60,000 units (the point of intersection of the old and new total-cost lines), the lower amount of operating leverage results in higher EBIT. Only at 60,000 units of sales is the level of EBIT identical for the two different levels of operating leverage.

4. At all points to the right of 60,000 units, EBIT is higher if the higher level of operating leverage is employed, since the vertical distance between the revenue line and the new total-cost line is always greater.

## Measuring the Degree of Operating Leverage

From the previous discussion (and Figure 8.8) it is apparent that the vertical distance between the revenue line and the total-cost line is greater at all levels of sales to the right of 60,000 units when greater operating leverage is employed. The farther to the right of 60,000 units the firm operates, the greater the difference is in EBIT for the two levels of operating leverage, since the two total-cost lines move farther apart.

Operating leverage can be viewed as the quickness with which the total-cost line diverges from the revenue line (how rapidly the profit wedge opens up). For example, assume that Cleaver Industries had sales last year of 110,000 units (see Figure 8.8) and expects next year's sales to be 120,000 units. Given this expected 9.1 percent increase in sales, what would be the percentage increase in EBIT if the lower amount of operating leverage is employed? Table 8.5 illustrates the calculation of EBIT for Cleaver Industries at 110,000 units ($70,000) and 120,000 units ($80,000). The percentage increase in the EBIT going from $70,000 to $80,000 is determined as follows:

$$\text{percentage change in EBIT} = \frac{\$80,000 - \$70,000}{\$70,000}$$

$$= 14.3\%$$

Therefore, a 9.1 percent increase in sales results in a 14.3 percent increase in EBIT. The *degree of operating leverage (DOL)* measures this relationship as follows:

$$DOL = \frac{\text{percentage change in EBIT}}{\text{percentage change in sales}} \qquad (8.4)$$

In our example, the degree of operating leverage is

$$DOL = \frac{14.3\%}{9.1\%} = 1.57$$

A degree of operating leverage of 1.57 indicates that for every 1 percent change in sales, EBIT changes by 1.57 percent. Since Cleaver Industries

**TABLE 8.5   Calculation of EBIT at Two Levels of Sales: Cleaver Industries**

|  | Level of Sales | |
|---|---|---|
|  | **110,000 Units** | **120,000 Units** |
| Sales revenue ($pQ$) | $440,000 | $480,000 |
| Less: Fixed costs ($F$) | 40,000 | 40,000 |
| Less: Variable costs ($vQ$) | 330,000 | 360,000 |
| EBIT | $ 70,000 | $ 80,000 |

expects sales to increase by 9.1 percent, then EBIT should increase by 1.57 times that amount, or 14.3 percent. Operating leverage is symmetrical, so that if sales decrease by 9.1 percent, EBIT also decreases by 14.3 percent.

What about the degree of operating leverage for the more highly lever-aged situation considered earlier (fixed costs of $100,000 and variable cost per unit of $2.00)? Going from 110,000 units to 120,000 units of sales, the degree of operating leverage is 1.84 (calculate the degree of operating leverage using Equation 8.4 to make certain the procedure is understood).

## The Special Case of Linear Revenue and Total-Cost Lines

Equation 8.4 can be used to find the degree of operating leverage whenever the percentage change in sales and the corresponding percentage change in EBIT is given or can be calculated. This includes those situations where the total revenue and total-cost lines are curved. When they are linear, the following equation can be used to find the degree of operating leverage beginning at some level of sales $(Q)$:[2]

$$DOL \text{ at point } Q = \frac{Q(p - v)}{Q(p - v) - F} \tag{8.5}$$

The degree of operating leverage for Cleaver Industries can be found using Equation 8.5. In the following calculation, the lower level of operating leverage is assumed.

---

2. Equation 8.5 is derived from Equation 8.4 as follows. The value of $Q(p - v) - F$ represents EBIT. Since the variables, $p$, $v$, and $F$ are constant, the change in EBIT can be stated as $\Delta Q(p - v)$, where the symbol $\Delta$ indicates change. Therefore, the numerator of Equation 8.4 can be restated as

$$\frac{\Delta Q(p - v)}{Q(p - v) - F}$$

and the denominator can be stated as

$$\frac{\Delta Q}{Q}$$

It follows that

$$DOL = \frac{\dfrac{\Delta Q(p - v)}{Q(p - v) - F}}{\dfrac{\Delta Q}{Q}}$$

$$= \left(\frac{\Delta Q(p - v)}{Q(p - v) - F}\right)\left(\frac{Q}{\Delta Q}\right)$$

$$= \frac{Q(p - v)}{Q(p - v) - F}$$

$$DOL \text{ at } 110,000 \text{ units} = \frac{110,000 \, (\$4 - \$3)}{110,000 \, (\$4 - \$3) - \$40,000}$$

$$= 1.57$$

Notice that future sales do not need to be estimated when using this equation. Since the revenue and total-cost lines are linear, the degree of operating leverage is the same between 110,000 units and any other level of sales, in either direction. If, however, the base level of sales changes, the degree of operating leverage also changes as a result of an increase in the denominators of the growth-rate calculations. For example, the degree of operating leverage for Cleaver Industries using 100,000 units of sales as the base point results in *DOL* of 1.67.

## Relationship between Breakeven Analysis and Operating Leverage

Breakeven analysis and operating leverage are very closely related. When management makes a decision on the amount and type of machinery to use in the production process, it is influencing both fixed costs and variable costs, both of which influence the breakeven point. Additionally, the same factors influence the sensitivity of EBIT to changes in the level of sales, which is operating leverage.

## Determining the Level of Operating Leverage

Several factors influence the decision on the appropriate level of operating leverage.

**The Nature of the Production Process**    Some firms produce products that require skilled craftsmanship, such as in the furniture manufacturing industry. In such labor-intensive industries, expensive plant and equipment may not be necessary. Consequently, variable cost per unit may be fairly high and fixed costs fairly low. Other firms operate in industries where extensive investment in plant and equipment is required, such as in the electric power generating industry. In these capital-intensive industries, variable cost per unit may be low while fixed costs are high.

**Intensity of Competition**    Different industries are characterized by different levels of competition. When the competition is intense, the competitors may be forced to update their production facilities frequently to keep variable costs (and total costs) low. If they cannot or do not modernize their productive facilities, they may suffer the consequences of reduced profit margins and/or reduced sales.

**Management's Attitude toward Risk and Return**    Regardless of how labor- or capital-intensive the industry in which a firm operates, management can generally influence the relationship between fixed costs and variable costs. How management elects to influence that relationship depends,

## FINANCIAL MANAGEMENT IN PRACTICE

### OPERATING LEVERAGE IN THE HOTEL INDUSTRY

Different industries have different characteristics of production and sales that affect their operating leverage. The hotel industry is an interesting example because of the high fixed costs necessary to operate a hotel and because of the volatility of demand for the industry's product. The high fixed costs are in the form of hotel rooms, and the volatility of sales results from the cyclical nature of sales, plus the fluctuations that result from changes in seasons, economic activity, and other factors.

The maximum amount of revenues for a hotel is constrained by the number of rooms available. The more rooms constructed, the higher the potential revenue is during peak demand periods. However, the more rooms constructed, the larger the investment required by the hotel, and many of those rooms may be unoccupied during slack periods. Some hotels attempt to improve the efficiency of asset use by reducing their prices during slack periods. This may attract more business for some hotels at the expense of other hotels. If, however, all hotels in an area reduce their prices, total demand may increase. A hotel may benefit from renting its rooms at a price below its total costs, provided revenue covers all of the variable costs plus part of the fixed costs. By covering part of fixed costs, the firm will lose less money on each room than if the rooms remain unoccupied.

Another strategy followed by some hotels is to simply shut down during slack periods. This action reduces the variable costs such as the labor and utilities associated with operating the hotel, but, of course, it cannot reduce the fixed cost of investment in the facilities.

---

in part, on its willingness to accept additional increments of risk for additional increments of expected return.

There are three components of additional risk assumed by a firm when it incorporates more operating leverage into its operations. First, a higher breakeven point occurs, which increases the risk of incurring operating losses. Second, greater volatility of EBIT results, which is perceived by investors as more risky, leading them to increase their required rates of return on the firm's securities and thus lowering the securities' prices. Third, at lower levels of sales, the level of the firm's operating losses will be magnified.

These increased risks must be weighed against the higher potential returns. The likelihood of realizing higher returns can be analyzed by evaluating sales forecasts.

**Level of Firm Risk Contributed by Other Factors**   Before deciding on the level of operating leverage, firms must consider the level of risk contributed by other factors. One major factor is sales volatility, which varies greatly depending on the industry in which the firm operates. For example, the demand for automobiles is more volatile than for many other products. Accordingly, automobile manufacturers may be unwilling to assume additional risks related to high levels of operating leverage.

A second major source of risk is a firm's *financial leverage,* which involves the use of fixed-cost sources of financing (debt and preferred stock) in place of common equity financing. When a firm issues large amounts of debt and preferred stock to raise funds, it has a high degree of financial leverage. This increases the volatility of the firm's *earnings per share (EPS)*. That is, the firm's **EPS** is more sensitive to changes in EBIT when the firm has more financial leverage. Since common stockholders view this increased volatility as being more risky, a firm with a high degree of financial leverage may want to offset the risk associated with that financial leverage by maintaining a low level of operating leverage. Conversely, a firm with a low degree of financial leverage may be more willing to assume a high degree of operating leverage. Thus, in determining the level of operating leverage, management should consider the degree of financial leverage. Chapter 13 elaborates on the concept of financial leverage, and its relationship to operating leverage.

## SUMMARY

The analysis of a firm's breakeven point and operating leverage are interrelated since both concepts involve the interaction of revenue, fixed operating costs, and variable operating costs. The breakeven point is the level of sales required for the firm to cover its fixed and variable operating costs. The breakeven point can be determined on the basis of unit sales or dollar volume of sales. The cash breakeven point indicates the level of sales necessary for the firm to generate sufficient revenue to cover its cash expenses for the period.

Breakeven analysis can be used to help an individual or group of individuals decide whether or not to start a business. It can also be used by existing firms that are considering whether to add a new product line, or whether to incur new fixed costs in order to reduce variable costs. Potential creditors and equity investors may use breakeven analysis to help decide whether to make an investment in the firm.

Factors such as the existence of semi-variable costs, expenses that provide long-term benefits, the sale of multiple products that share fixed costs, and nonlinear cost or revenue functions can complicate breakeven analysis. However, techniques are available that take these factors into consideration.

Operating leverage refers to the use of fixed operating costs in place of variable operating costs. When more operating leverage is added to the firm, EBIT becomes more sensitive to changes in the level of sales. If a firm increases its operating leverage, the changes in its fixed and variable costs also increase the breakeven point. In deciding on the appropriate level of operating leverage, management must consider the impact of the leverage on the firm's risk and return.

## KEY TERMS

**Breakeven point** The level of sales that generates EBIT of zero for the firm. It can be stated in terms of units of sales or dollar volume of sales.
**Cash breakeven point** The level of sales that generates sufficient revenue for the firm to pay its cash expenses.

**Contribution margin** The dollar amount remaining from the sale of each unit after variable costs have been covered. The remaining amount is available to cover fixed costs. When fixed costs have been covered, the contribution margin increases EBIT dollar for dollar. The contribution margin can also be stated as the percent of each sales dollar remaining after variable costs have been covered.

**Fixed operating costs** Costs incurred by the firm that do not change as the level of production and sales change.

**Operating leverage** The extent to which a firm uses fixed costs. Higher operating leverage results in greater sensitivity of EBIT to changes in sales.

**Operating profit** The operating earnings remaining after subtracting all operating expenses from operating revenue. It is equal to *earnings before interest and taxes (EBIT)* when the firm has no income or expenses from nonoperating sources.

**Total variable operating costs** Costs incurred by the firm that vary directly with the level of production and sales.

## EQUATIONS

**Equation 8.1**    **Breakeven Quantity**

$$Q_b = \frac{F}{(p - v)}$$    **(p. 231)**

where $Q_b$ = breakeven quantity of sales
$F$ = fixed operating costs
$p$ = selling price per unit
$v$ = variable operating cost per unit

This equation is used to find the level of sales (in units) necessary for the firm to generate sufficient revenue to cover all operating expenses. At this level of production and sales, EBIT is zero.

**Equation 8.2**    **Cash Breakeven Quantity**

$$CQ_b = \frac{F - NE}{(p - v)}$$    **(p. 234)**

where $CQ_b$ = cash breakeven quantity
$NE$ = noncash operating expenses

The cash breakeven quantity indicates the quantity of sales necessary for the firm to generate sufficient revenues to cover its cash expenses.

**Equation 8.3**    **Dollar Breakeven Point**

$$D = \frac{F}{1 - \dfrac{TV}{S}}$$    **(p. 236)**

where $D$ = dollar breakeven point
$TV$ = total variable costs
$S$ = sales revenue

When firms produce and sell numerous products, it can be difficult to determine the breakeven quantity for each product separately. Equation 8.3 helps determine the total dollar volume of sales of all products necessary for the firm to cover its operating expenses.

**Equation 8.4**    **Degree of Operating Leverage: General Formula**

$$DOL = \frac{\text{percentage change in EBIT}}{\text{percentage change in sales}}$$    **(p. 244)**

where $DOL$ = degree of operating leverage.

This equation provides the analyst with a measure of the sensitivity of a firm's operating profit (EBIT) to changes in the level of sales. This sensitivity is affected by fixed costs, variable costs, and selling price per unit.

**Equation 8.5**    **Degree of Operating Leverage: Given Linear Functions**

$$DOL = \frac{Q(p - v)}{Q(p - v) - F}$$    **(p. 245)**

When the revenue, fixed costs, and variable costs functions are linear, Equation 8.5 can be used to determine the degree of operating leverage. When one or more of these functions is nonlinear, Equation 8.4 must be used to find the degree of operating leverage between two specific points.

## QUESTIONS

**Q8-1.** How would you classify the following expenses for a manufacturing firm? (variable costs, fixed costs, or semi-variable costs).

**a.** Secretarial salaries
**b.** Electricity
**c.** Depreciation
**d.** Telephone bills
**e.** Cost of raw materials

**Q8-2.** Describe the relationship between the operating breakeven point and the earnings per share for a firm.

**Q8-3.** What is the difference between the contribution margin for a firm operating below the breakeven point and for one operating above the breakeven point?

**Q8-4.** Under what circumstances would the profit breakeven point be greater than the cash breakeven point, and vice versa?

**Q8-5.** What types of decisions can breakeven analysis help management make?

**Q8-6.** How do expense items with long-term benefits (such as advertising) affect breakeven analysis?

**Q8-7.** Why might a firm's fixed costs, revenue, or variable costs not be linear functions?

**Q8-8.** Describe what typically happens to variable cost per unit, fixed costs, and the breakeven point when a firm purchases new labor-saving equipment.

**Q8-9.** What factors do managers consider when determining the appropriate level of operating leverage?

**Q8-10.** What are the major sources of uncertainty involved in estimating a firm's EBIT?

## SELF-TEST PROBLEMS

Solutions to self-test problems appear on p. S1.

**SP8-1.** Abbott, Inc., produces one model of television set and sells it for $250. Abbott's variable cost per unit is $90, and its fixed costs are $1,600,000.

**a.** What is the breakeven point in units for Abbott, Inc.?
**b.** Draw a graph of the breakeven point.
**c.** If Abbott has annual depreciation expense of $600,000, what is its cash breakeven point?
**d.** Add a graph of the cash breakeven point to the graph you drew in Part b.
**e.** Last year Abbott had sales of 8,000 units. What was its EBIT?

**SP8-2.** Abel Industries had sales of 112,500 units last year and EBIT of $1,450,000. Next year it expects to have sales of 120,000 units and EBIT of $1,700,000. What is Abel's degree of operating leverage?

**SP8-3.** Abrams Enterprises produces and sells orange crates to citrus growers for $3.20 each. In the most recent year, Abrams sold 400,000 units and incurred $160,000 in fixed costs. Variable cost per unit was $2.40.

**a.** What is the degree of operating leverage for Abrams Enterprises at 400,000 units?
**b.** Abrams is considering purchasing an automated wood-cutting machine that would reduce variable cost per unit to $2.25 while increasing fixed costs to $209,000. Calculate the degree of operating leverage at 400,000 units if the machine is purchased.
**c.** Calculate the breakeven point if the machine is not purchased and if it is purchased.
**d.** Calculate EBIT at sales of 225,000 units if the machine is not purchased and if it is purchased.

## PROBLEMS

**P8-1.** Baggett, Inc., produces and sells just one product for $9,500 per unit. Baggett's variable cost per unit is $4,000, and fixed costs are $5,500,000.

**a.** What is Baggett's profit breakeven point in units?
**b.** If Baggett's noncash expenses (depreciation) are $2,000,000, what is its cash breakeven point?
**c.** Graph both breakeven points on the same graph.

**P8-2.** Caldwell Corporation produces and sells fourteen different wood products. In the year just completed, Caldwell incurred $520,000 of fixed costs and $1,300,000 of variable costs. Total sales last year were $1,729,000.

**a.** What is Caldwell Corporation's dollar breakeven point based on last year's revenues and costs?
**b.** What was Caldwell's EBIT last year?

**P8-3.** Consolidated Drake Corporation had EBIT of $63 million last year on sales of 52 million units. Consolidated expects to generate EBIT next year of $79 million on sales of 57 million units. What is the firm's degree of operating leverage?

**P8-4.** Bob and Ray Eastman are considering manufacturing and selling a car muffler that fits all small cars. They estimate that they can sell up to 100,000 mufflers per year with fixed costs of $300,000. Variable cost per unit is estimated to be $12 per muffler. They expect to price the mufflers at $18 each.

**a.** What would be the degree of operating leverage and EBIT of the business if it sells 60,000 mufflers?
**b.** Calculate and graph the firm's breakeven point.
**c.** Bob and Ray are considering starting the business with less automated equipment than was originally planned. If they do so, the firm's fixed costs will decline to $200,000 per year, while variable cost per unit will increase to $13. What will be the firm's degree of operating leverage and EBIT at 60,000 mufflers?
**d.** If Bob and Ray use less operating leverage as indicated in Part c, what would be the firm's breakeven point?

**P8-5.** Furguson & Fay, Inc., is a local firm that is considering adding a new product (replacement fanbelts) to its existing product line. This new product would require $150,000 of new fixed costs annually and $3.10 in variable costs for each unit produced. The firm expects to sell the new product for $3.60 per unit.

**a.** What is the firm's profit breakeven point?
**b.** If $50,000 of the fixed costs are depreciation, what is the firm's cash breakeven point?

**P8-6.** You are considering acquiring a small business that produces and sells three different products. From the firm's income statement, you can tell that the business's fixed costs were $350,000 last year while its total variable costs were $210,000. Although the firm incurred a loss in terms of net income, its sales were $520,000.

**a.** What is the business's dollar breakeven point?
**b.** What was the business's EBIT last year?

**P8-7.** L. L. Gabriel Corporation is uncertain of next year's sales and EBIT. It expects EBIT of $5.5 million if sales are at 370,000 units, or $6.1 million if sales are 470,000 units. What is the degree of operating leverage implied by this information, using 370,000 units as the base point?

**P8-8.** Hagen & Hall Corporation produces and sells just one type of grandfather clock. Since much of the work is done by hand, fixed costs have remained relatively low at about $400,000 per year. Bob Hall has suggested to the other major stockholder in the firm, Walt Hagen, that they purchase several new pieces of equipment to help them reduce variable cost per unit. Bob has prepared the following information to support this argument:

|  | Without the New Equipment | With the New Equipment |
|---|---|---|
| Fixed costs | $400,000 | $770,000 |
| Variable costs per unit | 2,100 | 1,800 |
| Sales price | 2,500 | 2,500 |
| Units sold | 1,500 | 1,500 |

**a.** What is the degree of operating leverage for Hagen & Hall Corporation at 1,500 units of sales under the current situation? What would it be if the firm purchases the new equipment?
**b.** What would be the firm's EBIT with and without the new equipment?
**c.** What is the breakeven point for the firm with and without the new equipment?
**d.** Assume that Hagen & Hall forecast sales of 1,200 units each year in the future. What justification could be offered for purchasing the equipment?

**P8-9.** Fixed costs for Ingram Enterprises totaled $410 million last year. Ingram's EBIT was $200 million on sales of $1 billion. Total units sold were 28,000, and non-cash expenses totaled 30 percent of fixed costs.

**a.** Find Ingram Enterprises' breakeven point in units.
**b.** What is Ingram Enterprises' cash breakeven point?

**P8-10.** Jackson Enterprises produces and sells sterile adhesive tape for use in hospitals. The firm forecasts the *average total cost* per unit at $3.37 when production is at 1 million units. The selling price and total fixed costs are $4.09 per unit and $245,000, respectively.

**a.** What is Jackson's dollar breakeven point?
**b.** If Jackson has sales of 900,000 units, what will be its EBIT?

**P8-11.** Kaplan Corporation had EBIT of $735,000 last year on sales of 6,125 units. It expects EBIT next year of $588,000 on sales of 5,818 units.

**a.** What is Kaplan's degree of operating leverage?
**b.** Using your answer to Part a, what would Kaplan's EBIT be if sales are 6,900 units?

**P8-12.** Lafleur, Inc., produces and sells home air fresheners for $23.50 per unit. Its fixed costs are $880,000, and variable cost per unit is $19.10. Lafleur is considering purchasing new equipment that will reduce variable costs per unit to $16.80 and increase fixed costs to $1,407,000.

**a.** Calculate Lafleur's breakeven point if it does not purchase the new equipment and if it does purchase the equipment.
**b.** Draw the two different breakeven points on the same graph.
**c.** At what level of sales is EBIT identical for the two different levels of operating leverage?
**d.** What is Lafleur's EBIT and degree of operating leverage at 175,000 units of sales, assuming it does not purchase the equipment?
**e.** What arguments can be made for not purchasing the equipment and for purchasing the equipment if sales are 205,000 units? 220,000 units? 240,000 units?

**P8-13.** Lehigh Company produces and sells fidgets for $300 each. Its variable cost per unit is $180, and fixed costs are $800,000.

**a.** What is Lehigh's profit breakeven point in units?
**b.** If Lehigh's noncash expenses (depreciation) are $40,000, what is its cash breakeven point?

**P8-14.** Summer Corporation had EBIT of $139 million on sales of 100 million units. It expects to generate EBIT next year of $151 million on sales of 106 million units. What is Summer's degree of operating leverage?

**P8-15.** Hein Company has fixed costs of $100 million last year. Its EBIT was $60 million on sales of $200 million. Total units sold was 53,000 and noncash expenses were 20 percent of fixed costs.

a. What is Hein's breakeven point in units?
b. What is Hein's cash breakeven point?

**P8-16.** Chatfield Industries produces three main products. The proportion of sales generated by each product, and the contribution percentage $[1 - (v/p)]$ of each product is as follows:

| Product | Percent of Total Sales Revenue | Contribution Margin |
|---------|--------------------------------|---------------------|
| A | 50% | 20% |
| B | 30 | 30 |
| C | 20 | 40 |

Sales next year are forecasted to be $10 million. The sales mix is expected to remain unchanged, and fixed costs will be $3 million.

a. For each product, estimate sales, total variable costs, and the contribution margin in dollars.
b. What is the breakeven point in dollars?
c. What is the expected level of EBIT next year?

## COMPUTER-ASSISTED PROBLEMS

**CP8-1. a. Sensitivity of Breakeven Point to Fixed and Variable Costs**   Bryant Corporation has developed estimates of its maximum and minimum expected variable and fixed costs for the next year:

|  | High Estimate | Low Estimate |
|---|---------------|--------------|
| Fixed costs | $8.3 million | $7.8 million |
| Variable costs | $64 per unit | $57 per unit |

Bryant sells its product for $95 per unit. Using this information, determine the most optimistic and most pessimistic breakeven points.

**b. Probability Distribution of Fixed and Variable Costs**   Bryant Corporation has developed probability distributions for its fixed and variable costs as follows:

| Fixed Costs | Probability | Variable Costs | Probability |
|-------------|-------------|----------------|-------------|
| $7.8 million | 10% | $57 per unit | 20% |
| 8.0 million | 70 | 61 per unit | 50 |
| 8.3 million | 20 | 64 per unit | 30 |

Assuming a product price of $95 once again, determine the probability distribution that applies to the breakeven point. What is the probability that the breakeven point will be less than 250,000 units?

**CP8-2. Simulation**   Assume that the fixed costs for Carr Corporation are estimated to be somewhere between $1 million and $1.1 million, while variable costs are estimated to be between $11 and $13 per unit. Carr Corporation sells its product for $23 per unit. Assume that it will continue producing the product of concern only if its breakeven point is less than 95,000 units. What is your recommendation to Carr Corporation? Explain.

**CP8-3.  Probability Distribution**   Boston Industries had EBIT of $90 million last year on sales of 20 million units. Its degree of operating leverage is 2.5. It has also forecasted next year's sales as follows:

| Scenario | Probability | Sales in Units |
|----------|-------------|----------------|
| Strong economy | 30% | 25 million |
| Moderate economy | 60 | 22 million |
| Weak economy | 10 | 16 million |

Determine the probability distribution of EBIT for next year. What is the probability that Boston Industries will achieve its goal of EBIT of at least $85 million?

## REFERENCES

Adar, Zvi, Amir Barnea, and Baruch Lev. "A Comprehensive Cost-Volume-Profit Analysis under Uncertainty." *Accounting Review* 52 (January 1977): 137–49.

Bowlin, Oswald D., John D. Martin, and David F. Scott, Jr. *Guide to Financial Analysis*, chap. 8. New York: McGraw-Hill, 1980.

Gahlon, James M., and James A. Gentry. "On the Relationship between Systematic Risk and the Degrees of Operating and Financial Leverage." *Financial Management* 11 (Summer 1982): 15–23.

Ghandi, J. K. S. "On the Measurement of Leverage." *Journal of Finance* 21 (December 1966): 715–26.

Gritta, Richard D. "The Effect of Financial Leverage on Air Carrier Earnings: A Break-Even Analysis." *Financial Management* 8 (Summer 1979): 53–60.

Haslem, John A. "Leverage Effects on Corporate Earnings." *Arizona Business Review* 19 (March 1970): 7–11.

Lev, Baruch. "On the Association between Operating Leverage and Risk." *Journal of Financial and Quantitative Analysis* 9 (September 1974): 627–42.

Levy, Haim, and Robert Brooks. "Financial Break-Even Analysis and the Value of the Firm." *Financial Management* 15 (Autumn 1986): 22–26.

Mandelker, Gershon N., and S. Ghon Rhee. "The Impact of the Degrees of Operating and Financial Leverage on Systematic Risk of Common Stock." *Journal of Financial and Quantitative Analysis* 19 (March 1984): 45–58.

Needles, Belverd E., Jr., Henry R. Anderson, and James C. Caldwell. *Principles of Accounting.* Boston: Houghton Mifflin Co., 1981.

Percival, John R. "Operating Leverage and Risk." *Journal of Business Research* 2 (April 1974): 223–27.

Shalit, Sol S. "On the Mathematics of Financial Leverage." *Financial Management* 4 (Spring 1975): 57–66.

# PART 4

# LONG-TERM INVESTMENT DECISIONS

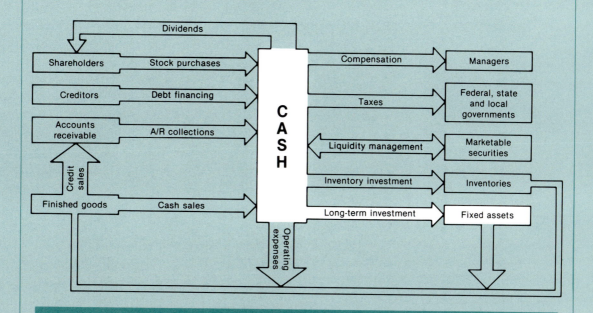

Chapters 9 through 11 focus on the acquisition of long-term (or fixed) assets. Decisions to acquire fixed assets normally require a substantial investment and cannot be reversed without great expense. Accordingly, the procedures used in making decisions about the acquisition of such assets are critical to the firm's long-term performance. Chapter 9 demonstrates how the relevant cash flows of a proposed capital project can be estimated. This process can be complicated by the impact of depreciation and taxes on cash flows.

Chapter 10 shows how the estimated cash flows of a proposed investment can be evaluated and how alternative projects can be compared directly to each other. Chapter 11 explains how risk can be accounted for when making decisions about the acquisition of long-term investments.

# CHAPTER 9

# FUNDAMENTALS OF CAPITAL BUDGETING

## CASH FLOW FORECASTING IN PERSPECTIVE

In May 1987, Detroit Edison Company revised its estimate of the cost of developing its Fermi II plant upward to $4.43 billion. Additionally, the firm predicted that for each month of development beyond the originally scheduled start-up date of May 1, 1987, the estimated cost of the plant would increase by $30 to $40 million.

In this situation, cash flow estimates made by Detroit Edison regarding the initial cost of adopting a capital budgeting project proved to be highly inaccurate. Large deviations of the actual cash flows from the estimated cash flows associated with the initial cost of a project can result in the adoption of unprofitable projects and financial distress for the firm.

In 1987, Mobil Corporation announced plans to move its corporate headquarters from New York City to Fairfax, Virginia. The move was motivated by the high rental and operating costs in New York. Mobil expects to save $40 million each year in operating expenses as a result of the move.

Here the cash flows in question are realized annually. Clearly, inaccurate estimates of these cash flows also have the potential of causing the adoption of unprofitable projects and financial distress for the firm.

What components of cash flow must be considered in the cash flow forecasts? Should incremental financing costs be considered? How do taxes affect the cash flows of a project? This chapter provides a framework that can be used to estimate the cash flows associated with capital budgeting projects such as those undertaken by Detroit Edison and Mobil Corporation.

All firms purchase fixed assets such as machinery and equipment for use in their operations. To finance the purchase of fixed assets they generally use long-term sources of funds, which are referred to as *capital funds* (retained earnings, long-term debt, preferred stock, and common stock). Since most firms have a limited amount of capital available to them, a critical decision involves how to allocate the limited capital available for the purchase of fixed assets. **Capital budgeting** is the procedure used to make this decision. Consider the task of financial managers in charge of capital expenditures for large corporations. As requests for the purchase of fixed assets are submitted by various departments, they must be able to distinguish between projects that will be financially profitable and those that will not. Poor capital budgeting decisions can lower firm profitability or increase risk, either of which can result in a lower price of the firm's common stock. Since the goal of management is to maximize shareholder wealth, it is important that managers make the right capital budgeting decisions.

This chapter explains why capital budgeting is important to firms, describes the various types of capital budgeting projects, and reviews the steps employed in the capital budgeting process. One of the most important and difficult steps in this process involves estimating the relevant cash flows generated by a project. Guidelines are presented for estimating these cash flows, and an example is provided to illustrate how this is done.

## IMPORTANCE OF CAPITAL BUDGETING

Capital budgeting is widely recognized as one of the most important corporate functions. Table 9.1 illustrates its importance by specifying the volume of capital expenditures of some selected corporations during their 1986 fiscal years. With such a substantial volume of funds allocated to capital budgeting, it is understandable that corporations make a concerted effort to correctly distinguish between profitable and unprofitable projects. Figure 9.1 illustrates the level of capital expenditures of U.S. corporations during the period 1978 to 1986. This period is characterized by a general increase in capital expenditures by all industries in the aggregate, except in 1980 due to a mild recession and in 1982–83 due to a severe recession. Notice that the capital expenditures of nonmanufacturing firms were at least 50 percent higher than those of manufacturing firms during this period. Figure 9.1 also suggests that the capital expenditures of the manufacturing sector are more sensitive to recessions. Yet, even during these periods, a substantial level of capital spending continues. Due to the large amount of capital spending, capital budgeting decisions can have a significant impact on corporate performance.

Even very small firms with only a single fixed asset can be significantly affected by capital budgeting decisions. If a poor decision is made, large amounts of funds may be tied up for long periods of time in a fixed asset of questionable value. For example, a typist who establishes his own business by taking out a loan to purchase expensive word-processing equipment could be adversely affected if a more efficient version of the equipment is marketed shortly thereafter. The typist could be at a competitive disadvantage because of the greater productive capacity of the newer

**TABLE 9.1**    **Capital Expenditures of Selected Corporations: 1986**

| Corporation | Capital Expenditures (Millions of Dollars) |
|---|---|
| Du Pont | $2,900 |
| Texaco | 2,900 |
| Procter & Gamble | 1,069 |
| Pillsbury | 309 |
| Caterpillar | 294 |
| General Mills | 245 |
| Quaker Oats | 147 |

**FIGURE 9.1**
**Capital Expenditure Level over Time**

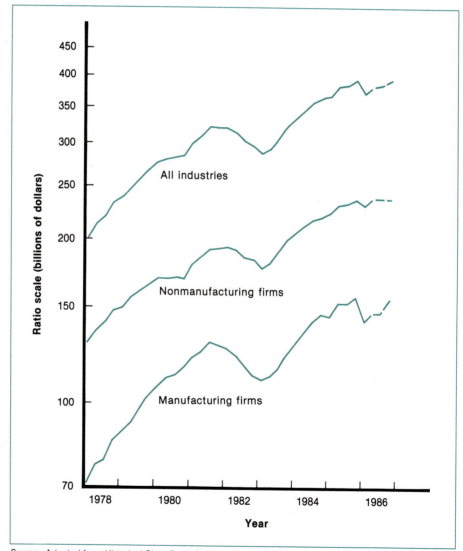

*Source:* Adapted from *Historical Chart Book,* Board of Governors, Federal Reserve System, p. 16.
*Note:* The solid lines indicate actual plant and equipment spending; the dashed lines indicate anticipated plant and equipment spending.

equipment. Because fixed assets generally require a substantial outlay of funds and can affect profitability for long periods of time, they must be chosen wisely.

In addition to requiring a substantial outlay, fixed assets often are hard to liquidate without substantial loss to the seller. Consider the typist once again. Reselling the word-processing equipment to the dealer would likely result in a significant loss, even if the equipment is only a few weeks old. On a larger scale, consider a corporation that constructs a new manufacturing plant and later decides the project is a mistake. Since an active market does not exist for manufacturing plants, capital expenditures normally are reversible only at a great cost to the seller. Due to the generally large outlay of funds necessary for most capital expenditures, and the irreversible nature of the adoption decision, proper capital budgeting analysis is critical to the firm's performance.

## CLASSIFICATION OF CAPITAL EXPENDITURES

The types of potential capital expenditures considered by firms can be broadly classified into the following four categories.

### Expansion of Current Business

If a firm's sales continue to increase, fixed assets eventually must be increased to support those rising sales. Thus, additional machinery, similar to existing machinery, normally is purchased to accommodate the increased demand for the firm's products.

### Development of New Business

Firms frequently expand into the production and sale of new products. Even when these products are related to current products, different types of capital equipment may be required. If the new product is unrelated to the existing business, of course, the need to purchase new and different machinery is inevitable.

### Replacement of Old Plant and Equipment

Machines wear out or become technologically obsolete over time. The decision to replace fixed assets is just as important to the firm as the decision to expand production, since both require large expenditures and are difficult to reverse. It should not be surprising that younger firms tend to allocate more of their capital expenditures to expansionary ventures, while older firms typically allocate more of their capital expenditures for the replacement of worn-out or obsolete plant and equipment.

### Other Capital Expenditures

While most capital expenditures can be classified into the preceding three categories, some cannot. For example, a firm may be considering the expenditure of a large sum of money on research and development or on an advertising campaign. When such expenditures are to benefit the firm for more than a one-year period of time, they are generally subjected to the capital budgeting evaluation process. Other expenditures may have intangible benefits, making them more difficult to evaluate—for example, a project to build a cafeteria or gym for the benefit of employees. While the firm benefits from such expenditures indirectly, those benefits are not easily quantified.

## PHASES OF CAPITAL BUDGETING

The process of capital budgeting can be broadly described in terms of six main functions:

- Planning new projects
- Estimating project cash flows
- Evaluating projects
- Selecting among proposed projects
- Implementing accepted projects
- Post-auditing implemented projects

### Planning New Projects

The planning phase of capital budgeting generally involves corporate planning for the expansion of ongoing business, development of new types of products, or the replacement of worn-out or obsolete assets. Planning normally is initiated within the firm as various corporate departments or divisions make requests for new capital equipment. In some cases, planning is dictated by changes in consumer demand or in manufacturing technology that force the firm to consider the purchase of new plant and equipment in order to produce new products or adopt the new technology.

### Estimating Project Cash Flows

Each potential project affects the after-tax cash flows of the firm. Estimating these cash flows is an important part of the capital budgeting process and is discussed in detail later in this chapter. The decision on whether to make a capital expenditure is based on an evaluation of the anticipated change in the cash flows of the firm if the project is adopted. Thus, it is critical that cash flows be estimated properly.

### Evaluating Projects

Once potential capital budgeting projects have been identified and their cash flows estimated, the projects must be evaluated. Specific techniques available to assess the profitability of projects based on their expected cash flows are described thoroughly in Chapter 10. Even if the cash flows generated by a proposed project are forecasted with perfect accuracy, a firm may make an incorrect decision about a project if it improperly evaluates the cash flows.

## Selecting among Proposed Projects

Once the evaluation of all projects is completed, the firm must select those projects benefiting the firm most. In some cases, a decision must be made between two projects designed for the same purpose. Such projects are said to be **mutually exclusive** when only one can be accepted. For example, a firm may be considering the purchase of a computer system for its accounting department. If there are three alternative systems from which to choose, these three systems are mutually exclusive capital budgeting projects since the purchase of one system precludes the purchase of the other two.

When the decision on whether to adopt a project has no bearing on the adoption of other projects, the project is said to be **independent.** For example, the purchase of a truck to enhance delivery capabilities and the purchase of a large computer system to handle payroll processing are independent projects. That is, the acceptance (or rejection) of one project does not influence the acceptance (or rejection) of the other project.

The authority to select projects varies among firms. Larger capital expenditures normally are reviewed by top management. Committees sometimes are organized to select among alternative projects. Smaller capital expenditures may be made by division managers.

## Implementing Accepted Projects

Once the firm has determined which projects to accept and which to reject, it must focus on implementing the accepted projects. All accepted projects should be prioritized so that those addressing immediate needs can be implemented first. As part of the implementation process, the firm must procure the necessary funds to finance the projects. The procurement of funds is discussed in a subsequent chapter.

## Post-Auditing Implemented Projects

Even after a project has been implemented, the capital budgeting process is not complete. The project should be monitored, or **post-audited,** in order to compare the project's actual costs and benefits to those estimated in the planning phase. One purpose of post-auditing is to detect errors in either estimation or evaluation of a project's cash flows. If any errors are detected, the employees responsible for planning and evaluation should be informed of the problem so that future projects can be assessed more accurately. A second purpose of post-auditing is to detect and correct inefficiencies in the current operation of the project. Finally, post-auditing can help determine if and when a project should be abandoned (liquidated) by the firm.

The six phases of capital budgeting are summarized in Table 9.2. If any single phase is not completed correctly, incorrect capital budgeting decisions may result. For example, if the cash flow estimates are inaccurate, a poor capital budgeting decision may result even if all other phases of the capital budgeting process are completed properly.

**TABLE 9.2   Phases of Capital Budgeting**

| | |
|---|---|
| Planning | Develop new ideas for expansion, and monitor the replacement requirements of existing capital equipment. |
| Estimating | Make estimates of changes in the after-tax cash flow that will result from each proposed project. |
| Evaluating | Use all data developed in the planning phase to estimate how much each project will benefit the firm. |
| Selecting | Based on the evaluation of each project, select all independent projects that will benefit the firm. For mutually exclusive projects, select those projects that will benefit the firm the most. |
| Implementing | Prioritize all accepted projects according to need, obtain funds, and begin operation. |
| Post-auditing | Assess implemented projects to determine whether project evaluation was accurate, and identify any sources of estimates that need to be improved in the future. |

The most challenging phases are the estimation of cash flows, project evaluation, and project selection. The estimation process is discussed thoroughly in this chapter, while evaluation and selection phases are discussed in the following chapter.

## GUIDELINES FOR ESTIMATING PROJECT CASH FLOWS

The term *cash flow* refers to the actual flow of cash into and out of the firm. This amount can differ from expenses and revenues since, under accrual accounting, expenses and revenues can be recognized without the actual exchange of cash. Capital budgeting projects are evaluated based on their cash flows, which reflect all of the dollars coming into the firm that the firm can reinvest, including depreciation and other noncash expenses (recall from Chapter 2 that depreciation is a source of funds). For our purposes, cash flows are equal to net income plus depreciation.

There are three important rules to follow when estimating the cash flows resulting from a project:

■ Consider incremental (or marginal) cash flows only
■ Consider cash flows on an after-tax basis
■ Postpone consideration of financing costs

### Consider Incremental Cash Flows Only

Projects should be evaluated according to how they change the cash flow of the firm. This requires comparison of the estimated cash flow stream if the project is not adopted against the estimated cash flow stream if the project is adopted. For example, if a firm is considering the replacement of an old machine with a new one, the relevant cash flow to consider is not the cash flow generated by the new machine, since some of that would have been realized if the old machine were retained. Only the *increased* cash flow attributable to using the replacement machine should be considered. These **incremental cash flows** should be measured during all phases of the project's life, including the initial outlay, the periodic cash flows that may be realized during the life of the project, and any cash flows that are realized when the project is terminated. These different phases of the project's life are discussed in detail later in this chapter.

### Consider Cash Flows on an After-Tax Basis

Only the cash flows generated by capital budgeting projects that remain after the payment of taxes can be used by the firm. Therefore, only after-tax cash flows are considered in capital budgeting. This is true for all phases of the project's life. The more common tax provisions influencing cash flows involve the taxing of gains and losses from the sale of old fixed assets, and the tax deduction available for depreciation. These provisions are discussed shortly. The point to be made here is that if a firm considers untaxed revenues generated by a project, it will overestimate the benefit of the project to the firm.

### Postpone Consideration of Financing Costs

It seems only natural to consider the cost of financing new projects (such as interest on debt) as part of the cash outflows related to the adoption of the projects. However, consideration of the financing costs is commonly postponed until the evaluation phase of the capital budgeting process. If the estimated cash flows of a project were to reflect the cost of financing the project, and if those costs were considered again in the evaluation phase, these costs would be counted twice. This will become more clear when the discounting techniques of capital budgeting project evaluation are described in Chapter 10.

Selecting a specific source of funds to finance capital budgeting projects (debt, retained earnings, common stock, or preferred stock) is also an important decision that must be made by the firm. This financing decision, however, is made separately from the investment (capital budgeting) decision.

## EXAMPLE OF ESTIMATING PROJECT CASH FLOWS

The incremental cash flows of a project can be classified into three categories:

- Initial outlay
- Periodic cash flows
- Terminal cash flow

It should be stressed that only incremental or marginal cash flows resulting from a given project are relevant. Therefore, future references made to initial outlay, periodic cash flows, and terminal cash flows are understood to be incremental amounts.

## Initial Outlay

The initial outlay for a given project reflects the immediate net cash outflows (after taxes) necessary to implement the project. It consists of three key cash flow components, two of which typically result in outlays, and one of which typically reduces the initial outlay. The following paragraphs describe these components and provide an example illustrating how they are combined to determine the initial outlay.

**Direct Cost of the Project**   A project's direct cost includes the actual purchase price of assets associated with the project, plus any installation and transportation costs. Any other direct expenses resulting from the purchase of assets would also be included. All such costs are considered on an after-tax basis.

**Indirect Cost of the Project**   Many projects cause firms to incur some indirect costs for such things as increasing working capital. Although this may cause an immediate cash outflow, at the termination of the project, the need for working capital may decrease, resulting in a cash inflow. As an example, an increase in raw materials may be necessary to undertake and operate a new project. When the project is terminated, the firm's raw materials can be reduced to their original level, resulting in a one-time cash inflow when they are liquidated.

**Cash Inflows from the Sale of Old Capital Equipment**   Under conditions where a new asset replaces an old asset, the estimated revenues from the sale of the old asset represent a cash inflow that helps offset the initial outlay.

The sale of the old equipment also may result in a tax liability (or tax saving), which adds to (or reduces) the initial outlay. Recall from Chapter 2 that the tax implications from the sale of a depreciable asset depend on the relationship between the selling price and the book value of the old asset. The three possible scenarios are summarized briefly in Table 9.3.

**Example of Calculating the Initial Outlay**   Logar Corporation is considering replacing an old machine with a new one. The replacement machine has a purchase price of $300,000 and requires an additional expenditure of $10,000 for delivery and installation. The old machine currently has a

**TABLE 9.3**   **Tax Effects of the Sale of Depreciable Assets**

| Scenario | Tax Effect |
|---|---|
| 1. Selling price = book value | No tax consequences. |
| 2. Book value < selling price | The amount by which selling price exceeds book value is subject to income tax, since the asset is being sold for more than its cost to the firm. |
| 3. Selling price < book value | The amount by which book value exceeds selling price reflects a loss that can be used to offset operating income. Thus, the firm realizes a tax savings equal to the loss times the firm's ordinary tax rate. |

book value of $250,000 and was purchased five years earlier for $500,000. It can be sold now for $100,000 but will have no salvage value if used for five more years (its remaining life). If the new asset is purchased and used for five years (its expected life), it is expected to have a salvage value of $35,000. In order to use the new machine, inventories must be increased by $20,000. The firm's marginal tax rate is 34 percent. Calculation of the initial outlay is as follows:

| Initial Outlay | |
| --- | --- |
| Purchase price | $300,000 |
| Plus: delivery and installation | 10,000 |
| Plus: increased working capital | 20,000 |
| Minus: proceeds from the sale of the old machine | 100,000 |
| Minus: tax savings from the sale of the old machine[1] ($250,000 − $100,000)(34%) | 51,000 |
| Initial outlay | $179,000 |

Notice from the preceding example that the computation of the initial outlay incorporates all of the cash flow components described earlier. Once the initial outlay is determined, the next step is to identify and compute the periodic cash flows.

## Periodic Cash Flows

Periodic incremental after-tax cash flows (hereafter referred to simply as *periodic cash flows*) normally occur in every year of the life of a project. Although the cash flows may occur daily or weekly, most firms estimate them over annual intervals. The annual interval is used for convenience, since cash flows on a daily or weekly basis are extremely difficult to estimate and do not add much accuracy to the analysis.

Some aspects of a project may increase the firm's periodic cash flow, while other aspects may decrease it. For example, a new, more efficient machine may decrease the labor cost associated with producing each unit of the firm's product. This in turn increases net income and cash flow. However, the same machine also may use more energy, increasing the cost of electricity and thereby decreasing net income and cash flow. When depreciation increases, it reduces net income but increases cash flow.

One way of forecasting the periodic cash flows is to begin with a forecast of what the firm's annual income statements would be if the project were adopted (hence, all expense changes are recognized). Next, a forecast is made of the annual income statements that would result if the project were rejected. From here, the cash flow under each scenario can be found easily by adding the appropriate amount of depreciation to the net income figures. This must be done for each year of the life of the asset. Since

---

1. If a machine is sold for more than its book value, the amount of tax paid on the gain would be added here instead of subtracting a tax savings.

the objective is to identify the incremental cash flows, the difference between the cash flows with and without project adoption is determined for each year.

Alternatively, the change in cash flow can be measured by analyzing the effect that adoption of the project would have on each income-statement item. Then, the total impact on firm cash flows can be estimated by determining how the changes in income statement items affect net income and cash flow. Both of these methods are described here using an example.

**Example of Calculating Periodic Cash Flows**    The previous example concerning the replacement of an old machine by Logar Corporation can be expanded to demonstrate the calculation of periodic cash flows. Assume that if the new machine is purchased, annual sales are expected to increase from $700,000 to $730,000 due to the greater productive capacity it provides. In addition, cost of goods sold will decrease from $500,000 to $480,000 because of a reduction in the amount of labor required to produce each unit of product, and depreciation will increase from $50,000 to $62,000 in each of the five years of the equipment's life. (*Because of its importance in capital budgeting, depreciation is considered as a separate expense in this chapter as opposed to being included as part of operating expenses.*)

The amount of annual depreciation is calculated throughout this chapter using a *simplified straight-line method*. Please note that this method is not recognized by professional accountants or the IRS as a valid method of depreciating assets (recognized methods were discussed in Chapter 2). It is, however, a simple method that permits us to concentrate our efforts on identifying relevant cash flows as opposed to spending our time and effort calculating annual depreciation. Annual depreciation is determined here by dividing $n$ into the depreciable basis of the asset, where $n$ is the number of years of life of the asset. The depreciable basis is defined as the purchase price plus transportation and installation costs. In this example, the life of the asset is five years, the price is $300,000, and the cost of installation and delivery is $10,000. Annual depreciation is calculated as follows:

$$\text{annual depreciation} = \frac{\$300,000 + \$10,000}{5}$$

$$= \$62,000$$

Given the preceding information, the firm can estimate the cash flows that will be realized if the new equipment is purchased and also if it is not. This information is reflected in the two abbreviated income statements appearing in Table 9.4. These two income statements were developed using the information previously specified concerning sales, cost of goods sold, and depreciation. Since the changes in revenue and expenses are assumed to be the same in each year of the life of the project, just one set of comparative income statements is necessary to represent all five years of the life of the project. The two income statements reveal that the firm's net income is expected to be $44,880 per year if the new machine is acquired, but only $19,800 per year if Logar Corporation continues to use the old machine. The cash flows under both situations are found by adding de-

**TABLE 9.4  Estimating Periodic Cash Flows: Logar Corporation**

|  | Using Old Machine | Using New Machine |
|---|---|---|
| Sales | $700,000 | $730,000 |
| Less: Cost of goods sold | 500,000 | 480,000 |
| Less: Operating expenses | 100,000 | 100,000 |
| Less: Depreciation | 50,000 | 62,000 |
| Operating income | 50,000 | 88,000 |
| Less: Interest expense | 20,000 | 20,000 |
| Taxable income | 30,000 | 68,000 |
| Less: Taxes (34%) | 10,200 | 23,120 |
| Net income | 19,800 | 44,880 |
| Plus: Depreciation | 50,000 | 62,000 |
| Cash flow | $ 69,800 | $106,880 |
| Periodic cash flow | $37,080 | |

preciation to net income. These income statements reveal that the expected cash flow is $106,880 per year if the new machine is purchased and only $69,800 per year if the firm continues to use the old machine. The difference between cash flows, $37,080, represents the periodic, incremental after-tax cash inflow each year for five years if the firm buys the new machine.

This same figure can be found using the alternative method described earlier. This is done by determining how the difference in each income statement item affects the firm's net income and cash flow. Table 9.5 demonstrates this technique using the Logar Corporation project once again. Notice that the changes that are *given* in this example are indicated in the second column, and the changes that must be *calculated* are indicated in the third column. The change in *operating income* reflects the changes in sales, cost of goods sold, and depreciation. That is, the increased sales and decreased cost of goods sold increases operating income by a total of $50,000, while the increase in depreciation decreases operating income by

**TABLE 9.5  Estimating Periodic Cash Flows (Alternative Approach): Logar Corporation**

|  | Change Given | Change Calculated |
|---|---|---|
| ΔSales | +$30,000 | |
| ΔCost of goods sold | −$20,000 | |
| ΔOperating expenses | No change | |
| ΔDepreciation | +$12,000 | |
| ΔOperating income | | +$38,000 [(ΔSales − ΔCost of goods sold) − ΔDepreciation] |
| ΔInterest expense | | Not considered |
| ΔTaxable income | | +$38,000 |
| ΔTaxes (34%) | | +$12,920 (34% × $38,000) |
| ΔNet income | | +$25,080 ($38,000 − $12,920) |
| ΔDepreciation | | +$12,000 |
| ΔCash flow | | +$37,080 ($25,080 + $12,000) |

$12,000. The net effect is an increase of $38,000 in operating income. Since there is no change in *interest expense* (financing costs are not considered here), the change in *taxable income* remains an increase of $38,000. If taxable income increases by $38,000, *taxes* will increase by 34 percent of $38,000, or $12,920. What remains ($25,080) represents an increase in *net income.* Since net income increases by $25,080, and depreciation increases by $12,000, the increase in *cash flow* is $37,080 ($25,080 + $12,000). This is the same periodic, incremental after-tax cash flow found using the other method.

The analyst must be particularly careful when adding the change in depreciation to the change in net income to arrive at the change in cash flow. If the change in depreciation is an increase, but the change in net income is a decrease, the change in cash flow may be either an increase or a decrease depending on which component changed the most. For example, if a project were to increase depreciation by $10,000 but decrease net income by $4,000, cash flow would increase by $6,000 ($10,000 − $4,000). Conversely, if depreciation increases by $15,000 and net income decreases by $18,000, cash flow would decrease by $3,000.

Again, financing costs are not included in the calculation of periodic cash flows. As indicated earlier, such costs are incorporated into the analysis during the evaluation phase of capital budgeting. Thus far, we have estimated the initial cash outlay and periodic cash flows of a project. The last relevant cash flow is the terminal cash flow resulting from the project.

## Terminal Cash Flow

The incremental after-tax terminal cash flow (hereafter called the *terminal cash flow*) generated by a project may include several components, one of which is frequently an increase or decrease in after-tax cash flow received from selling any depreciable assets upon termination of the project. It is important to identify the *incremental cash flow* since the firm may realize a terminal cash flow from the sale of old equipment (if the project is not adopted) or from the sale of the new equipment (if the project is adopted). Of course, the tax effects of selling a depreciable asset, as discussed earlier and summarized in Table 9.3, also must be considered when an asset is sold at the termination of the project.

In addition to recognizing cash flows resulting from the sale of disposable assets at the end of the expected life of the project, the firm may also realize a cash inflow from a reduction in working capital. Both aspects are described in the following example.

**Example of Calculating Terminal Cash Flow**   Continuing with our earlier example, recall that the old equipment will have no salvage value after five more years of use, but the new machine can be sold for an estimated $35,000 after five years. Since the book value at that time would be zero, the firm would pay income tax on the entire $35,000 gain. Given Logar's 34 percent tax rate, it will only keep 66 percent of the gain (100% − 34%). Also, recall that the firm must invest $20,000 more in inventories (part of the initial outlay) if the new machine is acquired. At the end of the five-year life of the project, those inventories will no longer be needed. There-

## SELECTION AND POST-AUDITING OF CAPITAL BUDGETING PROJECTS

A 1982 study conducted by Gitman and Mercurio reported the results of a questionnaire that had been mailed to 1,000 of the nation's largest firms.[1] Two questions in the survey had particular relevance to the material covered in this chapter. One question asked the respondents about the method they use to grant final approval of projects. More than 70 percent indicated that "the appropriate responsible manager must approve each project." However, 82.5 percent also indicated that the level at which the decision is made depends on the size of the required initial outlay.

A second area of inquiry concerned the procedures for evaluating the performance of adopted projects. Fifty-six percent of the respondents indicated that they have formal post-auditing procedures, and another 32 percent have informal procedures. The remaining 12 percent do not conduct post-audits.

A 1985 study by Gitman and Maxwell also provides some insight into the current practices of financial managers.[2] The responses made to this survey by the chief financial officers of the largest U.S. firms indicated the relative importance of various capital expenditure activities. The activities and the rank in terms of relative importance are presented in the following table (the activity descriptions have been altered to correspond with the terminology used in this text).

| Rank in Declining Order of Importance | Capital Expenditure Activity |
|---|---|
| 1 | Evaluating and selecting projects |
| 2 | Implementing projects |
| 3 | Planning new projects |
| 4 | Estimating project cash flows |
| 5 | Post-auditing implemented projects |

1. Lawrence J. Gitman and Vincent A. Mercurio, "Cost of Capital Techniques Used by Major U.S. Firms: Survey and Analysis of Fortune's 1000," *Financial Management* 11 (Winter 1982): 21–29.

2. Lawrence J. Gitman and Charles E. Maxwell, "Financial Activities of Major U.S. Firms: Survey and Analysis of Fortune's 1000," *Financial Management* 14 (Winter 1985): 57–65.

fore, it is assumed that inventories will be returned to normal, making that $20,000 available to the firm (a cash inflow). As a result, the terminal cash flow for this project is determined as follows:

| | |
|---|---|
| After-tax cash flow from salvage [$35,000(1 − .34)] | $23,100 |
| Reduction of inventory | 20,000 |
| Total | $43,100 |

It should be noted that if the old machine is expected to have a salvage value after five more years, the difference between the after-tax cash flows from salvaging the new equipment and the old equipment would be the appropriate figure to use. To illustrate, assume that in the example just presented the firm expects the old machine to have a salvage value of $8,000 after five more years, instead of the zero salvage value as previously specified. Also assume that the book value of the old equipment after five years would be zero. The terminal cash flow of $43,100 that was previously determined would no longer represent the *incremental* cash flow. Under

**FIGURE 9.2**

**Illustration of Relevant Cash Flows: Logar Corporation**

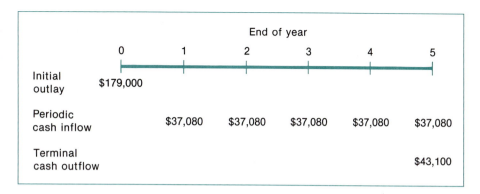

the new specifications, a cash flow of $5,280 [$8,000(1 − .34)] would be realized after five years if the project is not adopted. The incremental terminal cash flow if the project were adopted would be $37,820 ($43,100 − $5,280) in this case.

### Consolidating Cash Flow Estimates

The project used as an example throughout this chapter resulted in an estimated initial outlay of $179,000, periodic cash flows of $37,080 per year for five years, and a terminal cash flow of $43,100. These cash flows are displayed in Figure 9.2. This is the information that must be determined for every capital budgeting project under consideration. When all relevant cash flows have been identified, the evaluation phase of the capital budgeting process begins. The evaluation phase is the topic of Chapter 10.

## SUMMARY

Due to the large amount of funds involved in capital budgeting and the inability to reverse expenditure decisions once they are implemented, sound capital budgeting practices are crucial to the well-being of the firm. The process generally consists of six phases: (1) planning, (2) estimating, (3) evaluating, (4) selecting, (5) implementing, and (6) post-auditing. This chapter focused on the part of the planning process that involves identifying projects and estimating the relevant cash flows associated with those projects. To properly estimate the relevant cash flows, three important guidelines are (1) consider *incremental* cash flows only, (2) consider cash flows on an *after-tax* basis, and (3) postpone consideration of financing costs.

The relevant cash flows generated by a project can be classified as (1) initial outlay, (2) periodic cash flows, or (3) terminal cash flow. The initial outlay incorporates the purchase price, all indirect costs associated with the project, and any cash flows resulting from the sale of an old asset (if an old asset is being replaced). Periodic cash flows include changes in costs or revenues due to the new asset, and any tax-savings resulting from depreciation. The terminal cash flow reflects the difference between the after-tax salvage value of the new machine at the end of the project's expected life and the after-tax salvage value of the old machine at the same point in time (when an asset is being replaced). The terminal cash flow also reflects any cash flows realized by a decrease in working capital.

Once the relevant cash flows associated with a proposed project have been estimated, the next step is to assess those cash flows in order to determine whether the project should be adopted. Techniques to determine the value of a proposed project to the firm are discussed in the following chapter.

## KEY TERMS

**Capital budgeting** The process of identifying, evaluating, and deciding upon the implementation of proposed projects.

**Incremental cash flows** The change in cash flows resulting from a new project.

**Independent projects** When the accept/reject decision on one project has no bearing on the accept/reject decision on another project, the projects are said to be independent.

**Mutually exclusive projects** When the accep-

tance of any one project would prevent the acceptance of others, the projects are mutually exclusive.

**Post-auditing** Evaluation of a project after it has been implemented in order to (1) detect any inefficiencies that can be corrected, or (2) identify errors that were made in the cash flow estimation process in order to improve the accuracy of future project forecasts.

## QUESTIONS

**Q9-1.** Why is capital budgeting so important to firms?

**Q9-2.** Briefly describe the evaluation phase of capital budgeting.

**Q9-3.** If a project has already been accepted, why is the post-auditing phase relevant?

**Q9-4.** Explain the difference between independent projects and mutually exclusive projects.

**Q9-5.** Why shouldn't forecasted accounting profits be used for evaluating capital budgeting projects?

**Q9-6.** What are the three general guidelines to follow when estimating cash flows?

**Q9-7.** If a firm is considering the replacement of an old machine with a new one, what are the relevant cash flows that must be estimated?

**Q9-8.** Why aren't incremental financing costs considered when measuring the cash flows of a proposed project?

**Q9-9.** Explain the two different methods of estimating the periodic incremental after-tax cash flows for a project.

**Q9-10.** Terzer Corporation considered building a gym that its employees could use during lunch and after hours. The financial analyst in charge of analyzing this proposed project immediately rejected it since "the gym would require a large initial outlay and would generate no cash inflows to the firm." Comment on this situation.

**Q9-11.** Comment on the following statement: "Even if the estimation of cash flows phase of capital budgeting is improperly performed, the firm can resolve this deficiency if it properly performs the other phases."

**Q9-12.** A large machine being considered for purchase by Halix Corporation costs $30,000. This includes installation and transportation costs. Is $30,000 the initial outlay as defined in the text? Explain.

**Q9-13.** Assess the statement: "Depreciation is simply used for accounting purposes and can therefore be ignored when identifying relevant cash flows of a project."

## SELF-TEST PROBLEMS

Solutions to self-test problems appear on p. S1.

**SP9-1.** Collins Chrome Corporation may purchase a new machine for $500,000 to replace an existing machine. The old machine can be sold for $75,000 and has a book value of $50,000. Collins must pay an additional $6,000 for transportation and installation. In order to use the new machine, Collins must increase its working capital by $8,000. Collins has a 34 percent marginal tax rate.

**a.** What initial outlay is required for initiating this project?
**b.** If the old machine can be sold for only $25,000 instead of $75,000, what would be the initial outlay?

**SP9-2.** If Prince Cosmetics Company replaces an old machine, it can increase annual sales by $15,000. It will also increase annual cost of goods sold by $5,000, decrease operating expenses by $3,000, and increase annual depreciation by $6,000. Determine the periodic, incremental after-tax cash flow that would result from the purchase of the new machine.

**SP9-3.** Huey Lead Works is considering the purchase of some replacement equipment that it expects to use for a maximum of five years. During that time, Huey will have to increase its working capital by $8,000. The existing equipment should also last for five more years. At the end of five years, the old equipment can be sold for an estimated $10,000, although the book value at that time will be zero. If the replacement equipment is purchased, it is expected to be sold in five years for $39,000 although it, too, will have a book value of zero. If Huey has a 34 percent marginal tax rate, what is the incremental after-tax terminal cash flow associated with purchasing the replacement equipment?

## PROBLEMS

**P9-1.** Calculate the initial outlay for each of the following replacement projects. The firm has a 34 percent marginal tax rate. (Plus signs identify increases; minus signs identify decreases.)

| | Project | | | | |
|---|---|---|---|---|---|
| | A | B | C | D | E |
| Cost of new machine | $1,000,000 | $78,000 | $125,000 | $625,000 | $220,000 |
| Book value of old machine | 0 | 12,000 | 15,000 | 100,000 | 20,000 |
| Installation and transportation cost | 10,000 | 0 | 5,000 | 0 | 3,000 |
| Required change in working capital | +90,000 | −3,000 | 0 | +20,000 | +10,000 |
| Market value of old machine | 100,000 | 12,000 | 5,000 | 150,000 | 10,000 |

**P9-2.** Determine the periodic, incremental after-tax cash flow for the projects indicated below. All projects have five-year lives, the cash flows are identical in each year, and the firm's tax rate is 34 percent. (Plus signs identify increases; minus signs identify decreases.)

| | | | Project | | |
|---|---|---|---|---|---|
| *Annual Change in* | F | G | H | I | J |
| Cost of goods sold | −$ 6,000 | −$25,000 | −$100,000 | +$25,000 | −$200,000 |
| Depreciation | +3,000 | +25,000 | 0 | +40,000 | +30,000 |
| Sales | +12,000 | 0 | 0 | +50,000 | +30,000 |
| Operating expenses | −5,000 | +6,000 | −10,000 | +15,000 | 0 |

**P9-3.** Determine the incremental after-tax terminal cash flow for each of the following projects. Assume a 34 percent marginal tax rate. Also assume that the salvage values, book values, and working capital changes indicated below are at the end of the projects' lives. (Plus signs identify increases; minus signs identify decreases.)

| | | | Project | | |
|---|---|---|---|---|---|
| | K | L | M | N | O |
| Old equipment | | | | | |
| Salvage value | $ 75,000 | $10,000 | $25,000 | $ 5,000 | $125,000 |
| Book value | 0 | 0 | 0 | 10,000 | 75,000 |
| Replacement equipment | | | | | |
| Salvage value | 200,000 | 30,000 | 60,000 | 35,000 | 300,000 |
| Book value | 0 | 0 | 0 | 25,000 | 400,000 |
| Change in working capital | −10,000 | +5,000 | −65,000 | −6,000 | 0 |

**P9-4.** Jovi Bon Bon Company is considering the purchase of a new machine to replace a worn-out machine. The new machine costs $700,000 including transportation, but installation will require an additional expenditure of $12,000. This machine is expected to reduce annual operating expenses by $30,000, but Jovi will need to increase its working capital by $60,000 as long as the machine is in use. The old machine has a book value of $40,000 but it can be sold today for only $20,000. Jovi has a 34 percent marginal tax rate.

**a.** What initial outlay is required for this project?
**b.** If the old machine can be sold for $50,000, what is the initial outlay?

**P9-5.** Lauper Lamp Company may purchase a new machine at an installed cost of $300,000. The old machine is a 5-year class asset, was purchased one year earlier for $100,000, and is being depreciated under the modified ACRS system. If the old machine is sold for $20,000, what is the initial outlay?

**P9-6.** Beastie Toys, Inc., had sales last year of $2 million, cost of goods sold of $1.2 million, operating expenses of $400,000, depreciation expense of $200,000, interest expense of $100,000, and an average tax rate of 34 percent (this is also the firm's marginal tax rate). If Beastie purchases a new molding machine, it is expected to increase annual sales by $200,000, decrease annual cost of goods sold by $100,000, and increase annual depreciation expense by $150,000. Determine the periodic, incremental after-tax cash flows that would result from adopting the project. Calculate this value using two different methods.

**P9-7.** Madonna Horowitz is considering purchasing a new machine for her fabric company, Madonna's Material World. This new machine is expected to be used for ten years, at which time its market value is estimated to be $23,000 and its book value will be zero. If the old machine is not replaced, its book value and market value are expected to be zero ten years from today. If the firm's marginal tax rate is 34 percent, what is the incremental after-tax terminal cash flow for the project?

## REFERENCES

Bacon, Peter W. "The Evaluation of Mutually Exclusive Investments." *Financial Management* 6 (Summer 1977): 55–64.

Beardsley, G., and E. Mansfield. "A Note on the Accuracy of Industrial Forecasts of the Profitability of New Products and Processes." *Journal of Business* 51 (1978): 127–35.

Bierman, Harold, Jr., and Seymour Smidt. *The Capital Budgeting Decision*, 5th ed. New York: Macmillan, 1980.

Brown, K. C. "A Note on the Apparent Bias of Net Revenue Estimates for Capital Investment Projects." *Journal of Finance* 29 (September 1974): 1215–27.

Camillus, John C. "Designing a Capital Budgeting System That Works." *Long Range Planning* (April 1984): 103–10.

Ehrenreich, Keith B. "Postaudit Review of Capital Budgeting." *The Internal Auditor* (February 1983): 33–35.

Ferber, R. "Measuring the Accuracy and Structure of Businessmen's Expectations." *Journal of the American Statistical Association* (September 1953): 385–413.

Gitman, Lawrence J., and John R. Forrester, Jr. "Forecasting and Evaluation Practices and Performance: A Survey of Capital Budgeting." *Financial Management* 6 (Fall 1977): 66–71.

Hastie, K. L. "One Businessman's View of Capital Budgeting." *Financial Management* 3 (Winter 1974): 36–44.

Osteryoung, Jerome S. "A Survey into the Goals Used by Fortune's 500 Companies in Capital Budgeting Decisions." *Akron Business and Economic Review* (October 1975): 57–65.

Osteryoung, Jerome S., and Daniel E. McCarty. *Analytical Techniques for Financial Management*. New York: John Wiley & Sons, 1985.

Petty, J. William, David F. Scott, Jr., and Monroe M. Bird. "The Capital Expenditure Decision-Making Process of Large Corporations." *Engineering Economist* 20 (Spring 1975): 159–72.

Pinches, G. E. "Myopia, Capital Budgeting and Decision Making." *Financial Management* 11 (Autumn 1982): 6–19.

Schall, Laurence D., Gary L. Sundem, and William R. Geijsbeek, Jr. "Survey and Analysis of Capital Budgeting Methods." *Journal of Finance* 33 (March 1978): 281–87.

Schnell, James D., and Roy S. Nicholosi. "Capital Expenditure Feedback: Project Reappraisal." *Engineering Economist* 19 (Summer 1974): 253–61.

Smidt, Seymour. "A Bayesian Analysis of Project Selection and of Post-Audit Evaluations." *Journal of Finance* 34 (June 1979): 675–88.

Statman, Meir, and Tyzoon T. Tyebjee. "Optimistic Capital Budgeting Forecasts: An Experiment." *Financial Management* 14 (Autumn 1985): 27–32.

Weaver, James B. "Organizing and Maintaining a Capital Expenditure Program." *Engineering Economist* 20 (Fall 1974): 1–36.

# CHAPTER 10

# CAPITAL BUDGETING TECHNIQUES

## CAPITAL BUDGETING IN PERSPECTIVE

In 1987 the National Basketball Association (NBA) announced that it had approved four franchises for entrance into that league. Charlotte, North Carolina, and Miami, Florida, are to enter teams into the league in the 1988–89 season, while Minneapolis, Minnesota, and Orlando, Florida, are to enter teams in the 1989–90 season. The owners of each franchise paid $3.5 million upon approval of their franchise by the league; in December of the year before their team begins play, the owners must pay another $16 million; and in March of the year in which the team begins drafting players, the owners are required to pay a final $13 million. Thus, the owners of each franchise must pay a total of $32.5 million just to enter the league.

The organizations granted the rights to establish the new teams are committed to paying these large sums of money before their teams play even one game. With so much money involved, the franchise owners must give careful thought to whether sufficient revenue will be generated in future years to provide them with a reasonable return.

The methods potential NBA franchise owners use to determine if their large investments will result in a reasonable profit are the same methods used by firms to evaluate the purchase of new equipment, expenditures on advertising campaigns, the acquisition of subsidiaries, and so on. Certainly, as discussed in the previous chapter, the estimation of expected cash flows resulting from an investment is important. But how can those cash flows be evaluated to arrive at an accept or reject decision? This chapter provides the framework for making these decisions.

The preceding chapter demonstrated how to estimate the relevant cash flows associated with a proposed capital budgeting project. Once the net cash flows have been estimated, they must be evaluated to determine whether the project should be accepted or rejected. If a project is accepted when it should have been rejected, or vice versa, the firm's earnings may decline or its risk may rise, causing a decline in the value of the firm's common stock and shareholder wealth. Thus, proper capital budgeting techniques are essential to maximize shareholder wealth. This chapter describes the more popular techniques:

- Payback period
- Net present value
- Profitability index
- Internal rate of return

The pros and cons of each technique are discussed, and an example of each is provided.

## PAYBACK PERIOD

One of the more commonly used capital budgeting techniques is based on the **payback period,** which is the time necessary to recover the initial outlay from the cash flows generated by a project. This approach assumes that if the firm can recover its initial outlay quickly, it would be more inclined to adopt the project.

### Calculating the Payback Period

If the cash flows are identical for all years during the life of the project (an annuity situation), the payback period can be determined as follows:

$$\text{payback period} = \frac{\text{initial outlay}}{\text{annuity cash flows}} \tag{10.1}$$

**Example**

Assume the following information applies to a proposed project:

- Initial outlay is estimated to be $150,000.
- Cash flows are estimated to be $40,000 per year for five years.

Given this information, the payback period can be found as follows:

$$\text{payback period} = \frac{\$150,000}{\$40,000} = 3.75 \text{ years}$$

If the cash flows from a proposed project are expected to vary from year to year, Equation 10.1 cannot be used. Under these conditions, cumulative cash flows must be estimated for each successive year and compared to the initial outlay until the initial investment has been recovered. For example, assume the following information applies to a proposed project:

- Initial outlay = $70,000
- Cash flows are estimated as follows:

| Year | Annual Cash Flow |
|------|------------------|
| 1 | $30,000 |
| 2 | 40,000 |
| 3 | 30,000 |
| 4 | 35,000 |

Given this information, the cumulative cash flows for each year are as follows:

| Year | Cumulative Cash Flows |
|------|------------------------|
| 1 | $ 30,000 |
| 2 | 70,000 |
| 3 | 100,000 |
| 4 | 135,000 |

Since the initial outlay of $70,000 is recovered after two years, the project's payback period is two years.

If the initial outlay for the same project had been $120,000, then the payback period would have been 3.57 years. That is, after the third year, the firm would have recovered $100,000, and it would take some fraction of Year 4 to recover the remaining $20,000. This fraction is $20,000/$35,000, or .57 years. As employed here, this technique assumes that the cash flows are received evenly throughout the year.

## Decision Rule for the Payback Period

When using the payback-period approach, a firm must determine its maximum acceptable payback period for the project involved. This period could vary from firm to firm, and it could even vary within the firm based on the type of project being considered. There is no commonly accepted method of determining the maximum acceptable payback period, and it is generally determined subjectively. The maximum payback period is then compared to the expected payback period for specific projects, with the following decision rule being applied:

When payback period ≤ maximum acceptable payback period, accept the project.

When payment period > maximum acceptable payback period, reject the project.

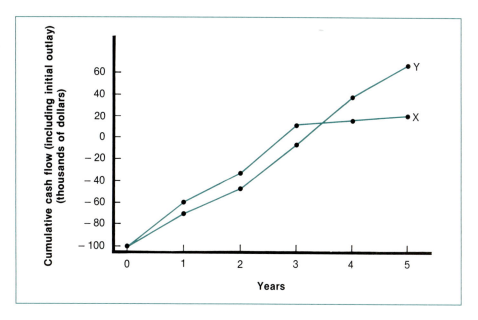

**FIGURE 10.1**

**Illustration of the Payback Period for Two Projects**

When mutually exclusive projects are being evaluated, the project with the shorter payback period is selected.

## Application of the Payback Period

Suppose a firm is evaluating two projects, X and Y. The schedule of cash flows for these projects is presented in Table 10.1. Using the technique described earlier, the payback period is determined to be 2.75 years for Project X and 3.25 years for Project Y. An illustration of the cumulative cash flows for each project is provided in Figure 10.1. If Projects X and Y were mutually exclusive, Project X would be selected over Project Y due to its shorter payback period. If the projects were independent, selection of either would depend on the maximum acceptable payback period. If this maximum period were specified as five years, both projects would be accepted. If it were three years, Project X would be accepted but not Project Y.

## Pros and Cons of Using the Payback Period

The payback-period technique is frequently used because it is easy to apply. It can be valuable for analyzing projects in which uncertainty increases rapidly over time (such as projects planned in politically unstable countries), since it evaluates how quickly the initial cost is recovered. Because of the emphasis the payback period technique places on the timing of cost recovery, it is frequently used in conjunction with other techniques presented here. The payback period approach partially recognizes the time value of money, since it favors projects that recapture the initial outlay quickly, but it does not fully consider the time value of money, as illustrated by the following example:

**TABLE 10.1   Calculation of the Payback Period for Two Separate Projects**

| | Project X Initial Cost = $100,000 | | Project Y Initial Cost = $100,000 | |
|---|---|---|---|---|
| Year | Annual Cash Flow | Cumulative Cash Flows | Annual Cash Flow | Cumulative Cash Flows |
| 1 | $40,000 | $40,000 | $30,000 | $30,000 |
| 2 | 30,000 | 70,000 | 20,000 | 50,000 |
| 3 | 40,000 | 110,000 | 40,000 | 90,000 |
| 4 | 5,000 | 115,000 | 40,000 | 130,000 |
| 5 | 5,000 | 120,000 | 30,000 | 160,000 |
| | Payback period for Project X = 2.75 years | | Payback period for Project Y = 3.25 years | |

**Example**

Projects A and B both require an initial outlay of $90,000. Their cash flows are as follows:

| Year | Cash Flow for Project A | Cash Flow for Project B |
|---|---|---|
| 1 | $50,000 | $20,000 |
| 2 | 30,000 | 30,000 |
| 3 | 10,000 | 40,000 |
| 4 | 40,000 | 10,000 |
| 5 | 40,000 | 10,000 |

These projects would be equally desirable as evaluated by the payback-period approach, since their estimated payback periods are identical (three years). Yet, Project A realizes larger cash flows in Year 1 than Project B, so because of the time value of money, Project A would be preferred.

A second and possibly more obvious disadvantage of using the payback-period approach is that it does not consider cash flows in periods after the initial outlay has been recovered. In the preceding example, Project A generates significantly higher cash flows than Project B in the two years following the payback period, yet this information is ignored.

## NET PRESENT VALUE

The **net present value (NPV)** of a project is its expected value in today's dollars after considering all costs. Naturally, firms wish to adopt projects with high *NPV*s.

### Calculating Net Present Value

The following equation can be used to calculate *NPV:*

$$NPV = \sum_{t=1}^{n} \frac{CF_t}{(1+k)^t} - I \qquad (10.2)$$

where $CF_t$ = cash flow in period $t$

$\qquad$ $k$ = the required rate of return on the project (cost of capital)

$\qquad$ $I$ = initial outlay

This formula can be restated in words as follows:

$\qquad$ $NPV$ = present value of cash flows − initial outlay

Recall from Chapter 9 that the incremental cash flows estimated for a project do not include incremental financing costs. The *NPV* method of evaluating projects, and the other methods that will be described here, consider the cost of financing projects as an integral part of the evaluation process. For the *NPV* method, using the cost of capital as the discount rate implicitly establishes the cost of financing the project as the minimum return that must be earned on the project. Since this technique involves discounting the cash flows back to present value, it is referred to as a *discounted cash flow* method. The remaining capital budgeting techniques discussed in this chapter are also discounted cash flow methods.

The cost of capital is the cost of the long-term funds for a firm. Since these funds are generally used to finance capital budgeting projects, the cost of capital is the appropriate discount rate to use in evaluating those projects. It is demonstrated in Chapter 11 that some projects may increase or decrease the risk of the firm. When this is true, the firm may want to use a discount rate that is higher or lower than the cost of capital. In this chapter, however, it is assumed that all capital budgeting projects have the same level of risk as the firm. Therefore, the firm's required rate of return on capital budgeting projects is the firm's cost of capital.

### Decision Rule for Net Present Value

If the *NPV* of a project is greater than zero, the project is expected to generate cash inflows that more than offset all costs (including the financing costs) associated with the project. Thus, the value of the firm should increase as a result of accepting the project. If the *NPV* is zero, the expected return on the project is technically equal to the required rate of return on the project, so the project should be adopted. If the *NPV* is negative, the present value of the cash flows is less than the initial outlay, indicating the project would reduce the value of the firm and should therefore be rejected. The decision rule for *NPV* analysis can be summarized as follows:

$\qquad$ When $NPV \geq 0$, accept the project.

$\qquad$ When $NPV < 0$, reject the project.

When two mutually exclusive projects have positive *NPV*s, the project with the higher *NPV* should be selected, because it will increase the value of the firm by a greater amount.

**TABLE 10.2** Calculation of Net Present Value for Two Separate Projects

| | Project X Initial Cost = $100,000 | | | Project Y Initial Cost = $100,000 | | |
|---|---|---|---|---|---|---|
| Year | Annual Cash Flow | Present Value Interest Factor (12%) | Discounted Cash Flow | Annual Cash Flow | Present Value Interest Factor (12%) | Discounted Cash Flow |
| 1 | $40,000 | .8929 | $35,716 | $30,000 | .8929 | $26,787 |
| 2 | 30,000 | .7972 | 23,916 | 20,000 | .7972 | 15,944 |
| 3 | 40,000 | .7118 | 28,472 | 40,000 | .7118 | 28,472 |
| 4 | 5,000 | .6355 | 3,177 | 40,000 | .6355 | 25,420 |
| 5 | 5,000 | .5674 | 2,837 | 30,000 | .5674 | 17,022 |
| | Total *PV* of cash flows | | $ 94,118 | Total *PV* of cash flows | | $113,645 |
| | Less: Initial outlay | | $100,000 | Less: Initial outlay | | $100,000 |
| | | *NPV* = | −$5,882 | | *NPV* = | $ 13,645 |

## Application of Net Present Value

Consider Projects X and Y once again, with initial outlays (*I*) and cash flows (*CF*) as presented in Table 10.2. Given a cost of capital of 12 percent, the *NPV* of these projects is determined to be −$5,882 for Project X and $13,645 for Project Y. If the projects were independent, Project Y would be adopted and Project X rejected. If they were mutually exclusive, Project Y would be selected according to the *NPV* criterion.

Recall that the payback-period approach preferred Project X over Project Y. Yet, according to *NPV* analysis, the selection of Project X would have been a mistake, since the present value of its cash flows is less than the initial outlay. These conflicting results can occur with the payback-period method because it neglects to fully consider the time value of money and all cash flows.

## Pros and Cons of Using Net Present Value

The *NPV* approach fully considers the time value of money since it is a discounted cash flow technique. In addition, the rate by which the cash flows are discounted reflects the firm's cost of raising funds to finance the project (cost of capital). These two characteristics help make the *NPV* approach theoretically sound and very useful for making capital budgeting decisions.

Perhaps the biggest disadvantage of using the *NPV* approach as the basis for capital budgeting decisions is the difficulty some managers have in interpreting the *NPV* estimate; that is, some managers relate better to measures of rates of return available on capital budgeting projects. There is an alternative technique available to assist in project selection that fully considers the time value of money and also reports the results in terms of a rate of return. This alternative technique, called the *internal-rate-of-return method*, is discussed in detail later in this chapter.

## PROFITABILITY INDEX

The **profitability index (PI)** is an alternative method of evaluating projects that considers the ratio of the present value of the project's cash flows to its initial outlay. Its use for evaluating projects is described below.

### Calculating the Profitability Index

The *PI* for a project can be computed as

$$PI = \frac{\sum_{t=1}^{n} \frac{CF_t}{(1+k)^t}}{I} \tag{10.3}$$

where $CF_t$ = cash flow in period $t$

$k$ = required rate of return (cost of capital)

$I$ = initial outlay

Equation 10.3 can be restated in words as follows:

$$PI = \frac{\text{present value of cash flows}}{\text{initial outlay}}$$

The same information used to determine *NPV* is used to determine the *PI*.

### Decision Rule for the Profitability Index

If the *PI* is greater than 1, the present value of cash flows exceeds the initial outlay, so the project should be adopted. If the *PI* is less than 1, the present value of cash flows is less than the initial outlay, so the project should be rejected. The basic decision rule can be written as follows:

When $PI \geq 1$, accept the project.

When $PI < 1$, reject the project.

This is perfectly consistent with the decision rule for *NPV*, except the *PI* is a ratio value where the decision centers around 1.0, and *NPV* is a dollar value with the decision centering around zero. The *PI* approach always indicates the same accept-reject decision for independent projects as the *NPV* approach. The *PI* approach, however, may rank mutually exclusive projects differently than the *NPV* approach, in which case, the *NPV* ranking is preferred. This difference will be addressed shortly.

### Application of the Profitability Index

The application of the *PI* method to Projects X and Y (discussed earlier) is displayed in Table 10.3, where the *PI* is .94 for Project X and 1.14 for Project Y. According to the decision rule for adopting independent projects,

**TABLE 10.3  Calculation of the Profitability Index (*PI*) for Two Different Projects**

| | Project X | | | Project Y | | |
|---|---|---|---|---|---|---|
| Year | Annual Cash Flow | Present Value Interest Factor (12%) | Discounted Cash Flow | Annual Cash Flow | Present Value Interest Factor (12%) | Discounted Cash Flow |
| 1 | $40,000 | .8929 | $35,716 | $30,000 | .8929 | $26,787 |
| 2 | 30,000 | .7972 | 23,916 | 20,000 | .7972 | 15,944 |
| 3 | 40,000 | .7118 | 28,472 | 40,000 | .7118 | 28,472 |
| 4 | 5,000 | .6355 | 3,177 | 40,000 | .6355 | 25,420 |
| 5 | 5,000 | .5674 | 2,837 | 30,000 | .5674 | 17,022 |
| | Total *PV* of cash flows | | $ 94,118 | Total *PV* of cash flows | | $113,645 |
| | Less: Initial outlay | | $100,000 | Less: Initial outlay | | $100,000 |

$$PI = \frac{94,118}{100,000} = .94118$$

$$PI = \frac{113,645}{100,000} = 1.13645$$

Project Y would be accepted since its *PI* is greater than 1, and Project X would be rejected since its *PI* is less than 1.

### Pros and Cons of Using the Profitability Index

The *PI* approach fully considers the time value of money (it is a discounted cash flow technique), and the discount rate employed reflects the firm's cost of capital. These favorable characteristics are shared with the *NPV* method. An additional advantage not shared with the *NPV* is that the *PI* indicates the return (present value of the cash flows) relative to the amount of capital invested. Thus, the value provided by the *PI* approach may be easier to interpret.

Perhaps the biggest disadvantage of the *PI* approach is its potential error in choosing between mutually exclusive projects.

**Example**

Consider Projects S and T:

| | Project S | Project T |
|---|---|---|
| Initial outlay | $10,000 | $100,000 |
| PV of cash flows | $12,000 | $110,000 |
| *NPV* | $ 2,000 | $ 10,000 |
| *PI* | 1.20 | 1.10 |

Project S would be preferred using the *PI* criteria, since Project S has the higher *PI*. This indicates that Project S generates higher *PV* of cash flows relative to the initial outlay. However, the *NPV* of Project T is greater than that of Project S. Since the *NPV* reflects the increase in the value of the firm after *all* costs have been considered (including financing costs), Project T is clearly the better project for the firm. Therefore, when the *PI* approach suggests making a different decision than that suggested by *NPV*, *NPV* is preferred.

## INTERNAL RATE OF RETURN

The **internal rate of return (*IRR*)** on a project is the rate of return that the firm expects to earn on the project. Mathematically, it is the discount rate that equates the present value of the cash flows to the initial outlay. Stated differently, the *IRR* is the discount rate at which *NPV* is equal to zero.

### Calculating the Internal Rate of Return

The *IRR* can be estimated once the initial outlay (*I*) and cash flows (*CF*) have been determined. It can be computed using the following equation:

$$I \stackrel{set}{=} \sum_{t=1}^{n} \frac{CF_t}{(1 + IRR)^t} \qquad (10.4)$$

where the *IRR* is the internal rate of return on the project and is unknown, and all other variables are known.

This equation can be rewritten as follows:

initial outlay = present value of cash flows (when *IRR* is used as the discount rate)

### Decision Rule for Using the Internal Rate of Return

When using the *IRR* approach for project evaluation, a firm should first establish its required rate of return, sometimes referred to as the *hurdle rate*. The cost of capital for the firm is commonly used as the firm's required rate of return since this is the cost of financing the project. If the estimated *IRR* is greater than the required rate of return, the project should be adopted because the firm will realize a return greater than its required return. Conversely, the firm should reject those projects having *IRR*s that are less than the required rate of return. This decision rule can be written as follows:

When *IRR* ≥ required rate of return, accept the project.

When *IRR* < required rate of return, reject the project.

### Application of the Internal Rate of Return

If a project is expected to generate an even stream of periodic cash flows throughout its lifetime (an annuity situation), the *IRR* can be computed easily using the present-value-of-an-annuity formula. For example, given annual cash flows of $30,000 during the five-year life of a project, and an initial outlay of $90,000, the IRR can be determined by solving for the discount rate that equates the present value of the cash flows ($30,000 annually for five years) to the initial outlay ($90,000). Substituting these values into the present-value-of-an-annuity formula results in

$$PVA = A(PVIFA_{k,n})$$

$$\$90{,}000 = \$30{,}000(PVIFA_{k=?,n=5})$$

$$3.0 = PVIFA_{k=?,n=5}$$

The left side of the equation is the present value interest factor of an annuity and can be found in Table D in the back of the text. Looking across the row for $n = 5$, you will see that the closest $PVIFA$ to 3.0 is 2.9906, found under the column headed by "20%." You can conclude that the $IRR$ for this project is approximately 20 percent. If the required rate of return for this project is below 20 percent, the project should be accepted.

The procedure described for determining the $IRR$ can be used only when there is an even stream of cash flows (an annuity). Unfortunately, the cash flows for many projects are uneven. While some calculators and computer programs can handle uneven cash flows, it is useful to work these problems manually to assure a thorough understanding of them. In so doing, one must apply different discount rates to the cash flows in a trial-and-error fashion until a discount rate is found that equates the present value of the cash flows to the initial outlay (this is the same technique that was used in Chapter 4 to determine the yield to maturity on a bond).

As an example, consider Project X introduced earlier in the chapter. Its cash flows are displayed in the second column of Table 10.4. Since the initial net outlay for the proposed project is $100,000, the objective is to find the discount rate at which the present value of cash flows is equal to $100,000. As indicated in Table 10.4, a discount rate of 7 percent generates a present value of cash flows equal to $103,618. Since this discount rate generates a higher value than desired, a higher discount rate is attempted in order to reduce the present value of cash flows. A discount rate of 8 percent generates a present value of cash flows equal to $101,585. Since this figure is still too high, a higher discount rate must be used. A 9 percent discount rate generates a present value of cash flows equal to $99,627. Thus, the $IRR$ for Project X is between 8 percent and 9 percent. By interpolation, the $IRR$ is determined to be approximately 8.8 percent. The implication is that Project X should be accepted only if the required rate of return on the project is 8.8 percent or less.

The computation of the $IRR$ for Project Y, also introduced earlier in the chapter, likewise appears in Table 10.4. First, a discount rate of 18 percent is attempted, for which the present value of cash flows is found to be $97,878. Since this figure is too low, a discount rate of 17 percent is attempted, for which the present value of cash flows is found to be $100,258. Since this figure is too high, the $IRR$ must be between 17 percent and 18 percent. Using interpolation, the $IRR$ is determined to be approximately 17.1 percent. Therefore, the project would be accepted only if the firm's required rate of return is less than or equal to 17.1 percent. If Projects X

**TABLE 10.4** Calculation of the Internal Rate of Return (*IRR*) for Projects with Uneven Cash Flows

Project X

| Year | Annual Cash Flow of Project X | Try a 7% Discount Rate Present Value Interest Factor | Discounted Cash Flow | Try an 8% Discount Rate Present Value Interest Factor | Discounted Cash Flow | Try a 9% Discount Rate Present Value Interest Factor | Discounted Cash Flow |
|---|---|---|---|---|---|---|---|
| 1 | $40,000 | .9346 | $37,384 | .9259 | $37,036 | .9174 | $36,696 |
| 2 | 30,000 | .8734 | 26,202 | .8573 | 25,719 | .8417 | 25,251 |
| 3 | 40,000 | .8163 | 32,652 | .7938 | 31,752 | .7722 | 30,888 |
| 4 | 5,000 | .7629 | 3,815 | .7350 | 3,675 | .7084 | 3,542 |
| 5 | 5,000 | .7130 | 3,565 | .6806 | 3,403 | .6499 | 3,250 |
| Total *PV* of Cash Flows | | | $103,618 | | $101,585 | | $99,627 |

*Conclusion:* The *IRR* of Project X is between 8% and 9% (8.8%, using interpolation).

Project Y

| Year | Annual Cash Flow of Project Y | Try an 18% Discount Rate Present Value Interest Factor | Discounted Cash Flow | Try a 17% Discount Rate Present Value Interest Factor | Discounted Cash Flow |
|---|---|---|---|---|---|
| 1 | $30,000 | .8475 | $25,425 | .8547 | $25,641 |
| 2 | 20,000 | .7182 | 14,364 | .7305 | 14,610 |
| 3 | 40,000 | .6086 | 24,344 | .6244 | 24,976 |
| 4 | 40,000 | .5158 | 20,632 | .5337 | 21,348 |
| 5 | 30,000 | .4371 | 13,113 | .4561 | 13,683 |
| Total *PV* of Cash Flows | | | $97,878 | | $100,258 |

*Conclusion:* The *IRR* of Project Y is between 17% and 18% (17.1%, using interpolation).

and Y are mutually exclusive, Project Y would be preferred because its *IRR* is greater than that of Project X. The procedure for calculating the *IRR* for projects having uneven cash flows is summarized in Figure 10.2.

## Pros and Cons of Using the Internal Rate of Return

As illustrated, the *IRR* method considers the timing of the cash flows over the entire life of the project (it is a discounted cash flow technique). This attribute is similar to that of the *NPV* and *PI* methods, and it makes *IRR* an acceptable technique for capital budgeting. The *IRR* method has the additional advantage of being stated in terms of a rate of return that is easily interpreted by management, an advantage not shared by the *NPV* and *PI* approaches.

There are also some disadvantages associated with the use of the *IRR*. First for projects lasting several periods and having uneven cash flows, the computation of the *IRR* without a computer or sophisticated calculator

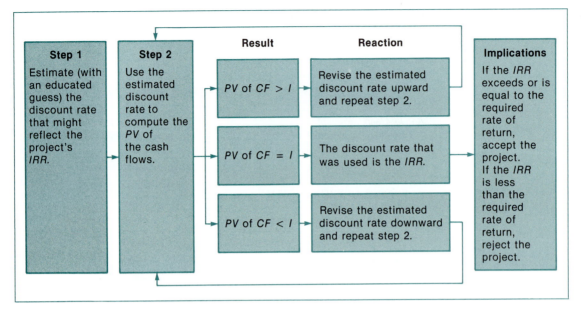

**FIGURE 10.2**
**Procedures for Calculating the *IRR* for a Project When Cash Flows Are Uneven**

can be quite difficult. Second, the *IRR* method implicitly assumes that the cash flows received can be reinvested at the internal rate of return for the project, but this assumption may not be realistic, particularly for projects with high *IRR*s. The result can be an estimate of the *IRR* that is higher than it should be. Third, and even more important, the *IRR* technique can lead to multiple solutions if the sign of the cash flows reverses from positive to negative or vice versa. The examples used earlier were not subject to this error since the signs of all the cash flows were positive. However, for projects where sign reversals occur, the firm should use an alternative capital budgeting technique.

## WHICH CAPITAL BUDGETING TECHNIQUE IS BEST?

Each technique has advantages and disadvantages. In terms of ease of application, the payback period may be easiest, while the *IRR* is the most difficult. Yet, given the availability of computers today, all techniques described in this chapter can be applied without great difficulty. Because of the importance of capital budgeting decisions, none of the capital budgeting techniques should be ruled out because of the tedious nature of the required calculations.

An overall comparison of capital budgeting techniques is provided in Table 10.5. Perhaps the most critical characteristic to compare among techniques is the ability it affords one to make a correct decision. In evaluating independent projects, the *NPV*, *PI*, and *IRR* approaches will lead to the same decision. The payback period approach is inferior because it ignores the timing of payments and thus sometimes leads to incorrect decisions when it is used as the sole criterion for decision making.

For comparing mutually exclusive projects, it was shown earlier that the *NPV* approach is superior to the *PI* approach. Additionally, the *NPV*

**TABLE 10.5** **Comparison of Capital Budgeting Techniques**

| Technique | Formula | Decision Rule of Project Acceptance | | Strengths | Weaknesses |
|---|---|---|---|---|---|
| Payback period for a project with even cash flows | $\dfrac{I}{\text{annuity cash flow}}$ | Payback period | $\leq$ maximum acceptable period | Easy to apply. Favors projects that generate cash quickly. | Does not fully account for timing of cash flows. Does not account for cash flows in periods after initial net outlay has been recovered. |
| Net present value (NPV) | $\displaystyle\sum_{t=1}^{n} \dfrac{CF_t}{(1+k)^t} - I$ | $NPV \geq 0$ | | Fully considers the time value of money. Discounting method incorporates firm's required rate of return. | Corporate managers have some difficulty relating to an NPV figure. They understand rate-of-return figures better, as provided by the IRR method. |
| Profitability index (PI) | $\dfrac{\displaystyle\sum_{t=1}^{n} \dfrac{CF_t}{(1+k)^t}}{I}$ | $PI \geq 1$ | | Fully considers the time value of money. Discounting method incorporates firm's required rate of return. | The PI approach can lead to improper decision when mutually exclusive projects are under consideration. |
| Internal rate of return (IRR) | $I \overset{\text{set}}{=} \displaystyle\sum_{t=1}^{n} \dfrac{CF_t}{(1+IRR)^t}$ | $IRR \geq$ required rate of return | | Fully considers the time value of money. | Implicitly assumes that funds generated by the project will be reinvested at the IRR, which may not be realistic. Multiple solutions for IRR can sometimes exist, which can result in incorrect decisions. |

approach and the *IRR* approach may rank mutually exclusive projects differently, which could lead to the selection of different mutually exclusive projects.

**Example**

Consider the comparison of Projects M and R, which have identical initial outlays but different expected cash flow streams, as indicated at the top of Table 10.6. The *NPV* of each project has been calculated and displayed in the lower part of Table 10.6 using twelve different discount rates. At a discount rate of 10 percent, the *NPV* of Project R is superior to that of Project M. Project R continues to have a higher *NPV* as the discount rate increases, until it reaches 17.5 percent. At that point,

**TABLE 10.6** Comparison of Two Projects Using *NPV* Method and Assuming Various Discount Rates

The initial outlay for both projects is $100,000.

| Year | Cash Flow for Project M | Cash Flow for Project R |
|------|------------------------|------------------------|
| 1 | $70,000 | $ 10,000 |
| 2 | 60,000 | 20,000 |
| 3 | 20,000 | 150,000 |

| Discount Rate | NPV of Project M | NPV of Project R | Preferred Project |
|---------------|------------------|------------------|-------------------|
| 10 % | $27,847 | $34,921 | R |
| 12 | 24,567 | 31,639 | R |
| 14 | 21,071 | 25,407 | R |
| 16 | 17,748 | 19,582 | R |
| 17.5 | 15,400 | 15,400 | — |
| 18 | 14,586 | 14,133 | M |
| 20 | 11,574 | 9,028 | M |
| 22 | 8,703 | 4,240 | M |
| 24 | 5,963 | −255 | M |
| 26 | 3,347 | −4,480 | M |
| 28 | 845 | −8,455 | M |
| 30 | −1,550 | −12,194 | Neither |

Project M has the same *NPV* as Project R. At discount rates above 17.5 percent, Project M has a higher *NPV* and is therefore preferred. This continues to be the case until the *NPV* of both projects becomes negative at a discount rate of close to 30 percent. At that point, neither project should be adopted.

The reason for the crossover of favorable projects at 17.5 percent is that higher discount rates favor projects that generate higher cash flows in the early years instead of late years. This relationship exists because the longer the period over which the cash flows must be discounted, the greater the impact of the high discount rate on the cash flows. Notice that Project R has an extremely large cash flow in the last year of the project's life.

Table 10.6 can also be used to evaluate projects M and R using the *IRR* method. Recall that the *IRR* is the discount rate that results in a present value of the cash flows equal to the initial outlay (where *NPV* is equal to zero). For Project M, the *IRR* is 28.7 percent. For Project R it is 23.9 percent. Therefore, Project M would be preferred if the two projects are mutually exclusive and if the *IRR* criterion is used. If the firm's required rate of return is higher than 17.5 percent, the *NPV* approach would suggest adopting the same project. However, if the required rate of return is lower than 17.5 percent, the *NPV* approach would suggest adoption of Project R instead.

The information in Table 10.6 is presented graphically in Figure 10.3. Each line intersects the horizontal scale at the *IRR* of the respective proj-

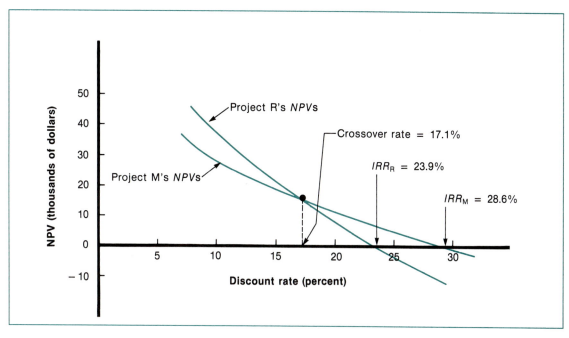

**FIGURE 10.3**
**The *NPV* of Projects M and R Using Various Discount Rates**

ects. At discount rates to the left of the crossover rate (17.5 percent), Project R has a higher *NPV*. To the right of the crossover point, Project M has the higher *NPV*.

The reason the *IRR* and *NPV* approaches may recommend different mutually exclusive projects centers around the assumption of the return that can be earned by the firm when it reinvests the cash flows from the project. The *NPV* approach implicitly assumes that cash flows can be reinvested at the firm's cost of capital (required rate of return), while the *IRR* approach assumes reinvestment of cash flows at the internal rate of return. The assumption of the *NPV* approach is generally perceived to be more realistic, since the firm can use funds generated by the project to earn a return equal to the cost of the capital by repaying the sources of capital. There is no assurance that cash flows can be reinvested at the *IRR* expected on the project generating those cash flows. In fact, the higher the *IRR* on a project, the less likely it is that the firm can reinvest the cash flows at the *IRR*. Therefore, when the two approaches conflict, the *NPV* approach is preferable.

## EVALUATING PROJECTS WITH UNEQUAL LIVES

When evaluating mutually exclusive projects that have unequal lives, the capital budgeting decision becomes more complex. To illustrate, consider a firm that is planning to purchase one of two alternative machines for the production of its product. The initial outlays (*I*) and periodic cash flows (*CF*) for the two machines are as follows:

| Year | Machine F (I = $5,000) CF | Machine G (I = $9,000) CF |
|------|------|------|
| 1 | $3,300 | $3,000 |
| 2 | 3,300 | 3,000 |
| 3 | 3,300 | 3,000 |
| 4 |  | 3,000 |
| 5 |  | 3,000 |
| 6 |  | 3,000 |

Assume the firm uses 10 percent as the required rate of return on capital budgeting projects and determines the NPV to be $3,203 for Machine F and $4,066 for Machine G. If the situation were such that neither machine would be replaced after its useful life has been expended (for example, if the product being made with the machine is to be discontinued when the machine wears out), selection of the machine that has the highest NPV would be appropriate. In this case, Machine G would be selected since it has the higher expected NPV. However, if the production and sale of the product is expected to continue indefinitely, Machine F will need to be re-placed after three years. This additional investment, and the cash flow it generates during Years 4 through 6 must be included in the evaluation. A comparison of the NPV generated by Machine G over a six-year period against the NPV generated by Machine F over only a three-year period would be unfair to Machine F.

One solution to this problem is to construct a **replacement chain** for Machine F. To construct a replacement chain, it is assumed that in the last year of Machine F's productive life, a cash outflow is incurred for the pur-chase of a new Machine F to replace the old one. This outflow will be par-tially offset by the cash inflows generated during that year (Year 3 in our example). The new replacement machine will generate another three years of identical cash flows. The project is now expected to have six years of cash inflows of $3,300 per year, plus a $5,000 outflow at the end of Year 3. This is in addition to the initial $5,000 outflow for the purchase of the first Machine F. The NPV of the replacement chain requires finding the present value of all the inflows, and the outflow, then subtracting the initial outlay. The expected cash flows related to the chain are

| Year | Machine F (I = $5,000) |
|------|------|
| 1 | $3,300 |
| 2 | 3,300 |
| 3 | 3,300 − 5,000 |
| 4 | 3,300 |
| 5 | 3,300 |
| 6 | 3,300 |

The NPV for the replacement chain of Machine F can be found as follows:

$$NPV = \$3,300(PVIFA_{k=10\%,n=6}) - \$5,000(PVIF_{k=10\%,n=3}) - \$5,000$$

$$= \$3,300(4.3553) - \$5,000(.7513) - \$5,000$$

$$= \$5,616$$

By using the replacement chain for Machine F, the lives of the two machines have been made equal, and their *NPV*s can now be compared. Because Machine F has a higher *NPV* over the six-year period, it is preferable to Machine G.

The major limitation of using the replacement-chain method is that numerous calculations may be necessary in some instances. For example, if one machine has a nine-year life and the other an eleven-year life, a ninety-nine-year chain is necessary for each machine in order to match their lives. Both chains must cover ninety-nine years, since ninety-nine is the lowest common denominator between nine years and eleven years.

An alternative method that is equally correct is to calculate the **annualized net present value (*ANPV*)** for both projects. This method adjusts the firm's *NPV* for the life of the project. A shorter life will be more highly valued, other things being equal. The *ANPV* is estimated as follows:

$$ANPV = \frac{NPV}{PVIFA_{k,n}} \qquad \textbf{(10.5)}$$

The denominator of Equation 10.5 is the present value interest factor of an annuity reflecting the number of years of the project's life and the required rate of return on the project. Note that the denominator is the present value interest factor of an annuity even if the project's cash flows are not an annuity.

By dividing the project's *NPV* by the present value interest factor of an annuity, one obtains the annual dollar benefit to the firm stated in terms of the time value of money. That is, two projects with equal *NPV*s but different lives will have different *ANPV*s. The project with the shorter life will have a higher *ANPV* since the total *NPV* is generated over a shorter period of time. The project with the higher *ANPV* is preferable. For Machines F and G, each *ANPV* is calculated as follows:

$$ANPV_F = \frac{NPV}{PVIFA_{10\%,3 \text{ yrs.}}}$$

$$= \frac{\$3,203}{2.487}$$

$$= \$1,288$$

$$ANPV_G = \frac{NPV}{PVIFA_{10\%,6 \text{ yrs.}}}$$

$$= \frac{\$4,066}{4.355}$$

$$= \$934$$

Machine F is preferable because of its higher *ANPV*. Although both the replacement-chain and *ANPV* techniques are useful (and they always agree in their recommendations) when comparing projects with unequal lives, the replacement chain is easier for corporate managers to understand. This advantage may be offset, however, by the ease with which the *ANPV* can be estimated.

## CAPITAL RATIONING

Up to this point, capital budgeting has been discussed using the assumption that a firm will accept all projects that are profitable (unless they are mutually exclusive) without concern about the level of total expenditures. In reality, firms often place a maximum limit on the funds available for adopting projects. Accordingly, such firms are forced to ration their limited capital.

One frequently cited reason for using **capital rationing** is a lack of qualified managers to oversee projects; the firm's management could be overwhelmed by the adoption of too many new projects. A second reason is management's unwillingness to issue the securities necessary to finance all the projects. In some cases, managers of smaller companies may not wish to sell new equity shares in the company for fear of losing control of the company. Other managers may be concerned about the increased risk the company incurs when it borrows large amounts to adopt projects.

A third possible reason for capital rationing is that the firm's securities may be temporarily depressed, and management wants to postpone the adoption of some projects until the firm can sell its securities at higher prices. Managers must be very cautious in using this strategy, however, since predicting future securities prices is extremely difficult.

When capital constraints exist, the firm may need to select only the best projects from a lengthy list of acceptable projects. The preferred method is to determine which combination of projects offers the highest combined *NPV* without exceeding the limit imposed by the capital budget. This approach is theoretically sound, since *NPV* indicates the net benefit realized by the firm from adopting the capital budgeting projects. For example, Table 10.7 lists five independent capital budgeting projects. Assuming the firm specifies a maximum capital budget of $100,000, the firm will be unable to adopt them all. Numerous combinations of projects are possible. For example,

| Project Combinations | Total Investment | Combined NPV |
|---|---|---|
| A & E | $100,000 | $38,750 |
| B, C, & D | 100,000 | 40,500 |
| C, D, & E | 85,000 | 23,750 |

The combination of projects that is expected to provide the firm with the highest combined *NPV* is B, C, and D. Therefore, those projects should be adopted.

**TABLE 10.7**  **Choice among Five Proposed Projects with Capital Rationing**

| Project | Initial Outlay | NPV | PI | IRR |
|---|---|---|---|---|
| A | $75,000 | $37,500 | 1.50 | 23% |
| B | 40,000 | 18,000 | 1.45 | 21 |
| C | 30,000 | 12,000 | 1.40 | 19 |
| D | 30,000 | 10,500 | 1.35 | 18 |
| E | 25,000 | 1,250 | 1.05 | 17 |

## FINANCIAL MANAGEMENT IN PRACTICE

### HOW IS CAPITAL BUDGETING CONDUCTED BY PRACTITIONERS?

A number of surveys have been conducted to determine how corporations conduct capital budgeting. While the specific findings vary, some general conclusions can be stated. First, the internal rate of return (*IRR*) is the most popular technique for assessing projects. One survey indicated that 54 percent of respondents use *IRR* as their primary method of project evaluation. Next in popularity were the average rate of return[1] (25 percent), net present value (10 percent), payback period (9 percent), and profitability index (3 percent) methods.

Most firms evaluate projects using more than one technique; many operate under the constraint of capital rationing. Fifty-two percent of surveyed firms indicated they employ capital rationing, the major cause being a limit imposed by management on the amount of debt the firm is willing to assume.[2] Although a considerable gap appears to exist between capital budgeting theory and practice, there is some evidence that the gap is narrowing.[3]

Regarding the division of time financial managers spend on various aspects of capital budgeting, one survey indicated that the greatest proportion of time is spent on analyzing and selecting projects (24 percent), followed by implementing projects (22 percent), planning capital expenditures (20 percent), defining and estimating project cash flows (19 percent), and project follow up and review (14 percent).[4]

1. The method using the average rate of return was not discussed in this chapter because there are numerous variations of it, and because it does not consider the time value of money.
2. Lawrence J. Gitman and John R. Forrester, Jr., "A Survey of Capital Budgeting Techniques Used by Major U.S. Firms," *Financial Management* 6 (Fall 1977): 66–71.

3. J. William Petty, David F. Scott, Jr., and Monroe M. Bird, "The Capital Expenditure Decision-Making Process of Large Corporations," *Engineering Economist* 20 (Spring 1975): 159–172.
4. Lawrence J. Gitman and Charles E. Maxwell, "Financial Activities of Major U.S. Firms: Survey and Analysis of Fortunes 1000," *Financial Management* 14 (Winter 1985): 57–65.

Two alternative approaches to capital rationing have been suggested by some analysts. One is to use profitability indexes to indicate the projects that will generate the largest present value of cash flows relative to the initial investment. The idea is to select the project with the highest *PI* first, the one with the next highest *PI* second, and so on.

Given the same five projects listed in Table 10.7, Project A would be selected first under this approach, but since only $25,000 remains to adopt other projects, Project E would be the only other project that could be adopted. This combination results in a lower combined *NPV* ($38,750) than the combination identified earlier. Therefore, this alternative approach may provide inferior results.

The other alternative is to begin by adopting the project with the highest *IRR* first, then the project with the next highest *IRR*, and so on. Once again, in our example this would result in the adoption of Projects A and E, which is not the optimal combination of projects.

While most firms specify maximum capital budgets, many firms allow for some flexibility in the budget. Therefore, if a proposed project appears extremely desirable and cannot be postponed, the budget may be increased to accommodate it.

A firm's capital budget is highly dependent on management's overall perception of the firm's economic environment. If economic conditions are expected to be favorable, a large number of profitable projects are likely to exist. As a result, management may authorize a large capital budget. Conversely, a relatively small capital budget may be established if unfavorable economic conditions exist. As an example, the capital budgets of many oil companies were revised downward in 1986 as a result of declining oil prices.

## SUMMARY

Given the estimated cash flows for a proposed project, a firm can use the capital budgeting techniques presented in this chapter to select specific projects for adoption. With the exception of the payback-period approach, the techniques presented here fully consider the time value of money.

The *NPV* approach discounts the expected incremental cash flows back to present value, using the firm's cost of capital as the discount rate. If the estimated present value exceeds the initial outlay, the project should be accepted. This approach is theoretically sound and has only one major disadvantage: some corporate managers have difficulty understanding how to interpret the results. The profitability index is the ratio of the present value of the incremental cash flows (discounted at the firm's required rate of return) divided by the initial outlay. While the accept-reject decision using *PI* is theoretically correct, using the *PI* index to evaluate mutually exclusive projects may result in incorrect decisions. The *IRR* approach involves calculating the rate of return the firm expects to earn on capital budgeting projects. If the rate of return exceeds the firm's cost of capital, the project should be adopted. While the *IRR* approach results in the same accept-reject decisions as both the *NPV* and *PI* approaches, it may result in incorrect decisions when used to select between mutually exclusive projects. This possible incorrect decision can result from the assumption that the cash flows realized from capital budgeting projects can be reinvested at the internal rate of return. Additionally, the *IRR* approach may identify two different expected rates of return for projects exhibiting cash outflows after the initial investment is made.

## KEY TERMS

**Annualized net present value** A measure used to evaluate mutually exclusive capital budgeting projects that have different lives.

**Capital rationing** The process of allocating a limited amount of available funds to alternative capital budgeting projects.

**Cost of capital** The cost of long-term funds to the firm.

**Internal rate of return** The rate of return that the firm expects to earn on its initial outlay.

**Net present value** A technique for evaluating capital budgeting projects. The net present value of a project is the expected value in today's dollars after accounting for all costs.

**Payback period** The length of time it takes for a firm to recover its initial outlay on a project.

**Profitability index** The ratio of the project's discounted cash flows to its initial outlay. This measure is used in capital budgeting project evaluation.

**Replacement chain** A method of comparing capital budgeting projects having unequal lives.

# EQUATIONS

See Table 10.5 for the equations describing each capital budgeting technique. The single equation not shown in this table follows.

**Equation 10.5**    **Annualized Net Present Value**

$$ANPV = \frac{NPV}{PVIFA_{k,n}}$$    **(p. 295)**

where    $ANPV$ = annualized net present value
$NPV$ = net present value
$PVIFA_{k,n}$ = present value interest factor of an annuity, given $k$ and $n$
$k$ = required rate of return
$n$ = number of periods

Equation 10.5 is used to evaluate mutually exclusive projects with unequal lives. After the annualized $NPV$s of the projects have been determined, the financial manager should adopt the project with the higher $ANPV$.

# QUESTIONS

**Q10-1.** What are the main limitations of the payback-period approach to capital budgeting?

**Q10-2.** How is the cost of financing a project accounted for when using the net present value approach?

**Q10-3.** If a project's $NPV$ is negative, what does that imply about the relationship between the present value of cash flows and the initial outlay? Does it suggest that you accept or reject the project?

**Q10-4.** If a project's $NPV$ is positive, what does that imply about a firm's required rate of return on the project relative to the estimated return on the project? Does it suggest that you accept or reject the project?

**Q10-5.** Assume you are deciding whether to go to the beach or snow skiing in the mountains for the entire spring break. Does the decision reflect independent or mutually exclusive opportunities? Explain.

**Q10-6.** Explain the relationship between net present value and profitability index. When will they give you the same solution? When will the solutions differ?

**Q10-7.** What does it mean to a firm if a project has a net present value of $75,000?

**Q10-8.** How are the internal rate of return and the net present value of a project affected if the firm's cost of capital increases?

**Q10-9.** Given the following information, which project is preferred when using the $PI$ approach? Which project is preferred using the $NPV$ approach? Which project should be accepted? Why?

|  | Project L | Project M |
|---|---|---|
| Initial outlay | $50,000 | $100,000 |
| PV of cash flows | 70,000 | 130,000 |

**Q10-10.** Explain the similarities and differences in decisions when using *NPV* versus *IRR*.

**Q10-11.** Why is *NPV* not appropriate for determining which of two mutually exclusive projects to adopt when they have unequal lives?

## SELF-TEST PROBLEMS

Solutions to self-test problems appear on p. S1.

**SP10-1.** La Rue Pizza Place has considered the purchase of an additional delivery van to expand its delivery area. The van costs $11,000 but is expected to generate additional cash flows as follows:

| Year | Cash Flow |
|---|---|
| 1 | $3,000 |
| 2 | 3,000 |
| 3 | 3,000 |
| 4 | 6,000 |

The cost of capital to La Rue is 14 percent.

**a.** Given a maximum payback period of three years required by La Rue, should the project be accepted or rejected? Explain.
**b.** Based on the estimated *NPV*, should the project be accepted or rejected? Explain.
**c.** Based on the estimated *IRR*, should the project be accepted or rejected? Explain.
**d.** Based on the estimated profitability index, should the project be accepted or rejected? Explain.

## PROBLEMS

**P10-1.** Scully Company is considering the purchase of some new equipment. The initial cost of the equipment is $1,200,000, and the firm's cost of capital is 15 percent. The estimated cash flows for this project are $300,000 per year for eight years. The salvage value is expected to be zero.

**a.** What is the project's payback period?
**b.** What is the project's *NPV?*
**c.** What is the project's *PI?*
**d.** What is the project's *IRR?*

**P10-2.** Laz Corporation is considering the purchase of a machine for $500,000. The firm's cost of capital is 17 percent, and the estimated cash flows resulting from the machine are as follows:

| Year | Cash Flow |
|------|-----------|
| 1 | $ 80,000 |
| 2 | 80,000 |
| 3 | 100,000 |
| 4 | 100,000 |
| 5 | 200,000 |
| 6 | 200,000 |
| 7 | 200,000 |

The salvage value is expected to be zero.

**a.** If Laz Corporation prefers a payback period of no more than four years, should it purchase the machine using the payback criterion? Justify your answer.
**b.** Based on the net present value (*NPV*) criterion, should Laz Corporation purchase the machine? Justify your answer.
**c.** Based on the profitability index (*PI*) criterion, should Laz Corporation purchase the machine? Justify your answer.
**d.** Based on the *IRR* criterion, should Laz Corporation purchase the machine? Justify your answer.

**P10-3.** Stuart Corporation plans to purchase a computer to reduce costs and therefore increase its cash flows over time. It is considering two computers. Computer C has an expected life of three years and would require an initial outlay of $10,000. Computer D has an expected life of four years and would require an initial outlay of $15,000. Stuart Corporation's cost of capital is 12 percent. Computer C's net present value is $30,000, while Computer D's net present value is $45,000. Based on the annualized net present value approach, which computer should be purchased? Justify your answer.

**P10-4.** Malex, Inc., is a small company that uses an aggressive strategy of growth through the acquisition of other businesses. It is currently evaluating five different businesses it is considering acquiring. For each business, it has estimated the initial outlay, profitability index, and net present value.

| Business | Initial Outlay | Profitability Index | Net Present Value |
|----------|----------------|---------------------|-------------------|
| Ajant Corporation | $200,000 | 1.60 | $120,000 |
| Carren Corporation | 200,000 | 1.30 | 60,000 |
| Garpen Foods | 100,000 | 1.10 | 10,000 |
| Hallmark Truckers | 200,000 | .95 | −10,000 |
| Voraxi Corporation | 100,000 | .90 | −10,000 |

**a.** Malex, Inc., has access to a maximum of $300,000. Which businesses should it purchase?
**b.** If Malex, Inc., had access to a maximum of $700,000, which businesses should it purchase?

**P10-5.** Abel Industries is evaluating two mutually exclusive projects whose expected annual cash flows are as follows:

| Year | Cash Flow for Project A | Cash Flow for Project B |
|------|------------------------|------------------------|
| 1 | $130,000 | $90,000 |
| 2 | 130,000 | 90,000 |
| 3 | 130,000 | 90,000 |
| 4 | 130,000 | 90,000 |
| 5 |  | 90,000 |
| 6 |  | 90,000 |
| 7 |  | 90,000 |
| 8 |  | 90,000 |

The initial outlay for Project A is $250,000, and for Project B it is $300,000. Using the replacement-chain approach, determine which project should be adopted. Abel has a 16 percent cost of capital.

**P10-6.** Dempsey Corporation is considering the purchase of either Machine A or Machine B for its production facilities. Both machines require an initial outlay of $170,000. The firm's cost of capital is 13 percent. The estimated cash flows for each machine are as follows:

| Year | Cash Flow for Machine A | Cash Flow for Machine B |
|------|------------------------|------------------------|
| 1 | $   0 | $20,000 |
| 2 | 60,000 | 80,000 |
| 3 | 100,000 | 90,000 |
| 4 | 130,000 | 90,000 |

The salvage value is expected to be zero.

**a.** Which machine is more desirable based on the payback criterion? Justify your answer.
**b.** Which machine is more desirable based on the *NPV* criterion? Justify your answer.
**c.** Which machine is more desirable based on the profitability index (*PI*) criterion? Justify your answer.
**d.** Which machine is more desirable based on the *IRR* criterion? Justify your answer.

**P10-7.** Flaim Flower Company is considering the purchase of a van for an initial outlay of $20,000 that would allow for more deliveries and increased sales. The firm's cost of capital is 19 percent. The estimated cash flows attributable to the van are as follows:

| Year | Cash Flow |
|------|-----------|
| 1 | $4,000 |
| 2 | 5,000 |
| 3 | 5,000 |
| 4 | 7,000 |
| 5 | 5,000 |

The after-tax salvage value is included in the last year's cash flow.

**a.** The company is only willing to purchase this van if the payback period is four years or less and if the van's NPV is positive. Given this criteria, should the company purchase the van? Justify your answer.

**b.** Should this project be accepted based on the probability index criterion? Justify your answer.

**c.** Should this project be accepted based on the internal rate of return criterion? Justify your answer.

**P10-8.** Streat, Inc., plans to purchase new machinery from either DISCOUNT WORLD or DELUXE WORLD. The initial outlay for the machinery is $100,000 at DISCOUNT WORLD versus $200,000 at DELUXE WORLD. The machinery will create additional cash flows of $80,000 per year, regardless of where it is purchased. The expected life of the machinery at DISCOUNT WORLD is three years versus five years at DELUXE WORLD. Find the annualized net present value (ANPV) for each machine. (Streat, Inc., has a cost of capital equal to 18 percent.)

**P10-9.** Huntington Corporation has six proposed projects that are all independent The relevant information for each project is as follows:

| Project | Initial Outlay | Net Present Value |
|---------|---------------|-------------------|
| A | $100,000 | $15,000 |
| B | 90,000 | 14,000 |
| C | 40,000 | 10,000 |
| D | 60,000 | 5,000 |
| E | 20,000 | 2,000 |
| F | 30,000 | 4,000 |

Which project(s) should it select if it has only $100,000 available for adopting projects?

**P10-10.** Bailey, Inc., is considering the adoption of three mutually exclusive projects. Bailey's cost of capital is 15 percent. The initial cost of each project is $30,000 for Project A, $50,000 for Project B, and $75,000 for Project C. The expected cash flows for each project are as follows:

| Year | Cash Flow for Project A | Cash Flow for Project B | Cash Flow for Project C |
|------|------------------------|------------------------|------------------------|
| 1 | $25,000 | $20,000 | $25,000 |
| 2 | 25,000 | 20,000 | 25,000 |
| 3 | | 20,000 | 25,000 |
| 4 | | 20,000 | 25,000 |
| 5 | | | 25,000 |
| 6 | | | 25,000 |

Determine which project to adopt using the replacement chain approach and the ANPV approach.

**P10-11.** Dorian, Inc., plans to purchase space and set up a business in one of two alternative shopping malls. The initial outlay for both locations would be $90,000. The business is expected to have a limited life of three years, and the firm's cost of capital is 16 percent. The cash flows attributable to each possibility are as follows:

| Year | Cash Flow for East Mall | Cash Flow for West Mall |
|------|-------------------------|-------------------------|
| 1 | $50,000 | $ 20,000 |
| 2 | 50,000 | 60,000 |
| 3 | 50,000 | 120,000 |

**a.** If the net-present-value method is used, which one of these mutually exclusive projects would be accepted? Justify your answer.
**b.** If the payback-period method is used, which project would be accepted? Justify your answer.
**c.** If the internal-rate-of-return method is used, which project would be accepted? Justify your answer.
**d.** If the profitability-index method is used, which project would be accepted? Justify your answer.

**P10-12.** Kalany Corporation is considering the purchase of an existing business as a subsidiary. The initial outlay required to purchase this business is $525,000, and Kalany's cost of capital is 15 percent. The estimated cash flows that would result from purchasing this business are as follows:

| Year | Cash Flow |
|------|-----------|
| 1 | $100,000 |
| 2 | 100,000 |
| 3 | 100,000 |
| 4 | 100,000 |
| 5 | 100,000 |
| 6 | 400,000 |

**a.** What is the *NPV* of the proposed project?
**b.** What is the *IRR* of the proposed project?
**c.** What is the *PI* of the proposed project?
**d.** What is the payback period of the proposed project?

**P10-13.** Fenton Industries is considering replacing an old machine with a new one. The replacement machine will cost $600,000, plus another $15,000 for installation. The book value of the old machine is $100,000, and it was purchased five years earlier for $500,000. It has five more years of life remaining and has a market value of $50,000. If it is used for five more years, it will have no salvage value. The new machine also has an expected life of five years. However, the expected salvage value after five years is $75,000.

In order to use the new machine, the firm must spend $35,000 to train its employees. If the new machine is purchased, annual sales will increase to $1,000,000 from $750,000. Cost of goods sold will also increase to $700,000 from $680,000, and annual depreciation will increase from $50,000 to $120,000. Fenton Industries has a 34 percent marginal tax rate.

**a.** Identify the initial outlay, periodic cash flows, and terminal cash flow associated with adopting this project.
**b.** Assuming a 14 percent required rate of return on the project, calculate the project's *NPV, IRR*, profitability index, and payback period.

## COMPUTER-ASSISTED PROBLEMS

**CP10-1.** SIU Corporation is considering adopting a project requiring an initial outlay of $4 million. The estimated annual cash flows from the project are $1 million per year for six years, and the project has an estimated salvage value of $2 million at the end of the sixth year. The appropriate discount rate for this project is 14 percent.

**a. Sensitivity of *NPV* to Annual Cash Flows** What is the *NPV* of this project based on the estimates provided above? Using the *NPV* estimate as the sole criterion, would you purchase the project? Explain.

SIU Corporation recognizes that the cash flows are uncertain. It feels that the annual cash flows could differ from the estimated $1 million. What is the *NPV* if the annual cash flows are $800,000 per year? $900,000 per year? $1.1 million per year? $1.2 million per year?

**b. Sensitivity of *NPV* to Salvage Value** Using the original information about SIU Corporation, how would the *NPV* be affected if the salvage value is actually $1.8 million? $1.9 million? $2.1 million? $2.2 million?

**c. Sensitivity of *NPV* to Annual Cash Flows and Salvage Value** Is the estimated *NPV* more sensitive to the uncertainty surrounding the annual cash flows or the salvage value? Explain.

**d. Sensitivity of *NPV* to Annual Cash Flows and Salvage Value** What would the *NPV* be under the most optimistic conditions regarding the annual cash flows and the salvage value? What would the *NPV* be under the most pessimistic conditions? Would the project be feasible under all possible conditions? Explain.

**e. Probability Distributions** Assume the following probability distributions:

| Annual Cash Flow | Probability | Salvage Value | Probability |
|---|---|---|---|
| $ 800,000 | 25% | $1,700,000 | 10% |
| 1,000,000 | 50 | 2,000,000 | 60 |
| 1,100,000 | 25 | 2,100,000 | 30 |

Should SIU Corporation accept this project if it requires at least an 80 percent probability that the project will be profitable? Explain.

**f. Simulation** Assume that annual cash flows will be somewhere between $700,000 and $1,200,000, while the salvage value will be between $1,700,000 and $2,200,000. Should SIU Corporation accept this project if it requires at least an 80 percent probability that the project will be profitable? Explain.

**g. Sensitivity of *IRR* to Annual Cash Flows and Salvage Value** Repeat Parts a through d, analyzing the *IRR* instead of the *NPV*.

## REFERENCES

Bacon, Peter W. "The Evaluation of Mutually Exclusive Investments." *Financial Management* 6 (Summer 1977): 55–58.

Gitman, Lawrence J., and John R. Forrester, Jr. "Forecasting and Evaluation Practices and Performance: A Survey of Capital Budgeting Used by Major U.S. Firms." *Financial Management* 6 (Fall 1977): 66–71.

Gitman, Lawrence J., and Charles G. Maxwell. "Financial Activities of Major U.S. Firms: Survey and Analysis of Fortune's 1000." *Financial Management* 14 (Winter 1985): 57–65.

Hoskins, Colin G., and Glen A. Mumey. "Payback: A Maligned Method of Asset Ranking?" *Engineering Economist* 25 (Fall 1979): 53–65.

————. "Current Capital Budgeting Practices." *Management Accounting* 28 (June 1981): 26–30.

Lorie, James H., and Leonard J. Savage. "Three Problems in Rationing Capital." *Journal of Business* 28 (October 1955): 229–39.

Pinches, George E. "Myopia, Capital Budgeting and Decision Making." *Financial Management* 11 (Autumn 1982): 6–19.

Rappaport, Alfred, and Robert A. Taggart, Jr. "Evaluation of Capital Expenditure Proposals under Inflation." *Financial Management* 11 (Spring 1982): 5–13.

Rosenblatt, Meir J. "A Survey and Analysis of Capital Budgeting Decision Process in Multi-Division Firms." *Engineering Economist* 25 (Summer 1980): 259–73.

Schall, Lawrence D., Gary L. Sundem, and William R. Geijsbeek. "Survey and Analysis of Capital Budgeting Methods." *Journal of Finance* 33 (March 1978): 281–87.

# CHAPTER 11

# CAPITAL BUDGETING UNDER UNCERTAINTY

## RISK-ADJUSTED CAPITAL BUDGETING IN PERSPECTIVE

In 1987 General Motors announced a goal of building a new four-door sport utility vehicle to be available to customers by 1990. To achieve its goal, GM plans to modify its assembly line operations at its plant in Moraine, Ohio, at an estimated cost of $40 million. In addition to making such investments for operational purposes, GM also frequently purchases U.S. Treasury bills as a temporary haven for cash that is not needed immediately.

Although both of these situations involve the investment of money by General Motors, a substantial difference in the level of risk of the two investments is evident. The money invested in the assembly line operation may be completely lost if the product produced at that facility is not accepted by the public. Conversely, if the demand for the proposed new vehicle is high, the return to GM on the money invested in assembly line modifica-

tion may be substantial. By contrast, the return on the money GM invests in U.S. government securities is known with virtual certainty.

GM may be considering numerous other projects that have risk levels that fall between the alternatives described here. Thus the company is constantly faced with the task of deciding how to allocate its funds among projects with various forecasted returns and degrees of risk.

How can firms measure and quantify the difference in the risk of alternative investments? How should the level of project risk be considered in evaluating capital budgeting projects? This chapter provides a framework that can be used to answer these and other questions about the risk of alternative investments.

The previous two chapters discussed how to estimate the cash flows for capital budgeting projects and how to make capital budgeting decisions based on an evaluation of those cash flows. There was an implicit assumption in both of these chapters that the projects are equally as risky as the firm. However, project risk may be more risky than the firm, and ignoring this uncertainty could lead to faulty decisions that might reduce the firm's profits or increase the firm's risk. Either of these might in turn reduce the value of the firm's common stock and thus prevent the maximization of shareholder wealth. This chapter demonstrates how to estimate and evaluate cash flows under conditions of uncertainty.

## WHY CAPITAL BUDGETING TECHNIQUES MUST ACCOUNT FOR UNCERTAINTY

Unwise capital budgeting decisions are likely if cash flows are inaccurately estimated. Incorrect forecasts of (1) the cost of the project, (2) the level of sales resulting from the project, (3) the price at which the firm's product can be sold, and (4) the periodic costs related to the project can skew the cash-flow estimates. A classic example of a project with considerable uncertainty is oil exploration. The cash flows resulting from such projects are particularly difficult to estimate because the quantity of oil to be extracted and the market price at which it will sell are so uncertain. Assume the cash flows from a potential drilling project are estimated based on a market price of oil of $25 per barrel. If oil is discovered, the actual cash flows could differ substantially from the estimated cash flows if the market price of oil decreases to $15 per barrel. Reduced cash inflows could cause this project to be unprofitable and reduce the value of the firm.

Other factors could also reduce the profitability of the project. Suppose that oil could be found only at an extremely high exploratory cost, or that production costs were higher than anticipated, or that oil is not found at all. These risks make it unlikely that a firm would be willing to evaluate this project in the same way it would evaluate an investment in, say, U.S. Treasury bonds. The difference in risk must be explicitly accounted for.

Since virtually all capital budgeting projects contain risk, firms must learn to measure risk and incorporate it into the analysis of projects before making investment decisions. Recall from the previous chapter that the net present value (*NPV*) and internal rate of return (*IRR*) methods are appropriate for evaluating projects having risk levels similar to that of the firm. These same techniques can also be used in modified form when future cash flows are uncertain. The focus of this chapter is on (1) modifying the *NPV* and *IRR* techniques to account for risk and (2) introducing several other techniques that are useful for evaluating risky capital budgeting projects. The main topics of this chapter include

- Risk-adjusted discount rates
- Certainty equivalent approach
- Decision trees

- Sensitivity analysis
- Simulation

Each of these topics is discussed in turn.

## RISK-ADJUSTED DISCOUNT RATES

Recall from Chapter 5 that investors in common stock require higher rates of return on stocks that have higher risk. This higher required rate of return compensates investors for assuming the higher risk. If the expected return on a stock is not sufficiently high to compensate for the risk, investors should not purchase the stock.

Similarly, capital budgeting projects containing high levels of risk must promise high rates of return in order to justify the investment of corporate funds. In Chapter 10 the cost of capital was used as the discount rate to determine the *NPV* of capital budgeting projects. This discount rate represents the firm's cost of raising long-term funds and reflects the risk of the firm itself. By using the cost of capital as the discount rate, the implicit assumption is made that the projects are equally as risky as the firm. In order to account for the specific risk of individual projects, the discount rate can be adjusted up or down to reflect the higher or lower risk of projects relative to the firm and the resulting higher or lower required rate of return on the projects.

When a firm uses a discount rate that reflects the risk of the project under consideration, it is said to be using a **risk-adjusted discount rate.** Although the use of risk-adjusted discount rates is justified based on the necessity of compensating for risk, it can also be justified based on the impact that high-risk projects can have on a firm's cost of capital. Since the cost of capital is the cost to firms of raising the long-term funds used to adopt capital projects, a firm adopting high-risk projects will realize an increase in the risk of the firm itself, and suppliers of long-term funds to the firm will require higher returns, increasing the firm's cost of capital. Therefore, the use of discount rates that differ from a firm's cost of capital is justified. The greater the risk exhibited by a project, the greater will be the required rate of return for the project, and the lower will be the *NPV* of the project, other things being equal.

### Steps Required When Using Risk-Adjusted Discount Rates

The risk-adjusted *NPV* of a proposed project is computed as

$$\text{risk-adjusted } NPV = \sum_{t=1}^{n} \frac{CF_t}{(1 + k^*)^t} - I \qquad (11.1)$$

where $CF_t$ = cash flow expected in period $t$

$I$ = initial outlay

$k^* =$ risk-adjusted discount rate

$n =$ life of the project

Solving this equation requires the use of steps similar to those used in computing *NPV* in the previous chapter.

*Step 1.* Determine the risk-adjusted discount rate ($k^*$) applicable to the project being evaluated.
*Step 2.* Discount the cash flows using $k^*$ as the discount rate, and subtract the initial cash outlay to arrive at the risk-adjusted *NPV*.
*Step 3.* Accept the project if risk-adjusted $NPV \geq 0$.

The application of the risk-adjusted discount rate may determine a project's risk-adjusted *NPV* to be negative, even though its *NPV* was positive when the cost of capital was used.

## Application of Risk-Adjusted Discount Rates

The following example illustrates how risk-adjusted discount rates can be applied.

**Example**

In the previous chapter, the *NPV* approach was applied to Project Y, where the future cash flows were assumed to be known with certainty, the cost of the project was $100,000, and the firm's cost of capital (12 percent) was used as the discount rate. Now assume these same cash flows are uncertain, and that the firm, after evaluating the risk of the project, has decided to use a risk-adjusted discount rate of 20 percent ($k^* = 20\%$).

Columns 3 and 4 of Table 11.1 illustrate the calculation of *NPV* for Project Y using the cost of capital as the discount rate. Here, the project's *NPV* is found to be

**TABLE 11.1  Use of Risk-Adjusted Discount Rates to Compute Net Present Value**

|  |  | Not Adjusted for Risk | | Adjusted for Risk | |
|---|---|---|---|---|---|
| (1) | (2) | (3) | (4) | (5) | (6) |
| End of Year | Expected Cash Flows | Present Value Interest Factor Using Cost of Capital of 12% | Discounted Cash Flows Using Cost of Capital of 12% | Present Value Interest Factor ($k^* = 20\%$) | Discounted Cash Flows ($k^* = 20\%$) |
| 1 | $30,000 | .8929 | $ 26,787 | .8333 | $ 24,999 |
| 2 | 20,000 | .7972 | 15,944 | .6944 | 13,888 |
| 3 | 40,000 | .7118 | 28,472 | .5787 | 23,148 |
| 4 | 40,000 | .6355 | 25,420 | .4823 | 19,292 |
| 5 | 30,000 | .5674 | 17,022 | .4019 | 12,057 |
|  |  | PV of cash flows = $113,645 | | PV of cash flows = $ 93,384 | |
|  |  | Less: Initial outlay = 100,000 | | Less: Initial outlay = 100,000 | |
|  |  | NPV = $ 13,645 | | Risk-Adjusted NPV = −$6,616 | |

positive ($13,645). In Columns 5 and 6, the project is reevaluated using $k^* = 20\%$. The result is a risk-adjusted *NPV* of $-$6,616. Since this value is negative, the project should be rejected. This example illustrates how a project may be acceptable when the cash flows are considered to be known with certainty, but unacceptable when the same cash flows are uncertain.

Risk-adjusted discount rates can also be used in an *IRR*-type framework. Recall that when the cost of capital is used to evaluate projects in an *IRR* framework, projects are to be accepted when the *IRR* is greater than or equal to the firm's cost of capital. Since the risk-adjusted discount rate represents the required rate of return on risky projects, the decision rule criteria are changed to

When $IRR \geq k^*$, accept the project.

When $IRR < k^*$, reject the project.

Here, the $k^*$ acts as a **hurdle rate,** meaning that for a project to be accepted, it must be able to "hurdle over" the required rate of return.

## Determining Risk-Adjusted Discount Rates

Although using a risk-adjusted discount rate is a fairly simple procedure, determining an appropriate discount rate can be very difficult. Generally, firms use their cost of capital as a reference point when determining an appropriate discount rate. If the risk of a potential project does not appear to differ substantially from that of the company itself, the cost of capital may suffice. An adjustment is normally made only if the risk of the project differs substantially. Determining an appropriate risk-adjusted discount rate involves (1) measuring the risk of the project and (2) determining an appropriate discount rate based on that level of risk.

One method of determining risk-adjusted discount rates is to use the capital asset pricing model (**CAPM**). Recall from Chapter 5 that the *security market line* (SML) specifies the relationship between the required rate of return and the level of systematic (non-diversifiable) risk of an asset. This relationship is as follows:

$$k_j = R_f + b_j(k_m - R_f) \qquad (11.2)$$

where  $k_j$ = required rate of return of asset $j$

$R_f$ = risk-free rate of return

$k_m$ = expected return on the market

$b_j$ = beta of asset $j$ (a measure of systematic risk)

A well-diversified firm that is concerned only with the systematic risk of projects (since unsystematic risk is eliminated or greatly reduced by diversification) may use the **SML** to estimate the required rate of return on projects, which then becomes the risk-adjusted discount rate.

| | |
|---|---|
| **Example** | As an example of the application of the SML in capital budgeting, assume the following information is being used to determine the required rate of return on Project Z: |

- Risk-free rate $(R_f) = 7\%$
- Expected return on the market $(k_m) = 14\%$
- Estimated beta of Project $Z = 1.1$

Given this information, the required rate of return on Project Z, using the SML is

$$k_Z = R_f + b_Z(k_m - R_f)$$
$$= 7\% + 1.1(14\% - 7\%)$$
$$= 7\% + 7.7\%$$
$$= 14.7\%$$

Thus, the risk-adjusted discount rate to use in evaluating Project Z is 14.7 percent.

While the CAPM may be an appropriate method of determining the required rate of return on projects, it has some disadvantages. First, determining the systematic risk of capital budgeting projects can be very difficult and subject to considerable error. Unlike publicly traded common stock, there is typically little data available about the historical returns on capital budgeting projects. Such information would be useful for forecasting project betas. Second, estimating the market rate of return is highly subjective and also subject to error. Finally, the application of the SML approach focuses only on systematic risk and ignores a project's unsystematic risk. If the firm is not sufficiently diversified in terms of the returns earned on its portfolio of assets, perhaps total risk should be considered. Despite its limitations, however, the SML is an acceptable method of determining the discount rate to use in some situations.

An alternative method of determining risk-adjusted discount rates is to measure the risk of projects using such measures as the variance, standard deviation, and coefficient of variation of expected returns. Or management may evaluate the risk of projects intuitively. Regardless of the risk measure used, each project can be assigned to a risk category that has been subjectively established. Each risk category can then be assigned a required rate of return relative to the firm's cost of capital. This method avoids the problem of having to establish a specific level of risk for each project and a specific discount rate for each level of risk. The following example illustrates such a classification system.

| Project Risk Classification | Discount Rate Relative to Firm's Cost of Capital |
|---|---|
| Low risk | +0% |
| Moderate risk | +2 |
| High risk | +4 |
| Very high risk | +6 |

Assuming this firm has a 13 percent cost of capital, low-risk projects would be evaluated using 13 percent as a discount rate. The same firm would evaluate moderate-risk projects using a 15 percent discount rate (13 percent + 2 percent). Although this appears to be a simple procedure, determining the discount-rate adjustments can be difficult. Unfortunately, no simple method exists.

### Advantages and Disadvantages of Using Risk-Adjusted Discount Rates

Using a risk-adjusted discount rate is a theoretically sound approach to accounting for risk in the capital budgeting decision-making process. It has the additional advantage of providing a single estimate of the risk-adjusted *NPV*, or hurdle rate, which can be used as the basis for making capital budgeting decisions. However, a disadvantage, as indicated earlier, is the lack of consensus on how to determine an appropriate risk-adjusted discount rate, a critical input variable. An improper discount rate can lead to incorrect decisions.

## CERTAINTY EQUIVALENT APPROACH

Whereas the risk-adjusted discount rate approach adjusts the discount rate according to the level of uncertainty, the **certainty equivalent** method adjusts the cash flows to reflect the uncertainty. After the uncertainty is removed from the cash flows, the risk-free rate can be used as the discount rate to find *NPV*. The difficult part of this approach involves the conversion of uncertain cash flows into certainty equivalent cash flows. This approach involves the evaluation of the riskiness of the cash flows and the subjective determination of an equivalent certain amount. That is, *certainty equivalent cash flows* represent the cash flows that the firm would accept with certainty in exchange for the uncertain cash flows. To illustrate the concept of certainty equivalent cash flows, consider the following situation.

Assume that your rich, eccentric uncle tells you he will flip a coin and pay you $100,000 if the coin comes up heads, but nothing if it comes up tails. The expected value of this gamble is, therefore, $50,000 as derived from the implied probability distribution (50 percent chance of receiving $100,000 and 50 percent chance of receiving nothing). He also gives you an alternative to the coin toss. Instead of tossing the coin, you can elect to receive $50 with no risk. You would probably have no trouble deciding to take your chances with the coin flip. However, if he offered you a choice between a certain $40,000 or the coin toss with its expected value of $50,000, you would probably elect to take the certain $40,000. Somewhere between $50 and $40,000 is an amount that would make it very difficult for you to decide. In fact, you could say that there is an amount known with certainty that is equivalent to the expected value of the coin toss. If that amount were $20,000, then $20,000 would be considered the certainty equivalent (to you) of the $50,000 expected value of the coin toss (each person may have a different certainty equivalent amount). This is the value the firm must decide upon as the certainty equivalent of each future expected cash flow from a capital budgeting project.

Frequently, firms express certainty equivalents in terms of *certainty equivalent coefficients,* which represent the ratios of the certain amount to the expected cash flow for each year. In the preceding example, since $20,000 is the certain amount, and $50,000 is the expected value, the certainty equivalent coefficient is .4 ($20,000/$50,000). It should be noted that the greater the uncertainty associated with a given cash flow, the lower the certainty equivalent coefficient (and cash flows). For example, assume your uncle is going to roll a die and pay you $150,000 if the number 1 or 2 comes up, but nothing if 3 through 6 comes up. The expected value is still $50,000 (33⅓ percent chance of receiving $150,000 and 66⅔ percent chance of receiving nothing). However, your risk is greater, since you have a 67 percent chance of receiving nothing. In this case, your certainty equivalent cash flow may be $10,000 (a certainty equivalent factor of .2).

If cash flows are known with certainty, the certainty equivalent coefficients are equal to 1.0. The inverse relationship between uncertainty and certainty equivalent coefficients exists because people are more willing to accept a lower percentage of the expected value with certainty than incur a higher level of risk. Since each cash flow can be adjusted using a different

**FIGURE 11.1**
**Uncertainty of Cash Flows over Time**

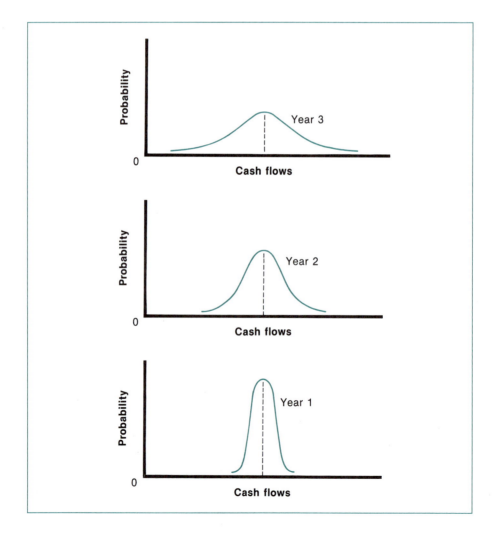

coefficient, the analyst can specifically take into consideration the change in risk over time. That is, the farther into the future a cash flow is expected to be realized, the greater the uncertainty of the cash flow.

This relationship between uncertainty and time is illustrated in Figure 11.1. Here, continuous probability distributions are displayed indicating the possible cash flows for a project in each of the three years of a project's life. The cash flows appear on the horizontal scale, and the corresponding probability of cash flows appears on the vertical scale. As shown in the figure, the farther into the future the cash flow distributions are, the wider the distributions tend to be. This indicates there is greater uncertainty in forecasting cash flows that are farther into the future. Such is generally the case since the economic conditions that affect cash flows are more uncertain for periods farther into the future.

### Steps Required When Using the Certainty Equivalent Approach

The certainty equivalent net present value (certainty equivalent *NPV*) of a proposed project can be estimated as:

$$\text{certainty equivalent } NPV = \sum_{t=1}^{n} \frac{CF_t(\alpha_t)}{(1 + R_f)^t} - I \tag{11.3}$$

where $CF_t$ = cash flow expected in period $t$

$\alpha_t$ = certainty equivalent coefficient for period $t$

$I$ = initial outlay

$R_f$ = risk-free rate of return

Because the cash flows are multiplied by the certainty equivalent coefficients, they are converted to values that are less than or equal to their original expected values. Notice that the discount rate applied to the certainty equivalent cash flows is the risk-free rate. This is because the riskiness of the cash flows has been effectively eliminated.

The following steps are necessary to evaluate independent projects using the certainty equivalent approach.

*Step 1.* Determine the certainty equivalent coefficients applicable to the cash flows and adjust the cash flows accordingly.
*Step 2.* Find the present value of the certainty equivalent cash flows using the risk-free discount rate, $R_f$, and subtract the initial outlay.
*Step 3.* Accept the project if the resulting value is greater than or equal to zero.

Other than adjusting the cash flows for risk and using the risk-free rate as the discount rate, the steps involved in the certainty equivalent approach are the same as those in the *NPV* approach. Because of the differences, however, it is possible that a project could be accepted if evaluated using *NPV* method but rejected using the certainty equivalent *NPV* method.

## Application of the Certainty Equivalent Approach

The following example illustrates the application of the certainty equivalent approach.

**Example**

The certainty equivalent approach is applied to the cash flows of Project Y in Table 11.2, where the certainty equivalent coefficients are given in Column 3. In this example, the coefficients assigned to the cash flows range from .9 for the first year down to .5 for the fifth year. The declining coefficients reflect the greater degree of uncertainty surrounding the estimated cash flows in later years. Multiplying the expected cash flows in Column 2 by the certainty equivalent coefficients in Column 3 results in certainty equivalent cash flows, which are then discounted at the risk-free rate. Summing the discounted cash flows and subtracting the initial outlay results in a certainty equivalent *NPV* of −$6,559 for Project Y. Therefore, this project would be rejected.

The certainty equivalent approach is easy to incorporate into capital budgeting analysis once appropriate coefficients have been determined for each period. However, determining appropriate coefficients can be very difficult; no prescribed method exists, so they must be estimated subjectively.

## Advantages and Disadvantages of Using the Certainty Equivalent Approach

The certainty equivalent approach is theoretically sound, and it leads to a single estimated value on which capital budgeting decisions can be made. Unfortunately, this approach has a major limitation: as previously mentioned, estimating the certainty equivalent coefficients is very difficult, and there is no generally accepted method of doing this. The accept/reject decision for a project is greatly affected by the coefficients selected.

**TABLE 11.2   Use of Certainty Equivalents to Compute Net Present Value**

| (1) End of Year | (2) Expected Cash Flows | (3) Certainty Equivalent Coefficients | (4) Certainty Equivalent Cash Flows | (5) Present Value Interest Factor ($R_f = 6\%$) | (6) Present Value of Certainty Equivalent CF |
|---|---|---|---|---|---|
| 1 | $30,000 | .9 | $27,000 | .9434 | $ 25,472 |
| 2 | 20,000 | .8 | 16,000 | .8900 | 14,240 |
| 3 | 40,000 | .7 | 28,000 | .8396 | 23,509 |
| 4 | 40,000 | .6 | 24,000 | .7921 | 19,010 |
| 5 | 30,000 | .5 | 15,000 | .7473 | 11,210 |

PV of cash flows = $ 93,441
Less: Initial outlay    100,000
Certainty equivalent *NPV* = −$6,559

## DECISION TREES

The use of **decision trees** permits firms to assess all the possible outcomes that may result for a particular project. This approach is particularly useful when the cash flows are conditional (when the cash flow in one period is influenced by the cash flow in the preceding period). When the probabilities of alternative cash flow streams can be determined, decision trees can display all possible *NPV* outcomes and their corresponding probabilities.

### Steps Required for Using Decision Trees

The following steps summarize the construction and use of decision trees:

*Step 1.* Identify possible cash flows that may result from a project, recognizing that the cash flow realized in one period may be related to the cash flow realized in the preceding period.

*Step 2.* Assign probabilities to each possible cash flow such that the probabilities of the cash flows for any given period sum to 1.0.

*Step 3.* Determine all possible *NPV*s that can result from all possible combinations of cash flows. Use the firm's cost of capital as the discount rate.[1]

*Step 4.* Calculate the probability of each possible *NPV* to determine the probability distribution of all possible *NPV*s.

*Step 5.* Using statistical measures such as expected value and standard deviation, evaluate the distribution of possible *NPV*s to be generated by the project in order to subjectively make the accept/reject decision.

### Application of Decision Trees

The way a decision tree is used is best illustrated by an example. Consider the following evaluation of Project R:

- Useful life of Project R is two years
- Initial outlay is estimated to be $500,000
- The firm's cost of capital is 13 percent
- The cash flow estimates and their probabilities for Project R are as displayed in Table 11.3.

Notice from Table 11.3 that the cash flow in Year 2 is conditional upon the cash flow in Year 1. In Year 1 the project will generate cash flows of either $500,000 (there is a 40 percent probability of that cash flow), or $300,000 (a 60 percent probability). If the higher cash flow is realized in the first year, then the cash flow in the second year is estimated to be either

---

1.   The appropriate discount rate to use is somewhat controversial. If the firm's cost of capital is used, the resulting expected *NPV* must be viewed in light of the expected risk of the project, which is also evaluated as part of the decision-tree analysis. Some analysts use the risk-free rate as the discount rate, reasoning that the decision tree helps to measure the risk of the project and is not designed to adjust for risk.

**TABLE 11.3**   Cash Flow Estimates and Probabilities: Project R

| Year 1 | Cash Flows | Probability |
|---|---|---|
| | $500,000 | .40 |
| | $300,000 | .60 |

| Year 2 | If the Cash Flow in Year 1 Is | The Cash Flow in Year 2 Will Be Either | Probability |
|---|---|---|---|
| | $500,000 | $700,000 | .70 |
| | | or | |
| | | $600,000 | .30 |
| | | $300,000 | .40 |
| | | or | |
| | $300,000 | $200,000 | .50 |
| | | or | |
| | | $100,000 | .10 |

$700,000 (a 70 percent probability) or $600,000 (a 30 percent probability). Conversely, if the lower cash flow is realized in the first year, the cash flow in the second year is more likely to be low. Three different cash flows are possible in the second year if the cash flow is $300,000 in the first year: $300,000, $200,000, or $100,000 with probabilities of 40 percent, 50 percent, and 10 percent, respectively.

All of the information presented in Table 11.3 is diagrammed on the decision tree in Figure 11.2. The initial outlay is indicated in Column 1, with the possible first-year cash flows and their probabilities in Columns 3 and 2, and the possible second-year cash flows and their probabilities in Columns 5 and 4. Columns 6 through 8 in Figure 11.2 display the analysis of this information. Column 6 indicates all possible *NPV*s that can result if the project is adopted. Each possible *NPV* outcome is calculated based on the initial outlay of $500,000 and the possible combinations of first- and second-year cash flows. The firm's cost of capital (13 percent) is used as a discount rate. The first possible *NPV* in Column 6 ($490,670) results from cash flows of $500,000 in Year 1 and $700,000 in Year 2. The second possible *NPV* ($412,360) results from cash inflows of $500,000 in Year 1 and $600,000 in Year 2. The other possible *NPV*s were calculated in a similar manner.

Column 7 displays the probabilities of each possible *NPV*. Each of these probabilities is the joint probability of the cash flows in Year 1 and Year 2 that were used to determine the *NPV*. For example, the probabilities of the cash flows for the top scenario in Figure 11.2 are 40 percent in Year 1 and 70 percent in Year 2. The joint probability is therefore 70 percent times 40 percent, or 28 percent. This is the probability that both cash flows will be realized and that the project's *NPV* will be $490,670.

Columns 6 and 7 combined represent the probability distribution of possible *NPV*s for Project R. From this probability distribution, the expected *NPV* can be estimated (as shown in Column 8), along with the stan-

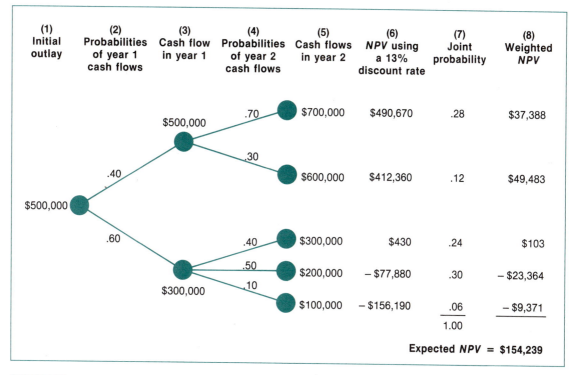

| (1) Initial outlay | (2) Probabilities of year 1 cash flows | (3) Cash flow in year 1 | (4) Probabilities of year 2 cash flows | (5) Cash flows in year 2 | (6) NPV using a 13% discount rate | (7) Joint probability | (8) Weighted NPV |
|---|---|---|---|---|---|---|---|
| | | | .70 | $700,000 | $490,670 | .28 | $37,388 |
| | | $500,000 | .30 | $600,000 | $412,360 | .12 | $49,483 |
| | .40 | | | | | | |
| $500,000 | | | | | | | |
| | .60 | | .40 | $300,000 | $430 | .24 | $103 |
| | | | .50 | $200,000 | − $77,880 | .30 | − $23,364 |
| | | $300,000 | .10 | $100,000 | − $156,190 | .06 | − $9,371 |
| | | | | | | 1.00 | |

Expected *NPV* = **$154,239**

**FIGURE 11.2**

**Example of a Decision Tree**

dard deviation and coefficient of variation of possible *NPV*s. For Project R, the standard deviation is $259,443, and the coefficient of variation is 1.7 (the calculation of each is illustrated in Table 11.4). These measures were discussed in detail in Chapter 5.

Another indicator of project risk is the probability that the project's *NPV* will be negative. In our example, the probability that the *NPV* will be negative is 36 percent, the sum of the probabilities of the two possible negative outcomes (30 percent + 6 percent) found in Figure 11.2. Likewise, the probability that the actual *NPV* will be positive is the sum of the probabilities of all possible positive outcomes (28 percent + 12 percent + 24 percent = 64 percent). Although this is a somewhat simplistic assessment of risk, it can be useful information to the decision maker.

The decision about whether or not to accept this project would be much easier if all possible *NPV*s were positive, since it would preclude the possibility of incurring losses from the project. Unfortunately, most projects have some probability of generating a negative *NPV*, making the decision more difficult. Thus, the final accept/reject decision may depend on the firm's degree of risk aversion.

## Advantages and Disadvantages of Using Decision Trees

The decision tree approach provides the decision maker with a probability distribution of possible *NPV*s for each project. This information can be used to determine the standard deviation or coefficient of variation of possible outcomes. Additionally, the probability of realizing a negative *NPV*

**TABLE 11.4   Calculation of Standard Deviation and Coefficient of Variation of Net Present Value Based on Decision-Tree Information**

Standard
deviation $= \sqrt{\sum[NPV_i - E(NPV)]^2 \, p_i}$
of NPVs

| (1) | (2) | (3) | (4) | (5) = (3) × (4) |
|---|---|---|---|---|
| Out-come | NPV for Each Outcome | Squared Deviation of Estimated NPV from Expected NPV | Probability of Each Outcome $(p_i)$ | Weighted Squared Deviation |
| 1 | $490,670 | $(490,670 - 154,239)^2$ | 28% | 31,692,029,000 |
| 2 | 412,360 | $(412,360 - 154,239)^2$ | 12 | 7,995,174,077 |
| 3 | 430 | $(430 - 154,239)^2$ | 24 | 5,677,656,206 |
| 4 | −77,880 | $(-77,880 - 154,239)^2$ | 30 | 16,163,769,000 |
| 5 | −156,190 | $(-156,190 - 154,239)^2$ | 6 | 5,781,969,842 |
| | | | 100% | 67,310,598,000 |

$$\text{Standard deviation} = \sqrt{67,310,598,000}$$
$$= \$259,443$$

$$\frac{\text{Coefficient of}}{\text{variation}} = \frac{\text{standard deviation of } NPVs}{\text{expected value of } NPV}$$

$$= \frac{\$259,443}{\$154,239}$$

$$= 1.7$$

can be determined from the probability distribution. Finally, the dependence of each year's cash flow on the prior year's cash flow can be explicitly recognized and incorporated into the decision-tree analysis.

There are some limitations in using a decision tree, however. First, the probabilities assigned to each possible outcome are subjective and difficult to estimate. Second, the information developed with a decision tree (expected *NPV*, standard deviation, and coefficient of variation) does not provide the firm with an accept or reject decision. Instead, the firm must evaluate the output for each project subjectively to make the decision. Third, when comparing two mutually exclusive projects, one cannot necessarily identify the superior project from decision-tree analysis, since one project may exhibit a higher expected *NPV* but also higher risk.

# SENSITIVITY ANALYSIS

The cash flows associated with projects are generally influenced by a number of key input variables, including sales, cost of raw materials, competition, and so forth. Many firms find it useful to calculate the expected *NPV* of a project, then change certain key input variables to determine how sensitive the project's *NPV* is to changes in these key variables. This procedure, called **sensitivity analysis,** allows the firm to identify a number of possible *NPV* outcomes and determine which factors affect the project's *NPV* the most. The next step is to determine whether the sensitivities revealed are acceptable. Sensitivity analysis allows the firm to concentrate its efforts on forecasting those factors that have the greatest impact on *NPV* and determine which projects are most sensitive to which key variables—information that can be very useful in the decision-making process.

## Steps Required When Using Sensitivity Analysis

The most common application of sensitivity analysis to capital budgeting can be summarized as follows:

*Step 1.* Determine the project's *NPV*, using the most likely estimates for initial outlay, cash flows (including terminal cash flow), and the appropriate discount rate (the firm's cost of capital or a risk-adjusted discount rate can be used).

*Step 2.* Make several revisions (one at a time) of one key input variable involved in estimating *NPV*, then reestimate *NPV* based on the revisions.

*Step 3.* Repeat the process described in Step 2, revising the estimate of each key variable one at a time.

*Step 4.* Evaluate the sensitivity of project *NPVs* to each variable, and consider the alternative *NPVs* that could result. Use this information to make a subjective accept/reject decision.

## Application of Sensitivity Analysis

Consider a manufacturing firm that plans to acquire a new piece of equipment that is expected to increase production and decrease costs. The firm develops forecasts of all the cash flows associated with this project, and it uses this information along with estimates of the initial outlay to estimate the *NPV* of the proposed project at $60,000. However, the firm is not convinced that this project should be adopted because of the uncertainty of the cash flows. Consequently, to gain a better understanding of the risk of the project, forecasts of some of the more critical factors that effect cash flows are revised, one at a time, and the project's *NPV* is reestimated after each revision. This process is illustrated in Table 11.5, which shows the impact of two variables on the project's *NPV*. The firm first analyzed the possibility of raw materials costs being higher or lower than originally estimated (see Lines 1 through 4 in Table 11.5). This resulted in *NPVs* ranging from −$40,000 to $160,000 (these values cannot be determined based on the information provided here). Next, the possibility of product demand being higher or lower than originally estimated was analyzed (Lines 5 through 8). The resulting *NPVs* based on those changing variables range from −$80,000 to $200,000. It is evident from the ranges of the possible outcomes indicated in Table 11.5 that the project's *NPV* is more sensitive to the product demand than to the cost of raw materials (the range of *NPVs* for changes in the cost of raw materials is −$40,000 to $160,000, compared to −$80,000 to $200,000 for changes in product demand).

The firm may wish to concentrate its efforts on researching product demand before making its final accept/reject decision on this project. The sensitivity analysis also reveals a number of different situations that can

**TABLE 11.5  Use of Sensitivity Analysis to Evaluate Capital Budgeting Projects (Expected *NPV* is $60,000)**

| If . . . | Then . . .<br>(Revised Estimate of *NPV:*) |
|---|---|
| 1. Raw materials cost is 5% more than originally estimated | $ 10,000 |
| 2. Raw materials cost is 5% less than originally estimated | 110,000 |
| 3. Raw materials cost is 10% more per year than originally estimated | −40,000 |
| 4. Raw materials cost is 10% less per year than originally estimated | 160,000 |
| 5. Product demand is 5% less than originally estimated | −5,000 |
| 6. Product demand is 5% more than originally estimated | 125,000 |
| 7. Product demand is 10% less than originally estimated | −80,000 |
| 8. Product demand is 10% more than originally estimated | 200,000 |

result in a negative *NPV*. This risk must be carefully considered before making the accept/reject decision.

## Advantages and Disadvantages of Using Sensitivity Analysis

The advantages of sensitivity analysis are (1) its ability to indicate which variables are expected to have the greatest impact on the *NPV* of a proposed project and (2) its ability to indicate the degree of variation (risk) of possible *NPV*s. A limitation of sensitivity analysis is that it generally requires considerable subjective input. Also, its very nature prevents probabilities from being assigned to alternative outcomes. As a result, it is difficult to quantify risk based on the results of sensitivity analysis. Also, sensitivity analysis does not offer a decision rule for making the accept/reject decision, but merely offers a method of evaluating risk.

# SIMULATION

Simulation requires that key input variables be defined in terms of probability distributions (except for those variables known with certainty). Next a value of each key variable is randomly selected from each distribution, and estimates of *NPV* are made based on the values chosen. This process is repeated many times in order to generate numerous estimates of *NPV*. Based on the distribution characteristics of the resulting *NPV* values, the analyst can determine the expected *NPV* as well as the standard deviation and coefficient of variation of possible outcomes. The analyst can also use the distribution of possible *NPV* outcomes to determine the probability that the project's *NPV* will be negative.

## Steps Required When Using Simulation

The following steps are required in using simulation to evaluate the risk of a capital budgeting project:

*Step 1.* Estimate the probability distributions describing the key variables that may affect a project's *NPV*.

*Step 2.* Randomly select one value for each variable based on the probability distributions that were previously determined. Calculate the cash flow and *NPV* based on these variables. Repeat this process numerous times (generally computers are used to perform this function).

*Step 3.* Evaluate the distribution of *NPV*s resulting from the simulation. Consider the expected value, standard deviation, and coefficient of variation of the project's possible *NPV*s in order to subjectively make the accept/reject decision. Also consider the probability of realizing a negative *NPV* on the project.

## Application of Simulation

Consider the same example used in the discussion of sensitivity analysis in which a firm plans to purchase a new piece of equipment. Since the firm was uncertain about the cost of raw materials and product demand, it would need to estimate probability distributions describing the possible values of each variable. The probability distributions relating to this example appear in Figure 11.3.

**FIGURE 11.3**
**Probability Distributions for Key Variables Used in Simulation Analysis**

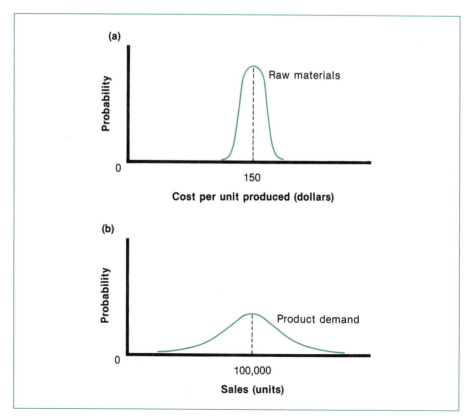

**FIGURE 11.4**
**Output from a
Capital Budgeting
Simulation Analysis**

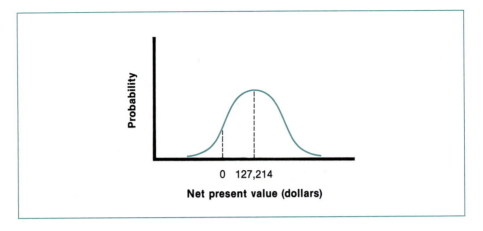

Net present value (dollars)

0   127,214

Assume the distributions specified in Figure 11.3 are expected to be realized in each year of the life of the project. The initial outlay and the discount rate to be used have been determined and, for simplicity, all other costs are assumed to be known with certainty. At this point, a value is randomly selected from each probability distribution where the probability of selecting a specific value is defined by the distribution. These randomly selected values are combined with the other known values in order to estimate the *NPV* of the project. Normally, a computer program is used to assist in conducting simulation analysis. Since the computer makes the random variable selections and calculates the resulting *NPV*, 100 or more iterations can be run very quickly. The results of each run can be tabulated and used to construct a final distribution of possible project *NPV*s. This distribution appears in Figure 11.4 for this example problem. By analyzing the resulting probability distribution of *NPV*s, management can determine the expected value and standard deviation of the project's *NPV*. It can also evaluate the probability of realizing a negative *NPV* on the project. This information is, of course, very useful in making the capital budgeting decision.

### Advantages and Disadvantages
### of Using Simulation

Simulation analysis is very easy to conduct with the assistance of computers. Since simulation generates a distribution of possible *NPV*s, the decision maker can measure the dispersion of possible *NPV*s in terms of a standard deviation or coefficient of variation in order to assess project risk. In addition, the probability that the *NPV* will be negative can be determined from this distribution.

A limitation of simulation is that there are no established decision rules on which to base the acceptance or rejection of a project. That is, simulation provides the decision maker with useful information concerning the expected risk and return of a project, but the final accept/reject decision is a subjective one.

**TABLE 11.6  Steps for Risk-Adjusted Capital Budgeting Techniques**

| Risk-Adjusted Capital Budgeting Technique | Steps for Using Technique | Output Generated by Technique |
|---|---|---|
| Risk-adjusted discount rates | 1. Determine the risk-adjusted discount rate ($k^*$) applicable to the project being evaluated.<br>2. Discount the cash flows using $k^*$ and subtract the initial cash outlay to arrive at the risk-adjusted *NPV*.<br>3. Accept the project if the risk-adjusted $NPV \geq 0$. | A single point estimate of *NPV* that has been adjusted for project risk. |
| Certainty equivalents | 1. Determine the certainty equivalent coefficients applicable to the cash flows, and adjust the cash flows accordingly.<br>2. Discount the certainty equivalent cash flows at the risk-free rate, and subtract the initial outlay.<br>3. Accept the project if $NPV \geq 0$. | A single point estimate of *NPV* that has been adjusted for project risk. |
| Decision trees | 1. Identify the cash flows that may occur in each period.<br>2. Assign a probability to each possible cash flow.<br>3. Determine the *NPV* for each possible combination of cash flows during the life of the project using the firm's cost of capital as the discount rate.<br>4. Calculate the probability of each possible *NPV*, and develop the probability distribution of *NPV*s.<br>5. Evaluate the distribution of *NPV*s, and determine whether the project should be accepted based on the risk-return relationship. | A probability distribution describing the *NPV*s that may result from the project. |
| Sensitivity analysis | 1. Estimate the cash flows that may occur in each period, and determine the *NPV* using the firm's cost of capital as a discount rate.<br>2. Revise one key variable several times to reflect possible outcomes, and determine project *NPV* after each revision.<br>3. Repeat Step 2, revising other key variables one at a time.<br>4. Evaluate the sensitivity of the project to each key variable, and use this information to make a subjective accept/reject decision. | A distribution of *NPV*s that may result from the project. |
| Simulation | 1. Estimate the probability distribution that describes the expected value of each factor that may significantly influence the *NPV* of the project.<br>2. Randomly select one value for each key variable based on the defined probability distributions. Calculate the cash flows and *NPV* that result from the selected values. Repeat this process numerous times.<br>3. Evaluate the distribution of *NPV*s resulting from the simulation. Consider the expected value and standard deviation of the project's possible *NPV*s to subjectively determine whether the project should be accepted. Also consider the probability of realizing a negative *NPV* on the project. | A distribution of possible *NPV*s that may result from the project. |

## COMPARISON OF RISK-ADJUSTED CAPITAL BUDGETING TECHNIQUES

A brief comparison of the risk-adjusted capital budgeting techniques is provided in Table 11.6. Of the five techniques discussed, all but the risk-adjusted discount rate method adjust the cash flows to reflect risk. Of the four capital budgeting techniques that adjust cash flows, all but the certainty equivalent approach incorporate a variety of cash flow scenarios and then estimate the *NPV* according to each scenario. The certainty equivalent approach adjusts the initial estimates of cash flows downward to reflect the level of risk in each cash flow estimate.

Decision trees, sensitivity analysis, and simulation generate a variety of possible *NPV*s, while the risk-adjusted discount rate and certainty equivalent techniques generate point estimates of *NPV*. Some managers may prefer to use point estimates of *NPV*, since the accept/reject decision follows directly from that value. The advantages and disadvantages of all the major techniques for considering risk in capital budgeting are compared in Table 11.7.

No single method of considering risk in capital budgeting is clearly superior to the others. The appropriate technique to use may depend on the situation. In the past, the risk-adjusted discount rate and certainty equivalent approaches have been given the most attention. However, through improved computer capabilities, sensitivity analysis and simulation are increasing in popularity.

**TABLE 11.7**   **Advantages and Disadvantages of Risk-Adjusted Capital Budgeting Techniques**

| Risk-Adjusted Capital Budgeting Technique | Advantages | Disadvantages |
|---|---|---|
| Risk-adjusted discount rates | Provides straightfoward decision rule of whether to accept the project once the analysis is completed. | Determining an appropriate risk-adjusted discount rate is subjective. |
| Certainty equivalents | Provides straightforward decision rule of whether to accept the project once the analysis is completed. | Determining appropriate certainty equivalent coefficients is subjective. |
| Decision trees | Provides a probability distribution describing *NPV*. This can be used to determine a number of risk and return measures. Also, contingent cash flows can be considered. | No decision rule is provided for accepting or rejecting projects. |
| Sensitivity analysis | Provides an indication of the sensitivity of project *NPV* to certain key variables. Also indicates alternative possible outcomes. | No probabilities of outcomes are provided. Also, no decision rule is provided for accepting or rejecting projects. |
| Simulation | Provides a probability distribution of possible outcomes from which a number of risk and return statistics can be calculated. | No decision rule is provided for accepting or rejecting projects. |

## PORTFOLIO RISK IN CAPITAL BUDGETING

The discussion in this chapter has focused on the risk of a single project with little consideration being given to the relationship between project risk and the firm's existing risk. We saw in Chapter 5 that when risky assets are added to a portfolio, the interaction of the returns on all of the assets in the portfolio affects the risk of the portfolio. The same concept can be applied to the adoption of capital budgeting projects. That is, firms may wish to consider how the adoption of a given project will affect the firm's overall risk. For example, a risky project whose returns are negatively correlated with the firm's current returns may actually reduce overall firm risk if adopted.

Considerable controversy surrounds the benefits to be derived by firm diversification. Some people argue that since investors can diversify their own portfolios, they are unwilling to pay more for the common stock of firms that have provided diversification for them. Others argue that by diversifying, a firm may be able to reduce its cost of debt; and if diversification prevents substantial earnings swings that would otherwise cause bankruptcy, the diversification would certainly prove beneficial.

## SUMMARY

The capital budgeting process is complicated by the fact that the future cash flows of most proposed projects are not known with certainty. Since the decision to accept a project is often irreversible, failure to recognize this uncertainty can result in poor project selection and financial distress to the firm. When firms adopt projects with high levels of risk, they must be rewarded with high levels of return—which is the reason that evaluating the riskiness of capital budgeting projects is so important.

Each method of considering risk in capital budgeting has both advantages and disadvantages. Despite the disadvantages, the likelihood of making poor capital budgeting decisions may be significantly reduced when using the techniques described in this chapter for risk evaluation and adjustment.

## KEY TERMS

**Certainty equivalent** A cash flow known with certainty that is deemed equal in desirability to a given uncertain cash flow.

**Decision tree** A graphical illustration of all possible cash flows from a project, and their probabilities, along with possible *NPV*s and their probabilities. Decision trees can provide information that is useful in making capital budgeting decisions under conditions of uncertainty.

**Hurdle rate** The minimum rate of return that must be earned on a capital budgeting project in order for it to be accepted.

**Risk-adjusted discount rate** A discount rate that reflects a project's risk and is used to determine the net present value of the project.

**Sensitivity analysis** Procedure used to determine how sensitive an outcome is to changes in the values of certain key input variables.

**Simulation** A procedure used to develop a distribution of possible outcomes based on probability distributions that describe the possible values of certain key input variables.

## EQUATIONS

**Equation 11.1**     **Risk-Adjusted Net Present Value**

$$\text{risk-adjusted } NPV = \sum_{t=1}^{n} \frac{CF_t}{(1 + k^*)^t} - I \qquad \textbf{(p. 309)}$$

where risk-adjusted $NPV$ = risk-adjusted net present value
$CF_t$ = cash flow expected in period $t$
$I$ = initial outlay
$k^*$ = risk-adjusted discount rate

Equation 11.1 is used to evaluate capital budgeting projects when they are more risky than the firm's overall risk. It determines the net present value of a project after adjusting the discount rate to reflect the amount of risk in the project.

**Equation 11.2**     **Security Market Line**

$$k_j = R_f + b_j(k_m - R_f) \qquad \textbf{(p. 311)}$$

where $k_j$ = required rate of return of asset $j$
$R_f$ = risk-free rate of return
$k_m$ = market rate of return
$b_j$ = beta of asset $j$

Equation 11.2 can be used to determine the required rate of return on a capital budgeting project, given the risk-free rate, market rate of return, and the project's beta. This return can then be used as the risk-adjusted discount rate in Equation 11.1.

**Equation 11.3**     **Certainty Equivalent Net Present Value**

$$\text{certainty equivalent } NPV = \sum_{t=1}^{n} \frac{CF_t(\alpha_t)}{(1 + R_f)^t} - I \qquad \textbf{(p. 315)}$$

where certainty equivalent $NPV$ = certainty equivalent net present value
$\alpha_t$ = certainty equivalent coefficient for period $t$

Equation 11.3 is used to adjust for risk in capital budgeting project evaluation. Here, the uncertain cash flows are converted to certainty equivalent cash flows, and the risk-free rate of return is used as a discount rate to find $NPV$.

## QUESTIONS

**Q11-1.** Explain the relationship between interest rates and the required rate of return on a project.

**Q11-2.** Explain the logic of using a higher discount rate to find the $NPV$ of projects containing higher risk.

**Q11-3.** Assume that a set of very uncertain cash flows for a proposed project is initially discounted at the firm's cost of capital to estimate the project's net present value. Then, the cash flows are discounted using a risk-adjusted discount rate. How will the estimated risk-adjusted net present value be affected? Why?

**Q11-4.** Explain why lower certainty equivalent coefficients are used for projects with higher risk.

**Q11-5.** What are the major limitations of the certainty equivalent approach?

**Q11-6.** Mendel Corporation planned the purchase of a new manufacturing plant. The person in charge of capital budgeting analysis estimated the *NPV* of this project to be negative and therefore recommended that the proposed project not be undertaken. While the estimation process was thought to be accurate under conditions of uncertainty, it did not incorporate any risk-adjusted capital budgeting technique. Consequently, higher-level management decided to hire an outside consultant to repeat the analysis, this time accounting for uncertainty using a risk-adjusted discount rate. Is a repeat of the analysis worthwhile in this case? Explain.

**Q11-7.** Okern Corporation uses a risk-adjusted discount rate to evaluate risky capital budgeting projects instead of sensitivity analysis or simulation because "sensitivity analysis and simulation do not always give enough direction as to the accept/reject decision; therefore, a firm will more likely make a wrong decision using such techniques." Do you agree with this statement? Explain.

**Q11-8.** Your friends plan to open a video store on campus after graduation with funds given to them by their parents. When your friends conducted a capital budgeting analysis of this project, they used a 3 percent risk-adjusted discount rate. They justified this rate as follows: since they did not need to borrow funds, the cost of obtaining funds was zero percent. They then added a 3 percent risk premium to their perceived cost of funds, resulting in a risk-adjusted discount rate of 3 percent. Comment on their reasoning. If you disagree with them, recommend your method for determining an appropriate discount rate.

**Q11-9.** A firm can attempt to avoid underestimating the risk of a project by lowering the certainty equivalent coefficients used for a project. What does this statement mean?

**Q11-10.** Some firms use a different discount rate to evaluate capital budgeting projects for each division. That is, each division may have a different discount rate assigned to it. What rationale might justify this action?

## SELF-TEST PROBLEMS

Solutions to self-test problems appear on p. S1.

**SP11-1.** Fargo, Inc., is considering purchasing some new equipment for $2 million. The anticipated cash flows resulting from this proposed project follow:

| Year | Cash Flow |
|------|-----------|
| 1 | $600,000 |
| 2 | 700,000 |
| 3 | 800,000 |
| 4 | 900,000 |

Assume that the risk-free rate of return is 7 percent and that Fargo's cost of capital is 15 percent.

**a.** Fargo assessed the uncertainty of this project's cash flows and feels that a 3 percent risk premium should be added to its cost of capital when evaluating this project. Determine whether this project is expected to be profitable for Fargo, Inc., using a risk-adjusted discount rate.

**b.** Find the certainty equivalent net present value of this project if the certainty equivalent coefficients are .8, .7, .6, and .5 in Years 1 through 4, respectively.

**c.** If this project has a beta of 1.5 and the expected return on the market is 13 percent, what risk-adjusted discount rate should be used according to the capital asset pricing model?

## PROBLEMS

**P11-1.** Carford Company plans to use a risk-adjusted discount rate to evaluate a proposed capital budgeting project. The risk-free rate of return is 9 percent, the expected return on the market is 14 percent, and the project's beta is 1.2. The anticipated cash flows of the two-year project are $100,000 in Year 1 and $200,000 in Year 2. The initial outlay of the project is $230,000.

**a.** Use the capital asset pricing model to determine the appropriate risk-adjusted discount rate to apply to this project.

**b.** Determine the risk-adjusted *NPV* of this project.

**c.** Should this project be accepted or rejected? Why?

**P11-2.** Milan Corporation is considering adopting a project that requires an initial outlay of $50,000. It has estimated cash flows as follows:

| Year | Cash Flow |
|------|-----------|
| 1 | $10,000 |
| 2 | 20,000 |
| 3 | 40,000 |

The risk-free rate of return is 8 percent, and Milan's cost of capital is 11 percent. The firm has decided to use certainty equivalent coefficients of .95, .83, and .71 for Years 1 through 3, respectively. Determine the certainty equivalent *NPV* for this project, and recommend whether the project should be accepted or rejected.

**P11-3.** Sadik, Inc., used a decision tree to evaluate a proposed capital budgeting project. It resulted in the following probability distribution:

| Probability | NPV |
|-------------|-----|
| .10 | −$24,000 |
| .21 | −7,000 |
| .42 | 59,000 |
| .19 | 102,000 |
| .08 | 160,000 |

a. What is the expected *NPV* of the project?
b. What is the standard deviation of possible *NPV*s?
c. What is the probability of a negative *NPV*?

**P11-4.** Burton Company is considering adopting a project that requires an initial outlay of $140,000. It has estimated the cash flows of this project to be $38,000 per year for the next six years. The beta of the project is .8, the risk-free rate of return is 6 percent, and the expected return on the market is 9.75 percent. Determine the risk-adjusted *NPV* for this project, and recommend whether the project should be accepted or rejected.

**P11-5.** Plak Corporation is considering adopting a project that is expected to generate cash flows of $70,000 in each of the next eight years and has an initial outlay of $300,000. Plak would be just as satisfied with 95 percent of the first year's cash flows, 90 percent of the second year's cash flows, 85 percent of the third year's cash flows, and so on. The risk-free rate is 4 percent, and Plak's cost of capital is 15 percent. Determine the certainty equivalent *NPV* for this project, and recommend whether to accept it.

**P11-6.** Yawman Corporation anticipates the following cash flows and probabilities for a proposed project where the cash flows in Year 2 are dependent upon the cash flows in Year 1:

| Year 1 | Probability | Year 2 | Probability |
|--------|-------------|--------|-------------|
|        |             | $60,000 | 40% |
| $50,000 | 80%        | | |
|        |             | $70,000 | 60% |
|        |             | $20,000 | 70% |
| $30,000 | 20%        | | |
|        |             | $10,000 | 30% |

The initial cost of this project is $45,000, and Yawman's cost of capital is 14 percent. Determine the probability distribution of *NPV*s for this project using a decision tree. Also specify the expected *NPV* and the probability that this project will generate a positive *NPV*.

**P11-7.** Nexter Company is considering adopting a project that would require an initial outlay of $900,000. It has estimated the cash flows resulting from the project to be as follows:

| Year | Cash Flow |
|------|-----------|
| 1 | $300,000 |
| 2 | 400,000 |
| 3 | 500,000 |

The beta for this project is 1.6, the risk-free rate of return is 5 percent, and the expected return on the market is 8.75 percent. Determine the *NPV* for this project using a risk-adjusted discount rate, and recommend whether the project should be accepted or rejected.

**P11-8.** Yankee Company has developed the following estimated cash flows and certainty equivalent coefficients for a proposed project:

| Year | Cash Flow | Certainty Equivalent Coefficient |
|------|-----------|----------------------------------|
| 1 | $200,000 | .95 |
| 2 | 300,000 | .90 |
| 3 | 500,000 | .80 |
| 4 | 900,000 | .70 |

If the project's initial outlay is $1,000,000, what is its certainty equivalent *NPV?* The risk-free rate of return is 5 percent, and Yankee's cost of capital is 13 percent.

**P11-9.** Perry Corporation used a decision tree to derive the following probability distribution of possible *NPVs* for a project:

| Probability | NPV |
|-------------|-----|
| .19 | −$47,000 |
| .23 | −19,000 |
| .31 | 12,000 |
| .15 | 20,000 |
| .12 | 31,000 |

a. What are the expected *NPV* and standard deviation of returns for the project?
b. What is the probability of realizing a negative *NPV?*

**P11-10.** Scanlon Company plans to use the risk-adjusted discount rate approach to evaluate a proposed project. The risk-free rate is 8 percent, the expected return on the market is 10 percent, and the project's beta is estimated to be 1.5. The anticipated cash flows of the project are expected to be $120,000 at the end of each of the next twelve years. The initial outlay of the project is $750,000.

a. Determine the appropriate risk-adjusted discount rate for this project using the capital asset pricing model.
b. Determine the risk-adjusted *NPV* of this project.
c. Should this project be accepted or rejected? Why?

**P11-11.** Spartan Electronics is considering the purchase of a new building at a cost of $2.3 million. The cash flows with corresponding certainty equivalent coefficients are as follows:

| Year | Cash Flow | Certainty Equivalent Coefficient |
|------|-----------|----------------------------------|
| 1 | $ 200,000 | .9 |
| 2 | 400,000 | .9 |
| 3 | 400,000 | .8 |
| 4 | 2,500,000 | .8 |

Spartan's cost of capital is 13 percent, and the risk-free rate is 7 percent. Determine the certainty equivalent *NPV* of the project.

**P11-12.** Mason Company is considering adopting a project that will last two years.

The first year's cash flow will be $100,000 under favorable conditions and $60,000 under unfavorable conditions. There is a 30 percent chance that the unfavorable conditions will occur. If they do occur, the second year's cash flow will be either $70,000 or $80,000, with an equal probability of either outcome. However, if favorable conditions occur in the first year, the second year's cash flow will be either $120,000 or $150,000 with an equal probability of each outcome. The initial outlay for this proposed project is $180,000, and Mason's cost of capital is 15 percent. Use a decision tree to determine the probability distribution of *NPV*s for this project, and specify the expected *NPV*, the probability that the project will have a positive *NPV*, and the standard deviation of possible *NPV*s.

## REFERENCES

Bey, Roger P. "Capital Budgeting Decisions When Cash Flows and Project Lives Are Stochastic and Dependent." *The Journal of Financial Research* 6 (Fall 1983): 175–87.

Bey, Roger P., and David A. Garvin. "Managing as if Tomorrow Mattered." *Harvard Business Review* 60 (May–June 1982): 71–9.

Hertz, David B. "Risk Analysis in Capital Investment." *Harvard Business Review* 42 (January–February 1964): 95–106.

———. "Investment Policies That Pay Off." *Harvard Business Review* 46 (January–February 1968): 96–108.

Hodder, James E., and Henry E. Riggs. "Pitfalls in Evaluating Risky Projects." *Harvard Business Review* 63 (January–February 1985): 128–35.

Schall, Lawrence D., and Gary L. Sundem. "Capital Budgeting Methods and Risk: A Further Analysis." *Financial Management* 9 (Spring 1980): 7–11.

Sick, Gordon A. "A Certainty-Equivalent Approach to Capital Budgeting." *Financial Management* 15 (Winter 1986): 23–32.

# PART 5

# LONG-TERM FINANCING DECISIONS

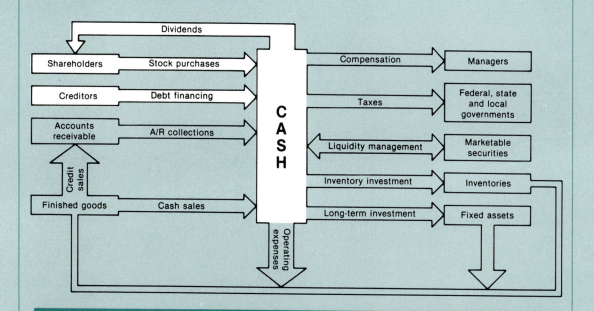

Chapters 12 through 14 focus on the acquisition of long-term financing (capital), including long-term debt, common equity, and preferred stock. Chapter 12 explains how the cost of each source of financing is estimated and how the overall cost of capital is determined. Chapter 13 illustrates how firms use the estimated cost of each source of capital to determine the optimal mix of long-term financing.

Chapter 14 explains how firms determine an appropriate dividend policy. Although the dividend policy is represented in the diagram above as a cash outflow, it also determines the amount of earnings to be retained. Because retained earnings is a source of equity capital to firms, dividend policy influences the amount and mix of long-term funds available to firms.

# CHAPTER 12

# COST OF CAPITAL

## COST OF CAPITAL IN PERSPECTIVE

In 1987 RJR Nabisco, Inc., sold Grand Metropolitan to Heublein, Inc., for $1.2 billion in cash. This money was then used to retire some long-term debt on which RJR Nabisco was paying 11.2% interest. It is also expected to redeem its Series B preferred stock on which it is paying $33 million annually in dividends. Two other preferred stock issues had been redeemed a year earlier. RJR Nabisco planned to consider the retirement of additional existing debt with future cash inflows.

During this same period, International Business Machines Corporation announced plans to repurchase about 4 million shares of its own common stock using cash generated from existing operations. This follows the repurchase of 9 million shares of its common stock in 1986.

The strategies of RJR Nabisco and IBM are similar in that they involve the use of internally generated cash to repurchase or repay sources of capital. However, RJR Nabisco chose to reduce its debt while IBM chose to reduce its common equity. Certainly, the cost of debt and equity to each firm were important determinants of which sources of capital were retired. Also of importance was the impact of the capital adjustments on the risk of the respective firms.

How do firms determine the cost of the various sources of capital? How does the amount of capital raised affect the cost of each source of capital? Is the cost of capital related to investor returns? This chapter provides a framework that can be used to address these questions.

In Chapter 10, the *cost of capital* was used as the discount rate to find the net present value of capital budgeting projects. It was also used as the *hurdle rate* when the internal rate of return method was employed to make capital budgeting decisions. In both applications, the cost of capital represents the minimum rate of return firms must earn on their projects in order for the projects to be adopted. The lower a firm's cost of capital is, the more projects the firm may be able to adopt (other things being equal). It is not just the project's internal rate of return, but the amount by which it exceeds the cost of capital that is critical. The greater this amount is, the greater the dollar return generated by the project and the higher the net income of the firm. It follows that higher net income helps maximize the value of the firm's common stock (other things being equal) and thus helps maximize shareholder wealth.

This chapter looks at the individual components of the cost of capital, considers how to combine these components into an overall measure, and provides further discussion on the use of the cost of capital in capital budgeting.

## BACKGROUND ON THE COST OF CAPITAL

Simply stated, the **cost of capital** is the firm's cost of long-term funds. The principal components of capital are long-term debt, preferred stock, and common equity.[1] Since a firm's capital structure normally includes more than one source of long-term funds, the cost of capital normally reflects the cost of each component of capital employed.

There are two important uses of the cost of capital. First, as previously discussed, the firm uses the cost of capital to help make capital budgeting decisions. Although firms may wish to use risk-adjusted discount rates instead of the cost of capital (as suggested in Chapter 11), this is appropriate only when the risk of the project under consideration is substantially different from that of the existing firm. When a risk-adjusted discount rate is employed, the firm may begin with its cost of capital and adjust that rate according to the level of project risk relative to firm risk. In most instances, however, the firm's cost of capital is used as the discount rate.

A second use of the cost of capital is to help determine the **capital structure** that is most beneficial to the firm.[2] The capital structure is the mix of long-term financing sources used to finance a firm's assets. For example, a firm's capital structure may consist of 30 percent long-term debt, 20 percent preferred stock, and 50 percent common equity. The capital structure that benefits the firm most is the one that minimizes the cost of capital. It can be determined by analyzing the impact of alternative capital structures on the firm's cost of capital.

---

1. Other, less important sources of capital, in terms of dollar volume of funds raised, are discussed in a later chapter.
2. Chapter 13 presents an opposing view that suggests capital structure does not affect the firm in any material way.

# DETERMINING THE COST OF EACH COMPONENT OF CAPITAL

To simplify the discussions of the cost of each component of capital, it is useful to assume that the **business risk** and **financial risk** of the firm are held constant. Business risk is the risk of being unable to cover operating costs. It can be measured in terms of the volatility of EBIT, and its sources are sales volatility and operating leverage. Financial risk is the risk of being unable to cover fixed financing costs. It results in greater volatility of EPS, and its source is financial leverage (the use of debt to finance the firm's assets). Keeping both sources of risk constant prevents the complications caused by risk-induced fluctuations in the cost of capital.

## Long-Term Debt

Most long-term debt is incurred by firms through the sale of bonds. Therefore, the discussion that follows specifically addresses the cost of bonds, although it applies generally to other forms of long-term debt such as term loans.

Bondholders receive interest payments by virtue of their bond ownership. At maturity, they receive the bond's par value, typically $1,000. Although there are some exceptions, most bonds are issued at or very close to their par value. If a bond investor pays the firm $1,000 for a bond and receives $100 in interest each year, the investors' expected return is 10 percent ($100/$1,000). This expected return to the investor is equal to the firm's before-tax cost of the bond, ignoring **flotation costs,** which are the costs associated with selling new securities to investors. These costs include the administrative cost of preparing to issue new securities, the fees or commissions paid to investment bankers, and any discounts offered to investors to induce them to purchase the new securities. Recall from Chapter 4 that the expected rate of return to bondholders is called the *yield to maturity* and that Equation 4.1 can be used to solve for the yield to maturity on a bond.

$$V_b = \sum_{t=1}^{n} I \left[ \frac{1}{(1 + k_b)^t} \right] + M \left[ \frac{1}{(1 + k_b)^n} \right] \quad \textbf{(4.1 restated)}$$

where $k_b$ = yield to maturity (expected return)

$V_b$ = value of a bond

$I$ = annual dollar amount of interest paid on the bond

$M$ = maturity value or par value of the bond

$n$ = number of years to maturity

$t$ = time

If the firm incurs flotation costs, it will not receive all of the money paid by the bondholders to purchase the bonds, and the cost of the bond issue to the firm will exceed the expected return (yield to maturity) of the bond-holder. Equation 4.1 can be adjusted to reflect the existence of flotation costs by substituting the net proceeds received by the firm from the sale of the bonds ($NP_b$) for the value of the bond ($V_b$). After this substitution is made, the firm can solve for $k_b$ in Equation 12.1 to determine its before-tax cost of debt.

$$NP_b = \sum_{t=1}^{n} I \left[ \frac{1}{(1 + k_b)^t} \right] + M \left[ \frac{1}{(1 + k_b)^n} \right] \qquad \textbf{(12.1)}$$

**Example**

Dillon, Inc., feels that, given current business and economic conditions, it must place a 7.8 percent coupon rate on the twenty-year bonds it wishes to sell (for simplicity, assume interest is to be paid annually). The bonds will be sold to investors at par value ($1,000), but the firm will incur a cost of $19.69 for each bond sold. Therefore, the net proceeds to the firm from the sale of each bond will be $980.31 ($1,000.00 − $19.69). The before-tax cost of debt is found by solving for $k_b$ in Equation 12.1 through trial and error. Try 8 percent as the discount rate, and see if the right side of equation 12.1 is equal to $980.31. If so, 8 percent is the before-tax cost of debt.

$$\$980.31 = \$78(PVIFA_{k=8\%, n=20}) + \$1,000(PVIF_{k=8\%, n=20})$$

$$= \$78(9.8181) + \$1,000(.2145)$$

$$= \$980.31$$

Since the present value of the interest payments and principal is equal to the net proceeds to the firm from the sale of the bond using an 8 percent discount rate, 8 percent is the before-tax cost of debt.

The before-tax cost of debt can be approximated by solving for $Ak_b$ in Equation 12.2. It should be emphasized, however, that this is a shortcut method that provides only an approximate answer since it does not consider the time value of money.

$$Ak_b = \frac{I + \dfrac{M - NP_b}{n}}{\dfrac{NP_b + M}{2}} \qquad \textbf{(12.2)}$$

where $Ak_b$ = approximate before-tax cost of debt

$I$ = annual dollar amount of interest payments

$M$ = maturity value or par value of the bond

$n$ = number of years to maturity

$NP$ = net proceeds from the sale of the bond

The numerator of Equation 12.2 reflects the annual interest paid by the firm, plus an additional cost (or benefit) resulting from the difference between the bond's par value, which the firm must pay at maturity, and the net proceeds from the sale of the bond. Typically, par value exceeds the net proceeds from issuing the bond. This difference represents an additional cost to the firm, which, when divided by the number of years over which the cost is spread (the life of the bond), becomes an annualized cost. The result is to have total annual costs (both cash and accrued expenses) included in the numerator. The denominator represents the average loan amount available to the firm during the life of the bond.[3] The average annual dollar cost divided by the average dollar amount of funds available to the firm results in the average annual percentage cost.

**Example**

Applying Equation 12.2 to the Dillon, Inc., bond used in the previous example results in an approximate before-tax cost of debt of 7.98 percent:

$$Ak_b = \frac{\$78 + \dfrac{\$1,000 - \$980.31}{20}}{\dfrac{\$980.31 + \$1,000}{2}}$$

$$= \frac{\$78.98}{\$990.16}$$

$$= 7.98\%$$

Notice that in this problem, the approximate before-tax cost is very similar to the cost determined by the approach that considers the time value of money. However, as the size of the interest payments and number of years until maturity increase, the difference between the answers also increases. Therefore, caution must be exercised when employing the short-cut method.

**Adjusting Before-Tax Cost of Debt for Taxes**   The before-tax cost of debt must be adjusted to reflect the fact that interest expense is tax-deductible for firms. This tax deduction reduces the firm's tax liability and has the effect of reducing the firm's cost of debt. The before-tax cost of debt can be adjusted to reflect this benefit using Equation 12.3.

$$k_i = k_b(1 - T) \tag{12.3}$$

where $k_i$ = after-tax cost of debt

---

3. This calculation recognizes that when the bond is first issued, the firm has $NP_b$ available to use. As the bond approaches maturity, the amount owed by the firm to bondholders approaches par value. The arithmetic average of those two amounts is the average amount of bondholder funds held by the firm during the life of the bond.

$$k_b = \text{before-tax cost of debt}$$

$$T = \text{marginal tax rate}$$

---

**Example**

Recall that the before-tax cost of debt for Dillon, Inc., is 8 percent. If Dillon has a marginal tax rate of 25 percent (used here for simplicity), the after-tax cost of debt is

$$k_i = k_b(1 - T)$$

$$= 8\%(1 - .25)$$

$$= 6\%$$

---

## Preferred Stock

The return earned by owners of preferred stock depends on the annual dividend paid by the firm and the price paid for the stock. As indicated in Chapter 4, the expected return on preferred stock can be expressed as

$$\hat{k}_p = \frac{D_p}{V_p} \qquad \text{(4.5 restated)}$$

where  $\hat{k}_p$ = expected return on preferred stock

$D_p$ = annual dollar amount of dividend paid on the preferred stock

$V_p$ = price of the preferred stock

The expected return on preferred stock, $\hat{k}_p$, also is the cost of preferred stock to the firm if there are no flotation costs. Since flotation costs normally are incurred by firms when preferred stock is issued, Equation 4.5 can be adjusted to reflect those costs by substituting the net proceeds from selling preferred stock for the price of the preferred stock. The hat is also left off $k_p$ to distinguish it from the expected return. The adjusted equation appears as Equation 12.4:

$$k_p = \frac{D_p}{NP_p} \qquad \text{(12.4)}$$

where   $k_p$ = cost of preferred stock

$NP_p$ = net proceeds from the sale of preferred stock

---

**Example**

Consider Dillon, Inc., again, which intends to issue preferred stock paying a $9.40 annual dividend. Assuming investors pay $99.50 for the stock, and the firm incurs flotation costs of $5.50 for every share it sells, the cost of the preferred stock can be determined as follows:

$$k_p = \frac{D_p}{NP_p}$$

$$= \frac{\$9.40}{\$99.50 - \$5.50}$$

$$= 10\%$$

The cost to Dillon, Inc., of issuing preferred stock is 10 percent. Since dividends on preferred stock are paid from after-tax profits, no adjustment is necessary for taxes.

## Common Equity

Firms raise common equity funds two ways. One method is to retain some of the *earnings available to common stockholders (EAC)* instead of paying them all out as dividends. This results in an increase in the firm's retained earnings account. The other method involves selling new shares of common stock.

**Cost of Retained Earnings**  A firm that retains some earnings effectively increases the investment of its common stockholders in the firm. The result is virtually the same as if the firm had paid those earnings to its stockholders as dividends and then sold new shares of common stock to those same stockholders. The only difference is that instead of issuing additional shares and increasing the "common stock" account on the balance sheet, the firm increases the equity account, "retained earnings" on the balance sheet. Of course, the common stockholders are not making a gift of these funds to the firm. They expect to be compensated in the form of higher dividends and higher stock prices in the future. Since the firm now has more funds to purchase additional productive assets, it should be able to pay higher dividends in the future. This increased earning power should also result in an increase in the price of the common stock.

The total expected return to stockholders, under the assumption of a constant dividend growth rate, is described in Chapter 4 as

$$\hat{k}_s = \frac{D_1}{P_0} + g \qquad \text{(4.11 restated)}$$

where  $\hat{k}_s$ = expected return to the common stockholder

$D_1$ = dividend in the coming period

$P_0$ = market price of the common stock today

$g$ = growth rate of the dividend in decimal form

Stockholders expect to earn the same return on retained earnings that they earn on their common stock. Recall that the before-tax cost of a bond to a firm is equal to the return earned on that bond by bondholders (ignoring flotation costs). A similar relationship exists for common equity. That is, the cost of common equity to the firm is equal to investors' returns on common equity, ignoring flotation costs. Since there are no flotation costs associated with retaining earnings, the cost of retained earnings is equal to the required rate of return on common stock without any adjustments for flotation costs. Additionally, since dividends are paid from after-tax profits, no adjustment for taxes is necessary. That is,

$$k_r = \hat{k}_s = \frac{D_1}{P_0} + g \qquad (12.5)$$

where $k_r$ = cost of retained earnings

If common stockholders receive less compensation than they expected (that is, if either $D_1$ or $g$ is lower than expected), they will sell the stock. The increased supply of the stock being sold combines with a decrease in demand for the stock (potential investors avoid buying it at its previous price), resulting in a lower stock price. The price will continue to decline until the expected return on the stock is equal to investors' required rates of return. Therefore, the cost of retained earnings may be viewed as the rate of return that must be earned by the stockholders in order to prevent the price of the stock from declining.

**Example**

Assume Dillon, Inc., expects to pay a $2.10 dividend next year. If the current price of the stock is $30.00 per share, and the dividend is expected to increase at a constant 5 percent rate annually, the cost of Dillon's retained earnings is determined as follows:

$$k_r = \frac{D_1}{P_0} + g$$

$$= \frac{\$2.10}{\$30.00} + .05$$

$$= 12\%$$

The cost of retained earnings for Dillon, Inc., is 12 percent.

**Cost of New Common Stock**    The difference between the cost of retained earnings and the cost of issuing new common stock is that the flotation costs incurred when new common stock is sold increase the cost to the firm. Generally, the firm must pay an underwriter to sell new stock, and investors are permitted to purchase the stock slightly below its current market price (this gives them an incentive to purchase new shares instead of old shares). These flotation costs increase the cost of new common stock to the firm as indicated in Equation 12.6.

$$k_n = \frac{D_1}{P_0 - f} + g \qquad (12.6)$$

where $k_n$ = cost of new common stock
$f$ = flotation cost in dollars per share

The value $(P_0 - f)$ in the denominator of Equation 12.6 represents the net proceeds available to the firm from the sale of new common stock.

---

**Example**

Assume that Dillon, Inc., wants to sell new common stock. In order to do so, it must sell each share to the public at $.75 below the current market price of $30.00 per share, and the underwriter will be paid $1.00 for each share it sells. The firm's cost of new common stock is

$$k_n = \frac{D_1}{P_0 - f} + g$$

$$= \frac{\$2.10}{\$30.00 - (\$.75 + \$1.00)} + .05$$

$$= 12.4\%$$

The cost to Dillon, Inc., of selling new common stock is 12.4 percent.

---

**Alternative Method of Determining Cost of Equity**   Recall that the cost of retained earnings is equal to the return stockholders require on their common equity investment. It was demonstrated in Chapter 5 that the capital asset pricing model (CAPM) can be used to determine the required rate of return on an investment when systematic risk is the relevant measure of risk. Since the CAPM can be used to determine the required rate of return on common stock, it can also be used to determine the cost of retained earnings to the firm. Equation 5.10, restated below as Equation 12.7, can be used to determine the cost of retained earnings.

$$k_j = R_f + b_j(k_m - R_f) \tag{12.7}$$

---

**Example**

Assume the risk-free rate of return $(R_f)$ is 6 percent, and the expected return on the market $(k_m)$ is 10 percent. The required rate of return $(k_j)$ on Dillon's common stock, which has a beta $(b_j)$ of 1.5, can be determined as follows:

$$k_j = 6\% + 1.5(10\% - 6\%)$$

$$= 12\%$$

Since the required rate of return on the firm's common stock is 12.0 percent, the firm's cost of retained earnings also equals 12 percent.

---

Studies have shown that the CAPM is not used as frequently as the dividend discount model to determine the cost of retained earnings. In 1986, however, Quaker Oats Company used the CAPM to determine its cost of equity. In doing so, it used the return on long-term U.S. Treasury securities as a measure of the risk-free return, it estimated a market risk premium $(k_m - R_f)$ of about 6 percent, and it estimated a beta of .80 for the firm. This resulted in a cost of equity for Quaker Oats of approximately 14 percent.

A major limitation of using the CAPM is that one cannot easily estimate the cost of selling new common stock, since there is no way to incorporate flotation costs directly into the model.

## DETERMINING COST OF CAPITAL

The cost of capital for a firm reflects the cost of every component in the capital structure. Normally, varying amounts of capital are raised from different sources, and the cost of capital is the weighted average of the cost of each of these sources, where the weights are the proportions of each component in the capital structure.

**Example**

Assume that Dillon, Inc., wishes to maintain a capital structure that includes 40 percent long-term debt, 10 percent preferred stock, and 50 percent common equity. Recall that the cost of retained earnings is 12 percent, and the after-tax costs of long-term debt and preferred stock are 6 percent and 10 percent, respectively. The weighted average cost of capital $(k_a)$ for Dillon can be found as follows:

| Component of Capital | Weight in Capital Structure | | After-Tax Cost | | Weighted Cost |
|---|---|---|---|---|---|
| Long-term debt | 40% | × | 6% | = | 2.4 |
| Preferred stock | 10 | × | 10 | = | 1.0 |
| Common equity (retained earnings) | 50 | × | 12 | = | 6.0 |
| | | | $k_a$ | = | 9.4% |

The weighted average cost of capital for Dillon, Inc., is 9.4 percent. Hereafter, the weighted average cost of capital is referred to as the **weighted cost of capital.**

### Timing of Financing Transactions

Most firms do not sell all three—bonds, preferred stock, and common stock—each year in order to raise new capital, but may instead sell one of them in a given year and the others separately in later years. The reason for this is that each financing transaction involves incurring certain fixed costs. The firm can minimize these fixed costs by reducing the total number of financing transactions it conducts.

Suppose Dillon, Inc., needs to raise $150 million gradually over the next three years. Also assume Dillon has sufficient retained earnings available to cover all needed equity. In order to maintain its target capital structure of 40 percent debt, 10 percent preferred stock, and 50 percent common equity, Dillon can retain $25 million worth of earnings and sell $20 million worth of bonds and $5 million worth of preferred stock in each of the next three years. This requires a total of six different external financing transactions (the firm must go to the market and sell bonds or preferred stock six different times). Instead, Dillon can elect to sell $60 million worth of bonds in the first year, $15 million worth of preferred stock in the second year, and retain $25 million worth of retained earnings in each of the three years. Although the needed funds are raised in the desired proportions over the three-year period, this method requires only two external financing transactions. Thus, total fixed transactions costs are reduced. Although this method may cause firms to deviate temporarily from their desired capital structure, such deviations may be desirable since they reduce transactions costs.

## Cost of Financing Specific Projects

If a firm knows it will sell bonds this year to finance its capital projects, it may be tempted to use the cost of debt as the measure of the firm's cost of capital. However, by issuing debt this year, the firm is expending some of its debt capacity. As a result, it must sell preferred or common stock in subsequent years to return to the desired capital structure. This means that capital raised in future years will be more expensive as a result of this year's financing. Using the weighted cost of capital effectively spreads these costs over all relevant periods.

Suppose Callihan Enterprises alternates raising funds between selling bonds at a cost of 7 percent and selling new common stock at a cost of 13 percent. The firm's desired capital structure includes 50 percent debt and 50 common equity. Assume Callihan sold bonds last year to finance projects promising an 8 percent return. Next year, Callihan must sell new common stock at a cost of 13 percent to raise funds. If Callihan expects the projects available for investment next year to generate a 12 percent return, it must reject the projects even though their expected return is four percentage points higher than the expected return on the projects adopted the previous year. Using a weighted cost of capital as the discount rate (or hurdle rate) helps avoid this problem.

## Target Weights versus Historic Weights

As indicated earlier, the weights used to find the cost of capital are the proportions of each component of capital in the capital structure. In this chapter, these weights are given, but in practice they would reflect **target weights** determined by the firm. They would not be **historic weights**, which refer to the proportion of total long-term funds raised in the past from each source of capital.

Historic weights can be identified by analyzing a firm's balance sheet. For example, consider the capital accounts for Baez Industries in Table 12.1. The first column of numbers indicates the *book value* of each capital account as it appears on the firm's balance sheet. These values indicate

**TABLE 12.1**   Historic Weights Based on the Balance Sheet: Baez Industries

| Capital Accounts | Book Value | Book Value Weights |
|---|---|---|
| Long-term debt | $400,000 | 40% |
| Preferred stock | 200,000 | 20 |
| Common equity | 400,000 | 40 |
| Total capital | $1,000,000 | 100% |

how capital was raised in the past, and they reflect the historic value of those accounts. The second column of numbers indicates the percent of total capital represented by each source based on these book values. To use these historic proportions as the weights assumes that market conditions and the firm's needs have not changed over time. Since the financial markets and individual firms are dynamic, such an assumption is generally invalid.

An alternative is to consider how the firm has raised capital in the past but also adjust the book values to reflect current market values. Yet, while this may improve the theoretical soundness of the weights, this approach still suffers from the strong influence of historic actions that may be inappropriate in the current environment.

Ideally, target weights should be determined according to the current environment for securities as well as the current situation of the firm. Chapter 13 discusses this procedure. Although target weights do not change frequently or by large amounts (there are exceptions to this), the potential need for changing them cannot be ignored, so they must be evaluated continuously.

## MARGINAL COST OF CAPITAL

The term **marginal cost of capital** refers to the cost of the next dollar of investment capital. For Dillon, Inc., the marginal cost of the first dollar of capital raised is 9.4 percent. This was determined earlier to be the weighted cost of capital using retained earnings as a source of common equity. The marginal cost of capital remains at 9.4 percent until the cost of one or more components of capital changes. In the case of Dillon, Inc., assume that Dillon has only a modest amount of retained earnings to use as a source of equity and must therefore issue new common stock to raise common equity funds once it has used up its retained earnings. As the firm is using its retained earnings, it is assumed to be maintaining its target capital structure by matching each $.50 of common equity funds with $.40 of long-term debt and $.10 of preferred stock financing. When Dillon begins to sell new common stock, it will continue to match each dollar of equity funds with appropriate amounts of long-term debt and preferred stock to maintain the target capital structure. However, the higher cost of selling new common stock (as opposed to the cost of retaining earnings) causes an increase in the firm's weighted cost of capital.

Shifting from the use of retained earnings to the sale of new common stock is not the only cause of changes in the cost of capital. Other changes occur as a result of increases in the cost of long-term debt, preferred stock, and new common stock as the firm sells more of each type of security within a short period of time. This increased cost results from the increased risk investors incur as the firm raises more and more capital. For example, the first bonds sold by a firm may be well secured by specific assets of the firm. Being well secured may mean being backed by $2 of assets for every $1 of debt. Since the firm has a limited amount of assets for securing its debt in this manner, eventually new bonds cannot be secured by specific assets. Bonds that are not secured by specific assets will be secured only by the general credit of the firm. Such bonds are more risky for investors to purchase. When investors incur greater risks, they require higher rates of return, and the firm's cost of capital increases. Therefore, when a firm has been issuing secured bonds but must begin issuing unsecured bonds, the cost of the long-term debt component of capital increases, and the firm's cost of capital also rises.

The relationship between the amount of debt capital raised and the cost of debt is similar to the relationship between the amount of other types of capital raised and their respective costs. That is, the more money that is raised in a short period of time from any source, the higher the cost of that component of capital will be to the firm.

## Marginal Cost of Capital (MCC) Line

The marginal cost of capital is the cost of an additional dollar of capital. This cost is illustrated for a firm by the *marginal cost of capital (MCC)* line. The MCC line for Dillon, Inc., appears in Figure 12.1. Notice that it intersects the vertical axis at 9.4 percent. The level of total financing at which there is a shift in the MCC line to a higher level is called a **breakpoint.** For Dillon, the first breakpoint in the MCC line occurs at point $X_1$. It is caused by the increase that occurs in the cost of equity financing when Dillon expends its retained earnings begins selling new common stock. Beginning at $X_1$, the MCC remains constant until the second breakpoint is reached at $X_2$. This break in the MCC line might be caused by the cost of debt rising as the firm begins to sell unsecured bonds rather than secured bonds. One final breakpoint occurs at $X_3$, which might be caused by the cost of preferred stock rising as the firm issues increasing amounts. This graph of the MCC shows management how much capital can be raised at different costs. Finding the values of $X_1$, $X_2$, and $X_3$, as well as the cost of capital at each level of the MCC, is the subject of the next section.

## Constructing the MCC Line

Assume that Dillon, Inc., is considering raising large amounts of capital next year. After consultation with its investment bank, Dillon constructs a schedule of costs for raising various amounts of capital. This schedule appears in Table 12.2, Columns 1, 2, and 3, and includes the costs of the components of capital determined earlier, as well as changes in the costs of

**FIGURE 12.1**

**Graph of the Marginal Cost of Capital (MCC): Dillon, Inc.**

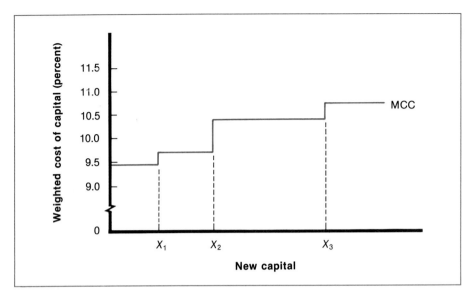

these components. Also indicated is the dollar amount of each component that can be raised at each cost. (This information is given here and cannot be calculated from other data presented earlier.)

Table 12.2 indicates that the firm expects to have $5,000,000 of retained earnings available to it during the next year at an estimated cost of 12 percent. Additional common equity capital can be raised (up to $30,000,000 more) at a cost of 12.4 percent, by selling new common stock. Up to $10,000,000 of long-term debt capital can be raised at an after-tax cost of 6 percent. However, if Dillon raises more than $10,000,000 through the sale of long-term debt, the after-tax cost of the additional debt increases to 8 percent. The cost of small amounts of preferred stock (up to $5,500,000) is 10 percent, but the cost increases to 12 percent when amounts in excess of $5,500,000 are raised.

It is evident from Table 12.2 that as larger amounts of capital are raised, the costs of the components of capital, and therefore the weighted cost of capital, also increases. Before calculating the weighted cost of capital before and after each breakpoint, it is useful to determine the levels of total capital at which the cost of various components change.

**TABLE 12.2**  **Cost of Each Component of Capital as Different Amounts Are Raised: Dillon, Inc.**

| (1) | (2) | (3) | (4) |
|---|---|---|---|
| Component of Capital | Amount Raised | After-Tax Cost | Breakpoint |
| Common equity | | | |
|   Retained earnings | $0–5,000,000 | 12.0% | $10,000,000 |
|   New common stock | 0–30,000,000 | 12.4 | 70,000,000 |
| Long-term debt | 0–10,000,000 | 6.0 | 25,000,000 |
| | 10,000,001–28,000,000 | 8.0 | 70,000,000 |
| Preferred stock | 0–5,500,000 | 10.0 | 55,000,000 |
| | 5,500,001–7,000,000 | 12.0 | 70,000,000 |

## Identifying Breakpoints in the MCC Line

It is important for firms to know the total amount of financing they can raise at various costs. For example, how much capital can Dillon, Inc., raise using retained earning before it must begin to sell more expensive new common stock? Recall that Dillon's target capital structure consists of 40 percent long-term debt, 10 percent preferred stock, and 50 percent common equity. While Dillon expects to have only $5 million of retained earnings available for use, in order to maintain the target capital structure the firm must also issue $4,000,000 of long-term debt and $1,000,000 of preferred stock. When these amounts are combined, the total capital raised is $10 million, and the target capital structure has been maintained. This is indicated in the following table.

| Component of Capital | Dollar Amount Raised | Percent of Total New Capital Raised |
|---|---|---|
| Long-term debt | $ 4,000,000 | 40% |
| Preferred stock | 1,000,000 | 10 |
| Common equity (retained earnings) | 5,000,000 | 50 |
| Total capital | $10,000,000 | 100% |

Ten million dollars is, therefore, the breakpoint associated with exhausting the availability of retained earnings. Stated differently, the firm can raise up to $10 million in new capital, supported by retained earnings plus the least expensive long-term debt and preferred stock. The cost of the next dollar of capital will be higher because of the need to sell common stock as a source of common equity. Equation 12.8 facilitates the calculation of breakpoints.

$$BP_i = \frac{TF_i}{PS_i} \qquad (12.8)$$

where $BP_i$ = breakpoint in the cost of capital line attributable to a change in the cost of source $i$

$TF_i$ = total financing available from source $i$ before the cost of source $i$ changes

$PS_i$ = proportion of source $i$ in the target capital structure, in decimal form

Employing Equation 12.8 to determine the breakpoint for Dillon, Inc., when retained earnings are exhausted results in the following calculation:

$$BP_i = \frac{TF_i}{PS_i}$$

$$= \frac{\$5,000,000}{.50}$$

$$= \$10,000,000$$

**TABLE 12.3  Weighted Cost of Capital before Each Breakpoint: Dillon, Inc.**

**Part A:** Prior to the first breakpoint at $10,000,000, the marginal cost of capital reflects the least expensive source of each component of capital.

| Component | Weight | After-Tax Cost | Weighted Cost |
|---|---|---|---|
| Long-term debt | 40% | 6% | 2.4 |
| Preferred stock | 10 | 10 | 1.0 |
| Common equity (retained earnings) | 50 | 12 | 6.0 |
| | | $k_a =$ | 9.4% |

**Part B:** After the first breakpoint, but prior to the second one at $25,000,000, the cost of common equity increases while the cost of long-term debt and preferred stock remain unchanged.

| Component | Weight | After-Tax Cost | Weighted Cost |
|---|---|---|---|
| Long-term debt | 40% | 6.0% | 2.4 |
| Preferred stock | 10 | 10.0 | 1.0 |
| Common equity (new common stock) | 50 | 12.4 | 6.2 |
| | | $k_a =$ | 9.6% |

**Part C:** After the second breakpoint, but before the third one at $55,000,000, the cost of debt rises to 8 percent while the costs of the other components remain unchanged from the previous calculation.

| Component | Weight | After-Tax Cost | Weighted Cost |
|---|---|---|---|
| Long-term debt | 40% | 8.0% | 3.2 |
| Preferred stock | 10 | 10.0 | 1.0 |
| Common equity (new common stock) | 50 | 12.4 | 6.2 |
| | | $k_a =$ | 10.4% |

**Part D:** After the third breakpoint, but before the fourth breakpoint at $70,000,000, the cost of each component is at its highest level.

| Component | Weight | After-Tax Cost | Weighted Cost |
|---|---|---|---|
| Long-term debt | 40% | 8.0% | 3.2 |
| Preferred stock | 10 | 12.0 | 1.2 |
| Common equity (new common stock) | 50 | 12.4 | 6.2 |
| | | $k_a =$ | 10.6% |

Since Table 12.1 indicates that $70,000,000 is the breakpoint for all three components, the cost of all three would increase. However, information concerning the cost of these components beyond $70,000,000 in total capital raised is not provided.

Other breakpoints in Dillon's MCC line occur when the firm exhausts the less expensive debt and when the firm exhausts the less expensive preferred stock. Using Equation 12.8, all of the breakpoints have been calculated for each component of capital and appear in Column 4 of Table 12.2 (note that the second breakpoint for common equity is found by dividing retained earnings plus new common stock, both of which are common equity components, by 50 percent).

Up to the first breakpoint at $10 million (this corresponds to point $X_1$ on Figure 12.1), the marginal cost of capital reflects the use of retained earnings as the common equity component of capital, plus the least expen-

**TABLE 12.4    Summary of Steps Required to Construct the Marginal Cost of Capital (MCC) Line**

Step 1. Identify the cost of each component of capital and the amounts of each component that can be obtained at each cost. This information appears in Table 12.2, Columns 2 and 3, for Dillon, Inc.

Step 2. Calculate the breakpoints for each source of capital using Equation 12.8. This information appears in Table 12.2, Column 4, for Dillon, Inc.

Step 3. Calculate the marginal cost of capital before and after each breakpoint. An example of this calculation for Dillon, Inc., appears in Table 12.3.

Step 4. Construct the weighted cost of capital (MCC) line using the information determined in Steps 2 and 3 above. An example of this for Dillon, Inc., appears in Figure 12.3.

sive long-term debt and preferred stock. The weighted cost of capital using these components was determined earlier in this chapter to be 9.4 percent. This has been calculated again in part A of Table 12.3. To the right of this breakpoint, the cost of common equity is 12.4 percent, and the cost of debt and preferred stock remain unchanged. (Table 12.2 indicates that the cost of debt does not increase until a total of $25 million of capital has been raised. It increases again after $70 million has been raised. The cost of preferred stock does not increase until a total of $55 million of capital has been raised. Like the cost of debt, it increases again after $70 million).

As a result of the increase in the cost of common equity after the first breakpoint, the weighted cost of capital increases to 9.6 percent as indicated in part B of Table 12.3. The next breakpoint is at $25 million (this corresponds to point $X_2$ on Figure 12.1), where the cost of debt increases to 8 percent. Part C of Table 12.3 indicates that the weighted cost of capital after $25 million has been raised is 10.4 percent until total capital of $55 million has been reached (this corresponds to point $X_3$ in Figure 12.1). After $55 million of total capital has been raised, the cost of preferred stock increases to 12 percent, and the weighted cost of capital increases to 10.6 percent (part D on Table 12.3). Since information has not been provided about the cost of the components of capital beyond $70 million of total capital raised, the MCC line cannot be constructed beyond that point. The steps necessary to derive a firm's MCC line are summarized in Table 12.4.

## USING THE MCC LINE IN CAPITAL BUDGETING

An ascending MCC line is normal for businesses seeking to raise new capital. However, it means the firm is faced with the potential problem of adopting projects that are acceptable at the lowest cost of capital but not at higher costs. To determine which projects are acceptable, the firm can compare its MCC line to its **investment opportunity schedule (IOS).** The IOS is a graph depicting the internal rate of return (*IRR*) and the level of investment required to adopt potential capital budgeting projects.

Table 12.5 displays relevant information about five capital budgeting projects being considered by Dillon, Inc. In order to simplify this discussion, it is assumed that all projects are independent and have the same level of risk as the firm itself. The information in Table 12.5 is used to con-

TABLE 12.5  **Information about Alternative Capital Budgeting Projects: Dillon, Inc.**

| Project | IRR | Initial Cost |
|---------|------|--------------|
| A | 11.00% | $21,000,000 |
| B | 11.25 | 17,000,000 |
| C | 9.5 | 12,000,000 |
| D | 11.50 | 11,000,000 |
| E | 10.00 | 9,000,000 |

struct the IOS displayed in Figure 12.2. Notice that the projects are arranged in descending order of their *IRR*. This places the most desirable projects on the left side of the graph. Here, Project D has an *IRR* of 11.5 percent and requires an investment of $11 million. Project B has an *IRR* of 11.25 percent and requires an investment of $17 million. The lower *IRR* is reflected by a shift downward in the IOS. The horizontal scale indicates the cumulative total investment required to adopt the projects—which is $28 million for Projects D and B together. Adopting the three most desirable projects (D, B, and A) requires a total investment of $49 million; the four most desirable projects, $58 million; and all five projects, $70 million.

Recall that the weighted cost of capital for Dillon, Inc. is expected to be 9.4 percent when small amounts of new capital are raised. If an unlimited amount of new capital could be raised at that cost, all five capital budgeting projects under consideration should be adopted since all five exhibit internal rates of return exceeding 9.4 percent (recall that independent projects are acceptable when their *IRR* is greater than or equal to the required rate of return).

However, the ascending MCC line shows that the weighted cost of capital rises as larger amounts of capital are raised. By plotting the MCC line and the IOS on the same graph (Figure 12.3) we can see how these two functions interact. The point of intersection of the IOS and the MCC lines

**FIGURE 12.2**
**Graph of the Investment Opportunity Schedule (IOS): Dillon, Inc.**

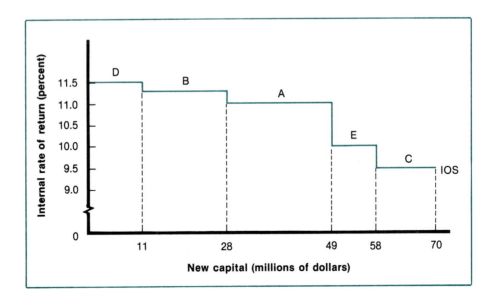

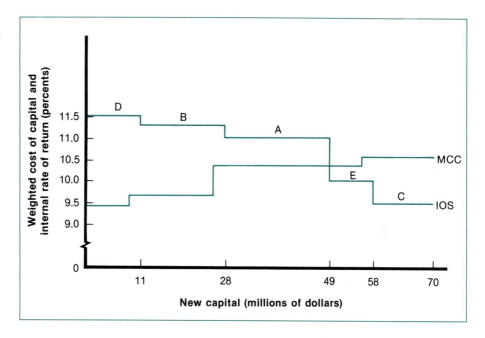

at $49 million provides useful information. At this point, the marginal revenue from the capital budgeting projects is equal to the marginal cost of financing those projects. To the left of the point of intersection, the expected rate of return earned on capital invested in projects exceeds the expected cost of capital used to finance these projects (marginal revenue exceeds marginal cost). To the right of the point of intersection, the expected cost of new capital exceeds the expected rate of return earned on the projects adopted with this capital (marginal cost exceeds marginal revenue). Therefore, the **optimal capital budget** is $49 million and includes the adoption of Projects D, B, and A only.

This analysis relies heavily on the *IRR* framework described in Chapter 10. When the net present value (*NPV*) approach is employed in capital budgeting, the appropriate discount rate to use is the weighted cost of capital that exists at the point of intersection of the IOS and the MCC line (assuming equal project risk). This follows from the fact that the *IRR* is the discount rate that yields an *NPV* of zero.

## Words of Caution

Management must be aware of the following complications associated with the concept of *cost of capital*.

**1.** Estimates of a firm's cost of capital are uncertain, because estimates of key input variables, such as investors' required rates of return and dividend growth rates for future periods, are uncertain. Moreover, as economic and business conditions change, so do these variables. Therefore, management must recognize that the estimated cost of capital may deviate from the actual cost of capital.

## FINANCIAL MANAGEMENT IN PRACTICE

### COST OF CAPITAL IN PRACTICE

A survey of large U.S. firms was conducted in 1982 to determine how businesses measure the cost of capital and use it in their operations.* Some of the more relevant findings are as follows:

**1.** Forty-two percent of the respondents indicated that they calculate the cost of capital using a weighted average method based on target capital structure weights. Seventeen percent of the firms use the cost of the specific source of financing planned for funding the project, and another 16 percent use a weighted average method based on book value weights. Twenty-nine percent use a weighted average method wherein the weights are based on the market value of the firm's current long-term obligations.

**2.** Most respondents (84 percent) calculate the cost of only one type of common equity rather than making a distinction between the cost of retained earnings and the cost of new common stock.

**3.** The methods used to estimate the cost of

*Lawrence J. Gitman and Vincent A. Mercurio, "Cost of Capital Techniques Used by Major U.S. Firms: Survey and Analysis of Fortune's 1000," *Financial Management* 11 (Winter 1982): 21–29.

common equity by the surveyed firms were many and varied. The most popular methods involve estimating the required rate of return of investors (36 percent), and using the Gordon model, in which the current dividend yield is added to the expected growth rate (26 percent). Surprisingly, 17 percent of the respondents use methods that do not reflect future expectations.

**4.** Half of the firms revise their cost of capital estimates "whenever environmental conditions change sufficiently to warrant it." Another 22 percent evaluate their cost of capital annually. Other responses were "less frequently than annually" (13 percent), "each time a major project is evaluated" (11 percent), and "quarterly or semiannually" (4 percent).

**5.** When asked how they use the cost of capital, 93 percent of the firms indicated it is used in project evaluation, 64 percent use it in making the leasing decision, 45 percent use it to make the decision on the abandonment of existing projects, 44 percent use it to help estimate the firm's value, and 35 percent use it to make bond refunding decisions.

**2.** The framework presented here assumes that the projects under consideration have the same risk as the firm itself. When this is not the case, it is appropriate to use a risk-adjusted discount rate to evaluate capital budgeting projects. This requires adjustment of the cost of capital.

**3.** The target weights used in this chapter were given. As seen in the next chapter, estimating target weights requires numerous estimates of other factors, again with a considerable degree of unavoidable uncertainty.

**4.** Privately owned firms and small businesses have additional complications associated with estimating the cost of capital. For example, when the common stock of a firm does not trade publicly, it is more difficult to estimate the cost of common equity, since there is no indication of the market value of the firm's common stock.

**5.** Sources of capital not previously addressed may be available to the firm. For example, depreciation is an important source of long-term funds to many firms. Deferred taxes also can be a source of long-term funds. That is, if the firm defers the payment of taxes through the use of accelerated depreciation, the result is similar to a short-term, interest-free loan to the firm made by the government. If the firm can defer taxes every year, this source of funds can be viewed as long-term or even permanent. When depreciation and/or deferred taxes are considered in calculating the weighted cost of capital, the cost of depreciation may be assigned a cost equal to the overall cost of the first dollar of capital to be raised. The cost of deferred taxes normally is considered to be zero.

## SUMMARY

Determining the cost of capital is important to the firm for two reasons. First, the cost of capital can be used to help select capital budgeting projects using either the *NPV* or *IRR* approach. Second, by analyzing the cost of capital, the firm may be able to determine the capital structure that minimizes the cost of capital and hence maximizes the value of the firm's common stock.

The cost of capital is a weighted average cost of each component of capital, wherein the target weights are determined by the firm. Historic weights should not be used, since the firm, the capital markets and the economy change over time, resulting in changing relative costs of the components of capital.

The cost of each component of capital is closely related to investors' required rates of return on the firm's securities. However, the cost of each component of capital may be higher due to the flotation costs associated with issuing securities. Flotation costs include the administrative cost of preparing to issue new securities, the fees or commissions paid to an investment banker, and any discounts offered to investors as enticement to purchase the firm's new securities. In addition, the before-tax cost of debt must be adjusted to reflect the tax-deductible nature of interest on debt.

As the firm raises larger amounts of capital relative to total firm assets, the cost of each component of capital increases, causing upward shifts in the cost of capital. These shifts appear as breaks in the marginal cost of capital (MCC) line. The MCC line is a graph of the cost of every dollar of investment capital raised by the firm.

The investment opportunity schedule (IOS) is a graph showing the expected internal rates of return on alternative capital budgeting projects (in descending order of *IRR*) and the cumulative level of investment required for project adoption. When the IOS is superimposed over the MCC line, the optimal capital budget is revealed, along with an indication of which projects to adopt.

## KEY TERMS

**Breakpoint** The level of total capital raised at which the marginal cost of capital increases.

**Business risk** The risk of being unable to cover operating costs. It is measured in terms of the volatility of EBIT and is caused by sales volatility and operating leverage.

**Capital structure** The mixture of long-term sources of financing, such as debt, preferred stock, and common stock, used by a firm.

**Cost of capital** The cost of long-term funds to the firm.

**Financial risk** The risk of being unable to cover

fixed financing costs. It results in volatility of EPS and is caused by the use of debt to finance the firm's assets.

**Flotation costs** The cost to the firm of selling new securities in the financial markets. This cost includes underwriting fees, registration fees, and so forth. It does not include interest and dividend compensation paid to the purchasers of the securities.

**Historic weights** The percent of each component of capital in the capital structure, based on the book value of previous capital raised.

**Investment opportunity schedule** A graph of the internal rate of return and the cumulative level of investment required for adopting potential capital budgeting projects.

**Marginal cost of capital** The cost to the firm of an additional dollar of capital.

**Optimal capital budget** The combination of capital projects that maximizes shareholder wealth. This budget is specified by the intersection of the marginal cost of capital (MCC) line and the investment opportunity schedule (IOS) and results in the adoption of all projects that are expected to increase the value of the firm.

**Target weights** The desired percent of each component of capital in the capital structure, based on current market conditions. Target weights are designed to minimize the firm's cost of capital.

**Weighted cost of capital** The cost of capital to a firm that reflects the cost of each component of capital in proportion to each component's weight in the capital structure.

## EQUATIONS

**Equation 12.1**    **Before-Tax Cost of Debt**

$$NP_b = \sum_{t=1}^{n} I\left[\frac{1}{(1 + k_b)^t}\right] + M\left[\frac{1}{(1 + k_b)^n}\right] \qquad \textbf{(p. 340)}$$

where   $k_b$ = before-tax cost of debt
$NP_p$ = net proceeds from the sale of the bond
$I$ = annual dollar amount of interest paid on the bond
$M$ = maturity or par value of the bond
$n$ = number of years to maturity
$t$ = time

By solving for the unknown, $k_b$, in Equation 12.1, the firm can determine the before-tax cost of issuing a bond. This cost considers all interest to be paid on the bond, the return of principal at maturity, and all flotation costs; however, it does not consider the tax-deductible nature of interest expense.

**Equation 12.2**    **Approximate Before-Tax Cost of Debt**

$$Ak_b = \frac{I + \dfrac{M - NP_b}{n}}{\dfrac{NP_b + M}{2}} \qquad \textbf{(p. 340)}$$

where $Ak_b$ = approximate before-tax cost of debt.

When only moderate accuracy is necessary in calculating the before-tax cost of debt, Equation 12.2 can be used. It has the advantage of being easily computed, but it has the disadvantage of not considering the time value of money. Therefore, it may be less accurate than using Equation 12.1.

**Equation 12.3**     **After-Tax Cost of Debt**

$$k_i = k_b(1 - T)$$     **(p. 341)**

where  $k_i$ = after-tax cost of debt
$k_b$ = before-tax cost of debt
$T$ = marginal tax rate of the firm

The before-tax cost of debt can be adjusted to reflect the tax-deductible nature of the interest expense by using Equation 12.3. It is this after-tax cost of debt that is used to calculate the firm's cost of capital.

**Equation 12.4**     **Cost of Preferred Stock**

$$k_p = \frac{D_p}{NP_p}$$     **(p. 342)**

where   $k_p$ = cost of preferred stock
$D_p$ = annual dollar amount of dividend paid on the preferred stock
$NP_p$ = net proceeds from the sale of preferred stock

Equation 12.4 can be used to determine the cost of preferred stock to the firm.

**Equation 12.5**     **Cost of Retained Earnings**

$$k_r = \frac{D_1}{P_0} + g$$     **(p. 344)**

where  $k_r$ = cost of retained earnings
$P_0$ = market price of the common stock
$g$ = growth rate of the dividend in decimal form
$D_1$ = dividend in the next year

Retained earnings represent earnings that belong to common stockholders but are not paid out to them as dividends. Retained earnings, therefore, represent an additional investment of stockholders in the firm. The return those stockholders require on their additional investment is the firm's *cost of retained earnings*. This cost can be found by using Equation 12.5.

**Equation 12.6**     **Cost of Selling New Common Stock**

$$k_n = \frac{D_1}{P_0 - f} + g$$     **(p. 344)**

where $k_n$ = cost of selling new common stock
$f$ = flotation cost in dollars per share

The only difference between the cost of selling new common stock and the cost of retained earnings (Equation 12.5) is that selling new common stock normally involves incurring flotation costs. Equation 12.6 reflects those flotation costs.

**Equation 12.7**      **Required Rate of Return: CAPM Framework**

$$k_j = R_f + b_j(k_m - R_f) \qquad \text{(p. 345)}$$

where   $k_j$ = required rate of return on stock $j$
         $R_f$ = risk-free rate of return
         $b_j$ = the beta (level of systematic risk) of stock $j$
         $k_m$ = return on the market

This equation was first introduced in Chapter 5 as Equation 5.10. It can be used to determine an investor's required rate of return on an asset within the capital asset pricing model framework.

**Equation 12.8**      **Breakpoint in the MCC Line**

$$BP_i = \frac{TF_i}{PS_i} \qquad \text{(p. 351)}$$

where   $BP_i$ = breakpoint in the MCC line attributable to a change in the cost of source $i$
         $TF_i$ = total financing available from source $i$ before the cost of source $i$ changes
         $PS_i$ = proportion of source $i$ in the capital structure in decimal form

When a firm raises large amounts of new capital, suppliers of that capital perceive their investments as being more risky. As a result, investors' required rates of return, and the cost of capital, tend to increase. Each time the cost of a given source of capital increases, it causes a break, or shift upward, in the MCC line. Equation 12.8 can be used to determine the level of total capital at which such breaks occur.

## QUESTIONS

**Q12-1.** What are the two principal functions of the cost of capital?

**Q12-2.** Explain why the actual cost of raising capital during a given period is not necessarily the firm's "cost of capital."

**Q12-3.** What factors might make a firm's target capital structure change?

**Q12-4.** How are investor returns on a financial asset similar and dissimilar to the issuing firm's cost of issuing the asset?

**Q12-5.** Under what circumstances might the approximate before-tax cost of debt as determined by the approximate method differ greatly from the cost as determined by the present value method? Why?

**Q12-6.** What are the two methods of calculating the firm's cost of retained earnings? Why might the answers differ?

**Q12-7.** Explain why the cost of a given source of capital tends to increase as more of that source is used within a short period of time (assume a constant capital structure).

**Q12-8.** What is the difference between a firm's *weighted* cost of capital and its *marginal* cost of capital?

**Q12-9.** Why do you agree or disagree with this statement? "A firm with a target capital structure of 50 percent debt and 50 percent equity should sell $1 of debt every time it raises $1 of equity."

**Q12-10.** How might each of the following affect a firm's cost of capital? Consider each separately.

**a.** Depreciation is a major source of funds to the firm.
**b.** Interest rates rise.
**c.** The firm changes its target capital structure to include more debt.
**d.** The firm has considerable deferred taxes on its balance sheet each year.
**e.** The firm's marginal tax rate declines.

**Q12-11.** If a firm can simply elect to retain some earnings as a source of capital, why is there a cost to the firm?

**Q12-12.** If the IOS schedule in Figure 12.4 were reversed so that projects with the lowest *IRR* were on the left and the IOS increases on the right, all projects would be above the MCC line. Why not do that and adopt all projects?

## SELF-TEST PROBLEMS

Solutions to self-test problems appear on p. S1.

**SP12-1.** B. Dawkins, Inc., is in the process of determining the cost of each component of its capital. The following information is provided about the securities that B. Dawkins is considering selling in the months to come.

*Bonds.* The bonds will have an $11\frac{1}{4}$ percent coupon and pay interest annually with twenty years to maturity. Their par value will be $1,000. Investors will pay $959 for each bond, and B. Dawkins must pay the underwriter $15 for each bond sold.

*Preferred stock.* The preferred stock will pay a dividend of $10.25 annually and will sell to the public for $100 per share. B. Dawkins must pay the underwriter $4 for each share sold.

*Common stock.* The current market price of B. Dawkins's common stock is $30 per share. The expected dividend for next year is $2.50, and the dividend is expected to grow at a constant 6 percent rate in the future. If new common stock is sold, investors will pay $28 per share; the underwriter will be paid $1.50 for each share sold.

If B. Dawkins has a 30 percent marginal tax rate, calculate the following:

**a.** The after-tax cost of long-term debt using the approximate method.
**b.** The after-tax cost of long-term debt considering the time value of money.
**c.** The cost of preferred stock.
**d.** The cost of retained earnings.
**e.** The cost of selling new common stock.

**SP12-2.** B. Dawkins, Inc., has a target capital structure of 45 percent common equity, 20 percent preferred stock, and 35 percent long-term debt. Dawkins expects the cost of each component of capital to increase as more of each type is raised. Information about the cost of each component of capital is as follows:

| Source of Capital | Amount at Indicated Cost | After-Tax Cost |
|---|---|---|
| Common equity | | |
| Retained earnings | $0–450,000 | 16% |
| New common stock | 0–540,000 | 17 |
| | above 540,000 | 18 |
| Preferred stock | 0–300,000 | 13 |
| | above 300,000 | 14 |
| Long-term debt | 0–525,000 | 9 |
| | above 525,000 | 10 |

a. Calculate the breakpoints for each source of capital.
b. Calculate the weighted cost of capital before and after each breakpoint.
c. Graph the MCC line.

SP12-3. B. Dawkins, Inc., has the following capital budgeting projects under consideration for adoption.

| Project | IRR | Cost |
|---|---|---|
| A | 13.8% | $200,000 |
| B | 12.5 | 500,000 |
| C | 14.5 | 300,000 |
| D | 13.0 | 600,000 |
| E | 14.0 | 900,000 |

a. Graph the projects on the same graph with the MCC line you developed in SP12-2.
b. Which projects should be adopted?

SP12-4. A young analyst at B. Dawkins wants to see how sensitive the firm's cost of retained earnings is to changes in certain economic factors. The analyst estimates the firm's beta to be .9 and the market return to be 16 percent. The current risk-free rate of interest is 6 percent.

a. What is the cost of retained earnings for B. Dawkins using the CAPM approach?
b. What is the cost of retained earnings if the estimate of the return on the market is 20 percent, and the risk-free rate is 11 percent?
c. What is the cost of retained earnings if the estimate of the market return changes to 5 percent, and the risk-free rate changes to 4 percent?

# PROBLEMS

P12-1. Campbell & Johnson Enterprises is considering selling bonds having $1,000 par value and a 13.25 percent coupon. These bonds would pay interest annually and mature in twenty years. Investors would pay $960 for the bonds, and Campbell & Johnson must pay an investment bank $9.64 for each bond sold. If the firm has a 34 percent marginal tax rate, what is the after-tax cost of debt using the approximate formula? Recalculate the after-tax cost using the more accurate formula that considers the time value of money.

P12-2. Morley Enterprises recently issued $10 million of $8.75 preferred stock. Investors paid $73.50 for each share purchased, and an investment banker was paid

$1.75 by Morley for each share sold. Par value of the preferred stock is $75. What is the cost of this preferred stock to the company?

**P12-3.** Craig Corporation is planning to sell some new common stock in the near future. The current price of the common stock is $4 per share, but the stock would be sold to investors at a discount, and Craig Corporation must pay an investment bank to assist in the sale. The fee and the discount are expected to total 5 percent of the current market value of the common stock. The dividend on the stock was $.20 last year and is expected to grow at a constant 6 percent.

a. What is the cost of Craig's retained earnings?
b. What is Craig's cost of issuing new common stock?

**P12-4.** Taylor & Hunt, Inc., are planning to issue new bonds that have twenty years to maturity. The firm's investment banker expects the bonds to have a 15.7 percent coupon (paid semiannually) and sell at par value ($1,000). After paying the investment banker, Taylor & Hunt expects to net $982 from each bond sold. Assuming a 34 percent marginal tax rate, what is the after-tax cost of this bond issue to Taylor & Hunt using the approximate method? Recalculate the after-tax cost using the method that considers the time value of money.

**P12-5.** Savage Enterprises is considering selling 10.5 percent preferred stock to the public. The stock will be sold to the public for $98.50 per share, and the firm's investment banker requires payment of $1.75 for each share sold. If the preferred stock has a $100 par value, what is the cost of preferred stock to Savage Enterprises?

**P12-6.** The common stock of Southern Enterprises currently sells for $122 per share. It paid a $6 dividend per share last year and has a beta of 1.3. The expected return on the market is 11 percent next year, and the risk-free rate of return is 6 percent. Southern Enterprises is considering selling new common stock at a 3 percent discount from the current market price. In addition, Southern must pay its investment banker $2.44 for each share sold. Investors expect the dividend on Southern common stock to continue to grow at a constant 7 percent rate in the future.

a. Based on the CAPM what is the cost of retained earnings for Southern Enterprises?
b. Using the dividend discount model, what is the cost of retained earnings for Southern Enterprises?
c. What is the cost of selling new common stock for Southern Enterprises?

**P12-7.** Klintworth Corporation has a target capital structure of 60 percent common equity and 40 percent long-term debt. Given the following information about the cost of raising various amounts of each type of capital, calculate the relevant breakpoints. Also calculate the weighted cost of capital before and after each breakpoint.

| Component of Capital | Amount Raised (in Millions) | After-Tax Cost |
|---|---|---|
| Long-term debt | $ 0–5 | 5.0% |
| | 5–10 | 5.5 |
| | 10–15 | 6.0 |
| Retained earnings | 0–3 | 9.0 |
| New common stock | 0–6 | 9.5 |
| | 6–12 | 10.0 |
| | above 12 | 10.5 |

**P12-8.** Welker Iron Works has six independent capital budgeting projects under consideration (see the information provided in the following table). It has already determined its weighted cost of capital at various levels of new financing (also indicated in the table).

**a.** Draw the MCC line and IOS on the same graph.
**b.** What is the optimal level of total capital expenditures?
**c.** Which projects should be adopted?
**d.** What would be the appropriate discount rate to use with the *NPV* approach to capital budgeting?

| Project | Cost | IRR |
|---------|------|-----|
| A | $20,000 | 11.0% |
| B | 40,000 | 10.0 |
| C | 60,000 | 12.0 |
| D | 70,000 | 10.5 |
| E | 30,000 | 12.5 |
| F | 50,000 | 11.5 |

| Capital Raised | Weighted Cost of Capital |
|----------------|--------------------------|
| $0–50,000 | 10.25% |
| 50,001–85,000 | 10.75 |
| 85,001–150,000 | 11.25 |
| 150,001–200,000 | 11.75 |
| 200,001–270,000 | 12.25 |

**P12-9.** Kilbride Corporation has a before-tax cost of debt of 9.5 percent, a cost of preferred stock of 11 percent, a cost of common equity of 13 percent, and a marginal tax rate of 34 percent.

**a.** Use the following information to determine the weighted cost of capital based on book value weights.

*Liability and Equity Accounts (from Balance Sheet)*

| | | |
|---|---|---|
| Long-term debt | | $2,000 |
| Preferred stock | | 1,000 |
| Common equity | | |
|    Common stock | $1,000 | |
|    Additional paid-in capital | 1,000 | |
|    Retained earnings | 3,000 | 5,000 |
| Total capital | | $8,000 |

**b.** What is the weighted cost of capital using the following target weights: 35 percent debt, 20 percent preferred stock, and 45 percent common equity?

**P12-10.** Raffa Industries just completed a year in which earnings available to common stockholders (EAC) was $5,250,000. Raffa's target capital structure includes 50 percent common equity, 30 percent long-term debt, and 20 percent preferred stock. Capital budgeting projects totaling $13 million have already been approved. Raffa expects to pay out half of its EAC in the form of a common stock dividend.

**a.** At what level of total financing would a break appear in the MCC line as a result of shifting from the use of retained earning to new common stock?

**b.** What dollar amount of the $13 million of financing would come from the sale of new common stock?

**c.** If the cost of retained earnings is 10 percent, the cost of new common stock is 10.5 percent, the cost of preferred stock is 9 percent, and the after-tax cost of debt is 7 percent, what is Raffa's weighted cost of capital to the left and right of the breakpoint?

**P12-11.** Xander Enterprises' current capital structure based on book value weights is also its target for the future:

| | |
|---|---|
| Long-term debt | $ 9,000,000 |
| Preferred stock | 4,000,000 |
| Common equity | 12,000,000 |
| | $25,000,000 |

Next year, Xander expects to add $1.44 million to its retained earnings. Xander's common stock sells for $35 per share, and the firm is expected to pay a $1.70 dividend per share next year. The dividend has increased at a constant rate over the past nine years and should continue at that rate in the future (nine years earlier the dividend was $1 per share). If Xander must sell new common stock next year, it will do so at $3.00 below the current market price. It must also pay a $2.00 per share commission.

Xander estimates that if it sells preferred stock next year, it will be 9 percent preferred with a par value of $100. Net proceeds from the sale of the preferred stock will be $97.50. Xander also estimates its before-tax cost of debt at 8 percent.

**a.** What is the cost of each component of capital? (Assume a 34 percent tax rate.)
**b.** How much total capital can Xander raise before it must sell new common stock?
**c.** What is the weighted cost of capital before and after the breakpoint?
**d.** Graph the MCC line and IOS for Xander based on the following additional information.

| Project | IRR | Cost |
|---|---|---|
| A | 9.3% | $3,000,000 |
| B | 9.5 | 2,000,000 |
| C | 8.7 | 3,000,000 |

**P12-12.** Fritz Corporation is planning now for its capital expenditures next year. Information about the securities that Fritz expects to issue next year is as follows:

*Preferred stock.* The preferred stock to be issued will pay a dividend of $9 per year and will sell to the public for $98.50 per share. In addition, the firm must pay an investment bank $1.75 for each share sold. Par value is $100.

*Common stock.* Fritz Corporation's common stock is currently priced at $4 per share. Last year it paid a dividend of $.20 per share, and the dividend is expected to grow at a constant rate of 5 percent. If new common stock is sold, it will be sold to the public at a 10 percent discount from its current market price. In addition, an investment bank will be paid $.12 per share for each share sold.

*Bonds.* Fritz Corporation expects its bonds to sell at par value with a yield to maturity of 11.8 percent. The bond would pay interest annually, it matures at ten years, and the Fritz Corporation would have to pay the investment bank $11 for each bond sold. Fritz has a marginal tax rate of 34 percent.

a. Calculate the cost of each component of capital.

b. The target capital structure for the Fritz Corporation is 55 percent common equity, 30 percent long-term debt, and 15 percent preferred stock. If the firm has $12 million to contribute to retained earnings next year, what total amount of capital can be raised without selling new common stock yet maintaining the target capital structure?

c. What is the weighted cost of capital to the left and right of the breakpoint?

**P12-13.** The following estimates of the cost of raising funds were made for E. Day Corporation.

| Source of Capital | Amount at Indicated Cost | After-Tax Cost |
|---|---|---|
| Retained earnings | $250,000 | 14.0% |
| New common stock | 0–1,750,000 | 15.0 |
| | 1,750,000–2,750,000 | 16.0 |
| Preferred stock | 0–500,000 | 11.5 |
| | 500,000–1,875,000 | 13.0 |
| Long-term debt | 0–1,225,000 | 8.0 |
| | 1,225,000–2,625,000 | 10.0 |

The target capital structure for E. Day Corporation is 40 percent common equity, 25 percent preferred stock, and 35 percent debt. The capital-budgeting projects currently under consideration are as follows:

| Project | Cost | IRR |
|---|---|---|
| A | $1,500,000 | 12.0% |
| B | 1,250,000 | 12.7 |
| C | 2,000,000 | 11.7 |
| D | 1,000,000 | 13.0 |
| E | 1,000,000 | 11.5 |
| F | 750,000 | 12.3 |

a. At what dollar amounts do breaks occur in the MCC line?

b. What is the weighted cost of capital before each breakpoint?

c. Graph the MCC schedule and the IOS on the same graph.

d. Which projects should be adopted?

e. What assumptions are implicit in this analysis?

# COMPUTER-ASSISTED PROBLEMS

**CP12-1.** Wizco Corporation is considering selling bonds and retaining some earnings next year. It expects to put a 12 percent coupon on the bonds and receive $1,000 net from the sale of each bond. The bonds will have a maturity of twenty years. Wizco expects the risk-free rate to be 7 percent and the return on the market to be 10 percent next year. The firm's beta is 1.0, and it has a 34 percent marginal tax rate.

a. **Sensitivity of the Cost of Debt to Changes in Net Proceeds** Wizco realizes that the sale price of its bonds may need to be adjusted for changes in market rates of interest. In fact, management feels that it may receive as little as $930 from the sale of each bond, or as much as $1,070. What would Wizco's after-tax cost of debt be under the three possible outcomes?

**b. Probability Distributions and the Expected Cost of Debt** After further analysis, Wizco has constructed the following probability distribution describing the expected net proceeds from the sale of each bond. What are all possible outcomes and the expected after-tax cost of debt?

| Probability | Net Proceeds from Sale of Each Bond |
|---|---|
| 10% | $ 930 |
| 25 | 965 |
| 35 | 1,000 |
| 25 | 1,035 |
| 5 | 1,070 |

**c. Sensitivity of the Cost of Equity to Changes in Interest Rates and Firm Risk** Wizco's management recognizes that some of the projects it has adopted in the past could increase investors' perception of the firm's risk, which could in turn increase the firm's cost of equity. Although Wizco's current beta is 1.0, it could increase to 1.1 or even 1.2 in the future. Wizco also recognizes that the risk-free rate may change from its current rate of 6 percent. The firm estimates the risk-free rate could change to either 5 percent or 7 percent. Find Wizco's cost of retained earnings for all possible combinations of beta and risk-free rate.

# REFERENCES

Aivazian, Varouj, and Jeffrey L. Callen. "Investment, Market Structure, and the Cost of Capital." *Journal of Finance* 34 (March 1979): 85–92.

Ang, James S. "Weighted Average versus True Cost of Capital." *Financial Management* 2 (Autumn 1973): 56–60.

Arditti, Fred D., and Milford S. Tysseland. "Three Ways to Present the Marginal Cost of Capital." *Financial Management* 2 (Summer 1973): 63–67.

Arditti, Fred D. "The Weighted Average Cost of Capital: Some Questions on Its Definition, Interpretation, and Use." *Journal of Finance* 28 (September 1973): 1001–07.

Beranek, William. "The Weighted Average Cost of Capital and Shareholder Wealth Maximization." *Journal of Financial and Quantitative Analysis* 12 (March 1977): 17–31.

———. "A little More on the Weighted Average Cost of Capital." *Journal of Financial and Quantitative Analysis* 5 (December 1975): 892–96.

Brennan, J.B. "A New Look at the Weighted Average Cost of Capital." *Journal of Business Finance* 5: 24–30.

Elliot, J. Walter. "The Cost of Capital and U.S. Investment." *Journal of Finance* 35 (September 1980): 981–1000.

Ezzel, John R., and R. Burr Porter. "Flotation Costs and the Weighted Average Cost of Capital." *Journal of Financial and Quantitative Analysis* 11 (September 1976): 403–14.

Gitman, Lawrence J., and Vincent A. Mercurio. "Cost of Capital Techniques Used by Major U.S. Firms: Survey and Analysis of Fortune's 1000." *Financial Management* 11 (Winter 1982): 21–29.

Haley, Charles. "Taxes, the Cost of Capital, and the Firm's Investment Decisions." *Journal of Finance* 20 (September 1971): 901–17.

Haley, Charles W., and Lawrence D. Schall. "Problems with the Cost of Capital." *Journal of Financial and Quantitative Analysis* 13 (December 1978): 847–70.

Lawrenz, David W. "The Effects of Corporate Taxation on the Cost of Equity Capital." *Financial Management* 5 (Spring 1976): 53–57.

Miles, J., and Ezzell, R. "The Weighted Average Cost of Capital, Perfect Capital Markets, and Project Life: A Clarification." *Journal of Financial and Quantitative Analysis* 15 (September 1980): 719–30.

Nantell, Timothy J., and C. Robert Carlson. "The Cost of Capital as a Weighted Average." *Journal of Finance* 30 (December 1975): 1343–55.

Scott, David F., Jr., and J. William Petty. "Determining the Cost of Common Equity Capital: The Direct Method." *Journal of Business Research* 8 (March 1980): 89–103.

# CHAPTER 13

# THE CAPITAL STRUCTURE DECISION

## CAPITAL STRUCTURE IN PERSPECTIVE

At year-end 1986, E. I. du Pont de Nemours & Co. (DuPont) had a debt to equity ratio of .25. This included $3.3 billion of long-term debt and $13.4 billion common equity. The debt to equity ratio for Humana, Inc., at year-end 1986 was 1.36 and included $1.2 billion of long-term debt and $.9 billion of common equity. At least partially because of this higher debt to equity ratio, Humana had a return on equity in 1986 of 20.6 percent versus just 11.5 percent for DuPont. Does this mean that all firms should maintain capital structures that contain large amounts of debt? Of course, it does not. Some firms have characteristics that permit them to maintain higher than average amounts of debt in their capital structures. In fact, some firms could literally not survive if they maintained low levels of debt. Conversely, other firms have characteristics that permit them to operate quite profitably with very low levels of debt. Some of these firms could not survive if their capital structures contained too much debt. Of course, the characteristics of a firm do not dictate the firm's capital structure. That is, there is considerable latitude for firms to determine the capital structure so that it reflects the attitudes of the owners and management.

Does capital structure affect the value of the firm, and if so, how? What are the characteristics of a firm that affect the firm's capital structure? Should a firm's capital structure change over time? What will make it change? The answers to these and other questions are addressed in this chapter.

The **capital structure** of a firm refers to its mixture of long-term sources of financing. This mixture frequently includes long-term debt, preferred stock, and common equity, but it can also include other long-term sources such as term loans and leases. In contrast to a firm's capital structure, its **financial structure** refers to its mixture of all sources of financing, both long-term and short-term. In order to closely examine the long-term sources of financing in this chapter, it is assumed that the proportion of total financing provided by short-term sources is held constant.

A firm's capital structure is important because it can affect the firm's cost of capital. As demonstrated in the previous chapter, the cost of capital must be minimized if the firm is to maximize shareholder wealth.

This chapter consists of four major sections. The first section introduces the concept of *financial leverage* and considers its effect on risk and return. The second section presents background information on the importance of capital structure to the firm and indicates how the firm can assess its capital structure. The third section provides the framework for capital structure management. The fourth and final section describes some practical tools used in managing the capital structure of a firm.

## FINANCIAL LEVERAGE

Chapter 8 described how operating leverage involves the use of fixed operating costs in place of variable costs. It also indicated that large amounts of operating leverage magnify the effects of changes in sales on EBIT; that is, when considerable operating leverage exists, even a small change in sales causes a large change in EBIT. This relationship between sales and EBIT is measured in terms of the *degree of operating leverage*, as illustrated in the top portion of the income statement in Table 13.1. Conversely, the bottom portion of the income statement (from EBIT to EPS) reflects **financial leverage,** which involves the use of fixed-cost sources of financing (as opposed to common equity) in an effort to magnify the firm's earnings per share (EPS). Notice in Table 13.1 that, given EBIT, the firm needs only to compensate creditors, pay taxes, and compensate preferred stockholders in order to arrive at earnings available to common stockholders (EAC).

**TABLE 13.1  Operating and Financial Leverage as Described on a Modified Income Statement**

| | |
|---|---|
| Sales (units) | |
| Sales revenue | Area of |
| Less: Variable costs | operating |
| Less: Fixed operating costs | leverage |
| EBIT | |
| Less: Interest | |
| EBT | |
| Less: Taxes | Area of |
| Net income | financial |
| Less: Preferred stock dividends | leverage |
| EAC | |
| Divided by shares of common stock | |
| EPS | |

**TABLE 13.2** **Right Side of Balance Sheet for Two Alternative Methods of Financing: Cleaver Industries**

| | Current Capital Structure (with Financial Leverage) | Proposed Capital Structure (without Financial Leverage) |
|---|---|---|
| Long-term debt (15%) | $300,000 | -0- |
| Preferred stock (10%) | 100,000 | -0- |
| Common equity ($20 par) | 100,000 (5,000 shares) | 500,000 (25,000 shares) |
| Total liability and equity | $500,000 | $500,000 |

Earnings per share results from dividing EAC by the number of shares of common stock outstanding.

When a firm employs financial leverage, it raises funds from fixed-cost sources (debt and preferred stock) and attempts to earn a return on those funds at a rate higher than their cost. The difference between the cost of the funds and the return generated by those funds goes to the common stockholders. When large amounts of financial leverage are employed, small changes in EBIT result in large changes in EPS; thus, the relationship between EBIT and EPS is measured in terms of the **degree of financial leverage.**

## An Example of Financial Leverage

Consider a simple case where Cleaver Industries (the same firm referred to extensively in Chapter 8) has total liabilities and equity of $500,000, consisting of 5,000 shares of common stock sold at $20 (par value), $300,000 of long-term debt with a 15 percent coupon, and $100,000 worth of 10 percent preferred stock. The firm is considering selling more common stock in order to retire all of its debt and all of its preferred stock. This swap would significantly change the capital structure, as indicated in Table 13.2.

Regardless of the capital structure of the firm, it is expected that Cleaver's EBIT will be either $70,000 (the same EBIT as in the previous year) or $80,000 next year. There is no reason to believe that the firm's EBIT would be different because of the source of funds used to finance the firm's assets. Table 13.3 shows the EPS that would result from the two possible levels of EBIT for both capital structures. For simplicity, an average tax rate of 20 percent is assumed. An analysis of Table 13.3 reveals a number of key characteristics of financial leverage.

1.   With the current high level of financial leverage, large financing costs (interest payments on debt and dividends on preferred stock) must be paid before common stockholders receive dividends. However, what remains for common stockholders after paying interest, taxes, and preferred stock dividends is divided among fewer shares of common stock.

2.   Under the proposed capital structure (no financial leverage) all of EBIT (except for taxes) belongs to the common stockholders. Although EAC is higher for the proposed financial structure under both possible levels of EBIT, it must be distributed among more shares of common stock.

**TABLE 13.3**   Earnings per Share under Two Different Financing Plans and
Two Different Levels of EBIT: Cleaver Industries

| | Current Capital Structure (with Financial Leverage) | | Proposed Capital Structure (without Financial Leverage) | |
|---|---|---|---|---|
| EBIT | $70,000 | $80,000 | $70,000 | $80,000 |
| Less: Interest | 45,000 | 45,000 | -0- | -0- |
| EBIT | $25,000 | $35,000 | $70,000 | $80,000 |
| Less: Taxes (20%) | 5,000 | 7,000 | 14,000 | 16,000 |
| Net income | $20,000 | $28,000 | $56,000 | $64,000 |
| Less: Dividend on preferred stock | 10,000 | 10,000 | -0- | -0- |
| EAC | $10,000 | $18,000 | $56,000 | $64,000 |
| Divided by number of shares of common stock | 5,000 | 5,000 | 25,000 | 25,000 |
| EPS | $2.00 | $3.60 | $2.24 | $2.56 |

**3.** At the lower level of EBIT in our example ($70,000), financing all assets with common equity (no financial leverage) provides higher EPS than financing with debt and preferred stock. The principal reason for this is that no fixed financing costs are required with common equity financing. If financial leverage is used, the majority of EBIT is needed to pay interest on debt and dividends on preferred stock, leaving little for common stockholders.

**4.** At higher levels of EBIT ($80,000 in our example), financing assets with debt and preferred stock results in higher EPS. This occurs because EBIT is sufficiently high to pay the fixed financing costs and still leave a large amount for the common stockholders. In addition, there are fewer shares of common stock outstanding among which the EAC must be divided.

**5.** EPS is more volatile when financial leverage is used. As EBIT changes, the EPS under the current capital structure (greater financial leverage) changes by a greater percentage than the EPS under the proposed capital structure (a smaller amount of financial leverage). This relationship is illustrated in the last row of Table 13.3. If EBIT were to increase from $70,000 to $80,000 (a 14.3 percent increase), EPS would increase from $2.00 to $3.60 (an 80 percent increase) for the leveraged capital structure. For the unleveraged structure, EPS would increase from $2.24 to $2.56 (only a 14.3 percent increase), given the same change in EBIT.

## Measuring Financial Leverage

There are a number of useful measures of financial leverage. In addition to the leverage ratios introduced in Chapter 6, the *degree of financial leverage* also is a measure of the amount of debt in the capital structure. Just as the degree of operating leverage measures the sensitivity of EBIT to changes in sales, the degree of financial leverage measures the sensitivity of EPS to changes in EBIT. Equation 13.1 can be used to find the degree of financial leverage (*DFL*) at a given base-level EBIT:

$$DFL = \frac{\text{percentage change in EPS}}{\text{percentage change in EBIT}} \qquad (13.1)$$

---

**Example**

Equation 13.1 can be used to determine the *DFL* for Cleaver Industries. If EBIT changes from $70,000 (the base-level EBIT) to $80,000, EPS will increase from $2.00 to $3.60 under the current capital structure, and the degree of financial leverage is

$$DFL = \frac{\dfrac{\$3.60 - \$2.00}{\$2.00}}{\dfrac{\$80,000 - \$70,000}{\$70,000}}$$

$$= \frac{80.0\%}{14.3\%}$$

$$= 5.6$$

---

Since the current financial structure contains large amounts of both debt and preferred stock, considerable financial leverage exists. A degree of financial leverage of 5.6 suggests that for every 1 percent change in EBIT, there would be a 5.6 percent change ($1\% \times 5.6$) in EPS. For example, a 3 percent increase in EBIT would result in a 16.8 percent increase ($3\% \times 5.6$) in EPS. This relationship is symmetrical, so a 3 percent decrease in EBIT would result in a 16.8 percent *decrease* in EPS. In the Cleaver Industries example, $70,000 of EBIT is the beginning, or base-level, EBIT. Starting from a different base-level EBIT would result in a different degree of financial leverage.

For the proposed capital structure, the *DFL* is 1.0, indicating there is no financial leverage with this structure. That is, for every 1 percent change in EBIT, a 1.0 percent change ($1\% \times 1.0$) in EPS is expected.

### Alternative Method of Calculating the Degree of Financial Leverage

It is possible to use Equation 13.2 to calculate the degree of financial leverage more directly using different information.

$$DFL = \frac{\text{EBIT}}{\text{EBIT} - I - [PSD/(1 - T)]} \qquad (13.2)$$

where  EBIT = earnings before interest and taxes

          $I$ = dollar amount of annual interest paid

     $PSD$ = annual preferred stock dividend

        $T$ = firm's tax rate

Since both EBIT and interest are before-tax amounts, the preferred stock dividend (which is paid from after-tax profits) also must be converted to a before-tax amount. In Equation 13.2, this is done by dividing the preferred stock dividend by $(1 - T)$.

---

**Example**

For Cleaver Industries' current capital structure, Equation 13.2 is used to find the degree of financial leverage at EBIT of $70,000 as follows:

$$DFL = \frac{\$70,000}{\$70,000 - \$45,000 - [\$10,000/(1 - .20)]}$$

$$= 5.6$$

For the proposed financial structure, the degree of financial leverage is

$$DFL = \frac{\$70,000}{\$70,000 - 0 - [0/(1 - .20)]}$$

$$= 1.0$$

The same answer results from both methods of calculation.

---

### Graphing the EBIT-EPS Trade-Off

A linear relationship exists between EBIT and EPS. A graph of this relationship for the capital structures used in the Cleaver Industries example is presented in Figure 13.1. Each line was constructed by plotting the data reported in Table 13.3. To derive the line for the current capital structure (with leverage), two points were plotted: one at EBIT of $70,000 and EPS of $2.00, and the other at EBIT of $80,000 and EPS of $3.60. A straight line was then drawn through these two points. The same procedure was followed to construct the EBIT-EPS line for the capital structure without leverage.

The steeper slope of the line for the current capital structure indicates greater financial leverage and greater volatility of EPS. That is, for a given change in EBIT, the percentage change in EPS (read from the vertical axis) is greater for the leveraged capital structure than for the unleveraged capital structure.

Point C on the graph indicates the only level of EBIT ($71,875) where EPS is identical for both capital structures ($2.30). If the firm's EBIT is less than $71,875, then EPS will be higher if the firm changes to the unleveraged capital structure. If EBIT is greater than $71,875, then EPS will be higher if the firm maintains its current leveraged capital structure. If EBIT is exactly $71,875, then the firm would be indifferent regarding the capital structure it selects, since EPS is the same for each. Point C is called the

**FIGURE 13.1**

A Graph of the
EBIT-EPS Trade-Off
for Two Possible
Capital Structures:
Cleaver Industries

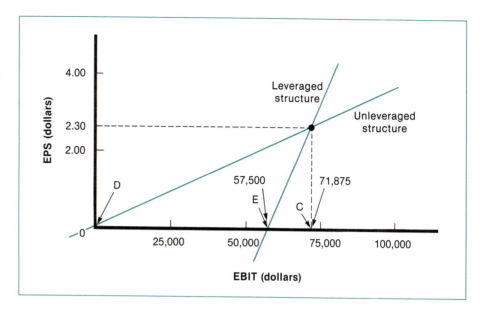

**financial indifference point.**[1] A word of caution is necessary here concerning the interpretation of the EBIT-EPS graph. There is a temptation to conclude that if the firm expects to have EBIT greater than the financial indifference point, then it should adopt the higher level of financial leverage. This may not be the correct decision even though it would result in higher EPS, since it would also result in more volatile EPS. This greater volatility could cause investors to increase their required rates of return, which could reduce the value of the firm's common stock.

In Figure 13.1, points D and E represent **financial breakeven points** in that they indicate the level of EBIT where EPS is equal to zero. For the

---

1. The financial indifference point can be determined algebraically by solving for EBIT in the following expression:

$$\frac{(1 - T)(\text{EBIT} - I_a) - PSD_a}{NS_a} = \frac{(1 - T)(\text{EBIT} - I_b) - PSD_b}{NS_b}$$

Here, $T$ is the firm's tax rate, $I$ is the annual interest paid on debt, $PSD$ is the preferred stock dividend, and $NS$ is the number of shares of common stock outstanding. The subscripts $a$ and $b$ represent two different capital structures. For the two capital structures being considered by Cleaver Industries,

$$\frac{(1 - .2)(\text{EBIT} - \$45,000) - \$10,000}{5,000} = \frac{(1 - .2)(\text{EBIT} - 0) - 0}{25,000}$$

$$25,000(.8\,\text{EBIT} - \$36,000 - \$10,000) = 5,000(.8\,\text{EBIT})$$

$$20,000\,\text{EBIT} - \$900,000,000 - \$250,000,000 = 4,000\,\text{EBIT}$$

$$16,000\,\text{EBIT} = \$1,150,000,000$$

$$\text{EBIT} = \$71,875$$

unleveraged capital structure, the firm has EPS of $.00 at an EBIT of $.00. For the leveraged capital structure, the firm has EPS of $.00 at an EBIT of $57,500. Therefore, $.00 is the financial breakeven point for the unleveraged capital structure, and $57,500 is the financial breakeven point for the leveraged capital structure.[2]

The significance of the financial breakeven point is that it indicates the minimum level of EBIT necessary for the firm to avoid a loss for the common stockholders. The firm may wish to compare these minimum levels of EBIT to forecasted levels of EBIT and their probabilities. The higher the probability that the firm will operate below the financial breakeven point for a given capital structure, the less desirable that structure is to the firm.

## IMPORTANCE OF CAPITAL STRUCTURE

It is evident from the preceding discussion that as the level of debt in the capital structure increases, the level of risk incurred by the creditors and stockholders of a firm also increases. Chapter 12 demonstrated that an increase in risk to investors results in higher required rates of return for investors, which increases the cost of funds for the firm. Since the firm has the ability to alter its capital structure, it may be able to influence the cost of the components of capital in order to minimize the overall cost of capital (a theory of capital structure that denies there is a relationship between capital structure and the cost of capital is described later in this chapter and in the appendix to this chapter).

By maintaining a low cost of capital, firms are more likely to accept proposed capital budgeting projects. For example, a firm would surely reject a proposed project that is expected to realize a 12 percent return if the firm's cost of capital is 14 percent. If, however, the firm can reduce its cost of capital to 11 percent by altering its capital structure, the project may be adopted and the profitability of the firm enhanced. In addition, a lower cost of capital can make adopted projects more profitable, since the margin between the return earned on projects and the cost of financing those projects will be greater. When the overall cost of capital is minimized, the value of the firm's common stock is maximized. The capital structure that

---

2. The financial breakeven point can be found algebraically as follows:

$$FBP = I + \frac{PSD}{1 - T}$$

Here, $FBP$ is the financial breakeven point, $I$ is the annual interest on debt, $PSD$ is the preferred stock dividend, and $T$ is the firm's tax rate. For the leveraged capital structure above, the $FBP$ is

$$FBP = \$45,000 + \frac{\$10,000}{1 - .2}$$

$$= \$57,500$$

maximizes the value of the firm's common stock, and thus shareholder wealth, is called the **optimal capital structure.**

## OPTIMAL CAPITAL STRUCTURE

In order to identify the capital structure that minimizes the cost of capital, management must first consider how the level of debt in the capital structure affects the cost of each component of capital. Figure 13.2 illustrates the relationship between the level of debt in the capital structure, as measured by the debt to equity ratio, and the after-tax cost of both debt ($k_i$) and common equity ($k_s$).

Notice that the cost of debt is lower than the cost of equity over the entire range of possible levels of leverage. This occurs for two reasons. First, the creditors of a firm incur less risk than the owners (equity investors) because creditors have a higher priority claim on the income and assets of the firm. The result is lower required rates of return for creditors than for owners. Second, interest is a tax-deductible expense to the firm, which reduces the after-tax cost of debt even further below the cost of equity (dividends paid on equity investments are not tax-deductible).

Also notice in Figure 13.2 that the cost of both debt and equity rise as the amount of leverage increases. The cost of equity begins to rise as small amounts of debt are added to the capital structure because the increased volatility of EPS caused by the leverage increases investors' required rates of return.

Small amounts of debt added to the capital structure do not cause an immediate increase in the cost of debt because the probability of default remains low when only small amounts of debt are added. However, as the level of debt increases, the cost of debt begins to rise and continues to rise as the probability of default rises. For simplification, the use of preferred stock is not included in this example. It should be recognized, however,

**FIGURE 13.2**

**Impact of Financial Leverage on the Cost of Debt and Equity**

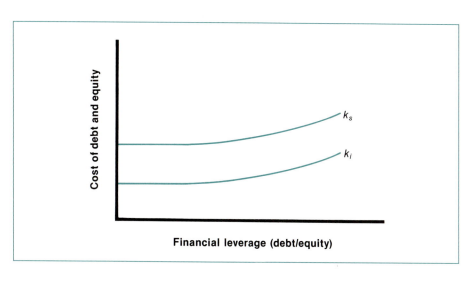

**TABLE 13.4**  Alternative Capital Structures and the Cost of Debt and Common Equity: Cleaver Industries

| (1) | (2) Long-Term Debt | (3) | (4) Common Equity | (5) |
|---|---|---|---|---|
| Debt to Equity Ratio | Implied Percent | $k_i$ | Implied Percent | $k_s$ |
| .0 | 0.0 | 6.0 | 100.0 | 12.0 |
| .5 | 33.3 | 6.0 | 66.7 | 13.0 |
| 1.0 | 50.0 | 6.5 | 50.0 | 14.0 |
| 1.5 | 60.0 | 8.0 | 40.0 | 16.0 |
| 2.0 | 66.7 | 12.0 | 33.3 | 20.0 |

that the cost of preferred stock also increases as the level of debt in the capital structure increases because the probability of default on the preferred stock also rises.

Firms may estimate the cost of each component of capital based on historical costs. Conversely, the cost of each component can be estimated based on subjective estimates made by the firm itself or those made by an outside firm such as an investment bank. Table 13.4 presents all the estimates needed to determine the optimal capital structure for Cleaver Industries. Here, Cleaver Industries is considering a capital structure that consists of only two components, long-term debt and common equity. Column 1 of Table 13.4 indicates several different debt to equity ratios. Columns 2 and 4 indicate the percentages of debt and common equity in the capital structure that are implied by the debt to equity ratios. For example, if a firm has $50,000 of long-term debt and $100,000 of common equity in its capital structure, the debt to equity ratio is .5 ($50,000/ $100,000). Given those same dollar amounts, debt represents 33.3 percent of total capital ($50,000/$150,000), and common equity represents 66.7 percent of total capital ($100,000/$150,000).

Column 3 indicates the cost of debt that has been estimated for each debt to equity ratio. At a ratio of zero, the cost of long-term debt is 6 percent. As debt is added to the capital structure (the debt to equity ratio increases), the after-tax cost of debt increases from 6 percent at low levels of debt to 12 percent at high levels of debt. A similar pattern of increasing costs exists for common equity, as indicated in Column 5. That is, at a debt to equity ratio of zero, the cost of common equity is 12 percent, but it increases to a high of 20 percent at a ratio of 2.0. The rising costs of debt and equity are consistent with the earlier discussion.

Given Table 13.4, the weighted cost of capital, $k_a$, can be determined at every level of debt to equity. For example, when the debt to equity ratio is zero, the weighted cost of capital, $k_a$, reflects 100 percent of the cost of equity and zero percent of the cost of debt. Since the cost of equity is 12 percent, the weighted cost of capital is 12 percent. At a debt to equity ratio of .5, the capital structure consists of 33.3 percent debt and 66.7 percent equity (see Table 13.4). Given these weights, the weighted cost of capital is found as follows:

FIGURE 13.3
**Weighted Cost of Capital at Various Levels of Debt to Equity: Cleaver Industries**

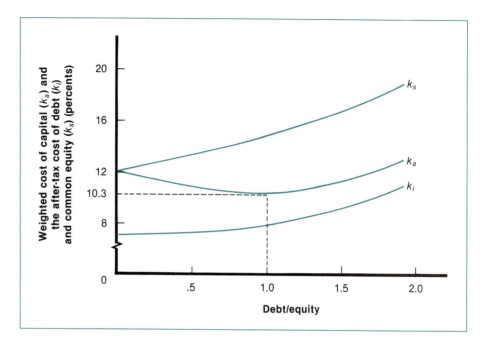

| Component | Percent of Capital Structure | | Cost (from Table 13.4) | | Weighted Cost |
|---|---|---|---|---|---|
| Common equity | 66.7% | × | 13.0% | = | 8.7% |
| Debt | 33.3 | × | 6.0 | = | 2.0 |
| | | | | $k_a =$ | 10.7% |

This same procedure can be followed to find the weighted cost of capital at every level of debt to equity. Table 13.5 displays this information for Cleaver Industries. Notice that the weighted cost of capital begins to decline when debt is first added to the capital structure. This occurs even though the cost of equity begins to rise as debt is added. The reason is that at low levels of debt, the increasing cost of equity is more than offset by the addition of low cost of debt to the capital structure. This relationship is illustrated in Figure 13.3, which is identical to Figure 13.2 except that a

TABLE 13.5 **Weighted Cost of Capital at Selected Debt to Equity Ratios: Cleaver Industries**

| Debt to Equity Ratio | $k_a$ |
|---|---|
| 0 | 12.0% |
| .5 | 10.7 |
| 1.0 | 10.3 |
| 1.5 | 11.2 |
| 2.0 | 14.7 |

line representing the weighted cost of capital has been added based on information presented in Table 13.5. Notice that at a debt to equity ratio of zero, $k_a$ is equal to the cost of equity, since there is no debt. As debt is added, the value of $k_a$ moves away from the cost of equity line and closer to the line representing the cost of debt. Since the costs of both debt and common equity are rising, eventually $k_a$ also must rise, and it does so in this example after a debt to equity ratio of 1.0.

Since the optimal capital structure is the one that minimizes the firm's cost of capital, this can be determined graphically on Figure 13.3 by identifying the low point on the weighted cost of capital line. As indicated earlier, the low point is directly above 1.0 on the horizontal scale, indicating that a debt to equity ratio of 1.0 is optimal. Drawing a horizontal line from the low point on the weighted cost of capital line to the vertical scale (a dashed line in Figure 13.3) reveals that the cost of capital at the optimal capital structure is 10.3 percent. This same information can be obtained from Table 13.5 by identifying the capital structure that minimizes the cost of capital, and the cost of capital at that capital structure.

### Relationship between Capital Structure and Common Stock Prices

As indicated earlier, maintaining the optimal capital structure both minimizes the firm's cost of capital and, at the same time, maximizes the price of the firm's common stock. Maximization of the price of common stock is considered here through the use of the constant growth valuation model. This model was originally presented in Chapter 4 as Equation 4.10 but is restated here as Equation 13.3.

$$P_0 = \frac{D_1}{k_s - g} \qquad \text{(13.3)}$$

where  $P_0$ = value of a share of common stock

$D_1$ = expected dividend on the common stock next year

$k_s$ = required rate of return on the common stock

$g$ = growth rate of the dividend

Maximizing the value of the firm's common stock is an important goal of management, since this is the best measure of management's success at maximizing shareholder wealth. In order for the value of a share of stock to rise, either the numerator of Equation 13.3 must increase or the denominator must decrease, or both. When a firm adds debt to its capital structure, both the expected dividend and the expected growth rate of the dividend increase (assuming that EBIT is to the right of the indifference point on the EBIT-EPS graph). Recall that higher amounts of financial leverage mean that even small changes in EBIT result in large changes in EPS. If the firm's EBIT is growing even modestly, EPS and dividends will grow more rapidly with the use of financial leverage. The higher dividend ($D_1$) increases the numerator of Equation 13.3, while an increase in the growth rate ($g$) decreases the denominator. Both of these changes tend to increase the value of the firm's common stock. At the same time, the increased volatility of EPS resulting from the increased financial leverage increases investors' required rates of return on the firm's common stock ($k_s$). This tends to increase the size of the denominator and decrease the price of the common stock.

The net effect of an increase in financial leverage on the value of the firm's stock depends on the relative size of the changes in $D_1$, $g$, and $k_s$. Generally, when only small amounts of debt are added to the capital structure, any increase in $k_s$ is more than offset by the increases in $D_1$ and $g$. The net result is an increase in the value of the firm's common stock. At some point, however, additional debt in the capital structure increases investors' required rates of return by so much that the resulting increases in $D_1$ and $g$ are overwhelmed by the increase in $k_s$. A decline in the value of the common stock results. Before this point is reached, the value of the firm increases as debt is added. Beyond this point, the value of the firm's common stock decreases. At this point, the value of the firm's common stock reaches its highest level, and the optimal capital structure has been determined.

**Example**

The relationship between capital structure and stock prices is described in Table 13.6 for Cleaver Industries. Notice that Column 1 lists the same debt to equity ratios that were used in the previous analysis of Cleaver's capital structure. Column 2 indicates the impact of rising financial leverage on the firm's EPS. Notice that EPS begins to increase at first, then peaks out and declines. The reason for the increases is that financial leverage magnifies EPS. The reason for the subsequent decline in EPS is that financing costs eventually become so large that they reduce net income. Column 3 indicates the size of the expected dividend in the next period based on an assumed dividend payout ratio of 40 percent (this indicates the percent of EPS paid out as dividends). Both the expected EPS and the dividend payout ratio are given here and cannot be determined from information previously presented. Column 4 indicates the expected future growth rate of the firm's earnings and dividends, which increases with the debt to equity ratio, since a higher degree of financial leverage magnifies EPS. These growth rates are also given here and cannot be determined based on previously supplied data.

The required rates of return on common stock (Column 5) increase as the debt

**TABLE 13.6**    Effect of Capital Structure on Stock Value: Cleaver Industries

| (1) | (2) | (3) | (4) | (5) | (6) | (7) |
|-----|-----|-----|-----|-----|-----|-----|
| Debt to Equity Ratio | Expected EPS | Expected $D_1$[a] | $g$ | $k_s$ (from Table 13.4) | Stock Price | $k_a$ (from Table 13.5) |
| 0.0 | $4.00 | $1.60 | 2% | 12.0% | $16.00 | 12.0% |
| .5 | 4.50 | 1.80 | 3 | 13.0 | 18.00 | 10.7 |
| 1.0 | 5.00 | 2.00 | 4 | 14.0 | 20.00 | 10.3 |
| 1.5 | 5.23 | 2.09 | 5 | 16.0 | 19.00 | 11.2 |
| 2.0 | 5.00 | 2.00 | 4 | 20.0 | 12.50 | 14.7 |

[a] A dividend payout ratio of 40 percent is assumed.

**FIGURE 13.4**
**Relationship between Capital Structure and EPS, $K_a$, and Stock Price: Cleaver Industries**

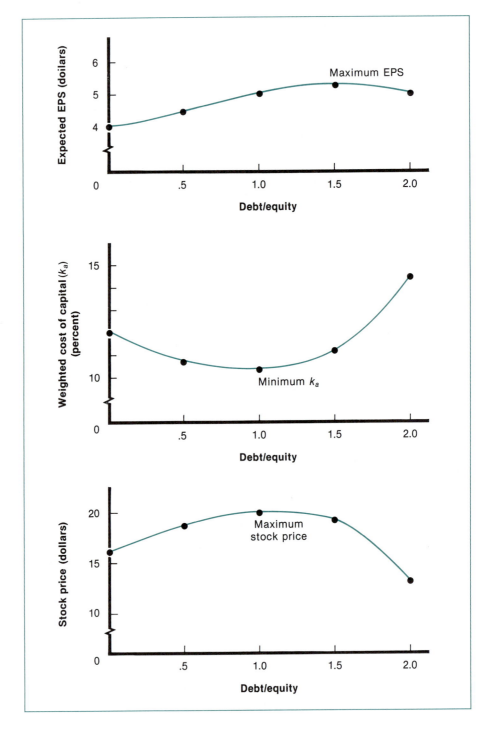

to equity ratio increases. In Column 6, the value of the firm's common stock has been determined using Equation 13.3. Notice that the value of the common stock increases as small amounts of debt are added to the capital structure. This occurs because the increases in the dividend and growth rate more than offset the increase in investors' required rates of return. Later, the value of the common stock decreases as large amounts of debt are added. This occurs because the increase in investors' required rates of return more than offsets the increases in the dividend and the growth rate. Thus, even though EPS is greater at a debt to equity ratio of 1.5 than at 1.0, the value of the common stock is higher at 1.0 than at 1.5 (see Column 5). The optimal capital structure is that which results in the highest value of the firm's common stock. For Cleaver Industries, the debt to equity ratio resulting in the highest value is 1.0.

Column 7 presents the weighted cost of capital for the various debt to equity ratios. This information is presented here so that it can be compared to the information in Column 6. Notice that the same capital structure (a debt to equity ratio of 1.0) that maximizes the stock price also minimizes the cost of capital. This information regarding the firm's EPS, stock price, and cost of capital is presented graphically in Figure 13.4.

## Taxes and Bankruptcy

The main reasons why the value of a firm's common stock increases as debt is added to the capital structure but then declines after considerable debt has been added are frequently described in terms of taxes and bankruptcy costs. Although debt tends to be a cheaper source of capital than equity, even without considering taxes, the tax-deductible nature of interest payments on debt makes the cost of debt lower than the cost of equity. As a result, when debt is added to the capital structure, the cost of capital declines, and the value of the firm's common stock rises.

However, as the amount of debt in the capital structure increases, it becomes more difficult for the firm to meet its fixed financing obligations, thus increasing the probability of default, and perhaps bankruptcy. If bankruptcy becomes a reality, the stockholders and the bondholders stand to lose much or all of their investment. Their losses are said to result from *bankruptcy-related costs*, which are largely legal expenses incurred in the liquidation or reorganization of the firm. Therefore, as debt is added to the capital structure, increasing the probability of incurring bankruptcy costs, the cost of both debt and equity begin to increase, eventually causing an increase in the firm's cost of capital.

## OPTIMAL CAPITAL STRUCTURE VERSUS TARGET CAPITAL STRUCTURE

In the previous examples, only five alternative capital structures were considered. There are actually many different capital structures possible for a single firm, even if common stock and bonds are the only components of capital being considered. Indeed, so many capital structures are possible, and the differences between them so small, that it is impractical for a firm to consider them all. And since all possible capital structures are not considered, the true optimal capital structure may never be known. The saucer-shaped weighted cost of capital line appearing in Figure 13.3 suggests, however, that, within a fairly wide range of debt to equity ratios, the cost of capital varies only slightly. Thus, even if the so-called optimal capital structure is not known, a capital structure can be identified and maintained that closely approximates the optimal capital structure; this is the **target capital structure** that firms attempt to maintain.

Once a firm determines its target capital structure, it generally uses this target as the midpoint of a range of capital structures, all of which achieve a low cost of capital. Although the target capital structure frequently is defined in terms of a single debt to equity ratio, a range of acceptable capital structures provides the firm with the flexibility necessary to operate in a real-world environment. That is, a firm currently operating at its target capital structure may elect to raise common equity funds without simultaneously raising debt funds. This would tend to move the actual capital structure to the left, away from the target structure, but may keep it within the range of acceptable capital structures. The next time additional capital is raised, the firm may use only debt as the source of capital, shifting the capital structure back to the right, perhaps past the target capital structure but still within the acceptable range. Firms normally use this strategy to reduce the frequency with which they raise each type of capital. Recall from Chapter 12 that some flotation costs are fixed, so total financing costs can be minimized by reducing the number of times the firm must issue each type of security in the capital markets.

For many firms experiencing rapid growth, the capital structure does not fluctuate around a target capital structure. Instead, a maximum level of debt is identified, and the firm attempts to stay below that level. For example, in 1985 Con Agra specified a maximum debt to total capitalization ratio of 35 percent. *Some firms that specify* a maximum level of debt find themselves violating those self-imposed limits when special circumstances exist. For example, in 1981 Cummins Engine Company found it necessary to increase its maximum debt to total capitalization ratio from 35 percent to 45 percent in order to finance large capital expenditures. Cummins elected to incur the additional financial risk in order to avoid the dilution of equity that would have resulted from selling new common stock at depressed prices. As a result, the increased risk contributed to a decline in the quality rating assigned to the bonds issued by Cummins.[3]

## SOME PRACTICAL ASPECTS OF CAPITAL STRUCTURE DECISION MAKING

Management of the capital structure in practice is generally consistent with the concepts presented above. That is, management seeks the capital structure that minimizes the cost of capital and maximizes the firm's common stock price. However, achieving this goal is not as simple as just plotting the cost of debt and equity at different debt to equity ratios and combining them to graph the weighted cost of capital line. A number of practical complications can make this a difficult process. These complications and some information to consider in estimating the cost of debt and equity are presented below.

---

3. Bond quality ratings provide a measure of the riskiness of bonds. They are discussed in detail in Chapter 15.

## Practical Complications in Determining the Capital Structure

1. The procedures described in this chapter ignored the use of preferred stock, term loans, and leases as sources of leverage for determining the target capital structure. The procedures also ignored short-term debt as a source of leverage since it is not part of the capital structure. Although consideration of these other sources of leverage complicates capital structure management, the same procedures that are used to analyze the use of long-term debt in the capital structure can be used to analyze the use of other sources of leverage. The major difference is that the analysis becomes more tedious due to the increased number of variables.

2. Earlier discussions about how to determine the target capital structure assumed that the goal of management is to maximize shareholder wealth. In practice, some managements may rank the goal of "self-preservation" above shareholder wealth maximization. When this is the case, management may try to avoid increasing firm risk by maintaining a capital structure that includes substantially less debt than called for in an optimal capital structure. This agency problem can arise because managements reason that stockholders are more likely to replace management if the firm incurs losses than if management fails to maximize the value of the firm.

3. Estimating the cost of debt, common equity, and preferred stock at various levels of financial leverage is very difficult. If management has little confidence in these estimates, it will have little confidence in the target capital structure it identifies.

4. Some firms are constrained by government regulations regarding the level of debt financing they can obtain. The most obvious example is electric utility companies that must receive permission from public service commissions before raising additional debt financing. Firms such as these may not be able to achieve a capital structure that is close to optimal.

5. The 1980s have witnessed an increase in mergers and acquisitions. Many of these combinations take the form of one firm purchasing another by using new debt to finance the purchase. This can result in a capital structure that contains greater leverage than desired based on the framework presented here. However, the acquiring firm may feel that the potential value of the assets being acquired is high enough to offset the negative impact of a higher than optimal level of debt in the capital structure. In addition, the acquiring firm may view the increased leverage as temporary and attempt to adjust its capital structure towards less debt in the future. Finally, the acquired firm may have excess debt capacity prior to the acquisition, and this capacity may be used to help finance the acquisition, thus preventing the acquiring firm's capital structure from including too much debt.

## Estimating the Costs of Debt and Equity

One of the most important tasks of capital structure management is estimating the overall cost of capital at various levels of financial leverage. In order to conduct this type of analysis, the firm (or its investment bank) must estimate the cost of each component of capital at various levels of debt to equity. These estimates are difficult to make and normally are based on subjective judgment. Management must ensure that as much information as possible is included in this analysis. It is suggested that, as a minimum, the following information be considered.

1. If the firm has existed for a number of years, it may have some *historical information* about the cost of its components of capital at various levels of leverage. This information should be analyzed to provide a historical perspective.

2. It is important for firms to consider the impact of various amounts of leverage on their *measures of financial leverage*. That is, firms considering several different capital structures should forecast the financial leverage ratios under each alternative structure and consider how these ratios would be viewed by potential owners and creditors. If the ratios are viewed unfavorably, the firm's cost of capital could rise. Comparing these ratios to industry norms is particularly useful, since substantial deviation from the norm (in either direction) may cause investor concern. Some principal measures of financial leverage discussed in Chapter 6 and earlier in this chapter are summarized in Table 13.7.

3. A third source of information to consider in estimating the cost of debt and equity for the firm at various levels of financial leverage is the EBIT-EPS trade-off. As indicated earlier in this chapter, the volatility of EPS is indicated by the slope of the EBIT-EPS line. An analysis of the EBIT-EPS trade-off can also reveal the financial breakeven points and the financial indifference point for alternative capital structures. However, the EBIT-EPS analysis should not be the sole criterion for developing the firm's capital structure, as it fails to consider several important aspects of risk.

4. Among the most important sources of information used to estimate the cost of a firm's components of capital at various levels of financial leverage are the characteristics of the company itself. A few of the more important characteristics are listed below.

a. *Sales stability.* The more stable the level of sales is for a firm, the lower

---

TABLE 13.7   **Summary of Measures of Financial Leverage**

- *Debt ratio* (ratio of total debt to total assets). This measure of leverage indicates the percent of total assets financed with debt. Since this measure includes both current liabilities and long-term debt, it is a measure of debt in the *financial structure*.

- *Debt to equity ratio* (ratio of long-term debt to equity). This is a measure of the level of debt relative to equity in the *capital structure*.

- *Times interest earned* (ratio of EBIT to annual interest expense). This ratio measures the ability of the firm to meet its interest payments, but does not measure the level of debt itself. This ratio provides an important indication of the level of risk incurred by creditors.

- *Fixed charge coverage ratio* (ratio of total funds available to service debt, lease, and preferred stock obligations, divided by annual debt, lease, and preferred stock obligations). This is a broad measure of the firm's ability to service its fixed financing costs and is used to assess the firm's level of financial risk.

- *Degree of financial leverage*. This measure indicates the volatility of EPS resulting from debt in the financial structure. This volatility is perceived as risk to both the owners and creditors of the firm.

the variability of EBIT, other things being equal. This lower variability of EBIT tends to keep the variability of EPS relatively low, which may permit the firm to assume more financial leverage.

**b.** *Degree of operating leverage.* Just as sales stability affects the volatility of EBIT, so too does the degree of operating leverage. Indeed, these two factors are the primary determinants of the volatility of EBIT. Because these factors affect the volatility of EBIT, they, along with the degree of financial leverage, are also key determinants of the volatility of EPS. Firms can influence their total risk by coordinating these three key sources of risk: sales volatility, operating leverage, and financial leverage. For example, firms in industries with low sales volatility may feel comfortable assuming a moderate or high level of operating and financial risk (this is typical of electric utilities). Conversely, firms in industries characterized by volatile sales and a need for substantial operating leverage (they may be capital intensive) may find it prudent to maintain an exceptionally low level of financial leverage. The interrelationship between operating leverage and financial leverage is presented in Appendix 13A.

**c.** *Firm's tax rate.* One of the major advantages of using debt rather than equity in the capital structure is that interest on debt is tax-deductible. Other things being equal, firms with high marginal tax rates benefit more from using debt. The result may be higher debt to equity ratios for firms with high marginal tax rates than for firms with low marginal tax rates.

**d.** *Ownership control.* For some firms, an individual stockholder or small group of stockholders may possess substantial control over the firm by virtue of owning a large proportion of the firm's total shares of common stock. These stockholders may be reluctant to authorize the sale of new shares of common stock for fear of weakening their control. The result may be a tendency toward greater debt in the capital structure.

**e.** *Market conditions.* The economic environment has been quite volatile in recent periods, encouraging firms to use more debt than normal in their capital structures during some periods and more equity in other periods. When common stock prices are high by historical standards, firms may want to sell new shares of common stock because they can raise relatively large amounts of funds by issuing relatively few new shares of stock. This action can prevent severe dilution of ownership and results in a decrease in the debt to equity ratio. Temporary changes in the capital structure resulting from extreme market conditions can be viewed as changes in the target capital structures themselves. Thus, there is a need for continual evaluation of the target capital structure as market conditions change.

**f.** *Firm profitability.* Firms that consistently generate high profits may be able to fulfill a large proportion of their financing needs with retained earnings. As a result, the capital structures of these firms may be dominated by equity.

## THEORETICAL APPROACHES TO CAPITAL STRUCTURE MANAGEMENT

The previous discussion suggests that capital structure affects the cost of capital and therefore the value of the firm. Actually, this premise has been debated for decades in the finance literature and continues to be debated

## FINANCIAL MANAGEMENT IN PRACTICE

### CAPITAL STRUCTURE DIFFERENCES

The capital structures of firms in the same industries tend to be similar because of the characteristics they share. Although their capital structures are similar, however, they are not identical, because the makeup of each firm is different and because each firm's management may have different attitudes towards risk. The following table indicates the debt to equity ratios for twenty-four selected industries. They are listed here in declining order of their ratios.

| Industry | Debt to Equity Ratio | Industry | Debt to Equity Ratio |
|---|---|---|---|
| Insurance | 78.3% | Auto—manufacturing | 63.1% |
| Advertising | 74.9 | Furniture—wholesale | 62.1 |
| Auto repair | 74.6 | Dairy products | 61.7 |
| Restaurants | 73.2 | Electronics—manufacturing | 60.4 |
| Auto sales | 70.7 | Physicians | 59.7 |
| Electronics—retail | 70.6 | Shoes—retail | 56.5 |
| Travel agents | 69.9 | Spirits—manufacturing | 56.0 |
| Petroleum—wholesale | 66.9 | Hardware—wholesale | 55.3 |
| Grocery stores | 64.3 | Department stores | 54.6 |
| Publishing—books | 63.9 | Steel—manufacturing | 50.7 |
| Fertilizer | 63.8 | Women's clothes—manufacturing | 50.4 |
| Men's clothing | 63.5 | Accounting firms | 48.0 |

Source: Annual Statement Studies, 1986 (Philadelphia: Robert Morris Associates, 1986).

today. Two theoretical approaches to capital structure, the net income (*NI*) approach and the net operating income (*NOI*) approach are at the heart of the controversy. These two theories were developed in the 1950s as a means of analyzing the relationship between a firm's capital structure and the value of the firm. In order to isolate the analysis on this basic relationship, a number of simplifying assumptions were made. Although some of these assumptions are unrealistic in terms of the true economic environment, many were later relaxed to determine how other variables affect the relationship between capital structure and the value of the firm.

The *NI* approach employs certain assumptions that lead to the conclusion that adding debt to the capital structure continually lowers the firm's cost of capital. Therefore, firms should have as much debt in their capital structure as they can obtain. The *NOI* approach employs a different set of assumptions and concludes that a firm's capital structure does not affect its cost of capital or the value of the firm. This latter approach concludes that financial managers should not search for an optimal capital structure for their firms, because the capital structure is irrelevant.

Although these two extreme approaches to capital structure conflict directly with the material presented in this chapter, they have proven invaluable in the development and understanding of the relationship between capital structure and the value of the firm. Indeed, many academicians and practitioners alike feel that an understanding of these two extreme positions is essential to understanding the task faced by financial managers in managing capital structures in the real-world environment. The reader is invited to read Appendix 13B to gain a more detailed, yet intuitive understanding of the *NI* and *NOI* approaches.

## SUMMARY

The capital structure of a firm refers to the mixture of the sources of long-term financing, including bonds, preferred stock, and common equity. The capital structure must be managed effectively since it can influence the firm's cost of capital and the value of the firm's common stock. Therefore, firms should attempt to identify and maintain the capital structure that minimizes their cost of capital and maximizes the value of their common stock.

As debt is added to the capital structure, financial leverage increases. The result of increased financial leverage is an increase in the financial breakeven point, the volatility of earnings per share, and usually the expected earnings per share.

For firms with common equity as their sole source of funds, the addition of debt to the capital structure normally reduces their cost of capital and increases the value of their common stock because of the lower cost of debt relative to common equity. When large amounts of debt are added to the capital structure, however, the cost of capital rises, and the value of the common stock begins to decline. These changes in the cost of capital result from the impact of debt on the firm's taxes and potential bankruptcy costs. That is, since interest payments on debt are tax-deductible to the firm, while dividends paid on common stock are not, the after-tax cost of debt is much lower than the after-tax cost of equity. Although debt tends to be inexpensive relative to equity sources, as larger amounts of debt are added to the capital structure, the firm's fixed financing costs increase, causing an increase in the variability of EPS and an increased probability of default. This increased probability of bankruptcy results in higher costs of both debt and equity to the firms, because investors increase their required rates of return. At some point, the benefit of adding less expensive debt to the capital structure is more than offset by the rising costs of debt and equity, and the cost of capital begins to rise.

## KEY TERMS

**Capital structure** The mixture of long-term sources of financing, such as debt, preferred stock, and common stock, used by a firm.

**Degree of financial leverage** A measure of the sensitivity of EPS to changes in EBIT.

**Financial breakeven point** The level of EBIT that results in EPS of zero.

**Financial indifference point** The level of EBIT at which the EPS is identical for two different capital structures.

**Financial leverage** The use of debt and preferred stock by a firm to magnify the effects of changes in EBIT on EPS.

**Financial structure** Mixture of all sources of financing used by a firm (the right side of a firm's balance sheet).

**Optimal capital structure** The capital structure that minimizes a firm's cost of capital and maximizes the value of the firm.

**Target capital structure** The capital structure that provides the firm with a low cost of capital and a high common stock value. Although the firm would like its target capital structure to be the optimal capital structure, the optimal structure generally is too difficult to determine.

**Weighted cost of capital** The firm's cost of capital, wherein the cost of each component of capital is considered in proportion to its percentage in the target capital structure.

## EQUATIONS

**Equation 13.1**       **Degree of Financial Leverage: General Form**

$$DFL = \frac{\text{Percentage change in EPS}}{\text{Percentage change in EBIT}} \qquad \textbf{(p. 373)}$$

where   $DFL$ = degree of financial leverage
        $EPS$ = earnings per share
       $EBIT$ = earnings before interest and taxes

When a firm has debt or preferred stock in its capital structure, changes in EBIT result in magnified changes in EPS. Equation 13.1 provides a measure of the degree of magnification.

**Equation 13.2**       **Degree of Financial Leverage: Alternative Form**

$$DFL = \frac{\text{EBIT}}{\text{EBIT} - I - [PSD/(1 - T)]} \qquad \textbf{(p. 373)}$$

where    $I$ = interest expense in dollars
       $PSD$ = preferred stock dividend
         $T$ = firm's tax rate

Equation 13.2 is used to find the degree of financial leverage when income statement data is available to the analyst.

**Equation 13.3**       **Value of Common Stock**

$$P_0 = \frac{D_1}{k_s - g} \qquad \textbf{(p. 380)}$$

where  $P_0$ = value of a share of common stock
       $D_1$ = expected dividend on the common stock next year
       $k_s$ = required rate of return on the common stock
        $g$ = growth rate of the dividend

This equation was used in Chapter 13 to illustrate the effects of changes in capital structure on the value of the firm's common stock. That is, as debt is added to the capital structure, the values, $D_1$, $k_s$, and $g$ are all affected. The objective of management is to determine the capital structure that maximizes $P_0$.

## QUESTIONS

**Q13-1.** What is the difference between a firm's financial structure and its capital structure?

**Q13-2.** Describe the relationship between financial leverage and each of the following: the cost of debt, the cost of equity, the weighted cost of capital.

**Q13-3.** Describe the relationship between financial leverage and the following variables: $D_1$, $k_s$, $g$, and $P_0$.

**Q13-4.** Describe the information provided to the analyst by an EBIT-EPS analysis.

**Q13-5.** If a firm replaces debt with common equity in the capital structure, which income statement items would you expect to change and in which way?

**Q13-6.** Distinguish between the financial breakeven point and the financial indifference point. Illustrate these concepts with a graph.

**Q13-7.** How do *taxes and bankruptcy* affect the capital structure of a firm?

**Q13-8.** There are a number of practical complications involved in determining capital structure. Briefly discuss each.

**Q13-9.** How are *measures of financial leverage* used in capital structure management?

**Q13-10.** List and briefly discuss five key company characteristics that affect the capital structure of a firm.

**Q13-11.** How might each of the following affect a firm's capital structure? Address each separately and assume all other variables remain unchanged.

**a.** The firm's marginal tax rate declines.
**b.** Stock prices in general decline (a bear market is experienced).
**c.** The inflation rate in the economy rises.
**d.** Investors become more risk-averse for all securities.

## SELF-TEST PROBLEMS

Solutions to self-test problems appear on p. S1.

**SP13-1.** McHone Enterprises had EBIT of $4 million and EPS of $2.57 per share in 1985. In 1986 the firm had EBIT of $4.2 million and EPS of $2.88 per share. What was McHone's degree of financial leverage?

**SP13-2.** Walters Enterprises has made the following forecasts of some key income statement items for next year.

- Sales: $45 million
- EBIT: $4.5 million
- Interest expense: $1.3 million
- Tax rate: 34%
- Dividends on preferred stock: $600,000
- Shares of common stock outstanding: 656,000 shares

**a.** What would be the degree of financial leverage for Walters Enterprises next year based on this information?

**b.** Using your answer to Part a, estimate the EPS for Walters Enterprises if EBIT increases to $5 million the following year (assume there is no change in the capital structure).

**SP13-3.** Richards, Inc., has estimated its cost of long-term debt and cost of common equity at various levels of financial leverage (see Table A).

**a.** Graph the firm's cost of debt and cost of equity functions. Place the debt to equity ratio on the horizontal scale.

**b.** Calculate the weighted cost of capital at each level of debt to equity under consideration.

**c.** Add the weighted cost of capital to the graph constructed in Part a.

**d.** What should Richards' target capital structure be and why?

### TABLE A
### COST OF DEBT AND EQUITY
### AT VARIOUS LEVELS OF LEVERAGE: RICHARDS, INC.

| Debt to Equity Ratio | Long-Term Debt % in Capital Structure | $k_i$ | Common Equity % in Capital Structure | $k_s$ |
|---|---|---|---|---|
| 0.00 | 0% | 8.0% | 100% | 14.0% |
| 0.18 | 15 | 8.0 | 85 | 14.5 |
| 0.43 | 30 | 8.5 | 70 | 15.0 |
| 0.82 | 45 | 9.0 | 55 | 16.0 |
| 1.50 | 60 | 10.0 | 40 | 17.5 |

**SP13-4.** White & Hosni Corporation currently has a capital structure consisting of 30 percent debt and 70 percent common equity. Table B lists the expected EPS that could be generated next year under several alternative capital structures.

**a.** What is the expected value of White & Hosni common stock for each alternative capital structure? Assume the firm will pay out 50 percent of its earnings as dividends. Also assume a constant dividend growth rate to infinity.

**b.** What debt to equity ratio would provide White & Hosni with the highest EPS? The highest growth rate? The highest stock price?

**c.** What should the target capital structure be for White & Hosni and why?

### TABLE B
### ESTIMATES OF EPS AND DIVIDEND GROWTH RATE
### UNDER VARIOUS CAPITAL STRUCTURES: WHITE & HOSNI CORPORATION

| Debt to Equity Ratio | Expected EPS | Expected Growth Rate | Investors' Required Rate of Return |
|---|---|---|---|
| 0.14 | $10.50 | 5.0% | 13.2% |
| 0.43 | 10.60 | 6.0 | 13.5 |
| 0.50 | 10.70 | 7.0 | 14.0 |
| 1.50 | 10.80 | 8.0 | 15.1 |

## PROBLEMS

**P13-1.** Some selected financial information about Boone Publishing Corporation is presented in the following table. Calculate the degree of financial leverage experienced by Boone Publishing from 1985 to 1986. Do the same for the period of 1986 to 1987.

| Year | EBIT | EPS |
|------|------|-----|
| 1985 | $67 million | $3.35 |
| 1986 | 71 million | 3.95 |
| 1987 | 76 million | 4.64 |

**P13-2.** The income statement of Davis & Joyce Industries reflected the following information last year:

- Sales: $60 million
- EBIT: $6 million
- Interest expense: $2 million
- Tax rate: 34%
- Dividends on preferred stock: $1 million
- Shares of common stock outstanding: 800,000 shares

a. What is the degree of financial leverage for Davis & Joyce?
b. Based on your answer to Part a, estimate the EPS for Davis & Joyce if EBIT increases to $6.3 million next year (assume there is no change in the capital structure).

**P13-3.** G. Paul Enterprises had EPS last year of $1.32 on EBIT of $975,000. The firm estimates it will earn $1.37 per share next year on EBIT of $1,072,500. What is G. Paul Enterprises' degree of financial leverage?

**P13-4.** The estimated after-tax cost of debt and common equity are indicated on the following table for Rubin & Gillett Corporation at various levels of financial leverage.

a. Construct a graph indicating the firm's cost of debt and cost of equity at the different levels of financial leverage.
b. What is the weighted cost of capital at each level of financial leverage?
c. Add the weighted cost of capital line to the graph constructed in Part a.
d. What should Rubin & Gillett's target capital structure be?

| Debt to Equity Ratio | **Long-Term Debt** | | **Common Equity** | |
|---|---|---|---|---|
| | % in Capital Structure | $k_i$ | % in Capital Structure | $k_s$ |
| 0.00 | 0% | 5.0% | 100% | 10.0% |
| 0.25 | 20 | 5.0 | 80 | 10.5 |
| 0.67 | 40 | 5.5 | 60 | 11.0 |
| 1.50 | 60 | 6.0 | 40 | 12.0 |
| 4.00 | 80 | 7.0 | 20 | 13.5 |

**P13-5.** Berry, Inc., is considering changing its current capital structure. It has estimated the EPS, dividend growth rate, and investors' required rates of return on common equity under different levels of financial leverage (see the following table). Berry expects to pay a dividend equal to 40 percent of its EPS; and it expects the growth rate to be constant to infinity once the capital structure has been determined.

a. Find the expected value of the common stock of Berry, Inc., for the different levels of financial leverage.
b. Identify the debt to equity ratio that maximizes EPS, the ratio that maximizes the dividend growth rate, and the ratio that maximizes the stock price.
c. What capital structure should Berry, Inc., maintain and why?

| Debt to Equity Ratio | Expected EPS | Expected Growth Rate | Required Return on Common Equity |
|---|---|---|---|
| 0.00 | $1.56 | 7.0% | 12.0% |
| 0.25 | 1.62 | 8.0 | 13.1 |
| 0.67 | 1.68 | 9.0 | 14.5 |
| 1.50 | 1.74 | 10.0 | 15.7 |

**P13-6.** Bogumil Industries expects EBIT to be $5 million next year, although it feels EBIT could be as high as $5.5 million. Bogumil is considering increasing its financial leverage soon by selling an additional $10 million of 10 percent bonds (it currently has $20 million of 10 percent bonds outstanding). The proceeds would be used to repurchase 300,000 of its 500,000 shares of common stock currently outstanding.

a. Determine Bogumil's EPS at both $5 million and $5.5 million of EBIT for the current financing and the proposed financing (assume a 34 percent tax rate).
b. Construct the EBIT-EPS graph for both capital structures.
c. What is the financial breakeven point for the two alternative capital structures?
d. What is the indifference level of EBIT for the two alternative capital structures?

**P13-7.** Winger Corporation's EPS last year was $1.23 on EBIT of $154 million. It expects EPS of $1.51 next year on EBIT of $162 million.

a. What degree of financial leverage is implied for Winger Corporation by this information?
b. What would Winger's EPS be if its EBIT is $144 million next year?

**P13-8.** Newman Enterprises had EBIT last year of $950,000. It incurred interest expense of $150,000, paid taxes at a 34 percent average rate, and paid a $3 dividend to each of the 100,000 shares of preferred stock it has outstanding. Newman also has 300,000 shares of common stock outstanding.

a. What is Newman's degree of financial leverage?
b. What was Newman's EPS last year?
c. If Newman's EBIT increases by 7 percent next year, what will its EPS be?

**P13-9.** Weaver Enterprises has estimated its after-tax cost of debt and cost of common equity to assist in determining its target capital structure. Those estimates are as follows:

| Debt to Equity Ratio | After-Tax Cost of Debt | Cost of Common Equity |
|---|---|---|
| 0.0 | 6.5 | 13.0% |
| 0.5 | 6.5 | 14.0 |
| 1.0 | 7.5 | 16.0 |
| 1.5 | 8.5 | 19.0 |
| 2.0 | 10.0 | 23.0 |

a. Construct a graph of Weaver's cost of debt and cost of equity at each level of financial leverage.
b. What is the weighted cost of capital at each level of financial leverage?
c. Add the weighted cost of capital line to the graph you constructed in Part a.
d. What should Weaver's target capital structure be?

**P13-10.** M. Brooks Corporation currently has 10 million shares of common stock outstanding in addition to 200,000 shares of $5.50 preferred stock and $50 million of 10 percent bonds. Brooks forecasts EBIT next year to be $12 million. However, if it loses one of its primary contracts, which is due for renewal, EBIT could shrink to $10 million. A proposal has been made to repurchase half of Brooks's bonds using the proceeds of the sale of 1 million more shares of common stock. Brooks has a 34 percent average and marginal tax rate.

**a.** Construct the EBIT-EPS graph for both capital structures.
**b.** What are the financial breakeven points for the two capital structures and the financial indifference point for Brooks?
**c.** Which capital structure would you recommend and why?

**P13-11.** Hanks Industries has estimated its EPS, dividend growth rate, and investors' required return on common equity at various debt to equity ratios. Use this information to determine Hanks's target capital structure. (Hanks pays a dividend equal to 50 percent of its earnings.)

| Debt to Equity Ratio | Expected EPS | Expected Dividend Growth Rate | Required Return on Common Equity |
|---|---|---|---|
| 0.0 | $1.25 | 4.0% | 14.0% |
| 0.5 | 1.50 | 5.0 | 15.0 |
| 1.0 | 1.75 | 6.0 | 17.0 |
| 1.5 | 1.90 | 7.0 | 20.0 |
| 2.0 | 1.80 | 6.0 | 24.0 |

## COMPUTER-ASSISTED PROBLEMS

**CP13-1.** Mizer, Inc. has made the following forecasts for next year:

- Tax rate: 34%
- Dividends on preferred stock: $800,000
- Shares of common stock outstanding: 1 million
- Interest expense: $1.2 million

Mizer is considering a proposal to replace some of the debt in its capital structure with equity. The proposed capital structure would result in 1.1 million shares of common stock outstanding, and next year's interest expense would be $1 million.

**a. Sensitivity of EPS to EBIT**   Use the M-V diskette to determine the forecasted EPS based on Mizer's existing capital structure. If Mizer expects EBIT to be $5 million, what is the forecasted EPS if Mizer revises its capital structure? How would the forecasted EPS for both capital structures be affected if EBIT is actually $4.5 million? What if EBIT is actually $5.4 million? If all three EBIT scenarios have an equal probability of occurring, what is the expected EPS for each of the capital structures?

**b. Sensitivity of EPS to EBIT**   Using the information in Part a, is the EPS more sensitive to possible outcomes of EBIT under the existing capital structure or the proposed capital structure? Why? What does this imply about the risk of the existing capital structure relative to that of the proposed capital structure? Does the proposed capital structure appear to be more attractive or less attractive than the existing capital structure? Explain.

**c. Probability Distributions**   Assume the following probability distribution describing Mizer's EBIT:

| EBIT | Probability |
|---|---|
| $4.2 million | 10% |
| 4.6 | 20 |
| 5.0 | 30 |
| 5.4 | 25 |
| 5.5 | 15 |

Using this information and the other information provided earlier, determine Mizer's EPS at each level of EBIT. Which capital structure would you select? Justify your answer.

## REFERENCES

Barnea, Amir, Robert A. Haugen, and Lemma W. Senbet. "Market Imperfections, Agency Problems, and Capital Structure: A Review." *Financial Management* 10 (Summer 1981): 7–49.

Belkaoui, Ahmed. "A Canadian Survey of Financial Structure." *Financial Management* 4 (Spring 1975): 74–79.

Castanias, Richard. "Bankruptcy Risk and Optimal Capital Structure." *Journal of Finance* 38 (December 1983): 1617–35.

Ferri, Michael G., and Wesley H. Jones. "Determinants of Financial Structure: A New Methodological Approach." *Journal of Finance* 34 (June 1979): 631–44.

Greenfield, Robert L., Maury R. Randall, and John C. Woods. "Financial Leverage and Use of the Net Present Value Investment Criterion." *Financial Management* 12 (Autumn 1983): 40–44.

Hamada, Robert S. "The Effect of the Firm's Capital Structure on the Systematic Risk of Common Stocks." *Journal of Finance* 27 (May 1972): 435–52.

Harris, John M., Jr., Rodney L. Roenfeldt, and Philip L. Cooley. "Evidence of Financial Leverage Clienteles." *Journal of Finance* 38 (September 1983): 1125–32.

Haugen, Robert A., and Lemma W. Senbet. "The Insignificance of Bankruptcy Costs to the Theory of Optimal Capital Structure." *Journal of Finance* 33 (May 1978): 383–93.

Hong, Hai, and Alfred Rappaport. "Debt Capacity, Optimal Capital Structure, and Capital Budgeting." *Financial Management* 7 (Autumn 1978): 7–11.

Jalilvand, Abolhassan, and Robert S. Harris. "Corporate Behavior in Adjusting to Capital Structure and Dividend Targets: An Econometric Study." *Journal of Finance* 39 (March 1984): 127–145.

Kim, E. Han. "A Mean-Variance Theory of Optimal Financial Structure and Corporate Debt Capacity." *Journal of Finance* 33 (March 1978): 45–64.

Kolodny, Richard, and Diane Rizzuto Schler. "Changes in Capital Structure, New Equity Issues, and Scale Effects." *Journal of Financial Research* 8 (Summer 1985): 127–136.

Litzenberger, Robert H. "Some Observations on Capital Structure and the Impact of Recent Recapitalizations on Share Prices." *Journal of Financial and Quantitative Analysis* 21 (March 1986): 59–72.

Mandelker, Gershon N., and S. Ghon Rhee. "The Impact of the Degrees of Operating and Financial Leverage on Systematic Risk of Common Stock." *Journal of Financial and Quantitative Analysis* 19 (March 1984): 45–58.

Marsh, Paul. "The Choice between Equity and Debt: An Empirical Study." *Journal of Finance* 37 (March 1982): 121–44.

Martin, John D., and David F. Scott, Jr. "A Discriminant Analysis of the Corporate Debt-Equity Decision." *Financial Management* 3 (Winter 1974): 71–79.

Melnyk, Z. Lew. "Cost of Capital as a Function of Financial Leverage." *Decision Sciences* 1 (July–October 1970): 327–56.

Miller, Merton H. "Debt and Taxes." *Journal of Finance* 32 (May 1977): 261–75.

Myers, Steward C. "Determinants of Corporate Borrowing." *Journal of Financial Economics* 5 (1977): 147–75.

Piper, Thomas R., and Wolf A. Weinhold. "How

Much Debt Is Right for Your Company?" *Harvard Business Review* 60 (July–August 1982): 106–14.

Pringle, John J. "Price/Earnings Ratios, Earnings per Share, and Financial Management." *Financial Management* 2 (Spring 1973): 34–40.

Scott, David F., Jr. "Evidence on the Importance of Financial Structure." *Financial Management* 1 (Summer 1972): 45–50.

Scott, David F., Jr., and Dana J. Johnson. "Financing Policies and Practices in Large Corporations." *Financial Management* 11 (Summer 1982): 51–59.

Scott, David F., Jr., and John D. Martin. "Industry Influence on Financial Structure." *Financial Management* 4 (Spring 1975): 67–73.

Scott, James H., Jr. "A Theory of Optimal Structure." *Bell Journal of Economics* 7 (Spring 1976): 33–54.

Titman, Sheridan. "The Effect of Forward Markets on the Debt-Equity Mix of Investor Portfolios and the Optimal Capital Structure of Firms." *Journal of Financial and Quantitative Analysis* 20 (March 1985): 19–28.

Walsh, Francis J., Jr. *Planning Corporate Capital Structures*, New York: The Conference Board, 1972.

# OPERATING AND FINANCIAL LEVERAGE COMBINED

Recall that Chapter 8 focused on operating leverage while Chapter 13 focused on financial leverage. Although these concepts were presented separately, they are related, and financial managers must be aware of this relationship when implementing certain policies.

Consider a firm that has large amounts of both operating leverage and financial leverage. If sales change just a little, the resulting change in EBIT is magnified by the operating leverage. This large change in EBIT causes an even larger change in EPS as a result of the firm's financial leverage. The change is favorable if sales are increasing. However, if sales decrease, the decrease in EBIT is magnified by the operating leverage, and the decrease in EPS is magnified by the financial leverage. For this reason (and some others not discussed here), firms with high levels of operating leverage often maintain low levels of financial leverage. Conversely, those with low levels of operating leverage often use a high level of financial leverage to magnify the impact of changing sales on EPS. Sometimes the level of operating leverage is heavily influenced by the product being manufactured and sold. As we will see, management's attitude toward risk, and other factors, also influence the levels of both types of leverage.

## AN EXAMPLE OF COMBINED LEVERAGE

Table 13A.1 presents some financial information about Cleaver Industries, the same firm used in the examples in Chapter 13, which can be used to analyze the relationship between operating and financial leverage.

The level of combined leverage for a firm is dependent upon the level of both operating and financial leverage and measures the sensitivity of EPS to changes in sales. If both operating and financial leverage are high, then the firm has a large amount of combined leverage, and changes in sales result in large changes in EPS. If both operating leverage and financial leverage are low, then the firm has a small amount of combined leverage, and small changes in sales result in small changes in EPS.

Table 13A.1 shows that if sales increase from 110,000 units (the current level) to 120,000 units (the expected level), EBIT increases from $70,000

**TABLE 13A.1**  **Key Financial Data during a Recent Fiscal Year: Cleaver Industries**

| | Current Year | Next Year (Expected) | |
|---|---|---|---|
| Sales (in units) | 110,000 | 120,000 | |
| Total revenue (at $4/unit) | $440,000 | $480,000 | Area of operating leverage (DOL = 1.57) |
| Less: Variable operating costs (at $3/unit) | 330,000 | 360,000 | |
| Less: Fixed operating costs | 40,000 | 40,000 | |
| EBIT | 70,000 | 80,000 | Area of combined leverage (DCL = 8.8) |
| Less: Interest | 45,000 | 45,000 | |
| EBT | 25,000 | 35,000 | Area of financial leverage (DFL = 5.6) |
| Less: Taxes (20%) | 5,000 | 7,000 | |
| Net income | 20,000 | 28,000 | |
| Less: Preferred stock dividends | 10,000 | 10,000 | |
| EAC | 10,000 | 18,000 | |
| EPS (5,000 shares outstanding) | $2.00 | $3.60 | |

to $80,000. This suggests a degree of operating leverage of 1.57, as determined using Equation 8.4.

$$DOL = \frac{\text{percentage change in EBIT}}{\text{percentage change in sales}} \qquad \textbf{(8.4 restated)}$$

$$= \frac{14.3\%}{9.1\%}$$

$$= 1.57$$

Similarly, when EBIT increases from $70,000 to $80,000, EPS increases from $2.00 to $3.60, and the degree of financial leverage is 5.6.

$$DFL = \frac{\text{percentage change in EPS}}{\text{percentage change in EBIT}} \qquad \textbf{(13.1)}$$

$$= \frac{80\%}{14.3\%}$$

$$= 5.6$$

The relationship between operating, financial, and combined leverage is formalized in Equation 13A.1:

$$DCL = DOL \times DFL \qquad \textbf{(13A.1)}$$

For Cleaver Industries, the DCL can be found as follows:

$$DCL = 1.57 \times 5.6$$

$$= 8.8$$

This can be interpreted as meaning that for every 1 percent change in sales, an 8.8 percent change in EPS will result. This relationship also holds for negative changes in sales.

## ALTERNATIVE METHODS OF CALCULATING *DCL*

If information about the degrees of operating and financial leverage is not available, one can calculate the *DCL* directly from more basic information using Equation 13A.2.

$$DCL = \frac{\text{percentage change in EPS}}{\text{percentage change in sales}} \qquad \textbf{(13A.2)}$$

This equation is very similar to the basic formulas for finding both the degree of operating leverage and the degree of financial leverage (*DOL* and *DFL*). It can be applied to the information in Table 13A.1 as follows:

$$DCL = \frac{\dfrac{\$3.60 - \$2.00}{\$2.00}}{\dfrac{120{,}000 \text{ units} - 110{,}000 \text{ units}}{110{,}000 \text{ units}}}$$

$$= \frac{80\%}{9.1\%}$$

$$= 8.8$$

Given even more fundamental information about the firm's operating and financial costs, Equation 13A.3 can be used to find the degree of combined leverage.

$$DCL = \frac{Q(p - v)}{Q(p - v) - F - I - \left(\dfrac{PSD}{1 - T}\right)} \qquad \textbf{(13A.3)}$$

where $DCL$ = degree of combined leverage

$\quad Q$ = number of units sold

$\quad p$ = price per unit sold

$\quad v$ = variable cost per unit sold

$\quad F$ = total fixed costs

$\quad I$ = dollar amount of interest on debt

$\quad PSD$ = preferred stock dividend

$\quad T$ = marginal income tax rate

Again using the information provided in Table 13A.1, and substituting this into Equation 13A.3, one can estimate the degree of combined leverage:

$$DCL = \frac{110,000(\$4 - \$3)}{110,000(\$4 - \$3) - \$40,000 - \$45,000 - \left(\frac{\$10,000}{1 - .20}\right)}$$

$$= \frac{\$110,000}{\$110,000 - \$40,000 - \$45,000 - \$12,500}$$

$$= 8.8$$

## PROBLEMS

**P13A-1.** O'Hara Corporation has a degree of operating leverage of 2.3 and a degree of combined leverage of 4.2. What is O'Hara's degree of financial leverage?

**P13A-2.** Glenn Industries had EPS of $1.87 last year on sales of 6 million units. If it expects to generate EPS of $2.00 next year on sales of 6,120,000 units, what is its degree of combined leverage?

**P13A-3.** Painter Steel Works had 30,000 units of sales last year and EPS of $5.00. It sells its product for $600 per unit. Its variable cost per unit is $200, and fixed costs are $9 million. Painter pays $1 million in interest each year and has a 34 percent average tax rate.

**a.** If the firm pays a preferred stock dividend of $320,000, what is its degree of combined leverage?
**b.** How many shares of common stock does Painter have outstanding?

**P13A-4.** Quant Corporation had EPS of $3.30 and EBIT of $90,000 last year on sales of 100,000 units.

**a.** If Quant has a degree of operating leverage of 3.1, what will its EBIT be next year?
**b.** If Quant has EPS next year of $4.95, what is its degree of financial leverage?

# CAPITAL STRUCTURE THEORY

As demonstrated in Chapter 13, a firm's capital structure affects its cost of capital and the value of the firm's common stock. If a firm has insufficient financial leverage, its dividend, as well as the growth rate of the dividend, will be lower than optimal, thus reducing the value of the firm's common stock. Conversely, too much financial leverage can increase the risk of the firm (and therefore investors' required rates of return) by so much that the value of the firm's common stock declines.

This appendix presents two theoretical approaches to capital structure that differ substantially from the more traditional approach described in Chapter 13. Each represents an extreme position, based on assumptions considered unrealistic in terms of the true economic environment. Nevertheless, the development of these approaches has contributed immensely to the existing body of knowledge concerning capital structure. Indeed, an understanding of these two theoretical approaches to capital structure and their assumptions contributes to an understanding of the more traditional approach presented in Chapter 13. The key assumptions are as follows:

1. There are no corporate or personal income taxes, and there are no bankruptcy costs.
2. The only source of capital is from the sale of bonds and common stock.
3. The securities markets are efficient.
4. All investors are rational and make the same forecasts of firm net operating income.

## NET INCOME (NI) APPROACH

A critical assumption of the net income (NI) approach is that creditors and stockholders of the firm do not increase their required rates of return as the amount of financial leverage increases (this assumption holds because bankruptcy costs are assumed absent). Instead, the after-tax cost of debt $(k_i)$ and the cost of common equity $(k_s)$ are constant over the total range of possible levels of financial leverage. The costs of these components of capi-

**FIGURE 13B.1**

**Cost of Capital
Using the Net In-
come Approach**

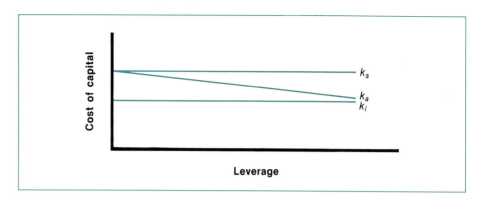

tal are represented by the horizontal lines in Figure 13B.1. Since the cost of debt is lower than the cost of equity (and the cost of both remains constant), as debt is added to the capital structure, the weighted cost of capital $(k_a)$ declines (See Figure 13B.1).

The NI approach assumes that the value of the firm's common stock is based on the firm's ability to generate net income for the stockholders. It implies that the appropriate capital structure for all firms includes as much debt as the firms can possibly obtain.

## NET OPERATING INCOME (NOI) APPROACH

The net operating income (NOI) approach to capital structure suggests that a firm's cost of capital and stock price are not affected by the firm's capital structure. This approach specifies that as debt is added to the capital structure, the increased financial leverage results in more risk to common stockholders through an increase in volatility of EPS. This higher risk causes investors in common stock to require higher rates of return. Meanwhile, in the absence of bankruptcy costs, the cost of debt is assumed to remain constant as financial leverage increases. The higher cost of equity is exactly offset by the addition of cheaper debt to the capital structure. As a result, the weighted cost of capital remains unchanged. Figure 13B.2 illustrates the impact of financial leverage on the cost of debt $(k_i)$, the cost of common equity $(k_s)$, and the overall cost of capital $(k_a)$, according to the NOI approach.

Notice that the cost of debt remains constant over the entire range of possible levels of financial leverage, while the cost of common equity increases as financial leverage increases. Since the cost of common equity increases by the same amount that the firm saves by adding less expensive debt to the capital structure, the overall cost of capital remains unchanged (it is a horizontal line in Figure 13B.2).

The NOI approach to capital structure is so named because it assumes that the value of a firm's common stock is derived indirectly from the firm's NOI. That is, NOI is available to compensate both the bondholders and stockholders of the firm. By dividing the firm's NOI by the overall cost of capital, we can determine the total value of the firm. Subtracting the

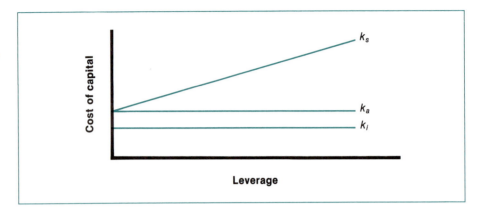

market value of the firm's debt from the total value of the firm leaves the value of the firm's equity as the residual.

Under the NOI approach to capital structure, the distribution of NOI between bondholders and stockholders does not affect the value of the firm, the value of the firm's common stock, or the firm's overall cost of capital. The NOI approach implies that any attempt to determine the optimal capital structure is wasted, since capital structure does not affect the value of the firm.[1]

---

1. For a more rigorous discussion of capital market theory, the reader is referred to David Durand, "The Cost of Debt and Equity Funds for Business," *The Management of Corporate Capital*, ed. Ezra Soloman (New York: Free Press, 1959), pp. 91–116; and Franco Modigliani and Merton H. Miller, "The Cost of Capital, Corporate Finance and the Theory of Investment," *American Economic Review* 48 (June 1958): 261–77. For a less rigorous yet comprehensive discussion of capital market theory, see Eugene F. Brigham and Louis C. Gapenski, *Intermediate Financial Management*, 2d ed. (New York: Dryden Press, 1987).

# CHAPTER 14

# DIVIDEND POLICY

## DIVIDEND POLICY IN PERSPECTIVE

During the period 1977 through 1986, Emerson Radio Corporation paid no dividends to its stockholders despite a 28.7% compound annual growth rate of its earnings. During the same period, International Business Machines Corporation paid dividends ranging from 38.1% to 66.7% of its annual earnings, which increased at a 5.5% compound annual rate during this period. The mean percentage payout for IBM during the ten-year period was 51.3%. Also during that period, Philadelphia Electric Company paid dividends ranging from a low of 81.5% to a high of 96.8% of its annual earnings, which increased at a 3.4% compound annual rate. The mean percentage payout for Philadelphia Electric was 88.1%.

As suggested by this data, there is a relationship between the percentage of earnings paid to stockholders as dividends and the growth rate of earnings. Growing firms must raise equity funds (as well as debt funds) to support their growth, and since internal equity is less expensive than external equity, rapidly growing firms frequently retain all or most of their earnings to support their growth. Conversely, slower growing firms have less need for expansion of assets and, therefore, are able to pay more of their earnings out as dividends.

What other factors affect a firm's dividend policy? What procedures do firms use to pay dividends? What are the tax implications of paying low dividends? Does the payment of dividends affect the value of the firm? This chapter addresses these and other questions about dividend policies.

The allocation of corporate earnings is an important decision. Although a firm's entire net income belongs to the stockholders, often only a portion is distributed to them in the form of dividends, and the remainder is reinvested in the firm as retained earnings. The dividends paid to stockholders represent partial compensation for the money they have invested in the firm. Although each firm determines its own dividend policy, some constraints, which will be discussed shortly, are common to all.

The constant growth valuation model for common stock presented in Chapter 4 indicates that the value of common stock is a function of the expected dividend in the next period, the growth rate of the firm's dividend, and the required rate of return on the stock; that is, $P_0 = D_1/(k_s - g)$. If a firm elects to pay a high dividend, this would increase the numerator of the equation and would tend to increase the value of the stock. However, by paying a high dividend, the firm must retain less earnings with which to purchase additional assets. And since an increasing asset base is necessary to help the firm grow, less retained earnings reduces the growth rate, thus increasing the denominator of the equation, which tends to lower the value of the stock.

In other words, paying high dividends results in conflicting forces that can either increase or decrease the value of the firm's common stock. The optimal dividend policy is the one that results in the highest possible value of the firm's common stock. Many factors must be considered in determining this optimal dividend policy. After discussing these factors, this chapter presents some alternative dividend theories and describes several dividend policies used in practice. Finally, dividend payment procedures and some special dividend topics are presented.

## FACTORS AFFECTING DIVIDEND POLICY

A number of shareholder-related and firm-related factors that affect dividend policy are summarized in Table 14.1 and are discussed in some detail in the following sections. Although lengthy, this list is not exhaustive. Throughout this text, reference to the size of the dividend paid refers to the **dividend payout ratio,** which is defined as the ratio of dividends to earnings and is interpreted as the percent of earnings paid out as dividends.

### Shareholder-Related Factors

Four major characteristics of shareholders that may affect their preferences for receiving dividends are (1) tax status, (2) need for current income, (3) attitude toward risk, and (4) concern about dilution of ownership.

**Tax Status**   The tax status of the firm's shareholders is particularly important to consider when the shareholders have high marginal tax rates. When stockholders receive dividends, they must declare them as income and pay taxes on them in the year received. Investors in high tax brackets may prefer smaller dividends, since they may not need the dividends to enhance their current consumption of goods and services and, of course, would prefer to avoid the tax liability resulting from a large dividend. If

**TABLE 14.1    Shareholder- and Firm-Related Factors Affecting Dividends**

|  | Conditions Favoring a Small or (Zero) Dividend | Conditions Favoring a Large Dividend |
|---|---|---|
| *Shareholder-related factors* | | |
| Tax status | Preference to defer taxes | No preference to defer taxes |
| Income needs | Income not needed | Income needed |
| Risk preferences | Willing to assume risk | Less willing to assume risk |
| Dilution of ownership | Concerned about dilution | Not concerned about dilution |
| *Firm-related factors* | | |
| Growth | Rapid | Slow |
| Debt capacity | Minimal | Substantial |
| Earnings stability | Unstable | Stable |
| Liquidity position | Low liquidity | High liquidity |

these investors own stocks that pay no dividends at all, they can select the appropriate time to sell their securities (theoretically at a higher price as a result of growing earnings supported by rapid increases in retained earnings), thus postponing any payment of taxes until profits are realized at the time of the sale. Currently, dividends and gains from the sale of appreciated securities are taxed at the same rate.

**Income Needs**   Some stockholders purchase common stock with the objective of supplementing their current income with dividend income. These investors have a preference for high dividends. Typically, they have low marginal tax rates, making the tax burden on dividends less severe.

**Attitude toward Risk**   Stockholders' preferences for particular dividend policies may also be affected by their attitudes towards risk. When a firm elects to retain say, $1 per share of earnings rather than paying that amount out as a dividend, investors expect to benefit in the future by selling that stock at a price that is at least $1 higher than if the dividend is paid. However, waiting to sell stock at a higher price is risky. Therefore, cautious investors may prefer to receive the cash dividend (the "bird in hand") than take a chance on the future sale price of the stock.

**Concerns about Dilution of Ownership**   Another influence on investors' preferences is a concern about the dilution of ownership. To the extent that firms can support their need for common equity financing by using retained earnings, they can avoid issuing new common stock and therefore avoid diluting each stockholder's proportionate ownership of the firm. This factor is particularly important to investors who own a substantial proportion of a firm's common stock.

## Firm-Related Factors

In addition to shareholder-related factors, there are a number of firm-related factors that also affect dividend policy.

**Firm Growth**   Firms experiencing rapid growth generally support that growth with both equity and debt financing. As shown in Chapter 12, the cost of the retained earnings component of equity is less expensive than the cost of issuing new common stock (recall that issuing new common stock involves incurring flotation costs). In order to keep the cost of capital as low as possible, rapidly growing firms are more likely to retain more earnings.

**Debt Capacity**   Some firms have less debt capacity than others, particularly small firms having few assets to use as collateral for loans. When debt capacity is low, growth must come from equity sources, and since retained earnings is a less expensive source of equity than the sale of new common stock, firms with low debt capacity are likely to retain more earnings and pay lower dividends.

**Earnings Stability**   When a firm's earnings are stable, it is more confident that net income will be available in future years to provide equity financing. As a result, such firms may be more willing to pay large dividends. Conversely, firms with less stable earnings may feel it is necessary to retain more of their earnings each year to hedge against the possibility of having little or no earnings in future years and thus no way to add to retained earnings.

**Liquidity Position**   It is not unusual for profitable firms as well as those experiencing financial difficulty to be without substantial amounts of cash in the bank. This is especially true of rapidly growing firms, which need all the cash they can raise to support their growth. Since dividends are paid with cash, a shortage can restrict the size of the dividend. This restriction may be offset, however, by the ability of the firm to borrow money.

## Other Factors

There are a number of factors that affect dividend policy that are not shareholder- or firm-related. Some of the more important factors are discussed below.

**Legal Constraints**   One of the broadest constraints on dividend policy is the impairment-of-capital rule, which specifies that a firm may not pay dividends in excess of its retained earnings. That is, firms may pay out all of their current year's net income and all of the net income that was retained from previous years (retained earnings), but they may not pay dividends from their common stock or paid-in capital accounts. This rule is designed to prevent firms that are experiencing financial difficulty from distributing their assets to the stockholders and forcing the creditors to absorb large losses.

**Loan Provisions**   Bond indentures and loan agreements frequently contain provisions limiting the payment of dividends to the level of current earnings. This is to ensure that the creditor's risk is not increased by the distribution of firm assets to the stockholders.

**Accumulated Earnings Tax**    Recall from Chapter 2 that firms incur a surtax on earnings retained in excess of "reasonable business needs." This penalty on accumulated earnings may act as a constraint on the level of earnings retained by firms. As a practical matter, however, privately owned firms are normally the only firms constrained by this tax provision.

**Level of Inflation**    During periods of high inflation, firms find it increasingly more expensive to purchase new fixed assets to replace old fixed assets. Although depreciation is designed to generate sufficient cash flows to replace old fixed assets, the higher replacement costs may make the level of depreciation insufficient. Therefore, firms may need additional financing just to replace old fixed assets during inflationary periods. One source of additional financing typically comes from equity sources; and since retained earnings is the least expensive source of equity financing, firms tend to pay less dividends (retain more earnings) during inflationary periods. Additionally, high levels of inflation are generally accompanied by high interest rates, making debt financing more costly. Consequently, firms tend to increase the proportion of total financing provided by equity sources during inflationary periods.

**Institutional Restrictions**    Many states specify that financial institutions such as banks, insurance companies, and pension funds operating within the state are prohibited from investing in the common stocks of companies that pay no regular dividends. These states publish *legal listings* indicating which stocks meet certain dividend requirements and other minimum standards of acceptability. Firms may be encouraged to pay a regular dividend in order to be included on the lists.

## IS DIVIDEND POLICY RELEVANT?

At the start of this chapter it was stated that a firm's dividend policy affects the value of its common stock. Actually, this relationship is a controversial one that is addressed frequently in the finance literature. The following discussion presents the major opposing views regarding the relevance of dividend policy.

### Dividend Irrelevance Theory

Much of the evidence suggesting that dividends are irrelevant (they do not affect the value of a firm's common stock) is drawn from the work of Merton Miller and Franco Modigliani (M&M).[1] They argue that the value of a firm is a function of the firm's net income and the level of business risk. The distribution of net income between dividends and retained earnings is irrelevant.

In developing their theory of **dividend irrelevance**, M&M make a number of assumptions, including the following:

---

1.   Merton Miller and Franco Modigliani, "Dividend Policy, Growth, and the Valuation of Shares," *Journal of Business* (October 1961).

1. No transactions costs are incurred by stockholders, and no flotation costs are incurred by firms.
2. Corporate and personal income taxes are nonexistent.
3. Financial leverage does not affect the cost of capital.

Although these assumptions are clearly not realistic, an understanding of the relationships specified by M&M is helpful in gaining an understanding of dividend policy.

Essentially, M&M argue that individuals are indifferent regarding the payment of dividends because they can create their own dividends, or they can reverse dividends that are paid. For example, assume an investor owns 100 shares of common stock priced at $10.10 per share. The company pays a dividend of $.10 per share, but the investor does not want the dividend. This investor can reverse the dividend by purchasing one new share of common stock with the cash dividend received. He or she will have enough money to purchase one share since, when a dividend is paid on common stock, the market price of the stock adjusts downward by the amount of the dividend—in this case, to $10.00 per share. Ten dollars is also the amount of dividend the investor received (100 shares × $.10 per share). The investor is no worse off or better off after the dividend than before the dividend (he or she paid no taxes, since taxes are nonexistent; he or she paid no transactions fees, since there are none; and the decrease in the market value of the stock is equal in value to the newly purchased stock). After the dividend, the investor owns 101 shares of common stock with a value of $10.00 per share for a total value of $1,010. This is equal in value to the 100 shares he or she owned worth $10.10 each before the dividend.

An investor who wants a dividend when the company does not pay one can create his own dividend by selling some shares of common stock equal to the amount of the desired dividend. Consider the firm in our previous example. Assume now that the firm does not pay a dividend, so an investor who wants a dividend sells one share of common stock. The investor will receive $10.10 in cash and retain 99 shares of common stock valued at $10.10 each for total wealth of $1,010. In this situation, the value of the common stock does not decline, since no cash dividend has been paid. In either instance, the investor ends up with total wealth of $1,010.

## Dividend Relevance Theory

Several arguments favor **dividend relevance** over dividend irrelevance. Perhaps the foremost argument concerns the difference in risk incurred by investors when they receive a cash dividend (low risk) as opposed to relying on the sale of common stock to receive a capital gain (high risk). This argument suggests that higher dividend-payout ratios result in higher stock values. M&M argue that this is a fallacy, because investors receiving dividends typically reinvest it in the same or similar stocks anyway, in which case they are assuming the same risk as if no dividend had been paid. A substantial amount of research has been conducted regarding this controversy, and the results have been inconclusive.

Real-world considerations appear to result in investor preferences either for or against particular dividend policies. These considerations in-

## FINANCIAL MANAGEMENT IN PRACTICE

### DO FIRMS THINK DIVIDEND POLICY IS RELEVANT?

Various arguments have been presented over the years as to whether dividend policy is relevant. A recent survey by Baker, Farrelly, and Edelman offers some interesting insight into the issue.* Most financial managers surveyed strongly believe that firms should avoid making changes in dividends if these changes may have to be reversed in a year or so, suggesting a policy of stable dividends per share is popular. Most financial managers also believe that any changes in a dividend policy should be adequately disclosed to investors, and that a firm should strive to maintain an uninterrupted record of dividend payments. Managers also believe

* H. Kent Baker, Gail E. Farrelly, and Richard B. Edelman, "A Survey of Management Views on Dividend Policy," *Financial Management* 14 (Autumn 1985): 78–84.

that shareholders interpret a firm's existing dividend policy as a signal about the future, so firms should avoid creating a situation in which the dividends may have to be decreased.

The survey disclosed considerable disagreement about whether dividends should be viewed as a residual after desired investments have been financed. The results of the study suggest that while firms allow some upward flexibility of their dividend payout, the first priority is to at least maintain the existing dollar dividend. Dividend increases should be made only if the new dividend level can be sustained. This helps avoid dividend cuts in future years. Overall, dividend policies tend to be very defensive (that is, geared to avoiding a dividend decrease), and the goal of achieving a higher dividend is secondary.

clude taxes that investors must pay on dividend income and transactions costs incurred when they buy or sell common stock. In addition, since firms incur flotation costs when they issue new common stock, the cost of capital is affected by dividend policy.

## OTHER THEORETICAL DIVIDEND ISSUES

Two other theories concerning the payment of dividends describe the *informational content of dividends* and the *clientele effect*.

### Informational Content of Dividends

Even before a firm announces the board of director's decision on the size of the next dividend payment, analysts and investors have developed expectations about what it will be. Assuming the announced dividend is equal to or very close to the expected dividend, the announcement should not affect the price of the stock. However, if the announced dividend is substantially higher or lower than the expected dividend, the price of the stock may increase or decrease in reaction to the announcement. Although this may seem to support the relevance of dividend theory, M&M argue that stock price changes in reaction to dividend announcements are a result of the **informational content** of the dividends. That is, when a firm announces a dividend that is unexpectedly high or low, investors view this announcement as having informational content about how management views the firm's future earnings prospects. An unexpectedly large dividend normally signals investors that management expects earnings to grow more rapidly in the future, while an unexpectedly small dividend may signal investors that management expects earnings to be weak for the foreseeable future.

Empirical tests of this relationship have proved inconclusive. Although most analysts agree with the basic premise outlined here, studies indicate that many variables are at work. For example, consider a situation where a firm unexpectedly decreases its dividend because it needs additional capital to adopt an exceptionally attractive capital budgeting project. In this case the dividend is decreased because of a decrease in the dividend payout ratio. Investors may view such a decrease favorably, resulting in an increase in the price of the stock.

### Clientele Effect

Recall that some investors prefer to receive high dividends while others prefer to realize the capital gains that should result when a firm retains its earnings. These differences are attributable to such factors as stockholders' desire for additional current income and the tax rate investors are subject to. The **clientele effect** suggests that investors seek out firms that have dividend policies consistent with their desires.

The clientele effect may help explain why stock prices change after an announced change in dividend policy. When a firm changes its policy, those stockholders who are unhappy with the new policy will sell the stock and then purchase stock of companies having dividend policies more to their liking. Investors who like the new policy may purchase the firm's stock from the discontented shareholders. If more investors like the new policy than dislike it, the net result of the clientele effect may be an increase in the price of the stock. If more investors dislike the new policy, the net result may be a decrease in the price of the stock.

## COMMON DIVIDEND POLICIES

The four most common dividend policies employed by firms are (1) the residual dividend policy, (2) stable, but growing dividend per share, (3) constant dividend payout ratio, and (4) small, regular dividend plus extras.

### Residual Dividend Policy

With a **residual dividend policy,** the amount of dividends paid is the *residual* (the amount left over) after the firm has used its net income to adopt all profitable capital budgeting projects. For example, consider Spring Company, which has the investment opportunity schedule (IOS) and marginal cost of capital (MCC) line indicated in Figure 14.1. Since the optimal capital budget is at the point of intersection of the IOS and the MCC, Spring Company should plan to adopt projects requiring a total capital budget of $4 million, as indicated on the horizontal scale. Assuming that Spring finances 30 percent of its investments with debt and 70 percent with

FIGURE 14.1

Optimal Capital
Budget: Spring
Company

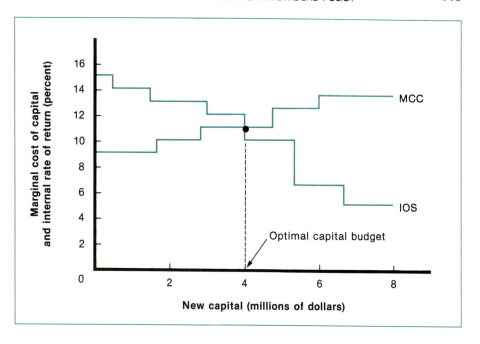

FIGURE 14.1

Optimal Capital Budget: Spring Company

equity, it must use $1.2 million of debt (30% × $4 million) and $2.8 million of equity (70% × $4 million) to finance the projects. If the firm generates $3 million of net income, a residual of $.2 million ($3 million − $2.8 million) will be available to pay dividends after financing the projects.

This approach assumes that investors prefer firms to retain and invest earnings if the return earned by the firm exceeds the return investors could earn on a cash dividend. The firm recognizes that its alternative to using retained earnings as a source of common equity is to sell new common stock. Since this is a more expensive source of equity, which will increase the firm's cost of capital, it may result in the adoption of fewer projects and lower profitability of the projects adopted.

A policy of paying dividends as a residual could result in large dividends during periods when earnings are high and investment opportunities poor, and small dividends during periods when earnings are low and investment opportunities are plentiful. As a result, the payment of dividends may be quite volatile over time.

Many rapidly growing companies pay no dividends at all since they need all of the capital they can raise to support their growth. The payment of no dividend may in many cases be classified as an application of a residual dividend policy where there is no residual.

## Stable but Growing Dividend per Share

The most popular dividend policy used by firms is to pay a **stable dividend per share** that is increased only when the firm becomes convinced that a higher dividend can be maintained in the future. Additionally, dividends are not normally decreased unless it is clearly evident that the current dividend cannot be maintained in the future. In an effort to avoid decreasing

FIGURE 14.2
History of Dividends and Profits for U.S. Firms in the Aggregate

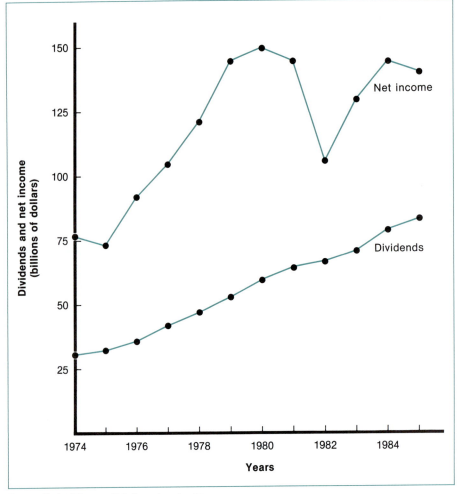

*Source: Federal Reserve Bulletin*, various issues.

their dividends during a year of low earnings, some firms elect to pay dividends that exceed their earnings per share.

Evidence of widespread use of a stable dividend policy is presented in Figure 14.2. This figure shows a graph of the aggregate after-tax profits and aggregate dividends of U.S. firms during the period 1974 through 1985. Most striking is the stability of the dividend line relative to the after-tax profit line. Although there have been some substantial declines in net income in some years, the level of dividends paid increased in all years. As a result, the dividend payout ratio has fluctuated substantially. The average ratio over this period was 42.8 percent, ranging from a low of 36.6 percent to a high of 62.8 percent.

Even more dramatic evidence of the effect of a policy of stable dividends on a firm's dividend payout ratio appears in Figure 14.3. Here, the earnings per share (EPS) and dividend per share (DPS) for Bell & Howell Company are displayed graphically for the period 1970 through 1986. The greater variability of EPS compared to DPS is clearly evident. Indeed, in several years, Bell & Howell's DPS exceeded its EPS, resulting in payout ratios

**FIGURE 14.3**

Earnings and Dividends per Share: Bell & Howell

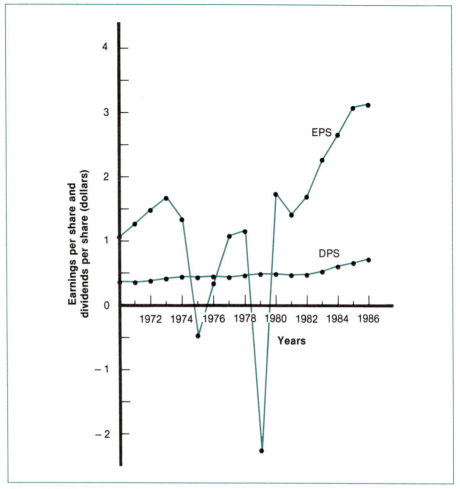

Source: *Value Line Investment Survey*, March 1987.

greater than 100 percent. However, Bell & Howell was able to avoid a decrease in DPS during these periods of temporary earnings decline.

There are several reasons why so many firms use a policy that involves stable dividends. First, many stockholders rely on dividends to provide a steady source of income to supplement their current consumption. If such investors are unable to rely on steady dividends from a firm, they are less likely to purchase the firm's stock.

Second, a policy of paying stable dividends is consistent with the requirements established by many states for being included on the states' legal listings. And being included on the legal listings can raise the demand for the shares of a firm's common stock.

## Constant Dividend Payout Ratio

Very few firms follow a policy of paying a dividend each period equal to a constant percent of earnings—a **constant dividend payout ratio.** Since the earnings of virtually all firms fluctuate, such a policy would result in equally volatile dividends. As indicated earlier, a policy resulting in volatile dividends would be unpopular with many investors.

Despite the impracticality of using a constant dividend payout ratio, most firms develop a target payout ratio. (For example, the 1986 annual report of Con Agra indicated that the firm's target dividend payout ratio is 30 to 35 percent.) A firm's actual dividend payout ratio may be higher or lower than the target in any given year, depending on corporate earnings and investment opportunities. Yet the long-run average should be near the target. A firm may revise its target ratio in response to changes in growth opportunities and other factors that can affect the need for retained earnings.

### Small, Regular Dividend plus Extras

A policy of paying a **small, regular dividend plus extras** (that is, an extra dividend may be paid at the end of the year based on the firm's performance), represents a compromise between paying a stable dividend per share and maintaining a constant dividend payout ratio. The small, regular dividend represents a stable dividend component that investors come to expect, while the extra dividend paid at the end of the year permits the firm to effectively increase the dividend for a year without the implicit need to continue that dividend in future years. During good earnings years, the total dividend paid may be large, and during poor earnings years, the total dividend may be small. As a result, the annual dividend may be quite volatile, with a base-level dividend established at a low level. General Motors is the most well-known firm electing to employ this dividend policy.

## DIVIDEND PAYMENT PROCEDURES

The board of directors of most firms meet quarterly or semiannually to review the firm's recent performance and determine the dividend to be paid based on that performance, expected future performance and anticipated needs. Although the board of directors actually makes the dividend decision, it considers the advice of senior management. In most firms, there is a tendency to pay the same dividend as in the prior period, unless there is overwhelming evidence that a change is justified.

The date on which the board of directors meets and decides on the size of the dividend is known as the **declaration date.** To be entitled to receive the dividend, an investor must be the **shareholder of record** on the **record date.** The board of directors establishes the record date, which may be a month or more after the declaration date. Four business days before the record date is the **ex-dividend date.** Investors must purchase the stock before this date in order to be the shareholder of record, because it takes five business days for stock transactions to be recorded on the firm's books. The **payment date** refers to the date when the firm mails the dividend checks to its shareholders. This is generally two to four weeks after the record date. Figure 14.4 presents a time line indicating the key dates in the payment of a regular quarterly dividend by a hypothetical corporation.

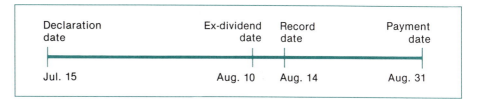

FIGURE 14.4
**Key Dates in the Payment of a Dividend by a Hypothetical Corporation**

## STOCK DIVIDENDS

**Stock dividends** (as opposed to cash dividends, which have been discussed thus far) are the payment of additional shares of common stock to the firm's existing shareholders. The amount of a stock dividend is normally stated as a percentage of the existing shares outstanding. For example, a 10 percent stock dividend means that the firm will increase its total shares outstanding by 10 percent, and every shareholder will be given one new share of stock for every ten shares currently owned.

From an accounting point of view, a stock dividend represents a transfer of amounts among the equity accounts, with no change in the overall level of owners' equity or in the asset and liability accounts. To illustrate, assume that E&W Industries expects to pay a 10 percent stock dividend. Also, assume that

- 1,000,000 shares of E&W common stock are currently outstanding
- par value of common stock is $4 per share
- paid-in capital is $10,000,000
- retained earnings is $15,000,000
- current stock price is $20 per share

The changes in equity accounts for E&W are indicated in Table 14.2. The 10 percent stock dividend calls for 100,000 new shares of common stock (10 percent of the 1,000,000 shares currently outstanding) to be issued to existing shareholders. In accounting for stock dividends, the pre-dividend market price of the stock is used as a basis for account transfers. Since 100,000 new shares are to be issued, and the pre-dividend market price is $20 per share, the balance sheet will reflect the movement of $2,000,000 between the equity accounts. This is accounted for on the balance sheet by

TABLE 14.2 **Impact of a Stock Dividend on Owners' Equity: E&W Enterprises**

|  | Before the Stock Dividend | After the Stock Dividend | Change Due to the Stock Dividend |
|---|---|---|---|
| Common stock ($4 par value, 1,000,000 shares)[a] | $ 4,000,000 | $ 4,400,000 | +$ 400,000 |
| Paid-in capital | 10,000,000 | 11,600,000 | +1,600,000 |
| Retained earnings | 15,000,000 | 13,000,000 | −2,000,000 |
| Total owners' equity | 29,000,000 | 29,000,000 | -0- |

[a]Shares increase to 1,100,000 after the stock dividend.

reducing retained earnings by $2,000,000, increasing the common stock account by the par value of the new shares issued (100,000 new shares × $4 per share or $400,000) and increasing paid-in capital by the difference between the change in the common stock account and the change in retained earnings ($1,600,000). The total value of owners' equity remains unchanged.

Essentially, a stock dividend increases the number of shares of stock outstanding but does not change the wealth of the shareholders, since total equity is unchanged, and each investor's proportionate ownership of the firm remains unchanged. Since no wealth has been created, the total value of each investor's common stock must also remain unchanged. Since each investor owns more shares of common stock, the market price of each share decreases. For example, an investor who owns 100 shares of E&W Enterprises common stock before the dividend owns stock worth $2,000 ($100 shares times $20 per share). After the stock dividend, the market value of the stock declines to $18.18 per share, other things being equal. This value is determined using Equation 14.1.

$$P_A = \frac{P_B}{1 + IS} \tag{14.1}$$

where $P_A$ = theoretical price of a stock after a stock dividend

$P_B$ = price of a stock before a stock dividend

$IS$ = percentage change in the number of shares of stock outstanding, in decimal form

For E&W Enterprises,

$$P_A = \frac{\$20}{1 + .10}$$

$$= \$18.18$$

Therefore the investor who owned 100 shares before the stock dividend will own 110 shares after the dividend valued at $18.18 each, for a total value of $1,999.80 (different from the $2,000 before the stock dividend only because of rounding).

If stock dividends have no effect on shareholder wealth, why do they exist? One reason is that paying a stock dividend while continuing to pay the same cash dividend per share effectively increases the cash dividend paid to stockholders. Therefore, this is a means of increasing the firm's cash dividend. A second reason is that a firm may wish to decrease the market value of its common stock to make it more attractive to more investors. Many firms feel that if the price per share of common stock is too high (above, say, $80 per share), or too low (below, say, $20 per share), some investors will not consider purchasing it. Stock dividends can be used to adjust the price downward. Firms continue to pay stock dividends for this reason despite the fact that there is little evidence to support the notion that an optimal price range for common stock exists.

**TABLE 14.3  Impact of a Stock Split on Owners' Equity: E&W Enterprises**

| | |
|---|---|
| *Before the split* | |
| Common stock ($4 par value, 1,000,000 shares) | $ 4,000,000 |
| Paid-in capital | 10,000,000 |
| Retained earnings | 15,000,000 |
| Total owners' equity | $29,000,000 |
| *After the split* | |
| Common stock ($2 par value, 2,000,000 shares) | $ 4,000,000 |
| Paid-in capital | 10,000,000 |
| Retained earnings | 15,000,000 |
| Total owners' equity | $29,000,000 |

## STOCK SPLITS

**Stock splits** are similar to stock dividends in that they affect the number of shares outstanding while not affecting the wealth of the stockholders. For example, a two-for-one stock split results in the issuance of one new share of stock for each outstanding share. The result is that stockholders have twice as many shares than before the split, and the value of each share is equal to half the pre-split value, other things being equal.

From an accounting standpoint, a stock split results in a proportionate decrease in par value and increase in the number of shares outstanding. For example, consider the effect on the equity accounts of E&W Enterprises if it implements a two-for-one stock split instead of paying a stock dividend. Table 14.3 indicates the necessary changes. Here, the total number of outstanding shares doubles to 2,000,000, and par value per share is reduced to $2. Thus, the value of the common stock account remains unchanged. Retained earnings and paid-in capital are also unaffected by the stock split.

Some firms split their stocks to obtain a market price they feel makes the stock more attractive to investors. Equation 14.1 (discussed earlier) can be used to determine the impact of stock splits on stock prices. Unlike stock dividends, stock splits are not normally used to increase the cash dividends per share.

## DIVIDEND REINVESTMENT PLANS

Many publicly traded firms offer **dividend reinvestment plans** (DRPs) to their stockholders. These plans enable stockholders to automatically purchase additional shares of the firm's common stock with the cash dividends they are entitled to receive. Although the stockholders receive additional shares of stock rather than cash, they must pay taxes on the amount of the dividend they were entitled to receive.

There are two types of dividend reinvestment plans. One type involves the use of a trustee selected by the firm, where the firm gives the trustee all dividends that are to be reinvested. These dividends (minus the trustee's fee and brokerage commissions) are used to purchase as much of the firm's stock on the open market as possible. The shares are then distributed to the shareholders on a pro rata basis. The main advantage of such a program is that stockholders can purchase stock automatically and at a low cost in terms of commissions (since the trustee purchases a large amount of stock at one time, the commissions are relatively low).

The other type of dividend reinvestment plan involves the firm issuing *new* shares of common stock to its stockholders through the automatic reinvestment of dividends. This has the advantage of generating new equity capital for the firm at regular intervals (whenever dividends are paid). It can also be an inexpensive method of issuing new common stock because of lower flotation costs. In many cases, this cost savings is reduced because some firms issue the stock at a discount from market value (frequently 5 percent). The stockholders benefit from both the discount and by avoiding brokerage commissions.

## STOCK REPURCHASES

As an alternative to paying cash dividends, some firms repurchase shares of their own common stock with funds that might otherwise be used to pay a larger cash dividend.[2] These stock repurchases are an alternative to paying dividends, because the stockholders benefit in a manner similar to receiving dividends. That is, by repurchasing shares of its own stock, the firm has fewer shares of stock outstanding. Assuming the firm's total earnings remain unaffected by the repurchase, earnings per share will rise, increasing the value of each share of the firm's common stock. This translates into capital gains for the stockholders, which can be taken at their own discretion. However, this advantage must be weighed against several disadvantages. First, stockholders may prefer the less risky alternative of receiving a cash dividend as opposed to waiting to take capital gains which are more uncertain. Second, the repurchase of a large number of shares can temporarily inflate the price of the firm's stock (other investors rushing to purchase shares to receive the benefits from the repurchase may also inflate the price). If the firm purchases much of the stock at a temporary inflated price, the wealth of the remaining shareholders could be adversely affected. Finally, it has been argued that unknowing shareholders who sell their stock to the company may be adversely affected since they do not participate in the resulting increased earnings per share of the firm. This has caused some ill will with stockholders in the past, some leading to lawsuits.

From the firm's perspective, stock repurchases offer several advantages. Since firms are reluctant to increase their dividends "temporarily," they can elect to repurchase stock using excess cash that would have been used to increase the dividend. Firms frequently have a need for additional shares of stock anyway to cover executive stock options and warrants that

---

2. There are other reasons why firms repurchase shares of their own common stock. For example, firms may repurchase their shares to adjust the capital structure or to help prevent hostile takeovers.

are exercised, and also to cover the conversion of convertible securities. Although new common stock can be used for these purposes, there is a limit to the amount of new common stock that can be sold before the shareholders must approve the issuance of more new shares.

The major disadvantages of stock repurchases to the firm involve the possible negative perceptions of such plans by the Internal Revenue Service (IRS) and the Securities and Exchange Commission (SEC). There is some danger that the IRS will view a particular program primarily as a means of helping stockholders avoid paying taxes on dividends. If so, firms could be subjected to the accumulated earnings tax mentioned earlier. Additionally, the SEC may suspect a firm of attempting to inflate the price of its stock through repurchases (price manipulation) in anticipation of future offerings of new stock. Both of these potential problems may be avoided if repurchases are structured properly.

Several common methods exist for firms to repurchase shares of their own stock. One method involves purchasing shares in the open market through a broker, in the same manner as an individual would purchase stock. A second method involves making a **tender offer** for shares of its stock. This involves making a public announcement that the firm will purchase a specified number of shares of its own stock at a specified price within a particular period of time (generally about two weeks). Stockholders can then "tender" (offer) their shares to the firm. If more shares are tendered than the firm wishes to purchase, it will purchase shares from investors on a pro rata basis. The third method of purchasing shares of its own stock involves purchasing a large block of stock on a negotiated basis from one shareholder. In doing so, the firm must demonstrate no favoritism in dealing with the shareholder. That is, the stock must be purchased at or very near its market price.

## SUMMARY

A firm's dividend policy reflects an important financing decision of the firm, since the amount of dividends paid affects the amount of earnings retained by the firm. A number of important factors affect a firm's dividend policy, some of which are shareholder-related, some firm-related, and some related to environmental factors.

The relevance of dividend policy continues to be debated in the finance literature. Those arguing that dividend policy is irrelevant suggest that, in the absence of flotation costs, commissions, and taxes, stockholders can generate their own dividends or offset cash dividends by selling or purchasing shares of stock. Those arguing that dividend policy is relevant suggest that investors prefer to receive cash dividends as opposed to capital gains because of the greater certainty associated with receiving the dividends. In addition, proponents of the relevance of dividends point out that, in the real world, flotation costs, commissions, and taxes do exist.

Two other theoretical issues concerning dividend policy are the informational content of dividends and the clientele effect. The informational content refers to the effect the announcement of an unexpectedly large or small dividend has on the price of a firm's stock. If the size of the dividend is unexpected, it may provide investors with new information about how management views the future earnings prospects of the firm. This can affect the price of the stock. The clientele effect suggests that a firm's dividend policy attracts investors who favor that policy.

The most common dividend policies include the residual dividend policy, a stable, but growing dividend per share, a constant dividend payout ratio, and a small, regular dividend plus extras. Although all of these policies are used in practice, a stable, but growing dividend per share is most popular.

Stock dividends and stock splits are similar in virtually every respect except for the method used to account for them on the firm's balance sheet. Essentially, both result in an increase in the number of shares of stock outstanding, both result in a proportionate decline in the market value of the stock, and neither affects shareholder wealth.

Stock repurchases conducted by firms are an alternative to paying cash dividends. When a firm repurchases shares of its own common stock, there is a tendency for the market price of the stock to increase, since each remaining investor owns a greater proportion of the total firm. Assuming the stock price rises, the gain realized by each stockholder can be viewed as a substitute for the dividend that could have been paid with the money used to repurchase the firm's stock.

## KEY TERMS

**Clientele effect** The tendency of investors to be attracted to firms that have a dividend policy they prefer.

**Constant dividend payout ratio** A dividend policy whereby the firm pays dividends equal to a fixed percentage of earnings.

**Declaration date** The date on which the dividend is declared by the firm.

**Dividend irrelevance theory** A theory suggesting that in the absence of transactions costs, flotation costs, and taxes, the dividend policy of a firm has no effect on the firm's value or the price of the firm's common stock.

**Dividend payout ratio** Ratio of dividends to net income.

**Dividend reinvestment plan** A program offered by some firms that permits shareholders to reinvest their dividends in additional shares of the firm's stock.

**Dividend relevance theory** A theory suggesting that the dividend policy of a firm affects the value of the firm because investors view the receipt of cash dividends as being less risky than waiting to benefit from a rising stock price that should result from retaining earnings.

**Ex-dividend date** Date prior to which an investor must purchase stock in order to receive the dividend.

**Informational content** Term referring to the fact that unexpected changes in firm dividends may contain information about management's expectations about future earnings.

**Record date** Investors who are listed as owners on the firm's records on this date are entitled to receive the dividend. The record date is four business days after the ex-dividend date.

**Residual dividend policy** A dividend policy specifying that dividends are to be paid from the earnings remaining after all needed funds have been used for the adoption of capital budgeting projects.

**Shareholder of record** Shareholders who are listed on the firm's books on a specified date are entitled to receive the dividend. These shareholders are called shareholders of record.

**Small, regular dividend plus extras** A dividend policy that permits firms to maintain a stable dividend yet retain the flexibility to distribute more dividends (as a bonus) to shareholders if money is available.

**Stable dividend per share** A dividend policy that attempts to maintain a constant dividend with periodic increases.

**Stock dividend** The payment of additional shares of stock by a firm to its shareholders.

**Stock repurchases** Purchases by a firm of a portion of its own common stock.

**Stock splits** When a company increases the number of shares of stock outstanding by some multiple (a two-for-one split turns each share of stock into two shares) by sending additional new shares to existing stockholders. A stock split is similar to a stock dividend except there is a greater percentage increase in the number of new shares outstanding, and it is accounted for differently on the balance sheet.

**Tender offers** A method of repurchasing stock whereby the firm announces its intention to purchase a specified number of shares of stock at a particular price. Investors can then tender (offer) their shares to the purchaser.

## EQUATIONS

**Equation 14.1**    **Theoretical Stock Price after a Stock Dividend or Stock Split**

$$P_A = \frac{P_B}{1 + IS}$$    **(p. 418)**

$P_B$ = price of a stock before a stock dividend or stock split

$IS$ = percentage change in the number of shares of stock outstanding, in decimal form

Equation 14.1 can be used to determine the theoretical impact on the market price of a share of stock when a firm increases the number of shares of stock outstanding through a stock dividend or stock split.

## QUESTIONS

**Q14-1.** For what reasons may some firms pay low or no dividends, even when they have funds available to pay high dividends?

**Q14-2.** Describe the argument made by Miller and Modigliani regarding why dividend policy may not be relevant to a firm.

**Q14-3.** If shareholders could create their own income stream at no cost (using the argument by Miller and Modigliani), what type of dividend policy would firms most likely use?

**Q14-4.** What is the clientele effect, and what implications does it have regarding a firm's dividend policy?

**Q14-5.** What characteristics affect shareholders' preferences for one dividend policy over another? How does each characteristic affect the preference?

**Q14-6.** What are the advantages of dividend reinvestment plans to firms and investors?

**Q14-7.** What characteristics of a firm affect its preference for one dividend policy over another? How does each characteristic affect the preference?

**Q14-8.** How can creditors affect a firm's dividend policy? Why do creditors prefer to place constraints on a firm's dividend policy?

**Q14-9.** Why do firms that target a stable dividend avoid boosting dividends when experiencing above-normal performance?

**Q14-10.** How is a stock repurchase similar and dissimilar to paying dividends?

**Q14-11.** Explain how a firm's repurchasing of its stock may affect its capital structure.

**Q14-12.** What is the impact of a stock dividend on (a) the overall level of owners' equity, (b) the firm's asset accounts, and (c) the firm's liabilities?

**Q14-13.** What is the impact of a stock split on (a) retained earnings and (b) paid-in capital?

**Q14-14.** Blatex Corporation has implemented a dividend reinvestment plan (DRP) so that shareholders can create the dividend stream that meets their individual desires. Blatex believes that this plan will satisfy shareholders as much as any other dividend policy offered by any other firm. Is there any reason why the Blatex DRP might not satisfy all shareholders as much as another firm's dividend policy? Explain.

**Q14-15.** Pick three corporations that you are interested in and look at their quarterly dividends and earnings for the last ten years. How would you describe these firms in terms of their dividend policies?

**Q14-16.** Rick Conaghan owns 60 percent of a Nemep Corporation stock. Nemep announces a stock dividend. Will Rick's fraction of ownership increase, decrease, or remain unaffected due to the stock dividend? Explain.

## SELF-TEST PROBLEMS

Solutions to self-test problems appear on p. S1.

**SP14-1.** Payton Company plans to use a residual dividend policy. It expects to need $2 million to finance investment opportunities and has generated $5 million of net income. It has determined that any new investments will be financed with 50 percent debt and 50 percent common equity. There are presently 8 million shares of Payton stock outstanding. How much will Payton Company pay as dividends on a per share basis?

**SP14-2.** Sellek Company has 2 million shares of common stock outstanding and retained earnings of $10 million. The par value of its common stock is $6 per share, the current market price is $10 per share, and paid-in capital is $20 million. Sellek plans to pay a 5 percent stock dividend. How would the following be affected: (a) par value, (b) paid-in capital, (c) retained earnings, (d) shareholder's equity, and (e) market price of the stock per share?

**SP14-3.** Sukey Company has 4 million shares of common stock outstanding with a par value of $10 per share and current market price of $20 per share. Paid-in capital is $30 million, while retained earnings is $12 million. Sukey plans to implement a two-for-one stock split. How would the following be affected: (a) number of outstanding shares, (b) par value per share, (c) par value of all shares, (d) paid-in capital, (e) retained earnings, (f) shareholder's equity, and (g) market price of the stock?

# PROBLEMS

**P14-1.** Wileman Company plans to spend $3 million to adopt capital budgeting projects. It recently generated $2 million of net income and expects to finance all projects with 40 percent debt and 60 percent common equity. There are presently 1 million shares of Wileman stock outstanding. If Wileman uses a residual dividend policy, what dividend per share will it pay?

Ruff Company has 1 million shares of common stock outstanding with par value of $8 per share and a market price of $16 per share. Retained earnings total $20 million, and paid-in capital is $15 million. If Ruff pays a 10 percent stock dividend, how would the following be affected: (a) par value, (b) paid-in capital, (c) retained earnings, (d) shareholder's equity, and (e) market price of the stock?

**P14-3.** Dickerson Company has 6 million shares of common stock outstanding with par value of $9 per share and market price of $14 per share. Paid-in capital is $20 million, and retained earnings are $13 million. Dickerson plans to implement a three-for-one stock split. How would the following be affected: (a) number of outstanding shares, (b) par value per share, (c) par value of all shares, (d) paid-in capital, (e) retained earnings, (f) shareholder's equity, and (g) market price of the common stock?

**P14-4.** Falcone Corporation presently pays dividends of $1.50 per share and has reported earnings of $4.50 per share. It is currently considering several alternative dividend policies that would result in paying dividends as indicated in the following table (forecasted EPS figures are also indicated). Each of the three dividend policies presented here is described in the text. Identify each policy by name.

| Year | Forecast EPS | Policy A | Policy B | Policy C |
|------|--------------|----------|----------|----------|
| 1 | $4.60 | $1.53 | $1.50 | $0.00 |
| 2 | 4.80 | 1.60 | 1.60 | 0.00 |
| 3 | 4.10 | 1.37 | 1.60 | 0.00 |
| 4 | 4.95 | 1.65 | 1.65 | 0.00 |

**P14-5.** Pinder Corporation recently generated net income of $7 million and expects to adopt $10 million of capital budgeting projects next year. What will Pinder's DPS be if it uses a residual dividend policy and has a target capital structure consisting of 60 percent debt and 40 percent common equity? Pinder currently has 6 million shares of common stock outstanding.

**P14-6.** Cattleback Corporation currently has 2,000,000 shares of stock outstanding with a par value of $3 per share and current market price of $10 per share. Paid-in capital is $12,000,000, and retained earnings are $13,000,000. How are each of these accounts affected if Cattleback Corporation offers a 5 percent stock dividend? How is the stock price affected?

**P14-7** Keystone Corporation has 500,000 shares of common stock outstanding with a par value of $6 per share. Paid-in capital is $7,000,000, and retained earnings are $6,000,000. How would these variables be affected if Keystone Corporation implements a one-for-five reverse stock split? How would the price of the stock be affected if it is currently $1.50 per share?

**P14-8.** Blazer Corporation plans to create a dividend reinvestment plan (DRP). It has projected its common stock dividends without a DRP to be $500,000 next year and $600,000 the following year. It has estimated DRP participation to be 10 percent of total dividends over the next two years. Determine the estimated additional equity for Blazer Corporation two years from now as a result of the DRP.

## REFERENCES

Arditti, Fred D., Haim Levy, and Marshall Sarnat. "Taxes Uncertainty and Optimal Dividend Policy." *Financial Management* 1 (Spring 1976): 46–52.

Asquith, Paul, and David W. Mullins, Jr. "The Impact of Initiating Dividend Payments on Shareholders' Wealth." *Journal of Business* 56 (January 1983): 77–96.

Baker, H. Kent, Gail E. Farrelly, and Richard B. Edelman. "A Survey of Management Views on Dividend Policy." *Financial Management* 14 (Autumn 1985): 78–84.

Baker, H. Kent, and Patricia L. Gallagher. "Management's View of Stock Splits." *Financial Management* 9 (Summer 1980): 73–7.

Bierman, Harold, Jr., and Jerome E. Hass. "Investment Cut-off Rates and Dividend Policy." *Financial Management* 12 (Winter 1983): 19–24.

Black, Fischer. "The Dividend Puzzle." *Journal of Portfolio Management* 2 (Winter 1976): 5–8.

Dann, Larry Y. "Common Stock Repurchases: An Analysis of Returns to Bondholders and Stockholders." *Journal of Financial Economics* 9 (June 1981): 113–38.

Dielman, Terry E., and Henry R. Oppenheimer. "An Examination of Investor Behavior During Periods of Large Dividend Changes." *Journal of Financial and Quantitative Analysis* 19 (June 1984): 7–216.

Fama, Eugene F. "The Empirical Relationships Between the Dividend and Investment Decisions of Firms." *American Economic Review* 64 (June 1974): 304–18.

Jalilvand, Abolhassan, and Robert S. Harris. "Corporate Behavior in Adjusting to Capital Structure and Dividend Targets: An Econometric Study." *Journal of Finance* 39 (March 1984): 127–46.

Litzenberger, Robert H., and Krishna Ramaswamy. "Dividends, Short Selling Restrictions, Tax Induced Investor Clienteles and Market Equilibrium." *Journal of Finance* 35 (May 1980): 469–82.

———. "The Effects of Dividends on Common Stock Prices: Tax Effects or Information Effects?" *Journal of Finance* 37 (May 1982): 429–44.

Masulis, Ronald W. "Stock Repurchases by Tender Offers: An Analysis of the Causes of Common Stock Price Changes." *Journal of Finance* 35 (May 1980): 305–19.

Miller, Merton H., and Franco Modigliani. "Dividend Policy, Growth, and the Valuation of Shares." *Journal of Business* 34 (October 1961): 411–33.

# PART 6

# SOURCES OF LONG-TERM FINANCING

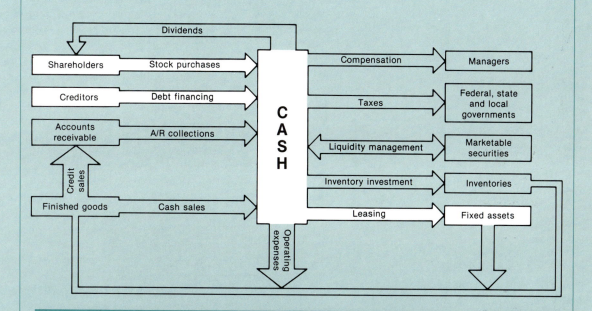

Even after a firm has decided to raise long-term funds through the sale of new bonds, preferred stock, or common equity, many related decisions must still be made before the financial transactions are completed. These include decisions about the nature of the issuing process, the potential target group that may purchase the securities issued, the specific characteristics of the securities issued, and so on. Chapter 15 describes how these factors relate to long-term debt, while Chapter 16 discusses how they relate to both preferred stock and common equity. Chapter 17 explains the role of financial intermediaries in placing these securities. Chapter 18 describes leasing, which is an alternative to raising long-term funds for the acquisition of assets. Chapter 18 also considers term loans as a source of long-term funds. Chapter 19 describes unique features of particular sources of long-term funds.

# CHAPTER 15

# LONG-TERM DEBT

## LONG-TERM DEBT IN PERSPECTIVE

On June 18, 1987, the following debt securities were issued:

■ Commonwealth Edison Company issued $140 million of first mortgage bonds that mature in June 1994. The bonds are rated single-A by Standard & Poor's Corporation and were priced to yield investors 8.92 percent.

■ BP North America, Inc., issued $200 million of sinking fund debentures that mature in the year 2017. The bonds are rated double-A by Standard & Poor's Corporation and were priced to yield investors 9.772 percent.

■ Joy Technologies, Inc., issued senior subordinated debentures that mature in 1999. These bonds are rated single B-minus by Standard & Poor's Corporation and were priced to yield investors 13.85 percent.

*Source: Wall Street Journal, June 18, 1987, p. 49.*

■ Olin Corporation issued $125 million of subordinated notes that mature in 1997. The notes are rated triple B-minus by Standard & Poor's Corporation and were priced to yield investors 9.558 percent.

Although these bonds were issued on the same day, there is a substantial difference in the yields available to investors on these bonds and, therefore, substantial differences in the cost to the issuing firms. What factors resulted in the different yields? Which of these factors can the issuing organization influence or control? Should all firms issue bonds that minimize the firm's interest expense? What features can provide the firm with greater financing flexibility and less risk? This chapter provides information about bonds that can be used to address these questions.

It was demonstrated in Chapter 13 that debt provides firms with financial leverage, which increases the firm's expected return and risk. The expected return is higher because the financing cost associated with debt as a source of capital is lower than the cost of equity. This low cost results from (1) the relatively low return normally required by bondholders, since the risk of investing in bonds is less than the risk of investing in common stock, and (2) the fact that interest payments on debt are deductible for tax purposes whereas dividends on stock are not. The higher risk incurred by firms using financial leverage results from the fixed nature of the financing costs.

Financial managers must be familiar with the many different aspects of debt financing in order to achieve a low cost of debt. The higher the cost of debt, the higher the cost of capital will be. If the cost of capital is too high, it will reduce profit margins and thus the value of the firm's common stock, resulting in reduced shareholder wealth. Maintaining a low cost of debt will help to minimize the firm's cost of capital, which will increase profit margins and thus increase the value of the firm's common stock. The result is increased shareholder wealth.

Firms can acquire long-term debt either by selling bonds or by obtaining long-term loans (called *term loans*) from lending institutions. This chapter introduces bond terminology, describes different types of bonds, and discusses bond ratings and bond yield spreads. Later in the chapter, the key characteristics of term loans are described.

## BOND TERMINOLOGY

Bonds are long-term promisory notes. When issued by corporations (they are also issued by governments), they represent agreements between the issuing firms and the bondholders whereby the bondholders lend money to the firms for a specified period of time during which the firms pay the bondholders a stated rate of interest. At the end of the agreed upon loan period, the loan principal is repaid by the firms. It is useful to begin our discussion of bonds by defining some key terms and explaining some important concepts that are commonly referred to in discussing bonds.

### Note

The term *note* can have two different meanings. A loan note is a signed, legal document providing evidence of debt. Another type of note is a debt instrument identical to a bond except that it has an intermediate-term maturity at the time it is issued.

### Funded Debt

The term **funded debt** is a synonym for long-term debt. Therefore, both bonds and term loans are funded debt.

## Maturity Date, Par Value, and Coupon Rate

As indicated in Chapter 4, the maturity date is the date on which the firm ceases to pay interest on the bond and the bondholder is entitled to receive the bond's par value. The par value is the stated value of the bond as specified in the bond indenture. The par value of corporate bonds is typically $1,000. The coupon rate indicates the annual interest paid on a bond as a percentage of the bond's par value. When the coupon rate is multiplied by the bond's par value, the product is the dollar amount of interest paid on the bond annually.

## Indenture

A bond **indenture** is a legal document specifying the rights and obligations of both the issuing firm and the bondholders. As suggested by the length of the document (normally several hundred pages), it is comprehensive in nature. In fact, it is designed to address all matters relating to the bond issue (collateral, payment dates, default provisions, call provisions, and so forth).

## Trustee

Federal law requires that a **trustee** be appointed for each bond issue of substantial size. The function of the trustee is to represent the bondholders in all matters concerning the bond issue. This is necessary because there are hundreds or thousands of bondholders for many bond issues. An important duty of the trustee is to monitor the activities of the issuing firm to ensure compliance with the terms of the indenture. If the terms of the indenture are violated, the trustee initiates legal action against the firm and represents the bondholders in that action. Bank trust departments frequently perform the duties of trustee for bond issues in return for a fee.

## Protective Covenants

Bond indentures normally place restrictions on the issuing firm that are designed to protect the bondholders from being exposed to increasing risk during the life of the bond. These **protective covenants** frequently limit the amount of dividends and corporate officers' salaries the firm can pay. They may also specify the level of working capital that must be maintained and may restrict the amount of additional debt the firm can issue, in addition to other restrictions.

## Sinking Fund Provisions

Bond indentures frequently include a **sinking fund provision,** which requires the issuing firm to retire a certain amount of the bond issue each year. This provision ensures that at maturity, the firm will not have to repay the entire bond issue all at once. As a result, there is less risk that the firm will incur difficulty retiring the bond issue—an advantage to those bondholders whose bonds are not retired early since the risk that the firm will be unable to repay principal at maturity is reduced.

Specific sinking fund provisions can vary greatly from bond issue to bond issue. For example, a bond with twenty years until maturity could have a provision to retire 5 percent of the bond issue each year. Alternatively, it could have a requirement to retire 5 percent of the bond issue each year beginning in the fifth year, with the remaining 20 percent to be retired at maturity.

The actual mechanics of retirement are carried out by the trustee. Normally, there are provisions that permit the trustee to either purchase the necessary bonds in the open market or to call the bonds, whichever is the least expensive to the firm. Bond call provisions are the subject of the following section.

## Call Provisions

Most bonds issued in recent years have included indenture provisions that permit the issuing firm to require bondholders to sell their bonds back to the firm. This **call provision** normally requires firms to pay a price above par value when the bonds are called. The difference between a bond's par value and its call price is the **call premium.** Call premiums are frequently one year's interest, although they may differ substantially from that.

Some indentures provide for call premiums that decline as the bond approaches maturity. Other bonds have two different call prices: a lower call price that applies when bonds are called for the purpose of meeting sinking fund requirements and a higher call price that is used if the firm calls the bond for any other reason.

There are two principal uses of call provisions. First, if market interest rates decline after a bond issue has been sold, the issuing firm may find itself paying a higher rate of interest than the prevailing rate. Under these circumstances, the firm may find it worthwhile to sell a new issue of bonds having a lower interest rate and use the proceeds to call the old bonds with the higher interest rates (retire them). This procedure is referred to as a *bond refunding* and is discussed later in this chapter, and in the chapter appendix. The second principal use of the call provision is to retire bonds as required by a sinking fund provision.

Call provisions are normally viewed as disadvantageous to bondholders since they can disrupt investment plans and reduce investment returns. For example, assume an investor purchases a twenty-year bond with a 12 percent coupon and a call price of $1,100. Assume further that the investor purchases the bond at par value and intends to hold the bond until maturity. The investor, therefore, expects to receive $120 every year for twenty years. If interest rates decline five years later to the point that bonds of comparable risk yield an 8 percent return, the value of the bond rises to $1,346 (ignoring the impact the call provision might have on the market price of the bond). If the firm calls the bond for $1,100, the investor will lose $246 of his investment ($1,346 minus $1,100). Additionally, the investor will not be able to reinvest the $1,100 in a bond of comparable risk and still receive $120 in interest each year but instead will receive a total return of only 8 percent (the going rate) on the new investment. Due to this effect that call provisions can have on bondholders' returns, firms must pay higher rates of interest on bonds that are callable.

## BOND COLLATERAL

Bonds can be classified according to whether or not they are secured by collateral. Secured bonds can also be classified by the nature of the collateral used to secure the bond issue.

### Secured Bonds

Most secured bonds are backed by a mortgage on **real property** (land and buildings). A **first mortgage bond** is one that has first claim on the specified assets. If the bond issue is an **open-ended mortgage bond,** the firm can issue additional bonds in the future using the same assets as collateral and giving the same priority of claim against those assets.

If a bond is a **closed-ended mortgage bond,** the firm is prohibited from issuing additional bonds using the same assets as collateral, unless the new bonds are given a lower priority of claim against the assets. Bonds having junior claims on specified assets are called *second mortgage bonds, third mortgage bonds,* and so on, depending on the priority of the claim. *Limited open-ended mortgage* bonds permit a limited amount of additional bonds to be issued having the same priority of claims against the assets.

In some cases, specific property is not designated as collateral against a bond issue. Instead, a **blanket mortgage** is used, which means the bond issue is backed by all of the firm's real property.

Bonds can also be secured with a **chattel mortgage** which is a mortgage secured by **personal property,** defined as all property other than real property. For example, **collateral trust bonds** are a special type of chattel mortgage bond that is normally secured by the common stock and/or bonds issued by subsidiaries of the issuing firm. These securities are held as collateral by a trustee and are to be liquidated if the issuing firm defaults on the collateral trust bonds. Table 15.1 presents some examples of collateral

**TABLE 15.1   Examples of Collateral Trust Bonds and Equipment Trust Certificates**

| Issuing Company | Coupon | Maturity | Call Price for Sinking Fund[a] | Call Price for Other Purposes[a] |
|---|---|---|---|---|
| *Collateral trust bonds* | | | | |
| Citizens Utilities | 8⅞ | 2005 | 100.00 | 105.35 |
| Potomac Edison Company | 8⅜ | 2001 | 101.41 | 104.89 |
| Ryder Systems | 9¼ | 1998 | 100.00 | 105.36 |
| *Equipment trust certificates* | | | | |
| Pullman Leasing | 12¼ | 2000 | 100.00 | 105.45 |
| World Airways | 11¼ | 1994 | 100.00 | 102.25 |
| Seaboard Coast Line Railroad | 11⅜ | 1995 | 100.00 | Not callable |

[a]Call prices are stated as a percentage of par value.
*Source: Bond Guide* (New York: Standard & Poor's Corporation), September 1986.

trust bonds and equipment trust certificates. Like collateral trust bonds, **equipment trust certificates** are secured by personal property. In this case, the securing property is normally equipment belonging to the borrowing firm. Notice in Table 15.1 that for five of the six bonds, the call price for sinking fund purposes is equal to par value, while the call price for other purposes is above par value (one of the equipment trust certificates is not callable). The fact that all three of the equipment trust certificates listed in Table 15.1 were issued by transportation firms is not a coincidence. Transportation firms are by far the largest issuer of that type of security. Conversely, electric utility companies are major issuers of collateral trust bonds, although they do not dominate that type of security.

### Unsecured Bonds

Bonds that are not secured by specific property are called **debentures.** These bonds are backed only by the general credit of the issuing firm. They are normally issued either by large, financially sound firms, whose ability to service the debt is not in question, or by firms that own very few mortgagable assets, perhaps because of the nature of their business. For example, finance companies and department stores have relatively few fixed assets with which to secure mortgage bonds.

### Subordinated Debentures

Debentures that have claims against a firm's assets that are junior to the claims of both mortgage bonds and regular debentures are called **subordinated debentures.** Owners of subordinated debentures receive nothing until the claims of mortgage bondholders and regular debenture owners have been satisfied.

## SPECIAL TYPES OF BONDS AND BOND PROVISIONS

Some bonds differ from the norm because of special provisions or characteristics they possess. Some of those provisions and characteristics are discussed in this section.

### Income Bonds

A firm is not required to pay interest to the owners of **income bonds** unless it generates sufficient operating income to do so. In contrast, interest must be paid to the owners of regular bonds in the amount specified in the indenture, or the firm will be in default and can be forced into bankruptcy. Interest payments that have been omitted on income bonds, however, normally accumulate, and no common or preferred stock dividends can be paid until all accumulated interest on the income bonds has been paid.

Income bonds are usually created as a result of corporate reorganizations following bankruptcy when the owners of more senior securities (mortgage bonds and debentures) are asked to exchange those securities for income bonds. The purpose of such exchanges is to reduce the firm's fixed financing costs. Frequently, income bonds are convertible into shares of common stock, an enticement that may be necessary to obtain investor acceptance of the exchange since it results in higher risk to the bondholders.

## Low or Zero Coupon Bonds

In recent years, some firms have issued bonds having coupons substantially lower than the market rate of interest and, in many cases, bonds with zero coupons. Due to the low or zero coupon rates, the bonds sell at prices well below par value. These bonds are frequently referred to as *deep-discount bonds.*

Some investors view the low coupons and deep discounts as an advantage, since their return is normally close to (or equal to in the case of **zero coupon bonds**) the yield to maturity at the time of the purchase, even during periods of rising or falling interest rates. This may not be true of bonds selling at or near their par values, since in order to realize the yield to maturity promised by a bond, investors must reinvest all interest payments received at that same rate (the yield to maturity). When interest rates are declining, investors may be forced to reinvest the interest received at lower rates of interest, resulting in an actual return to investors that is below the original yield to maturity. With zero coupon bonds, there are no interest payments to reinvest, since all the return to the investor comes from the difference between the purchase price of the bond and the maturity value of the bond. Therefore, the yield to maturity at the time of purchase is the actual return to the investor, provided the issuing firm does not default on the bond.

With low-coupon bonds, only a small amount of the investor's total return comes from the reinvestment of interest. Therefore, the realized return is close to, if not equal to, the yield to maturity during periods of declining (or rising) interest rates.

Other investors do not like low or zero coupon bonds because of the way interest is taxed on them. The return realized by investors in zero coupon bonds, and most of the return realized by investors in low coupon bonds, is not received until the bond matures. However, investors actually earn that return over the entire period of ownership. Therefore, the Internal Revenue Service specifies that investors must recognize the amount of interest earned (accrued) each year, and pay taxes on it, even though the interest is not actually received each year. As a result, these bonds are purchased mainly for investment accounts that are exempt from paying taxes (such as pension funds).

To the issuing firm, these bonds have the advantage of requiring little or no cash outflow during their life. Additionally, the firm is permitted to deduct the amortized discount as interest expense for federal income tax purposes, even though it does not pay the interest until maturity. This adds to the firm's cash flow. Finally, the demand for low and zero coupon bonds has been great enough that firms can in most cases pay lower rates

**TABLE 15.2**   Examples of Zero Coupon Bonds and Notes

| Issuing Company | Note or Bond | Maturity | Sinking Fund | Call[a] Price | Market[a] Price 9/86 | Yield to Maturity |
|---|---|---|---|---|---|---|
| Allied Corporation | Bond | 2009 | No | 100 | 14½ | 8.60 |
| McDonald's Corporation | Note | 1994 | No | 100 | 55½ | 8.18 |
| Intel Overseas Corporation | Note | 1995 | No | 100 | 45⅞ | 8.15 |
| J. C. Penney Company | Note | 1992 | No | 100 | 60 | 8.36 |

[a]Both the call prices and market prices are stated as a percentage of par value.
*Source: Bond Guide* (New York: Standard & Poor's Corporation), September 1986.

of interest on them than on regular bonds. The major disadvantage to the firm is that at maturity it must pay an amount equal to both principal and all accrued interest on the bond (the discount), which can be substantial. Making such a large payment at one time can strain a firm's financial situation and is viewed by some investors as imposing additional risk on the firm and the bond issue.

Table 15.2 provides some examples of zero coupon bonds. Notice the variety of characteristics present. Some of the issues are bonds and some are technically notes (notes have shorter original maturities than bonds). Notice that none of the "zeros" require sinking fund contributions, and the call prices are all at par value. These are typical zero coupon bond provisions. The prices of the bonds listed in Table 15.2 range from a low of $145 for the bond that matures in the year 2009 to $600 for the bond that matures in 1992. The price of each bond will approach $1,000 (par value) as the maturity date gets closer.

## Eurobonds

The difference between the other bonds presented in this chapter and **Eurobonds** is that Eurobonds are marketed in a European country. Despite their foreign flavor, Eurobonds are sold for U.S. dollars and pay both interest and principal in dollars. There are three principal reasons why many U.S. firms have chosen to sell Eurobonds. First, the interest rates have generally been lower than the rates paid on bonds sold in the United States. For example, Weyerhaeuser Company estimates it saved one-half of one percentage point in interest by selling $60 million of Eurobonds instead of domestic bonds in 1983. A second advantage of Eurodollar bonds is that European countries generally require less disclosure of corporate information to investors. And finally, Eurobonds do not need to be registered with the U.S. Securities and Exchange Commission. This results in less expense and less delay in the sale of the bond issue.

The reason why dollar-denominated bonds have been well accepted by European investors relates to the historic stability of the U.S. dollar and the U.S. economy. The continued acceptance of U.S. securities in foreign markets will certainly be affected by the future stability (or instability) of the dollar and the U.S. economy. Some examples of Eurobonds are given in Table 15.3. Once again, both bonds and notes are listed in the table. Few Eurobond issues have sinking funds, and most are callable, as suggested by the table.

**TABLE 15.3** Examples of Eurobonds

| Issuing Company | Note or Bond | Coupon | Maturity | Sinking Fund | Call Price |
|---|---|---|---|---|---|
| Procter & Gamble | Note | 10.00 | 1995 | No | 1010.00 |
| Tenneco | Bond | 6.88 | 1995 | No | 1020.00 |
| United Technology Corporation | Note | 7.375 | 1993 | No | Not callable |
| American Brands | Note | 12.00 | 1995 | No | 1002.40 |
| AMR Corporation | Bond | 5.25 | 2001 | No | 1020.00 |

*Source: Moody's Bond Record* (New York: Moody's Investors' Service, Inc.), September 1986.

## Industrial Development Bonds

In order to attract new industry into an area, state and local governments have assisted firms in financing industrial plants. A government can do this by selling an issue of its own bonds on which the interest received by investors is exempt from federal income tax. This makes the **industrial development bonds (IDBs)** so attractive that the rate of interest paid on the bonds by the government is very low. The state or local government then constructs the plant to meet the design specifications of the incoming firm, and the incoming firm agrees to lease the plant for an amount that covers the interest and principal payments on the debt. Alternatively, the government can lend the funds directly to the firm based on a pledge by the firm to make loan payments to the government in sufficient amounts for them to service the debt. The net result in either case is that the firm has the use of the plant at a lower than normal cost (the cost paid by the government).

Since this financing arrangement represents local government favors to select businesses, and since it also reduces federal tax revenues (investors pay no federal income tax on the interest they earn), the federal government has limited the use of industrial development bonds in recent years. The 1986 tax law limited the size of IDB issues that qualify for tax exemption, and it restricted the types of projects that can be financed with the funds raised by issuance. More restrictions may be placed on IDBs in the future.

The main point about IDBs is that their use can be an inexpensive source of financing that is available to some businesses. The top half of Table 15.4 provides some examples of IDBs currently outstanding. Although some of these bonds would not qualify for tax exemption if issued today, they all retain their tax exemption because they were issued under prior tax law. Notice that some of the bonds are issued by cities and some by states.

## Pollution Control Bonds

Like industrial development bonds, **pollution control bonds** are issued by local governments and the interest received by investors is exempt from federal income tax. The proceeds from the sale of pollution control bonds are made available to industrial firms to help them finance the acquisition of equipment designed to protect the environment from pollution. The local community benefits from the cleaner environment, and the firm

**TABLE 15.4** Examples of Industrial Development and Pollution-Control Bonds

| State or Municipality | Coupon | Maturity | Amount Issued (Millions) | Lessee or Guarantor |
|---|---|---|---|---|
| *Industrial development bonds* | | | | |
| City of Colorado Springs | 8.00 | 8/1/2000 | $ 1.0 | NCR Corporation |
| City of Huntsville | 5.375 | 10/1/1998 | 86.6 | PPG Industries |
| State of Ohio | 9.75 | 10/1/2010 | 7.0 | Dow Chemical |
| City of Chicago | 11.25 | 10/1/2013 | 62.7 | Delta Airlines |
| *Pollution-control bonds* | | | | |
| City of Mobile | 5.875 | 6/1/2007 | $17.3 | Scott Paper Company |
| Beaver County (PA) | 11.00 | 8/1/2001 | 5.1 | Atlantic Richfield |
| St. Louis | 10.375 | 12/1/2002 | 1.8 | Avon Products |
| City of Saginaw | 5.75 | 6/1/2005 | 13.3 | General Motors |

*Source: Moody's Bond Record* (New York: Moody's Investors' Service, Inc.), September 1986.

benefits from the low-cost financing of pollution-control equipment. The bottom half of Table 15.4 provides some examples of pollution control bonds currently outstanding. Notice the variety of large companies that have benefited from this method of raising funds.

## Variable-Rate Bonds

Conventional bonds have a stated coupon rate that does not change during the life of the bond, but the highly volatile interest rates experienced during the 1970s inspired the development of variable-rate bonds. These bonds reduce the risk to the borrowing firm that interest rates will decline after funds have been borrowed on a long-term basis. Additionally, they reduce the risk to the lender that interest rates will rise after making a long-term loan. Conversely, they cause lenders to earn less interest when interest rates are falling, and borrowers to pay higher rates of interest when interest rates are rising. During periods when interest rates are high, the risks of borrowing funds using fixed-rate obligations can be very high since the firm may find itself forced to pay high rates of interest for long periods of time. Although these risks may be reduced by borrowing funds on a short-term basis and then rolling the loan over every year at the prevailing rate, this may not be an appropriate source of funds for financing fixed assets. (The matching of the maturities of sources of funds with the life of the assets being financed is discussed in Chapter 20.)

It is interesting to note that most variable-rate bonds have intermediate-term maturities (ten to fifteen years) when initially issued. Also, variable-rate bonds remain the exception in long-term financing. Table 15.5 provides some examples of variable-rate bonds. Notice that all of them listed here were issued by firms in the financial services industry. Banks are well equipped to issue variable-rate bonds because they can offset a rise in the interest rates they must pay by charging their customers higher rates. The specific terms of interest-rate adjustment are different for each bond listed in Table 15.5, although all of the adjustment formulas listed here refer to

**TABLE 15.5    Examples of Variable-Rate Bonds**

| Issuing Company | Maturity | Terms of Interest Rate Adjustment | Sinking Fund |
|---|---|---|---|
| Norstar Bancorp | 1997 | Determined quarterly as the sum of ⅛ of 1% plus the average London interbank offered quotes for a recent 3-month period. | No |
| Irving Bank Corporation | 2004 | Determined semiannually as 1% above the current interest yield of the 6-month U.S. T-bill rate, subject to a maximum (after 4/30/89, the maximum is ¾% above the T-bill rate). | Yes |
| E. F. Hutton | 1994 | Determined and paid quarterly at the rate of ³⁄₁₆ of 1% above the average London interbank offered quotes for a recent 3-month period. | No |
| RepublicBank Corporation | 2004 | Determined semiannually as 1% above the interest yield of the 6-month U.S. T-bill rate subject to a maximum. | Yes |

*Source: Moody's Bank & Finance Manual* (New York: Moody's Investors' Service, Inc.), Vols. 1 and 2, 1986.

either the average London interbank rate or the rate on six-month Treasury bills.

## Convertible Bonds

Bonds that contain a special provision permitting the owners to exchange them for a stated number of shares of the firm's common stock, at the discretion of the investors, are called **convertible bonds.** This exchange or conversion feature offers investors the potential for high returns if the price of the firm's common stock rises, since the bondholder can convert the bond into common stock and sell the shares. Because of this potential benefit, investors are willing to accept a lower rate of interest on convertible bonds than on straight bonds, which can help the firm generate financing at a lower cost. For example, it is estimated that Hospital Corporation of America saves $7.5 million in interest payments annually because it issued convertible bonds instead of regular bonds in 1983 when it raised $450 million. Several other convertible bonds are illustrated in Table 15.6. The "Shares per Bond" column indicates the number of shares of common stock into which each bond is convertible. The conversion price of a bond represents the price the bond investor would pay for each share of common stock if he or she purchased the bond at par value and then immediately converted the bond into common stock.

## Bonds with Warrants Attached

A **warrant** is an option to purchase a stated number of shares of common stock at a specified price (the exercise price) within a specified period of time (normally two years or more from the date they are issued). As the

**TABLE 15.6**   Examples of Convertible Bonds

| Issuing Company | Coupon | Maturity | Sinking Fund | Recent Call Price | Conver- sion Price | Shares per Bond[e] |
|---|---|---|---|---|---|---|
| Union Pacific[a] | 4.75 | 1999 | No | $1,000.00 | $14.29 | 69.98 |
| Bally Manufacturing[b] | 6.00 | 2006 | Yes | 1,086.60 | 32.68 | 30.60 |
| Southwestern Energy[c] | 8.50 | 2010 | Yes | 1,085.00 | 32.38 | 30.88 |
| USAIR Group[d] | 8.75 | 2009 | Yes | 1,061.20 | 34.48 | 20.00 |

[a]Convertible debenture
[b]Convertible subordinated debenture
[c]Convertible senior debenture
[d]Convertible senior subordinated debenture
[e]Each bond has a par value of $1,000.
*Source: Moody's Bond Record* (New York: Moody's Investors' Service, Inc.), September 1986.

price of the underlying common stock rises above the exercise price, the value of the warrants increases rapidly because of the increasing profit potential. Since warrants have this potential value, investors are willing to accept lower rates of interest on bonds when warrants are attached to them. The warrants are said to provide a "sweetener" to the bond issue. Investors who do not wish to exercise the warrants can sell them to other investors.

## BOND RATINGS

A number of companies analyze the probability of firms defaulting on the bonds they issue, assign quality ratings to the bonds based on that probability, and sell this information to investors to help them evaluate the riskiness of the bonds they may purchase. The two best-known firms that provide this information are Moody's Investors' Service and Standard and Poor's Corporation (S&P). Both firms provide ratings for a wide range of corporate and state and local government bonds. Table 15.7 presents a description of the bond ratings assigned by Moody's and S&P, listed in declining order of quality. Ratings are very important to companies issuing bonds, since higher quality ratings indicate lower risk to investors, which means lower required rates of return for investors and lower costs of debt to the issuing firms.

Most institutional investors are prohibited from owning bonds unless they are **investment-grade bonds,** which includes those assigned one of the four highest quality ratings. Since most bonds are purchased by institutions, this classification is very important to the firms issuing bonds. If a firm's bonds are below investment grade, or even at the lower end of the investment-grade class, many potential buyers will not even consider purchasing the bonds (since bond ratings change, bonds at the lower end of the investment-grade class have greater potential of being lowered to the speculative class). If there are few potential buyers of a particular bond issue, it may be difficult to market the bonds unless the issuing firm pays a high rate of interest. This increases the cost of debt for the firm.

**TABLE 15.7**  Bond Ratings and Classifications

| Bond Classification | Ratings | | Description of Ratings[a] |
| --- | --- | --- | --- |
| | **Moody's** | **S&P** | |
| Investment grade | Aaa | AAA | Highest ratings. Very low risk of default. |
| | Aa | AA | High quality but not quite as strong as bonds possessing the highest rating. |
| | A | A | Good quality but susceptible to adverse economic conditions. |
| | Baa | BB | Good quality but even more susceptible to adverse economic conditions than the next higher rating. |
| Speculative | Ba | BB | Interest and principal payments are only moderately safe in all economic conditions. |
| | B | B | There is little assurance of interest and principal payment over the long term. |
| Default | Caa | CCC | Low quality. Bonds are either in default or near default. |
| | Ca | CC | Highly speculative. Bonds are in default. |
| | | C | Income bonds with interest not being paid. |
| | C | D | Extremely poor quality. Bonds are in default. Lowest rating. |

[a]Approximate definitions taken from *Bond Guide* (New York: Standard & Poor's Corporation), August 1986; and *Bond Record* (New York: Moody's Investors' Service), August 1986.

Although the companies that rate bonds do not reveal how the ratings are determined, it is known that both quantitative and qualitative factors are involved. Firms with the following characteristics tend to have bonds with the highest ratings: low financial leverage, high profitability, stable earnings, large size, and good coverage ratios. Not all bonds issued by a company have the same rating since the rating agencies consider the particular terms of each bond issue, the collateral backing the issue, and the priority of claims the bondholders have against the firm's assets.

It is important for financial managers to recognize the factors that affect bond ratings. Since a decline in the quality rating increases a firm's cost of debt and cost of capital, the financial manager must continually monitor the firm's performance in order to anticipate potential rating changes on existing or potential bond issues. If changes can be anticipated far enough in advance, corrective action may be taken to prevent a decline in rating.

## BOND YIELD SPREADS

The term *yield spread* refers to the difference in the return to investors from different bonds. Such differences can exist for any number of reasons: different maturities, different coupon rates, different taxing of distributions, and different investment quality.

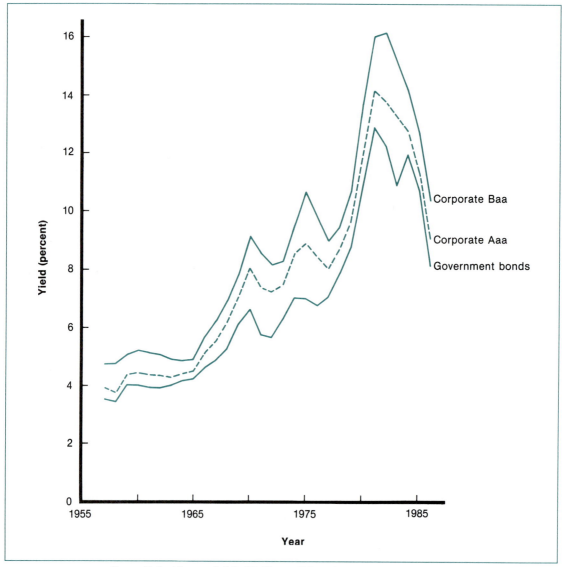

*Source: Federal Reserve Bulletin* (Washington, D.C., various issues).

**FIGURE 15.1**
**Yields on Bonds of Varying Quality**

Figure 15.1 illustrates the yields on bonds that result from differences in quality ratings. The yield spreads can be measured as the vertical distance between the bond yields indicated in the figure. Notice that the yields on all four quality groups move essentially in tandem. Despite this apparent correlation of yields, the yield spreads do change over time, suggesting that at certain times investors demand a higher (or lower) risk premium on high-risk bonds relative to low-risk bonds. Among the numerous possible reasons for such changes, certainly one important reason is that during periods of economic recession investors are less willing to hold high-risk securities due to the perceived higher probability of default. As a result, many investors sell their higher-risk securities, which tends to reduce the prices of those securities and increase their yields. If the proceeds are reinvested in higher-quality bonds, the prices of those bonds tend to rise, decreasing their yields. This combination of actions tends to increase the yield spread.

## CONSIDERATION OF DEBT AS A SOURCE OF CAPITAL

Making the decision on the level of long-term debt to maintain in the capital structure involves evaluating trade-offs just like other financial decisions. These trade-offs are briefly summarized in the following lists of the advantages and disadvantages of using long-term debt.

*Advantages:*
1. Debt provides the firm with financial leverage that can help earnings per share (EPS) grow more rapidly.
2. Bondholders normally have no voting rights, so the stockholders retain full control of the firm.
3. The cost of debt is lower than the cost of other sources of capital due to the lower risk incurred by creditors (as opposed to equity owners) and because of the tax-deductible nature of interest payments.
4. Flotation costs are typically lower for raising debt funds than for raising external equity funds.

*Disadvantages:*
1. The financial leverage gained by using debt increases the volatility of EPS, a measure of risk.
2. The use of debt results in increased fixed financing costs that, if not paid, can lead to bankruptcy.
3. Restrictive covenants normally included in indentures tend to reduce the flexibility of the firm in terms of being able to raise new debt funds, alter working capital, pay dividends, and so forth.

## REFUNDING A BOND ISSUE

Following a decline in market rates of interest, many firms find it beneficial to call in their old high-interest long-term debt and replace it with new lower-interest long-term debt. As mentioned previously, this is called **bond refunding.** Deciding whether or not to refund a bond issue can be complex since numerous cash flows may be affected. However, by identifying all relevant after-tax cash flows, the decision can be handled in much the same manner as a capital budgeting decision. That is, the firm can determine the present value of the incremental decrease in cash outflows (annual interest payments) and compare this to the initial outlay (in present value terms). If the present value of the incremental decrease in cash outflows exceeds the initial outlay, the refunding should be conducted. However, if the firm is confident that interest rates will continue to decline in the future, it may wish to postpone the refunding to take advantage of even

## FINANCIAL MANAGEMENT IN PRACTICE

### DEFEASANCE AS A TOOL OF FINANCIAL MANAGEMENT

One method of eliminating old *low-coupon* bonds from a firm's balance sheet in order to improve the firm's leverage ratios is to repurchase the bonds with the proceeds from the sale of new shares of common stock (selling new bonds to replace old bonds does not eliminate bonds from the balance sheet). A major disadvantage of this method is that earnings may be diluted by the increase in the number of shares of common stock outstanding. Another disadvantage of this approach is that some bondholders may not be willing to sell their bonds back to the firm. Although the firm may be able to call the bonds in, it will probably not wish to do so since low-coupon bonds typically sell at a discount from par value.

An alternative method, called *defeasance*, permits the firm to discharge its obligation to the bondholders without repurchasing or calling the bonds. This is accomplished by substituting a trustee (for example, a bank) as the debtor. To do this, the firm gives the trustee a portfolio of risk-free securities, generally U.S. Treasury bonds. The interest earned on the Treasury bonds is used by the trustee to pay interest on

the firm's bonds, and when the Treasury bonds mature, the principal is used to retire the firm's bond issue, which generally has a similar maturity. This procedure is worthwhile only when the interest rate available on Treasury bonds is substantially higher than the interest rate on the company's bonds, a situation that prevailed for many companies during the mid 1980s.

In addition to permitting a firm to extinguish its debt, this procedure can also increase the firm's profits. Since the trustee is paying interest on the firm's debt, the firm does not incur the interest expense. Since the coupon rates on the Treasury bonds are higher than on the firm's bonds, the firm's bonds are effectively retired at a discount from their face value. That is, Treasury bonds with a par value of $5,000 may be able to retire the firm's bonds having a par value of $7,000. Although the firm must pay taxes on this gain, it may be able to postpone payment until the firm's bonds are actually retired. If a firm elects to repurchase its bonds to eliminate them from its balance sheet, it must recognize the gain immediately and pay tax on the gain in the current year.

lower interest rates in the future. The appendix to this chapter presents a detailed discussion of the refunding decision.

## TERM LOANS

**Term loans,** discussed in detail in Chapter 18, are mentioned here only for comparison to bonds as a source of long-term debt. Term loan maturities range from two to thirty years and are typically in the three-to-fifteen-year range. These loans are generally provided by banks and insurance companies, although other financial institutions also make term loans. Under term loan agreements, the borrowing firms promise to repay the loan principal and make interest payments according to an agreed upon payment schedule. Most term loans are amortized so that the loan payments are equal over the life of the loan and include both principal and interest. While term loans can be used to finance almost anything, they are most frequently used to finance a permanent increase in working capital or to finance the purchase of fixed assets.

Term loans have two principal advantages over the sale of bonds. First, the administrative and flotation costs associated with obtaining term loans are lower. The lower costs result from less need for formal documentation, no need for registering the loan with the Securities and Exchange Commission, and no need for marketing securities (bonds) to the public. A second advantage term loans have over bonds is the greater flexibility they provide firms if changes in the loan agreement are necessary. Altering the provisions of an existing bond issue can be substantially more difficult, since generally hundreds or even thousands of different lenders are affected.

Today, most term loans have variable interest rates making the firm's interest obligation fluctuate with other market rates of interest. Where fixed interest rates apply, the rates are comparable to those paid on bond issues. Term loans are generally reserved for borrowing relatively small amounts of money, since term loan lenders normally place limits on the size of the loans they make to any one firm. Also, the cost to the firm of floating a small bond issue tends to be higher than the cost of floating a large bond issue on a cost-per-dollar-raised. This can make the term loan alternative more attractive when small amounts are involved.

## SUMMARY

Two principal sources of long-term debt are available to firms: (1) the sale of bonds (the primary subject of this chapter), and (2) negotiation of term loans with banks or other institutions. Firms may also lease plant and equipment as an alternative to borrowing money to purchase these assets.

The terms and provisions of a bond issue are spelled out in the bond indenture. This legal document specifies the maturity date, par value, and coupon rate. It also identifies the trustee for the bond issue, describes any protective covenants that may apply, and indicates any special provisions that may be included in the bond issue, such as call provisions, sinking fund provisions, collateral requirements, and so forth.

Secured bonds are generally backed by mortgages on real property. These bond issues may be first mortgage bonds, second mortgage bonds, and so on. They can also be open-ended, closed-ended, or limited open-ended mortgage bonds. Bonds secured by personal property include collateral trust bonds and equipment trust certificates. Unsecured bonds are called debentures. Subordinated debentures are junior in their claims on the firm's income and assets to regular debentures.

Some firms issue special types of bonds or bonds with special provisions. Among these special bonds and bond provisions are income bonds, low or zero coupon bonds, Eurobonds, industrial development bonds, pollution-control bonds, variable-rate bonds, convertible bonds, and bonds with warrants attached.

Several different companies publish bond quality ratings designed to estimate the probability of bonds going into default. Bonds with high quality ratings are perceived as having low risk. Investors require lower rates of return on bonds with low risk than on bonds with high risk. The difference between the yield to maturities on different bonds is called the yield spread. While yield spreads can result from differences in the riskiness of bonds, they can also result from differences in such things as maturity, coupon rate, and tax status.

Bond refunding is the process of issuing new bonds in order to raise money to retire an older bond issue prior to its maturity. Normally, this operation is worthwhile only when market rates of interest decline substantially after the older bonds have been issued.

## KEY TERMS

**Blanket mortgage** A loan or bond issue secured by all of the firm's real property, rather than by specific assets.

**Bond refunding** The process of selling a new bond issue in order to raise money to retire an old bond issue.

**Call premium** The dollar amount in excess of par value that a firm must pay bondholders when it calls its bonds.

**Call provisions** Provisions found in many bond indentures that permit the issuing firm to repurchase its bonds at the firm's discretion. Firms generally must pay a premium above par value when they call their bonds.

**Chattel mortgage** A mortgage secured by personal property (property other than real property).

**Closed-ended mortgage bonds** Bonds secured by assets that cannot be used to secure any other loans having the same or higher priority of claim against those assets.

**Collateral trust bonds** Bonds normally secured by the common stock and/or bonds of the issuing firm's subsidiaries.

**Convertible bonds** Bonds that can be exchanged for a fixed number of shares of common stock at the discretion of the bondholders.

**Debentures** Unsecured bonds backed only by the general credit of the issuing firm.

**Equipment trust certificates** Bond-like securities that use equipment as collateral.

**Eurobonds** U.S. dollar–denominated bonds sold in a European country. Interest and principal are paid in U.S. dollars.

**First mortgage bonds** Bonds that have the first claim on specified corporate assets being used as collateral against the bond issue.

**Funded debt** Long-term debt.

**Income bonds** Bonds on which the issuing firm has no legal obligation to pay interest if it has no earnings. Conversely, if the firm does have earnings from which it can pay interest, it must do so.

**Indenture** Legal document specifying the rights and obligations of the firm issuing bonds and the investors purchasing the bonds.

**Industrial development bonds** Tax-exempt bonds issued by state and local governments, the funds from which are made available to businesses at a low cost in order to attract businesses into the community. Their use is restricted by law.

**Investment-grade bonds** Bonds assigned one of the four highest quality ratings. The bond investments of many institutional investors are limited to investment-grade bonds.

**Open-ended mortgage bonds** Bonds secured by collateral wherein that same collateral can be used to secure subsequent bond issues having the same priority of claim on those assets. When there is a *limit* on the amount of additional bonds that can be issued having the same priority of claim on the same assets, the bond is called a *limited open-ended mortgage bond*.

**Personal property** All property that is not real property (land and buildings) is personal property.

**Pollution control bonds** Tax-exempt bonds issued by local governments. The funds raised by these bond issues are made available to firms at a low cost so they can purchase pollution control equipment.

**Protective covenants** Provisions in a bond indenture that are designed to protect the bondholders. They normally prohibit the firm from taking actions that could increase the bondholder's exposure to risk.

**Real property** Real property is defined as land and buildings.

**Sinking fund provisions** Provisions requiring firms to retire a certain amount of a bond issue each year. The effect is to reduce the size of the bond issue as maturity approaches.

**Subordinated debentures** Unsecured bonds having claims against the firm's assets that are junior to those of mortgage bonds and regular debentures.

**Term loans** Loans from a bank, insurance company, or other financial institution that have an original maturity in excess of one year.

**Trustee** An individual or company whose function is to act on behalf of the owners of a particular bond issue. Specific duties include monitoring the firm's compliance with the indenture and taking action against the firm when indenture provisions are violated.

**Warrants** Options to purchase a stated number of shares of common stock at a fixed price. They are normally issued as an attachment to bonds in order to make the bond issue more attractive.

**Zero coupon bonds** Bonds that pay no periodic interest to bondholders. Investors purchase zero coupon bonds at a considerable discount from maturity value. Investors' returns are the difference between the price they pay for the bond and the amount they receive at maturity (the maturity value).

## QUESTIONS

**Q15-1.** What are the advantages of financing with term loans as opposed to bonds?

**Q15-2.** Explain the following sentence: "The indenture of the debenture provided for a call provision that can be used to satisfy the sinking fund requirement."

**Q15-3.** Describe the difference between open-ended, closed-ended, and limited open-ended mortgage bonds.

**Q15-4.** Rank the following bonds in declining order of their claim against the firm's earnings.

>Second mortgage bond
>Debenture
>Income bond
>Subordinated debenture
>First mortgage bond

**Q15-5.** What are the advantages and disadvantages to the firm of issuing the following types of bonds?

>Zero coupon bonds
>Eurobonds
>Convertible bonds
>Bonds with warrants

**Q15-6.** Will each of the following factors tend to increase, decrease, or have no effect on the rating of a bond, and why?

**a.** The firm sells some new preferred stock.
**b.** The firm's net income declines.
**c.** The firm sells some new bonds with a higher claim against the firm's assets.
**d.** The firm acquires some new equipment that increases its operating leverage.
**e.** The firm leases a new facility for twenty years.

**Q15-7.** If a firm elects to retire a bond issue prior to maturity, what are its alternatives, and under what circumstances would each alternative be used?

**Q15-8.** Ideally, what characteristics would most investors want a warrant to have?

## SELF-TEST PROBLEMS

Solutions to self-test problems appear on p. S1.

**SP15-1.** Rader Corporation bonds have a $1,000 par value, a 12½ percent coupon and twenty years until maturity. The bonds are callable in five years at $1,100, and pay interest semiannually. If they currently sell for $1,158, what is the yield to call on the bonds? (Hint: Substitute the call price for par value, and the number of years until the bond is callable for the number of years until maturity, and solve for the discount rate that equates the expected cash flows to the cost of the bond.)

**SP15-2.** Salazan Industries recently issued $5 million worth of bonds that mature in twenty years and have an 11¾ percent coupon. The issue has a sinking fund provision that requires the firm to retire 5 percent of the entire bond issue at the end of each year beginning with the fifth year. The balance is to be paid at maturity.

**a.** What dollar amount of principal (plus call premium) must be paid each year if the bonds are to be called at $1,100 each?
**b.** How much interest must the firm pay on its bonds in Year 1, 10, and 20?

**SP15-3.** What is the value of a twenty-year $1,000 par value zero coupon bond if you require a 10 percent return on the bond?

## PROBLEMS

**P15-1**  You can purchase a $1,000 par value zero coupon bond for $235 that matures in eighteen years. How much income must you declare on that bond each year?

**P15-2.** You purchase a bond for $900 that is convertible into twenty-nine and one-half shares of common stock. One year later the market price of the bond is $1,100, and the price of the common stock into which the bond is convertible is $38. If you want to liquidate your investment, should you convert to common stock first? (Ignore transactions' costs.)

**P15-3**  What is the value of a zero coupon bond that matures in fifteen years if you require a 12 percent return? The bond has a par value of $1,000.

**P15-4.** Tanner Corporation recently issued 10,000 bonds, each having a par value of $1,000. The bonds mature in fifteen years, have an 11 percent coupon, and pay interest semiannually. The indenture calls for sinking fund retirement of 6 percent of the total bond issue at the end of each year beginning with Year 5.

**a.** What dollar amount of bonds must be retired each year?
**b.** What dollar amount of interest must Tanner pay on the bonds in Years 10 and 15?

Utt Corporation bonds mature in fifteen years, have a 12.6 percent coupon (paid semiannually), and a par value of $1,000. The bonds are callable in just three more years at 110 percent of par value and currently sell for $819. What is the bond's yield to call? (Hint: Substitute the call price for the par value, and the number of years until the bond is callable for the number of years until maturity, then solve for the discount rate that equates the expected cash flows to the cost of the bond.)

**P15-6.** You purchased a bond issued by Walker Corporation that had seventeen warrants attached, each of which can be used to purchase one share of Walker Corporation's common stock for $23 per share. At the time you purchased the bond, it sold at par value ($1,000) and Walker's common stock sold for $15 per share. Two years later the bond sells for $1,050, the common stock sells for $40 per share, and the warrants sell for $16 each. If you need to raise at least $250, what alternatives do you have, and how much would each alternative provide you with?

**P15-7.** A zero coupon bond that matures in twelve years currently sells for $287.50. What is the yield to maturity on the bond? On how much income must you pay taxes each year?

**P15-8.** A $1,000 par value bond issued by UBC Corporation is convertible into thirteen shares of UBC common stock. The common stock has a market price of $62 per share and the bond $825. If you want to purchase UBC common stock, would it be cheaper to purchase the bond and convert it, or purchase the stock directly? Explain. (Ignore transactions' costs.)

**P15-9.** Hill Enterprises has $500,000 of bonds outstanding with a $1,000 par value and 12 percent coupon. The bonds mature in twenty years and have a sinking fund requirement to retire 5 percent of the bond issue at the end of each year beginning with Year 6, with the balance to be repaid at maturity.

**a.** What dollar amount of bonds must be retired in each year?
**b.** What dollar amount of interest must Hill pay on the bonds in Years 3, 9, and 18?

**P15-10.** Hogue Corporation bonds mature in ten years, have an 11.5 percent coupon and are callable at 110 percent of par value, but not for four more years. The bonds currently sell for $893 and have a par value of $1,000. What is the bonds' yield to call if interest is paid semiannually?

**P15-11.** Horton Enterprises is issuing 10 percent coupon bonds at par value ($1,000). Each bond also has twenty warrants attached, each good for the purchase of Horton common stock at $9 per share. Assume that after you purchase one bond, the price of the stock increases to $15 per share from its current price of $6 per share, the price of the bond (without the warrants) declines to $925, and the warrants sell for $7 each. If you need to raise at least $100, what alternatives do you have? How much would each alternative provide you with?

## REFERENCES

Agmon, T., A. R. Ofer, and A. Tamir. "Variable Rate Debt Instruments and Corporate Debt Policy." *Journal of Finance* 36 (March 1981): 113–26.

Ang, James S. "The Two Faces of Bond Refunding." *Journal of Finance* 30 (June 1975): 869–74.

Barrett, W. Brian, Andrea J. Henson, and Robert W. Kolb. "The Differential Effects of Sinking Funds on Bonds Risk Premia." *Journal of Financial Research* 9 (Winter 1986): 303–312.

Bierman, Harold, Jr., and Amir Barnea. "Expected Short-Term Interest Rates in Bond Refunding." *Financial Management* 3 (Spring 1974): 75–79.

Billingsley, Randall S., Robert D. Lamy, and G. Rodney Thompson. "Valuation of Primary Issue Convertible Bonds." *Journal of Financial Research* 9 (Fall 1986): 251–260.

Bodie, Zvi, and Robert A. Taggart, Jr. "Future Investment Opportunities and the Value of the Call Provision on a Bond." *Journal of Finance* 33 (September 1978): 1187–1200.

Brennan, Michael J., and Eduardo S. Schwartz. "Savings Bonds, Retractable Bonds and Callable Bonds." *Journal of Financial Economics* 5 (1977): 66–88.

Cordes, Joseph J., and Steven M. Sheffrin. "Estimating the Tax Advantage of Corporate Debt." *Journal of Finance* 38 (March 1983): 95–106.

Dyl, Edward A., and Michael D. Joehnk. "Refunding Tax Exempt Bonds." *Financial Management* 5 (Summer 1976): 59–66.

Ederington, Louis. "Negotiated versus Competitive Underwritings of Corporate Bonds." *Journal of Finance* 31 (March 1976): 17–26.

Fabozzi, Frank J., and Richard R. West. "Negotiated versus Competitive Underwriting of Public Utility Bonds: Just One More Time." *Journal of Financial and Quantitative Analysis* 16 (September 1981): 323–39.

Finnerty, John D. "Refunding Discounted Debt: A Clarifying Analysis." *Journal of Financial and Quantitative Analysis* 21 (March 1986): 95–106.

———. "Evaluating The Economics of Refunding High-Coupon Sinking-Fund Debt." *Financial Management* 12 (Spring 1983): 5–10.

Halford, Frank A. "Income Bonds." *Financial Analysts Journal* 20 (January–February 1964): 73–79.

Kalotay, A. J. "On the Advanced Refunding of Discounted Debt." *Financial Management* 7 (Summer 1978): 14–18.

———. "An Analysis of Original Issue Discount Bonds." *Financial Management* 13 (Autumn 1984): 29–38.

———. "On the Management of Sinking Funds." *Financial Management* 10 (Summer 1981): 34–40.

———. "Sinking Funds and the Realized Cost of Debt." *Financial Management* 11 (Spring 1982): 43–54.

———. "On the Structure and Valuation of Debt Refunding." *Financial Management* 11 (Spring 1982): 41–42.

King, Raymond. "Convertible Bond Valuation: An Empirical Test." *Journal of Financial Research* 9 (Spring 1986): 53–70.

Marshall, William J., and Jess B. Yawitz. "Optimal Terms of the Call Provision on a Corporate Bond." *Journal of Financial Research* 2 (Fall 1980): 203–11.

Marr, M. Wayne, and G. Rodney Thompson. "The Pricing of New Convertible Bond Issues." *Financial Management* 13 (Summer 1984): 31–37.

McConnel, John J., and Gary G. Schlarbaum. "Returns, Risks, and Pricing of Income Bonds, 1956–76." *Journal of Business* 54 (January 1981): 33–57.

McDaniel, William R. "Convertible Bonds in Perfect and Imperfect Markets." *Journal of Financial Research* 6 (Spring 1983): 51–66.

Nunn, Kenneth P., Jr., Joanne Hill, and Thomas Schneeweis. "Corporate Bond Price Data Sources and Return/Risk Measurement." *Journal of Financial and Quantitative Analysis* 21 (June 1986): 197–208.

Riener, Kenneth D. "Financial Structure Effects on Bond Refunding." *Financial Management* 9 (Summer 1980): 18–23.

Smith, Clifford W., Jr., and Jerold B. Warner. "On Financial Contracting: An Analysis of Bond Covenants." *Journal of Financial Economics* 7 (June 1979): 117–61.

Stevenson, Richard A. "Retirement of Non-Callable Preferred Stock." *Journal of Finance* 25 (December 1970): 1143–52.

Van Horne, James C. "Called Bonds: How Does the Investor Fare?" *Journal of Portfolio Management* 6 (Summer 1980): 58–61.

Yawitz, Jess B., and Kevin J. Maloney. "Evaluating the Decision to Issue Original Issue Discount Bonds: Term Structure and Tax Effects." *Financial Management* 12 (Winter 1983): 36–46.

# APPENDIX 15A

# BOND REFUNDING

Following a decline in market rates of interest, many firms find it beneficial to call in their old high-interest long-term debt and replace it with new lower-interest long-term debt. The steep decline in interest rates during 1985 and 1986 led to a flood of refinancings in those years. For example, Florida Power & Light Company had $125 million of 16 percent bonds outstanding in 1986 before refinancing with 9.87 percent bonds.

In order for a bond refunding to benefit the firm financially, the present value of the incremental decrease in cash outflows (annual interest payments) must exceed the initial outlay. Table 15A.1 presents the major factors that must be considered in determining the initial outlay and the present value of the incremental annual cash outflows. In determining the present value of cash flows involved in refinancing debt, the appropriate discount rate to use is the *after-tax cost of the new debt*. Unlike capital budgeting where the incremental cash flows are uncertain, in refunding problems the difference between the interest payments required on the old bonds and the interest payments required on the replacement bonds is known. In fact, the only risk to the firm is the risk of defaulting on the bonds. Since this risk is reflected in the after-tax cost of the firm's debt, that figure is the most appropriate one to use as the discount rate.

Table 15A.1 describes the steps to take in evaluating a potential refunding situation. It is suggested that the reader review these steps before reading the refunding example that follows.

## Refunding Example

Shamberger Enterprises currently has $100 million of 16 percent coupon bonds outstanding. Those bonds originally had a twenty-five-year maturity but only twenty years remain. Shamberger incurred $4 million in flotation costs when it issued those bonds, and the flotation costs are being amortized on a straight-line basis over the life of the bond. The bond is callable at 12 percent over par value. Shamberger feels it can issue new twenty-year bonds at par with a 9.1 percent coupon, but it would cost an additional $4 million in flotation costs. The old bond would not be retired

**TABLE 15A.1 Expected Changes in Cash Flow Resulting from a Refunding Operation**

| Initial Outlay Components |
| --- |

1. *Call premium:* This is the amount paid above par value to call the old bonds in. Since it is a tax-deductible expense, it must be multiplied by $1 - T$ to determine the after-tax call premium.

2. *Flotation cost of issuing new bonds:* Although this amount will be paid at the time the new issue is sold, the firm will benefit annually from a tax deduction on the amortized portion of the flotation costs. The net flotation cost is therefore the total flotation cost minus the present value of the annual tax savings resulting from amortizing the flotation costs. The annual tax savings is the tax rate times the annual flotation expense (flotation costs divided by years to maturity). To find the present value of the annual tax savings, $n$ = the life of the bonds, and $k$ = the after-tax cost of new debt.

3. *Tax savings from expensing the remaining flotation costs on the old bonds:* When an old bond issue is called, all unamortized flotation costs associated with that issue can be expensed immediately. The tax savings to be realized today is equal to the firm's tax rate times total unamortized flotation costs. If the firm were to retain the old bond issue, it would have received a tax savings from expensing those benefits in the future. Therefore, the present value of the future tax benefits that would have been realized from amortizing the flotation costs in future years must be subtracted from the savings that will be realized if the entire amount is expensed today. The appropriate discount rate to use is the after-tax cost of new debt. The result is the net after-tax savings from the old bonds' flotation costs.

4. *Overlapping interest:* A firm will normally issue the new bonds prior to calling in the old bonds. This helps reduce the risk of a quick rise in interest rates or the inability to sell the new issue. The interest on the old bonds during this time represents overlapping interest and can be found by multiplying the principal times the rate times the time. This amount must then be adjusted to reflect the tax-deductible nature of interest payments.

| Present Value of the Incremental Annual Cash Outflows |
| --- |

Comparison of annual after-tax bond interest: Subtract the annual after-tax interest on the new bonds from that of the old bonds. Find the present value of this annual amount over the life of the bonds, using the firm's after-tax cost of debt as the discount rate.

until one month after the new bond was issued, so for one month interest charges would be incurred on both bond issues. Assuming Shamberger's tax rate is 34 percent, should it refund the old bond issue? The following steps correspond to those described in Table 15A.1.

*Initial outlay components (in present-value terms):*

1. Call premium: Since the bonds are callable at 12 percent over par value, Shamberger must pay a call premium of

$$(\$100,000,000 \text{ par value})(.12) = \$12,000,000$$

After-tax call premium: Since the call premium is tax-deductible, the after-tax cost is

$$(1 - .34)(\$12,000,000) = \$7,920,000$$

**2.** Annual amortized flotation cost of the new bonds: Given that total flotation costs of $4 million must be amortized over a twenty-year period, the flotation expense realized each year is

$$\frac{\$4,000,000 \text{ flotation costs}}{20 \text{ years}} = \$200,000 \text{ per year}$$

Annual tax savings from the flotation costs: Since the flotation cost is tax deductible, it will result in an annual tax savings of

$$(\$200,000)(.34) = \$68,000 \text{ per year}$$

Present value of the tax savings: Given a $68,000 annual tax savings for twenty years, the present value can be determined using the after-tax cost of debt as the appropriate discount rate. The after-tax cost of debt is 6 percent, found as follows: $9.1\%(1 - T)$. Therefore, the present value interest factor of an annuity that follows reflects 6 percent and twenty years.

$$PVA = \$68,000 \ (11.470)$$

$$= \$779,960$$

Net flotation cost from issuing new bonds: This is the dollar cost of issuing the new bonds minus the tax savings realized by the annual tax deductions.

$$\text{net flotation cost} = \text{gross flotation cost} - \text{present value of the tax savings}$$

$$= \$4,000,000 - \$779,960$$

$$= \$3,220,040$$

**3.** Net tax savings on the old bond's flotation costs: The firm is permitted to expense the remaining flotation cost of the old bonds when it calls that issue in. This provides the firm with a tax savings that is partially offset by the present value of the annual tax savings that would be realized if the firm does not call the old bond issue in.

$$\text{annual flotation cost on the old bonds} = \frac{\$4,000,000}{25 \text{ years}}$$

$$= \frac{\$160,000}{\text{year}}$$

Tax savings today from expensing the remaining unamortized flotation cost on the old bond issue in the current year:

$$(20 \text{ years})(\$160,000)(.34) = \$1,088,000$$

Present value of the future tax benefits that would have been realized from amortizing the remaining flotation costs on the old bonds (if they are not called) in future years ($n = 20$, $k = 6\%$):

$$PVA = [(\$160,000)(.34)](11.470)$$
$$= \$623,968$$

Net after-tax savings on the old bonds' flotation costs:

$$\$1,088,000 - \$623,968 = \$464,032$$

**4.** The overlapping interest paid on the old debt for one month can be found as follows:

$$(\$100,000,000)(16\%)\left(\frac{1}{12}\right) = \$1,333,333$$

*Summary of initial outlay components:*

| | |
|---|---:|
| After-tax call premium | $ 7,920,000 |
| Plus: Net flotation costs, new bonds | 3,220,040 |
| Minus: Net tax saving on old bonds' flotation costs | (464,032) |
| Plus: Overlapping interest | 1,333,333 |
| Net initial outlay | $12,009,341 |

*Present value of the incremental annual cash outflows:*

**1.** Annual after-tax outflow (interest) on the new bonds:

$$\$100,000,000(.091)(1 - .34) = \$6,006,000$$

Annual after-tax outflow (interest) on the old bonds:

$$\$100,000,000(.16)(1 - .34) = \$10,560,000$$

Decreased annual after-tax outflow (interest):

$$\$10,560,000 - \$6,006,000 = \$4,554,000$$

Present value of the decreased annual after-tax outflow ($n = 20$, $k = 6\%$):

$$PVA = \$4,554,000 \, (11.470)$$
$$= \$52,234,380$$

**The Refunding Decision**   Since the benefit expected from the refunding operation ($52,234,380) exceeds the cost of the refunding ($12,009,341), the firm should proceed with the refunding. Notice that in this example, the remaining life of the old bond and the original life of the new bonds are equal. The problem was designed this way to simplify the solution. If the lives of the two bonds were different, a replacement-chain type of analysis similar to that used in capital budgeting (Chapter 10) might be necessary.

## SELF-TEST PROBLEMS (Appendix 15A)

Solutions to self-test problems appear on p. S1.

**SP15A-1.** T. Sale Corporation has a $75 million bond issue outstanding. The bond issue has a 14 percent coupon rate, and it matures in fifteen more years (it originally had a twenty-year maturity). The $3 million flotation cost that was incurred when the bond issue was originally sold is being amortized on a straight-line basis over the original twenty-year life of the bond. The bond is callable at a 14 percent premium above par value. T. Sale Corporation is considering a refunding operation that would involve replacing the existing bond issue with a new fifteen-year bond issue of the same size but having a 10 percent coupon. Issuing the new bond would involve an additional $3 million of flotation costs, and interest would overlap for one month. T. Sale Corporation is subject to a 30 percent tax rate.

**a.** What is the size of the after-tax call premium?
**b.** What are the net flotation costs expected from issuing the new bonds?
**c.** What is the net after-tax savings from the old bonds' flotation costs if the refunding takes place?
**d.** How much overlapping interest must be paid?
**e.** What is the net initial outlay?
**f.** What is the present value of the decreased annual after-tax cash flow?
**g.** Should T. Sale Corporation go through with the bond refunding?

## PROBLEMS (Appendix 15A)

**P15A-1.** Ten years ago Sherrerd Industries issued $80 million of thirty-year bonds with a 12 percent coupon. Since that time, market interest rates have declined to the point where a new issue of twenty-year bonds would carry only a 9 percent coupon today. The old bonds cost $2,000,000 to issue, and the cost is being amortized using the straight-line method. Sherrerd expects the flotation cost of issuing $80 million of bonds today to remain the same ($2,000,000). The firm is subject to a 34 percent tax rate.

**a.** What is the size of the after-tax call premium?
**b.** What is the net flotation cost expected from issuing the new bonds?
**c.** What is the net after-tax savings on the old bonds' flotation costs?
**d.** How much overlapping interest must be paid?
**e.** What is the net initial outlay?
**f.** What is the present value of the decreased annual after-tax cash flow?
**g.** Should Sherrerd Industries go through with the bond refunding?

**P15A-2.** Now that interest rates have declined, G. Meed Enterprises is considering refunding the $25 million 11.5 percent bond issue it had sold five years earlier. There are twenty years remaining until that bond issue matures. G. Meed feels it can replace that old issue with a new $25 million issue having a $9\frac{1}{4}$ percent coupon and maturing in twenty years. The underwriting cost to sell the new issue is expected to be $1 million, which is $250,000 less than it cost to issue the old bonds. G. Meed amortizes the cost of issuing bonds on a straight-line basis. If the firm is subject to a 34 percent tax rate, should it refund the old bond issue?

# CHAPTER 16

# COMMON STOCK AND PREFERRED STOCK FINANCING

## COMMON STOCK IN PERSPECTIVE

A 1987 study by the Securities and Exchange Commission (SEC) found that when companies announce their intention to issue dual classes of common stock with unequal voting rights, there is little immediate effect on the price of the firm's stock. However, once the dual issues have traded for a while, the stocks with the lower voting rights may trade 2 to 8 percent below stocks with higher voting rights. The study was conducted in response to the New York Stock Exchange's earlier proposal to permit firms to list their shares on that exchange, even if they have dual classes of common stock outstanding. The study concluded that dual-class common stock can be a useful tool for growing firms that want to raise equity capital without reducing the voting control of existing share-

holders. Further, the issuance of dual-class stock may not adversely affect shareholder wealth. However, the SEC warned that the stockholders of slow growing companies or those that are not characterized by substantial insider control may experience significant reductions in wealth as a result of the issuance of dual classes of common stock. The SEC took this study into account when it proposed preventing stock exchanges from listing the shares of companies that would reduce the voting rights of existing stockholders.

What are the rights and responsibilities of common stock ownership? What are the advantages and disadvantages to firms when they issue common stock? What special characteristics can firms give to common stock issues? The answers to these and other questions are addressed in this chapter.

*Source:* "Firm's Plans for Unequal Classes of Stock Hardly Affect the Price, SEC Study Finds," *Wall Street Journal,* June 26, 1987, p. 4.

Both *common stock* and *preferred stock* are **equity** sources of financing because they represent ownership of the firm. Therefore, any net income generated by the firm belongs to the owners of the common and preferred stock. Normally, some of these profits are paid out in the form of dividends, and some are retained within the firm to support its growth. Despite the fact that both common and preferred stock are equity sources of capital, there are some important differences between them, and these differences must be considered when deciding how to raise new equity capital. Factors such as the level and volatility of **earnings available to common stockholders (EAC)** and the risk of bankruptcy are affected by the mix of equity capital (although firms must use common equity as a source of funds, the use of preferred stock is optional).[1] Since these factors can affect the value of the firm's common stock, they can also affect the wealth of the owners of common stock. As emphasized before, anything that affects the maximization of shareholder wealth must be fully understood by management.

## CHARACTERISTICS OF COMMON STOCK

All corporations have common stock outstanding. A look at the balance sheet of a firm can provide some interesting information about its common stock. Table 16.1 illustrates the common equity accounts for Haltiner Industries. The first row (labeled "Common stock") indicates that the firm's common stockholders have authorized the sale of 20 million shares of common stock. Thus far, however, the firm has sold only 15 million shares at $1 par value per share. The total book value of the common stock account is therefore $15 million. Remember, though, that the total book value of a firm's common stock may differ substantially from the total market value of its common stock. Total market value can be determined by multiplying the number of shares of common stock outstanding by the market price per share. For example, if the common stock of Haltiner Industries currently sells for $25 per share, the total market value of Haltiner's common stock is $25 times 15 million shares, or $375,000,000.

The second line in Table 16.1, "Additional paid-in capital," indicates that when the common stock was originally sold, investors paid more than $1 per share for at least some of the shares. In fact, the firm has received a total of $60 million (the sum of the common stock and additional paid-in capital accounts) from the sale of its common stock. Of that amount, $15 million represents par value, and $45 million represents additional capital that was received by the firm. The firm may have sold common stock at different times and at different prices, but we cannot tell from the information presented what the breakdown was on the number of shares sold, at what time, and for how much.

The retained earnings account for Haltiner Industries (Table 16.1) currently has a value of $180 million. Every year the firm's board of directors must decide how much of the firm's EAC to pay out to common stock-

---

1. EAC is defined as net income minus dividends paid on preferred stock. For firms with no preferred stock outstanding, EAC is equal to net income.

TABLE 16.1   **Common Equity Accounts: Haltiner Industries**

| | |
|---|---:|
| Common stock (20 million shares authorized, 15 million shares outstanding, $1 par) | $ 15,000,000 |
| Additional paid-in capital | 45,000,000 |
| Retained earnings | 180,000,000 |
| Total common stockholders' equity | $240,000,000 |

holders as a dividend and how much to retain within the firm. Even if the firm retains some or all of the firm's EAC, stockholders expect to benefit from it. By retaining earnings, the firm has more funds with which to purchase additional assets, which in turn can be used to generate even more profits and pay even higher dividends in future years.

## Rights of Common Stockholders

By virtue of their ownership of common stock, stockholders have a number of rights that are not available to other investors. Several key rights are discussed here.

**Voting Right**   Normally, only the owners of common stock are permitted to vote on certain key matters concerning the firm. Among those key matters are the election of the board of directors, authorization to issue new shares of common stock, approval of amendments to the corporate charter, adoption of by-laws, approval of merger proposals, etc. While this exercise of control is important to the stockholders of smaller firms, it is frequently unimportant to the stockholders of large firms because they are usually asked by management to transfer their right to vote to management. Many investors comply by assigning their vote to management through the use of a **proxy.** Many others simply fail to vote at all. As a result, management normally ends up with the majority of the votes and can elect its own candidates as directors.

If investors become dissatisfied with the firm's performance, they can compete with management in the solicitation of proxy votes in what is known as a **proxy fight.** If the dissident stockholders can gain enough votes, they can elect one or more directors who share their views. Since the firm's board of directors has the responsibility and authority to make strategic decisions for the firm, including the hiring and firing of corporate officers, key managers may be replaced. In this case, stockholders are truly exercising their control. Voting procedures are elaborated on later in this chapter.

**Right to Income**   The owners of common stock have a right to the firm's EAC. Since all creditors and owners of preferred stock must be compensated before the owners of common stock, the latter are said to have a **residual claim** on firm income. EAC can be distributed in two ways. All or part of it can be paid out in the form of cash dividends. Any remaining portion is then reinvested in the firm and appears on the balance sheet as an increase in retained earnings, which increases the level of firm assets, enabling the firm to increase future income and dividends. The expectation of higher future dividends should result in a more rapid rise in the market price of the firm's common stock. Therefore, stockholders normally benefit from both the payment of dividends and the retention of earnings.

**Preemptive Right**   The right (but not obligation) of existing stockholders to purchase all new shares of common stock being sold by firms is called the **preemptive right.** Many states require firms chartered in the state to include the preemptive right in their charters. In other states it is optional. The purpose of this right is to prevent existing stockholders from unwillingly losing their proportionate ownership of the firm. For example, assume you own 1,000 shares of a firm's total of 10,000 shares of common stock. If the firm decides to sell an additional 10,000 shares to other investors, your ownership would decline from 10 percent (1,000 shares/10,000 shares) to 5 percent (1,000 shares/20,000 shares) of the firm's common stock. Under the preemptive right, the firm must present you with the opportunity to purchase 10 percent of all new shares sold. If you purchase them, your proportionate ownership of the firm remains unchanged.

**Other Rights**   Among other rights of stockholders is the right to inspect the firm's books, although severe limitations are placed upon this right where it concerns minority stockholders since some information could be of value to the firm's competitors. In addition, investors with only a small investment in the firm could cause considerable disruption of the business environment if they were permitted to visit the firm on a whim to "check out the books."

Owners of common stock also have the right, in the event of bankruptcy, to receive the assets remaining after the claims of all other parties have been satisfied. Normally, however, there is little (if anything) remaining from a bankrupt firm after the claims of all creditors and preferred stockholders have been met.

Finally, stockholders have the right to transfer their ownership interest to other individuals or groups. Recall from Chapter 2 that the corporate form of business organization has an advantage over the other forms of business in the ease of transfer of ownership. A stockholder can transfer ownership by signing the back of the stock certificate and directing the firm's transfer agent (normally a bank) to transfer ownership to another individual or firm. Most ownership transfers are completed through stockbrokers who handle all dealings between the buyer, the seller, and the transfer agent. Table 16.2 summarizes the rights of common stockholders.

## Voting Procedures

As indicated earlier, the owners of common stock have the right to vote on certain key matters concerning the firm. Investors receive one vote for each share of common stock owned. Therefore, the more stock owned by an individual, the greater the influence that stockholder can have on the firm, other things being equal. Election of members of the firm's board of directors generally involves either majority voting or cumulative voting. The difference can be explained with an example. Consider a situation where there are two directors' positions to be filled and four candidates

TABLE 16.2   **Summary of the Rights of Common Stockholders**

| Rights | Comment |
|---|---|
| Voting right | One vote for each share owned. Vote on key matters: election of the board of directors, issuance of new shares of common stock, approval of amendments to the corporate charter, adoption of by-laws, etc. |
| Right to income | Residual claim on the firm's income after the claims of all creditors and preferred stockholders have been satisfied. |
| Preemptive right | The right of current stockholders to purchase shares of a new issue of the firm's stock in proportion to their existing ownership. The purpose is to prevent dilution of ownership. |
| Right to inspect the firm's books | The right of stockholders to information about the firm that will help them evaluate how good a job management is doing. This right is somewhat restricted, however, to avoid disruption of the firm's operations and to prevent competitive firms from gaining confidential information about the firm. |
| Right to assets if the firm is liquidated | Residual claim on the firm's assets in the event of firm liquidation. That is, after all the claims of creditors and preferred stockholders have been satisfied, common stockholders receive what remains. |
| Right to transfer ownership | The right of the stockholder to transfer ownership of common stock to another individual or organization at his or her discretion. |

running for those positions. You own 100 shares of stock, which entitle you to cast 100 votes for each position to be filled, or a total of 200 votes. Assume that you want to elect Candidates A and B, whereas the only other stockholder in the company, who owns 125 shares, wants to elect Candidates C and D. Under **majority voting,** you cannot cast more votes for a candidate than the number of shares you own. Therefore, you must divide your 200 votes between two different candidates so that Candidates A and B each receive 100 votes. However, the other stockholder can cast 125 votes for Candidate C and 125 votes for Candidate D, thus, electing both of her candidates.

Under **cumulative voting,** you can cast all 200 of your votes (100 shares times 2, for the two positions to be filled) for one candidate (say, Candidate A). Since two candidates are to be elected, the other stockholder would be unable to prevent the election of Candidate A as a director. That is, the other stockholder cannot give both Candidates C and D sufficient votes to exceed the 200 votes you can give to Candidate A. Cumulative voting is permitted by law in some states, and required in others. The purpose of cumulative voting is to give individual minority stockholders (those with less than 50 percent of the voting shares) or small groups of minority stockholders the ability to gain representation on the board of directors.

## Classes of Common Stock

Some firms choose to issue more than one class of common stock. When this happens, the different types of stock are generally designated as Class A, Class B, and so on. Firms can define each class of stock as they wish, al-

---

## FINANCIAL MANAGEMENT IN PRACTICE

### SPECIAL CLASSES OF STOCK

One thing that makes finance an interesting field is that, despite all the principles, conventions, and rules of thumb, there is always room for creativity. Such creativity is continually being demonstrated by the development of new types of securities designed to meet the special needs of investors and issuing firms alike. An excellent example is the 1984 issuance of General Motors' Class E common stock.

General Motors found itself faced with special circumstances calling for innovative financing when it acquired Electronic Data Systems (EDS) for $2.5 billion. In addition to needing money to finance the transaction, it also was concerned about the possibility of losing key EDS employees who feared the loss of autonomy of EDS. The solution was for General Motors

to purchase all common shares of EDS common stock, paying a combination of cash and shares of General Motors' Class E common stock (GME). Most GME shares went to EDS employees, although many additional shares have since been sold to the public. By purchasing part of the EDS shares with GME stock, the company reduced the amount of cash required for the acquisition, another advantage.

Additionally, General Motors stated its intention to account for EDS earnings separately and to pay 25 percent of the subsidiary's earnings out as dividends. Since the majority of the GME stockholders were EDS employees, this policy was designed as an incentive for them to remain with the firm and permitted them to carry on in their customary entrepreneurial style.

---

though the distinction normally centers around voting rights and the payment of dividends. Some firms designate Class A shares as being identical to Class B shares in all respects except Class A shares have no voting right. Other firms designate Class A shares as normal shares and Class B shares as shares on which no dividend is paid until the company becomes better established. In the latter case, the Class B shares are normally held by the firm's founders as a sacrifice to make the Class A shares more attractive to potential investors.

## KEY DECISIONS IN ISSUING COMMON STOCK

Most new businesses begin as proprietorships or partnerships because of the low cost and ease of organization. Those firms meeting with some success may subsequently decide to switch to the corporate form of business because of the advantages it offers (such as limited liability). Normally this involves some legal documentation and the issuing of common stock to the individuals who founded the firm. If the firm continues to grow, the need for additional equity funds may force the firm's owners to issue additional shares of common stock to friends and relatives on a limited basis. At this point, the firm is still a *closely held* corporation (the common stock is not widely distributed). If additional large amounts of external financing are needed to support rapid growth, the firm may eventually sell stock to outsiders to raise the necessary equity funds.

### Going Public

The term **going public** refers to the sale of part (or all) of the firm's common stock to the public, normally with the help of an investment banker. The decision to go public is not an easy one to make since it involves both advantages and disadvantages to the firm's owners. (These factors are discussed in Chapter 17.) Clearly, the decision to go public is an important one that affects the very nature of the firm. In some cases, firms that go public subsequently reverse themselves and *go private*. That is, a small group of employees and other interested parties repurchase all, or nearly all, of the firm's outstanding shares of common stock. There are a variety of reasons why firms go private. In recent years, numerous managements have taken their firms private with the objective of improving the firm, then reselling the firm's stock at a higher price.

### Raising Venture Capital

**Venture capital** refers to money invested in small, unproven firms where the risks and potential returns are particularly high. While this description may apply to many types of firms, today venture capital is normally invested in firms that are developing new high-technology products. In most instances, these firms have the management skills to develop, produce, and sell their products, but little money to support rapid growth. Venture capitalists (those providing venture capital) purchase large amounts of common stock in such firms as investments, hoping to earn large enough returns on a few good investments to more than offset the considerable losses that they may incur on investments that prove unprofitable.

Venture capitalists include units of investment banking firms, commercial banks, insurance companies, public corporations, private partnerships, and proprietorships. Firms willing to use venture capital as a source of equity financing must be willing to forfeit considerable control of the firm. However, venture capitalists seldom participate in the management of the firm, preferring to hold the stock only until the price has risen high enough to give them a satisfactory return.

## ISSUING STOCK THROUGH A RIGHTS OFFERING

The preemptive right was described earlier as the right of existing stockholders to purchase new shares of common stock in proportion to their current ownership. When a firm issues new shares of common stock subject to the preemptive right, it is done so through a **rights offering** whereby each stockholder is given one **right** for each share of stock owned. The stockholders are then permitted to redeem these rights for the purchase of one new share of common stock at a price below the stock's current market price. The firm announces the number of rights that must be redeemed in order to purchase each new share. As we will see, this number is based on the relationship between the number of pre-offering shares of common stock outstanding and the number of new shares to be issued. Rights have value because they permit investors to purchase stock at below market prices and because they are transferable; consequently, stockholders who do not wish to purchase additional stock can sell their rights to other investors.

## Mechanics of a Rights Offering

The best way to describe a rights offering is through the use of an example. Consider Johnson Enterprises, which currently has 5 million shares of common stock outstanding and had net income and earnings per share last year of $10 million and $2, respectively. The stock currently sells for $25 a share. Johnson wants to raise $25 million of additional common equity capital by selling new shares of common stock. To entice investors to purchase the new shares, it elects to sell them at $20 a share through a rights offering. Therefore, it must sell 1,250,000 new shares ($25 million divided by $20 per share). The price that the owner of the rights must pay to purchase a share of stock is called the **subscription price** or **exercise price.**

The number of rights an existing stockholder must redeem in order to purchase one new share at the discounted price can be determined by dividing the number of shares outstanding by the number of new shares to be issued:

$$N_r = \frac{N_o}{N_n} \tag{16.1}$$

where $N_r$ = number of rights (old shares) needed to purchase one new share of stock

$N_o$ = number of old shares outstanding

$N_n$ = number of new shares to be sold

For Johnson Enterprises, the number of rights necessary to purchase one new share of common stock through the rights offering is

$$N_r = \frac{5 \text{ million}}{1.25 \text{ million}}$$

$$= 4 \text{ shares}$$

Therefore, the owner of four rights can purchase one new share of common stock for $20.

When a firm announces a rights offering, it designates a **holder-of-record date.** Whoever owns the stock on that date receives the rights. Since an investor does not own stock until five business days after purchasing it, an investor who wants to own the stock on the holder-of-record date must purchase it five business days or more before that date. Four days before the holder-of-record date is called the **ex-rights** date because the stock sells without being accompanied by the rights. Prior to the ex-rights date, the stock is said to sell **rights-on.** Rights normally expire after a few months and a specific *expiration date* is declared by the firm. The period during which the rights can be exercised is called the *subscription period.*

## Effect of Rights Offering on Stock Price

Consider our previous example again. Before Johnson Enterprises issues the new common stock, the market value of the firm is $125 million (5 million shares of common stock outstanding times the market price per share of $25). Assume that the market value of the firm increases by $25 million as a result of the stock offering. This increase in market value is equal to the total of the new equity raised through the rights offering (in reality, the market value of the firm would go up even higher than that, although the exact increase is difficult to estimate). As a result, the market value of the firm increases to $150 million after the offering. Dividing the new market value of the firm by the total number of shares outstanding after the new common stock is issued (6,250,000), provides an estimate of the market value of the common stock after the new shares have been sold.

$$\frac{\$150,000,000}{6,250,000} = \$24 \text{ per share}$$

We can conclude that the market price of Johnson Enterprises' common stock will decline from $25 a share to $24 a share as a result of the rights offering. The actual price adjustment will take place at the time the stock begins selling ex-rights, since the ex-rights price will reflect the anticipated value of the stock after completion of the new issue. While the stock trades rights-on, the market value of the stock should remain at $25, other things being equal. Figure 16.1 illustrates the timing of key rights-offering dates and the effect of the rights offering on the price of Johnson Enterprises' common stock.

## Theoretical Value of Rights

After a stock begins selling ex-rights, the difference between the stock's price and the subscription price reflects the discount available to investors. Since it may require the ownership of several rights to purchase stock at a discount, in order to determine the theoretical value of one right, the

**FIGURE 16.1
Example of Key
Rights Offering
Dates: Johnson
Enterprises**

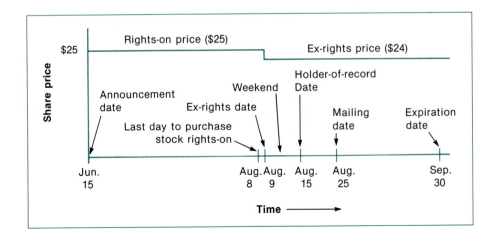

discount must be divided by the number of rights required to obtain the discount. That is,

$$V_r = \frac{P_e - S_p}{N_r} \qquad (16.2)$$

where $V_r$ = theoretical value of a right

$P_e$ = price of the stock, ex-rights

$S_p$ = subscription price of the stock

$N_r$ = number of rights needed to purchase one share of stock

For Johnson Enterprises,

$$V_r = \frac{P_e - S_p}{N_r}$$

$$= \frac{\$24 - \$20}{4}$$

$$= \$1$$

Therefore, one right has a theoretical value of $1. As the market price of the common stock changes, the value of the right also changes, because the size of the discount (the amount in the numerator of Equation 16.2) is affected. If the stock is actively traded, this value can change from minute to minute.

There are several reasons why the market value of a right may differ from its theoretical value. First, when investors sell their rights in the open market, the market price of the rights is determined by the supply and demand for those rights, which in turn is heavily influenced by investors' expectations about the future price of the common stock during the subscription period. This can result in the market value of rights being either above or below the theoretical value. A second reason why the market value of a right may differ from its theoretical value is that the transactions' costs necessary to buy and sell rights may be relatively large. This means that the buyer may be unwilling to pay the full theoretical value to purchase the rights.

During a short period after a firm has announced a rights offering but while the stock still sells rights-on, the calculation of theoretical value is somewhat different. Since the price of the stock reflects both the ex-rights value of the stock and the value of a right (the right has not begun to sell separately), the difference between the rights-on price and subscription price reflects the theoretical value of two rights. Therefore, this difference must be divided by the number of rights required to subscribe to a share of stock, plus 1.

$$V_r = \frac{P_r - S_p}{N_r + 1} \qquad (16.3)$$

where $P_r$ = price of the stock, rights-on

Applying Equation 16.3 to the rights offering of Johnson Enterprises yields

$$V_r = \frac{P_r - S_p}{N_r + 1}$$

$$= \frac{\$25 - \$20}{4 + 1}$$

$$= \$1$$

## Impact of Rights Offering on Current Stockholders

Theoretically, a rights offering will not affect the wealth of existing stockholders, provided they either exercise their rights or sell them. For example, an investor who owns 100 shares of Johnson Enterprises priced at $25 a share has $2,500 of wealth. If the investor subsequently receives 100 rights, she can purchase 25 additional shares at $20 a share. If she subscribes to the offering, she must invest an additional $500, after which she will own 125 shares, with a total market value of $3,000 (125 shares at $24 a share based on the ex-rights value). Since the investor began with $2,500 of stock and spent an additional $500 to purchase more stock, the $3,000 market value of the stock does not represent a change in the wealth of the stockholder.

If the investor does not purchase the new shares but sells the rights, she will receive $1 for each right (the theoretical value), for a total of $100. Since the market price of the stock declines to $24 a share, her total wealth remains unchanged at $2,500 ($100 received from selling the rights and $2,400 worth of stock). If however, the investor does not sell the rights or exercise them, she will lose money, since her 100 shares will be worth only $2,400 after the rights offering. This discussion is based on theoretical values, and transactions costs are ignored. In any given situation, the investor may realize either an increase or decrease in wealth.

## Cost of Issuing Stock through a Rights Offering

One might expect a rights offering to be an inexpensive method of selling new stock to the public because the firm is selling stock to current stockholders. This is not so (except in the case of closely held firms), since rights offerings do not eliminate the need for the assistance of an investment bank, which normally issues the rights, handles the administrative aspects of the issue, and in most cases, promises to purchase and resell all stock not subscribed. The greater the dispersion of stock ownership, the greater the cost of distribution because of the greater administrative burden. Also, the smaller the amount of money to be raised with an issue, the higher the flotation cost as a percent of new financing. This relationship exists because some of the flotation costs are fixed and thus are lower on a per share basis when spread over more shares being issued. Indeed, the flotation cost can exceed 7 percent of the money being raised when the issue is for less than $1 million.

### Undersubscriptions

Except in very unusual situations, rights offerings go undersubscribed, meaning not all of the rights are exercised and therefore not all of the stock is sold. The issuing firm can plan for this contingency by arranging for its investment banks to purchase all shares not sold. Another alternative is to include an undersubscription privilege, which permits current stockholders to purchase additional unsold shares at the subscription price. When this provision is in effect, the unsold shares are sold to interested stockholders on a pro rata basis.

## CHARACTERISTICS OF PREFERRED STOCK

Preferred stock differs from common stock in a number of ways including the order of claims on assets and income, and its cost to the firm. The major characteristics of preferred stock are discussed below.

### Prior Claim on Assets

When a firm is liquidated as a result of bankruptcy (or for any other reason), before common stockholders receive anything, the owners of preferred stock are repaid an amount approximating their initial investment. The amount of payment made to preferred stockholders is based on either the *par value* or the *liquidation value* of the preferred stock. One value or the other is stated when the preferred stock is initially issued. This value is frequently $25 or $100 a share. The liquidation value represents the maximum amount that investors will receive at liquidation. They may receive less because all creditors must be paid the principal and interest owed to them before preferred stockholders receive anything. What remains after the claims of all creditors and preferred stockholders have been satisfied belongs to the common stockholders.

### Prior Claim on Income

The dividend promised to the owners of preferred stock must be paid to them before any dividend can be paid to the owners of common stock. Conversely, all interest must be paid to creditors before the owners of preferred stock can receive a dividend. If the firm does not have sufficient earnings from which to pay the preferred stock dividends, it may omit the dividend without fear of being forced into bankruptcy by the owners of the preferred stock. That is, unlike creditors, who can force the liquidation of the firm in order to satisfy their claims, preferred stockholders technically share the ownership of the firm with common stockholders and are therefore compensated only when earnings have been generated. However, most preferred stock has a **cumulative dividend provision** that states that no dividends can be paid on common stock until all preferred stock dividends (both current and those previously omitted) have been paid.

The dividend paid to the owners of preferred stock is normally a fixed amount paid in quarterly increments. This amount can be stated as a *percent of par value*, or as a *dollar amount*. For example, Bissell, Inc., could issue a $9.50 preferred stock, or it could issue a $9\frac{1}{2}$ percent preferred stock with a par value of $100. In either case, investors would receive $9.50 in dividends each year for each share of Bissell's preferred stock they own.

## Risk and Cost of Preferred Stock to the Firm

Firms assume less risk when they issue preferred stock than when they issue bonds, since the payment of dividends on preferred stock can be omitted without the risk of being forced into bankruptcy. In addition, by issuing preferred stock, the firm may be in a better position to issue more bonds in the future, because preferred stock acts as a cushion for creditors in that money raised through the sale of preferred stock can be used by the firm to purchase assets that will generate income. Since creditors have a more senior claim on the firm's income and assets than stockholders, this income must be used to pay the creditors first. If a firm does issue preferred stock and then omits the payment of preferred stock dividends, it will generally be unable to raise new capital until the previously omitted dividends have been paid. Investors are reluctant to make new investments in a firm that is unable to compensate its existing sources of capital.

From a cost perspective, preferred stock is a more expensive source of capital than bonds. One reason for this is that investors normally incur more risk when they purchase preferred stock than when they purchase bonds (preferred stockholders' claims against a firm's income and assets are junior to those of bondholders), so in order to entice investors to assume the risk of investment in preferred stock, the firm must pay a relatively high dividend. A second reason why preferred stock is an expensive source of capital is that preferred stock dividends are technically compensation to owners of the firm. Consequently, the payment of preferred stock dividends is not a tax-deductible expense to the firm (whereas interest on bonds is tax-deductible).

Although the cost of preferred stock is higher than the cost of debt, it is lower than the cost of common equity. This is because common stockholders have the last claim (residual claim) on the firm's assets and income. For assuming this risk, common stockholders require higher rates of return.

## Risk and Return to Owners of Preferred Stock

As indicated previously, the risk of investing in preferred stock is greater than the risk of investing in bonds but less than the risk of investing in common stock. For this reason, the after-tax return on preferred stock tends to be higher than the after-tax return on bonds but lower than the after-tax return on common stock. Emphasis is given here to the *after-tax* return because of the unusual way preferred stock is taxed to corporate owners. Beginning in 1988, 80 percent of all dividends earned by corporations on preferred and common stock is exempt from federal income tax.[2] Since there is no such exemption on the *interest* earned by corporations, many companies with funds available for investment purchase preferred stock rather than bonds.

As a result of this attractive feature, the price of preferred stock is generally bid up fairly high, making the before-tax return relatively low. In fact, in recent years, the before-tax yields on high-grade preferred stocks have actually been lower than the before-tax yields on high-grade corporate bonds, despite the higher risk of preferred stock investments. Because this special tax feature is not available to individual investors, individuals generally receive higher after-tax returns and incur lower risk by investing in bonds rather than preferred stock.

## Special Preferred Stock Provisions

There are several other characteristics of preferred stock worthy of mention here, some common to most preferred stock issues and others less frequently found.

**1.** Nearly all preferred stock is subject to a **call provision,** which permits the issuing firm to retire the issue at its discretion. This provision means that although preferred stock is considered to be a permanent source of financing, many firms can easily retire their preferred stock by calling it in. The issuing firm is normally required to pay a premium above the preferred stock's par value in order to call it.

**2.** Preferred stockholders are not normally given *voting rights* unless the firm fails to pay preferred stock dividends for a designated number of quarters. When this happens, the preferred stockholders may be permitted to elect a minority of the members of the firm's board of directors. Unless the preferred stockholders are permitted to elect the majority of directors (which is rare), however, the voting right provides little benefit to preferred stockholders.

**3.** Less than half of all preferred stock sold in recent years has been *convertible* into common stock (convertible securities are discussed in Chapter 19). Since this option is a benefit to owners of preferred stock, investors must pay for the privilege by accepting a lower dividend on convertible preferred stock.

**4.** While it is very rare to see preferred stock with a *maturity date*, it is fairly common to have a **sinking fund provision.** This provision requires the firm to retire a certain proportion of its preferred stock at regular intervals. The net effect is to eliminate the entire preferred stock issue over time.

**5.** Occasionally an issue of preferred stock has a **participating feature.**

---

2. Until 1988, 85 percent of all corporate dividend income was exempt from federal income tax.

**TABLE 16.3** Examples of Adjustable Rate Preferred Stock

| Issuing Firm | Shares Outstanding | Terms of Dividend Adjustment | Recent Dividend Rate | Minimum and Maximum Dividend Rates |
|---|---|---|---|---|
| Chemical N.Y. Corporation | 4.0 million | Adjusted quarterly to be .5% plus the highest of the T-bill rate, 10-year T-bond rate, or the 20-year T-bond rate. | 8.60% | 7.50%–16.25% |
| Enserch Corporation | 1.5 million | Adjusted quarterly to be .1% below the highest of the 3-month T-bill rate, 10-year T-bond rate or 20-year T-bond rate. | 7.50% | 7.50%–15.50% |
| Citicorp | 3.9 million | Adjusted quarterly to be 4.125% less than the highest rate between the 3-month T-bill rate, 10-year T-bond, and the 20-year T-bond rate. | 6.00% | 6.00%–12.00% |
| Burlington Northern | 6.6 million | Adjusted quarterly to be .75% less than the highest rate between the T-bill rate, 10-year T-bond rate, and the 20-year T-bond rate. | 8.75% | 8.75%–12.50% |

*Source: Moody's Bank & Finance Manual*, vol 1; and *Moody's Transportation Manual* (New York: Moody's Investors' Services, Inc.), 1986.

This provides for the payment of monetary compensation to preferred stockholders in excess of the stated dividend. That is, the preferred stockholders "participate" in the good fortune (high profits) of the company. When this feature exists, the extent of the participation is clearly spelled out in a mathematical formula.

**6.** In response to the increased volatility of interest rates during the 1970s, a number of firms issued preferred stock with dividends that fluctuate with market rates of interest. This arrangement protects investors during periods of rising interest rates and also benefits the issuing firm during periods of declining interest rates. Banks have found *adjustable rate* preferred stock to be a particularly useful source of funds since it helps reduce their cost of funds during periods when the returns on their loan portfolios decline.

Table 16.3 provides some examples of adjustable rate preferred stock. Notice that the terms of dividend adjustment for each of the preferred stocks listed are based on the rates being paid on U.S. Treasury securities, and the dividends on all stocks listed in Table 16.3 are adjusted quarterly. The last column indicates a minimum and maximum dividend rate, indicating that although the dividends are flexible, the issuing firms are protected from paying extremely high dividends, and the preferred stockholders are protected from receiving extremely low dividends.

**TABLE 16.4  Examples of Preferred Stock with Various Characteristics**

| | (1) | (2) | (3) | (4) | (5) | (6) | (7) | (8) |
|---|---|---|---|---|---|---|---|---|
| | Issuing Firm | S&P Rating | Dividend Rate | Cumula- tive | Convert- ible | Voting Right | Sinking Fund | Callable |
| Allegheny International | | CCC | $11.25 | Yes | Yes | Yes | No | Yes |
| Allied Signal, Inc. | | BBB | $12.00 | Yes | Yes | No | Yes | Yes |
| Amerada Hess | | B | $3.50 | Yes | Yes | Yes | No | Yes |
| Kansas City Southern Indiana | | A | 4% | No | No | Yes | No | No |

Source: *Stock Guide* (New York: Standard and Poor's Corp.), September 1986.

Table 16.4 provides examples of preferred stock that have a number of the different features just described. Column 2 indicates the quality rating assigned to each preferred stock issue. These ratings are identical in interpretation to the bond ratings discussed in the prior chapter. Column 3 shows that most of the preferred stock listed here specifies the dividend in dollars, while one specifies the dividend as a percentage of par value. While most preferred stock listed here has a cumulative feature, the preferred stock issued by Kansas City Southern Indiana does not (Column 4). It is also the only preferred stock listed here that is not convertible (Column 5) and not callable (Column 8). Three of the issues have voting rights (Column 6), and just one has a sinking fund provision (Column 7).

## COMPARISON OF PREFERRED STOCK TO COMMON STOCK AND BONDS

As suggested in the previous discussion, some characteristics of preferred stock are very similar to those of common stock. For example, they both provide a protective cushion for the firm's creditors (all interest must be paid to creditors before dividends can be paid to the owners of common and preferred stock). Also, the owners of both common and preferred stock are unable to force the firm into bankruptcy for failure to pay dividends, since they are "owners" of the firm. Another similarity between common and preferred stock is that both pay dividends to their respective stockholders as opposed to interest, which is paid to creditors. A final similarity between common and preferred stock is that both are permanent sources of financing. That is, neither has a maturity date (there are some exceptions to this for preferred stock).

In addition to sharing some key characteristics with common stock, preferred stock also shares some characteristics with bonds. First, preferred stock provides financial leverage to the owners of common stock in a manner similar to that provided by bonds. Second, the owners of preferred stock typically do not have voting rights and thus lack control of the firm. Third, the owners of preferred stock normally do not participate in the profits of the firm beyond the stated fixed annual dividend. Instead, all profits above those needed to pay dividends on preferred stock belong to the owners of common stock. One might describe preferred stock as a cross between common stock and bonds.

## SUMMARY

Both common and preferred stock are sources of equity financing. All corporations have common stock outstanding, and most companies have additional paid-in capital and retained earnings, which also represent common equity financing.

The owners of common stock have numerous rights of ownership, including control of the firm through voting, a residual claim on income and assets, the right to purchase new shares of stock issued by the firm (pre-emptive right), the right to inspect the firm's books, and the right to sell their ownership of the firm.

Firms must decide whether to have more than one class of common stock and whether or not to sell the firm's common stock to the general public. When firms issue additional new shares of common stock, they normally do so through a rights offering. This procedure permits existing shareholders to purchase new shares at a price below the existing market price. If the stockholders elect not to purchase new shares, they can sell their rights to someone else.

Preferred stock is similar to common stock in that both are compensated by the payment of dividends, both have claims against the firm's income and assets that are junior to those of creditors, neither common nor preferred stockholders can force the firm into bankruptcy for nonpayment of dividends, and both are considered to be permanent sources of financing. On the other hand, preferred stock is similar to long-term debt in that both provide financial leverage to common stockholders, neither has voting power (normally), and neither participates in the profits of the firm beyond the stated interest or dividend payment.

## KEY TERMS

**Call provision** Nearly all preferred stock has this provision, which permits the issuer of the preferred stock to repurchase those shares, normally at a price above par value.

**Cumulative dividend provision** A provision frequently found in preferred stock requiring that any preferred stock dividends that were previously omitted must be paid before dividends can be paid on common stock.

**Cumulative voting** The maximum number of votes stockholders can cast for any one candidate is equal to the number of shares owned times the number of positions being filled on the board of directors. This system can give minority stockholders representation on the board of directors.

**Earnings available to common stockholders (EAC)** The net income remaining after payment of preferred stock dividends.

**Equity** An investment in a firm representing ownership. There are two general types: preferred stock and common equity.

**Ex-rights** A stock sells ex-rights if it is sold after the holder-of-record date. The purchaser of stock is not entitled to receive rights if he purchases the stock ex-rights.

**Going public** When a firm elects to sell its common stock to the general public as opposed to being owned by a small group of investors.

**Holder-of-record date** During a rights offering, the owner of the stock on the holder-of-record date will receive the rights.

**Majority voting** The maximum number of votes stockholders can cast for any one candidate is equal to the number of shares owned.

**Participating feature (on preferred stock)** Occasionally a firm will issue preferred stock that participates in the firm's net income beyond the minimum stated dividend amount.

**Preemptive right** The right of existing stockholders to purchase new shares of common stock being issued by the firm. Each stockholder is permitted (but not required) to purchase shares in proportion to their current ownership.

**Proxy** A written instrument by which stockholders can transfer their voting rights to other individuals or organizations.

**Proxy fight** When two or more parties compete with each other to obtain the voting rights of stockholders.

**Residual claim** The claim of common stockholders on all of the income and assets remaining after the claims of the creditors and preferred stockholders have been satisfied.

**Right** An intangible asset given to existing stockholders that permits them to purchase additional shares of common stock at a discount from the market price. Generally investors receive one right for each share of stock they own, and more than one right is usually required to purchase stock at a discount.

**Rights offering** The process whereby a firm sells new common stock to existing stockholders.

**Rights-on** A stock sells rights-on when the purchaser is entitled to receive rights that are to be subsequently issued.

**Sinking fund provision (preferred stock)** A provision requiring the issuing firm to retire a certain amount of preferred stock each year until the entire issue has been retired.

**Subscription price (exercise price)** The dollar price that investors must pay to purchase stock through a rights offering.

**Venture capital** Money invested in small, unproven firms where the potential returns and risk are high. Individuals and firms that make venture capital investments are called *venture capitalists*.

## EQUATIONS

**Equation 16.1**    **Number of Rights Needed to Purchase One New Share of Stock**

$$N_r = \frac{N_o}{N_n}$$

(p. 463)

where  $N_r$ = number of rights needed to purchase one new share of stock
$N_o$ = number of old shares outstanding
$N_n$ = number of new shares to be sold

In a rights offering the number of rights needed to purchase one new share of stock is based on the ratio of the number of old shares outstanding to the number of new shares to be sold. The firm must determine this value, issue the rights, and notify the existing stockholders how to purchase new shares.

**Equation 16.2**    **Theoretical Value of a Right Based on the Ex-Rights Price of the Stock**

$$V_r = \frac{P_e - S_p}{N_r}$$

(p. 465)

where  $V_r$ = theoretical value of a right
$P_e$ = price of the stock, ex-rights
$S_p$ = subscription price of the stock
$N_r$ = number of rights needed to purchase one share of stock

Equation 16.2 can be used to find the theoretical value of a right based on the ex-rights price of the stock. The theoretical value is the dollar discount available to the purchaser divided by the number of rights necessary to take advantage of the discount.

**Equation 16.3**    **Theoretical Value of a Right Based on the Rights-on Price of the Stock**

$$V_r = \frac{P_r - S_p}{N_r + 1}$$

**(p. 465)**

where $P_r$ = price of the stock, rights-on.

Equation 16.3 is similar to Equation 16.2 except it is based on the rights-on price of the stock. Both equations result in the same theoretical value of a right.

## QUESTIONS

**Q16-1.** Describe the difference between the following financial statement items: common stock, additional paid-in capital, retained earnings, net income, and earnings available to common stockholders.

**Q16-2.** Describe five rights of ownership available to common stockholders.

**Q16-3.** Discuss the differences between majority voting and cumulative voting.

**Q16-4.** When a firm has different classes of common stock, what are typically the differences?

**Q16-5.** What are the advantages and disadvantages to a firm of issuing preferred stock as opposed to common stock?

**Q16-6.** What is venture capital, and what types of firms normally provide it?

**Q16-7.** What is the effect on the wealth of a stockholder who receives rights if he (1) sells the rights, (2) exercises the rights, or (3) lets the rights expire? Explain each.

**Q16-8.** Is a rights offering a cheaper way to issue new common stock? Why?

**Q16-9.** Why does the theoretical value of a right often differ from the market value?

**Q16-10.** For what reasons is the cost of preferred stock lower than the cost of equity and higher than the cost of debt?

**Q16-11.** What characteristics of preferred stock are shared with common stock, and what characteristics are shared with bonds?

## SELF-TEST PROBLEMS

Solutions to self-test problems appear on p. S1.

**SP16-1.** Cherico Industries is planning to issue 2 million new shares of common stock at $11 a share through a rights offering. There are currently 6 million shares outstanding with a market price of $14 a share. Cherico earned $10 million last year.

**a.** How many rights must a stockholder own in order to purchase one new share of common stock at $11 a share?
**b.** Find the theoretical value of a right using the rights-on price.
**c.** What will be the value of the firm's common stock after the new stock offering? (Assume the value of the firm will increase by the amount of the new offering.)
**d.** Find the theoretical value of a right using the ex-rights price.

**SP16-2.** Thiele Enterprises has capital accounts as follows:

THIELE ENTERPRISES
CAPITAL ACCOUNTS
YEAR ENDED 1987

| | |
|---|---:|
| *Long-term debt* | |
|    Twenty-year 12% debentures due December 31, 2001 | $700,000 |
| *Stockholders' equity* | |
|    Preferred stock: 12,000 shares of 9% preferred ($25 par value) | 300,000 |
|    Common stock: 50,000 shares of $10 par value | 500,000 |
|    Additional paid-in capital | 100,000 |
|    Retained earnings | 400,000 |
|      Total equity | $1,300,000 |
|      Total capital | $2,000,000 |

**a.** What was the total amount paid to the firm for the purchase of the firm's common stock?
**b.** If Thiele Enterprises has net income of $130,000, what is its earnings available to common stockholders (EAC) and earnings per share (EPS)?

# PROBLEMS

**P16-1.** The common stock of Upton Industries currently sells for $50 a share. Upton had net income of $55 million last year and EPS of $4. It is planning to sell 3 million new shares of common stock at $45 a share through a rights offering.

**a.** How many rights must a stockholder own in order to purchase one new share of common stock?
**b.** Find the theoretical value of a right using the rights-on price.
**c.** What will be the value of Upton Industries' common stock after the new stock offering? (Assume the value of the firm will increase by the amount of the new offering.)
**d.** Find the theoretical value of a right using the ex-rights price.

**P16-2.** Olney Enterprises pays a common stock dividend equal to half its EAC. Olney expects to have earnings before interest and taxes next year of $450,000. Use the capital accounts that follow to answer Questions a and b about Olney Enterprises. Assume Olney has no short-term debt and has an average tax rate of 34 percent.

**a.** How much money will Olney pay out as dividends on preferred stock? What will be the amount of the common stock dividend?
**b.** If Olney wants to sell 10,000 new shares of common stock through a rights offering, how many rights would it take to purchase one new share?

## OLNEY ENTERPRISES
## CAPITAL ACCOUNTS
## YEAR ENDED DECEMBER 31, 1986

| | |
|---|---:|
| *Long-term debt* | |
| Fifteen-year 11% debentures due December 31, 1996 | $300,000 |
| *Stockholders' equity* | |
| Preferred stock: 10,000 shares of $2.25 preferred ($25 par value) | 250,000 |
| Common stock: 100,000 shares of $1 par value | 100,000 |
| Additional paid-in capital | 350,000 |
| Retained earnings | 400,000 |
| Total equity | $1,100,000 |
| Total capital | $1,400,000 |

**P16-3.** Ginger Corporation is planning to raise $100 million next year from common equity sources. The following information about Ginger Corporation can be used to answer Questions a through f.

- Sales for Ginger Corporation next year are estimated to be $300 million.
- There are currently 20 million shares of common stock outstanding.
- The market price of Ginger Corporation's common stock is $7 a share.
- The net profit margin is estimated to be 6 percent next year.
- Ginger expects to have a dividend payout ratio next year of 30 percent.

**a.** How much of the needed $100 million will be provided by retained earnings?
**b.** If Ginger specifies a subscription price of $6.25 per share, how many additional shares must it issue?
**c.** How many rights will it take to purchase one new share of common stock?
**d.** What is the theoretical value of a right based on the rights-on price?
**e.** What will be the value of Ginger's common stock after the new stock offering? (Assume the value of the firm will increase by the amount of the new offering.)
**f.** Find the theoretical value of a right using the ex-rights price.

**P16-4.** Curry Corporation expects to retain $5 million of its earnings next year and pay the remainder out as a dividend. It expects to have earnings before interest and taxes next year of $50 million. Assume an average tax rate of 34 percent. Curry's balance sheet appears as follows (it has no current liabilities):

## CURRY CORPORATION
## CAPITAL ACCOUNTS
## YEAR ENDED DECEMBER 31, 1987

| | |
|---|---:|
| *Long-term debt* | |
| 14% first mortgage bonds due June 30, 1990 | $50,000,000 |
| 13.25% debentures due February 15, 2005 | 40,000,000 |
| *Stockholders' equity* | |
| Preferred stock: 100,000 shares of 10.25% preferred ($100 par value) | 10,000,000 |
| Common stock: 10,000,000 shares at $4 par value | 40,000,000 |
| Additional paid-in capital | 23,816,000 |
| Retained earnings | 272,584,000 |
| Total equity | $346,400,000 |
| Total capital | $436,400,000 |

**a.** What will be Curry's earnings available to common stockholders?
**b.** What will be the dividend per share of common stock?
**c.** What will be Curry's earnings per share?

**d.** When Curry issued new common stock in the past, what was the average price that investors paid per share?

**P16-5.** BHI Industries expects to raise $630 million next year by selling new common stock. BHI currently has 30 million shares of stock outstanding selling at $48 a share and paying an annual dividend of $.50 a share. New stock will be issued at a 12.5 percent discount from the current price.

**a.** If BHI issues new shares of stock in a rights offering, how many rights must a stockholder own in order to purchase one new share of common stock?
**b.** Calculate the theoretical value of a right using the rights-on price.
**c.** What will be the value of the firm's common stock after the new offering? (Assume the value of the firm increases by the amount of money raised through the offering.)
**d.** Calculate the theoretical value of a right using the ex-rights price.

**P16-6.** Mann, Inc., has capital accounts as follows:

MANN, INC.
CAPITAL ACCOUNTS
YEAR ENDED 1987

*Long-term debt*
| 11% first mortgage bonds due July 15, 2006 | $40,000,000 |
|---|---|
| *Stockholders' equity* | |
| Preferred stock: 100,000 shares of $9.75 preferred ($100 par value) | 10,000,000 |
| Common stock: 10 million shares of $1 par value | 10,000,000 |
| Additional paid-in capital | 30,000,000 |
| Retained earnings | 110,000,000 |
| Total equity | $150,000,000 |
| Total capital | $200,000,000 |

**a.** If Mann, Inc., has earnings before interest and taxes of $4 million next year, what will be its net income, earnings available to common stockholders, and earnings per share? (Assume Mann has no short-term debt and has a 34 percent average tax rate.)
**b.** What average amount was paid by common stockholders in the past for the purchase of each share of Mann's common stock?

# REFERENCES

Bhagat, Sanjai, James A. Brickley, and Ronald C. Lease. "The Authorization of Additional Common Stock: An Empirical Investigation." *Financial Management* 15 (Autumn 1986): 45–53.

Bildersee, John S. "Some Aspects of the Performance of Non-Convertible Preferred Stocks." *Journal of Finance* 28 (December 1973): 1187–1202.

Elsaid, Hussein H. "The Function of Preferred Stock in the Corporate Financial Plan." *Financial Analysts Journal* 25 (July–August 1969): 112–17.

Fooladi, Iraj, and Gordon S. Roberts. "On Preferred Stock." *The Journal of Financial Research* IX (Winter 1986): 319–324.

Furst, Richard W. "Does Listing Increase the Market Price of Common Stocks?" *Journal of Business* 43 (April 1970): 174–80.

Ibbotson, R. R. "Price Performance of Common Stock New Issues." *Journal of Financial Economics* 2 (September 1975): 235–72.

Keane, S. M. "The Significance of Issue Price in Rights Issues." *Journal of Business Finance* 4 (September 1972): 40–45.

McDaniel, William R. "Sinking Fund Preferred Stock." *Financial Management* 13 (Spring 1984): 45–52.

Sanger, Gary C., and John J. McConnell. "Stock Exchange Listings, Firm Value, and Security Market Efficiency: The Impact of NASDAQ." *Journal of Financial and Quantitative Analysis* 21 (March 1986): 1–26.

Smith, David B. "A Framework for Analyzing Nonconvertible Preferred Stock Risk." *The Journal of Financial Research* 6 (Summer 1983): 127–40.

White, R. W., and P. A. Lusztig. "The Price Effects of Rights Offerings." *Journal of Financial and Quantitative Analysis* 15 (March 1980): 25–40.

Winger, Bernard J., Carl R. Chen, John D. Martin, J. William Petty, and Steven C. Hayden. "Adjustable Rate Preferred Stock." *Financial Management* 15 (Spring 1986): 48–57.

# CHAPTER 17

# RAISING FUNDS IN THE CAPITAL MARKETS

## RAISING FUNDS IN PERSPECTIVE

The October 12, 1987 issue of *Barron's* listed the securities of eighteen corporations as being probable corporate offerings for the coming week. Included in this list of securities were common stocks, notes, subordinated debentures, and zero coupon notes. The list included almost 63 million shares of common stock worth an estimated $1.5 billion and approximately $900 million worth of debt issues. Included in the list of firms issuing their securities were large well-known firms such as Bethlehem Steel Corporation and Wilson Sporting Goods Company. In addition, smaller less well-known firms such as ECRM Incorporated and Topps Company could also be found on the list.

The securities listed in *Barron's* were all being brought to the market with the assistance of investment banking firms, including such well-known firms as Salomon Brothers, Merrill Lynch, Drexel Burnham Lambert, Lazard Freres, Donaldson Lufkin & Jenrette, and Kidder Peabody. During the same week, many other securities were also being issued, but by private placement. That is, the securities were sold to a single investor or a small group of investors rather than to the public. Generally, private placements also involve the assistance of investment banking firms, although some do not.

Chapter 17 looks closely at the services provided by investment banking firms, considers the decisions that must be made by firms raising funds in the capital markets, and discusses the mechanics of issuing new securities.

This chapter identifies the various methods by which corporations can obtain long-term funds. After firms have determined which of the various alternative sources best fits their needs in order to minimize their cost of financing and maximize the wealth of their shareholders, they must enter the financial markets to raise the needed funds. Funds can be raised in either **money markets,** where short-term securities are sold, or **capital markets,** where long-term securities are sold. Because this chapter is concerned with long-term funds, it focuses on the capital markets.

## ROLE OF CAPITAL MARKETS

Individuals are, in the aggregate, the primary supplier of long-term funds to firms. They rarely provide funds directly to firms, however, because they typically lack knowledge about which firms need funds and are unable to assess the creditworthiness and potential equity returns of those firms.

Financial intermediaries channel the savings of many individuals to firms in need of funds. Individuals generally prefer short maturities and save relatively small amounts. Firms may need large amounts and for long periods. Financial intermediaries must therefore repackage the savings of individuals to create the types of loans and equity investments desired by firms. The performance of loans and equity investments is susceptible both to the economic environment and factors affecting the individual firm. As investment experts, these institutions are able to evaluate and manage the risks they incur.

## INSTITUTIONAL SOURCES OF FUNDS IN THE CAPITAL MARKETS

Many different financial institutions participate in the capital markets, including commercial banks, insurance companies, pension funds, and mutual funds.

### Commercial Banks

Commercial banks accept deposits in various sizes and maturities. They use a portion of the deposits to provide loans to firms. Before extending a loan, they must evaluate the creditworthiness of loan applicants. Their credit analysts obtain financial data on each applicant and attempt to determine the applicant's default risk. If the bank approves the loan, the credit evaluation will influence the rate of interest to be charged. When appropriate, the commercial bank may require the borrowing firm to pledge assets (collateral) to back the loan. In the event that the firm is unable to repay the loan, the bank has claim to those assets.

Beyond providing loans, banks also purchase corporate bonds. Again, a credit check of the company issuing the bonds is necessary. The purchase of the bonds is similar to providing a long-term commercial loan, except that bonds have standardized provisions whereas a bank loan can include provisions tailored to the bank's desires. Through both loans and purchases of corporate bonds, commercial banks play a major role in channeling funds from individuals (depositors) to corporations.

## Insurance Companies

Insurance companies provide insurance in the event of accidents, illness, or death. Some of the insurance premiums paid by individuals are needed to cover existing claims and expenses, and the remaining funds are invested until they are needed. Much of these funds are used to purchase corporate stocks and bonds. In this way, insurance companies act as a key supplier of funds to corporations.

## Pension Funds

Many corporations and government agencies participate in pension plans for the benefit of their employees. Periodic payments are made into pension funds by employees, the employer, or both. The funds are invested so that assets can accumulate until the time of the employees' retirement. Common investments include corporate stocks and bonds. Thus, pension funds effectively serve as financial intermediaries by channeling funds from corporate or government employees to other firms that issue stocks and bonds.

## Mutual Funds

Mutual funds also act as financial intermediaries between individuals and corporations. They sell shares to individuals and use the funds to purchase corporate stocks and/or bonds. While individuals could purchase stocks or bonds directly, purchasing mutual funds can be advantageous for several reasons. First, they often require just a small initial investment (such as $1,000 or $2,500). This allows individuals to obtain a diversified portfolio with just a minimal amount of funds. In addition, the composition of the portfolio is left to the responsibility of investment professionals (mutual fund managers). Because a variety of mutual funds are available, individuals can invest in a fund that best suits them.

The stocks and bonds managed by mutual funds indirectly belong to the individuals who purchased shares of the mutual funds. This differs from commercial banks, insurance companies, and pension funds, which assume the risk of ownership of the securities they purchase (with exception of trust accounts managed by commercial banks).

An overview of the four key institutional sources of funds in the capital markets is provided in Figure 17.1. While each institution performs different functions, all four institutions supply long-term funds to corporations.

## PRIMARY CAPITAL MARKETS

When firms need long-term funds, they often choose between issuing bonds or stock. This decision was discussed in other chapters. Once they make their decision, the new issues of bonds and/or stock are sold in the **primary capital markets.** These are markets where new security issues are first distributed to investors. The *primary market* is not a visible trading exchange or location, but instead represents a telecommunications network where new securities are sold.

Table 17.1 summarizes the volume of new stocks and bonds issued by firms in various industries from 1979 through 1986. The manufacturing and real estate/financial industries have dominated the new-issues market for both bonds and stocks. Figure 17.2 illustrates the value of new bond issues as a percentage of new capital market securities issued. In the early 1980s the ratio was relatively low, as corporations attempted to avoid issuing long-term bonds with high interest rates. By 1984 the ratio shifted significantly as interest rates decreased and corporations were more willing to lock in lower interest rates for long periods.

**FIGURE 17.1**
**Key Sources of Funds in the Capital Markets**

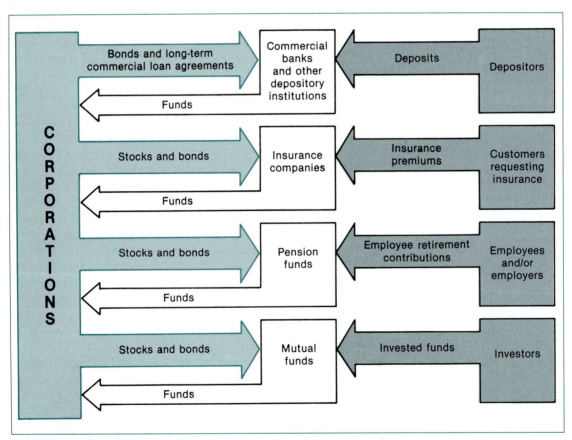

**TABLE 17.1**  Value of New Corporate Securities Issued by Firms in Various Industries (Millions of Dollars)

|  | 1979 | 1980 | 1981 | 1982 | 1983 | 1984 | 1985 | 1986 |
|---|---|---|---|---|---|---|---|---|
| *Bonds* | $40,211 | $53,205 | $44,642 | $54,076 | $68,493 | $109,683 | $166,236 | $313,228 |
| Industry group: | | | | | | | | |
| Manufacturing | 9,678 | 15,409 | 12,325 | 12,822 | 16,851 | 24,607 | 52,278 | 78,584 |
| Commercial and miscellaneous | 3,948 | 6,693 | 5,229 | 5,442 | 7,540 | 1,372 | 15,215 | 37,277 |
| Transportation | 3,119 | 3,329 | 2,054 | 1,491 | 3,833 | 4,694 | 5,743 | 9,734 |
| Public utility | 8,153 | 9,557 | 8,963 | 12,327 | 9,125 | 10,679 | 12,957 | 31,058 |
| Communication | 4,219 | 6,683 | 4,280 | 2,390 | 3,642 | 2,997 | 10,456 | 15,489 |
| Real estate and financial | 11,094 | 11,534 | 11,793 | 19,604 | 27,502 | 52,980 | 69,587 | 141,086 |
| *Stocks* | 11,325 | 20,489 | 25,349 | 30,562 | 51,579 | 22,628 | 35,515 | 61,830 |
| Industry group: | | | | | | | | |
| Manufacturing | 1,679 | 4,839 | 5,073 | 5,649 | 14,135 | 4,054 | 5,700 | 14,234 |
| Commercial and miscellaneous | 2,623 | 5,245 | 7,557 | 7,770 | 13,112 | 6,277 | 9,149 | 9,252 |
| Transportation | 255 | 549 | 779 | 709 | 2,729 | 589 | 1,544 | 2,392 |
| Public utility | 5,171 | 6,230 | 5,577 | 7,517 | 5,001 | 1,624 | 1,966 | 3,791 |
| Communication | 303 | 567 | 1,778 | 2,227 | 1,822 | 419 | 978 | 1,504 |
| Real estate and financial | 1,293 | 6,059 | 4,585 | 6,690 | 14,780 | 9,665 | 16,178 | 30,657 |

*Source: Federal Reserve Bulletin, various issues.*

**FIGURE 17.2**
Value of New Bond Issues as a Percentage of Total New Capital Raised

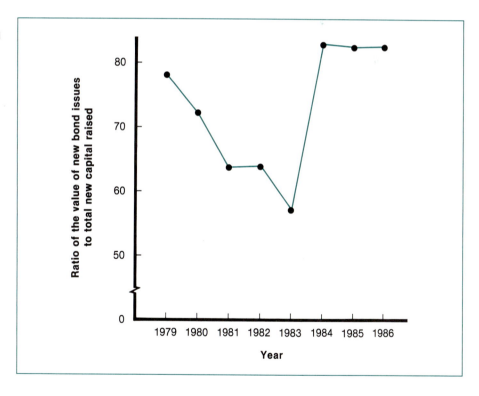

## PUBLIC OFFERING

When a corporation issues stocks or bonds, it must choose between a public offering or private placement. A **public offering** involves selling the securities to the general public. Typically, many different investors purchase the securities, and the offering normally involves the use of **investment banking firms** (IBFs) and possibly brokerage firms to place the securities with purchasers. Conversely, a **private placement** involves selling the entire issue to one or a few large investors.

In a public offering, the IBF acts as an intermediary between the corporation issuing securities and the purchasers. Specifically, the IBF has four main functions:

- Origination
- Underwriting
- Distribution
- Advising

Each task is described in the following sections.

### Origination

Once a corporation decides to publicly issue new securities, it contacts an IBF. The IBF may recommend the appropriate amount of securities to issue, since it can anticipate the amount of securities the market could absorb without causing a reduction in the security price. If a corporation issued an excessive amount of new stock, it could possibly depress the market value of its stock. Alternatively, if it issued an excessive amount of bonds, it might have to accept a relatively low price in order to assure a complete sale. A low price received on newly issued stocks or bonds implies a high cost of obtaining funds. The IBF helps determine the maximum amount of capital to be raised at any particular point in time.

Once the IBF and the corporation agree on the amount of securities to be issued, the specifics of the security are determined. For bonds, a maturity date must be specified along with the coupon rate, collateral, payment dates, and so forth. For stocks, it must be specified when they will be issued, how they will be distributed, to whom they will be issued, and so forth.

If bonds are being issued, the IBF evaluates the corporation's financial condition to determine the appropriate price for the newly issued securities. The final determination of price is based on negotiation between the corporation and IBF. Determination of price involves a trade-off. If the original asking price on the securities is too high, the securities will not sell; but if the price is too low, the issuing corporation will receive less funds for the securities than deserved. The price is influenced by the issuing firm's risk characteristics and by other terms specified for the securities. The greater the issuing firm's risk is, the lower the price at which it can sell its securities, other things being equal.

If a corporation plans to issue new stock, its selling price should be similar to the market price of its outstanding stock. If it has not issued stock to the public before, determination of the selling price is much more difficult. The firm's financial characteristics may be compared with other similar firms in the same industry that have stock outstanding, and from this comparison, the IBF can estimate the price at which the stock could be sold. Alternatively, the IBF can employ the valuation techniques described in Chapter 4. The price at which bonds can be sold is determined by analyzing the returns being earned on bonds with similar characteristics.

Once a price is established for the securities to be issued, the issuing corporation registers the issue with the Securities and Exchange Commission (SEC). All information relevant to the security and the agreement between the firm and the IBF must be provided within the registration statement. This registration requirement is intended to assure that sufficient information is disclosed about the issuing corporation and the securities to be issued. Some publicly issued securities do not require registration if the issue is very small or sold entirely within a particular state.

Approval by the SEC does not guarantee safety of the securities to be issued, but merely acknowledges that the firm is disclosing sufficient information about itself and the new issue. Included within the required registration information is the **prospectus,** which summarizes the relevant financial information about the firm and the new issue. This new document is also made available to prospective investors. The prospectus can be issued to prospective investors only after the registration is approved, which typically takes twenty to forty days.

In some cases, the issuing corporation will accept competitive bids from various IBFs on the price of its securities rather than selecting and negotiating with a particular IBF. The IBF with the highest competitive bid will then be selected to issue the securities. The advantage of competitive bidding is that the issuing firm receives the highest possible price on its securities. In general, competitive bidding is used by the very largest firms since most IBFs are unwilling to bid on smaller firms' issues. They feel the expense of developing bids on lesser known firms is too great. These smaller firms must select an IBF that has performed well for them in the past or that has a good reputation.

## Underwriting

An **underwriting arrangement** is one in which the IBF purchases the securities to be issued, then sells them to investors. The risk of the new issue not selling well is borne by the IBF. The **underwriting spread** is the difference between the price at which the IBF is willing to purchase the securities and the price at which it expects to sell the securities. In essence, the underwriting spread represents a commission to the IBF for selling the securities. The actual commission earned from selling the securities may be lower if the securities are sold by the IBF at a lower price than anticipated.

As an example, assume that Z Corporation planned to issue 1 million shares of new stock. An IBF guaranteed a selling price of $9.70 per share and then sold the stock for $10 per share. The underwriting spread earned by the IBF is 30 cents for every share sold at $10, or 3 percent. The underwriting spread on a percentage basis will average around 3 percent for large issues of stocks and as high as 10 percent or more on small issues. For newly issued bonds, the underwriting spreads are typically lower. Bonds can be sold by IBFs in large blocks to financial institutions, whereas the distribution of stock is more time-consuming since it is typically sold in smaller amounts to more investors.

The IBF may form an *underwriting syndicate* of IBFs, in which each participating IBF agrees to sell a portion of the securities. Each earns the underwriting spread and assumes the risk for the portion of securities it has agreed to sell. Thus, the risk to the *lead* or *managing* IBF is reduced to only the securities it is responsible for selling. If the securities sell for a price lower than expected, the managing IBF will not suffer as great a loss, since the loss is shared by the other IBFs. A syndicate may be composed of just a few IBFs for a relatively small issue, or as many as fifty or more for a large issue.

For securities issued by relatively risky corporations, IBFs may not be willing to act as underwriters. Instead, they may offer to issue the securities on a "best efforts" basis. In a **best-efforts agreement** the IBF does not guarantee a price to the issuing corporation. In this event, the issuing corporation bears the risk rather than the IBF. If an issuing corporation's financial performance is questionable or unproven, it may have to accept a best-efforts agreement.

## Distribution

Once all agreements between the issuing firm, the managing IBF, and other participating IBFs are complete, and the registration is approved by the SEC, the distribution process begins. The prospectus is first distributed to all potential investors, and the issue is advertised to the public. Once the actual selling begins, some issues sell out within hours. However, if the issue does not sell quickly, the underwriting syndicate will likely have to reduce the price to complete the sale.

The demand for the securities is influenced somewhat by the efforts of the IBF's sales force. Sometimes the underwriting syndicate will ask for the assistance of other sales organizations (securities dealers). Although they are not part of the underwriting syndicate, these organizations receive allotments of stock from the syndicate at wholesale prices and effectively earn commissions on the shares they sell. However, they do not incur the risk of underwriting the issue. The underwriting syndicate plus the securities dealers constitute the *selling group*. The involvement of the managing IBF, the underwriting syndicate, and the sales force is displayed in Figure 17.3.

When a corporation publicly places securities, it incurs **flotation costs,** or costs of placing the securities. These costs include the underwriting spread paid to the underwriters who guarantee the issuing firm a set price for the securities and administrative costs such as printing, legal, registration, and accounting expenses. Because these costs are not significantly affected by the size of the issue, flotation costs as a percentage of the value of securities issued are lower for larger issues.

Flotation costs are highest for common stock and lowest for bonds, with the cost of issuing preferred stock falling in between. Flotation costs

**TABLE B  Present Value of $1 Due at the End of n Periods**

$$PVIF_{k,n} = \frac{1}{(1+k)^n}$$

| Period n | 1% | 2% | 3% | 4% | 5% | 6% | 7% | 8% | 9% | 10% | 11% | 12% | 13% | 14% | 15% | 16% | 17% | 18% | 19% | 20% | 25% | 30% | 35% | 40% | 50% |
|---|---|---|---|---|---|---|---|---|---|---|---|---|---|---|---|---|---|---|---|---|---|---|---|---|---|
| 1 | 9901 | 9804 | 9709 | 9615 | 9524 | 9434 | 9346 | 9259 | 9174 | 9091 | 9009 | 8929 | 8850 | 8772 | 8696 | 8621 | 8547 | 8475 | 8403 | 8333 | 8000 | 7692 | 7407 | 7143 | 6667 |
| 2 | 9803 | 9612 | 9426 | 9246 | 9070 | 8900 | 8734 | 8573 | 8417 | 8264 | 8116 | 7972 | 7831 | 7695 | 7561 | 7432 | 7305 | 7182 | 7062 | 6944 | 6400 | 5917 | 5487 | 5102 | 4444 |
| 3 | 9706 | 9423 | 9151 | 8890 | 8638 | 8396 | 8163 | 7938 | 7722 | 7513 | 7312 | 7118 | 6931 | 6750 | 6575 | 6407 | 6244 | 6086 | 5934 | 5787 | 5120 | 4552 | 4064 | 3644 | 2963 |
| 4 | 9610 | 9238 | 8885 | 8548 | 8227 | 7921 | 7629 | 7350 | 7084 | 6830 | 6587 | 6355 | 6133 | 5921 | 5718 | 5523 | 5337 | 5158 | 4987 | 4823 | 4096 | 3501 | 3011 | 2603 | 1975 |
| 5 | 9515 | 9057 | 8626 | 8219 | 7835 | 7473 | 7130 | 6806 | 6499 | 6209 | 5935 | 5674 | 5428 | 5194 | 4972 | 4761 | 4561 | 4371 | 4190 | 4019 | 3277 | 2693 | 2230 | 1859 | 1317 |
| 6 | 9420 | 8880 | 8375 | 7903 | 7462 | 7050 | 6663 | 6302 | 5963 | 5645 | 5346 | 5066 | 4803 | 4556 | 4323 | 4104 | 3898 | 3704 | 3521 | 3349 | 2621 | 2072 | 1652 | 1328 | 0878 |
| 7 | 9327 | 8706 | 8131 | 7599 | 7107 | 6651 | 6227 | 5835 | 5470 | 5132 | 4817 | 4523 | 4251 | 3996 | 3759 | 3538 | 3332 | 3139 | 2959 | 2791 | 2097 | 1594 | 1224 | 0949 | 0585 |
| 8 | 9235 | 8535 | 7894 | 7307 | 6768 | 6274 | 5820 | 5403 | 5019 | 4665 | 4339 | 4039 | 3762 | 3506 | 3269 | 3050 | 2848 | 2660 | 2487 | 2326 | 1678 | 1226 | 0906 | 0678 | 0390 |
| 9 | 9143 | 8368 | 7664 | 7026 | 6446 | 5919 | 5439 | 5002 | 4604 | 4241 | 3909 | 3606 | 3329 | 3075 | 2843 | 2630 | 2434 | 2255 | 2090 | 1938 | 1342 | 0943 | 0671 | 0484 | 0260 |
| 10 | 9053 | 8203 | 7441 | 6756 | 6139 | 5584 | 5083 | 4632 | 4224 | 3855 | 3522 | 3220 | 2946 | 2697 | 2472 | 2267 | 2080 | 1911 | 1756 | 1615 | 1074 | 0725 | 0497 | 0346 | 0173 |
| 11 | 8963 | 8043 | 7224 | 6496 | 5847 | 5268 | 4751 | 4289 | 3875 | 3505 | 3173 | 2875 | 2607 | 2366 | 2149 | 1954 | 1778 | 1619 | 1476 | 1346 | 0859 | 0558 | 0368 | 0247 | 0116 |
| 12 | 8874 | 7885 | 7014 | 6246 | 5568 | 4970 | 4440 | 3971 | 3555 | 3186 | 2858 | 2567 | 2307 | 2076 | 1869 | 1685 | 1520 | 1372 | 1240 | 1122 | 0687 | 0429 | 0273 | 0176 | 0077 |
| 13 | 8787 | 7730 | 6810 | 6006 | 5303 | 4688 | 4150 | 3677 | 3262 | 2897 | 2575 | 2292 | 2042 | 1821 | 1625 | 1452 | 1299 | 1163 | 1042 | 0935 | 0550 | 0330 | 0202 | 0126 | 0051 |
| 14 | 8700 | 7579 | 6611 | 5775 | 5051 | 4423 | 3878 | 3405 | 2992 | 2633 | 2320 | 2046 | 1807 | 1597 | 1413 | 1252 | 1110 | 0985 | 0876 | 0779 | 0440 | 0254 | 0150 | 0090 | 0034 |
| 15 | 8613 | 7430 | 6419 | 5553 | 4810 | 4173 | 3624 | 3152 | 2745 | 2394 | 2090 | 1827 | 1599 | 1401 | 1229 | 1079 | 0949 | 0835 | 0736 | 0649 | 0352 | 0195 | 0111 | 0064 | 0023 |
| 16 | 8528 | 7284 | 6232 | 5339 | 4581 | 3936 | 3387 | 2919 | 2519 | 2176 | 1883 | 1631 | 1415 | 1229 | 1069 | 0930 | 0811 | 0708 | 0618 | 0541 | 0281 | 0150 | 0082 | 0046 | 0015 |
| 17 | 8444 | 7142 | 6050 | 5134 | 4363 | 3714 | 3166 | 2703 | 2311 | 1978 | 1696 | 1456 | 1252 | 1078 | 0929 | 0802 | 0693 | 0600 | 0520 | 0451 | 0225 | 0116 | 0061 | 0033 | 0010 |
| 18 | 8360 | 7002 | 5874 | 4936 | 4155 | 3503 | 2959 | 2502 | 2120 | 1799 | 1528 | 1300 | 1108 | 0946 | 0808 | 0691 | 0592 | 0508 | 0437 | 0376 | 0180 | 0089 | 0045 | 0023 | 0007 |
| 19 | 8277 | 6864 | 5703 | 4746 | 3957 | 3305 | 2765 | 2317 | 1945 | 1635 | 1377 | 1161 | 0981 | 0829 | 0703 | 0596 | 0506 | 0431 | 0367 | 0313 | 0144 | 0068 | 0033 | 0017 | 0005 |
| 20 | 8195 | 6730 | 5537 | 4564 | 3769 | 3118 | 2584 | 2145 | 1784 | 1486 | 1240 | 1037 | 0868 | 0728 | 0611 | 0514 | 0443 | 0365 | 0308 | 0261 | 0115 | 0053 | 0025 | 0012 | 0003 |
| 21 | 8114 | 6598 | 5375 | 4388 | 3589 | 2942 | 2415 | 1987 | 1637 | 1351 | 1117 | 0926 | 0768 | 0638 | 0531 | 0443 | 0370 | 0309 | 0259 | 0217 | 0092 | 0040 | 0018 | 0009 | 0002 |
| 22 | 8034 | 6468 | 5219 | 4220 | 3418 | 2775 | 2257 | 1839 | 1502 | 1228 | 1007 | 0826 | 0680 | 0560 | 0462 | 0382 | 0316 | 0262 | 0218 | 0181 | 0074 | 0031 | 0014 | 0006 | 0001 |
| 23 | 7954 | 6342 | 5067 | 4057 | 3256 | 2618 | 2109 | 1703 | 1378 | 1117 | 0907 | 0738 | 0601 | 0491 | 0402 | 0329 | 0270 | 0222 | 0183 | 0151 | 0059 | 0024 | 0010 | 0004 | 0001 |
| 24 | 7876 | 6217 | 4919 | 3901 | 3101 | 2470 | 1971 | 1577 | 1264 | 1015 | 0817 | 0659 | 0532 | 0431 | 0349 | 0284 | 0231 | 0188 | 0154 | 0126 | 0047 | 0018 | 0007 | 0003 | 0001 |
| 25 | 7798 | 6095 | 4776 | 3751 | 2953 | 2330 | 1842 | 1460 | 1160 | 0923 | 0736 | 0588 | 0471 | 0378 | 0304 | 0245 | 0197 | 0160 | 0129 | 0105 | 0038 | 0014 | 0006 | 0002 | 0000 |
| 26 | 7720 | 5976 | 4637 | 3607 | 2812 | 2198 | 1722 | 1352 | 1064 | 0839 | 0663 | 0525 | 0417 | 0331 | 0264 | 0211 | 0169 | 0135 | 0109 | 0087 | 0030 | 0011 | 0004 | 0002 | 0000 |
| 27 | 7644 | 5859 | 4502 | 3468 | 2678 | 2074 | 1609 | 1252 | 0976 | 0763 | 0597 | 0469 | 0369 | 0291 | 0230 | 0182 | 0144 | 0115 | 0091 | 0073 | 0024 | 0008 | 0003 | 0001 | 0000 |
| 28 | 7568 | 5744 | 4371 | 3335 | 2551 | 1956 | 1504 | 1159 | 0895 | 0693 | 0538 | 0419 | 0326 | 0255 | 0200 | 0157 | 0123 | 0097 | 0077 | 0061 | 0019 | 0006 | 0002 | 0001 | 0000 |
| 29 | 7493 | 5631 | 4243 | 3207 | 2429 | 1846 | 1406 | 1073 | 0822 | 0630 | 0485 | 0374 | 0289 | 0224 | 0174 | 0135 | 0105 | 0082 | 0064 | 0051 | 0015 | 0005 | 0002 | 0001 | 0000 |
| 30 | 7419 | 5521 | 4120 | 3083 | 2314 | 1741 | 1314 | 0994 | 0754 | 0573 | 0437 | 0334 | 0256 | 0196 | 0151 | 0116 | 0090 | 0070 | 0054 | 0042 | 0012 | 0004 | 0001 | 0001 | 0000 |
| 35 | 7059 | 5000 | 3554 | 2534 | 1813 | 1301 | 0937 | 0676 | 0490 | 0356 | 0259 | 0189 | 0139 | 0102 | 0075 | 0055 | 0041 | 0030 | 0023 | 0017 | 0004 | 0001 | 0000 | 0000 | 0000 |
| 40 | 6717 | 4529 | 3066 | 2083 | 1420 | 0972 | 0668 | 0460 | 0318 | 0221 | 0154 | 0107 | 0075 | 0053 | 0037 | 0026 | 0019 | 0013 | 0010 | 0007 | 0001 | 0000 | 0000 | 0000 | 0000 |
| 45 | 6391 | 4102 | 2644 | 1712 | 1113 | 0727 | 0476 | 0313 | 0207 | 0137 | 0091 | 0061 | 0041 | 0027 | 0019 | 0013 | 0009 | 0006 | 0004 | 0003 | 0000 | 0000 | 0000 | 0000 | 0000 |
| 50 | 6080 | 3715 | 2281 | 1407 | 0872 | 0543 | 0339 | 0213 | 0134 | 0085 | 0054 | 0035 | 0022 | 0014 | 0009 | 0006 | 0004 | 0003 | 0002 | 0001 | 0000 | 0000 | 0000 | 0000 | 0000 |

TABLE D  Present Value of an Annuity of $1 per Period for n Periods

$$PVIFA_{k,n} = \frac{1 - \frac{1}{(1+k)^n}}{k}$$

| Period n | 1% | 2% | 3% | 4% | 5% | 6% | 7% | 8% | 9% | 10% | 11% | 12% | 13% | 14% | 15% | 16% | 17% | 18% | 19% | 20% | 25% | 30% | 35% | 40% | 50% |
|---|---|---|---|---|---|---|---|---|---|---|---|---|---|---|---|---|---|---|---|---|---|---|---|---|---|
| 1 | 0.9901 | 0.9804 | 0.9709 | 0.9615 | 0.9524 | 0.9434 | 0.9346 | 0.9259 | 0.9174 | 0.9091 | 0.9009 | 0.8929 | 0.8850 | 0.8772 | 0.8696 | 0.8621 | 0.8547 | 0.8475 | 0.8403 | 0.8333 | 0.8000 | 0.7692 | 0.7407 | 0.7143 | 0.6667 |
| 2 | 1.9704 | 1.9416 | 1.9135 | 1.8861 | 1.8594 | 1.8334 | 1.8080 | 1.7833 | 1.7591 | 1.7355 | 1.7125 | 1.6901 | 1.6681 | 1.6467 | 1.6257 | 1.6052 | 1.5852 | 1.5656 | 1.5465 | 1.5278 | 1.4400 | 1.3609 | 1.2894 | 1.2245 | 1.1111 |
| 3 | 2.9410 | 2.8839 | 2.8286 | 2.7751 | 2.7232 | 2.6730 | 2.6243 | 2.5771 | 2.5313 | 2.4869 | 2.4437 | 2.4018 | 2.3612 | 2.3216 | 2.2832 | 2.2459 | 2.2096 | 2.1743 | 2.1399 | 2.1065 | 1.9520 | 1.8161 | 1.6959 | 1.5889 | 1.4074 |
| 4 | 3.9020 | 3.8077 | 3.7171 | 3.6299 | 3.5460 | 3.4651 | 3.3872 | 3.3121 | 3.2397 | 3.1699 | 3.1024 | 3.0373 | 2.9745 | 2.9137 | 2.8550 | 2.7982 | 2.7432 | 2.6901 | 2.6386 | 2.5887 | 2.3616 | 2.1662 | 1.9969 | 1.8492 | 1.6049 |
| 5 | 4.8534 | 4.7135 | 4.5797 | 4.4518 | 4.3295 | 4.2124 | 4.1002 | 3.9927 | 3.8897 | 3.7908 | 3.6959 | 3.6048 | 3.5172 | 3.4331 | 3.3522 | 3.2743 | 3.1993 | 3.1272 | 3.0576 | 2.9906 | 2.6893 | 2.4356 | 2.2200 | 2.0352 | 1.7366 |
| 6 | 5.7955 | 5.6014 | 5.4172 | 5.2421 | 5.0757 | 4.9173 | 4.7665 | 4.6229 | 4.4859 | 4.3553 | 4.2305 | 4.1114 | 3.9975 | 3.8887 | 3.7845 | 3.6847 | 3.5892 | 3.4976 | 3.4098 | 3.3255 | 2.9514 | 2.6427 | 2.3852 | 2.1680 | 1.8244 |
| 7 | 6.7282 | 6.4720 | 6.2303 | 6.0021 | 5.7864 | 5.5824 | 5.3893 | 5.2064 | 5.0330 | 4.8684 | 4.7122 | 4.5638 | 4.4226 | 4.2883 | 4.1604 | 4.0386 | 3.9224 | 3.8115 | 3.7057 | 3.6046 | 3.1611 | 2.8021 | 2.5075 | 2.2628 | 1.8829 |
| 8 | 7.6517 | 7.3255 | 7.0197 | 6.7327 | 6.4632 | 6.2098 | 5.9713 | 5.7466 | 5.5348 | 5.3349 | 5.1461 | 4.9676 | 4.7988 | 4.6389 | 4.4873 | 4.3436 | 4.2072 | 4.0776 | 3.9544 | 3.8372 | 3.3289 | 2.9247 | 2.5982 | 2.3306 | 1.9220 |
| 9 | 8.5660 | 8.1622 | 7.7861 | 7.4353 | 7.1078 | 6.8017 | 6.5152 | 6.2469 | 5.9952 | 5.7590 | 5.5370 | 5.3282 | 5.1317 | 4.9464 | 4.7716 | 4.6065 | 4.4506 | 4.3030 | 4.1633 | 4.0310 | 3.4631 | 3.0190 | 2.6653 | 2.3790 | 1.9480 |
| 10 | 9.4713 | 8.9826 | 8.5302 | 8.1109 | 7.7217 | 7.3601 | 7.0236 | 6.7101 | 6.4177 | 6.1446 | 5.8892 | 5.6502 | 5.4262 | 5.2161 | 5.0188 | 4.8332 | 4.6586 | 4.4941 | 4.3389 | 4.1925 | 3.5705 | 3.0915 | 2.7150 | 2.4136 | 1.9653 |
| 11 | 10.368 | 9.7868 | 9.2526 | 8.7605 | 8.3064 | 7.8869 | 7.4987 | 7.1390 | 6.8052 | 6.4951 | 6.2065 | 5.9377 | 5.6869 | 5.4527 | 5.2337 | 5.0286 | 4.8364 | 4.6560 | 4.4865 | 4.3271 | 3.6564 | 3.1473 | 2.7519 | 2.4383 | 1.9769 |
| 12 | 11.255 | 10.575 | 9.9540 | 9.3851 | 8.8633 | 8.3838 | 7.9427 | 7.5361 | 7.1607 | 6.8137 | 6.4924 | 6.1944 | 5.9176 | 5.6603 | 5.4206 | 5.1971 | 4.9884 | 4.7932 | 4.6105 | 4.4392 | 3.7251 | 3.1903 | 2.7792 | 2.4559 | 1.9846 |
| 13 | 12.134 | 11.348 | 10.635 | 9.9856 | 9.3936 | 8.8527 | 8.3577 | 7.9038 | 7.4869 | 7.1034 | 6.7499 | 6.4235 | 6.1218 | 5.8424 | 5.5831 | 5.3423 | 5.1183 | 4.9095 | 4.7147 | 4.5327 | 3.7801 | 3.2233 | 2.7994 | 2.4685 | 1.9897 |
| 14 | 13.004 | 12.106 | 11.296 | 10.563 | 9.8986 | 9.2950 | 8.7455 | 8.2442 | 7.7862 | 7.3667 | 6.9819 | 6.6282 | 6.3025 | 6.0021 | 5.7245 | 5.4675 | 5.2293 | 5.0081 | 4.8023 | 4.6106 | 3.8241 | 3.2487 | 2.8144 | 2.4775 | 1.9931 |
| 15 | 13.865 | 12.849 | 11.938 | 11.118 | 10.380 | 9.7122 | 9.1079 | 8.5595 | 8.0607 | 7.6061 | 7.1909 | 6.8109 | 6.4624 | 6.1422 | 5.8474 | 5.5755 | 5.3242 | 5.0916 | 4.8759 | 4.6755 | 3.8593 | 3.2682 | 2.8255 | 2.4839 | 1.9954 |
| 16 | 14.718 | 13.578 | 12.561 | 11.652 | 10.838 | 10.106 | 9.4466 | 8.8514 | 8.3126 | 7.8237 | 7.3792 | 6.9740 | 6.6039 | 6.2651 | 5.9542 | 5.6685 | 5.4053 | 5.1624 | 4.9377 | 4.7296 | 3.8874 | 3.2832 | 2.8337 | 2.4885 | 1.9970 |
| 17 | 15.562 | 14.292 | 13.166 | 12.166 | 11.274 | 10.477 | 9.7632 | 9.1216 | 8.5436 | 8.0216 | 7.5488 | 7.1196 | 6.7291 | 6.3729 | 6.0472 | 5.7487 | 5.4746 | 5.2223 | 4.9897 | 4.7746 | 3.9099 | 3.2948 | 2.8398 | 2.4918 | 1.9980 |
| 18 | 16.398 | 14.992 | 13.754 | 12.659 | 11.690 | 10.828 | 10.059 | 9.3719 | 8.7556 | 8.2014 | 7.7016 | 7.2497 | 6.8399 | 6.4674 | 6.1280 | 5.8178 | 5.5339 | 5.2732 | 5.0333 | 4.8122 | 3.9279 | 3.3037 | 2.8443 | 2.4941 | 1.9986 |
| 19 | 17.226 | 15.678 | 14.324 | 13.134 | 12.085 | 11.158 | 10.336 | 9.6036 | 8.9501 | 8.3649 | 7.8393 | 7.3658 | 6.9380 | 6.5504 | 6.1982 | 5.8775 | 5.5845 | 5.3162 | 5.0700 | 4.8435 | 3.9424 | 3.3105 | 2.8476 | 2.4958 | 1.9991 |
| 20 | 18.046 | 16.351 | 14.877 | 13.590 | 12.462 | 11.470 | 10.594 | 9.8181 | 9.1285 | 8.5136 | 7.9633 | 7.4694 | 7.0248 | 6.6231 | 6.2593 | 5.9288 | 5.6278 | 5.3527 | 5.1009 | 4.8696 | 3.9539 | 3.3158 | 2.8501 | 2.4970 | 1.9994 |
| 21 | 18.857 | 17.011 | 15.415 | 14.029 | 12.821 | 11.764 | 10.836 | 10.017 | 9.2922 | 8.6487 | 8.0751 | 7.5620 | 7.1016 | 6.6870 | 6.3125 | 5.9731 | 5.6648 | 5.3837 | 5.1268 | 4.8913 | 3.9631 | 3.3198 | 2.8519 | 2.4979 | 1.9996 |
| 22 | 19.660 | 17.658 | 15.937 | 14.451 | 13.163 | 12.042 | 11.061 | 10.201 | 9.4424 | 8.7715 | 8.1757 | 7.6446 | 7.1695 | 6.7429 | 6.3587 | 6.0113 | 5.6964 | 5.4099 | 5.1486 | 4.9094 | 3.9705 | 3.3230 | 2.8533 | 2.4985 | 1.9997 |
| 23 | 20.456 | 18.292 | 16.444 | 14.857 | 13.489 | 12.303 | 11.272 | 10.371 | 9.5802 | 8.8832 | 8.2664 | 7.7184 | 7.2297 | 6.7921 | 6.3988 | 6.0442 | 5.7234 | 5.4321 | 5.1668 | 4.9245 | 3.9764 | 3.3254 | 2.8543 | 2.4989 | 1.9998 |
| 24 | 21.243 | 18.914 | 16.936 | 15.247 | 13.799 | 12.550 | 11.469 | 10.529 | 9.7066 | 8.9847 | 8.3481 | 7.7843 | 7.2829 | 6.8351 | 6.4338 | 6.0726 | 5.7465 | 5.4509 | 5.1822 | 4.9371 | 3.9811 | 3.3272 | 2.8550 | 2.4992 | 1.9999 |
| 25 | 22.023 | 19.523 | 17.413 | 15.622 | 14.094 | 12.783 | 11.654 | 10.675 | 9.8226 | 9.0770 | 8.4217 | 7.8431 | 7.3300 | 6.8729 | 6.4641 | 6.0971 | 5.7662 | 5.4669 | 5.1951 | 4.9476 | 3.9849 | 3.3286 | 2.8556 | 2.4994 | 1.9999 |
| 26 | 22.795 | 20.121 | 17.877 | 15.983 | 14.375 | 13.003 | 11.826 | 10.810 | 9.9290 | 9.1609 | 8.4881 | 7.8957 | 7.3717 | 6.9061 | 6.4906 | 6.1182 | 5.7831 | 5.4804 | 5.2060 | 4.9563 | 3.9879 | 3.3297 | 2.8560 | 2.4996 | 1.9999 |
| 27 | 23.560 | 20.707 | 18.327 | 16.330 | 14.643 | 13.211 | 11.987 | 10.935 | 10.027 | 9.2372 | 8.5478 | 7.9426 | 7.4086 | 6.9352 | 6.5135 | 6.1364 | 5.7975 | 5.4919 | 5.2151 | 4.9636 | 3.9903 | 3.3305 | 2.8563 | 2.4997 | 2.0000 |
| 28 | 24.316 | 21.281 | 18.764 | 16.663 | 14.898 | 13.406 | 12.137 | 11.051 | 10.116 | 9.3066 | 8.6016 | 7.9844 | 7.4412 | 6.9607 | 6.5335 | 6.1520 | 5.8099 | 5.5016 | 5.2228 | 4.9697 | 3.9923 | 3.3312 | 2.8565 | 2.4998 | 2.0000 |
| 29 | 25.066 | 21.844 | 19.188 | 16.984 | 15.141 | 13.591 | 12.278 | 11.158 | 10.198 | 9.3696 | 8.6501 | 8.0218 | 7.4701 | 6.9830 | 6.5509 | 6.1656 | 5.8204 | 5.5098 | 5.2292 | 4.9747 | 3.9938 | 3.3317 | 2.8567 | 2.4999 | 2.0000 |
| 30 | 25.808 | 22.396 | 19.600 | 17.292 | 15.372 | 13.765 | 12.409 | 11.258 | 10.274 | 9.4269 | 8.6938 | 8.0552 | 7.4957 | 7.0027 | 6.5660 | 6.1772 | 5.8294 | 5.5168 | 5.2347 | 4.9789 | 3.9950 | 3.3321 | 2.8568 | 2.4999 | 2.0000 |
| 35 | 29.409 | 24.999 | 21.487 | 18.665 | 16.374 | 14.498 | 12.948 | 11.655 | 10.567 | 9.6442 | 8.8552 | 8.1755 | 7.5856 | 7.0700 | 6.6166 | 6.2153 | 5.8582 | 5.5386 | 5.2512 | 4.9915 | 3.9984 | 3.3330 | 2.8571 | 2.5000 | 2.0000 |
| 40 | 32.835 | 27.355 | 23.115 | 19.793 | 17.159 | 15.046 | 13.332 | 11.925 | 10.757 | 9.7791 | 8.9511 | 8.2438 | 7.6344 | 7.1050 | 6.6418 | 6.2335 | 5.8713 | 5.5482 | 5.2582 | 4.9966 | 3.9995 | 3.3332 | 2.8571 | 2.5000 | 2.0000 |
| 45 | 36.095 | 29.490 | 24.519 | 20.720 | 17.774 | 15.456 | 13.606 | 12.108 | 10.881 | 9.8628 | 9.0079 | 8.2825 | 7.6609 | 7.1232 | 6.6543 | 6.2421 | 5.8773 | 5.5523 | 5.2611 | 4.9986 | 3.9998 | 3.3333 | 2.8571 | 2.5000 | 2.0000 |
| 50 | 39.196 | 31.424 | 25.730 | 21.482 | 18.256 | 15.762 | 13.801 | 12.233 | 10.962 | 9.9148 | 9.0417 | 8.3045 | 7.6752 | 7.1327 | 6.6605 | 6.2463 | 5.8801 | 5.5541 | 5.2623 | 4.9995 | 3.9999 | 3.3333 | 2.8571 | 2.5000 | 2.0000 |

**TABLE C**  Future Value of an Annuity of $1 per Period for n Periods

$$FVIFA_{k,n} = \frac{(1+k)^n - 1}{k}$$

| Period n | 1% | 2% | 3% | 4% | 5% | 6% | 7% | 8% | 9% | 10% | 11% | 12% | 13% | 14% | 15% | 16% | 17% | 18% | 19% | 20% | 25% | 30% | 35% | 40% | 50% |
|---|---|---|---|---|---|---|---|---|---|---|---|---|---|---|---|---|---|---|---|---|---|---|---|---|---|
| 1 | 1.0000 | 1.0000 | 1.0000 | 1.0000 | 1.0000 | 1.0000 | 1.0000 | 1.0000 | 1.0000 | 1.0000 | 1.0000 | 1.0000 | 1.0000 | 1.0000 | 1.0000 | 1.0000 | 1.0000 | 1.0000 | 1.0000 | 1.0000 | 1.0000 | 1.0000 | 1.0000 | 1.0000 | 1.0000 |
| 2 | 2.0100 | 2.0200 | 2.0300 | 2.0400 | 2.0500 | 2.0600 | 2.0700 | 2.0800 | 2.0900 | 2.1000 | 2.1100 | 2.1200 | 2.1300 | 2.1400 | 2.1500 | 2.1600 | 2.1700 | 2.1800 | 2.1900 | 2.2000 | 2.2500 | 2.3000 | 2.3500 | 2.4000 | 2.5000 |
| 3 | 3.0301 | 3.0604 | 3.0909 | 3.1216 | 3.1525 | 3.1836 | 3.2149 | 3.2464 | 3.2781 | 3.3100 | 3.3421 | 3.3744 | 3.4069 | 3.4396 | 3.4725 | 3.5056 | 3.5389 | 3.5724 | 3.6061 | 3.6400 | 3.8125 | 3.9900 | 4.1725 | 4.3600 | 4.7500 |
| 4 | 4.0604 | 4.1216 | 4.1836 | 4.2465 | 4.3101 | 4.3746 | 4.4399 | 4.5061 | 4.5731 | 4.6410 | 4.7097 | 4.7793 | 4.8498 | 4.9211 | 4.9934 | 5.0665 | 5.1405 | 5.2154 | 5.2913 | 5.3680 | 5.7656 | 6.1870 | 6.6329 | 7.1040 | 8.1250 |
| 5 | 5.1010 | 5.2040 | 5.3091 | 5.4163 | 5.5256 | 5.6371 | 5.7507 | 5.8666 | 5.9847 | 6.1051 | 6.2278 | 6.3528 | 6.4803 | 6.6101 | 6.7424 | 6.8771 | 7.0144 | 7.1542 | 7.2966 | 7.4416 | 8.2070 | 9.0431 | 9.9544 | 10.946 | 13.188 |
| 6 | 6.1520 | 6.3081 | 6.4684 | 6.6330 | 6.8019 | 6.9753 | 7.1533 | 7.3359 | 7.5233 | 7.7156 | 7.9129 | 8.1152 | 8.3227 | 8.5355 | 8.7537 | 8.9775 | 9.2068 | 9.4420 | 9.6830 | 9.9299 | 11.259 | 12.756 | 14.438 | 16.324 | 20.781 |
| 7 | 7.2135 | 7.4343 | 7.6625 | 7.8983 | 8.1420 | 8.3938 | 8.6540 | 8.9228 | 9.2004 | 9.4872 | 9.7833 | 10.089 | 10.405 | 10.730 | 11.067 | 11.414 | 11.772 | 12.142 | 12.523 | 12.916 | 15.073 | 17.583 | 20.492 | 23.853 | 32.172 |
| 8 | 8.2857 | 8.5830 | 8.8923 | 9.2142 | 9.5491 | 9.8975 | 10.260 | 10.637 | 11.028 | 11.436 | 11.859 | 12.300 | 12.757 | 13.233 | 13.727 | 14.240 | 14.773 | 15.327 | 15.902 | 16.499 | 19.842 | 23.858 | 28.664 | 34.395 | 49.258 |
| 9 | 9.3685 | 9.7546 | 10.159 | 10.583 | 11.027 | 11.491 | 11.978 | 12.488 | 13.021 | 13.579 | 14.164 | 14.776 | 15.416 | 16.085 | 16.786 | 17.519 | 18.285 | 19.086 | 19.923 | 20.799 | 25.802 | 32.015 | 39.696 | 49.153 | 74.887 |
| 10 | 10.462 | 10.950 | 11.464 | 12.006 | 12.578 | 13.181 | 13.816 | 14.487 | 15.193 | 15.937 | 16.722 | 17.549 | 18.420 | 19.337 | 20.304 | 21.321 | 22.393 | 23.521 | 24.709 | 25.959 | 33.253 | 42.619 | 54.590 | 69.814 | 113.33 |
| 11 | 11.567 | 12.169 | 12.808 | 13.486 | 14.207 | 14.972 | 15.784 | 16.645 | 17.560 | 18.531 | 19.561 | 20.655 | 21.814 | 23.045 | 24.349 | 25.733 | 27.200 | 28.755 | 30.404 | 32.150 | 42.566 | 56.405 | 74.697 | 98.739 | 171.00 |
| 12 | 12.683 | 13.412 | 14.192 | 15.026 | 15.917 | 16.870 | 17.888 | 18.977 | 20.141 | 21.384 | 22.713 | 24.133 | 25.650 | 27.271 | 29.002 | 30.850 | 32.824 | 34.931 | 37.180 | 39.581 | 54.208 | 74.327 | 101.84 | 139.23 | 257.49 |
| 13 | 13.809 | 14.680 | 15.618 | 16.627 | 17.713 | 18.882 | 20.141 | 21.495 | 22.953 | 24.523 | 26.212 | 28.029 | 29.985 | 32.089 | 34.352 | 36.786 | 39.404 | 42.219 | 45.244 | 48.497 | 68.760 | 97.625 | 138.48 | 195.93 | 387.24 |
| 14 | 14.947 | 15.974 | 17.086 | 18.292 | 19.599 | 21.015 | 22.550 | 24.215 | 26.019 | 27.975 | 30.095 | 32.393 | 34.883 | 37.581 | 40.505 | 43.672 | 47.103 | 50.818 | 54.841 | 59.196 | 86.949 | 127.91 | 187.95 | 275.30 | 581.86 |
| 15 | 16.097 | 17.293 | 18.599 | 20.024 | 21.579 | 23.276 | 25.129 | 27.152 | 29.361 | 31.772 | 34.405 | 37.280 | 40.417 | 43.842 | 47.580 | 51.660 | 56.110 | 60.965 | 66.261 | 72.035 | 109.69 | 167.29 | 254.74 | 386.42 | 873.79 |
| 16 | 17.258 | 18.639 | 20.157 | 21.825 | 23.657 | 25.673 | 27.888 | 30.324 | 33.003 | 35.950 | 39.190 | 42.753 | 46.672 | 50.980 | 55.717 | 60.925 | 66.649 | 72.939 | 79.850 | 87.442 | 138.11 | 218.47 | 344.90 | 541.99 | 1311.7 |
| 17 | 18.430 | 20.012 | 21.762 | 23.698 | 25.840 | 28.213 | 30.840 | 33.750 | 36.974 | 40.545 | 44.501 | 48.884 | 53.739 | 59.118 | 65.075 | 71.673 | 78.979 | 87.068 | 96.022 | 105.93 | 173.64 | 285.01 | 466.61 | 759.78 | 1968.5 |
| 18 | 19.615 | 21.412 | 23.414 | 25.645 | 28.132 | 30.906 | 33.999 | 37.450 | 41.301 | 45.599 | 50.396 | 55.750 | 61.725 | 68.394 | 75.836 | 84.141 | 93.406 | 103.74 | 115.27 | 128.12 | 218.04 | 371.52 | 630.92 | 1064.7 | 2953.8 |
| 19 | 20.811 | 22.841 | 25.117 | 27.671 | 30.539 | 33.760 | 37.379 | 41.446 | 46.018 | 51.159 | 56.939 | 63.440 | 70.749 | 78.969 | 88.212 | 98.603 | 110.28 | 123.41 | 138.17 | 154.74 | 273.56 | 483.97 | 852.75 | 1491.6 | 4431.7 |
| 20 | 22.019 | 24.297 | 26.870 | 29.778 | 33.066 | 36.786 | 40.995 | 45.762 | 51.160 | 57.275 | 64.203 | 72.052 | 80.947 | 91.025 | 102.44 | 115.38 | 130.03 | 146.63 | 165.42 | 186.69 | 342.94 | 630.17 | 1152.2 | 2089.2 | 6648.5 |
| 21 | 23.239 | 25.783 | 28.676 | 31.969 | 35.719 | 39.993 | 44.865 | 50.423 | 56.765 | 64.002 | 72.265 | 81.699 | 92.470 | 104.77 | 118.81 | 134.84 | 153.14 | 174.02 | 197.85 | 225.03 | 429.68 | 820.22 | 1556.5 | 2925.9 | 9973.8 |
| 22 | 24.472 | 27.299 | 30.537 | 34.248 | 38.505 | 43.392 | 49.006 | 55.457 | 62.873 | 71.403 | 81.214 | 92.503 | 105.49 | 120.44 | 137.63 | 157.41 | 180.17 | 206.34 | 236.44 | 271.03 | 538.10 | 1067.3 | 2102.3 | 4097.2 | 14962 |
| 23 | 25.716 | 28.845 | 32.453 | 36.618 | 41.430 | 46.996 | 53.436 | 60.893 | 69.532 | 79.543 | 91.148 | 104.60 | 120.20 | 138.30 | 159.28 | 183.60 | 211.80 | 244.49 | 282.36 | 326.24 | 673.63 | 1388.5 | 2839.0 | 5737.1 | 22443 |
| 24 | 26.973 | 30.422 | 34.426 | 39.083 | 44.502 | 50.816 | 58.177 | 66.765 | 76.790 | 88.497 | 102.17 | 118.16 | 136.83 | 158.66 | 184.17 | 213.98 | 248.81 | 289.49 | 337.01 | 392.48 | 843.03 | 1806.0 | 3833.7 | 8033.0 | 33666 |
| 25 | 28.243 | 32.030 | 36.459 | 41.646 | 47.727 | 54.865 | 63.249 | 73.106 | 84.701 | 98.347 | 114.41 | 133.33 | 155.62 | 181.87 | 212.79 | 249.21 | 292.10 | 342.60 | 402.04 | 471.98 | 1054.8 | 2348.8 | 5176.5 | 11247 | 50500 |
| 26 | 29.526 | 33.671 | 38.553 | 44.312 | 51.113 | 59.156 | 68.676 | 79.954 | 93.324 | 109.18 | 128.00 | 150.33 | 176.85 | 208.33 | 245.71 | 290.09 | 342.76 | 405.27 | 479.43 | 567.38 | 1319.5 | 3054.4 | 6989.3 | 15747 | 75752 |
| 27 | 30.821 | 35.344 | 40.710 | 47.084 | 54.669 | 63.706 | 74.484 | 87.351 | 102.72 | 121.10 | 143.08 | 169.37 | 200.84 | 238.50 | 283.57 | 337.50 | 402.03 | 479.22 | 571.52 | 681.85 | 1650.4 | 3971.8 | 9436.5 | 22047 | * |
| 28 | 32.129 | 37.051 | 42.931 | 49.968 | 58.403 | 68.528 | 80.698 | 95.339 | 112.97 | 134.21 | 159.82 | 190.70 | 227.95 | 272.89 | 327.10 | 392.50 | 471.38 | 566.48 | 681.11 | 819.22 | 2063.9 | 5164.3 | 12740 | 30867 | * |
| 29 | 33.450 | 38.792 | 45.219 | 52.966 | 62.323 | 73.640 | 87.347 | 103.97 | 124.14 | 148.63 | 178.40 | 214.58 | 258.58 | 312.09 | 377.17 | 456.30 | 552.51 | 669.45 | 811.52 | 984.07 | 2580.9 | 6714.6 | 17200 | 43214 | * |
| 30 | 34.785 | 40.568 | 47.575 | 56.085 | 66.439 | 79.058 | 94.461 | 113.28 | 136.31 | 164.49 | 199.02 | 241.33 | 293.20 | 356.79 | 434.75 | 530.31 | 647.44 | 790.95 | 966.71 | 1181.9 | 3227.2 | 8730.0 | 23222 | 60501 | * |
| 35 | 41.660 | 49.994 | 60.462 | 73.652 | 90.320 | 111.43 | 138.24 | 172.32 | 215.71 | 271.02 | 341.59 | 431.66 | 546.68 | 693.57 | 881.17 | 1120.7 | 1426.5 | 1816.7 | 2314.2 | 2948.3 | 9856.8 | 32423 | * | * | * |
| 40 | 48.886 | 60.402 | 75.401 | 95.026 | 120.80 | 154.76 | 199.64 | 259.06 | 337.88 | 442.59 | 581.83 | 767.09 | 1013.7 | 1342.0 | 1779.1 | 2360.8 | 3134.5 | 4163.2 | 5529.8 | 7343.9 | 30089 | * | * | * | * |
| 45 | 56.481 | 71.893 | 92.720 | 121.03 | 159.70 | 212.74 | 285.75 | 386.51 | 525.86 | 718.90 | 986.64 | 1358.2 | 1874.2 | 2590.6 | 3585.1 | 4965.3 | 6879.3 | 9531.6 | 13203 | 18281 | * | * | * | * | * |
| 50 | 64.463 | 84.579 | 112.80 | 152.67 | 209.35 | 290.34 | 406.53 | 573.77 | 815.08 | 1163.9 | 1668.8 | 2400.0 | 3459.5 | 4994.5 | 7217.7 | 10436 | 15090 | 21813 | 31515 | 45497 | * | * | * | * | * |

*Interest factors exceed 99,999

**TABLE A  Future Value of $1 at the End of n Periods**

$$FVIF_{k,n} = (1 + k)^n$$

| Period n | 1% | 2% | 3% | 4% | 5% | 6% | 7% | 8% | 9% | 10% | 11% | 12% | 13% | 14% | 15% | 16% | 17% | 18% | 19% | 20% | 25% | 30% | 35% | 40% | 50% |
|---|---|---|---|---|---|---|---|---|---|---|---|---|---|---|---|---|---|---|---|---|---|---|---|---|---|
| 1 | 1.0100 | 1.0200 | 1.0300 | 1.0400 | 1.0500 | 1.0600 | 1.0700 | 1.0800 | 1.0900 | 1.1000 | 1.1100 | 1.1200 | 1.1300 | 1.1400 | 1.1500 | 1.1600 | 1.1700 | 1.1800 | 1.1900 | 1.2000 | 1.2500 | 1.3000 | 1.3500 | 1.4000 | 1.5000 |
| 2 | 1.0201 | 1.0404 | 1.0609 | 1.0816 | 1.1025 | 1.1236 | 1.1449 | 1.1664 | 1.1881 | 1.2100 | 1.2321 | 1.2544 | 1.2769 | 1.2996 | 1.3225 | 1.3456 | 1.3689 | 1.3924 | 1.4161 | 1.4400 | 1.5625 | 1.6900 | 1.8225 | 1.9600 | 2.2500 |
| 3 | 1.0303 | 1.0612 | 1.0927 | 1.1249 | 1.1576 | 1.1910 | 1.2250 | 1.2597 | 1.2950 | 1.3310 | 1.3676 | 1.4049 | 1.4429 | 1.4815 | 1.5209 | 1.5609 | 1.6016 | 1.6430 | 1.6852 | 1.7280 | 1.9531 | 2.1970 | 2.4604 | 2.7440 | 3.3750 |
| 4 | 1.0406 | 1.0824 | 1.1255 | 1.1699 | 1.2155 | 1.2625 | 1.3108 | 1.3605 | 1.4116 | 1.4641 | 1.5181 | 1.5735 | 1.6305 | 1.6890 | 1.7490 | 1.8106 | 1.8739 | 1.9388 | 2.0053 | 2.0736 | 2.4414 | 2.8561 | 3.3215 | 3.8416 | 5.0625 |
| 5 | 1.0510 | 1.1041 | 1.1593 | 1.2167 | 1.2763 | 1.3382 | 1.4026 | 1.4693 | 1.5386 | 1.6105 | 1.6851 | 1.7623 | 1.8424 | 1.9254 | 2.0114 | 2.1003 | 2.1924 | 2.2878 | 2.3864 | 2.4883 | 3.0518 | 3.7129 | 4.4840 | 5.3782 | 7.5938 |
| 6 | 1.0615 | 1.1262 | 1.1941 | 1.2653 | 1.3401 | 1.4185 | 1.5007 | 1.5869 | 1.6771 | 1.7716 | 1.8704 | 1.9738 | 2.0820 | 2.1950 | 2.3131 | 2.4364 | 2.5652 | 2.6996 | 2.8398 | 2.9860 | 3.8147 | 4.8268 | 6.0534 | 7.5295 | 11.391 |
| 7 | 1.0721 | 1.1487 | 1.2299 | 1.3159 | 1.4071 | 1.5036 | 1.6058 | 1.7138 | 1.8280 | 1.9487 | 2.0762 | 2.2107 | 2.3526 | 2.5023 | 2.6600 | 2.8262 | 3.0012 | 3.1855 | 3.3793 | 3.5832 | 4.7684 | 6.2749 | 8.1722 | 10.541 | 17.086 |
| 8 | 1.0829 | 1.1717 | 1.2668 | 1.3686 | 1.4775 | 1.5938 | 1.7182 | 1.8509 | 1.9926 | 2.1436 | 2.3045 | 2.4760 | 2.6584 | 2.8526 | 3.0590 | 3.2784 | 3.5115 | 3.7589 | 4.0214 | 4.2998 | 5.9605 | 8.1573 | 11.032 | 14.758 | 25.629 |
| 9 | 1.0937 | 1.1951 | 1.3048 | 1.4233 | 1.5513 | 1.6895 | 1.8385 | 1.9990 | 2.1719 | 2.3579 | 2.5580 | 2.7731 | 3.0040 | 3.2519 | 3.5179 | 3.8030 | 4.1084 | 4.4355 | 4.7854 | 5.1598 | 7.4506 | 10.604 | 14.894 | 20.661 | 38.443 |
| 10 | 1.1046 | 1.2190 | 1.3439 | 1.4802 | 1.6289 | 1.7908 | 1.9672 | 2.1589 | 2.3674 | 2.5937 | 2.8394 | 3.1058 | 3.3946 | 3.7072 | 4.0456 | 4.4114 | 4.8068 | 5.2338 | 5.6947 | 6.1917 | 9.3132 | 13.786 | 20.107 | 28.925 | 57.665 |
| 11 | 1.1157 | 1.2434 | 1.3842 | 1.5395 | 1.7103 | 1.8983 | 2.1049 | 2.3316 | 2.5804 | 2.8531 | 3.1518 | 3.4785 | 3.8359 | 4.2262 | 4.6524 | 5.1173 | 5.6240 | 6.1759 | 6.7767 | 7.4301 | 11.642 | 17.922 | 27.144 | 40.496 | 86.498 |
| 12 | 1.1268 | 1.2682 | 1.4258 | 1.6010 | 1.7959 | 2.0122 | 2.2522 | 2.5182 | 2.8127 | 3.1384 | 3.4985 | 3.8960 | 4.3345 | 4.8179 | 5.3503 | 5.9360 | 6.5801 | 7.2876 | 8.0642 | 8.9161 | 14.552 | 23.298 | 36.644 | 56.694 | 129.75 |
| 13 | 1.1381 | 1.2936 | 1.4685 | 1.6651 | 1.8856 | 2.1329 | 2.4098 | 2.7196 | 3.0658 | 3.4523 | 3.8833 | 4.3635 | 4.8980 | 5.4924 | 6.1528 | 6.8858 | 7.6987 | 8.5994 | 9.5964 | 10.699 | 18.190 | 30.288 | 49.470 | 79.371 | 194.62 |
| 14 | 1.1495 | 1.3195 | 1.5126 | 1.7317 | 1.9799 | 2.2609 | 2.5785 | 2.9372 | 3.3417 | 3.7975 | 4.3104 | 4.8871 | 5.5348 | 6.2613 | 7.0757 | 7.9875 | 9.0075 | 10.147 | 11.420 | 12.839 | 22.737 | 39.374 | 66.784 | 111.12 | 291.93 |
| 15 | 1.1610 | 1.3459 | 1.5580 | 1.8009 | 2.0789 | 2.3966 | 2.7590 | 3.1722 | 3.6425 | 4.1772 | 4.7846 | 5.4736 | 6.2543 | 7.1379 | 8.1371 | 9.2655 | 10.539 | 11.974 | 13.590 | 15.407 | 28.422 | 51.186 | 90.158 | 155.57 | 437.89 |
| 16 | 1.1726 | 1.3728 | 1.6047 | 1.8730 | 2.1829 | 2.5404 | 2.9522 | 3.4259 | 3.9703 | 4.5950 | 5.3109 | 6.1304 | 7.0673 | 8.1372 | 9.3576 | 10.748 | 12.330 | 14.129 | 16.172 | 18.488 | 35.527 | 66.542 | 121.71 | 217.80 | 656.84 |
| 17 | 1.1843 | 1.4002 | 1.6528 | 1.9479 | 2.2920 | 2.6928 | 3.1588 | 3.7000 | 4.3276 | 5.0545 | 5.8951 | 6.8660 | 7.9861 | 9.2765 | 10.761 | 12.468 | 14.426 | 16.672 | 19.244 | 22.186 | 44.409 | 86.504 | 164.31 | 304.91 | 985.26 |
| 18 | 1.1961 | 1.4282 | 1.7024 | 2.0258 | 2.4066 | 2.8543 | 3.3799 | 3.9960 | 4.7171 | 5.5599 | 6.5436 | 7.6900 | 9.0243 | 10.575 | 12.375 | 14.463 | 16.879 | 19.673 | 22.901 | 26.623 | 55.511 | 112.46 | 221.82 | 426.88 | 1477.9 |
| 19 | 1.2081 | 1.4568 | 1.7535 | 2.1068 | 2.5270 | 3.0256 | 3.6165 | 4.3157 | 5.1417 | 6.1159 | 7.2633 | 8.6128 | 10.197 | 12.056 | 14.232 | 16.777 | 19.748 | 23.214 | 27.252 | 31.948 | 69.389 | 146.19 | 299.46 | 597.63 | 2216.8 |
| 20 | 1.2202 | 1.4859 | 1.8061 | 2.1911 | 2.6533 | 3.2071 | 3.8697 | 4.6610 | 5.6044 | 6.7275 | 8.0623 | 9.6463 | 11.523 | 13.743 | 16.367 | 19.461 | 23.106 | 27.393 | 32.429 | 38.338 | 86.736 | 190.05 | 404.27 | 836.68 | 3325.3 |
| 21 | 1.2324 | 1.5157 | 1.8603 | 2.2788 | 2.7860 | 3.3996 | 4.1406 | 5.0338 | 6.1088 | 7.4002 | 8.9492 | 10.804 | 13.021 | 15.668 | 18.822 | 22.574 | 27.034 | 32.324 | 38.591 | 46.005 | 108.42 | 247.06 | 545.77 | 1171.4 | 4987.9 |
| 22 | 1.2447 | 1.5460 | 1.9161 | 2.3699 | 2.9253 | 3.6035 | 4.4304 | 5.4365 | 6.6586 | 8.1403 | 9.9336 | 12.100 | 14.714 | 17.861 | 21.645 | 26.186 | 31.629 | 38.142 | 45.923 | 55.206 | 135.53 | 321.18 | 736.79 | 1639.9 | 7481.8 |
| 23 | 1.2572 | 1.5769 | 1.9736 | 2.4647 | 3.0715 | 3.8197 | 4.7405 | 5.8715 | 7.2579 | 8.9543 | 11.026 | 13.552 | 16.627 | 20.362 | 24.891 | 30.376 | 37.006 | 45.008 | 54.649 | 66.247 | 169.41 | 417.54 | 994.66 | 2295.9 | 11223 |
| 24 | 1.2697 | 1.6084 | 2.0328 | 2.5633 | 3.2251 | 4.0489 | 5.0724 | 6.3412 | 7.9111 | 9.8497 | 12.239 | 15.179 | 18.788 | 23.212 | 28.625 | 35.236 | 43.297 | 53.109 | 65.032 | 79.497 | 211.76 | 542.80 | 1342.8 | 3214.2 | 16834 |
| 25 | 1.2824 | 1.6406 | 2.0938 | 2.6658 | 3.3864 | 4.2919 | 5.4274 | 6.8485 | 8.6231 | 10.835 | 13.585 | 17.000 | 21.231 | 26.462 | 32.919 | 40.874 | 50.658 | 62.669 | 77.388 | 95.396 | 264.70 | 705.64 | 1812.8 | 4499.9 | 25251 |
| 26 | 1.2953 | 1.6734 | 2.1566 | 2.7725 | 3.5557 | 4.5494 | 5.8074 | 7.3964 | 9.3992 | 11.918 | 15.080 | 19.040 | 23.991 | 30.167 | 37.857 | 47.414 | 59.270 | 73.949 | 92.092 | 114.48 | 330.87 | 917.33 | 2447.2 | 6299.8 | 37877 |
| 27 | 1.3082 | 1.7069 | 2.2213 | 2.8834 | 3.7335 | 4.8223 | 6.2139 | 7.9881 | 10.245 | 13.110 | 16.739 | 21.325 | 27.109 | 34.390 | 43.535 | 55.000 | 69.345 | 87.260 | 109.59 | 137.37 | 413.59 | 1192.5 | 3303.8 | 8819.8 | 56815 |
| 28 | 1.3213 | 1.7410 | 2.2879 | 2.9987 | 3.9201 | 5.1117 | 6.6488 | 8.6271 | 11.167 | 14.421 | 18.580 | 23.884 | 30.633 | 39.204 | 50.066 | 63.800 | 81.134 | 102.97 | 130.41 | 164.84 | 516.99 | 1550.3 | 4460.1 | 12348 | 85223 |
| 29 | 1.3345 | 1.7758 | 2.3566 | 3.1187 | 4.1161 | 5.4184 | 7.1143 | 9.3173 | 12.172 | 15.863 | 20.624 | 26.750 | 34.616 | 44.693 | 57.575 | 74.009 | 94.927 | 121.50 | 155.19 | 197.81 | 646.23 | 2015.4 | 6021.1 | 17287 | * |
| 30 | 1.3478 | 1.8114 | 2.4273 | 3.2434 | 4.3219 | 5.7435 | 7.6123 | 10.063 | 13.268 | 17.449 | 22.892 | 29.960 | 39.116 | 50.950 | 66.212 | 85.850 | 111.06 | 143.37 | 184.68 | 237.38 | 807.79 | 2620.0 | 8128.5 | 24201 | * |
| 35 | 1.4166 | 1.9999 | 2.8139 | 3.9461 | 5.5160 | 7.6861 | 10.677 | 14.785 | 20.414 | 28.102 | 38.575 | 52.800 | 72.069 | 98.100 | 133.18 | 180.31 | 243.50 | 328.00 | 440.70 | 590.67 | 2465.2 | 9727.9 | 36449 | * | * |
| 40 | 1.4889 | 2.2080 | 3.2620 | 4.8010 | 7.0400 | 10.286 | 14.974 | 21.725 | 31.409 | 45.259 | 65.001 | 93.051 | 132.78 | 188.88 | 267.86 | 378.72 | 533.87 | 750.38 | 1051.7 | 1469.8 | 7523.2 | 36119 | * | * | * |
| 45 | 1.5648 | 2.4379 | 3.7816 | 5.8412 | 8.9850 | 13.765 | 21.002 | 31.920 | 48.327 | 72.890 | 109.53 | 163.99 | 244.64 | 363.68 | 538.77 | 795.44 | 1170.5 | 1716.7 | 2509.7 | 3657.3 | 22959 | * | * | * | * |
| 50 | 1.6446 | 2.6916 | 4.3839 | 7.1067 | 11.467 | 18.420 | 29.457 | 46.902 | 74.358 | 117.39 | 184.56 | 289.00 | 450.74 | 700.23 | 1083.7 | 1670.7 | 2566.2 | 3927.4 | 5988.9 | 9100.4 | 70065 | * | * | * | * |

*Interest factors exceed 99.999

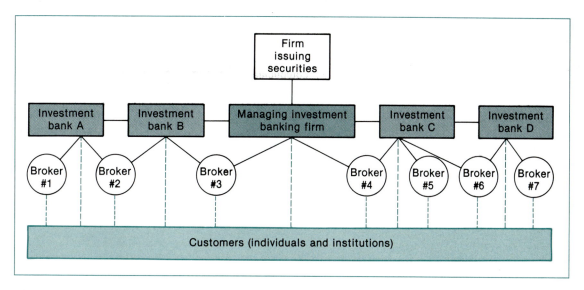

**FIGURE 17.3**
**Illustration of a Public Placement of Securities**

may range from 2 to 15 percent or more for common stock and from .5 to 3 percent for bonds.

Consider the impact of large flotation costs on a firm that issues stock worth $10 million with flotation costs of 10 percent. This firm will receive only 90 percent ($9 million) of the value of stock issued, leaving the other parties (IBFs, lawyers, printers, and so forth) with the other $1 million.

### Advising

Even after the new securities are issued, the IBF may continue to provide advice on the timing, amount, and terms of future financing. This role of advising includes recommendations on the appropriate type of financing (bonds, stocks, or long-term commercial loans). Table 17.2 summarizes the role of the IBF in helping a firm raise long-term funds.

## OTHER ASPECTS OF PUBLIC OFFERINGS

### Privileged Subscription

When the issuing corporation elects to give its existing stockholders the first opportunity to purchase any new securities to be issued, it is called a **privileged subscription.** In many cases, corporate charters include a **preemptive right** provision giving existing stockholders the right to purchase any new shares of common stock issued on a pro rata basis. Some states require that corporations chartered with them have the preemptive right in their charters. The preemptive right is designed to protect existing shareholders from having their proportionate ownership diluted when a firm issues new common stock. The existing shareholders can benefit from these rights either by exercising them during the subscription period (which normally lasts a month or less) or by selling the rights to someone else.

**TABLE 17.2** Functions of an Investment Banking Firm during Public Placement

| Task | Description |
|------|-------------|
| 1. Organization | ▪ Preliminary discussion between issuing firm and IBF on appropriate amount of securities to issue and the terms involved.<br>▪ Determination of price that IBF will guarantee the issuing firm.<br>▪ Registration with the SEC. |
| 2. Underwriting | ▪ The IBF, acting as the managing underwriter, forms an underwriting syndicate.<br>▪ Each participant is allocated a portion of the newly issued securities and assumes the risk of that portion. |
| 3. Distribution | ▪ The issue is advertised.<br>▪ A prospectus is distributed to potential purchasers.<br>▪ A sales force sells new securities to investors. |
| 4. Advising | ▪ The IBF, acting as the managing underwriter, advises during the origination stage and continues to advise the issuing firm on various matters, such as future financing. |

## Shelf-Registration

Due to a 1982 SEC rule allowing **shelf-registration,** corporations can publicly issue securities without the time lag often caused by registering with the SEC. By this means, the corporation fulfills SEC registration requirements up to two years before issuing new securities. The registration statement identifies securities that may be issued over the upcoming two years. The securities are, in a sense, "shelved" until the firm needs to issue them or feels the market is "right" to bring out the new issue. When the securities are sold, the registration can be quickly amended using current information.

Shelf registrations allow firms quick access to funds without repeatedly being slowed by the registration process. Those corporations anticipating higher market interest rates can quickly lock in their financing cost now by issuing bonds now. While this is beneficial to issuing corporations, it can be misleading to potential purchasers unless they realize that the information disclosed in the registration statement may reflect some information that is somewhat dated.

## PRIVATE PLACEMENT

When a new issue of securities is sold to one (or just a few) large investors, it is known as a **private placement.** In some cases, the services of an IBF are used to help identify potential investors and/or to help make key decisions about the features of the new issue. In other cases, the issuing firm does not seek the assistance of an IBF in order to reduce the cost of issuing the securities. Where the services of an IBF are not used, it is referred to as a *direct issue.* Potential purchasers of securities through a private placement are large enough to buy an entire issue (or a substantial portion of it), and include insurance companies, commercial banks, pension funds, and mutual funds. Private placements are more common for issuing bonds than for stocks.

Figure 17.4 illustrates the volume of privately placed bond issues relative to total bond issues during the period 1974 through 1986. The percentage of privately placed issues was lowest during the early 1980s, but increased to about 33 percent of total bond placements by 1984. Since that time, the percentage has declined. Private placement has the disadvantage to investors of providing lower liquidity of the securities in the secondary market. As a result, the issuing firm must typically pay a higher rate of interest on the bonds. The provisions within a privately placed issue can be tailored to the desires of the purchaser involved. This differs from a public offering in which the provisions are more standardized to accommodate all types of potential purchasers.

Private placement entails some possible disadvantages. Demand for a privately placed issue may not be as strong as for a public offering since only a fraction of the market is targeted as potential buyers. This could force a lower price for the securities, which could result in a higher cost of financing for the issuing firm. In addition, securities issued in private placements are generally less marketable in the secondary markets because of fewer interested buyers and sellers. This reduced marketability is another reason why privately placed securities may sell at a lower price than publicly placed securities.

**FIGURE 17.4**
**Dollar Volume of Privately Placed Bonds as a Percentage of Total Bond Placements**

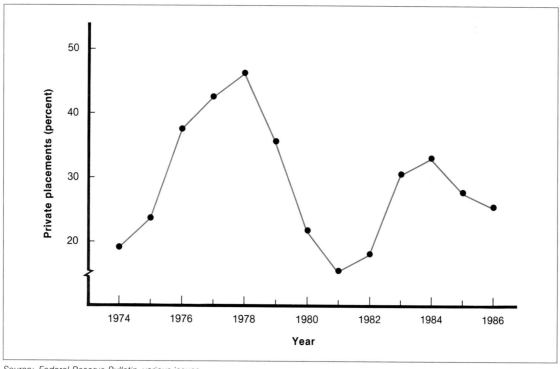

Source: *Federal Reserve Bulletin,* various issues.

## DECISION TO GO PUBLIC

Most firms are created as proprietorships or partnerships. If they are successful and plan to expand, their ability to grow is limited to their borrowing capacity and the ability of the owners/partners to make additional equity investments. At some point, firms must decide whether to *go public* (issue stock to the public). Going public has both advantages and disadvantages. The appropriate decision on whether to go public depends on the relative importance of these advantages and disadvantages as they relate to the firm's characteristics.

The primary advantage of going public is the ability to obtain more long-term funds. A firm that obtains all funds internally or through borrowing is limited in the amount of financial support it can receive. As a result, the firm's liquidity can be reduced as all available funds may be necessary to promote expansion. In addition, the cost of borrowing may become high as a firm approaches its debt capacity. A firm that goes public can obtain additional funds without approaching its debt capacity because going public involves issuing new shares of common stock. Another result of going public is that a market price may be established if the stock is subsequently traded publicly. This can be useful for the settlement of estates and when stock options are given to employees as incentive compensation (those with options to purchase stock at a fixed price will be able to determine the market value of the stock).

One of the main disadvantages of going public is the dilution of ownership that results. Generally, owner-managers of privately owned firms exercise a great deal of autonomy. Once many new owners are brought into the firm, this autonomy can disappear.

A second disadvantage is the expense incurred in filing financial reports with the SEC and state officials. Also undesirable is the fact that the public has access to considerably more information about the firm. Because some reports filed by publicly traded firms state the number of shares held by directors and major stockholders, they inform the public about the financial wealth of some of the owners. In addition, competitors and employees would have access to more information about the company. Such information can be kept confidential by not going public.

A third disadvantage is that if the firm remains relatively small after the public stock offering, secondary trading of the stock may be inactive. This can result in an artificially low market price of the common stock.

Finally, the objective of maintaining a maximum share price may force the firm to make decisions differently than if it were family-owned because the original owners' decisions would be monitored by the new shareholders. Thus, the autonomy of the original owners is reduced. For example, the decision of a family-owned business to expand in order to create management jobs for other family members would not necessarily satisfy the new owners (shareholders).

## SECONDARY MARKETS

In some cases, the individuals or institutions that purchase newly issued stocks and bonds later decide to sell these securities. This is accomplished in the **secondary markets,** where existing stocks and bonds are traded on trading floors of security exchanges (such as the New York Stock Exchange) and in the over-the-counter market (discussed later in the chapter). Stocks and bonds trading in the secondary market are as valuable as newly issued securities, other things being equal.

### Trading on Security Exchanges

To facilitate secondary market transactions, **organized security exchanges** were developed. The larger exchanges are the New York Stock Exchange, the American Stock Exchange, the Midwest Stock Exchange, and the Pacific Stock Exchange. The New York Stock Exchange is by far the largest, controlling 80 percent of the volume of all exchange transactions in the United States. Over 2,300 different stocks are traded there, with an average of over 100 million shares sold each day. Each of the exchanges has a trading floor, where the buying and selling of securities take place.

Individuals or firms that purchase *seats* on the exchange are provided the right to trade securities on the exchange. The term *seat* is somewhat misleading since all trading is carried out by individuals standing in groups. Each brokerage firm that owns a seat on the exchange can purchase or sell securities requested by their clients. Some individuals and firms own seats so that they can trade for their own accounts, and others sell their services to brokerage firms that are too busy to handle all of their customers' transactions.

The trading that takes place on the floor of an exchange resembles an auction. Those members of the exchange attempting to sell a client's stock strive to achieve the highest price possible, while members purchasing stock for their clients attempt to obtain it at the lowest possible price. When a member on the floor of the exchange announces the sale of 100 shares of XYZ stock, the member receives bids for that stock by other members who wish to purchase that stock. The seller will accept the highest bid, unless that bid is not considered high enough (in which case the seller may hold the stock until an acceptable bid is made).

If firms desire to have their stock traded on an exchange, they must have it *listed*. Each exchange has its own listing requirements generally involving a specified minimum number of outstanding shares, a minimum market value of outstanding shares, and numerous other firm characteristics. In addition to satisfying exchange requirements, the firm must satisfy SEC requirements as well.

Two advantages of exchange listing follow:

**1.** Listing a company's stock on an exchange is thought to enhance the prestige of the firm, which could result in increased demand for the firm's products. It follows that increased product demand could increase earnings and result in a higher stock price and lower cost of capital. However, the evidence is not clear on this issue.

2. Some institutional investors are permitted to purchase only shares of listed securities. Therefore, listing could increase the demand for a firm's stock, resulting in a higher stock price and a lower cost of capital for the firm. Once again, the evidence is not clear on whether this actually happens.

Two disadvantages of exchange listing follow:

1. Stock exchanges require the payment of fees and the filing of additional reports, which add to the firm's expenses.

2. Exchanges can require the publication of more information about the firm than the firm might otherwise need to expose to the public (and its competitors).

### Trading Over-the-Counter

In addition to the organized exchanges that have been described here, the **over-the-counter** (OTC) **market** also facilitates secondary market transactions. Unlike the organized exchanges, the OTC market does not have a trading floor. The buy and sell orders for stocks trading in the OTC market are completed through a telecommunications network connecting brokers (those acting as intermediaries between buyers and sellers) and dealers (firms maintaining inventories of securities from which they sell securities and for which they purchase securities). Over 90 percent of all bonds are traded in this market.

Because the OTC market does not have a trading floor, it is not necessary for participants to purchase a seat in order to trade in this market. However, it is necessary for brokers and dealers to register with the SEC or the National Association of Securities Dealers in order to trade securities in the OTC market. Securities not listed on exchanges are traded here.

### Regulation of Trading on Security Exchanges

The Securities Exchange Act of 1934 was enacted in order to prevent unfair or unethical trading practices on security exchanges. This act gave the SEC the authority to monitor these exchanges and required listed companies to file a registration statement and financial reports with the SEC and the exchanges. In addition, directors and major stockholders of firms were required to file monthly reports on any changes in their personal stock holdings.

## SUMMARY

A corporation that needs additional external capital can either increase its debt level or issue new stock. If it chooses to increase debt, it may either borrow directly from a bank or other lender or issue bonds. The bonds can be issued publicly through IBFs, or privately to one or a few financial institutions.

If the corporation decides to issue stock in order to obtain long-term funds, it will likely use the services of an IBF to publicly place the stock. The IBF will recommend the size and other provisions relating to the stock issue, and it may act as underwriter by guaranteeing the issuing firm a set price for the stock. The IBF then forms a syndicate in order to help sell the stock to investors. The flotation costs to the issuing corporation are higher for stocks than for bonds and are lower on a percentage basis for larger issues.

While the secondary market for securities is not used by corporations to issue new securities, it creates liquidity for securities originally sold in the primary market. This broadens the market for potential purchasers of newly issued securities. Increasing the demand for these securities allows corporations to issue their securities at a higher price, therefore reducing their cost of raising long-term funds.

## KEY TERMS

**Best-efforts agreement** A promise by the investment banking firm that it will do its best to sell the new securities without guaranteeing a price.

**Capital markets** Markets where long-term securities are issued or traded.

**Flotation costs** The initial costs of placing securities, including the underwriting spread and other administrative costs.

**Investment banking firm** Acts as an intermediary between the corporation issuing securities and the purchasers of these securities.

**Money markets** Markets where short-term securities are issued and traded.

**Over-the-counter market** A telecommunications network used for secondary market transactions involving unlisted securities.

**Preemptive rights** The right of existing stockholders to purchase new shares of stock in proportion to their current ownership of the firm.

**Primary markets** Markets where new securities are issued.

**Private placement** The sale of a new issue of securities to a single investor or a small group of investors.

**Privileged subscription** The sale of securities to a specific group of people.

**Prospectus** A written disclosure of a firm's financial data and provisions applicable to the security the firm plans to issue.

**Public offering** The distribution and sale of a new issue of securities to the general public.

**Secondary markets** Markets where existing securities are traded.

**Security exchanges** Physical trading places where the buying and selling of listed securities takes place.

**Shelf-registration** Allows a corporation to fulfill SEC registration requirements up to two years before issuing securities.

**Underwriting** The process of issuing new securities where an investment bank purchases the securities from the issuing firm and sells them to other investors. The investment bank assumes the risk that all of the securities will not be sold.

**Underwriting spread** The difference between what an investment banking firm pays for a new issue of securities and the price it receives (or expects to receive) for the securities.

## QUESTIONS

**Q17-1.** Distinguish among commercial banks, insurance companies, pension funds, and mutual funds as to how they obtain most of their funds.

**Q17-2.** Distinguish among commercial banks, insurance companies, pension funds, and mutual funds as to how they use the funds they receive.

**Q17-3.** Describe a situation where a corporation would utilize the primary market. Also describe a situation where a corporation would utilize the secondary market.

**Q17-4.** What payment obligation does an issuing firm have to purchasers of new bonds versus purchasers of new common stock?

**Q17-5.** Does trading on the New York Stock Exchange represent primary or secondary market transactions? Why?

**Q17-6.** What are the typical requirements for a corporation that has its stock listed on an exchange?

**Q17-7.** How does the over-the-counter (OTC) market differ from the New York Stock Exchange?

**Q17-8.** Define the tasks involved in the origination phase of issuing new securities.

**Q17-9.** When an IBF underwrites securities for a corporation, it assumes risk. Describe this risk, and explain why the IBF is willing to assume the risk.

**Q17-10.** Assume that Kattleman Corporation issued 2 million shares of new stock and was guaranteed a price of $12.00 per share by an IBF. The IBF sold the shares for $12.50. What is the underwriting spread on a percentage basis?

**Q17-11.** Why would an IBF form an underwriting syndicate rather than simply keep all the business (and profits) to itself?

**Q17-12.** Explain the difference in the risk to an IBF that offers a best-efforts agreement versus one that acts as underwriter.

**Q17-13.** Describe the costs incurred by a corporation that issues new securities.

**Q17-14.** Why would a firm planning to issue securities possibly prefer a privileged subscription?

**Q17-15.** Why would a firm consider shelf-registration prior to issuing its securities?

**Q17-16.** Belko Corporation is a growing corporation that could easily satisfy the listing requirements to have its stock traded on a securities exchange. Yet, it has avoided organized exchanges, ascribing to the philosophy that it obtains necessary funds by issuing new stock in the primary market and therefore has no use for organized exchanges. Comment on this philosophy.

**Q17-17.** Zooflow Corporation received a recommendation by an IBF to issue new stock at $11 per share, and to issue no more than 1 million shares. Zooflow felt that it would have nothing to lose by asking $13 per share. In addition, it desired to sell 1.5 million shares. Comment on its strategy.

**Q17-18.** Gondolic Corporation has decided on a private placement rather than public offering of bonds. What reasons might this firm have for using a private placement?

**Q17-19.** Henke Corporation called Kraig Investment Banking Company, requesting some advice on issuing bonds. Kraig offered to underwrite the bonds for Henke Corporation. Henke decided to decline but asked Kraig for advice on what companies might be interested if it conducted a private placement. Kraig identified three large insurance companies that might be interested. Henke called these companies but was unable to sell its bonds successfully through a private placement. Consequently, it blamed Kraig for poor advice. Is Henke justified in its criticism of Kraig?

**Q17-20.** Three of your friends have been successful at their own businesses in recent years. They are now confident that they can now go public. They consider hiring you as an employee and ask you to list any reasons why they should not go public. Your answer will determine whether they hire you.

## REFERENCES

Baron, David P., and Bengt Holmstrom. "The Investment Banking Contract For New Issues under Asymmetric Information: Delegation and the Incentive Problem." *Journal of Finance* 35 (December 1980): 1115–38.

Bhagat, Sanjai. "The Effect of Pre-emptive Right Amendments on Shareholder Wealth." *Journal of Financial Economics* 12 (November 1983): 289–310.

Dyl, Edward A., and Michael D. Joehnk. "Competitive Versus Negotiated Underwriting of Public Utility Debt." *Bell Journal of Economics* 7 (Autumn 1976): 680–90.

Fabozzi, Frank J., and Richard R. West. "Negotiated vs. Competitive Underwritings of Public Utility Bonds: Just One More Time." *Journal of Financial and Quantitative Analysis* 15 (September 1981): 323–39.

Hansen, Robert S., and John M. Pinkerton. "Direct Equity Financing: A Resolution of a Paradox." *Journal of Finance* 37 (June 1982): 651–65.

Hess, Alan C., and Peter A. Frost. "Tests for Price Effects of New Issues of Seasoned Securities." *Journal of Finance* 37 (March 1982): 11–26.

Joehnk, Michael D., and David S. Kidwell. "Comparative Costs of Competitive and Negotiated Underwriting in the State and Local Bond Market." *Journal of Finance* (June 1979): 725–31.

———. "The Impact of Market Uncertainty on Municipal Bond Underwriter Spread." *Financial Management* 13 (Spring 1984): 37–44.

Kidwell, David S., M. Wayne Marr, and G. Rodney Thompson. "SEC Rule 415: The Ultimate Competitive Bid." *Journal of Financial and Quantitative Analysis* 19 (June 1984): 183–96.

Logue, D. E., and R. A. Jarrow. "Negotiation vs. Competitive Bidding in the Sale of Securities by Public Utilities." *Financial Management* 7 (Fall 1978): 31–39.

Sorensen, Eric H. "The Impact of Underwriting Method and Bidder Competition upon Corporate Bond Interest." *Journal of Finance* 34 (September 1979): 863–71.

Zwick, Burton. "Yields on Privately Placed Corporate Bonds." *Journal of Finance* 35 (March 1980): 23–9.

# CHAPTER 18

# TERM LOANS
# AND LEASES

## LEASING IN PERSPECTIVE

In June 1987, Texas Air announced that it planned to acquire as many as two hundred aircraft from Boeing Company over a period of years. The total value of the aircraft was close to $6 billion. At the time of the planned acquisition, Texas Air already had a relatively high level of debt and was concerned that it would be unable to secure the additional debt financing needed to acquire the aircraft or that additional debt financing would be too expensive in terms of either the direct dollar cost or the indirect costs (for example, greater risk) associated with assuming additional debt financing. Texas Air decided to explore the possibility of leasing the aircraft. The most likely leasing arrangement in this case would involve the leasing of the aircraft from the manufacturer, Boeing Company, on a short-term basis. In this way, Boeing assumes the risk of financing the actual owner-ship of the aircraft while the risk to Texas Air is substantially lower as a result of the short-term lease commitment. Boeing also benefits, however, since it will effectively find a market for two hundred of its aircraft that might not exist without the lease arrangement.

There is some precedent for such lease arrangements. In March 1987, American Airlines used a similar short-term lease arrangement to acquire fifteen Boeing and twenty-five Airbus Industrie aircraft.

What factors should firms consider in making lease decisions? How can a lease alternative be compared to the alternative of borrowing money to purchase assets? What qualitative factors should be considered in making a decision to lease assets? This chapter provides a framework that can be used to address these and other questions about the leasing decision.

Earlier chapters discussed long-term sources of financing (long-term debt, common stock, and preferred stock). In a later chapter, a number of short-term sources of financing are discussed (such as bank loans and commercial paper). This chapter presents a discussion of two *intermediate-term* sources of financing: term loans and leases.

Although term loans and leases provide a smaller proportion of total financing than some of the other sources, some businesses use them almost exclusively. In certain situations, they can be the least expensive source of financing, helping to keep the firm's cost of capital low and contributing to the maximization of shareholder wealth.

## TERM LOANS

**Term loans** are loans made to businesses that have original maturities in excess of one year. The primary term loan lenders are financial institutions such as commercial banks, insurance companies (mostly life insurance), and pension funds. Other lenders include commercial finance companies, equipment manufacturers, the SBA (Small Business Administration), SBICs (Small Business Investment Companies), and regional development companies.[1]

Term loan agreements normally are negotiated directly between the borrower and the lender, a major advantage to the borrower since it can keep the cost of obtaining borrowed funds low. In contrast, when firms sell bonds to the public, the bond issue must be registered with the Securities and Exchange Commission, and an investment banker normally is hired to help sell the bonds—both costly activities. (There are exceptions to this.)

Another advantage of raising funds with term loans as opposed to issuing bonds is the increased flexibility resulting from the shorter time necessary to negotiate term loans and the fact that if their provisions need to be altered the firm can negotiate directly with a single lender in most cases. This increased flexibility in altering term loan agreements can benefit the firm in the event of financial hardship. In the case of a bond issue, making changes in the indenture normally is more difficult due to the large number of lenders (bondholders) involved.

The contract covering a term loan specifies all the provisions of the loan, including the interest rate, maturity, method of repayment, collateral, and restrictive covenants.

### Interest Rates

Interest rates charged on term loans are comparable to the rates paid on bonds. Both, of course, reflect market rates of interest and the riskiness of the borrower. Although the vast majority of bonds have fixed interest rates, a substantial proportion of term loans have variable rates. Variable rates

---

1. Regional development companies are organizations formed to promote increased business development in certain geographic areas. One way they do this is by making loans to firms that promise to locate in their area.

may be tied to the prime interest rate charged by banks, or a similar measure of market rates of interest, so that increases or decreases in market rates are matched by similar changes in the rate charged on term loans.[2] For example, an institution may charge a firm the prime rate plus 2 percent. As the prime rate fluctuates, so does the interest rate on the term loan. Variable rate loans help protect lenders from earning lower than market rates of interest on their investments during periods when their cost of funds is rising.

## Maturity

The original maturities of term loans normally range from three to fifteen years, although some term loans are made for periods as long as thirty years. Commercial banks tend to make term loans in the three- to twelve-year range, and insurance companies tend to make term loans in the ten- to twenty-year range. This difference in maturity reflects the generally longer-term liabilities of insurance companies as compared to banks. Matching the maturities of assets (loans) and liabilities helps these lenders manage their cash flows.

## Repayment Method

Most term loans are amortized. That is, they are repaid in equal, regular installments that include both interest and principal. The payment interval can be monthly, quarterly, semiannually, or annually. Amortization of a loan results in a gradual reduction of the loan balance over time. Repayment of term loan principal over time is particularly appropriate when the loan is used to purchase equipment, since the increased cash flows generated over time by the equipment can be used to repay the loan.

In some cases, term loan repayments are made with small, regular payments covering only interest, or interest plus a small amount of principal. At maturity, the firm is faced with a *balloon payment* equal to the total loan principal or a large portion of the loan principal. This arrangement increases the risk that the firm will be unable to repay the loan at maturity, so when balloon payments are required, the borrower may agree to make deposits into a sinking fund that will be used to make the balloon payment at maturity.

## Collateral

Commercial banks require collateral on the majority of the term loans they make. Conversely, insurance companies make more of their term loans on an unsecured basis. Equipment, machinery, stocks, bonds, and natural resources owned by the borrowers commonly are used as collateral.

---

2. A bank's prime rate is normally the lowest rate of interest the bank charges to its best corporate customers.

## Restrictive Covenants

**Restrictive covenants** are loan provisions that either prevent borrowers from taking certain actions or require them to take certain actions that are designed to prevent an increase in firm risk during the life of the loan. Some of the more common restrictive covenants included in term loan agreements are as follows:

**Financial Statements**   The borrower must generally provide the lender with either annual or quarterly financial statements. In this way, the lender can easily monitor the financial situation of the borrower and assure compliance with other restrictive covenants.

**Working Capital**   The lender may require the borrower to maintain a specified minimum current ratio, quick ratio, or net working capital. This requirement is designed to ensure that adequate liquidity is available to make payments of principal and interest to the lender.

**Additional Debt**   In order to protect the lender's claim against the borrower's assets, a common term loan provision is to prohibit the borrower from incurring additional debt (or lease obligations) without prior approval of the lender. The lender may also require any additional debt to be subordinated to the existing debt.

**Payment of Dividends**   The lender may place restrictions on the amount of dividends the firm can pay, since the payment of dividends could reduce the ability of the borrower to make principal and interest payments.

**Management Provisions**   A common provision in term loan agreements is to require lender approval of any changes in key management personnel. Additionally, some agreements require life insurance on key personnel with the proceeds designated for the repayment of the loan.

**Equity Options**   Although not a typical term-loan provision, there has been a trend in recent years toward granting lenders the option to purchase some shares of the borrower's common stock at a fixed price. This represents additional compensation to the lender. It also means giving up part of the ownership of the firm, which can be a significant sacrifice for the owners of a small firm. Since this additional compensation to the lender is undesirable from the borrower's perspective, it normally is agreed to only by small, less financially sound firms that are unable to raise funds on more attractive terms.

## LEASING

Leasing assets can be viewed as a substitute for borrowing money to purchase assets. A **lease** is a source of financing, since firms obtain the use (but not the ownership) of the leased assets for a specified period of time in return for the promise to make periodic lease payments. Although leases can technically last for up to thirty years according to IRS rules, generally they do not extend beyond ten years and therefore are considered to be an intermediate-term source of financing.

A *lessor* is the individual or organization that owns the asset being leased. The *lessee* is the firm or individual that is making lease payments in order to secure the use of the asset. The largest lessors in terms of dollar value of assets leased are the manufacturers of leased assets. For example, although Xerox Corporation sells many of its copiers, it also makes a lease option available to its customers.

Commercial banks are the second largest lessor group. When a bank leases property, it normally assumes ownership (but not physical possession) of the leased asset for the sole purpose of leasing that asset to a customer. Leasing services are also provided by specialized leasing companies.

## Types of Leases

There are two basic types of leases: **financial leases** and **operating leases.** Financial leases (also called *capital leases*) resemble debt obligations more than operating leases. Under a typical financial lease, the lessee agrees to make lease payments for a fixed period of time. Generally, the period of the lease is about the same as the life of the leased asset, and most financial leases cannot be cancelled. When the expected salvage value of the leased property is close to zero, the lease payments will exceed the value of the asset, and the excess amount compensates the lessor for the money it has invested in the asset.

As with a debt obligation, failure to make lease payments can result in legal action against the firm. Many lease contracts provide the lessee with an option to purchase the leased asset upon completion of the lease obligation. Typical assets leased under financial lease obligations include equipment, machinery, and buildings.

An **operating lease** is similar to a financial lease in that the lessee pays the lessor for the use of the lessor's property. However, an operating lease typically has a shorter life (five years or less is normal), and the lease generally can be cancelled by the lessee (although the lessee may have to pay a cancellation fee). Although the life of an operating lease tends to be shorter than that of a financial lease, the expected life of the leased assets may not be shorter. As a result, assets under an operating lease are expected to have substantial value remaining at the end of the lease period. Therefore, the lessor can either lease the asset to another lessee or sell the asset. Sometimes the original lessee has the option of purchasing the leased asset at the end of the lease period.

Since the asset is expected to have substantial value to the lessor beyond the original lease period, the sum of the lease payments is generally less than the value of the leased asset. The lessor realizes profits by either selling the asset or leasing it to a second lessee. Computers, automobiles, and apartments are commonly leased under operating leases.

## Leasing Provisions

In addition to the two basic types of leases, financial and operating, there are numerous alternative lease provisions and lease characteristics. Some of the more important ones follow:

**Sale and Leaseback versus Direct Lease**     There are two different ways the lessor can assume ownership of leased assets. Under a **sale and leaseback** arrangement, a firm that already owns an asset sells it to the lessor, which then leases the asset back to the seller (lessee). This arrangement is designed to help a lessee raise funds that are needed elsewhere in the firm. A sale and leaseback arrangement generally results in a financial lease.

Under a **direct lease,** the lessor has either manufactured the asset to be leased, or it has purchased the asset directly from the manufacturer at the request of the lessee. Under this arrangement, the lessee does not own the asset prior to the lessor owning it. Operating leases are generally direct leases, but financial leases can also be direct (as well as sale and leaseback).

**Maintenance of Leased Assets**     Operating leases typically include a provision for the lessor to provide all necessary maintenance on the leased assets, especially when the lessor is the manufacturer of the asset. When maintenance is provided by the lessor, the cost of maintenance is built into the lease payments. One reason why the lessor typically provides all maintenance on operating leases is that this type of lease tends to be short relative to financial leases, making it fairly easy for the lessor to estimate the maintenance costs required during the operating lease period. Also, the fact that the lessor expects to profit from the sale or subsequent leasing of the asset after the original lease has expired provides the lessor with motivation for maintaining the asset in good condition.

There are several reasons why financial leases seldom provide for maintenance of leased assets. First, financial leases tend to be longer than operating leases, so maintenance costs are more difficult to forecast. Second, banks and other financial institutions are frequently the lessors in financial leases, and these institutions are unqualified to provide the required maintenance. Third, the lessor does not normally need to sell the leased asset after the lease period to make a profit, since the original lessee fully compensates the lessor for its investment in the asset during the lease period. Therefore, even if the asset is poorly maintained, the return to the lessor is not substantially affected.

**Renewal Options**     Many lease contracts provide the lessee with the option to renew the lease upon expiration of the original contract. This is a particularly common provision in operating leases, since the original lease period is likely to be shorter than the useful life of the asset. Renewal lease payments are generally lower than the initial lease payments, reflecting the lower value of the leased asset.

**Leveraged Lease**     The lessor borrows a portion of the money used to acquire the leased assets in a **leveraged lease.** The leased assets are then used as collateral to secure the loan; thus, they are owned by the lessor, but the lessor's creditors have a lien against them. The fact that a lease is leveraged allows the lessor to magnify its profits on the lease transactions. However, it does not affect the lessee in any way.

## IRS Lease Requirements

Properly structured leases can provide tax advantages (discussed later in this chapter) to both the lessee and the lessor. In order to qualify for these tax advantages, a lease must have certain characteristics that distinguish it from an installment loan. If a transaction does not meet the following requirements, it may not qualify as a lease.

**1.** The term of a lease must be less than 75 percent of the useful life of the asset.
**2.** The lease payments must be sufficient to provide the lessor with a return comparable to the return on a loan. That is, a bona fide lease transaction offers the lessor more than just tax benefits.
**3.** Any renewal option cannot favor the lessee over other potential customers. However, the lessee can be given the option to match any outside offers for renewal.
**4.** The lessee should not have the option to purchase the asset at the end of the lease at a below-market price. If a purchase option is granted, the lessee must compete fairly with other outside buyers.

The reason why IRS regulations do not permit transactions with the aforementioned provisions to qualify as leases is to prevent firms from taking an installment sale and calling it a lease. Firms may wish to do that in order to accelerate depreciation beyond what is allowed by law. While the modified ACRS provisions provide for accelerated depreciation, consider the effect on a firm's taxes if it is permitted to lease an asset over a three-year period that has been classified as a five-year asset. Since lease payments are fully tax deductible, the firm would in effect be depreciating the asset over a three-year period.

## Accounting for Leases

The Financial Accounting Standards Board (FASB) issued Statement #13 in 1976, specifying how firms are to record leases on their financial statements. Financial leases are to be capitalized and appear on the firm's balance sheet as an asset (leased property under capital leases) and as a liability (capital lease obligations). The amount of the asset and liability recorded is the present value of the future contractual lease payments using the lower of either the firm's before-tax cost of debt or the lessor's implicit interest rate as the discount rate. Each year, the value of both the asset and liability are reduced as the lease payments are made, and the asset is used up.

The rationale behind putting financial leases on firms' balance sheets involves their similarity to debt obligations. Both can lead to the bankruptcy of the firm if it fails to make payments in accordance with the governing contract. Therefore, analysts and investors view financial leases as if they are debt obligations. By requiring firms to report financial leases on their balance sheets, the public is less likely to overlook those obligations. Operating leases are less similar to debt and are, therefore, not required to be capitalized. However, current accounting rules require that the key provisions of all operating leases be fully disclosed in the footnotes of the firm's financial statements.

FASB Statement #13 specifies that a lease having any one or more of the following conditions is a capital lease. All other leases are deemed to be operating leases.

**1.** The leased asset is transferred to the lessee at the conclusion of the lease period.
**2.** A provision exists for the lessee to purchase the leased asset at a bargain price.
**3.** The lease period is greater than or equal to 75 percent of the life of the asset.
**4.** The present value of the lease payments is greater than or equal to 90 percent of the value of the asset.

## Factors Affecting the Lease-versus-Purchase Decision

Firms seeking to acquire new assets are frequently faced with the decision of whether to lease the asset or borrow money to purchase it. In the discussion that follows, both financial and nonfinancial considerations are addressed. The final section presents an example of how the financial considerations can be quantified.

**Tax Considerations**  When a firm borrows money to purchase an asset, both the interest on the borrowed funds and depreciation on the asset are tax-deductible expenses. Conversely, when an asset is leased, the entire amount of each lease payment is a tax-deductible expense. A method of explicitly considering the impact of this difference on the firm is discussed later in this chapter.

Tax considerations are generally recognized as the most important reason why leasing is a popular method of financing. Both the lessor and the lessee can benefit from a lease agreement at the expense of government tax revenues. Consider a manufacturing firm with a marginal tax rate of 20 percent and a lessor with a 45 percent marginal tax rate (this includes both federal and state taxes). If the manufacturing firm purchases needed equipment, it will benefit from the tax deductions provided by the interest expense and depreciation. Tax deductions of $100,000 in the first year will reduce the firm's tax bill by 20 percent of $100,000, or $20,000. If, however, the lessor receives those same tax deductions, its tax bill will be reduced by 45 percent of $100,000, or $45,000. A properly structured lease can transfer these annual tax benefits to the lessor, and the lessor can then share these benefits with the lessee. Essentially, the lessor purchases the equipment and receives the interest and depreciation deductions. In addition, the lessor receives payments from the lessee of sufficient size to cover its cost of funds and provide it with a rate of return commensurate with the risk it incurs. The lessee may find that the lessor has received sufficient tax benefits from the transaction that the cost of the lease is below the cost of borrowing money to purchase the asset. As suggested by the previous discussion, firms with low marginal tax rates may find that leasing presents considerable advantages. Conversely, firms with high marginal tax rates may find leasing less attractive.

**Residual Value of the Asset**   Since the lessee does not own the leased asset, the lessee is not entitled to the residual value of the asset at the end of the lease period (the residual value is the value remaining after the lease period). Conversely, if a firm borrows money to purchase an asset, the residual value of the asset (after a comparable time period) belongs to the firm. In situations where a firm expects the residual value to be large, purchasing the asset may be preferred. When an asset is likely to have a very low residual value, as in the case of computer hardware that could be rendered obsolete in a short period of time, firms may prefer to lease the asset. Of course the lessor also considers the expected residual value of the asset and prices the lease accordingly.

**Impact on Financial Ratios**   Since financial leases appear on a firm's balance sheet, they can be conveniently reflected in the firm's leverage ratios. However, operating leases appear in footnotes and are frequently omitted from the firm's ratios (although they should be included in most cases). When leases are not reflected in the firm's ratios, the firm may appear to have less financial leverage than it actually has, which could increase the firm's debt capacity. Many analysts feel this is not truly an advantage.

**Favorable Financing Provisions**   Firms can frequently finance 100 percent of the value of an asset if the asset is leased from the manufacturer. That is, a firm may have an asset installed and begin using it upon making the first lease payment (lease payments generally are made in advance of the period they cover). Conversely, when purchasing an asset, a lender will normally lend only a percentage of the cost of the asset (perhaps 80 or 90 percent) and require the firm to pay the remaining amount.

**Restrictive Covenants**   A final consideration is that lease contracts generally have few of the restrictive covenants that a loan obtained to purchase the asset would have; thus, greater flexibility is preserved for the firm.

## Procedure for Making the Lease-versus-Purchase Decision

Although all of the considerations discussed in the previous section cannot be quantified, many of them can be. When a firm is faced with the decision of whether to lease an asset or borrow money to purchase the asset, it can compare the *present value of the after-tax cost* of each method and select the method resulting in the lower cost.[3] All costs must be adjusted to reflect the impact of taxes, and the present value of all costs must be determined.

Making the decision to lease or purchase an asset can be described in three steps: (1) find the present value of the cost of leasing, (2) find the present value of the cost of borrowing and purchasing the asset, and (3) select the approach having the lower present value cost. It should be noted that there are many different approaches to solving lease-purchase problems. The three-step approach described here is one of the more popular methods.

G. Paul Industries (GPI) has decided to acquire a new machine by either leasing it or borrowing money to purchase it. Notice that the decision on whether to acquire the asset is made separately from and in advance of the decision on whether to lease or purchase it.

If the machine is purchased, it will cost a total of $1,000,000, including transportation and installation. GPI can borrow the $1,000,000 from a bank at 10 percent interest and repay the loan by making five equal installments of interest and principal at the end of each year. The machine would be depreciated using modified ACRS, and since it is in the 5-year class, it would be depreciated over a six-year period. (GPI expects to continue using the machine even after it is fully depreciated.)

If the machine is leased, GPI must sign a lease contract promising to pay $216,000 at the beginning of each of the next six years. The size of the lease payments was determined by the lessor, who stated that $216,000 was the "lowest possible lease payment" he could offer. The lease payment reflects the lessor's required rate of return on the money it must invest in the asset.

The lessor will give GPI the option of purchasing the asset at its fair market value at the end of the lease period (GPI expects to exercise this option if it leases the machine). It is estimated that the fair market value will be $50,000. The lessor agrees to pay all insurance costs and provide all maintenance on the machine. If GPI decides to purchase the machine, instead, the cost of maintenance and insurance will be $30,000 per year. This cost is known with certainty since GPI can obtain a service contract on the asset and has shopped for insurance. For simplicity, assume GPI has a flat tax rate of 30 percent.

**Present Value of the Cost of Leasing**   Table 18.1 displays the information necessary to determine the present value of the cost of leasing. Column 2 indicates the before-tax lease payment required each year. Notice that the lease payments are made at the beginning of each of the next six years. To be consistent with the format used in earlier chapters, the cash flows are identified in Table 18.1 as being paid at the *end* of each of six years. The

---

3.   Some firms may also have the option of using existing cash to purchase the asset. If they do, however, they incur an opportunity cost of not applying those funds elsewhere. Since most firms have long-term debt outstanding at all times, the opportunity cost can be viewed as the cost of not repaying this debt. Under these conditions, the cost of using excess cash to purchase an asset is equal to the cost of borrowing money to purchase the asset.

**TABLE 18.1   Determining Present Value of the Cost of Leasing: G. Paul Industries**

| (1) | (2) | (3) | (4) | (5) |
|---|---|---|---|---|
| End of Year | Lease Payment | After-Tax Lease Payment: $(1-.30) \times (2)$ | PVIFs for 7% | Present Value of Each Lease Payment $(3) \times (4)$ |
| 0 | $216,000 | $151,200 | 1.0000 | $151,200 |
| 1 | 216,000 | 151,200 | .9346 | 141,312 |
| 2 | 216,000 | 151,200 | .8734 | 132,058 |
| 3 | 216,000 | 151,200 | .8163 | 123,425 |
| 4 | 216,000 | 151,200 | .7629 | 115,350 |
| 5 | 216,000 | 151,200 | .7130 | 107,806 |
| 6 | 50,000 | 50,000 | .6663 | 33,315 |
| | | | PV of the cost of leasing = | $804,466 |

first payment is made at the end of Year 0, which is the same as the beginning of Year 1. The final lease payment is therefore made at the end of Year 5 (beginning of Year 6).

The $50,000 payment indicated at the end of the sixth year is the assumed purchase of the machine from the lessor. Column 3 indicates the after-tax lease payment. Given GPI's 30 percent tax rate, the $216,000 annual lease payments are reduced to $151,200 on an after-tax basis by multiplying each payment by 1 minus the firm's tax-rate $(1 - .30)$. The final payment of $50,000 for the purchase of the machine is not tax deductible, so the after-tax cost is equal to the before-tax cost. Column 4 indicates the present value interest factor to be applied to each after-tax cash outflow.

The selection of an appropriate discount rate to use is important. Recall from earlier discussions of capital budgeting and valuation that discount rates are selected according to the uncertainty of the cash flows. The same concept can be applied here. Since the lease payments are fixed by contract, the before-tax cash flows are known with considerable certainty (uncertainty exists because the firm's future tax rate could vary, causing changes in the after-tax lease payments). In addition, the firm is fairly certain it will exercise the option to purchase the equipment at the end of the lease period. Because of the relative certainty of the cash flows under a typical lease contract, there is little risk. Consequently, most analysts suggest using a fairly low discount rate, such as the after-tax cost of debt. The after-tax cost of debt has been used in this example to discount the cash flows associated with lease payments, where the after-tax cost of debt for GPI is 10 percent (the before-tax cost of debt) times $(1 - .30)$, or 7 percent. The same discount rate is used to discount the costs associated with the borrow-and-purchase alternative, for similar reasons. That is, the cash flows involved are fairly certain.

Notice that the first outflow in Column 3 is already in today's dollars and does not need to be discounted. Column 5 reflects the present values of the cash flows, which are found by multiplying Column 3 by Column 4. When summed, the result is the present value of the cost of leasing the equipment, $804,466.

**TABLE 18.2  Loan Amortization Schedule for the Purchase of an Asset: G. Paul Industries**

| (1)<br>End of<br>Year | (2)<br>Loan<br>Payment | (3)<br><br>Interest | (4)<br>Principal<br>Payment | (5)<br>Remaining<br>Balance |
|:---:|:---:|:---:|:---:|:---:|
| 1 | $263,797 | $100,000 | $163,797 | $836,203 |
| 2 | 263,797 | 83,620 | 180,177 | 656,026 |
| 3 | 263,797 | 65,603 | 198,194 | 457,832 |
| 4 | 263,797 | 45,783 | 218,014 | 239,818 |
| 5 | 263,797 | 23,982 | 239,818 | -0- |

**Present Value of the Cost of Purchasing**  Table 18.2 presents the loan amortization schedule for GPI if it borrows money to purchase the asset (loan amortization schedules were discussed in Chapter 4). The size of the loan payments is determined by solving for the annuity amount using the present value of an annuity equation (Equation 3.5), where the *PVIFA* reflects 10 percent interest and five payments:

$$PVA = A(PVIFA_{k,n})$$

$$\$1,000,000 = A(3.7908)$$

$$A = \$263,797$$

The loan payment amount is $263,797. Column 2 of Table 18.2 identifies this amount as the before-tax cash outflow each year. Column 3 indicates the interest portion of each payment, which is the only portion that is tax deductible. Column 4 indicates the amount of principal included in each loan payment and is determined by subtracting the interest paid from the loan payment. Column 5 indicates the balance of the loan outstanding after each loan payment has been made. The information presented in Table 18.2 is necessary to determine the cost of purchasing the asset, since the size of the loan payments (Column 2) and the tax benefits provided by the interest payments (Column 3) affect the firm's after-tax cash flows.

Table 18.3 is used to calculate the depreciation that can be expensed by GPI each year if it purchases the asset. The ACRS depreciation percentages appearing in Column 2 were taken from Chapter 2, Table 2.8. These percentages are multiplied by the assets' depreciable basis (Table 18.3, Column 3) to determine the depreciation expense the firm can use as a tax deduction each year (Column 4). The loan payments, interest expense, and depreciation expense each year have been transferred from Tables 18.2 and 18.3 to Columns 2, 3, and 4 in Table 18.4. This table is then used to determine the present value of the cost of purchasing the asset.

Column 5 of Table 18.4 indicates the maintenance expenses each year, while Column 6 indicates the sum of all the tax-deductible expenses GPI would incur each year as a result of purchasing the asset—including interest, depreciation, and maintenance. The tax savings realized by GPI each

TABLE 18.3  **Depreciation Schedule: G. Paul Industries**

| (1) | (2) | (3) | (4) |
|-----|-----|-----|-----|
| Year | ACRS Depreciation Percentage | Depreciable Basis | Dollar Amount of Depreciation |
| 1 | 20.00% | $1,000,000 | $200,000 |
| 2 | 32.00 | 1,000,000 | 320,000 |
| 3 | 19.20 | 1,000,000 | 192,000 |
| 4 | 11.52 | 1,000,000 | 115,200 |
| 5 | 11.52 | 1,000,000 | 115,200 |
| 6 | 5.76 | 1,000,000 | 57,600 |
|   |   |   | $1,000,000 |

year from these tax-deductible expenses are indicated in Column 7 and are found by multiplying the sum of the tax-deductible expenses in Column 6 by the firm's tax rate (30 percent). Then the tax savings in Column 7 are subtracted from the total cash outflows, which include the amounts in Columns 2 (total loan payments) and 5 (maintenance costs). The result, which is the annual net cash outflows that would result from purchasing the machine, appears in Column 8.

The next step is to find the present value of the annual net cash outflows. The discount rate used for the borrow-and-purchase alternative is the same one used for the lease option since the uncertainty of the cash

TABLE 18.4  **Determining the Present Value of the Cost of Purchasing an Asset: G. Paul Industries**

| (1) | (2) | (3) | (4) | (5) |
|-----|-----|-----|-----|-----|
| End of Year | Loan Payment (from Table 18.2) | Interest (from Table 18.2) | Depreciation (from Table 18.3) | Maintenance Cost |
| 1 | $263,797 | $100,000 | $200,000 | $30,000 |
| 2 | 263,797 | 83,620 | 320,000 | 30,000 |
| 3 | 263,797 | 65,603 | 192,000 | 30,000 |
| 4 | 263,797 | 45,783 | 115,200 | 30,000 |
| 5 | 263,797 | 23,982 | 115,200 | 30,000 |
| 6 |  | -0- | 57,600 | 30,000 |

| (1) | (6) | (7) | (8) | (9) | (10) |
|-----|-----|-----|-----|-----|-----|
| End of Year | Tax-Deductible Expenses (3) + (4) + (5) | Tax Savings: 30% × (6) | Net Cash Outflow from Purchasing (2) + (5) − (7) | PVIFs for 7% | Present Value of Each Year's Cost of Purchasing (8) × (9) |
| 1 | $330,000 | $ 99,000 | $194,797 | .9346 | $182,057 |
| 2 | 433,620 | 130,086 | 163,711 | .8734 | 142,985 |
| 3 | 287,603 | 86,281 | 207,516 | .8163 | 169,395 |
| 4 | 190,983 | 57,295 | 236,502 | .7629 | 180,427 |
| 5 | 169,182 | 50,755 | 243,042 | .7130 | 173,289 |
| 6 | 87,600 | 26,280 | 3,720 | .6663 | 2,479 |
|   |   |   | PV of the cost of purchasing = | | $850,632 |

## FINANCIAL MANAGEMENT IN PRACTICE

### HOW PRACTITIONERS EVALUATE LEASES

The framework used in this text to evaluate leases is sometimes referred to as the *net advantage to leasing (NAL)* approach. Essentially, this approach assumes that capital budgeting projects are adopted first, and then the method of acquiring the necessary assets (lease versus purchase) is considered separately. The disadvantage of using this method is that it fails to recognize that an attractive leasing arrangement could salvage a project that has been rejected under normal capital budgeting analysis.

An alternative to the NAL approach is to consider leasing assets within the capital budgeting framework. That is, determine the net present value or internal rate of return of projects using the net cash flows that are estimated for the project assuming the project is leased. This approach has the disadvantage, however, of considering the cost of financing both in the cash flows and in the discounting process.

A 1982 survey conducted by O'Brien and Nunnally reports that 75 percent of the firms participating in a survey indicated that if a project is rejected based on regular capital budgeting criteria (assuming purchase), it is not reconsidered under a leasing alternative.* Once projects have been adopted, the majority of the firms use the NAL approach, rather than the capital budgeting approach, to evaluate the lease-versus-purchase decision.

Of the respondents who use the NAL approach, 77 percent use the cost of debt as a discount rate applied to cash flows as opposed to using the weighted average cost of capital. This is consistent with the theoretically justified discount rate used in this text.

* Thomas J. O'Brien and Bennie H. Nunnally, Jr., "A 1982 Survey of Corporate Leasing Analysis," *Financial Management* 12 (Summer 1983): 30–36.

---

flows is similar. That is, the loan payments are fixed, the maintenance cost is fixed by contract, depreciation expense is unlikely to change, and a change in the tax laws is unlikely to alter the tax savings substantially. Because of the relative certainty (low risk) of the cash flows associated with the borrow-and-purchase alternative, most analysts recommend using the after-tax cost of debt as the discount rate. The present value interest factors reflecting GPI's after-tax cost of debt appear in Column 9, and the present value of the net cash outflows appear in Column 10. The sum of the figures in Column 10 indicates that the present value of the cost of borrowing money and purchasing the machine is $850,632.

**Final Step in the Lease-versus-Purchase Decision**   Many factors enter into the final lease-versus-purchase decision. The quantitative analysis conducted here provides very important input, but it is not the only input that should be considered. Based on this analysis alone, GPI should elect to lease the machine, since the present value of the cost of that alternative ($804,466) is less than the present value of the cost of borrowing money and purchasing the machine ($850,632). However, other factors discussed earlier can influence the decision. For example, management may feel that the firm has more flexibility if it purchases the asset since it would be easier to terminate the project if necessary. Other factors such as this are usually less important than the quantitative analysis but cannot be ignored.

## SUMMARY

Two important sources of intermediate-term financing for businesses are term loans and leases. Term loans are loans having original maturities in excess of one year. They are generally made by financial institutions such as banks, insurance companies, and pension funds. Advantages to the borrower are their low flotation costs, the flexibility they offer in terms of the time necessary to raise borrowed funds, and the relative ease of making revisions in loan provisions if necessary. The interest rate on term loans is similar to that on bonds, and term loan maturities normally range from three to fifteen years. Most term loans are amortized and collateralized. Restrictive covenants are frequently included in term loan agreements to prevent firms from taking action that could adversely affect the ability of the borrower to repay the loan.

Leasing assets is a substitute for borrowing money to purchase assets. It is a source of financing since it provides a means by which firms can obtain the use of assets. Financial leases typically provide for the payment of rents and use of an asset for a period comparable to the life of the asset. Normally financial leases cannot be cancelled, and the lessee generally has responsibility for maintaining the asset. Most operating leases are for periods shorter than the life of the assets being leased. They can normally be cancelled by the lessee, and the lessor generally maintains the assets.

Leases may benefit both the lessee and the lessor, since they can effectively shift tax-deductible expenses from a lessee with a low tax rate to a lessor with a high tax rate. The lessor can then share with the lessee the benefits realized from the tax savings.

The lease-versus-purchase decision can be made by analyzing both alternatives in a capital budgeting type of framework. Specifically, the firm estimates the net cash outflows associated with each alternative. Next, the present value of the net cash outflows is calculated for each alternative, using the after-tax cost of debt as the discount rate. The firm then selects the alternative that has the lowest expected present value cost.

## KEY TERMS

**Direct lease** A lease arrangement wherein the lessor has either manufactured the leased asset or has purchased the asset directly from the manufacturer at the lessee's request.

**Financial lease** A long-term lease that cannot be cancelled and that normally makes the lessee responsible for all maintenance.

**Lease** An agreement between two parties wherein the owner of an asset (the lessor) permits the other party (the lessee) to use the asset in return for a fee.

**Leveraged lease** When the lessor borrows a portion of the money used to acquire a leased asset.

**Operating lease** A relatively short-term lease that normally can be cancelled. The lessor is typically responsible for all maintenance.

**Restrictive covenants** Loan provisions that may prevent borrowers from taking certain actions or require them to take certain actions.

**Sale and leaseback** When the owner of an asset sells the asset to the lessor, who leases the asset back to the original owner.

**Term loans** Loans made to businesses, generally by financial institutions, that have original maturities in excess of one year.

## QUESTIONS

**Q18-1.** What are the differences between using term loans and selling bonds as sources of financing?

**Q18-2.** Explain the following statement: "Variable rate loans can be both advantageous and disadvantageous to lenders and borrowers."

**Q18-3.** What advantages does a loan requiring a balloon payment have for the lender and the borrower?

**Q18-4.** Describe the key differences between financial and operating leases.

**Q18-5.** What relationship might you expect to find between the type of lease (financial versus operating) and the type of lessor (financial institution versus manufacturer)?

**Q18-6.** How does a leveraged lease affect the lessee? The lessor?

**Q18-7.** Explain the following statement: "In many cases, both the lessor and lessee benefit from a lease at the expense of Uncle Sam."

**Q18-8.** Describe the major steps one would take to make a lease-versus-purchase decision.

**Q18-9.** How would each of the following most likely affect the lease versus purchase decision? Why?

**a.** The lessee's tax rate increases.
**b.** Congress approves more rapid depreciation of assets.
**c.** Market rates of interest rise.

## SELF-TEST PROBLEMS

Solutions to self-test problems appear on p. S1.

**SP18-1.** Edberg Trucking Company is considering leasing a small fleet of trucks at a cost of $42,000 per year for six years (each payment is to be made at the beginning of the year). At the end of the lease period, Edberg will be given the option to purchase the trucks at their fair market value. Edberg estimates this will be $20,000, and it expects to exercise this option if it leases the trucks. Alternatively, Edberg may borrow $250,000 from a bank at 11 percent interest, amortized over five years with the proceeds to be used to purchase the trucks. Edberg estimates annual maintenance on the trucks to be $10,000, but if the trucks are leased, the lessor will provide all maintenance. The trucks are in the 5-year class and will be depreciated using the modified ACRS method if they are purchased. Assume that Edberg has a marginal tax rate of 27 percent.

**a.** What is the present value of the cost of leasing the trucks for Edberg?
**b.** Construct the loan amortization schedule that applies to Edberg's proposed loans.
**c.** Determine the dollar amount of depreciation Edberg can take on the trucks if it elects to purchase them.

**d.** What is the present value of the cost of borrowing money to purchase the trucks?

**e.** Should Edberg lease or purchase the trucks? Why?

## PROBLEMS

**P18-1.** Becker Construction Company is negotiating with a bank for a $170,000 loan to purchase some earth-moving equipment. The two alternative loan provisions now under consideration are as follows:

*Loan A:* A loan at 14 percent interest to be amortized over a seven-year period.

*Loan B:* A loan at 13 percent interest with payments amortized over a ten-year period, but with a balloon payment due after five years.

Construct the loan repayment schedules for the two loans, including a breakdown of interest and principal amounts.

**P18-2.** Connors Industries has decided to acquire a machine costing $700,000. The machine is in the 3-year class, and Connors expects to use the modified ACRS method of depreciation. The estimated maintenance cost is $15,000 per year, and Connors has a 31 percent marginal tax rate. Connors can borrow the needed funds at 13 percent interest with the loan to be amortized over three years, and with payments due at the end of each year.

Alternatively, Connors can lease the machine by making payments of $210,000 per year at the beginning of each of the next four years. The lessor will maintain the equipment during the term of the lease, and Connors will be given an option to purchase the machine at its fair market value at the end of the lease period. The estimated future market value of the machine is $50,000, and Connors expects to exercise this purchase option.

**a.** What is the present value of the cost of borrowing money to purchase the machine?

**b.** What is the present value of the cost of leasing the machine?

**c.** What decision should Connors make? Why?

**P18-3.** Noah Boatworks has decided to expand its current production facilities. The expansion will require the purchase or lease of $400,000 of new equipment. To finance the new equipment, Noah can either lease it or purchase it. The following information concerning the two alternative financing methods is to be used to make the lease-versus-purchase decision.

- Estimated maintenance cost on the equipment is $25,000 per year. Noah must pay for maintenance regardless of the financing method elected.
- If the equipment is purchased, Noah can borrow the necessary funds at 15 percent interest, and the loan will be amortized over a five-year period.
- The equipment is in the 5-year class, and Noah will use the modified ACRS method of depreciation if the equipment is purchased.
- The lease arrangements call for payments of $95,000 to be paid at the beginning of each of the next five years.
- The lessor will permit Noah to purchase the equipment at the end of the lease period at its fair market value. Noah estimates that value to be $30,000.
- Noah has a 40 percent marginal tax rate.

**a.** Determine the present value of the cost of leasing the equipment.

**b.** Determine the present value of the cost of purchasing the equipment.

**c.** What decision should Noah make based on the information presented here?

**P18-4.** Gomez Enterprises has decided to renovate an old production facility and equip it with all new machinery. Gomez can borrow the entire $5 million it needs to purchase the machinery at 10 percent from a bank, to be amortized over five years. The machinery is all in the 5-year class and is to be depreciated using the modified ACRS method. If purchased, maintenance will cost $50,000 per year.

As an alternative to purchasing the machinery, Gomez is considering leasing it. The lease payments are to be $1,000,000 per year, for six years, and each payment is to be made in advance. Gomez estimates that it can purchase the equipment at the end of the lease period for $200,000. However, this is subject to considerable uncertainty. Gomez has a 30 percent marginal tax rate. Maintenance is included in the lease.

**a.** What is the present value of the cost of leasing?
**b.** What is the present value of the cost of the purchase alternative?
**c.** If Gomez decides to recognize the greater uncertainty of the purchase price of the asset at the end of the lease period by using a different discount rate than that used for other cash flows, should it be a higher discount rate or a lower one? Why?
**d.** If Gomez knows now that it will discontinue the use of the assets after six years, how would this change the analysis?

## REFERENCES

Anderson, Paul F., and John D. Martin. "Lease versus Purchase Decisions: A Survey of Current Practices." *Financial Management* 6 (Spring 1977): 41–47.

Athanasopoulas, Peter J., and Peter W. Bacon. "The Evaluation of Leveraged Leases." *Financial Management* 9 (Spring 1980): 76–80.

Bayless, Mark E., and J. David Diltz. "An Empirical Study of the Debt Displacement Effects on Leasing." *Financial Management* 15 (Winter 1986): 53–60.

Bower, Richard S. "Issues in Lease Financing." *Financial Management* 2 (Winter 1973): 25–34.

Copeland, Thomas E., and J. Fred Weston. "A Note on the Evaluation of Cancellable Operating Leases." *Financial Management* 11 (Summer 1982): 60–67.

Crawford, Peggy J., Charles P. Harper, and John J. McConnel. "Further Evidence on the Terms of Financial Leases." *Financial Management* 10 (Autumn 1981): 7–14.

Doenges, R. Conrad. "The Cost of Leasing." *Engineering Economist* 17 (Fall 1971): 31–44.

Dyl, Edward A., and Stanley A. Martin, Jr. "Setting Terms for Leveraged Leasing." *Financial Management* 6 (Winter 1977): 20–27.

Gordon, Myron J. "A General Solution to the Buy or Lease Decision: A Pedagogical Note." *Journal of Finance* 29 (March 1974): 245–54.

Grimlund, Richard A., and Robert Capettini. "A Note on the Evaluation of Leveraged Leases and Other Investments." *Financial Management* 11 (Summer 1982): 68–72.

Hochman, Shalom, and Ramon Rabinovitch. "Financial Leasing Under Inflation." *Financial Management* 13 (Spring 1984): 17–26.

Johnson, Robert W., and Wilbur G. Lewellen. "Analysis of the Lease or Buy Decision." *Journal of Finance* 27 (September 1972): 815–23.

Levy, Haim, and Marshall Sarnat. "Leasing, Borrowing, and Financial Risk." *Financial Management* 8 (Winter 1979): 47–54.

Martin, John D. "Leasing" in *Financial Analysts Handbook*, ed. Edward Altman. New York: John Wiley, 1981.

Middleton, J. William. "Term-Lending—Practical and Profitable." *Journal of Commercial Banking Lending* 50 (August 1968): 31–43.

Miller, Merton H., and Charles W. Upton. "Leasing, Buying, and the Cost of Capital Services." *Journal of Finance* 31 (June 1976): 761–86.

O'Brien, Thomas J., and Bennie H. Nunnally, Jr. "A 1982 Survey of Corporate Leasing Analysis." *Financial Management* (Summer 1983): 30–36.

Roenfeldt, Rodney L., and Jerome S. Osteryoung. "Analysis of Financial Leases." *Financial Management* 2 (Spring 1973): 74–87.

Rogers, Dean E. "An Approach to Analyzing Cash Flow for Term Loan Purposes." *Bulletin of the Robert Morris Associates* 48 (October 1965): 79–85.

Smith, Bruce D. "Accelerated Debt Repayment in Leveraged Leases." *Financial Management* (Summer 1982): 73–80.

Smith, Clifford W., Jr., and Wakeman L. McDonald. "Determinants of Corporate Leasing Policy." *Journal of Finance* 40 (July 1985): 896–908.

Smith, Pierce R. "A Straightforward Approach to Leveraged Leasing." *Journal of Commercial Bank Lending* (July 1973): 19–39.

# CHAPTER 19

# CONVERTIBLE SECURITIES, WARRANTS, AND OPTIONS

## CONVERTIBLE BONDS IN PERSPECTIVE

USAir Group, Inc., is the ninth largest U.S. aircarrier. As of March 1987, it had the following securities outstanding (among others):

- $1.3 million of $5\frac{3}{4}$ percent subordinated debentures due in 1993, each convertible into 43.17 shares of common stock at $23.20 per share.

- $1.6 million of 6 percent subordinated debentures due in 1993, each convertible into 18.1 shares of common stock at $55.25 per share.

- $50 million of 7 percent subordinated debentures due in 1998, each convertible into 28.7 shares of common stock at $34.875 per share.

- $100 million of $8\frac{3}{4}$ percent subordinated debentures due in 2009, each convertible into 29 shares of common stock at $34.48 per share.

- 35,000 shares of $3 preferred (liquidation value of $50 per share), each convertible into 3 shares of common stock.

- 476,645 warrants, each good for the purchase of 1.04 shares of common stock at $17.31 per share.

In addition, put options (good for the sale of USAir common stock at a fixed price) and call options (good for the purchase of USAir common stock at a fixed price) are listed on the Pacific Exchange.

Why do firms issue convertible securities and warrants? What are put and call options and how do they benefit investors? What factors does the market consider in determining the price of these securities? These and other questions are addressed in this chapter.

Firms attempt to raise funds at the lowest possible cost since minimizing the cost of funds is an important ingredient in maximizing shareholder wealth. By making some securities convertible into common stock and attaching warrants good for the purchase of stock (potentially at a discount) to others, firms may be able to minimize the cost of long-term funds. This chapter discusses the characteristics of both convertible securities and warrants. It also presents a brief overview of stock options, which have become an important investment vehicle for many individuals and institutions.

## CONVERTIBLE SECURITIES

Some bonds and preferred stock are **convertible securities** in that they contain provisions that permit their conversion into a fixed number of shares of common stock of the issuing firm.[1] In some cases, the number of shares into which a security can be converted decreases over time. Virtually all convertible securities provide for adjustment of the number of shares into which the security can be converted if the firm takes action that artificially reduces the market price of the firm's stock (that is, if it pays a stock dividend or splits the stock).[2] For example, if a firm's common stock has a market price of $50 a share, and its convertible bond is convertible into twenty shares of stock, the owners of the bond would be adversely affected if the firm took action that reduced the stock's price to $25 a share. Provided that the price reduction was artificial (did not affect the wealth of existing shareholders), the convertible bond would then be convertible into forty shares of common stock.

### Advantages of Convertible Securities:
### Investors' Perspective

Convertible securities offer investors potentially high returns from conversion into a fixed number of shares of common stock, which has no limit to its potential price appreciation. In addition, convertible securities offer protection against declining securities prices since they derive their value from two different sources. That is, even if the market value of the issuing firm's common stock declines, the value of a convertible bond retains its value as a straight bond. Conversely, if the value of straight bonds declines due to rising interest rates, the market value of convertible bonds may remain high due to the potential for conversion into common stock. Since this combination of attributes is attractive to investors, convertible se-

---

1. Generally, convertible securities are convertible into common stock, however, they can also be convertible into other types of securities.
2. A *stock dividend* involves the issuance of additional shares of common stock to the current owners. Although the owners subsequently own more shares of common stock, each investor's proportionate ownership of the firm remains unchanged. Therefore, the price per share of common stock adjusts downward so that, other things being equal, the market value of an investor's total shares after the stock dividend remains the same as the value of the smaller number of shares held before the stock dividend. A *stock split* involves a similar arrangement, except (1) more new shares are issued, and (2) it is accounted for on the firm's balance sheet differently.

curities typically sell at a premium above the price of comparable non-convertible securities.

## Advantages of Convertible Securities: Firms' Perspective

Since investors generally pay a premium for convertible securities over straight securities, firms issuing securities with the conversion option can raise capital at a lower cost. For example, a firm may have to offer a 13 percent coupon on a straight bond issued at par value. However, if it adds a conversion feature to that bond, it may be able to place a 12 percent coupon on the bond and still sell the bond at par value.

A second important reason why firms may sell convertible securities instead of straight securities is to help issue new common stock at a price above the current price. For example, assume Martin Enterprises needs to raise some capital for expansion. Its common stock has a market price of $40 per share, which is lower than the firm feels it should be. To raise $10,000,000 of new capital, Martin would need to sell 250,000 new shares of common stock, and Martin fears that this will excessively dilute the ownership of the firm. Martin may be willing, however, to issue new common stock for $50 per share, since it would have to sell only 200,000 new shares at that price to raise the $10 million.

If Martin sells 10,000 straight bonds to raise the funds, it expects to put a 13 percent coupon on the bonds and sell them at par value ($1,000). Instead of doing either, Martin may be able to sell convertible bonds with a 12 percent coupon, where each bond is convertible into twenty shares of common stock. This will reduce the firm's interest expense, and when the firm's common stock rises above $50 per share, investors will begin to convert the bonds to common stock.

Since Martin received $1,000 per bond sold, and each bond is convertible into twenty shares of common stock, it is as if Martin were selling shares for $50. This is true regardless of the market price of the stock at the time of the conversion, since each $1,000 paid by the investors to purchase convertible bonds is subsequently converted into twenty shares of common stock. Therefore, the cost of each share to investors is $1,000 divided by twenty shares, or $50 per share. After all bonds have been converted, Martin is left with 200,000 new shares of common stock outstanding (10,000 bonds × 20 shares per bond) and no convertible bonds.

To increase the probability that the bonds will be converted, Martin can make the bonds callable. If and when the value of twenty shares of Martin common stock exceeds the call price of the bond, Martin can announce it is calling the bonds. This will force the bondholders to convert to common stock since that value would exceed the amount received if the bond is called.

## Valuation of Convertible Securities

The following hypothetical convertible bond and preferred stock help illustrate the factors affecting the value of convertible securities.

■ *Convertible bond issued by Brian Corporation.* Par value is $1,000, the coupon rate is 10 percent, and the maturity is ten years. The bond is convertible into twenty-five shares of common stock, and the common stock currently sells for $30 per share. The market price of the bond is $900.

■ *Preferred stock issued by Petri Corporation.* Par value is $100, the annual dividend is $10, and each share of preferred stock is convertible into two shares of common stock. The price of Petri's common stock is currently $40 per share, and the preferred stock sells for $110.

**Conversion Ratio**    The number of shares of common stock into which the security can be converted is the **conversion ratio.** For the Brian Corporation convertible bond and Petri Corporation convertible preferred stock, the conversion ratios are 25 and 2, respectively.

**Conversion Price**    The implied price investors would pay to purchase the common stock of a company if they purchase the convertible security at *par value* and convert it into common stock is the **conversion price.** It is calculated as follows:

$$CP = \frac{M}{CR} \tag{19.1}$$

where  $CP$ = conversion price

$M$ = maturity value (par value) of the convertible security

$CR$ = conversion ratio (number of shares of common stock into which the security is convertible)

For the Brian Corporation convertible bond and Petri Corporation convertible preferred stock, the conversion prices are

$$CP_{Bond} = \frac{\$1,000}{25}$$

$$= \$40$$

and

$$CP_{Pfd} = \frac{\$100}{2}$$

$$= \$50$$

**Conversion Parity Price**    The price investors pay for shares of a firm's common stock if they purchase the convertible security at the *market price* and convert it into common stock is the **conversion parity price.** It is calculated as follows:

$$CPP = \frac{MC}{CR} \tag{19.2}$$

where $CPP$ = conversion parity price

$MC$ = market price of the convertible security

$CR$ = conversion ratio (number of shares of common stock into which the security is convertible)

For the Brian Corporation convertible bond and Petri Corporation convertible preferred stock, the conversion parity prices are

$$CPP_{Bond} = \frac{\$900}{25}$$

$$= \$36$$

and

$$CPP_{Pfd} = \frac{\$110}{2}$$

$$= \$55$$

**Investment Value**   The value of a convertible security if it did not have the conversion option is its **investment value.** It can be calculated by determining the present value of all the future cash flows. The appropriate discount rate to use in discounting the cash flows is the required rate of return on nonconvertible securities with similar characteristics. This rate can be estimated by determining the expected rate of return on bonds or preferred stock having similar coupons or dividends, default risk, maturities, and other similar provisions.

Assume the expected returns on nonconvertible bonds and preferred stock with characteristics similar to the Brian bond and Petri preferred stock are 12 percent and 9 percent, respectively. The value of the Brian Corporation convertible bond and Petri Corporation convertible preferred stock can be determined using Equations 4.4 and 4.6 from Chapter 4. These equations are restated here as Equations 19.3 and 19.4:

$$V_b = \frac{I}{2}(PVIFA_{k_{b/2},2n}) + M(PVIF_{k_{b/2},2n}) \tag{19.3}$$

$$= \frac{\$100}{2}(PVIFA_{k=6\%,n=20}) + 1,000(PVIF_{k=6\%,n=20})$$

$$= 50(11.4699) + \$1,000(.3118)$$

$$= \$885.30$$

and

$$V_p = \frac{D_p}{k_p} \tag{19.4}$$

$$= \frac{\$10}{.09}$$

$$= \$111.11$$

Notice that the investment value of each convertible security is less than the respective market price. This is normal, since the conversion option has value that is reflected in the price of the convertible securities.

**Conversion Value**   The market value of the common stock that would be received if a convertible security were immediately converted is its **conversion value.** It can be calculated with Equation 19.5:

$$CV = (CR)(MP) \qquad \textbf{(19.5)}$$

where   $CV$ = conversion value of a convertible security

$\quad CR$ = conversion ratio of the security (the number of shares of stock into which the security can be converted)

$\quad MP$ = market price of the common stock into which the security can be converted

For the Brian Corporation convertible bond and Petri Corporation convertible preferred stock described earlier, the conversion values are

$$CV_{Bond} = (25)(\$30)$$
$$= \$750$$

and

$$CV_{Pfd} = (2)(\$40)$$
$$= \$80$$

**Market Value**   As illustrated in Figure 19.1, the *market value* (price) of a convertible security is a function of its investment value, its conversion value, and the value of the conversion option. Here, using the Brian Corporation convertible bond as an example, the value of the bond is on the vertical scale, and the value of the firm's common stock is on the horizontal scale. The *conversion value* of the bond is represented by a straight line beginning at the origin of the graph and sloping upward to the right, showing that as the value of the underlying common stock rises, so too does the bond's conversion value. The slope of this line is 25, the conversion ratio.

The horizontal line intersecting the vertical scale at $885.30 represents the *investment value* of the bond. This value would remain constant over the life of the bond, provided market rates of interest and the default risk of the bond remain unchanged (this assumption is made here). The *market value* of the convertible bond is represented by the dashed line, which intersects the vertical scale just above the investment value of the bond and curves upward to the right, approaching but not intersecting the conversion value of the bond. The vertical distance between the dashed line and the investment value or conversion value (whichever is higher) represents the value of the conversion option, called the **conversion premium.**

When the price of Brian Corporation common stock is low, the investment value of the convertible bond is much higher than the conversion

FIGURE 19.1
**Graphical Illustration of the Value of a Convertible Bond**

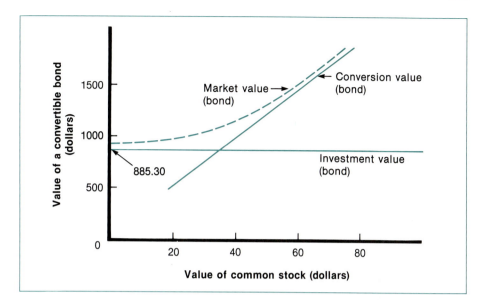

value. Under these circumstances, the market price of the bond reflects the investment value plus a small conversion premium. The premium exists because there is some probability, although small, that the stock price will rise sufficiently to increase the conversion value above the investment value.

As the price of the common stock rises, the conversion value approaches the investment value, increasing the probability that the conversion option will benefit the bondholder. As a result, the market price reflects the investment value plus a larger conversion premium. The larger conversion premium reflects the higher probability that the conversion value will subsequently rise above the investment value. If it does, the market price of the bond will reflect the conversion value plus a small conversion premium. Once again the conversion premium is small because the market value of the bond now reflects the market value of the common stock. The only reason why investors may be willing to pay a premium for this bond under these circumstances is to obtain the floor value provided by the bond's investment value. The greater the difference between the conversion value and investment value, the lower the probability is that the investment value will be needed to provide a floor price. Therefore, the conversion premium declines.

When investors estimate the value of a convertible bond, they must determine the investment value or the conversion value (whichever is higher), plus the conversion premium. The following factors tend to increase the value of the conversion premium:

**1.** The conversion privilege does not expire for a long time, giving investors a long time to take advantage of it.
**2.** The prospects for price appreciation of the common stock are good, making potential profits from converting the security greater.

**3.**  When the conversion value and investment value are very close, the value of the conversion option is greater, since the probability that the investor will benefit by converting the security to common stock increases. Additionally, the potential for benefiting from the floor value represented by the investment value of the security is high, since it is close to the market price of the bond.

## WARRANTS

**Warrants** are options to purchase a fixed number of shares of a firm's common stock at a specified price, called the *exercise price*. Although the exercise price is generally fixed when the warrants are issued, in some cases it increases over time. A rising exercise price encourages conversion of the warrants when the market price of the stock exceeds the exercise price of the warrants.

When a warrant is exercised, the investor purchases shares of stock directly from the issuing firm. The life of a warrant is typically three or more years from the time it is issued, although some warrants are issued with no expiration date. Generally, warrants are created when a firm sells a new issue of bonds or preferred stock and elects to attach warrants to each unit. The warrants act as sweeteners to the issue to induce investors to accept lower interest rates on the bonds or smaller dividends on the preferred stock. Most warrants can be detached from the bond or preferred stock and either exercised or sold separately. Some are listed on exchanges and enjoy an active secondary market.

### Advantages of Warrants: Investors' Perspective

Since the ownership of a warrant provides investors with an option to purchase a fixed number of shares of common stock at a specified price, the value of a warrant can increase rapidly if the market value of the common stock increases. For example, suppose Cramden Industries issued bonds with thirty warrants attached to each. Cramden has specified that investors can purchase one share of common stock for $25 plus one warrant. If the market value of Cramden's common stock is currently $20 per share, the warrants have little value. But assume that the Cramden warrants can be sold to other investors who expect the price of Cramden Industries common stock to rise above the $25 exercise price. Assume further that each warrant can be sold for $.50. If the price of Cramden common stock subsequently rises to $30 per share, the price of the warrants is likely to increase to $5 per share or more, since the exercise price of the warrant is $5 less than the market price of the stock. Based on a warrant value of $5, the leverage provided by warrants magnifies the impact of the assumed 50 percent increase in the price of the stock (from $20 to $30) by causing a 900 percent increase in the price of the warrant (from $.50 to $5.00).

Investors can receive the benefits of leverage even when the market price of the stock exceeds the exercise price of the warrant. However, the greater the amount by which the price of the stock exceeds the exercise price, the smaller the amount of leverage is. For example, if the price of Cramden common stock increases from $30 per share to $45 per share, while the value of the warrant increases from $5 to $20, the 50 percent rise in the price of the stock results in only a 300 percent rise in the price of the warrant—considerably less than the 900 percent increase realized in the earlier example.

### Advantages of Warrants: Firms' Perspective

Firms issue warrants for three principal reasons. First, when warrants are attached to bonds or preferred stocks, the firm can pay a lower rate of interest or a smaller dividend than it would otherwise have to pay. This can reduce the firm's cost of capital and help maximize shareholder wealth. (Of course, it can also dilute the firm's earnings per share after conversion, since the number of shares of common stock outstanding increases.)

Second, attaching warrants can be a means by which the firm issues new shares of common stock on a delayed basis, and at a price that is higher than the current market price. In addition, the firm is not required to conduct a separate underwriting for the sale of the new shares of common stock, although if the market price of the common stock fails to surpass the exercise price of the warrants, no new stock will be issued.

A third use of warrants concerns risky firms that may be required to issue warrants to lenders as part of their loan agreements. The warrants represent potential returns to the lenders that are in addition to interest on the loans. If the warrants are converted, it may result in significant dilution of earnings per share and in the ownership of the firm. For this reason, only risky firms, which have no other sources of loanable funds, are likely to agree to these terms. Many recent issuers of warrants are firms seeking to restructure existing loans.

Notice that the use of warrants to help delay an issue of common stock differs from the use of convertible securities in a very important way. With convertible securities, conversion results in the automatic retirement of the convertible bonds or convertible preferred stock. When warrants are exercised, the original securities to which they were attached continue to remain in circulation until they mature or are otherwise retired by the firm. In addition, the issuing firm receives the exercise price of the warrant for each new share of common stock sold under the warrant issue. With convertible securities, no additional funds flow into the firm when the securities are converted into common stock.

### Value of Warrants

In discussing the value of warrants it is useful to refer to the earlier example of Cramden Industries. Recall that one Cramden warrant and $25 (the exercise price) is necessary to purchase one share of Cramden common stock, which currently sells for $30 per share.

**Theoretical Value of Warrants**   The theoretical value of a warrant might be described as the dollar savings to an investor who exercises one warrant. The dollar savings to an investor is a function of the current price of the common stock ($P_0$), the exercise price of the warrant ($EP$), and the number of shares the warrant entitles the investor to purchase ($N$). The theoretical value of a warrant ($TV$) is determined as follows:

$$TV = (P_0 - EP)N \qquad \textbf{(19.6)}$$

For the Cramden example, the theoretical value of the warrant is

$$TV = (\$30 - \$25)(1)$$
$$= \$5$$

It should be noted that $TV$ has a lower boundary of zero, since a warrant cannot have a negative value (no one would pay you to purchase a warrant). Also note that in some cases one warrant entitles the owner to purchase more or less than one share of common stock. For example, assume that one Cramden warrant entitled the owner to purchase 1.5 shares of common stock instead of one share as assumed in the previous example. If the stock can be purchased with warrants for $25 per share when the market price of the stock is $30, the theoretical value of the warrant would be

$$TV = (\$30 - \$25)(1.5)$$
$$= \$7.50$$

**Market Value of Warrants**  Generally, the theoretical value of a warrant is lower than its market value (price). Indeed, the theoretical value often is viewed as a minimum value of a warrant, and the market price equals the theoretical value plus a warrant premium. The **warrant premium** is the price investors are willing to pay for the leverage provided by the warrant. That is, since warrants offer investors potentially high returns from leverage, they normally sell at a premium above their theoretical values, even when the exercise price of a warrant is well above the market price of the stock.

Figure 19.2 is a graphical illustration of the value of a warrant using Cramden Industries as an example. The theoretical value is represented by the solid line and the market value of the warrant by the dashed line. Both warrant values change with the value of the firm's common stock, which appears on the horizontal scale, and both values can be read from the vertical axis.

When the price of the common stock is well below $25 (the exercise price of the warrant), the theoretical value of the warrant is zero, and the warrant premium (the price above the theoretical value) is low, because of the low probability that the warrant will ever be exercised. When the value of the common stock is $25, the theoretical value of the warrant is still zero, but the warrant premium is at or near its highest value because the probability is high that the warrant will be exercised and because the leverage provided by the warrant is substantial. The market value of the warrant continues to increase as the value of the common stock rises, because of the increasing theoretical value of the warrant. However, the war-

**FIGURE 19.2**
Graphical Illustration of the Value of a Warrant

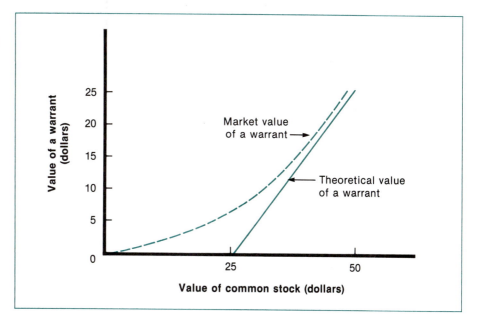

rant premium declines due to the decrease in leverage available to the owner of the warrant. As the stock price rises and the warrant premium approaches zero, the market value of the warrant approaches the theoretical value of the warrant.

## EFFECTS OF ISSUING CONVERTIBLES AND WARRANTS ON FIRM EARNINGS

The Securities and Exchange Commission (SEC) imposes special *earnings per share (EPS)* reporting requirements for firms with convertibles and warrants outstanding. Instead of reporting simple EPS as other firms do, firms with convertibles and warrants outstanding must report two other earnings figures: primary and fully diluted EPS (when only small differences between these two figures exist, the firm is exempt from the requirement). **Primary EPS** is determined by dividing *earnings available to common stockholders* by the average number of shares of common stock that would have been outstanding during the year if certain securities had been converted and warrants exercised. The firm does not need to assume that all outstanding convertibles and warrants are converted or exercised, only those that are likely to be converted or exercised in the near future. The determination of whether they are "likely to be converted or exercised" is spelled out very clearly by the SEC. When the conversion of a bond is assumed, interest paid on the bond during the year (adjusted for the tax effect by multiplying by one minus the tax rate) is added back to net income (or EAC).

The second earnings figure that must be reported is **fully diluted EPS.** This figure differs from the primary EPS figure in that the number of shares outstanding is adjusted to reflect all possible dilution from convertibles and warrants, regardless of how likely it is that they actually will be converted or exercised.

These two earnings figures can differ substantially. When they do, investors need to know what the two figures are so that they can determine the potential impact that the convertible securities and warrants may have on the firm's earnings in the future. Any decline in firm EPS can cause a decline in the price of the stock and thus a decline in shareholder wealth.

## OPTIONS

An *option* is the right to purchase (or sell) an asset at a specified price within a specified period of time. Warrants, discussed in this chapter, and stock rights, discussed in Chapter 16, are both options to purchase common stock that are issued by the firm. A third option issued by firms is incentive stock options, granted to key corporate executives to encourage them to perform well. The reasoning behind these options is that if executives perform well, the price of the firm's common stock should rise, benefiting the firm's shareholders as well as the executives, who can exercise their stock options by purchasing stock at the lower specified price.

*Puts* and *calls* are also options that are very popular in today's financial markets. A **call option** is an option to purchase the common stock of a firm at a specified price within a specified period. Consider a call option on 100 shares of Norton Enterprises common stock. The stock currently sells for $50 per share and the option expires in six months (normally, nine months is the maximum life of put and call options). The **striking price** of the option (the price the owner of the option must pay to purchase the stock) is $55, and the market price of the option is $400. If the price of Norton Enterprises common stock rises to $60 per share, it would not be surprising to see the price of the option increase to $1,300. The leverage obtained by the owner is apparent from the 225 percent rise in the price of the call option caused by just a 20 percent rise in the price of the common stock. This is similar to the leverage available from the purchase of warrants. Most investors who purchase call and put options sell their options for a profit (or loss) rather than exercising them.

A **put option** gives the option owner the right to sell common stock to someone else at a specified price within a specified period. Assume that a put option on Norton Enterprises common stock has a striking price of $55 and sells for $1,000. If the price of Norton enterprises declines from its current price of $50 per share to, say, $40 per share, the owner of the option can benefit by purchasing the stock in the open market for $40 per share and then exercising the put option (selling the stock) at $55 per share. By exercising the put, the investor is forcing someone else (someone who has sold that option or an identical option) to purchase the stock at the striking price of $55 per share. The lower the stock's price goes, the more valuable the put option becomes. An alternative to exercising the put option to make a profit is to sell it for a higher price than was paid for it. As indicated earlier, investors normally sell options to take profits (and losses), rather than exercising them.

Put and call options differ from the other options discussed earlier in that anyone can write them (sell them). For example, after establishing a brokerage account, you could tell your broker to sell a call option on IBM stock. You do not need to own the stock in order to do this. You just need to maintain a certain balance in your brokerage account. If you sell this call, however, you must be prepared to fulfill your obligation to sell 100 shares of IBM common stock at the striking price to the person who purchases the option from you. If you do not own 100 shares that you can deliver, you may be forced to purchase 100 shares of IBM stock at a high market price, and then sell those shares at a lower striking price. Of course, you would not sell a call option if you were confident that the price of the stock would rise above the striking price. In fact, most investors who sell call and put options expect the market price of the underlying stock to remain fairly stable. In this way, the investors keep the proceeds from the sale of the options without ever being forced to buy or sell the stock.

Firms on whose stock the puts and calls are written have nothing to do with those options. That is, when puts and calls are exercised, the firm is not involved. Instead, the exchange of money and securities takes place between the parties who bought and sold the options. This differs from the case of warrants, which are issued by the firms whose stock can be purchased and which, when exercised, bring money into the firm.

## SUMMARY

By issuing convertible securities and warrants, firms can realize several advantages. First, when a firm makes securities convertible or attaches warrants to new securities, it reduces the after-tax cost of those sources of financing. Second, convertible securities are converted into common stock at prices that are higher than the firm's stock price at the time the convertible securities were issued. Conversion can be forced in many cases if the conversion value of the security exceeds the call price. When conversion takes place, the original security is simultaneously retired. Third, when warrants are exercised, they bring additional capital into the firm. Additionally, the firm issues the new common stock at a higher price than the price of the stock at the time the warrants were issued.

When a firm issues convertibles or warrants, it must reveal to its investors the potential dilution effect those securities can have on earnings per share (EPS). This is done by reporting both primary EPS and fully diluted EPS in the firm's financial statements. Primary EPS essentially reflects the EPS that would have resulted if the convertible securities and warrants that are likely to be converted and exercised in the near future had already been converted and exercised. Fully diluted EPS reflects the EPS that would have resulted if all convertible securities had been converted and all warrants had been exercised.

Stock options are securities that grant the owner the right to purchase or sell common stock at a specified price within a specified period of time. Call options are similar to warrants in that the owner can purchase stock at a specified price. However, call options are written (sold) by investors who have no connection with the firm on which the options are written.

When a call is exercised, the stock is purchased directly from the seller of the option.

A put option gives the owner the right to sell stock to the writer of the put at a specified price within a specified period of time. If the market price of the stock is very low, the owner of a put option can purchase the stock at the low price and force the writer to purchase the stock at the higher exercise price.

## KEY TERMS

**Call option** An option to purchase shares of common stock at a fixed price during a specified period.

**Conversion parity price** The implied price investors would pay for shares of a firm's common stock if they purchased the firm's convertible securities at the market price and converted them.

**Conversion premium** The dollar value of a convertible security attributable to the conversion privilege.

**Conversion price** The implied price investors would pay to purchase the common stock of a firm if they purchase the firm's convertible securities at par value and convert them.

**Conversion ratio** The number of shares of common stock for which a convertible security can be exchanged.

**Conversion value** The market value of the securities that would be received if a convertible security were converted.

**Convertible securities** Bonds and preferred stock that are convertible into the common stock of the issuing firm at the discretion of the investor.

**Fully diluted EPS** Earnings per share of a firm, determined by dividing earnings available to common stockholders by the average number of shares of common stock that would have been outstanding if all convertible securities and warrants had been converted or exercised. Interest paid on the debt is added back into the firm's earnings before dividing by the number of shares.

**Investment value** The value a convertible security would have if it were not convertible (its value as a straight bond or preferred stock).

**Primary EPS** The earnings per share of a firm, determined by dividing earnings available to common stockholders by the average number of shares of common stock that would have been outstanding during the year if certain convertible securities and warrants had been converted or exercised. Only those convertibles or warrants that are likely to be converted or exercised in the near future are assumed to be converted or exercised. Interest paid on debt assumed to be converted is added back into the firm's earnings before dividing by the number of shares.

**Put option** An option to sell shares of common stock at a fixed price during a specified period.

**Striking price** The purchase price or sale price per share of common stock specified in an option contract.

**Warrant** An option to purchase the common stock of a company at a fixed price. It is issued by the firm on which the options can be exercised and generally comes attached to new bonds.

**Warrant premium** The price of a warrant in excess of its theoretical value. Investors are willing to pay this premium for the leverage provided by the warrant.

## EQUATIONS

**Equation 19.1**      **Conversion Price**

$$CP = \frac{M}{CR}$$      **(p. 518)**

where $CP$ = conversion price
$M$ = par value of the convertible security
$CR$ = conversion ratio (number of shares of common stock into which the security is convertible)

This equation is used to determine the price investors would pay for a firm's common stock if they purchased the firm's convertible security at par value and then converted it.

**Equation 19.2**    **Conversion Parity Price**

$$CPP = \frac{MC}{CR}$$                    **(p. 518)**

where $CPP$ = conversion parity price
$MC$ = market price of the convertible security
$CR$ = conversion ratio (number of shares of common stock into which the security is convertible)

Equation 19.2 can be used to determine the price investors would pay for shares of a firm's common stock if they purchased the firm's convertible security at the market price and converted it.

**Equation 19.3**    **Investment Value of a Bond**

$$V_b = \frac{I}{2}\,(PVIFA_{k_{b/2},2n}) + M(PVIF_{k_{b/2},2n})$$                    **(p. 519)**

where      $V_b$ = value of a bond (investment value as used here)
$I$ = annual interest paid on the bond in dollars
$M$ = maturity value of the bond
$n$ = number of years until the bond matures
$k_b$ = investors' required rate of return on the convertible bond if the bond were not convertible
$PVIFA$ = present value interest factor of an annuity
$PVIF$ = present value interest factor of a lump sum

The investment value of a convertible bond is the value the bond would have if it were not convertible. To determine this value, the analyst must find the present value of the interest payments and maturity value using a discount rate reflecting the rate of return investors can earn on straight bonds of similar risk, maturity, and coupon. Equation 19.3 can be used to calculate this value.

**Equation 19.4**    **Investment Value of Preferred Stock**

$$V_p = \frac{D_p}{k_p}$$                    **(p. 519)**

where  $V_p$ = investment value of convertible preferred stock
$D_p$ = dividend on the convertible preferred stock
$k_p$ = required rate of return on the preferred stock if it did not have the conversion privilege

The investment value of a convertible preferred stock is the value the stock would have if it were not convertible. To determine this value, the analyst must find the present value of all future dividend payments discounted at a rate reflecting the return investors can earn on straight preferred stock of similar risk. Equation 19.4 can be used to calculate this value.

**Equation 19.5**     **Conversion Value**

$$CV = (CR)(MP) \qquad \text{(p. 520)}$$

where  $CV$ = conversion value of a convertible security
$CR$ = conversion ratio of the security (the number of shares of stock into which the security can be converted)
$MP$ = market price of the common stock into which the security can be converted

The conversion value of a convertible security is derived from the market value of the underlying common stock. Equation 19.5 can be used to calculate this value.

**Equation 19.6**     **Theoretical Value of a Warrant**

$$TV = (P_0 - EP)N \qquad \text{(p. 524)}$$

where $TV$ = theoretical value of a warrant
$P_0$ = market price of the common stock underlying the warrant
$EP$ = exercise price of the warrant
$N$ = number of shares of common stock each warrant entitles the investor to purchase

The theoretical value of a warrant reflects the dollar saving to an investor who exercises the warrant. Equation 19.6 reflects that value. When the value of $TV$ is negative, the theoretical value of the warrant is considered to be zero rather than negative.

## QUESTIONS

**Q19-1.** What types of securities are convertible, and what types of securities are they convertible into?

**Q19-2.** From the firm's perspective, what are the advantages of issuing convertible securities?

**Q19-3.** Explain why the following quotation may be correct: "Convertible bonds may provide unlimited returns and limited losses, but the risk-return relationship is not sufficiently favorable for me to invest in them."

**Q19-4.** How are a convertible bond's conversion ratio and conversion price related?

**Q19-5.** If you were providing investment advice to someone else, would you advise them to be more concerned with the conversion price or the conversion parity price of a convertible bond? Why?

**Q19-6.** What steps would you take to determine the discount rate to use in determining a convertible bond's investment value?

**Q19-7.** Describe the interrelationships between a convertible bond's investment value, conversion value, and market value.

**Q19-8.** List the similarities between call options and warrants.

**Q19-9.** What advantages are there for firms to issue warrants?

**Q19-10.** What factors affect the market value of a warrant, and what effect does each factor have?

**Q19-11.** How do warrants and convertibles affect firm earnings?

**Q19-12.** How would each of the following most likely affect the value of a put option and a call option?

**a.** The price of the underlying common stock increases.
**b.** The expiration date is very near.
**c.** The volatility of the price of the underlying stock increases.

## SELF-TEST PROBLEMS

Solutions to self-test problems appear on p. S1.

**SP19-1.** The convertible bonds issued by Astro Enterprises have a par value of $1,000, coupon rate of 9.8 percent (paid semiannually), and twenty years until maturity. The bonds are convertible into forty shares of common stock, which currently sell for $20 per share. The market price of the bonds is $840.

**a.** What is the bond's conversion price?
**b.** What is the bond's conversion parity price?
**c.** What is the bond's investment value if straight bonds with similar characteristics sell to yield 16 percent?
**d.** What is the bond's conversion value?

**SP19-2.** Bolte Corporation's common stock currently sells for $46 per share. Warrants, good for the purchase of 2.5 shares of Bolte Corporation's common stock at $40 per share, currently sell for $17 per warrant.

**a.** What is the theoretical value of one Bolte Corporation warrant?
**b.** If you own twenty-five Bolte Corporation warrants, how much money would it cost you to exercise all of your warrants? What would be the total market value of all the shares you own after the purchase?

**SP19-3.** Colbourn, Inc., had earnings available to common stockholders of $6 million in a recent year. The average number of shares of common stock outstanding during the year was 4.5 million. Colbourn also had 1 million warrants outstanding, each of which is good for the purchase of one share of common stock. These warrants are considered likely to be exercised in the near future. In addition, Colbourn had $70 million (par value) of bonds outstanding during the year. Each $1,000 par value bond is convertible into fifty shares of common stock, but conversion is not considered likely in the near future (the bonds have a 6 percent coupon). What are Colbourn's primary and fully diluted earnings per share if its tax rate is 34 percent?

## PROBLEMS

**P19-1.** The convertible preferred stock of Zook Corporation currently sells for $91 per share and pays an $8 annual dividend. It has a $100 par value, and each share is convertible into three shares of Zook common stock, currently priced at $28 per share.

a. What is the conversion price of Zook convertible preferred stock?
b. What is the preferred stock's conversion parity price?
c. What is the preferred stock's investment value if straight preferred stocks having similar characteristics sell to yield 9.5 percent?
d. What is the conversion value of Zook preferred stock?

**P19-2.** Wyatt, Inc., has 2 million warrants outstanding, each of which can be used to purchase 3.5 shares of Wyatt common stock. The stock currently sells for $4 per share, but the warrants permit the purchase of shares at $3 per share.

a. What is the theoretical value of one Wyatt, Inc., warrant?
b. What would be the theoretical value of a warrant if the price of the stock declined to $2.50 per share?
c. If you purchase two warrants today at their theoretical value and exercise them when the price of Wyatt common stock reaches $6.75 per share, what will be your dollar profit?

**P19-3.** Twitchell Enterprises has the following securities outstanding:

- *Long-term debt*
  Convertible bonds: 11 percent coupon due 2002. Par value is $100 million, and the conversion ratio is 25.
- *Common stock:* 9.2 million shares at $1 par value.
- *Warrants:* 100,000 outstanding, each of which can be used to purchase 1.5 shares.

Twitchell has earnings before interest and taxes of $4 million and a 34 percent flat tax rate. What are Twitchell's primary and fully diluted earnings per share if the bonds are likely to be converted but the warrants are not likely to be converted? (Assume Twitchell has no short-term debt.)

**P19-4.** Taylor Corporation has a bond issue outstanding with a 12.75 percent coupon that matures in fifteen years. It has a par value of $1,000 and is convertible into sixty shares of common stock. Taylor common stock currently sells for $22 per share, and the bond is callable at 112 percent of par value; the bond has a market price of $1,350.

a. What is the bond's conversion price?
b. What is the bond's conversion parity price?
c. What is the bond's investment value if straight bonds with similar characteristics sell to yield 14 percent?
d. What is the bond's conversion value?
e. Would calling the bonds force conversion?

**P19-5.** Trew Enterprises is about to issue bonds having a combined par value of $50 million. Each bond will have a par value of $1,000, and Trew intends to attach one warrant to each bond. Trew's common stock currently sells for $25 per share, but the firm feels the stock is really worth $30 per share. It would like to raise $100 million of equity funds by attaching warrants to the bonds, exercisable at $30 per share.

a. How many shares can be purchased with each warrant?
b. What is the theoretical value of a warrant?

**P19-6.** The capital accounts of Vega Corporation are as follows:

VEGA CORPORATION
CAPITAL ACCOUNTS
YEAR–END 1987

| | |
|---|---:|
| *Long-term debt* | |
| 11.6% bonds due 1999 (par value is $1,000) | $50,000,000 |
| 9.5% convertible bonds due 2010 (par value is $1,000, and the conversion ratio is 50) | 30,000,000 |
| *Preferred stock* | |
| 100,000 shares of 8.75% convertible preferred (par value is $50, the conversion ratio is 1.0) | 5,000,000 |
| *Common equity* | |
| Common stock (32 million shares at $1 par value) | 32,000,000 |
| Paid-in capital | 16,000,000 |
| Retained earnings | 100,000,000 |
| Total capital | $233,000,000 |

In addition to the preceding, Vega has 250,000 warrants outstanding, each one good for the purchase of 1.5 shares of common stock at $21 per share. The convertible bonds are likely to be converted shortly but the preferred stock and warrants are unlikely to be exercised in the near future. If Vega's earnings before interest and taxes totaled $50 million in 1987, what are its primary and fully diluted earnings per share? (Assume a 34 percent average tax rate.)

## REFERENCES

Alexander, Gordon J., and Roger D. Stover. "The Effect of Forced Conversion on Common Stock Prices." *Financial Management* 9 (Spring 1980): 39–45.

———. "Pricing in the New Issue Convertible Debt Market," *Financial Management* 6 (Fall 1977): 35–39.

Alexander, Gordon J., Roger D. Stover, and David B. Kuhnau. "Market Timing Strategies in Convertible Debt Financing." *Journal of Finance* 34 (March 1979): 143–55.

Baumol, William J., Burton G. Malkiel, and Richard E. Quandt. "The Valuation of Convertible Securities." *Quarterly Journal of Economics* 80 (February 1966): 48–59.

Black, Fisher, and Myron Scholes. "Pricing of Options and Corporate Liabilities." *Journal of Political Economy* 81 (May–June 1973): 637–59.

Brennan, M. J., and E. S. Schwartz. "Convertible Bonds: Valuation and Optimal Strategies for Call and Conversion." *Journal of Finance* 32 (December 1977): 1699–1715.

Brennan, M. J., and E. Schwartz. "Analyzing Convertible Bonds." *Journal of Financial and Quantitative Analysis* 15 (November 1980): 907–29.

Brigham, Eugene F. "An Analysis of Convertible Debentures: Theory and Some Empirical Evidence." *Journal of Finance* 21 (March 1966): 35–54.

Evnine, Jeremy, and Andrew Rudd. "Index Options: The Early Evidence." *Journal of Finance* 40 (July 1985): 743–55.

Galai, Dan, and Mier I. Schneller. "Pricing of Warrants and the Value of the Firm." *Journal of Finance* 33 (December 1978): 1333–42.

Pinches, George E. "Financing with Convertible Preferred Stocks, 1960–1967." *Journal of Finance* 25 (March 1970): 53–64.

Schwartz, Eduardo S. "The Valuation of Warrants: Implementing a New Approach." *Journal of Financial Economics* 4 (January 1977): 79–93.

Solofsky, Robert M. "Yield Risk Performance of Convertible Securities." *Financial Analysts Journal* 39 (March–April 1971): 61–65.

Weil, Roman L., Jr., Joel E. Segall, and David Green, Jr. "Premiums on Convertible Bonds." *Journal of Finance* 23 (June 1968): 445–63.

# PART 7

# WORKING CAPITAL MANAGEMENT

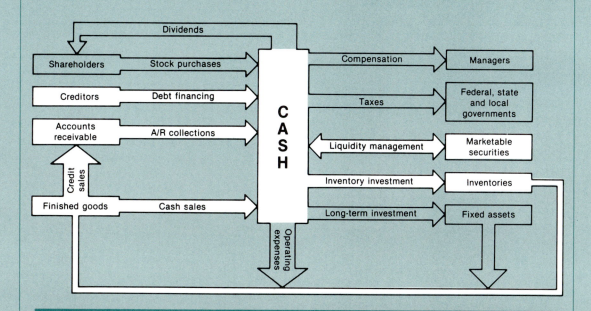

Chapters 20 through 23 focus on the management of the firm's current assets and current liabilities. Chapter 20 presents a broad overview of the risk-return relationships that exist in managing current assets and liabilities and discusses how these balance sheet accounts are interrelated.

Chapter 21 discusses the key factors to consider in managing cash and marketable securities and also describes some techniques for managing these assets. Chapter 22 discusses the key factors to consider in managing two other key assets, inventories and accounts receivable. Chapter 23 discusses some important considerations in managing short-term sources of financing and describes the main characteristics of alternative sources of short-term funds.

# CHAPTER 20

# WORKING CAPITAL MANAGEMENT

## WORKING CAPITAL MANAGEMENT IN PERSPECTIVE

In June 1987, Geriatric & Medical Centers, Inc., planned to issue as much as $452 million in commercial paper (short-term promissory notes) backed by a bank's letter of credit. An initial offering of $37 million was targeted with flexibility to issue more if needed. The proceeds were to be used to increase the firm's current assets and to retire some long-term fixed-rate debt that had been issued at a time when interest rates were relatively high. The replacement of the long-term debt was intended to reduce the firm's overall cost of financing, and the increase in current assets was to support a higher level of sales. This plan would also increase the risk of the firm since the additional short-term financing would reduce the firm's current ratio and quick ratio, other

things being equal. This financing decision illustrates a decision on the part of management to become more aggressive in managing its working capital (current assets and current liabilities) by attempting to decrease interest expense in exchange for accepting greater risk through reduced liquidity.

How would this strategy affect a firm's financing costs if interest rates decline in the future? What if interest rates rise in the future? Are a firm's earnings more or less uncertain as a result of an increase in short-term financing? How will this change in financing affect the firm's creditworthiness? This chapter explains how working capital management can affect a firm's risk and potential return.

**Working capital management** refers to the management of current assets and current liabilities. It requires the evaluation of a risk-return trade-off in which risk is measured by the level of firm liquidity, risk of stock-outs, and variability of firm earnings, and return is measured by the level and growth rate of earnings and dividends. If management elects to employ high levels of risk in managing working capital in an effort to maximize profits, it must be aware of the effects this can have on investors' required rates of return. Decisions that minimize investors' required rates of return and maximize the level and growth rate of the dividend will increase the firm's stock value and thus maximize shareholder wealth.

## THE IMPORTANCE OF WORKING CAPITAL MANAGEMENT

One reason why working capital management is such an important aspect of financial management is that, for the average manufacturing firm, the level of current assets exceeds 50 percent of total assets, and the level of current liabilities represents nearly 30 percent of total financing. Also, the relationship between current assets and current liabilities is an important indication of the firm's liquidity (the ability of the firm to pay its bills when they come due). Many firms fail because they do not maintain adequate liquidity, even though they have a good product and growing sales. (As indicated in Chapter 6, the adequacy of liquidity can be measured using the current ratio, quick ratio, and net working capital.) A final reason why working capital management is important is that the level of current assets and current liabilities can be quite volatile, leading to either excess liquidity or a liquidity deficiency. Financial managers normally spend the bulk of their time managing working capital in an effort to avoid these excesses and deficiencies.

The purpose of this chapter is to explain how managerial decisions affect the level of **net working capital** (current assets minus current liabilities) and the firm's risk and return. The basic working capital decisions involve determining the overall level of current assets and the level of total debt financing provided by current liabilities as opposed to long-term debt. It is important to recognize that the level of equity financing is held constant throughout our discussion of working capital management. Therefore, any reduction in current liabilities is assumed to be replaced with long-term debt, and vice versa. The issue of debt versus equity was addressed in Chapter 13.

The three chapters that follow provide a detailed analysis of each of the major types of current assets and current liabilities. Chapters 21 and 22 discuss how to determine the appropriate level of investment in each of the major current assets (cash, marketable securities, accounts receivable, and inventory). Chapter 23 discusses the principal sources of short-term funds (current liabilities) and how to determine which sources to use. While the determination of each current asset and each current liability separately results in a given level of net working capital, it is important to evaluate the combined effect of these separate decisions on the firm. This combined effect is discussed in this chapter so that the student can begin with a broad overview of working capital management.

## THE CASH FLOW CYCLE

The **cash flow cycle** is critical to understanding working capital management. Essentially, the cash flow cycle describes the movement of funds out of the firm for the purchase of raw materials and labor (and for other required expenditures) and then back into the firm from the sale of the firm's product. A simplified view of this cycle is presented in Table 20.1. The six "periods" in the table are not assumed to be of equal length. In this example, the firm realizes an increase in both current assets and current liabilities during Periods 1 and 2 with no additional outside financing required. The increase in current assets results from the purchase of raw materials, and the increase in the value of inventories occurs as labor is applied to the raw materials. Meanwhile, the firm's accounts payable and accrued wages also increase assuming the firm purchases the raw materials on credit and the firm's employees have not yet been paid. This increase in accounts payable and wages payable represents a source of short-term financing to the firm since the firm has received the use of assets without having paid for them.

During Periods 3 and 4, the firm finally pays for the materials and labor it purchased, so accounts payable and wages payable are no longer sources of financing. At this point, the firm's need for additional financing is at its maximum level, since it has invested its cash in raw materials and labor but has not yet sold its product and received payment from the sale. In Period 5, the firm sells its product, but it is not until Period 6, when the customer finally pays for the product it had purchased earlier, that the cash spent earlier flows back into the firm. At the end of the sixth period, the firm has funds available with which to purchase more raw materials

**TABLE 20.1** **A Simplified View of the Cash Flow Cycle**

| | | Effect on Firm's | | |
|---|---|---|---|---|
| Period | Action Taken by Firm | Cash | Current Assets | Current Liabilities |
| 1 | Purchase raw materials using trade credit | No change | Raw materials inventory increases | Accounts payable increase |
| 2 | Apply labor to materials to produce finished goods | No change | Value of inventories increases | Wages payable increase |
| 3 | Pay for the raw materials purchased earlier | Outflow | Cash decreases | Accounts payable decrease |
| 4 | Pay for the labor used to produce the product | Outflow | Cash decreases | Wages payable decreases |
| 5 | Sell the product on trade credit | No change | Inventory decreases; accounts receivable increase | No change |
| 6 | Collect on the account receivable | Inflow | Accounts receivable decrease; cash increases | No change |

and labor. Of course, firms normally do not view the cash flow cycle in discrete increments like this. Instead, each phase of the cycle is conducted continuously throughout the year.

A firm with level sales may be able to maintain a stable level of current assets over time as it continuously purchases raw materials and labor and continuously sells its product. However, most firms experience fluctuations in the demand for their product. These fluctuations can result from seasonal demand changes, cyclical demand fluctuations, or for other reasons. When product demand temporarily increases, the amount of raw materials and labor purchased by the selling firm also increases, which may cause the firm to borrow funds temporarily to pay for raw materials and labor (Period 4 on the table) until cash has been received from the sale of the product (Period 6). The decision on how to finance a temporary increase in assets affects the firm's level of net working capital and its risk and return.

## THE RISK-RETURN TRADE-OFF

The risk-return trade-off may be discussed in terms of maintaining either a low or high net working capital.

### Maintaining a Low Level of Net Working Capital

Two strategies exist for maintaining a low level of net working capital. Both affect the risk and return of the firm. The first is to *maintain a low level of current assets.* Any investment in current assets results in an additional financing expense to the firm. That is, for every dollar of cash, marketable securities, accounts receivable, and inventory that the firm adds to the left side of its balance sheet, an equivalent value must be added to the right side of the balance sheet. Since the firm incurs a cost for items on the right side of its balance sheet,[1] financing costs increase when more assets are maintained. This increase in financing costs may adversely affect the value of the firm's common stock and thus shareholder wealth.

If the firm elects to keep current assets low, however, it will incur certain risks as a result. Recall that current assets provide the liquidity necessary for the firm to pay its bills. Therefore, an inadequate level of cash (or marketable securities that can be converted quickly into cash) can prevent the firm from paying its bills on time. A low level of accounts receivable normally means the firm has either a low level of sales (not a desirable situation) or a shorter average collection period, which may be desirable, but action taken to reduce the collection period can result in lower sales (this relationship is discussed in detail in Chapter 22).

When a firm maintains low levels of inventories, it risks incurring a shortage of raw materials or work-in-process inventory that can shut down

---

1. Firms may not incur a cost for some accruals and accounts payable. However, there is a limit to how much of a firm's assets can be financed with these liabilities.

the production process. Low levels of finished goods inventory can result in lost sales, lower and more volatile earnings, higher required rates of return to investors, and a lower value of the firm's common stock. The financial manager must weigh the risks described here in deciding whether to keep current assets at a very low level.

Pillsbury Company was confronted with evaluating its working capital policy in the early 1980s as a result of what it felt was inefficient utilization of current assets. Despite some concerns that a reduction in current assets might cause a shortage of cash or inventory or that some customers may be lost (as a result of a tight credit policy used to reduce accounts receivable), Pillsbury elected to decrease its current assets. This action proved successful as Pillsbury was able to increase its sales for the next five years while maintaining current assets at the same level it had maintained three years earlier.

The second strategy for maintaining a low level of working capital is to *maintain a high level of current liabilities* by substituting short-term financing for long-term financing. This action may increase the firm's profits, because the cost of short-term financing tends to be lower than the cost of long-term financing. Although there have been some notable exceptions to this during the 1970s, early 1980s, and at other times throughout history, long-term financing generally costs more.

Figure 20.1 illustrates two possible relationships between the cost of financing (assumed here to be equal to the yield to lenders) and the maturity of debt obligations. The graph of this relationship is called a **yield curve.** The ascending yield curve describes the relationship that normally exists: that is, firms borrowing funds for longer periods incur higher financing costs. Therefore, by financing more of the firm's assets with short-term liabilities, the cost of financing can usually be kept lower.

While financing more assets with current liabilities tends to increase potential profits, there are two major risks associated with such a strategy. First, the firm may be unable to roll its short-term debt over when it comes due. Some firms borrow money for a short period, despite needing the funds for a longer period; and when the short-term loan is repaid, a new loan of the same amount is obtained by the firm. Firms needing to "roll their debt over" risk being unable to obtain a new loan for any of a number of reasons, such as the existence of a credit crunch in the economy or problems developing within the firm that make it a poor credit risk. If firms finance their assets with long-term funds to begin with, they do not need to roll their debt over.

A second risk of financing with current liabilities is that the firm's interest expense will be less certain. Although short-term interest rates are normally lower than long-term rates, this is not always the case. Notice the descending yield curve in Figure 20.1. When a descending yield curve exists, short-term interest rates are higher than long-term interest rates.[2] In addition, Figure 20.1 illustrates that short-term interest rates are more volatile than long-term interest rates (compare the range of short-term interest rates to the range of long-term interest rates for the two periods il-

---

2. Appendix A to this chapter describes the determinants of the yield curve.

**FIGURE 20.1**

**Hypothetical Yield Curves at Two Different Points in Time**

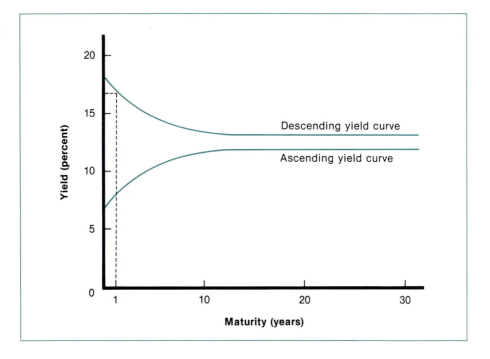

lustrated). If a firm rolls its short-term debt over every year, its interest expense is subject to considerable variability. In contrast, the interest expense for borrowing long-term funds does not change until the long-term debt matures.

Consider a firm that uses significant amounts of short-term financing when the yield curve is ascending (the lower curve in Figure 20.1). If it borrows money with a one-year maturity it will pay 7 percent interest. Assume that interest rates increase over time until the descending yield curve exists. The firm is now faced with extremely high costs of borrowing if it borrows for one year again (17 percent). Firms financing large amounts of assets using short-term debt could experience reduced earnings due to the extremely high interest expense. Of course, these firms could switch to long-term financing. However, when the yield curve is descending, even long-term interest rates tend to be relatively high. Switching to long-term debt at that time could lock the firm into relatively high interest rates for a long period of time.

## Maintaining a High Level of Net Working Capital

Just as there are two approaches to maintaining a low level of net working capital, there are also two strategies for maintaining a high level. The first is to *maintain a large amount of current assets*, and the second is to *maintain a low level of current liabilities*.

If the firm maintains a high level of net working capital, it may avoid the risks described in the previous section that are related to holding small amounts of current assets and financing with current liabilities. That is, the firm may experience less difficulty in meeting its short-term obligations, and such a policy is consistent with a high level of sales, which results in a high level of accounts receivable. Furthermore, high levels of inventory reduce the danger of stock-outs. If the firm elects to finance with long-term debt rather than with current liabilities, its exposure to volatile interest rates will be lower. Finally, exposure to the other risks associated with rolling over short-term debt each year will also be reduced.

While the strategy of maintaining a high level of net working capital reduces risk, it may also reduce potential returns. Higher financing costs are associated with maintaining high levels of current assets and with using long-term sources of funds rather than short-term sources. Of course, the specific costs and benefits of any given situation must be considered before management can make a final decision. While this decision is generally based on the subjective judgment of management, the following discussion provides a framework that management can use to make working capital decisions.

## DETERMINING THE APPROPRIATE LEVEL OF NET WORKING CAPITAL

Management's willingness to accept risk in return for higher expected returns is a critical determinant of the level of net working capital. However, other factors must also be considered by the firm in making this decision.

### Determining the Level of Current Assets

The level of current assets maintained by a firm is affected by the *level of uncertainty* surrounding the firm's operations. In a world of certainty, management would maintain only enough cash to make required payments and only enough inventory to continue production and fill known orders (the delivery time for raw materials and the demand for the firm's product would be known with certainty). Accounts receivable would be at a level consistent with an optimal credit policy for the firm, assuming no uncertainty about collections. In other words, there would be no need for the firm to hold any excess current assets. Therefore, the *minimum* level of current assets is the level necessary to continue operations in the absence of uncertainty.

However, businesses operate in a world of uncertainty, although the level of uncertainty may vary from firm to firm. For example, firms with substantial uncertainty about their level of sales may find it necessary to maintain a large finished goods inventory, while firms with substantial uncertainty regarding the reorder time for raw materials may require a large raw materials inventory. Uncertainty in other areas of operations may require higher levels of work-in-process inventory, cash, or accounts receivable. The result is a higher level of working capital.

In addition to the level of uncertainty, a second key factor that may affect the level of current assets maintained is loan *provisions*, which frequently require the firm to hold a minimum level of specific current assets (cash, for example), a minimum level of total current assets, or a minimum level of net working capital. A third factor is *stockholder pressure*. Stockholders generally recognize the risk and return implications associated with the level of current assets maintained by firms, and they may view excessive or insufficient levels of current assets as an indication of poor management. Therefore, stockholders place an implicit upper and lower limit on the level of current assets maintained by the firm. Although, the attitudes of stockholders are not likely to influence daily operations, they can establish broad limits of acceptability.

## Determining the Level of Current Liabilities

Management's attitude toward risk and return is a key determinant of the level of current liabilities, but other factors also influence this decision—notably, the *asset structure of the firm*. A strategy known as the **hedging principle** suggests that the maturity of the sources of financing should be matched with the life of the assets being financed. For example, to finance a temporary increase in inventories, a firm should borrow short-term funds. Upon the receipt of cash from the sale of the inventory, funds will be available to repay the loan. Conversely, when a firm acquires a fixed asset with a twenty-year life, it can use cash flows generated over the twenty years to gradually repay a long-term loan used to finance the asset. If that asset were financed with short-term debt, the firm would incur the risk of being unable to roll the debt over every year (a smaller amount each year), or it might be forced to pay a much higher rate of interest when it rolls the loan over.

Figure 20.2 illustrates the matching of the financing source with the life of the asset. In this example, it is assumed that there is no long-run upward trend in the firm's sales so that the complicating factor of increasing fixed assets is eliminated. The vertical scale shows the dollar investment in assets, and the horizontal scale measures time. The horizontal line representing the level of fixed assets indicates that they remain constant. The level of current assets fluctuates over time in this example due to either short-run seasonal changes in product demand, the unsystematic variability of demand for the firm's product, or some other reason.

Recall that a temporary increase in demand for a firm's product results in a temporary increase in the firm's current assets. This is illustrated in Figure 20.2a by a rise in the top line representing total assets, as time passes from $X_1$ to $X_2$. The increase in current assets is the result of increased investment in inventory as more raw materials and labor are purchased (this corresponds to Period 2 in Table 20.1). Subsequently, accounts receivable replace inventory when the finished product is sold. Finally, the need for current assets decreases as cash is received from the sale of the firm's product (moving from $X_2$ to $X_3$) and is used to repay short-term sources.

All current assets might not be financed with short-term sources, however. Even though all current assets have short lives, there is a minimum level of current assets the firm always expects to maintain; that is, the firm will always have some cash, inventory, and accounts receivable, although the specific inventory items and accounts receivable change over time. This minimum level of current assets is referred to as **permanent current**

**FIGURE 20.2**
Illustration of the
Hedging Principle

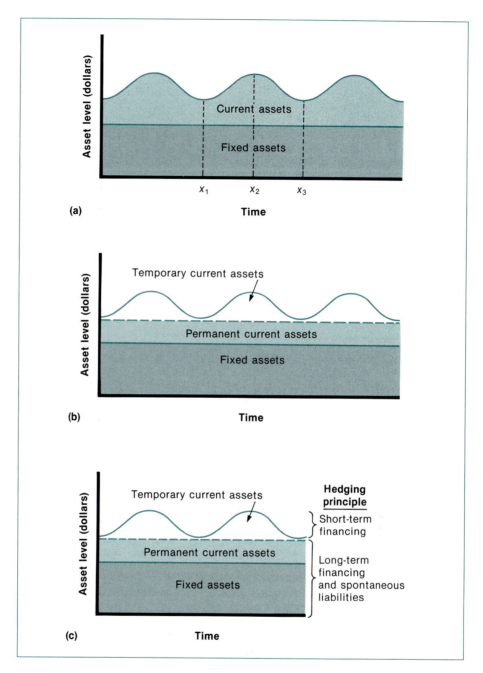

**assets** and appears in Figure 20.2b below the broken line but above the fixed assets. The hedging principle suggests that firms should finance permanent current assets with long-term sources and **spontaneous liabilities**, which are liabilities that increase automatically in the course of business, such as accounts payable and accruals. There are three reasons why the firm should finance permanent current assets with long-term sources and spontaneous liabilities. First, although spontaneous liabilities are technically short-term liabilities, a certain level will generally remain on the firm's balance sheet at all times. Therefore, these current liabilities can be considered permanent current liabilities, analogous to the permanent current assets discussed earlier. Second, the firm would assume too much risk if it had to roll over temporary short-term debt each year to finance assets that are critical to the firm's continued operations (permanent current assets). The consequences are less severe if a firm is unable to borrow funds to finance a temporary increase in current assets to meet a temporary increase in product demand. The third reason why firms should finance permanent current assets with long-term sources and spontaneous liabilities is that lenders may be unwilling to lend short-term funds for such purposes.

According to the hedging principle, firms should finance temporary current assets (those which increase a firm's total financing requirements for only a short time) with short-term sources of financing, and permanent current assets and fixed assets with long-term sources of financing. This situation is illustrated in Figure 20.2c. While the hedging principle acts as a guide for asset financing, firms may be justified in deviating from it. Some firms elect to be more aggressive in their approach to financing their assets while others elect to be more conservative. A more aggressive approach involves financing more than just temporary current assets with short-term liabilities. That is, some permanent current assets are financed with short-term liabilities, as is illustrated in Figure 20.3. This strategy requires the firm to roll over its short-term debt every year to finance some of its permanent current assets. The main reason for financing in this manner is to benefit from the typically lower cost of short-term debt.

A more conservative approach involves financing most or even all of the firm's assets with long-term sources and spontaneous liabilities, thereby using little or no temporary short-term financing. This approach is illustrated in Figure 20.4. At certain times a conservative firm will have excess financing (point $X$ on Figure 20.4, for example), because total long-term sources and spontaneous liabilities exceed the requirement for total assets. During these periods, the firm can make short-term investments using the excess funds it has available. Although the firm can earn interest on the invested funds, it incurs a net loss on them, since the cost of raising long-

**FIGURE 20.3**
**Aggressive Financing Strategy**

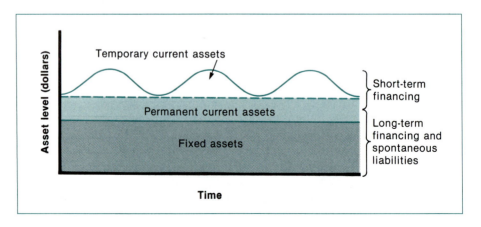

**FIGURE 20.4**

**Conservative Financing Strategy**

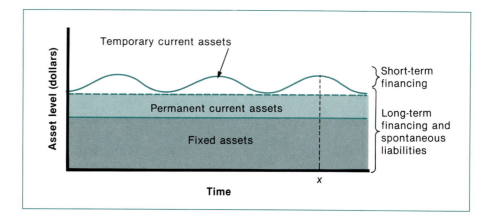

term funds is normally higher than the return the firm can earn by investing those funds in short-term securities.

## Estimating the Cost of Alternative Approaches to Asset Financing

Although it is very difficult to quantify the difference in risk involved with using short-term versus long-term financing, estimating the cost difference is fairly simple and may help in making the financing decision. The principal variables necessary to estimate the cost differential include the estimated future cost of short-term borrowing, the estimated future return on short-term investments, the current cost of long-term funds, and the level of assets required by the firm on a monthly basis (or biweekly, weekly, and so on).

Consider Ryan Enterprises, which has an estimated average annual cost of short-term financing of 11 percent and an estimated cost of long-term financing of 15 percent. This firm expects to earn an 8 percent return on its portfolio of marketable securities. The information concerning the future financing needs of Ryan Enterprises appears in Columns 1 and 2 of Table 20.2. The firm expects to need $100,000 of assets during January. From February through June, there is an increasing need for assets, reaching a peak of $160,000 in June. It is apparently a temporary need, however, since total required assets are expected to decline from June through December, when the need reaches its beginning level of $100,000. This pattern of total asset requirements is typical of a firm with seasonal sales. Since the buildup of assets is temporary, the lowest level of total assets ($100,000) represents fixed assets plus permanent current assets in our example.

Column 3 reveals the level of long-term financing the firm will need if it takes the extremely conservative approach of using no short-term debt (for simplicity, spontaneous liabilities are ignored in this example). The firm would need a maximum of $160,000 of long-term financing, since this is the maximum level of assets required in any given month. At an annual cost of long-term financing of 15 percent, the total financing cost for Ryan Enterprises using the conservative strategy would be $24,000

**TABLE 20.2**   Analysis of Conservative and Aggressive Approaches to Debt Financing:
Ryan Enterprises

| (1) | (2) | (3) | (4) | (5) | (6) |
|---|---|---|---|---|---|
| | Required Assets | Conservative Financing | | Hedging Principle | |
| Month | | Long-Term | Excess Funds | Long-Term | Short-Term |
| January | $100,000 | $160,000 | $60,000 | $100,000 | -0- |
| February | 120,000 | 160,000 | 40,000 | 100,000 | $20,000 |
| March | 130,000 | 160,000 | 30,000 | 100,000 | 30,000 |
| April | 140,000 | 160,000 | 20,000 | 100,000 | 40,000 |
| May | 150,000 | 160,000 | 10,000 | 100,000 | 50,000 |
| June | 160,000 | 160,000 | -0- | 100,000 | 60,000 |
| July | 150,000 | 160,000 | 10,000 | 100,000 | 50,000 |
| August | 140,000 | 160,000 | 20,000 | 100,000 | 40,000 |
| September | 130,000 | 160,000 | 30,000 | 100,000 | 30,000 |
| October | 120,000 | 160,000 | 40,000 | 100,000 | 20,000 |
| November | 110,000 | 160,000 | 50,000 | 100,000 | 10,000 |
| December | 100,000 | 160,000 | 60,000 | 100,000 | -0- |
| Totals | | | $370,000 | | $350,000 |

($160,000 × 15 percent). However, at least part of the $160,000 can be invested during periods when the total financing available exceeds total required assets. For example, in January the firm has $160,000 of funds available to it but needs only $100,000 of assets. The excess $60,000 can be used to purchase marketable securities on which the firm can earn an 8 percent return. Column 4 indicates the amount of excess funds available each month. The total of the excess monthly funds available ($370,000) is indicated at the bottom of Column 4. By dividing this total by 12 (the number of months being considered), we can find the average amount of excess funds available for investment each month ($370,000/12 = $30,833). Invested over a twelve-month period, the total dollar return to the firm would be $2,467 ($30,833 × 8 percent). This will partially offset the cost of financing the firm's assets using all long-term sources and will result in a net cost of $21,533 ($24,000 − $2,467).

If the firm takes a more moderate approach to financing by using the hedging principle, only $100,000 of long-term financing is required. This is the level of fixed assets plus permanent current assets, since it is the minimum level of total assets needed during the year. The cost of financing these permanent assets for the year is $15,000 (15 percent × $100,000). Column 6 indicates the amount of short-term financing necessary each month using the hedging principle. This amount is the difference between required assets (Column 2) and the level of long-term financing recommended by the hedging principle (Column 5). The average monthly short-term financing required can be found by dividing the total of the monthly short-term financing requirements ($350,000) by the number of months in the analysis (12). The result is $29,167, which when multiplied by the cost of short-term financing (11 percent), indicates the cost of short-term financing for the year ($3,208). The total financing cost for the firm using the hedging principle is therefore $18,208 ($15,000 + $3,208). This compares

## FINANCIAL MANAGEMENT IN PRACTICE

### HOW DO PRACTITIONERS MANAGE WORKING CAPITAL?

Most of working capital management is conducted at the individual asset level. That is, management determines the appropriate level of each asset individually and then manages current liabilities to accomplish a desired current ratio. Managers rarely decide to increase or decrease current assets as a whole. One exception to this occurs during periods of low earnings when the firm needs to generate additional profits even at the expense of temporarily increasing risk. Another exception occurs during periods when the firm needs to "dress up" its financial statements for year-end reporting, or when additional financing is needed. Under these circumstances, the firm may temporarily increase current assets to make the balance sheet more attractive.

In a recent survey, "managing working capital" ranked second only to "financial planning" and "budgeting" in terms of the amount of time spent on financial activities by financial managers.* This same survey indicated that approximately 60 percent of the financial manager's time is spent on short-term activities as opposed to long-term activities. When the working capital activities are divided into those oriented toward current assets and those oriented toward current liabilities, the financial manager's time is divided up roughly 65 percent and 35 percent, respectively.

*Lawrence J. Gitman and Charles E. Maxwell, "Financial Activities of Major U.S. Firms: Survey and Analysis of Fortune's 1000," *Financial Management* 14 (Winter 1985): 57–65.

favorably with the net cost of financing the firm's assets using the extremely conservative approach ($21,533).

Recall that the lower expected financing costs resulting from an aggressive approach are only half the story. The risks incurred by firms using large amounts of short-term financing, described earlier, must be considered. Subjective analysis of these risks should be weighed against the expected benefit.

## THE NET WORKING CAPITAL DECISION

After the firm has tentatively determined the level of current assets and the level of current liabilities to maintain, it must evaluate the risk-return aspects of the combined decisions. As indicated earlier, the impact of these two decisions can be analyzed according to their expected impact on the firm's current ratio (a measure of liquidity risk), return on equity (a measure of return), and the volatility of return on equity (a measure of total risk).

For example, given a tentative decision on the level of current assets and current liabilities, the firm can construct pro forma income statements based on possible levels of future sales that may result in view of the expected probability of stock-outs, demand changes, and so forth. From these pro forma income statements, the firm can measure the potential return on equity (ROE), variability of ROE, and the implied current ratio that would exist under each scenario. The next step is to estimate the overall impact of these factors on the growth rate of the firm, investors' required rates of return, and the value of the firm's common stock. A sensitivity analysis such as this permits the firm to consider a number of possible levels of current assets and current liabilities in order to identify the combination that is expected to maximize the price of the firm's common stock.

## An Example of the Working Capital Decision

The impacts of two alternative levels of net working capital on a firm's risk and return are analyzed in Table 20.3. Here, Glenn Industries is considering changes in working capital that will decrease current assets and in-

**TABLE 20.3  The Effect of Different Levels of Current Assets and Current Liabilities on Risk and Return: Glenn Industries (Dollar Figures Are in Thousands)**

| Line | | Conservative Structure (High Current Assets, Low Current Liabilities) | Aggressive Structure (Low Current Assets, High Current Liabilities) |
|---|---|---|---|
| 1 | Current assets | $1,600 | $1,200 |
| 2 | Fixed assets | 1,000 | 1,000 |
| 3 | Total assets | $2,600 | $2,200 |
| 4 | Current liabilities | 100 | 1,100 |
| 5 | Long-term liabilities | 1,200 | 0 |
| 6 | Equity (50% of total assets) | 1,300 | 1,100 |
| 7 | Total financing | $2,600 | $2,200 |
| 8 | Current ratio | 16.0 | 1.1 |
| | *Period A* | | |
| | Cost of current liabilities = 10%<br>Cost of long-term liabilities = 15% | | |
| 9 | EBIT | $360 | $340 |
| 10 | Less: Interest | 190 | 110 |
| 11 | EBT | 170 | 230 |
| 12 | Less: Taxes (40%) | 68 | 92 |
| 13 | Net income | $102 | $138 |
| 14 | Return on equity | 7.8% | 12.5% |
| | *Period B* | | |
| | Cost of short-term financing = 25%<br>Cost of long-term liabilities = 20%<br>  (however, the firm locked in a rate of<br>  15% in Period A) | | |
| 15 | EBIT | $330 | $265 |
| 16 | Less: Interest | 265 | 275 |
| 17 | EBT | 65 | (10) |
| 18 | Less: Taxes (40%) | 26 | (4) |
| 19 | Net income | $39 | ($6) |
| 20 | Return on equity | 3.0% | (.5%) |

crease current liabilities (as indicated in Lines 1 and 4 of the table). Both of these actions tend to increase the firm's risk and potential return. The increased risk is readily apparent as one compares the current ratio of 16.0 under the current conservative structure to 1.1 under the proposed aggressive structure (Line 8). Notice that the proportion of total assets financed with equity is assumed to remain the same in both situations in order to avoid introducing different levels of financial leverage into the problem (Line 6).

In Period A where relatively low financing costs exist, the expected EBIT is higher for the conservative firm (Line 9) since the higher level of current assets makes it less likely the firm will incur stock-outs that reduce sales or increase operating expenses. However, the conservative structure also results in higher interest expense (Line 10) due to both the higher level of current assets being financed and the higher cost of financing those assets with long-term financing. The net result is a lower net income (Line 13) and lower return on equity (Line 14) if the conservative structure is used.

In Period B interest rates have increased substantially. As a result, total interest expense is higher for the aggressive structure than for the conservative structure (Line 16) due to the high rate of interest that must be paid. This is true even though more current assets must be financed under the conservative structure. The net result is that the firm has higher net income (Line 19) and higher return on equity (Line 20) during this period under the conservative structure. The greater variability of interest expense, net income, and return on equity between Periods A and B are a direct result of using short-term debt for financing. The use of short-term debt also contributes to the low current ratio of the aggressive structure.

An additional risk incurred under the aggressive structure is that the firm may not be able to roll its short-term debt over. All of the risk and return aspects described in this example must be considered by the financial manager when making working capital decisions.

## SUMMARY

Management of working capital involves managing both current assets and current liabilities, a very important task since current assets represent a large investment for most firms, and current liabilities are an important source of funds to most firms. In addition, the level of net working capital is an important measure of a firm's ability to pay its bills when due.

The cash flow cycle refers to the circular flow of funds out of the firm for the purchase of raw materials and labor, subsequent conversion of inventories to accounts receivable, and finally the recapture of those funds from the collection of accounts receivable. Firms with fluctuating product demand experience a changing need for current assets as the need to invest funds in inventories and accounts receivable changes.

Firms wishing to maintain a low level of net working capital can keep current assets low, current liabilities high, or both. Such an aggressive approach results in relatively high expected returns due to low financing costs. These low financing costs result from (1) having a low level of assets to finance and (2) from the lower financing costs normally associated with using short-term financing as opposed to long-term financing. While expected returns are higher when net working capital is low, the risks are also higher because there is less liquidity available for paying bills. Using high levels of current liabilities to finance assets can increase a firm's risk because of the need to roll its debt over when it comes due, resulting in more volatile interest expense for the firm.

In order to decide on an appropriate level of net working capital, a firm's management should determine the level of each current asset and each current liability and then evaluate the desirability of the resulting level of net working capital. Desirability can be evaluated in terms of the current ratio, ROE, and the variability of ROE. If these measures of risk and return are unacceptable, the firm can change either (or both) the level of current assets or (and) the level of current liabilities.

## KEY TERMS

**Cash flow cycle** The movement of funds out of the firm for the purchase of raw materials and labor (and other required expenditures) and then back into the firm from the sale of the firm's product.

**Hedging principle** An approach to financing assets whereby the maturity of the financing source is matched to the expected life of the asset.

**Net working capital** Current assets minus current liabilities.

**Permanent current assets** The minimum level of current assets held by the firm.

**Spontaneous liabilities** Current liabilities that increase automatically with an increase in sales. They include accounts payable and accruals.

**Temporary current assets** An amount of current assets that represents a temporary increase in total assets.

**Working capital management** The management of current assets and current liabilities.

**Yield curve** A graph of the relationship between the yield available to investors on fixed income securities and the maturity of those securities at a point in time.

## QUESTIONS

**Q20-1.** How does *working capital management* differ from *management of current assets?*

**Q20-2.** Describe three measures of firm liquidity.

**Q20-3.** Describe the change in cash, current assets, and current liabilities associated with the cash flow cycle.

**Q20-4.** What two actions can a firm take to minimize net working capital?

**Q20-5.** What are the risk and return consequences of maintaining a low level of current assets?

**Q20-6.** What are the risk and return consequences of maintaining a high level of current liabilities?

**Q20-7.** In addition to the willingness of management to accept higher risks in order to generate higher returns, what other factors influence the level of current assets maintained by the firm?

**Q20-8.** How would a conservative firm and an aggressive firm finance their fixed assets, permanent current assets, and temporary current assets?

**Q20-9.** If a firm switches from a high level of current assets and a low level of current liabilities to a low level of current assets and a high level of current liabilities, what is the likely impact on total assets, the current ratio, net working capital, EBIT, interest expense, net income, ROE, and the variability of ROE?

## SELF-TEST PROBLEMS

Solutions to self-test problems appear on p. S1.

**SP20-1.** A. Montgomery Corporation currently finances all of its temporary current assets with short-term sources and its permanent current assets and fixed assets with long-term sources and spontaneous current liabilities. Montgomery's financial manager is considering changing to a more conservative approach by financing all assets with long-term sources and spontaneous liabilities. Montgomery estimates the average cost of long-term and spontaneous sources of financing is 14 percent versus 9 percent for short-term sources. In addition, Montgomery expects to earn 6 percent interest on its marketable securities. Table A indicates the level of total assets needed by Montgomery during the coming twelve months.

**a.** Calculate Montgomery's total cost of financing assets next year if it continues to use the current approach.
**b.** Calculate Montgomery's total financing cost if it switches to the more conservative approach.

### TABLE A
### A. MONTGOMERY CORPORATION'S EXPECTED TOTAL FINANCING:
### (IN MILLIONS OF DOLLARS)

| Month | Required Assets | Month | Required Assets | Month | Required Assets |
|-------|-----------------|-------|-----------------|-------|-----------------|
| Jan | $41.1 | May | $50.0 | Sep | $51.4 |
| Feb | 43.2 | Jun | 52.5 | Oct | 48.9 |
| Mar | 45.3 | Jul | 55.1 | Nov | 43.9 |
| Apr | 47.6 | Aug | 54.7 | Dec | 41.1 |

**SP20-2.** Table B on p. 554 presents two simplified balance sheets for W. Reilly Enterprises. One is the current balance sheet and the other is a proposed balance sheet, containing more current assets. W. Reilly Enterprises has a tax rate of 35 percent, a cost of long-term debt of 16 percent, and a cost of current liabilities of 11 percent. Compare the current ratio, net income, and return on equity if EBIT is $6 million under the current balance sheet and $6.5 million under the proposed balance sheet (greater sales should result when current assets are increased). Explain the reason for each difference.

**SP20-3.** G. Shaw International is considering a change in its financing. Table C on p. 554 presents the firm's current and proposed balance sheets, reflecting a shift toward more long-term financing. It has an average tax rate of 38 percent (this includes state income tax), a cost of long-term liabilities of 15 percent, and a cost of short-term debt of 9 percent. Compare G. Shaw's current ratio, net income, and return on equity under the two structures if EBIT is $85,000 (since both structures have the same amount of assets, EBIT would be identical). Explain the reasons for each difference.

**TABLE B**
**CURRENT AND PROPOSED BALANCE SHEETS:**
**W. REILLY ENTERPRISES (IN THOUSANDS OF DOLLARS)**

|  | Current | Proposed |
|---|---|---|
| Current assets | $31,000 | $36,000 |
| Fixed assets | 28,000 | 28,000 |
| Total assets | $59,000 | $64,000 |
| Current liabilities | 17,700 | 19,200 |
| Long-term liabilities | 17,700 | 19,200 |
| Equity (40% of total assets) | 23,600 | 25,600 |
| Total financing | $59,000 | $64,000 |

**TABLE C**
**CURRENT AND PROPOSED BALANCE SHEETS:**
**G. SHAW INTERNATIONAL**

|  | Current | Proposed |
|---|---|---|
| Current assets | $737,000 | $737,000 |
| Fixed assets | 692,000 | 692,000 |
| Total assets | $1,429,000 | $1,429,000 |
| Current liabilities | 457,280 | 114,320 |
| Long-term liabilities | 114,320 | 457,280 |
| Equity (40% of total assets) | 857,400 | 857,400 |
| Total financing | $1,429,000 | $1,429,000 |

# PROBLEMS

**P20-1.** Table A indicates the level of total assets that Newhouse, Inc., expects to need during each of the next twelve months. The asset buildup that begins after March is a result of seasonal sales, and Newhouse expects the level of assets to return to $344,000 by the following March. Due to rather weak earnings the previous year, Newhouse is considering taking a more aggressive approach to financing by financing only fixed and permanent current assets with long-term and spontaneous sources, as opposed to the current policy of financing all assets with long-term sources. The objective of this change would be to reduce financing costs, since long-term and spontaneous sources have an average cost of 15 percent while short-term sources cost only 10 percent. Newhouse can earn 7 percent on its marketable securities.

**TABLE A**
**EXPECTED TOTAL ASSETS FOR NEXT YEAR: NEWHOUSE, INC.**

| Month | Assets | Month | Assets | Month | Assets |
|---|---|---|---|---|---|
| Jan | $368,000 | May | $383,000 | Sep | $439,000 |
| Feb | 350,000 | Jun | 410,000 | Oct | 404,000 |
| Mar | 344,000 | Jul | 442,000 | Nov | 385,000 |
| Apr | 361,000 | Aug | 482,000 | Dec | 372,000 |

a. Calculate the net cost of financing Newhouse's assets next year if the conservative approach is used.

b. Calculate the net cost of financing Newhouse's assets if the firm switches to the more aggressive approach.

**P20-2.** Tuchi Instruments is faced with the prospect of selling common stock in order to finance its rapid growth as a manufacturer of precision instruments. To make its balance sheet look better, Tuchi is considering increasing its current assets, but is uncertain what impact this will have on net income and return on equity. Calculate the current ratio, net income, and return on equity for Tuchi Instruments if the change indicated in Table B is instituted. Calculate the same financial measures if the change is not made. Table C provides additional information needed to solve this problem. What does this analysis show?

**TABLE B**
CURRENT AND PROPOSED BALANCE SHEETS:
TUCHI INSTRUMENTS (IN THOUSANDS OF DOLLARS)

|  | Current | Proposed |
|---|---|---|
| Current assets | $5,000 | $7,000 |
| Fixed assets | 5,000 | 5,000 |
| Total assets | $10,000 | $12,000 |
| | | |
| Current liabilities | $3,000 | $3,600 |
| Long-term liabilities | 1,000 | 1,200 |
| Equity (60% of total assets) | 6,000 | 7,200 |
| Total financing | $10,000 | $12,000 |

**TABLE C**
MISCELLANEOUS INFORMATION ABOUT TUCHI INSTRUMENTS

| | |
|---|---|
| Average tax rate | = 40% (includes state income tax) |
| Cost of long-term debt | = 17% |
| Cost of short-term debt | = 12% |
| Expected EBIT | |
|   without the change | = $2,000,000 |
|   with the change | = $2,100,000 |

**P20-3.** Scherr Enterprises has made extensive use of short-term financing in recent years, but it is concerned that interest rates will increase over the next several years. It is therefore considering locking in more long-term financing now at 15 percent before interest rates have an opportunity to rise. Table D on p. 556 indicates the current and proposed financing plans. If short-term interest rates average 18 percent over the next two years, what would be the net income, return on equity and current ratio for Scherr Enterprises for each financial structure? Assume EBIT will be $100 million and a 45 percent tax rate applies (this includes state income tax). Work this problem again assuming short-term interest rates average 12 percent over the next two years. What does this analysis show?

**P20-4.** Young Industries finances 80 percent of its fixed assets and permanent current assets with long-term sources and spontaneous current liabilities. The average cost of these sources is 15 percent. The remaining financing requirements are met by using short-term sources at a cost of 10 percent. Table E on p. 556 indicates Young's expected total financing requirements (total assets) for next year.

## TABLE D
### CURRENT AND PROPOSED BALANCE SHEETS:
### SCHERR ENTERPRISES (IN MILLIONS OF DOLLARS)

|  | Current | Proposed |
|---|---|---|
| Current assets. | $150 | $150 |
| Fixed assets | 150 | 150 |
| Total assets | $300 | $300 |
| | | |
| Current liabilities. | 100 | 50 |
| Long-term liabilities | 50 | 100 |
| Equity | 150 | 150 |
| Total financing. | $300 | $300 |

## TABLE E
### EXPECTED TOTAL FINANCING: YOUNG INDUSTRIES
### (IN THOUSANDS OF DOLLARS)

| Month | Required Assets | Month | Required Assets | Month | Required Assets |
|---|---|---|---|---|---|
| Jan | $600 | May | $600 | Sep | $500 |
| Feb | 650 | Jun | 550 | Oct | 500 |
| Mar | 700 | Jul | 500 | Nov | 500 |
| Apr | 650 | Aug | 500 | Dec | 550 |

a. Calculate Young's total cost of financing next year if it continues to use the same financing pattern.

b. Young's economic consultant is forecasting the possibility of volatile financial markets for the next five to ten years. This has motivated Young Industries to consider a more conservative approach to financing that would involve financing 80 percent of the firm's maximum level of total assets with long-term sources and the remaining amounts with short-term sources. Assuming the same interest rate forecasts given earlier, what would be the cost of financing the firm's assets under this alternative method? Young can earn 8 percent interest on its marketable securities.

**P20-5.** Wyman Corporation is considering changing its working capital accounts to reflect a more aggressive policy. The current and proposed balance sheets for Wyman are presented in Table F.

## TABLE F
### CURRENT AND PROPOSED BALANCE SHEETS:
### WYMAN CORPORATION

|  | Current | Proposed |
|---|---|---|
| Current assets | $1,500,000 | $1,000,000 |
| Fixed assets. | 1,500,000 | 1,500,000 |
| Total assets | $3,000,000 | $2,500,000 |
| | | |
| Current liabilities | $500,000 | $1,250,000 |
| Long-term liabilities | 1,000,000 | -0- |
| Equity (50% of total assets). | 1,500,000 | 1,250,000 |
| Total financing. | $3,000,000 | $2,500,000 |

If the change is made, sales are expected to decrease from $6 million annually to $5.6 million as a result of stock-outs. The level of EBIT is estimated to be $1 million and $900,000, respectively. Wyman's cost of long-term debt is 13 percent, and short-term debt is 9 percent. The firm has a 34 percent average tax rate.

**a.** Calculate the current ratio, net income, and return on equity for Wyman under the current and proposed balance sheets.

**b.** If short-term interest rates rise to 16 percent and all else remains the same, what are the current ratios, net income, and return on equity for Wyman under the two alternative balance sheets?

**c.** Would you recommend the change?

## COMPUTER-ASSISTED PROBLEMS

**CP20-1. a. Sensitivity of Financing Costs to Interest Rate Changes** Use the computer package to work P20-1, Parts a and b, in the "Problems" section. Next, assume that management feels there is a positive probability that interest rates will rise next year. What is the cost of financing under the conservative and aggressive approaches next year if the cost of short-term sources of financing increases to 12 percent and the rate Newhouse, Inc., can earn on marketable securities increases to 9 percent?

Newhouse, Inc., recognizes that interest rates could also decline next year, causing the firm's cost of short-term financing to decline to 8 percent and the return it earns on its marketable securities to 5 percent. Under these circumstances, what is the cost to Newhouse of using the conservative and aggressive approaches to financing?

**b. Simulation** Assume that Newhouse, Inc., expects its cost of short-term financing next year to be between 8 percent and 16 percent and its return on marketable securities to be between 5 percent and 13 percent. What is the expected total cost of financing Newhouse's assets next year using the conservative and aggressive approaches? What is the range of possible financing costs using the conservative and aggressive approaches?

**CP20-2. Sensitivity of Ratios to Asset and Liability Mix** Use the computer package to work P20-2 in the "Problems" section. Next, assume that Tuchi Instruments wishes to consider other financial structures and asset combinations. For each of the following situations determine the current ratio, net income, and return on equity that would result.

**a.** Beginning with the current financial structure, current assets are increased to $6,000,000, and fixed assets are reduced to $4,000,000. EBIT declines to $1,900,000.

**b.** In addition to the situation in Part a, Tuchi may decrease current liabilities to $2,000,000 and increase long-term liabilities to $2,000,000. Expected EBIT is $1,900,000.

**c.** Beginning with the situation in Part b, fixed assets are increased to $6,000,000, and long-term liabilities are increased to $4,000,000. Expected EBIT is $2,000,000.

## REFERENCES

Knight, W. D. "Working Capital Management: Satisficing versus Optimization," *Financial Management* 1 (Spring 1972): 33–40.

Mehta, Dileep. "Working Capital Management." Englewood Cliffs, N.J.: Prentice-Hall, 1974.

Merville, L. J., and L. A. Tavis. "Optimal Working Capital Policies: A Chance-Constrained Programming Approach." *Journal of Financial and Quantitative Analysis* 8 (January 1973): 47–60.

Sartoris, William L., and Ned C. Hill. "A Generalized Cash Flow Approach to Short-Term Financial Decisions." *Journal of Finance* 38 (May 1983): 349–60.

Smith, Keith V. *Readings on the Management of Working Capital.* 2d ed. New York: West Publishing Company, 1980.

Van Horne, James C. "A Risk-Return Analysis of a Firm's Working Capital Position." *Engineering Economist* 14 (Winter 1969): 71–89.

Walker, Ernest W. "Towards a Theory of Working Capital." *Engineering Economist* 9 (January–February 1964): 21–35.

# THE TERM STRUCTURE OF INTEREST RATES

The relationship between the cost of debt and its maturity is called the *term structure of interest rates* and is normally described with the help of a *yield curve*. The yield curve graphs the relationship between the yield earned by investors on fixed-income securities and the maturity of those fixed-income securities at a given point in time. Since the yield earned by investors is equal to the cost paid by the issuer (except for any transactions costs that may be required), the yield can be used as a proxy for the cost of borrowing.

In constructing the yield curve, analysts normally use U.S. Treasury securities in order to control the level of business risk. Thus, if a bond issued by Company C that has a one-year maturity is compared to a bond issued by Company D that has a two-year maturity, the difference in yield may be due to a difference in the riskiness of the companies rather than the difference in the maturity of the bonds.

Figure 20A.1 illustrates the shape of an ascending yield curve and an inverted, or descending, yield curve. Given the shape of the ascending yield curve, the firm may elect to keep its financing costs low by using short-term liabilities. Conversely, if the yield curve is inverted (the descending yield curve in the figure), the cost of short-term financing is higher, and the firm must decide whether or not to finance short term at high rates of interest or long term at what are currently lower rates of interest.

Since the yield curve affects the firm's cost of financing, financial managers should have an understanding of the factors that affect its shape. The following discussion introduces those factors. A more detailed discussion can be found in most money and banking texts.

Three main theories attempt to explain the shape of the yield curve:

1. The *liquidity-preference theory* argues that short-term investments are less risky to investors, who are therefore willing to lend money for shorter periods at lower rates of interest. Risk is lower because the lender does not incur much risk that a rise in interest rates will cause a decline in the value of the investment (recall that Chapter 4 explains why the prices of short-

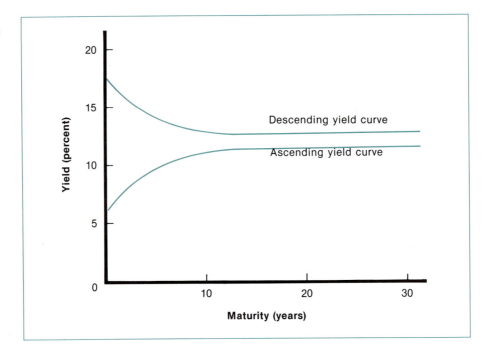

term securities are less sensitive to changes in market interest rates than the prices of long-term securities). In addition, it is less likely that the borrower will default on short-term securities than on long-term securities. Investors who are willing to assume the greater risk of buying assets with longer maturities (less liquidity) require higher returns (yields) as compensation. Conversely, some borrowers are willing to pay higher rates of interest to long-term lenders so that they can avoid the risks associated with short-term borrowing (these risks were explored earlier in this chapter). As a result of lender preferences for liquidity and borrower preferences for long-term financing, the cost of borrowing short-term is less expensive than the cost of borrowing long-term.

2. The *expectations theory* suggests that long-term interest rates reflect the average of the expected short-term interest rates over the life of the investment. Suppose that an investor wants to invest funds for two years and is considering investing in a bond with a 10 percent yield that matures in one year. When the bond matures, the proceeds can be reinvested for a second year at the market rate of interest existing at that time. If the investor expects the interest rate on one-year bonds to decline to 5 percent next year, resulting in an average return over the two-year period of 7.5 percent, and other investors have the same expectations, supply and demand forces will adjust bond prices in such a way that bonds with two years until maturity will have yields of 7.5 percent. Since the yield on one-year securities is currently 10 percent in this example, while the yield on a two-year security is 7.5 percent, a descending yield curve results. If interest rates are expected to rise in the future, long-term interest rates would exceed short-term interest rates, and an ascending yield curve would result.

3. The *segmented markets theory* explains the shape of the yield curve by recognizing that some lenders prefer to lend short-term (such as banks),

while others prefer to lend long-term (such as pension funds). Conversely, some borrowers prefer to borrow short-term (such as business for temporary needs), while others prefer to borrow long-term (such as individuals when purchasing a home). Given these preferences, the market for fixed income securities is actually segmented into numerous smaller markets for securities with varying maturities. The interest rate in each market is determined by the supply and demand for borrowed funds in that market. If lenders in the longer-term markets have an excess of loanable funds relative to the demand for longer-term funds, long-term interest rates will be low. If lenders in the shorter-term markets do not have much money to lend, while the borrowers in the shorter-term markets have a large demand for funds, short-term interest rates will be high. The combined result will be an inverted yield curve.

While the debate still continues over which theory best explains the shape of the yield curve, we can generalize the results of numerous studies on the subject. Basically, each theory appears to contribute to our understanding of the yield curve. At times, the liquidity-preference theory seems to dominate the yield curve, while at other times, the expectations theory or segmented markets theory seems to be the dominant force. The liquidity-preference theory explains the yield curve well when interest rates are not abnormally high but cannot by itself explain the inverted yield curve. The expectations theory appears to explain an inverted yield curve when interest rates are abnormally high and investors expect interest rates to fall. Yet even under this scenario the shape of the yield curve would still be influenced by liquidity preferences and by particular demand-and-supply conditions in different maturity markets.

# CHAPTER 21

# MANAGEMENT OF CASH AND MARKETABLE SECURITIES

## CASH AND MARKETABLE SECURITIES MANAGEMENT IN PERSPECTIVE

Ford Motor Company's cash and marketable securities were estimated to be about $9.4 billion as of June 1987. This balance was substantially above the level Ford normally holds and resulted from the record earnings in 1985 and 1986. It is expected that the level of cash and marketable securities will grow to $11 billion by the end of 1987. Since this money is invested in highly liquid assets, Ford is probably earning only about 5 percent interest on it after paying taxes. Since Ford's stockholders are not likely to approve of maintaining an exceptionally high level of current assets without a reason, some analysts speculate that Ford will repurchase large amounts of its own common stock (this would benefit the stockholders much the same as paying a cash dividend). Other analysts speculate that Ford will acquire one or more other companies as subsidiaries (this could provide diversification and reduce Ford's vulnerability to business cycles). Meanwhile, the United Auto Workers consider this cash buildup to be an indication of Ford's ability to return to workers the concessions they had granted the firm during the recession in 1982.

How much cash and marketable securities should a firm maintain? How should these liquid assets be divided between cash and marketable securities? What types of marketable securities should firms purchase? This chapter provides a framework that can be used to answer these and other questions about the management of cash and marketable securities.

*Source:* "Ford Accumulates $9.4 Billion in Cash," *Wall Street Journal*, June 23, 1987, p. 4.

The previous chapter established the importance of properly managing working capital and explored the major decisions involved in that endeavor. In this chapter, and in the two that follow, the management of specific types of current assets and current liabilities is described—cash and marketable securities in this chapter, inventories and accounts receivable in the next, and current liabilities in the following chapter. It is important for firms to maintain an adequate level of **cash,** defined as currency plus demand deposits, since the inability of firms to pay their bills can cause embarrassment, legal problems, and even bankruptcy. It is also important for firms to maintain an adequate level of marketable securities, since their main function is to provide additional cash to the firm when it is needed (they can generally be converted to cash very quickly).

Firms can reduce the risk of being unable to pay their bills by holding excess cash and marketable securities, but this practice ties up assets that could be earning a higher return elsewhere. As a result, the firm's income, dividends, and the growth rate of dividends may suffer, reducing the value of the firm's stock and thus preventing the maximization of shareholder wealth.

If a low level of cash and marketable securities is maintained, the firm's income, dividends, and growth rate may all be higher, but the risk of bankruptcy and loss to stockholders will also be greater. This higher risk could result in higher required rates of return to investors and lower stock values, thus reducing shareholder wealth. The financial manager must attempt to balance the risk and return to keep the stock value at the highest possible level and therefore maximize shareholder wealth.

Although management of cash and marketable securities has always been important to firms, the high interest rates experienced in the late 1970s and early 1980s increased the opportunity cost of holding these liquid assets. Under these conditions, businesses looked for new methods of reducing their cash and marketable securities. They were also more willing to spend money to purchase the expertise and employ the techniques necessary to effectively manage these assets. Some of these techniques are too costly to employ when interest rates are low, while others have become a permanent part of the cash management practices of many firms.

## REASONS FOR HOLDING CASH

Businesses, individuals, and governments hold cash for several reasons, the major one being to *conduct transactions* such as purchasing raw materials, paying for labor, and purchasing fixed assets. Also, because businesses do not always know in advance exactly when payments must be made or when cash will be received, they generally hold an excess amount of cash called *precautionary balances.* The greater the uncertainty regarding the cash needed for transactions, the greater the required level of precautionary balances is.

Still another reason for holding cash is for *speculative purposes.* Most businesses are constantly looking for unusually good deals that may become available on the purchase of raw materials and equipment, and excess cash balances may be held by a firm to take advantage of these opportunities. Most firms today, however, rely on bank credit or hold marketable securities to provide the liquidity necessary for speculative purposes. In this way they can minimize the opportunity cost of holding cash.

In addition to these three traditional motives for holding cash, a fourth reason is frequently cited: the need for **compensating balances.** Financial institutions that lend money to firms (or provide them with services) may require those firms to hold a stated minimum level of cash in a checking account at the institution. These balances are intended to provide the lending institution with additional compensation, which is the reason they are called "compensating" balances. This subject is discussed in detail in Chapter 23.

## DETERMINANTS OF THE TARGET LEVEL OF CASH TO MAINTAIN

Although no single formula can indicate the optimal level of cash for a firm to maintain, it is useful to explore the key factors that influence a firm's decision on the level of cash to maintain. One general consideration is the *risk-return trade-off* associated with holding cash. The most serious risk of not maintaining adequate cash is that the firm may be unable to pay its bills when due. This situation could result in embarrassment, a damaged reputation, loss of trade credit, higher interest rates on future loans, loss of bank credit, legal action against the firm, or even bankruptcy. Each of the above consequences is serious and has the potential of causing severe or even fatal damage to the firm.

A second risk of not maintaining an adequate cash balance is that the firm may be unable to take advantage of unexpected purchasing opportunities that may arise. Such opportunities might permit the firm to make a cash purchase of used equipment, slightly damaged raw materials, or other assets at a very low price. A third risk is that the company will not have enough cash to take advantage of trade discounts that may be available.

Of course, the firm must also consider the impact of holding cash on its returns. Maintaining large cash balances (or **near-cash** balances, which are marketable securities that can be quickly converted into cash) can be expensive in terms of financing costs. The firm might be able to repay some of its debts if it is willing to reduce cash balances, and the resulting reduction in interest expense could increase profits. Even if firms maintain excess balances in marketable securities, firms earn less interest on their marketable securities than they pay on borrowed funds. This relationship is described in greater detail later in this chapter.

In addition to the general risk-return trade-off, there are a number of firm-specific factors that influence the level of cash maintained. These firm-specific factors are discussed briefly below and summarized in Table 21.1.

**TABLE 21.1** Determinants of the Target Level of Cash and Near-Cash

| If the following determinant is high . . . | Cash needs tend to be |
|---|---|
| Level of sales | high |
| Variability of sales | high |
| Credit availability | low |
| Level of interest rates | low |
| Management's risk tolerance | low |
| Compensating balance requirements | high |
| Ability to forecast irregular expenditures | low |

## Level of Sales

As the level of sales increases, the dollar amount of transactions conducted by a firm also increases. The more transactions a firm conducts, the more cash must be available to conduct those transactions.

## Variability of Sales

Sales provide the main source of cash flowing into the firm. If sales are volatile, the cash coming into the firm is also volatile, and the need to hold excess cash balances to pay bills is greater. High variability of sales can also affect the need to temporarily invest more cash in raw materials inventories and accounts receivable. To reduce the need to borrow such necessary funds, firms can hold excess cash.

## Credit Availability

If a firm has established lines of credit or other sources of cash, the need to hold excess cash is lower. In recent years, credit has been increasingly used as a substitute for holding cash.

## Level of Interest Rates

When interest rates are low, it is less expensive to hold excess cash since the rate of interest paid on borrowed funds is low. In addition, the opportunity cost of tying up funds in cash is low when interest rates are low. When interest rates are high, the cost of holding excess cash is high.

## Management's Tolerance of Risk

Most business decisions reflect management's attitude toward risk and potential return, and the decision to hold cash is no exception. The greater the willingness of a firm's management to bear risk while striving for a high return, the less cash the firm holds.

## Compensating Balance Requirements

As indicated earlier, compensating balances are frequently required as a loan provision. If a compensating balance requirement is greater than the balance a firm would otherwise maintain, this could be the dominant factor that determines the level of cash held by the firm.

## Ability to Forecast Irregular Expenditures

Irregular expenditures can arise for numerous reasons, including such things as the repair of equipment. If these irregular expenditures are large and difficult to forecast with accuracy, the firm may need to maintain larger cash balances.

# CASH MANAGEMENT TECHNIQUES

An analysis of the preceding factors, and other factors peculiar to the firm can help management determine the desired level of cash (and near-cash). This level may change frequently as the level of sales or other factors change. It is this desired level of cash that is used in the cash budget as the minimum level of operating cash.

Although the *cash budget* was described earlier as a tool used in financial planning, it is also a valuable cash management tool. By analyzing the cash budget, the firm can evaluate the degree of synchronization of its cash inflows and outflows in order to determine when the level of cash will be lower or higher than desired. When it is lower than desired, the firm must plan to secure additional cash. When it is higher than desired, the firm can plan for investment of the excess cash or for the repayment of loans.

Some cash management techniques help the firm hold its cash longer and collect cash more quickly. Recall the cash flow cycle that was presented in the previous chapter. It describes the purchase of raw materials and labor, the cash payment for raw materials and labor, the sale of the firm's product, and the subsequent receipt of payment from the sale. Cash must be available to flow through this cycle.

Consider an extreme case where a firm receives cash from the sale of its product on the same day that it must pay for the raw materials and labor it used to produce that product. This situation would mean the firm could avoid the short-term borrowing that might be necessary to carry it through the period after it pays for the raw materials and labor but before cash has been received from the sale of the product. By reducing the borrowing period as much as possible, the firm will pay less interest on needed debt. Or, if the firm sells some marketable securities to carry it through this period, keeping the period short will minimize the forgone interest on those securities. Keeping this period short can be accomplished by either delaying disbursements, accelerating collections, or reducing the average age of inventory. The first two methods are discussed here. The third will be discussed in Chapter 22.

## Delaying Disbursements

Some techniques that can be employed to slow disbursements and accelerate collections follow. While some of these techniques can be accomplished with little or no additional expense, others can be costly to implement, so firms should determine whether the financial benefits of these techniques exceed the cost.

**Use Float**   The difference between what a firm's checkbook indicates it has in the bank and what the bank's records indicate is **float.** Assume a firm has $1,000 in its checking account today, and that this amount agrees with the bank's records. If the firm subsequently writes a check for $5,000 and mails it to a supplier, the firm's checkbook immediately indicates that the firm has a negative balance of $4,000 in the account. Meanwhile, the bank's records still indicate the firm has $1,000. This difference will remain until the check clears through the banking system.

To take advantage of float, the firm that wrote the check can estimate when that check will be presented to its bank for payment and then deposit $5,000 into the account just in time to cover the check. In the interim period, the firm can keep the money invested in marketable securities that earn interest. Of course, float can also work against the firm on the collections side. That is, when the firm receives checks and deposits them in its bank account, its checkbook indicates larger balances than the bank's records indicate. This can be a problem, since the firm cannot spend those funds until its bank collects them. Some techniques used to speed collections are discussed later in this chapter.

**Increase Accruals**   Accrued wages and taxes represent money that the firm owes to employees or to the U.S. government that is still in the possession of the firm. Therefore, accruals represent interest-free loans to the firm. There is little a firm can do to increase accrued taxes except to avoid early payment of taxes and to ensure that quarterly tax payments are no larger than necessary.

Regarding accrued wages, when employees are paid less frequently, the disbursements are slower and the firm's average accrued wages are higher. Conversely, when employees are paid more frequently, the disbursements are faster and the average accrued wages are lower. For example, if a firm pays its employees a total of $100,000 at the end of each two-week period, the firm has an average of $50,000 of employee money available to it that it can invest during that period. That is, starting the first day (Week 0 on the horizontal scale of Figure 21.1a) the firm owes employees nothing, but accrued wages grow to $100,000 at the end of Week 2. Notice that at the end of each two-week period, accrued wages return to zero. The average amount owed to employees is halfway between zero and $100,000, or $50,000. If the firm changes to paying employees every four weeks as illustrated in Figure 21.1b, then the size of the payroll increases to $200,000, and the average amount of employee money held by the firm is $200,000/2, or $100,000.

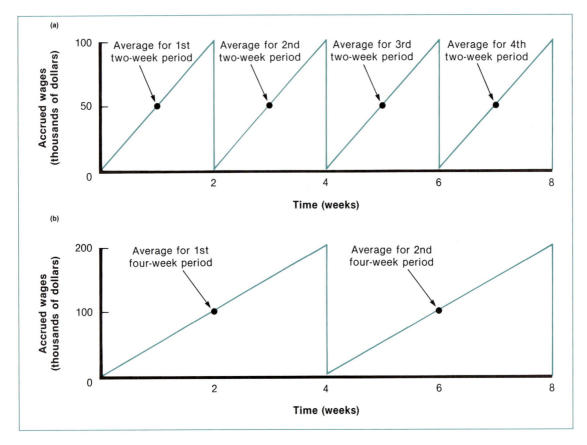

**FIGURE 21.1**

**Pattern of Accrued Wages and the Determination of Average Accrued Wages**

**Analyze Check Clearing**  Given the frequency with which a firm's employees are paid, the firm can analyze its payroll check-clearing pattern in an effort to utilize its money to the maximum extent possible. That is, a firm can determine the percent of payroll checks that normally clear its checking account on payday, and on each day thereafter. If only 15 percent of a firm's employees normally cash their checks at the firm's bank on payday, then perhaps the firm only needs to have 15 percent of the payroll amount (plus perhaps 5 percent more for safety) in its checking account. Each subsequent day can be similarly analyzed, with an appropriate amount of cash deposited to cover the paychecks that are expected to clear.

To illustrate the analysis of check clearing, a simple example is provided in Table 21.2. Here, all payroll checks normally clear through Drake Enterprises' checking account within four days of payday. Drake normally makes deposits early each morning in sufficient quantity to cover the payroll checks expected to clear plus 5 percent of payroll, until 100 percent of the payroll has been deposited. This 5 percent is designed to cover payroll checks that clear through the checking account earlier than expected. The greater the volatility of the collection pattern, the greater the safety amount should be.

Given the percent of the payroll that is expected to clear on payday (Day 0), Drake should deposit $55,000 into its account on payday (6 per-

**TABLE 21.2** Check Clearing Analysis: Drake Enterprises (Given a $500,000 Payroll)

| (1) | (2) | (3) | (4) |
|---|---|---|---|
| Days after Payday | Percent Expected to Clear | Percent of Payroll to be Deposited | Dollar Amount Deposited |
| 0 | 6% | 6% + 5% | $ 55,000 |
| 1 | 43 | 43% | 215,000 |
| 2 | 29 | 29 | 145,000 |
| 3 | 14 | 14 | 70,000 |
| 4 | 8 | 8% − 5% | 15,000 |
| | | | Total $500,000 |

cent + 5 percent of $500,000). On Day 1, the firm should deposit $215,000 (43 percent of $500,000). It is not necessary to deposit an additional 5 percent of payroll as a safety amount, since that amount was deposited on Day 0 and remains in the account. This pattern continues until the final day, when the amount deposited is the amount remaining from the original $500,000 payroll. That is, after 14 percent of the payroll is deposited on Day 3, 97 percent of the total payroll has been deposited. Therefore, only 3 percent or $15,000 remains to be deposited on Day 4.

This system can help prevent the firm from maintaining large unused balances in its checking account. In addition to analyzing payroll check clearing, the firm can use a similar approach to analyze the clearing of cash dividend checks sent to stockholders.

**Delay Payment of Bills**   Some firms are so concerned about how they are viewed by their suppliers that they actually pay their bills early. However, most firms delay paying their bills until they absolutely must. When they "must" is interpreted differently by different firms, but the general principle is, do not pay so late, or so consistently late, that you lose access to trade credit or damage your firm's credit rating.

**Pay with Drafts**   Instead of writing checks, some companies make payments by issuing **drafts.** Although drafts look very much like checks, they are drawn on the company itself instead of being drawn on the company's bank. Therefore, after the draft clears through the banking system, it is returned to the firm for its approval before funds are released. This additional step permits the firm to hold its funds longer, and it simultaneously delays access to those funds by the firm or individual receiving the draft.

The main purpose of drafts is to increase the control a home office has on payments made by regional offices. If the home office feels a particular disbursement is improper, it can stop payment on the draft. This system has proven effective in the insurance industry, where claims agents can make preliminary settlement on a claim, with the home office approving the payment (draft) before the funds are released.

The payment-by-draft system has been used by some firms in the past for the sole purpose of delaying the disbursement of funds. One company even paid its employees with drafts. Recently, however, the Federal Reserve ruled that when drafts clear through the Federal Reserve system, funds must be transferred from the bank upon receipt of the draft (before approval by the firm). Therefore, most banks now charge drafts against firm checking accounts before firm approval. Despite this requirement, legal payment still does not take place until after the draft has been approved (meaning that payment can be stopped before that point if desired).

**Use Zero Balance Accounts (ZBAs)**   Though not a method of slowing disbursements, **zero balance accounts** (ZBAs) can assist large companies to maintain lower cash balances by making cash disbursements more efficient. This system normally is used when a firm has several divisions that write checks against their own separate accounts. If a firm has five divisions, each with its own demand deposit account, each division will need to maintain a positive balance in its account at all times. These positive balances represent *nonworking assets*. With ZBAs, each division continues to maintain its own demand deposit account, but the accounts are tied to the firm's master checking account. All division accounts are located in the same bank as the master account. Only the master account maintains a positive balance, while the division accounts maintain zero balances. Each day, checks clearing against the division accounts result in negative balances; and at the end of each day, funds are transferred from the master account into the division accounts in whatever amount is necessary to bring them up to a zero balance (see Figure 21.2).

Zero balance accounts have several advantages. First, since only one account maintains a positive balance (a safety stock of cash), the total level of excess cash held by the firm is lower than if each division held excess cash. Second, the task of managing the cash, marketable securities, and bank credit can be centralized in one office instead of taking place in each division. This should result in more efficient management of the disbursement function. Of course, continuous input from the divisions is necessary to ensure that adequate liquidity is maintained. Third, the divisions can maintain their authority over the disbursement of cash, while the main

**FIGURE 21.2**
**Illustration of a Zero Balance Account for a Firm with Two Divisions**

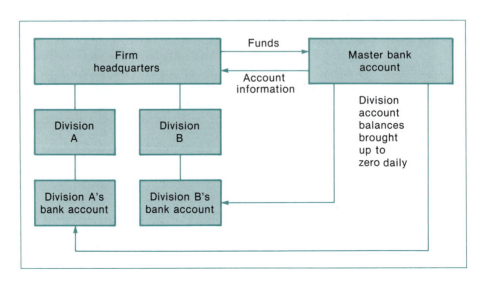

office can monitor those disbursements and maintain central control over them. Fourth, the float available to the firm may be increased, since checks must be cleared through the bank where the master account and division accounts are located. This may be farther from the division's payees than a local bank that would have been used, since division suppliers tend to be located near the divisions they service.

## Accelerating Collections

Accelerating cash receipts can be just as effective a cash management tool as slowing disbursements, since cash received quickly can reduce the need to borrow money or liquidate securities in order to pay some of the firm's bills. Or, if the funds are not needed immediately, they can be invested in additional marketable securities sooner. There are a number of strategies firms can use to accelerate cash inflows. Once again, firms should weigh the cost and risks of using these techniques against the expected benefits of adopting them. Some of the major approaches follow:

**Tighten Credit Polices**   Firms can affect the time it takes to collect accounts receivable by altering their credit policies. For example, if a firm wants to collect accounts receivable more quickly, it can (1) extend trade credit to only the most creditworthy customers, (2) offer credit terms that require payment in a shorter period of time, and/or (3) aggressively collect past-due accounts. Although all of these strategies will help reduce the collection period, they also tend to reduce sales. This trade-off is addressed in detail in Chapter 22.

**Use a Lock-Box System**   A popular tool for reducing both the mail time and the processing time required to collect funds from customers is the **lock-box system.** It is typically used by large corporations with nationwide sales to move the collection point closer to the customer. Consider a large company that receives hundreds of checks daily from across the country. It may take three days for the U.S. mail to deliver checks from customers located on the West Coast of the United States to the firm's headquarters in Atlanta. Upon receipt of those checks, the firm must process the paperwork before depositing the checks in its bank account. Assuming the customers' checks are written on West Coast banks, another two days will pass before the checks clear through the banking system and the funds are made available to the firm. In total, it could take six business days or more from the time the customer puts the check in the mail until the money is in the firm's bank account.

To initiate a lock-box system, the firm in this example might ask its local bank to help establish a nationwide system. The bank would then advise the firm regarding how many regional lock-boxes would be required and where they should be located to provide collection services for the firm's customers in each region. Perhaps one lock-box would be established in San Francisco to handle all the West Coast customers. If so, all West Coast customers would be directed to send their payments to a specific post office box (lock-box) in San Francisco instead of to the Atlanta office. A San Francisco bank would then check the lock-box as often as eight or ten times a day (or more) to pick up customer checks. The bank would then return the mail to its offices, where it would examine the contents, make copies of all enclosed documents, and deposit the checks in the firm's account at that bank.

The firm would be informed daily about the dollar amounts deposited in its San Francisco bank account, and these funds would become available to the firm in about a day. Copies of all documents would be forwarded to the firm's headquarters in Atlanta at the end of each day although the money would be available to the firm to spend even before the firm received the documentation indicating who the money is from and what it is for. This system can reduce collection time by three days or more.

Lock-box systems can be expensive to establish and maintain. Generally, only large firms with many collections find such arrangements financially worthwhile. To make the decision on whether to use a lock-box system, firms must estimate the cost of the system and compare this to the expected financial benefit. The financial benefit is based on the increased amount of cash made available to the firm for investment elsewhere. For example, suppose a firm has sales of $1 million a day, and a lock-box system is expected to reduce collection time by two days. If the firm can earn 8 percent interest on excess cash, what annual savings would result?

Under the lock-box system, the firm would have available to it every day an additional $2 million ($1 million per day multiplied by two days) on which it can earn 8 percent interest.[1] The total savings for the firm would be $160,000 per year ($2 million × 8 percent). To make the decision on whether or not to use the lock-box system, the firm must compare this estimated annual savings to the annual cost of operating the system.

Table 21.3 presents a comparison of the timing involved in collecting funds from customers using an ordinary collection system versus using a lock-box system.

**Employ Concentration Banking** The system of **concentration banking** has some characteristics similar to a lock-box system, but it is less elaborate and less expensive to operate. Concentration banking is used by large firms with numerous sales offices throughout the country where each regional office is given responsibility for collections in their respective regions. Customers are instructed to send payment checks directly to the regional office in their area, and all collections are deposited in regional banks. Instead of each regional bank holding the deposits, however, funds are regularly (perhaps daily) forwarded by wire to one or more concentration banks. The main advantage of concentration banking is that funds collected locally can be transferred immediately to the firm's main bank

---

1. Without the lock-box system, the firm in this example receives $1 million on Tuesday, Wednesday, and Thursday. With the lock-box system, the firm would still receive $1 million on Tuesday, but it is the $1 million that would not have been received until Thursday. The firm would also have available to it on Tuesday $1 million that would not have been received until Wednesday (but was actually received on Monday). All told, the firm has $2 million more on Tuesday than it would have had without the lock-box. On Wednesday, the firm will still have $2 million more available to it than it would have had without the lock-box (not only the $1 million it would have had without the lock-box, but also the money it would have had to wait for until Thursday and Friday).

**TABLE 21.3**    **Ordinary Collection System Versus a Lock-Box System**

| Day | Ordinary Collection System | Lock-Box System |
|-----|---------------------------|-----------------|
| 1 | Customer mails check. | Customer mails check. |
| 2 | | Check delivered to lock-box. Bank collects checks and deposits them. |
| 3 | Check received and delivered to accounting department. | Check begins the clearing process. |
| 4 | Check deposited in the bank. | Firm notified that funds are available for use. |
| 5 | Check begins the clearing process. | |
| 6 | | |
| 7 | Firm notified that funds are available for use. | |

through the use of *wire transfers*. When the amounts to be transferred are too small to make wire transfers economical, less expensive (though slower) forms of transfer are available.

**Arrange for Preauthorized Payments (PAPs)**    Given the special circumstances whereby a firm receives payments from the same customers at regular intervals, **preauthorized payments** (PAPs) may speed collections. These special circumstances are typical of lending institutions, leasing firms, insurance companies, and utility companies. Under a PAP arrangement, customers authorize the firm to draw payments directly against their checking accounts. Then, when a payment is due from a customer, the firm sends a magnetic tape with all of the PAP information on it (customer identification, dollar amounts, firm identification and account numbers, and so forth) to the customer's bank. The bank then either creates checks drawn on the customer accounts and deposits them into the firm's demand deposit account, or it electronically debits customer accounts and credits the firm's account.

There are several major advantages to using PAPs. First, the timing of receipts from PAP customers is highly predictable. Second, the mail time required to receive a check sent by a customer is eliminated. Third, the processing time is eliminated, since the firm does not have to process the check before it is deposited in its account. Fourth, the clerical expense associated with handling customer checks may be reduced. However, these savings are at least partially offset by the increased cost of the PAP system. The firm must weigh the costs of the system against its benefits before making a final decision.

## ALTERNATIVES TO HOLDING CASH

Some alternative sources of liquidity are available to firms, so that a low level of excess cash can be maintained. One alternative is to establish access to credit (loans) at commercial banks or other lending institutions and then borrow against that credit when additional funds are needed. More information about bank credit lines is presented in Chapter 23.

A second alternative to holding excess cash is to purchase marketable securities that provide the firm with interest income while they are owned but can be converted to cash quickly when cash is needed. Unfortunately, the interest rate earned by firms on their marketable securities is normally lower than the cost of raising those funds initially. Therefore, firms do not hold more marketable securities than is necessary, since they could benefit from selling the securities and using the proceeds to repay sources of financing. The remainder of this chapter is devoted to a discussion of marketable securities.

## MANAGEMENT OF MARKETABLE SECURITIES

The primary role of marketable securities is as a *substitute for cash*. This role implies that marketable securities, along with cash, provide the liquidity necessary to conduct both anticipated and unanticipated transactions. A second reason why firms hold marketable securities is as a *temporary investment*. For example, a firm may accumulate cash over an extended period of time in anticipation of making large payments on the purchase of plant or equipment. Since the firm does not want to make the required payments before it is necessary, it will normally purchase and hold marketable securities until the payments are due. Assuming the firm knows the size and date of the required payments, securities can be purchased that have maturity dates matching the payment dates.

Firms also hold marketable securities as a temporary investment following the sale of a new issue of securities. Immediately after the sale, money is available for which there is no current need, so temporary investments are made in marketable securities until the cash is needed.

Firms that use marketable securities as a substitute for cash are constantly faced with the decision as to how much cash to invest in marketable securities and how much cash to hold for transactions purposes. A number of cash management models have been developed to help make this decision. Two such models are presented in Appendix A to this chapter.

## DESIRABLE CHARACTERISTICS OF MARKETABLE SECURITIES

The reason for holding marketable securities helps determine what characteristics are desired in those securities. When marketable securities are held as either a substitute for cash or as a temporary investment, which are the usual reasons, the following characteristics are generally sought:

- Low interest rate risk
- Low default risk
- Low market liquidity risk
- Appropriate taxability

Notice that a high return is not included on this list. This is relegated to secondary importance because the main objective of the marketable securities portfolio is to provide a source of cash to the firm when needed.

## Low Interest Rate Risk

The risk that the market value of a security will decline substantially if interest rates rise is called **interest rate risk.** As demonstrated in Chapter 4, the prices of securities having long maturities are more sensitive to interest rate changes than the prices of securities having short maturities. Therefore, to avoid the risk of incurring large losses when interest rates rise, firms generally hold securities with short maturities. This is true despite the fact that firms normally earn a lower rate of return on short-maturity securities than on securities with longer maturities.

## Low Default Risk

**Default risk** is the risk that the issuer will be unable to pay interest and principal when due. Businesses purchasing marketable securities as a cash substitute want to keep this risk as low as possible, because if the issuer were to default, the firm could incur considerable financial loss. In fact, even if the issuing firm does not default on its securities, just the hint of increasing default risk could reduce the market value of the issuer's securities.

Although a firm can earn higher returns by investing in securities with substantial default risk, most firms prefer to accept a lower return in order to keep risk in their marketable securities portfolio low.

## Low Market Liquidity Risk

The risk of being unable to quickly convert a security into cash at or near its true value is known as **market liquidity risk.** If certain market characteristics do not exist (such as the existence of many interested buyers and sellers of that security) considerable time and expense might be necessary to find a buyer. In fact, the buyer that is found may be willing to purchase the security only with a considerable price concession. The result may be substantial loss to the selling firm.

Firms that are willing to purchase securities with higher liquidity risk can earn higher rates of interest. However, given that the primary objective of the marketable securities portfolio is to provide a source of ready cash to the firm, and not to earn high returns, a high level of market liquidity risk is unacceptable.

## Appropriate Taxability

Firms having very low marginal tax rates may not be interested in the tax advantages offered by some securities, but those with high marginal tax rates should evaluate alternative securities based on the *after-tax* return they provide. One simple method of calculating this return is to reduce the before-tax return by the proportion that would be paid in taxes. This can be accomplished with the help of Equation 21.1:

$$R^* = R(1 - T) \qquad \textbf{(21.1)}$$

where $R^*$ = after-tax return

$R$ = before-tax return

$T$ = firm's marginal tax-rate

---

**EXAMPLE**

Consider a firm that will purchase one of two marketable securities having equal default risk and maturity (one year). The before-tax return on Security A is 10 percent, but it is fully taxable at the firm's 34 percent marginal tax rate. Security B promises a before-tax return of 7 percent, but the entire return is tax-free. The after-tax return of both securities can be determined using Equation 21.1:

Security A

$$R^* = 10\%(1 - .34)$$
$$= 6.6\%$$

Security B

$$R^* = 7\%(1 - .00)$$
$$= 7\%$$

Based on the results of these two calculations, the firm should select Security B, since it offers a higher after-tax return to the firm.

---

The readers should recognize that adjustment for taxes is normally more complex than described here, and the taxing of returns on securities can be very complex, since returns on some securities are subject to one or more of the following taxes: federal income tax, state property tax, state income tax, and city income tax. Further discussion of the taxing of securities' returns is beyond the scope of this text.

## MEASURING RETURNS ON SHORT-TERM SECURITIES

Unless stated otherwise, the interest rate quoted on marketable securities is an annual rate even if the security matures in less than one year. Determining the rate of return on long-term investments was addressed in Chapter 3. The following discussion centers on how to determine the dollar amount of interest on short-term investments.

First, consider a security promising the investor a 10 percent return and that matures in one year. If a firm has $10,000 to invest in this security, it will earn $1,000 in interest for the one year period (10% × $10,000). If, however, the firm purchases a security that promises 10 percent interest but matures in six months, the firm will earn only $500 in interest (6/12 × 10% × $10,000). In the previous calculation, the annual rate of interest was adjusted by multiplying it by the fraction of the year that the money is to be invested (six-twelfths of a year). If the same $10,000 is to be invested at 10 percent interest for thirty-seven days, the dollar amount of interest the firm would earn is $102.78 (37/360 × 10% × $10,000).

## MARKETABLE SECURITIES HELD BY FIRMS

Although most firms hold marketable securities as a substitute for cash or as a temporary investment, other reasons are possible. For example, some firms purchase the securities of other firms as a speculative investment with the main objective of short-term gains. Firms may also purchase the securities of other firms in order to influence the management of those firms. The discussion that follows highlights a number of securities that are commonly held as a substitute for cash.

### U.S. Treasury Bills

U.S. Treasury bills are widely held by businesses. Their main characteristics include a maximum maturity of one year and excellent liquidity, and they are free of default risk. The lack of default risk stems from the fact that they are direct obligations of the U.S. government, which has the power to tax and print money. As such, they are the only securities considered to be riskless.

Treasury bills sell on a discounted basis and therefore pay interest only at maturity. That is, the interest paid is the difference between the purchase price (which is always below par value) and par value, which the owner receives at maturity. Table 21.4 presents a summary of key characteristics of marketable securities, including information about the tax treatment and minimum investment amounts of Treasury bills and other securities.

### Federal Agency Securities

These securities are issued by agencies of the U.S. government, such as the Federal Home Loan Bank, the Federal National Mortgage Association, and the Federal Land Bank (there are numerous other issuers). Securities issued by these agencies have maturities as long as fifteen years, although most mature in less than five years, and many mature within one year. Agency securities do contain some default risk. Although the issuing agencies were created by the U.S. government, their securities are not guaranteed by the government. However, many experts feel the government would back these securities if necessary.

**TABLE 21.4**   Alternative Marketable Securities for Firm Investment

| Security | Typical Maturity | Default Risk | Market Liquidity | Minimum Investment | Approximate Yield May 22, 1987 | Tax Treatment |
|---|---|---|---|---|---|---|
| U.S. Treasury bills | 7 to 365 days | Riskless | Excellent | $ 10,000 | 6.4% | Pay federal income tax only |
| Federal agency securities | Up to 15 years | Low | Good | 1,000 | 9.1 | Pay federal income tax only |
| Commercial paper | Up to 270 days | Low | Moderate | 25,000 | 7.0 | Fully taxable |
| Negotiable CDs | Up to 1 year | Low | Good | 100,000 | 6.6 | Fully taxable |
| Repurchase agreements | 1 to 30 days | Low | Good | 100,000 | 6.5 | Fully taxable |
| Bankers' acceptances | 30 to 180 days | Low | Good | 25,000 | 7.1 | Fully taxable |
| Money market mutual funds | None | Low | Excellent | 1,000 | 5.7 | Fully taxable |
| U.S. Treasury notes and bonds | Up to 30 years | Riskless | Good | 1,000 | 8.9 | Pay federal income tax only |
| Corporate bonds (AAA-rated) | Up to 30 years | Low | Poor | 1,000 | 9.4 | Fully taxable |
| Municipal bonds (AAA-rated) | Up to 30 years | Low | Poor | 5,000 | 8.5 | May pay state income tax only |
| Eurodollar market time deposits | 1 month to 1 year | Low | Moderate | 100,000 | 7.3 | Fully taxable |
| Money market deposit accounts | None | Low | Excellent | 2,500 | 5.4 | Fully taxable |

The liquidity of agency securities is fairly good in general, but it is not good for all agency securities. Most pay interest semiannually.

## Commercial Paper

**Commercial paper** is a short-term, unsecured promissory note issued by a large, financially sound firm. Firms sell commercial paper to raise short-term funds. The main purchasers of commercial paper are other businesses that have a short-term surplus of cash. The maximum maturity of commercial paper is 270 days (with some exceptions), because securities with longer maturities must go through the cumbersome process of being registered with the Securities and Exchange Commission. Default risk on commercial paper is fairly low since commercial paper is generally issued only by financially sound firms.

No active secondary market for commercial paper exists. Therefore, the purchaser must be fairly certain that it will not need the invested funds until maturity. This restriction reduces the usefulness of commercial paper as a substitute for cash when the firm requires maximum liquidity. Commercial paper sells at a discount from par value and has no coupon.

## Negotiable Bank Certificates of Deposit (CDs)

**Negotiable bank certificates of deposit (CDs)** represent loans made to large money-center banks. The lender (purchaser of the CD) receives a certificate that can be sold in the secondary market if cash is needed before the CD matures. Although the maturities can be as long as eighteen months, most negotiable CDs have maturities of less than four months. They are backed by the banking institution that has issued them, and the first $100,000 of each CD is normally insured by the Federal Deposit Insurance Corporation. While the large money-center banks that issue negotiable CDs tend to be financially sound, default risk is still present, and the interest rate earned on CDs is therefore higher than on Treasury bills.

Negotiable CDs pay all interest at maturity (like Treasury bills and commercial paper), but they do not sell at a discount (unlike Treasury bills and commercial paper). That is, one purchases a CD at par value and, at maturity, receives par value plus interest.

## Repurchase Agreements (Repos)

A **repurchase agreement** (repo) is created when a commercial bank or securities dealer elects to sell some securities to raise needed cash but simultaneously promises to buy them back (repurchase them) in the future. The repurchase price is equal to the original purchase price plus interest on the dollar amount received from the original sale. The date of repurchase is normally specified. Businesses wishing to invest funds temporarily are key participants in this market on the purchase side of the transaction.

Maturities on repos tend to be shorter than for most other money market securities, usually just one or two days. This short maturity is considered an advantage of repos over most other short-term investments. When firms have funds available for very short periods and do not want to incur the interest rate risk associated with purchasing a security one day and selling it the next, they can enter into a repurchase agreement.

The risk of entering a repurchase agreement can be measured in terms of the risk of the asset purchased. Since most of the assets used in repurchase agreements are of high quality (Treasury bills and U.S. agency securities), default risk is very low. There is no secondary market for repos, and interest is paid at maturity.

## Bankers' Acceptances

**Bankers' acceptances** are normally created to assist firms engaged in international trade. For example, assume a U.S. firm is importing goods from a foreign manufacturer and does not want to pay for those goods until they have been received, but the exporter does not want to ship the goods until it is certain of payment. The U.S. firm can have its bank send a letter of credit to the exporter authorizing the exporter's bank to create a draft drawn on the U.S. bank. This has the effect of substituting the bank's credit for that of the U.S. firm, which promises to pay the bank the amount of the draft plus a commission at a later date.

The draft will be payable on a specified date, perhaps ninety days after issuance. Since the exporter normally wants the money sooner, it can sell the draft at a discount to its bank, which in turn presents the draft to the U.S. firm's bank for verification. At this point, the U.S. firm's bank stamps the draft "accepted," thus creating the bankers' acceptance. The foreign bank may now wish to sell the bankers' acceptance in the secondary market, again at a discount from its face (par) value, but at a price greater than it had paid. It is at this point that other businesses may wish to purchase the bankers' acceptance to add to their portfolios of marketable securities.

While ninety days is the most common maturity for bankers' acceptances, other common maturities range from thirty to one hundred eighty days. There is normally very little default risk associated with bankers' acceptances, since they are backed by both the importer and its commercial bank.

There is a secondary market for bankers' acceptances, although it is less active than that for Treasury bills. Like Treasury bills, bankers' acceptances are sold on a discounted basis, with interest being received at maturity. The face value of a bankers' acceptance is based on the purchase price of the goods being imported. As a result, face values are normally not in round numbers.

### Money Market Mutual Funds (MMMFs)

**Money market mutual funds** (MMMFs) sell their own shares to many investors, then invest the proceeds in money market–type securities (such as Treasury bills, negotiable CDs, and commercial paper). Investors in MMMFs indirectly own part of all the securities purchased by the mutual fund. As the value of the securities in the portfolio rise and fall, so does the value of the shares issued by the MMMF.

There are three major advantages of purchasing MMMF shares. First, investors with small amounts of money to invest can earn interest rates normally available only on large-denomination securities (the minimum investment in Treasury bills is $10,000). A second advantage is the diversification an investor can obtain by purchasing MMMFs, as opposed to investing directly in other marketable securities. Although diversification may not be important to an investor in Treasury bills, it can be important to investors in other types of securities. A third advantage is that smaller firms may lack the expertise to manage a marketable securities portfolio. If so, they can let the mutual fund do it for them.

MMMFs hold securities with average maturities of from one week to one year; however, to the firm investing in MMMFs, there is no maturity, since the proceeds from maturing securities are used to purchase replacement securities. The risk of investing in MMMFs varies with the fund, although in general they are relatively safe investments. Some funds attempt to attract investors by paying high yields, but in order to do so, they may invest in securities with considerable default risk and/or longer maturities (up to one year). Other MMMFs prefer to keep risk low, investing only in Treasury bills having very short maturities.

The liquidity of MMMFs is excellent, since each fund stands ready to redeem shares upon request by investors. Most funds provide checkbooks on which investors can write checks against their accounts. Most also permit redemptions by telephone and will even wire redemption proceeds to the investor's bank account, making funds available to the investor within one business day.

## FINANCIAL MANAGEMENT IN PRACTICE

### MANAGEMENT OF CASH AND MARKETABLE SECURITIES

A survey of corporate financial managers reported some of their common practices related to the management of cash and marketable securities.* The questionnaire was sent to the corporate financial managers of the 150 largest and the 150 smallest firms included in the list of *Fortune 1000* firms (these are the 1,000 largest firms in terms of sales). This study offered the following conclusions:

1. The average number of banks from which firms borrow money is sixteen, the average number of banks in which firms maintain checking accounts is thirty-two, and the average number of banks used for customer collections is seventy-seven.

2. All of the responding firms use bank wire transfer services, and 68 percent have zero-balance accounts.

3. Eighty-five percent of responding firms maintain compensating balances as one means of paying banks for services provided.

* Lawrence J. Gitman, Edward A. Moses, and I. Thomas White, "An Assessment of Corporate Cash Management Practices," *Financial Management* (Summer 1979): 32–41.

4. Responding banks ranked cash management policies as follows in order of importance (the first is most important):

- Speeding collection of accounts receivable
- Minimizing bank balances
- Minimizing investment in inventory
- Slowing payment of accounts payable

5. The most frequently used systems to speed collection of accounts receivable are lock-box systems (used by 90 percent of the responding firms), and concentration banking (used by 61 percent of the firms). Many firms use both systems.

6. The most frequently held marketable securities are as follows:

| | *Percent of Firms Owning Each* |
|---|---|
| Commercial paper | 78% |
| Repurchase agreements | 75 |
| Treasury securities | 72 |
| Negotiable CDs | 69 |
| Bankers acceptances | 58 |
| Federal agency securities | 46 |

### Other Securities

These seven different securities commonly held by businesses in their marketable securities portfolios are not the only securities held by businesses. Not described here are long- and intermediate-term securities that are nearing maturity, such as U.S. Treasury notes and bonds, corporate bonds, and municipal bonds, and short-term securities such as Eurodollar market time deposits and money market deposits at banks and other institutions. Generally, each of these securities is lacking at least one of the characteristics desired of securities held as a substitute for cash (low interest rate risk, low default risk, and/or good liquidity).

## SELECTING MARKETABLE SECURITIES

Within the framework described in this chapter, firms have considerable latitude in terms of selecting specific securities. Some take the very conservative approach of holding only U.S. Treasury bills of very short maturity, rolling them over into new Treasury bills as they mature. This strategy keeps risk relatively low, but it also keeps the return relatively low. More aggressive firms seek the higher returns expected from securities containing higher levels of default and liquidity risk.

Some firms have large enough portfolios of marketable securities to make the employment of an investment specialist economical. An investment specialist can seek out attractive investment opportunities, engage in active trading (buying and selling), evaluate the risk of specific investments, and constantly monitor investment performance. The details of such strategies are normally discussed in investments classes and are beyond the scope of this text.

## SUMMARY

It is important for firms to maintain adequate liquidity in the form of cash and marketable securities. Insufficient liquidity can result in the inability of a firm to pay bills when they are due, which can lead to a loss of future access to credit, or even legal action and bankruptcy. However, the risk of not maintaining adequate liquidity must be weighed against the higher costs associated with maintaining excess cash and marketable securities. The level of cash a firm maintains normally depends on the firm's level and volatility of sales, the firm's access to borrowed funds, the level of interest rates, management's attitude toward risk, the need for compensating balances, and the ability of the firm to forecast irregular expenditures.

In managing the cash position, firms should attempt to slow disbursements and accelerate collections. There are a number of tools available to help firms do this, including such things as float, zero-balance accounts, lock-box systems, concentration banking, and preauthorized payments.

The most desirable characteristics of securities held as a substitute for cash are short maturities, low risk of default, and high market liquidity. Numerous securities meet these requirements, including U.S. Treasury bills, commercial paper, negotiable certificates of deposit, and money market mutual funds.

## KEY TERMS

**Bankers' acceptance** A security backed by the creditworthiness of both an importing firm and the firm's bank. It can be bought or sold in the secondary market.

**Cash** Currency plus demand deposits.

**Commercial paper** Unsecured promissory notes issued by large financially sound firms.

**Compensating balance** Non-interest-earning bank deposit that a firm must maintain as a provision of a loan agreement.

**Concentration banking** A collection system whereby customers are directed to send payments to a sales office in their region. Regional offices then forward collected funds to the firm's main (concentration) bank.

**Default risk** The risk that the issuer of a fixed income security will be unable to pay interest and principal when due.

**Drafts** Check-like instruments drawn against the draft writer as opposed to the writer's bank account.

**Float** Bank balances against which checks have been written but from which funds have not yet been removed.

**Interest rate risk** The risk that the value of an investment will fall when interest rates rise.

**Lock-box system** A system to speed the collection of customer payments whereby customers send checks to regional post office boxes. These boxes are accessed by regional banks for collection and forwarding to the firm's main bank.

**Market liquidity risk** The risk that the owner of a security will be unable to convert that security into cash at its true value.

**Money market mutual fund** An investment in which the owner indirectly owns a small part of many money market securities held in a portfolio that is managed by the mutual fund.

**Near-cash** Marketable securities that can be quickly converted into cash.

**Negotiable bank certificates of deposit (CDs)** Securities representing short-term loans made to large money-center banks.

**Preauthorized payments (PAPs)** A collection system whereby customers authorize a firm to access their checking account directly.

**Repurchase agreement** A contract whereby the seller of a security promises to buy back the same security at a later date at a specified higher price.

**Zero balance accounts** A group of bank accounts whereby funds in a master account are used to make deposits in a number of related accounts when the balance in those accounts deviates from zero.

## EQUATIONS

**Equation 21.1**     **After-Tax Return**

$$R^* = R(1 - T)$$     **(p. 576)**

where $R^*$ = after-tax return
$R$ = before-tax return
$T$ = marginal tax rate

This equation can be used to determine the return on an investment after taxes have been paid.

## QUESTIONS

**Q21-1.** Discuss the four reasons why firms hold cash.

**Q21-2.** What are the risks incurred by a firm if it keeps cash at a very low level?

**Q21-3.** List seven factors that influence the target level of cash, and indicate how they affect the level of cash.

**Q21-4.** Discuss five techniques for slowing cash disbursements.

**Q21-5.** What alternative methods are available to a firm to slow the check clearing process, the mailing time, and the check processing time?

**Q21-6.** Describe how a lock-box system can be used to speed collections.

**Q21-7.** Explain why concentration banking might be preferred by a firm over a lock-box system.

**Q21-8.** How does a preauthorized payments system work?

**Q21-9.** What are the advantages and disadvantages associated with holding marketable securities and using bank credit as a substitute for holding excess cash?

**Q21-10.** List and describe the four major characteristics of marketable securities that business firms generally seek.

**Q21-11.** Describe the major investment characteristics of U.S. Treasury bills, federal agency securities, commercial paper, negotiable CDs, repurchase agreements, bankers' acceptances, and money market mutual funds.

## SELF-TEST PROBLEMS

Solutions to self-test problems appear on p. S1.

**SP21-1.** A firm's union has proposed that all employees be paid weekly. The firm currently has a $600,000 payroll, which it pays every two weeks. If it incurs an administrative expense of $2,000 with each payroll, and if it can earn 8 percent interest on marketable securities, what additional cost would the firm incur annually if it makes the change?

**SP21-2.** Sparks Corporation is planning to send $5,000,000 in cash dividends to its stockholders on April 15. Historical records indicate that none of the checks clear through the firm's bank until the fourth day after mailing, and it generally takes another five days for the balance of the checks to clear (see the following table for the pattern). The firm's policy is to put into its checking account each day the amount that is expected to clear, plus 4 percent of the total payroll as a safety amount. How much should the firm deposit each day?

| Days since Mailing | Percent Expected to Clear This Day |
|:---:|:---:|
| 4 | 5% |
| 5 | 18 |
| 6 | 31 |
| 7 | 25 |
| 8 | 14 |
| 9 | 7 |
| | 100% |

**SP21-3.** A firm is considering implementing a lock-box system at an annual cost of $100,000. The firm has annual collections of $210,000,000 and can earn 7 percent interest on its marketable securities. If the system can reduce collection time by two days, should the firm adopt it?

**SP21-4.** Lucas Enterprises has some excess cash with which to purchase marketable securities. If it can earn 9.35 percent interest on a fully taxable security or 6.05 percent interest on a tax-exempt security, which should it purchase, and why? (Lucas Enterprises has a 35 percent marginal tax rate.)

**SP21-5.** WWR Corporation expects to have $50,000 of excess cash available for the next two weeks. If it can earn 6 percent annual interest on marketable securities but must pay a total of $125 in transactions costs, should WWR Corporation invest the money for two weeks? For three weeks?

## PROBLEMS

**P21-1.** After two years of earnings losses, SSG Corporation is on the verge of gaining some concessions from its union. One proposal is to begin paying employees on a monthly basis as opposed to the current weekly basis. The firm has a weekly payroll of $200,000, and it incurs a $5,000 administrative cost with each payroll. If it can earn 7 percent interest on marketable securities, how much money would this proposal save the firm each year?

**P21-2.** Dewitt, Ltd., pays a $750,000 payroll every two weeks. The following table indicates the pattern of check clearing by Dewitt's employees. If Dewitt's policy is to deposit only the amount expected to clear its checking account, plus 5 percent of payroll, how much should be deposited each day?

| Days since Payday | Percent Expected to Clear This Day |
|:---:|:---:|
| 1 | 43% |
| 2 | 38 |
| 3 | 16 |
| 4 | 3 |

**P21-3.** Babb Company expects its total disbursements to equal $40,000,000 next year, and it is instituting several programs that should help delay disbursements by an average of two days. If the firm can earn 6 percent interest on marketable securities, by what dollar amount will it benefit from these programs? (Hint: This can be handled in a manner similar to speeding collections by using a lock-box system.)

**P21-4.** What is the after-tax return on the following securities given the tax rates indicated?

| Security | Before-Tax Return | Applicable Tax Rate |
|:---:|:---:|:---:|
| A | 9% | 34% |
| B | 6 | Tax-exempt |
| C | 8 | 25% |
| D | 5.5 | 39% |

**P21-5.** Find the dollar amount of interest a firm would earn on securities given a $25,000 investment in each of the securities indicated below.

| Security | Maturity | Stated Interest Rate |
|:---:|:---:|:---:|
| E | 5 months | 8% |
| F | 192 days | 7 |
| G | 1 year | 11 |
| H | 14 weeks | 9 |

**P21-6.** SKV Corporation is about to open a new assembly plant in El Paso, Texas. Instead of paying its employees weekly, as it does at its main facility near Boston, SKV would like to pay its employees biweekly (every other week). If SKV can earn 6 percent interest on marketable securities, expects a biweekly payroll of $300,000, and if it costs $1,000 in administrative costs for each payroll, how much would the firm save annually if it uses a biweekly payroll in El Paso?

**P21-7.** Austin Company is considering a policy change involving the payment of employees every two weeks rather than every week. It has a weekly payroll of $125,000 and incurs an administrative cost of $3,000 with each payroll. If Austin can earn 9 percent on marketable securities, what annual savings would result from the proposed policy?

**P21-8.** Coleman, Inc., pays a $200,000 payroll every two weeks. The pattern of check clearing is as follows:

| Days since Payday | Percent Expected to Clear This Day |
|:---:|:---:|
| 1 | 35% |
| 2 | 30 |
| 3 | 19 |
| 4 | 16 |

If Coleman plans to deposit only the amount expected to clear its checking account, plus 10 percent of the payroll, how much should be deposited each day?

**P21-9.** Hazle Company plans to purchase marketable securities. It is considering tax-exempt securities that offer a before-tax return of 8 percent, and taxable securities that offer a before-tax return of 11 percent. The risk of both types of securities is identical. If Hazle has a 34 percent marginal tax rate, which type of security should it purchase? Explain.

**P21-10.** Trunk Enterprises expects total disbursements of $13 million next year, and it can earn 8 percent interest on marketable securities. If it can delay disbursements by an average of one day, what dollar benefit would Trunk realize?

**P21-11.** In negotiating with its union, Alexander Enterprises feels that if it gives in to one of the union's two remaining demands, an agreement can be reached. One demand is for the firm to pay its employees each week instead of once every four weeks, and the other is to contribute an additional $10 per employee each week into the firm's pension fund. Given the following information, determine which demand Alexander should agree to, and justify your answer. (Ignore taxes.)

- The current payroll is $432,000 every four weeks.
- The number of employees affected by the decision is 450.
- The fixed administrative cost associated with each payroll is $500.
- Alexander earns 6 percent interest on its marketable securities.

**P21-12.** Bailey Corporation is preparing to pay its shareholders a dividend of $.75 per share. An analysis of historical check clearing patterns reveals a fairly stable pattern of check clearing when dividends were paid in the past (last quarter's pattern of check clearing was typical and appears in the table below). The firm's policy is to deposit an amount into the checking account that is sufficient to cover the checks that are expected to clear, plus 5 percent of the total payroll as a safety amount. How much money must be deposited each day if there are 100 million shares of stock outstanding?

| Days since Mailing | Dollar Amount Cleared Each Day (Last Quarter) |
|---|---|
| 4 | $2,100,000 |
| 5 | 5,600,000 |
| 6 | 7,700,000 |
| 7 | 15,400,000 |
| 8 | 18,200,000 |
| 9 | 13,300,000 |
| 10 | 6,300,000 |
| 11 | 1,400,000 |
| | $70,000,000 |

**P21-13.** Canter Corporation wishes to implement a lock-box system to help accelerate its collections. Each of its seven regional offices receives an average of $250,000 in collections monthly. If Canter can earn 6.5 percent interest on marketable securities, what would be the maximum amount it would be willing to pay for the system if it reduces collection time by one and one-half days?

**P21-14.** As treasurer of a corporation, you must select one of the following marketable securities as a short-term investment. All are identical in every way except for their before-tax returns and the tax-rates that apply to the returns. Security A is subject to state income taxes only, Security B is subject to federal income taxes only, and Security C is subject to both state and federal income taxes. Which should your firm purchase?

| Security | Before-Tax Return | Applicable Tax Rate |
|---|---|---|
| A | 6.1% | 15% |
| B | 7.6 | 34 |
| C | 9.8 | 49 |

**P21-15.** Elgin Transporation Corporation has $250,000 of excess funds available for short-term investment. It can earn a 7.5% annual return on marketable securities, but must pay a total commission of $1,950 to purchase and sell them. How long must Elgin hold the securities in order to make the investment worthwhile?

## COMPUTER-ASSISTED PROBLEMS

**CP21-1.** Yoder Industries is considering implementing a lock-box system at an annual cost of $30,000. Yoder expects to have annual collections of $95 million next year. It also expects to earn 8 percent interest on its marketable securities, and the lock-box is expected to reduce collection time by one day. Use the computer program to determine the net benefit the firm will realize if it initiates the lock-box system.

**a. Sensitivity of Lock-Box Net Benefits to Annual Collections** Yoder is uncertain about the size of its collections next year. It has forecasted several possible sales levels that would result in annual collections of $75 million, $85 million, $95 million, $105 million, or $115 million. What is the expected net benefit to the firm under each scenario?

**b. Sensitivity of Lock-Box Net Benefits to Market Rates of Interest** Yoder recognizes that interest rates may not be 8 percent as forecasted. In fact, they could be as low as 6 percent or 7 percent, or as high as 9 percent or 10 percent. Assuming annual collections are $95 million, what is the net benefit under each possible level of interest rates?

**c. Sensitivity of Lock-Box Net Benefits to Annual Collections and Interest Rates** Based on your previous analysis, is the net benefit of a lock-box more sensitive to Yoder's sales or to interest rates? What is the net benefit Yoder can expect to obtain from the lock-box system if the collections and interest rates are most favorable to the firm? What is the lowest possible net benefit?

**d. Probability Distributions** Yoder has developed probability distributions to describe its expectations about future collections and future interest rates. Determine the probability distribution that applies to the net benefit provided to Yoder Industries by the lock-box system.

| Annual Collections | Probability | Interest Rates | Probability |
|---|---|---|---|
| $85 million | 25% | 7% | 20% |
| 95 million | 55 | 8 | 55 |
| 105 million | 20 | 9 | 25 |

**e. Simulation** Yoder has revised its estimates of annual collections and interest rates. It now forecasts annual collections of $85 million to $105 million and interest rates of 7 percent to 9 percent. Use simulation analysis to determine the probability that the lock-box system will result in a net benefit to the firm.

## REFERENCES

Batlin, C. A., and Susan Hinko. "Lockbox Management and Value Maximization." *Financial Management* 10 (Winter 1981): 39–44.

Baumol, William J. "The Transactions Demand for Cash: An Inventory Theoretic Approach." *Quarterly Journal of Economics* 65 (November 1952): 545–56.

Cook, Timothy Q., and Bruce J. Summers, eds. *Instruments of the Money Market.* 5th ed. Richmond: Federal Reserve Bank of Richmond, 1981.

Daellenbach, Hans G. "Are Cash Management Optimization Models Worthwhile?" *Journal of Financial and Quantitative Analysis* 9 (September 1974): 607–26.

Ferguson, Daniel M. "Optimize Your Firm's Lock-box Selection System." *Financial Executive* 51 (April 1983): 8–19.

Gilmer, R. H., Jr. "The Optimal Level of Liquid Assets: An Empirical Test." *Financial Management* 14 (Winter 1985): 39–43.

Gitman, Lawrence J., E. A. Moses, and I. T. White. "An Assessment of Corporate Cash Management Practices." *Financial Management* 8 (Summer 1979): 32–41.

Gitman, Lawrence J., D. Keith Forrester, and John R. Forrester, Jr. "Maximizing Cash Disbursement Float." *Financial Management* 5 (Summer 1976): 15–24.

Gitman, Lawrence J., and Mark D. Goodwin. "An Assessment of Marketable Securities Management Practices" *Journal of Financial Research* 2 (Fall 1979): 161–69.

Johnson, James M., David R. Campbell, and Leonard M. Savoie. "Corporate Liquidity: A Comparison of Two Recessions." *Financial Executive* 51 (October 1983): 18–22.

Maier, Steven F. "What Lockbox and Disbursement Models Really Do." *Journal of Finance* 38 (May 1983): 361–72.

Maier, Steven F., David W. Robinson, and James H. Vander Weide. "A Short-Term Disbursement Forecasting Model." *Financial Management* 10 (Spring 1981): 9–20.

Maier, Steven F., and James H. Vander Weide. "A Practical Approach to Short-Run Financial

Planning." *Financial Management* 7 (Winter 1978): 10–16.

Miller, Merton H., and Daniel Orr. "A Model of the Demand for Money by Firms." *Quarterly Journal of Economics* 80 (August 1966): 413–35.

Richards, Verlyn D., and Eugene J. Laughlin. "A Cash Conversion Cycle Approach to Liquidity Analysis." *Financial Management* 9 (Spring 1980): 32–38.

Shim, Jae K. "Estimating Cash Collection Rates from Credit Sales: A Lagged Regression Approach." *Financial Management* 10 (Winter 1981): 28–30.

Van Horne, James C. *Financial Market Rates and Flows.* 2d ed. Englewood Cliffs, N.J.: Prentice-Hall, 1984.

———, and Ned C. Hill. "Cash Transfer Scheduling for Efficient Cash Concentration." *Financial Management* 9 (Autumn 1980): 35–43.

———, and Robert A. Wood. "Daily Cash Forecasting: A Simple Method for Implementing the Distribution Approach." *Financial Management* 6 (Fall 1977): 40–50.

Vickson, R. G. "Simple Optimal Policy for Cash Management: The Average Balance Requirement Cash." *Journal of Financial and Quantitative Analysis* 20 (September 1985): 353–370.

# CASH MANAGEMENT MODELS

William Baumol adapted an inventory control model (the EOQ model discussed in the next chapter) to help firms determine the distribution of assets between marketable securities and cash.[1] This model, called the *Baumol model*, assumes that cash outflows and inflows are both constant and steady, with the outflows exceeding the inflows. As a result of this constant drain of cash from the firm, the firm needs to replenish cash periodically by selling marketable securities. Figure 21A.1 illustrates this process. At Time 0 (zero), the firm has just sold marketable securities, bringing the level of cash up to Level C. Since cash outflow exceeds inflow, and both flows are steady, the level of cash declines to zero by Time 1. At this point marketable securities are sold, and the level of cash is brought back up to Level C.

The Baumol model considers the trade-off made by the firm when it must liquidate securities to raise cash. This trade-off involves the fixed cost of selling securities and the interest income forgone by holding cash. If the firm liquidates only small amounts of marketable securities to replenish that cash, it must conduct numerous securities transactions and incur large transactions expenses. However, the firm will also keep its cash balances low, minimizing the opportunity cost of holding cash. If it takes the other approach and sells large amounts of securities in each transaction, fewer transactions are required and total transaction costs will be lower. However, the firm's average cash balance will be greater, as will the opportunity cost of holding cash. In order to determine the optimal amount of securities to be sold ($C^*$) each time cash is needed, the following input is required: the fixed cost of selling securities ($F$), the interest rate that can be earned on the securities ($k$), and the total expected net cash outflow during a given time period ($TCF$). The relationship is such that

$$C^* = \sqrt{\frac{2F(TCF)}{k}} \qquad \textbf{(21A.1)}$$

---

1. William J. Baumol, "The Transactions Demand for Cash: An Inventory Theoretic Approach," *Quarterly Journal of Economics* 65 (November 1952): 545–56.

**FIGURE 21A.1**
**Graphical Description of the Baumol Model**

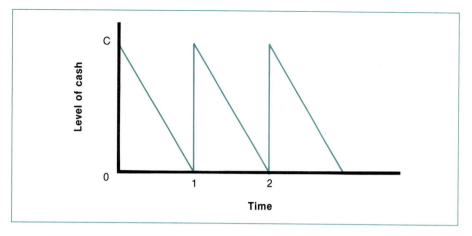

**Example**

Consider Company Y that expects to have a net cash outflow of $800,000 during a one-year period. The firm expects to earn 10 percent annual interest on its marketable securities, but it will cost the firm $25 each time securities are sold. Equation 21A.1 can be used to determine the optimal amount of securities to liquidate each time cash is needed:

$$C^* = \sqrt{\frac{(2)(\$25)(\$800,000)}{.10}}$$

$$= \$20,000.$$

This analysis indicates that every time the firm sells securities, it should sell $20,000 worth. Since the firm will spend a total of $800,000 during the period, it will need to sell securities a total of forty times during the year ($800,000/$20,000), an average of one time each nine days (360 days/40 liquidations). The average amount of cash the firm will hold during the year is $10,000. That is, since the firm begins each nine-day period with $20,000 and ends with zero, the average amount it holds is $20,000/2.

While the Baumol model may have some application as a practical tool, the necessary assumptions about having smooth cash inflows and outflows limit its usefulness.

The unrealistic assumptions implicit in the Baumol model led to its expansion by Merton Miller and Daniel Orr.[2] Their model, the *Miller-Orr model*, assumes random changes in cash inflows and outflows and, therefore, in cash balances. Basically, the Miller-Orr model establishes maximum and minimum levels of cash a firm should hold, shown on Figure 21A.2 as levels $u$ and $q$ respectively. If and when the level of cash reaches $u$

---

2. Merton H. Miller and Daniel Orr, "A Model for the Demand for Money By Firms," *Quarterly Journal of Economics* 80 (August 1966): 413–435.

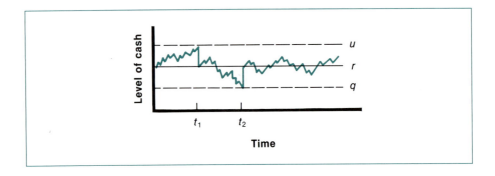

(at point $t_1$ on the figure), the firm purchases marketable securities in sufficient quantity to reduce cash balances to level $r$. If and when cash reaches
level $q$ (as it does at point $t_2$ on the figure), the firm sells marketable securities in sufficient quantity to return cash balances back to level $r$. Thus,
this model specifies an acceptable range of cash holdings.

The minimum level of cash, $q$, is arrived at subjectively by the firm. The
return point, level $r$, and the maximum level, $u$, are established so that the
total costs to the firm are minimized. These costs include transaction
costs, $F$, and the daily opportunity cost of investment in cash, $i/360$. Here, $i$
is equal to the annual opportunity cost. Also of importance in determining
points $r$ and $u$ is the variance of the cash balances, $\sigma^2$. The greater the variance is, the higher the return point and the maximum level, since greater
variance would tend to result in more transactions unless the return point
and maximum level are relatively high. When there is an equal probability
of an increase and decrease in the cash balance during a planning period,
the following relationships exist:

$$r = \left[ \frac{3F\sigma^2}{4(i/360)} \right]^{1/3} + q \qquad \text{(21A.2)}$$

$$u = 3r \qquad \text{(21A.3)}$$

**Example**

To illustrate the Miller-Orr model, assume Company G has an annual opportunity
cost of investment in cash of 7.2 percent, an established lower cash limit of $1,000,
variance of cash balances of $250,000, and transaction costs of $50. The return
point, $r$, and the upper limit, $u$, can be found as follows:

$$r = \left[ \frac{3(\$50)(\$250,000)}{4\left(\dfrac{.072}{360}\right)} \right]^{1/3} + \$1,000$$

$$= \left[ \frac{\$37,500,000}{.0008} \right]^{1/3} + \$1,000$$

$$= \$4,606$$

$$u = 3(\$4,606)$$

$$= \$13,818$$

The Miller-Orr model has been used in practice and has proven to be as effective or more effective than more intuitive approaches. It is not without its limitations, however. The most serious limitation is the assumption of random movement of cash balances. If cash balances do not move randomly, some other approach to cash management may provide superior results.

## PROBLEMS (Appendix 21A)

**P21A-1.** Spudeck Enterprises expects to have a steady net outflow of funds over the next year and currently has enough marketable securities to cover that outflow. What dollar amount of securities should be liquidated each time cash is needed if it costs Spudeck $30 each time it sells securities, Spudeck earns 6 percent interest on its marketable securities and expects the net outflow to total $100,000 over the next year?

**P21A-2.** Hardin & Hardin Corporation wants to maintain a minimum of $10,000 in cash during the coming period, and it expects cash balances to move randomly. Use the Miller-Orr model to determine the maximum level of cash and the return point for cash. The variance of cash balances is expected to be $100,000, transactions costs are fixed at $45 per transaction, and the firm can earn 8 percent interest on marketable securities.

**P21A-3.** RES Corporation currently has $250,000 of marketable securities that it expects to liquidate gradually over the next year in order to cover a steady net cash outflow during that period. If RES Corporation can earn 7.5 percent interest on its marketable securities, what dollar amount should it liquidate each time cash is needed? RES Corporation incurs a $45 cost each time it sells securities.

**P21A-4.** Klock Corporation is unhappy about the current management of its cash position. Since its cash balances move randomly, it would like to use the Miller-Orr model to determine the maximum level of cash to hold and the return level of cash. Determine those values for Klock Corporation if it wants to maintain a minimum level of cash of $6,000, pays $50 for each securities transaction, estimates the variance of cash flows to be $19,000, and can earn 7 percent interest on marketable securities.

# CHAPTER 22

# MANAGEMENT OF INVENTORY AND ACCOUNTS RECEIVABLE

## ACCOUNTS RECEIVABLE AND INVENTORY MANAGEMENT IN PERSPECTIVE

In 1986 Corning Glass Works underwent a reorganization designed to improve the firm's efficiency. One aspect of the move toward greater efficiency involved reducing the lead time necessary for procuring raw materials inventory from six weeks to two weeks. This increased efficiency meant that less work-in-process and finished goods inventories were needed. As a result, Corning realized a one-time savings of $150,000 on its work-in-process inventory and $400,000 on its finished goods inventory.

Separately, the inventories of Claire's Stores, Inc., were increased by 65 percent over a four-month period in 1987 as a result of its strategy of capitalizing on bargain prices in overseas markets. This onetime reduction in the cost of purchasing inventory saved Claire's Stores a substantial amount that contributed to increased firm earnings.

The events described here suggest that effective management of a firm's inventories can involve either an increase or a decrease in the level of inventories. A similar situation exists for accounts receivable; that is, some firms may be able to benefit from actions that increase their accounts receivable, while others benefit from actions that reduce their accounts receivable.

How can managers increase the inefficiency with which they manage inventories and accounts receivable? What are the risks involved with maintaining too much inventory and accounts receivable? This chapter provides a framework that can be used to answer these and other questions about the management of these important current assets.

*Source: Wall Street Journal,* October 13, 1986, and May 21, 1987.

The importance of inventory and accounts receivable to a firm is evidenced by the fact that the typical firm holds about 8 percent of its total assets in the form of inventory and 25 percent in the form of accounts receivable. Moreover, the level of these two current assets involves a risk-return trade-off that affects the firm's profits. By minimizing its investment in inventory and accounts receivable in order to use funds more productively elsewhere, a firm may increase its income, dividend, and growth rate, resulting in a higher common stock value and increased shareholder wealth. However, certain risks may also increase, such as the risk of running out of raw materials and being forced to close down production. And if the higher level of risk increases investors' required rates of return, it could *decrease* the value of the firm's common stock and *reduce* shareholder wealth. The financial manager must carefully balance the risk and return associated with these decisions.

As explained in the discussion of the cash flow cycle in Chapter 20, accounts receivable are created by the sale of inventory. This relationship between inventory and accounts receivable is important. If the firm decides to increase sales, perhaps by extending trade credit to more customers, both sales and accounts receivable will increase. Although inventories may decrease in the *short run* as finished goods inventory is sold off, the firm will probably need to increase its inventories above the original level in order to support the higher level of sales. Thus, when sales increase, both inventories and accounts receivable normally increase in the *long run* as well. Conversely, if the firm denies trade credit to more customers, sales and accounts receivable will decrease, and the firm will realize an involuntary increase in inventories in the short run. However, eventually the firm will need to reduce inventories to a lower level to avoid excess inventories. Clearly, this relationship between accounts receivable and inventories must be recognized and coordinated within the firm.

Managers must make numerous decisions about ordering and maintaining inventories. In the following sections, the risk-return trade-off is analyzed as it applies to inventories, and some inventory-control models and other techniques used in inventory management are discussed.

## RISK-RETURN TRADE-OFF FOR VARIOUS TYPES OF INVENTORY

Inventory can be classified as raw materials, work-in-process, or finished goods inventory. Most firms prefer to keep each type at a level sufficient to reduce the risk of stock-outs, which occur when a firm has no more inventory from which to make sales or continue production. However, in order to reduce the opportunity cost of investing funds in inventories, firms also like to maintain inventory at a low level. For example, Apple Computer Company attributed much of its significant improvement in gross margin during 1986 to its ability to reduce inventories by 35 percent over 1985's inventory level. A discussion of the risk-return relationship for each type of inventory follows.

## Raw Materials Inventory

An inventory of raw materials is needed by manufacturing firms as input into the production process. A large inventory can be costly in terms of storage, insurance, and the opportunity cost of tying up funds in inventory. However, the production manager normally favors maintaining a large raw materials inventory to avoid the possibility of a shortage that could close down the production process. Since some costs rise as the level of inventory rises, the financial manager typically advocates maintaining lower levels of inventory than desired by the production manager.

A number of variables must be considered in determining the appropriate level of raw materials inventory to maintain. The following conditions would suggest maintaining a large raw materials inventory, other things being equal:

■ A large amount of raw materials is needed for production.
■ The price of raw materials is low.
■ The cost of storing raw materials is low.
■ The cost of placing orders for raw materials is high (so to avoid placing numerous orders, the firm should order a large amount at one time).
■ No substitutes are available for the raw materials in the production process.
■ Delivery time of new raw materials is highly uncertain.

## Work-in-Process Inventory

Work-in-process inventory represents partially completed products in manufacturing firms. A key determinant of the level of this type of inventory is the length of the production process. If it is a very slow process, the work-in-process inventory will tend to be large, and vice versa. Consider a firm that produces two units of finished goods per week, using two slow production lines. At any point in time, the work-in-process inventory is equal to the material that is being used to produce the two units. If the firm were to switch to a single, faster production line that produces one unit each half-week, it would still produce the same number of units, but the work-in-process inventory at any point in time would be equal to the materials used to produce just one unit. Therefore, for firms having a simple production process, inventory can normally be reduced only by reducing the length of the production process.

A second determinant of work-in-process inventory is the complexity of the production process. Firms with complex production processes hold excess work-in-process inventory to "uncouple" the individual production steps. For example, if production requires five separate steps, and the machine used in the first step breaks down, all five steps may be forced to shut down. If, however, a reserve of partially completed items (work-in-process inventory) is held at each step of production, temporary stoppage at one stage will not close down all phases of production.

For firms holding excess inventory to prevent chain-reaction shutdowns, considerable thought must go into deciding the appropriate level of work-in-process inventory to maintain. Some of the key factors that tend to keep work-in-process inventory large are as follows:

- The cost of the inventory items is low.
- The production equipment is difficult to replace quickly should it break down.
- The production equipment is subject to frequent and/or lengthy downtime.
- The cost of storing the inventory items is low.

In firms with complex production processes, the production manager generally prefers to maintain considerable excess work-in-process inventory at each level of production. The financial manager must balance this need against the need to keep inventory financing and carrying costs low. Both goals must be considered in making the final decision on the level of work-in-process inventory to maintain.

### Finished Goods Inventory

Finished goods inventory is inventory that is ready for sale but has not yet been sold. It serves to uncouple the production and sales functions by providing a reservoir of the firm's product from which rapid delivery can be made after a sale.

If the finished goods inventory is too low, a slowing or stoppage of production could result in lost sales. Certainly sales could be lost on any unexpectedly large orders to be filled on short notice. Firms unwilling to assume the risk of lost sales, however, incur the higher costs associated with financing and carrying a large finished goods inventory.

Financial managers must consider many different factors in evaluating the risk-return trade-off regarding the level of finished goods inventory. Factors that warrant a large finished goods inventory are as follows:

- The production process is subject to lengthy slowdowns or stoppages.
- The demand for the firm's product is volatile.
- The cost of the finished goods is low.
- The cost of storing the finished goods is low.

The marketing manager typically favors a large finished goods inventory because the level of sales is influenced by the firm's ability to deliver finished goods promptly. The financial manager, on the other hand, must consider all the costs as well as the benefits of any given inventory levels in determining the appropriate level of finished goods inventory to maintain.

## INVENTORY ACQUISITION AND USE

The preceding discussion of the three types of inventory illustrates that inventory flows through the firm from (1) raw materials, to (2) work-in-process, and finally to (3) finished goods inventory before being sold. In

**FIGURE 22.1**

**The Pattern of Inventory Levels over Time**

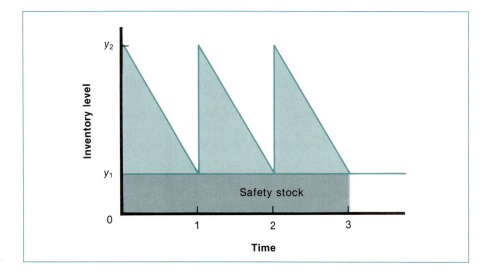

this section a simplified view of inventory flowing into and out of the firm is presented as a foundation for understanding the various techniques described later for managing inventory.

Figure 22.1 illustrates changes in the level of inventory over time. Although the subject of this specific analysis is raw materials inventory, the same type of analysis applies to the finished goods inventory being sold by a nonmanufacturing firm.

In order to simplify the analysis, it is assumed that there is no work-in-process inventory or finished goods inventory. However, since both work-in-process and finished goods inventories may remain fairly constant over time for a manufacturing firm, they could be added to this analysis very easily. When inventory is acquired at Time 0 in Figure 22.1, it is at its highest level, $y_2$. This level represents newly acquired inventory $(y_2 - y_1)$ plus a **safety stock** of inventory $(y_1)$. Safety stock is inventory that the firm does not expect to use but maintains in case of an unforeseen need.

The level of inventory subsequently declines from $y_2$ to $y_1$ between Time 0 and Time 1. In this example, the decline is represented by a straight line, indicating that the inventory is used up evenly over time. At Time 1, it has declined to the point where only the safety stock remains. However, a new shipment of inventory is received at that point, and the process is repeated.

## Average Inventory

Given this sawtooth pattern of inventory levels, the average level of inventory can be easily determined. Ignoring the safety stock for now, the average level of inventory is equal to an amount halfway between $y_2$ (starting inventory) and $y_1$ (ending inventory). The amount $(y_2 - y_1)$ represents the size of each order of inventory placed and received. Average inventory can be found by dividing this order quantity by 2. When the safety stock is considered, average inventory increases by the level of safety stock, since it is not expected to fluctuate in size like the regular inventory. Average inventory for the firm can be found as follows:

$$AI = \frac{OQ}{2} + SS \qquad \textbf{(22.1)}$$

where  $AI$ = average inventory

$OQ$ = order quantity of inventory

$SS$ = safety stock

---

**Example**

The average inventory of a firm that orders 1,000 units at a time and requires a safety stock of 200 units can be found as follows:

$$AI = \frac{1,000 \text{ units}}{2} + 200 \text{ units}$$

$$= 700 \text{ units}$$

---

## Inventory Reorder Level

A firm is rarely able to reorder inventory and receive it instantaneously. Therefore, when an order is placed for new inventory, the firm must make certain that it has enough inventory on hand to use between the time the firm places the order and the time the new inventory is received. This is an amount in addition to the safety stock. The level of inventory at which the firm should reorder (the **reorder level**) is therefore

$$RL = \left(\frac{U}{360}\right)RP + SS \qquad \textbf{(22.2)}$$

where $RL$ = reorder level of inventory

$U$ = annual usage

$RP$ = reorder period in days

The first component ($U/360$) is the daily usage, and it assumes even usage during the year. The result of multiplying daily usage by the reorder period is the amount of inventory the firm expects to use during the reorder period.

---

**Example**

Using Equation 22.2, at what level of inventory should the firm reorder inventory if it has a safety stock of 200 units, annual usage of 50,400 units, and a reorder period of ten days?

$$RL = \left(\frac{50,400}{360}\right)10 + 200$$

$$= 1,600 \text{ units}$$

### More on the Safety Stock

Even if the firm does not use its safety stock, the items constituting safety stock normally are rotated. That is, when a new order of inventory is received, the items previously identified as safety stock are used and replaced as safety stock by newer inventory.

Although firms do not expect to use their safety stock under normal conditions, the possibility of abnormal conditions is reason enough to maintain it. For example, demand may be higher than anticipated during the reorder period. Alternatively, the reorder period could be longer than expected due to transportation delays (resulting from bad weather, labor strikes in the transportation industry, and so forth) or problems with suppliers (such as a strike by a supplier's production workers). The greater the possibility of abnormal product sales and/or an extended reorder period, the greater the need for safety stock.

## TECHNIQUES FOR MANAGING INVENTORY

Various techniques are available to help manage inventories. Some of the more common techniques are described here.

### Economical Ordering Quantity (*EOQ*) Model

The economical ordering quantity (*EOQ*) model is popular for determining the amount of inventory to order each time an order is placed. Essentially, the *EOQ* model balances the high cost of carrying large inventories that result from placing just a few large orders against the high cost of placing numerous small orders. That is, some costs rise as order quantity increases (when a firm places fewer orders), such as the cost of storing and insuring the inventory, the cost of deterioration and obsolescence of inventory that is held for long periods, and the cost of financing inventory. Other costs decrease as order quantity rises, such as the administrative cost of placing an order, processing the paperwork, and receiving and checking the order (all fixed costs). Large orders minimize the total fixed ordering costs (since they are incurred less frequently) but increase average inventory.

Figure 22.2 illustrates both the carrying costs and the ordering costs. Also shown is the total-costs line (carrying costs plus ordering costs). The lowest point on the total-costs line lies directly above the order quantity that provides the firm with the lowest total costs associated with ordering and carrying inventory. This quantity is the **economical ordering quantity,** or *EOQ*. The point of intersection of the carrying-costs line and ordering-costs line also lies directly above the *EOQ*. This latter relationship exists, however, only when carrying costs are a linear function of order quantity.

While this graphical illustration of the *EOQ* model is useful to gain an understanding of the *EOQ* concept, determining the *EOQ* in a given situation is much easier using the following equation.

**FIGURE 22.2**
*Graphical Representation of the EOQ* Model

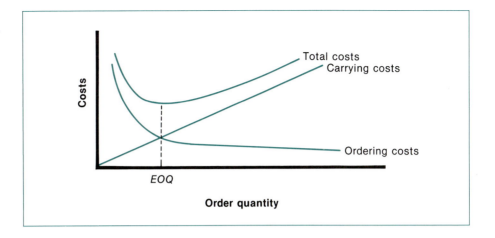

$$EOQ = \sqrt{\frac{2SO}{C}} \qquad (22.3)$$

where  $S$ = usage in units per period

$O$ = order cost in dollars (per order placed)

$C$ = carrying cost in dollars per unit per period

---

**Example**

Reiff Corporation is a retail store that expects to sell 8,100 units of its main product during the next year. What is the firm's economical ordering quantity if the cost of placing each order is $50 and the carrying cost is $1 per unit?

$$EOQ = \sqrt{\frac{2(8,100)(50)}{1}}$$

$$= \sqrt{810,000}$$

$$= 900 \text{ units}$$

---

The *EOQ* model has practical application for both the purchase of raw materials by a manufacturing firm and for the purchase of finished goods inventory by a retail or wholesale firm. In both situations, the firm incurs higher carrying costs as the order size increases, and it incurs certain fixed costs associated with placing orders for inventory.

The *EOQ* model assumes accurate sales forecasts and even distribution of sales over the designated period. If the first assumption is not valid, it may be necessary to analyze the *EOQ* periodically as sales forecasts are revised. If the second assumption does not hold, the use of smaller planning periods that are not subject to significant fluctuation in product demand may be appropriate.

### ABC System

While the *EOQ* model can help the firm determine how much inventory to order, the **ABC system** helps the firm establish a priority system for controlling inventory. Although firms normally consider all of their inventory to be important, some inventory items are generally more important than others. Relative importance may be judged in terms of dollar value, frequency of use, seriousness of problems caused by stock-outs, reorder period, or other criteria. Those inventory items that are judged to be most important to the firm are classified as A items. Because of their importance, the firm is willing to spend considerable time and expense keeping track of these inventory items, monitoring their usage, and frequently evaluating reorder criteria. At an automobile assembly plant, car engines would certainly be classified as A items.

Other inventory items would be classified as B items if they are of moderate importance to the firm. These items are afforded less attention than the A items but more attention than the C items, which are of minor importance to the firm. In the case of an automobile assembly plant, the B items might include hub caps that have only moderate value and can be replaced fairly easily without loss of production. C items might include ordinary nuts and bolts that are used routinely in the production process. They have little individual value and can be replaced quickly.

This system of inventory classification permits the firm to concentrate its efforts on monitoring the items that are most important. It also ensures that resources will not be wasted on monitoring items of little importance to the firm.

### Computerized Inventory Control Systems

Many firms, both large and small, use computers to help control inventory. Essentially, these firms begin with a computer-stored record of the quantity of each inventory item on hand. Each time an item is used, this information is inputted into the computer so that the record of inventory quantity is adjusted. For example, at many grocery store checkout counters, the clerk passes each item sold over a code reader, which adds the price of the item to the cash register tape while simultaneously deducting one unit of inventory from the computer's memory. Regardless of whether such information is recorded manually or automatically (as in the grocery store example), a computer can monitor the level of inventory and notify the firm when each item has declined to its reorder level. In many cases, the computer is programmed to place an order for new inventory automatically when the reorder level is reached.

## BENEFITS OF GOOD INVENTORY MANAGEMENT

The preceding pages discussed some methods of ordering and controlling inventory that can help a firm maintain a relatively low but adequate level of inventory. The benefits of good inventory management are low inventory financing costs, minimal inventory losses from deterioration and obsolescence, infrequent work stoppages resulting from stock-outs, and a minimum of lost sales from stock-outs. All of these benefits contribute to high profit margins, high earnings, low risk, and a higher common stock value.

## FROM INVENTORY TO ACCOUNTS RECEIVABLE

The sale of inventory results in (1) an immediate cash inflow when the sale is for cash or (2) the creation of accounts receivable when trade credit is granted. In terms of the cash flow cycle, the creation of accounts receivable represents a loan made by selling firms to their customers. A change in a firm's credit policy can affect not only the levels of sales and accounts receivable, but also the level of inventory. In the short run, either more (or less) inventory is sold, and in the long run, there is a resulting need to maintain higher (or lower) levels of inventory to support the new level of sales. Conversely, if the firm elects to change its level of finished goods inventory, this could have an impact on the timely delivery of firm sales, which could affect the amount of firm sales and, therefore, the level of accounts receivable.

## ACCOUNTS RECEIVABLE MANAGEMENT

Firms would not have accounts receivable if they sold all of their products for cash. Many customers, however, who expect to receive trade credit when purchasing goods would change suppliers if it were denied. Consequently, a competitive environment may require firms to extend trade credit, even though it entails an expense for the selling firm (it represents the delivery of goods and services to customers without receipt of payment).

Firms face a risk-return trade-off in managing their accounts receivable that is similar to that faced in managing inventories. Essentially, the higher the level of accounts receivable, the greater the opportunity cost is of financing those receivables. Yet if actions are taken to reduce accounts receivable, the firm could incur the risk of lower sales.

A firm's *credit policies* describe how it manages its accounts receivable. Credit policies can be described as having three components:

■ *Credit standards.* The specifications of how creditworthy customers must be in order to receive trade credit.
■ *Credit terms.* The terms of payment given to customers who purchase goods on credit.
■ *Collection policies.* The approach taken by management in collecting overdue accounts receivable.

## HOW FIRMS ARE AFFECTED BY THEIR CREDIT POLICY

When firms make decisions regarding any aspect of accounts receivable management, there is likely to be an effect on one or more key variables: level of sales (and gross profit), the cost of financing accounts receivable, bad debt expense, and discount costs. Before discussing how specific changes in credit policy affect these key variables, a look at the procedure used to estimate the cost of a change in each variable is in order. Later in this chapter the effect of credit-policy adjustments on each variable and firm costs is presented in detail. If the firm can accurately forecast how a change in credit policy will affect each of the following variables, it can forecast the net change in the firm's profits.

## Level of Sales

When a firm changes its credit standards, credit terms, or collection policies, sales are frequently affected. The analyst must therefore evaluate the expected effect of the change in sales on profits. If the change in sales does not affect fixed costs, the change in gross profit is the difference between the selling price per unit ($p$) and variable cost per unit ($v$) for each additional unit sold (or not sold). Given the change in the number of units sold ($\Delta Q$), the change in gross profit ($CGP$), before considering discounts and bad debt expense, can be found as follows:

$$CGP = \Delta Q(p - v) \tag{22.4}$$

In the long run, fixed costs may rise to support higher sales. If so, the change in gross profit is $\Delta Q(p - v) - \Delta F$, where $\Delta F$ represents the change in fixed costs. For simplicity, the problems in this text assume that excess capacity exists (that is, fixed costs do not need to be increased in order to increase sales), or that excess capacity is permitted to exist if sales decline.

## Cost of Financing Accounts Receivable

Some credit-policy decisions affect the cost of financing accounts receivable. This can result from either a change in sales or a change in average collection period. To determine the cost of financing accounts receivable for a firm, the following equation can be employed:

$$CFAR = \left[ \frac{(Q)(v) + F}{360} \right](ACP)(OC) \tag{22.5}$$

where $CFAR$ = cost of financing accounts receivable

$Q$ = annual sales in units

$v$ = variable cost per unit

$F$ = total fixed costs

$ACP$ = average collection period

$OC$ = opportunity cost of financing accounts receivable

The numerator in the first component of Equation 22.5 represents the firm's cost of goods sold. Dividing the cost of goods sold by 360 results in the cost of goods sold per day. Multiplying that figure by the average collection period indicates the average investment in accounts receivable throughout the year. To find the cost of financing accounts receivable, the average level of investment in accounts receivable is multiplied by the opportunity cost of investment in accounts receivable.

Since the objective normally is to estimate the change in the cost of financing accounts receivable that would result from a given policy change, the expected cost of carrying accounts receivable after the change must be calculated separately and compared to the cost if the change is not made. The difference is the *change* in the cost of financing accounts receivable.

## Bad Debt Expense

Most firms that extend trade credit to their customers incur some bad debt expense, meaning they are unable to collect some accounts receivable. Some changes in credit policies tend to increase the bad debt expense while others tend to decrease it. To determine the dollar cost of bad debts[1] to the firm, Equation 22.6 can be used.

$$BDE = (PBD)(Q)(p) \qquad \textbf{(22.6)}$$

where $BDE$ = bad debt expense in dollars

$PBD$ = percentage of bad debts expected

To determine the *change* in bad debt expense resulting from a change in credit standards, credit terms or collection policies, the firm must estimate the bad debt expense without the change and compare it to the expected figure if the change is made.

## Discount Costs

Many firms offer discounts to customers who pay for their purchases early. The purpose of the discounts is to encourage early payment, which reduces the firm's cost of financing accounts receivable. However, discounts also reduce profit by the dollar amount of the discounts taken. This discount cost (reduction in profit) can be determined as follows:

$$DC = (Q)(p)(PTD)(D) \qquad \textbf{(22.7)}$$

where   $DC$ = discount costs in dollars

$PTD$ = percent of customers taking the discount

$D$ = discount in decimal form

To determine the change in discount costs, the firm must compare the discount costs without the proposed change to the forecasted discount costs if the change is made.

---

1. This cost includes both the loss of dollars invested in the product sold (cost of goods sold) and also the loss of profit that would have been earned had the account been collected.

## THE DECISION ON CREDIT STANDARDS

As indicated earlier, credit standards are one of the three major decision areas in managing accounts receivable. The credit standards of a firm refer to how creditworthy the customers must be in order to obtain trade credit. In general, several changes are expected to result when a firm adopts more liberal credit standards:

1.  Sales are expected to increase, since customers that would otherwise need to shop elsewhere for trade credit could now purchase goods from the firm in question.
2.  The cost of financing accounts receivable is expected to increase for two reasons. First, a larger level of credit sales will directly increase the level of accounts receivable. Second, by extending trade credit to less creditworthy customers, the firm will lengthen its average collection period, since marginally creditworthy customers tend to pay later.
3.  Bad debt expense is expected to increase as a result of extending trade credit to less creditworthy firms.
4.  Discount costs are expected to increase, provided that the firm offers discounts and that some of the new credit customers take advantage of them.

The exact opposite of the preceding results can be expected when credit standards are tightened. Table 22.1 summarizes the likely effects on the key variables of a change in credit standards in either direction.

### Marginal Analysis of Changes in Credit Standards

The following example illustrates how marginal analysis can be used to determine whether to change credit standards. Graham Corporation sells its product for $4 per unit, has variable cost per unit of $3, and total fixed costs of $40,000. Current sales volume is 60,000 units, bad debt expense is 2 percent of sales, and the average collection period is forty-five days. The firm offers no discount for early payment.

The current policy of Graham Corporation is to extend trade credit only to firms in Risk Classes A and B (Graham Corporation places all customers into five different risk classes, A through E, based on the results of credit analysis). The firm is considering easing its credit standards to in-

TABLE 22.1  **The Effect of Changes in Credit Standards on Key Variables**

| Change in Credit Standards | Sales | Cost of Financing Accounts Receivable | Bad Debt Expense | Discount Costs |
|---|---|---|---|---|
| More stringent | Decrease | Decrease | Decrease | Decrease |
| Less stringent | Increase | Increase | Increase | Increase |

clude the extension of trade credit to firms in Risk Class C. It expects that such a change would result in a 10 percent increase in sales, an increase in bad debt expense to 3 percent of total sales, and an increase in average collection period to fifty-five days. Should the firm make this change if the opportunity cost of financing accounts receivable is 12 percent?

Given these expected changes, we can use Equations 22.4 through 22.6 to calculate the expected net effect of the proposed change in credit standards on the profits of the firm.

- Change in gross profit

$$CGP = \Delta Q(p - v) \tag{22.4}$$

$$= (10\%)(60,000 \text{ units})(\$4 - \$3)$$

$$= \$6,000 \text{ increase}$$

- Change in the cost of financing accounts receivable

$$CFAR \text{ without the change} = \left[\frac{(Q)(v) + F}{360}\right](ACP)(OC) \tag{22.5}$$

$$= \left[\frac{60,000 \text{ units}(\$3) + \$40,000}{360}\right](45 \text{ days})(12\%)$$

$$= \$3,300$$

$$CFAR \text{ with the change} = \left[\frac{66,000 \text{ units}(\$3) + \$40,000}{360}\right](55 \text{ days})(12\%)$$

$$= \$4,363$$

$$\text{change in } CFAR = CFAR \text{ with change} - CFAR \text{ without the change}$$

$$= \$4,363 - \$3,300$$

$$= \$1,063 \text{ increase}$$

- Change in bad debt expense

$$BDE \text{ without the change} = (PBD)(Q)(p) \tag{22.6}$$

$$= 2\%(60,000 \text{ units})(\$4)$$

$$= \$4,800$$

$$BDE \text{ with the change} = 3\%(66,000 \text{ units})(\$4)$$

$$= \$7,920$$

$$\text{change in } BDE = BDE \text{ with change} - BDE \text{ without the change}$$

$$= \$7,920 - \$4,800$$

$$= \$3,120 \text{ increase}$$

■ Change in discount costs

none indicated

■ Net effect of the change

| | |
|---|---:|
| Gross profit increases by | $6,000 |
| Less: Increased cost of financing accounts receivable | 1,063 |
| Less: Increased bad debt expense | 3,120 |
| Net benefit | $1,817 |

Given an expected net benefit of $1,817 from the proposed easing of credit standards, the firm should elect to extend credit to customers in Risk Class C.

## Credit Analysis

The foregoing example refers to the placement of potential credit customers into risk classes. This can be done by evaluating the degree of risk that the customer will not pay for its purchases, an evaluation based on detailed information about the firm that the credit manager must procure and analyze, although this function can also be purchased from an outside firm for a fee. The creditworthiness of customers can change over time so it should be evaluated periodically, using updated information. Major sources of such information are as follows:

**1.** *The firm being evaluated.* Each firm applying for trade credit is normally asked to provide audited financial statements dating back three or more years (for smaller firms, tax returns may be used in lieu of audited financial statements). The credit department of the selling firm can use this data to perform ratio analysis concentrating on the firm's liquidity, financial strength, stability of sales and profits, and ability to service debt.
**2.** *Credit associations.* Local organizations composed of credit managers who exchange information about their credit customers are called **credit associations.** These local groups, in turn, have organized the Credit Interchange for the purpose of sharing information about the past performance of debtor firms on a broader scale.
**3.** *Credit-reporting agencies.* Firms that collect and sell credit information are called **credit-reporting agencies.** The leading firm in this industry is Dun & Bradstreet, which offers several different credit-information services. One service involves the sale of reference books containing financial and credit information on 3 million North American firms. Dun & Bradstreet indicates their own opinion about the creditworthiness of each firm covered. A second service offered by Dun & Bradstreet provides more detailed credit information through the sale of Business Information Reports, each of which covers one particular firm.

The type of information collected about a customer should be both quantitative and qualitative. The quantitative information consists of financial data, and the qualitative information concerns the character of the firm's management. Since customers frequently find legal means to avoid paying their obligations, creditors look for evidence of moral integrity that would prompt the customer to satisfy the credit obligation. This moral character of the firm may be more difficult to judge than financial creditworthiness, but it may be equally as important.

While there is normally plenty of information available with which to judge a firm's creditworthiness, evaluation of this information is generally subjective. Evaluation of creditworthiness normally involves conducting ratio analysis on the firm, talking with the managers, analyzing the past credit history of the firm, and perhaps even visiting the firm's physical plant. Today statistical tools such as *discriminant analysis* are increasingly being used. In discriminant analysis, potential customer's financial data are compared to similar historical data for firms that have proven to be creditworthy and for firms that have not. Essentially, the credit manager attempts to determine which type of firm the customer resembles most. Given the increasing access to computers, the use of statistical tools in evaluating creditworthiness is likely to become more popular in the future.

## THE DECISION ON CREDIT TERMS

Frequently, the major competitors in an industry offer credit terms identical to each other. If one firm makes its credit terms more attractive, the others follow suit to avoid being at a competitive disadvantage. But not all firms follow the lead of the major firms in an industry. Instead, some smaller firms seeking to increase market share can gain a competitive advantage by offering more attractive credit terms. To illustrate the probable impact on a firm when it changes its credit terms, consider a firm that offers terms of 1/10, net 30. The first number is the cash discount, the second is the discount period, and the third is the net payment period. For this firm, customers are offered a 1 percent discount on all purchases paid for by the tenth day of the billing cycle. If not paid by the tenth day, customers must pay the full amount by the thirtieth day of the billing cycle. If any of these three variables is altered, changes in one or more of the following variables would be expected.

- Level of sales
- Cost of financing accounts receivable
- Bad debt expense
- Discount costs

How these variables react to changes in credit terms can be forecasted by the firm. These forecasts can then be used as the basis for estimating the marginal benefit or cost to the firm of making a change in its credit terms. The analysis is very similar to that used to evaluate changes in credit standards discussed earlier.

### Effect of a Change in the Cash Discount

An increase in the cash discount is likely to affect the firm in the following ways: Sales would increase as customers are lured away from competitors by the higher discounts (assuming retaliatory action is not taken). At the same time, the cost of financing accounts receivable could either increase or decrease, since two forces would tend to counteract each other. First, higher sales would tend to increase the firm's investment in accounts receivable and therefore increase the cost of financing accounts receivable. Second, the average collection period would tend to decrease as the larger discounts encourage more customers to pay early. This would tend to decrease the cost of financing accounts receivable. The net effect of these two forces depends on the individual circumstances surrounding the change.

Also, bad debt expense could decrease. Any reduction in the average collection period tends to reduce bad-debt expense since, as a rule, customers are less likely to default on their obligations when they are encouraged to pay their bills sooner. Furthermore, discount costs would increase because (1) the size of the cash discount has increased, (2) total sales on which the discount is taken will increase even if the percentage of customers taking the discount remains unchanged, and (3) a greater percentage of customers may take the discount.

The previous discussion indicated the likely impact of an increase in the cash discount; a decrease would tend to have the opposite impact on the same variables.

### Effect of a Change in the Cash-Discount Period

An increase in the cash-discount period tends to *increase sales* by attracting more customers. Meanwhile, the cost of financing accounts receivable could either increase or decrease, since two forces tend to counteract each other. First, some customers that previously did not pay early to take the discount would do so now since they can pay later and still qualify for the discount. This would tend to *reduce* the average collection period (*ACP*) and therefore reduce the cost of financing accounts receivable. Second, customers that previously took the discount could now pay later and still be eligible for the cash discount. This would tend to *increase* the *ACP* and therefore increase the cost of financing accounts receivable. In addition, the increased sales resulting from the increase in the discount period would tend to increase accounts receivable and therefore the cost of financing accounts receivable.

The effect on bad debt expense is uncertain in this case, since the level of bad debt expense is influenced by the *ACP*, and the effect of an increase in the cash-discount period on *ACP* is uncertain. Discount costs would increase, because total sales would increase, and because the proportion of sales on which the discount is taken would increase. A decrease in the cash-discount period would have the opposite affect on all of these variables.

### Effect of a Change in the Net Payment Period

An increase in the net-payment period tends to increase sales because customers would be attracted by the longer time they can hold their money before paying. At the same time, the cost of financing accounts receivable increases because of the increased sales and because the average collection

**TABLE 22.2** The Effect of Changes in Credit Terms on Key Variables

| | Sales | Financing Accounts Receivable | Bad Debt Expense | Discount Costs |
|---|---|---|---|---|
| *Cash Discount* | | | | |
| Increased | Increase | Uncertain | Decrease | Increase |
| Decreased | Decrease | Uncertain | Increase | Decrease |
| *Cash-Discount Period* | | | | |
| Increased | Increase | Uncertain | Uncertain | Increase |
| Decreased | Decrease | Uncertain | Uncertain | Decrease |
| *Net-Payment Period* | | | | |
| Increased | Increase | Increase | Increase | Decrease |
| Decreased | Decrease | Decrease | Decrease | Increase |

period would increase. Not only would those who normally forgo the discount pay later, but fewer customers would take the discount because they are able to use the funds even longer given an extended payment period.

Bad debt expense would increase as a result of the increase in *ACP* (when customers pay later, there is a greater likelihood they will default on their obligation). Discount costs would tend to decrease because more firms would find it beneficial to forgo the discount in order to keep their money longer. A decrease in the net-payment period would have the opposite effect on all these variables.

Table 22.2 summarizes the likely effects of changes in credit terms on the key variables that affect the firm's decision on whether to make a change.

## Marginal Analysis of Changes in Credit Terms

Given forecasts of changes in the key variables that are affected by changes in credit terms, the firm can estimate the net effect on the firm's profits in much the same manner as it can evaluate changes in credit standards discussed earlier. That is, Equations 22.4 through 22.7 can be applied to the forecasts in order to estimate the net cost or net benefit of a proposed change in credit terms.

For example, assume Modani Corporation currently has credit terms of 1/10, net 30, and is considering increasing the cash discount from 1 percent to 2 percent. The firm estimates that such a change will increase sales by 8 percent. In addition, the percentage of firms taking the discount would increase from 40 percent to 60 percent, the average collection period would decrease from eighty-five days to seventy-five days, and bad debt expense would decrease from 3 percent to 2 percent. Modani Corporation currently has sales of 10,000 units, price per unit of $100, variable cost per unit of $80, total fixed cost of $100,000, and its opportunity cost of investment in accounts receivable is 14 percent. The net cost or benefit of making the proposed change is determined as follows:

■ Change in gross profit

$$CGP = \Delta Q(p - v) \qquad \textbf{(22.4)}$$
$$= (.08)(10,000)(\$100 - \$80)$$
$$= \$16,000$$

■ Change in the cost of financing accounts receivable

$$CFAR \text{ without the change} = \left[\frac{(Q)(v) + F}{360}\right](ACP)(OC) \qquad \textbf{(22.5)}$$
$$= \left[\frac{10,000(\$80) + \$100,000}{360}\right](85)(.14)$$
$$= \$29,750$$

$$CFAR \text{ cost with the change} = \left[\frac{10,800(\$80) + \$100,000}{360}\right](75)(.14)$$
$$= \$28,117$$

$$\text{change in } CFAR = \$29,750 - \$28,117$$
$$= \$1,633 \text{ decrease}$$

■ Change in bad debt expense

$$BDE \text{ without the change} = (PBD)(Q)(p) \qquad \textbf{(22.6)}$$
$$= (.03)(10,000)(\$100)$$
$$= \$30,000$$

$$BDE \text{ with the change} = (.02)(10,800)(\$100)$$
$$= \$21,600$$

$$\text{change in } BDE = \$21,600 - \$30,000$$
$$= \$8,400 \text{ decrease}$$

■ Change in discount costs

$$DC \text{ without the change} = (Q)(p)(PTD)(D) \qquad \textbf{(22.7)}$$
$$= (10,000)(\$100)(.40)(.01)$$
$$= \$4,000$$

$$DC \text{ with the change} = (10,800)(\$100)(.60)(.02)$$
$$= \$12,960$$

$$\text{change in } DC = \$12{,}960 - \$4{,}000$$

$$= \$8{,}960 \text{ increase}$$

■ Net effect of the change

| | |
|---|---:|
| Gross profit increases by | $16,000 |
| Plus: Decrease cost of financing accounts receivable | 1,633 |
| Plus: Decrease in bad debt expense | 8,400 |
| Minus: Increased discount costs | 8,960 |
| Net benefit (cost) | $17,073 |

Given an expected net benefit from the proposed change in the cash discount, the firm should elect to increase the cash discount to 2 percent.

## THE DECISION ON COLLECTION POLICIES

Every firm should have a policy describing the collection of accounts receivable, although policies will differ from firm to firm. Without such policies, a firm will undoubtedly experience a longer average collection period

**TABLE 22.3**   **The Effect of Changes in Collection Policies on Key Variables**

| Change in Collection Policy | Sales | Financing Accounts Receivable | Bad Debt Expense | Discount Costs | Cost of Collections |
|---|---|---|---|---|---|
| More aggressive | Decrease | Decrease | Decrease | Unchanged | Increase |
| Less aggressive | Increase | Increase | Increase | Unchanged | Decrease |

and higher bad debt expense than is optimal. A trade-off is involved in instituting collection policies. If collection efforts are increased, *bad debt expense* should decrease, although the firm's increased aggressiveness in collecting accounts receivable may anger some customers who tend to pay late, causing an eventual decline in sales. It is also possible, however, that no repercussions will be experienced by the firm except to lose the customers who would have eventually been written off as bad debt expenses anyway.

An increase in collection efforts typically causes the cost of financing accounts receivable to decrease due to a decrease in the average collection period. If sales also decline, the cost of financing accounts receivable will be further reduced. Discount costs are not likely to change much, if at all, since the customers taking the discounts would not be affected by the new collection policy. The cost of collection, however, would increase as the firm increases its collection efforts.

Table 22.3 summarizes the likely effects of a change in collection policy on certain key variables. If the firm can estimate how a change in collection efforts will affect these variables, it can forecast the net benefit or cost of making a change in its collection policy. The analysis is very similar to that conducted earlier in this chapter.

## Collection Procedures

The steps taken by the firm to collect accounts receivable are referred to as *collection procedures*. Collection begins when the firm notifies the customer of the credit terms and indicates when payment is due. If and when an account becomes delinquent (past due), follow-up procedures begin, normally in the form of gentle reminders, but they can end with legal action. The timing of the action taken is very important and varies with the firm. The following steps are listed in the order that they are normally taken by firms. Each subsequent step is taken once it appears that the previous step did not work.

1. Polite letter notifying the customer of the overdue account.
2. Letter with a more serious tone requesting immediate payment.
3. Telephone calls to the management of the delinquent company.
4. A personal visit to the company by a collection person or salesperson. This step is omitted in some cases.
5. Referral of the delinquent account to a collection agency. This is generally expensive due to the fees required.

**6.** An alternative to turning the account over to a collection agency is to have the firm's attorney attempt to collect the account through the courts. This procedure can be expensive. Furthermore, if the debtor firm declares bankruptcy, the account may never be paid.

## Monitoring Accounts Receivable

Firms must monitor their accounts receivable to assure that their collection policies are adequate and that they are being followed by employees. This task involves determining if the receivables are being collected in a timely manner. The three main tools used by credit departments to monitor accounts receivable are used by upper-level management to monitor the performance of the credit department.

**Average Collection Period** The average collection period (ACP), discussed in Chapter 6 and referred to earlier in this chapter, is a tool for monitoring accounts receivable. It indicates the average time it takes the firm to collect its accounts receivable. Significant deviations of the ACP from the firm's stated credit terms and from the industry average may indicate the development of a problem. It is very important to watch this ratio over time to detect problems early.

**Aging Schedule** Another tool, **aging schedules,** can be developed periodically by the credit department to reveal the percentage of total receivables that are current and the percent that are past due by varying amounts of time.

Table 22.4 illustrates the aging schedule for Cheney Corporation. If this firm requires full payment by the sixtieth day, 22.6 percent of its accounts receivable are past due (12.9% + 6.5% + 3.2%). In addition, 9.7 percent are past due by more than thirty days. Unfortunately, the information revealed by the aging schedule can be distorted when a firm has declining (or rising) sales, which may occur annually for firms with seasonal sales. That is, if recent sales have been low, the proportion of total credit sales that are "up in age" will automatically tend to be high. Consequently, care must be taken to interpret the aging schedule correctly.

**TABLE 22.4  Aging Schedule: Cheney Corporation (Terms: Net Sixty Days)**

| Age of Accounts Receivable | Amount Outstanding (Thousands of Dollars) | Percent of Total |
|:---:|:---:|:---:|
| 0–30 days | $1,456 | 51.6% |
| 31–60 | 728 | 25.8 |
| 61–90 | 364 | 12.9 |
| 91–120 | 182 | 6.5 |
| 121–150 | 91 | 3.2 |
| Total | $2,821 | 100.0% |

**TABLE 22.5  Payments Pattern Schedule: Cheney Corporation**

| Age of Accounts Receivable | Credit Sales (Thousands of Dollars) | Amount Outstanding (Thousands of Dollars) | Percent of Month's Sales Not Yet Collected |
|---|---|---|---|
| 0–30 Days | $1,592 | $1,456 | 91.5% |
| 31–60 | 1,384 | 728 | 52.6 |
| 61–90 | 1,203 | 364 | 30.3 |
| 91–120 | 1,047 | 182 | 17.4 |
| 121–150 | 910 | 91 | 10.0 |

**Payments Pattern Analysis**  Because of the false signals that can be given by the aging schedule during periods of declining (or rising) sales, some firms now use the **payments pattern approach.** Basically, this approach replaces the percent of total sales figures with the percent of sales for each month (or other period) that has not yet been collected. Table 22.5 illustrates the payments pattern approach for Cheney Corporation. Here, it is evident that sales have increased significantly during the period covered, resulting in a different view of the status of accounts receivable. A full 10 percent of all accounts receivable that were generated over 120 days earlier have not been collected. This suggests a problem may exist, although the aging schedule did not reveal it (see Table 22.4).

## Using Computers to Manage Accounts Receivable

Since management of accounts receivable requires the collection, analysis, and presentation of a considerable amount of information, the computer has proven to be a real benefit in a number of ways.

1. *Credit analysis.* A firm's computer can be programmed to screen financial data about firms applying for trade credit. Based on preestablished criteria, a computer program can evaluate the creditworthiness of customers and recommend whether or not to approve the extension of credit to customers.
2. *Monitoring individual accounts.* By storing all purchase and payment information about each account in the computer, the computer can keep track of overdue accounts. When predetermined time limits have been exceeded, the computer can notify the credit department.
3. *Record keeping.* The computer memory can be used to store all relevant data about a customer's payment record, financial data, credit limit, and so forth. This provides the credit department easy access to data for periodic account review.
4. *Report generation.* The computer can quickly produce all reports necessary to help the company monitor the performance of its credit department.

## SUMMARY

When determining the level of inventories and accounts receivable, managers must carefully consider the trade-off between risk and return. Although a low level of inventory can keep certain expenses low, it can also result in a shutdown of the production process and/or lost sales due to stock-outs. Decisions made by management to reduce the level of accounts receivable and, therefore, the cost of financing receivables also may result in lost sales. This may occur when a firm imposes a more stringent credit policy, offers less attractive terms of trade credit, or increases its aggressiveness in collecting overdue accounts. Conversely, a high level of inventory and accounts receivable represents a large investment in assets that the firm must finance. These financing costs can reduce the firm's profitability. Additionally, large accounts receivable that result from inadequate collection procedures can quickly turn into a large bad debt expense for the firm.

A number of tools are available to help the firm manage its inventories. The more common tools include the *EOQ* model, the ABC system, and computerized inventory control systems. In managing accounts receivable, the firm must make certain decisions regarding the firm's credit standards, credit terms, and collection policy. These decisions affect the level of sales, cost of financing accounts receivable, bad debt expense, and the cost of discounts.

## KEY TERMS

**ABC system** An inventory control system that classifies each inventory item according to its importance to the firm. The amount of attention given to controlling each item is based on its classification.

**Aging schedule** A tool used to monitor accounts receivable. It indicates the percentage of total receivables that are current and the percentage that are past due by varying amounts of time.

**Credit associations** Local organizations composed of credit managers who exchange information about their customers.

**Credit-reporting agencies** Firms that collect and sell credit information. Dun & Bradstreet is the leading credit-reporting agency.

**Credit standards** The level of creditworthiness a customer must have in order to be extended trade credit.

**Credit terms** The provisions of trade credit extended to a firm's customers.

**Economical ordering quantity** The amount of inventory the firm should order to minimize total carrying costs plus ordering costs.

**Payments pattern approach** An alternative to the aging schedule for analyzing accounts receivable. It avoids the false impression the aging schedule may give during periods of rising or falling sales.

**Reorder level** The level of inventory at which the firm must order replacement inventory so as not to run out.

**Safety stock** Inventory that the firm does not expect to use but maintains in case of an unforeseen need.

## EQUATIONS

**Equation 22.1**    **Average Inventory**

$$AI = \frac{OQ}{2} + SS \qquad \textbf{(p. 599)}$$

where  $AI$ = average inventory
         $OQ$ = order quantity of inventory
         $SS$ = safety stock

This equation can be used to determine average raw materials inventory (or finished goods inventory) held by firms.

**Equation 22.2**         **Reorder Level of Inventory**

$$RL = \left(\frac{U}{360}\right)RP + SS \qquad\qquad \textbf{(p. 599)}$$

where $RL$ = reorder level of inventory
         $U$ = annual usage
         $RP$ = reorder period in days

As the firm uses up its raw materials inventory (or finished goods inventory in some cases), it will need to reorder inventory prior to running out. This equation identifies the level of inventory at which replacement items must be ordered.

**Equation 22.3**         **Economical Ordering Quantity**

$$EOQ = \sqrt{\frac{2SO}{C}} \qquad\qquad \textbf{(p. 601)}$$

where $EOQ$ = economical ordering quantity
         $S$ = usage in units per period
         $O$ = order cost in dollars (per order placed)
         $C$ = carrying cost in dollars per unit per period

As the order quantity increases, some costs rise (carrying costs) and some decline (order costs). The $EOQ$ model identifies the order quantity that minimizes total costs.

**Equation 22.4**         **Change in Gross Profit**

$$CGP = \Delta Q(p - v) \qquad\qquad \textbf{(p. 604)}$$

where $CGP$ = change in gross profit
         $\Delta Q$ = change in units sold
         $p$ = price per unit
         $v$ = variable cost per unit

When a firm initiates a change in credit standards, credit terms, or collection policies, the level of gross profit (before considering discounts and bad debt expenses) will also change by the difference between price per unit and variable cost per unit for each unit sold (or not sold).

**Equation 22.5**         **Cost of Financing Accounts Receivable**

$$CFAR = \left[\frac{(Q)(v) + F}{360}\right](ACP)(OC) \qquad\qquad \textbf{(p. 604)}$$

where $CFAR$ = cost of financing accounts receivable
$\quad Q$ = annual sales in units
$\quad v$ = variable cost per unit
$\quad F$ = total fixed costs
$\quad ACP$ = average collection period
$\quad OC$ = opportunity cost of financing accounts receivable

When a change in credit standards, credit terms, or collection policies affects sales or average collection period, the cost to the firm of financing accounts receivable can change. Equation 22.5 can be used to determine the cost with and without the change in standards, terms, or policies. A comparison of the two costs indicates the incremental cost.

**Equation 22.6**  **Bad Debt Expense**

$$BDE = (PBD)(Q)(p)$$   (p. 605)

where $BDE$ = bad debt expense in dollars
$\quad PBD$ = percentage bad debts expected
$\quad Q$ = annual sales in units
$\quad p$ = price per unit

To determine the effect of a change in credit standards, credit terms, or collection policies on the firm's bad debt expense, the firm can compare its current dollar amount of bad debt expense to the expected bad debt expense if a change is made. Equation 22.6 can be used to estimate both current and expected bad debt expense.

**Equation 22.7**  **Discount Cost**

$$DC = (Q)(p)(PTD)(D)$$   (p. 605)

where $\quad DC$ = discount cost
$\quad Q$ = annual sales in units
$\quad p$ = price per unit
$\quad PTD$ = percent of customers taking the discount
$\quad D$ = discount in decimal form

Some changes a firm makes in credit terms can affect the dollar amount of discounts taken by the firm's customers. Equation 22.7 can be used to determine the current cost of discounts, the expected cost of discounts, and the change in the cost of discounts if a change in credit terms is instituted.

## QUESTIONS

**Q22-1.** Describe the risk-return relationships that apply to raw materials inventory, work-in-process inventory, and finished goods inventory.

**Q22-2.** What factors might encourage a firm to maintain a low level of each type of inventory?

**Q22-3.** If a firm increases its safety stock by 100 units, what will the effect be on the firm's reorder level and average inventory?

**Q22-4.** Under what conditions is the point of intersection of the carrying-costs line and ordering-costs line directly above the *EOQ?* Graph this relationship.

**Q22-5.** Give some examples of A items and C items of inventory (under the ABC system) for a firm that makes furniture.

**Q22-6.** What are the likely effects on a firm's sales, bad debt expense, and so forth, if it makes its credit standards more restrictive?

**Q22-7.** List and briefly describe the three major sources of credit information about customers.

**Q22-8.** What are the most likely effects on sales, discount costs, and so forth, of the following credit-term changes (consider each separately):

**a.** The discount is reduced.
**b.** The discount period is reduced.
**c.** The net-payment period is reduced.

**Q22-9.** Why is it important for firms to act consistently in applying their collection procedures?

**Q22-10.** Describe the difference between an aging schedule and a payment pattern schedule.

**Q22-11.** List and briefly describe four applications of computers to the management of accounts receivable.

## SELF-TEST PROBLEMS

Solutions to self-test problems appear on p. S1.

**SP22-1.** UNC Corporation uses 200,000 units of raw materials annually. The annual carrying costs for the raw materials are $.20 per unit, ordering costs are $75 per order, and the price per unit of inventory is $7. UNC Corporation maintains a 2,000-unit safety stock, and the reorder period is fourteen days.

**a.** What is the economical ordering quantity?
**b.** What is UNC's average inventory?
**c.** What is the reorder level of inventory?

**SP22-2.** FIU Corporation currently has sales of 1 million units per year at $1.25 per unit, total fixed costs of $400,000, and a variable cost per unit of $.60. FIU is considering increasing the discount it offers to customers paying early from 1 percent to 2 percent. It estimates that this change would increase sales by 5 percent, increase the percentage of customers taking the discount to 60 percent from 45 percent, decrease the bad debt expense to 2.5 percent from 3 percent, and decrease the average collection period to sixty-five days from seventy-eight days. FIU's opportunity cost of carrying accounts receivable is 11 percent. If the discount is increased, what would be

**a.** The change in gross profit?
**b.** The change in discount costs?

c. The change in bad debt expense?
d. The change in the cost of financing accounts receivable?
e. The net benefit or cost to FIU of making the change?

**SP22-3.** USD Corporation is experiencing 3 percent bad debt expense. In order to reduce that, USD plans to increase its collection efforts at a cost of about $25,000 per year. These efforts are expected to reduce the bad debt expense to 2 percent, reduce the average collection period to seventy-two days from eighty-five days, and reduce sales to 6,000 units from 6,500 units. Given that USD sells its product for $300 per unit, has total fixed costs of $200,000, has a variable cost per unit of $225, and has an opportunity cost of financing accounts receivable of 13 percent, determine the following:

a. The change in gross profit.
b. The change in the cost of financing accounts receivable.
c. The change in bad debt expense.
d. The net benefit or cost to the firm of the proposed change in collection policy.

**SP22-4.** Dominick Industries would like to analyze its accounts receivable by evaluating the aging schedule and payments pattern schedule. Construct both for Dominick Industries using the following information:

| No. of Days Since Sales Were Made | Credit Sales (Thousands of Dollars) | Collections (Thousands of Dollars) |
|---|---|---|
| 0–30 | $5,822 | $2,387 |
| 31–60 | 5,110 | 2,708 |
| 61–90 | 4,637 | 2,875 |
| 91–120 | 3,904 | 2,733 |
| 121–150 | 3,223 | 2,417 |

# PROBLEMS

**P22-1.** Light Bulb City purchases light bulbs at wholesale prices and sells them retail in two local stores. It purchases all bulbs from one manufacturer and sells 30,000 bulbs each year for $1 each. While ordering costs are $200 per order, carrying costs are only $.04 per bulb per year. The firm wishes to hold a 1,000-unit safety stock. Reorder time is three weeks. (Assume 360 days in a year.)

a. What is the economical ordering quantity?
b. What is the firm's average inventory?
c. What is the reorder level of inventory?

**P22-2.** JMC Corporation manufactures and sells fiberglass fishing rods. Each rod produced involves a variable cost of $11, but the firm sells the rods for $14 each to retail stores. JMC Corporation's fixed costs are $28,000, its average collection period (*ACP*) is sixty-five days, and its opportunity cost of investment in accounts receivable is 14 percent. If the firm eases its credit standards, it expects sales to rise from 25,000 units to 29,000 units, *ACP* to increase to seventy days, and bad debt expense to increase from 2 percent of sales to 3 percent. Conduct a marginal analysis to determine if JMC Corporation should make the change.

**P22-3.** DRK, Inc., is considering reducing the net-payment period required of its customers to forty-five days from fifty days. All relevant information concerning the current situation appears in Column 1 of Table A. In addition, the effects of the proposed change are presented in Column 2 (you may ignore Columns 3 and 4 for now). What would be the net benefit or cost to DRK if the change is made?

**TABLE A**

|  | (1) Current | (2) | (3) | (4) |
|---|---|---|---|---|
| Current credit terms | 1/15, net 50 | 1/15, net 45 | 2/15, net 50 | 1/20, net 50 |
| Percent of customers taking the discount | 55% | 60% | 70% | 65% |
| Average collection period | 110 days | 103 days | 90 days | 100 days |
| Bad debt expense | 2.5% | 2% | 1.5% | 2% |
| Sales | 40,000 units | 38,000 units | 45,000 units | 45,000 units |
| Price per unit | $57 | unch | unch | unch |
| Variable cost per unit | $41 | unch | unch | unch |
| Total fixed costs | $120,000 | unch | unch | unch |
| Opportunity cost of carrying accounts receivable | 9% | unch | unch | unch |

**P22-4.** DRK, Inc. (see Problem 22-3), is considering increasing the size of its discount from 1 percent to 2 percent. All relevant information concerning the current situation appears in Column 1 of Table A, while the expected effects of the proposed change are presented in Column 3. What would be the net benefit or cost to DRK if the change is made?

**P22-5.** DRK, Inc. (see Problem 22-3), is considering increasing the length of its discount period from fifteen days to twenty days. All relevant information concerning the current situation appears in Column 1 of Table A, while the expected effects of the proposed change are presented in Column 4. What would be the net benefit or cost to DRK if the change is made?

**P22-6.** RPD Corporation had sales and collections for the past five months as follows. Construct the payments pattern schedule and the aging schedule for the firm, and interpret both.

| No. of Days Since Sales Were Made | Credit Sales (Thousands of Dollars) | Collections (Thousands of Dollars) |
|---|---|---|
| 0–30 | $235 | $ 59 |
| 31–60 | 290 | 122 |
| 61–90 | 310 | 264 |
| 91–120 | 389 | 354 |
| 121–150 | 427 | 414 |

**P22-7.** Hogan Corporation manufactures and sells wooden chairs. Each chair produced has a variable cost of $40 and sells for $52 to retail stores. Hogan's fixed costs are $80,000, its average collection period (*ACP*) is fifty days, and its opportunity cost of investment in accounts receivable is 12 percent. If Hogan eases its credit standards, it expects sales to rise from 50,000 units to 60,000 units, *ACP* to increase to sixty days, and bad-debt expense to increase from 10 percent of sales to

12 percent. Conduct a marginal analysis to determine if Hogan Corporation should make the change.

**P22-8.** Mag Company has inventory-ordering costs of $300 per order and carrying costs of $.20 per unit of inventory. Mag wishes to hold a 3,000-unit safety stock. Reorder time is four weeks, and Mag uses 600,000 units annually. (Assume 360 days in a year.)

a. What is the economical ordering quantity?
b. What is the Mag's average inventory?
c. What is the reorder level of inventory?

**P22-9.** Cowan Company is considering changing its credit terms from 1/15, net 30, to 1/15, net 45. Its average collection period is currently twenty-three days and its bad debt expense is 1 percent. Sales are 120,000 units, unit price is $8, variable cost is $3 per unit, and total fixed costs are $200,000. The opportunity cost of investment in accounts receivable is 7 percent, and 50 percent of its customers currently take the discount. Cowan Company estimates that, if the change is made, 40 percent of the customers will take the discount, the average collection period will increase to thirty-nine days, and the bad-debt expense will increase to 1.5 percent. Sales will increase to 130,000 units and all other variables will remain unchanged. Should Cowan Company revise its credit terms? Explain.

**P22-10.** Boca Company is considering a decrease in the length of its discount period from fifteen days to ten days. Based on this revision, the following variables would be affected as indicated:

| | Current Policy | Proposed Policy |
|---|---|---|
| Discount | 2% | 2% |
| Percent of customers taking the discount | 60% | 50% |
| Average collection period | 31 days | 39 days |
| Bad debt expenses | 1% | 1.5% |
| Sales | 50,000 units | 48,000 units |
| Price per unit | $30 | $30 |
| Variable cost per unit | $21 | $21 |
| Total fixed cost | $150,000 | $150,000 |
| Opportunity cost of financing accounts receivable | 8% | 8% |

Determine the net benefit or cost to Boca Company if it implements the proposed policy. Should Boca Company implement this policy?

**P22-11.** Delray, Inc., is considering a change in its credit terms from 1/20, net 50, to 2/20, net 50. The expected effects of such a change are as follows:

| | Present Policy | Proposed Policy |
|---|---|---|
| Percent of customers taking the discount | 30% | 75% |
| Average collection period | 48 days | 30 days |
| Bad debt expense | 2% | 1.5% |
| Sales | 30,000 units | 33,000 units |
| Price per unit | $20 | $20 |
| Variable cost per unit | $14 | $14 |
| Total fixed cost | $100,000 | $100,000 |
| Opportunity cost of financing accounts receivable | 10% | 10% |

Determine the net benefit or cost of implementing the proposed policy. Should Delray, Inc., implement the policy?

## COMPUTER-ASSISTED PROBLEMS

**CP22-1.** Tish Enterprises has retail stores that sell 1 million tennis rackets annually at $70 each. Tish purchases the rackets directly from a manufacturer. Ordering costs are $100 per order, and carrying costs are $4 per racket. Tish desires to hold a 4,000-unit safety stock. Reorder time is thirty days. (Assume 360 days in a year.)

**a. Sensitivity of *EOQ* to Carrying Costs**  Tish recognizes that ordering costs and carrying costs can change over time. Based on the preceding information, how would the economical ordering quantity be affected if carrying costs decreased to $3.80 a unit? $3.60 a unit? What if the costs increase to $4.20 a unit? $4.40 a unit? What does this suggest about the relationship between carrying costs and economical ordering quantity?

**b. Sensitivity of *EOQ* to Ordering Costs**  Using the original information presented in the problem, determine how the economical ordering quantity would be affected if ordering costs decreased to $90 per order. $80 per order. What if the costs increase to $120 per order? $140 per order? What does this suggest about the relationship between the ordering cost and the economical ordering quantity?

**c. Sensitivity of *EOQ* to Carrying Costs and Ordering Costs**  Is the economical ordering quantity more sensitive to the carrying-cost estimates or the ordering-cost estimates presented here?

**d. Probability Distributions**  Assume the following probability distributions:

| Ordering Costs | Probability | Carrying Costs | Probability |
|---|---|---|---|
| $ 70 | 20% | $3.60 per unit | 20% |
| 100 | 50 | 4.00 per unit | 50 |
| 140 | 30 | 4.40 per unit | 30 |

Determine the probability distribution for the economical ordering quantity based on this information.

## REFERENCES

Altman, Edward I. "Financial Ratios, Discriminant Analysis and the Prediction of Corporate Bankruptcy." *Journal of Finance* 23 (September 1968): 589–609.

Atkins, Joseph C., and Yong H. Kim. "Comment and Correction: Opportunity Cost in the Evaluation of Investment in Accounts Receivable." *Financial Management* 6 (Winter 1977): 71–74.

Brick, Ivan E. "The Effect of Taxes on the Trade Credit Decision." *Financial Management* 13 (Summer 1984): 24–30.

Celec, Stephen E., and Joe D. Icerman. "A Comprehensive Approach to Accounts Receivable Management." *Financial Review* 15 (Spring 1980): 23–34.

Christie, George N., and Albert E. Bracuti. *Credit Management.* Lake Success, N.Y.: Credit Research Foundation, 1981.

Dyl, Edward A. "Another Look at the Evaluation of Investments in Accounts Receivable." *Financial Management* 6 (Winter 1977): 67–70.

Gentry, James A. "A Generalized Model for Monitoring Accounts Receivable." *Financial Management* 14 (Winter 1985): 28–38.

Halloren, John A., and Howard P. Lanser. "The Credit Policy Decision in an Inflationary Environment." *Financial Management* 10 (Winter 1981): 31–38.

Hill, Ned C., and Kenneth D. Riener. "Determining the Cash Discount in the Firm's Credit Policy." *Financial Management* 8 (Spring 1979): 68–73.

Kim, Yong H., and Joseph C. Atkins. "Evaluating Investments in Accounts Receivable: A Wealth Maximization Framework." *Journal of Finance* 33 (May 1978): 403–12.

Long, Michael S. "Credit Screening System Selection." *Journal of Financial and Quantitative Analysis* 11 (June 1976): 313–28.

Oh, John S. "Opportunity Cost in the Evaluation of Investment in Accounts Receivable." *Financial Management* 6 (Summer 1976): 32–36.

Peterson, Richard L. "Creditors' Use of Collection Remedies." *Journal of Financial Research* 9 (Spring 1986): 71–86.

Sachdeva, Kanwal S. "Accounts Receivable Decisions in a Capital Budgeting Framework." *Financial Management* 10 (Winter 1981): 45–49.

Sartoris, William L., and Ned C. Hill. "A Generalized Cash Flow Approach to Short-Term Financial Decisions." *Journal of Finance* 38 (May 1983): 349–60.

Smith, Keith V. *Management of Working Capital.* New York: West Publishing, 1980.

Stone, Bernell K. "The Payments-Pattern Approach to the Forecasting and Control of Accounts Receivable." *Financial Management* 5 (Autumn 1976): 65–82.

Walia, Tirlochan S. "Explicit and Implicit Cost of Changes in the Level of Accounts Receivable and the Credit Policy Decision of the Firm." *Financial Management* 6 (Winter 1977): 75–78.

Weston, J. Fred, and Pham D. Tuan. "Comment on Analysis of Credit Policy Changes." *Financial Management* 9 (Winter 1980): 59–63.

# Chapter 23

# SHORT-TERM FINANCING

## SHORT-TERM FINANCING IN PERSPECTIVE

In May 1986, General Motors Acceptance Corporation (GMAC) announced that it would soon begin raising short-term funds in the Euro–commercial paper market. GMAC, the financing unit of General Motors Corporation, was already the largest issuer of commercial paper in the U.S. market, with about 10 percent of the total of $30 billion outstanding. Commercial paper, which is an unsecured short-term promissory note, is considered to be an alternative to bank loans as a source of short-term financing for businesses.

GMAC had been reluctant to enter the Euro–commercial paper market earlier because of an apparent lack of liquidity in that market and the substantially higher interest rates in the Euromarket as compared to the U.S. market. In the past two years, however, the liquidity in the European market has improved, and the difference between European and U.S. interest rates has narrowed. By the spring of 1987, the volume of European commercial paper outstanding had risen to more than $6 billion, and the difference between the interest rate on European and U.S. commercial paper had narrowed to .25 percent.

The stated reason why GMAC wants to borrow short-term funds in both markets is to diversify its sources of financing. That is, if GMAC relies too heavily on one market as a short-term source of financing, any problems that may develop in that market can have a direct impact on the firm. If, however, GMAC has several different sources of short-term financing, problems that arise in one market may be circumvented by going to the others. For the same reason, most firms that rely heavily on the commercial paper market also borrow from banks in order to keep that source of financing active and readily available.

What are the advantages of raising funds in the commercial paper market as opposed to borrowing from a bank? What are the disadvantages? What other sources of short-term financing are available to firms, and how do they compare to the commercial paper market? These and other questions are addressed in this chapter.

Short-term financing refers to funds that must be repaid by the firm within one year. Therefore, sources of short-term financing appear on the firm's balance sheet as current liabilities. The major factors influencing the proportion of a firm's current assets financed with current liabilities were discussed in Chapter 20. It was concluded that financing with high levels of current liabilities increases the risk of the firm while simultaneously increasing potential return. The use of low levels of current liabilities decreases both risk and potential return. Financial managers must determine the levels of risk and return that will keep the required rates of return to stockholders low relative to the growth rate of the firm's earnings and dividends so that the firm's common stock will have a high value and shareholder wealth will be maximized. This chapter describes the characteristics of the alternative current liabilities that are used to finance current assets.

Table 23.1 lists all major current liabilities. Accounts payable and accrued wages and taxes are called **spontaneous current liabilities** because they increase automatically as firm sales increase. While these sources of short-term credit are not characterized by cash flowing into the firm, they do represent the use of someone else's money, since it is money that has been prevented from flowing out of the firm. Therefore, these sources of financing provide funds to the firm the same way bank loans do. **Discretionary current liabilities,** on the other hand, increase only if the firm takes specific action to increase them, such as taking out a loan. A description of the major current liabilities follows.

## ACCOUNTS PAYABLE

The current liability, accounts payable, arises when firms purchase goods from a supplier but do not pay for those goods until sometime after receiving them. Accounts payable represent the primary source of short-term funds for the typical firm for two reasons. First, trade credit normally is free for a limited time and thus very desirable. In order to be granted trade credit, a firm must establish and maintain creditworthiness by maintaining acceptable financial ratios and by paying its bills in a timely manner.

**TABLE 23.1    Types of Current Liabilities**

| **Spontaneous Current Liabilities** |
| --- |
| Accounts payable |
| Accrued wages and taxes |

| **Discretionary Current Liabilities** |
| --- |
| Bank loans |
| Loans from commercial finance companies |
| Commercial paper |
| Other (customer advances and private loans) |

Second, trade credit is convenient. Once a firm has established trade credit with a supplier, it can normally use that source of credit indefinitely, or until either the purchasing firm or the selling firm encounters some financial difficulty. As the firm's sales increase, its credit purchases and accounts payable increase simultaneously. For firms making purchases continuously throughout the year, some accounts payable are always outstanding. Thus, some accounts payable become a permanent source of credit to the firm.

After the limited time that trade credit is free, trade credit is like a loan on which the firm incurs an interest charge. Consider MRV Corporation, which purchased $1,000 worth of goods from a supplier and was extended trade credit of 2/10, net 45. MRV can pay just $980 for those goods if it pays for them by the tenth day (a 2 percent discount from the $1,000 purchase price), and should therefore consider $980 to be the purchase price of the goods. MRV is being given free credit of $980 for ten days. If, however, it elects to pay *after* the tenth day, it must pay $20 more, or $1,000. This $20 should be viewed by the firm as an interest expense incurred for borrowing the $980 from the tenth day (the firm borrowed the $980 interest-free until the tenth day) until the forty-fifth day (a thirty-five-day period). This $20 of interest can be expressed as a percent of the amount borrowed ($980), and it can be annualized as follows:

$$\left(\frac{\$20}{\$980}\right)\left(\frac{360}{35}\right) = 21.0\%$$

This figure, 21.0 percent, represents the annualized rate of interest the firm must pay to borrow money using trade credit during the thirty-five-day period. If the firm can borrow money from other sources at a lower cost, it should do so and pay for its purchases by the tenth day to obtain the discount. Of course, if the firm has excess cash balances, it should pay by the tenth day and take the discount since it does not need to borrow the money.

The cost of trade credit after the discount period has ended can be found directly using Equation 23.1:

$$CTC = \left(\frac{D}{1 - D}\right)\left(\frac{360}{N}\right) \qquad \textbf{(23.1)}$$

where $CTC$ = cost of trade credit

   $D$ = trade discount in decimal form

   $N$ = number of days between when the discount must be taken and when the net payment is due

The first component of Equation 23.1, $D/(1 - D)$, converts the discount from purchase price into the equivalent of an interest rate paid to the lender (in this case, the supplier of goods). The second component of the equation annualizes the interest rate so it can be compared to other annual rates of interest.

**Example**

To demonstrate the application of Equation 23.1, consider the cost of trade credit for Gopher Industries after the interest-free period has ended. If Gopher has credit terms of 1/15, net 30, the cost of trade credit after day 15 is

$$CTC = \left(\frac{.01}{1 - .01}\right)\left(\frac{360}{30 - 15}\right)$$

$$= .242, \text{ or } 24.2\%$$

If Gopher has other sources of credit available to it at a cost lower than 24.2 percent, it should take the discount and rely on those other sources for borrowed funds. From the first to the fifteenth day, the credit is free and should be used.

### Stretching Accounts Payable

In order to increase accounts payable as a source of short-term financing, some firms *stretch* their trade credit beyond the period desired by the supplier. Firms can do this by simply paying their bills late. For example, MRV (discussed earlier) could decide to pay $980 on the fifteenth day instead of the tenth day. It might feel that this unauthorized extension of the discount period is too short for the supplier to be concerned about. Alternatively, MRV Corporation might pay the *net* amount on the fifty-fifth day, instead of the forty-fifth day, again reasoning that the unauthorized extension of the credit period is too short to upset the supplier.

While stretching the credit period can produce inexpensive credit, it also introduces a risk to the purchasing firm. The risk is that the supplier may begin to view the purchasing firm negatively, which could lead to revoking the firm's trade credit. Firms concerned about their image within the industry are not likely to stretch accounts payable by much, if at all.

## ACCRUED WAGES AND TAXES

Accruals are interest-free loans made to businesses by employees and governments. Although businesses would like to increase accruals as much as possible, there is generally very little a firm can do to increase them. For **accrued taxes** (income taxes, employee withholding taxes, and sales taxes) federal and state governments specify payment amounts and the timing of those payments. All the firm can do is avoid making payments earlier than necessary.

Firms can create a nonspontaneous increase in **accrued wages** (one caused by factors other than an increase in wage expense) by making less frequent payments to employees (for example, paying employees monthly as opposed to biweekly). Since payroll frequency is influenced greatly by industry standards, state laws, and labor unions, it is difficult for a firm to increase accrued wages.

For analysis and planning purposes, however, the firm can easily determine the average level of accrued wages it maintains as a source of short-term credit. Assume UND, Inc., pays its employees a total of $200,000 every two weeks. This firm has an average of $100,000 in employee funds available to it during each two-week period and, therefore, throughout the year (recall from Chapter 21 that average accrued wages is equal to the payroll divided by 2). If the frequency with which employees are paid is decreased to once every three weeks, the size of each payroll would increase to $300,000. This would increase the average accrued wages of UND, Inc., to $150,000 ($300,000/2). This increase in accrued wages results from a discretionary management decision. An example of a spontaneous increase in accrued wages would be an increase in the payroll that results from hiring more employees. If UND's payroll were still being paid every two weeks, but the size of the payroll increased to $300,000 as a result of hiring of new employees (or paying the existing ones higher wages), the average accrued wages would still increase to $150,000. In short, any increase in accrued wages will benefit the firm since it represents a free source of short-term financing.

## BANK LOANS

Short-term loans from banks are the second most important source of short-term credit to businesses, and they are the most important *discretionary* source. Firms that borrow funds to support a temporary increase in working capital (cash, inventory, or accounts receivable) generally seek financing from a bank first. Bank loans appear on borrower balance sheets as the current liability, **notes payable.**

### Types of Bank Loans

There are numerous ways to categorize bank loans. (Table 23.2 summarizes the major characteristics of various types.) In terms of the timing of principal and interest payments, *single-payment loans* are repaid in one large payment, while *installment loans* are repaid in a series of payments throughout the life of the loan. With regard to the purpose of a loan, a *transaction loan* is a loan obtained to finance a specific transaction, while a *line of credit* is a preapproved loan amount that the firm can borrow whenever the funds are needed and for whatever purpose the firm wishes.

A **line of credit** can be either informal or guaranteed. With an *informal line of credit*, the bank approves a maximum amount the firm can borrow over a specified future period of time (perhaps one year). However, if the bank does not have the requested funds available at the time the firm wants to borrow them, the bank is under no obligation to loan the funds.

With a *guaranteed line of credit* (also known as a *revolving line of credit*), the bank guarantees that the preapproved funds will be available to the firm when needed. The firm must pay the bank a commitment fee on the funds promised but not yet borrowed. This commitment fee is designed to compensate the bank for maintaining the liquidity necessary to permit the firm to borrow money on short notice. (Maintaining this liquidity involves an opportunity cost to the bank.) Assume UND, Inc., arranges a $100,000

TABLE 23.2 **Summary of Bank-Loan Characteristics**

| Characteristic | Alternatives | |
|---|---|---|
| Number of payments | *Single payment.* One payment made at maturity. | *Installment.* Periodic payments over the life of the loan. |
| Purpose | *Transaction loan.* Loan made for a specific purpose. | *Line of credit.* Credit made available for whatever purpose firm wishes. |
| Maturity | *Short-term loan.* One year or less. | *Term loan.* Greater than one year. |
| Bank compensation | *Interest only.* No additional costs. | *Interest plus compensating balance.* Both compensate the bank; however, the former is direct, the latter indirect. |
| Interest rate | *Fixed.* The interest rate does not change over the life of the loan. | *Floating rate.* The interest rate changes at regular intervals to reflect market conditions. |
| Collateral | *When required.* Most common assets are inventory, accounts receivable, stocks and bonds, plant, and equipment. | *When not required.* Interest rate tends to be lower, since only low-risk borrowers can borrow without collateral. |

guaranteed line of credit with Citizen's Bank for one year at 12 percent annual interest. This agreement also requires a commitment fee of one-half of 1 percent per year on any part of the line of credit not borrowed. If UND, Inc., borrows $25,000 during a given month, it will pay $250 in interest ($25,000 × 12% × 1/12 of a year) *plus* $31.25 in commitment fees on the part that was not borrowed during the month ($75,000 × .005 × 1/12 of a year). Note that the cost to the firm was found by multiplying the amount times the annual interest rate, times an adjustment for time. Unless stated otherwise, it is normally assumed that the interest rates and commitment fee rates quoted by lending institutions are annual rates. If the period of the loan or commitment is less than one year, the rate must be multiplied by the fraction of the year being considered (in this case one-twelfth of a year).

Bank lines of credit provide firms with the opportunity to reduce their investment in working capital while maintaining access to liquidity. For example, Pillsbury Company felt secure in reducing its net working capital from $177 million in 1985 to $24 million in 1986 because it had established lines of credit totaling approximately $475 million to accommodate its liquidity needs.

## Bank Loan Maturity

Most bank loans mature in one year or less, although some loans, called *term loans,* are made for more than one year. Frequently, loans are made to businesses for a period of ninety days and then renewed for successive ninety-day periods if needed.

Many businesses rely on bank loans every year to help them finance seasonal increases in current assets. To ensure that firms are using their short-term funds for temporary financing needs, lending banks frequently require firms to "clean up" their short-term loans (be completely free of the loans) for at least one month every year.

## Compensating Balances

Many banks require borrowers to maintain checking account balances equal to a certain percentage (normally 10 percent to 20 percent) of the face value of the loans, called **compensating balances**. These balances provide additional compensation to the bank for making the loan. That is, the bank continues to hold part of the money it has loaned to the firm and can lend that money to someone else. In this way, it can earn interest on the same money from two different borrowers simultaneously.

Compensating balances increase the effective (or true) rate of interest firms pay on bank loans. If a firm borrows $10,000 at 10 percent interest but must maintain a 15 percent compensating balance ($1,500), the firm pays interest on $10,000 but can remove only $8,500 from the bank. Of course, if the borrowing firm normally maintains a $1,500 checking account balance, it would not reduce the amount of money available to the borrower, nor would it increase the borrower's effective rate of interest. A discussion of the effective rate of interest is presented below.

## Interest Rates on Bank Loans

The interest rates charged on bank loans depend on the overall level of market interest rates and the risk of the borrower. The greater the risk is to the bank that the borrower will default on the loan, the higher the interest rate charged by the bank.

The interest rate charged by banks to their most creditworthy customers is called the bank's **prime rate.** (There are exceptions to this in that some banks have been known to lend at rates below their own stated prime rate.) Other borrowers will pay the prime rate plus an additional amount based on the riskiness of the borrower. For example, a fairly risky firm may be charged as much as the prime rate plus 5 percent. Firms with moderate amounts of risk may be charged the prime rate plus 2 percent or 3 percent.

Banks can specify a *fixed rate* of interest on loans or a *floating rate*. While the rate of interest charged on a fixed rate loan does not change during the life of the loan, the interest rate charged on a floating rate loan may be changed periodically, reflecting changes in the bank's cost of obtaining funds.

There are essentially three different ways banks charge interest on loans. The following discussion demonstrates how the borrower can calculate the **effective rate of interest** (true rate of interest) on a bank loan regardless of which way interest is charged. In each case, the effective rate of interest determined is an annual rate.

$$ERI = \left(\frac{I}{LP}\right)\left(\frac{360}{N}\right) \tag{23.2}$$

where $ERI$ = effective rate of interest

$I$ = dollar amount of interest

$LP$ = loan proceeds available to the borrower during the life of the loan

$N$ = number of days the money is available to the borrower

**Regular Interest**   When interest is paid only on the principal borrowed and at the time the loan is repaid, it is called **regular interest** or **simple interest.** Consider a $10,000 loan for ninety days, where the borrower pays 12 percent annual interest at maturity.

$$ERI = \left[\frac{(\$10,000)(12\%)(90/360)}{\$10,000}\right]\left(\frac{360}{90}\right)$$

$$= 12.0\%$$

**Discounted Interest**   When interest is paid in advance (at the time the loan is obtained), it is said to be discounted interest. The *ERI* is higher on a discounted loan than on a loan where interest is paid at maturity. This higher interest rate results from a decrease in the amount of the loan available to the borrower (the borrower pays interest from the borrowed amount). Consider the loan in the preceding example, but now assume the loan is discounted. In this case, the borrowing firm will have $10,000 minus the interest payment available to it during the life of the loan.

$$ERI = \left[\frac{(\$10,000)(12\%)(90/360)}{\$10,000 - \$300}\right]\left(\frac{360}{90}\right)$$

$$= 12.4\%$$

**Loans with Compensating Balances**   When a borrower is required to maintain a compensating balance (discussed earlier) the amount of the compensating balance is not available for use during the life of the loan. This increases the *ERI* on the loan. Once again, consider a 12 percent, $10,000 loan for ninety days. Assume, however, that the firm must maintain a 15 percent compensating balance. Assume further that the loan is discounted. The firm currently maintains a checking account balance of zero.

$$ERI = \left[\frac{(\$10,000)(12\%)(90/360)}{\$10,000 - \$300 - \$10,000(15\%)}\right]\left(\frac{360}{90}\right)$$

$$= 14.6\%$$

Notice that both the interest and the compensating balance are based on the face value of the loan. If the loan were not discounted, the *ERI* would be

$$ERI = \left[ \frac{(\$10{,}000)(12\%)(90/360)}{\$10{,}000 - \$10{,}000(15\%)} \right] \left( \frac{360}{90} \right)$$

$$= 14.1\%$$

### Secured Bank Loans

Most bank loans are *secured*, which means the borrowers pledge collateral against the loans. This collateral is intended to reduce the lender's loss in the event that the borrower defaults on the loan, because the lender will have first claim on the assets that have been pledged against the loan. It should be noted, however, that lenders have a strong preference for being repaid without having to liquidate collateral, since to do so involves legal fees, liquidation expenses, and time. Additionally, collateral that appears to have sufficient value to secure a loan frequently proves inadequate to provide enough cash to repay the entire loan when it is liquidated.

Secured loans tend to have higher interest rates for two reasons. First, the fact that the lender requires collateral on the loan implies that there is a significant amount of default risk associated with the borrower (financially sound firms can borrow on an unsecured basis). This higher risk calls for a higher interest rate. Second, there are administrative costs associated with securing loans (legal documentation), and the lender will make the borrower pay these costs by charging a higher rate of interest.

Many different types of property are used as loan collateral on short-term loans, including financial assets (stocks and bonds), plant, equipment, inventory, and accounts receivable. Inventory and accounts receivable are by far the most common forms of collateral for short-term loans. Borrowing against inventory and accounts receivable is so important that loans secured by those assets are discussed in two separate sections later in this chapter. Although technically not collateral, some loans are co-signed by a third party who has a vested interest in seeing the firm receive a loan (such as a major stockholder). These **comaker loans** provide greater security to the lender, who can require repayment of the loan by the co-signer if the borrower defaults on the loan.

## LOANS BY COMMERCIAL FINANCE COMPANIES

Commercial finance companies are similar to banks in that they primarily make loans to businesses. Unlike banks, however, commercial finance companies do not accept demand deposits or time deposits. Instead, they raise funds mostly by selling their own securities in the financial markets and by borrowing money from commercial banks at wholesale rates. Their cost of funds is generally higher than that of banks, and the loans they make are generally more risky. Thus, they normally charge borrowers higher rates of interest. Commercial finance companies make both short-term and long-term loans, virtually all of which are secured by either accounts receivable (their most frequently held collateral), inventories, or equipment. The discussion about accounts receivable and inventory financing at the end of this chapter relates to borrowing from commercial finance companies as well as commercial banks.

## COMMERCIAL PAPER

Commercial paper was discussed in Chapter 21 from the perspective of an investor. In this chapter, commercial paper is viewed from the perspective of the issuer. Recall that commercial paper is a short-term, unsecured promissory note issued by a large, financially sound firm.

The effective rate of interest paid by the seller (borrower) is normally lower than the prime rate, since the ultimate lender may purchase commercial paper directly from the ultimate borrower. In a bank loan, the bank earns a return for being an intermediary between the ultimate lender (bank depositor) and the ultimate borrower. As a result, the commercial paper market competes very effectively with commercial banks in providing short-term business financing.

It should be emphasized, however, that only a small percentage of firms are large enough and financially sound enough to issue commercial paper. Even firms that are able to issue commercial paper still borrow from banks for convenience and also to maintain good banking relationships, which are valuable to a firm. Such relationships are not likely to disappear when the firm experiences some financial difficulties. In contrast the commercial paper market can be impersonal, and the availability of commercial paper funds to a given firm disappears at the first sign of financial distress.

In addition to the lower rates of interest the firm pays on commercial paper as compared to borrowing from a bank, there are several other advantages. First, there is no regulatory limit to the amount of money that can be raised by selling commercial paper, whereas banks are limited in the size of the loans they can make. Second, firms borrowing in the commercial paper market need not maintain compensating balances. Finally, the ability to sell commercial paper implies financial strength, which can enhance the prestige of the firm.

Commercial paper is sold mainly to other corporations that have a temporary surplus of funds. It can be issued with the help of a *commercial paper dealer* for a fee. However, the majority of commercial paper is sold directly to the ultimate investors by the issuing firm.

### Calculating Rates of Interest on Commercial Paper

Equation 23.2 can be used to calculate the rate of interest on commercial paper, just as it was used to calculate the effective rate of interest on bank loans. For example, assume UND, Inc., is planning to sell $5 million of 180-day commercial paper. It expects to pay $50,000 to a commercial paper dealer in placement fees and $250,000 in interest on a discounted basis. The effective rate of interest on the commercial paper is

$$ERI = \left(\frac{I}{LP}\right)\left(\frac{360}{N}\right) \qquad \textbf{(23.2 restated)}$$

$$= \left(\frac{\$250,000 + \$50,000}{\$5,000,000 - \$250,000 - \$50,000}\right)\left(\frac{360}{180}\right)$$

$$= 12.8\%$$

Notice that the placement fees incurred by the firm are handled just the same as if they were interest payments.

## OTHER SOURCES OF SHORT-TERM FINANCING

Two other sources of short-term financing that deserve mention are *customer advances* and *private loans*. One characteristic that both of these sources have in common is that they are typically used only by small firms.

Customer advances are sometimes made when a small firm agrees to produce an expensive item that has been custom-designed for the purchasing firm. By requiring an advance payment, the selling firm receives some assistance in financing the cost of producing the product, while simultaneously receiving a tangible commitment from the purchasing firm that it will purchase the item. Customer advances are also common when a larger firm relies on a small supplier for a key component of its operation. Under this arrangement, the purchasing firm has a vested interest in the continued financial success of the smaller firm. These larger firms occasionally help the smaller firms by providing this financing assistance.

Private loans are made to businesses by the firm's own employees, owners, relatives of owners, or friends. For example, a small firm may experience a temporary need for financing but be unable to borrow the needed funds from traditional sources. Wealthy investors or key employees may be willing to lend the firm money to help it through the period of need.

## ACCOUNTS RECEIVABLE AND INVENTORY AS COLLATERAL

As indicated earlier, commercial banks and commercial finance companies are major sources of short-term credit to businesses, and collateral is frequently required on loans made by those institutions. The two assets most commonly used as collateral against short-term loans are accounts receivable and inventories.

### Accounts Receivable as Collateral

There are two ways a firm can use its accounts receivable to obtain short-term funds: (1) pledging them and (2) factoring them. **Pledging accounts receivable** involves the use of accounts receivable as collateral against a loan. **Factoring accounts receivable** involves the sale of accounts receivable. However, most factoring agreements also permit the seller to receive advanced payments on the factored receivables, which makes it a form of a short-term loan to the firm. Table 23.3 provides a summary of the key characteristics of both pledging and factoring.

**Pledging**   When accounts receivable are pledged as collateral against a loan, the firm uses the revenues generated by those accounts to pay off the loan. However, the firm has the ultimate responsibility of repaying the

## FINANCIAL MANAGEMENT IN PRACTICE

### SHORT-TERM FINANCING

Short-term financing is an important component of a firm's total activities. It is not the type of activity that dominates the financial manager's time, however, because the firm normally establishes sources of short-term credit that are used repeatedly, bringing only gradual changes. Most changes that occur are a result of changes in the firm's creditworthiness or growth. For example, when a firm is initially created, very little short-term credit is available, since the firm has not yet demonstrated it is capable of generating profits on a continuous basis. In addition, the character of the firm has not yet been established. In these early stages, short-term sources are normally available only through comaker loans. After the firm has operated for sufficient time to demonstrate both a willingness and an ability to pay its bills, suppliers may begin extending trade credit to the firm. As the firm's financial strength and credit history grow, the ability of the firm to borrow from commercial finance companies and commercial banks on its own merit also can be established. The relationships established with these institutions are important and generally are nurtured so that during periods of temporary financial distress the firm will not be abandoned by the lending institution. Instead, the institution can act as financial advisor to the firm and assist it through difficult periods.

Accounts receivable and inventory loans may be used as a source of financing at any time by a firm, provided there are a sufficient quantity and quality of accounts receivable and/or appropriate inventory. Although relatively few firms ever achieve the size and level of financial strength that enable them to sell commercial paper to raise short-term funds, this is a very important source of funds to large corporations.

At each phase of the firm's growth, considerable effort may be necessary to establish new short-term sources of financing. However, once those sources are established, maintaining them takes little additional effort. This was illustrated by the results of a survey of financial managers in which, on average, the time spent managing current liabilities was less than the time spent managing current assets.* In fact, out of eight different working capital activities considered, the three concerned with current liabilities were ranked fourth (managing banking relationships), fifth (managing accounts payable), and eighth (short-term borrowing). Combined, these three activities occupy about 18 percent of the financial manager's total work time. In addition, the same financial managers indicated that the management of accounts payable requires the least skill out of eight separate activities (both long-term and short-term) that were considered.

*Lawrence J. Gitman and Charles E. Maxwell, "Financial Activities of Major U.S. Firms: Survey and Analysis of Fortune's 1000," *Financial Management* 14 (Winter 1985): 57–65.

loan regardless of what happens to the pledged accounts. That is, even if the accounts receivable are never collected, the borrower still is obligated to repay the loan and all accrued interest on the loan.

There are two ways for the lender to identify which receivables it is willing to accept as collateral. The *selective method* requires the lender to review all receivables and select those it feels have an acceptable level of risk. This differs from a *general line,* in which the lender accepts all of the firm's receivables as collateral. The latter approach is normally used when a firm has numerous small customers, which would make the evaluation of each receivable uneconomical. Regardless of how the accounts receivable

**TABLE 23.3**  **Summary of Pledging and Factoring Characteristics**

| Characteristic | Pledging | Factoring |
|---|---|---|
| Asset involved. | Accounts receivable | Accounts receivable |
| Transaction. | A/R used as collateral | A/R sold but used as collateral until payment is due |
| Who incurs a loss if the A/R is not collected? | Borrowing firm | Factoring firm |
| Method of identifying acceptable accounts receivable. | Selective or general line | Selective only |
| Are customers notified to change payment designee? | No | Yes |
| Continuous or periodic source? | Either | Either |
| Other services offered the borrower (seller). | Credit analysis, billing, collection | Credit analysis, billing, collection |

are identified, the collateral is normally held on a non-notification basis. That is, customers of the borrowing firm are unaware that their accounts have been pledged, and payment is still made to the borrowing firm.

Pledging can be done on a *periodic* basis or on a *continuous* basis. If done on a periodic basis, the firm must reach an agreement with the lending institution each time a loan is needed. This agreement specifies the loan amount, and the borrower promises to repay the loan as the pledged receivables are liquidated. If done on a continuous basis, the firm may maintain a fairly constant loan amount outstanding, replacing old receivables that have been collected with new receivables that have not.

In some cases, the lender may provide additional services to the borrower, such as credit analysis, billing, and/or collection services. This type of arrangement transfers some administrative functions from the borrower to the lender, thus reducing some of the borrower's administrative costs. Of course, the lender will pass its increased costs along to the borrower in the form of service fees.

After identifying the receivables against which it will lend money, the lender must specify the percent of face value of those receivables it is willing to lend. When the lender has selectively chosen the receivables, up to 90 percent of the face value of the collateral may be loaned. In the case of a general line, the loan amount normally would not exceed 75 percent.

The cost of borrowing when accounts receivable are pledged as collateral tends to be relatively high. The borrowing firm typically pays interest on the loan principal equal to two to five percentage points above the prime rate if the loan is from a bank. The interest rate may be even higher if the firm borrows from a commercial finance company. In addition to interest charges, the borrower may incur a service charge anywhere from 1 percent to 3 percent of the value of the pledged receivables (as opposed to the value of the loan).

The following example illustrates how to calculate the effective rate of interest on a loan where receivables have been pledged as collateral. ECU Enterprises has an average level of accounts receivable during the year of $100,000 and wishes to pledge all of them to a lender as collateral on a loan. The lender agrees to lend ECU 80 percent of the face value of the receivables at a cost of 3 percent above the prime rate, which is currently 10 percent, and interest is to be paid at the end of each 60-day loan period. The lender also charges a 1 percent processing charge on all pledged receivables. The firm's credit terms are net 60 days.

The calculations that follow can be used to determine the amount of money that can be borrowed by the firm and the total cost of borrowing each 60 days.

| | |
|---|---|
| Face value of pledged receivables, each 60 days | $100,000 |
| Times: Percent of face value to be loaned | 80% |
| Loan amount each 60 days | $80,000 |
| Processing charge each 60 days (1% × $100,000) | $1,000 |
| Interest on the loan each 60 days ($80,000)(13%)(60/360) | $1,733 |

Equation 23.2 can again be used to determine the effective rate of interest on this loan:

$$ERI = \left(\frac{I}{LP}\right)\left(\frac{360}{N}\right) \qquad \textbf{(23.2 restated)}$$

$$= \left(\frac{\$1,733 + \$1,000}{\$80,000}\right)\left(\frac{360}{60}\right)$$

$$= 20.5\%$$

Several observations can be made regarding these calculations. First, all calculations were based on a sixty-day loan (the assumed time until each account receivable will be collected and the loan repaid). This assumption is not necessary if the pledging is to be done on a continuous basis because as some receivables are liquidated, new receivables replace them. Second, if the preceding calculations were made for a one-year period, the numerator of the first component would contain one year's interest and service charges, but the denominator would be unchanged. The second component of the equation would be changed to 360/360. The final answer would be unchanged:

$$ERI = \left(\frac{\$10,400 + \$6,000}{\$80,000}\right)\left(\frac{360}{360}\right)$$

$$= 20.5\%$$

Third, the borrower may be able to save money by eliminating some duplicate costs associated with credit analysis, billing, and collection. When this is the case, the amount of savings (sixty days' worth in the first calculation and one year's worth in the second) should be subtracted from the numerator, reducing the effective rate of interest. Calculation of the effective rate of interest using sixty-day data, and adjusting for the savings (assumed here to be $700 for each sixty-day period) is as follows:

$$ERI = \left(\frac{\$1,733 + \$1,000 - \$700}{\$80,000}\right)\left(\frac{360}{60}\right)$$

$$= 15.2\%$$

**Factoring**   As indicated earlier, factoring actually represents the sale of accounts receivable. However, there is generally a provision for the seller to receive advances on the factored receivables, which represents a short-term loan to the firm. The factoring firms (called *factors*) include some of the same firms that lend money against pledged receivables (banks and commercial finance companies). In addition, there are a number of other firms that specialize in factoring.

Since receivables that have been factored actually are sold, the purchaser of the receivables generally has *no recourse* if the receivables remain uncollected; that is, the firm purchasing the receivables cannot seek payment from the seller. For this reason, each receivable is analyzed by the factoring firm prior to purchasing it.

Firms that routinely sell all of their accounts receivable can avoid the expense of maintaining their own credit department by directing all credit applications to the factoring firm. In addition to credit analysis, the factoring firm generally provides billing and collection services to the firm, for a fee. Since factors actually purchase the receivables, customers are advised to send their payments directly to the factor. Frequently, however, the name and address of the factor are disguised so the customer does not know the account has been sold. This action is taken because selling receivables could imply financial weakness of the selling firm.

After an account receivable has been sold, the seller is not normally entitled to receive its money until either the account has been collected by the factor, or until *payment is due* from the customer, whichever occurs first. For example, assume a firm sells a $1,000 receivable to a factor for $950. If that receivable is not required to be paid for thirty days, the seller is not entitled to the $950 until thirty days later, or until the account has been collected. The seller may borrow that $950 in advance, however. If the account is paid fifteen days later, the $950 advance (loan) converts to a payment from the factor to the selling firm. The selling firm must now pay the factor interest for a fifteen-day loan (actually, interest on such loans are discounted, and any excess interest is returned to the borrowing firm at the time the account is cleared). If the receivable is not paid by the thirtieth day as required, the loan is converted to a payment for the receivable anyway, and interest stops accruing. That is, the factor is not normally obligated to pay the seller for the account receivable until the last day of the customer's credit period, or until the receivable is collected, if earlier.

Firms that factor their accounts receivable are not required to borrow against the factored accounts. When they do not, everything remains as just described, except the seller incurs no interest charge and receives the

$950 only after the receivable has been collected or after the thirtieth day, whichever occurs first.

To determine the effective rate of interest on an advance from a factor, consider the following example. Lynch Corporation is evaluating the cost of borrowing from a factor that charges 15 percent interest (discounted) on advances and a fee of 2 percent of the factored receivables for servicing the account and for assuming the risk of default (this fee is typically between 1 percent and 2 percent). This 2 percent fee is also discounted. In addition, the factor requires Lynch Corporation to maintain an 8 percent reserve to cover returned merchandise (factor reserves generally range from 10 percent to 40 percent). Funds held in this reserve will be returned to Lynch, provided the merchandise that was sold creating the receivable is not returned. Lynch Corporation has $100,000 worth of receivables that are due in sixty days. From this information, the firm can calculate the maximum advance it can obtain from the factor and also the effective rate of interest on advances from the factor.

| | |
|---|---:|
| Face value of receivables factored | $100,000 |
| Less: Service charge (2%) | 2,000 |
| Less: Reserve (8%) | 8,000 |
| Gross loan amount | 90,000 |
| Less: Interest (15%): | |
| ($90,000 × .15 × 60/360) | 2,250 |
| Net amount available to borrower | $87,750 |

The effective rate of interest on a loan from the factor can now be calculated.

$$ERI = \left(\frac{\$2,250 + \$2,000}{\$87,750}\right)\left(\frac{360}{60}\right)$$

$$= 29.1\%$$

The numerator on the left side of the equation represents total dollar costs associated with the loan, including both interest charges and service fees. If the firm expects to use the factor on a continuous basis for all of its receivables, it should reduce the numerator by the dollar amount of savings expected from not having to evaluate and service the receivables itself. Additionally, if a firm uses a factor as part of its operation without normally taking advances, the cost of borrowing periodically should not reflect the service charge, since it would have been incurred anyway.

## Inventory as Collateral

Inventory is also frequently used as collateral for loans. Some types of inventory are more suitable for this than others, and some are not suitable at all. Those that are suitable have the following characteristics:

■ *Physical durability.* Without physical durability, inventory cannot be used as collateral. For example, a bank would not wish to hold perishable food as collateral.

- *Small size.* Small inventory items can be transported and stored easily and are therefore preferred as collateral.
- *Good marketability.* Although the lender hopes never to liquidate collateral in order to collect on a loan, good marketability will ensure this can be done easily if necessary.
- *Stable price.* A stable price (value) of the collateral means the lender need not worry about losing money should it become necessary to liquidate the collateral. If an asset is subject to becoming obsolete or losing value for some other reason, it is less desirable as collateral.

There are three basic types of inventory loans: floating inventory liens, trust receipts, and warehouse receipts. Table 23.4 summarizes their characteristics. A **floating inventory lien** (also called a *blanket lien*) means the lender holds a lien, or claim, against all of the borrower's inventory. Specific inventory items are not specified in the loan documents, and the borrower can sell the inventory (collateral) without prior permission and replace it with new inventory as it conducts its normal business operations. Because the lender lacks control over the inventory, however, it usually lends less than half the value of the inventory to the borrower.

A **trust receipt** agreement involves a more formal arrangement than the floating lien. Here, the lender files a lien against specific inventory items, all identified by serial number. Automobile dealers frequently use this arrangement when financing autos on their showroom floors. While the borrower is free to sell the inventory, it is obligated to notify the lender when it sells each inventory item. The seller must then remit the amount of proceeds from the sale to the lender. In essence, the borrower holds the inventory in trust for the lender. Since the lender has more control over the inventory using trust receipts than when using a floating inventory lien, firms can generally borrow from 80 percent to 100 percent of the value of the inventory and also pay a lower rate of interest because the risk to the lender is lower.

A major disadvantage of this arrangement to the borrowing firm is that it incurs the administrative expense associated with keeping track of inventory (inspections, handling, trust receipts, and so forth). A major disadvantage to the lender is that although it has some control, it does not

**TABLE 23.4**  Summary of Characteristics of Three Types of Inventory Loans

|  | Floating Inventory Lien | Trust Receipt | Warehouse Receipt |
|---|---|---|---|
| Are specific inventory items identified? | Sometimes | Yes | Yes |
| Who maintains possession of collateral? | Borrower | Borrower | Third party |
| Can inventory be sold by borrower without prior permission? | Yes | Yes | No |
| Quality of lender's control | Bad | Moderate | Good |
| Administrative expense involved | Low | Moderate | High |

have tight control over the inventory (the borrower could sell inventory without the lender's knowledge).

A **warehouse receipt** agreement involves third-party control over inventory that is being used as loan collateral. That is, items pledged as collateral are removed from the possession of the borrower and placed in a public warehouse under the control of an agent hired by the lender. Inventory items are not released to the borrower until the loan (or part of the loan) has been repaid. As more of the loan is repaid, more inventory is released. While this approach to inventory financing provides the lender with its greatest control over inventory, it is also the most expensive to operate due to the need for the services of a third party.

While the use of public warehouses is appropriate for controlling easily transported and stored items such as canned goods and liquor, it may be very inconvenient for bulky items that are difficult to transport, such as lumber and raw steel. In such cases, a portion of the *borrower's facility* or outdoor property is sometimes isolated with a fence, rope, or other means. This area is then controlled by the third party. These guarded areas become *field warehouses*.

A number of firms specialize in establishing field warehouses. Once a field warehouse has been established, the lender will normally extend credit of 75 percent to 90 percent of the value of the collateral. As an alternative to releasing inventory only after part of the loan has been repaid, the lender may release finished goods inventory to the borrower upon receiving evidence of an order for the finished goods. This can occur before the lender receives a payment on the loan, although the borrower must agree to remit the proceeds of the sale to the lender.

While warehouse receipts offer the lender the greatest control over loan collateral, this control is expensive to maintain, and these costs are ultimately borne by the borrower. As a consequence, only large-volume deals (perhaps involving a minimum of $1,000,000 in inventory) are economical.

## SUMMARY

A firm's short-term financing sources appear on its balance sheet as current liabilities. Some of these current liabilities increase automatically (spontaneously) as the firm grows, providing the firm with a timely source of funds. The two main spontaneously increasing current liabilities are accounts payable and accrued wages and taxes.

Accounts payable provide the greatest source of short-term funds to the average firm. While part of a firm's accounts payable represents free credit (the amount owed prior to the end of the discount period), any accounts payable extending beyond the discount period incur an interest charge. The firm can determine the cost of the non-free credit using Equation 23.1. Some firms stretch accounts payable in order to slow disbursements, but care must be taken not to damage the firm's creditworthiness. Firms have little control over accrued wages and taxes as a source of financing.

Bank loans are the most important discretionary source of short-term financing to the average business. Although most are made for a period of less than one year, some are made for longer periods. The effective rate of interest on a bank loan depends on the stated rate of interest, compensating balance requirements, and the timing of the interest payments.

Loans from commercial finance companies and short-term borrowing from the sale of commercial paper are also very important sources of short-term funds to businesses. Customer advances and private loans are somewhat less important sources of short-term funds.

Accounts receivable and inventory are frequently used as collateral for business loans. When accounts receivable are used as collateral, they are either pledged or factored. When inventories are used as collateral, the loan agreement is generally in the form of a floating inventory lien, a trust receipt, or a warehouse receipt.

## KEY TERMS

**Accrued taxes** Tax liabilities that have been incurred by a firm but have not yet been paid.

**Accrued wages** Wages that have been earned by a firm's workers but have not yet been paid by the firm.

**Comaker loan** A loan to a firm that is guaranteed by an individual who promises to repay the loan if the firm defaults.

**Compensating balances** Cash balances maintained by firms in non–interest-earning bank accounts for the purpose of compensating the bank for a loan or other service provided.

**Discounted interest** When interest on a loan is paid at the time the loan is made rather than when the loan is repaid.

**Discretionary current liabilities** Current liabilities that do not change in size unless the firm takes specific action to change them.

**Effective rate of interest** The true rate of interest paid by a borrower on a loan.

**Factoring accounts receivable** The sale of accounts receivable. This arrangement may involve a loan to the selling firm from the purchaser in the form of an advance on the accounts receivable being sold.

**Floating inventory lien** When a lender holds a claim against all of the borrower's inventory as collateral for a loan. Also called a *blanket lien*.

**Line of credit** A preapproved maximum loan amount for a stated period of time, against which a firm can borrow if and when it so desires.

**Notes payable** A balance sheet account indicating the dollar amount of short-term bank loans outstanding.

**Pledging accounts receivable** Using accounts receivable as collateral against a loan.

**Prime rate** The rate of interest charged by banks to their most creditworthy customers.

**Regular interest** When interest is paid only on the principal borrowed and at the time the loan is repaid, it is called regular interest. It is also called simple interest.

**Spontaneous current liabilities** Current liabilities that change automatically, and directly, with sales (accounts payable and accruals).

**Trust receipt** When a lender files a lien against specific inventory items being used as loan collateral, all identified by serial number.

**Warehouse receipt** When a third party takes physical possession of inventory being used as loan collateral. Inventory is released to the borrower as the loan is repaid.

## EQUATIONS

**Equation 23.1**        **Cost of Trade Credit**

$$CTC = \left(\frac{D}{1-D}\right)\left(\frac{360}{N}\right)$$          **(p. 628)**

where $CTC$ = cost of trade credit
       $D$ = discount in decimal form

$N$ = number of days between when the discount must be taken and when the net payment is due

Up until the discount period has ended, trade credit is free. After that point, the firm incurs a cost for extending trade credit. Equation 23.1 helps determine the cost of trade credit on an annualized basis.

**Equation 23.2**    **Effective Rate of Interest**

$$ERI = \left(\frac{I}{LP}\right)\left(\frac{360}{N}\right)$$

**(p. 633)**

where $ERI$ = effective rate of interest
$I$ = interest in dollars
$LP$ = loan proceeds available to the borrower during the life of the loan
$N$ = number of days the money is available to the borrower

This equation can be used to determine the effective rate of interest on any loan of one year or less. When the borrower incurs costs in addition to interest, those costs are generally handled as if they were interest. That is, they are added to the numerator and/or deducted from the denominator of the left component of Equation 23.2.

## QUESTIONS

**Q23-1.** What is the difference between spontaneous and discretionary current liabilities?

**Q23-2.** What is meant by the statement, "Part of trade credit is normally free, while the other part is not free"?

**Q23-3.** In determining the cost of trade credit, why is the discount divided by 1 minus the discount?

**Q23-4.** Describe the risk-return trade-off involved in *stretching* accounts receivable.

**Q23-5.** Briefly describe the rationale for, and impact of, compensating balances.

**Q23-6.** On average, is the interest rate on secured loans higher or lower than on unsecured loans? Why?

**Q23-7.** Why do loans from commercial finance companies tend to carry a higher rate of interest than loans from commercial banks?

**Q23-8.** Briefly list the major characteristics of commercial paper.

**Q23-9.** Under what circumstances are customer advances and private loans normally used as sources of short-term financing?

**Q23-10.** Compare the characteristics of pledging with those of factoring.

**Q23-11.** How would you rate the following types of inventory in terms of their suitability as collateral?

- Textbooks
- Farm tractors
- Industrial robots
- Canned vegetables

**Q23-12.** How do the three major types of inventory loans compare in terms of lender control and administrative expense?

## SELF-TEST PROBLEMS

Solutions to self-test problems appear on p. S1.

**SP23-1.** What is the cost to the firm of not taking the trade discount for each of the following credit terms?

**a.** 1/10, net 30
**b.** 1/20, net 60
**c.** 2/15, net 45

**SP23-2.** What is the effective rate of interest on a $22,000 loan under the following conditions?

**a.** 13 percent regular interest for ninety days.
**b.** 12 percent discounted interest for one hundred ninety-two days.
**c.** 11 percent regular interest for one hundred eighty-five days and a 15 percent compensating balance.
**d.** 10 percent discounted interest for 10 weeks and a 10 percent compensating balance.

**SP23-3.** UAB International is considering selling commercial paper with a face value of $1,000,000. It expects to receive $965,000 from the sale and must pay a broker $15,000 in placement fees. If the commercial paper matures in 210 days, what is the effective rate of interest to UAB International?

**SP23-4.** M. H. Davis Beverage Company has just been presented with terms by which it can pledge its accounts receivable. Davis offers credit terms of net 45 and wishes to pledge all its receivables on a continuous basis. It averages $150,000 of accounts receivable during the year. The lender will charge 16 percent interest on loans and will lend only 75 percent of the value of the pledged receivables. In addition, the lender will charge a 2 percent processing fee on the value of the pledged receivables.

**a.** How much money will M. H. Davis be able to borrow?
**b.** What is the effective rate of interest on the loan arrangement if Davis realizes no reduction in the cost of operating its credit department?

**SP23-5.** Tinari Corporation is considering establishing a factoring arrangement on a continuing basis for the $400,000 of accounts receivable that remain on its books daily (that is the average level of receivables during the year). The factor charges 3 percent for servicing the account and 17 percent on any advances taken. Both charges are made on a discounted basis. In addition, the factor requires a 6 percent reserve to cover returned items. If Tinari offers terms of net 45,

**a.** What is the amount of advances the firm can expect to have on a continuing basis?

**b.** What is the effective rate of interest on the factoring arrangement if Tinari does not realize a reduction in the cost of operating its credit department?

## PROBLEMS

**P23-1.** If a firm pays 13 percent interest to borrow from a bank, should it do so in order to take trade discounts on the following accounts?

a. 2/15, net 90
b. 1/10, net 45
c. 1/30, net 60

**P23-2.** What is the effective rate of interest on the following loans?

**a.** $15,000 at 14 percent discounted interest for thirty days.
**b.** $50,000 at 13 percent regular interest for ninety days and a 20 percent compensating balance.
**c.** $175,000 at 15 percent regular interest for ten months.
**d.** $200,000 at 12 percent discounted interest for four months and a 10 percent compensating balance.

**P23-3.** FIT Enterprises just sold $3,000,000 worth of ninety-day commercial paper for $2,880,000. What is the effective rate of interest if FIT paid a $20,000 commission on the transaction?

**P23-4.** Strode Industries is considering pledging its accounts receivables on a continuous basis. Strode's average accounts receivable is $1,200,000 and credit terms of net 30 are offered to its customers. Strode expects to pledge all of its receivables in a general line and anticipates being able to borrow 70 percent of total receivables at 18 percent interest. There is a 1 percent servicing fee applied to all pledged receivables.

**a.** What is the maximum amount that Strode could borrow?
**b.** What is the effective rate of interest on the loan arrangement?

**P23-5.** G. Hyatt Corporation is considering factoring its accounts receivable on a continuous basis to provide a needed source of short-term credit. If it elects to do so, it can save $750,000 annually by reducing the size of its credit department. Hyatt currently extends credit terms of net 75 and has an average accounts receivable of $7,500,000. The factor would charge Hyatt 11 percent on advances and a 3 percent processing charge. In addition, Hyatt must maintain a 7 percent factoring reserve. Interest is paid on a discounted basis.

**a.** What is the maximum amount of advances Hyatt can expect to receive?
**b.** What is the effective rate of interest on advances? (Note: Be sure to consider the savings to Hyatt by reducing its credit department.)

**P23-6.** Marsite Company must pay 11 percent interest to borrow funds from a bank. It has been given credit terms of 2/15, net 40, by its main supplier. Should Marsite take the trade discount if it must borrow money to do so? Explain.

**P23-7.** Sloan, Inc., needs to borrow $100,000 for ninety days. It has been offered the following alternative loan terms by various banks:

- 9 percent discounted interest
- 8 percent interest paid at maturity and a 20 percent compensating balance requirement
- 10 percent interest paid at maturity

What is the effective rate of interest on each alternative?

**P23-8.** Watte Company plans to issue $4 million worth of 180-day commercial paper for $3.8 million. Watte must pay a commission of $30,000 on the transaction. What is the effective rate of interest on the commercial paper transaction?

**P23-9.** Scap Company plans to pledge its accounts receivable on a continuous basis. Its average accounts receivable is $1 million, and credit terms of net 45 are extended to its customers. Scap will pledge all of its receivable in a general line, and it could borrow 80 percent of total receivable at 13 percent interest. A 1.5 percent service fee applies to all pledged receivables.

a. What is the maximum amount that Scap could borrow?
b. What is the effective rate of interest on the loan arrangement?

**P23-10.** Peters, Inc., plans to factor its accounts receivable on a continuous basis to provide a needed source of short-term credit. This would reduce credit department expenses by $1.2 million annually. Peters currently extends credit terms of net 50 and has an average accounts receivable of $12 million. The factor would charge Peters 10 percent on advances and a 3 percent processing charge. Peters must also maintain an 8 percent factoring reserve. Interest is paid on a discounted basis.

a. What is the maximum amount of advances Peters can expect to receive?
b. What is the effective rate of interest on advances (be sure to account for the savings due to the reduction in credit department expenses).

**P23-11.** Sessions Industries needs to borrow $250,000 for a three-month period. Its bank will lend Sessions the needed amount, but will require 14 percent annual interest paid on a discounted basis, plus a 15 percent compensating balance.

a. If Sessions wants to have $250,000 available to it, how much must it borrow?
b. What is the dollar amount of interest Sessions must pay?
c. What is the effective rate of interest on the loan?
d. If Sessions normally maintains a $10,000 account balance at the bank, how does this change your answers to Parts a through c of this problem?

**P23-12.** June Corporation is considering selling $5 million (face value) of commercial paper maturing in 200 days. If June must pay an effective rate of interest of 9 percent on the paper, how much will it receive from selling the issue? (Ignore commissions.)

## COMPUTER-ASSISTED PROBLEM

**CP23-1. Effective Rate of Interest**   Yarnell, Inc., has visited a number of banks to determine the loan provisions available to it on future loans. Since Yarnell expects to borrow $2 million for 315 days next year, all terms indicated in the following table apply to loans of that amount and for that period. Yarnell will shift its checking account to the bank where the loan is made. The average checking account balance is maintained close to zero.

| Loan | Annual Rate of Interest | Compensating Balance Requirement | Discounted? |
|------|------------------------|----------------------------------|-------------|
| A | 13% | none | Yes |
| B | 12 | none | No |
| C | 14 | 20 | No |
| D | 15 | 20 | Yes |
| E | 16 | 15 | No |
| F | 16 | 15 | Yes |
| G | 17 | 10 | No |
| H | 17 | 10 | Yes |

Use the computer to determine the effective rate of interest Yarnell would pay for each loan.

## REFERENCES

Abraham, A. B. "Factoring—The New Frontier for Commercial Banks." *Journal of Commercial Bank Lending* 53 (April 1971): 32–43.

Abraham, A. B., and Harold T. Shapiro. "Compensating Balance Requirements: The Results of a Survey." *Journal of Finance* 19 (September 1964): 483–96.

Daniels, F., S. Legg, and E. C. Yueille. "Accounts Receivable and Related Inventory Financing." *Journal of Commercial Bank Lending* 52 (July 1970): 38–53.

Hayes, D. A. *Bank Lending Policies: Domestic and International.* Ann Arbor: University of Michigan, 1971.

Moskowitz, L. A. *Modern Factoring and Commercial Finance.* New York: Crowell, 1977.

Quarles, J. C. "The Floating Lien." *Journal of Commercial Bank Lending* 52 (November 1970): 51–58.

Schadrack, Frederick C., Jr. "Demand and Supply in the Commercial Paper Market." *Journal of Finance* 25 (September 1970): 837–52.

Stone, Bernell K. "The Cost of Bank Loans," *Journal of Financial and Quantitative Analysis.* 7 (December 1972): 2077–86.

# PART 8

# SPECIAL TOPICS

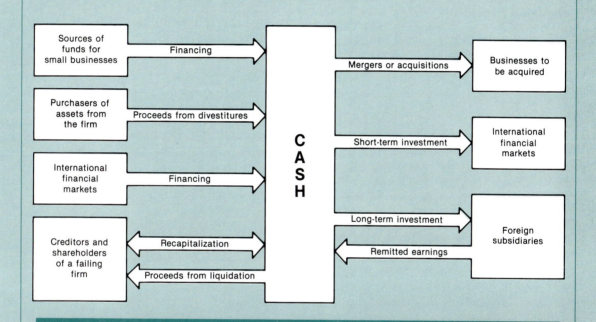

Each chapter in Part 8 focuses on a topic of special interest to managers in particular situations. Chapter 24 discusses how financial management concepts presented thus far apply to small business. Chapter 25 focuses on mergers and acquisitions. Although this topic is similar to the decision to acquire other fixed assets, special provisions apply.

Every year, thousands of businesses fail. Chapter 26 explains the alternative approaches to dealing with failure and bankruptcy. Finally, Chapter 27 explains how financial management is conducted by firms engaged in international business.

# CHAPTER 24

# SMALL BUSINESS

## SMALL BUSINESS FINANCIAL MANAGEMENT IN PERSPECTIVE

Kelly's Flower Shop was in business for twenty years and experienced substantial growth in sales during that time. The current owner decided to sell the shop and let the purchaser use the shop's name and customer list. It decided that the appropriate price for the business would be the market value of all existing physical assets, including the building, all inventory and equipment, and the delivery vehicles. Using this procedure, the value of the business was estimated to be $480,000.

The flower shop was subsequently sold to a group of finance majors who had recently graduated from a local university. The students believed the small business should be valued as the present value of the firm's expected future cash flows. Given that the shop would continue to use the same name and customer list, the students forecasted that cash flows would continue to grow at the same rate as they did in the past. Using a discount rate that is appropriate for retail stores listed on the New York Stock Exchange, the students determined the value of the firm to be $1 million. Thus, the shop appeared to the students to be grossly undervalued by the current owner, and they purchased it for $480,000.

Was the previous owner correct in valuing the business based on the value of the firm's assets? Could the discount rate the students used be inappropriate for the flower shop? What characteristics of small businesses could cause the use of a higher discount rate? This chapter identifies some general differences in risk and potential return between large and small businesses. Such differences must be recognized in order to value and manage a small business properly.

A common criticism of financial management textbooks is insufficient coverage of small business. The focus is commonly centered on large corporations, even multinationals. The financial management concepts introduced throughout this text, however, can be applied to any size business. This chapter briefly summarizes how the more important concepts specifically relate to the small business. First, the background, goals, and risk-return trade-offs of the small business are discussed. Second, the financial management functions are identified. Finally, the impact of growth on the financial structure of a small business is discussed.

## GOAL OF THE SMALL BUSINESS

The objective of a small business, like that of a larger business, is to maximize the wealth of the firm's owners (whether the firm is owned by shareholders or a single proprietor). It is generally easier for small businesses than larger businesses to ensure that the financial managers will maximize the wealth of the owners, as there are fewer managers to watch over. Indeed, in many cases, the owner acts as the financial manager and makes all the financial decisions. Of course, in that event, all managerial decisions will be consistent with the owner's objectives, and agency costs will not exist.

## RETURN AND RISK OF A SMALL BUSINESS

Research has found that small businesses have more flexibility to grow at a higher rate during favorable economic conditions.[1] Research has also found that small businesses have historically generated higher risk-adjusted returns than larger firms (assuming that the models applied to measure risk-adjusted returns have properly assessed risk).[2] These characteristics encourage investors to seriously consider investing in small businesses. But while the potential return is high, so is the risk. A large percentage of small businesses fail.

A common reason for the failures of small businesses is their inability to diversify, exposing them to unsystematic risk. Any event that affects their single industry (such as a strike by workers of a supplier firm or an economic slowdown in the town where they are located) can have just as much impact as some national event that systematically affects all firms. In addition, the death or retirement of a key manager can have a greater impact on a small business. Larger businesses have a more diversified managerial structure, so no one person is irreplaceable.

Since investors recognize the higher risk of small businesses, they will invest in them only if the potential for high returns outweighs that risk. Creditors will lend to small businesses only if they can charge an interest rate that properly reflects the risk. For these reasons, the cost of capital for a small business is generally higher than for a large corporation.

---

1. See R. Richardson Pettit and Ronald F. Singer, "Small Business Finance: A Research Agenda," *Financial Management* 14 (Autumn 1985): 47–60.
2. Ibid.

Small businesses are not only unable to diversify away their unsystematic risk, but also have a higher degree of systematic risk. This has been substantiated by the higher estimated betas of smaller businesses.[3]

The risk of a small business is often more difficult for outsiders to estimate than the risk of larger firms for two reasons. First, the asset structure of many small businesses can be substantially modified within a short period of time. For example, investment in a new machine that produces a new product may significantly affect the firm's cash flows. Or the hiring of one manager may drastically alter the firm's attitude toward risky ventures. Consequently, the risk of a small business is more likely to change without an obvious signal to shareholders or creditors than in the case of a large business. Second, because many small firms do not provide audited financial statements, their managers may have information that outsiders do not. This concept, commonly referred to as **asymmetric information,** can exist for large firms as well. However, asymmetric information is typically more important for small firms since their financial statements are less revealing to outsiders.

## FINANCIAL MANAGEMENT FUNCTIONS OF A SMALL BUSINESS

Their exposure to risk makes financial management particularly important to small businesses. Some of the more common financial management functions of a small business are

- Financial planning
- Capital budgeting
- Working capital management
- Financing
- Capital structure
- Operating leverage

Each of these functions as related to small business is discussed in turn.

### Financial Planning

For both investing and financing decisions, small businesses depend on financial analysis and planning. Financial analysis is less complicated for the small business since its financial characteristics (such as its recent sales volume and profitability) can be easily monitored on a daily or weekly basis. Furthermore, the small business's list of potential opportunities is constrained by a limited amount of funds.

Like large corporations, small businesses must assess seasonal demand and additional cash requirements for the replacement or addition of new machinery. However, small businesses cannot withstand a temporary shortage of cash because they have less access to funds. Consequently, they must be very accurate in forecasting potential cash deficiencies.

---

3. Ibid.

## Capital Budgeting

The capital budgeting processes of small businesses are somewhat similar to that of large corporations. Yet, because small businesses generally have a higher cost of capital, they need to apply a higher discount rate to a proposed project's cash flows. Also, their capital budgeting decision is more influential on their overall performance. One wrong decision could be devastating. (The risk adjustment for proposed projects by small businesses should account for this risk.) Furthermore, capital rationing is more common for small businesses, since their access to funds is so limited.

## Working Capital Management

The working capital management of small businesses should be conducted with risk in mind. Being less able to withstand a sudden, substantial increase in bad debt expense, small businesses must maintain a somewhat conservative credit policy. Likewise, their inventory and cash levels should be conservatively managed. An inventory shortage could stop production and/or sales of the products they specialize in. A cash shortage could create severe liquidity problems, since they do not normally have extensive lines of credit available.

## Financing

Small businesses generally start up with some capital provided by the owners, along with a loan from a commercial bank or finance company. Over time, they depend on retained earnings as a key source of funds. When retained earnings are not sufficient to finance ongoing operations or growth, they may attempt to borrow additional funds from a financial institution. Because they are not widely known, they are unable to issue securities. Even if they could issue their own securities, the typical amount of funds borrowed through the issuance of securities would exceed the appropriate debt capacity for some small businesses.

Creditors fear that any firm will become more risky after credit is provided. Yet, this fear is greater for the smaller firms, since they are more likely to change their asset structure and thus their risk within a short period of time. While a potential benefit of increased risk is higher return, creditors are not appropriated any share of higher returns.

Creditors may attempt to prevent an increase in risk by enforcing protective covenants on a variety of financial policies. These covenants are meant to prevent managers from making decisions that benefit shareholders at the expense of creditors. They limit the flexibility of small businesses and maintain risk to a level that can be tolerated by creditors. As a result, the potential return to shareholders is also more limited. Such covenants tend to make the small business's risk-return characteristics more similar to those of larger firms.

Small businesses commonly need funds to finance accounts receivable and to finance a seasonal buildup of inventories. These situations require short-term loans. To finance the purchase of fixed assets, a small business would likely request a term loan (maturing in one year or longer). As the small business grows, it commonly obtains funds from either a commercial bank, a *venture capital firm*, or by *going public*. An explanation of each of these alternatives follows.

**Commercial Banks**   While commercial banks frequently provide loans to small businesses, they represent businesses themselves. Thus, they should not use their funds for any purpose unless the potential return is large enough to compensate for the risk involved. For this reason, they first assess the creditworthiness of a small business as determined by several factors, including (1) the character of the borrower, (2) the borrower's planned use of funds to be borrowed, (3) the borrower's planned loan repayment schedule, (4) the financial condition of the business, (5) the outlook of the industry or environment in which the business is involved, and (6) the available collateral of the business. Because the bank needs to assess the financial condition of any business it lends to, it requires financial statements (often including pro forma statements). From this analysis, the bank will attempt to determine whether the business has maintained the appropriate level of cash and inventories, fixed assets, and so forth. In addition, it will evaluate the existing assets to determine their value as collateral for backing any loans provided.

While financial statements are useful for monitoring the financial condition, small businesses and their lending institutions give special attention to the cash budget, since it indicates the anticipated cash flows over time and reveals whether the business will be generating as much cash as it needs. Because small businesses tend to have volatile cash flows, they can easily experience periods of negative cash flow.

When their reputation has not been proven, small businesses may be forced to pledge a portion of their assets as collateral. For example, the bank could require that the maximum loan provided be equal to no more than 50 percent of inventory value, where the entire amount of inventory would be required as collateral. In the event that the business fails, the bank would be allowed to liquidate the inventory in order to obtain the funds owed to it. Other forms of collateral include accounts receivable, equipment, and assets of the business owner (such as the cash value of a life insurance policy, personal savings accounts, and marketable securities).

**Venture Capital Firms**   If a small business is willing to give up a portion of its ownership, it can submit a proposal to **venture capital firms** for obtaining funds (called **venture capital**). These firms are commonly composed of wealthy individuals who manage a portion of their own funds by investing in small businesses. Venture capital firms want to act as an investor rather than a creditor. They expect a share of the business they invest in. Their investments support projects with potential for high return but also high risk. Because of the risk involved, many of the projects may generate little or no return. However, the providers of venture capital hope that the successful projects will more than make up for any unsuccessful projects they invested in.

Projects considered by venture capital firms are commonly in the range of $250,000 to $1,500,000. Smaller projects are not popular because their potential return is not worth the time involved in assessing their feasi-

**TABLE 24.1**   **Estimated Cost of $10 Million Initial Offering**

| | |
|---|---:|
| Underwriting commissions | $850,000 |
| Legal fees | 120,000 |
| Printing and engraving | 90,000 |
| Accounting | 80,000 |
| Other | 42,000 |
| Total | $1,182,000 |

*Source:* "Special Report on Small Business," *Wall Street Journal*, Supplement, May 15, 1987, 13D.

bility. A large proportion of the project proposals received by venture capital firms will be quickly screened out, allowing more time to evaluate the more attractive projects.

**Going Public**   If a small privately held business desires to obtain additional funds, it may consider an initial offering of stock to the public, called **going public.** Because this procedure allows for additional funds without boosting the existing debt level, it deserves consideration. Furthermore, it may cause the company to become better known and may even be able to attract key personnel through the use of stock-related bonuses.

Firms that plan to go public should estimate the costs involved. Table 24.1 summarizes the more significant explicit expenses. The total expenses can be more than 10 percent of funding. There are also some indirect costs. After going public, the firm is responsible for informing shareholders of its financial condition, an expensive procedure that may divulge certain information the business prefers to keep confidential.

Some companies prefer to make decisions without having to be concerned with how investment analysts will react. For these companies, going public is not an attractive option. As an example, Silicon Compilers, Inc., considered going public in 1987 but decided against it for fear of being constantly monitored and evaluated by investment analysts.[4] Another disadvantage of going public is that the original owners lose a portion of the ownership and therefore may not retain complete control over the firm. Also, when small businesses attempt to obtain funding from the public, they may have difficulty in informing the public about their business opportunities. This limits the amount of funding that can be obtained from a public offering. It also forces the firm to sell part of the ownership at a relatively low cost. When the original owners permit partial ownership to other investors at a bargain price, their cost of capital is high. Under these conditions, they may attempt to avoid selling shares, as they are not being adequately compensated for them.

During stock market boom periods, small firms are more willing to go public. They expect a stronger demand for their shares and have a greater chance of obtaining the necessary funding. Many firms are not convinced that they can attract funds, as they have only a household name in a single town or geographic area.

---

4. See *Fortune*, February 23, 1987, 64.

Firms that see evidence of potential strong performance will often attempt to keep entire ownership to themselves. They therefore finance with borrowed funds until they reach their debt capacity. Additional funds are generated over time through retained earnings. If over time, there is sufficient evidence of continued strong performance, the firm may go public, since it will be able to sell its shares for a reasonable price. This does not mean that only the successful firms will go public. Some firms that have very uncertain cash flows will go public as well. Owners of these firms may be unable to obtain loans due to the risk, so they have no choice but to go public. Some investors still consider such firms since the shares may be purchased at very low prices, offering a potential return that compensates for the high risk.

When business owners invest their own funds, financing costs are still incurred since these funds could have generated a certain return if they had not been used for the business. Even if the owners are not forced to bankruptcy, the business should be voluntarily closed if it cannot generate a return that exceeds the owners' opportunity cost of tying up their funds.

Some small businesses may not even expect to become large enough to go public. In these cases, additions to the equity portion of their capital is constrained by the amount of earnings generated. The ability to increase debt is also constrained by the amount of collateral available. Over time, the equity percentage should rise as earnings are retained and reinvested back into the company, enabling a greater investment in assets, additional available collateral, and increased debt capacity.

## Capital Structure

The capital structure of small businesses is partially influenced by some of the characteristics mentioned earlier. Recall that small businesses are sometimes unable to inform investors of their investment opportunities (asymmetric information). Consequently, they are encouraged to use a debt-intensive capital structure. However, a heavy dosage of debt can result in substantial restrictions enforced by creditors and less management flexibility.

Small businesses vary in their ability to inform the public about investment opportunities. Small businesses that are capable of informing the public about their investment opportunities, but are severely restricted by covenants, normally prefer an equity-intensive capital structure. Conversely, firms that are less able to inform the public about investment opportunities and are less affected by covenants normally prefer a debt-intensive capital structure. Therefore, the optimal capital structure varies from one small business to another.

## Operating Leverage

Because small businesses have limited access to funds and experience volatile sales patterns, they usually prefer to invest only in fixed assets that can be fully utilized. However, this is easier said than done. Most ma-

### FINANCIAL MANAGEMENT IN PRACTICE

## CHARACTERISTICS OF SMALL BUSINESS OWNERS

Results of a recent survey of small businesses revealed that 42 percent of small business owners derived their idea for creating a small business from a prior job, and 18 percent pursued an idea that evolved from their own personal interests.* Other sources of ideas are shown in the following table.

| Source of Idea for Establishing a Business | Percentage of Respondents Citing This Source |
|---|---|
| Prior job | 42% |
| Personal interest | 18 |
| Suggestion | 8 |
| Education | 6 |
| Family business | 6 |
| Other | 20 |

The previous occupations of small business owners are summarized in the next table. Forty-six percent of the owners were previously employed by small firms. Only 16 percent of owners were previously employed by large firms.

*"Special Report on Small Business," *Wall Street Journal*, Supplement, May 15, 1987, 13D; and the National Federation of Independent Business.

| Previous Employers of Owners | Percentage of Respondents Citing This Source |
|---|---|
| Small firms | 46% |
| Medium firms | 12 |
| Large firms | 16 |
| Other | 26 |

The initial investment by small business owners is displayed in the following table. Seventeen percent of the owners began their business with less than $5,000. At the other extreme, 11 percent began with more than $100,000. Twenty-six percent of the owners began with at least $50,000.

| Initial Investment | Percentage of Respondents Investing This Amount[a] |
|---|---|
| Under $5,000 | 17% |
| $5,000–19,999 | 30 |
| 20,000–49,999 | 25 |
| 50,000–99,999 | 15 |
| 100,000 or more | 11 |

[a]Numbers do not sum to 100% because of rounding.

chinery and equipment do not allow for add-on parts later as production requirements increase over time. Thus, small businesses must forecast future demand and invest in enough machinery to satisfy forecasted demand. While such planning for growth avoids the cost of replacing machinery, it requires a greater initial investment.

## IMPACT OF GROWTH ON THE FINANCIAL STRUCTURE OF A SMALL BUSINESS

To illustrate how characteristics of a small business can differ from a larger corporation, the following discussion focuses on a sole proprietorship that develops into a corporation. Throughout the firm's evolution, significant changes in the firm's asset and liability structure, investment and financing strategies, potential return, and risk are identified.

**Example**

Consider the case of Don Toland who purchased a computer system for $5,000 and provided computer services (word processing, spreadsheets, and so forth) from his home. His main investment in the business was the computer system. It was financed by funds that he had saved in previous years. Over the first year, Toland generated sales of $20,000 through a large volume of small jobs provided to customers. He felt that while such a volume might be maintained, it would not grow much because friends and referrals made up the entire customer base. Consequently, he decided to set up a computer services shop along a busy street of town. This strategy was expected to attract a wide variety of customers and significantly increase revenues. Toland moved his computer system from his house to his shop. The rent and utilities bills amounted to $900 per month. Although he expected revenues to more than cover this expense, he borrowed $50,000 from a local bank in order to build up an inventory of supplies, advertise his services in the newspaper, hire one employee, and maintain extra cash for unanticipated expenses.

Business volume increased substantially once the retail outlet shop, called Toland Computer Services (TCS), was opened. Toland was forced to provide credit to some customers since other competitors provided credit. This required an investment in accounts receivable. In addition, one computer system was not sufficient to handle all business, so he purchased a second high-speed computer system for $5,000. To run the second computer, he hired an additional employee.

While business was steady, it was only a matter of time before other competitors set up shop nearby. Furthermore, there was unused space in the shop that Toland wanted to use efficiently. He began to use this space by setting up displays of blank diskettes, packaged programs, and other related products for sale but doing so required a large investment in inventory. Toland borrowed additional funds to finance this investment, and he also was granted a limited amount of credit by the suppliers.

As Toland became more knowledgeable about the computer services business, he set up an additional shop at the other end of town. He borrowed an additional $70,000 from the bank to set up a second shop. His revenues increased by a greater proportion than his expenses, partially because he advertised both stores in the same ad, and he could switch inventory between stores whenever one store was short. This strategy reduced the likelihood of an inventory shortage or a cash flow squeeze. TCS was then given additional credit on supplies purchased since suppliers felt that its ability to cover its accounts payable had improved. In addition, TCS was able to purchase supplies at lower prices than before because of the large amount of supplies ordered. All of these factors contributed to a higher degree of efficiency.

After five successful years, Toland decided to set up two more TCS outlets around town, but he decided to purchase these stores rather than rent them. The purchases were financed through additional loans from his local bank. His investment in fixed assets was now substantial. Due to the growth, he became a preferred customer of suppliers and was allowed a generous credit policy.

The dangerously high debt load of TCS motivated Toland to incorporate. TCS was able to issue stock and used the funds to retire some of its debt.

Many small businesses start out like TCS, as a one-person, one-product operation, later evolving into multiple outlets and multiple products. The

**TABLE 24.2** Changing Financial Characteristics over Growth Stages of a Small Business: TCS, Inc.

|  | Business from Home | First Stage of Expansion | Second Stage of Expansion | Decision to Go Public |
|---|---|---|---|---|
| Relative investment in inventory | Minor | Minor | Increasing | No direct impact |
| Relative investment in accounts receivable | Minor | Increasing | Increasing | No direct impact |
| Relative investment in net fixed assets | Major | Decreasing | Increasing | No direct impact |
| Degree of operating leverage | High | Decreasing | Increasing | No direct impact |
| Degree of asset utilization | Moderate | Moderate | Increasing | Increasing |
| Relative level of accounts payable | Minor | Minor | Increasing | Increasing |
| Relative level of debt | Minor | Increasing | Increasing | Decreasing |
| Relative level of equity | Major | Decreasing | Decreasing | Increasing |
| Degree of financial leverage | Low | Increasing | Increasing | Decreasing |
| Overall risk-return assessment | Low risk; low potential return | High risk; higher potential return | Higher risk; potential for very high return if revenues are high | Lower risk as interest payments on debt are reduced |

evolution normally changes the asset and liability composition. The relative importance of short-term assets such as accounts receivable and inventory tend to increase over time. The relative importance of net fixed assets generally declines except for abrupt, periodic increases when a new investment in a building or machinery is made. Asset utilization for a small business continues to improve as it grows and is often the main reason for the firm's desire to grow. Debt tends to grow with the firm, supporting the increased investment in assets. Yet, retained earnings will typically be a major source of funds to the small business during its growth stages.

Table 24.2 summarizes how the various financial characteristics of TCS, Inc., changed as it grew. Its asset and liability structures were significantly affected by the various business strategies identified at the top of each column. Its riskiest stage was its large investment in fixed assets, financed with additional debt. This resulted in a high degree of financial leverage and a low degree of liquidity. If sales were to drop during such a period, the firm's asset utilization and ability to meet its interest payments on debt would have been severely reduced. A much safer strategy would have been renting rather than purchasing the additional stores, since the rental payments would be much smaller than the payments on the debt that financed the purchase of the stores. An alternative strategy would have been to finance the purchase with stock instead of additional debt. While these alternative strategies would have maintained debt at a more tolerable level, they also would reduce the potential return.

The previous discussion illustrates how a small business is confronted with the same types of financial decisions as larger firms. An understanding of the main concepts covered throughout this text is essential to successfully run a small business.

## SUMMARY

Small businesses have some different characteristics than larger businesses. They generally have less access to funds and more exposure to unsystematic risk. They typically do not utilize economies of scale, are less diversified, have a higher cost of capital, and experience more volatile cash flows. The risks are obviously higher for small businesses than larger businesses in the same industry. Yet, for those small businesses that survive, the potential return to the owners is greater. Most concepts in this textbook can be related to small business. When these concepts are applied to the unique characteristics of a small business, the policy decisions may be affected. Nevertheless, the concepts themselves hold true, regardless of firm size.

## KEY TERMS

**Asymmetric information** Discrepancy between information about a firm known by its managers versus that known by potential investors.
**Going public** The original offering of stock by a firm to the public.
**Venture capital** Funds provided by venture capi-

tal firms to support mostly small business ventures; they are generally used to purchase a portion of the firm's ownership.
**Venture capital firms** Firms that invest funds (venture capital) in a variety of businesses.

## QUESTIONS

**Q24-1.** What is the objective of a small business?

**Q24-2.** How do small businesses differ from larger businesses with respect to unsystematic risk?

**Q24-3.** Would the cost of capital of a small business be higher or lower than a larger business in the same industry? Why?

**Q24-4.** Should a small business use a more or less conservative cash management policy than larger businesses in the same industry? Why?

**Q24-5.** Why does a commercial bank assess the market value of assets of a small business that has applied for a loan?

**Q24-6.** What is the general strategy of a venture capital firm?

**Q24-7.** Why do venture capital firms often avoid small projects?

**Q24-8.** What is a primary reason for small businesses to consider going public in order to support their growth?

**Q24-9.** What are the major disadvantages of going public?

**Q24-10.** Would the existence of asymmetric information tend to favor more debt or equity in the capital structure of a small business? Explain.

**Q24-11.** Why may the existence of asymmetric information discourage a firm from going public?

**Q24-12.** Why would a small business be concerned with overinvesting in fixed assets?

**Q24-13.** When a business owner moves a business from the home to a store, how are the major income statement items affected?

**Q24-14.** When a small business is in its growth stage, what happens to its asset utilization?

**Q24-15.** Sam Scrumentie invested $2 million to start up a small business. This business was expected to generate $70,000 per year in profits and would not require any additional financing. The business used rented space in a shopping mall. Sam felt very successful, since he would earn $70,000 per year from the business. Do you think this business is highly successful, moderately successful, or unsuccessful? Explain.

## REFERENCES

Cooley, Phillip L., and Charles E. Edwards. "Ownership Effects on Managerial Salaries in Small Business." *Financial Management* 11 (Winter 1982): 5–9.

Huntsman, Blaine, and James P. Hoban Jr. "Investment in New Enterprise: Some Empirical Observations on Risk, Return, and Market Structure." *Financial Management* 9 (Summer 1980): 44–51.

Pettit, Richardson R., and Ronald F. Singer. "Small Business Finance: A Research Agenda." *Financial Management* 14 (Autumn 1985): 47–60.

Walker, Ernest W., and J. William Petty II. "Financial Differences Between Large and Small Firms." *Financial Management* 7 (Winter 1978): 61–68.

# CHAPTER 25

# MERGERS AND DIVESTITURES

## MERGERS AND DIVESTITURES IN PERSPECTIVE

Following is a sampling of the merger activity that took place in 1987: Amoco Corporation outbid Exxon and Trans Canada by paying $3.87 billion for Dome Petroleum. Chrysler Corporation pursued the acquisition of American Motors and, in the process, increased its bid from $4 per share to $4.50 per share. Rupert Murdoch offered $65 per share for Harper & Row Publishers, Inc., more than two times the market price just a few months earlier. All of these events represent the attempted acquisition of businesses.

While some companies were growing through acquisitions in 1987, other companies were attempting to divest, or sell off, some of their assets. Divestiture decisions were particularly common in 1987 for companies with subsidiaries in South Africa as many sold their South African units in re-sponse to political problems experienced there. Other firms divested themselves of subsidiaries that were not as profitable as had been expected. In other cases, subsidiaries were sold to generate cash flows that were needed elsewhere. In all cases, the managements involved felt that shareholder wealth could be enhanced by selling the subsidiaries.

What motivates one company to acquire another? How does a company know how much to pay for an acquisition? How can companies determine whether to divest themselves of a subsidiary or other assets? What is the minimum price they should accept for assets they are trying to sell? This chapter provides a framework that can be used to answer these and other questions about mergers and divestitures.

A business combination can reflect either a **merger** or an **acquisition.** Although these terms may carry different legal meanings, they are used interchangeably in this chapter to describe a combination of two corporations whereby one loses its identity. Some mergers are designed to increase returns to the shareholders, while others are designed to reduce the risk to shareholders. This chapter first provides a brief background on merger transactions. Then corporate motives for mergers are identified, and the steps involved in enacting a merger are explained. Within this discussion, takeover battles are discussed.

Following the discussion of mergers, the act of divesting (selling) assets is presented. Motives for divestitures are identified, and a method for analyzing divestiture proposals is provided. Some divestitures occur as a result of a leveraged buyout. Advantages and risks to a business formed from a leveraged buyout are identified.

## BACKGROUND ON MERGERS

Table 25.1 illustrates U.S. merger activity in recent years. A dramatic increase in mergers occurred in 1981 and again in 1984, following recessionary periods. Merger activity was generally lowest during recessions. These tendencies existed not only during the 1980s, but for the last forty years. In 1986 the number and value of merger transactions was higher than any other year.

Some of the more publicized mergers during 1986 are summarized in Table 25.2. Thirty-one mergers had an acquisition value of $1 billion or more in 1986. Some companies significantly revised their operations and financial structure as a result of frequent merger activity. Table 25.3 identifies the companies most actively involved in mergers. Dart and Kraft was the leader, with eighteen different mergers in 1986. Numerous companies engaged in five or more mergers in 1986.

When mergers in 1986 are classified by industry, the banking industry is the most active, with 307 mergers and a combined value of about $9.5 billion. The retailing industry experienced fewer but larger mergers. Its 210 merger transactions are valued at over $25 billion in aggregate. Other industries whose mergers totalled more than $10 billion in aggregate dur-

**TABLE 25.1** Mergers Involving U.S. Companies

| Year | Number of Mergers | Dollar Value of Mergers (in Millions) | Annual Percentage Change in Value |
|---|---|---|---|
| 1980 | 1,565 | $ 32,958.9 | −3.6% |
| 1981 | 2,326 | 67,208.9 | +103.9 |
| 1982 | 2,297 | 60,402.3 | −10.1 |
| 1983 | 2,385 | 52,535.5 | −13.0 |
| 1984 | 3,144 | 125,693.0 | +139.3 |
| 1985 | 3,397 | 144,283.5 | +14.8 |
| 1986 | 4,024 | 190,512.3 | +32.0 |

*Source: Mergers & Acquisitions* 21 (May–June 1987):57.

**TABLE 25.2** Sample of Large Mergers (Acquisitions) during 1986

| Acquiring Company | Acquired/Merged Company | Dollar Value of Mergers (in Millions) |
|---|---|---|
| Kohlberg, Kravis, Roberts & Company | Beatrice Company, Inc. | $6,250.0 |
| General Electric | RCA Corporation | 6,141.9 |
| Kohlberg, Kravis, Roberts & Company | Safeway Stores, Inc. | 5,335.5 |
| Burroughs Corporation | Sperry Corporation | 4,432.1 |
| Campeau Corporation | Allied Stores Corporation | 3,608.0 |
| Capital Cities Communications, Inc. | American Broadcasting Company, Inc. | 3,529.9 |
| U.S. Steel Corporation | Texas Oil & Gas Company | 2,996.6 |
| May Department Stores | Associated Dry Goods Corporation | 2,386.2 |

Source: *Mergers & Acquisitions* 21 (May–June 1987):47.

**TABLE 25.3** U.S. Firms Most Actively Involved in Mergers in 1986

| Firm | Number of Transactions |
|---|---|
| Dart & Kraft, Inc. | 18 |
| Macmillan, Inc. | 15 |
| McGraw-Hill, Inc. | 12 |
| Sudbury Holdings, Inc. | 12 |
| Gulf & Western, Inc. | 11 |
| Coca Cola Company | 10 |
| Merchants National Corporation | 10 |

Source: *Mergers & Acquisitions* 21 (May–June 1987):57.

**TABLE 25.4** Breakdown of Mergers by Size in 1986

| Price Paid (in Millions) | Percentage of Transactions |
|---|---|
| $ 1.0– 5.0 | 25.9% |
| 5.1–10.0 | 14.3 |
| 10.1–15.0 | 8.4 |
| 15.1–25.0 | 10.8 |
| 25.1–50.0 | 11.4 |
| 50.1–99.9 | 9.1 |
| 100.0 and over | 20.1 |

Source: *Mergers & Acquisitions* 21 (May–June 1987):61. The figures are based on 1,822 transactions in which price data were revealed.

ing 1986 include communications, food and allied products, and electrical machinery.

Table 25.4 provides a breakdown on mergers by size. It reveals that the smaller companies were the most popular takeover targets. For the mergers in which price data was available, about 26 percent had an acquisition price of less than $5 million. At the other extreme, about 20 percent had an acquisition price of over $100 million.

With regard to international mergers, acquisitions of U.S. firms by non–U.S. firms were valued at over $23 billion in 1986. Acquisitions of non–U.S. firms by U.S. firms were valued at less than $2 billion. The significant difference was partially attributed to the dollar's value in foreign markets. During 1986 the dollar weakened substantially, which reduced the acquisition cost to non–U.S. firms that acquired U.S. firms. British companies were the most active acquirers of U.S. firms in 1986, followed by companies from Canada, Japan, Hong Kong, and Sweden.

Mergers can be classified into one of three general types. A **horizontal merger** is the combination of firms that engage in the same line of business. For example, the combination of two hospital supply companies, two hospitals, or two publishing companies represents a horizontal merger. A **vertical merger** is the combination of a firm and a potential supplier. For example, the combination of a hospital and a hospital supply company represents a vertical merger. A **conglomerate merger** is the combination of two firms in unrelated businesses. For example, the combination of a hospital supply company and a publishing company is a conglomerate merger.

## CORPORATE MOTIVES FOR MERGERS

Mergers normally occur due to the aggressive effort of the acquiring firm. Such an aggressive nature commonly results from one of the following motives for mergers:

- Immediate-growth objective
- Economies of scale
- Greater managerial expertise
- Unused tax shields
- Increased debt capacity
- Diversification

Each of these corporate motives is discussed in turn.

### Immediate-Growth Objective

A firm that plans for growth may prefer to achieve its objective immediately through a merger. Suppose a firm whose production capacity cannot fully satisfy demand for its product needs two years to expand its production facilities. To avoid a delay in increased production, it may search for a company that owns the appropriate facilities. By acquiring either part or all of such a company, it can achieve immediate growth in its business.

Some firms desire immediate growth in order to increase market share and reduce competition. For example, in 1987 Reebok International, Ltd., acquired a competitor, AVIA Group International, for $180 million. Reebok's stock increased by more than 10 percent shortly after the announcement. It should be mentioned that antitrust laws prohibit mergers that would significantly reduce competition. These laws limit the degree of market share that can be attained from mergers.

## Economies of Scale

Growth may also be desirable in order to achieve economies of scale. Some products can be produced at a much lower cost per unit if a larger amount is produced. Economies of scale are especially achievable for assembly line products, where fixed costs represent a large proportion of total production costs. A merger could allow for increased production, thereby achieving a lower production cost per unit.

Firms may be able to reduce other costs of operation as well through mergers. For example, if a merger allows for the nationwide distribution of a product, the advertising cost per unit will likely decrease. In addition, if a merger can avoid duplication in various costs, it can increase efficiency. This results in so-called **synergistic benefits.** When efficiency can be improved from merging, synergy exists, and the value of the merged firm can exceed the sum of the values of the two individual businesses.

## Greater Managerial Expertise

Mergers can be feasible when one firm's management has greater related expertise than the other. Consider a firm that has performed well in the past but lost some of its key personnel. It may search for a potential partner firm that is knowledgeable in the business and could provide the needed management. As a second example, consider a firm with strong management that identifies a poorly managed company in the same industry. If the firm detecting the other company's weak management believes this characteristic to be the only weakness, it may attempt to acquire that company. The acquisition price may be low due to the poor historical performance. Yet, performance could be improved if properly managed.

## Unused Tax Shields

Corporations reporting negative earnings are sometimes attractive candidates for mergers because of potential tax advantages. The previous losses incurred by the company prior to the merger can be carried forward to offset earnings of the acquiring corporation. While the losses of the acquired firm have occurred prior to the acquisition, they reduce the taxable income and therefore the taxes of the newly merged corporation.

## Increased Debt Capacity

A corporation can borrow funds at a relatively lower cost if it has not already borrowed extensively. A high degree of existing debt is risky, and may restrict or at least discourage a firm from expanding. To alleviate such a problem, the firm may attempt to acquire a company that has relatively low debt and therefore extra borrowing capacity. The merger can allow for additional borrowing, since the combined periodic interest expenses would not be excessive relative to the combined cash flows of the two businesses.

## Diversification

Firms often attempt to diversify their businesses so that their overall performance will not be totally dependent on the demand for one or a few products. It may be argued that diversification can benefit shareholders if it results in more stable returns (less risk) over time. As an example, the recent merger between Monsanto Company and G. D. Searle & Company resulted in a more diversified company. Monsanto was previously concentrated in oil and gas, plastics, agricultural business, fibers, and chemicals. The acquisition of Searle represented diversification into prescription drugs and consumer products.

An argument against the diversification motive is that shareholders can create their own diversification (homemade diversification) by purchasing shares of various firms. Therefore, the firm does not need to diversify for them. This argument ignores the potential benefit of a lower cost of capital by a diversified firm. Lower financing costs could occur, since creditors are more confident of getting repaid by a more diversified firm that has more stable cash flows. Thus, diversification can be an appropriate reason for a merger.

Some firms may consider diversifying to reduce their bankruptcy costs, which are costs associated with the possibility of going bankrupt, such as higher rates charged by creditors or protective covenants enforced by creditors. If a firm's diversification strategy stabilizes cash flows to a degree that reduces its probability of bankruptcy, then bankruptcy costs could be reduced.

## MERGER ANALYSIS

Merger analysis involves the necessary steps to complete a successful merger, as follows:

1. Determine the company's long-run objectives.
2. Select potential merger prospects.
3. Evaluate potential merger prospects.
4. Make the merger decision.

A description of these steps follows.

### Determine the Company's Long-Run Objectives

Each company has its own long-run objectives. Before evaluating any potential merger prospects, it is necessary for the firm to establish some direction. Some of the more common questions that a firm should consider are as follows:

1. Could future earnings be improved by reducing competition through a merger?
2. Is there any expertise within the firm that is not being fully utilized?

**3.** Would there be an advantage in having manufacturing or warehouses at additional locations?

**4.** Are there other locations where the product line is currently not available?

Answers to the preceding questions will determine the type of growth best suited for the firm. If the firm plans for growth in its current line of products, it will consider acquiring firms in the same business. If it needs to restructure its production process, it may attempt to acquire a supplier. If it desires a more diversified product line, it may attempt to acquire firms in unrelated businesses. The point here is that the company's long-run objectives dictate the types of firms to be considered for a merger. The company should not consider only firms that have been publicized by the media to be attractive merger prospects. The attractiveness of any prospect is dependent on the characteristics and objectives of the firm planning a merger.

## Select Potential Merger Prospects

Firms attempt to identify potential merger prospects that may help them achieve their policy objectives. This involves identifying firms with desirable characteristics, such as the appropriate lines of business. The size of firms is also a relevant criterion, since some firms may be too small to achieve the desired objectives, while others may be too large to acquire. The location is another possible criterion, since a firm's product demand, transportation costs, and local tax status are dependent on its location.

## Evaluate Potential Merger Prospects

An evaluation of certain characteristics of firms that are prospects for merger—such as line of business, size, and location—is sufficient for an initial screening. Yet, many prospects could meet these basic criteria. A more thorough analysis is necessary, using publicly available financial statements and reports. Such a financial analysis may detect inadequate liquidity, excessive borrowing, or other problems that would eliminate some prospects from further consideration. (However, firms with deficiencies that could be corrected should still be considered.) Along with the financial aspects, additional characteristics of each firm must be assessed, including its reputation, competitors, and labor-management relations. From this assessment, problems that may have gone unnoticed on financial statements can be detected.

If the firm still appears to be an attractive merger prospect, an evaluation of its specific characteristics is necessary, such as its facilities, its dependency on particular suppliers, and pending lawsuits. Unfortunately, the firm planning a merger may not be able to complete a full evaluation of such specific characteristics unless the prospect provides the information. Many of the mergers in recent years have been initiated without the approval of the prospect's management. In such cases, management of the prospect firms may not provide all of the relevant details.

Once the firm has sufficiently reduced its merger prospect list down to one or a few possibilities, it should conduct a capital budgeting analysis on the remaining prospects. Each prospect can be viewed as an asset that may be purchased. The initial outlay to purchase a prospect can be compared to the anticipated incremental cash inflows that would be generated over time due to this purchase. The term *incremental* implies the difference between cash flows (after taxes) that would occur with the merger versus without the merger. Once the cash flows have been estimated, the net present value of the proposed acquisition (denoted as $NPV_a$) can be computed as follows:

$$NPV_a = -PP + \sum_{t=1}^{n} \frac{CF_t}{(1 + k)^t} \qquad \textbf{(25.1)}$$

where  $PP$ = estimated purchase price for the prospect
$CF_t$ = estimated incremental after-tax cash flows
$k$ = required rate of return to acquire the prospect

If the *NPV* is positive, the prospect should be acquired. Under conditions where two mutually exclusive prospects are analyzed for a similar purpose, and both prospects exhibit positive *NPV*s, the acquiring firm must choose between them. To make this choice, an *NPV* comparison is inappropriate since one prospect may have a greater *NPV* but also require a much larger purchase price. In this case, the merger decision must take into account all other projects that have been proposed and then determine the combination of purchases that will generate the highest overall *NPV*.

**TABLE 25.5**  Acquisition Analysis: Acquire, Inc.

| Year | Cash Flow | Present Value Factor at 14 Percent | Present Value |
|------|-----------|-----------------------------------|---------------|
| 0 | $(14,000,000) | 1.0000 | $(14,000,000) |
| 1 | 9,000,000 | .8772 | 7,894,800 |
| 2 | 6,000,000 | .7695 | 4,617,000 |
| 3 | 3,000,000 | .6750 | 2,025,000 |
| | | | $NPV_a = \$536,800$ |

Like any other project, the future cash flows of a merger prospect are uncertain. Due to the expense of acquiring a firm and the irreversibility of such a decision, the capital budgeting analysis is critical to the acquiring firm's future performance. While the acquiring firm cannot escape uncertainty about the merger prospect's future cash flows, it should at least incorporate the uncertainty in the capital budgeting analysis. There is no perfect method to account for the uncertainty of a merger prospect's future cash flows. Any of the risk-adjusted capital budgeting techniques discussed in Chapter 11 can be applied.

**Example**

As an example, assume Acquire, Inc., has plans to acquire its main supplier, Target Company, for $14 million. Acquire, Inc., expects that the acquisition would provide incremental cash flows of $9 million per year in the first year, $6 million in the second year, and $3 million in the third year. After evaluating the risk involved, Acquire, Inc., uses a risk-adjusted discount rate of 14 percent. The analysis is shown in Table 25.5. Based on the estimated NPV, the acquisition of Target Company appears to be feasible.

## Make the Merger Decision

Once the risk-adjusted capital budgeting analysis is completed, the firm must make its decision. If a specific company is judged by the risk-adjusted capital budgeting method to be a feasible purchase and preferable to the alternative of internal growth, the firm should attempt to acquire the company. The procedures necessary to complete the acquisition will be described shortly. An alternative consequence of the analysis is that internal growth is judged by the analysis to be feasible and preferable to an acquisition. In this case, the firm should carry out the necessary steps to implement this strategy. Finally, the analysis might determine that neither an acquisition nor internal growth is feasible. This would imply that the company would not benefit by achieving its growth objectives, and that it should therefore revise these objectives.

## How the Evaluation of Mergers Differs from Other Projects

While the prospect firm can be viewed like any other asset to determine whether it should be purchased, some distinctions should be realized when applying the capital budgeting analysis. First, the purchase price of a single asset such as a machine is known in advance. The purchase price of a prospect firm is not necessarily known, since the acquiring firm will need to negotiate with the prospect's management or shareholders (as discussed in the following section). Thus, the purchase price, like the other cash flows, is uncertain.

As a second distinction, the expenses of a single asset such as a machine can sometimes be easily forecasted over time. Such expenses include the labor cost required to run the machine and the necessary overhead. The expenses of a merger prospect may involve hundreds or thousands of machines and employees. Thus, the net cash flows are often more difficult to estimate for a merger prospect than a single asset.

As a third distinction, the salvage value of a single asset can typically be forecasted with more accuracy than the salvage value of a merger prospect. The prospect never terminates, as the components making it up are continuously replaced over time. The acquiring firm can estimate the salvage value of a prospect for any future point in time as the projected price at which the prospect could be sold.

## MERGER PROCEDURES

If an attempt is made to acquire a prospect, that prospect becomes the *target*. It is set apart from all the other prospects that were considered. To enact the acquisition, corporations normally hire an investment bank (such as First Boston, Morgan Stanley, or Solomon Brothers) for guidance. Some firms that continuously acquire or sell businesses may employ their own merger department to handle the necessary tasks. Most tasks can be classified as one of the following:

- Financing the merger
- Tender offer
- Integrating the businesses
- Post-merger evaluation

A discussion of each procedure follows.

### Financing the Merger

A merger normally requires a substantial amount of long-term funds. One common method of financing a merger is to issue additional stock. As new stock is sold to the public, the funds received are used to purchase the target's stock. Alternatively, the acquiring firm may trade its new stock to the shareholders of the target firm in exchange for their stock at some negotiated exchange ratio. This alternative method achieves the same ultimate result.

Instead of issuing new stock, the acquiring firm can attempt to borrow the necessary funds. This has been a popular method for financing mergers in the 1980s. The use of debt to finance mergers represents a trade of borrowed funds in exchange for the target firm's stock. Consequently, the capital structure of acquiring firms using this financing approach becomes more debt-intensive.

When one company acquires all of the common stock or net assets of another company, a **statutory merger** results. In this case, the acquiring company retains its name, while the acquired company no longer exists as a separate legal entity. If the combination of two or more companies forms a new company, this is known as a **statutory consolidation.** Under this type of combination, both companies cease to exist as legal entities, and the shareholders of each become shareholders of a newly formed corporation. As a final possibility, the acquiring company could purchase more than 50 percent of the voting stock of another company. In this case, the acquiring company acts as a parent to the acquired company, which is now a subsidiary. Yet, the acquired company remains as a separate legal entity.

In the case of a statutory merger, shareholders of the acquired firm may be able to exchange their shares for that of the acquiring firm at a predetermined **exchange ratio** (**ER**). This ratio represents the number of the acquiring firm's shares received by the shareholders of the acquired firm for every share surrendered. It is computed as

$$ER = \frac{P_s}{P_r} \qquad \qquad (25.2)$$

where $P_s$ = market price per share surrendered
$P_r$ = market price per share to be received

---

**Example**

To illustrate, consider the proposed acquisition of Target Company by Acquire, Inc. The price of Acquire's stock is $30 per share. The company has offered $12 per share for Target's stock. The ratio of exchange would be

$$ER = \frac{\$12}{\$30}$$

$$= .4$$

Thus, shareholders of Target Company will receive .4 shares of Acquire's stock in exchange for each of their existing shares of Target stock.

---

## Tender Offer

If the acquiring firm contacts management of the target firm to negotiate a merger, but the two firms cannot come to terms, the acquiring firm may attempt a **tender offer.** This is a direct bid by the acquiring firm for the shares of the target firm. It does not require prior approval of the target firm's management, so a tender offer could accomplish a merger even if management of the target firm disapproves.

The acquiring firm must decide the price at which it is willing to purchase the target firm's shares and then officially extend this tender offer to the shareholders. This decision should have been made during the merger analysis, since the estimated purchase price of the target firm is dependent on the price to be paid per share of its stock. The tender offer sometimes represents a premium of 10 percent or more above the prevailing market price to encourage the shareholders of the target firm to sell their shares. The acquiring firm can achieve control of the target firm only if enough of the target firm's shareholders are willing to sell their shares. The acquiring firm must decide how long to maintain the offer and whether to obtain all or a portion of the target firm's outstanding shares.

## Integrating the Businesses

If a merger is achieved, the departments within the two companies must be restructured. The key to successfully integrating the management of two companies is to clearly communicate the long-run objectives of the firm, as well as the roles of each corporate department and position. This includes identifying the person (that is, the position) to whom each subordinate person (or position) will report and the positions accountable for various tasks. While this strategy may seem easy to apply, it is often neglected by those in charge. If the roles are not clearly defined up front, the newly integrated management will not function cohesively, and mutual trust will be lacking.

Tensions are especially high in the beginning stages of a newly formed merger, since the employees may not be fully aware of the acquiring firm's plans. The personnel involved in the initial evaluation of the target firm should aid in the integrating of the businesses once the merger has occurred. For example, if the primary reason for a horizontal merger was to reduce duplication of some managerial functions, management of the newly formed firm should make sure that the potential benefits that initiated the merger are realized.

A newly formed merger typically requires a so-called *incubation* period, during which production, transportation, cash management, financing, inventory management, capital structure, and dividend policies are reevaluated. Policies are commonly revised to conform to the newly formed company's characteristics. For example, inventory of the combined firm will need to be larger than for either original business (although perhaps not as large as the sum of both businesses) to deal with the larger volume of sales. Long-term financing decisions will be affected by the newly formed company's current mix of debt versus equity. The incubation period may last a few years. In some cases, the fine-tuning takes longer than expected or never achieves the efficiency that potentially exists. On paper, it is often easy to identify ways by which a merger could be beneficial. Fully capitalizing on those benefits without creating any new problems, however, can be difficult. As a final point, the process of creating the merger can also be much more expensive than originally anticipated, and it often places a financial strain on the acquiring company (especially when a takeover battle erupts).

### Post-Merger Evaluation

After the merger, the firm should periodically assess the merger's costs and benefits. Were the benefits as high as expected? Were there any hidden costs involved in the merger that were not anticipated? Was the analysis of the target firm too optimistic? Once the merger takes place, it cannot be easily reversed. However, lessons can be learned from any errors detected in the analysis that led to the merger, so that future merger prospects can be more accurately assessed. In addition, some post-merger evaluations may encourage a firm to abandon the business it recently purchased. The decision to abandon or *divest* a business is discussed later in this chapter.

## DEFENSE AGAINST TAKEOVER ATTEMPTS

In some cases, managers of a target firm may not approve of the takeover attempt by the acquiring firm. They may feel that the price offered for their firm is below what it is worth, or they may believe that the firm has higher potential if not acquired. Under such conditions where the takeover attempt is hostile, management of the target firm can choose from a variety of so-called *shark repellents* to defend itself:

- A plea to existing shareholders to hold their shares
- Repurchasing shares of stock
- Private placement of stock
- Golden parachutes
- Legal action
- Search for a more suitable acquirer

### Plea to Shareholders

As soon as managers of the target firm are aware of the takeover attempt, they may immediately attempt to convince shareholders to retain their shares. The plea may be in the form of newspaper advertisements or personal letters. While communication by management is sometimes effective, its success depends on the willingness to pass up a sell-off of stock at perhaps 10 percent or more above the market value. A stronger defense can be built by using other tactics just in case this communication is not effective.

### Repurchasing Shares of Stock

Another defensive tactic for the target firm is to repurchase some of its own shares. This may drive up the market price of the stock, making the premium offered by the potential acquiring firm look less attractive. As an example, in 1985 CBS, Inc., announced that it would buy back a portion of its outstanding stock at a significant premium above market value. This action was in defense of Ted Turner's attempt to acquire CBS. As a second example, Colgate Palmolive Company offered to buy back some of its outstanding shares in 1985 in order to discourage any possible takeover attempts that were anticipated.

In some cases, the target firm will bid for any of its stock that is held by the firm attempting the takeover. Obviously, the firm attempting the takeover would be willing to sell this stock only if the bid price were high enough to give up the takeover plan. Unocal Corporation, for example, became the target of T. Boone Pickens, Jr. To resist the takeover attempt, Unocal bid for its stock held by Pickens. The bid was high enough to cause Pickens to sell holdings of Unocal stock to Unocal Corporation.

Although repurchasing shares may prevent a takeover, it can also be very expensive. The repurchasing of shares by CBS, Inc., to resist Ted Turner's takeover attempt required an increase in debt to obtain the necessary cash. The recapitalization plan more than doubled CBS's degree of financial leverage, and the price of its bonds plummeted as a result of the increased probability of default. The ratings of CBS bonds fell from AA to A during this period.

The case of CBS, Inc., illustrates how existing bondholders can be affected by takeover attempts. The bondholders of Unocal Corporation were affected in a similar manner as Unocal built up its debt level in order to repurchase shares. A perception of higher risk caused a decline in Unocal's bond ratings from AA to BBB during this period. Unocal estimated its cost of resisting the takeover attempt at $60 million.

In 1986 and 1987 several corporations planned or implemented some form of the recapitalization plan just described to prevent hostile takeovers. FMC Corporation, Colt Industries, Owens-Corning, Holiday Corporation, Allegis Corporation, Harcourt Brace Jovanovich, Inc., and Caesar's World were among these corporations. The stock prices generally reacted favorably to the recapitalization strategy. For example, the stock price of Owens-Corning at the time of recapitalization was $12.12 per share. In June 1987 the price reached $25, representing a 106 percent increase in about seven months.

A common form of recapitalization is to use debt proceeds for a large, one-time cash dividend payment to existing shareholders. In this way shareholders benefit without selling their shares. The firm's amount of equity is reduced because of the cash dividends paid to shareholders. Because the firm's capital structure becomes more debt-intensive, it must be very efficient in order to service the debt. Yet, the increase in financial leverage can magnify the impact of strong operating performance on shareholder returns.

## Private Placement of Stock

A third defensive tactic for a target firm to avoid a merger is a private placement of stock. By selling these shares directly (privately) to specific institutions, the target firm can reduce the acquiring firm's chances of obtaining the sufficient percentage of shares to gain controlling interest. The more shares outstanding in the market, the larger is the number of shares that must be purchased by the acquiring firm in order to gain controlling interest.

### Golden Parachutes

Some companies grant special provisions to their executives called **golden parachutes,** which are intended to maintain the stability of upper management. Because they can prevent a replacement of management, these provisions discourage takeover attempts by other firms. As an example, in 1987 directors of UAL, Inc., awarded special provisions to eight of their top executives that entitled them to receive their current annual compensation on an annual basis until April 30, 1992 (or until their retirement if that occurred first). In addition, severance payments of one to three times the base salary were to be awarded to thirty-seven other executives if they were fired or if they resigned for good reason after any change in the control of UAL, Inc.

### Legal Action

A fifth defensive tactic is for the target firm to take legal action against the acquiring firm. It may claim that the acquiring firm has not satisfied all the SEC requirements prior to its attempted takeover. Or it may claim that the merger would violate sections of the Sherman Act or Clayton Act that prohibit any takeovers that would create a monopoly or significantly reduce competition.

### Search for a More Suitable Acquirer

A sixth defensive tactic is for the target firm to find a more suitable company, called a **white knight,** that would be willing to acquire it. The white knight rescues the target firm from the initial attempts of the potential acquiring firm by acquiring the target firm itself. While the target firm no longer retains its independence, it may prefer being acquired by the white knight firm.

Even if a firm is armed with anti-takeover ammunition, hostile takeovers can occur. A high enough bid can often sway shareholders, regardless of the defense built against a takeover. As an example, Spectradyne, a pay-movie supplier, accepted a bid of $46 per share on May 26, 1987. This price was 57 percent higher than its price as of May 1, 1987.

## WHO BENEFITS FROM MERGERS?

The motives for mergers (discussed earlier in the chapter) suggest that firms can benefit by acquiring other firms, although the target firms may not be willing to be acquired. Do mergers benefit both the acquired and the acquiring firm? Shareholders of acquired firms are usually able to sell their shares at a significant premium above the market price. Yet, if the benefits are so appealing, why do target firms often attempt to avoid a takeover? Perhaps they believe that they would perform better if they could remain independent or be acquired by some alternative firm. It is difficult to estimate how the share price would have changed if the firm had remained independent. Therefore, it is impossible to say with assurance that the acquired firm's shareholders are better off as a result of the merger. Most studies on this topic find that shareholders of acquired firms have benefited from mergers.

The benefits to shareholders may be greater for firms in which there are two or more corporations attempting to take it over. Research by Walking and Edmister found that the bid premium on takeover targets was 30 percent higher on average when two or more bidders were competing for the target firm.

There is some evidence that shareholders of target firms may be adversely affected by their firm's anti-takeover tactics. A study by the Securities and Exchange Commission's office of the chief economist analyzed 649 anti-takeover tactics between January 1979 and May 1985 and found that these attempts caused an average decline in stock prices of 1.31 percent.[1] Some types of tactics were more harmful than others.

From the perspective of the acquiring firm, the evidence is also not clear as to whether shareholders benefit. The results tend to vary with the merger of concern. When examining all mergers in aggregate, there does not appear to be an abnormal increase in share price subsequent to a merger that can be attributed to the merger itself. The results are inconclusive, since it is difficult to measure what the performance of the acquiring firms would have been if they had not made acquisitions.

Examples of the stock price reaction to merger activity are shown in Figure 25.1. The top chart represents Texaco's takeover of Getty Oil Company. The stock price of Getty Oil began to rise dramatically about 25 days prior to the announcement of a takeover attempt. It rose substantially more than the stock price of Texaco, Inc. (the acquirer), both before and after the announcement date.

The lower chart in Figure 25.1 represents Standard Oil's takeover of Gulf Corporation. Again, the stock price of the target firm is more favorably affected by the merger than the stock price of the acquirer. While all mergers would not show the same results, the more favorable advantage to the target firm has been common in recent mergers.

An example of a merger that did not go as smoothly as expected was Du Pont's takeover of Conoco in the early 1980s. Initially, Mobil Oil and Seagram battled for the acquisition of Conoco. Then Du Pont entered the battle as a *white knight*, expecting to obtain Conoco at a bargain price. It was thought that Conoco could be beneficial to Du Pont, as it would provide a relatively cheaper source of petroleum feedstock for its chemical output than foreign oil. As Du Pont became involved in the takeover battle, Conoco's stock price was $77 per share. Du Pont's initial bid for Conoco was about $79.52 per share. By the time the acquisition was accomplished,

---

1. See "Shark Repellents Said to Affect Value Slightly," *Wall Street Journal*, October 11, 1985, 60.

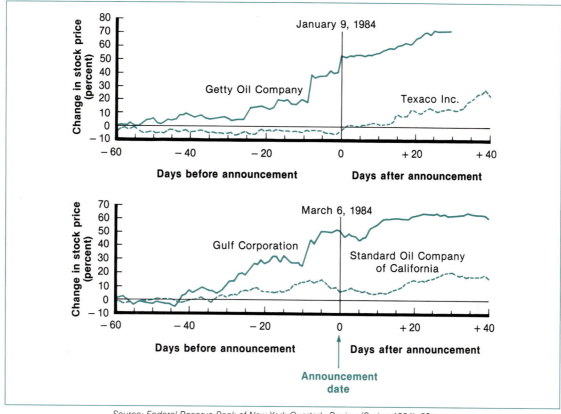

Source: Federal Reserve Bank of New York Quarterly Review (Spring 1984): 28.

**FIGURE 25.1**
**Stock Prices'**
**Reactions to**
**Merger Activity**

the offer price was $98 a share, since Du Pont had to outbid the other firms attempting the takeover. To follow through on the purchase of Conoco's stock, Du Pont more than tripled its debt at a time when interest rates were very high. While the merger may offer Du Pont sufficient benefits over time to warrant the merger, this example illustrates the potential costs from engaging in a merger.

## DIVESTITURES

Up to this point, the discussion has focused on the desire to grow and/or diversify. Yet, some firms often attempt to become smaller through **divestiture,** or selling a portion of their assets. Some of the larger divestitures in recent years include

■ Sale of seven television stations by Metromedia, Inc., to News Corporation, Ltd., for over $1.9 billion.
■ Sale of a battery division by Union Carbide to Ralston Purina for about $1.4 billion.
■ Sale of Utah International Company by General Electric to Broken Hill Proprietary Company for $2.4 billion.

**TABLE 25.6    Breakdown of Divestitures by Size in 1986**

| Selling Price (in Millions) | Percentage of Divestitures |
|---|---|
| $ 1.0– 5.0 | 12.2% |
| 5.1–10.0 | 11.4 |
| 10.1–15.0 | 7.6 |
| 15.1–25.0 | 11.0 |
| 25.1–50.0 | 14.9 |
| 50.1–99.9 | 10.7 |
| 100.0 and over | 32.2 |

*Source: Mergers & Acquisitions* 21 (May–June 1987):65.

■ Sales of Aminoil, Inc., and Geysers Geothermal Company to Phillips Petroleum Company for $1.7 billion.
■ Sale of CIT Financial Corporation by RCA Corporation to Manufacturers Hanover Corporation for $1.51 billion.

A breakdown of divestitures by size is displayed in Table 25.6. About 12 percent of all divestitures in 1986 in which price data were available had a sales price of $5 million or less. At the other extreme, about 32 percent of all divestitures were priced at over $100 million. In 1986 alone, more than 500 divisions and subsidiaries were sold.

## Motives for Divestitures

Divestitures are enacted to improve corporate performance and increase shareholder wealth. Some firms may have mistakenly diversified into businesses for which they did not have managerial expertise. Divestitures allow a firm to concentrate on what it does best. As an example, RCA divested in 1985 in order to concentrate on its main businesses. Gulf & Western sold over fifty businesses during the 1983–1985 period in order to concentrate on its entertainment, information, and financial services businesses. ITT Corporation sold over sixty businesses in recent years to better capitalize on its main lines of business.

A second motive for divesting is to sell facilities that do not appear to have much potential. As technology improves, old-fashioned production facilities are sold.

A third motive for divesting is a need for increased liquidity. A divestiture can generate cash while avoiding additional debt. From a balance sheet perspective, financing is obtained by reducing assets rather than by increasing liabilities. In some cases, funds obtained from divestitures are used to buy back outstanding stock as a defense against potential takeovers by acquiring firms. To illustrate, Colgate Palmolive Company and CBS, identified earlier in examples of defending against takeovers by buying back their outstanding stock, divested some of their businesses to obtain some of the necessary funds. While CBS also used debt to finance its takeover defense strategy, it later used divestitures to reduce the debt. Its debt level was reduced from $1.2 billion at the end of 1985 to $687 million at the end of 1986.

A fourth motive for divesting is that the so-called *break-up value* of a firm is sometimes believed to be worth more than the firm as a whole. In other words, the sum of a firm's individual asset liquidation values exceeds the combined market value of the firm's assets. This so-called **reverse synergy** encourages firms to sell that which would be worth more when liquidated than retained.

## Valuation of a Divestiture

Like any investment in real assets, a decision to divest real assets normally involves a significant amount of funds. Moreover, the decision is irreversible. Thus, a poor divestiture decision can have a long-lasting adverse impact on the firm. For this reason a thorough divestiture analysis is necessary before making the decision.

As with assets that are considered for future purchase, assets to be sold can be evaluated using capital budgeting methods. However, the application of capital budgeting to proposed divestitures is unique to itself. A divestiture creates an initial inflow of funds. Because the assets sold will no longer generate the periodic cash flows for the firm, the divestiture has an opportunity cost, which is the value of cash flows that would have been received if the assets had not been sold. This opportunity cost would be measured as periodic cash outflows. Therefore, the net present value of a divestiture would compare the initial cash received from selling the assets to the present value of cash flows forgone due to selling the assets. That is, the *NPV* of a proposed divestiture (denoted as $NPV_d$) can be expressed as:

$$NPV_d = SP - \sum_{t=1}^{n} \frac{CF_t}{(1 + k)^t} \qquad \textbf{(25.3)}$$

where  $SP$ = estimated selling price of the assets
$\quad CF_t$ = estimated incremental after-tax cash flows forgone as a result of selling the assets
$\quad\quad k$ = required rate of return to divest the assets

---

**Example**

Skid Company has considered selling one of its businesses to a large manufacturing firm. It has received a bid of $4.9 million for the business. By selling the business, Skid expects to forgo $1 million in each of the next three years, and $2 million in the fourth and fifth years. Assume Skid's required rate of return for this proposed divestiture is 12 percent. The divestiture analysis is shown in Table 25.7. Because the initial cash received exceeds the present value of forgone cash flows, the *NPV* of the proposed divestiture would be positive, implying that the divestiture is feasible.

---

As with the purchase of assets, a divestiture has uncertain costs and benefits. The firm must estimate the price at which it can sell the assets, as well as the cash flows that are forgone if the assets are sold. The analysis of a proposed divestiture must account for the uncertainty involved.

**TABLE 25.7**  **Divestiture Analysis: Skid Company**

| Year | Cash Flow | Present Value Factor at 12 Percent | Present Value |
|:---:|:---:|:---:|:---:|
| 0 | $ 4,900,000 | 1.0000 | $4,900,000 |
| 1 | (1,000,000) | .8929 | (892,900) |
| 2 | (1,000,000) | .7972 | (797,200) |
| 3 | (1,000,000) | .7118 | (711,800) |
| 4 | (2,000,000) | .6355 | (1,271,000) |
| 5 | (2,000,000) | .5674 | (1,134,800) |
| | | | $NPV_d$ = $92,300 |

## Searching for an Appropriate Acquirer

Just as companies planning for growth often seek out firms to acquire, a company deciding to divest some of its assets should search for an appropriate acquirer. The search process is worthwhile, since the selling price will likely be much higher if firms that could potentially benefit from the acquisition are aware that the assets are for sale. The divesting firm should attempt to identify corporations that exhibit characteristics that would benefit from acquiring the assets for sale. Then these corporations should be notified of the planned sale, and a bidding war will follow. As the bidding ensues, the divesting firm must consider the assessed value of the assets from its perspective. If the bid prices are lower than the perceived present value of these assets, the firm may be better off canceling the divestiture plan and retaining the assets.

## Are Divestitures Beneficial?

As in the case of mergers, determining whether past divestitures were beneficial is difficult since it is not known how the firm would have performed if it had retained the assets. A study of large companies found that divested businesses have performed better under their new owners.[2] Other research has examined recent divestitures by all types of firms and has generally concluded that firms have benefited from divesting.[3]

# LEVERAGED BUYOUTS

Some divestitures occur as a result of a **leveraged buyout** (LBO), which represents a purchase of a company (or the subsidiary of the company) by an investor group with borrowed funds. The investors are often the previous managers of the business. For example, consider a diversified conglomerate firm that plans to sell its financial services division in order to

---

2.  See "Splitting Up," *Business Week*, July 1, 1985, 50–55.
3.  See the articles by Jain; Kudla; and McIntish; Miles and Rosenfeld; and Rosenfeld, all listed in the references to this chapter.

**TABLE 25.8     Leveraged Buyout Trends**

| Year | Number of Deals | Dollar Value (in Millions) |
|------|-----------------|----------------------------|
| 1981 | 99  | $ 3,093.1 |
| 1982 | 164 | 3,451.8 |
| 1983 | 230 | 4,519.0 |
| 1984 | 251 | 18,631.4 |
| 1985 | 253 | 19,339.9 |
| 1986 | 308 | 40,910.5 |

Source: Mergers & Acquisitions 21 (May–June 1987): 70.

generate cash. The management of this division may attempt to obtain personal loans to purchase the subsidiary. In this case, the managers would represent the owners. The newly owned business is highly leveraged, since little equity is used to support the business.

Table 25.8 shows LBO activity over time. There has been a consistent increase in the number of LBO deals each year. In addition, the market value of all LBO deals has increased each year. The majority of LBOs result from a corporate sale of a division or subsidiary, although some result when the entire corporation goes private (becomes privately owned).

Any business with characteristics that can adequately operate with a large amount of borrowed funds is a potential candidate for a LBO. Such characteristics include established product lines, stable cash flow, low level of debt (prior to the LBO), and no need for additional fixed assets. These characteristics increase the probability that a sufficient amount of net cash flows will consistently be forthcoming to cover periodic interest payments on the debt. Growth is not normally a primary goal, since the firm does not have excess cash to expand and may have already borrowed up to its capacity. While the LBO can place a strain on cash, it offers the advantage of restricting ownership of the business to a small group of people. All profits can be allocated to this group (although most profits will likely be reinvested in the business in the early years). As is expected for such high-leverage businesses, high risk exists (in meeting the high interest payments), but the potential for high return also exists.

Agency costs are generally reduced for businesses purchased through a leveraged buyout. Since the managers tend to become part-owners, there is less chance of them behaving in a manner that would not maximize the wealth of the owners. Another advantage of LBOs is that managers tend to improve operating efficiency, possibly because, as part-owners, they can directly benefit from their performance.

Some companies that have experienced an LBO go public at a future point in time. For example, in 1984 Tiffany & Company was purchased from Avon & Company by its managers for $105 million. The purchase was financed with $10 million in cash and $95 million in debt. In 1987 Tiffany & Company went public, raising more than ten times the original $10 million investment by the managers.

Various financial institutions have participated in LBOs, including some investment companies, insurance companies, and pension funds. The popularity of LBOs is partially due to the substantial amount of investment by these companies.

## SUMMARY

The recent wave of mergers is the result of various benefits that they can generate. Some of the more common benefits are immediate growth, economies of scale, greater managerial expertise, tax shields, increased debt capacity, and diversification. When a firm is considering a merger, it should initially develop its objectives and then determine whether a merger with any prospective firms could help meet these objectives. If a takeover attempt is feasible, financing must be arranged, a tender offer should be submitted, and the businesses must be integrated (if the takeover attempt is successful). Because takeover candidates are armed with so-called shark repellents, some hostile takeover attempts are unsuccessful or become much more expensive than originally expected.

Divestitures have also become very popular lately because they allow a firm to concentrate on one or a few key businesses. It is not unusual for a firm to divest a portion of assets that it recently acquired. Many firms are simultaneously involved in mergers and divestitures in their attempt to create the optimal composition of assets that will maximize shareholder wealth.

## KEY TERMS

**Acquisition** Act of one firm obtaining a controlling interest in another firm, so that the acquired firm loses its identity. (This term is used interchangeably with the term *merger* in this chapter.)

**Conglomerate merger** Combination of two or more corporations with unrelated businesses.

**Divestiture** A firm's sale of a portion of its assets.

**Exchange ratio** The number of the acquiring firm's shares received by the shareholders of the acquired firm for every share surrendered.

**Golden parachutes** Special provisions granted by companies to executives, usually intended to maintain stability of management and/or prevent hostile takeovers.

**Horizontal merger** Combination of firms that engage in the same line of business.

**Leveraged buyout** Purchase of a company (or a subsidiary of the company) by an investor group with borrowed funds.

**Merger** Act of one firm obtaining a controlling interest in another firm, so that the acquired firm loses its identity. (This term is used inter-

changeably with the term *acquisition* in this chapter.)

**Reverse synergy** Exists when the sum of a firm's individual asset liquidation values exceeds the combined value of the firm's assets.

**Statutory consolidation** Combination of two or more corporations to form a new corporation.

**Statutory merger** Acquisition by one company of all of another company's common stock or net assets.

**Synergistic benefits** Also called *synergy*, a combination that is valued at an amount exceeding the sum of the individual values of the components combined.

**Tender offer** Direct bid by the acquiring firm for the shares of the target firm.

**Vertical merger** Combination of a corporation and a potential supplier or customer.

**White knight** Company that rescues the target firm by acquiring it, thereby preventing the acquisition attempt by another firm.

# EQUATIONS

**Equation 25.1**     **Net Present Value of a Proposed Acquisition**

$$NPV_a = -PP + \sum_{t=1}^{n} \frac{CF_t}{(1+k)^t}$$     **(p. 672)**

where  $PP$ = estimated purchase price for the prospect
$CF_t$ = estimated incremental after-tax cash flows
$k$ = required rate of return to acquire a prospect

This equation can be used to determine whether a particular acquisition prospect should be acquired.

**Equation 25.2**     **Exchange Ratio**

$$ER = \frac{P_s}{P_r}$$     **(p. 675)**

where $P_s$ = market price per share surrendered
$P_r$ = market price per share to be received

This equation determines the number of shares an acquired firm will receive in exchange for each of their existing shares.

**Equation 25.3**     **Net Present Value of a Proposed Divestiture**

$$NPV_d = SP - \sum_{t=1}^{n} \frac{CF_t}{(1+k)^t}$$     **(p. 683)**

where  $SP$ = estimated selling price of the assets
$CF_t$ = estimated incremental after-tax cash flows forgone as a result of selling the assets
$k$ = required rate of return to divest the assets

This equation can be used to determine whether a particular asset or set of assets should be sold by the company.

# QUESTIONS

**Q25-1.** What is the relationship between merger activity and business cycles?

**Q25-2.** Of the common motives for mergers, which motive would be more likely for a conglomerate merger than a vertical or horizontal merger? Why?

**Q25-3.** Why would a firm with negative earnings attract potential acquiring firms?

**Q25-4.** Briefly discuss the general steps involved in merger analysis.

**Q25-5.** How can a company's long-term objectives dictate the type of merger desired by a firm?

**Q25-6.** Relate the use of capital budgeting to analyzing a merger prospect. How are they related?

**Q25-7.** If a firm finances the acquisition of another company by borrowing funds, how does this affect the capital structure and financial leverage of the acquiring firm?

**Q25-8.** What is the underlying reason why hostile takeovers still occur, even with all the anti-takeover ammunition available?

**Q25-9.** Why do tender offers often involve bid prices that exceed market prices by 10 percent or more? After all, the stock should be available in the market at the market price.

**Q25-10.** Explain the meaning of *synergy,* and identify the types of mergers (vertical, horizontal, or conglomerate) in which it would frequently serve as a motive.

**Q25-11.** When a firm diversifies, it can reduce the variability of its returns. Yet, it can be argued that shareholders can diversify on their own by purchasing shares of a variety of firms, and that diversification by a firm provides no special advantage to shareholders. Comment on this statement.

**Q25-12.** Transit Corporation has seriously considered an attempt to acquire Beltway Corporation. Transit has planned a takeover attempt but is waiting for a bearish stock market before implementing it. What is the justification for such a strategy?

**Q25-13.** Pluto Corporation has just repurchased 20 percent of its outstanding shares of stock. Thus, Pluto becomes a more likely takeover target, since there is less outstanding stock necessary for a firm to gain control of in order to acquire it. Do you agree or disagree with this statement? Explain.

**Q25-14.** Explain in general terms how a proposed divestiture can be analyzed to determine whether it is feasible.

**Q25-15.** Comment on the following statement: "Divestitures that reduce a firm's degree of diversification increase risk and reduce the value of the firm."

## SELF-TEST PROBLEMS

Solutions to self-test problems appear on p. S1.

**SP25-1.** Ortego Corporation plans to acquire Hester Company for $25 million if this acquisition would generate a rate of return of at least 16 percent. Ortego believes that this acquisition would generate incremental cash flows of $15 million, $10 million, $5 million, and $4 million over the next four years, respectively. The assets of Hester Company will have completely deteriorated by the end of the fourth year. Should Ortego acquire Hester Company? Justify your answer.

**SP25-2.** Kemp Company plans to acquire Haden Company. The market price of Kemp's stock is $16. Kemp has offered $12 per share for Haden's stock. Determine the ratio of exchange, and explain the meaning of this ratio.

**SP25-3.** BYU Company has considered selling one of its businesses. It has received a bid for $19 million. If it sells the businesses, it expects to forgo cash flows of $6 million in the first year, $8 million in the second year, and $12 million in the third year. Given that BYU has a required rate of return of 14 percent, should it divest the business? Justify your answer.

## PROBLEMS

**P25-1.** Bernazard Company is considering the acquisition of Dotson Company for $11 million. Bernazard's plans are to use the resources of Dotson Company for two years and then sell the company. It expects to generate incremental cash flows of $2 million from Dotson at the end of each of the two years, and then it expects to sell Dotson Company for $8 million at the end of the second year. Bernazard would require a rate of return of 18 percent on this acquisition. Should Bernazard acquire Dotson Company? Justify your answer.

**P25-2.** Landry Company plans to acquire Utep Company. The market price of Landry's stock is $20. Landry has offered $5 per share for Utep's stock. Determine the ratio of exchange, and explain the meaning of this ratio.

**P25-3.** ASU Company considers selling one of its businesses for $4 million. It expects to forgo $1 million in each of the next four years as a result of selling the business now. Should ASU Company sell its business if it has a 20 percent required rate of return? Justify your answer.

## REFERENCES

Alexander, Gordon J., P. George Benson, and Joan M. Kampmeyer. "Investigating the Valuation Effects of Announcements of Voluntary Corporate Selloffs." *Journal of Finance* 39 (June 1984): 503–517.

Ashton, D. J., and D. R. Atkins. "A Partial Theory of Takeover Bids." *Journal of Finance* 39 (March 1984): 167–84.

Asquith, Paul. "Merger Bids, Uncertainty, and Stockholder Returns." *Journal of Financial Economics* 11 (April 1983): 51–84.

Asquith, Paul, and E. Han Kim. "The Impact of Merger Bids on the Participants Firms' Security Holders." *Journal of Finance* 37 (December 1982): 1209–28.

Asquith, Paul, Robert F. Bruner, and David W. Mullins, Jr. "The Gains to Bidding Firms from Merger." *Journal of Financial Economics* 11 (April 1983): 121–40.

Baron, David P. "Tender Offers and Management Resistance." *Journal of Finance* 38 (May 1983): 331–347.

Becketti, Sean. "Corporate Mergers and the Business Cycle." *Economic Review,* Federal Reserve Bank of Kansas City (May 1986): 13–26.

Bianco, Anthony. "Can the Corporate Raider Be Stopped in His Tracks?" *Business Week,* December 23, 1985, 65.

Choi, Dosoung, and George C. Philippatos. "An Examination of Merger Synergism." *Journal of Financial Research* 6 (Fall 1983): 239–56.

Davidson, Kenneth M. "Looking at the Strategic Impact of Mergers." *Journal of Business Strategy* 2 (Summer 1981): 13–22.

DeAngelo, Harry, and Edward M. Rice. "Antitakeover Charter Amendments and Stockholder Wealth." *Journal of Financial Economics* 11 (April 1983): 329–60.

Dodd, Peter. "Merger Proposals, Management Discretion and Stockholder Wealth." *Journal of Financial Economics* 5 (November 1977): 351–73.

"Goodrich: Something very drastic . . . had to be done." *Business Week,* July 1, 1985, 27.

Halpern, Paul. "Corporate Acquisitions: A Theory of Special Cases? A Review of Event Studies Applied to Acquisitions." *Journal of Finance* 38 (May 1983): 297–318.

Hearth, Douglas, and Janis K. Zaima. "Voluntary Corporate Divestitures and Value." *Financial Management* 13 (Spring 1984): 10–16.

Hoffmeister, J. Ronald, and Edward A. Dyl. "Predicting Outcomes of Cash Tender Offers." *Financial Management* 10 (Winter 1981): 50–58.

Jain, Prem C. "The Effect of Voluntary Sell-off Announcements on Shareholder Wealth." *Journal of Finance* 60 (March 1985): 209–24.

Keown, Arthur J., and John M. Pinkerton. "Merger Announcements and Insider Trading Activity: An Empirical Investigation." *Journal of Finance* 36 (September 1981): 855–70.

Kudla, Ronald J., and Thomas McIntish. "Valuation Consequences of Corporate Spin-offs." *Review of Business and Economic Research* (Winter 1983): 71–77.

Leontiades, Milton. "Rationalizing the Unrelated Acquisition." *California Management Review* 24 (Spring 1982): 5–14.

Lewellen, Wilbur G., and Michael G. Ferri. "Strategies for the Merger Game: Management and the Market." *Financial Management* 12 (Winter 1983): 25–35.

Linn, Scott C., and John J. McConnell. "An Empirical Investigation of the Impact of Antitakeover Amendments on Common Stock Prices." *Journal of Financial Economics* 11 (April 1983): 361–99.

Little, Royal. "Conglomerates Are Doing Better Than You Think." *Fortune*, May 28, 1984, 50–60.

"Merger Ethics, Anyone?" *Newsweek*, December 9, 1985, 46–47.

Miles, James A., and James D. Rosenfeld. "The Effect of Voluntary Spin-off Announcements on Shareholder Wealth." *Journal of Finance* (December 1983): 1597–1606.

Pittel, Leslie. "Smaller Can Be Prettier." *Forbes*, June 17, 1985, 206–208.

Pozdena, Randall J. "Takeovers: Good or Evil." *Federal Reserve Bank of San Francisco Weekly Letter*, January 3, 1986.

Rosenfeld, James D. "Additional Evidence on the Relation Between Divestiture Announcements and Shareholder Wealth." *Journal of Finance* 39 (December 1984): 1437–1448.

Ruback, Richard S. "The Cities Service Takeover: A Case Study." *Journal of Finance* 38 (May 1983): 319–330.

Salter, Malcolm S., and Wolf A. Weinhold. "Diversification via Acquisition: Creating Value." *Harvard Business Review* (July–August 1978): 166–76.

"Shark Repellents Said to Affect Value of Stock Slightly." *Wall Street Journal*, October 11, 1985, 60.

Sharp, J. Franklin. "Find the Right Partner for Your Company." *Financial Executive* (June 1983): 23–6.

"Splitting Up." *Business Week*, July 31, 1985, 50–55.

"Takeovers and Buyouts Clobber Blue-Chip Bondholders." *Business Week*, November 11, 1985, 113–14.

Walking, Ralph A., and Robert O. Edmister. "Determinants of Tender Offer Premiums." *Financial Analysts Journal* 41 (January–February 1985): 27–37.

Wansley, James W., William R. Lane, and Ho C. Yang. "Abnormal Returns to Acquired Firms by Type of Acquisition and Method of Payment." *Financial Management* 12 (Autumn 1983): 16–22.

Wansley, James W., Rodney L. Roenfeldt, and Philip L. Cooley. "Abnormal Returns from Merger Profiles." *Journal of Financial and Quantitative Analysis* 18 (June 1983): 149–62.

# CHAPTER 26

# FINANCIAL FAILURE

## FINANCIAL FAILURE IN PERSPECTIVE

In April 1986, Gearhart Industries, Inc., defaulted on $141.8 million of secured notes held by several insurance companies. In June 1987, Gearhart defaulted on an additional $54 million of unsecured bank loans by failing to make the required interest payments. The banks then exercised their right to demand immediate repayment of the entire loan principal. However, the banks did not immediately take legal action through the court system. Although the insurance companies had not demanded repayment of the notes, Gearheart announced that it does not have sufficient assets to repay all creditors

*Source:* "Gearhart Receives Demand by Banks for Debt Repayment," *Wall Street Journal,* June 23, 1987, p. 16.

and that it may be forced to seek protection under the federal bankruptcy laws.

Gearhart officials then met with representatives of its creditors to determine if an agreement can be reached that might involve one or more of the following provisions: (1) permit the repayment of principal over an extended period of time, (2) add collateral backing to the loan, or (3) permit the replacement of some debt with equity.

What other solutions might Gearhart and its lenders consider? If Gearhart does file for bankruptcy, what happens to Gearhart, the banks, and the insurance companies? What would happen to Gearhart's suppliers and employees? What are the different forms of bankruptcy? This chapter addresses these and other questions about financial failure.

The biggest challenge in financial management is dealing with risk. Some firms use conservative management to minimize risk, but this can cause returns to be insufficient. At the other extreme, some firms strive for very high returns and therefore are highly exposed to risk. The extreme adverse consequence of risk is failure. This chapter discusses the history of business failures, as well as their causes, symptoms, and remedies. The remedy chosen to deal with failure can have significant implications for both creditors and shareholders.

## FORMS OF FAILURE

There are varying degrees of business failure. **Economic failure** implies that the firm's operations are not providing an adequate return to shareholders to justify continued business. The opportunity cost of the shareholders' investment is to forgo alternative investments. If alternative investments offer a higher return without more risk, or lower risk without lower returns, shareholders are not receiving an adequate return. Thus, the solution is to liquidate the business, either in parts or in aggregate.

**Technical insolvency** is another type of failure, which implies that the firm can no longer meet contractual obligations to creditors. This is more severe than economic failure since the technically insolvent firm cannot continue unless creditors allow it to. Even if the book value of its assets exceeds liabilities, a firm could be technically insolvent due to a lack of liquidity. If creditors expect that the liquidity problem is temporary, they may be willing to let the business continue without forcing it into bankruptcy. However, when the market value of a firm's assets is less than its liabilities, the situation is more serious than just a lack of liquidity. A firm in this condition, known as **insolvency in bankruptcy,** cannot completely meet all of its liabilities even if it sells all of its assets.

## THE FAILURE RECORD

Figure 26.1 illustrates the trend in the number of business failures in the United States. Notice the increase in bankruptcies during recessionary periods such as 1974–1975 and 1982–1983. This indicates the susceptibility of firms to economic business cycles. The large increase in failures in 1978 is mainly due to the Bankruptcy Reform Act of 1978, which made it easier for firms to qualify for bankruptcy. In fact, some firms that were not actually failing qualified for bankruptcy anyway, leading to widespread abuse of this act. Consequently, in 1984 Congress amended the act with the Bankruptcy Amendments and Judgeship Act of 1984, which was designed to discourage such abuse.

In 1986 there were 61,183 business failures in the United States. A breakdown of failures by broad industry classes is shown in Table 26.1. More failures occurred in the commercial service industry than any other industry. In addition, the percentage increase in commercial service failures from 1985 was higher than that of any other industry.

**FIGURE 26.1**
**Annual Business
Failure Rate**

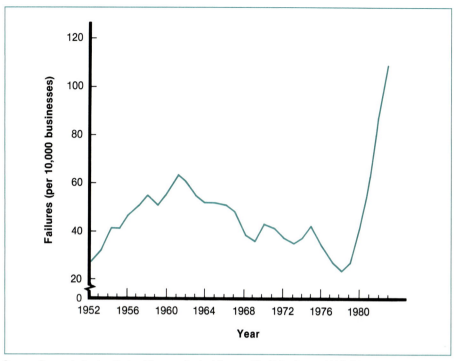

*Source: Economic Review,* Federal Reserve Bank of Kansas City (July–August 1984):34.

**TABLE 26.1  Classification of Business Failures**

| | Number of Business Failures | Percentage of Total Failures |
|---|---|---|
| Commercial service | 20,911 | 34.2% |
| Construction | 7,035 | 11.5 |
| Manufacturing and mining | 5,641 | 9.2 |
| Retail trade | 13,509 | 22.1 |
| Wholesale | 4,808 | 7.9 |
| Other | 9,279 | 15.2 |
| | 61,183 | 100.0% |

*Source:* U.S. Department of Commerce, *Survey of Current Business* 67 (April 1987):S–5.

## CHARACTERISTICS AFFECTING
## THE PROBABILITY OF FAILURE

Some of the more obvious financial management functions that if improperly managed could lead to financial failure are

- Financial leverage
- Inventory management
- Credit policy

- Dividend policy
- Diversification of sales

## Financial Leverage

A firm that obtains most of its funds through debt as opposed to equity incurs large periodic interest payments. The ability to cover these payments depends on the stability of cash flows. Some firms are overly optimistic about future cash inflows and therefore incur more debt than is reasonably safe. Yet, if a firm primarily obtains funds through equity rather than debt, it forgoes the tax benefits from interest expenses.

## Inventory Management

While an excessive inventory can avoid stock-outs, it ties up the funds that are used to support it. Thus, excessive inventories often require additional financing and place pressure on a firm's cash flow. A low level of inventory ties up less funds but can reduce cash inflows through lost sales if stock-outs occur.

## Credit Policy

Even if sales are strong, a cash squeeze can occur due to a long time lag between sales and cash inflows. Cash, not accounts receivable, is necessary to pay the bills. Firms that maintain a very relaxed credit policy may not only have a long time lag in generating cash, but may also experience bad debts.

## Dividend Policy

If a firm pays excessive dividends to its shareholders, it requires a greater amount of external financing for its operations, which may increase the cost of capital. Yet, if a firm pays low or no dividends, it may not satisfy shareholders and may therefore increase the rate of return required by shareholders (assuming that shareholders prefer some amount of dividends).

## Diversification of Sales

If a firm concentrates all of its resources on a single business, its performance will be highly susceptible to the factors affecting that business. By diversifying into a variety of businesses, aggregate sales, and therefore cash flow, can be stabilized. However, a firm must know its limitations. An attempt to diversify into areas in which the firm has no expertise could fail due to poor management and poor performance. Besides, diversification cannot eliminate the variability of cash flows caused by systematic factors such as economic conditions.

## Summary of Characteristics Causing Failure

In summary, cash inflows can be slowed or reduced due to a poor credit policy or inadequate product diversification. Cash outflows can be excessive due to poor management of financial leverage, inventories, and dividends. Any improper financial management decisions can force cash outflows to consistently exceed inflows and eventually lead to failure.

The possible reasons listed here for not meeting contractual obligations are especially harmful when they occur simultaneously. For example, a firm with volatile sales that has a large investment in assets, mostly supported by debt, is destined for failure. The preceding discussion implies that firms should assess their operating characteristics and then implement policies that will generate a sufficient amount of cash to cover contractual obligations.

Beyond general financial characteristics that are commonly monitored by all firms, a company's unique situation may make it more susceptible to failure. For this reason, the firm should ask itself the following questions:

- Will the firm's performance be greatly affected if competitors make technological advances?
- Will the managerial expertise of the firm be greatly affected if any particular manager dies or resigns?
- Are management and labor typically able to agree to terms without serious conflict?
- Can the firm survive if its major supplier cuts off supplies, or if a labor strike occurs?
- Can the firm survive a recession?

These questions do not definitively reveal whether a firm will fail, but they at least measure the firm's likelihood of failure should a disastrous event occur. Management is responsible for developing policies that will minimize the impact of adverse events on the firm's performance. Because such events are inevitable from time to time, financial managers must be prepared to deal with them.

## FORECASTING FAILURE

An efficient system for detecting symptoms of failure requires a complete data base to measure and monitor financial characteristics. The individual firm identifies the financial characteristics to be monitored and the financial ratios that can be used to measure those characteristics. For example, the firm may choose to use the debt ratio to monitor its debt levels over time, the sales to fixed assets ratio to determine whether fixed assets are excessive, and so on.

While it is useful to track these ratios using historical data, pro forma financial statements can also be valuable. From these statements, the anticipated financial ratios for the future can be derived. Even if symptoms of failure have not yet occurred, they may show up in the pro forma statements. Forecasting the financial variables reveals potential weaknesses of the firm, allowing it to take corrective action now in order to reduce the chances of failure. The sensitivity of the relevant financial ratios that measure the firm's financial health to future economic conditions should also be evaluated.

Consider the actual case of W. T. Grant, which filed for bankruptcy in October 1975.[1] After 1969 Grant became a continual net user of funds each year until it declared bankruptcy. That is, its operations could not generate a positive cash flow. In 1973 Standard & Poors downgraded Grant's bond issues. In the first quarter of 1974, Grant reduced its quarterly dividend. It then eliminated dividends altogether two quarters later.

In late 1974 Grant requested an extension on debt that was to come due in December. In addition, high-level management personnel were reorganized, and Grant's corporate operations were restructured during 1974. Even though Grant was experiencing serious financial problems prior to 1974, it apparently did not take major steps to correct the problems at that time.

## Z-Score Models for Forecasting Failure

To detect symptoms of failure, a variety of computer models are available. One of the most popular models is **discriminant analysis,** which can be used to identify financial characteristics that distinguish between successful firms and failing firms. While there are various ways in which discriminant analysis can be applied, one of the more common ways is illustrated in the following example. McMahon, Inc., a manufacturing company, desires to evaluate its financial condition. It assembles a list of firms that have been in a somewhat similar line of business and obtains financial ratios for all these firms. It also identifies those firms that are still healthy versus those firms that are not. Then, it applies discriminant analysis to the data in an attempt to identify the financial ratios that tend to differ significantly between the group of firms that are still healthy versus the group of firms that are not. In addition, the analysis is intended to imply the general size of these critical variables for the firms that are experiencing financial problems. For example, if firms in the industry of concern that had a liquidity ratio of less than .8 failed within three years after that point, the implication for McMahon is that it should maintain its liquidity ratio above .8.

Other ratios included in the discriminant analysis determine which ratios are significantly different (and therefore can discriminate) between the two groups of firms. The firm will then use these ratios to assess its own financial condition. By combining all the relevant financial ratios in a single equation, the firm can compute a single overall score (often referred to as a *Z-score*). This **Z-score model** was developed by Professor Edward Altman (see References at the end of this chapter) and is now used in some form by several firms.

---

1.    The information on W. T. Grant was adapted from Gary A. Giroux and Casper E. Wiggins, "Chapter XI and Corporate Resuscitation," *Financial Executive* 51 (December 1983): 37–41.

The equation generated by McMahon's analysis is

$$Z = 1.0X_1 + 0.1X_2 + .5X_3 - 3.0X_4 + 10.0X_5$$

where $X_1$ = current assets/current liabilities
$X_2$ = cost of goods sold/inventory
$X_3$ = sales/total assets
$X_4$ = debt/total assets
$X_5$ = earnings after taxes/sales

It is possible that some additional financial ratios were initially considered within the analysis but turned out to be similar for both healthy and weak firms. If so, these ratios are not useful for measuring the firm's financial condition, and are therefore omitted from the Z-score equation.

Assume that most of the healthy firms in the sample had a Z-score of 2.0 or better, while the weak firms generally had a Z-score of .9 or less. The zone of Z-scores representing only weak companies is sometimes referred to as the *danger zone*. Assume that there were a few healthy firms as well as a few weak firms that exhibited Z-scores within the range of .9 to 2.0. This may be called the *gray zone;* the model cannot discriminate between the healthy and weak firms that exhibit Z-scores within this range.

Once the firm has determined the Z-score ranges, it could compute its own Z-score and determine whether it is classified as healthy, weak, or in the gray (unclear) zone. Assume the following values for McMahon, Inc., based on the most recent financial statements:

$$X_1 = 1.5$$
$$X_2 = 8$$
$$X_3 = 2$$
$$X_4 = .5$$
$$X_5 = .07$$

Given this information, the Z-score is computed as

$$Z = 1.0(1.5) + .1(8) + 0.5(2) - 3.0(.5) + 10.0(.07)$$
$$= 1.5 + .8 + 1 - 1.5 + .7$$
$$= 2.5$$

Recall that a Z-score of 2.0 or higher classifies a firm as healthy. Thus, the Z-score model gives McMahon, Inc., a favorable evaluation over this year. However, consider the possibility that the company applied the Z-score model to the relevant ratios computed from the next five years of pro forma financial statements. Assume that the relevant ratios have been computed as shown in Table 26.2. Given this information, the Z-score has been computed for each of the next five years and is also displayed in Table 26.2. Figure 26.2 provides an illustration of the expected trend in the Z-score. Notice that by the third year, the Z-score is expected to be less than 2.0,

**TABLE 26.2   Assumed Ratios Based on Pro Forma Financial Statements: McMahon, Inc.**

| Variable | Current | Years Ahead | | | | |
|---|---|---|---|---|---|---|
| | | 1 | 2 | 3 | 4 | 5 |
| $X_1$ (current assets/current liabilities) | 1.50 | 1.40 | 1.30 | 1.30 | 1.20 | 1.20 |
| $X_2$ (cost of goods sold/ inventory) | 8.00 | 7.00 | 8.00 | 7.00 | 7.00 | 6.00 |
| $X_3$ (sales/total assets) | 2.00 | 2.00 | 2.00 | 1.60 | 1.40 | 1.20 |
| $X_4$ (debt/total assets) | .60 | .60 | .60 | .70 | .80 | .80 |
| $X_5$ (earnings after taxes/sales) | .07 | .08 | .07 | .05 | .05 | .03 |
| Z-score | 2.20 | 2.10 | 2.00 | 1.20 | .70 | .30 |

**FIGURE 26.2**
**Trend of Expected Z-Score over Time: McMahon, Inc.**

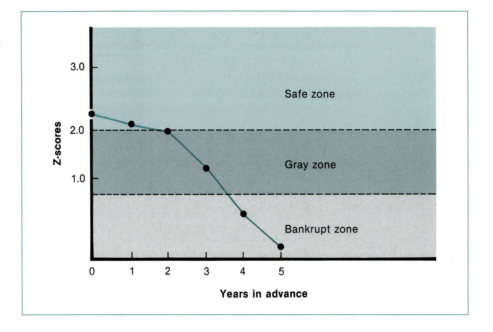

placing McMahon, Inc., into the gray zone. By the fourth year, the Z-score is expected to be below .9, thereby classifying McMahon, Inc., as a weak company.

By evaluating the expected Z-score over time, McMahon, Inc., is warned that its financial condition will be weakening by the third year and that it may fail by the fourth or fifth year. Knowing this information in advance, it can attempt to revise its operating plans in order to improve its projected financial conditions.

The Z-score model provides an overall rating of a firm as a measurement of the firm's health. In addition, it can forecast the firm's health over time (if pro forma financial statements are available). A review of Table 26.2 suggests that the main reasons for potential deterioration in McMahon's health are

- Reduction in liquidity
- Reduction in the efficiency by which inventories are converted into sales
- Reduction in the efficiency by which total assets are used to generate sales
- Increase in the debt level
- Reduction in earnings relative to assets

Firms can complement their normal financial planning tasks with some form of a failure-forecasting model that aggregates all financial characteristics into a single overall score or rating for the firm.

## Limitations of Failure-Forecasting Models

While failure-forecasting models can be useful, their limitations should be recognized. First, firms vary in characteristics even if they are in the same industry. Therefore, one firm may be able to live with higher debt ratio than another firm. Alternatively, some firms may experience serious problems even though they have avoided the generalized danger zones specified by the model. A ratio that at one time is not perceived as a problem can become a problem later. For example, a debt ratio of a certain size may have been acceptable in the past. Yet, if interest rates rise dramatically and the debt has variable rates that adjust to market conditions, the debt ratio could become the primary cause of failure.

## Research on Failure-Forecasting Models

Due to the importance of predicting financial failure, much research has attempted to determine whether failure could have been anticipated by the failure-forecasting models. Studies have often differed with respect to the time period analyzed, the industries analyzed, and the exact model applied to the data. Thus, it is difficult to generalize the results. However, much of the research found evidence that failing firms can be identified by these models one to two years prior to actual failure. The financial ratios commonly able to discriminate between failing and surviving firms include

- Working capital/total assets
- Net cash flow/total liabilities
- Current assets/current liabilities
- Working capital/sales
- Sales/total assets

While financial ratios measuring efficiency, leverage, and profitability are obviously very important, they were not always capable of predicting failure in the samples of firms examined. However, a recent study by Rose and Giroux found these types of ratios to be valuable indicators of future failure.

Most of the studies examining the ability to forecast financial failure used financial ratios of firms to develop the forecasts. Yet, one recent study by Giroux and Wiggins used particular events to forecast whether a firm would fail in the future. They found that the following events commonly occurred prior to failure.

- Requests by the firm to extend or reschedule its debt payments to creditors
- Reduction or complete elimination of dividends by firms
- Reporting of net losses by firms

While both surviving firms and firms that later failed reported these events, they were much more prevalent for the failing firms. Consequently, they could serve as signals of probable failure in the near future. Unfortunately, by the time these events occur, the firm is very likely already aware of its fate. After all, firms are not likely to request debt rescheduling or eliminate their dividend payout unless they are faced with serious cash flow problems.

### Failure Forecasting from a Creditor's Perspective

Not only is each individual firm concerned about avoiding failure, but its creditors are concerned as well. They are well aware that if the firm fails, only a portion of their loan will be repaid, or maybe not even a portion. Any firms that commonly provide credit will staff a credit analysis department to assess whether a loan should be granted. Their key decisions are whether the potential borrower is creditworthy and what interest rate to charge (if the loan is to be offered). Their decisions are based on an evaluation of the firm's historical and pro forma financial statements. When creditors detect one or a few major problems that could lead the borrowing firm to failure, they will provide a loan only if the borrowing firm is able to correct these deficiencies. If a loan is granted, one of the typical provisions is that the firm periodically update its financial statements so that its financial condition can be monitored. It is hoped that the combined efforts of the firm and its creditors will detect symptoms of failure in time to cure any potential deficiency. However, even with these efforts, some firms will still be unable to meet their contractual payments. In these cases, some of the following remedies may be considered.

## INFORMAL REMEDIES FOR A FAILING FIRM

When a debtor firm and its creditors realize that it is experiencing financial difficulties, they may consider the following informal remedies:

- Extension
- Composition
- Private liquidation

### Extension

If a debtor is having difficulty in meeting payments owed to creditors, these creditors may allow for an **extension,** providing additional time for the firm to generate the necessary cash. Obviously, creditors would prefer their repayment on time, but receiving late payments in full may be preferred to receiving only a portion of their loans back if the firm goes bankrupt and its assets are liquidated. An extension should be considered only if creditors believe that the firm's financial problems are temporary and can be resolved. If formal bankruptcy is inevitable, an extension may only stall the liquidation process and possibly reduce the liquidation value of the firm's assets.

If creditors allow an extension, they may require that the debtor firm abide by various stipulations. For example, they may disallow dividend payments, so that the firm will retain enough funds to repay its loans, if given enough time. The firm will likely agree to any stipulations required for an extension, since the alternative could be bankruptcy.

No creditor is forced to go along with an extension. Creditors who would prefer some alternative action must be paid off in full if an extension is to be allowed. If too many creditors disapprove of an extension, it would not be feasible to enact, as all disapproving creditors would first need to be paid what they are owed.

## Composition

If creditors decide that an extension is not feasible, they can negotiate with the debtor to a **composition** agreement, which will provide them with a pro rata settlement. For example, the agreement may call for creditors to receive seventy cents on every dollar owed to them. This partial repayment may be as much or more than creditors would receive from formalized bankruptcy proceedings. In addition, the debtor firm may be able to survive, since its interest payments are reduced by the agreement. As with an extension, any creditors dissatisfied with a composition agreement must be paid in full.

## Private Liquidation

With either an extension or a composition, the agreement between the debtor firm and the creditors allows the firm to continue its business. If neither alternative is feasible, the creditors may request that the firm liquidate its assets and distribute the funds received from liquidation to them, a procedure called **private liquidation.** While this can be achieved through formalized bankruptcy proceedings, it can also be accomplished informally outside the court system—in less time and at less cost, as it avoids excessive legal fees.

All creditors must agree to a private liquidation, or else an alternative remedy is necessary. To enact the process, an outside party with expertise in liquidation is normally assigned to liquidate the failing firm's assets; and once the assets are liquidated, the remaining funds are distributed to the creditors on a pro rata basis.

## FORMAL REMEDIES FOR A FAILING FIRM

If creditors cannot agree to any of the informal remedies, the solution to the firm's financial problems will be worked out formally in the court system. The formal remedies are either *reorganization* or *liquidation under bankruptcy* (both defined later in this section). Whether a debtor firm should reorganize or liquidate depends on its estimated value under each alternative. If the debtor firm's estimated value as a going concern is clearly above the liquidation value, it should be reorganized. Otherwise it should be liquidated.

## Reorganization

In the case of **reorganization** (often referred to as *Chapter 11*), the debtor or the creditors must file a petition. The bankruptcy court then appoints a committee of creditors (usually the seven creditors with the largest claims against the firm) to restructure the debtor firm's operations and possibly its capital structure as well. Legal and financial liabilities are frozen while management develops a restructuring plan for the firm's operations and/or capital position. Any revision in capital structure would likely involve a greater use of equity (through issuing new common stock) and a corresponding reduction in debt in order to alleviate the pressure of periodic interest payments on cash flow. No change is required in managerial structure, although some managers may decide to resign. Once the restructuring plan is completed, it is submitted to the court for approval. The restructuring plan must be approved by the creditors holding two-thirds of the dollar value of claims.

Creditors often have different objectives and therefore disagree on the reorganization decision. Institutional creditors such as commercial banks typically prefer to recover their claims as quickly as possible and may therefore prefer alternatives to reorganization. Trade creditors, however, may have a greater interest in preserving the failing firm as a customer and consequently prefer that the firm be reorganized.

Once a reorganization plan is approved, a trustee will then allocate new securities to the old security holders. In some cases, the current management acts as the trustee. The procedure for allocating new securities must be viewed as fair and equitable by all involved, or it will not be initiated. Frequent updates on financial data and forecasts are usually required by creditors, even after the reorganization is official.

Some of the more recent filings for Chapter 11 include Endotronics, Inc.; Air Atlanta; Sharon Steel; and Dunes Hotel & Casinos (all in 1987). The most publicized recent filing was by Texaco, Inc., in April 1987, as a result of its legal battle with Pennzoil Company.

Several filings for Chapter 11 in recent years have raised concern about whether the bankruptcy laws are used in the way they were intended. One example is Johns-Manville Corporation, which in 1982 was liable for damage claims relating to asbestos. By filing for Chapter 11, the company was able to continue its normal operations while it created a special fund that would compensate victims over time.

A second classic filing for Chapter 11 led to the court case *National Labor Relations Board v. Bildisco and Bildisco, Inc.,* in 1984. The U.S. Supreme Court ruled in this case that a company undergoing Chapter 11 may modify its collective bargaining agreements under certain conditions. Later in that year, Congress added amendments to the Bankruptcy Code

## FINANCIAL MANAGEMENT IN PRACTICE

### TURNAROUND SPECIALISTS: A LAST-RESORT REMEDY FOR FAILING FIRMS

A failing firm that prefers to avoid liquidation will typically attempt to reorganize. A group of businesses that specialize in helping firms reorganize are called "turnaround specialists" because of their ability to turn a failing firm into a success. Of course, they cannot guarantee that the failing firm can be saved. If it is, the failing firm either pays the turnaround specialist a salary or sometimes offers part of its equity (shares of stock) as compensation.

Turnaround specialists typically have been involved in business consulting for a number of years or have previously been executives of successful corporations. Some executives opt for early retirement and act as a turnaround specialist on a part-time basis.

One of the more difficult tasks of a turnaround specialist is suggesting changes that will adversely affect employees. For example, a common suggestion to a failing firm may be to sell off a division to another firm or to discontinue production of particular products. These decisions can cause a shift in the tasks performed by various employees and may even result in some firings.

*Source: USA Today, June 23, 1987, 6B.*

Well-known turnaround specialists include Gresanti, Galef, and Goldress, Inc.; Hambrecht & Quist, Inc.; Victor Palmerieri; Sanford C. Sigoloff; and Stanley Hiller, Jr. Hiller was hired to "turn around" Borg-Warner Corporation's York International Corporation in 1986. Hiller was hired by Bekins Company in 1978 and helped Bekins achieve an operating profit of $8.5 million by 1983. He earned $1.25 million on his stock options compensation. Sigoloff was hired by Wickes Company in 1982, three weeks before it filed for reorganization. By 1983 Wickes had improved and dropped its petition for reorganization. Sigoloff was retained as one of its managers. In 1985 Wickes generated a net income of $76.1 million, and Sigoloff received $1.5 million in salary and bonuses.

Other well-known firms that have used turnaround specialists include Penn Central, CMX Corporation, Nutritional Foods Corporation, and Baldwin-United Corporation. Many failing firms elect not to use a turnaround specialist, either because they are unaware of their problems, believe they can resolve the problem without help, or believe that there is no hope for a remedy. Also, some failing firms may not be willing to pay the high fees charged by turnaround specialists.

that established standards for whether collective bargaining agreements can be rejected.

In April 1983 Wilson Foods filed a petition for Chapter 11 and then rejected collective bargaining agreements covering two-thirds of its employees. Its wages were reduced by 40 to 50 percent. Wilson's petition showed a net worth of more than $67 million.

In September 1983 Continental Airlines filed a petition for Chapter 11 and then rejected contracts with several unions. Some employees were laid off and wages were reduced by as much as 50 percent for some positions.

The preceding examples suggest that companies may be able to use petition for reorganization as a method of reducing operating costs. Until bankruptcy laws are revised, this method will probably be used more frequently in the future.

## Liquidation under Bankruptcy

When debtors and creditors cannot reach some informal agreement, and reorganization is not an attractive solution, **liquidation under bankruptcy** (often referred to as *Chapter 7*) is the only choice left. As with reorganization, a petition must be filed by either the debtor or the creditors. The liquidation procedures for bankruptcy are listed under Chapter 7 of the Bankruptcy Reform Act.

The failing firm is obligated to file a list of creditors along with up-to-date financial statements. A trustee is appointed to sell existing assets and allocate the funds received to the creditors. Secured creditors are paid with the proceeds from the sales of any assets serving as their collateral. Unsecured debt is paid in the following order of priority:

**1.** Expense of administering the firm's bankruptcy proceedings (court costs, accounting, and legal fees).
**2.** Unsecured claims after the bankruptcy petition is filed but before a trustee is appointed.
**3.** Wages (up to $2,000 per employee) owed over the ninety days prior to filing for bankruptcy.
**4.** Taxes owed to federal, state, and local governments.
**5.** Claims of unsecured creditors.

Remaining funds (if there are any) after covering all of the claims in the preceding list would be used to pay preferred stockholders (up to the par

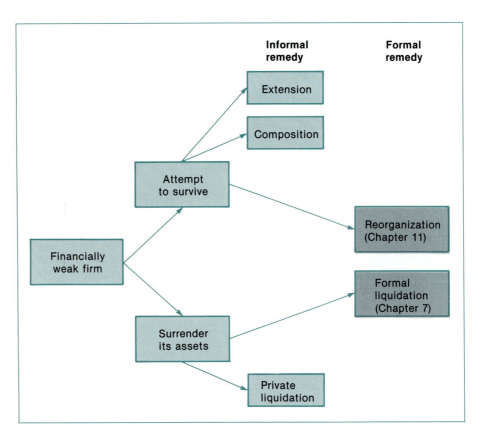

**FIGURE 26.3**

**Possible Remedies for a Failing Firm**

**TABLE 26.3** Comparison of Remedies for a Failing Firm

| Remedies | Description of Remedy |
|---|---|
| **Informal remedies** | |
| ■ Extension | Debtor continues operations and is granted additional time to make payment. |
| ■ Composition | Debtor continues operations and agrees to pay creditors only a portion of what it owes them, on a pro rata basis. |
| ■ Private liquidation | Debtor's assets are liquidated, and proceeds are distributed to creditors according to an informal agreement. |
| **Formal remedies** | |
| ■ Reorganization | Debtor continues operations and reorganizes its operations and possibly its capital structure in an attempt to resolve existing financial problems. |
| ■ Liquidation under bankruptcy | Debtor's assets are liquidated, and proceeds are distributed to creditors in order of priority according to Chapter 7 of the Bankruptcy Reform Act. |

value). Should there be anything left after paying preferred stockholders, it would go to common stockholders on a per share basis.

Figure 26.3 summarizes the remedies for a firm experiencing financial problems. It may first attempt to work out an informal arrangement with creditors. If an agreement cannot be reached, formalized court proceedings are likely. The possible solutions for the firm are compared in Table 26.3. Under liquidation (whether private or through the court system), the firm is terminated. Under the other alternatives, the operations continue.

## SUMMARY

Many causes of financial failure can be related to financial management. While some uncontrollable economic factors (such as the economy's strength) are influential, the firm's management must be held responsible for maintaining exposure to such outside factors to a tolerable degree. If the firm's management dedicates sufficient resources toward monitoring and evaluating its key financial characteristics, it should be able to detect and cure any weakness of the firm before it becomes too serious. Should the firm experience serious financial difficulties, it must work out an arrangement with its creditors to improve its financial health. As a last resort, it can liquidate its assets, leaving the creditors with the market value of what remains.

## KEY TERMS

**Composition** Informal agreement whereby creditors accept a pro rata partial repayment on credit provided.

**Discriminant analysis** Statistical model commonly used to detect financial characteristics distinguishing between a group of failing firms and a group of non-failing firms.

**Economic failure** When a firm's operations are

not providing a return to shareholders adequate to justify continued business.

**Extension** Additional time allowed for a failing firm to meet payment obligations of its creditors.

**Insolvency in bankruptcy** When the market value of a firm's assets are less than its liabilities.

**Liquidation under bankruptcy** Formalized solution to bankruptcy in which a failing firm files a list of creditors and a trustee is appointed to sell off existing assets and allocate funds received to the creditors.

**Private liquidation** When creditors request a failing firm to informally liquidate its assets and distribute the funds received from liquidation to them.

**Reorganization** A formalized solution to bankruptcy in which a committee of creditors works with the bankruptcy court to restructure the firm's operations and capital structure.

**Technical insolvency** When a firm can no longer meet contractual obligations to creditors.

**Z-score model** Used to rate a firm in order to determine whether it is approaching failure.

## QUESTIONS

**Q26-1.** What is the difference between economic failure and technical insolvency?

**Q26-2.** Describe the breakdown of failures by industry classification.

**Q26-3.** Look at any business periodical that identifies firms which have recently failed. What are the most common explanations as to why these firms failed?

**Q26-4.** How can poor inventory management cause a firm to fail?

**Q26-5.** How can poor credit policies cause a firm to fail?

**Q26-6.** Why would a firm apply a failure-forecasting model to its own pro forma statements?

**Q26-7.** What are some limitations of failure-forecasting models?

**Q26-8.** Describe the use of an extension to deal with financial difficulties.

**Q26-9.** What is the key difference between a *private liquidation* and *composition?*

**Q26-10.** What are the alternative formal remedies for bankruptcy, and how would creditors decide which formal remedy to use (assuming that the informal remedies could not be agreed upon)?

**Q26-11.** Why is a *private liquidation* sometimes preferred over *liquidation under bankruptcy?*

**Q26-12.** How would *reorganization* possibly make a failing firm successful?

**Q26-13.** What is the meaning of the "gray zone" when analyzing results of a failure-forecasting model?

**Q26-14.** Why should failure-forecasting models be developed from a sample of firms that have similar business characteristics of the firm in question?

**Q26-15.** If you, as a creditor to a failing firm, desire to get whatever you can as soon as possible, would you prefer a *composition* or an *extension?* Why?

# REFERENCES

Aharony, Joseph, Charles P. Jones, and Itzhak Swary. "An Analysis of Risk and Return Characteristics of Corporate Bankruptcy Using Capital Market Data." *Journal of Finance* 35 (September 1980): 1001–16.

Altman, Edward I. "Exploring the Road to Bankruptcy." *Journal of Business Strategy* 4 (Fall 1983): 36–41.

———. "Financial Ratios, Discriminant Analysis and the Prediction of Corporate Bankruptcy." *Journal of Finance* 23 (September 1968): 589–609.

———. "A Further Empirical Investigation of the Bankruptcy Cost Question." *Journal of Finance* 39 (September 1984): 629–42.

Altman, Edward I., and Menachem Brenner. "Information Effects and Stock Market Response to Signs of Firm Deterioration." *Journal of Financial and Quantitative Analysis* 16 (March 1981): 35–52.

Altman, Edward I., Robert G. Haldeman, and P. Narayanan. "Zeta Analysis: A New Model to Identify Bankruptcy Risk of Corporations." *Journal of Banking and Finance* 1 (June 1977): 29–54.

Altman, Edward I., and Joseph Spivack. "Predicting Bankruptcy: The Value Line Relative Financial Strength System vs. the Zeta Bankruptcy Classification Approach." *Financial Analysts Journal* 39 (November–December 1983): 60–67.

Ang, James S., Jess H. Chua, and John J. McConnell. "The Administrative Costs of Corporate Bankruptcy: A Note." *Journal of Finance* 37 (March 1982): 219–26.

Clark, Truman A., and Mark I. Weinstein. "The Behavior of the Common Stock of Bankrupt Firms." *Journal of Finance* 38 (May 1983): 489–504.

Collins, Robert A. "An Empirical Comparison of Bankruptcy Prediction Models." *Financial Management* 9 (Summer 1980): 52–57.

Evans, Ben. "Accountants' Signals of Approaching Bad Debts." *Credit & Financial Management* 86 (September 1984): 27–30.

Giroux, Gary A., and Casper E. Wiggins. "An Events Approach to Corporate Bankruptcy." *Journal of Bank Research* 15 (Autumn 1984): 179–187.

———. "Chapter XI and Corporate Resuscitation." *Financial Executive* (December 1983): 37–41.

Grimmig, Robert J. "Corporate Bankruptcy." *Journal of Commercial Bank Lending* 63 (November 1981): 2–11.

Kalaba, Robert E., Terence C. Langetieg, Nima Rasakhoo, and Mark I. Weinstein. "Estimation of Implicit Bankruptcy Costs." *Journal of Finance* 39 (July 1984): 629–42.

Rohrer, Julie. "The Imperfect Art of Forecasting Bankruptcies." *Institutional Investor* 16 (September 1982): 145–150.

Rose, Peter S., and Gary A. Giroux. "Predicting Corporate Bankruptcy: An Analytical and Empirical Evaluation." *Review of Business and Economic Research* 19 (Spring 1984): 1–12.

Scott, James. "The Probability of Bankruptcy." *Journal of Banking and Finance* 5 (September 1981): 317–44.

Scott, James H., Jr. "Bankruptcy, Secured Debt, and Optimal Capital Structure." *Journal of Finance* 32 (March 1977): 1–21.

Warner, Jerold B. "Bankruptcy Costs: Some Evidence." *Journal of Finance* 32 (May 1977): 339–49.

White, Michelle J. "Bankruptcy Costs and the New Bankruptcy Code." *Journal of Finance* 38 (May 1983): 477–88.

# CHAPTER 27

# INTERNATIONAL FINANCIAL MANAGEMENT

## INTERNATIONAL FINANCIAL MANAGEMENT IN PERSPECTIVE

The following performance results of companies were partially attributable to the U.S. dollar's weakness during 1986 and 1987:

- Tobacco-related revenues of Phillip Morris Companies, Inc., increased by $887 million in 1986.
- Campbell Soup Company's international earnings increased by 38 percent in 1986.
- Polaroid Corporation's international sales increased by 22 percent in the first quarter of 1987.
- Chrysler Corporation's sales were strong in the first quarter of 1987, at least in part because comparably equipped Japanese models were selling in the United States for as much as $2,000 more than Chrysler automobiles.

Not all U.S. companies were favorably affected, however. The Limited, Inc., which imports fifty percent of the products it sells in the United States, incurred higher costs as a result of the weak dollar. It responded by using more domestic sources of apparel. Some U.S. companies that had financed with foreign currencies were also adversely affected by the weak dollar.

Why does a weak dollar favorably affect companies such as Phillip Morris, Campbell Soup, and Polaroid? How would a strong dollar affect these companies? Why are some companies affected in different ways by a change in the value of the dollar? How would a firm's investment and financing strategies be influenced by expectations of a strong or weak dollar? This chapter addresses these questions.

Over the last two decades, multinational corporations (MNCs) have established subsidiaries throughout the world. MNCs such as Exxon, Dow Chemical, American Brands, Colgate-Palmolive, and Gillette typically generate more than half of their sales from outside the United States. Even smaller companies have increased their import or export business over time. Firms frequently reduce their cost of production by purchasing cheaper foreign supplies or by establishing a subsidiary where labor and land costs are low. In addition, they may be able to generate higher revenues by marketing their products in foreign markets. They may stabilize their cash flows, as well, by diversifying their business among foreign markets.

Along with the potential benefits, international business may also expose a firm to exchange rate movements and other types of risk. This chapter first provides a background of the international financial markets utilized by corporations and then describes what determines a corporation's exposure to exchange rate fluctuations. Finally, it explains how financial management policies are influenced by international conditions. Corporations that capitalize on benefits while minimizing exposure to the risks of international business may be able to increase shareholder wealth.

## EUROMARKETS

Firms engaged in international business may find reason to either borrow or invest in foreign currencies. For example, they may invest in a foreign security so that upon maturity, the proceeds can be used to cover a payable due in that same currency. Conversely, they may invest or borrow a foreign currency because the foreign interest rate is more attractive than the domestic interest rate. Numerous commercial banks accept deposits and provide loans in a variety of foreign currencies. These banks make up the **Eurocurrency market.** It became popular in the 1960s, when U.S. regulations restricted loans from U.S.-based banks to foreign subsidiaries of U.S. corporations, forcing subsidiaries to borrow from banks near their location (primarily Europe). In addition, other U.S. regulations such as interest rate ceilings and bank reserve requirements encouraged both banking and nonbanking corporations to do business in the Eurocurrency market, where regulations did not exist.

Deposits and loans in the Eurocurrency market are normally of large denomination (the equivalent of $1 million or more). Thus, the Eurocurrency market is sometimes described as a *wholesale market*. The maturities of the deposits and loans are short-term, typically one year or less. However, longer-term loans called **Eurocredit loans,** which commonly have maturities of five to seven years, can be obtained from the banks.

If firms prefer long-term financing, they can utilize the **Eurobond market,** where bonds are denominated in a variety of currencies and sold to investors in numerous countries. Large well-known corporations use the Eurobond market as a source of funds. Ford Motor Credit Company issued bonds in the Eurobond market in May 1987; Toyota Motor Credit Company issued bonds in this market in June 1987. Investment bankers act as financial intermediaries in the Eurobond market by placing bonds of the issuing firm with investors.

If corporations can use these Euromarkets to either generate more interest income on short-term funds or reduce their financing costs, they can improve their returns and therefore increase shareholder wealth. Corporations may also conduct investment or financing transactions in the Euromarkets to hedge against exchange rate movements, as will be explained shortly.

## FOREIGN EXCHANGE MARKETS

When firms participate in international business, they commonly need to buy or sell foreign currencies. A foreign exchange market is available to accommodate such needs. Numerous banks participate in this market, acting as intermediaries between firms that want to buy or sell specific currencies. They quote exchange rates, or the number of one currency needed to purchase another currency. The market is not visible in the way that stock

**FIGURE 27.1**
**Exchange Rate Movements of Major Foreign Currencies**

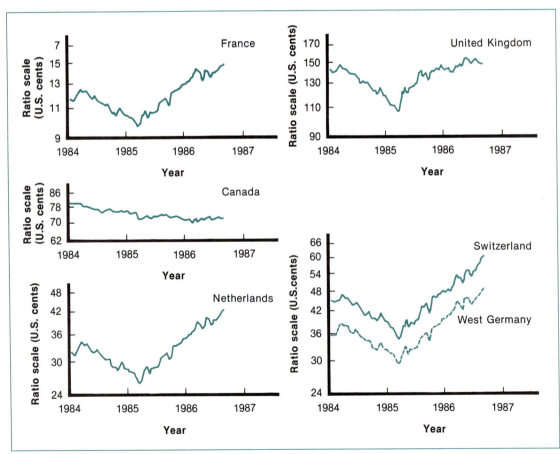

Source: Adapted from *Federal Reserve Chart Book.* Board of Governors, Federal Reserve System.

exchanges are, where trading floors exist. Instead, currency transactions are negotiated over a telecommunications network.

Banks participating in the foreign exchange market offer currencies on a *spot* and a *forward* basis. The **spot rate** refers to the rate quoted for immediate exchange, while the **forward rate** refers to the rate quoted for exchange at some specified future date. Figure 27.1 shows recent movements in the spot exchange rate of major foreign currencies against the dollar. Most foreign currencies were generally **depreciating** (declining in value) during the early 1980s until 1985, when they began to **appreciate** (increase in value). As shown in the figure, movements in European currencies are highly correlated.

A change in the exchange rate is important to firms that engage in international trade, since it affects the prices paid for goods denominated in foreign currencies.

| Example | If a U.S. car dealer is charged 40,000 German marks for each BMW automobile, and a mark is worth $.50, the price per car paid by the dealer is $20,000 (40,000 marks × $.50 per mark). However, if the mark value changes to $.60, the price paid for each BMW by the dealer would be $24,000 (40,000 marks × $.60 per mark). The increased payment is not due to the BMW manufacturer changing its price, but to the change in the exchange rate. |
|---|---|

This example illustrates why exchange rates are closely monitored by firms that import foreign goods. As exchange rates change, exporters can be affected as well, even if their bill is invoiced in their home currency. In the preceding example, the BMW manufacturer could lose business to U.S. customers as the appreciation of the mark raises the price paid by U.S. customers.

## DETERMINANTS OF EXCHANGE RATES

Exchange rates are determined by market forces. For example, if the demand for foreign currency by U.S. firms and consumers suddenly becomes much greater than the supply of that foreign currency for sale, this causes a shortage of that currency in the foreign exchange market. Like any commodity, a currency's price will rise in reaction to the shortage. Conversely, if the supply of a foreign currency exceeds demand, the equilibrium price of the currency decreases. Some of the more common factors affecting the supply of and demand for a currency are

- Relative inflation rates
- Relative interest rates
- Central bank intervention
- Relative income levels
- Government trade barriers

Each factor is briefly discussed here.

## Relative Inflation Rates

Given two countries that trade extensively with each other, the country that experiences higher inflation tends to increase its demand for the other country's goods, since the prices of foreign goods may appear to be lower. In addition, the foreign demand for goods in the high inflation country tends to decrease because of the inflated prices. Thus, a currency in a highly inflated country is expected to depreciate, other things being equal.

Figure 27.2 illustrates the inflation differential between the United States and other countries. The inflation differential is calculated here as the average U.S. inflation rate minus the foreign inflation rate. During the late 1970s the U.S. inflation rate was generally higher than foreign inflation rates (as represented by the positive differential), and the dollar was weakening. Conversely, in 1982 and 1983 the U.S. inflation rate was lower than that of many foreign countries, and the dollar was strengthening. In some other periods, the link between the inflation differential and dollar value was counteracted by one of the other factors that affect the dollar.

Some currencies of less developed countries such as Mexico and Argentina have weakened substantially over time. For example, in 1985 it took 250 pesos to purchase a U.S. dollar. By 1987 the exchange rate was 1,000 pesos per dollar. The high inflation rate of Mexico and other less developed countries was a major reason for depreciation of their currencies.

## Relative Interest Rates

High interest rates can attract foreign funds and therefore create a demand for the local currency. The relatively high interest rate in the United States compared to other countries during the early 1980s encouraged firms and individual investors in foreign countries to purchase U.S. securities. This was a major reason for dollar appreciation during the early 1980s.

## Central Bank Intervention

The central bank of a particular country may prefer to adjust the value of its currency in order to influence the economy. For example, the strong U.S. dollar during the 1981–1984 period adversely affected U.S. exporting firms. Foreign customers reduced their demand for U.S. goods because the dollar was expensive, thereby causing a reduction in U.S. production and employment. In response, the U.S. government chose to weaken the dollar in order to create more foreign demand for U.S. goods and therefore more U.S. jobs. To this end, the Federal Reserve Bank periodically intervened in the foreign exchange markets and sold U.S. dollars in exchange for foreign currencies. The Federal Reserve Bank flooded the foreign exchange market with dollars and thus placed downward pressure on the dollar's value. Yet, this impact is sometimes only temporary when other factors (such as those mentioned earlier) force the dollar's movement in the other direction.

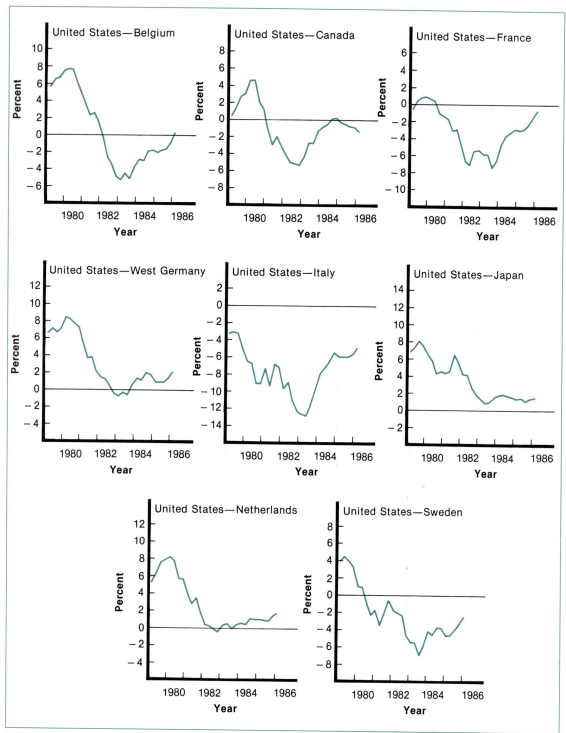

**FIGURE 27.2**
**Inflation Differential
between the
United States and
Major Countries**

*Source:* Adapted from *International Economic Conditions,* Federal Reserve Bank of St. Louis, August 1986, p. 4.

* Comparison of rates of change in consumer price index over corresponding four-quarter periods. For example, the U.S.–Belgium inflation differential for 1/77 (the first quarter of 1977) is computed by subtracting the percentage change in the Belgian CPI over the 1/76–1/77 period from the percentage change in the U.S. CPI over the same four-quarter period. Data are seasonally adjusted.

### Relative Income Levels

Given two countries that trade with each other, a country that experiences a relatively large increase in national income will likely increase its demand for foreign goods. This places upward pressure on the foreign currency's value and downward pressure on the local currency's value. Thus, a currency in a country experiencing relatively strong growth in national income is expected to depreciate, other things being equal.

### Government Trade Barriers

If the domestic government imposes trade barriers that effectively reduce local demand for a foreign country's goods, the domestic country's demand for the foreign currency decreases. This places downward pressure on the value of the foreign currency (assuming that there is no retaliation by the foreign government). One of the more common trade barriers used is a **quota,** which limits the amount of a particular good that can be imported. An alternative trade barrier is a **tariff,** which is a tax imposed on imported goods. Either type of trade barrier can influence the volume of trade transactions, which in turn affects a currency's value.

Because exchange rates are influenced by several factors, they are difficult to forecast. For example, even though a country experiences relatively high inflation, its currency may appreciate due to other factors (such as high interest rates and the imposition of trade barriers) that offset the impact of high inflation.

MNCs monitor all these factors discussed here in order to anticipate future movements in the foreign currencies that they will be purchasing or receiving. Their forecasts of future exchange rates determine whether they should attempt to *hedge,* or insulate against exchange rate fluctuations. The measurement and management of exchange rate risk is discussed in the following section.

## IDENTIFICATION OF EXCHANGE RATE RISK

The motives for conducting international business are obvious. To capitalize on these potential advantages, however, often requires that a firm expose itself to various forms of exchange rate risk.

### Transaction Exposure

Firms that conduct international business experience **transaction exposure,** or exposure of international transactions to exchange rate fluctuations. The overall impact of a weak or strong currency depends on the firm's characteristics. A weak dollar can benefit U.S. exporting firms by reducing the prices paid by foreign customers for U.S. goods. For example, a Swiss company would pay 5,000 Swiss francs for a $2,000 computer if a franc were worth $.40 ($2\frac{1}{2}$ francs per dollar) but only 4,000 francs for the computer if a franc were worth $.50 (2 francs per dollar). Foreign demand for the computers is likely to be higher when the Swiss franc is stronger (and therefore when the dollar is weaker).

A weak dollar can also be beneficial to U.S. firms that have invested in foreign financial assets, since the currency denominating the investment would be worth more dollars over time.

| | |
|---|---|
| **Example** | Consider a firm that converted $300,000 to British pounds to purchase British Treasury bills, when the spot rate of the pound was $1.50. The firm obtained 200,000 pounds ($300,000/$1.50 per pound) from this conversion. If the Treasury bills offered a yield of 10 percent, the firm's investment would be worth 220,000 pounds at the end of one year (200,000 pounds × 1.1). If the pound appreciated to, say, $1.70 by the end of the year, the pounds would convert back to $374,000 (220,000 pounds × $1.70 per pound), resulting in a return of 24.67 percent (gain of $74,000 relative to the initial investment of $300,000). |

A weak dollar also boosts the dollar amount of earnings remitted by subsidiaries to the U.S.–based parent. For example, if a British subsidiary of a U.S. firm remitted 1 million pounds to the U.S. parent when the pound's spot rate was $1.50, the U.S. parent would receive $1.5 million. Yet, if the pound were worth $1.70, the U.S. parent would receive $1.7 million.

A weak dollar can also adversely affect U.S. firms under various conditions. U.S. firms that import materials must pay more dollars in exchange for a particular amount of a foreign currency. The BMW example provided earlier demonstrates how prices of U.S. imports can be affected by a weak dollar.

A weak dollar can also raise the cost of financing to corporations that borrowed a foreign currency.

| | |
|---|---|
| **Example** | Consider a U.S. firm that wishes to borrow $1 million. Rather than borrow dollars at the prevailing 9 percent interest rate, it borrows 2 million German marks at the prevailing German interest rate of 6 percent and immediately converts them into $1 million at the spot exchange rate of $.50 per mark (2 marks per dollar). A year later, it plans to repay the loan plus interest of 2.12 million marks (2 million marks × 1.06). By this time, the dollar has weakened to be worth 1.67 marks ($.60 per mark). Consequently, the firm needs $1,272,000 (2.12 million marks × $.60 per mark) to repay the loan. The effective interest rate paid on this loan is 27.2 percent ($272,000/$1,000,000). Thus, even though the firm pays a lower interest rate by borrowing marks instead of dollars, this advantage is more than offset by the weak dollar. |

Because MNCs are involved in a wide variety of international transactions, the impact of a weak or strong dollar on their performance can be difficult to determine. It is nearly impossible to assess the magnitude by which a strong or weak dollar affects each of the firm's operations. Some operations may be affected favorably while others are affected unfavorably by a change in the dollar's value. The *net* impact depends on the composition of international business operations conducted by the firm. For example, Honeywell exports more than it imports from its foreign operations and therefore benefits overall from a weaker dollar. Eastman Kodak also benefits from a weaker dollar and was adversely affected by a strong dollar over the 1980–84 period. It estimated that if 1980 exchange rates remained constant up to 1985, its earnings would have been about $3.5 billion higher over this five-year period.

## Economic Exposure

Firms must also be concerned with **economic exposure,** which represents any exposure of cash flows to exchange rate fluctuations. Transaction exposure is a subset of economic exposure. However, a firm can still be subject to economic exposure even if it is not subject to transaction exposure. For example, a U.S. firm that exports goods to Great Britain is not subject to transaction exposure if it requests payment in U.S. dollars. Nevertheless, its cash flows will still likely be affected by a change in the British pound's exchange rate. If the British pound appreciates against the dollar, British companies may increase their demand for the goods. In like manner, a weakened British pound will reduce the British demand for the goods. Thus, the cash flows generated by the U.S. firm are affected by exchange rate movements, even though transaction exposure does not exist.

## Translation Exposure

A third form of exposure to exchange rate fluctuations is **translation exposure,** which represents the sensitivity of a firm's consolidated financial statements to exchange rate movements. An MNC's financial statement is a consolidation of its subsidiaries' financial statements. Because the MNC's balance sheet and income statement items from all subsidiaries are translated into a single currency, the values of many items are affected by exchange rate fluctuations. This can make profits overseas look more favorable when foreign currencies have strengthened, since the profits are translated at higher exchange rates. Conversely, weakened foreign currencies cause profits to be translated at relatively low exchange rates and make the consolidated earnings of the MNC appear less favorable. For example, the 1985 annual reports of Sperry, United Brands, NCR, Eastman Kodak, Goodyear, General Foods, and several other U.S.–based MNCs explain that their reported profits were adversely affected because foreign currencies weakened. The 1986 annual reports of many U.S. corporations identified the strengthening of these currencies as a reason for their high reported profits.

## MANAGEMENT OF EXCHANGE RATE RISK

Even if a firm could clearly determine how exchange rate movements would affect its overall performance, it could not be sure of future exchange rates. Because of this uncertainty, the firm may prefer to reduce its exposure to exchange rate fluctuations.

The ability to eliminate or reduce exchange rate risk varies with the firm's characteristics as well as the form of exchange rate risk involved. Transaction exposure can often be eliminated through **forward contracts.**

**Example**

Consider a U.S. firm that needs 50,000 British pounds in ninety days to pay for supplies sent by a British firm. The U.S. firm could negotiate a forward contract with a bank, whereby the firm agrees to purchase 50,000 pounds in ninety days at today's ninety-day forward rate. The advantage of the forward contract is that it locks in the price to be paid for the pounds, regardless of how the exchange rate changes over time. The potential disadvantage of a forward contract is that it obligates the firm to buy the pounds at the contracted forward rate, even if the spot rate turns out to be more attractive on the settlement date of the forward contract.

Some companies, such as Phillip Morris Companies, Inc., commonly use forward exchange contracts. Other companies, such as Coca Cola, generally do not use forward contracts, but rather engage in other hedging activities designed to minimize potential losses on foreign currency cash flows.

**Currency futures contracts** are also used by corporations to hedge against exchange-rate movements. They provide a service similar to that of forward contracts but are not offered by banks. Instead, they are traded among firms and individuals with the help of brokers. Because they are traded on an exchange, they are standardized to expedite transactions; and in this respect they differ from the more personalized forward contracts, which can be tailored to the firm's specific amount and maturity desired.

Forward contracts and currency futures contracts are normally available for only the widely used currencies. For other currencies, firms can hedge by attempting to match liabilities and assets in the same currency. For example, if they need a particular currency in the future, they can obtain the currency at the spot rate immediately and invest it until needed. In this way, they are not exposed to future movements in the exchange rate.

Firms that engage in international business cannot completely eliminate exposure to exchange rate movements, since they cannot fully hedge economic exposure. They can at least reduce exposure, however, by diversifying international business across countries. In this way, a particular currency's movement will have only a minor impact on total cash flows. Recall that U.S. exporters can be adversely affected by the weakening of a foreign currency. If the majority of the U.S. exporter's goods are purchased by customers in a single country, the exposure can be substantial. Yet, this firm could reduce its economic exposure by expanding sales within the

United States as well as other foreign countries. In this way, cash flows are less exposed to movements in a single foreign currency.

Some firms believe that translation exposure does not need to be hedged because it does not affect cash flows. Other firms believe that their stock price is adversely affected when translation with a weak foreign currency reduces the reported consolidated earnings. Some MNCs use hedging methods to keep their consolidated reported earnings from being significantly affected by translation. However, when firms hedge against their translation exposure, they usually increase their transaction exposure.

The translation process can even affect the company's balance sheet and financial ratios. For example, consider a U.S.–owned MNC that has a large research and development center in West Germany. If the German mark strengthens, the translated amount of fixed assets increases. This places downward pressure on the asset-turnover ratio (sales/assets) and on the return-on-investment ratio (net profit/assets). This impact is especially large when the numerator of a ratio is not simultaneously affected in the same direction. The research and development center is unlikely to generate much sales or profits, since it is used merely to develop, not sell, new products. Thus, ratios computed from consolidated financial statements can be significantly affected by exchange rate movements.

Creditors and investors (potential or existing shareholders) should attempt to account for any translation effects on financial statements, since ignoring such effects can distort the financial evaluation of companies. The financial statements of companies with a greater proportion of direct foreign investment (in subsidiaries) will typically be more vulnerable to translation effects.

When a firm is evaluating itself over time, it can attempt to disentangle changes in financial ratios that are real from those that are due to translation effects. One way to accomplish this is to maintain separate financial statements for each subsidiary based on the primary currency used by that subsidiary. In this way, each particular subsidiary's financial performance can be evaluated over time. Because these financial statements are not translated into some other currency, they more closely represent the performance of each particular subsidiary. Of course, these statements cannot be used for an annual report, since there are specific accounting guidelines to be used, and consolidated statements (including all subsidiaries) are required. Yet, a breakdown of financial statements for each subsidiary enables MNCs to identify the financial strengths and weaknesses of their individual subsidiaries.

# INTERNATIONAL FINANCIAL MANAGEMENT POLICIES

Although international financial management is similar to domestic financial management, it entails some additional aspects for consideration in carrying out the following financial functions: (1) financial planning, (2) working capital management, (3) capital budgeting, (4) capital structure policy, (5) financing with debt, and (6) financing with equity.

## Financial Planning

An MNC's cash budget relies on forecasted sales. These sales projections must consider all national economies where the MNC does business. The national economies of concern will also have to be evaluated when assessing cash disbursements, since the costs of doing business in these countries is influenced by their inflation rates and interest rates.

The particular characteristics of the MNC's cash management approach determines how the MNC develops its cash budget. If the MNC's headquarters has complete responsibility for meeting the cash deficiencies of subsidiaries or accepting excess cash of subsidiaries, it should first create a separate cash budget to determine an ending cash balance per subsidiary. Then the ending cash balance is converted to the currency desired by headquarters at the exchange rate existing at that time. This exchange rate has to be forecasted. Finally, the individual subsidiary's ending cash balances are consolidated to determine the overall ending cash balance of the entire MNC.

If the headquarters does not use a centralized cash management system, each subsidiary maintains its own cash budget. The individual subsidiary's ending cash balances still need to be determined, but they do not have to be converted to another currency. If a subsidiary is expected to consistently generate more cash than it needs, it can inform headquarters so that the cash can be sent somewhere else (to be used more properly). Conversely, if a subsidiary expects to experience a cash deficiency, it can inform headquarters so that funds can be transferred to the subsidiary (perhaps from another subsidiary with excess funds). Even when headquarters does not implement a centralized cash budget, it still plays a role in shifting funds from subsidiaries with excess funds to subsidiaries in need of funds.

Some subsidiaries with excess cash may be requested by headquarters to make early payment on imports from other subsidiaries. This so-called **leading strategy** is an effective financing arrangement for the exporting subsidiaries that need funds. If the importing subsidiaries need funds, headquarters may approve a **lagging strategy,** allowing them to delay their payments on imports—an effective financing arrangement for the importing subsidiaries in need of funds.

Intersubsidiary financing arranged by leading and lagging strategies can often benefit the MNCs, since it reduces the amount of external financing (from financial institutions) and therefore reduces financing costs. Unfortunately, these strategies are sometimes prohibited by country governments.

An MNC's pro forma statements represent a consolidation of the parent and all subsidiary pro forma statements, all translated into a single currency. This requires forecasts of not only all income statement and balance sheet items, but also exchange rates. These statements are then examined to detect any potential problem areas. Separate evaluations of the individual subsidiary pro forma statements may be useful, since when all subsidiary pro forma statements are combined, one subsidiary's anticipated poor performance may be overshadowed by another subsidiary's anticipated above-normal performance. Individual evaluations are better for detecting individual problems.

In order to reduce currency conversion costs, the MNC may employ **netting**, in which intersubsidiary payments due within a given period of time are "netted out" to determine the net amount owed by one subsidiary to the other. Because netting reduces the amount of currency to be exchanged, it reduces the transaction cost associated with converting one currency into another.

## Working Capital Management

When an MNC has excess short-term funds available, it considers not only the type of investment instrument, but the appropriate country for purchasing the instrument. This location decision is critical, since the interest rate of a given money market instrument can vary substantially among locations. This is verified in Figure 27.3, which shows the interest rate movements in three different countries over time. Such wide interest rate differentials may encourage firms to consider investing in foreign money market instruments that exhibit a more attractive interest rate.

Because foreign money market instruments are denominated in foreign currencies, firms are usually exposed to exchange rate movements (as discussed earlier). Since the effective (exchange rate–adjusted) yield of a foreign instrument is not known until the investment period is over, there is a risk that the foreign investment may provide a lower effective yield than what is available domestically. Because of this risk, some firms may prefer to avoid investing in foreign money market instruments. On the other

**FIGURE 27.3**
**Short-Term Interest Rates over Time (Monthly Average)**

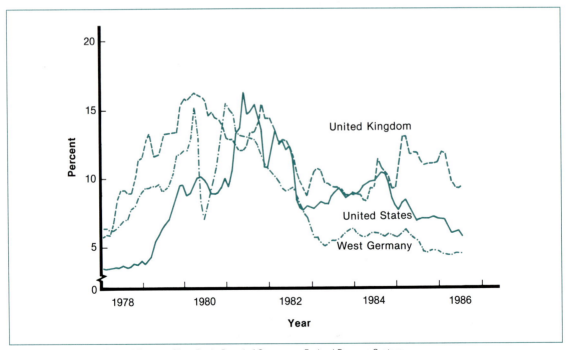

*Source:* Adapted from *Federal Reserve Chart Book. Board of Governors, Federal Reserve System.*

hand, other firms may be willing to accept the risk with the objective of generating higher yields than are possible domestically.

The management of accounts receivable by MNCs is complicated by the greater uncertainties involved in collecting money from foreign customers. MNCs often search for methods to ensure future payment for the goods they sell to foreign customers. One method is to sell the accounts receivable to a factor at a discount, so that the factor assumes full responsibility for collecting the receivables.

Another method of reducing the risk of bad debts from foreign customers is to require a *letter of credit,* or a promise by the customer's bank that guarantees payment. A letter of credit essentially substitutes the bank's credit for that of the customer. The exporter may prefer to have its local bank "confirm" the letter of credit, providing a guarantee that payment will be made. In this case, two banks are guaranteeing payment to the seller.

Multinational management of inventories sometimes requires more planning than domestic inventory management. An MNC that uses foreign materials to produce its final products tends to keep a larger safety stock on hand. This allows production to continue in the event of transportation delays, which are more likely when foreign suppliers are distant.

## Capital Budgeting

When a company evaluates a proposed foreign project, it must recognize the international aspects that could influence the project's relevant cash flows. First, the company must decide whether to estimate the cash flows from its perspective or from the perspective of the subsidiary administering the project. The relevant cash flows will vary with the perspective, since any cash flows to the subsidiary that are remitted to the parent may be subject to additional taxes. Also, funds remitted to the parent are usually converted into the parent's home currency, and if the foreign currency unexpectedly strengthens or weakens over time, the cash flows remitted to the parent may be much larger or smaller than expected. A project that initially appeared to be feasible could even exhibit a negative return under these conditions. If the parent of the company provides funds to a foreign subsidiary to administer the project, it should analyze the project from its own perspective.

It is sometimes suggested that because MNCs conduct business in so many countries, they diversify away the impact of exchange rate fluctuations. While a given volume of foreign business in several currencies will usually represent less exchange rate exposure than that same amount of business volume in a single foreign currency, exchange rate risk still exists. Because the dollar tends to move in the same direction against most currencies, a perfect offsetting effect does not occur.

Some additional considerations necessary when evaluating a foreign project are related to **country risk,** broadly defined here to describe any characteristics of a foreign country that affect a firm's value. When a firm invests in a foreign country, it must consider how the various forms of country risk could affect its investment. Country risk can influence a firm's investment in real assets (such as establishment of a foreign subsidiary) or in financial assets (such as foreign bank deposits or Treasury securities).

The most extreme form of country risk is expropriation by the foreign government of a firm's subsidiary or a freeze of financial assets without compensation. Many less devastating but significant forms of country risk exist as well. Consider a U.S. firm that plans to establish a subsidiary in the hypothetical foreign country of Zenland. Forms of country risk possible other than expropriation by the Zenland government are as follows. First, the political relationship between the United States and Zenland could affect demand for the subsidiary's products and the people's willingness to work there. Second, future economic conditions of Zenland could affect the subsidiary's sales performance. Third, Zenland's corporate tax laws could influence the after-tax earnings generated by the subsidiary. Fourth, withholding taxes could possibly be imposed on earnings remitted by the subsidiary to the headquarters. Fifth, funds remitted to the headquarters in the United States could be subject to currency restrictions on the conversion of Zenland's currency into dollars. All of these forms of country risk, not applicable to a purely domestic firm, could dramatically influence a firm involved in international business. Although these forms of risk should not prevent a firm from considering international business, they must be accounted for when determining whether an international project is feasible.

The characteristics of some foreign projects may cause companies to adjust how they traditionally use capital budgeting techniques. For example, consider a firm that plans to establish a manufacturing subsidiary in a less developed country. Because the firm believes it can hire labor there for one-tenth its domestic labor cost, it expects the subsidiary to be a profitable venture. However, the project could backfire if political turmoil causes the foreign government to take over the subsidiary. Some takeovers are friendly and may result in a payment to the parent company. Other takeovers are hostile and do not result in any foreign government payment to the parent. Given the substantial risk of developing a subsidiary, the parent company struggles with the trade-off of a potentially high risk for potentially high returns.

To account for the risk that the subsidiary could be taken over by the foreign government, the company may determine not only the net present value (*NPV*), but also the payback period. Its criteria may be that the *NPV* must exceed zero and, in addition, the payback period must be shorter than a specified number of years. If the company can achieve payback quickly, any future takeover possibility beyond the payback period is less of a concern.

Another method of evaluating such a foreign project is to ignore cash flows after the point at which a takeover may occur. The cash flows up to this point may be evaluated using *NPV*. If this project is feasible even when excluding cash flows beyond that point, it should be undertaken by the firm.

The initial outlay of a foreign project depends on the existing currency value in that country. The weak dollar in 1986 and 1987 caused U.S. investments overseas to be relatively expensive. However, the weak dollar also caused foreign investment in the United States to be relatively inexpensive. In 1987 Bridgestone Corporation, Japan's largest producer of tires, announced plans to invest $70 million in a truck-tire plant outside Nashville, Tennessee. The project was attractive to Bridgestone because of the weak U.S. dollar. In addition, Bridgestone planned to market its product at the various Japanese-owned automobile manufacturing plants based in the United States.

Some foreign governments may allow a project to continue in their respective countries for only a specified period of time, at which point they may purchase the existing project at some agreed upon price. Under these conditions, the company should use that price as the estimated *terminal* (or *salvage*) *value* of the project, which would likely be converted into the company's home currency at whatever exchange rate exists at that time.

## Capital Structure Policy

Since MNCs have many characteristics that differ from domestic corporations, they may find it both necessary and desirable to maintain a different type of capital structure. Factors that tend to stabilize cash flows permit firms to use more debt in their capital structure. Because MNCs typically sell their products in countries that have different business cycles, their aggregate cash flows may be more stable than those of purely domestic firms. This particular characteristic favors a debt-intensive capital structure.

Since MNCs often conduct some business in foreign currencies, their cash flow is more susceptible to currency fluctuations than the cash flow of domestic firms. Yet, MNCs can use various strategies to hedge against the possible adverse impact of currency fluctuations on cash flow. However, it is virtually impossible to completely eliminate this type of risk; and exposure to exchange rate risk and country risk can make future cash flows of MNCs less certain than those of purely domestic firms. This disadvantage favors more equity in the capital structure of MNCs. If MNCs adequately diversify their operations across countries, the impact of any single adverse event in a foreign country (such as a government takeover of a subsidiary or a recession) is reduced, and the MNCs could maintain more stable cash flows and absorb a larger percentage of debt.

Another factor worth considering is the mix of currencies in which MNCs do business. If they generate substantial cash flows in any foreign currencies that have low interest rates, they can issue bonds denominated in those currencies and use foreign cash inflows to repay the debt. Thus, MNCs having this characteristic may favor a debt-intensive capital structure, since they can obtain funds at a low cost and simultaneously hedge their foreign cash inflows (by using them to repay foreign debt). The optimal capital structure for MNCs, as with domestic corporations, depends on their operating characteristics. Each MNC should evaluate its own characteristics to determine the most appropriate capital structure.

## Financing with Debt

When corporations issue bonds, the key characteristic of concern is the yield they offer. The yield will be somewhat similar to prevailing long-term yields offered on other bonds at that time. Because long-term yields can

## FINANCIAL MANAGEMENT IN PRACTICE

### HOW DO FIRMS CONDUCT INTERNATIONAL FINANCIAL MANAGEMENT?

Several surveys of multinational corporations (MNCs) have been conducted to determine how international financial management is practiced. A brief summary of the results of two recent surveys follows:[*]

With regard to exchange rate exposure, MNCs have historically perceived translation exposure to be more important than transaction exposure. By the late 1970s, however, transaction exposure became a greater concern as MNCs began to believe that if translation effects were properly communicated to investors via the annual report, there would be little reason to hedge that exposure. Such a strategy would also prevent additional transaction exposure that could result from hedging translation exposure.

With regard to capital budgeting, some recent surveys found that net present value and internal rate of return techniques are used for foreign projects just as they are used for domestic projects. However, the payback approach is more frequently used to evaluate foreign projects than domestic projects. Despite the limitations of

[*]Suk H. Kim, Edward J. Farragher, and Trevor Crick, "Foreign Capital Budgeting Practices Used by the U.S. and Non–U.S. Multinational Companies," *Engineering Economist* 30 (Spring 1984): 207–15; and Marjorie T. Stanley and Stanley B. Block, "A Survey of Multinational Capital Budgeting," *Financial Review* 19 (March 1984): 36–54.

the payback approach, it may be especially useful for evaluating international projects that have a high probability of being quickly terminated.

One survey found that 49 percent of MNCs use the parent's cost of capital to evaluate foreign projects, while 32 percent use the subsidiary's cost of capital. The cost of capital used may depend on whether the foreign project is to be financed by the parent or the subsidiary.

The same survey found that 52 percent of MNCs evaluated projects from either the parent's perspective or a combination of parent's and the subsidiary's perspective. The remaining 48 percent of MNCs evaluate projects strictly from the perspective of the subsidiary. Based on a comparison of surveys over time, there appears to be an increasing tendency toward considering projects from the parent's perspective.

With regard to foreign financing, a separate survey found that 34 percent of the MNCs consider expected changes in the foreign currency value when calculating the cost of foreign debt. It may seem surprising that exchange rate fluctuations are not explicitly accounted for in all foreign financing decisions of MNCs. However, these fluctuations are so uncertain that incorporating forecasted exchange rates does not necessarily improve the forecast of the cost of foreign debt.

vary significantly among countries, corporations may consider issuing bonds in a foreign country if they can reduce their financing cost. Figure 27.4 illustrates the differences in long-term yields of three countries over time. While the specific differential between country yields does not remain constant over time, some countries (such as Switzerland and Germany) consistently have low yields in comparison to many other countries. Corporations may consider placing their bonds in these countries in order to obtain a low yield. Some U.S. corporations commonly follow this strategy. As an example, Intel Corporation issued 12.5 billion yen (approximate U.S. dollar equivalent of $49 million) in bonds in 1985.

**Example**

Assume a U.S. firm needs dollars and considers issuing bonds in either the U.S. or West Germany. Assume that the prevailing yield on dollar-denominated bonds is 12 percent, while the required yield on a bond denominated in German marks in West Germany is 8 percent. If the U.S. firm decides to issue bonds in West Germany, it would receive marks and convert them into dollars for use in the United States. Assuming the mark was initially valued at $.50, and the firm needed $5 million, it would have issued an amount of bonds that would attract 10 million marks. If the bonds sold at par value and the coupon rate was 8 percent, the U.S. firm would make annual coupon payments of .8 million marks to the German bondholders every year. Given a fixed value of $.50 per mark, it would take $.4 million to obtain .8 million marks in order to make annual coupon payments. This reflects an 8 percent cost of financing over the life of the bond.

Because the mark/dollar exchange rate changes over time, so does the number of dollars needed to obtain the .8 million marks. Therefore, the U.S. firm's cost of financing will change. If the mark depreciates against the dollar over time, fewer dollars are needed to obtain the .8 million marks, and the actual cost of financing is reduced (below 8 percent). Conversely, if the mark appreciates against the dollar over time, more dollars are needed to obtain the .8 million marks, and the cost of financing increases. Should the mark appreciate substantially over time, the cost of financing with mark-denominated bonds could turn out to be higher than if dollar-denominated bonds were sold in the United States. Because future exchange rates are not known with certainty, the cost of bond financing in a foreign currency is not known until the period is over.

**FIGURE 27.4**
**Long-Term Bond Yields over Time (Monthly Average)**

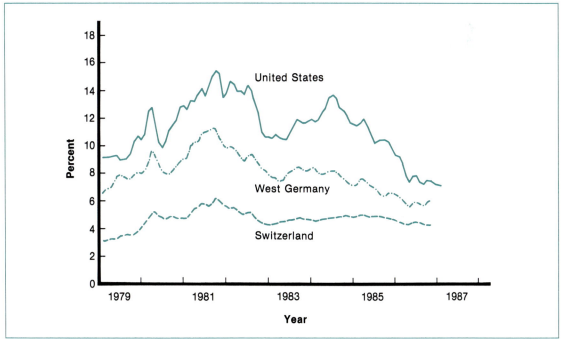

*Source:* Adapted from *Federal Reserve Chart Book.* Board of Governors, Federal Reserve System.

In many cases, U.S.–based MNCs need foreign currencies to finance their subsidiary operations. They frequently borrow foreign currencies to finance these needs. If this type of financing is repaid with foreign currency revenues, it does not expose the MNCs to exchange rate risk. Black and Decker, Coca Cola, Procter & Gamble, and many other MNCs finance much of their foreign operations with the corresponding foreign currencies.

When companies place their bonds in the Eurobond market, the bonds are typically underwritten by a multinational syndicate. Some of the *investment banking firms* (IBFs) participating in this syndicate have their headquarters in the United States and maintain foreign branches overseas.

The underwriting process in the Eurobond market can be summarized as follows. A group of IBFs known as the *managing syndicate* performs the origination, including any necessary advisory services. This syndicate identifies another group of IBFs (although some may be in the managing syndicate) that underwrites the bond issue. These underwriters may distribute portions of the issue to other IBFs to diversify the underwriting process. If some IBFs do not sell their portion, the managing syndicate is forced to redistribute these unsold portions to other IBFs or to sell the portions directly to investors. To avoid this situation, the managing syndicate often distributes large portions of the issue to IBFs that fulfilled their commitments on previous bond underwritings. Eurobonds purchased by investors can be resold before maturity due to the existence of a secondary market.

## Financing with Equity

There are advantages to issuing new stock in foreign rather than local equity markets. Non–U.S. corporations may place new issues in the United States since secondary markets in the United States are so liquid. If these non–U.S. firms place their equity in their domestic markets, the marketability of the stock may not be as strong over time, due to relatively inactive secondary markets in non–U.S. countries. New issues may sell for a lower price in foreign markets, reflecting the relatively low degree of marketability. Non–U.S. corporations have increasingly used the U.S. markets for issuing new stocks.

While U.S. stock markets are more active, they also enforce more restrictive regulations, which can discourage non–U.S. corporations from issuing stock in the United States. In fact, even some U.S. firms may be discouraged by the regulations and place their stock in foreign markets.

The decision by a firm to place stock in U.S. or foreign markets involves a trade-off between marketability and regulatory costs. Corporations that can easily meet the regulatory provisions prefer the U.S. markets. Other corporations that find U.S. regulations excessive prefer the foreign markets. Only companies that are well-known in foreign countries attempt to place their stock there. Smaller companies have no choice but to place their stock locally.

Some large MNCs place their stock in their domestic market as well as in foreign markets. The secondary trading of such stock takes place in each of the different markets (local and foreign) where it was initially issued.

## SUMMARY

International business offers the potential to increase production efficiency, reduce production costs, and increase sales. However, it also presents some additional forms of risk. Effective international financial management capitalizes on the advantages of international business while maintaining the risks at a tolerable level. This requires an initial identification of the risks to which the firm is exposed and then a measurement of the degree of exposure. Finally, the firm must determine which forms of exposure should be reduced or avoided.

The financial management of a MNC is similar to that of a purely domestic firm except that additional aspects must be considered. If these aspects are ignored, poor policy decisions may result. The degree to which these aspects influence financial management policies depends on the particular characteristics of the MNC.

## KEY TERMS

**Appreciate** Currency rising in value.

**Country risk** Broadly defined as any characteristic of a foreign country that can affect a firm's value.

**Currency futures contract** A standardized contract traded on exchange that allows one to receive a specified amount of a currency for a specified exchange rate and at a specified future point in time.

**Depreciate** Currency declining in value.

**Economic exposure** The exposure of a firm's cash flows to exchange rate fluctuations.

**Eurobond market** The market where bonds denominated in various currencies are traded.

**Eurocredit loans** Loans provided by banks in various currencies for an intermediate term, such as five to seven years.

**Eurocurrency market** A market made up of numerous banks that accept short-term deposits and offer short-term loans in various currencies.

**Forward contract** A contract between a business and a bank to exchange a specified amount of currency at a specified forward rate and at a specified future point in time.

**Forward rate** A rate quoted for exchange at some specified future date.

**Lagging strategy** A delay by one subsidiary in paying another subsidiary for trade, thereby receiving an implicit form of financing.

**Leading strategy** An early payment by a subsidiary in paying another subsidiary for trade, thereby providing an implicit form of financing.

**Netting** Determining the net balance owed between subsidiaries; the payments due are netted out so that only the net balance is paid; netting is used to reduce currency conversion costs.

**Quota** A limit imposed on the amount of a particular good that can be imported.

**Spot rate** An exchange rate quoted for immediate exchange or delivery.

**Tariff** A tax imposed on imported goods.

**Transaction exposure** The exposure of a firm's international transactions to exchange rate fluctuations.

**Translation exposure** The exposure of a firm's financial statements to exchange rate fluctuations.

## QUESTIONS

**Q27-1.** How can corporations use the Eurocurrency market to improve their performance?

**Q27-2.** How would a jump in U.S. inflation and reduced German inflation affect the value of the German mark, other things being equal?

**Q27-3.** How would high U.S. interest rates and lower German interest rates affect the value of the German mark, other things being equal?

**Q27-4.** How is the imposition of a quota on British goods expected to affect the value of the British pound, other things being equal?

**Q27-5.** Explain how the Federal Reserve can use government intervention to weaken the U.S. dollar.

**Q27-6.** Explain how a weak dollar can affect a U.S. firm's (a) exporting business, (b) importing business, (c) foreign investment in money market instruments, and (d) foreign financing.

**Q27-7.** Explain the meaning of transaction exposure. How does it differ from economic exposure?

**Q27-8.** Mag Company is in the business of exclusively exporting furniture from the United States to Great Britain. It invoices its exports in U.S. dollars. Is this firm experiencing transaction exposure? Economic exposure? Translation exposure? Explain each of your answers.

**Q27-9.** How can a firm use a forward contract to reduce its exchange rate risk?

**Q27-10.** Compare and contrast forward contracts and currency futures contracts.

**Q27-11.** How does accounts receivable management for an MNC differ from that of a purely domestic firm?

**Q27-12.** How does an MNC's inventory management differ from that of a purely domestic firm?

**Q27-13.** Explain why cash flows of a project differ when viewed from a subsidiary's perspective versus the parent's perspective.

**Q27-14.** Provide some examples of how a subsidiary is exposed to country risk.

**Q27-15.** Describe the international characteristics of an MNC that may favor a more debt-intensive capital structure. Explain how each characteristic favors more debt.

## PROBLEMS

**P27-1.** Chanie Computers is a U.S. company that purchases 1,000 printers from West Germany every month. The price per printer is 1,200 German marks. While the currency value of the mark is $.50, it is expected to average about $.40 over the next three years. How will this affect Chanie Computers? Be precise.

**P27-2.** Armack Company is a U.S. company that needs $5 million in financing for one year. It can borrow dollars at 9 percent. Alternatively, it can borrow Swiss francs and convert the francs into dollars. A Swiss franc loan can be obtained at 6 percent. The Swiss franc's spot rate is $.50. In one year, the spot rate is forecasted to be $.48. What would be the effective (exchange rate–adjusted) rate of borrowing Swiss francs? What would the effective rate be if the spot rate is $.55 in one year? If there is a fifty-fifty chance of either outcome occurring, would you borrow Swiss francs or dollars? Explain.

**P27-3.** Banta Corporation is a U.S. company that has $10 million in excess cash. It considers purchasing one-year U.S. Treasury bills that offer a yield of 8 percent. Alternatively, it considers purchasing Canadian Treasury bills that offer a yield of 10 percent. The Canadian dollar's spot rate is $.80. What would Banta's effective (exchange rate–adjusted) yield on the Canadian Treasury bills be if the Canadian dollar's spot rate remains unchanged? What if the Canadian dollar's spot rate is $.82 by the end of the year? What if it is $.79 by the end of the year? If there is an equal probability of any of these outcomes occurring, should Banta Corporation purchase the U.S. Treasury bills or Canadian Treasury bills? Explain.

**P27-4.** Migrane Company is a U.S. company that issued a ten-year bond denominated in German marks six years ago. The par value of the bond is 100 million marks. Coupon payments in marks are made at the end of each year, and the coupon rate is 7 percent. Determine the dollar cash outflows that would be necessary to pay coupon payments and the principal if the spot rate of the mark is forecasted as follows:

| Years from Now | Forecasted Spot Rate of German Mark |
|:---:|:---:|
| 1 | $.48 |
| 2 | .53 |
| 3 | .47 |
| 4 | .49 |

If Migrane Company could be guaranteed a low spot rate on the mark in any one of those four years, which year would it choose? Why? Suggest whether Migrane's cost of financing would be higher or lower if the mark consistently appreciated over this four-year period. Explain.

## REFERENCES

Adler, Michael, and Bernard Dumas. "International Portfolio Choice and Corporate Finance: A Synthesis." *Journal of Finance* 38 (June 1983): 925–84.

Aggarwal, R. "International Differences in Capital Structure Norms: An Empirical Study of Large European Companies." *Management International Review* 21 (1981): 75–88.

Calderon-Rossell, Jorge R. "Covering Foreign Exchange Risks of Single Transactions." *Financial Management* 8 (Autumn 1979): 78–85.

Chrystal, K. Alec. "A Guide to Foreign Exchange Markets." *Review* 66 (March 1984): 5–18.

Cohn, Richard A., and Donald R. Lessard. "The Effect of Inflation on Stock Prices: International Evidence." *Journal of Finance* 36 (May 1981): 277–90.

Cornell, Bradford. "Inflation, Relative Price Changes, and Exchange Risk." *Financial Management* 9 (Autumn 1980): 30–34.

Cornell, Bradford, and Marc R. Reinganum. "Forward and Futures Prices: Evidence from the Foreign Exchange Markets." *Journal of Finance* 36 (December 1981): 1035–45.

Levy, Haim. "Optimal Portfolio of Foreign Currencies with Borrowing and Lending." *Journal of Money Credit and Banking* 13 (August 1981): 326–41.

Logue, Dennis E., and George S. Oldfield. "Managing Foreign Assets When Foreign Exchange

Markets Are Efficient." *Financial Management* 6 (Summer 1977): 16–22.

Madura, Jeff. *International Financial Management*, 1st ed. St. Paul, Minnesota: West Publishing Co., 1986.

Oblak, David J., and Roy J. Helm, Jr. "Survey and Analysis of Capital Budgeting Methods Used by Multinationals." *Financial Management* 11 (Winter 1982): 74–87.

Robichek, Alexander A., and Mark R. Eaker. "Debt Denomination and Exchange Risk in International Capital Markets." *Financial Management* 5 (Autumn 1976): 11–18.

Rodriguez, Rita M. "Corporate Exchange Risk Management: Theme and Aberrations." *Journal of Finance* 36 (May 1981): 427–38.

Shapiro, Alan C. "Exchange Rate Changes, Inflation, and the Valuation of the Multinational Corporation." *Journal of Finance* 30 (May 1975): 485–502.

Taggart, Robert A. "Capital Budgeting and the Financing Decision." *Financial Management* 6 (Summer 1977): 59–64.

# PART 9

# SYNTHESIS

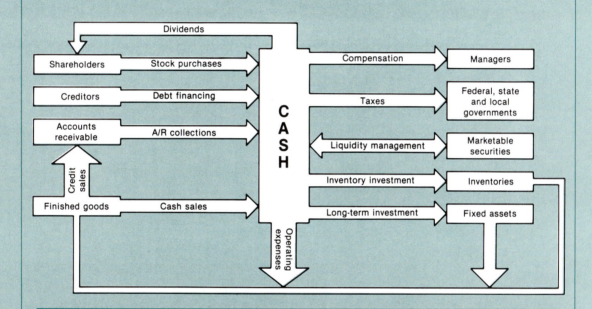

Part 9 is designed to illustrate the interrelationships between the major aspects of financial management. For example, financial management can be thought of as a series of investment problems. The firm must invest in current and fixed assets in such a way that profits are high and risk is low. The specific assets selected affect the firm's cost of raising funds. Conversely, the cost of funds affects the firm's decision as to which assets to acquire. Chapter 28 emphasizes these relationships and provides a comprehensive review of the major aspects of financial management.

# CHAPTER 28

# SYNTHESIS OF FINANCIAL MANAGEMENT POLICIES

## INTEGRATED FINANCIAL MANAGEMENT IN PERSPECTIVE

In 1987 a substantial number of shareholders of Allegis Corporation became dissatisfied with the firm's strategy of developing a full-service travel company. They did not perceive synergistic benefits from the recent combining of Westin Hotels, Hilton International Company, Hertz Rent-a-Car, and United Airlines. In June 1987, the chairman of the board resigned.

At this writing, plans to divest part or all of Westin Hotels, Hilton International Company, and Hertz Rent-a-Car are being considered. The main objective underlying these plans is to concentrate the firm's efforts in its main line of business. The divestitures would significantly change Allegis's asset structure. In addition, a recapitalization plan to increase the proportion of debt is also being consid-

ered. Such a strategy would significantly change Allegis's liability and shareholders' equity structure.

The planned changes in Allegis's balance sheet can have a major effect on its cash flows and therefore influence its risk and return. If these plans are implemented, how will cash flow be affected? How will the company's risk as perceived by both shareholders and credit rating agencies be affected? Will the company's cost of capital change? Will its dividend policy be affected? Would future projects be assessed differently as a result of the company's revised financial and operating structure? This chapter provides a framework that can be used to integrate many of the important financial questions.

This chapter reexamines the most relevant financial management policies that have been described throughout the text and emphasizes the relationships between these policies. In order to make policy decisions that maximize shareholder wealth, financial managers must consider the ramifications of any proposed policy or other existing policies.

## DISTINGUISHING BETWEEN INVESTMENT AND FINANCING POLICIES

Many financial management functions can be classified as either investment or financing policies, as shown in Table 28.1. Each investment policy is described, followed by a summary of each financing policy.

### Investment Policies

The initial investment to establish a business, and subsequent decisions to expand, are commonly determined by capital budgeting. While this is the most obvious investment decision, there are other more subtle yet relevant investment decisions as well. Any use of funds that results in additional assets represents an investment, even if the funds are used to purchase marketable securities or maintain cash balances.

Inventory management is also considered an investment decision because funds are used to invest in the inventory. Credit policy is also an investment decision, since the investment in accounts receivable becomes larger as the credit terms are relaxed.

Each type of investment decision must be reevaluated periodically throughout the life of the firm. Projects that were at one time deemed unfeasible may become feasible due to the changing nature of the characteristics relevant to the capital budgeting decision. Cash flow forecasts of a proposed project will adjust over time to changing economic and industry-specific conditions. The firm's required rate of return for a particular project will also change over time, since changes in technology and competition often affect the project's degree of risk. Even if the project's risk were to remain constant, the required rate of return for a particular project may change due to changes in the cost of capital. This could cause a project that was previously rejected to become acceptable.

Along with capital budgeting, the other policies relating to investment of funds must also be continually reevaluated. The level of cash, securities,

**TABLE 28.1**   Classifying Financial Management Functions as Investment or Financing Policies

| Investment Policies | Financing Policies |
| --- | --- |
| Capital budgeting | Financial leverage |
| Cash management | Short-term financing |
| Marketable securities management | Capital structure |
| Inventory management | Dividend policy |
| Accounts receivable management | |

and inventory needed to support corporate operations will be revised in response to changing economic conditions and sales projections. Accounts receivable management is also revised periodically. Yet, it tends to differ from the management of cash, marketable securities, and inventory in that it is adjusted to act as an *influence on sales* rather than as a *reaction to changes in sales*.

Some investment decisions cause a decrease in assets. For example, the assessment of an existing project may result in the divestiture of that project. An analysis of existing credit policy may result in the tightening of credit and a reduction in accounts receivable. A reduction in assets results when the opportunity cost of forgoing alternative uses of funds becomes higher than the benefits provided by the assets.

All investment decisions should be made with the intention of maximizing shareholder wealth. These decisions involve trade-offs of higher risk in order to achieve higher potential returns, or lower potential returns in order to reduce risk. Decisions to reduce the investment in cash, marketable securities, and inventory will generally offer higher potential returns, since less funds are tied up. Yet, these decisions can cause a reduction in the firm's liquidity and an increased likelihood of lost sales due to stockouts, causing a higher level of risk.

Managers may consider implementing policies that satisfy their own preferred risk-return trade-off rather than the shareholders' preferred tradeoff. Agency costs are incurred by the firm as managers are pressured to place shareholder goals above their own.

## Financing Policies

In addition to the investment policies just described, financing policies are also shown in Table 28.1. Capital structure policy specifies the composition of long-term financing and has a direct impact on the cost of capital. Dividend policy represents a financing decision, since it influences the amount of financing that must be obtained externally. Firms that pay dividends even when they need financing do not perceive dividends to be a residual after all necessary financing is provided by recent earnings. In fact, dividends are perceived by some firms as an automatic cash outflow, as if they were required.

Dividend policy and capital structure policy are interrelated. The greater the amount of earnings distributed as dividends, the less the amount of retained earnings available for future financing. Thus, a firm that uses a high dividend payout is likely to have a debt-intensive capital structure and a higher degree of financial leverage. As an example, Toledo Edison Company implemented a large capital spending program in the 1980s (mainly on two nuclear plants) and also continued to offer high dividends. These policies absorbed internally generated funds and caused Toledo Edison to issue more long-term debt. Consequently, its capital structure has become more debt-intensive.

The relationship between the dividend policy and capital structure may vary if firms adjust their volume of shares outstanding. For example, firms can achieve high dividend payout and an equity-intensive capital structure if they issue new stock in the capital markets. In addition, they can achieve low dividend payout and a debt-intensive capital structure by using retained earnings to repurchase some of their outstanding stock.

The cost of financing with retained earnings is the opportunity cost of forgone opportunities to shareholders. When managers cannot use available funds to generate the return required by shareholders, they should consider distributing the funds as dividends. However, shareholders could become accustomed to the higher dividends and mistakenly interpret a future dividend cut (perhaps to finance a new investment) as a signal that the firm is experiencing problems. Such a misinterpretation results from asymmetric information, as the managers have more information than the shareholders. If managers cannot inform shareholders of their investment plans, they may decide to avoid any reductions in dividends.

Financing decisions, like investment decisions, should be made with the intention of maximizing shareholder wealth. They also involve the same type of risk-return trade-off. Decisions to finance with debt are often linked with maximizing potential return, since there is a tax advantage of debt not applicable to equity financing. Yet, too much debt may force excessive periodic cash outflows in the form of interest payments. With this trade-off in mind, firms seek the proper balance of debt and equity that attracts funds at the lowest possible required return. Each type of financing decision must be reevaluated periodically throughout the life of the firm. As economic conditions change, the market interest rates and the risk premiums adjust. Consequently, the optimal financial structure may change as well.

## INTEGRATION OF INVESTMENT AND FINANCING POLICIES

Because investment in fixed assets can influence cash flow patterns, it can affect the capital structure as well. For example, consider a firm that decides to diversify into a variety of new businesses. It expects that its new diversified asset structure will generate more stable cash flows over time. In anticipation of a more stable cash flow pattern, the firm may finance the acquisition of these new businesses with a relatively high proportion of debt (since it is more capable of meeting periodic interest payments). The adjustment in capital structure to accommodate a new asset structure can be difficult, since the firm is forced to make a financing decision before it can determine the cash flow patterns generated by the new asset structure.

While capital budgeting decisions influence the capital structure, they are also influenced by the capital structure. The capital structure affects the cost of capital, which can influence the accept/reject decision for the acquisition of new fixed assets.

Capital budgeting decisions can influence cash management, inventory, and accounts receivable decisions. Any investment in cash, inventory, and accounts receivable resulting from a new project should be incorporated in the capital budgeting evaluation. Normally, these factors are included as required additions to the initial outlay.

Firms sometimes finance an investment in assets by divesting existing fixed assets rather than financing with additional debt or equity. They may even obtain some financing by selling accounts receivable, reducing cash balances, or selling marketable securities. These possibilities illustrate the integration of investment and financing decisions. Investment decisions that cause a reduction in assets represent a method of financing.

Divestitures of assets are feasible if the proceeds to be received exceed the present value of forgone cash flows attributable to the assets to be divested. This does not imply that firms willing to purchase these divested assets are making a mistake. Because these firms plan to make better use of the assets, their assessment of future expected cash flows attributable to the assets is more favorable. Also, if these firms have a lower cost of capital, the cash flows attributable to the assets of concern will be discounted at a relatively low rate, increasing the likelihood that the purchase of these assets is feasible.

Divestitures have become a very popular method of financing. Alcoa Corporation commonly divests assets that no longer serve its needs. This policy has generated over $300 million for Alcoa in recent years. IC Industries generated $400 million from ten divestitures in 1985. During the 1980s the Coca-Cola Company divested assets that were no longer generating acceptable returns, selling businesses engaged in wine, coffee and tea, water purification, pasta, and plastics. This divestiture policy was intended to concentrate on remaining businesses, and it created a significant source of financing. In 1987 Unisys divested a substantial amount of assets in order to focus on its remaining businesses.

The risk-return trade-off applied to investment and financing decisions is displayed in Table 28.2. In general, financial managers following a philosophy of high return and high risk strive for a relatively low level of assets (compared to other firms in the same line of business) in order to achieve optimal asset utilization. In addition, a relatively high level of liabilities is used to support these assets, reflecting a high degree of financial

**TABLE 28.2   Classifying Financial Management Decisions by Return and Risk**

| Decision | Goal | |
|---|---|---|
| | *Potential for High Return (High Risk)* | *Potential for Lower Return (Low Risk)* |
| *Asset management* | | |
| Accounts receivable | Loosen credit standards | Tighten credit standards |
| Cash and marketable securities | Maintain low level | Maintain high level |
| Inventory | Maintain low level | Maintain high level |
| Fixed assets | Maintain low level | Maintain high level |
| *Liability management* | | |
| Accounts payable | Maintain high level | Maintain low level |
| Notes payable | Maintain high level | Maintain low level |
| Long-term debt | Maintain high level | Maintain low level |
| *Equity accounts* | | |
| Common stock outstanding | Maintain low level | Maintain high level |

**TABLE 28.3** **Potential Dangers from Improper Management of Assets, Liabilities, and Equity**

| | Danger of Maintaining Excessive Amount | Danger of Maintaining Insufficient Amount |
|---|---|---|
| *Asset management* | | |
| Accounts receivable | Large amount of funds tied up; potentially high bad-debt expense | Forgone sales if credit policy is too restrictive |
| Cash and marketable securities | Large amount of funds tied up; high opportunity cost | Insufficient liquidity; may cause excessive borrowing |
| Fixed assets | Sales would not be large enough to support the investment in fixed assets; inefficient use of fixed assets | Production would not keep up with demand, and forgone sales would result |
| Inventory | Large amount of funds tied up; high opportunity cost | Production and/or level of finished goods would not satisfy demand, and forgone sales would result |
| *Liability management* | | |
| Accounts payable | Suppliers cut off firm's credit line; credit rating deteriorates | Firms do not utilize an available source of temporary funds and must therefore borrow more funds (and incur additional interest expenses) |
| Notes payable | Strain on cash flow due to large interest payments required on debt | Firms forced to rely more on long-term sources of funds |
| Long-term debt | Strain on cash flow due to large interest payments required on debt; perceived risk may be high, forcing creditors and shareholders to require a high rate of return | Firms forced to rely more on equity funding, which can be more expensive; in addition, it can cause firms to flood the market with stock, which places downward pressure on the stock prices |
| *Management of equity accounts* | | |
| Dividend payments (and retained earnings) | If excessive dividends are paid, the firms may be forced to obtain most of their financing from sources other than retained earnings; this could force a high degree of financial leverage or an excessive supply of stock in the market | If insufficient dividends are paid, those shareholders that prefer to receive a high level of dividends may become dissatisfied; also, any decrease in dividend payments may signal to shareholders that the firms are experiencing financial problems |
| Common stock outstanding | A large supply of stock tends to place downward pressure on the stock price | Firms are forced to obtain most of their funds from retaining earnings (which limits the dividend payments) or long-term debt (which causes a high degree of financial leverage) |

leverage. In contrast, a more conservative philosophy of low return and low risk allows for a greater investment in assets relative to anticipated sales, compared to other firms in the same line of business. These assets are supported by a relatively low level of liabilities and a high level of equity, reflecting a low degree of financial leverage.

Table 28.3 describes the potential dangers involved with maintaining a relatively low or relatively high level of various assets, liabilities, and equity. The risky strategy of accepting a high level of accounts receivable can result in excessive bad-debt expense. A relatively low level of other assets, such as cash and inventory, can result in shortages. A relatively high level of liabilities can force a strain on cash flow, especially when a small amount of liquid assets is maintained.

A more conservative strategy of maintaining a larger level of assets requires a larger investment to generate a given level of sales. In addition, the conservative strategy of maintaining a low level of liabilities requires that assets must be supported with a relatively high degree of equity. Thus, every dollar of return is more widely distributed to the shareholders, reflecting a lower rate of return to the shareholders.

## CASH FLOW AND THE INTEGRATION OF POLICY OBJECTIVES

Assume that the newly hired chief executive officer (CEO) of a growing firm intends to substantially improve the firm's performance. The CEO has created the following list of corporate goals for this year:

- Increase sales by 10 percent
- Reduce inventory by 8 percent
- Reduce accounts receivable balances by 10 percent
- Increase dividends per share by 20 percent
- Reduce debt by 10 percent
- Repurchase 15 percent of outstanding shares
- Significantly reduce the firm's financial leverage
- Increase expenditures on fixed assets by 20 percent

Many of these goals are interrelated. Consequently, they may not all be achieved simultaneously, regardless of how optimistic future conditions might be. The following discussion identifies these inconsistencies.

If financial managers reduce investment in accounts receivable and inventory according to the CEO's goals, they may not be able to increase sales (due to less credit sales and more stockouts). In addition, the firm's cash inflows will not be sufficient to simultaneously support higher dividends, debt reduction, stock repurchases, and increased investment in fixed assets. If additional cash is used for stock repurchases and extra dividend payments, there will be no internally generated funds for the firm's capital budget.

The key to the problem at hand is cash flow. The CEO's plans emphasize spending funds but ignore the need for additional financing. In fact, the existing levels of debt and outstanding stock are to be reduced by 10 percent and 15 percent, respectively. Other potential sources of funds such as reducing dividend payments or divesting fixed assets are not conceivable, since the CEO plans to use more funds to increase dividends and fixed assets. All of the CEO's goals require additional funds. These goals can be achieved only if the proposed policies are combined with non-conflicting policies that generate funds.

# INTEGRATION OF POLICIES THAT AFFECT PERFORMANCE

Financing and investing decisions affect the firm's performance, which can be measured by earnings, return on equity, return on assets, stock price, or some other criterion. The following discussion focuses on how financial management affects return on equity, one of the most popular measures of performance.

The return on equity (ROE) is determined by three factors. First, what level of assets is supported by the existing equity? Second, what level of sales is generated by the existing assets? Finally, what level of earnings results from the level of sales? If the company's actual ROE does not reach the targeted ROE, it is because of at least one of the following reasons. First, the firm's profit margin may not be adequate. Second, asset turnover may be too low. Third, the equity multiplier may be too low (not enough financial leverage). Finally, if all of these ratios are adequate, but the ROE is not, the ROE target must be inappropriate.

**Example**

Consider a firm that intends to boost its return on assets, and specifies the following goals:

- Profit margin (net income/sales) of 3 percent
- Asset turnover (sales/assets) of 2.5
- Debt ratio (debt/assets) of 50 percent
- Return on equity (net income/equity) of at least 20 percent

If debt supports 50 percent of assets, then the equity supports the other 50 percent, and the equity multiplier (which equals assets/equity) is 2.0. The ROE can be decomposed into the products of the profit margin, the asset turnover, and the equity multiplier (as was illustrated in Chapter 6). The product of these ratios is 15 percent (computed as 3% × 2.5 × 2.0). Thus, even if each ratio is achieved, the return on equity target is not. Performance goals should be developed with consideration of the individual policies that affect them. Otherwise, the goals may be unrealistic, as illustrated in this example.

The consolidation of financial decisions that affect product pricing, efficiency in utilizing assets, and capital structure will determine the firm's ROE. In the preceding example, the firm could attempt to increase its ROE by increasing its prices (profit margin). While such a pricing policy may achieve a higher profit margin, it can reduce the asset turnover if there is a corresponding reduction in sales. Consequently, any increase in the profit margin may be more than offset by a decrease in the asset turnover, so that ROE might even decrease.

As an alternative solution, the firm may consider reducing its assets in order to increase asset turnover and therefore ROE. Yet, the firm may not be able to maintain the same sales level with less assets. Attempts to increase asset turnover expose the firm to more risk.

Another possible solution is to increase the debt proportion of the capital structure in order to increase ROE. While this magnifies the impact of the return on investment (assets) on ROE, it also places a greater strain on cash flow. Once again, higher potential return is achieved only at the expense of higher risk.

Corporate goals extend beyond a target ROE. Some goals are applied to individual policies, with the underlying objective to improve corporate performance. Still, the relationships between these policies must be recognized when establishing individual goals.

## MONITORING FINANCIAL CHARACTERISTICS OF MULTI-DIVISION FIRMS

Existing financial policies are evaluated over time to assess managerial decision making. Because financial policies are integrated, it is difficult to evaluate any single policy by itself. It is especially difficult to evaluate a multi-division firm. When some divisions are performing above par while other divisions are performing below par, the overall performance may appear reasonable, and problems of the subpar divisions may go unnoticed.

This dilemma can be resolved by evaluating the firm on a divisional basis. That is, every division can be considered as a separate entity. For example, a firm with thirty retail outlets across the nation can analyze each outlet separately. This method is useful for detecting any problems unique to an individual outlet or division. In many cases, the divisions to be monitored are not directly comparable, in that some divisions may focus on manufacturing, for example, while others focus on warehousing or retailing. Nonetheless, divisions can be analyzed in comparison to industry norms related to each division or to goals previously established for each division. As an example of multi-division monitoring, the management of Quaker Oats Company analyzes divisional financial characteristics in order to determine which divisions are generating low returns. This type of analysis has helped Quaker Oats identify businesses that should be divested. It recently divested several businesses as a result, including Needlecraft and Magic Pan Restaurant.

In many cases, divisions are dependent on each other, which causes a division's performance to be distorted for reasons it cannot control. For example, a retail division may experience reduced sales because of inventory problems at a warehouse division. Financial analysis on a divisional basis is also useful for this type of situation. The initial analysis would detect problems at the retail division, but further investigation would identify the warehouse as the real culprit.

# INTEGRATED FINANCIAL MANAGEMENT AT GEORGIA-PACIFIC CORPORATION

Relationships among financial management policies can best be understood by evaluating an existing company. The following discussion focuses on Georgia-Pacific (G-P) Corporation, which does business in the forest products industry and has generated annual sales of over $6 billion in recent years. Its 1986 annual report provided a summary of its financial condition and a discussion of financial policies. A summary of this information follows. The integration between G-P's policies is noted where appropriate.

## Capital Budget

G-P spent more than $2 billion on property, plant, and equipment during the 1981–85 period. For 1986 it spent about $482 million on projects, with the primary intent of reducing operating costs and improving product lines. G-P's recent annual reports verify that proposed projects are evaluated on the basis of after-tax cash flow rather than accounting income. In addition, its estimated initial outlay on proposed projects includes any requirements for additional working capital along with the explicit cost of the projects. The annual report also verifies that G-P's accept/reject decision for each proposed project is based on the internal rate of return (*IRR*).

G-P categorizes its projects as "defensive" or "high return." Its defensive projects are undertaken to adequately maintain existing operations. They may generate high returns but are implemented primarily to avoid operating complications rather than to boost returns. G-P's high-return projects are assessed with the intention of improving its return on equity.

G-P post-audits its high-return projects in order to determine whether these projects are achieving their respective targeted returns. It also post-audits any businesses that have been acquired. In this way, the previous decisions made by G-P's financial managers are assessed, and future capital budgeting decisions may be improved. Also, existing projects that should be divested may be identified.

Capital expenditures of $600 million were projected in 1987. Since G-P planned to finance these expenditures with funds generated from continuing operations, these investments were not expected to require additional debt financing.

As a result of the Tax Reform Act of 1986, the federal tax rate of corporate ordinary income was reduced to 34 percent (as of 1988). This increases the expected after-tax cash flows of projects. However, the act's repeal of the investment tax credit increases the initial outlay on projects. G-P expected that the advantages and disadvantages of the tax law will be offset to a degree. Therefore, the Tax Reform Act is not expected to have a significant impact on G-P's capital budget or its project decisions.

## Capital Structure

G-P has a target debt-to-equity range of 30 to 35 percent. The 1986 annual report states:

> We believe that managing Georgia-Pacific's capital structure within a 30 to 35 percent range of total debt-to-capital will keep the company's cost of capital

competitive while ensuring access to most major capital markets. This access will provide the needed flexibility to take advantage of internal and external investment opportunities, as they arise.

This statement implies that the company's debt level is high enough to benefit from the relatively low cost of debt, yet low enough to issue bonds without necessarily exceeding the company's debt capacity or raising its cost of capital.

The capital structure target provides direction for future financing decisions. The use of a range rather than a precise target offers some flexibility for new financing. G-P planned to finance most of its needs in 1987 internally (cash from ongoing operations). If any external financing was necessary, it planned to use debt rather than equity, because of the lower cost of debt to G-P at that time. Because G-P's capital structure affects its cost of capital, it also influences its accept/reject decisions on proposed capital expenditures. Consequently, G-P's capital budget of $600 million for 1987 is related to its present capital structure.

G-P's total debt-to-capital ratios in recent years are shown in the following table:

| Year | Georgia-Pacific's Total Debt-to-Capital Ratio |
|------|-----------------------------------------------|
| 1982 | 42.1% |
| 1983 | 37.4 |
| 1984 | 35.7 |
| 1985 | 32.0 |
| 1986 | 26.3 |

The decline in the ratio is mainly attributable to a reduction in total debt from $1.9 billion in 1982 to $1.2 billion in 1986. G-P's total debt-to-capital level fell below its 30 to 35 percent target range in 1986, allowing the company substantial flexibility to finance future investments with debt. Since internal funds are expected to finance planned capital expenditures, additional debt could be used for other purposes.

G-P is in a position to finance a greater degree of growth than it has planned. Yet, it will not attempt additional growth simply to achieve an increase in its debt level. If it does not find additional feasible investment opportunities, it could leave its debt level as is (below the target) until such opportunities do occur. If it prefers to achieve its target debt ratio soon, it could revise its capital structure by issuing new debt and using the proceeds to retire outstanding stock. G-P's management has been authorized by its board of directors to purchase some of its outstanding common stock in order to achieve its target capital structure. As of December 31, 1986, G-P had a shelf registration of $250 million in debt securities with the Securities and Exchange Commission—which will allow the company to rapidly revise its capital structure when conditions are favorable.

## Financing with Debt

In June 1985 G-P issued $195 million worth of debentures with relatively short maturities and with interest rates ranging from 8.55 percent to 10.30

percent. The net proceeds were used to pay off term loans that had an effective interest cost of 10.31 percent.

During 1986 G-P implemented the following strategies to revise its capital structure and reduce its cost of capital:

- Issued $150 million of $9\frac{1}{4}$ percent sinking fund debentures at par, due in the year 2016.
- Retired $24 million of 12 percent notes due at various dates beginning in the year 2006.
- Purchased $50 million of redeemable preferred stock.
- Retired $65 million of $14\frac{5}{8}$ percent notes due in 1987.
- Retired $100 million of $12\frac{1}{4}$ percent sinking-fund debentures due in the year 2013.
- Retired $150 million of 10.10 percent notes due in 1990.
- Retired $14 million of zero coupon debentures due in 1986.
- Called $87 million of $5\frac{1}{4}$ percent convertible subordinated debentures due in 1996 for redemption.

G-P's refinancing strategies were designed to take advantage of low prevailing interest rates and reduce the cost of capital. Such a strategy can increase the number of attractive projects and also affect the size of its capital budget.

## Dividends

G-P uses a policy of paying about one-third of its earnings as dividends. In 1983 it had reduced dividends in response to depressed earnings over previous years. As a result of improved performance, dividend payments per share were increased in each of the next three years.

While G-P has a target dividend payout ratio, it also considers future capital needs, other cash requirements, and prospective returns on its equity when determining the dividend payout. Its 1985 and 1986 annual reports state that its dividend policy is implemented with the objective of maximizing total shareholder returns over the long term.

## Divestitures

G-P has divested assets that were performing below targeted levels or were unrelated to the core business. The proceeds received from the divestitures were used to reduce debt, replace worn-out assets, and invest in new projects. In general, the divestitures allowed G-P to increase its concentration in the forest products business and reduce its degree of financial leverage.

## Cash Flow

A summary of G-P's cash flow position is shown in Table 28.4. Over the 1981–85 period, G-P obtained 64 percent of its funds internally and 36 percent externally. The primary internal source of funds was continuing operations. The primary source of external funds was debt.

**TABLE 28.4  Sources and Uses of Funds: Georgia-Pacific Corporation (Millions of Dollars)**

| | 1981–1985 | | 1986 | |
|---|---|---|---|---|
| | Total Amount in Dollars | Percent of Total | Total Amount in Dollars | Percent of Total |
| *Sources of funds* | | | | |
| Internal Sources: | | | | |
| Continuing operations | $2,383 | 49.0% | $ 575 | 43.4% |
| Sales of discontinued operations[a] | 345 | 7.1 | 182 | 13.7 |
| Discontinued operations prior to sale | 156 | 3.2 | | 0.0 |
| Other | 230 | 4.7 | | 0.0 |
| Total internal sources | 3,114 | 64.0% | 757 | 57.1 |
| External Sources: | | | | |
| Debt additions | 1,717 | 35.3 | 555 | 41.9 |
| Stock issued for acquisitions | 32 | .7 | 0 | 0.0 |
| Other | 0 | 0 | 14 | 1.0 |
| Total external sources | 1,749 | 36.0% | 569 | 42.9% |
| Total sources of funds | $4,863 | 100.0% | $1,326 | 100.0% |
| | | | | |
| *Uses of funds* | | | | |
| Internal Uses: | | | | |
| Capital expenditures | $2,356 | 48.5% | $ 482 | 36.3% |
| Cash on hand | 30 | .6 | 18 | 1.4 |
| | 2,386 | 49.1 | 500 | 37.7 |
| External Uses: | | | | |
| Debt and preferred stock repayments | 1,876 | 38.6 | 715 | 53.9 |
| Dividends | 507 | 10.4 | 97 | 7.3 |
| Other | 94 | 1.9 | 14 | 1.1 |
| | 2,477 | 50.9 | 826 | 62.3 |
| Total uses of funds | $4,863 | 100.0% | $1,326 | 100.0% |

[a] Includes discontinued operations prior to sale and liquidation of investments.

During the 1981–85 period, G-P allocated its funds evenly between internal and external uses. Its main internal use was capital expenditures, while its main external uses were debt and preferred stock repayments, and dividend payments.

In 1986 the relative composition of G-P's sources and uses of funds changed significantly. Its continuing operations generated a smaller percentage of total funds in 1986 than in the previous five-year period. However, its divestment of operations became a more important source of funds in 1986. G-P used a larger proportion of funds for debt and preferred stock repayments in 1986 than in the previous five-year period. However, it used a smaller proportion of funds for capital expenditures. In fact, the debt and preferred stock repayments became the primary use of funds in 1986. This suggests that some of the investment opportunities available to G-P would not adequately compensate shareholders. Consequently, the use of funds to reduce debt offered a higher return to shareholders than additional investment in assets.

## Liquidity

At the start of 1987 G-P had domestic and foreign bank lines of credit amounting to $700 million. Approximately $275 million of this amount was being used to back commercial paper and other short-term instruments.

G-P's liquidity as measured by its current ratio recently declined. Nevertheless, because the main reason for the decline was reduced accounts receivable and inventory, liquidity was still adequate. Furthermore, the company's substantial lines of credit enhance its ability to obtain funds quickly.

## Return

G-P has substantially improved its returns over the 1980s. Table 28.5 illustrates the reason for the improvement over the last three years. Its net profit margin increased from 1.78 percent in 1984 to 4.10 percent in 1986. Since its asset turnover was stable in these years, G-P's return on assets in 1986 more than doubled the 1984 level. Because of the firm's continual debt-reduction strategy over this period, the assets-equity ratio declined. Its reduced degree of financial leverage dampened the 1986 return on equity. Yet, its return on equity in 1986 was still more than double the 1984 level. While G-P might have been able to achieve a higher return on equity in 1986 with a more debt-intensive capital structure, it would not have had as much future financing flexibility.

## Agency Aspects

G-P's annual reports clearly state its primary goal of maximizing shareholder wealth over the long run. To assure that its managers strive for this objective, G-P offers an incentive program that compensates managers according to return on equity, so that the goals of managers are similar to those of shareholders.

The return-on-equity measure can be influenced by capital structure decisions. Thus, it may be possible for managers to increase financial leverage in an effort to boost return on equity and therefore their amount of

**TABLE 28.5**   Decomposition of Return on Equity: Georgia-Pacific Corporation

|  | 1984 | 1985 | 1986 |
|---|---|---|---|
| Net income (in millions) | $ 119 | $ 187 | $ 296 |
| Sales (in millions) | 6,682 | 6,716 | 7,223 |
| Assets (in millions) | 4,785 | 4,866 | 5,114 |
| Equity (in millions) | 2,035 | 2,147 | 2,452 |
| Net profit margin (Net income/Sales) | 1.78% | 2.78% | 4.10% |
| Asset turnover (Sales/Assets) | 1.40 | 1.38 | 1.41 |
| Return on assets (Net income/Assets) | 2.49 | 3.84 | 5.79 |
| Assets/equity | 2.35 | 2.27 | 2.09 |
| Return on equity (Net income/Equity) | 5.84 | 8.71 | 12.07 |

incentive compensation. This strategy could increase risk and reduce the price of the firm's common stock, meaning that the managers would benefit at the expense of shareholders. However, G-P has a target capital structure that limits the ability of managers to implement a financing policy that would be in their own best interests rather than shareholder interests.

### Economic Aspects

G-P's performance depends on economic factors that affect the demand for its products. It attributes recent improved performance to changes in the housing industry. Lower interest rates have stimulated demand for single-family construction and remodeling—and consequently, demand for G-P's building products. The Tax Reform Act of 1986, however, reduced the tax benefits on rental property and may therefore reduce the construction of multi-family dwellings, which could adversely affect demand for G-P's products.

The weakening of the U.S. dollar in 1986 caused an increased foreign demand for some U.S. products, and G-P's sales volume was favorably affected by the weak dollar. G-P's future growth is somewhat dependent on interest rates, tax laws, the value of the dollar, and other factors that influence economic conditions. The firm is financially positioned to grow if conditions are favorable.

## INTEGRATION OF FINANCIAL MANAGEMENT WITH OTHER BUSINESS DISCIPLINES

The main financial management decisions are not only interrelated but are also closely related to all other business disciplines. Marketing strategies have a strong influence on sales, which in turn affect all investing and financing decisions. Marketing strategies also determine which particular operations generate excess cash versus those operations that require additional financing.

When economies of scale result from a high level of production, marketing may be used to assure a high sales volume. Such a marketing strategy allows firms to achieve increased efficiency and higher returns. For example, Quaker Oats Company uses marketing to develop an image of brand strength. This results in high demand, efficient production, and high returns.

Most decisions are based on projections of future sales and costs. Given the impact of economic factors (such as inflation, interest rates, and economic growth) on a firm's sales and costs, the use of economic projections to forecast sales and costs is quite common. Future cash flows, the cost of capital, operating leverage, and financial leverage are all affected by economic variables such as inflation and interest rates. Corporate economists provide forecasts of the economic variables, which are used as input to set financial management policies.

Since firms attempt to maximize the long-term value of their stock price (a goal consistent with maximizing shareholder wealth), they must continually inform existing and prospective shareholders of their financial condition. Accountants facilitate this process by converting the firm's past earnings performance and current balance sheet characteristics into standardized financial statements. Accountants also audit the firm's operations to detect any possible inefficiencies.

To more fully appreciate the interaction between the various business disciplines, consider an evaluation of a proposed investment in additional machinery. Forecasted cash flows to be generated by the machine are dependent on sales, which in turn are influenced by economic factors such as future interest rates, inflation, and consumer income. A primary role of the economist is to forecast how these factors will influence sales. In addition, any changes in industry-specific characteristics (such as competition) must be projected, along with the impact of these changes on sales.

In addition to economic and industry-specific factors, firm-specific factors such as pricing, reputation, current market share, and the advertising budget will influence sales. These firm-specific factors must be considered in conjunction with economic factors in order to appropriately assess future sales volume. Even if all economic factors were favorable, future sales could be highly overestimated if unfavorable firm-specific factors such as overpricing and a low advertising budget are not considered. Therefore, economists should utilize pricing and advertising information from the marketing department when forecasting sales.

The potential increase in sales to be generated from additional machinery is constrained by the amount of products the machinery can produce. The production department must provide input on production capacity and costs of operating the additional machinery, including additional labor, greater investment in inventory, and increased energy usage.

The economists, marketing agents, and managers use historical information provided by accountants. Historical financial statements may enable the various departments to determine the sensitivity of sales volume to various economic and firm-specific factors and also to determine the additional production costs associated with operating additional machinery.

The input from various departments is used to forecast net cash flows generated from the additional machinery. Financial managers use this information along with their required rate of return to determine whether the machinery should be purchased. Their required rate of return may be influenced by the economist's interest-rate projections and the degree of uncertainty surrounding the cash flow projections. The input provided by other departments is just as important as the capital budgeting analysis in order to make the proper decision.

The preceding discussion is simplified to the extent that it does not totally integrate all business disciplines. Yet, even a simplified overview illustrates the dependencies on every discipline and how financial management fits into the overall picture.

## SUMMARY

Every financial management policy is affected by other policies. Thus, even if financial managers concentrate on a particular decision, they must recognize the relationships between policies. Well-trained financial managers are exposed to all types of policies so that they can understand how their decisions influence other financial characteristics of the firm.

Financial managers who do not consider the integrative characteristics of a financial management decision are unable to maximize shareholder wealth. To the extent that these managers are penalized by their employers for such subpar performance, they are unable to maximize their own wealth as well.

## QUESTIONS

**Q28-1.** Classify the following as either an investment or financing decision, and justify your classifications:

- Inventory management
- Capital structure policy
- Marketable securities management
- Dividend policy

**Q28-2.** Classify the following decisions as to whether they have a direct impact on sales or are affected by sales.

- Accounts receivable management
- Cash management
- Inventory management
- Marketable securities management

**Q28-3.** Why would a proposed capital expenditure that was once unfeasible become feasible in a subsequent period?

**Q28-4.** Describe some general differences in the balance sheet structure between low-risk and high-risk firms.

**Q28-5.** What is the main disadvantage of maintaining an excessive amount of cash, marketable securities, and inventory?

**Q28-6.** What is the main disadvantage of maintaining insufficient inventory and fixed assets?

**Q28-7.** How can the capital structure decision affect a firm's capital budget?

**Q28-8.** Explain how a firm can adjust its capital structure in an attempt to boost its return on equity.

**Q28-9.** What is the purpose of conducting a financial analysis of each division within a firm?

**Q28-10.** The CEO of Higgins Corporation has implemented a plan to boost the company's return on equity by 30 percent. The plan involves increasing asset utilization and increasing the profit margin. Comment on why these goals may not easily be achieved at the same time.

**Q28-11.** Explain in general terms how the capital budgeting decision, dividend policy, and existing cash flow can affect the capital structure decision.

**Q28-12.** In order to generate funds, Melnyk Corporation has discontinued its dividend payments, credit to customers, and new projects. Do you think these policies should be used to obtain temporary financing? Explain.

**Q28-13.** Lynde Corporation plans to purchase some divisions of other firms over the next year. All of these divisions are significantly different from one another in terms of their product offerings and other characteristics. Although Lynde Corporation will not make its investment decisions until later in the year, it wants to determine how to finance these investments now. Since it plans to utilize $400 million for these purchases, it has decided to develop its long-term capital structure target now. Comment on this strategy.

**Q28-14.** Obtain the most recent annual report of a firm assigned by your professor. Use this annual report to address the following questions.

**a.** Determine the firm's main sources and uses of funds for each of the last two years. Estimate the relative proportion of funds obtained from each source. Estimate the relative proportion of funds allocated for each use. Discuss why the relative proportion of individual sources and uses changed over time.
**b.** How has the firm's capital budget amount changed over the last two years? Explain why it may have changed. What is the planned capital budget for the following year? Why is this budget different from last year's budget?
**c.** What is the relationship between the firm's net income and its dividends, if any?
**d.** How has the firm's return on equity changed in recent years? Break down the return on equity into profit margin, asset turnover, and assets/equity. Explain which components caused the most significant adjustments in return on equity recently.
**e.** Does the firm have lines of credit as a source of liquidity? What is the dollar amount of these lines?
**f.** Does the firm have a target capital structure? If so, what is it? How has the firm's capital structure changed in recent years? Explain why the firm may have changed its capital structure.
**g.** Does the annual report suggest any managerial incentives to assure that managerial and shareholder goals are similar? If so, what are the incentives based on?
**h.** Identify any industry-specific factors and economic factors that may have a strong influence on the firm's future performance. Based on projections of these factors (calculated by yourself or obtained from business periodicals), provide a general forecast of the firm's future financial performance.

## REFERENCES

Beck, P. W. "Corporate Planning for an Uncertain Future." *Long Range Planning* 15 (August 1982): 12–23.

Donaldson, Gordon. "Financial Goals and Strategic Consequences." *Harvard Business Review* 63 (May–June 1985): 57–66.

Lynch, Thomas E. "Business Divisions: A Performance Evaluation." *Financial Executive* 52 (November 1984): 30–43.

Nauert, Roger C. "Jumping the Hurdles to Strategic Planning." *Healthcare Financial Management* 37 (August 1983): 26–30.

Tandon, Rajiv. "Strategic Planning in an Era of Uncertainty." *Journal of Business Strategies* 5 (Winter 1985): 94–97.

# APPENDIX

## TABLE A    Future Value of $1 at the End of *n* Periods

$$FVIF_{k,n} = (1 + k)^n$$

| Period n | 1% | 2% | 3% | 4% | 5% | 6% | 7% | 8% | 9% | 10% | 11% | 12% |
|---|---|---|---|---|---|---|---|---|---|---|---|---|
| 1 | 1.0100 | 1.0200 | 1.0300 | 1.0400 | 1.0500 | 1.0600 | 1.0700 | 1.0800 | 1.0900 | 1.1000 | 1.1100 | 1.1200 |
| 2 | 1.0201 | 1.0404 | 1.0609 | 1.0816 | 1.1025 | 1.1236 | 1.1449 | 1.1664 | 1.1881 | 1.2100 | 1.2321 | 1.2544 |
| 3 | 1.0303 | 1.0612 | 1.0927 | 1.1249 | 1.1576 | 1.1910 | 1.2250 | 1.2597 | 1.2950 | 1.3310 | 1.3676 | 1.4049 |
| 4 | 1.0406 | 1.0824 | 1.1255 | 1.1699 | 1.2155 | 1.2625 | 1.3108 | 1.3605 | 1.4116 | 1.4641 | 1.5181 | 1.5735 |
| 5 | 1.0510 | 1.1041 | 1.1593 | 1.2167 | 1.2763 | 1.3382 | 1.4026 | 1.4693 | 1.5386 | 1.6105 | 1.6851 | 1.7623 |
| 6 | 1.0615 | 1.1262 | 1.1941 | 1.2653 | 1.3401 | 1.4185 | 1.5007 | 1.5869 | 1.6771 | 1.7716 | 1.8704 | 1.9738 |
| 7 | 1.0721 | 1.1487 | 1.2299 | 1.3159 | 1.4071 | 1.5036 | 1.6058 | 1.7138 | 1.8280 | 1.9487 | 2.0762 | 2.2107 |
| 8 | 1.0829 | 1.1717 | 1.2668 | 1.3686 | 1.4775 | 1.5938 | 1.7182 | 1.8509 | 1.9926 | 2.1436 | 2.3045 | 2.4760 |
| 9 | 1.0937 | 1.1951 | 1.3048 | 1.4233 | 1.5513 | 1.6895 | 1.8385 | 1.9990 | 2.1719 | 2.3579 | 2.5580 | 2.7731 |
| 10 | 1.1046 | 1.2190 | 1.3439 | 1.4802 | 1.6289 | 1.7908 | 1.9672 | 2.1589 | 2.3674 | 2.5937 | 2.8394 | 3.1058 |
| 11 | 1.1157 | 1.2434 | 1.3842 | 1.5395 | 1.7103 | 1.8983 | 2.1049 | 2.3316 | 2.5804 | 2.8531 | 3.1518 | 3.4785 |
| 12 | 1.1268 | 1.2682 | 1.4258 | 1.6010 | 1.7959 | 2.0122 | 2.2522 | 2.5182 | 2.8127 | 3.1384 | 3.4985 | 3.8960 |
| 13 | 1.1381 | 1.2936 | 1.4685 | 1.6651 | 1.8856 | 2.1329 | 2.4098 | 2.7196 | 3.0658 | 3.4523 | 3.8833 | 4.3635 |
| 14 | 1.1495 | 1.3195 | 1.5126 | 1.7317 | 1.9799 | 2.2609 | 2.5785 | 2.9372 | 3.3417 | 3.7975 | 4.3104 | 4.8871 |
| 15 | 1.1610 | 1.3459 | 1.5580 | 1.8009 | 2.0789 | 2.3966 | 2.7590 | 3.1722 | 3.6425 | 4.1772 | 4.7846 | 5.4736 |
| 16 | 1.1726 | 1.3728 | 1.6047 | 1.8730 | 2.1829 | 2.5404 | 2.9522 | 3.4259 | 3.9703 | 4.5950 | 5.3109 | 6.1304 |
| 17 | 1.1843 | 1.4002 | 1.6528 | 1.9479 | 2.2920 | 2.6928 | 3.1588 | 3.7000 | 4.3276 | 5.0545 | 5.8951 | 6.8660 |
| 18 | 1.1961 | 1.4282 | 1.7024 | 2.0258 | 2.4066 | 2.8543 | 3.3799 | 3.9960 | 4.7171 | 5.5599 | 6.5436 | 7.6900 |
| 19 | 1.2081 | 1.4568 | 1.7535 | 2.1068 | 2.5270 | 3.0256 | 3.6165 | 4.3157 | 5.1417 | 6.1159 | 7.2633 | 8.6128 |
| 20 | 1.2202 | 1.4859 | 1.8061 | 2.1911 | 2.6533 | 3.2071 | 3.8697 | 4.6610 | 5.6044 | 6.7275 | 8.0623 | 9.6463 |
| 21 | 1.2324 | 1.5157 | 1.8603 | 2.2788 | 2.7860 | 3.3996 | 4.1406 | 5.0338 | 6.1088 | 7.4002 | 8.9492 | 10.804 |
| 22 | 1.2447 | 1.5460 | 1.9161 | 2.3699 | 2.9253 | 3.6035 | 4.4304 | 5.4365 | 6.6586 | 8.1403 | 9.9336 | 12.100 |
| 23 | 1.2572 | 1.5769 | 1.9736 | 2.4647 | 3.0715 | 3.8197 | 4.7405 | 5.8715 | 7.2579 | 8.9543 | 11.026 | 13.552 |
| 24 | 1.2697 | 1.6084 | 2.0328 | 2.5633 | 3.2251 | 4.0489 | 5.0724 | 6.3412 | 7.9111 | 9.8497 | 12.239 | 15.179 |
| 25 | 1.2824 | 1.6406 | 2.0938 | 2.6658 | 3.3864 | 4.2919 | 5.4274 | 6.8485 | 8.6231 | 10.835 | 13.585 | 17.000 |
| 26 | 1.2953 | 1.6734 | 2.1566 | 2.7725 | 3.5557 | 4.5494 | 5.8074 | 7.3964 | 9.3992 | 11.918 | 15.080 | 19.040 |
| 27 | 1.3082 | 1.7069 | 2.2213 | 2.8834 | 3.7335 | 4.8223 | 6.2139 | 7.9881 | 10.245 | 13.110 | 16.739 | 21.325 |
| 28 | 1.3213 | 1.7410 | 2.2879 | 2.9987 | 3.9201 | 5.1117 | 6.6488 | 8.6271 | 11.167 | 14.421 | 18.580 | 23.884 |
| 29 | 1.3345 | 1.7758 | 2.3566 | 3.1187 | 4.1161 | 5.4184 | 7.1143 | 9.3173 | 12.172 | 15.863 | 20.624 | 26.750 |
| 30 | 1.3478 | 1.8114 | 2.4273 | 3.2434 | 4.3219 | 5.7435 | 7.6123 | 10.063 | 13.268 | 17.449 | 22.892 | 29.960 |
| 35 | 1.4166 | 1.9999 | 2.8139 | 3.9461 | 5.5160 | 7.6861 | 10.677 | 14.785 | 20.414 | 28.102 | 38.575 | 52.800 |
| 40 | 1.4889 | 2.2080 | 3.2620 | 4.8010 | 7.0400 | 10.286 | 14.974 | 21.725 | 31.409 | 45.259 | 65.001 | 93.051 |
| 45 | 1.5648 | 2.4379 | 3.7816 | 5.8412 | 8.9850 | 13.765 | 21.002 | 31.920 | 48.327 | 72.890 | 109.53 | 163.99 |
| 50 | 1.6446 | 2.6916 | 4.3839 | 7.1067 | 11.467 | 18.420 | 29.457 | 46.902 | 74.358 | 117.39 | 184.56 | 289.00 |

*(Continued on next page)*

**TABLE A**    Future Value of $1 at the End of *n* Periods (*Continued*)

$$FVIF_{k,n} = (1 + k)^n$$

| 13% | 14% | 15% | 16% | 17% | 18% | 19% | 20% | 25% | 30% | 35% | 40% | 50% |
|---|---|---|---|---|---|---|---|---|---|---|---|---|
| 1.1300 | 1.1400 | 1.1500 | 1.1600 | 1.1700 | 1.1800 | 1.1900 | 1.2000 | 1.2500 | 1.3000 | 1.3500 | 1.4000 | 1.5000 |
| 1.2769 | 1.2996 | 1.3225 | 1.3456 | 1.3689 | 1.3924 | 1.4161 | 1.4400 | 1.5625 | 1.6900 | 1.8225 | 1.9600 | 2.2500 |
| 1.4429 | 1.4815 | 1.5209 | 1.5609 | 1.6016 | 1.6430 | 1.6852 | 1.7280 | 1.9531 | 2.1970 | 2.4604 | 2.7440 | 3.3750 |
| 1.6305 | 1.6890 | 1.7490 | 1.8106 | 1.8739 | 1.9388 | 2.0053 | 2.0736 | 2.4414 | 2.8561 | 3.3215 | 3.8416 | 5.0625 |
| 1.8424 | 1.9254 | 2.0114 | 2.1003 | 2.1924 | 2.2878 | 2.3864 | 2.4883 | 3.0518 | 3.7129 | 4.4840 | 5.3782 | 7.5938 |
| 2.0820 | 2.1950 | 2.3131 | 2.4364 | 2.5652 | 2.6996 | 2.8398 | 2.9860 | 3.8147 | 4.8268 | 6.0534 | 7.5295 | 11.391 |
| 2.3526 | 2.5023 | 2.6600 | 2.8262 | 3.0012 | 3.1855 | 3.3793 | 3.5832 | 4.7684 | 6.2749 | 8.1722 | 10.541 | 17.086 |
| 2.6584 | 2.8526 | 3.0590 | 3.2784 | 3.5115 | 3.7589 | 4.0214 | 4.2998 | 5.9605 | 8.1573 | 11.032 | 14.758 | 25.629 |
| 3.0040 | 3.2519 | 3.5179 | 3.8030 | 4.1084 | 4.4355 | 4.7854 | 5.1598 | 7.4506 | 10.604 | 14.894 | 20.661 | 38.443 |
| 3.3946 | 3.7072 | 4.0456 | 4.4114 | 4.8068 | 5.2338 | 5.6947 | 6.1917 | 9.3132 | 13.786 | 20.107 | 28.925 | 57.665 |
| 3.8359 | 4.2262 | 4.6524 | 5.1173 | 5.6240 | 6.1759 | 6.7767 | 7.4301 | 11.642 | 17.922 | 27.144 | 40.496 | 86.498 |
| 4.3345 | 4.8179 | 5.3503 | 5.9360 | 6.5801 | 7.2876 | 8.0642 | 8.9161 | 14.552 | 23.298 | 36.644 | 56.694 | 129.75 |
| 4.8980 | 5.4924 | 6.1528 | 6.8858 | 7.6987 | 8.5994 | 9.5964 | 10.699 | 18.190 | 30.288 | 49.470 | 79.371 | 194.62 |
| 5.5348 | 6.2613 | 7.0757 | 7.9875 | 9.0075 | 10.147 | 11.420 | 12.839 | 22.737 | 39.374 | 66.784 | 111.12 | 291.93 |
| 6.2543 | 7.1379 | 8.1371 | 9.2655 | 10.539 | 11.974 | 13.590 | 15.407 | 28.422 | 51.186 | 90.158 | 155.57 | 437.89 |
| 7.0673 | 8.1372 | 9.3576 | 10.748 | 12.330 | 14.129 | 16.172 | 18.488 | 35.527 | 66.542 | 121.71 | 217.80 | 656.84 |
| 7.9861 | 9.2765 | 10.761 | 12.468 | 14.426 | 16.672 | 19.244 | 22.186 | 44.409 | 86.504 | 164.31 | 304.91 | 985.26 |
| 9.0243 | 10.575 | 12.375 | 14.463 | 16.879 | 19.673 | 22.901 | 26.623 | 55.511 | 112.46 | 221.82 | 426.88 | 1477.9 |
| 10.197 | 12.056 | 14.232 | 16.777 | 19.748 | 23.214 | 27.252 | 31.948 | 69.389 | 146.19 | 299.46 | 597.63 | 2216.8 |
| 11.523 | 13.743 | 16.367 | 19.461 | 23.106 | 27.393 | 32.429 | 38.338 | 86.736 | 190.05 | 404.27 | 836.68 | 3325.3 |
| 13.021 | 15.668 | 18.822 | 22.574 | 27.034 | 32.324 | 38.591 | 46.005 | 108.42 | 247.06 | 545.77 | 1171.4 | 4987.9 |
| 14.714 | 17.861 | 21.645 | 26.186 | 31.629 | 38.142 | 45.923 | 55.206 | 135.53 | 321.18 | 736.79 | 1639.9 | 7481.8 |
| 16.627 | 20.362 | 24.891 | 30.376 | 37.006 | 45.008 | 54.649 | 66.247 | 169.41 | 417.54 | 994.66 | 2295.9 | 11223. |
| 18.788 | 23.212 | 28.625 | 35.236 | 43.297 | 53.109 | 65.032 | 79.497 | 211.76 | 542.80 | 1342.8 | 3214.2 | 16834. |
| 21.231 | 26.462 | 32.919 | 40.874 | 50.658 | 62.669 | 77.388 | 95.396 | 264.70 | 705.64 | 1812.8 | 4499.9 | 25251. |
| 23.991 | 30.167 | 37.857 | 47.414 | 59.270 | 73.949 | 92.092 | 114.48 | 330.87 | 917.33 | 2447.2 | 6299.8 | 37877. |
| 27.109 | 34.390 | 43.535 | 55.000 | 69.345 | 87.260 | 109.59 | 137.37 | 413.59 | 1192.5 | 3303.8 | 8819.8 | 56815. |
| 30.633 | 39.204 | 50.066 | 63.800 | 81.134 | 102.97 | 130.41 | 164.84 | 516.99 | 1550.3 | 4460.1 | 12348. | 85223. |
| 34.616 | 44.693 | 57.575 | 74.009 | 94.927 | 121.50 | 155.19 | 197.81 | 646.23 | 2015.4 | 6021.1 | 17287. | * |
| 39.116 | 50.950 | 66.212 | 85.850 | 111.06 | 143.37 | 184.68 | 237.38 | 807.79 | 2620.0 | 8128.5 | 24201. | * |
| 72.069 | 98.100 | 133.18 | 180.31 | 243.50 | 328,00 | 440.70 | 590.67 | 2465.2 | 9727.9 | 36449. | * | * |
| 132.78 | 188.88 | 267.86 | 378.72 | 533.87 | 750.38 | 1051.7 | 1469.8 | 7523.2 | 36119. | * | * | * |
| 244.64 | 363.68 | 538.77 | 795.44 | 1170.5 | 1716.7 | 2509.7 | 3657.3 | 22959. | * | * | * | * |
| 450.74 | 700.23 | 1083.7 | 1670.7 | 2566.2 | 3927.4 | 5988.9 | 9100.4 | 70065. | * | * | * | * |

*Interest factors exceed 99,999.

**TABLE B    Present Value of $1 Due at the End of *n* Periods**

$$PVIF_{k,n} = \frac{1}{(1 + k)^n}$$

| Period n | 1% | 2% | 3% | 4% | 5% | 6% | 7% | 8% | 9% | 10% | 11% | 12% |
|---|---|---|---|---|---|---|---|---|---|---|---|---|
| 1 | .9901 | .9804 | .9709 | .9615 | .9524 | .9434 | .9346 | .9259 | .9174 | .9091 | .9009 | .8929 |
| 2 | .9803 | .9612 | .9426 | .9246 | .9070 | .8900 | .8734 | .8573 | .8417 | .8264 | .8116 | .7972 |
| 3 | .9706 | .9423 | .9151 | .8890 | .8638 | .8396 | .8163 | .7938 | .7722 | .7513 | .7312 | .7118 |
| 4 | .9610 | .9238 | .8885 | .8548 | .8227 | .7921 | .7629 | .7350 | .7084 | .6830 | .6587 | .6355 |
| 5 | .9515 | .9057 | .8626 | .8219 | .7835 | .7473 | .7130 | .6806 | .6499 | .6209 | .5935 | .5674 |
| 6 | .9420 | .8880 | .8375 | .7903 | .7462 | .7050 | .6663 | .6302 | .5963 | .5645 | .5346 | .5066 |
| 7 | .9327 | .8706 | .8131 | .7599 | .7107 | .6651 | .6227 | .5835 | .5470 | .5132 | .4817 | .4523 |
| 8 | .9235 | .8535 | .7894 | .7307 | .6768 | .6274 | .5820 | .5403 | .5019 | .4665 | .4339 | .4039 |
| 9 | .9143 | .8368 | .7664 | .7026 | .6446 | .5919 | .5439 | .5002 | .4604 | .4241 | .3909 | .3606 |
| 10 | .9053 | .8203 | .7441 | .6756 | .6139 | .5584 | .5083 | .4632 | .4224 | .3855 | .3522 | .3220 |
| 11 | .8963 | .8043 | .7224 | .6496 | .5847 | .5268 | .4751 | .4289 | .3875 | .3505 | .3173 | .2875 |
| 12 | .8874 | .7885 | .7014 | .6246 | .5568 | .4970 | .4440 | .3971 | .3555 | .3186 | .2858 | .2567 |
| 13 | .8787 | .7730 | .6810 | .6006 | .5303 | .4688 | .4150 | .3677 | .3262 | .2897 | .2575 | .2292 |
| 14 | .8700 | .7579 | .6611 | .5775 | .5051 | .4423 | .3878 | .3405 | .2992 | .2633 | .2320 | .2046 |
| 15 | .8613 | .7430 | .6419 | .5553 | .4810 | .4173 | .3624 | .3152 | .2745 | .2394 | .2090 | .1827 |
| 16 | .8528 | .7284 | .6232 | .5339 | .4581 | .3936 | .3387 | .2919 | .2519 | .2176 | .1883 | .1631 |
| 17 | .8444 | .7142 | .6050 | .5134 | .4363 | .3714 | .3166 | .2703 | .2311 | .1978 | .1696 | .1456 |
| 18 | .8360 | .7002 | .5874 | .4936 | .4155 | .3503 | .2959 | .2502 | .2120 | .1799 | .1528 | .1300 |
| 19 | .8277 | .6864 | .5703 | .4746 | .3957 | .3305 | .2765 | .2317 | .1945 | .1635 | .1377 | .1161 |
| 20 | .8195 | .6730 | .5537 | .4564 | .3769 | .3118 | .2584 | .2145 | .1784 | .1486 | .1240 | .1037 |
| 21 | .8114 | .6598 | .5375 | .4388 | .3589 | .2942 | .2415 | .1987 | .1637 | .1351 | .1117 | .0926 |
| 22 | .8034 | .6468 | .5219 | .4220 | .3418 | .2775 | .2257 | .1839 | .1502 | .1228 | .1007 | .0826 |
| 23 | .7954 | .6342 | .5067 | .4057 | .3256 | .2618 | .2109 | .1703 | .1378 | .1117 | .0907 | .0738 |
| 24 | .7876 | .6217 | .4919 | .3901 | .3101 | .2470 | .1971 | .1577 | .1264 | .1015 | .0817 | .0659 |
| 25 | .7798 | .6095 | .4776 | .3751 | .2953 | .2330 | .1842 | .1460 | .1160 | .0923 | .0736 | .0588 |
| 26 | .7720 | .5976 | .4637 | .3607 | .2812 | .2198 | .1722 | .1352 | .1064 | .0839 | .0663 | .0525 |
| 27 | .7644 | .5859 | .4502 | .3468 | .2678 | .2074 | .1609 | .1252 | .0976 | .0763 | .0597 | .0469 |
| 28 | .7568 | .5744 | .4371 | .3335 | .2551 | .1956 | .1504 | .1159 | .0895 | .0693 | .0538 | .0419 |
| 29 | .7493 | .5631 | .4243 | .3207 | .2429 | .1846 | .1406 | .1073 | .0822 | .0630 | .0485 | .0374 |
| 30 | .7419 | .5521 | .4120 | .3083 | .2314 | .1741 | .1314 | .0994 | .0754 | .0573 | .0437 | .0334 |
| 35 | .7059 | .5000 | .3554 | .2534 | .1813 | .1301 | .0937 | .0676 | .0490 | .0356 | .0259 | .0189 |
| 40 | .6717 | .4529 | .3066 | .2083 | .1420 | .0972 | .0668 | .0460 | .0318 | .0221 | .0154 | .0107 |
| 45 | .6391 | .4102 | .2644 | .1712 | .1113 | .0727 | .0476 | .0313 | .0207 | .0137 | .0091 | .0061 |
| 50 | .6080 | .3715 | .2281 | .1407 | .0872 | .0543 | .0339 | .0213 | .0134 | .0085 | .0054 | .0035 |

*(Continued on next page)*

**TABLE B**   Present Value of $1 Due at the End of *n* Periods (*Continued*)

$$PVIF_{k,n} = \frac{1}{(1 + k)^n}$$

| 13% | 14% | 15% | 16% | 17% | 18% | 19% | 20% | 25% | 30% | 35% | 40% | 50% |
|---|---|---|---|---|---|---|---|---|---|---|---|---|
| .8850 | .8772 | .8696 | .8621 | .8547 | .8475 | .8403 | .8333 | .8000 | .7692 | .7407 | .7143 | .6667 |
| .7831 | .7695 | .7561 | .7432 | .7305 | .7182 | .7062 | .6944 | .6400 | .5917 | .5487 | .5102 | .4444 |
| .6931 | .6750 | .6575 | .6407 | .6244 | .6086 | .5934 | .5787 | .5120 | .4552 | .4064 | .3644 | .2963 |
| .6133 | .5921 | .5718 | .5523 | .5337 | .5158 | .4987 | .4823 | .4096 | .3501 | .3011 | .2603 | .1975 |
| .5428 | .5194 | .4972 | .4761 | .4561 | .4371 | .4190 | .4019 | .3277 | .2693 | .2230 | .1859 | .1317 |
| .4803 | .4556 | .4323 | .4104 | .3898 | .3704 | .3521 | .3349 | .2621 | .2072 | .1652 | .1328 | .0878 |
| .4251 | .3996 | .3759 | .3538 | .3332 | .3139 | .2959 | .2791 | .2097 | .1594 | .1224 | .0949 | .0585 |
| .3762 | .3506 | .3269 | .3050 | .2848 | .2660 | .2487 | .2326 | .1678 | .1226 | .0906 | .0678 | .0390 |
| .3329 | .3075 | .2843 | .2630 | .2434 | .2255 | .2090 | .1938 | .1342 | .0943 | .0671 | .0484 | .0260 |
| .2946 | .2697 | .2472 | .2267 | .2080 | .1911 | .1756 | .1615 | .1074 | .0725 | .0497 | .0346 | .0173 |
| .2607 | .2366 | .2149 | .1954 | .1778 | .1619 | .1476 | .1346 | .0859 | .0558 | .0368 | .0247 | .0116 |
| .2307 | .2076 | .1869 | .1685 | .1520 | .1372 | .1240 | .1122 | .0687 | .0429 | .0273 | .0176 | .0077 |
| .2042 | .1821 | .1625 | .1452 | .1299 | .1163 | .1042 | .0935 | .0550 | .0330 | .0202 | .0126 | .0051 |
| .1807 | .1597 | .1413 | .1252 | .1110 | .0985 | .0876 | .0779 | .0440 | .0254 | .0150 | .0090 | .0034 |
| .1599 | .1401 | .1229 | .1079 | .0949 | .0835 | .0736 | .0649 | .0352 | .0195 | .0111 | .0064 | .0023 |
| .1415 | .1229 | .1069 | .0930 | .0811 | .0708 | .0618 | .0541 | .0281 | .0150 | .0082 | .0046 | .0015 |
| .1252 | .1078 | .0929 | .0802 | .0693 | .0600 | .0520 | .0451 | .0225 | .0116 | .0061 | .0033 | .0010 |
| .1108 | .0946 | .0808 | .0691 | .0592 | .0508 | .0437 | .0376 | .0180 | .0089 | .0045 | .0023 | .0007 |
| .0981 | .0829 | .0703 | .0596 | .0506 | .0431 | .0367 | .0313 | .0144 | .0068 | .0033 | .0017 | .0005 |
| .0868 | .0728 | .0611 | .0514 | .0443 | .0365 | .0308 | .0261 | .0115 | .0053 | .0025 | .0012 | .0003 |
| .0768 | .0638 | .0531 | .0443 | .0370 | .0309 | .0259 | .0217 | .0092 | .0040 | .0018 | .0009 | .0002 |
| .0680 | .0560 | .0462 | .0382 | .0316 | .0262 | .0218 | .0181 | .0074 | .0031 | .0014 | .0006 | .0001 |
| .0601 | .0491 | .0402 | .0329 | .0270 | .0222 | .0183 | .0151 | .0059 | .0024 | .0010 | .0004 | .0001 |
| .0532 | .0431 | .0349 | .0284 | .0231 | .0188 | .0154 | .0126 | .0047 | .0018 | .0007 | .0003 | .0001 |
| .0471 | .0378 | .0304 | .0245 | .0197 | .0160 | .0129 | .0105 | .0038 | .0014 | .0006 | .0002 | .0000 |
| .0417 | .0331 | .0264 | .0211 | .0169 | .0135 | .0109 | .0087 | .0030 | .0011 | .0004 | .0002 | .0000 |
| .0369 | .0291 | .0230 | .0182 | .0144 | .0115 | .0091 | .0073 | .0024 | .0008 | .0003 | .0001 | .0000 |
| .0326 | .0255 | .0200 | .0157 | .0123 | .0097 | .0077 | .0061 | .0019 | .0006 | .0002 | .0001 | .0000 |
| .0289 | .0224 | .0174 | .0135 | .0105 | .0082 | .0064 | .0051 | .0015 | .0005 | .0002 | .0001 | .0000 |
| .0256 | .0196 | .0151 | .0116 | .0090 | .0070 | .0054 | .0042 | .0012 | .0004 | .0001 | .0000 | .0000 |
| .0139 | .0102 | .0075 | .0055 | .0041 | .0030 | .0023 | .0017 | .0004 | .0001 | .0000 | .0000 | .0000 |
| .0075 | .0053 | .0037 | .0026 | .0019 | .0013 | .0010 | .0007 | .0001 | .0000 | .0000 | .0000 | .0000 |
| .0041 | .0027 | .0019 | .0013 | .0009 | .0006 | .0004 | .0003 | .0000 | .0000 | .0000 | .0000 | .0000 |
| .0022 | .0014 | .0009 | .0006 | .0004 | .0003 | .0002 | .0001 | .0000 | .0000 | .0000 | .0000 | .0000 |

**TABLE C**  Future Value of an Annuity of $1 per Period for *n* Periods

$$FVIFA_{k,n} = \frac{(1 + k)^n - 1}{k}$$

| Period *n* | 1% | 2% | 3% | 4% | 5% | 6% | 7% | 8% | 9% | 10% | 11% | 12% |
|---|---|---|---|---|---|---|---|---|---|---|---|---|
| 1 | 1.0000 | 1.0000 | 1.0000 | 1.0000 | 1.0000 | 1.0000 | 1.0000 | 1.0000 | 1.0000 | 1.0000 | 1.0000 | 1.0000 |
| 2 | 2.0100 | 2.0200 | 2.0300 | 2.0400 | 2.0500 | 2.0600 | 2.0700 | 2.0800 | 2.0900 | 2.1000 | 2.1100 | 2.1200 |
| 3 | 3.0301 | 3.0604 | 3.0909 | 3.1216 | 3.1525 | 3.1836 | 3.2149 | 3.2464 | 3.2781 | 3.3100 | 3.3421 | 3.3744 |
| 4 | 4.0604 | 4.1216 | 4.1836 | 4.2465 | 4.3101 | 4.3746 | 4.4399 | 4.5061 | 4.5731 | 4.6410 | 4.7097 | 4.7793 |
| 5 | 5.1010 | 5.2040 | 5.3091 | 5.4163 | 5.5256 | 5.6371 | 5.7507 | 5.8666 | 5.9847 | 6.1051 | 6.2278 | 6.3528 |
| 6 | 6.1520 | 6.3081 | 6.4684 | 6.6330 | 6.8019 | 6.9753 | 7.1533 | 7.3359 | 7.5233 | 7.7156 | 7.9129 | 8.1152 |
| 7 | 7.2135 | 7.4343 | 7.6625 | 7.8983 | 8.1420 | 8.3938 | 8.6540 | 8.9228 | 9.2004 | 9.4872 | 9.7833 | 10.089 |
| 8 | 8.2857 | 8.5830 | 8.8923 | 9.2142 | 9.5491 | 9.8975 | 10.260 | 10.637 | 11.028 | 11.436 | 11.859 | 12.300 |
| 9 | 9.3685 | 9.7546 | 10.159 | 10.583 | 11.027 | 11.491 | 11.978 | 12.488 | 13.021 | 13.579 | 14.164 | 14.776 |
| 10 | 10.462 | 10.950 | 11.464 | 12.006 | 12.578 | 13.181 | 13.816 | 14.487 | 15.193 | 15.937 | 16.722 | 17.549 |
| 11 | 11.567 | 12.169 | 12.808 | 13.486 | 14.207 | 14.972 | 15.784 | 16.645 | 17.560 | 18.531 | 19.561 | 20.655 |
| 12 | 12.683 | 13.412 | 14.192 | 15.026 | 15.917 | 16.870 | 17.888 | 18.977 | 20.141 | 21.384 | 22.713 | 24.133 |
| 13 | 13.809 | 14.680 | 15.618 | 16.627 | 17.713 | 18.882 | 20.141 | 21.495 | 22.953 | 24.523 | 26.212 | 28.029 |
| 14 | 14.947 | 15.974 | 17.086 | 18.292 | 19.599 | 21.015 | 22.550 | 24.215 | 26.019 | 27.975 | 30.095 | 32.393 |
| 15 | 16.097 | 17.293 | 18.599 | 20.024 | 21.579 | 23.276 | 25.129 | 27.152 | 29.361 | 31.772 | 34.405 | 37.280 |
| 16 | 17.258 | 18.639 | 20.157 | 21.825 | 23.657 | 25.673 | 27.888 | 30.324 | 33.003 | 35.950 | 39.190 | 42.753 |
| 17 | 18.430 | 20.012 | 21.762 | 23.698 | 25.840 | 28.213 | 30.840 | 33.750 | 36.974 | 40.545 | 44.501 | 48.884 |
| 18 | 19.615 | 21.412 | 23.414 | 25.645 | 28.132 | 30.906 | 33.999 | 37.450 | 41.301 | 45.599 | 50.396 | 55.750 |
| 19 | 20.811 | 22.841 | 25.117 | 27.671 | 30.539 | 33.760 | 37.379 | 41.446 | 46.018 | 51.159 | 56.939 | 63.440 |
| 20 | 22.019 | 24.297 | 26.870 | 29.778 | 33.066 | 36.786 | 40.995 | 45.762 | 51.160 | 57.275 | 64.203 | 72.052 |
| 21 | 23.239 | 25.783 | 28.676 | 31.969 | 35.719 | 39.993 | 44.865 | 50.423 | 56.765 | 64.002 | 72.265 | 81.699 |
| 22 | 24.472 | 27.299 | 30.537 | 34.248 | 38.505 | 43.392 | 49.006 | 55.457 | 62.873 | 71.403 | 81.214 | 92.503 |
| 23 | 25.716 | 28.845 | 32.453 | 36.618 | 41.430 | 46.996 | 53.436 | 60.893 | 69.532 | 79.543 | 91.148 | 104.60 |
| 24 | 26.973 | 30.422 | 34.426 | 39.083 | 44.502 | 50.816 | 58.177 | 66.765 | 76.790 | 88.497 | 102.17 | 118.16 |
| 25 | 28.243 | 32.030 | 36.459 | 41.646 | 47.727 | 54.865 | 63.249 | 73.106 | 84.701 | 98.347 | 114.41 | 133.33 |
| 26 | 29.526 | 33.671 | 38.553 | 44.312 | 51.113 | 59.156 | 68.676 | 79.954 | 93.324 | 109.18 | 128.00 | 150.33 |
| 27 | 30.821 | 35.344 | 40.710 | 47.084 | 54.669 | 63.706 | 74.484 | 87.351 | 102.72 | 121.10 | 143.08 | 169.37 |
| 28 | 32.129 | 37.051 | 42.931 | 49.968 | 58.403 | 68.528 | 80.698 | 95.339 | 112.97 | 134.21 | 159.82 | 190.70 |
| 29 | 33.450 | 38.792 | 45.219 | 52.966 | 62.323 | 73.640 | 87.347 | 103.97 | 124.14 | 148.63 | 178.40 | 214.58 |
| 30 | 34.785 | 40.568 | 47.575 | 56.085 | 66.439 | 79.058 | 94.461 | 113.28 | 136.31 | 164.49 | 199.02 | 241.33 |
| 35 | 41.660 | 49.994 | 60.462 | 73.652 | 90.320 | 111.43 | 138.24 | 172.32 | 215.71 | 271.02 | 341.59 | 431.66 |
| 40 | 48.886 | 60.402 | 75.401 | 95.026 | 120.80 | 154.76 | 199.64 | 259.06 | 337.88 | 442.59 | 581.83 | 767.09 |
| 45 | 56.481 | 71.893 | 92.720 | 121.03 | 159.70 | 212.74 | 285.75 | 386.51 | 525.86 | 718.90 | 986.64 | 1358.2 |
| 50 | 64.463 | 84.579 | 112.80 | 152.67 | 209.35 | 290.34 | 406.53 | 573.77 | 815.08 | 1163.9 | 1668.8 | 2400.0 |

*(Continued on next page)*

**TABLE C** Future Value of an Annuity of $1 per Period for *n* Periods (*Continued*)

$$FVIFA_{k,n} = \frac{(1+k)^n - 1}{k}$$

| 13% | 14% | 15% | 16% | 17% | 18% | 19% | 20% | 25% | 30% | 35% | 40% | 50% |
|---|---|---|---|---|---|---|---|---|---|---|---|---|
| 1.0000 | 1.0000 | 1.0000 | 1.0000 | 1.0000 | 1.0000 | 1.0000 | 1.0000 | 1.0000 | 1.0000 | 1.0000 | 1.0000 | 1.0000 |
| 2.1300 | 2.1400 | 2.1500 | 2.1600 | 2.1700 | 2.1800 | 2.1900 | 2.2000 | 2.2500 | 2.3000 | 2.3500 | 2.4000 | 2.5000 |
| 3.4069 | 3.4396 | 3.4725 | 3.5056 | 3.5389 | 3.5724 | 3.6061 | 3.6400 | 3.8125 | 3.9900 | 4.1725 | 4.3600 | 4.7500 |
| 4.8498 | 4.9211 | 4.9934 | 5.0665 | 5.1405 | 5.2154 | 5.2913 | 5.3680 | 5.7656 | 6.1870 | 6.6329 | 7.1040 | 8.1250 |
| 6.4803 | 6.6101 | 6.7424 | 6.8771 | 7.0144 | 7.1542 | 7.2966 | 7.4416 | 8.2070 | 9.0431 | 9.9544 | 10.946 | 13.188 |
| 8.3227 | 8.5355 | 8.7537 | 8.9775 | 9.2068 | 9.4420 | 9.6830 | 9.9299 | 11.259 | 12.756 | 14.438 | 16.324 | 20.781 |
| 10.405 | 10.730 | 11.067 | 11.414 | 11.772 | 12.142 | 12.523 | 12.916 | 15.073 | 17.583 | 20.492 | 23.853 | 32.172 |
| 12.757 | 13.233 | 13.727 | 14.240 | 14.773 | 15.327 | 15.902 | 16.499 | 19.842 | 23.858 | 28.664 | 34.395 | 49.258 |
| 15.416 | 16.085 | 16.786 | 17.519 | 18.285 | 19.086 | 19.923 | 20.799 | 25.802 | 32.015 | 39.696 | 49.153 | 74.887 |
| 18.420 | 19.337 | 20.304 | 21.321 | 22.393 | 23.521 | 24.709 | 25.959 | 33.253 | 42.619 | 54.590 | 69.814 | 113.33 |
| 21.814 | 23.045 | 24.349 | 25.733 | 27.200 | 28.755 | 30.404 | 32.150 | 42.566 | 56.405 | 74.697 | 98.739 | 171.00 |
| 25.650 | 27.271 | 29.002 | 30.850 | 32.824 | 34.931 | 37.180 | 39.581 | 54.208 | 74.327 | 101.84 | 139.23 | 257.49 |
| 29.985 | 32.089 | 34.352 | 36.786 | 39.404 | 42.219 | 45.244 | 48.497 | 68.760 | 97.625 | 138.48 | 195.93 | 387.24 |
| 34.883 | 37.581 | 40.505 | 43.672 | 47.103 | 50.818 | 54.841 | 59.196 | 86.949 | 127.91 | 187.95 | 275.30 | 581.86 |
| 40.417 | 43.842 | 47.580 | 51.660 | 56.110 | 60.965 | 66.261 | 72.035 | 109.69 | 167.29 | 254.74 | 386.42 | 873.79 |
| 46.672 | 50.980 | 55.717 | 60.925 | 66.649 | 72.939 | 79.850 | 87.442 | 138.11 | 218.47 | 344.90 | 541.99 | 1311.7 |
| 53.739 | 59.118 | 65.075 | 71.673 | 78.979 | 87.068 | 96.022 | 105.93 | 173.64 | 285.01 | 466.61 | 759.78 | 1968.5 |
| 61.725 | 68.394 | 75.836 | 84.141 | 93.406 | 103.74 | 115.27 | 128.12 | 218.04 | 371.52 | 630.92 | 1064.7 | 2953.8 |
| 70.749 | 78.969 | 88.212 | 98.603 | 110.28 | 123.41 | 138.17 | 154.74 | 273.56 | 483.97 | 852.75 | 1491.6 | 4431.7 |
| 80.947 | 91.025 | 102.44 | 115.38 | 130.03 | 146.63 | 165.42 | 186.69 | 342.94 | 630.17 | 1152.2 | 2089.2 | 6648.5 |
| 92.470 | 104.77 | 118.81 | 134.84 | 153.14 | 174.02 | 197.85 | 225.03 | 429.68 | 820.22 | 1556.5 | 2925.9 | 9973.8 |
| 105.49 | 120.44 | 137.63 | 157.41 | 180.17 | 206.34 | 236.44 | 271.03 | 538.10 | 1067.3 | 2102.3 | 4097.2 | 14962. |
| 120.20 | 138.30 | 159.28 | 183.60 | 211.80 | 244.49 | 282.36 | 326.24 | 673.63 | 1388.5 | 2839.0 | 5737.1 | 22443. |
| 136.83 | 158.66 | 184.17 | 213.98 | 248.81 | 289.49 | 337.01 | 392.48 | 843.03 | 1806.0 | 3833.7 | 8033.0 | 33666. |
| 155.62 | 181.87 | 212.79 | 249.21 | 292.10 | 342.60 | 402.04 | 471.98 | 1054.8 | 2348.8 | 5176.5 | 11247. | 50500. |
| 176.85 | 208.33 | 245.71 | 290.09 | 342.76 | 405.27 | 479.43 | 567.38 | 1319.5 | 3054.4 | 6989.3 | 15747. | 75752. |
| 200.84 | 238.50 | 283.57 | 337.50 | 402.03 | 479.22 | 571.52 | 681.85 | 1650.4 | 3971.8 | 9436.5 | 22047. | * |
| 227.95 | 272.89 | 327.10 | 392.50 | 471.38 | 566.48 | 681.11 | 819.22 | 2064.0 | 5164.3 | 12740. | 30867. | * |
| 258.58 | 312.09 | 377.17 | 456.30 | 552.51 | 669.45 | 811.52 | 984.07 | 2580.9 | 6714.6 | 17200. | 43214. | * |
| 293.20 | 356.79 | 434.75 | 530.31 | 647.44 | 790.95 | 966.71 | 1181.9 | 3227.2 | 8730.0 | 23222. | 60501. | * |
| 546.68 | 693.57 | 881.17 | 1120.7 | 1426.5 | 1816.7 | 2314.2 | 2948.3 | 9856.8 | 32423. | * | * | * |
| 1013.7 | 1342.0 | 1779.1 | 2360.8 | 3134.5 | 4163.2 | 5529.8 | 7343.9 | 30089. | * | * | * | * |
| 1874.2 | 2590.6 | 3585.1 | 4965.3 | 6879.3 | 9531.6 | 13203. | 18281. | 91831. | * | * | * | * |
| 3459.5 | 4994.5 | 7217.7 | 10436. | 15090. | 21813. | 31515. | 45497. | * | * | * | * | * |

*Interest factors exceed 99,999.

**TABLE D**   **Present Value of an Annuity of $1 per Period for *n* Periods**

$$PVIFA_{k,n} = \frac{1 - \dfrac{1}{(1 + k)^n}}{k}$$

| Period *n* | 1% | 2% | 3% | 4% | 5% | 6% | 7% | 8% | 9% | 10% | 11% | 12% |
|---|---|---|---|---|---|---|---|---|---|---|---|---|
| 1 | 0.9901 | 0.9804 | 0.9709 | 0.9615 | 0.9524 | 0.9434 | 0.9346 | 0.9259 | 0.9174 | 0.9091 | 0.9009 | 0.8929 |
| 2 | 1.9704 | 1.9416 | 1.9135 | 1.8861 | 1.8594 | 1.8334 | 1.8080 | 1.7833 | 1.7591 | 1.7355 | 1.7125 | 1.6901 |
| 3 | 2.9410 | 2.8839 | 2.8286 | 2.7751 | 2.7232 | 2.6730 | 2.6243 | 2.5771 | 2.5313 | 2.4869 | 2.4437 | 2.4018 |
| 4 | 3.9020 | 3.8077 | 3.7171 | 3.6299 | 3.5460 | 3.4651 | 3.3872 | 3.3121 | 3.2397 | 3.1699 | 3.1024 | 3.0373 |
| 5 | 4.8534 | 4.7135 | 4.5797 | 4.4518 | 4.3295 | 4.2124 | 4.1002 | 3.9927 | 3.8897 | 3.7908 | 3.6959 | 3.6048 |
| 6 | 5.7955 | 5.6014 | 5.4172 | 5.2421 | 5.0757 | 4.9173 | 4.7665 | 4.6229 | 4.4859 | 4.3553 | 4.2305 | 4.1114 |
| 7 | 6.7282 | 6.4720 | 6.2303 | 6.0021 | 5.7864 | 5.5824 | 5.3893 | 5.2064 | 5.0330 | 4.8684 | 4.7122 | 4.5638 |
| 8 | 7.6517 | 7.3255 | 7.0197 | 6.7327 | 6.4632 | 6.2098 | 5.9713 | 5.7466 | 5.5348 | 5.3349 | 5.1461 | 4.9676 |
| 9 | 8.5660 | 8.1622 | 7.7861 | 7.4353 | 7.1078 | 6.8017 | 6.5152 | 6.2469 | 5.9952 | 5.7590 | 5.5370 | 5.3282 |
| 10 | 9.4713 | 8.9826 | 8.5302 | 8.1109 | 7.7217 | 7.3601 | 7.0236 | 6.7101 | 6.4177 | 6.1446 | 5.8892 | 5.6502 |
| 11 | 10.368 | 9.7868 | 9.2526 | 8.7605 | 8.3064 | 7.8869 | 7.4987 | 7.1390 | 6.8052 | 6.4951 | 6.2065 | 5.9377 |
| 12 | 11.255 | 10.575 | 9.9540 | 9.3851 | 8.8633 | 8.3838 | 7.9427 | 7.5361 | 7.1607 | 6.8137 | 6.4924 | 6.1944 |
| 13 | 12.134 | 11.348 | 10.635 | 9.9856 | 9.3936 | 8.8527 | 8.3577 | 7.9038 | 7.4869 | 7.1034 | 6.7499 | 6.4235 |
| 14 | 13.004 | 12.106 | 11.296 | 10.563 | 9.8986 | 9.2950 | 8.7455 | 8.2442 | 7.7862 | 7.3667 | 6.9819 | 6.6282 |
| 15 | 13.865 | 12.849 | 11.938 | 11.118 | 10.380 | 9.7122 | 9.1079 | 8.5595 | 8.0607 | 7.6061 | 7.1909 | 6.8109 |
| 16 | 14.718 | 13.578 | 12.561 | 11.652 | 10.838 | 10.106 | 9.4466 | 8.8514 | 8.3126 | 7.8237 | 7.3792 | 6.9740 |
| 17 | 15.562 | 14.292 | 13.166 | 12.166 | 11.274 | 10.477 | 9.7632 | 9.1216 | 8.5436 | 8.0216 | 7.5488 | 7.1196 |
| 18 | 16.398 | 14.992 | 13.754 | 12.659 | 11.690 | 10.828 | 10.059 | 9.3719 | 8.7556 | 8.2014 | 7.7016 | 7.2497 |
| 19 | 17.226 | 15.678 | 14.324 | 13.134 | 12.085 | 11.158 | 10.336 | 9.6036 | 8.9501 | 8.3649 | 7.8393 | 7.3658 |
| 20 | 18.046 | 16.351 | 14.877 | 13.590 | 12.462 | 11.470 | 10.594 | 9.8181 | 9.1285 | 8.5136 | 7.9633 | 7.4694 |
| 21 | 18.857 | 17.011 | 15.415 | 14.029 | 12.821 | 11.764 | 10.836 | 10.017 | 9.2922 | 8.6487 | 8.0751 | 7.5620 |
| 22 | 19.660 | 17.658 | 15.937 | 14.451 | 13.163 | 12.042 | 11.061 | 10.201 | 9.4424 | 8.7715 | 8.1757 | 7.6446 |
| 23 | 20.456 | 18.292 | 16.444 | 14.857 | 13.489 | 12.303 | 11.272 | 10.371 | 9.5802 | 8.8832 | 8.2664 | 7.7184 |
| 24 | 21.243 | 18.914 | 16.936 | 15.247 | 13.799 | 12.550 | 11.469 | 10.529 | 9.7066 | 8.9847 | 8.3481 | 7.7843 |
| 25 | 22.023 | 19.523 | 17.413 | 15.622 | 14.094 | 12.783 | 11.654 | 10.675 | 9.8226 | 9.0770 | 8.4217 | 7.8431 |
| 26 | 22.795 | 20.121 | 17.877 | 15.983 | 14.375 | 13.003 | 11.826 | 10.810 | 9.9290 | 9.1609 | 8.4881 | 7.8957 |
| 27 | 23.560 | 20.707 | 18.327 | 16.330 | 14.643 | 13.211 | 11.987 | 10.935 | 10.027 | 9.2372 | 8.5478 | 7.9426 |
| 28 | 24.316 | 21.281 | 18.764 | 16.663 | 14.898 | 13.406 | 12.137 | 11.051 | 10.116 | 9.3066 | 8.6016 | 7.9844 |
| 29 | 25.066 | 21.844 | 19.188 | 16.984 | 15.141 | 13.591 | 12.278 | 11.158 | 10.198 | 9.3696 | 8.6501 | 8.0218 |
| 30 | 25.808 | 22.396 | 19.600 | 17.292 | 15.372 | 13.765 | 12.409 | 11.258 | 10.274 | 9.4269 | 8.6938 | 8.0552 |
| 35 | 29.409 | 24.999 | 21.487 | 18.665 | 16.374 | 14.498 | 12.948 | 11.655 | 10.567 | 9.6442 | 8.8552 | 8.1755 |
| 40 | 32.835 | 27.355 | 23.115 | 19.793 | 17.159 | 15.046 | 13.332 | 11.925 | 10.757 | 9.7791 | 8.9511 | 8.2438 |
| 45 | 36.095 | 29.490 | 24.519 | 20.720 | 17.774 | 15.456 | 13.606 | 12.108 | 10.881 | 9.8628 | 9.0079 | 8.2825 |
| 50 | 39.196 | 31.424 | 25.730 | 21.482 | 18.256 | 15.762 | 13.801 | 12.233 | 10.962 | 9.9148 | 9.0417 | 8.3045 |

*(Continued on next page)*

**TABLE D**  Present Value of an Annuity of $1 per Period for *n* Periods (*Continued*)

$$PVIFA_{k,n} = \frac{1 - \dfrac{1}{(1 + k)^n}}{k}$$

| 13% | 14% | 15% | 16% | 17% | 18% | 19% | 20% | 25% | 30% | 35% | 40% | 50% |
|---|---|---|---|---|---|---|---|---|---|---|---|---|
| 0.8850 | 0.8772 | 0.8696 | 0.8621 | 0.8547 | 0.8475 | 0.8403 | 0.8333 | 0.8000 | 0.7692 | 0.7407 | 0.7143 | 0.6667 |
| 1.6681 | 1.6467 | 1.6257 | 1.6052 | 1.5852 | 1.5656 | 1.5465 | 1.5278 | 1.4400 | 1.3609 | 1.2894 | 1.2245 | 1.1111 |
| 2.3612 | 2.3216 | 2.2832 | 2.2459 | 2.2096 | 2.1743 | 2.1399 | 2.1065 | 1.9520 | 1.8161 | 1.6959 | 1.5889 | 1.4074 |
| 2.9745 | 2.9137 | 2.8550 | 2.7982 | 2.7432 | 2.6901 | 2.6386 | 2.5887 | 2.3616 | 2.1662 | 1.9969 | 1.8492 | 1.6049 |
| 3.5172 | 3.4331 | 3.3522 | 3.2743 | 3.1993 | 3.1272 | 3.0576 | 2.9906 | 2.6893 | 2.4356 | 2.2200 | 2.0352 | 1.7366 |
| 3.9975 | 3.8887 | 3.7845 | 3.6847 | 3.5892 | 3.4976 | 3.4098 | 3.3255 | 2.9514 | 2.6427 | 2.3852 | 2.1680 | 1.8244 |
| 4.4226 | 4.2883 | 4.1604 | 4.0386 | 3.9224 | 3.8115 | 3.7057 | 3.6046 | 3.1611 | 2.8021 | 2.5075 | 2.2628 | 1.8829 |
| 4.7988 | 4.6389 | 4.4873 | 4.3436 | 4.2072 | 4.0776 | 3.9544 | 3.8372 | 3.3289 | 2.9247 | 2.5982 | 2.3306 | 1.9220 |
| 5.1317 | 4.9464 | 4.7716 | 4.6065 | 4.4506 | 4.3030 | 4.1633 | 4.0310 | 3.4631 | 3.0190 | 2.6653 | 2.3790 | 1.9480 |
| 5.4262 | 5.2161 | 5.0188 | 4.8332 | 4.6586 | 4.4941 | 4.3389 | 4.1925 | 3.5705 | 3.0915 | 2.7150 | 2.4136 | 1.9653 |
| 5.6869 | 5.4527 | 5.2337 | 5.0286 | 4.8364 | 4.6560 | 4.4865 | 4.3271 | 3.6564 | 3.1473 | 2.7519 | 2.4383 | 1.9769 |
| 5.9176 | 5.6603 | 5.4206 | 5.1971 | 4.9884 | 4.7932 | 4.6105 | 4.4392 | 3.7251 | 3.1903 | 2.7792 | 2.4559 | 1.9846 |
| 6.1218 | 5.8424 | 5.5831 | 5.3423 | 5.1183 | 4.9095 | 4.7147 | 4.5327 | 3.7801 | 3.2233 | 2.7994 | 2.4685 | 1.9897 |
| 6.3025 | 6.0021 | 5.7245 | 5.4675 | 5.2293 | 5.0081 | 4.8023 | 4.6106 | 3.8241 | 3.2487 | 2.8144 | 2.4775 | 1.9931 |
| 6.4624 | 6.1422 | 5.8474 | 5.5755 | 5.3242 | 5.0916 | 4.8759 | 4.6755 | 3.8593 | 3.2682 | 2.8255 | 2.4839 | 1.9954 |
| 6.6039 | 6.2651 | 5.9542 | 5.6685 | 5.4053 | 5.1624 | 4.9377 | 4.7296 | 3.8874 | 3.2832 | 2.8337 | 2.4885 | 1.9970 |
| 6.7291 | 6.3729 | 6.0472 | 5.7487 | 5.4746 | 5.2223 | 4.9897 | 4.7746 | 3.9099 | 3.2948 | 2.8398 | 2.4918 | 1.9980 |
| 6.8399 | 6.4674 | 6.1280 | 5.8178 | 5.5339 | 5.2732 | 5.0333 | 4.8122 | 3.9279 | 3.3037 | 2.8443 | 2.4941 | 1.9986 |
| 6.9380 | 6.5504 | 6.1982 | 5.8775 | 5.5845 | 5.3162 | 5.0700 | 4.8435 | 3.9424 | 3.3105 | 2.8476 | 2.4958 | 1.9991 |
| 7.0248 | 6.6231 | 6.2593 | 5.9288 | 5.6278 | 5.3527 | 5.1009 | 4.8696 | 3.9539 | 3.3158 | 2.8501 | 2.4970 | 1.9994 |
| 7.1016 | 6.6870 | 6.3125 | 5.9731 | 5.6648 | 5.3837 | 5.1268 | 4.8913 | 3.9631 | 3.3198 | 2.8519 | 2.4979 | 1.9996 |
| 7.1695 | 6.7429 | 6.3587 | 6.0113 | 5.6964 | 5.4099 | 5.1486 | 4.9094 | 3.9705 | 3.3230 | 2.8533 | 2.4985 | 1.9997 |
| 7.2297 | 6.7921 | 6.3988 | 6.0442 | 5.7234 | 5.4321 | 5.1668 | 4.9245 | 3.9764 | 3.3254 | 2.8543 | 2.4989 | 1.9998 |
| 7.2829 | 6.8351 | 6.4338 | 6.0726 | 5.7465 | 5.4509 | 5.1822 | 4.9371 | 3.9811 | 3.3272 | 2.8550 | 2.4992 | 1.9999 |
| 7.3300 | 6.8729 | 6.4641 | 6.0971 | 5.7662 | 5.4669 | 5.1951 | 4.9476 | 3.9849 | 3.3286 | 2.8556 | 2.4994 | 1.9999 |
| 7.3717 | 6.9061 | 6.4906 | 6.1182 | 5.7831 | 5.4804 | 5.2060 | 4.9563 | 3.9879 | 3.3297 | 2.8560 | 2.4996 | 1.9999 |
| 7.4086 | 6.9352 | 6.5135 | 6.1364 | 5.7975 | 5.4919 | 5.2151 | 4.9636 | 3.9903 | 3.3305 | 2.8563 | 2.4997 | 2.0000 |
| 7.4412 | 6.9607 | 6.5335 | 6.1520 | 5.8099 | 5.5016 | 5.2228 | 4.9697 | 3.9923 | 3.3312 | 2.8565 | 2.4998 | 2.0000 |
| 7.4701 | 6.9830 | 6.5509 | 6.1656 | 5.8204 | 5.5098 | 5.2292 | 4.9747 | 3.9938 | 3.3317 | 2.8567 | 2.4999 | 2.0000 |
| 7.4957 | 7.0027 | 6.5660 | 6.1772 | 5.8294 | 5.5168 | 5.2347 | 4.9789 | 3.9950 | 3.3321 | 2.8568 | 2.4999 | 2.0000 |
| 7.5856 | 7.0700 | 6.6166 | 6.2153 | 5.8582 | 5.5386 | 5.2512 | 4.9915 | 3.9984 | 3.3330 | 2.8571 | 2.5000 | 2.0000 |
| 7.6344 | 7.1050 | 6.6418 | 6.2335 | 5.8713 | 5.5482 | 5.2582 | 4.9966 | 3.9995 | 3.3332 | 2.8571 | 2.5000 | 2.0000 |
| 7.6609 | 7.1232 | 6.6543 | 6.2421 | 5.8773 | 5.5523 | 5.2611 | 4.9986 | 3.9998 | 3.3333 | 2.8571 | 2.5000 | 2.0000 |
| 7.6752 | 7.1327 | 6.6605 | 6.2463 | 5.8801 | 5.5541 | 5.2623 | 4.9995 | 3.9999 | 3.3333 | 2.8571 | 2.5000 | 2.0000 |

# SOLUTIONS TO SELF-TEST PROBLEMS

## CHAPTER 2

**SP2-1.**

| Firm | Tax Liability | Average Tax Rate | Marginal Tax Rate |
|------|---------------|------------------|-------------------|
| A | ($50,000 × 15%) +($24,500 × 25%) = $13,625 | $\dfrac{\$13,625}{\$74,500} = 18.3\%$ | 25% |
| B | $350,000 × 34% = $119,000 | $\dfrac{\$119,000}{\$350,000} = 34\%$ | 34% |
| C | ($50,000 × 15%) +($25,000 × 25%) +($10,000 × 34%) = $17,150 | $\dfrac{\$17,150}{\$85,000} = 20.2\%$ | 34% |
| D | ($50,000 × 15%) +($25,000 × 25%) +($25,000 × 34%) +($110,000 × 39%) = $65,150 | $\dfrac{\$65,150}{\$210,000} = 31.0\%$ | 39% |

**SP2-2.**

**a.**

| (1) Year | (2) Depreciation Percentage | (3) Depreciable Basis | (4) (2) × (3) Depreciation in Dollars |
|----------|------------------------------|------------------------|----------------------------------------|
| 1 | 14.28% | $2,500,000 | $357,000 |
| 2 | 24.49 | 2,500,000 | 612,250 |
| 3 | 17.49 | 2,500,000 | 437,250 |
| 4 | 12.49 | 2,500,000 | 312,250 |
| 5 | 8.93 | 2,500,000 | 223,250 |
| 6 | 8.93 | 2,500,000 | 223,250 |
| 7 | 8.93 | 2,500,000 | 223,250 |
| 8 | 4.46 | 2,500,000 | 111,500 |
| | | | $2,500,000 |

**b.**

| (1) Years | (2) Depreciation Fraction | (3) Depreciable Basis | (4) (2) × (3) Depreciation in Dollars |
|---|---|---|---|
| 1 | 1/2 of 1/7 | $2,500,000 | $178,571 |
| 2–7 | 1/7 | 2,500,000 | 357,143 |
| 8 | 1/2 of 1/7 | 2,500,000 | 178,571 |
| | | | $2,500,000 |

**SP2-3.**

| | | |
|---|---|---|
| Sales | | $2,000,000 |
| Less: Cost of goods sold | | 1,200,000 |
| Gross profit | | 800,000 |
| Less: Operating expenses | | 320,000 |
| Operating profit | | 480,000 |
| Other income and expenses | | |
| Interest income | $100,000 | |
| Dividend income[a] | 10,000 | |
| Sale of machine | 20,000 | |
| Interest expense | (150,000) | (20,000) |
| Profit before taxes | | 460,000 |
| Taxes (34%) | | 156,400 |

[a] Eighty percent of dividend income is exempt from federal income taxes.

# CHAPTER 3

**SP3-1.**   This is a present value of a mixed stream problem. The present value is determined as follows:

**Step 1.** Determine the appropriate *PVIF* for the years in which payments are to be received. See Column 3 in the table that follows.

**Step 2.** Multiply the *PVIF* by the corresponding payment for each year. See Column 4 in the table.

**Step 3.** Sum the present value of each year's payments. See the bottom of Column 4.

| (1) End of Year | (2) Payment | (3) PVIF (Using k = 12%) | (4) Present Value of Payment |
|---|---|---|---|
| 1 | $    0 | .8929 | $     0 |
| 2 | 0 | .7972 | 0 |
| 3 | 25,000 | .7118 | 17,795 |
| 4 | 40,000 | .6355 | 25,420 |
| 5 | 40,000 | .5674 | 22,696 |
| 6 | 60,000 | .5066 | 30,396 |
| 7 | 70,000 | .4523 | 31,661 |
| | | | PV = $127,968 |

**SP3-2.**   This is a future value of an annuity problem. The annuity is $1,000 for eight years. The future value of the annuity is determined as follows:

**Step 1.** Given a 9% interest rate and an eight-year period, determine the appropriate *FVIFA:*

$$FVIFA_{k=9\%,n=8} = 11.028$$

**Step 2.** Multiply the annuity amount by the appropriate *FVIFA* to determine the future value:

$$FVA = A(FVIFA_{k=9\%,n=8})$$
$$= \$1,000(11.028)$$
$$= \$11,028$$

(Eq. 3.4)

**SP3-3.** The number of years needed to accumulate a specified future lump sum can be determined by solving for the value of $n$ in Equation 3.1.

$$FV = P(1 + k)^n$$ (Eq. 3.1)
**a.** $\$100,000 = \$9,000(1 + .11)^n$
$\quad 11.111 = (1 + .11)^n$
From Table A, $n$ is slightly above twenty-three years (23.07 years).
**b.** $\$100,000 = \$12,000(1 + .11)^n$
$\quad 8.333 = (1 + .11)^n$
From Table A, $n$ is between twenty and twenty-one years (20.3 years).
**c.** $\$100,000 = \$22,000(1 + .06)^n$
$\quad 4.5455 = (1 + .06)^n$
From Table A, $n$ is approximately twenty-six years (25.985 years).

**SP3-4.** **a.** $FV = P(FVIF_{k,n})$ (Eq. 3.1)
$\quad = \$7,000(FVIF_{k=9\%,n=4})$
$\quad = \$7,000(1.4116)$
$\quad = \$9,881$

**b.** $FV = P(FVIF_{k,n})$ (Eq. 3.1)
$\quad \$11,000 = P(FVIF_{k=9\%,n=4})$
$\quad \$11,000 = P(1.4116)$
$\quad \$7,793 = P$

**c.** $FV = P(FVIF_{k,n})$ (Eq. 3.1)
$\quad \$11,000 = \$7,000(FVIF_{k=?,n=4})$
$\quad 1.57 = FVIF_{k=?,n=4}$
$\quad k = \text{about } 12\%$

**SP3-5.** **a.** $PVA = A(PVIFA_{k,n})$ (Eq. 3.5)
$\quad = \$50,000(PVIFA_{k=14\%, n=3})$
$\quad = \$50,000(2.3216)$
$\quad = \$116,080$

**b.** $PVA = A(PVIFA_{k,n})$ (Eq. 3.5)
$\quad \$110,000 = \$50,000(PVIFA_{k=?,n=3})$
$\quad 2.2 = PVIFA_{k=?,n=3}$
$\quad k = \text{about } 17\%$

**c.** $PVA = A(PVIFA_{k,n})$ (Eq. 3.5)
$\quad \$110,000 = A(PVIFA_{k=14\%,n=3})$
$\quad \$110,000 = A(2.3216)$
$\quad \$47,381 = A$

**SP3-6.**     Present value of cash flows from years 1–7:

$$PVA = A(PVIFA_{k,n}) \qquad \textbf{(Eq. 3.5)}$$
$$= \$8,000(PVIFA_{k=16\%,n=7})$$
$$= \$8,000(4.0386)$$
$$= \$32,309$$

Present value of cash flows from years 8–12:

$$PVA = A(PVIFA_{k,n}) \qquad \textbf{(Eq. 3.5)}$$
$$= \$12,000(PVIFA_{k=16\%,n=5})$$
$$= \$12,000(3.2743)$$
$$= \$39,292$$

This represents the present value as of the start of the second annuity stream (end of Year 7). Its present value is determined as follows:

$$P = FV\left[\frac{1}{(1+k)^n}\right] \qquad \textbf{(Eq. 3.3)}$$

$$= \$39,292\left[\frac{1}{(1+.16)^7}\right]$$

$$= \$39,292(.3538)$$
$$= \$13,902$$

Present value of combined streams = \$32,309 + \$13,902
$$= \$46,211$$

**SP3-7.**     $PVA = A(PVIFA_{k,n})$                **(Eq. 3.5)**
$$= \$8,000(PVIFA_{k=17\%,n=10})$$
$$= \$8,000(4.6586)$$
$$= \$37,269$$

**SP3-8.**

| End of Year | Cash Flow | PVIF (at 20%) | Discounted Cash Flow |
|---|---|---|---|
| 1 | $25,000 | .8333 | $20,833 |
| 2 | 40,000 | .6944 | 27,776 |
| 3 | 55,000 | .5787 | 31,829 |
|   |   |   | $80,438 |

Because the present value of the investment is \$80,438, Jayhawk Corporation should pay no more than this amount.

# CHAPTER 4

**SP4-1.**     a. $V_b = I(PVIFA_{k_b,n}) + M(PVIF_{k_b,n})$        **(Eq. 4.2)**
$$= \$146(PVIFA_{14\%,20\text{yrs}}) + \$1,000(PVIF_{14\%,20\text{yrs}})$$
$$= \$146(6.6231) + \$1,000(.0728)$$
$$= \$1,039.77$$

**b.** $V_b = \dfrac{I}{2} (PVIFA_{k_b/2,2n}) + M(PVIF_{k_b/2,2n})$ **(Eq. 4.4)**

$= \dfrac{\$146}{2} (PVIFA_{7\%,40\text{periods}}) + \$1,000(PVIF_{7\%,40\text{periods}})$

$= \$73(13.3317) + \$1,000(.0668)$

$= \$1,040.01$

**c.** $V_b = I(PVIFA_{k_b,n}) + M(PVIF_{k_b,n})$ **(Eq. 4.2)**

$\$917.00 = \$146(PVIFA_{?\%,20\text{yrs}}) + \$1,000(PVIF_{?\%,20\text{yrs}})$

Try $k_b = 16\%$.

$= \$146(5.9288) + \$1,000(.0514)$

$= \$917.00$

**d.** $V_b = \dfrac{I}{2} (PVIFA_{k_b/2,2n}) + M(PVIF_{k_b/2,2n})$ **(Eq. 4.4)**

$\$1,195.58 = \dfrac{\$146}{2} (PVIFA_{?\%,40\text{periods}}) + \$1,000(PVIF_{?\%,40\text{periods}})$

Try $k_b = 12\%$ (note that $k_b/2 = 6\%$).

$= \$73(15.0463) + \$1,000(.0972)$

$= \$1,195.58$

**SP4-2.**

**a.** $V_p = \dfrac{D_p}{k_p} = \dfrac{\$12.35}{.105} = \$117.62$ **(Eq. 4.6)**

**b.** $\hat{k}_p = \dfrac{D_p}{V_p} = \dfrac{\$12.35}{\$137.50} = 9.0\%$ **(Eq. 4.7)**

**SP4-3.**

**a.** $P_0 = \dfrac{D_1}{k_s - g} = \dfrac{\$.43}{.13 - .09} = \$10.75$ **(Eq. 4.10)**

**b.** $\hat{k}_s = \dfrac{D_1}{P_0} + g = \dfrac{\$.43}{\$8.25} + .09 = 14.2\%$ **(Eq. 4.11)**

**SP4-4.**

**a.** The growth rate for each year indicated is 7 percent. For example,

Most recent year's growth $= \dfrac{\$2.45 - \$2.29}{\$2.29} = 7.0\%$

Prior year's growth $= \dfrac{\$2.29 - \$2.14}{\$2.14} = 7.0\%$

$D_1$ is needed to determine the value of common stock. We can estimate $D_1$ by calculating a 7 percent increase over last year's dividend.

$D_1 = \$2.45(1 + .07) = \$2.62$

$P_0 = \dfrac{D_1}{k_s - g} = \dfrac{\$2.62}{.16 - .07} = \$29.11$ **(Eq. 4.10)**

**b.** $\hat{k}_s = \dfrac{D_1}{P_0} + g = \dfrac{\$2.62}{\$32.75} + .07 = 15.0\%$      **(Eq. 4.11)**

# CHAPTER 5

**SP5-1.**

**a.** Expected return for Y $= .3(30\%) + .4(10\%) + .3(-10\%)$      **(Eq. 5.1)**
$= 10.0\%$
Expected return for Z $= .3(16\%) + .4(9\%) + .3(1\%)$
$= 8.7\%$

**b.** Standard deviation of returns for Y      **(Eq. 5.3)**
$= \sqrt{(30\% - 10\%)^2\,(.3) + (10\% - 10\%)^2\,(.4) + (-10\% - 10\%)^2\,(.3)}$
$= \sqrt{120\% + 0 + 120\%}$
$= \sqrt{240\%}$
$= 15.5\%$

Standard deviation of returns for Z
$= \sqrt{(16\% - 8.7\%)^2\,(.3) + (9\% - 8.7\%)^2\,(.4) + (1\% - 8.7\%)^2\,(.3)}$
$= \sqrt{15.99\% + .04\% + 17.79\%}$
$= \sqrt{33.81\%}$
$= 5.82\%$

**c.** Coefficient of variation for Y $= \sigma/\hat{k}$      **(Eq. 5.4)**
$= 15.5\%/10\%$
$= 1.55$

Coefficient of variation for Z $= \sigma/\hat{k}$
$= 5.82\%/8.7\%$
$= .67$

**d.** $k_p = 60\%(10.0\%) + 40\%(8.7\%)$      **(Eq. 5.5)**
$= 6.0\% + 3.5\%$
$= 9.5\%$

**SP5-2.**

**a.** $k_p = 80\%(15\%) + 20\%(25\%)$      **(Eq. 5.5)**
$= 17\%$

**b.** $\sigma_p = \sqrt{(.8)^2\,(.03)^2 + (.2)^2\,(.05)^2 + 2\,(.8)(.2)(.03)(.05)(.9)}$      **(Eq. 5.6)**
$= \sqrt{.000576 + .0001 + .000432}$
$= \sqrt{.001108}$
$= .03329$ or $3.3\%$

**SP5-3.**

**a.** Expected return of Lancer stock $= 9\% + 1.3(14\% - 9\%)$      **(Eq. 5.8)**
$= 15.5\%$
Expected return of Rudi stock $= 9\% + 1.8(14\% - 9\%)$
$= 18\%$

**b.** Risk premium of Lancer stock $= 15.5\% - 9\%$      **(Eq. 5.9)**
$= 6.5\%$
Risk premium of Rudi stock $= 18\% - 9\%$
$= 9\%$

# CHAPTER 6

**SP6-1.**

**a.** Current ratio $= \dfrac{\text{current assets}}{\text{current liabilities}} = \dfrac{\$2,300,000}{\$1,500,000} = 1.53$

**b.** Quick ratio $= \dfrac{\text{current assets} - \text{inventories}}{\text{current liabilities}}$

$= \dfrac{\$2,300,000 - \$450,000}{\$1,500,000} = 1.23$

**c.** Inventory turnover $= \dfrac{\text{cost of goods sold}}{\text{inventory}} = \dfrac{\$8,000,000}{\$450,000} = 17.78$

**d.** Total asset turnover $= \dfrac{\text{sales}}{\text{total assets}} = \dfrac{\$12,000,000}{\$6,300,000} = 1.90$

**e.** Debt ratio $= \dfrac{\text{total debt}}{\text{total assets}} = \dfrac{\$3,300,000}{\$6,300,000} = 52\%$

**f.** Debt to equity ratio $= \dfrac{\text{long-term debt}}{\text{owners' equity}} = \dfrac{\$1,800,000}{\$3,000,000} = .60$

**g.** Times interest earned $= \dfrac{\text{earnings before interest and taxes}}{\text{annual interest expense}}$

$= \dfrac{\$1,000,000}{\$400,000} = 2.5$

**h.** Gross profit margin $= \dfrac{\text{gross profits}}{\text{sales}} = \dfrac{\$4,000,000}{\$12,000,000} = 33.3\%$

**i.** Net profit margin $= \dfrac{\text{net income}}{\text{sales}} = \dfrac{\$400,000}{\$12,000,000} = 3.3\%$

**j.** Return on investment $= \dfrac{\text{net income}}{\text{total assets}} = \dfrac{\$400,000}{\$6,300,000} = 6.3\%$

**k.** Return on equity $= \dfrac{\text{net income}}{\text{owners' equity}} = \dfrac{\$400,000}{\$3,000,000} = 13.3\%$

**SP6-2.**

The company's debt level is excessive. Its debt to equity ratio is well above the industry norms. This has committed the company to a relatively large level of periodic interest payments and increases the probability that the company will be unable to meet these payments. A comparison of the company's times interest earned ratio to the industry norm confirms this. The company's liquidity is higher than the industry norms, and the company should investigate whether it has excessive liquidity. The company's asset utilization is better than the industry's, and its profitability is slightly below the norm when measured by net profit margin, return on investment, and return on equity.

**SP6-3.**

$$\frac{\text{return on}}{\text{equity}} = \frac{\text{net profit}}{\text{margin}} \times \frac{\text{asset}}{\text{turnover}} \times \frac{\text{equity}}{\text{multiplier}}$$

$$= \frac{\text{net income}}{\text{sales}} \times \frac{\text{sales}}{\text{total assets}} \times \frac{\text{total assets}}{\text{owners' equity}}$$

$$\frac{\text{ROE (Kassel}}{\text{Corp.)}} = \frac{\$400,000}{\$12,000,000} \times \frac{\$12,000,000}{\$6,300,000} \times \frac{\$6,300,000}{\$3,000,000}$$

$$= \quad 3.33\% \quad \times \quad 1.9 \quad \times \quad 2.1$$

$$= \quad 13.3\%$$

$$\frac{\text{ROE}}{\text{(Industry)}} = \quad 4.00\% \quad \times \quad 1.7 \quad \times \quad 1.79$$

$$= \quad 12.2\%$$

Kassel Corporation differs from the industry in that its net profit margin is slightly lower while its total asset turnover and equity multiplier are both higher than the industry average. Therefore, Kassel is able to generate a higher level of sales per dollar of assets, and it finances more of its assets with debt. These two combine to offset the lower net profit margin resulting in higher ROE.

**SP6-4.**

KASSEL CORPORATION
COMMON-SIZE INCOME STATEMENT
YEAR ENDING DECEMBER 31, 19X9
(THOUSANDS OF DOLLARS)

|  |  | Actual Value | Value as a Percent of Sales |
|---|---|---|---|
| Net sales |  | $12,000 | 100.00% |
| Less: Cost of goods sold |  | 8,000 | 66.66 |
| Gross profit |  | 4,000 | 33.33 |
| Less: Selling expense | $1,400 | | 11.67% |
| Depreciation expense | 600 | | 5.00 |
| General and administrative | 1,000 | | 8.33 |
| Total operating expenses |  | 3,000 | 25.00 |
| Earnings before interest and taxes |  | 1,000 | 8.33 |
| Less: Interest expense |  | 400 | 3.33 |
| Earnings before taxes |  | 600 | 5.00 |
| Less: Taxes |  | 200 | 1.67 |
| Net income |  | 400 | 3.33 |

## KASSEL CORPORATION
## COMMON-SIZE BALANCE SHEET
## AS OF DECEMBER 31, 19X9
## (THOUSANDS OF DOLLARS)

| Assets | | Percentage of Total Assets |
|---|---|---|
| Current assets | | |
| Cash | $    50 | .79% |
| Marketable securities | 700 | 11.11 |
| Accounts receivable | 1,100 | 17.46 |
| Inventory | 450 | 7.14 |
| Total current assets | 2,300 | 36.50 |
| Fixed assets | | |
| Plant and equipment | 5,000 | 79.36 |
| Less: Accumulated depreciation | 1,000 | 15.87 |
| Net fixed assets | 4,000 | 63.49 |
| Total assets | $6,300 | 100.00% |

| Liabilities and owners' equity | | |
|---|---|---|
| Current liabilities | | |
| Accounts payable | $   700 | 11.11% |
| Notes payable | 500 | 7.93 |
| Accrued expenses | 100 | 1.59 |
| Other current liabilities | 200 | 3.17 |
| Total current liabilities | $1,500 | 23.80 |
| Long-term liabilities | | |
| Long-term debt | 1,800 | 28.57 |
| Owners' equity | | |
| Common stock—par value | 300 | 4.76 |
| Additional paid-in capital | 700 | 11.11 |
| Retained earnings | 2,000 | 31.75 |
| Total owners' equity | $3,000 | 47.62 |
| Total liabilities and owners' equity | $6,300 | 100.00% |

# CHAPTER 7

**SP7-1.** **a.** The schedule of anticipated cash receipts is as follows (numbers are in thousands of dollars):

| | Dec 19X8 | Jan 19X9 | Feb 19X9 | Mar 19X9 | Apr 19X9 | May 19X9 | June 19X9 | July 19X9 |
|---|---|---|---|---|---|---|---|---|
| Total forecasted sales | $10,000 | $12,000 | $10,000 | $14,000 | $16,000 | $16,000 | $14,000 | $12,000 |
| Cash sales (40% of total) | | 4,800 | 4,000 | 5,600 | 6,400 | 6,400 | 5,600 | |
| Credit sales (60% of total: 1-month lag) | | 6,000 | 7,200 | 6,000 | 8,400 | 9,600 | 9,600 | |
| Total cash receipts | | $10,800 | $11,200 | $11,600 | $14,800 | $16,000 | $15,200 | |

**b.** The schedule of anticipated cash disbursements is as follows (numbers are in thousands of dollars):

|  | Dec 19X8 | Jan 19X9 | Feb 19X9 | Mar 19X9 | Apr 19X9 | May 19X9 | June 19X9 | July 19X9 |
|---|---|---|---|---|---|---|---|---|
| Forecasted sales | $10,000 | $12,000 | $10,000 | $14,000 | $16,000 | $16,000 | $14,000 | $12,000 |
| Materials purchased (50% of next month's sales) | 6,000 | 5,000 | 7,000 | 8,000 | 8,000 | 7,000 | 6,000 | |
| Cash purchases (60% of material purchases) | 3,600 | 3,000 | 4,200 | 4,800 | 4,800 | 4,200 | 3,600 | |
| Credit purchases (40% paid in the month after purchases) | | 2,400 | 2,000 | 2,800 | 3,200 | 3,200 | 2,800 | |
| Wages (10% of next month's sales) | | 1,000 | 1,400 | 1,600 | 1,600 | 1,400 | 1,200 | |
| Fixed operating expenses | | 1,000 | 1,000 | 1,000 | 1,000 | 1,000 | 1,000 | |
| Capital expenditures | | 4,000 | 3,000 | | | | | |
| Tax payments | | | | 600 | | | 600 | |
| Total cash disbursements | | $11,400 | $11,600 | $10,800 | $11,600 | $ 9,800 | $ 9,200 | |

c. The cash budget for Gable Company is as follows:

### GABLE COMPANY
### CASH BUDGET
### JANUARY 19X9 THROUGH JUNE 19X9
### (THOUSANDS OF DOLLARS)

|  | Jan | Feb | Mar | Apr | May | June |
|---|---|---|---|---|---|---|
| 1. Net cash gain (loss) for the month | (600) | (400) | 800 | 3,200 | 6,200 | 6,000 |
| 2. Minus: Interest on prior month's short-term debt | 0 | 6 | 10 | 2 | 0 | 0 |
| 3. Plus: Beginning cash (before short-term borrowing) | 1,000 | 400 | (6) | 784 | 3,982 | 10,182 |
| 4. Ending cash (before short-term borrowing) | 400 | (6) | 784 | 3,982 | 10,182 | 16,182 |
| 5. Minus: Desired level of cash | 1,000 | 1,000 | 1,000 | 1,000 | 1,000 | 1,000 |
| 6. Cumulative short-term borrowing | 600 | 1,006 | 216 | | | |
| 7. Excess cash | | | | 2,982 | 9,182 | 15,182 |

**SP7-2.**  Construction of the pro forma income statement for 19X9 is shown below.

MULFORD COMPANY
INCOME STATEMENTS
YEARS ENDING DECEMBER 31
(THOUSANDS OF DOLLARS)

| | 19X8 | Percentage of Sales for Items Dependent on Sales | Forecast for 19X9 | Source of the Estimate |
|---|---|---|---|---|
| Sales | $200,000 | | $220,000 | Given |
| Less: Cost of goods sold | 100,000 | 50% | 110,000 | 50% of sales |
| Less: Depreciation | 18,000 | 9 | 19,800 | 9% of sales |
| Gross profit | 82,000 | | 90,200 | |
| Less: Operating expense | | | | |
| Fixed | 28,000 | | 28,000 | Fixed (will not change) |
| Variable | 20,000 | | 22,000 | 10% of sales |
| Total | 48,000 | | 50,000 | |
| Earnings before interest and taxes | 34,000 | | 40,200 | |
| Less: Interest expense | 4,000 | 2 | 4,400 | 2% of sales |
| Earnings before taxes | 30,000 | | 35,800 | |
| Less: Taxes | 10,200 | | 12,172 | 34% tax rate |
| Net income | 19,800 | | 23,628 | |
| Cash dividend | 7,000 | | 7,000 | Given |
| To retained earnings | 12,800 | | 16,628 | |

The pro forma balance sheet for 19X9 is as follows:

MULFORD COMPANY
BALANCE SHEETS
AS OF DECEMBER 31
(THOUSANDS OF DOLLARS)

| Assets | 19X8 | Forecast for 19X9 | Source of the Estimate |
|---|---|---|---|
| Current assets | | | |
| Cash | $ 2,000 | $ 2,200 | 1% of sales |
| Marketable securities | 1,000 | 1,000 | Given: No change |
| Accounts receivable | 7,000 | 7,700 | 3.5% of sales |
| Inventories | 20,000 | 22,000 | 10% of sales |
| Total current assets | 30,000 | 32,900 | |
| Fixed assets | | | |
| Gross fixed assets | $150,000 | $183,000 | Given a $33 million increase |
| Less: Accumulated depreciation | 90,000 | 109,800 | From pro forma income statement |
| Net fixed assets | 60,000 | 73,200 | |
| Total assets | $ 90,000 | $106,100 | |
| | | | |
| Liabilities and owners' equity | | | |
| | | | |
| Current liabilities | | | |
| Accounts payable | $ 3,000 | $ 3,300 | 1.5% of sales |
| Notes payable | 1,450 | 1,450 | Given: No change |
| Taxes payable | 2,550 | 3,043 | 25% of 19X9 taxes |
| Other current liabilities | 8,000 | 8,000 | Given: No change |
| Total current liabilities | 15,000 | 15,793 | |
| Long-term debt (13.33%) | 25,000 | 25,000 | Given: No change |
| Owners' equity | | | |
| Common stock—par value | $ 4,000 | $ 4,000 | Given: No change |
| Additional paid-in capital | 14,000 | 14,000 | Given: No change |
| Retained earnings | 32,000 | 48,628 | From pro forma income statement |
| Total owners' equity | 50,000 | 66,628 | |
| Total liabilities and owners' equity | $ 90,000 | $107,421 | |

**SP7-3.** Total liabilities and owners' equity are expected to exceed total assets by $1,321,000 in 19X9 ($107,421,000 − $106,100,000). Therefore, Mulford will be able to repay some of its existing debt, pay a higher dividend, or otherwise apply the expected excess funds.

# CHAPTER 8

**SP8-1.** a. $Q_b = \dfrac{F}{p - v} = \dfrac{\$1,600,000}{\$250 - \$90} = 10{,}000$ units   **(Eq. 8.1)**

**b.**

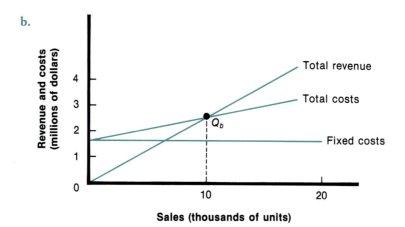

**Sales (thousands of units)**

**c.** $CQ_b = \dfrac{F - NE}{p - v} = \dfrac{\$1,600,000 - \$600,000}{\$250 - \$90} = 6,250$ units          **(Eq. 8.2)**

**d.**

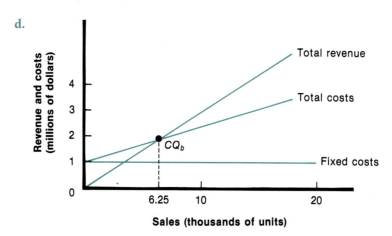

**Sales (thousands of units)**

**e.**

| | |
|---|---:|
| Sales revenue (8,000 units times $250 per unit) | $2,000,000 |
| Less: Fixed costs | 1,600,000 |
| Less: Variable costs (8,000 units times $90) | 720,000 |
| EBIT | ($320,000) |

**SP8-2.**          $\text{DOL} = \dfrac{\text{percentage change in EBIT}}{\text{percentage change in sales}}$          **(Eq. 8.4)**

$$= \dfrac{\dfrac{\$1,700,000 - \$1,450,000}{\$1,450,000}}{\dfrac{\$120,000 - 112,500}{112,500}} = \dfrac{17.2\%}{6.7\%} = 2.57$$

**SP8-3.**          **a.** $\text{DOL} = \dfrac{Q(p - v)}{Q(p - v) - F}$          **(Eq. 8.5)**

$$= \dfrac{400,000(\$3.20 - \$2.40)}{400,000(\$3.20 - \$2.40) - \$160,000}$$

$$= 2.0$$

**b.** $\text{DOL} = \dfrac{Q\,(p - v)}{Q\,(p - v) - F}$    **(Eq. 8.5)**

$\quad\quad = \dfrac{400{,}000\,(\$3.20 - \$2.25)}{400{,}000\,(\$3.20 - \$2.25) - \$209{,}000}$

$\quad\quad = 2.22$

**c.** If the machine is not purchased

$Q_b = \dfrac{F}{(p - v)} = \dfrac{\$160{,}000}{\$3.20 - \$2.40} = 200{,}000 \text{ units}$    **(Eq. 8.1)**

If the machine is purchased

$Q_b = \dfrac{F}{(p - v)} = \dfrac{\$209{,}000}{\$3.20 - \$2.25} = 220{,}000 \text{ units}$    **(Eq. 8.1)**

**d.**

|  | If the Machine | |
|---|---|---|
|  | Is Not Purchased | Is Purchased |
| Sales revenue $(p \times Q)$ | $720,000 | $720,000 |
| Less: Fixed costs $(F)$ | 160,000 | 209,000 |
| Less: Variable costs $(v \times Q)$ | 540,000 | 506,250 |
| EBIT | $ 20,000 | $   4,750 |

# CHAPTER 9

**SP9-1.**

**a.**

| | |
|---|---|
| Purchase price | $500,000 |
| Plus: Delivery and installation | +6,000 |
| Plus: Increased working capital | +8,000 |
| Minus: Proceeds from old machine | −75,000 |
| Plus: Tax from sale of old machine | |
| ($75,000 − $50,000) (34%) | +8,500 |
| Initial outlay | $447,500 |

**b.** If the machine is sold for $25,000, Collins will incur a $25,000 loss from the sale ($25,000 − $50,000). This loss would create a tax savings of $8,500 ($25,000 × 34 percent), which would be *subtracted* from the purchase price instead of being added. The result is an initial outlay of $430,500.

**SP9-2.**

| | | |
|---|---|---|
| Change in sales | Increase by | $15,000 |
| Change in cost of goods sold | Increase by | 5,000 |
| Change in operating expense | Decrease by | 3,000 |
| Change in depreciation | Increase by | 6,000 |
| Change in operating income | Increase by | 7,000 |
| Change in interest expense | Not considered | |
| Change in taxable income | Increase by | 7,000 |
| Change in taxes (34%) | Increase by | 2,380 |
| Change in net income | Increase by | 4,620 |
| Change in cash flow | Increase by | $10,620 |

**SP9-3.**

| | |
|---|---|
| After-tax cash flow from salvage ($39,000 − $10,000) (1 − .34) | $19,140 |
| Reduction of inventory | 8,000 |
| | $27,140 |

# CHAPTER 10

**SP10-1.**

**a.** To help determine the payback period, the cumulative cash flows are listed here along with the annual cash flows:

| Year | Annual Cash Flow | Cumulative Cash Flow |
|---|---|---|
| 1 | $3,000 | $ 3,000 |
| 2 | 3,000 | 6,000 |
| 3 | 3,000 | 9,000 |
| 4 | 6,000 | 15,000 |

The payback period is three and one-third years. Given a maximum payback period of three years, the project should be rejected.

**b.** The *NPV* is determined as follows:

**Step 1.** Determine the present value (*PV*) of the periodic cash flows using the cost of capital (14 percent) as the discount rate.

| Year | Cash Flow | PVIF (14%) | Discounted Cash Flow |
|---|---|---|---|
| 1 | $3,000 | .8772 | $ 2,632 |
| 2 | 3,000 | .7695 | 2,309 |
| 3 | 3,000 | .6749 | 2,025 |
| 4 | 6,000 | .5921 | 3,553 |
| | | | PV = $10,519 |

**Step 2.** Subtract the initial outlay from the present value of cash flows to obtain the *NPV*:

$$NPV = \$10,519 - \$11,000$$
$$= -\$481$$

The project should be rejected because the *NPV* is negative.

**c.** The *IRR* can be estimated using trial and error. Since a 14 percent discount rate resulted in a present value that was slightly higher than the initial outlay (see part b above), we will try 12%.

| Year | Cash Flow | PVIF (12%) | Discounted Cash Flow |
|---|---|---|---|
| 1 | $3,000 | .8929 | $ 2,679 |
| 2 | 3,000 | .7972 | 2,392 |
| 3 | 3,000 | .7118 | 2,135 |
| 4 | 6,000 | .6355 | 3,813 |
| | | | PV = $11,019 |

Since the 12 percent discount rate results in a present value of cash flows that is slightly higher than the initial outlay, the *IRR* is slightly higher than 12 percent.

The project should be rejected because the *IRR* is less than the firm's cost of capital.

d. The *PI* is determined as follows:

$$PI = \frac{\text{present value of cash flows}}{\text{initial outlay}}$$

The present value of the cash flows was determined in part a to be $10,519 using a 14 percent discount rate. The initial outlay of $11,000 was given. Thus, the profitability index is

$$PI = \frac{\$10,519}{\$11,000}$$

$$= .956$$

The project should be rejected since the *PI* is less than 1.00.

# CHAPTER 11

**SP11-1.**  a. Given a 3 percent risk premium, the appropriate risk adjusted discount rate is 18 percent.

| End of Year | Expected Cash Flows | Present Value Interest Factor for 18% | Discounted Cash Flows |
|---|---|---|---|
| 1 | $600,000 | .8475 | $ 508,200 |
| 2 | 700,000 | .7182 | 502,600 |
| 3 | 800,000 | .6086 | 487,200 |
| 4 | 900,000 | .5158 | 464,400 |

PV of cash flows = $1,962,340
Less: Initial outlay = $2,000,000
NPV = −$37,660

Because the *NPV* is negative, the project should not be adopted.

b.

| End of Year | Expected Cash Flows | Certainty Equivalent Coefficients | Certainty Equivalent Cash Flows | Present Value Interest Factor for 7% | Present Value of Certainty Equivalent Cash Flows |
|---|---|---|---|---|---|
| 1 | $600,000 | .80 | $480,000 | .9346 | $ 448,608 |
| 2 | 700,000 | .70 | 490,000 | .8734 | 427,966 |
| 3 | 800,000 | .60 | 480,000 | .8163 | 391,824 |
| 4 | 900,000 | .50 | 450,000 | .7629 | 343,305 |

PV of cash flows = $1,611,703
Less: Initial outlay = $2,000,000
NPV = −$388,297

c. $k_j = R_f + b_j(k_m - R_f)$  **(Eq. 11.2)**
  $= 7\% + 1.5(13\% - 7\%)$
  $= 16\%$

# CHAPTER 12

**SP12-1.**

a. $Ak_b = \dfrac{I + \dfrac{M - NP_b}{n}}{\dfrac{NP_b + M}{2}}$      **(Eq. 12.2)**

$= \dfrac{\$112.50 + \dfrac{\$1,000 - \$944}{20}}{\dfrac{\$944 + \$1,000}{2}}$

$= 11.9\%$

$k_i = k_b(1 - T)$      **(Eq. 12.3)**
$\phantom{k_i} = 11.9\%(1 - .30)$
$\phantom{k_i} = 8.3\%$

b. $NP_b \overset{set}{=} \sum\limits_{t=1}^{n} I\left[\dfrac{1}{(1 + k_b)^t}\right] + M\left[\dfrac{1}{(1 + k_b)^n}\right]$      **(Eq. 12.1)**

Try 12%.

$\$944 \overset{?}{=} \sum\limits_{t=1}^{20} \$112.50\left[\dfrac{1}{(1 + .12)^t}\right] + \$1,000\left[\dfrac{1}{(1 + .12)^{20}}\right]$

$= \$112.50(PVIFA_{k=12\%, n=20}) + \$1,000(PVIF_{k=12\%, n=20})$
$= \$112.50(7.4694) + \$1,000(.1037)$
$= \$944$

Since the present value of the cash flows is equal to the net proceeds using a 12 percent discount rate, 12 percent is the before-tax cost of debt.

$k_i = k_b(1 - T)$      **(Eq. 12.3)**
$\phantom{k_i} = 12\%(1 - .30)$
$\phantom{k_i} = 8.4\%$

c. $k_P = \dfrac{D_P}{NP_P} = \dfrac{\$10.25}{\$100 - \$4} = 10.7\%$      **(Eq. 12.4)**

d. $k_r = \dfrac{D_1}{P_0} + g = \dfrac{\$2.50}{\$30} + .06 = 14.3\%$      **(Eq. 12.5)**

e. $k_n = \dfrac{D_1}{P_0 - f} + g = \dfrac{\$2.50}{\$28 - \$1.50} + .06 = 15.4\%$      **(Eq. 12.6)**

**SP12-2.**

a. $BP_i = \dfrac{TF_i}{PS_i}$      **(Eq. 12.8)**

Common equity breakpoints

1. $BP_i = \dfrac{\$450,000}{.45} = \$1,000,000$

2. $BP_i = \dfrac{\$450,000 + \$540,000}{.45} = \$2,200,000$

Preferred stock breakpoint

$$BP_i = \frac{\$300,000}{.20} = \$1,500,000$$

Long-term debt breakpoint

$$BP_i = \frac{\$525,000}{.35} = \$1,500,000$$

**b.** Up to the first breakpoint at $1,000,000, the cost of capital for B. Dawkins, Inc., reflects the least expensive cost of each component.

| Component of Capital | Weight | After-Tax Cost | Weighted Cost |
|---|---|---|---|
| Common equity | 45% | 16% | 7.20% |
| Preferred stock | 20 | 13 | 2.60 |
| Long-term debt | 35 | 9 | 3.15 |
| | | $k_a = $ | 12.95% |

After $1,000,000, the cost of common equity increases to 17 percent. There are no additional changes in the cost of each component until total capital reaches $1,500,000 (the second breakpoint). Between $1,000,000 and $1,500,000, the cost of capital is as follows:

| Component of Capital | Weight | After-Tax Cost | Weighted Cost |
|---|---|---|---|
| Common equity | 45% | 17% | 7.65% |
| Preferred stock | 20 | 13 | 2.60 |
| Long-term debt | 35 | 9 | 3.15 |
| | | $k_a = $ | 13.40% |

After $1,500,000 of total capital has been raised, the cost of both preferred stock and long-term debt increase to 14 percent and 10 percent, respectively. The cost of capital after $1,500,000, but before $2,200,000 (the third and final breakpoint), can be found as follows:

| Component of Capital | Weight | After-Tax Cost | Weighted Cost |
|---|---|---|---|
| Common equity | 45% | 17% | 7.65% |
| Preferred stock | 20 | 14 | 2.80 |
| Long-term debt | 35 | 10 | 3.50 |
| | | $k_a = $ | 13.95% |

After the final breakpoint at $2,200,000, the cost of equity increases to 18 percent. Therefore, the weighted cost of capital for capital raised above $2,200,000 is as follows:

| Component of Capital | Weight | After-Tax Cost | Weighted Cost |
|---|---|---|---|
| Common equity | 45% | 18% | 8.1% |
| Preferred stock | 20 | 14 | 2.8 |
| Long-term debt | 35 | 10 | 3.5 |
| | | $k_a =$ | 14.4% |

## Summary of MCC

| Capital Raised | Cost |
|---|---|
| 0–$1,000,000 | 12.95% |
| $1,000,000–$1,500,000 | 13.40 |
| $1,500,000–$2,200,000 | 13.95 |
| $2,200,000+ | 14.40 |

**c.**

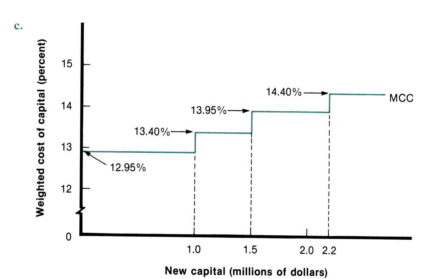

**SP12-3.**    **a.**

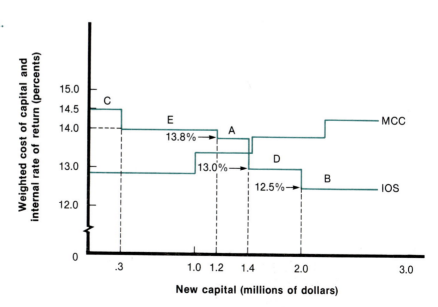

**b.** By observation, the graph presented in part a identifies Projects C, E, and A as being worthy of adoption since those projects have *IRR*s that exceed their cost of financing.

**SP12-4.**  **a.** $k_j = R_f + b_j(k_m - R_f)$  **(Eq. 12.7)**
$$= 6\% + .9(16\% - 6\%)$$
$$= 6\% + 9\%$$
$$= 15\%$$

**b.** $k_j = 11\% + .9(20\% - 11\%)$
$$= 11\% + 8.1\%$$
$$= 19.1\%$$

**c.** $k_j = 4\% + .9(5\% - 4\%)$
$$= 4\% + .9\%$$
$$= 4.9\%$$

# CHAPTER 13

**SP13-1.**  $\text{DFL} = \dfrac{\text{Percentage change in EPS}}{\text{Percentage change in EBIT}}$  **(Eq. 13.1)**

$$\text{DFL} = \dfrac{\dfrac{\$2.88 - \$2.57}{\$2.57}}{\dfrac{\$4.2\text{ mil} - \$4\text{ mil}}{\$4\text{ mil}}}$$

$$= \dfrac{12.1\%}{5.0\%}$$

$$= 2.42$$

**SP13-2.**  **a.** $\text{DFL} = \dfrac{\text{EBIT}}{\text{EBIT} - I - PSD/(1 - T)}$  **(Eq. 13.2)**

$$\dfrac{\$4.5\text{ mil}}{\$4.5\text{ mil} - \$1.3\text{ mil} - \$600{,}000/(1 - .34)}$$

$$= \dfrac{\$4.5\text{ mil}}{\$2{,}290{,}909}$$

$$= \$1.96$$

**b.** An increase in EBIT to $5 million represents an 11.1 percent increase. Given a degree of financial leverage of 1.96 (see Part a), Walter's EPS should increase by 1.96 times 11.1 percent, or 21.8 percent, to $2.80 in the following year.

Forecasted EPS next year:

| | |
|---|---|
| EBIT | $4,500,000 |
| Less: Interest | 1,300,000 |
| EBT | 3,200,000 |
| Less: Taxes | 1,088,000 |
| Net income | 2,112,000 |
| Less: Preferred stock dividend | 600,000 |
| EAC | $1,512,000 |
| Divided by common shares outstanding | 656,000 |
| EPS | $2.30 |

**SP13-3.**          **a** and **c.**

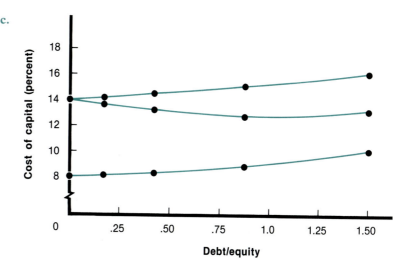

**b.**

| Debt to Equity Ratio | % Debt | | Cost Debt | | % Equity | | Cost of Equity | | $k_a$ |
|---|---|---|---|---|---|---|---|---|---|
| 0.00 | ( 0% | × | 8.0%) | + | (100% | × | 14.0%) | = | 14.0% |
| 0.18 | (15% | × | 8.0%) | + | ( 85% | × | 14.5%) | = | 13.5% |
| 0.43 | (30% | × | 8.5%) | + | ( 70% | × | 15.0%) | = | 13.1% |
| 0.82 | (45% | × | 9.0%) | + | ( 55% | × | 16.0%) | = | 12.9% |
| 1.50 | (60% | × | 10.0%) | + | ( 40% | × | 17.5%) | = | 13.0% |

**d.** The target capital structure should be a debt to equity ratio of .82 since the weighted cost of capital is lowest at that point.

**SP13-4.**          **a.** *Debt/Equity*

.14          $P_0 = \dfrac{\$5.25}{.132 - .050} = \$64.02$          **(Eq. 13.3)**

.43          $P_0 = \dfrac{\$5.30}{.135 - .060} = \$70.67$

.50          $P_0 = \dfrac{\$5.35}{.140 - .070} = \$76.43$

1.50          $P_0 = \dfrac{\$5.40}{.151 - .080} = \$76.06$

**b.**                        *Debt/Equity*

| | |
|---|---|
| Highest EPS | 1.50 |
| Highest growth rate | 1.50 |
| Highest stock price | .50 |

**c.** The target capital structure should include a debt to equity ratio of .50 since it will maximize the value of the firm's common stock.

# CHAPTER 14

**SP14-1.**    Amount of investment to be financed with equity = ($2,000,000) (50%) = $1,000,000

Residual = $5,000,000 − $1,000,000 = $4,000,000

$$\text{Dividend per share} = \frac{\text{residual}}{\text{number of shares outstanding}} = \frac{\$4,000,000}{8,000,000} = \$.50 \text{ per share.}$$

**SP14-2.**

| | Before Stock Dividend | After Stock Dividend | Change Due to Stock Dividend |
|---|---|---|---|
| Common stock ($6 par value, 2 million shares outstanding)[a] | $12,000,000 | $12,600,000 | +$ 600,000 |
| Paid-in capital | 20,000,000 | 20,400,000 | +400,000 |
| Retained earnings | 10,000,000 | 9,000,000 | −1,000,000 |
| Owners' Equity | 42,000,000 | 42,000,000 | 0 |

[a]  The number of shares outstanding increases to 2,100,000.

Theoretically, the market price per share changes as follows:

$$P_A = \frac{P_B}{1 + IS} = \frac{\$10}{1 + .05} = \$9.52 \qquad \text{(Eq. 14.1)}$$

**SP14-3.**    *Before the split*

| | |
|---|---|
| Common stock ($10 par value, 4 million shares outstanding) | $40,000,000 |
| Paid-in capital | 30,000,000 |
| Retained earnings | 12,000,000 |
| Total owners' equity | $82,000,000 |

*After the split*

| | |
|---|---|
| Common stock ($5 par value, 8 million shares outstanding) | $40,000,000 |
| Paid-in capital | 30,000,000 |
| Retained earnings | 12,000,000 |
| Total owners' equity | $82,000,000 |

**a.** The number of outstanding shares increases to 8 million.

**b.** Par value decreases to $5 per share.

c. Total par value remains unchanged.

d. Paid-in capital remains unchanged.

e. Retained earnings remains unchanged.

f. Shareholders' equity remains unchanged.

g. Theoretically, the market price of the stock decreases as follows:

$$P_A = \frac{P_B}{1 + IS} = \frac{\$20}{1 + 1.0} = \$10$$

# CHAPTER 15

**SP15-1.**

Try 10 percent (find the present value of all interest payments and the call price using a 10 percent annual discount rate but assuming semiannual compounding).

$$= \frac{\$125}{2}(PVIFA_{k_b/2=5\%,n=10}) + \$1,100(PVIF_{k_b/2=5\%,n=10})$$

$$= \$62.50(7.7217) + \$1,100(.6139)$$
$$= \$1,157.90$$

Since the present value of the interest payments and call price is equal to the price of the bond, 10 percent is the yield to call.

**SP15-2.**

Given that 5 percent of the bond issue ($250,000) is to be retired each year beginning at the end of the fifth year, the balance of the issue outstanding each year is as follows:

| Year | Bonds Outstanding During the Year | Year | Bonds Outstanding During the Year |
|------|-----------------------------------|------|-----------------------------------|
| 1–5 | $5,000,000 | 13 | $3,000,000 |
| 6 | 4,750,000 | 14 | 2,750,000 |
| 7 | 4,500,000 | 15 | 2,500,000 |
| 8 | 4,250,000 | 16 | 2,250,000 |
| 9 | 4,000,000 | 17 | 2,000,000 |
| 10 | 3,750,000 | 18 | 1,750,000 |
| 11 | 3,500,000 | 19 | 1,500,000 |
| 12 | 3,250,000 | 20 | 1,250,000 |

a. Since $250,000 of bonds must be retired each year beginning at the end of the fifth year at a premium of 10 percent above par value, the total annual principal payment (including the call premium) is ($250,000)(110%) = $275,000

b. Year  1: $5,000,000 × 11¾% = $587,500
Year 10: $3,750,000 × 11¾% = $440,625
Year 20: $1,250,000 × 11¾% = $146,875

**SP15-3.**

Find the present value of a $1,000 lump sum discounted back twenty years at 10 percent interest:

$$PV = \$1,000(PVIF_{k=10\%,n=20})$$
$$= \$1,000(.1486)$$
$$= \$148.60$$

## APPENDIX 15A

**SP15A-1.**   **a.** Call premium:

($75,000,000)(.14) = $10,500,000

After-tax call premium:

(1 − .30)($10,500,000) = $7,350,000

**b.** Annual amortized flotation cost (new bonds):

$3,000,000/15 yrs. = $200,000

Annual tax-saving from flotation costs:

$200,000 (.30) = $60,000

Present value of the tax savings ($n = 15, k = 7\%$):

$PVA$ = $60,000(9.108)
     = $546,480

Net flotation cost (new bonds):

= $3,000,000 − $546,480
= $2,453,520

**c.** Annual amortized floatation costs (old bonds):

($3,000,000/20) = $150,000

Tax savings today for expensing the remainder of the old bonds' flotation costs in the current year:

($150,000)(15 yrs.)(.30) = $675,000

Present value of the future tax benefits that would have been realized from amortizing the flotation costs on the old bonds in future years ($n = 15, k = 7\%$).

$PVA$ = ($150,000)(.30)(9.1079)
     = $409,856

Net after-tax savings on flotation costs (old bonds):

$675,000 − $409,856 = $265,144

**d.** Overlapping interest (old bonds):

($75,000,000)(.14)(1/12) = $875,000

**e.** Net initial outlay:

| | |
|---|---:|
| After-tax call premium | $ 7,350,000 |
| Plus: Net flotation cost (new bonds) | 2,453,520 |
| Minus: Net tax-saving on flotation cost (old bonds) | 265,144 |
| Plus: Overlapping interest | 875,000 |
| | $10,413,376 |

**f.** Annual after-tax interest on the new bonds:

$75,000,000(.10)(1 - .30) = \$5,250,000$

Annual after-tax interest on the old bonds:

$75,000,000(.14)(1 - .30) = \$7,350,000$

Decreased annual after-tax interest:

$\$7,350,000 - \$5,250,000 = \$2,100,000$

Present value of the decreased annual after-tax interest ($n = 15, k = 7\%$):

$PVA = \$2,100,000(9.108)$
$\quad\quad = \$19,126,800$

**g.** Yes, since the benefit expected from the refunding ($19,126,800) exceeds the net initial outlay ($10,413,376), Johnson Corporation should go through with the refunding.

# CHAPTER 16

**SP16-1.**

**a.** $N_r = \dfrac{N_0}{N_n} = \dfrac{6 \text{ million}}{2 \text{ million}} = 3 \text{ rights}$  **(Eq. 16.1)**

**b.** $V_r = \dfrac{P_r - S_P}{N_r + 1} = \dfrac{\$14 - \$11}{3 + 1} = \$.75$  **(Eq. 16.3)**

**c.** Current value of the firm:

6 million shares × $14 a share = $84 million

Add: Increase in value of the firm:

2 million shares × $11 a share = $22 million

Value of the firm after issuing the new stock = $106 million

New value of the common stock:

$\dfrac{\$106 \text{ million}}{8 \text{ million shares}} = \$13.25$

d. $V_r = \dfrac{P_e - S_P}{N_r} = \dfrac{\$13.25 - \$11.00}{3} = \$.75$            **(Eq. 16.2)**

**SP16-2.**

a. The total amount paid for the firm's common stock is equal to the amount in the common stock account plus additional paid-in capital: $500,000 + $100,000 = $600,000.

b.
| | |
|---|---:|
| Net income | $130,000 |
| Less: Dividend on preferred stock | 27,000 |
| EAC | $103,000 |

$$\text{EPS} = \frac{\text{EAC}}{\text{no. of common stock shares}}$$

$$= \frac{\$103,000}{50,000}$$

$$= \$2.06$$

# CHAPTER 18

**SP18-1.**

a.

| (1) End of Year | (2) Lease Payment | (3) After-Tax Lease Payment: $(1-30\%) \times (2)$ | (4) PVIFs for 8% | (5) Present Value of Each After-Tax Payment $(3) \times (4)$ |
|---|---|---|---|---|
| 0 | $42,000 | $29,400 | 1.000 | $ 29,400.00 |
| 1 | 42,000 | 29,400 | .9259 | 27,221.46 |
| 2 | 42,000 | 29,400 | .8573 | 25,204.62 |
| 3 | 42,000 | 29,400 | .7938 | 23,337.72 |
| 4 | 42,000 | 29,400 | .7350 | 21,609.00 |
| 5 | 42,000 | 29,400 | .6806 | 20,009.64 |
| 6 | 20,000 | 20,000 | .6302 | 12,604.00 |

PV of the Cost of Leasing = $159,386.44

b.

| (1) End of Year | (2) Loan Payment[a] | (3) Interest | (4) Principal Payment | (5) Remaining Balance |
|---|---|---|---|---|
| 1 | $67,643 | $27,500 | $40,143 | $209,857 |
| 2 | 67,643 | 23,084 | 44,559 | 165,298 |
| 3 | 67,643 | 18,183 | 49,460 | 115,838 |
| 4 | 67,643 | 12,742 | 54,901 | 60,937 |
| 5 | 67,643 | 6,703 | 60,940 | 0 |

[a] $PVA = A(PVIFA)$
$250,000 = A(3.6959)$
$A = $67,643

**c.**

| (1) Year | (2) ACRS Depreciation Percentage | (3) Depreciable Basis | (4) Dollar Amount of Depreciation |
|---|---|---|---|
| 1 | 20.00% | $250,000 | $50,000 |
| 2 | 32.00 | 250,000 | 80,000 |
| 3 | 19.20 | 250,000 | 48,000 |
| 4 | 11.52 | 250,000 | 28,800 |
| 5 | 11.52 | 250,000 | 28,800 |
| 6 | 5.76 | 250,000 | 14,400 |

**d.**

| (1) End of Year | (2) Maintenance Costs | (3) Depreciation | (4) Tax-Deductible Expenses: Interest + Maintenance + Depreciation | (5) Tax Savings 27% × (4) |
|---|---|---|---|---|
| 1 | $10,000 | $50,000 | $ 87,500 | $23,625 |
| 2 | 10,000 | 80,000 | 113,084 | 30,533 |
| 3 | 10,000 | 48,000 | 76,183 | 20,569 |
| 4 | 10,000 | 28,800 | 51,542 | 13,916 |
| 5 | 10,000 | 28,800 | 45,503 | 12,286 |
| 6 | 10,000 | 14,400 | 24,400 | 6,588 |

| (6) Net Cash Outflow from Purchase: Loan Payments + Maintenance − Tax Savings | (7) PVIF for 8% | (8) Present Value of Each Year's Cost of Purchasing: (6) × (7) |
|---|---|---|
| $54,018 | .9259 | $ 50,015 |
| 47,110 | .8573 | 40,387 |
| 57,074 | .7938 | 45,305 |
| 63,727 | .7350 | 46,839 |
| 65,357 | .6806 | 44,482 |
| 71,055 | .6302 | 44,779 |
| | | $271,807 |

# CHAPTER 19

**SP19-1.**

**a.** $CP = \dfrac{M}{CR} = \dfrac{\$1,000}{40} = \$25$     **(Eq. 19.1)**

**b.** $CPP = \dfrac{MC}{CR} = \dfrac{\$840}{40} = \$21$     **(Eq. 19.2)**

**c.** $V_b = \dfrac{I}{2}(PVIFA) + M(PVIF)$     **(Eq. 19.3)**

$\qquad = \dfrac{\$98}{2}(11.9246) + \$1,000(.0460) = \$630.31$

**d.** $CV = (CR)(MP) = (40)(\$20) = \$800$     **(Eq. 19.5)**

**SP19-2.**

**a.** $TV = (P_0 - EP)N = (\$46 - \$40)2.5 = \$15$     **(Eq. 19.6)**

**b.** Total cost = (25 warrants)(2.5 shares per warrant)($40 per share)

$$= \$2,500$$

Market value = (62.5 shares)($46 per share)

$$= \$2,875$$

**SP19-3.**

Primary EPS = $6 mil/(4.5 mil + 1 mil shares)

$$= \$1.09$$

Fully diluted EPS $= \dfrac{\$6 \text{ mil} + \$4.2 \text{ mil}(1 - .34)}{4.5 \text{ mil} + 1 \text{ mil} + 3.5 \text{ mil}} = \$.97$

# CHAPTER 20

**SP20-1.**

**a.** Cost of long-term financing:

($41.1 mil)(14%) = $5,754,000

Sum of required assets for each month: $574.8 million

Average required assets per month:

$$\frac{\$574.8 \text{ mil}}{12} = \$47.9 \text{ mil}$$

Average required short-term financing (monthly):

$47.9 mil − $41.1 mil (long-term financing) = $6.8 mil

Cost of short-term financing:

($6.8 mil)(9%) = $612,000

Total cost of financing:

$5,754,000 + $612,000 = $6,366,000

**b.** Cost of long-term financing:

($55.1 mil)(14%) = $7,714,000

Average required assets per month:

$47.9 mil (from Part a)

Average excess assets per month:

$55.1 mil − $47.9 mil = $7.2 mil

Interest earned on excess assets:

($7.2 mil)(6%) = $432,000

Net cost of financing:

$7,714,000 − $432,000 = $7,282,000

**SP20-2.**

| | Current (in Thousands) | Proposed (in Thousands) |
|---|---|---|
| EBIT | $6,000 | $6,500 |
| Less: Interest | | |
| Short-term | 1,947 | 2,112 |
| Long-term | 2,832 | 3,072 |
| EBT | 1,221 | 1,316 |
| Less: Taxes (35%) | 427 | 461 |
| Net income | $ 794 | $ 855 |
| ROE | 3.4% | 3.3% |
| Current ratio | 1.8 | 1.9 |

**a.** The current ratio is higher under the proposed balance sheet because of the increase in current assets, even though some of this increase was financed with current liabilities.

**b.** Net income is higher under the proposed balance sheet because of the higher sales that result. This is true despite the higher financing costs.

**c.** ROE is higher under the current balance sheet because the level of equity investment is smaller. Equity was increased under the proposed balance sheet.

**SP20-3.**

| | Current | Proposed |
|---|---|---|
| EBIT | $85,000 | $85,000 |
| Less: Interest | | |
| Short-term | 41,155 | 10,289 |
| Long-term | 17,148 | 68,592 |
| EBT | 26,697 | 6,119 |
| Less: Taxes (38%) | 10,145 | 2,325 |
| Net income | $16,552 | $ 3,794 |
| ROE | 1.9% | .4% |
| Current ratio | 1.6 | 6.4 |

**a.** The current ratio under the proposed balance sheet is higher as a result of replacing short-term debt with long-term debt.

**b.** Net income is higher under the current balance sheet since more assets are financed with less expensive short-term liabilities.

**c.** The return on equity is higher for the current structure because of the lower financing costs.

# CHAPTER 21

**SP21-1.**

The firm would incur two additional costs.

**a.** Increased administrative cost.

| | | |
|---|---|---|
| Current annual cost: (26 payrolls)($2,000) | = | $ 52,000 |
| Expected annual cost: (52 payrolls)($2,000) | = | $104,000 |
| Increased annual cost | | $ 52,000 |

**b.** Loss of interest on accrued wages.

Current average accrued wages: $600,000/2 = $300,000
Expected average accrued wages: $300,000/2 = $150,000

Decreased accrued wages                    $150,000

Lost interest = ($150,000)(.08) = $12,000

Total expected increased annual cost =
$52,000 + $12,000 = $ 64,000

**SP21-2.**

| Days after Checks Are Mailed | Percent Expected to Clear | Percent of Payroll to Be Deposited | Dollar Amount Deposited |
|---|---|---|---|
| 4 | 5% | 5% + 4% | $   450,000 |
| 5 | 18 | 18 | 900,000 |
| 6 | 31 | 31 | 1,550,000 |
| 7 | 25 | 25 | 1,250,000 |
| 8 | 14 | 14 | 700,000 |
| 9 | 7 | 7% − 4% | 150,000 |
| | | | $5,000,000 |

**SP21-3.**     Daily collections:

$$\frac{\$210,000,000}{365} = \$575,342$$

Average increase in cash available to the firm:

(2 days)($575,342) = $1,150,684

Annual interest that can be earned on the increased cash balance:

($1,150,684)(.07) = $80,548

Since the lockbox will provide annual interest income that is lower than the annual cost, the system should not be adopted.

**SP21-4.**     $R^* = R(1 - T)$                                                    **(Eq. 21.1)**
        $= 9.35\%(1 - .35)$
        $= 6.08\%$

Since the after-tax return on the taxable security exceeds the return on the tax-exempt security, Lucas Enterprises should purchase the taxable security.

**SP21-5.**     Interest earned for two weeks:

$$(\$50,000)(.06)\left(\frac{2 \text{ weeks}}{52 \text{ weeks}}\right) = \$115.38$$

The firm should not purchase the securities since transactions costs exceed the interest earned.

Interest earned for three weeks:

$$(\$50,000)(.06)\left(\frac{3\text{ weeks}}{52\text{ weeks}}\right) = \$173.08$$

The firm should purchase the securities since the interest earned exceeds transactions costs.

## CHAPTER 22

**SP22-1.**

a. $EOQ = \sqrt{\dfrac{2SO}{C}}$                                                **(Eq. 22.3)**

$$= \sqrt{\frac{2(200,000)(75)}{.20}}$$

$$= \sqrt{150,000,000}$$

$$= 12,247 \text{ units}$$

b. $AI = \dfrac{OQ}{2} + SS = \dfrac{12,247}{2} + 2,000 = 8,124 \text{ units}$          **(Eq. 22.1)**

c. $RL = \dfrac{U}{360}\,RP + SS = \dfrac{200,000}{360}\,(14) + 2,000 = 9,778 \text{ units}$       **(Eq. 22.2)**

**SP22-2.**

a. $CGP = \Delta Q\,(p - v)$                                           **(Eq. 22.4)**
     $= .05\,(1,000,000 \text{ units})(\$1.25 - \$.60)$
     $= \$32,500 \text{ increase}$

b. $DC = (Q)(p)(\text{PTD})(D)$
current $DC = (1,000,000 \text{ units})(\$1.25)(.45)(.01)$          **(Eq. 22.7)**
        $= \$5,625$
forecasted $DC = (1.05)(1,000,000 \text{ units})(\$1.25)(.60)(.02)$
         $= \$15,750$
change in $DC = \$15,750 - \$5,625 = \$10,125 \text{ increase}$

c. $BDE = (PBD)(Q)(p)$                                       **(Eq. 22.6)**
current $BDE = (.03)(1,000,000 \text{ units})(\$1.25)$
        $= \$37,500$
forecasted $BDE = (.025)(1.05)(1,000,000 \text{ units})(\$1.25)$
         $= \$32,812.50$
change in $BDE = \$32,812.50 - \$37,500 = \$4,687.50 \text{ decrease}$

d. $CFAR = \left[\dfrac{(Q)(v) + F}{360}\right](ACP)(OC)$          **(Eq. 22.5)**

current $CFAR = \dfrac{(1,000,000)(\$.60) + \$400,000}{360}\,(78 \text{ days})(.11)$

$$= \$23,833.33$$

forecasted $CFAR = \dfrac{(1.05)(1,000,000 \text{ units})(\$.60) + \$400,000}{360}\,(65 \text{ days})(.11)$

$$= \$20,456.94$$

change in $CFAR = \$20,456.94 - \$23,833.33 = \$3,376.39 \text{ decrease}$

e. $CGP$     +\$32,500.00[a]
   $DC$      − 10,125.00
   $BDE$     +  4,687.50
   $CFAR$    +  3,376.39
           \$30,438.89 net benefit

[a]   Costs are indicated by a minus sign, benefits by a plus sign.

**SP22-3.**

a. $CGP = \Delta Q(p - v)$                     **(Eq. 22.4)**
       $= (500 \text{ units})(\$300 - \$225)$
       $= \$37,500 \text{ decrease}$

b. $CFAR = \left[\dfrac{(Q)(v) + F}{360}\right] (ACP)(OC)$       **(Eq. 22.5)**

current $CFAR = \dfrac{(6,500 \text{ units})(\$225) + \$200,000}{360} (85 \text{ days})(.13)$

            $= \$51,029.51$

forecasted $CFAR = \dfrac{(6,000 \text{ units})(\$225) + \$200,000}{360} (72)(.13)$

            $= \$40,300$

change in $CFAR = \$40,300 - \$51,029.51 = \$10,729.51 \text{ decrease}$

c. $BDE = (PBD)(Q)(p)$                   **(Eq. 22.6)**
current $BDE = (.03)(6,500 \text{ units})(\$300)$
            $= \$58,500$
forecasted $BDE = (.02)(6,000 \text{ units})(\$300)$
            $= \$36,000$
change in $BDE = \$36,000 - \$58,500 = \$22,500 \text{ decrease}$

d. $CGP$            − \$37,500.00[a]
   $CFAR$       +  10,729.51
   $BDE$        +  22,500.00
   Collection cost   −  25,000.00
               \$29,270.49 net cost

[a]   Costs are indicated by a minus sign, benefits by a plus sign.

**SP22-4.**

### AGING SCHEDULE

| Age of Accounts Receivable | Amount Outstanding (Thousands of Dollars) | | Percent of Total |
|---|---|---|---|
| 0–30 days | \$3,435 | (\$5,822 − \$2,387) | 35.9% |
| 31–60 days | 2,402 | (5,110 − 2,708) | 25.1 |
| 61–90 days | 1,762 | (4,637 − 2,875) | 18.4 |
| 91–120 days | 1,171 | (3,904 − 2,733) | 12.2 |
| 121–150 days | 806 | (3,223 − 2,417) | 8.4 |
| Total | \$9,576 | | 100.0% |

| Age of Accounts Receivable | Credit Sales (Thousands of Dollars) | Amount Outstanding (Thousands of Dollars) | Percent of Month's Sales Not Yet Collected |
|---|---|---|---|
| 0–30 days | $5,822 | $3,435 | 59.0% |
| 31–60 days | 5,110 | 2,402 | 47.0 |
| 61–90 days | 4,637 | 1,762 | 38.0 |
| 91–120 days | 3,904 | 1,171 | 30.0 |
| 121–150 days | 3,223 | 806 | 25.0 |

# CHAPTER 23

**SP23-1.**

$$CTC = \left(\frac{D}{1-D}\right)\left(\frac{360}{N}\right) \qquad \text{(Eq. 23.1)}$$

a. $CTC = \left(\frac{.01}{1-.01}\right)\left(\frac{360}{30-10}\right) = 18.2\%$

b. $CTC = \left(\frac{.01}{1-.01}\right)\left(\frac{360}{60-20}\right) = 9.1\%$

c. $CTC = \left(\frac{.02}{1-.02}\right)\left(\frac{360}{45-15}\right) = 24.5\%$

**SP23-2.**

$$ERI = \left(\frac{I}{LP}\right)\left(\frac{360}{N}\right) \qquad \text{(Eq. 23.2)}$$

a. $ERI = \left[\frac{(.13)(\$22,000)(90/360)}{\$22,000}\right]\left[\frac{360}{90}\right]$

$= \left(\frac{\$715}{\$22,000}\right)\left(\frac{360}{90}\right)$

$= 13.0\%$

b. $ERI = \left[\frac{(.12)(\$22,000)(192/360)}{\$22,000 - (.12)(\$22,000)(192/360)}\right]\left(\frac{360}{192}\right)$

$= \left(\frac{\$1,408}{\$20,592}\right)\left(\frac{360}{192}\right)$

$= 12.8\%$

c. $ERI = \left[\frac{(.11)(\$22,000)(185/360)}{\$22,000 - (.15)(\$22,000)}\right]\left(\frac{360}{185}\right)$

$= \left(\frac{\$1,243.61}{\$18,700}\right)\left(\frac{360}{185}\right)$

$= 12.9\%$

d. $ERI = \left[\frac{(.10)(\$22,000)(10/52)}{\$22,000 - (.10)(\$22,000)(10/52) - (.10)(\$22,000)}\right]\left(\frac{52}{10}\right)$

$= \left(\frac{\$423.08}{\$22,000 - \$423.08 - \$2,200}\right)\left(\frac{52}{10}\right)$

$= 11.4\%$

**SP23-3.**

$$ERI = \left(\frac{I}{LP}\right)\left(\frac{360}{N}\right)$$    **(Eq. 23.2)**

$$= \left(\frac{\$1,000,000 - \$965,000 + \$15,000}{\$965,000 - \$15,000}\right)\left(\frac{360}{210}\right)$$

$$= \left(\frac{\$50,000}{\$950,000}\right)(1.71)$$

$$= 9.0\%$$

**SP23-4.**

**a.** Face value of pledged receivables,

| | |
|---|---:|
| each 45 days | $150,000 |
| Times: Percent of face value to be loaned | 75% |
| Loan amount each 45 days | $112,500 |

**b.**

| | |
|---|---:|
| Processing charge each 45 days (2%)($150,000) | $3,000 |
| Interest on the loan each 45 days ($112,500)(16%)(45/360) | 2,250 |

$$ERI = \left(\frac{I}{LP}\right)\left(\frac{360}{N}\right)$$    **(Eq. 23.2)**

$$= \left(\frac{\$3,000 + \$2,250}{\$112,500}\right)\left(\frac{360}{45}\right)$$

$$= 37.3\%$$

**SP23-5.**

**a.**

| | |
|---|---:|
| Face value of receivables factored | $400,000 |
| Less: Service charge (3%) | 12,000 |
| Less: Reserve (6%) | 24,000 |
| Gross loan amount | 364,000 |
| Less: Interest (.17)($364,000)(45/360) | 7,735 |
| Net amount available to the borrower | $356,265 |

**b.** $$ERI = \left(\frac{I}{LP}\right)\left(\frac{360}{N}\right)$$    **(Eq. 23.2)**

$$= \left(\frac{\$7,735 + \$12,000}{\$356,265}\right)\left(\frac{360}{45}\right)$$

$$= 44.3\%$$

# CHAPTER 25

**SP25-1.**

| Year | Cash Flow | Present Value Factor at 16% | Present Value |
|---|---|---|---|
| 0 | ($25,000,000) | 1.0000 | ($25,000,000) |
| 1 | 15,000,000 | .8621 | 12,931,500 |
| 2 | 10,000,000 | .7432 | 7,432,000 |
| 3 | 5,000,000 | .6407 | 3,203,500 |
| 4 | 4,000,000 | .5523 | 2,209,200 |
| | | | $NPV_a$ = ($776,200) |

Because the *NPV* of the proposed acquisition is negative, the acquisition should not be attempted.

**SP25-2.**    The exchange ratio is

$$ER = \frac{P_s}{P_r} = \frac{\$12}{\$16} = .75 \tag{Eq. 25.2}$$

An exchange ratio of .75 implies that the shareholders of Haden Company (the target) will receive .75 shares of Kemp's stock in exchange for each of their existing shares of Haden's stock.

**SP25-3.**

| Year | Cash Flow | Present Value at 14% | Present Value |
|------|-----------|----------------------|---------------|
| 0 | $19,000,000 | 1.0000 | $19,000,000 |
| 1 | (6,000,000) | .8772 | (5,263,200) |
| 2 | (8,000,000) | .7695 | (6,156,000) |
| 3 | (12,000,000) | .6750 | (8,100,000) |
| | | | $NPV_d$ = ($519,200) |

Because the *NPV* is negative, the proposed divestiture is not feasible.

# ANSWERS TO SELECTED PROBLEMS

## CHAPTER 2

**1.a.** $100,250; $20,550
  **b.** 33.4%; 21.6%
  **c.** 39%; 34%
**3.** Year 1: $150,000
  Years 2–5: $300,000
  Year 6: $150,000
**4.** 1983: $500,000
  1984: zero
  1985: zero
  1986: $400,000
  1987: zero
  1988: zero
  1989: zero
  1990: zero
  1991: $800,000
  1992: $1,000,000
**5.a.** $62,050
  **b.** $68,000
**9.** $28,889

## CHAPTER 3

**1.** $9,869
**3.** 14.5%
**6.** $38,475
**8.** $24,911.20
**10.** Between 10% and 11%
**11.** $81,393
**14.** $9,653
**16.** $36,363.64
**19.** $72,108.45
**20.** 15%
**22.** $14,741.77
**24.** $56,502
**27.** $47,555
**30.** $325,206
**32.** Approximately 3%
**33.** $1,527,107
**36.** $691,813.98
**38.** $383,490

## CHAPTER 4

**1.a.** $846.76
  **b.** $845.13
  **c.** Approximately 13%
  **d.** 10%
**3.a.** $48.75
  **b.** 16.8%
**6.** 10.3%
**10.** 9.73%
**11.** 18%
**13.** $77.25
**14.a.** 11.76%
  **b.** $25.00
**18.** Between 2% and 14%
**19.** $63.64

## CHAPTER 5

**2.a.** 13.6%
  **b.** 7.24%
  **c.** .5324
**4.** Project 5 is preferred since it has
  the lowest coefficient of
  variation.
**5.a.** 11%; 19%
  **b.** 7%; 23%
  **c.** 3%; 27%
**7.a.** 14.8%
  **b.** .0327
**9.a.** 6%
  **b.** 13%
  **c.** 4.5%; 11.5%
  **d.** 5%; 12.5%
  **e.** 10%; 17%

## CHAPTER 6

**2.a.** Current ratio: 1.8
  Inventory turn: 5.9
  Net profit margin: 1.4%
  ROE: 6.5%
  Debt ratio: .57
  Quick ratio: 1.0

Total asset turn: 2.0
Times interest: 1.8
ROI: 2.8%
**2.c.** Beginning cash:    $1,700
  Sources
    Net income      784
    Depreciation     500
    Inventory       500
    Accounts pay    500
    Notes pay       500
  Uses
    Fixed assets    3,084
    Dividends       200
  Ending cash:      $1,200

## CHAPTER 7

**1.a.** J: $20,600
  F: $21,900
  M: $21,000
  A: $18,300
  M: $18,400
  J: $20,800
  **b.** J: $21,150
  F: $17,500
  M: $17,200
  A: $16,900
  M: $19,800
  J: $18,900
  **c.** J: ($550)
  F: $3,844
  M: $7,644
  A: $9,044
  M: $7,644
  J: $9,544
**4.a.** $125,698
  **b.** 19X8: $140,000
  19X9: $150,000

## CHAPTER 8

**2.a.** $691,489
  **b.** −$91,000

**3.** 2.64
**5.a.** 300,000 units
  **b.** 200,000 units
**8.a.** 3.0 and 3.75
  **b.** $280,000 and $200,000
  **c.** 1100 units
    1000 units
  **d.** EBIT is higher with the new
    equipment.
**11.a.** 4.0
  **b.** $1,106,910
**13.a.** 6,667 units
  **b.** 6,333 units
**14.** 1.44
**15.a.** 33,125 units
  **b.** 26,499 units

## CHAPTER 9

**1.** A: $1,034,000
  B: $63,000
  C: $121,600
  D: $512,000
  E: $219,600
**2.** F: $16,200
  G: $15,760
  H: $72,600
  I: $20,200
  J: $162,000
**3.** K: $29,500
  L: $8,200
  M: $102,950
  N: $30,900
  O: $258,000
**6.** $249,000

## CHAPTER 10

**1.a.** 4 years
  **b.** $146,190
  **c.** 1.12
  **d.** 18% to 19%
**3.** C = $12,491
  D = $14,816
**4.a.** Ajant and Garpen
  **b.** Ajant, Carren, and Garpen
**8.** Discount: $34,008
  Deluxe: $16,045
**10.** Chain: $35,486
        $13,477
        $28,093
  *ANPV:* $6,546
        $2,487
        $5,182
**12.a.** $16,860
  **b.** Approximately 14%
  **c.** .97
  **d.** 5.06 years

## CHAPTER 11

**1.a.** b = 15%
  **b.** $8,180
  **c.** Adopt
**2.** −$4,456
**4.** b = 9%
  *NPV* = $30,464
**9.a.** −$2,860
    $\sigma$ = $26,730
  **b.** 42%
**11.** −$30,332

## CHAPTER 12

**1.** 9.11%
  9.24%
**2.** 12.2%
**6.a.** 12.5%
  **b.** 12.3%
  **c.** 12.5%
**9.a.** 11.09%
  **b.** 10.24%
**10.a.** $5,250,000
  **b.** $3,875,000
  **c.** 8.9%
    9.2%
**12.a.** Preferred: 9.3%
    R.E.: 10.3%
    New common: 11.0%
    Debt: 7.9%
  **b.** $21,818,181
  **c.** 9.44%
    9.82%

## CHAPTER 13

**1.** 2.99 and 2.48
**2.a.** 2.41
  **b.** $2.05
**6.a.** $8.25 and $6.60
  **c.** $2 million and $3 million
  **d.** $3,666,667
**7.a.** 4.39
  **b.** $.88
**8.a.** 2.75
  **b.** $.76
  **c.** $.91
**9.b.** .0: 13.00%
    .5: 11.50%
    1.0: 11.75%
    1.5: 12.70%
    2.0: 14.33%
  **d.** D/E = .5

## CHAPTER 14

**1.** $.20
**2.a.** $8
  **b.** $15,800,000
  **c.** $18,400,000
  **d.** $43 million
  **e.** $14.55

**3.a.** 18 million
  **b.** $3
  **c.** $54 million
  **d.** $20 million
  **e.** $13 million
  **f.** $87 million
  **g.** $4.67
**7.a.** Unaffected
  **b.** $7.50

## CHAPTER 15

**1.** $42.50
**3.** $182.70
**4.a.** $600,000
  **b.** $770,000
    $440,000
**5.** 16%
**7.** $59.37

## CHAPTER 16

**1.a.** 4.58 rights
  **b.** $.90
  **c.** $49.10
  **d.** $.90
**2.a.** $22,500
    $126,360 or $1.26 per share
  **b.** 5 rights
**3.a.** $12,600,000
  **b.** 13,984,000 shares
  **c.** 1.43 rights
  **d.** $.31
  **e.** $6.69
  **f.** $.31
**16.a.** $23,857,000
  **b.** $1.89
  **c.** $2.39
  **d.** $6.38

## CHAPTER 18

**2.a.** $550,463
  **b.** $547,120
  **c.** Lease
**3.a.** $280,081 (ignoring maint.)
  **b.** $273,284 (ignoring maint.)
  **c.** Purchase

## CHAPTER 19

**1.a.** $33.33
  **b.** $30.33
  **c.** $84.21
  **d.** $84.00
**2.a.** $3.50
  **b.** zero
  **c.** $19.25
**5.a.** 67 shares
  **b.** zero

## CHAPTER 20

**1.a.** $66,210
  **b.** $56,700

**2.** Current ratio: 1.67 and 1.94
Net income: $882,000 and $878,400
ROE: 14.7% and 12.2%
**3.** Net income: $40,970,000 and $41,800,000
ROE: 27.3% and 27.9%
Current ratio: 1.5 and 3.0
**4.a.** $76,250
**b.** $84,860

## CHAPTER 21

**1.** $223,333
**3.** $13,151
**5.** E: $2,000
F: $933.33
G: $2,750
H: $605.77
**8.** #1: $90,000
#2: $60,000
#3: $38,000
#4: $12,000
**13.** $5,609.59/year

**14.** A: 5.2%
B: 5.0%
C: 5.0%
Purchase A
**15.** 30 days

## CHAPTER 22

**1.a.** 17,321 units
**b.** 9,661 units
**c.** 2,750 units
**3.** Cost: $13,585
**4.** Benefit: $79,342
**5.** Benefit: $80,842
**8.a.** 42,426 units
**b.** 24,213 units
**c.** 49,667 units

## CHAPTER 23

**1.a.** 9.8%
**b.** 10.4%
**c.** 12.1%
**3.** 19.6%

**7.** 9.2%
10.0%
10.0%
**9.a** $800,000
**b.** 43.0%
**10.a.** $10,591,000
**b.** 19.2%
**12.** $4,761,905

## CHAPTER 25

**1.** $NPV_a$ = $2,123,000
Therefore, reject.
**2.** .25
**3.** $NPV_d$ = $578,600
Therefore, divest.

## CHAPTER 27

**2.** 1.8%; 16.6%
U.S. dollars
**3.** 10.0%; 12.8%; 8.6%
Canadian T-bills

# INDEX TO KEY TERMS

---

* The number in boldface type indicates the chapter in which the term is discussed; the second number indicates the page where the term is defined in a list of key terms.

# INDEX

# Present Value of an Annuity of $1 per Period for n Periods

$$PVIFA_{k,n} = \frac{1 - \dfrac{1}{(1 + k)^n}}{k}$$

| Period n | 1% | 2% | 3% | 4% | 5% | 6% | 7% | 8% | 9% | 10% | 11% | 12% |
|---|---|---|---|---|---|---|---|---|---|---|---|---|
| 1 | 0.9901 | 0.9804 | 0.9709 | 0.9615 | 0.9524 | 0.9434 | 0.9346 | 0.9259 | 0.9174 | 0.9091 | 0.9009 | 0.8929 |
| 2 | 1.9704 | 1.9416 | 1.9135 | 1.8861 | 1.8594 | 1.8334 | 1.8080 | 1.7833 | 1.7591 | 1.7355 | 1.7125 | 1.6901 |
| 3 | 2.9410 | 2.8839 | 2.8286 | 2.7751 | 2.7232 | 2.6730 | 2.6243 | 2.5771 | 2.5313 | 2.4869 | 2.4437 | 2.4018 |
| 4 | 3.9020 | 3.8077 | 3.7171 | 3.6299 | 3.5460 | 3.4651 | 3.3872 | 3.3121 | 3.2397 | 3.1699 | 3.1024 | 3.0373 |
| 5 | 4.8534 | 4.7135 | 4.5797 | 4.4518 | 4.3295 | 4.2124 | 4.1002 | 3.9927 | 3.8897 | 3.7908 | 3.6959 | 3.6048 |
| 6 | 5.7955 | 5.6014 | 5.4172 | 5.2421 | 5.0757 | 4.9173 | 4.7665 | 4.6229 | 4.4859 | 4.3553 | 4.2305 | 4.1114 |
| 7 | 6.7282 | 6.4720 | 6.2303 | 6.0021 | 5.7864 | 5.5824 | 5.3893 | 5.2064 | 5.0330 | 4.8684 | 4.7122 | 4.5638 |
| 8 | 7.6517 | 7.3255 | 7.0197 | 6.7327 | 6.4632 | 6.2098 | 5.9713 | 5.7466 | 5.5348 | 5.3349 | 5.1461 | 4.9676 |
| 9 | 8.5660 | 8.1622 | 7.7861 | 7.4353 | 7.1078 | 6.8017 | 6.5152 | 6.2469 | 5.9952 | 5.7590 | 5.5370 | 5.3282 |
| 10 | 9.4713 | 8.9826 | 8.5302 | 8.1109 | 7.7217 | 7.3601 | 7.0236 | 6.7101 | 6.4177 | 6.1446 | 5.8892 | 5.6502 |
| 11 | 10.368 | 9.7868 | 9.2526 | 8.7605 | 8.3064 | 7.8869 | 7.4987 | 7.1390 | 6.8052 | 6.4951 | 6.2065 | 5.9377 |
| 12 | 11.255 | 10.575 | 9.9540 | 9.3851 | 8.8633 | 8.3838 | 7.9427 | 7.5361 | 7.1607 | 6.8137 | 6.4924 | 6.1944 |
| 13 | 12.134 | 11.348 | 10.635 | 9.9856 | 9.3936 | 8.8527 | 8.3577 | 7.9038 | 7.4869 | 7.1034 | 6.7499 | 6.4235 |
| 14 | 13.004 | 12.106 | 11.296 | 10.563 | 9.8986 | 9.2950 | 8.7455 | 8.2442 | 7.7862 | 7.3667 | 6.9819 | 6.6282 |
| 15 | 13.865 | 12.849 | 11.938 | 11.118 | 10.380 | 9.7122 | 9.1079 | 8.5595 | 8.0607 | 7.6061 | 7.1909 | 6.8109 |
| 16 | 14.718 | 13.578 | 12.561 | 11.652 | 10.838 | 10.106 | 9.4466 | 8.8514 | 8.3126 | 7.8237 | 7.3792 | 6.9740 |
| 17 | 15.562 | 14.292 | 13.166 | 12.166 | 11.274 | 10.477 | 9.7632 | 9.1216 | 8.5436 | 8.0216 | 7.5488 | 7.1196 |
| 18 | 16.398 | 14.992 | 13.754 | 12.659 | 11.690 | 10.828 | 10.059 | 9.3719 | 8.7556 | 8.2014 | 7.7016 | 7.2497 |
| 19 | 17.226 | 15.678 | 14.324 | 13.134 | 12.085 | 11.158 | 10.336 | 9.6036 | 8.9501 | 8.3649 | 7.8393 | 7.3658 |
| 20 | 18.046 | 16.351 | 14.877 | 13.590 | 12.462 | 11.470 | 10.594 | 9.8181 | 9.1285 | 8.5136 | 7.9633 | 7.4694 |
| 21 | 18.857 | 17.011 | 15.415 | 14.029 | 12.821 | 11.764 | 10.836 | 10.017 | 9.2922 | 8.6487 | 8.0751 | 7.5620 |
| 22 | 19.660 | 17.658 | 15.937 | 14.451 | 13.163 | 12.042 | 11.061 | 10.201 | 9.4424 | 8.7715 | 8.1757 | 7.6446 |
| 23 | 20.456 | 18.292 | 16.444 | 14.857 | 13.489 | 12.303 | 11.272 | 10.371 | 9.5802 | 8.8832 | 8.2664 | 7.7184 |
| 24 | 21.243 | 18.914 | 16.936 | 15.247 | 13.799 | 12.550 | 11.469 | 10.529 | 9.7066 | 8.9847 | 8.3481 | 7.7843 |
| 25 | 22.023 | 19.523 | 17.413 | 15.622 | 14.094 | 12.783 | 11.654 | 10.675 | 9.8226 | 9.0770 | 8.4217 | 7.8431 |
| 26 | 22.795 | 20.121 | 17.877 | 15.983 | 14.375 | 13.003 | 11.826 | 10.810 | 9.9290 | 9.1609 | 8.4881 | 7.8957 |
| 27 | 23.560 | 20.707 | 18.327 | 16.330 | 14.643 | 13.211 | 11.987 | 10.935 | 10.027 | 9.2372 | 8.5478 | 7.9426 |
| 28 | 24.316 | 21.281 | 18.764 | 16.663 | 14.898 | 13.406 | 12.137 | 11.051 | 10.116 | 9.3066 | 8.6016 | 7.9844 |
| 29 | 25.066 | 21.844 | 19.188 | 16.984 | 15.141 | 13.591 | 12.278 | 11.158 | 10.198 | 9.3696 | 8.6501 | 8.0218 |
| 30 | 25.808 | 22.396 | 19.600 | 17.292 | 15.372 | 13.765 | 12.409 | 11.258 | 10.274 | 9.4269 | 8.6938 | 8.0552 |
| 35 | 29.409 | 24.999 | 21.487 | 18.665 | 16.374 | 14.498 | 12.948 | 11.655 | 10.567 | 9.6442 | 8.8552 | 8.1755 |
| 40 | 32.835 | 27.355 | 23.115 | 19.793 | 17.159 | 15.046 | 13.332 | 11.925 | 10.757 | 9.7791 | 8.9511 | 8.2438 |
| 45 | 36.095 | 29.490 | 24.519 | 20.720 | 17.774 | 15.456 | 13.606 | 12.108 | 10.881 | 9.8628 | 9.0079 | 8.2825 |
| 50 | 39.196 | 31.424 | 25.730 | 21.482 | 18.256 | 15.762 | 13.801 | 12.233 | 10.962 | 9.9148 | 9.0417 | 8.3045 |